Essentials of Finance: An Integrated Approach

George W. Gallinger

Arizona State University

Jerry B. Poe

Arizona State University

Prentice Hall, Englewood Cliffs, New Jersey 07632

Library of Congress Cataloging-in-Publication Data

Gallinger, George W.
    Essentials of finance : an integrated approach / George W. Gallinger, Jerry B. Poe.
      p. cm.
    Includes bibliographical references and index.
    ISBN 0-13-013566-6
    1. Finance. 2. Corporations—Finance. 3. Business enterprises—Finance. I. Poe, Jerry B. II. Title.
HG173.G25 1995
658.15—dc20   94-22595
                                                        CIP

Editorial/Production Supervision: Lisa Kinne
Acquisitions Editor: Leah Jewell
Editor-in-Chief: Valerie Ashton
Development Editor: Patricia Nealon
Assistant Editor: Teresa Cohan
Managing Editor: Frances Russello
Copy Editor: Donna Mulder
Interior and Front Matter Designs: Donna Wickes
Cover Design: Patricia H. Wosczyk
Design Directors: Patricia H. Wosczyk and Linda Fiordilino
Manufacturing Buyer: Patrice Fraccio
Marketing Manager: Patti Arneson
Proofreader: Karen E. Bosch
Editorial Assistant: Eileen Deguzman
Production Assistant: Renee Pelletier

Cover Illustration by Nicholas Wilton

 ©1995 by Prentice Hall, Inc.
A Simon & Schuster Company
Englewood Cliffs, New Jersey 07632

Printed in the United States of America
10 9 8 7 6 5 4 3 2 1

ISBN 0-13-013566-6

Prentice-Hall International (UK) Limited, *London*
Prentice-Hall of Australia Pty. Limited, *Sydney*
Prentice-Hall Canada Inc., *Toronto*
Prentice-Hall Hispanoamericana, S.A., *Mexico*
Prentice-Hall of India Private Limited, *New Delhi*
Prentice-Hall of Japan, Inc., *Tokyo*
Simon & Schuster Asia Ptd. Ltd., *Singapore*
Editora Prentice-Hall do Brasil, Ltda., *Rio de Janeiro*

▼▼▼▼▼▼▼▼▼▼▼

To our wives, Susan Gallinger and Carol Poe

Brief Contents

Table of Contents

PART IV   VALUE OF THE FIRM

11   CREATING SHAREHOLDER VALUE

12   THE COST OF CAPITAL

Preface

Why did we write this book? There are many good textbooks available for the introductory finance class, but we believe that these books are missing an important point. Consider the fact that most business students take only one finance class in their curriculum—the required course. Instructors usually teach the class from a managerial, or corporate, finance perspective because that is the focus of the major books. Indeed, the title of many of these textbooks includes the word *managerial* or *corporate.* However, as a discipline the subject of finance is much broader. Finance encompasses financial markets and institutions, and investments, in addition to managerial finance.

We agree that managerial finance should be the emphasis of the introductory course. However, we also believe that by exposing students to broader coverage of financial markets and investments, they will have a better understanding of the role of managerial finance in the financial environment. Nonfinance specialists need to have more knowledge of financial institutions and financial decision making than is traditionally covered in most texts. The reengineering of corporate America is resulting in people from different specialties forming teams to solve problems. A broader exposure to finance provides the marketing, management, or production team player with improved insight about how to create shareholder value and the impact of changing financial markets on this value.

THE MODEL MOST AUTHORS FOLLOW

Our textbook offers a fresh approach. But to provide some perspective, let's look at the pattern, or close derivative, that most comprehensive books follow. In the first few chapters there is a brief discussion of basic accounting and financial markets. Next, there is an examination of risk and time value of money concepts, which they use to value financial securities. However, rather than building on these valuation principles, the authors often interrupt the flow by changing the discussion to financial statement analysis and forecasting. After this digression, they return to the valuation issue by examining capital budgeting topics. However, in the transition back to valuation they fail to discuss the value of the firm and how to create shareholder value. The discussion then proceeds to examine decisions related to investment banking, long-term debt, preferred stock, mergers, divestitures, holding companies and leveraged buyouts. (Some authors place many of these topics at the end of the book as special topics.) Following these topics, the texts often discuss cost of capital, leverage, and dividend policy. Issues examined in the last chapters usually relate to working capital management without any connection to investment decisions discussed earlier. In summary, there is an overall lack of a logical, consistent flow from one topic to another. There is little in the way of building blocks.

 ## OUR APPROACH

Our text differs from the traditional managerial finance textbook. We lay a broad foundation based on macrofinance topics and proceed in a logical order to microfinance topics. In this way, we explain the environment in which managers operate as they attempt to create value for shareholders. We present the topics as a cohesive body of knowledge, rather than as a series of seemingly unrelated pieces of information. As a result, students obtain a more thorough survey of the subject matter.

We divide our nineteen chapters into six parts. Part I provides for a quick review of prerequisite concepts studied in accounting and economics, two courses that are important for understanding finance. In Part II, we lay the foundation for understanding valuation through discussion of time value of money and risk-return concepts. Part III shows the value of financial securities and examines the important concept of efficient markets. In Part IV, we extend the valuation of securities to the valuation of the corporation and discuss how to create shareholder value. Part V examines specific techniques for evaluating both long-term and short-term investment opportunities for enhancing shareholder value. Part VI concludes our systematic progression by examining financial statement analysis and forecasting. Financial statement analysis shows the impact of management's investment, financing, and operating decisions on the financial position of the firm. With an understanding of what has happened, stakeholders can forecast the future financial position of the firm for enhancing shareholder value. The following annotated table of contents provides a more detailed overview.

ANNOTATED TABLE OF CONTENTS

PART I – INTRODUCTION

1. **Introduction to Finance**
   The introductory chapter lays out the principles that are important to finance, and introduces many key concepts studied in later chapters. We relate the finance function to the other functional areas of business management.

2. **Review of Financial Statements**
   This chapter provides an accounting review from a different perspective than found in most texts. We discuss the difference between accounting and economic profits and explain the importance of understanding cash flows. Much of the chapter revolves around discussing the annual report of Kellogg Company.

3. *An Overview of the Financial System*

The emphasis here is on why financial markets exist and the importance of interest rates and risk in the valuation of assets. An understanding of this chapter enhances students' understanding of time value of money in Chapter 4.

PART II – DETERMINANTS OF VALUE

4. *The Time Value of Money*

The focus of this chapter is on the fundamental principle of finance: Money has a time value represented by the interest cost. We solve extensive examples using formulas, tables, and calculators.

5. *Risk, Return, and the CAPM*

This chapter provides an understandable explanation of modern portfolio theory with several practical examples to keep students interested. The discussion includes problems associated with beta.

PART III – SECURITIES: MARKETS AND VALUATION

6. *Financial Markets*

The institutional framework for the issuance and trading of financing securities is the topic of this chapter.

7. *Fixed-Income Securities*

This chapter is full of real world examples from *The Wall Street Journal*. We discuss who issues and buys fixed-income securities and why. We also explain the tax treatment of debt interest versus the multiple taxation of dividends.

8. *Valuation of Fixed-Income Securities*

The basic concepts for understanding bond valuation are the focus in this chapter. Our discussion of duration is simple, but effective in showing students how it measures the sensitivity of bonds to interest rate changes.

9. *Common Stock and Its Valuation*

The strength of this chapter is that it successfully introduces common stock valuation concepts without becoming unnecessarily technical. We examine the debate about dividend relevancy in this chapter.

10. *Efficient Financial Markets*

Current theoretical and practical issues about market efficiency are the focus in this chapter. The discussion is straightforward so that students can understand the arguments for and against efficient markets.

PART IV – VALUE OF THE FIRM

11. *Creating Shareholder Value*

Here we extend the discussion of security valuation to the valuation of the firm. The underlying theme revolves around the creation of shareholder value in a principal-agent paradigm.

12. *The Cost of Capital*

This chapter builds on the concepts of Chapter 11 by integrating value creation, cost of capital, and capital structure management in a simple but effective fashion. Illustrations show that the cost of capital is a derivative of the firm's value, and not vice versa.

13. Capital Structure Management

This chapter views the management of capital structure from a practical perspective. We examine capital structure changes in both healthy and distressed firms.

PART V – INVESTMENT DECISIONS

14. Capital Budgeting: Decision Process and Models

Models for aiding the value-creating decision process are the theme of this chapter. We stress the advantage of net present value analysis over other approaches.

15. Capital Budgeting: Identifying Relevant Cash Flows

This chapter allows students to understand the relevant cash flows in a variety of capital budgeting situations. It is a chapter of applications.

16. Short-Term Business Investment

The focus of this chapter is twofold. First, we present value-enhancing decision models for determining investment in cash, accounts receivable, and inventory. Second, we examine techniques for monitoring the investment in these accounts.

17. Short-Term Financing

This chapter discusses the use of operating, seasonal, and bridge loans to support the firm's short-term investments. There is extensive discussion of the use of financial ratios to measure liquidity risk of the firm.

PART VI – FINANCIAL ANALYSIS AND FORECASTING

18. Financial Statement Analysis

The discussion of financial statement analysis in this chapter helps tie together many concepts discussed earlier in the text. By waiting until the last part of the text to study financial statement analysis, students have a better appreciation of the underlying concepts and interpretation of the statements and ratios.

19. Financial Planning

This concluding chapter utilizes many of the financial ratios and techniques discussed earlier in the text to show how to forecast the firm's financial performance and position over the near future. The discussion reminds students of the importance of the economic and financial environments, and the guideposts to use in directing management decisions in the shareholder value-enhancing process.

 IMPORTANT FEATURES

Now that you have a better understanding of our approach to the introductory finance class, let us point out some important features you will find in the book.

- Each chapter begins with learning objectives and concludes with a detailed summary for students to review chapter contents quickly.
- There are only 19 chapters, thereby eliminating topics most instructors seldom cover in the introductory course (for example, mergers and acquisitions, and derivative securities).

- The vocabulary is readable and understandable to the average student. We bold-face key terms when we first use them, and also define them in the margin.

- *Comprehension Checks* at the end of each major section in a chapter allow students to check their understanding of the material.

- There is extensive use of graphs, tables, and illustrations to help demonstrate concepts and minimize the use of complex formulas. We explain all formulas by means of illustrations.

- Each chapter has at least one *Financial Reality* reading that allows students to see the importance of finance through articles published in leading business journals and newspapers.

- All but two chapters have an *Executive Commentary* that outlines a practicing executive's view of some aspect of finance discussed in the chapter.

- The use of a valuation approach, rather than a balance sheet approach, allows us to link concepts to the shareholder wealth-maximization principle. For example, we show that cost of capital is a derivative of firm value and not vice versa as implied in many texts.

- We introduce financial ratios as needed, as opposed to discussing all of them early in the text without showing their relationship to important financial concepts.

- International finance topics appear throughout the text, rather than isolated in appendices or boxes, and are highlighted by global icons.

- Each chapter has an average of 35 problems, including library assignments and *Disclosure* database assignments. Each chapter (except the first) has a comprehensive problem that integrates concepts and issues examined in the chapter.

SUPPLEMENTAL MATERIALS

There is the usual complement of supplemental materials accompanying this book. In addition, there are two new features: electronic transparencies for instructors who are computerizing their classroom delivery, and a computerized study guide for students who want access to a multitude of practice problems. A brief description of the supplemental materials follows.

Instructor's Manual   The instructor's manual provides a lecture outline, teaching tips, quizzes designed to easily test students' comprehension of content, and detailed problem solutions which have been independently checked for accuracy.

Text Bank   Prentice Hall Test Manager provides individual tailoring of midterm and final examinations from a database of over 2000 questions and problems. This computerized test bank allows you to add and edit test questions, and assemble and save tests. Test scrambling options provide an almost infinite number of test versions.

Transparencies   Over 100 transparencies are available to facilitate instruction and learning by making it easy for instructors to present key concepts from the text.

Electronic Transparencies   *Designed by Darrell Crutchley, Auburn University.* Each chapter's *Comprehensive Problem* is on electronic transparencies. An instructor can teach the major concepts of the chapter using the comprehensive problem set. Many of the transparencies overlay to show the buildup of important concepts and answers.

Study Guide   *Written by Stanley Jacobs, Central Washington University.* The study guide is consistent in question content and structure with the text. Each chapter contains suggestions for chapter study, a summary of key concepts, illustrative examples, multiple-choice and true-false questions keyed to chapter objectives in the text, problems keyed to objectives, and fully worked solutions to study guide problems.

Finance A+   This electronic study guide operates in the Microsoft Windows© environment. Students can test their understanding of concepts and problems through true-false, multiple choice, numerical, and graphical questions. The software provides hints for correcting wrong answers. It also automatically grades performance and lists topics needing further study.

ABC/Prentice Hall Video Library Cases   *Written by John Byrd, Fort Lewis College.* All but two chapters have video cases specifically written for the chapter. Each case's discussion questions relate the video to concepts and issues discussed in the textbook.

 ## ACKNOWLEDGMENTS

Writing a textbook requires more than a major commitment of time by the authors. There are many people involved in the process of shaping a vision into a successful product. We want to express our gratitude to these people. The following list of names indicates people involved in the process in one manner or another. Some people reviewed the prospectus, others provided comments on selected chapters or took time to respond to a survey, a few people reviewed the entire manuscript, and six people participated in a focus group. Generally, the feedback was positive and encouraging. However, if you have ever written a book, you know it is impossible to satisfy everyone. We made every effort to incorporate as many suggestions as possible without changing our vision of the text.

Robert J. Angell	North Carolina A&T State University
Nasser Arshadi	University of Missouri, St. Louis
Allen B. Atkins	University of Arizona
Robert T. Aubey	University of Wisconsin, Madison
Thomas A. Bankston	Angelo State University
William L. Beedles	University of Kansas
John S. Bildersee	New York University
Paul J. Bolster	Northeastern University
G. Geoffrey Booth	Louisiana State University
Jerry D. Boswell	Metropolitan State College of Denver
Helen M. Bowers	University of Notre Dame
Robert E. Chatfield	University of Nevada, Las Vegas
Ji Chen	University of Colorado at Denver
K.C. Chen	California State University, Fresno
J. Jay Choi	Temple University
John H. Crockett, Jr.	George Mason University
R. Michael Cudd	Southeastern Louisiana University
Brent B. Dalrymple	University of Texas—Pan American
James O. Desreumaux	Corpus Christi State University
Les Dlabay	Lake Forest College
Eugene F. Dunham, Jr.	University of South Florida
Donald Ray Escarraz	University of North Dakota
Eugene Furtado	University of San Diego
James A. Gentry	University of Illinois, Champaign
Waldemar M. Goulet	Wright State University

Alan E. Grunewald	Michigan State University
Kathleen T. Hevert	Boston College
Robert F. Hodgin	University of Houston, Clear Lake
Robert D. Hollinger	Kansas State University
Alfred L. Kahl	University of Ottawa
William F. Kennedy	University of North Carolina at Charlotte
Hal S. Kerr	Washington State University
Robert Kieschnick, Jr.	George Mason University
Robert T. Kleiman	Oakland University
Duncan Kretovich	University of Michigan, Flint
V. Sivarama Krishnan	Case Western Reserve University
Morris A. Lamberson	University of Central Arkansas
Martin Laurence	William Paterson College
Edward C. Lawrence	University of Missouri, St. Louis
Anthony J. Lerro	Stetson University
S.K. Mansinghka	San Francisco State University
Elizabeth M. Maynes	York University
Edward M. Miller	University of New Orleans
John B. Mitchell	Central Michigan University
Diane Morrison	University of Wisconsin at La Crosse
William E. Muhs	Montana State University
Donald A. Nast	Florida State University
Henry M. Okleshen	Mankato State University
Robert A. Olsen	California State University, Chico
Richard Osborne	The American University
Pamela P. Peterson	Florida State University
James B. Pettijohn	Southwest Missouri State University
Eugene O. Poindexter	West Georgia College
William B. Riley	West Virginia University
Hadi Salavitabar	SUNY at New Paltz
Gary C. Sanger	Louisiana State University
William L. Sartoris	Indiana University
Frederick P. Schadler	East Carolina University
John W. Settle	Portland State University
Richard A. Shick	Canisius College
Ronald E. Shrieves	University of Tennessee
Gerald E. Smolen	University of Toledo
Richard H. Stanton	University of California—Berkeley
Edward J. Stendardi	St. John Fisher College
Jerry L. Stevens	University of Richmond
A. Charlene Sullivan	Purdue University
Amir Tavakkol	Kansas State University
David E. Upton	Virginia Commonwealth University
Howard E. Van Auken	Iowa State University
Pieter A. Vandenberg	San Diego State University
James A. Verbrugge	University of Georgia
Michael R. Vetsuypens	Southern Methodist University
Joe Walker	University of Alabama at Birmingham
Michael C. Walker	University of Cincinnati
Samuel C. Weaver	Lehigh University
Marianne Westerman	University of Colorado at Denver
C. Don Wiggins	University of North Florida

J. Daniel Williams	University of Akron
Joseph W. Wilson	California State University, Fresno
Daniel T. Winkler	University of North Carolina, Greensboro
Walter J. Woerheide	Rochester Institute of Technology
Edward R. Wolfe	Western Kentucky University
Steve B. Wyatt	University of Cincinnati

The following people deserve special recognition. They willingly agreed to class test the manuscript. Although we had class tested an earlier version of the manuscript, these people still taught from a product that was far from polished. Thank you, and thanks to your students.

Peggy J. Crawford	George Mason University
Frank T. Griggs	Grand Valley State University
Joe Walker	University of Alabama at Birmingham
Marianne Westerman	University of Colorado at Denver

A frustration often encountered with a first edition text is errors in the problem sets. The following people have painstakingly checked many of the problems. We appreciate their attention to detail and are confident that you will not find errors a concern.

Stanley Jacobs	Central Washington University
Victoria B. McWilliams	Arizona State University, West Campus
Joe Walker	University of Alabama at Birmingham
Marianne Westerman	University of Colorado at Denver

We are truly indebted to the team of professionals at Prentice Hall. Will Ethridge, formerly vice president–editorial and marketing director, was willing to take a chance on a manuscript that deviated from the mainstream introductory corporate finance textbook. Garret White, former publisher of business and economics, Leah Jewell, finance and economics editor, and Charlotte Morrissey, the local sales representative at the time, were strong advocates in making sure we understood senior management's commitment to our manuscript.

We are especially appreciative of two people: Leah Jewell and Trish Nealon. Leah was tenacious in her support of our manuscript and was the most influential person in our signing with Prentice Hall. We could not have asked for a better editor; she made things happen. Trish, our developmental editor, shaped the manuscript into a textbook in which we take a great deal of pride. Stamped all over this book are the creative talents of Leah and Trish.

Several other people deserve recognition. Eileen Deguzman, Leah's assistant, coordinated much of the activity associated with taking the manuscript from rough draft to production. Lisa Kinne, our production editor, shepherded the manuscript through an extremely tight time schedule. Teresa Cohan managed activities associated with the supplements. Patti Arneson was responsible for designing advertisements to catch your attention about the important features of our book.

Another person who deserves thanks is Penny Beintema, a former student of one of the authors. As a student, she took time to provide feedback about the manuscript when it was in a very early stage. Her comments provided a student's view and helped shape the product.

Enjoy the book.

George W. Gallinger
Jerry B. Poe

CHAPTER 1

Introduction to Finance

Do you intend to make a career in marketing, purchasing, production, or human resources management? Possibly you want to be an economist, an attorney, a tax expert, a public relations specialist, or your goal is your own communications firm. No matter which field you choose, you will be involved with finance in one way or another. Let's look at a few of these careers to see how each may incorporate finance. Decisions by marketing managers influence growth in sales; as a result, there may be a need for increased funds to support further investment in plant and equipment. Purchasing managers must know whether sufficient funds exist to take advantage of volume discounts. Lower material costs increase profits, and increased profits may result in higher value of the firm. Public relations specialists must know about the financial strengths and weaknesses of the business so they can carry on informed discussions with inquiring reporters and investors. Attorneys are involved in corporate fund raising or in litigation in which the value of a company may be at stake. As an owner of a small business, an entrepreneur has complete financial responsibility and must closely manage money and credit.

An understanding of finance can do more than enhance your career. It can also sharpen your day-to-day grasp of current events and give you a better handle on your personal finances. How much of today's morning business broadcast or financial page of the newspaper did you understand? Chances are you found the glut of facts too much to absorb in one sitting. If you did make the effort to comprehend the material about "bulls and bears," the Dow Jones Industrial Average, interest rates, money supply, and so on, you possibly came away wondering how the information will affect you. If this describes your reaction, you are not unusual. Most people have difficulty applying the meaning of financial data to their own situations. For instance, they do not know:

- How actions of the Federal Reserve affect the level of interest rates.
- How interest rates affect investments.
- How to calculate effective interest rates charged on their credit cards.
- How to evaluate the risk of an investment.

- How bonds or stocks are valued, or how to buy them.
- How to read annual reports issued by companies.

And so people often make decisions about financial matters without really understanding what financial news means and how finance operates.

Let's begin the study of finance by discussing the origins of the finance discipline. The meaning of the word *finance* is derived from the Latin word *finis*. During Roman times, *finis* meant the completion of a contract between parties with either a transfer of money or barter (exchange) or a credit agreement. The word *finance* has much the same meaning today. However, we must conceptualize the discipline of finance in broader terms. **Finance** encompasses the analysis of, the issuance of, the distribution of, and the purchase of financial contracts written against **real assets.** Implicit in these activities is the determination of *value;* finance involves a process of deciding what something is worth.

The issuers, or suppliers, of financial contracts include individuals, business corporations, and government agencies located worldwide. The issuers must use the funds efficiently to provide satisfactory returns to investors who buy the contracts in financial markets. The efficient use of funds requires that the issuers administrate and manage investors' funds efficiently; they must practice sound financial decision making.

This brief introduction to finance suggests that it is a multifaceted discipline, international in scope, and bound together by contracts. It includes the areas of managerial finance, investments, and financial markets. These areas are closely related for a very simple reason: *the most widely accepted financial objective of a company is maximization of its market value.* Management's actions can influence the market value, but they are unable to determine the value completely. The simultaneous interplay of supply and demand for financial securities (ownership claims) in financial markets determines market value. Through the mechanism of these financial markets, other companies also participate as suppliers of securities, and a great number of investors participate as demanders for these securities. The study of finance provides an explanation of how securities are valued and how investors behave by taking into account the relationships among these investors' decisions. The interactions of the demands of all investors determine market values.

Finance in its broadest terms is an integrated body of knowledge built around the guiding principles of wealth maximization, time value of money, expected return versus risk, leverage, and diversification. We examine these principles shortly. You will see how they help to integrate the areas of managerial finance, investments, and financial markets.

When you have completed this chapter, you should understand:

- Some of the differences and similarities among managerial finance, investments, and financial markets.
- The dominant guiding principles of finance.
- Common elements of finance that cross all the subareas of the discipline.
- How finance is integrated with and depends on other areas of business.
- Ethical issues that are important to finance.

 1.1 TRADITIONAL FINANCE AREAS

Finance and many other business disciplines were originally part of the field of economics. By the turn of the century, as a result of the growth of industry engendered by the Industrial Revolution, a greater need for study of detailed business problems and processes arose. About this time business schools began, and managerial finance, or

Finance. The study and practice of making money-denominated decisions. As a discipline, finance can be classified into three areas: managerial, investments, and markets and institutions.

Real assets. Land, buildings, plant and equipment, inventories, and consumer durable goods.

THE IMPORTANCE OF THE STUDY OF FINANCE
by Edward N. Basha, Jr., Chairman of the Board, Bashas' Inc.

My family business started from humble beginnings in 1932 with a single store south of Chandler, Arizona. Today, we are 68 stores strong and still growing. Our phenomenal growth is a result of many things, one of which is a fundamental understanding of the role of finance in business. From the early days, my father, Eddie Sr. and Uncle Ike were well grounded in money matters, even though money was scarce during the darkest days of the Depression. Understanding finance allowed them to provide quality products to customers at the lowest possible price, and still make a profit. In addition, it also allowed them to experience consistent growth, which in turn provided jobs and security for others.

Today, the Phoenix, Arizona, market for retail grocers is one of the most competitive in the nation. This market allows grocers to take home only about one cent for each dollar spent at the register. With this small margin, it is incumbent on every Bashas' employee (whom we call members) *to always* think *finance,* regardless of position or title. Our courtesy clerks' main concerns are packing groceries with maximum efficiency and safety for our customers. Our deli and bakery members not only think about preparing products that are pleasing and nutritious, but that will sell at a sufficient margin to cover a large overhead. The same can be said for the meat and produce department members. They all market their respective products to minimize shrink and waste and at the same time to hold down costs. Store management, on the other hand, is concerned with product mix, merchandising, and maximizing gross margin dollars, while keeping labor costs and supplies under control. Our buyers and merchandisers deal with purchasing, maintaining, and setting prices for the 25,000 items or more in each of our stores. All functions, regardless of size, require fundamental financial considerations.

At the corporate level, our members are also concerned with financial matters. Maintaining cash flow is critical with millions of dollars coming in and going out every day. Good cash management is a must. The ability to evaluate financial investments is also important. Everything from the purchase of a copy machine to the acquisition of a chain of stores needs to be analyzed from a financial viewpoint to be successful in our business. Procuring the financing and negotiating the terms and conditions are also important ingredients.

We have survived and prospered over the years due to the understanding and application of financial principles to business on the part of every Bashas' member. The resultant prosperity, in turn, is shared with our families, communities, and our great state of Arizona. Other businesses are not so fortunate. My observation is that more businesses fail because of deficient financing than from deficient products or services.

Your college finance course can act as a catalyst in defining issues and selecting solutions to financial matters. I invite each of you, in your respective careers, to view the principles of finance as a tool in reaching your own goals—whatever they may be. Good luck!

corporate finance as it was called more generally, was one of the first specialties to be taught separately from economics. The principal emphasis in economics first was on institutions and institutional arrangements. The economics of the individual firm had not yet been developed as a focal point of economic inquiry. Within this general context, the purpose of the newly defined area of managerial finance was to describe and document the rapidly evolving, complex nature of financial market institutions, instruments, and practices. Rather than correspond to managerial finance as we know it today, these studies precede the modern-day finance subareas of financial markets and investments. Thus, managerial finance began as a descriptive, legalistic, and institutional subject with little focus on financial decision making within the firm.

The study of finance changed little until the 1940s, when critics questioned the lack of interest in day-to-day problems of financial management such as those pertaining to cash, accounts receivable, and inventory. However, it was not until the late 1950s and early 1960s that finance began to evolve into the dynamic field of study called *financial economics*. Academicians in economics and mathematics, namely, Harry Markowitz, Merton Miller, Franco Modigliani, and William Sharpe, provided the impetus for this change. Each of these founders of modern finance has received the Nobel Prize in economics in recognition for their contributions. Their insights and research contributions are the basis for today's valuation concepts. The following Financial Reality article by Professor Jarrell summarizes the important contributions of these Nobel laureates.

The areas of managerial finance, investments, and financial markets are used frequently to classify financial topics. Managerial finance deals with financial decisions in the business organization. It is usually the area that receives the most emphasis in the finance class required of all business students. The area of investments primarily relates to the valuation of financial securities and their grouping to satisfy an investor's objectives. Financial markets represent the channels for transferring funds from savings into investment. Taken together, a study of managerial finance, investments, and financial markets provides a strong understanding of the financial system.

1.1.1 Managerial Finance

Managerial finance has evolved from its early beginning as a descriptive, institutional subject to the dynamic study of decision making on financial issues pertaining to the firm. Specifically, **managerial finance** addresses the following issues:

- What investments should the firm make?
- What type of financing should be used to pay for the investments?
- How should daily financial activities be managed to satisfy cash requirements?

We can classify the first two issues, which pertain to investment and financing alternatives, as **strategic decisions.** These decisions select from among investment and financing alternatives that offer long-term opportunities for management to increase the value of the firm. An example is General Motors Corporation's decision in early 1993 to close several assembly plants in an effort to return to profitability. Another example is Ford Motor Company's decision of whether to build a new assembly plant or buy an existing plant that GM abandons. The third issue, concerning daily financial activities, such as management of cash, accounts receivable, inventories, and short-term liabilities, applies to **tactical decisions.** These decisions concern managing resources, including money, to ensure the firm meets customer demand.

The financial manager must worry about the interrelationships between strategic and tactical decisions and the effect these decisions may have on the value of the firm. For example, if Ford buys a plant from GM, can Ford generate enough cash from operations to pay back any debt borrowed to finance the acquisition? The Financial Reality article on page 7 provides evidence of the important role the chief financial officer (CFO) plays within the organization.

There is little difference in most types of decisions domestic and international financial managers face. However, two significant financial problems confront firms competing in foreign markets. Managers cannot ignore two constant risks: currency risks and political risks. An unexpected currency devaluation or expropriation of the

Managerial finance. One of the three areas of finance. It deals with management decisions relating to obtaining funds and assets for the firm, controlling costs, and managing the firm's cash flows.

Strategic decisions. The set of decisions resulting in the formulation and implementation of strategies, or plans, designed to achieve the objectives of the organization.

Tactical decisions. The set of decisions designed to carry out daily activities to meet strategic objectives.

▼▼▼▼▼▼▼▼▼▼▼▼▼▼

EN-NOBELING FINANCIAL ECONOMICS

What a great day for financial economists! The announcement of the Nobel Prize for economics to Merton Miller, William Sharpe, and Harry Markowitz finally acknowledges that the field of financial economics is a genuine science. It is in the same league with physics and mathematics.

Largely thanks to these three fathers of finance, academics who study corporate finance, investment management, and financial markets can walk a little taller around their campuses. Finance has been instrumental in defining the contributions of other Nobel-winning economists, such as James Tobin, Paul Samuelson, and Franco Modigliani. But, finance was not the central subject for these men and their contributions to the field of finance were not responsible for their awards. Messrs. Miller, Markowitz, and Sharpe are pureblood financial economists and their prize-winning contributions are strictly on the subject of finance. What are these contributions to financial knowledge?

Historically, portfolio theory focused on picking "winners." All sorts of ad hoc ideas about security pricing, many found in the still popular book *Security Analysis* by Benjamin Graham and David Dodd, supported the central investment goal of attempting to pick undervalued stocks to beat the market. Harry Markowitz, a mathematician by training and an expert on statistical theory, began thinking about the statistical properties of security returns around 40 years ago. He published an article called "Portfolio Selection" in the *Journal of Finance* in 1952 and a book by the same title the same year.

PORTFOLIO RISK

Mr. Markowitz defined the risk to owning securities as variance, a familiar statistical concept, and rigorously developed the principles governing how portfolio variance, or risk, is affected by adding and subtracting the individual securities from a portfolio, which is simply a combination of securities. The major lesson implied by this math is that portfolios offer far superior returns for given risk (variance) than do individual securities. This insight flew in the face of the conventional practice of emphasizing individual securities in an effort to pick winners. Mr. Markowitz showed that eschewing diversification was enormously risky and could only be justified economically as a general approach if financial markets were unbelievably inefficient.

William Sharpe was the most notable of several financial economists, including names like Treynor, Lintner, Mossin, and Black, who extended Mr. Markowitz's powerful insights and created the revolutionary theories of asset pricing based on Mr. Markowitz's mathematical treatment of security returns and variances. Specifically, William Sharpe, in his 1964 *Journal of Finance* article, "Capital Asset Prices: A Theory of Market Equilibrium under Conditions of Risk," assumed that all investors looked at security risk and return as did Mr. Markowitz. Under these assumptions, Mr. Sharpe developed a model of market equilibrium that showed how the risk of individual securities would be priced in a "Markowitz world."

The main insight here was that only the so-called systematic risk of individual securities (the famous beta risk) would be priced in such a market. The holding of unsystematic risk, which is variance in returns to individual securities that could be eliminated through diversification, would earn no additional return. So, in such a market, diversification was imperative to sensible and successful investing. Refusing to diversify exposed one to additional risk with no market-based prospect for reward.

These contributions were the genesis of a revolution in finance, leading to an explosion of theoretical and empirical advances that has yet to run its course. The emphasis on diversification and portfolio management is at the heart of practical investment management today. Indeed, even program trading, which is really another innovation developed to heighten the efficiency of portfolio management, is a direct descendant of the theoretical innovations of Messrs. Markowitz and Sharpe. Benjamin Graham, the co-author of *Security Analysis*—often called the bible of Wall Street—reportedly repudiated the stock-picking principles underlying his book in a 1974 interview in reaction to the compelling new thinking on efficient capital markets generated by the Markowitz-and-Sharpe revolution of finance.

Merton Miller won his share of the Nobel prize for his contributions to the field of corporate finance, which is mainly the study of corporations' debt and dividend payout policies. Mr. Miller's seminal contribution came in an article co-authored with Franco Modigliani, entitled "The Cost of Capital, Corporate Finance, and the Theory of Investment," which appeared in the *American Economic Review* in June 1958.

Corporate finance before Mr. Miller was in very sad shape. The study of corporate debt and dividend policies amounted to a series of rules of thumb that simply described widespread practice and justified them logically in consistent, normative assertions. Financial economists in academia were treated as second-class citizens at universities, and their weak, unpromising body of knowledge deserved this treatment. Mr. Miller's article applied the physics principle of conservation of matter to the study of the value and riskiness of the corporate entity. In his theory the corporation was a stream of expected future cash flows, or profits from operations. These were independent of the financial policies and dividend payout policies of the firm.

RIGOROUS ANALYSIS

This approach allowed Mr. Miller and his followers to apply rigorous mathematical analysis in understanding how increasing long-term debt levels or changing dividend payout rates affected the overall value of the firm. Two revolutionary principles, called irrelevance propositions, emerged from this early work. First, that the value of the firm is independent of the degree of financial leverage employed by the firm (debt levels are irrelevant to firm value). Second, that the value of the firm is independent of the level of dividends chosen by the firm (dividends, too, are irrelevant). These two propositions, derived mathematically, were completely counterintuitive and caused an enormous academic debate.

In hindsight, it was no contest. Mr. Miller, armed with enormous intelligence, humor, energy, and a genius of a co-author, won over the finance profession and started the field on its way to becoming rich with scientifically rigorous theories and statistically sophisticated empirical knowledge. Mr. Miller has not been the retiring father on the sidelines. Far from it. He remains today the king of corporate finance, paving the way to understanding the important role of taxes in corporate policy and how financial markets for securities and derivative instruments operate in arbitrage equilibriums.

The Nobel Committee has sifted through the hundreds of contributors to the field of financial economics and has succeeded in selecting the genuine founding fathers of the theories on which all of this modern knowledge is based. Many others have made enormous contributions, such as Gene Fama, Myron Scholes, and Robert Merton. These people too deserve serious consideration for future Nobel Prizes. But every academic in the field of financial economics will work a little harder and teach with a little more conviction, for the Nobel Committee has just said to the world that our science is legitimate and important. Congratulations to Merton Miller, Harry Markowitz, and William Sharpe and, from all of us, thank you very much indeed.

Adapted from Gregg A. Jarrell, "En-Nobeling Financial Economics," *The Wall Street Journal,* October 17, 1990, p. A14. Reprinted by permission of *The Wall Street Journal,* © 1990 Dow Jones & Company, Inc. All Rights Reserved Worldwide.

THE BIG PICTURE CFO COMES OF AGE

Corporations have been talking about integrating business and finance since the 1960s. Now they are starting to actually do it.

Six weeks into his new job as chief financial officer of Campbell Soup Company, Frank Weise dropped into the office of market research chief Anthony Adams and peppered him with questions about a potential acquisition. How were the company's brands positioned? What were the demographics of its customer base? Was there room for incremental volume? Could the product name be extended?

"He asked how we could take this company and grow it on a consumer and brand franchise basis; he didn't just ask the due-diligence questions," Adams recalls. "I've been in this game 30 years and worked with four CFOs. I've never had a conversation like this before."

Although marketing has always been key to a consumer goods company like Campbell, Adams says, communication between marketing and finance was often confused—like people looking at the same thing through opposite ends of a telescope. "This guy obviously looks from multiple points of view," he says. "I see Frank as part of a new generation of strategic thinking CFOs."

Weise says he considers himself a marketing person first and a financial person second. "A financial guy can be penny-wise and pound-foolish. It's easy to wring costs out, but you have to reinvest in businesses, in people, in capital, and in the consumer base—that's advertising. A purely financial guy can come in and say, 'I'll cut $1 billion out of marketing.' If you do that, you're dead."

Consultants and headhunters say that corporations seeking CFOs increasingly require a candidate who will go beyond counting the beans and raising the dough: they have to understand the market dynamics of their companies, participate in general management, help to devise business strategy and work closely with operations.

"I haven't been a bean counter in 25 years," insists Texaco CFO Allen Krowe. "Be it marketing, developing, manufacturing or exploration, the CFO should be involved, if he is talented enough and interested enough."

Eric Olsen, vice president in the shareholder value planning practice at the Boston Consulting Group, says: "You can't have this tension between the guy who doesn't do the numbers and just thinks creatively and the group that myopically looks at the numbers and ignores the things you can't quantify, like strategic position and competitive response."

Adapted from Miriam Bensman, "The Big Picture CFO Comes of Age," *Institutional Investor*, May 1992, p. 29. This copyrighted material is reprinted with permission from Institutional Investor, Inc. 488 Madison Avenue, New York, NY 10022

company's foreign facilities by an unfriendly government can wipe out profit margins on sales to foreign clients.

A major difference exists between financial management practices in developed countries and in developing countries. In the major developed countries, financial markets are very sophisticated and market participants usually engage in independent corporate financial decision making. However, even within the leading world economies, significant differences exist. For example, investment and financing decisions by German and Japanese firms often involve more communications between bankers and firms' managers than do similar decisions in Britain, Canada,

JAPAN'S KEIRETSU AND KOREA'S CHAEBOL

A distinguishing characteristic of the Japanese economy is the prominence of *keiretsu*, large corporate groups each centered around a major commercial bank. Many of Japan's blue-chip companies, such as Nissan Motors, Mitsubishi Electric, and NEC, belong to one of these groups. Such groupings are not an industrial structure unique to Japan, however. For example, leading companies in Korea, such as Samsung, Hyundai, and Daewoo, belong to large and diversified groups called *chaebol*.

Major keiretsu groups typically consist of firms in diverse industries centered around a main bank; hence they are sometimes called financial keiretsu. There are currently six large financial keiretsu in Japan: Mitsui, Mitsubishi, Sumitomo, Fuyo, Sanwa, and Dai-Ichi Kangyo.

Although no single clear-cut criterion defines a given firm's membership to any one particular keiretsu, group-affiliated firms generally share three characteristics. First, firms within a given keiretsu tend to hold interlocking shares. Second, close consultation is maintained by keiretsu firms on business concerns and policies of mutual interest. Third, firms in keiretsu tend to rely heavily for financing on the main commercial bank and financial institutions, such as insurance companies and trust banks. These financial institutions generally hold equity in the firms to which they lend.

Almost half of the 200 largest firms in Japan are members of a major keiretsu. Evidence suggests that keiretsu firms do not tend to cut back on investment as sharply in response to a cash shortfall as do firms without close bank ties. There is also evidence that the close bank-industry tie within keiretsu confers greater flexibility in financing.

The chaebol groups in Korea consist of diversified business firms with a concentrated ownership structure. The emergence and growth of chaebol is closely linked to government intervention in Korea's economic development. In its bid to accelerate Korea to an industrialized economy, the government adopted a strategy of supporting growth in existing firms rather than encouraging the formation of new firms. The rationale was that growth through diversification of existing firms would economize on scarce entrepreneurial talent and technical knowledge.

Commercial banks in Korea by law are not allowed to be a part of chaebol groups. To a large extent, therefore, the government has been the main conduit of finance to chaebol firms. Due to the dominant role of the Korean government in the allocation of credit, banks have had less discretion and relatively little incentive to monitor lending compared to main banks in Japan's financial keiretsu.

Adapted from Chan Guk Huh and Sun Bae Kim, "Japan's Keiretsu and Korea's Chaebol," *FRBSF Weekly Letter*, Number 93-25, July 16, 1993. Used by permission.

Investments. One of the three areas of finance. It deals with the commitment of funds toward the purchase of securities or assets issued by firms, governments, or individuals.

or the United States. In less developed economies, the governments and financial institutions play a significant role in corporate financial decision making. The above Financial Reality reading provides insight into the decision making process in Japan and Korea.

1.1.2 Investments

The financial area of **investments** includes investors' activities and decision rules about the selection and management of assets, such as stocks, bonds, gold, and real estate.

When a group of assets is held by an investor, the collection is called a **portfolio**. The portfolio can be arranged to lessen total risk for a targeted expected return.

The *expected return versus risk concept* is central. An underlying assumption of this concept is the existence of **efficient financial markets;** that is, markets in which competition is as fierce and extreme as possible. Investors act quickly and efficiently to incorporate any new information in the determination of each asset's price. Because all investors respond in a similar manner, no investor can consistently earn **excess profits**—returns more than necessary to compensate for risk. In finance, we call such markets *informationally* efficient markets.[1] Asset prices set in informationally efficient financial markets reflect the market's assessment of managerial performance. The broadest measure of a firm's achievements over time is the extent to which the firm develops its future earnings potential while controlling the risk.

Sometimes the amount and quality of information in financial markets can be a problem. Often there is a scarcity of information about young firms or foreign firms. Also, accounting philosophies vary among countries, and this can result in difficulty interpreting information about companies. Regulatory monitoring of financial markets also varies drastically from one country to another. The protection afforded investors in the United States does not exist in every financial market in the world.

Investment decisions involve asset selection and portfolio formation with respect to longer-term risk and return relationships. Another important aspect of investments is the art of *trading assets*. Trading is a complex activity separate from investing. **Trading** involves the implementation of investment decisions and buying and selling assets in an attempt to profit from weekly, daily, hourly, or shorter, price swings. The New York Stock Exchange (NYSE) is the most renowned securities marketplace in the world for trading shares of over 1800 companies from around the world.

1.1.3 Financial Markets

Financial markets consist of *money markets* and *capital markets*. If financial contracts are for one year or less, they have a short-term duration and trade in **money markets**. The most important money markets are in New York and London. Financial contracts with durations in excess of one year are long term and trade in **capital markets**, with the largest markets located in Tokyo and New York. Financial markets are the channels whereby savings are translated into investment—into accumulation of assets. There are three broad ways in which investment takes place:

- Households (individuals and families) buy assets.
- Firms buy assets and finance them by selling stocks and bonds to households.
- Firms buy assets and finance them by loans from *financial intermediaries*, who in turn take in households' savings.

Financial intermediaries are firms whose principal business is taking deposits, making loans, and buying securities. The best known type of financial intermediary is a commercial bank, such as Citibank. The financial markets for stocks and bonds coordinate the actions of households, firms, and financial intermediaries. **Stock markets,** like the New York Stock Exchange, are markets in which shares (commonly called *stocks*) representing ownership of firms, such as Home Shopping Network, Inc., trade. The **bond market** is the market in which debts issued by firms like CSX Corporation and local, state, or national governments trade.

[1]In Chapter 10, we discuss technical analysis. Technicians do not believe in informationally efficient markets.

Portfolio. A combination of multiple securities that attempts to obtain the best balance between risk and return.

Efficient financial market. Prices for traded securities embody all currently available relevant information. Characteristics of efficient markets include low transaction costs, freely accessible information, many investors, and quick price corrections.

Excess profits. Returns in excess of profits required to satisfy the investor for the amount of risk involved.

Investment decisions. Decisions pertaining to the selection and diversification of the purchase of assets.

Trading. The buying and selling of securities to take advantage of price swings.

Financial markets. One of the three areas of finance. Markets of the economy in which both short-term and long-term securities are dealt in.

Money markets. Financial markets for trading debt securities with one year or less to maturity.

Capital markets. Financial markets for trading equity and debt securities with maturities beyond one year.

Financial intermediaries. Financial institutions that serve as middlemen between lenders and borrowers. They create and issue financial claims against themselves in order to acquire financial claims against others.

Stock market. The financial market for trading ownership claims (shares) of a firm.

Bond market. Financial market for trading long-term debt instruments issued by firms and governments; bonds represent promises to repay specified amounts.

FIGURE 1.1
GLOBAL STOCK TRADING

When the Tokyo stock market opens at 9 a.m. Tokyo time, it's 2 a.m. in Johannesburg and 7 p.m. in New York. When the Tokyo market closes, it's 8 a.m. in Johannesburg and 1 a.m. in New York, and the London market opens in three hours.

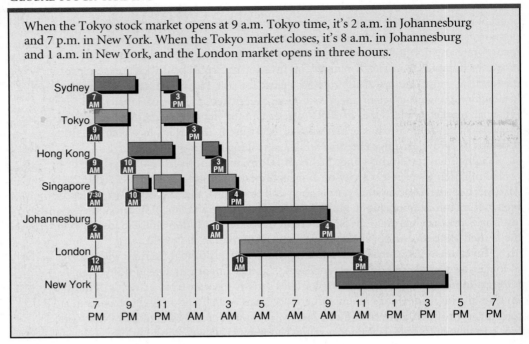

An important function of financial markets is to provide a means to measure the smallest return investors should expect to earn when they exchange their funds for financial contracts. Information is important for determining the appropriate return. Fortunately, competitive financial markets in leading world economies process information efficiently. Advances in computer technology have resulted in quick dissemination of news and the globalization of trading. The reporting of events is nearly simultaneous with their occurrence.[2] Today, stock prices trade continuously, as they electronically move around the world. When stock trading ends in one city, it soon continues in another city, causing stocks to travel around the world every 24 hours. Figure 1.1 shows a 24-hour chart of the stock market.

 Comprehension Check

1. Discuss the contribution to modern-day finance by each of the following persons: Harry Markowitz, William Sharpe, Merton Miller, and Franco Modigliani.
2. Describe the three areas that make up the discipline of finance.
3. What are the three important issues addressed by managerial finance?

[2]The importance of news is critical to well-functioning financial markets. On June 18, 1815, Napoleon was defeated at Waterloo. A carrier pigeon took news of the British victory to Nathan Rothschild in London. In a single day, Rothschild reaped a fortune by buying shares from uninformed, and quite frightened, traders. Rothschild's profit was not due to the news. It was due to his having received the news first.

4. What are two significant problems concerning financial managers in foreign operations?
5. What are financial markets?
6. Why are financial markets important for both investors and business firms?

1.2 GUIDING PRINCIPLES OF FINANCE

Managerial finance, investments, and financial markets are integrated under the broad heading of finance through shared principles. These important principles are: *maximization of wealth, time value of money, expected return versus risk trade-off, leverage,* and *diversification.* We will review each principle and how it affects financial decision making.

1.2.1 Maximization of Wealth

The most important guiding principle is *wealth maximization,* which is the creation of as much wealth as possible with the resources available. A wealth-maximizing goal looks beyond the short run and explicitly seeks to incorporate the entire future stream of cash flows that will be generated by the decision. Needless to say, the principle assumes that wealth is created lawfully and ethically.

Many people would temper a goal of wealth maximization to include a goal of social responsibility, which is generally defined as a consciousness for the good of all people in society and a respect for the environment on the part of the corporation. Social responsibility can extend as far as the role of corporations in funding social programs. While many individuals may see this as a noble goal to embrace, we must remember that we are dealing with the role of the business entity. Nobel laureate economist Milton Friedman argues that when investors bring a corporation into existence through buying stock, they do so on the condition that corporate managers will follow their wishes—usually, to make a profit.[3] A moral obligation is thus generated for managers, namely, to serve as agents for profit-seeking investors. It follows that using the investors' money otherwise is equivalent to stealing. Theodore Levitt states that if business were to become a protector of the welfare society, the result could be disastrous.[4] Levitt argues that because corporate officials are not democratically elected business should stick to business. It has no holy mission and it ought not become a new "church." Yet there are some business managers, such as those of Tom and Jerry's Ice Cream, who disagree with this position and take active roles to promote through financial incentives the opening of franchises in minority urban neighborhoods. We will come to see that there is room for much firm-specific decision making—on all levels— within the financial discipline.

The wealth-maximization goal has broad applicability to the areas of managerial finance, investments, and financial markets. For the financial manager, maximization of wealth means operating the firm with the goal of increasing shareholders' wealth. Financial management decisions, such as buying new equipment or extending credit to customers, are all subject to decision rules whose aim it is to **maximize shareholders' wealth,** that is, to maximize the long-run stock price.

From an investment perspective, it is clear that investors choose financial contracts expecting to increase wealth. The decision to invest in different types of assets or

> **Maximize shareholders' wealth.** The theoretical objective management should follow to increase the long-term value of the company's common stock.

---

[3]Milton Friedman, "The Social Responsibility of Business Is to Increase Its Profits," *New York Times Magazine,* September 13, 1970, p. 33.

[4]Theodore Levitt, "The Dangers of Social Responsibility," *Harvard Business Review* (September–October 1958), p. 49.

combinations of assets into a portfolio is a simple example. Deciding whether to invest in low-risk, low-expected-return assets versus high-risk, high-expected-return assets is another case.

Financial markets provide individuals and firms with the means to make wealth-increasing decisions by efficiently transacting financial contracts. Efficient financial markets provide buyers and sellers with more opportunities to select securities that satisfy their needs.

1.2.2 Time Value of Money

The principle of *time value of money* is central to financial decision making. **Time value of money** means that funds have an opportunity cost because alternative uses for the funds exist. Should opportunity number one or opportunity number two be taken? Managers and investors evaluate potential wealth-increasing decisions using an interest rate called the *opportunity cost of money* to value *all* future cash flows.

A technique called **future value analysis** finds the value of funds to be received in the future. If the opportunity rate is 8 percent, $1 received two periods from now is worth $1 \times (1 + 0.08) \times (1 + 0.08) = \$1.166$. Because interest paid on money can itself earn interest, there is a multiplicative growth dimension to the future amount. The growth dimension is called **compounding.** As the interest rate increases, a dollar invested today appreciates faster to some future value. For example, if the Native Americans who sold Manhattan for $24 had invested this money at 6 percent compounded annually, it would be worth about $74 billion at the end of 1994.

We can also use the opportunity rate to convert *future* cash flows into a *present* value to determine if the wealth-maximization goal is satisfied. More present value dollars are sought rather than fewer. The present value process is called **discounted cash flow analysis.** For example, $1 received one year from now is worth $0.926 today if the opportunity cost of money is 8 percent: $1 \div (1 + 0.08) = \$0.926$. If the opportunity cost of money is 10 percent, the value of that same $1 is about $0.909 today. Check this number. The present worth declines as the interest rate, or opportunity cost of money, increases.

1.2.3 Expected Return versus Risk Trade-off

The principle that ties finance together is the *expected return versus risk trade-off concept.* The **expected return-risk principle** states that if investments A and B have the same risk, the investment with the greater expected return, B, should be chosen. Or consider a firm that issues additional debt, which causes risk to increase. Investors' expected return must increase to compensate for the higher risk. Figure 1.2 shows these relationships.

The cornerstone of managerial finance and investments is the application of discounted cash flow analysis and expected return and risk concepts to the **valuation** (that is, finding the present value) of financial claims. We will learn in Chapter 3 that the opportunity rate used to discount cash flows is the same rate we could have expected to earn from alternative investments of equal risk.

A necessary assumption of the expected return-risk principle is that market *equilibrium prices* exist in financial markets. A market **equilibrium price** is the price at which the quantity demanded of financial instruments equals the quantity supplied. At the equilibrium price, opposing forces exactly balance each other. Trust officers at Wells Fargo & Company, investment officers employed by Metropolitan Life Insurance Company, money managers hired by CalPERS to invest pension funds, specialized deal-

---

Time value of money. A principle stating that dollars at different points in time can only be directly compared when they are first adjusted by the interest rate representing the opportunity cost of money.

Future value analysis. The determination of the future worth of a series of cash flows. This process is the opposite of discounted cash flow analysis.

Compounding. Process by which a given amount of money (called the principal) accumulates forward in time. Interest earned in one period earns additional interest in all subsequent periods.

Discounted cash flow analysis. The process of converting future cash flows to their present values. This process is the opposite of future value analysis.

Expected return-risk principle. Given the risk exposure, securities are priced to provide investors with a return that compensates for the risk.

Valuation. The worth of an economic asset.

Equilibrium price. Price of a commodity or service determined in the market by the intersection of supply and demand; the price at which the market clears.

FIGURE 1.2

EXPECTED RETURN-RISK TRADE-OFF

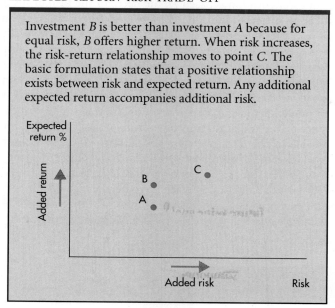

Investment *B* is better than investment *A* because for equal risk, *B* offers higher return. When risk increases, the risk-return relationship moves to point *C*. The basic formulation states that a positive relationship exists between risk and expected return. Any additional expected return accompanies additional risk.

ers on the floor of the stock exchange, individual investors, and thousands of other organizations constantly trade financial securities, thereby maintaining equality between demand and supply.

1.2.4 Leverage

Some costs are constant, or **fixed,** over a range of business activity. Other costs are **variable** and change in direct response to changes in business activity. The linkage, or *leverage,* between the fixed and variable costs offers significant financial gains or losses. There are two types of leverage: *operating* and *financial.*

The particular choice of fixed and variable *operating costs* existing within a firm is a result of the production technology chosen by management to compete in the industry. **Operating costs** are the necessary outlays incurred in producing the product or service. A business like Intel Corporation uses highly advanced technology to produce state-of-the-art computer chips. The result is relatively high fixed operating costs, which result in relatively high **operating leverage.** Operating leverage is favorable if sales (the activity) expand faster than additional fixed costs. Operating leverage is unfavorable if sales decline faster than any reduction in fixed costs.

Financial leverage is the use of debt financing to support income-earning investments. The commitment of the firm or investor to pay interest on borrowed funds (that is, the leverage portion) is not (usually) related to the amount of product or services produced by the assets financed. As business activity improves without any changes in fixed costs, financial leverage causes profits to increase. A change in the opposite direction causes losses. Profits improve if debt-financed investments earn more than the cost of debt. Conversely, losses increase if the cost of debt exceeds the return earned by the assets. The financial leverage relationship holds true for all participants in the financial system, whether they be managers, individuals, or financial institutions.

Fixed cost. A cost that remains relatively constant regardless of the volume of operations. Examples: rent, depreciation, and property taxes.

Variable cost. A cost that moves directly with a firm's output, rising as output increases over a full range of production. Examples: raw materials and sales commissions.

Operating costs. Expenses incurred in operating a business, excluding all financing expenses.

Operating leverage. The effect of fixed operating costs on earnings when sales revenue changes.

Financial leverage. The effects of debt financing on shareholders' claims on earnings.

1.2.5 Diversification

The principle of diversification is based on the need for the firm or investor to reduce risk. **Diversification** means to introduce variety into the portfolio. The maxim stating "Don't put all your eggs in one basket" describes the concept of diversification.

Too much or too little of one type of investment can be detrimental at any time. For example, Artisoft, Inc. produces and sells local area networks (LANS). Artisoft's LANS may be very profitable when that product is in demand. However, if consumers stop buying LANS, Artisoft may become unprofitable and eventually cease to exist. A similar result can happen if competitors take market share away from an undiversified firm selling a product or service that is similar to many other firms. Casualties in the airline industry in recent years provide an example. American West, Eastern, TWA, and Continental airlines filed bankruptcy. Likewise, if an investor's retirement income is dependent on a single financial security, say IBM stock, that person is more likely to find that not enough money exists in the retirement account upon reaching retirement age than if he or she invested in several securities. A prudent person invests in several different assets to diversify risk. The finance terminology is that the person seeks an efficient portfolio.

Comprehension Check

1. Discuss the five guiding principles common to all three fields of finance.
2. Define: maximization of shareholders' wealth, discounted cash flow analysis, compounding, valuation, equilibrium price, operating leverage, financial leverage.

1.3 ELEMENTS COMMON TO THE THREE AREAS OF FINANCE

Common elements are woven throughout the areas of managerial finance, investments, and financial markets helping to integrate the discipline. These elements include: *investment decision rules, financial analysis, organizational form, taxes,* and *politics.* We examine each of these elements in the following sections.

1.3.1 Investment Decision Rules

Investment decision rules specify the desired standards of financial decision making. The most widely accepted investment decision standard is the maximization of wealth. From an investment perspective, the investor seeks to invest in and trade securities that result in the greatest appreciation in long-term value of the portfolio.

From a managerial finance perspective, shareholders are the owners of the firm and the investment rule states that a financial decision that adds to the net wealth position of shareholders is a good decision. An unwise decision is one that knowingly causes shareholders' wealth to deteriorate. If several actions increase shareholders' wealth, the more desirable action is the one that results in greater wealth with equal or less risk. Sales maximization, profit maximization, and firm size maximization, among others, are sometimes used as investment decision standards. These standards are inferior to maximization of shareholders' wealth; generally, they tend to make managers more happy than they do shareholders.

1.3.2 Financial Analysis

Managerial finance relies on economic and quantitative analysis to fulfill the goal of increasing wealth of shareholders. The financial manager must have the analytical skills and insights that reveal ways to reduce costs and increase revenues and thus lead to improved profitability for the company. In the areas of investments and financial markets, financial analysis helps investors by providing guidelines for evaluating the risk versus expected return trade-off.

Financial analysis takes its meaning from the study of the financial interrelationships that exist in a particular problem. You cannot assume that these relationships are constant from problem to problem. For example, common stock issued by BankAmerica Corporation, a financial institution, is more sensitive to interest rate changes than is common stock issued by Cincinnati Milacron Inc., a manufacturer. The reason is that financial institutions have significant investments in debt securities (financial assets) whose values move inversely to interest rates. Manufacturing firms invest heavily in physical, or real, assets such as plant and equipment. Values of investments in physical assets are less affected by changes in interest rates. Ignoring expected changes in interest rates when analyzing stock prices of financial institutions will result in questionable conclusions.

Techniques we use to explore financial interrelationships are the basic mathematical tools of financial analysis. The dominant analytical tools are financial ratio analysis, statistical models to analyze expected return versus risk, and operations research models to determine the acceptability of investments. Imagination and ability are proving the only limits to recently developed techniques for financial analysis.

1.3.3 Organizational Form

Economic organizations are entities through which people interact to reach individual and collective economic goals. The economic system consists of networks of people and organizations linked together. The highest-level organization is the economy as a whole. At the next level are entities more traditionally regarded as organizations: business organizations, labor unions, and government agencies. A key characteristic of an organization at this level is its legal identity. For example, consider the definition of a **business organization** in a broad context. It means the set of contracts between an entity, called the firm (for example, Club Med, Inc.), and its *stakeholders*. **Stakeholders** are those who have an interest in the welfare of the firm, including the firm's creditors, customers, employees, governments, managers, shareholders, and suppliers. Laws and legal remedies help to enforce the contracts between stakeholders.

Three primary forms of business organizations exist: the sole proprietorship, the partnership, and the corporation. Most firms operating in the world are proprietorships. However, most of the dollar value of sales is attributed to corporations like Exxon and The Home Depot. State governments charter corporations to do business. In chartering a corporation, the state grants to it certain rights and privileges, and imposes certain duties and obligations. By demanding that corporations act responsibly and in a legal manner, states attempt, through the chartering process, to bring any corporate abuse under control. A problem arises if one state, Texas for example, decides to impose more stringent duties upon corporations chartered in its state. The corporations could move to a state where the laws are less demanding. Today, most of the major corporations are established in Delaware, a state with the least restrictive chartering laws.

Business organization. An institution that buys material and labor and organizes them to produce and sell goods and services.

Stakeholders. Claimants on cash flows of the firm.

TABLE 1-1

FORMS OF BUSINESS ORGANIZATIONS

	Proprietorship	Partnership	Corporation
Taxation of profits	Individual	Individual	Corporation; individual for dividend receipts
Liability	Unlimited	General partners: unlimited Limited partners: limited to contributions to partnership	Shareholders only liable up to the amount of their ownership investment
Life of the entity	Ceases with proprietor	Terminates when general partner dies or withdraws	Unlimited life; ownership easily transferred in the capital markets
Ownership versus control	Proprietor controls	General partner exercises control	Ownership by shareholders is separate from control by management
Raising capital	Limited to proprietor's personal wealth	Equity contribution generally limited to partners' contributions	Able to issue ownership claims to raise new equity capital

Table 1.1 summarizes distinguishing features of business organizations along the dimensions of taxation, liability of the owners, survivability of the business form, control of business decisions, and ability to raise capital.

The issue of ownership versus control shown in Table 1.1 is an important topic in finance. When ownership and control in the corporation are separate, a *principal-agent problem* exists. The important issue centers on whether corporate managers (**agents**) have the proper incentives for them to act in the interests of stakeholders (**principals**). The **principal-agent problem** assumes that managers, if left alone, will operate in their own self-interest, not in the interest of the stakeholders. Critics make the following claims:

- Managers invest a firm's earnings in low-value projects to expand their empires when the funds would be better distributed to the shareholders to invest for themselves.
- Managers supposedly hang on to badly performing operations when new managers could run them more profitably.
- Managers pay themselves exorbitantly and lavish expensive perquisites upon themselves.
- Managers resist attempts to force more profitable operations, especially by resisting takeovers that threaten their jobs.

All these alleged misdeeds serve the interests of the managers themselves, not the interests of the firm's owners. Agents' actions may be detrimental to the wealth of principals. For example, consider the actions of senior management of Pinnacle West Capital Corporation, a firm whose securities trade on the New York Stock Exchange.

Agent. A person who performs activities for another person, called a principal. Managers are agents of the firm.

Principal. An individual who establishes a compensation scheme to motivate an agent to choose activities advantageous to the principal. Shareholders are principals of the firm.

Principal-agent problem. The possibility that an agent will act in her or his own self-interest to the detriment of the principal for whom she or he is acting.

We have excerpted the following passage from pages 11 and 12 of the company's *Notice and Proxy Statement*, dated April 17, 1992:

> Effective January 1, 1992 the Company established a supplemental executive benefit plan to provide certain benefits to directors and officers of the Company and its subsidiaries upon the occurrence of certain events, which generally include **bankruptcy,** . . .

Management is protecting its own future even if its actions result in bankruptcy of the firm! Ask yourself: If I am a shareholder, a supplier, a creditor, or an employee, would I feel protected if Pinnacle West became bankrupt? As a shareholder your stock would lose much of its value, as a supplier or creditor you would likely not receive full value on your claims, and as an employee you could lose your job. The need for a sense of trust is an integral part of the business relationship. Ethical decisions (or unethical ones) affect the world of finance as much as they do any aspect of business. Hence, an awareness of the principal-agent problem should improve our study of finance.

1.3.4 Taxes

Tax rules legislated by governments affect the rates of return investments earn both before and after any taxes. Before-tax rates of return differ because domestic and foreign federal, state, and local taxing authorities are not consistent in their application of taxes. They tax returns to different types of investments differently. Different jurisdictions tax similar investments differently. We will also find that returns to similar investments within the same jurisdiction are taxed differently depending upon the organizational form; corporations are taxed differently than partnerships. Finally, returns to similar investments located in the same jurisdiction and owned by the same type of organization receive differential tax treatment if the operating histories of the organizations differ.

As an example of the problem managers face, consider the Italian federal corporate tax system. Italian tax authorities assume that no corporation operating in Italy would submit a tax return showing its true profits. The presumption is that firms understate actual profits 30 to 70 percent. They are essentially correct. Thus, about six months after the deadline for filing tax returns, the tax authorities issue an "invitation to discuss" the tax return to each corporation. At the meeting, the Italian revenue authorities state the amount of corporate income tax which it believes is due. The authorities and the corporation then proceed through several rounds of bargaining until they reach a settlement.

The area of taxes is a highly specialized topic and subjected to frequent changes by governmental attempts to raise revenues to fund government programs or stimulate the economy. Later chapters will discuss taxes on an "as-needed" basis, particularly when we examine investment and financing decisions.

1.3.5 Politics

Most discussions about finance leave politics to the politicians. However, it can be said that politics is an inseparable facet of many financial decisions. Historically, times of business depression and social unrest have periodically given rise to attacks upon "big corporations" by those who hope to gain public support and political office. Yet surprisingly little has been done to inhibit the use of the corporate form of business. Many corporations maintain offices in a country's capital city not only to influence legislation, but also to help management predict changes in government policy.

Financial markets, via the buying and selling actions of investors, are constantly responding to either real or anticipated changes in legislation. The attitudes of government can seriously affect certain business segments. For instance:

- Expectations of decreased demand for defense contributed to General Dynamics Corporation, Northrop Corporation, and other American firms cutting back on making investment decisions in their defense businesses.
- The Tax Reform Act of 1986 reversed some incentives given to real estate investors a few years earlier. The new act greatly reduced the attractiveness of investing in real estate.

Multinational firm. A business with investments and operating facilities in more than one country.

Politics and economic policy are more complex when we consider international financial markets. Actions of many governments become part of the decision-making process. Integrating political considerations into managerial finance are particularly appropriate in **multinational firms,** such as Pepsico, Inc., Motorola, Inc., and Caterpillar, Inc., which build facilities in both domestic and foreign markets. The development of multinational firms is partially a response to world conditions that do not allow free movement of labor, materials, goods, and services between countries. The reason for many of the barriers is understandable from a political perspective. For instance, international trade agreements between countries exist because of import restrictions and other politically motivated arguments.

Comprehension Check

1. Discuss the five common elements integrating managerial finance, investments, and financial markets.
2. Discuss the advantage of the corporate form of business organization. What are the drawbacks?
3. What is the principal-agent problem?
4. Why are taxes an important issue?
5. Why is it necessary to consider politics and economic policy in financial decisions?

1.4 RELATIONSHIP OF FINANCE TO OTHER DISCIPLINES

Finance incorporates information from the disciplines of economics, management, accounting, and quantitative methods. Figure 1.3 depicts the relationships. Economics provides the underlying theory for financial decision making, whereas accounting provides a form for much of the data used to analyze financial decisions through various quantitative techniques. The field of management provides an understanding of organizational psychology that enhances decision making.

1.4.1 Economics

Finance is said to represent applied microeconomics. For example, the rule a financial manager uses to decide to accept or reject a proposed project or investment is essentially the same as the economist's *marginal revenue versus marginal cost rule.* The financial decision rule says: Accept all projects whose expected rates of return are greater than the

FIGURE 1.3

RELATIONSHIP OF FINANCE WITH OTHER DISCIPLINES

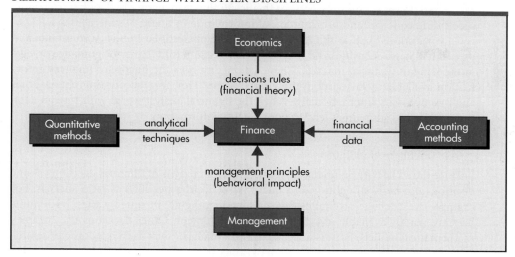

opportunity cost of capital; or simply, accept projects whose marginal revenues exceed marginal costs.

Another interplay between economics and finance has to do with the economic concept of an *efficient market,* which we explore more fully in Chapter 10. The basis for modern financial theory is a belief in efficient financial markets, which is adapted from the economist's concept of perfect competition. As stated earlier, an efficient financial market is one in which investors cannot consistently earn excess returns because essentially everyone has access to the same information, which is reflected in security prices.

1.4.2 Management

In all areas of finance, decisions are unmistakably affected by behavioral issues, both on the parts of individuals and as a consequence of organizational form. A key element of managerial finance is *decision making,* and decisions are made by *people who are managers.* Financial managers oversee the efficient use of resources within the firm. A manager's understanding of organizational psychology can be an important factor in motivating employees to produce quality products and improving the firm's performance.

From an investor's perspective, knowledge of the psychology of behavior applied to an aggregation of investors can influence decisions about buying and selling securities. This knowledge may entail anything from a "sense" or "feel" some investors might have to large-scale predictions about behavior. For example, many professional investors take the position that when most investors see "good times" ahead, it is time to sell securities. The idea is that the euphoria about the financial market is likely wrong and securities soon may decline significantly in value.

1.4.3 Accounting

Good accounting data are necessary for both the financial manager and the investor to make informed financial decisions. Financial statements accompanied by complete notes explaining the accounting rules followed allow a better understanding of how management derived items like sales, profits, and assets. However, comparison of accounting information from one firm to another can often be difficult because generally accepted accounting principles (known as *GAAP* and pronounced *gap*) allow alternative methods for management to choose from to record transactions. We briefly touch back to the accounting basis of finance in the next chapter by looking over some accounting concepts and presentation of information in financial statements.

Institutions such as the American Institute of Certified Public Accountants and the United States Securities and Exchange Commission (SEC) provide guidance or legal monitoring of financial markets. These actions improve the quality of financial information available to investors in the United States. However, accounting philosophies and practices vary internationally. When the financial analyst works with foreign data, these variations sometimes lead to poor-quality information.

1.4.4 Quantitative Methods

Finance draws heavily on quantitative methods for analysis of financial decisions. Some decisions use fairly straightforward quantitative approaches such as ratio analysis. For example, we calculate profitability of sales by dividing net income by sales. Both numbers are readily available in a firm's income statement. Other decisions use complex mathematical models. For instance, a portfolio manager may use a quadratic programming model to decide on the allocation of funds among several securities to be included in a portfolio. In another case, a financial analyst for a manufacturing firm may use a linear programming model to recommend which of several projects to select, given future cash flows and a limited amount of money to invest.

 Comprehension Check

1. How does the field of finance relate to economics, management, accounting, and quantitative methods?

 ## 1.5 ETHICS AND FINANCE

A theoretical discussion of finance implicitly assumes that participants conduct activities and relationships in an ethical manner. Unfortunately, this is not always the case. In 1980, *Fortune* magazine surveyed 1,043 large companies.[5] A total of 117 of the corporations satisfied *Fortune's* definition of law violation—conviction on criminal charges or consent decrees for bribery, criminal fraud, illegal political contributions, tax evasion, and criminal antitrust.

In some cases, it is easy to understand why corporate managers may act unethically. Consider a company on the brink of bankruptcy. Can the president be expected to reject an ethically objectionable but potentially lucrative last-minute gamble to save the company on the grounds that, because it is unethical, it will be unprofitable in the long run? The president may reason that unless the gamble is taken, there will be no long run.

Or consider the many activities of securities brokers. They execute transactions in financial markets for clients, examine the securities of various companies as possible investments, and recommend securities to individual clients. Financial institutions with brokerage offices may also be in the business of investment banking. **Investment bankers** help companies sell their financial securities to investors. As brokers try to per-

Investment banker. A financial organization that specializes in selling newly issued securities. Investment bankers also advise clients on financial matters, negotiate mergers and takeovers, and sell previously issued securities.

[5]"How Lawless Are Big Companies?" *Fortune,* December 1, 1980, p. 57.

form all these functions, especially the provision of financial advice, there is room for serious questions of professional ethics. One legitimate ethics question involves the objectivity of research about a public company. Consider what can happen when an investment banking division of a large financial institution such Merrill Lynch & Company takes a firm public in an initial public offering of stock (called an IPO) and then passes its research on to the brokers. The investment banking division receives a large fee for taking the firm public. The brokers, in turn, try to convince investors to buy the public company's securities. Brokerages are typically reluctant to issue sell recommendations about stocks. What does this imply about the investment banking-brokerage relationship?

Another question about ethics in securities markets addresses the distinction between investments, speculation, and gambling.[6] Is the only distinction the degree of risk involved in a particular transaction? Stock exchange officials react in horror to the commonly voiced opinion that Wall Street is "the biggest casino in the world." Yet, some say, the grounds for distinction are not clear. There are relatively safe bets available to gamblers and extremely risky propositions in securities markets, such as the new issues of a young firm.

Of the many ethical issues surrounding financial markets, the most intriguing and publicized in recent years is *insider trading*. The common definition of **insider trading** is trading in which someone buys or sells securities using information that is not publicly available to all investors. Thus, instead of the financial markets being efficient in the sense that all investors have equal access to information, a significant market imperfection exists. *Asymmetric information* exists; information is known only to certain people. The presence of asymmetric information inhibits the accurate valuation of assets.

Insider trading is extremely difficult to define legally, however. Securities and Exchange Commission (SEC) officials have frequently refused to define the term. Former SEC Commissioner Irving Pollock said at a Congressional hearing: "I see it in the same way the Supreme Court Justice Stewart saw pornography. You can't define insider trading, but you know it when you see it."[7]

Another very contentious issue is the responsibility that management has to shareholders of the company; this is the principal-agent problem that we discussed earlier. Managers have been known to use many tactics to protect their positions, including issuance of voting stock to friendly shareholders, the nomination of a slate of directors that is friendly to management, and the use of *golden parachutes,* or employment contracts that provide large severance pay if senior managers lose their jobs because of an unfriendly takeover by another firm. For instance, the chief executive officer of Pinnacle West Capital Corporation has a severance agreement calling for severance benefits of about three times his average annual compensation over the preceding five years if there is change of control of the company.

> **Insider trading.** Process of trading in a company's stock to profit from information that is not available to the public.

Comprehension Check

1. Outline the ethical issues in the three areas of finance introduced in this chapter.

2. Why are ethical considerations important for those involved in finance?

---

[6]See the interview with Gary Bielfeldt in the book by Jack D. Schwager, *Market Wizards: Interviews with Top Traders* (New York: NYIF Corporation, 1989), p. 150.

[7]"Defining Insider Trading," *Dun's Business Month* (February 1984), p. 11

1.6 THE NEXT STEP: CHECKING BACK TO ACCOUNTING AND ECONOMICS

Like most first chapters, this one provides a sketchy outline of topics to be examined in later chapters. We've defined finance as consisting of different areas tied together by several guiding principles. These principles will continue to surface throughout the text as we explain the various topics within an integrated study of finance.

The next two chapters will help you to integrate your knowledge of accounting and economics with finance. Chapter 2 reviews differences between accounting profit, economic profit, and cash flows. The chapter also examines the presentation of accounting information. Chapter 3 augments our definition of finance, presented in the introduction to this chapter, by emphasizing the importance of a smoothly operating financial system and the mechanism of interest rates within the system, for maximizing wealth. You've been exposed to many of Chapter 3's concepts in introductory economics. Hopefully, a review of these concepts will allow you to better understand the importance of finance and how it influences decisions related to marketing, production, human resources management, investments, and many other aspects of the business world.

SUMMARY ▼▼▼▼▼▼▼▼▼▼▼

TRADITIONAL FINANCE AREAS

- The traditional finance areas are managerial finance, investments, and financial markets.
- Managerial finance addresses what investments to make, how these investments should be financed, and how daily financial activities should be managed.
- Investments relate to activities and decision rules about selecting, managing, and trading assets, such as stocks and bonds. The underlying theory is that assets trade in perfect markets so that investors earn profits consistent with their risk exposure.
- Financial markets—money and capital markets—are the channels which direct funds to their most profitable use. These markets determine the appropriate risk-adjusted rate to evaluate investments.

GUIDING PRINCIPLES OF FINANCE

- Five guiding principles integrate the three areas of finance:
  1. Maximization of wealth
  2. Time value of money
  3. Expected return versus risk trade-off
  4. Leverage
  5. Diversification
- Maximization of wealth principle provides the necessary focus for evaluating decisions.
- The principles of time value of money and expected return versus risk trade-off are critical for determining value and maximizing wealth.

- Leverage allows output or wealth to expand for a fixed input.
- The principle of diversification is investing in more than one asset to reduce risk.

ELEMENTS COMMON TO THE THREE AREAS OF FINANCE

- The subject of finance uses the common elements of financial analysis, investment decision rules, organizational form, taxes, and politics.
- Finance, as a quantitative subject, relies on insightful analysis to make wealth-maximization decisions.
- Organizational form influences these decisions. Proprietors, as owners, are responsible for creating their own wealth. At the other extreme, nonowner managers' decisions affect the wealth of the stakeholders of the business, including the shareholders, who are the real owners of the corporation. In this latter case, principal-agent problems can arise.
- Investors and managers make decisions based on both taxes and legal concerns.

RELATIONSHIP OF FINANCE TO OTHER DISCIPLINES

- The discipline of finance relies on economics, accounting, quantitative methods, and management.
- Economics provides theoretical foundations for assessing wealth-creating decisions.
- Accounting provides much of the data necessary to evaluate decisions.
- Quantitative methods offer several techniques for analyzing the data.
- The area of management provides skills for understanding people, as they behave in organizations, who ultimately carry out the wealth-creating decisions.

ETHICS AND FINANCE

- The role of ethics in finance is significant in several areas. Investment in securities is a major area of concern, and managers also can make decisions that are ethically objectionable.
- Insider stock trading clearly is unethical. There are several gray areas a student of finance must evaluate as well, such as corporate decisions that injure local economies in the interest of short-term profit and unrealistically high executive compensation or severance packages.

FURTHER READING ▼▼▼▼▼▼▼▼▼▼▼

Donaldson, Gordon, *Managing Corporate Wealth: The Operation of a Comprehensive Financial Goals System,* New York: Praeger Publishers, 1984. This book furnishes an interesting real-world view of how senior managers think about their business and its financial challenges.

Mokhiber, Russell, *Corporate Crime and Violence: Big Business and the Abuse of the Public Trust,* San Francisco: Sierra Club Books, 1989. The book examines several case histories of companies valuing short-term economic profits above human lives, community safety, or long-term health of the environment.

Rappaport, Alfred, *Creating Shareholder Value: The New Standard for Business Performance,* New York: The Free Press, 1986. This book provides managers with a practical standard for measuring their efforts in strategic planning, competitiveness, asset control, and other areas.

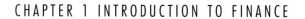

Scholes, Myron S., and Mark A. Wolfson, *Taxes and Business Strategy: A Planning Approach,* Englewood Cliffs, NJ: Prentice Hall, 1992. The book renders a bridge between tax theory and practice.

Stewart, James B., *Den of Thieves,* New York: Simon & Schuster, 1991. This book reports in detail the full story of insider trading that nearly destroyed Wall Street.

PROBLEM	▼▼▼▼▼▼▼▼▼▼▼

LIBRARY ASSIGNMENT

1-1. Look over the business news for the next month to see what questionable ethical practices happen. Keep a brief journal of the instances and examine their financial implications.

Video Case 1

General Motors Takes A Sharp Turn

from *Business World,* November 8, 1992

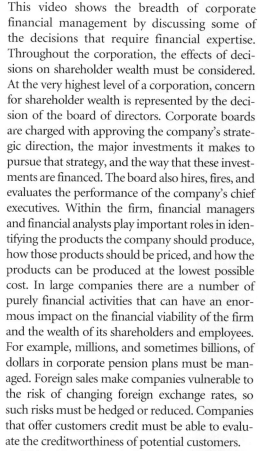

This video shows the breadth of corporate financial management by discussing some of the decisions that require financial expertise. Throughout the corporation, the effects of decisions on shareholder wealth must be considered. At the very highest level of a corporation, concern for shareholder wealth is represented by the decision of the board of directors. Corporate boards are charged with approving the company's strategic direction, the major investments it makes to pursue that strategy, and the way that these investments are financed. The board also hires, fires, and evaluates the performance of the company's chief executives. Within the firm, financial managers and financial analysts play important roles in identifying the products the company should produce, how those products should be priced, and how the products can be produced at the lowest possible cost. In large companies there are a number of purely financial activities that can have an enormous impact on the financial viability of the firm and the wealth of its shareholders and employees. For example, millions, and sometimes billions, of dollars in corporate pension plans must be managed. Foreign sales make companies vulnerable to the risk of changing foreign exchange rates, so such risks must be hedged or reduced. Companies that offer customers credit must be able to evaluate the creditworthiness of potential customers.

This video case touches on many of these aspects of corporate finance. Because of several years of poor performance, the board felt compelled to find a new management team to head General Motors. Over the past several years the board approved a diversification strategy that included buying EDS, Ross Perot's company, and Hughes Aircraft. This diversification strategy, and the profits these subsidiaries generate, helped GM weather poor years in its core business, the auto industry. The video also mentions the $10 billion in cash that GM holds. This cash must be invested, which requires dozens of investment managers.

Recently GM issued $2.2 billion of new stock, then had to reduce the dividend it pays to shareholders. These decisions—to raise more capital and how capital is to be distributed to securityholders—are examples of corporate financial decisions. In making these decisions, the GM board or GM financial managers must decide the amount, timing, and attributes of the stock issue, and how it will affect current shareholders. A dividend cut usually implies bad news to investors—it signals that something is wrong—so the decision to cut dividends is not made lightly.

Possibly the most important decision made at most companies involves choosing the products to produce. As the video says, in the auto industry poor product design takes a toll on workers, shareholders, and in this case, the CEO. Careful financial analysis of new-product introductions, by combining information from marketing research and manufacturing, must be completed to avoid new-product disasters. As you can see, many corporate decisions have financial aspects, so an understanding of finance will help you to compete successfully in today's corporate world.

Study Questions

1. In corporations, the board of directors hires, fires, and determines the pay of CEO, but the CEO often selects board members (who, by the way, are very well paid). Do you see any problems with the design of this oversight mechanism? Why don't shareholders participate more actively in monitoring the managers of corporations?

2. The choosing of new products or modifying the features of existing products seems like a marketing function—ask potential customers what they want and make it. Where does financial analysis enter into such new-product decisions?

CHAPTER 2

Review of Financial Statements

Every company has a history—good, bad, or neutral—that is important to managers and potential investors, bankers, or creditors. The firm's history is its track record of accomplishments and the measure of its financial virtue. From a financial perspective, we measure this history by the company's principal financial statements—the balance sheet, the income statement, and the statement of cash flows. These statements evolved from the accrual accounting process, following accepted principles, procedures, and standards of the accounting profession. Accounting is an important part of the language of finance. We must understand this language to analyze the financial condition and profitability of the firm. The difference is that an understanding of the information conveyed by accounting statements is based predominantly in the past by what already has happened, while financial decisions are made in the present with a view to the future.

In our discussion we assume you have a working knowledge of elementary accounting. Our purpose in this chapter is not to review basic elements of accounting but to provide a slightly different view of accounting, that of chief financial officers, creditors, or investors. They are the principal users of accounting data and the principal decision makers who influence the future of the firm. As part of this review, we look at the financial information presented by companies in the document called the *annual report*. We use Kellogg Company as a model. Our discussion provides some indication of what information the annual report reveals, as well as what it does *not* reveal. When you have completed this chapter, you should understand:

- The difference between income and funds.
- How book value differs from economic and market values.
- The various parts of the firm's annual report and what each reveals.
- How management can compromise the integrity of the financial statements to show improved accounting income.

2.1 THE ACCOUNTING VERSUS FINANCE PERSPECTIVE

From a financial perspective, the firm is a unit through which **funds** (financial resources) flow in and flow out. A major concern of the company's financial officer is to manage these flows in order to increase the long-run market value of the company. In the short run, management tries to balance the inflows and outflows of funds so that the company is able to meet demands for cash by creditors, as well as satisfy investment needs within the company.

When a firm invests funds, it expects to recover those funds plus increase its income by selling products or services. The accountant records and classifies financial transactions of the firm and prepares reports that summarize those transactions and interpret their effects on the firm's financial position.

The expression *income versus funds* explains a significant difference between the accounting and financial points of view of financial data. A major objective of accounting is the development and application of a consistent, logical procedure for estimating income in a given time period. Think of **income** as the net addition to the accounting value of the company as a result of its operations for a given period after deducting the costs of material, labor, and overhead required for operations from revenues. If we measure income from the beginning of the firm's life until the day the company goes out of business, it is not hard to determine income exactly. In this case, when the company ceases operations its debts would be paid off. Any value remaining in excess of the amount that the owners committed to the business is the true income for the period, assuming that no other (nonwage) payments, such as **cash dividends,** had been made to the owners.

Two problems arise with this picture. First, most companies do not begin with planning to go out of business at some specific future date! Companies are initiated with the hope of operating forever. And, second, financial data must be current to be useful. Yet it is impossible to measure income precisely over any period less than the life of the company. It is absurd to suppose that managers, investors, and creditors can wait until the firm ceases operations to know whether it operated at a profit or at a loss. For financial data to be useful, then, management must make *estimates* of income over a period shorter than the life of the business. This period can be annually, quarterly, monthly, or less, depending on the needs of management.

Estimation of income requires management to make assumptions about what the future will hold. These assumptions may or may not prove to be true. The amount of revenues and costs that can properly be assigned to a given period are a matter of judgment. Much of accounting's technical logic is based on rules for assigning revenues and costs to arbitrary accounting periods. The accountant's formal definition of income is "the amount by which realized . . . revenue for a period exceeds the historical cost . . . of the assets used up to obtain the revenue."[1] This concept of income allows management to make periodic estimates of the company's results of operations. But there is no denying that the figure arrived at is still an estimate:

> The preparation of statements within a business continuity . . . normally involves both estimates and exercises of judgment. Such statements must be recognized as no more than tentative reports or "test readings," since the full story is yet to be told and the future may modify the inferences made in the periodic analyses.[2]

Funds. Any means of payment.

Income. Revenues for the period minus the costs for the period.

Cash dividend. Cash payment from the firm to its shareholders.

---

[1]Robert K. Jaedicke and Robert T. Sprouse, *Accounting Flows: Income, Funds and Cash,* Prentice-Hall Foundations of Finance Series (Englewood Cliffs, NJ: Prentice-Hall, Inc., 1965), p. 1.

[2]Wilbert E. Karrenbock and Harry Simons, *Intermediate Accounting,* 3rd ed. (Cincinnati, OH: South-Western Publishing Company, 1958), p. 6.

Estimating income leads to another accounting problem: the distinction between return *of* investment and return *on* investment. Accountants must distinguish between the part of revenue which represents a recapture of amounts spent in the process of generating the revenue (*return of investment*) and amounts that may be validly considered to be a surplus over the amounts spent (income, or *return on investment*). By contrast, the financial manager and creditor are both interested in *funds,* regardless of whether or not the resources represent income.

Funds, as distinct from income, may be derived from the firm's operations, from credit advanced by suppliers, from monies received from lenders, from new investment by owners, or from the sale of assets. A central duty of the financial manager is to control and manipulate the flow of funds to ensure that the firm always will have sufficient funds on hand to meet demands for payment. These demands may originate externally, from creditors, or from within the company to take advantage of favorable investment opportunities. The point is that the *financial manager does not pay creditors with income.* Bills must be paid with funds. A high level of income does not guarantee that adequate funds will be available to meet these demands for payment.

A central theme of this book is that management's decisions are directed toward increasing the value of the firm. However, we must carefully define what value means. Accounting often refers to *book value of assets.* This term has little meaning in finance. Instead, finance uses *economic value* and *market value.* Let's define these terms.

Book value of assets represents the original or historical cost, less depreciation on the fixed assets of the firm, plus the book value of current assets, such as receivables and inventories. Book value may bear no recognizable relationship to either economic value or market value. The recorded assets of the firm may have increased in terms of both economic and market value, as is often the case with land, or they may have become obsolete and have little economic or market value despite the fact that the assets appear on the firm's financial statements.

Economic value refers to the fundamental, going-concern value of the firm. To calculate economic value, we discount the anticipated stream of cash benefits at an interest rate that reflects the uncertainty associated with the expected cash benefits. This process is called **capitalizing cash flows.** It is possible for the economic value of the firm to differ from the sum of the book values of the individual component assets. If economic value exceeds book value, it is because the momentum of the firm possesses value apart from the accounting value of the assets used in the business. For example, the economic value of Wal-Mart Stores Limited is greater than the book value of its inventories and buildings because of the excellent service and value customers feel they receive.

Market value is the price the firm's assets will bring on the market. This definition has a certain intuitive appeal. It is direct and does not involve any estimates. In addition, it includes the value of the organization's personnel, competitive strategies, and reputation, plus the value of the assets themselves. Theoretically, in a market where all participants have the same information and expectations, market value equals economic value. But theory does not always hold, and economic and market values can and do diverge from each other.

Book values fail to satisfy two requirements of economic or market value: a future cash flow stream generated by the assets and the opportunity cost of funds (the interest rate) used to capitalize cash flows. As we know from economics, the opportunity cost implies that management could use the funds elsewhere to earn income. By not investing elsewhere, management sacrifices the opportunity to earn income from these investments. Thus, both economic and market values of an asset reflect the future cash stream that the asset is expected to produce. Book values simply reflect the past. Because

Book value of assets. Historical value of the assets adjusted for depreciation of fixed assets and other asset write-downs.

Economic value of assets. The expected value of an asset derived by capitalizing future cash flows at an appropriate interest rate. See *capitalizing cash flows.*

Capitalizing cash flows. The process of dividing future cash flow amounts by an interest rate representing the minimum return the cash flows should earn; for example, if future cash flow is $10 per year in perpetuity and the interest rate is 4 percent, the cash flows have a capitalized (economic) value of $10 ÷ 0.04 = $25. Chapter 4 discusses this and other types of calculations to capitalize cash flows.

Market value of assets. The value exchanged in an arm's-length transaction between a willing buyer and a willing seller.

opportunities only exist in the future, not in the past, book values are not very meaningful in decision making. Book values only tell us where the firm has been. They represent decisions made in the past.

With this brief background of some of the different perspectives between accounting and finance, the remainder of the chapter consists of a discussion of the financial information released by public firms in their annual reports.

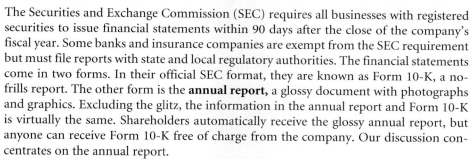

Comprehension Check

1. What is the concern from a finance perspective about the difference between income and funds?
2. Describe the distinction between return of investment and return on investment.
3. How does book value differ from economic value and market value?
4. What is the difference between economic value and market value?

2.2 AN OVERVIEW OF THE ANNUAL REPORT

The Securities and Exchange Commission (SEC) requires all businesses with registered securities to issue financial statements within 90 days after the close of the company's fiscal year. Some banks and insurance companies are exempt from the SEC requirement but must file reports with state and local regulatory authorities. The financial statements come in two forms. In their official SEC format, they are known as Form 10-K, a no-frills report. The other form is the **annual report,** a glossy document with photographs and graphics. Excluding the glitz, the information in the annual report and Form 10-K is virtually the same. Shareholders automatically receive the glossy annual report, but anyone can receive Form 10-K free of charge from the company. Our discussion concentrates on the annual report.

The annual report is a company's public face; its presentation is geared to enhance the corporate image. Many people believe the independent certified public accountant, commonly called the CPA, is responsible for the annual report. Not true. The annual report is fashioned by accountants and lawyers, as well as marketers and executives, and costing major companies as much as $250,000 to $750,000 to publish. Management is ultimately responsible for writing and issuing the annual report. Thus, we must "read between the lines" when reviewing the document.

The SEC requires management to divulge certain information. However, management may write the story to tone down any unfavorable news. For this reason, some professional security analysts are extremely critical of annual reports. They claim that annual reports are too self-serving and not worth reading. No doubt there is some truth to that assertion. However, keeping that bias in mind, the annual report can serve as an important primary source of information to actual or potential creditors and investors. It can be an important source of information about companies that do not have a large following of researchers, brokers, analysts, and financial publications. The annual report gives a quick overview of the company and what it is gearing up to accomplish in the next year. Since the annual report is as close as most investors will ever get to the company's facilities, the report is a window to the firm's operations.

Included in the annual report are key data with which to analyze a company, appearing in distinct sections:

Annual report. The formal financial statement issued yearly by a corporation. The annual report shows assets, liabilities, income, and how the company stood at the close of the business year. It usually includes other information of interest to shareholders as well.

- Financial highlights
- Message to shareholders
- Business overview
- Financial information
- Financial statements
- Notes to financial statements
- Report of independent public accountant
- Other information

 The preceding listing represents the order in which this information is presented in most companies' annual reports. We use excerpts from the 1991 annual report of Kellogg Company to show how management presents each part of the report. Although the Kellogg annual report is relatively straightforward, Marcia Berss warns in the nearby Financial Reality reading that investors need considerable creativity to understand many foreign firm's financial reports.

Financial Reality

MAPPING THE GLOBAL WILDERNESS

Investors should proceed with care as they read the financial reports of foreign corporations. Reporting requirements vary substantially from country to country and most do not satisfy disclosure standards required of U.S. corporations.

Two things to remember about investing abroad: Information about foreign equities is tough to come by, and when you do get financial results, they probably won't be up to U.S. disclosure standards. No big deal, says Robert Henry, international tax partner at Coopers & Lybrand, the Big Eight accounting firm. Henry believes foreign investing novices need not get in a sweat trying to understand French inventory valuation or Korean depreciation principles. "The big leap to make is not the different accounting, it's the different cultural milieu," he says. He means understanding that German companies are more highly leveraged than U.S. companies because of their close relationship to their banks, or realizing that Japanese balance sheets are presented in a different format.

That aside, Henry warns U.S. investors of two fundamental differences in overseas accounting. First, many foreign countries do not require consolidated statements. Second, many foreign outfits with less than 50 percent stakes in other companies don't include these in their own accounts. They will stash a 40 percent holding in a nonconsolidated subsidiary. Still, Henry notes that more foreign companies are moving into line with international accounting standards, which are based on the U.S. generally accepted accounting principles. Here, the Dutch, British, and Japanese are leaders, and the Italians and French are laggards.

Understanding the numbers is one thing; getting them is something else. The big portfolio managers use such computer databases as Dun & Bradstreet's Datastream, which costs $15,000 a year for the financial results of some 20,000 worldwide companies.

Of course, you can turn to your broker for information on foreign stocks. Many U.S. brokerage houses are adding security analysts to cover foreign stocks.

Adapted from Marcia Berss, "Mapping the Global Wilderness," *FORBES*, July 29, 1985, p. 153.
Reprinted by permission of *FORBES* magazine ©, FORBES, Inc., 1985.

2.2.1 Financial Highlights

The *highlights* greet us at the beginning of the annual report. Often including charts and other graphics, they present basic information in a clear, comparative way. Usually, we should expect to find the company's total sales and net income, among other items, shown for the past two or three years. Upward trends in any graphs are usually positive and downward trends are usually negative. But it is important to understand that the company and its public relations advisors can include here whatever information they feel will create the desired impression on the reader. Hence, we can expect to find highlights that add up to a positive impression—statistics of which the company is the most proud, as Figure 2.1 shows for Kellogg.

2.2.2 Message to Shareholders

The *message to shareholders* is a letter from the chairperson of the company. It purports to be a serious comment on the year's results and their financial impact, a report that puts into perspective the major developments affecting shareholders, a statement of management's position on relevant social issues, and an expression of management's plans for the company's future. Other information included frequently in the message is an overview or summary of specific operations, new products, acquisitions or divestitures, and management changes. The information is often upbeat and positive, brimming with confidence, as is the report issued by Chairman Arnold G. Langbo of Kellogg (see Figure 2.2).

An impressive letter is one that compares past predictions with actual results and explains in a candid way the successes as well as the disappointments. Beware of the chairperson who never mentions any problems or areas of concern. If there were failures, there should be logical explanations and not clichés with double meanings. For example:

- The message says, "The year was difficult and challenging." The message likely means: Sales and profits were off, but expenses were up.
- The message says, "Management has taken steps to strengthen market share." The message likely means: We're underselling our competitors to drive them out of the market.
- The message says, "Management worked diligently to preserve a strong financial position." The message likely means: We barely broke even but were able to avoid new debts.

Much of the meaning of the message to shareholders is between the lines. Management is not always right in its decisions, but in financial matters, frankness is the investor's base for confidence.

2.2.3 Business Overview

The *business overview* section of the annual report consists of pictures and prose and often occupies the bulk of the pages of the annual report. Frequently slick, oriented toward public relations, and designed to impress a corporation's various publics, the overview can nonetheless be a valuable source of information about the company's products, services, facilities, and future direction. There are usually little, if any, meaningful data on the company's financial condition. However, in Figure 2.3 we see in the last sentence that Kellogg's inventory control and customer service programs have been

FIGURE 2.1
FINANCIAL HIGHLIGHTS OF KELLOGG'S ANNUAL REPORT

Financial Highlights

(dollar amounts in millions, except per share data)	**1991**	**Change**	1990	Change	1989	Change
Net sales	**$5,786.6**	**+12%**	$5,181.4	+11%	$4,651.7	+ 7%
Net earnings	**606.0**	**+21%**	502.8	+ 7%	470.2	− 2%
Earnings per share	**2.51**	**+21%**	2.08	+ 8%	1.93	− 1%
Dividends per share	**1.075**	**+12%**	.96	+12%	.86	+13%
Cash provided by operations	**934.4**	**+14%**	819.2	+54%	533.5	+ 8%
Capital expenditures	**333.5**	**+ 4%**	320.5	−37%	508.7	− 5%
Return on average equity	**30%**		28%		30%	
Debt to total capital	**18%**		26%		34%	
Average shares (millions) outstanding	**241.2**		241.6		244.2	

Share and per share amounts have been restated to reflect the two-for-one stock split, effective December 4, 1991.

Net earnings for 1989 include $48.1 million ($.20 per share) resulting from the adoption of Statement of Financial Accounting Standards No. 96, "Accounting for Income Taxes," as of January 1, 1989.

Annual Report 1991

Kellogg Company, headquartered in Battle Creek, Michigan, is the world's leading producer of ready-to-eat cereal products. The Company also manufactures frozen pies and waffles, toaster pastries, cereal bars, and other convenience foods.

Founded in 1906, Kellogg Company has a heritage of excellence and a reputation for products that contribute to a healthy diet. Kellogg products are manufactured in 17 countries and distributed in more than 150 countries.

Source: 1991 Annual Report of Kellogg Company. ®, ™ Kellogg Company. © 1992 Kellogg Company. Used by permission.

FIGURE 2.2

KELLOGG'S MESSAGE TO SHAREHOLDERS

TO OUR SHAREHOLDERS

Your Company achieved record results in 1991 and prepared globally to take advantage of unprecedented opportunities for long-term growth. Sales increased for the 47th consecutive year, earnings were up for the 39th time in 40 years, and dividends were raised for the 35th straight year. The per-share value of Kellogg stock increased significantly during 1991 and the stock split two-for-one, effective December 4. In response to the Company's continued financial strength and growth prospects, the Board of Directors authorized management to purchase up to $150 million in shares of Kellogg stock during 1992.

Worldwide consumption of ready-to-eat cereal now exceeds 5 billion pounds per year, with Kellogg Company commanding a 44 percent share of the market. Consumption is growing steadily due to ever-increasing recognition by consumers of the nutritional value, good taste, and convenience of this unique category of products. Further enhancing this growth potential are favorable political and economic developments in high-potential markets around the globe.

More than 85 years of investment in our ready-to-eat cereal business has yielded a global manufacturing, sales, marketing, and distribution infrastructure that is poised to meet growing competition and provides a solid platform for future growth. Our greatest growth potential is in new and developing markets in Europe, Asia, and Latin America. However, considerable potential still exists in more developed markets such as the United States, Canada, the United Kingdom, and Australia.

To best position Kellogg Company for the future, our global operations were restructured, effective January 1, 1992, into four operating divisions, each headed by an area director who reports directly to the chairman. The four divisions and their directors are Kellogg North America – Gary E. Costley; Kellogg Europe – Thomas A. Knowlton; Kellogg Australasia – Donald G. Fritz; and Kellogg Latin America – William A. Camstra. Mr. Knowlton, Mr. Fritz, and Mr. Camstra were promoted to executive vice president of Kellogg Company, a position already held by Dr. Costley. The pages that follow describe the performance and growth potential of each division.

2

Source: 1991 Annual Report of Kellogg Company. ®, ™ Kellogg Company. © 1992 Kellogg Company. Used by permission.

FIGURE 2.3

A BUSINESS OVERVIEW OF KELLOGG

NORTH AMERICA

**LEVERAGING LEADERSHIP
IN A COMPETITIVE MARKET**

Comprised of Kellogg USA (formerly the U.S. Food Products Division) and Kellogg Canada, Kellogg North America is leveraging its leadership position to achieve growth in a highly competitive market environment.

During 1991, Kellogg USA's aggressive marketing programs led to volume increases by the six top Kellogg's brands – *Kellogg's Corn Flakes,® Kellogg's Frosted Flakes,® Kellogg's®* Raisin Bran, *Rice Krispies,® Froot Loops,®* and *Frosted Mini-Wheats.®* All but *Rice Krispies* also gained market share. More importantly, our carefully targeted marketing support further strengthened consumer loyalty to these and other key brands.

Consistent with strong consumer interest in health and fitness, Kellogg USA markets 24 fat-free cereal products, more than any other manufacturer. Late in 1991, the Company announced the national introduction of *Kellogg's Frosted Bran™* and *Kellogg's®* Low-Fat Granola cereals and the West Coast introduction of *Kellogg's® Nutri-Grain®* Nuggets. This followed the launches of *Kellogg's®* Cinnamon Mini Buns and *Kellogg's® Double Dip Crunch™* cereals earlier in the year.

Kellogg Canada also marketed its major brands vigorously during 1991 and continued to achieve gains in volume and market share. Particular emphasis was placed on volume growth in Quebec, where the ready-to-eat cereal category traditionally has been underdeveloped. The introduction of *Kellogg's® Cruncheroos™* toasted oat cereal in two varieties broadened Kellogg Canada's product lineup.

To meet long-term production needs and improve effectiveness, Kellogg North America continued to invest in all six of the division's cereal plants – at London, Ontario; Battle Creek, Michigan; Omaha, Nebraska; Memphis, Tennessee; Lancaster, Pennsylvania; and San Leandro, California – and its convenience foods plant at Muncy, Pennsylvania. Also during 1991, Kellogg further sharpened its foodservice marketing, inventory control, and customer service programs, underscoring an intense, unrelenting commitment to leadership and long-term growth in North America.

5

improved. The result of these changes should be improved future profitability for Kellogg.

2.2.4 Financial Information

The first section of the annual report to contain useful information for analyzing the company is the *financial information* section. This part of the report includes management's discussion of financial performance and historical data.

MANAGEMENT DISCUSSION AND ANALYSIS. The discussion of financial performance, usually called *management discussion and analysis (MDA)*, is the only section containing predictive material in an otherwise historical corporate report. The Securities and Exchanges Commission requires a section in which management is more forthcoming about what it sees in the company's future, and this is the MDA section. The discussion largely pertains to this year's operations versus last year's, and last year's operations versus two years ago. This section is essentially a summary. We could derive most of the numbers given in this section ourselves from analyzing the company's financial statements. Nevertheless, the report provides a clear look at management's officially stated interpretation of what has happened over the past three years. Figure 2.4 shows excerpts of this information from the Kellogg report, which refers to the MDA section as "Financial Review."

Investors take the MDA report seriously, and full disclosure by the company is important. In one instance, the MDA report led to a problem for management of Caterpillar, Inc. In April 1992, the SEC charged that Caterpillar violated its duty to adequately inform investors of expected future events in its published MDA. The explicit charge was that the statement failed to inform investors that a high proportion of Caterpillar's 1989 earnings came from its Brazilian unit and that such strong profit probably would not recur the next year. At the time the annual report was issued, management apparently was discussing the problem in detail with the board of directors.[3] The omission was costly to Caterpillar investors in 1990, when management announced that steps taken by the new Brazilian government would hurt earnings. The stock price plummeted 16 percent on the day of the announcement.

HISTORICAL INFORMATION. The annual report usually shows historical information, which provides a snapshot of financial trends. Among the more important trends this section often shows are:

- Direction and consistency of sales fluctuations.
- The trend of income, particularly in relation to sales and the economy.
- The trend of income as a percent of sales.
- The trend of income on a per share basis (earnings per share).
- The trend of dividends.

In Kellogg's case (see Figure 2.5), notice that the compound growth in net earnings (11 percent) is greater than the compound growth in sales (10 percent). Investors would look upon this comparison as favorable. The historical data also

[3]Kevin G. Salwen, "SEC Charges Caterpillar Failed to Warn Holders of Earning Risk Posed by Unit," *The Wall Street Journal,* April 2, 1992, pp. A3–A6.

FIGURE 2.4

KELLOGG'S FINANCIAL REVIEW

Financial Review

Operations

Strong growth in both our international and domestic cereal markets led to record sales and earnings during 1991. Earnings reached $606 million, up 21 percent from 1990. This followed a 19 percent increase in 1990 earnings over 1989 (before the effect of an accounting change). In 1990, by comparison, a strong international business contributed significantly toward the 19 percent increase. In 1989 (before the effect of an accounting change), earnings fell 12 percent, the first decline in 38 years.

Sales totaled $5.8 billion in 1991, up 12 percent, marking the 47th consecutive year of increased sales. Cereal volume for international and the United States grew by 8 percent and 6 percent, respectively. During 1990, growth of 8 percent in international cereal volume more than offset a 4 percent decline in the United States. Increases in both years were aided by higher worldwide selling prices. European currency exchange rates negatively impacted 1991, but positively impacted 1990. In 1989, sales rose by 7 percent as worldwide cereal volume grew 2 percent.

After minimal growth in 1990, the United States ready-to-eat cereal category grew almost 3 percent in 1991. This level of growth represents a return to levels typical of the last decade. The Company's market share of the domestic ready-to-eat cereal category was 37.5 for 1991, unchanged from 1990. With the market share now stabilized over the last two years, the Company is well positioned to continue volume growth and rebuild market share.

Worldwide noncereal volume increased 5 percent and 2 percent in 1991 and 1990, respectively. Toaster pastries and frozen waffles in the United States were the largest contributors to these increases. Consumer interest in convenience foods and development of new products continue to strengthen these markets.

Sales in Europe increased 9 percent in 1991, consistent with an 8 percent increase in cereal volume. The increased volume together with higher prices were partially offset by unfavorable currency exchange rates. European sales in 1990 increased 32 percent. Cereal volume growth of 9 percent, higher prices, and favorable currency exchange rates all contributed to this strong increase. In 1989, a 4 percent rise in European sales occurred due to increases in prices and cereal volume, partially offset by unfavorable currency exchange rates. Sales in other geographic areas increased 14 percent in 1991 and 15 percent in 1990 on the strength of a 7 percent rise in cereal volume for both years. In 1989, higher volume and prices resulted in a 14 percent increase in sales.

Cost of goods sold as a percentage of sales was 49 percent in 1991, the lowest in the last decade. Improved volume, worldwide productivity gains in factory operations, timely price increases, and improved inventory management are among the factors that contributed to this lower ratio. This ratio was 52 percent in both 1990 and 1989.

Selling and administrative expense was 33 percent of each sales dollar in 1991, compared to 31 percent in 1990 and 32 percent in 1989. Increased investment in domestic marketing led to the higher percent in 1991. The introduction of new products worldwide is expected to continue in 1992, with each of the products having undergone a rigorous testing process and supported by strong marketing programs.

Geographic operating segments – covered by Report of Independent Accountants

Net sales (millions)	1991	Percent Change	1990	Percent Change	1989	Percent Change
United States	$3,411.0	+ 12	$3,043.8	+ 4	$2,940.5	+ 6
% of total	59%		59%		63%	
Europe	1,447.0	+ 9	1,321.5	+ 32	999.4	+ 4
% of total	25%		26%		21%	
Other areas	928.6	+ 14	816.1	+ 15	711.8	+ 14
% of total	16%		15%		16%	
Consolidated	$5,786.6	+ 12	$5,181.4	+ 11	$4,651.7	+ 7

Net earnings (millions)	1991	Percent Change	1990	Percent Change	1989	Percent Change
United States	$388.3	+ 19	$325.4	+ 4	$312.6	− 11
% of total	64%		65%		66%	
Europe	130.1	+ 20	108.1	+ 12	96.6	+ 11
% of total	21%		21%		21%	
Other areas	87.6	+ 26	69.3	+ 14	61.0	+ 40
% of total	15%		14%		13%	
Consolidated	$606.0	+ 21	$502.8	+ 7	$470.2	− 2

Identifiable assets (millions)	1991	Percent Change	1990	Percent Change	1989	Percent Change
United States	$1,859.6	+ 1	$1,835.3	+ 4	$1,770.9	+ 8
% of total	47%		49%		52%	
Europe	1,110.8	+ 1	1,096.8	+ 25	879.0	+ 5
% of total	28%		29%		26%	
Other areas	767.4	+ 8	707.9	+ 9	652.2	+ 5
% of total	20%		19%		19%	
Corporate assets	188.0	+ 72	109.4	+ 24	88.3	− 54
% of total	5%		3%		3%	
Consolidated	$3,925.8	+ 5	$3,749.4	+ 11	$3,390.4	+ 3

FIGURE 2.5
SUMMARY OF HISTORICAL RESULTS FOR KELLOGG

Eleven-Year Summary
(dollar amounts in millions, except per share data)

Summary of Operations

	Net Sales	% Growth	Pretax Earnings	% Growth	Net Earnings	% Growth
10-year Compound Growth Rate	10%		10%		11%	
1991	**$5,786.6**	**12**	**$984.2**	**21**	**$606.0**	**21**
1990	5,181.4	11	814.7	22	502.8	7
1989	4,651.7	7	667.0	(14)	470.2	(2)
1988	4,348.8	15	774.7	16	480.4	21
1987	3,793.0	14	665.7	13	395.9	24
1986	3,340.7	14	586.6	11	318.9	13
1985	2,930.1	13	527.4	11	281.1	12
1984	2,602.4	9	476.1	7	250.5	3
1983	2,381.1	1	444.0	8	242.7	7
1982	2,367.1	2	410.9	9	227.8	11
1981	2,321.3	8	378.6	12	205.4	12

Other Information and Financial Ratios

	Property, Net	Capital Expenditures	Depreciation	Total Assets	Number of Employees
1991	**$2,646.5**	**$333.5**	**$222.8**	**$3,925.8**	**17,017**
1990	2,595.4	320.5	200.2	3,749.4	17,239
1989	2,406.3	508.7	167.6	3,390.4	17,268
1988	2,131.9	538.1	139.7	3,297.9	17,461
1987	1,738.8	478.4	113.1	2,680.9	17,762
1986	1,281.1	329.2	92.7	2,084.2	17,383
1985	1,035.9	245.6	75.4	1,726.1	17,082
1984	856.0	228.9	63.9	1,667.1	17,239
1983	743.2	156.7	62.8	1,467.2	18,293
1982	682.2	121.1	55.9	1,297.4	19,290
1981	658.4	146.4	49.1	1,279.1	20,260

Net earnings for 1989 include $48.1 million ($.20 per share) resulting from the adoption of Statement of Financial Accounting Standards No. 96, "Accounting for Income Taxes," as of January 1, 1989.

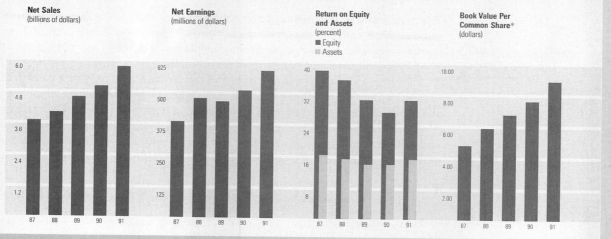

Net Sales (billions of dollars)

Net Earnings (millions of dollars)

Return on Equity and Assets (percent)
■ Equity
▨ Assets

Book Value Per Common Share* (dollars)

show that cash provided by operations (that is, cash profits) has grown steadily from $293.3 million in 1981 to $934.4 million in 1991. (See Figure 2.8).

2.2.5 Financial Statements

The basic financial statements of every annual report include the *income statement,* the *balance sheet,* and the *statement of cash flows.*[4] These statements evolved from the accrual accounting process, following generally accepted accounting principles (GAAP), procedures, and standards of the accounting profession.

The objective of accounting rules and conventions is to provide a consistent and objective account of the firm's financial status based on historical costs, where revenues and expenses are matched over the appropriate time periods. Despite the degree of precision implied by financial statements, amounts reported in them are estimates based on accounting rules and conventions.[5] And there is another limitation of the usefulness of financial statements. They provide mostly historical information, while most finan-

---

[4]A fourth statement included in the annual report is the *statement of change in stockholders' equity.* We ignore it because it is unimportant to our discussion.

[5]For example, the allowance for doubtful accounts in the balance sheet is an approximation of the amount of accounts receivable expected to go uncollected.

cial statement users want information about the future. Economists, investment analysts, and others criticize accounting rules for distorting corporate income. But accountants counter that they are justified, given the complexities of business and the objectivity they get by using documented historical cost. Objectively, however, we can conclude that financial statements are a good place at least to begin a study of finance, depending on how we interpret them.

INCOME STATEMENT. The aim of the **income statement** is to present a "true and fair picture" of results of operations during the accounting period. The accounting profession follows GAAP with the intent of obtaining the accounting income number. Analysts and the financial press devote much attention to reported accounting income. This attention to income is based on the fact that many managers believe investors consider income of paramount importance. Managers often feel compelled to satisfy investors' perceived desire for income. In this quest, managers have been known to resort to time-consuming and, in some cases, questionable accounting practices. The nearby Financial Reality box summarizes "creative" accounting of six companies.

    Income is difficult to measure for two reasons. First, prices for labor and materials change. Second, the *original cost rule* maintains that the resources used up in the production and sale of a product should be expensed at their original or historical cost. This rule is designed to provide objectivity to accounting practice. Attributing historical cost to a resource whose replacement or current cost is higher (or lower) has the effect of overstating (or understating) income—if not in an accounting sense, then at least in an economic sense. Income is overstated because it costs more to replace the consumed resource than was shown on the accounting income statement.

    We can also see the misplaced focus people have on accounting income by direct example. Accountants make journal entries to expense the excess of the purchase price over the revised book value of the assets, called **goodwill,** or set up a warranty reserve. These entries have no effect on cash and, thus, have no effect on economic value. In other cases, accountants make accounting entries to record income as a liability. For example, to a magazine publisher, the offsetting journal entry for cash received for a subscription that expires in 24 months is to an *unearned income liability account.* The accountant records amounts as sales sometime in the future by reducing the balance in the unearned income account. However, the true value to the company improves with the receipt of the cash and not when the company later records the sale.

    Kellogg's income statement, shown in Figure 2.6, shows sales have increased $1.1 billion during the last two years. Net income has increased $125.8 million during this same two-year period. Also note that in 1989 Kellogg recorded income of $48.1 million when it changed accounting to adopt new rules for income taxes. No cash was received by Kellogg—the $48.1 million was simply a paper profit. Thus, no additional value was created by the $48.1 million accounting entry.

BALANCE SHEET. The aim of the *balance sheet* is to present a "true and fair picture" of the accounts of a business at the close of the accounting period. The balance sheet records what has happened; it does not show the future. Often, however, financial analysts use balance sheet information to get some idea of what the future holds. The **balance sheet** lists the kinds and amounts of a firm's *assets* (what it owns) as well as *liabilities* and *equity* (what and to whom it owes) as of a given date. Assets always equal liabilities plus equity. Even if a firm were *insolvent* (owed more than it had in assets), assets would be equalized to liabilities and equity by showing negative equity.

    GAAP requires accountants to record asset values at their original acquisition cost and liabilities at what they were when originally incurred. Such figures are normally

Income statement. Financial statement of a firm showing its revenues, costs, and profit during a given period. Also known as a profit-and-loss statement.

Goodwill. The excess of the purchase price over the assessed value of the tangible assets acquired.

Balance sheet. Statement of a firm's financial position on a given date. Shows what the firm owns (its assets), what it owes (its liabilities), and the residual or equity of the owners (the net worth).

FIGURE 2.6

KELLOGG'S INCOME STATEMENT

Kellogg Company and Subsidiaries

Consolidated Earnings and Retained Earnings

Year ended December 31,

(millions)	1991	1990	1989
Net sales	**$5,786.6**	$5,181.4	$4,651.7
Interest revenue	**20.9**	17.8	14.5
Other revenue (deductions), net	**(6.3)**	(22.9)	(31.7)
	5,801.2	5,176.3	4,634.5
Cost of goods sold	**2,828.7**	2,676.6	2,413.8
Selling and administrative expense	**1,930.0**	1,618.8	1,505.4
Interest expense	**58.3**	66.2	48.3
	4,817.0	4,361.6	3,967.5
Earnings before income taxes and cumulative effect of accounting change	**984.2**	814.7	667.0
Income taxes	**378.2**	311.9	244.9
Earnings before cumulative effect of accounting change	**606.0**	502.8	422.1
Cumulative effect of change in method of accounting for income taxes – $.20 a share			48.1
Net earnings – $2.51, $2.08, $1.93 a share	**606.0**	502.8	470.2
Retained earnings, beginning of year	**2,542.4**	2,271.4	2,011.1
Dividends paid – $1.075, $.96, $.86 a share	**(259.3)**	(231.8)	(209.9)
Retained earnings, end of year	**$2,889.1**	$2,542.4	$2,271.4

See notes to financial statements.

QUOTH THE BANKER, "WATCH CASH FLOW"

Once upon a midnight dreary as I pondered weak and weary
Over many a quaint and curious volume of accounting lore,
Seeking gimmicks (without scruple) to squeeze through some new tax loophole,
Suddenly I heard a knock upon my door,
    Only this, and nothing more.

Then I felt a queasy tingling and I heard the cash a-jingling
As a fearsome banker entered whom I'd often seen before
His face was money-green and in his eyes there could be seen
Dollar-signs that seemed to glitter as he reckoned up the score.
    "Cash flow," the banker said, and nothing more.

I had always thought it fine to show a jet black bottom line.
But the banker sounded a resounding, "No.
Your receivables are high, mounting upward toward the sky;
Write-offs loom. What matters is cash flow."
    He repeated, "Watch cash flow."

Then I tried to tell the story of our lovely inventory
Which, though large, is full of most delightful stuff.
But the banker saw its growth, and with a mighty oath
He waved his arms and shouted, "Stop! Enough!
    Pay the interest, and don't give me any guff!"

Next I looked for non-cash items which could add ad infinitum
To replace the ever-outward flow of cash,
But to keep my statement black I'd held depreciation back,
And my banker said that I'd done something rash.
    He quivered, and his teeth began to gnash.

When I asked him for a loan, he responded, with a groan,
That the interest rate would be just prime plus eight,
And to guarantee my purity he'd insist on some security —
All my assets plus the scalp upon my pate.
    Only this, a standard rate.

Though my bottom line is black, I am flat upon my back,
My cash flows out and customers pay slow.
The growth of my receivables is almost unbelievable;
The result is certain—unremitting woe!
And I hear the banker utter an ominous low mutter,
    "Watch cash flow."

Source: Reprinted from *Publishers Weekly*, January 13, 1975, published by
R. R. Bowker Company. Copyright © 1975 Herbert Bailey, Jr.; reprinted
with the permission of the author, Herbert Bailey, Jr.

referred to as book values, which we discussed earlier. These dollar amounts are maintained on the accounting books as long as the corresponding assets and liabilities remain in existence, with two exceptions. First, accountants reduce depreciable assets, such as buildings, in value each year by the amount of depreciation taken. Second, accountants reduce loans for partial payment. Figure 2.7 shows the balance sheet for Kellogg Company.

FIGURE 2.7

KELLOGG'S BALANCE SHEET

Kellogg Company and Subsidiaries

Consolidated Balance Sheet

At December 31,

(millions)	1991	1990
Current assets		
Cash and temporary investments	$ 178.0	$ 100.5
Accounts receivable, less allowances of $5.8 and $4.8	420.0	430.2
Inventories:		
Raw materials and supplies	173.2	174.8
Finished goods and materials in process	227.9	184.9
Deferred income taxes	63.5	70.4
Prepaid expenses	110.4	80.6
Total current assets	1,173.0	1,041.4
Property		
Land	40.4	41.0
Buildings	1,045.5	1,026.9
Machinery and equipment	2,635.5	2,462.8
Construction in progress	168.3	141.3
Accumulated depreciation	(1,243.2)	(1,076.6)
Property, net	2,646.5	2,595.4
Intangible assets	49.8	62.9
Other assets	56.5	49.7
Total assets	$3,925.8	$3,749.4
Current liabilities		
Current maturities of long-term debt	$ 260.7	$ 102.3
Notes payable	188.4	280.3
Accounts payable	289.8	247.1
Accrued liabilities:		
Income taxes	129.7	103.7
Salaries and wages	86.2	73.2
Advertising and promotion	252.6	153.7
Other	117.0	149.3
Total current liabilities	1,324.4	1,109.6
Long-term debt	15.2	295.6
Other liabilities	87.5	95.4
Deferred income taxes	338.9	347.0
Shareholders' equity		
Common stock, $.25 par value		
Authorized: 330,000,000 shares in 1991 and 165,000,000 in 1990		
Issued: 309,771,940 shares in 1991 and 154,501,434 in 1990	77.4	38.6
Capital in excess of par value	60.2	81.2
Retained earnings	2,889.1	2,542.4
Treasury stock, at cost: 69,309,231 and 33,843,183 shares	(880.9)	(797.3)
Currency translation adjustment	14.0	36.9
Total shareholders' equity	2,159.8	1,901.8
Total liabilities and shareholders' equity	$3,925.8	$3,749.4

See notes to financial statements.

Problems with the original cost rule occur because many assets and liabilities are held for a considerable period of time, during which prices can and do change. If they change significantly, then the historical figures shown on the balance sheet can be very misleading indeed. Any cash already invested in an asset is irrelevant for computing value. The amount of cash that has gone previously into the acquisition of an asset does not determine its market value; rather its value is determined by the amount of expected future cash flow from the asset. For example, Kellogg's balance sheet shows land valued at $40.4 million. This amount is likely grossly undervalued in terms of the market price Kellogg could receive if it sold the land. Because Kellogg's balance sheet reflects historical, or book, value and not market value, the $40.4 million for land is useless for all practical purposes.

STATEMENT OF CASH FLOWS. A **cash flow statement** shows the various sources and uses of financial resources within the business. The statement reconciles the change in the cash account on the balance sheet from one period to the next by taking information from both the balance sheet and the income statement. Table 2.1 shows the underlying concept of the statement of cash flow.

The first section of the cash flow statement takes the accountant's accrual-based income statement and converts it to a cash-based income statement. *Cash flow from operating activities* is cash income. The second section of the statement is *cash flow from investing activities*. This section summarizes the purchases and sales of investments in the firm to maintain or enhance its productive activities. The final section is the *cash flow from financing activities*. Included in this section is the issuance and retirement of securities the firm uses to finance assets.

Figure 2.8 shows the statement of cash flow for Kellogg. We can see that in 1991 Kellogg reported accounting income of $606 million. The company's cash income was $934.4 million. In this case, there are two primary reasons for the difference between accounting and cash incomes—the noncash charge for depreciation of $222.8 million, and the accrued liabilities of $105.6 million, which are recorded for accounting purposes but not yet paid.

Statement of cash flows. An accounting statement that traces the sources and uses of cash as a result of organizational activity.

TABLE 2.1

CONCEPT BEHIND THE STATEMENT OF CASH FLOWS

Cash Inflows		Cash Outflows
Generation of cash from normal operations	*Cash flow from operating activities*	Expenditure of funds in normal operations
	+	
Sale of assets	*Cash flow from investing activities*	Purchase of assets
	+	
Issuance of financial securities	*Cash flow from financing activities*	Retirement of financial securities
	=	
	Change in cash	

FIGURE 2.8

KELLOGG'S STATEMENT OF CASH FLOWS

Kellogg Company and Subsidiaries

Consolidated Statement of Cash Flows

Year ended December 31,

(millions)	1991	1990	1989
Operating activities			
Net earnings	**$ 606.0**	$ 502.8	$ 470.2
Items in net earnings not requiring (providing) cash:			
Depreciation	**222.8**	200.2	167.6
Cumulative effect of change in method of accounting for income taxes			(48.1)
Deferred income taxes	**(5.4)**	45.6	32.0
Other	**16.8**	17.7	25.1
Change in operating assets and liabilities:			
Accounts receivable	**10.2**	(75.0)	49.4
Inventories	**(41.4)**	34.3	(31.8)
Prepaid expenses	**(22.9)**	(74.4)	34.8
Accounts payable	**42.7**	(3.8)	(114.4)
Accrued liabilities	**105.6**	171.8	(51.3)
Cash provided by operations	**934.4**	819.2	533.5
Investing activities			
Additions to properties	**(333.5)**	(320.5)	(508.7)
Property disposals	**25.2**	18.0	15.0
Other	**(11.6)**	(7.9)	(1.5)
Cash used by investing activities	**(319.9)**	(310.4)	(495.2)
Financing activities			
Borrowings of notes payable	**182.1**	367.8	268.9
Reduction of notes payable	**(274.0)**	(463.7)	(199.9)
Issuance of long-term debt	**4.3**	24.2	202.5
Reduction of long-term debt	**(126.0)**	(102.4)	(135.2)
Issuance of common stock	**17.7**	8.4	9.5
Purchase of treasury stock	**(83.6)**	(86.9)	(78.6)
Cash dividends	**(259.3)**	(231.8)	(209.9)
Other	**1.1**	(6.5)	(.5)
Cash used by financing activities	**(537.7)**	(490.9)	(143.2)
Effect of exchange rate changes on cash	**.7**	2.3	.2
Increase (decrease) in cash and temporary investments	**77.5**	20.2	(104.7)
Cash and temporary investments at beginning of year	**100.5**	80.3	185.0
Cash and temporary investments at end of year	**$ 178.0**	$ 100.5	$ 80.3

See notes to financial statements.

Source: 1991 Annual Report of Kellogg Company. ®, ™ Kellogg Company. © 1992 Kellogg Company. Used by permission.

Note that for the years 1990 and 1991, Kellogg was able to generate enough cash from operations to pay for all investments, pay down its borrowings, and pay dividends to shareholders. After satisfying all cash requirements in 1990, Kellogg still had a $20.2 million increase in its cash account. In 1991, the cash balance increased $77.5 million after paying for investments, debts, and dividends.

Many analysts consider the statement of cash flow more important than either the income statement or the balance sheet. The "Quoth the Banker" poem on page 41 lends an interesting touch to cash flow. If more managers truly understood the important message of this poem, their companies would have fewer financial problems.

2.2.6 Notes to Financial Statements

At the end of the annual report are *notes* explaining various facets of the firm's accounting procedures. The reports themselves are kept concise and condensed and, therefore, any explanatory matter that cannot be abbreviated readily is set out in greater detail in notes. Generally, the notes include information about:

- Summary of significant accounting policies
- Leases
- Long-term debt and capital stock
- Pension plans and their status
- Current and deferred income taxes payable
- Related party transactions
- Lines of business
- Other material information

Read these notes carefully because they can point up problems.

Figure 2.9 is an example of what to expect. A later note (not shown in Figure 2.9) discusses "Employers' Accounting for Postretirement Benefits Other Than Pensions." This note indicates that if Kellogg had adopted the new accounting rule SFAS 106 as of December 1991, its long-term liabilities would have increased about $400 million and net income would have declined about $254 million. Management is admitting that according to the new accounting standards, net income for 1991 was overstated and liabilities were understated. The $400 million represents an *off-balance sheet liability;* that is, it is not shown on the balance sheet but the company is obligated for it.

We need a sound knowledge of financial accounting to understand fully all the notes. It's almost as if we must be financial detectives to compare one company closely with other companies. Different companies often follow different accounting procedures, at least for some accounts. We must search for clues in the notes to the financial statements. It is not enough simply to check net income, rather we need to be wary of the many accounting conventions that can overstate or understate income, often significantly. Most likely, we need to adjust some accounting items that distort income.

As Table 2.2 reveals, management is quite willing to juggle income, or earnings. The practice borders on or is sometimes unethical; at least it is questionable.[6] A study of allegedly fraudulent activities of public firms reveals that 87 percent of the frauds are

---

[6]Ethics in the accounting profession is such a concern that the National Association of Accountants has produced a video tape on the subject.

FIGURE 2.9
NOTES TO KELLOGG'S FINANCIAL STATEMENTS

Kellogg Company and Subsidiaries

Notes to Financial Statements

Note 1 Accounting policies

Consolidation

The consolidated financial statements include the accounts of Kellogg Company and its wholly owned subsidiaries. Intercompany balances and transactions are eliminated.

Cash and temporary investments

Temporary investments that are highly liquid with original maturities of less than three months are considered to be cash equivalents.

Inventories

Inventories are valued at the lower of cost (principally average) or market.

Property

Fixed assets are recorded at cost and depreciated over estimated useful lives using straight-line methods for financial reporting and accelerated methods for tax reporting. Interest cost capitalized as part of the construction cost of capital assets amounted to $2.4 million in 1991, $18.3 million in 1990, and $24.3 million in 1989.

Intangible assets

Intangible assets represent the unamortized excess of cost over fair market value of net assets of businesses acquired by purchase (goodwill), trademarks, and the underfunded amount of certain pension plans. Trademarks and goodwill are being amortized by the straight-line method over periods up to 40 years.

Net earnings per share

Net earnings per share is determined by dividing net earnings by the weighted average number of common shares outstanding. All per share amounts have been restated to reflect the two-for-one stock split, effective December 4, 1991.

Note 2 Leases

Operating leases generally are for equipment and warehouse space. Rent expense on all operating leases, which generally are renewable at the Company's option, amounted to $39.3 million in 1991, $39.8 million in 1990, and $38.7 million in 1989. There are no significant future minimum rental commitments under non-cancelable leases.

Note 3 Research and development

Research and development costs charged to earnings approximated $34.7 million in 1991, $38.3 million in 1990, and $42.9 million in 1989.

Note 4 Divestments

During the first quarter of 1992, the Company sold its wholly owned subsidiary, Fearn International Inc. The disposal resulted in a pretax gain of approximately $60 million.

Note 5 Foreign currency translations

Most effects of exchange rate changes are reflected as a currency translation adjustment in shareholders' equity.

Exchange adjustments attributable to operations in highly inflationary economies are reflected in earnings along with the exchange adjustments related to foreign currency transactions that affect cash flows.

The currency translation adjustment included in shareholders' equity consists of the following components.

(millions)	1991	1990
Balance, January 1,	$ 36.9	$(38.0)
Exchange adjustments	(22.9)	72.8
Income tax effect of the adjustments		2.1
Balance, December 31,	$ 14.0	$ 36.9

Note 6 Debt

Notes payable consists of borrowings in the United States of $165.5 million at 4.9 percent at December 31, 1991, $232.0 million at 8.3 percent at December 31, 1990, and bank loans of foreign subsidiaries at competitive market rates.

Information on long-term debt follows.

(millions)	1991	1990
9½% Eurodollar Notes due 1992	$200.2	$201.1
9⅛% Eurodollar Notes due 1991		100.3
9% Canadian Dollar Notes due 1992	43.3	43.1
Other	32.4	53.4
	275.9	397.9
Less current maturities	260.7	102.3
Balance, December 31,	$ 15.2	$295.6

Principal payments are due as follows (in millions): 1993 – $2; 1994 – $2; 1995 – $1; 1996 – $1.

Interest paid, net of amounts capitalized, approximated interest expense in each of the three years ended December 31, 1991.

The Company has credit agreements providing for borrowing an aggregate of approximately $616 million on an unsecured basis, $587 million of which is unused at December 31, 1991. In 1988, the Company filed a "shelf registration" of $290 million of debt securities with the Securities and Exchange Commission. Under this registration statement, the Company issued $100 million of 10.3 percent short-term notes in March 1989 that matured in March 1990. In April 1991, the remaining $190 million on the 1988 shelf registration was increased to $300 million.

Note 7 Common stock and other capital

On December 3, 1991, shareholders approved an increase in the authorized shares of common stock from 165 million to 330 million and approved a two-for-one stock split to shareholders of record on December 4, 1991. The stated par value per share of common stock was not changed from $.25. All share and per share amounts have been restated to retroactively reflect the stock split.

In 1991 the Company purchased 1,515,600 shares of its common stock at an average cost of $52; in 1990, purchased 2,766,200 shares at an average cost of $31; and in 1989, purchased 2,464,200 shares at an average cost of $32. All purchases are included in treasury stock. A summary of capital stock transactions follows.

(millions)	Common stock	Capital in excess of par value	Treasury stock
Balance, January 1, 1989	$38.5	$63.3	$631.8
Stock options exercised	.1	9.5	
Treasury stock purchased			78.6
Balance, December 31, 1989	38.6	72.8	710.4
Stock options exercised		8.4	
Treasury stock purchased			86.9
Balance, December 31, 1990	38.6	81.2	797.3
Stock options exercised	.1	17.7	
Two-for-one stock split	38.7	(38.7)	
Treasury stock purchased			83.6
Balance, December 31, 1991	$77.4	$60.2	$880.9

TABLE 2-2

Managing Reported Earnings

	% of Managers Who Judge the Manipulation Practice		
	Ethical	Questionable or a Minor Infraction	Unethical or Serious Infraction
• Managing short-term earnings by changing or manipulating operating decisions or procedures:			
When the result is to reduce earnings	79%	19%	2%
When the result is to increase earnings	57	31	12
• Managing short-term earnings by changing or manipulating accounting methods:			
When the change in earnings is small	5	45	50
When the change in earnings is large	3	21	76
• Managing short-term earnings by deferring discretionary expenditures into the next accounting period:			
To meet an interim quarterly budget target	47	41	12
To meet an annual budget target at year end	41	35	24
• Increasing short-term earnings to meet a budget target:			
By selling excess assets and realizing a profit	80	16	4
By ordering overtime work at year end to ship as much as possible	74	21	5
By offering customers special credit terms to accept delivery without obligation to pay until the following year	43	42	15

Reprinted from William J. Burns, Jr. and Kenneth A. Merchant, "The Dangerous Morality of Managing Earnings," Management Accounting (August 1990), pp. 22–25. Copyright by Institute of Management Accountants, Montvale, NJ.

accomplished through the use of misleading financial information. High-level managers are involved in 66 percent of the alleged frauds.[7]

Because of the flexibility in applying accounting principles, we should be aware of the most common areas in which accounting changes may occur.

[7]S. Raab, "Detecting and Preventing Financial Statement Fraud: The Roles of the Reporting Company and The Independent Auditor," *Yale Law & Policy Review* 5 (1987), p. 527.

READ THE FOOTNOTES

by Patricia McConnell, C.P.A., Managing Director, Tax and Accounting Research, Bear, Stearns & Company

When I started my career about 20 years ago, financial statements, particularly the footnotes, were much shorter because there were fewer accounting rules to follow. Today there are so many rules that it is almost impossible for a professional accountant, let alone a financial analyst, to keep track of what the rules even are. And I am only talking about U.S. rules. If you analyze foreign companies' financial statements, you need to be familiar with GAAP of the home country as well as standards issued by an international board. Some footnotes are so extensive, they require a page or more of text. It has led some analysts to say that financial statements are no longer useful. I disagree. While the FASB still has not addressed every accounting problem, and I can find fault with some aspect of every rule the FASB has issued, I have to admit that on the whole the rules that have been issued in the last 20 years make financial statements more comparable, more economically representative, and more useful, not less so.

You no longer need to take the reported results on faith. There are notes explaining accounting policies and a note giving interest rates and maturities of long-term debt. Notes provide the fair value of financial assets and liabilities both on and off the balance sheet. There are notes on income taxes, notes on leases, and notes on employee benefits. In addition, the SEC-mandated MD&A requires management to explain its results and current position as well as future liquidity needs. Analysts can use these extensive notes to undo the financial accounting the FASB has mandated, but in most cases they should not undo the accounting. The supplemental information should be used primarily to make comparisons when necessary, to calculate core earnings, to access the quality of the core earnings, and to make forecasts of future earnings and cash flows.

In fact, many of the rules issued by the FASB in the last 20 years have made financial statements easier to compare by eliminating many alternatives or free choices in accounting. Unfortunately, many free choices still exist. In the oil and gas industry, "successful efforts" and "full cost" accounting live side by side, thanks to the lobbying efforts of the oil industry which led to Washington's intervention in the accounting rule-making game. And companies still have choices of LIFO, FIFO, and average for inventories. Companies still are able to use accelerated or straight-line depreciation without an economic justification for the choice. Many other examples exist.

Ironically, another source of noncomparability in financial statements is the transition provisions in the new FASB pronouncements themselves. For example, companies were allowed to adopt the new rules on pension accounting anytime between 1985 and 1987, thereby causing three years where comparisons among companies were distorted. New rules on accounting for retiree medical benefits were issued in December 1990, but firms were not required to follow the rules until January 1, 1993. Companies could decide to adopt anywhere during that period, resulting in another period of noncomparability. To make matters even worse, companies had a choice of how to implement the new retiree medical benefit rules. A company could record its total unfunded retiree health-care liability by taking a one-time cumulative charge in the income statement. Alternatively, it could choose to write the liability off as an expense over 20 years. Now we are talking about 20 years of noncomparability—that's a long time!

The FASB justifies its rules by requiring companies to make sufficient disclosures so that analysts can make the necessary correcting adjustments. Of course, this means analysts need to understand how the rules work and where to look for the information. Analysts also need the time to make the adjustments and time, unfortunately, is a scarce and very valuable commodity in this business. Still, 20 years ago we would not even have known that these accounting differences existed much less have sufficient information to make adjustments. Now we know we have a comparability problem and worry about how to handle it. Read the footnotes. They are good for you.

- Management may switch its inventory flow assumption from "last-in, first-out" (LIFO) to "first-in, first-out" (FIFO), or vice versa. During a period of rising prices for materials, FIFO leads to higher accounting income but lower cash income. The reverse situation occurs if prices are falling.

- Significant changes in expenses for advertising, marketing, or research and development also may indicate that management is searching for income, especially if these amounts have declined from the prior period's levels. Changes in allowance for doubtful accounts and depreciation and amortization expense as a percentage of fixed assets should send up a flag as well.

- A switch to a different independent certified public accounting firm to perform the audit of the financial statements may be due to accounting policy differences between the former accounting firm and management.

- If the independent public accounting firm should qualify a company's financial statement or not give an opinion, it is a signal of real or potential problems.

There are additional concerns with foreign companies' financial statements.

- Foreign firms treat as assets some expenditures that U.S. firms expense immediately. Research and development (R&D) cost is an example. Some foreign firms show R&D on the balance sheet as an asset. They write R&D off over time regardless of the final profitability of the product developed. American firms must expense R&D when incurred.

- Income of many foreign companies is subject to a wide latitude of interpretation. In Europe, accepted accounting principles are merely "in accordance with legal provisions." Many European companies prepare their financial statements to show tax authorities how little income was made, not to show stockholders how much income was made. There are about as many statement formats as there are companies.

- Different laws and practices in other countries can conceal asset or liability valuation, performance data, and even sales data. Subsidiaries' and parent firm's incomes are not combined in many foreign businesses. Fully disclosed and freely available financial reports are the exception rather than the rule in many countries. The extent of disclosure, or rather the lack thereof, can be appalling by U.S. standards.

Currently, the SEC requires all publicly held companies whose securities trade in the United States to disclose any material legal proceedings other than ordinary routine litigation incidental to the business. Rarely do corporations report problems with federal enforcement agencies. And management is not above making false statements. In one instance, B.F. Goodrich, General Tire and Rubber, and Goodyear all filed sworn affidavits in the U.S. Supreme Court claiming that new standards for the chemical benzene would shut down their tire manufacturing operations. Next, the companies told their shareholders that the standard would have no material impact on their operations or told them nothing at all.[8]

---

[8]Russell Mokhiber, *Corporate Crime and Violence: Big Business Power and the Abuse of the Public Trust* (San Francisco: Sierra Club Books, 1989), p. 61.

2.2.7 Report of Independent Public Accountants

The audit report, or the *report by the independent public accountants,* states whether the financial statements conform to generally accepted accounting principles. Most auditors' statements take no more than a few standard short sentences. Unfortunately, investors referring to the audit report usually are not sufficiently skilled to decipher the financial reports. The average investor needs objective and comparable data, not stilted language and expressions only accountants can understand.

Most investors look to the audit report as affirmation that no fraud exists in the company. The good news is that over 99 percent of all reports certified by independent public accountants (who act as auditors) are free of financial fraud.[9] The bad news is that the auditors do not uncover most fraudulent activity. One cynic states that, when auditors sign a financial report, they claim: *"We took a look; we did a few tests; the financials are probably OK; and if they are not OK, we did not write the financials—management did."*[10] The courts have determined that adherence to the accountant's GAAP standards does not conclusively protect the accountant from being answerable to clients, investors, and creditors.[11]

Management may demonstrate a pronounced willingness to change auditors for a variety of reasons, including the desire to obtain more favorable accounting treatment regarding a particular issue or transaction. When a company substitutes auditors in an effort to improve the reported financial position of the firm, or surveys several public accounting firms to gain their views to select a desired option, the firm has probably engaged in *opinion shopping.* As employed by the SEC, opinion shopping involves an attempt by a company to:

- Find a public accountant who will approve management's proposed accounting treatment.
- Make its decision about which auditor to engage contingent upon receiving the desired answer from a consulting accountant.
- Use an accounting method in a way that frustrates the true reporting objectives of financial statements.

Figure 2.10 presents the auditor's report for Kellogg. The company received what is called a *clean opinion.* This means that Price Waterhouse, the independent accounting firm, satisfied itself that Kellogg followed generally accepted accounting principles and the company's financial statements fairly represent the financial condition. If there were phrases such as "except for" or "subject to" in the report, be wary. These phrases can signal the inability of the CPA to get accurate information.

Also note that Price Waterhouse wants the reader of the statements to clearly understand that management, not the auditors, put the financial statements together: "These financial statements are the responsibility of the Company's management; our

---

[9]S. Raab, "Detecting and Preventing Financial Statement Fraud: The Roles of the Reporting Company and the Independent Auditor," *Yale Law and Policy Review* 5 (1987), 514

[10]Patrick Finegan, Jr., *Master Financial Statements* (Washington, DC: Palindrome Press, 1991), p. 16.

[11]The Supreme Court, in *United States* v. *Arthur Young & Company* (465 U.S. 805 (1984)) has typecast the accountant as a "public watchdog," whose "ultimate allegiance [is] to the . . . [firm's] creditors and stockholders, as well as to the investing public . . . [and such] function demands that the accountant maintain total independence from the client at all times and requires complete fidelity to the public trust." The Supreme Court reasoned that the public accountant's responsibility to detect, not merely search for, errors and irregularities is based on the accountant's being in a better position and more skilled to detect errors and irregularities than anyone else, and on society's significant reliance on the accuracy of information provided by the accountant.

FIGURE 2.10

INDEPENDENT AUDITOR'S REPORT

Report of Independent Accountants

Price Waterhouse

To the Shareholders and Board of Directors of Kellogg Company

In our opinion, the accompanying consolidated balance sheet and the related consolidated statements of earnings and retained earnings and of cash flows present fairly, in all material respects, the financial position of Kellogg Company and its subsidiaries at December 31, 1991 and 1990, and the results of their operations and their cash flows for each of the three years in the period ended December 31, 1991, in conformity with generally accepted accounting principles. These financial statements are the responsibility of the Company's management; our responsibility is to express an opinion on these financial statements based on our audits. We conducted our audits of these statements in accordance with generally accepted auditing standards which require that we plan and perform the audit to obtain reasonable assurance about whether the financial statements are free of material misstatement. An audit includes examining, on a test basis, evidence supporting the amounts and disclosures in the financial statements, assessing the accounting principles used and significant estimates made by management, and evaluating the overall financial statement presentation. We believe that our audits provide a reasonable basis for the opinion expressed above.

As discussed in Note 9 to the financial statements, the Company changed its method of accounting for income taxes in 1989.

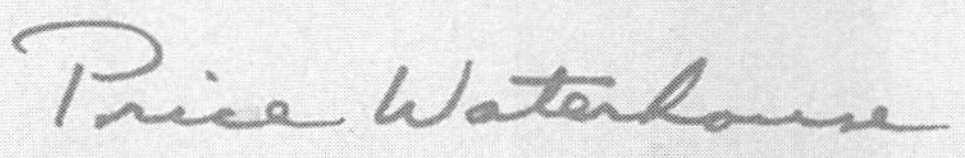

Price Waterhouse

Battle Creek, Michigan
February 5, 1992

Source: 1991 Annual Report of Kellogg Company. ®, ™ Kellogg Company. © 1992 Kellogg Company. Used by permission.

responsibility is to express an opinion on these financial statements based on our audits."

2.2.8 Miscellaneous Information

The annual report may include additional matter about the historical pattern of the company's stock price and payments to shareholders (dividends), and the roster of directors and corporate executives. Figure 2.11 is an example from Kellogg's report. A quick look at the roster reveals how many directors hold management positions in the company. The board of directors is supposed to represent the shareholders and provide oversight of management. If too many directors are employees, it clearly is questionable how much oversight they provide. Of Kellogg's 14-member board, three directors are employees of Kellogg and a fourth person is the immediate past chairperson. On balance, Kellogg's board is well represented by nonemployees.

With this discussion of miscellaneous information, we have completed our review of information released by the firm to the public. Later chapters use the financial state-

FIGURE 2.11
KELLOGG'S ROSTER OF DIRECTORS

Board of
Directors

Charles M. Bliss
*Chairman of the Board and
Chief Executive Officer, Retired*
Harris Trust and Savings Bank
Chicago, Illinois

Charles W. Elliott
*Executive Vice President
Administration
Chief Financial Officer*
Kellogg Company

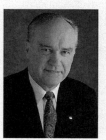

Arnold G. Langbo
*Chairman of the Board
Chief Executive Officer*
Kellogg Company

Philip Caldwell
Senior Managing Director
Shearson Lehman Brothers Inc.
New York, New York
*Chairman and
Chief Executive Officer, Retired*
Ford Motor Company

Claudio X. Gonzalez
*Chairman of the Board
Chief Executive Officer*
Kimberly-Clark de Mexico,
S.A. de C.V.
Mexico City, Mexico

Theodore Cooper
*Chairman of the Board
Chief Executive Officer*
The Upjohn Company
Kalamazoo, Michigan

FIGURE 2.11 (CONTINUED)

Gordon Gund
President and
Chief Executive Officer
Gund Investment Corporation
Princeton, New Jersey

Ann McLaughlin
Visiting Fellow
The Urban Institute
Washington, D.C.

William E. LaMothe
Chairman Emeritus
Kellogg Company

J. Richard Munro
Chairman of the
Executive Committee
Time Warner Inc.
New York, New York

Russell G. Mawby
Chairman of the Board and
Chief Executive Officer
W. K. Kellogg Foundation
Battle Creek, Michigan

Donald Rumsfeld
Chairman and
Chief Executive Officer
General Instrument Corporation
Chicago, Illinois

Timothy P. Smucker
Chairman
The J.M. Smucker Company
Orrville, Ohio

Dolores D. Wharton
President
The Fund for Corporate
Initiatives, Inc.
New York, New York

Committees

Executive Committee
Arnold G. Langbo *(Chairman)*
Charles M. Bliss
Theodore Cooper
Gordon Gund
William E. LaMothe
Russell G. Mawby

Audit Committee
Gordon Gund *(Chairman)*
Claudio X. Gonzalez
Ann McLaughlin
J. Richard Munro
Timothy P. Smucker

**Committee on
Social Responsibility**
Charles M. Bliss *(Chairman)*
Philip Caldwell
Charles W. Elliott
Arnold G. Langbo
Russell G. Mawby
Ann McLaughlin
Dolores D. Wharton

Compensation Committee
Russell G. Mawby *(Chairman)*
Theodore Cooper
J. Richard Munro
Donald Rumsfeld
Dolores D. Wharton

**Employee Benefits
Advisory Committee**
Dolores D. Wharton *(Chairman)*
Charles W. Elliott
Claudio X. Gonzalez
Gordon Gund
J. Richard Munro
Timothy P. Smucker

Finance Committee
Donald Rumsfeld *(Chairman)*
Charles M. Bliss
Philip Caldwell
Charles W. Elliott
Claudio X. Gonzalez
Arnold G. Langbo
Timothy P. Smucker

Nominating Committee
Philip Caldwell *(Chairman)*
Theodore Cooper
William E. LaMothe
Ann McLaughlin
Donald Rumsfeld

ments as a basis to monitor management's activities, assess the risk of the firm, and derive the firm's market value.

 Comprehension Check

1. Why does the Securities and Exchange Commission require corporations to issue 10-K reports? How may the 10-K report be useful to interested parties outside the firm?

2. What information do the following sections of the annual report provide: the chairperson's message to shareholders, the business overview discussion, and the financial information discussion?

3. What information is provided in the corporation's annual report by the balance sheet, the income statement, and the cash flow statement?

4. Why is it important to understand the notes to the financial statements?

5. What is the purpose of the report by the independent accounting firm?

SUMMARY ▼▼▼▼▼▼▼▼▼▼▼

ACCOUNTING VERSUS FINANCE PERSPECTIVE

- Accounting is more concerned with presenting income, whereas finance is more concerned with understanding the funds flow of a company.

- Income cannot be measured with precision. In the derivation of income, management uses many estimates for revenues and costs.

- *Return of investment* is the recapture of the initial investment, whereas *return on investment* is the surplus of revenues over costs generated by investments.

- Funds represent financial resources the firm uses to buy inputs (material, labor, and assets) and pay investors. Money represents funds, but so does buying on credit.

- Book value of an investment is a figure of historical cost only; it has little relevance to financial decision making.

- Both economic and market value of an investment are based on forward-looking projections of expected cash flows.

AN OVERVIEW OF THE ANNUAL REPORT

- The annual report provides a summary of activity that took place in the firm during the past year. The report consists of several parts:
  1. Highlights
  2. Message to shareholders
  3. Business overview
  4. Financial information, including history, balance sheets, income statements, and cash flow statements
  5. Notes explaining accounting methodology and information not contained in the financial statements

6. Auditor's report

7. Miscellaneous information

- The statement of cash flows is extremely important. It provides information as to where funds came from and how they were used.

- Readers of financial statements must be aware that sometimes management purposefully misrepresents information to show higher income.

FURTHER READING ▼▼▼▼▼▼▼▼▼▼▼

Boyadjian, Haig J., and James F. Warren, *Risks: Reading Corporate Signals,* New York: John Wiley & Sons, Ltd., 1987. This book is highly critical of financial information presented in annual reports.

Briloff, Abraham J., *More Debits Than Credits,* New York: Harper & Row, Publishers, 1976 and *The Truth About Corporate Accounting,* New York: Harper & Row, Publishers, 1981. These two books reveal many creative accounting practices.

Gordon, Gus, *Understanding Financial Statements,* Cincinnati, OH: South-Western Publishing Company, 1992. The author explains accounting in understandable language.

SELF-TEST PROBLEMS ▼▼▼▼▼▼▼▼▼▼▼

ST2-1. The following table presents balance sheets on December 31, Year 1 and December 31, Year 2, an income statement for Year 2, and a statement of cash flows for Year 2. Compute the amounts of each of the missing items labeled a through k in the table.

Balance Sheet	Yr. 1	Yr. 2	Income Statement	Yr. 2	Cash Flows	Yr. 2
Cash	$ 200	$ 440	Sales	$ 3000	Collections	$ 2950
Receivables	a	300	Cost of sales	(2080)	Purchases	(2280)
Inventories	300	500	Wages expense	(400)	Increase in	
Fixed assets	700	d	Interest expense	(30)	trade payables	c
Total	$1450	$2140	Income tax	f	Wages paid	j
			Other expenses	g	Interest paid	h
Trade payables	$ 190	$ 350	Depreciation	(100)	Income tax paid	(30)
Wages payable	30	40	Net income	$ 120	Other expenses	
Interest payable	10	20			paid	(280)
Taxes payable	20	30			Cash from	
Other payables	150	100			operations	110
Bonds payable	100	b			Fixed assets	
Common stock	500	700			acquired	e
Retained						
earnings	450	i			Bonds issued	300
Total	$1450	$2140			Common stock	
					issued	k
					Dividends paid	(70)
					Change in cash	$ 240

ST2-2. Organize the following accounts according to the basic financial statement in which they would be located. List these accounts in proper order with headings for the income statement, balance sheet, or statement of cash flows.

Sales	Inventories	Wages payable
Cash	Depreciation expense	Income tax
Bonds payable	Fixed assets (gross)	Collections
Wages paid	Accumulated depreciation	Trade payables
Bonds issued	Dividends paid	Other payables
Wages paid	Other expenses paid	Interest expense
Purchases	Interest payable	Interest paid
Common stock	Wages expense	Receivables
Taxes payable	Retained earnings	Net fixed assets
Other expenses	Fixed assets acquired	Cost of sales
Income tax paid	Common stock issued	Increase in trade payables

PROBLEMS ▼▼▼▼▼▼▼▼▼▼▼▼

THE ACCOUNTING VERSUS FINANCE PERSPECTIVE

2-1. Requiring annual financial statements seems to create problems of measurement and of deciding when revenues and expenses should be recognized. Why do you suppose annual financial statements are necessary?

2-2. Are the dollar amounts shown in financial statements the actual amounts related to the specific item, such as cash, accounts receivable, and inventory?

AN OVERVIEW OF THE ANNUAL REPORT

2-3. State your reaction to the statement that "Corporations' annual reports are simply slick picture books designed by management to give themselves a pat on the back."

2-4. What is the overall purpose of the chairperson's letter in a corporation's annual report?

2-5. Identify five important pieces of information divulged in Kellogg's letter "To Our Shareholders" (Figure 2.2).

2-6. What is the purpose of the management's discussion and analysis of financial condition and results of operations?

2-7. What is the primary message of Kellogg's "Business Overview: North America" shown in Figure 2.3?

2-8. How does the management's discussion and analysis of financial condition and results of operations benefit investors?

2-9. What is the purpose of Kellogg's "Financial Review" shown in Figure 2.4?

2-10. List some relevant information revealed by the 11-year history (Figure 2.5) of Kellogg's financial results.

2-11. What are the basic financial statements found in every annual report? Briefly discuss the limits on the usefulness of these financial statements for outside users such as lenders and investors.

2-12. Why is it difficult to measure income precisely over any period less than the life of the company?

2-13. Figure 2.6 shows three years of income data. Without doing any numerical analysis, what do these data convey to you?

2-14. Kellogg's balance sheet in Figure 2.7 shows the two most recent years of data. Without doing any calculations, what useful information is revealed by this balance sheet?

2-15. Without doing any calculations, what does Kellogg's statement of cash flows in Figure 2.8 reveal?

2-16. What is the purpose of notes to financial statements? Why should the reader of a corporation's annual report always read these footnotes?

2-17. Kellogg's "Notes to Financial Statements" in Figure 2.9 contain important information for the analyst to understand the financial statements. What are some items the figure reveals?

2-18. Are the three financial statements discussed in this chapter related or unrelated? Discuss.

2-19. Briefly discuss some of the concerns encountered when analyzing foreign companies' financial statements.

2-20. What does the auditor's opinion paragraph prepared by independent public accountants imply when it states that generally accepted accounting principles were applied on a consistent basis?

2-21. Figure 2.10 shows the external auditors' report for Kellogg. Does it disclose any information useful to an outsider who is reading Kellogg's financial statements?

2-22. "The financial statements of a company are management's, not the accountant's." Discuss the implications of this statement.

2-23. In some cases there has been publicity in the financial press concerning lawsuits against firms of certified public accountants (CPAs). Should investors place reliance on the financial statements that were audited by a CPA firm that is involved in a lawsuit?

2-24. Other information about Kellogg shown in Figure 2.11 reveals the makeup of the board of directors and the committee assignments. What useful information is provided by this figure?

2-25. As a potential shareholder, why should you look at financial reports when you can easily get a stockbroker to advise you as to what companies you might invest in?

2-26. Assume that you own common stock in a particular company. Why would you read the financial reports issued by that company? Won't your broker advise you as to whether you should continue to maintain the investment or sell out?

DISCLOSURE ASSIGNMENTS

2-27. Use the *Disclosure* database to answer the following questions pertaining to Nike, Inc. and Reebok International Ltd.

a. Briefly discuss the major concerns of the management as revealed in the president's letter to shareholders.

b. From the footnotes to the financial statements, determine the following: How is revenue recognized for reporting in the income statement? What rule is used to classify investments as belonging in the cash account? How are fixed assets depreciated and over what period of time? Do any contingent liabilities exist? Have any accounts been reclassified to conform to new accounting rules and, if so, what impact did these changes have on either the income statement or the balance sheet?

LIBRARY ASSIGNMENTS

2-28. Obtain the address of a corporation of interest to you by checking Moody's *Industrial Manual, Value Line Investment Survey,* or some other source available in your library. Write to the corporate secretary or the director of shareholder relations for a copy of the corporation's most recent annual report. Based on the management discussion and analysis section of the report, write a one-page summary of management's views for the corporation's future.

2-29. Review the corporate annual report files in your library (or visit a stock brokerage company or the trust department of a commercial bank in your area) for an annual report in which the audit report by the certified public accountant contains a "qualified opinion." Discuss the circumstances that gave rise to the qualifications and suggest what the company might have done differently to obtain a "clean opinion."

2-30. Find a recent story in a business magazine or newspaper that discusses how management of a particular firm used creative accounting (maybe fraud) to increase the income of the company.

COMPREHENSIVE PROBLEMS ▼▼▼▼▼▼▼▼▼▼▼

2-31. The following table presents balance sheets on December 31, Year 1 and December 31, Year 2, an income statement for Year 2, and a statement of cash flows for Year 2. Compute the amounts of each of the missing items labeled *a* through *j* in the table.

Balance Sheet	Yr. 1	Yr. 2	Income Statement	Yr. 2	Cash Flows	Yr. 2
Cash	$ 100	$ 160	Sales	$2000	Collections	$ 1700
Receivables	200	a	Cost of sales	b	Purchases	(1300)
Inventories	300	400	Salary expense	(400)	Increase in	
Fixed assets	600	740	Interest expense	(20)	trade payables	40
Total	$1200	$1800	Income tax	(35)	Wages paid	c
			Other expenses	e	Interest paid	(20)
Trade payables	$ 180	$ 220	Depreciation	(60)	Income tax paid	(40)
Wages payable	30	40	Net income	$ 35	Other expenses	
Interest payable	d	10			paid	(220)
Taxes payable	20	15			Cash from	
Other payables	115	145			operations	f
Bonds payable	200	400			Fixed assets	
Common stock	h	600			acquired	g
Retained						
earnings	345	i			Bonds issued	200
Total	$1200	$ j			Common stock	
					issued	300
					Dividends paid	(10)
					Change in cash	$ 60

2-32. The following table presents balance sheets on December 31, Year 1 and December 31, Year 2, an income statement for Year 2, and a statement of cash flows for Year 2. Compute the amounts of each of the missing items labeled a through k in the table.

Balance Sheet	Yr. 1	Yr. 2	Income Statement	Yr. 2	Cash Flows	Yr. 2
Cash	$ 100	$ b	Sales	$ 2500	Collections	$ 2200
Receivables	300	600	Cost of sales	(1520)	Purchases	(1620)
Inventories	400	500	Salary expense	(500)	Increase in	
Fixed assets	700	c	Interest expense	f	trade payables	h
Total	$1500	$1950	Income tax	(20)	Wages paid	i
			Other expenses	g	Interest paid	(70)
Trade payables	$ 220	$ 220	Depreciation	(70)	Income tax paid	j
Wages payable	70	80	Net income	$ 50	Other expenses	
Interest payable	50	20			paid	(300)
Taxes payable	10	15			Cash from	
Other payables	200	200			operations	(295)
Bonds payable	400	325			Fixed assets	
Common stock	250	800			acquired	(170)
Retained						
earnings	a	e			Bonds issued	(75)
Total	$ d	$1950			Common stock	
					issued	k
					Dividends paid	(60)
					Change in cash	$ (50)

ST2-1.
a: $250 — Difference in total and other Year 1 assets

b: $400 — $100 Year 1 bonds payable + $300 bonds issued from cash flows statement

c: $160 — Difference in $190 Year 1 trade payables and $350 Year 2 trade payables

d: $900 — Difference in Year 2 total and other Year 2 assets

e: ($300) — $900 Year 2 fixed assets − $700 Year 1 fixed assets + $100 depreciation (income statement)

f: ($40) — $30 Year 2 taxes payable + $30 income taxes paid − $20 Year 1 taxes payable

g: ($230) — $280 other expenses paid − $150 other payables Year 1 + $100 other payables Year 2

h: ($20) — $30 interest expense − $10 increase in interest payable from balance sheets

i: $500 — $450 retained earnings Year 1 + $120 net income Year 2 − $70 dividends paid Year 2

j: ($390) — $400 wages expense − $10 increase in wages payable from balance sheets

k: $200 — Increase in common stock account from Year 1 to Year 2 in the balance sheets

ST2-2.

Balance Sheet as of (Date)

Current assets:		Current liabilitites:	
Cash		Trade payables	
Receivables		Wages payable	
Inventories		Interest payable	
Total current assets	_____	Taxes payable	
	_____	Others payable	
Gross fixed assets		Total current liabilities	_____
Less accumulated depreciation	_____		_____
Net fixed assets	_____	Long-term liabilities:	
		Bond payable	
		Stockholders' equity:	
		Common stock	
	_____	Retained Earnings	_____
Total assets	=====	Total liabilities and equity	=====

Income Statement for the Year		Statement of Cash Flows for the Year	
Sales		Operating activities:	
Cost of sales	_____	Collections	
Gross income		Purchases	
Selling, general and		Increase in trade payables	
administrative expenses:		Depreciation	
Wages expense		Wages paid	
Depreciation expense		Interest paid	
Other expenses	_____	Other expenses paid	
Operating income		Income tax paid	_____
Interest expense	_____	Cash flow from operations	_____
Taxable income			
Income tax	_____	Investing activities:	
Net income	=====	Fixed assets acquired	_____
		Cash flow from investing	_____
		Financing activities:	
		Bonds issued	
		Common stock issued	
		Dividends paid	_____
		Cash flow from financing	_____
		Net cash flow	
		Beginning cash balance	_____
		Ending cash balance	=====

Video Case 2

How Taxes Drive Business Decisions

from *Business World,* October 1, 1989

Chapter 2 reviews the basic accounting statements of the corporation. Finance is not an accounting course, but it does rely on accounting information, particularly estimates of after-tax cash flows. Later in the text we use such cash flows to choose among potential investments. The profitability of some investments depends on a favorable tax treatment. Thus, it is important to understand the basics of accounting, particularly the computation of after-tax cash flows.

Politicians recognize the importance of taxes in business decision making and modify the tax code to stimulate certain types of behavior. When the economy needs a boost, legislators often insert some form of the investment tax credit (ITC) into the tax code. By reducing the cost of investing in productive assets, this change encourages companies to invest in new capital and helps generate more jobs. President Carter's energy policy included tax credits on solar energy and energy conservation. Since tax laws emerge from a political process, it should surprise no one that politicians use them to achieve their political ends—to satisfy strong constituent groups.

A recent example of both types of tax reform occurred during the Congressional debate on the capital gains tax cut. To increase tax revenues the administration proposed lowering the capital gains tax from 33 percent to 19.6 percent for a two-year period. After two years the rate returns to the 33 percent level. The capital gains tax applies to profits investors earn from price appreciation on their investments. Proponents of the plan argue that the lower rate on capital gains income will stimulate investors to sell those assets, take their profits, and, most importantly from the administration's perspective, pay taxes on those profits, albeit at the lower rate. Having this lower rate expire in just two years encourages investors to sell and be taxed now rather than later.

Tax laws do not favor just wealthy investors and the interests of big business. The most commonly used tax advantage is probably the deductibility of the interest on home mortgage payments. Homeowners benefit from this tax law by reducing their taxable income by the amount of mortgage interest paid, which effectively reduces the cost of financing their home. Another example of a commonly used tax benefit is the IRA or individual retirement account. IRAs allow people to make tax-deductible deposits into a retirement account. If the funds are left in the account until retirement age (defined as age $59\frac{1}{2}$) no taxes are paid on either the original deposit or earnings on the investment. Keogh plans and 401(k) plans offer similar tax shelter advantages.

Invariably, changes in the tax laws create winners and losers. In the case of the capital gains tax cut, one likely winner is the brokerage industry. Stockbrokers benefit because investors with large gains on investments will sell, generating brokerage commissions from the sale and from the subsequent reinvestment of the funds.

Study Questions

1. To understand the importance of taxes, consider the decision to raise additional funds for a growing corporation. The company must choose between borrowing $1 million or issuing additional stock. Suppose interest on the debt will be $100,000 per year and that annual dividends on the new shares will be $70,000 per year. If the company's marginal tax rate is 34 percent, will the company's after-tax cash flow be higher with debt or equity?

2. Invariably, changes in the tax laws create winners and losers. In the case of the capital gains tax cut, list a winner and describe why the winner benefits from the tax change.

An Overview of the Financial System

Our economy is built upon the principle of exchange, which creates markets for goods, services, and financial instruments, such as money; the goal is the formation of satisfying patterns of consumption and resource allocation. As economic beings in a free-market system we consume as well as produce, save as well as spend, and make decisions to maximize our wealth. We often take for granted the importance of a working, free-market economic system. What would it be like to live in a country where goods and services were restricted or where it was difficult to exchange them? What would it be like to live in a place where it is difficult to borrow or lend money? In such an environment, any consumption, investment, production, and financing decisions would be very different from what we now experience.

We begin this chapter by discussing how the market economy system forms the basis for the financial market system. Just as the product and service economy is an aggregate result of business and individual supply and demand for products and services, the financial system is an aggregation of institutions, markets, and relationships that enables funds to flow through the economy. Some participants want to invest, others want to borrow, and the financial markets are the forums for the exchange of financial resources to fulfill the financial goal of maximization of wealth. Once we lay the economic foundation for the financial system, we build on it by examining interest rates and factors influencing them. The role of the Federal Reserve System is of particular importance. Its management of the nation's money supply directly affects interest rates and, thus, the profitability of investments by investors and businesses.

After you have studied this chapter, you should have a better understanding of:

- Why wealth increases when financial markets and production opportunities exist.
- The importance of interest rates in creating wealth.
- How the Federal Reserve System's monetary policy affects interest rates.

- Why monitoring the actions of the Federal Reserve System may be helpful in determining the direction of interest rates and financial markets.
- The global influences on domestic interest rates and why they are important.

3.1. THE ECONOMIC SYSTEM

As defined in Chapter 1, the goal of finance is to maximize the value of cash flows generated by an investment. This is accomplished through good decision making. Investors seek securities that appreciate in value. Businesses seek projects that earn returns greater than their costs. Financial institutions seek ways to reinvest money deposits so they can earn profits. Each financial player or participant pursues its goals within the *economic system*. The **economic system** allows for the exchange of goods or services and money; it consists of business, government, and household sectors of the economy, all of which interact with each other. While all societies or countries have such sectors, they relate in very different ways in different countries. For example, the government sector is much more predominant in determining outcomes of the economic system in China or Cuba than it is in the United States.

Implementation of *fiscal policy* and *monetary policy* are means the government sector uses to alter economic activity of households and businesses. **Fiscal policy** refers to policies or laws that affect the government budget. **Monetary policy** involves changes in the economy's money supply, which is the responsibility of the nation's central bank. Although the government plays a major role in the economy, it is not necessary to concentrate on the government sector to show how financial markets allow the economic system to operate more effectively. Therefore, we exclude discussion of the government sector now. Then, in the next section of the chapter, we consider the significant influence of monetary policy on the financial system.

3.1.1 The Simplest Economic System: No Production, Exchange, Financial Markets

Instead of looking into the real world with all its complexity and detail in this section, we build a model economy to clarify the forces that shape finance. Our economy initially has just one person, Robinson, who lives on a deserted island. Robinson's wealth consists of 100 pounds of seed corn that must meet his needs both now and in the near future. No opportunity exists to produce or increase Robinson's initial wealth position, nor can he exchange goods or services with anyone else. Robinson must decide how to allocate his wealth between consumption of corn this period and consumption next period. The rules dictate that he cannot save corn past the next period (it would rot).

The decision of how much consumption to defer to the next period is the same as determining how much to save this period. However, in this economy, one cob of corn saved this period is still only one cob of corn next period—nothing more, nothing less. The interplay of Robinson's satisfaction for consumption (and survival) now versus investing for future consumption determines his **time preference rate.** (See Figure 3.1.) He tries to maximize total satisfaction over the two periods.[1]

---

[1]An introductory microeconomics course refers to this exercise as maximizing an individual's *utility for consumption.* Economists often use utility curves to illustrate this point.

Economic system. Relationship between the components of an economy (such as its households, firms, and government) and the institutional framework of laws and customs within which these components operate.

Fiscal policy. Deliberate exercise of government's power to tax and spend in order to achieve price stability, help dampen the swings of business cycles, and bring the nation's output and employment to desired levels.

Monetary policy. Deliberate exercise of a country's monetary authority's (for example, Federal Reserve's) power to induce expansions or contractions in the money supply in order to help dampen the swings of business cycles and bring the nation's output and employment to desired levels.

Time preference rate. Human desire for a good in the present as opposed to the future. The rate is reflected by the price people are willing to pay for immediate possession of the good, as opposed to the price they are willing to pay for future possession.

FIGURE 3.1

TIME PREFERENCE FOR CONSUMPTION

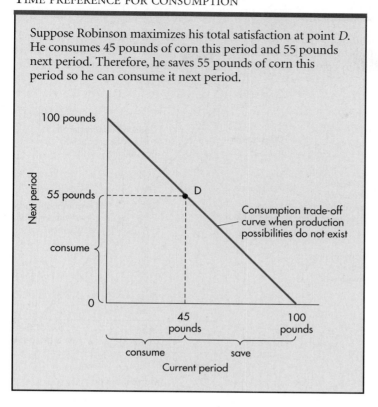

Suppose Robinson maximizes his total satisfaction at point *D*. He consumes 45 pounds of corn this period and 55 pounds next period. Therefore, he saves 55 pounds of corn this period so he can consume it next period.

100 pounds

55 pounds

Next period

D

Consumption trade-off curve when production possibilities do not exist

consume

0

45 pounds

100 pounds

consume   save

Current period

3.1.2 Introducing Production into the Economic System

Let's introduce *production opportunities* into this one-person economy. The introduction of **production opportunities** means that instead of simply saving some wealth for later consumption, Robinson actually invests some wealth now so that future consumption increases. The ability to produce allows him to enjoy the same current consumption but increase his future consumption. For instance, assume that for each pound of seed corn planted this period, Robinson can harvest 1.25 pounds of seed corn next period. The 0.25 portion of the multiplier represents the **rate of return,** that is, the increase in output from investing one unit of input.

Earlier, we decided that Robinson gets the greatest satisfaction by consuming 45 pounds of corn this period. Hence, by planting (that is, *investing*) 55 pounds of seed corn, he will have 68.75 pounds (= 55 pounds × 1.25) available for consumption next period. Total available corn increases 13.75 pounds, or 25 percent, over the earlier situation of no production opportunities. The rate of return from producing exceeds his time preference rate for consumption by 25 percent. Robinson's total future consumption can be stated as:

Production opportunities. The diversion of some present wealth into activities which result in increased future wealth.

Rate of return. In a financial framework, it is the interest rate that equates the present value of cash returns on an investment with the present value of the cash expenditures relating to the investment.

$$\text{Future consumption} = \text{Investment in production} \times (1 + \text{rate of return}) \quad (3.1)$$

$$= 55 \times (1 + 0.25)$$

$$= 68.75 \text{ pounds}$$

FIGURE 3.2
RETURN TO INVESTMENT

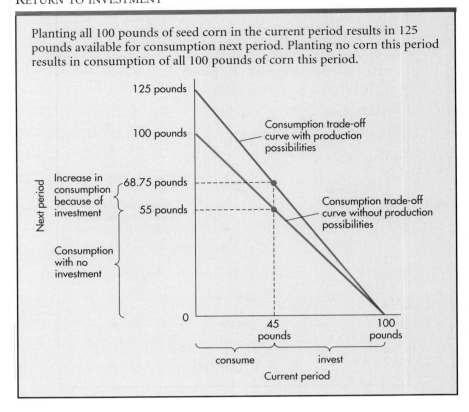

Planting all 100 pounds of seed corn in the current period results in 125 pounds available for consumption next period. Planting no corn this period results in consumption of all 100 pounds of corn this period.

125 pounds

100 pounds

Consumption trade-off curve with production possibilities

Next period

Increase in consumption because of investment

68.75 pounds

55 pounds

Consumption trade-off curve without production possibilities

Consumption with no investment

0

45 pounds

100 pounds

consume

invest

Current period

As Figure 3.2 shows, production opportunities cause Robinson's consumption opportunity curve to change to the production possibilities curve. *The availability of production leads to greater overall wealth.*

3.1.3 Introducing Exchange into the Economic System

Now we assume that other people enter Robinson's economy with similar or different commodities. Each person maximizes her or his satisfaction by allocating resources between current and future consumption. But since individuals are not homogeneous in their attitudes toward savings and consumption decisions, they possess different time preference rates for consumption. Soon they decide to trade among themselves. For example, Robinson exchanges seed corn that he does not consume this period for another person's surplus wheat, and so on.

With the growth in the number of people, the single-sector economy divides into two sectors: a *business sector* and a *household sector*. The **business sector** produces goods and services. The **household sector** purchases goods and services from the business sector and provides inputs to the business sector so that it can produce the goods and services. To facilitate exchanges of goods and services between the sectors, all participants in the economy agree on a form of money (see Figure 3.3).

After a period of satisfying basic consumption needs, households begin to actually save some of their income. But because no financial security exists for them to buy with their savings, they simply hoard it. In addition, businesses do not sell all their out-

Business sector. Part of the economy that consists of units that produce and provide goods and services to households and other businesses.

Household sector. Part of the economy that consists of units that consume and provide funds and labor to business sector. Households purchase goods and services from business sector.

FIGURE 3.3
TWO-SECTOR ECONOMY WITH PRODUCTION

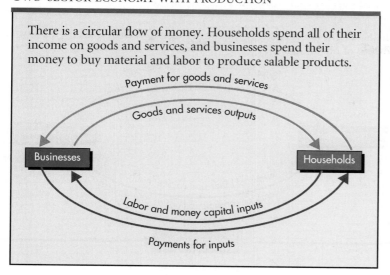

There is a circular flow of money. Households spend all of their income on goods and services, and businesses spend their money to buy material and labor to produce salable products.

Payment for goods and services

Goods and services outputs

Businesses

Households

Labor and money capital inputs

Payments for inputs

Investment goods.
Additions to the economy's real capital stock; that is, all final purchases of capital equipment (machinery, tools), all construction, both residential and non-residential, and changes in inventory.

Surplus (saving) units. Net savers, who save more than they spend. The household sector is considered a net surplus sector.

Deficit (borrowing) units. Net borrowers, who spend more than they save. The business sector is considered a net deficit unit.

put to households. Some firms produce plant and equipment, called **investment goods,** which they sell to other businesses. Figure 3.4 displays the developing economy.

3.1.4 Introducing a Financial System into the Economic System

To focus on the essentials, consider the two-sector economy shown in Figure 3.4. Let's assume that households are **surplus (saving) units;** they earn more than they spend. Businesses are **deficit (borrowing) units;** they spend more than they earn and borrow

FIGURE 3.4
TWO-SECTOR ECONOMY WITH SAVINGS AND INVESTING

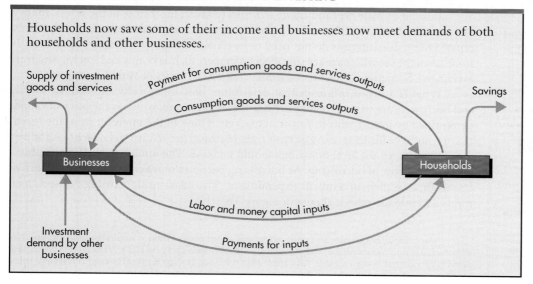

Households now save some of their income and businesses now meet demands of both households and other businesses.

Supply of investment goods and services

Payment for consumption goods and services outputs

Consumption goods and services outputs

Savings

Businesses

Households

Investment demand by other businesses

Labor and money capital inputs

Payments for inputs

FIGURE 3.5
ECONOMY WITH A FINANCIAL SYSTEM

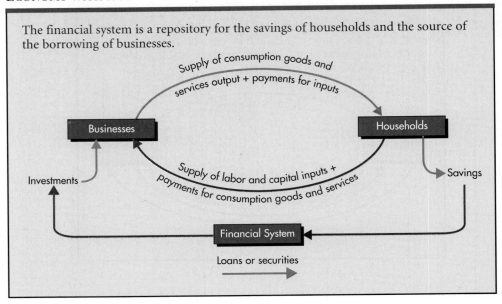

The financial system is a repository for the savings of households and the source of the borrowing of businesses.

Supply of consumption goods and services output + payments for inputs

Businesses

Households

Supply of labor and capital inputs + payments for consumption goods and services

Investments

Savings

Financial System

Loans or securities

to finance the deficit.[2] What do households do with their savings? Where do businesses borrow the money that allows them to spend more than they earn? The answer to both of these questions is the *financial system.*

The function of the **financial system** is to accept the excess money of savers and lend it to deficit units which need to borrow. This function is made more important by the fact that methods of production often require a volume of money greater than can be generated by the producing firm itself in its early stages of production. For example, a firm needs to construct or lease buildings and equipment to manufacture a product. The financial system meets the needs of such firms by locating, securing, and channeling money to them (see Figure 3.5).

Businesses issue *debt* and *equity securities* to savers for the use of the savers' money. We can view a **debt security** as the business providing an IOU to savers for funds it must repay. Ownership interests do not need to be repaid and are called **equity securities.** In some cases the securities are actually pieces of paper, such as bonds and stocks, which are exchanged. Sometimes a security is simply a signed contract or verbal agreement.

What is a major influence that determines how much savers are willing to save and borrowers are willing to borrow? It is the **interest rate,** which is the price of money determined by participants in financial markets. Think of the interest rate as the incentive for households to save. As interest rates increase, the reward to households for savings is greater, so the level of savings should increase. The interest rate is also the business sector's cost of borrowing. As borrowing becomes more costly, businesses borrow less to finance their investment expenditures. The relationship existing between loan funds and interest rates is shown in Figure 3.6.

Financial system. The channel through which the savings of surplus sectors flow to the deficit sectors that wish to borrow.

Debt security. Agreement to pay a specified sum (called the principal) either at a future date or over the course of a loan, during which time interest may be paid on certain dates.

Equity security. Security which provides ownership in the firm issuing it. The security has no maturity date.

Interest rate. The price paid for borrowing money. It is the rate of exchange of present consumption for future consumption, or the price of current dollars in terms of future dollars.

[2]Depicting all households as surplus sectors and all businesses as deficit sectors is a simplification. Not all households earn more than they spend—some spend more than they earn and are deficit units. Some businesses also generate more earnings than they invest and are surplus units. However, households taken together earn more than they spend. Businesses, in the aggregate, spend more than they earn.

▼▼▼▼▼▼▼▼▼▼▼▼▼▼

THE EFFECT OF INTEREST RATES ON SMALL BUSINESS LENDING

by Earl Nau, President and CEO, First City National Bank

First City National Bank was chartered in July 1984. The bank is located in Springfield, Missouri, a community of about 150,000. When we began business, the prime interest rate was at 13.5 percent. For the next four years, the rate steadily declined to 9.5 percent in June 1988. During this time, our bank experienced rapid growth and heavy demand in small business loans, as well as federally guaranteed Small Business Administration (SBA) loans. The SBA loans amounted to one-third of our business at that time, placing First City National Bank in the top 100 banks in the nation, out of approximately 13,000 banks, relative to dollars loaned on SBA loans. For the next 18 months, the prime increased, eventually reaching 11 percent. During this time, we saw a slight decrease in the demand for money for business loans, even though inflation was only in the 4.4 percent to 6.1 percent range. Loan demand didn't increase because of interest rate uncertainty in the economy as perceived by the borrowing public.

In January 1991, the prime interest rate started a quick descent from 10 percent, reaching 6.5 percent within 12 months. A falling prime rate brought an increase in the demand for SBA loans, as well as other small business loans. Most of our SBA loans were to small manufacturing startups, expansions, and acquisitions. A small amount of loan business was booked for retailing and professional persons, such as lawyers, dentists, accountants, and veterinarians, establishing or expanding offices.

As the prime rate has been relatively stable at 6 percent to 6.5 percent for the past two years, increased demand for money has been consistent and First City National Bank has maintained an average loan-to-deposit ratio ranging from 78 percent to 85 percent. This ratio is considered moderate to aggressive by most examining authorities and bank analysts. Because of this increase in business, we were able to increase SBA loans in 1992 and 1993. SBA lending still accounts for about one-third of the bank's overall business. Direct loans of the bank also increased in concert with SBA loans.

The banking industry as a whole has not experienced a great increase in commercial loan demand over the last year, although there has been a moderate increase. The decreasing interest rates and overall strengthening of the economy helped reduce loan charge-offs in 1993 to a low level within the banking industry, as well as helping to reduce the level of troubled debt.

Inasmuch as we are primarily a commercial lender, we don't have extensive experience in refinancing of real estate or real estate loan purchases, although any one month will show us with ten to twenty real estate deals in progress. However, the lowering of interest rates over the last two years has brought about a crescendo of real estate refinancing and purchases, as well as new home construction.

It is our experience with borrowers and businesspeople who lived through the prime rate spike to 22 percent in the early 1980s that borrowers begin to batten down the hatches relative to expansion, acquisition, and new business borrowing when the prime interest rate begins to shift upward. Conversely, level or slowly declining interest rates appear to stimulate the risk-taking behavior of entrepreneurs who own and operate their own businesses, thereby increasing demand for small business loans.

We characterize investment and saving as the present sacrifice of certain current consumption for uncertain future benefit. For businesses and households to defer current consumption for investment or savings yielding uncertain benefits, they must expect the value of their investments or savings at the end of the holding period to exceed their initial value. This idea is the concept of time preference rate we discussed

FIGURE 3.6

SᴜᴘᴘLY ᴀɴᴅ ᴅᴇᴍᴀɴᴅ ғᴏʀ ғᴜɴᴅs

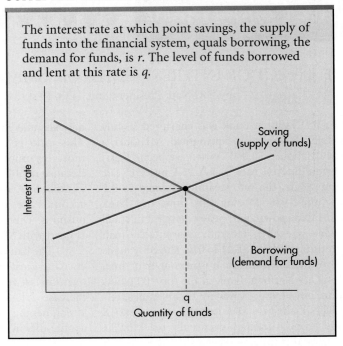

The interest rate at which point savings, the supply of funds into the financial system, equals borrowing, the demand for funds, is *r*. The level of funds borrowed and lent at this rate is *q*.

earlier (see Equation 3.1). More specifically, the idea is the *time value of money principle*, which will be developed fully in the next chapter. Illustration 3.1 provides an example of the principle in the context of how financial markets aid the allocation of funds between consuming, investing, and saving.

ILLUSTRATION 3.1

Resource allocation decisions

Robinson has $100 to allocate between consuming, investing, and saving. He can earn 7 percent on his savings and also borrow any needed funds at 7 percent. Different businesses seek to borrow from him to finance their riskless one-year projects.

Projects	% Return	Cost	Total Return	Total Return from Investing in Savings at 7%	Project Return Minus Savings Return
Fiero	10.0%	$10	$ 11.00	$10.70	$0.30
DeGrazia	7.5	15	16.13	16.05	0.08
Spyder	6.0	30	31.80	32.10	(0.30)
BHS	4.0	20	20.80	21.40	(0.60)
Edsel	1.1	25	25.28	26.75	(1.47)
		$100	$105.01		

Note: Total project return = Cost x (1 + % project return/100).
     Total savings return = Cost x (1 + 7/100)

The owner of the Fiero project seeks $10 and offers a return of 10 percent plus the return of Robinson's original $10 investment after one year. Since this project's return exceeds the 7 percent savings rate, he invests $10 in it. He likewise invests $15 in the DeGrazia project, since its return exceeds the 7 percent savings rate. Robinson rejects all remaining projects because they earn less than 7 percent.

Now that Robinson has made his investment decision, costing $25, he must decide how much to consume and save this period. The following table indicates several alternatives for his remaining endowment of $75: consume it all (line 2), save it all (line 5), consume some and save some (lines 3 and 4), and consume all $75 plus borrow $25.35 against the *present value* ($10.28 + $15.07) of the future cash flows of his investments in Fiero and DeGrazia and consume it (line 1).

	This Period				Consumption Next Period from			Consumption for 2 Periods
	Consume	Borrow	Save	Invest	Saving	Investing	Total	
1.	$100.35	$25.35	$ 0	$25	$ 0.00	$ 0.00	$ 0.00	$100.35
2.	75.00	0.00	0	25	0.00	27.13†	27.13	102.13
3.	50.00	0.00	25	25	26.75*	27.13	53.88	103.88
4.	25.00	0.00	50	25	53.50	27.13	80.63	105.63
5.	0.00	0.00	75	25	80.25	27.13	107.38	107.38

Note:

*Consumption next period from saving = Amount saved this period x (1 + 0.07)
= $25 x (1.07)
= $26.75

†Consumption next period from investing = Amount invested this period in Fiero x (1 + 0.10)
+ amount invested this period in DeGrazia x (1 + 0.075)
= $10 x 1.10 + $15 x 1.075
= $27.13

Let's analyze line 1, the borrowing alternative. Fiero returns $11 at the end of one year. How much is the future $11 worth today if Robinson can borrow money at 7 percent?[3] In other words, how much does he need to invest today at a 7 percent interest rate for it to be worth $11 one year from now? The amount he needs to invest today is the *present value amount:*

Present value amount $\times$ (1 + 0.07) = $11

Solving for present value amount results in:

Present value amount = $11 $\div$ (1.07) = $10.28

Robinson can borrow $10.28 against Fiero's next period cash flow of $11 to increase current consumption. Similarly, he

[3]We are solving for the *present value* of the future cash flow. Chapter 4 addresses this and other time value of money problems.

can borrow $15.07 against DeGrazia's next period cash flow of $16.13 (that is, $16.13 ÷ 1.07).

Thus, Robinson can consume $100.35 this period: $100 initial endowment - $25 investment in the two projects + $25.35 he borrows against the two projects (= $10.28 + $15.07). Next period, he uses the $27.13 cash flow he receives from Fiero ($11) and DeGrazia ($16.13) to pay off the loan of $25.35 plus its interest of $1.78: $25.35 × 0.07 = $1.78. By consuming $100.35 this period, Robinson has no cash flow to consume next period.

Depending on his desire for current consumption, Robinson will choose a combination of consuming, investing, and borrowing or saving that provides him with the greatest satisfaction.

Illustration 3.1 reveals several important features of having financial markets available.

- *The investment decision is separate from the consumption decision.* We should invest in all assets with expected returns equal to or greater than the interest rate determined by market participants. Alternatively, think of the process as investing in all projects whose monetary return exceeds the minimum monetary return the funds could earn.
- *If wealth-enhancing investments require more funds than we have available, we should borrow from the financial market.* For example, if Robinson's initial endowment in Illustration 3.1 is only $4, he should borrow $21 from the financial market to invest in Fiero and DeGrazia. He borrows at 7 percent and earns a 10 percent rate of return on Fiero and 7.5 percent on DeGrazia.
- *Financial markets allow us to borrow against future cash flows to satisfy our current consumption needs.* The future cash flows provide the necessary funds to repay the loan.
- *Financial markets permit us to transfer wealth across time to increase satisfaction.*

Illustration 3.1 also shows the importance of interest rates determined in the financial marketplace. For example, if the interest rate is 12 percent, none of the projects in the illustration are worthy. Each project would earn less than the 12 percent Robinson could earn through savings.

▶ **Comprehension Check**

1. Explain what is meant by a person's time preference rate for consumption.
2. How is future consumption affected by the introduction of production opportunities?
3. How does a wealth maximizer determine the balance between production (investing) and current consumption?
4. How does the introduction of financial markets affect an economy? What is the role of the market interest rate?
5. Describe how you should allocate resources between the current period and a future period so as to maximize your satisfaction.

3.2 STRUCTURE OF INTEREST RATES

Let's continue our discussion of financial markets and the broader economic system by examining interest rates. The interest rate is a reflection of the time value of money, or the cost of money as stated earlier. Many factors, including inflation and the risk of default by the borrower, influence the time value of money. Central to this discussion is *money* and its effect on interest rates. We distinguish between *nominal interest rates* and *real interest rates.* And although our discussion mainly refers to the interest rate, there are in fact several different interest rates: money rates, consumer savings rates, government treasury rates, government agency rates, and corporate rates, among others. Generally, these interest rates all move in the same direction in response to economic activity.

3.2.1 Nominal versus Real Interest Rates

There have been significant fluctuations in interest rates in countries' economies over the years. In the early 1960s, U.S. corporations borrowed in the financial markets at interest rates of about 5 percent a year. By the end of the 1960s, the borrowing rate was nearly 8 percent a year. During the 1970s and early 1980s, the borrowing rate steadily advanced, reaching the low twenties, before retreating to single digits during the late 1980s and early 1990s.

Why do interest rates fluctuate so much? The answer to this question lies in understanding the difference between nominal interest rates and real interest rates. **Nominal interest rates** are those rates actually paid and received in the financial market. **Real interest rates** are the rates that nominal interest rates translate into when the effects of *inflation* are removed. **Inflation** is the increase in the supply of money and *credit* beyond the proportion of available goods and services, resulting in a sharp and continuing rise in price levels.[4] **Credit** represents an amount of funds someone agrees to lend.

Figure 3.7 shows the close relationship between inflation and money growth for selected countries. There is much evidence that the inflation rate in one country is dependent on inflation rates in other countries. The interdependency of countries' interest rates is of particular importance among the major currencies used for business transactions—the U.S. dollar, the German mark, and the Japanese yen. The appendix to this chapter outlines this interdependency in terms of a concept called *interest rate parity.*

The nominal interest rate, r_N, consists of two parts:

- real rate of interest, r_R
- expected inflation premium, Δp

When participants in the economic system correctly anticipate changes in the supply of money and credit relative to the supply of goods and services, there is *expected inflation.* Unanticipated changes in the supply of money and credit relative to the supply of goods and services produce *unexpected inflation.* The **expected inflation premium** pays investors for the loss of purchasing power of their money expected to occur over the life

Nominal interest rate. The observed rate of interest, uncorrected for inflation. *Nominal* means in name only, and thus is likely not the effective rate of interest.

Real interest rate. The observable (nominal) rate of interest minus the rate of inflation.

Inflation. Rise in the general price level of all goods and services — or equivalently, a decline in the purchasing power of a unit of money (such as the dollar).

Credit. Arrangement that allows a customer to take goods or services and delay making payment for them.

Expected inflation premium. The premium investors require to compensate them for the expected eroding effect of inflation on the value of money.

---

[4]We often hear the following arguments. Labor leaders vaguely attribute inflation to the "greed" or "exorbitant profits" of manufacturers. And most business executives are similarly eager to pass the buck. The retailer throws the blame for higher prices on the wholesaler, the wholesaler on the manufacturer, and the manufacturer on the raw material supplier and on labor costs.

FIGURE 3.7

MONEY GROWTH AND INFLATION ACROSS COUNTRIES, 1986-1990

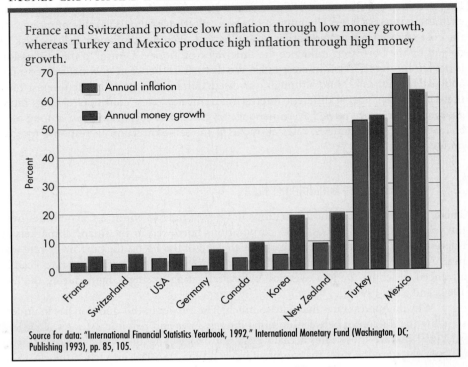

France and Switzerland produce low inflation through low money growth, whereas Turkey and Mexico produce high inflation through high money growth.

Source for data: "International Financial Statistics Yearbook, 1992," International Monetary Fund (Washington, DC; Publishing 1993), pp. 85, 105.

of the security. Hence, we can think of the real interest rate as the nominal rate quoted if the expected inflation rate were zero.

Mathematically, the relationship between the nominal rate, the real rate, and the risk adjustment for expected inflation is:[5]

Nominal interest rate

$$= (1 + \text{real interest rate}) \times (1 + \overset{\text{expected}}{\text{inflation premium}}) - 1 \qquad (3.2)$$

$$r_N = (1 + r_R) \times (1 + \Delta p) - 1$$

The nominal interest rate is observable; it is the rate paid and received in the financial market. The expected rate of inflation is indirectly observable by observed price changes from year to year. However, we cannot observe the real rate of interest. (See Illustration 3.2.) We calculate it by rearranging Equation 3.2 as:

$$r_R = \frac{(1 + r_N)}{(1 + \Delta p)} - 1 \qquad (3.3)$$

[5]The nominal interest rate (Equation 3.2) is written frequently as:

Nominal interest rate = Real interest rate + expected inflation premium

$$r_N = r_R + \Delta p$$

This formulation is not mathematically correct because it ignores the cross-product term $r_R \times \Delta p$ when Equation 3.2 is expanded. However, this simpler equation does provide a good approximation.

FIGURE 3.8

AVERAGE REAL RATES OF INTEREST DURING THE 1980S

The real returns are quite variable over the ten-year period. Overall, U.S. Treasury bills averaged 3.8 percent, long-term U.S. Treasury bonds averaged 7.5 percent, and long-term high-grade U.S. corporate bonds averaged 7.9 percent. On occasion real rates for Treasury and corporate bonds were negative. Notice that the real return for long-term corporate bonds in 1982 averaged 38.4 percent. This return consisted of a 43.8 percent nominal return and a 3.9 percent inflation rate: $(1 + 0.438) \div (1 + 0.039) - 1 = 0.384$. The 1982 real rate of return on the Treasury bonds was 35.0 percent. Check this number, given a nominal rate of 40.3 percent for government bonds.[6]

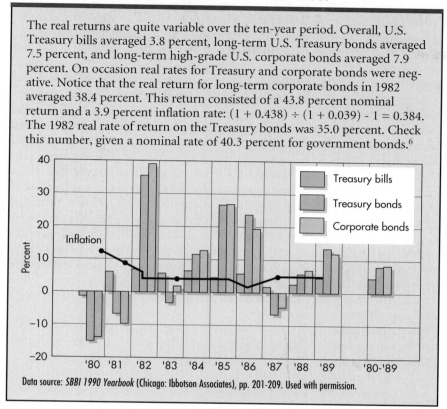

Data source: *SBBI 1990 Yearbook* (Chicago: Ibbotson Associates), pp. 201-209. Used with permission.

ILLUSTRATION 3.2

Real interest rates

A financial security pays 10 percent interest; thus, a $100 investment in the security grows to $110 after one year. A loaf of bread costs $1.88 today but is expected to cost $2.05 the following year. The price increase for a loaf of bread is expected to be ($2.05 ÷ $1.88) − 1 = 0.0904, or 9.04 percent. If this rate is representative of overall inflation, $\Delta p = 0.0904$ with the result that the real interest rate earned on the security is 0.88 percent.

$$r_R = \frac{(1 + 0.10)}{(1 + 0.0904)} - 1$$
$$= 0.0088 \text{ or } 0.88 \text{ percent}$$

Inflation erodes just about all of the security's nominal return.

Figure 3.8 shows real interest rates for U.S. Treasury bills and bonds and corporate bonds over the decade of the 1980s. In these years investors lost purchasing power since real returns were less than inflation.

[6]Solution: $(1.403 \div 1.039) - 1 = 0.35$ or 35 percent.

3.2.2 Risk Premia

The average annual interest rate difference between government bonds and corporate bonds arises from risk premia. Most financial securities face *default risk,* many securities face *reinvestment risk* if not held to maturity, all securities face *market risk* and *purchasing power risk,* and some securities face *currency risk.* These risks affect different securities differently.

Default risk, also called **credit risk,** is the chance the investor takes that the issuer of the security will be unable to meet its financial obligations to pay interest and principal payments, either out of dishonesty or true inability to do so. This being the case, the security will lose much, or all, of its value. **Reinvestment risk,** also called **interest rate risk,** is the risk of having to accept a lower interest rate when the investor uses the funds in another investment. Reinvestment risk is a function of general interest rates and the state of the economy. **Market risk** is risk associated with a security that cannot be eliminated. It influences in varying degrees all securities, as we will discuss in Chapter 5. **Purchasing power risk** is the risk that, due to unexpectedly high inflation, the future cash receipts will have less purchasing power than the lender anticipated at the time of the loan. **Currency risk** is the risk involved when investors buy foreign securities denominated in a foreign currency. Currency exchange rates between countries can be very volatile. From 1980 to 1988, U.S. investors of Mexican stocks realized a 50 percent currency exchange rate loss because the peso weakened against the dollar. When investors converted pesos back to dollars, they received fewer dollars and realized significantly lower returns.

Thus, the nominal interest rate, as defined in Equation 3.2, should include a term for risk premia to account for bearing all forms of risk. To simplify this discussion, let's rewrite Equation 3.2 in a form that approximates an adjustment for all risk premia r_{RP} as:

$$\begin{aligned}
\text{Nominal interest rate} \\
= \text{Real interest rate} + \text{expected inflation premium} + \text{risk premia} \\
= \text{Risk-free rate} + \text{risk premia} \qquad (3.4)
\end{aligned}$$

$$r_N = r_f + r_{RP}$$

The nominal interest rate r_N is a function of the *risk-free rate r_f* and risk premia r_{RP}. The **risk-free rate** represents the **pure time value of money** of a federal government security—*real interest rate + expected inflation premium.*

Figure 3.9 shows several factors affecting nominal interest rates and the relationships of the factors to one another. Factors affecting the r_f rate include governmental fiscal and monetary policies, inflation expectations, and the need for and availability of loanable funds. The mix of governments' fiscal and monetary policies influence the composition of aggregate demand in their economies. For instance, governments often use fiscal policy to stimulate employment by construction projects, such as building a bridge. However, the bridge has to be paid for out of taxes. For every dollar spent on the bridge, a dollar is taken away from taxpayers. If the bridge costs $10 million, the taxpayers will lose control of $10 million. If the bridge is not paid for by higher taxes, then more money or credit must be created to pay for the bridge. If any increase in the money supply or credit exceeds the demand for goods and services, inflation will result, which causes the pure time value of money to increase and, in turn, causes the nominal interest rate to increase.

Default (credit) risk. The chance that interest or principal on a debt security will not be paid on a payment date and in the promised amount.

Reinvestment (interest rate) risk. Uncertainty about the rate of return that will be earned by future cash flows from an investment.

Market risk. The risk inherent in the ownership of any security because the market fluctuates. This risk cannot be eliminated.

Purchasing power risk. The risk that an investment's principal and income will lose their purchasing power because of inflation.

Currency risk. The risk that fluctuating exchange rates will adversely affect the investment.

Risk-free rate. The interest rate for an asset that is virtually riskless. For example, debt issued by the government maturing in one year has a precisely predictable rate of return for one year.

Pure time value of money. Theoretical interest rate on a long-term, riskless loan, where the interest payments are made solely for the use of someone else's money. In practice, this rate is often approximated by the interest rate on negotiable government bonds.

FIGURE 3.9

FACTORS AFFECTING THE NOMINAL RATE OF INTEREST

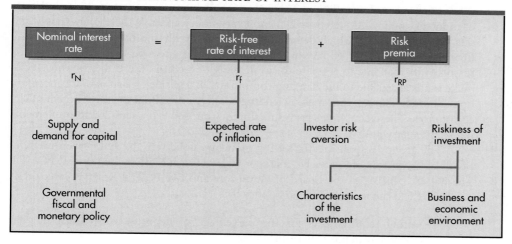

Factors affecting risk premia are investor *risk aversion,* the general state of national and international economies, and riskiness of the investment. **Risk aversion** means that risk matters and is disliked; thus, investors must be paid a premium to take on risk.

Risk aversion. It is a dislike for risk. Higher risk requires higher expected return.

Comprehension Check

1. Distinguish between the nominal interest rate and the real interest rate. What is the precise formula for calculating the nominal rate of interest? How is the real rate of interest calculated?
2. Explain which interest rate should have the most significance to you as an investor.
3. Why are interest rates on U.S. Treasury bonds different from corporate bonds for issues having similar dates of maturity?
4. Define default risk, reinvestment risk, market risk, purchasing power risk, and currency risk.
5. What does the risk-free rate of interest represent?

3.3 FEDERAL RESERVE SYSTEM

Interest rates in an economy are critically influenced by the nation's central bank. In the United States, the **Federal Reserve Bank** (commonly called the **Fed**) is the central bank with responsibility for monetary policy, which affects interest rates. The Federal Reserve System was born out of the financial panic of 1907, when the U.S. Congress determined that it was necessary to provide emergency liquidity to the banking system. Twelve regional banks were chartered, and the Federal Reserve Board was created in 1913 as an independent government agency.

Federal Reserve Bank (Fed). One of the 12 banks (and branches) which make up the Federal Reserve System. Each serves as a "banker's bank" for the member banks in its district by acting as a source of credit and a depository of resources.

Congress gave the Fed the responsibility of providing a flow of money and credit for the nation and to foster orderly economic growth and stable prices.[7] The expression *stable prices* means low inflation. The Fed tries to achieve this objective through the use of monetary policy. As stated earlier, monetary policy controls the money supply and sets key interest rates, which determine the cost of credit and has implications for all financial markets. The Fed has an ongoing and major effect on financial securities by reason of its mandate to regulate the availability of credit in the U.S. economy. It can make funds accessible to the banking community in a trickle or a stream. Or it can dry up the money sources, thus making lending possible only under the most urgent of circumstances. These consequences result simply from the Fed's setting and implementing its monetary policy.

The groups responsible for setting monetary policy are the Fed's seven-member Board of Governors of the twelve-member Federal Open Market Committee (FOMC). The FOMC consists of the Board of Governors and five Federal Reserve Bank presidents. The Fed carries out monetary policy by:

- Setting requirements for the percentage of deposits banks must hold as reserves by depository institutions.
- Changing the interest rate, called the **discount rate,** charged for bank borrowing from the Fed's *discount window*.[8] The discount rate influences the **federal funds rate,** which is the borrowing rate charged among banks for overnight loans to adjust banks' reserve positions.
- Directing open-market operations that involve the purchase or sale of federal government securities.

These actions affect businesses and individuals, which in turn result in changes in economic activity. Let's examine them.

3.3.1 Bank Reserves and Creation of Money

Banks operate using a **fractional reserve banking system:** Banks keep only a fraction of customers' deposits in the form of actual cash reserves. Banks lend most deposits to a variety of borrowers or invest the deposits in other assets to earn income. Loans are typically for the purchase of automobiles, short-term and long-term business needs, home improvements, and home mortgages. If a bank invested all of its deposits, there would be no funds available to honor requests by depositors who desire to withdraw their money.

The Fed's Board of Governors sets the **reserve requirements.** The Fed has learned from experience that reserves of about 10 percent are adequate for ordinary business needs. Periodically, the Fed changes reserve requirements.[9] Figure 3.10 shows the intended effect of increases and decreases in bank reserves. When reserve requirements

---

Discount rate. Interest rate charged to member banks on their loans from the Federal Reserve Banks. It is so called because the interest on a loan is discounted when the loan is made, rather than collected when the loan is repaid.

Federal funds rate. Interest rate at which banks borrow excess reserves from other banks' accounts at the Fed, usually overnight, to keep required reserves from falling below the legal level. In general, the lower the volume of excess reserves, the higher the federal funds rate. Therefore, the federal funds rate is an important indicator that the Fed watches to decide whether to add to banks' reserves or take away from them.

Fractional reserve banking system. The practice of keeping only a fraction of the deposits of depository institutions as cash reserves.

Reserve requirements. Minimum amount of legal reserves that a bank is required by law to keep behind its deposit liabilities.

---

[7]Countries with central banks that have greater legal independence in setting monetary policy tend to have relatively lower average inflation rates. The Fed and the German Bundesbank are good examples of such central banks. However, in early 1993, Senator Sarbanes of Maryland and Representative Gonzalez of Texas proposed changing the structure of U.S. monetary policy decision making. Although the proposal failed to get support, their intent was to provide greater political control over the conduct of monetary policy, and thus interest rates, by increasing the role of the president in determining who makes the decisions about monetary policy.

[8]The discount window gets its name from the earlier practice of banks bringing to a Fed teller's cage, or window, customer notes against which they borrowed. The Fed "discounted" the notes, in effect lending the banks an amount less than the face value of the notes.

[9]Historically, when the Fed reduces reserve requirements, the action foretells a rise in stock prices over the next 12 to 18 months. An increase in reserve requirements has the opposite effect.

FIGURE 3.10

EFFECTS OF CHANGE IN RESERVE REQUIREMENTS

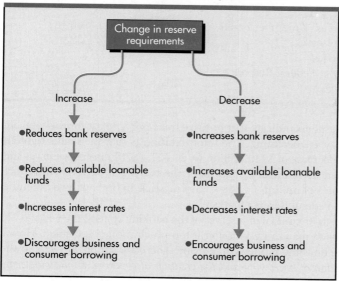

increase, banks must hold more funds in reserve against their deposits. Therefore, banks have less funds available to lend. The intent of higher reserves is to reduce the money supply, increase interest rates, and reduce inflationary pressure in the economy through lower economic activity. The Fed hopes that a decrease in reserves has opposite effects. Reserves are kept either as vault cash at the bank or as deposits with a regional Federal Reserve Bank.[10]

Many banks hold more than the required level of reserves to accommodate any outflows of funds. We call these additional reserves **excess reserves.** The amount of excess reserves held by banks will depend on differences between the interest rates banks can charge borrowers and the federal funds rate banks must pay to borrow reserves from other banks, or the discount rate banks must pay to borrow reserves from the Fed. Often banks short of necessary reserves are large money-center banks; these banks have greater investing and lending opportunities than banks in small communities.

When the collective excess reserves of banks are larger than the total borrowing of reserves from each other or the regional Federal Reserve Banks, a positive **free reserve** position exists. Normally, when free reserves exist in the banking system, interest rates are falling as the Fed attempts to stimulate the economy. When collective free reserves are negative, banks' excess reserves are smaller than their actual Fed borrowing. Such a situation suggests that the Fed is pursuing a tight monetary policy, which usually causes interest rates to increase in the short term.

We can determine the aggregate reserve position of U.S. banks by looking in Friday's edition of *The Wall Street Journal.* For example, on April 8, 1994, various numbers reported on page C15 related to the banking industry allowed us to make the following tabulations:

Excess reserves. Quantity of a bank's legal reserves over and above its required reserves. Excess reserves are the key to a bank's lending power.

Free reserves. Excess banking reserves minus reserves borrowed from the Federal Reserve by depository institutions.

---

[10]Historically, bank reserves consisted of gold and silver specie safely stored in vaults. Today, the *reserves are nothing more than checking accounts* that the banks have on deposit with the Fed. These checking accounts are similar to yours.

Daily Average in $Millions	1994 March 30	March 16
Total reserves of member banks	$60,462	$60,696
– Required reserves	59,612	59,635
Excess reserves	$ 850	$ 1,061
– Borrowing at Federal Reserve banks	68	39
Free reserves	$ 782	$ 1,022

The numbers indicate that positive free reserves exist for the total banking system, although they are declining. The interpretation is that the Fed is tightening monetary policy. The decrease of $240 million (= $1,022 – $782) in free reserves suggests that the Fed tightened its monetary policy over the two-week period. This conclusion is supported by the $29 million (= $68 – $39) increase in borrowing by member banks from the regional Federal Reserve banks.

Through its control of reserves of the banking system, the Fed can "create money," a process which may cause inflation if too much money is created. How is money created? Where does the money come from? There are simple answers to these questions. *The stimulation of borrowing and the creation of checking accounts determine the money supply.* This statement reveals the critical significance of the money supply. The **money supply** is a measurement of the increase in demand made possible by bank lending.

Table 3.1 shows the money-creation process. It begins with a $10,000 cash deposit by Gary in Banc One. The bank needs to hold only $1000, or 10 percent, of the deposit,

Money supply. Money is a medium of exchange. The money supply measures the amount of the exchange medium available.

TABLE 3-1

THE CREATION OF MONEY

Bank	Depositor	Borrower	New Deposits	New Loans	New Reserves	Increase in Money
Banc One	Gary	Patrick	$ 10,000	$ 9,000	$ 1,000	$ 0
Bank of America	Susan	Bob	9,000	8,100	900	9,000
Scottsdale Bank	Andrea	Herb	8,100	7,290	810	8,100
Far West Bank	Eric	Jim	7,290	6,561	729	7,290
Utah First Bank	Marie	Glenn	6,561	5,905	656	6,561
Seafirst Bank	John	Rick	5,905	5,314	591	5,905
Wells Fargo Bank	Frank	Linda	5,314	4,783	531	5,314
Union Bank	Trish	Leah	4,783	4,305	478	4,783
Citibank	Dick	George	4,305	3,874	431	4,305
Banc One	Jerry	Francis	3,874	3,487	387	3,874
.	.	.	.	.	.	.
All other transactions			34,868	31,381	3,487	34,868
Total for all transactions			$100,000	$90,000	$10,000	$90,000

A $10,000 initial deposit causes deposits to increase by $100,000 (= $10,000 ÷ 0.10), loans to increase by $90,000 (= $9000 ÷ 0.10), and reserves to increase by $10,000 (= $1000 ÷ 0.10).

in reserve. Banc One lends $9000 of the deposit to Patrick by increasing the balance in his checking account. He uses the loan to buy goods from Susan by writing her a check on his Banc One checking account. Susan deposits the $9000 check in Bank of America. The bank withholds $900 to satisfy reserve requirements and lends $8100 to Bob by increasing the balance in his checking account. Bob then writes a check for $8100 on his account to pay for advertising provided by Andrea. She deposits the check in her bank and the process continues. Each new loan is for a smaller amount, as shown in the table.

The banks have created money by making loans. The quantity of new money created is $90,000—the same amount as the new loans. Notice that real money does not change hands with each loan and each subsequent purchase. The only limits to the money supply are:

- The Fed's willingness to provide the banks with reserves.
- The banks' ability to find borrowers.

3.3.2 Changing the Discount Rate

The discount rate is the interest rate at which member banks borrow from the Federal Reserve. The Fed considers use of the discount window a last resort for members that are in urgent need of additional reserves. Economists consider any changes in the discount rate as a signal of policy intent by the Fed. As Figure 3.11 outlines, the Fed views an increase in the discount rate as a discouragement to bank lending with the ultimate objective of discouraging business and consumer borrowing. A decrease in the discount

FIGURE 3.11

EFFECTS OF CHANGE IN THE DISCOUNT RATE

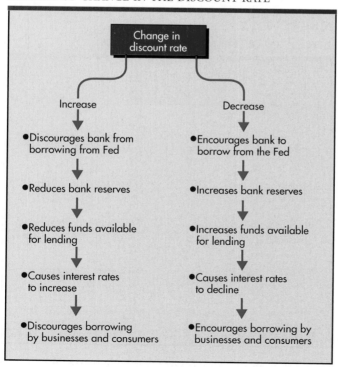

rate has the intended opposite effect by encouraging borrowing through lower interest rates.

In reality the discount rate appears to have little policy significance because the Fed has generally kept this rate *below* the market rate for money. As a result, the discount rate has become a preferred borrowing rate for the banks. It is not a penalty rate at all.

3.3.3 Fed Open-Market Operations

The Federal Open Market Committee (FOMC) meets every six weeks and provides guidelines to the Federal Reserve Bank of New York, which actually carries out FOMC decisions. **Open-market operations (OMO)** represent the New York Fed buying and selling U.S. Treasury securities. The New York Fed increases the banking system's reserves by buying securities in the financial market. It decreases the system's reserves by selling securities in the financial market. Figure 3.12 outlines the objectives of OMO. The nearby Financial Reality article provides a narrative of carrying out policy.

The buying of securities by the Fed causes the banking system to respond as we examined earlier in the discussion on the creation of money. When the Fed buys securities, the seller deposits the proceeds of the sale in a bank account, thereby increasing bank reserves. And because the bank needs to hold only a fraction of the deposit in reserve, the balance can be lent to borrowers. This action creates new checking account balances which, in turn, increase the money supply. When the Fed sells securities, the buyer pays with funds withdrawn from the bank. The withdrawal decreases bank reserves and, therefore, the money supply. Higher reserves make it easier for banks to lend. This lending stimulates the economy. Lower reserves make it more difficult for banks to lend, which restrains the economy. However, banks cannot change their reserves through their own actions.

> **Open-market operations.** Purchases and sales of government securities by the Federal Reserve System. Purchases of securities are expansionary because they add to commercial banks' reserves; sales of securities are contractionary because they reduce commercial banks' reserves.

FIGURE 3.12

EFFECTS OF OPEN-MARKET OPERATIONS

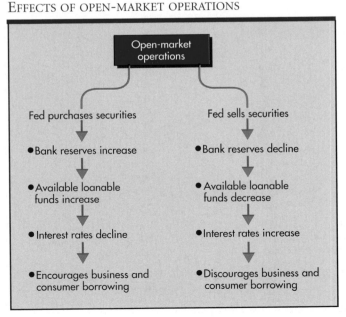

OPEN-MARKET OPERATIONS

Few areas seem to mystify the general public more than Federal Reserve open-market operations in U.S. government securities. It is through the trading of U.S. government securities in the open market that the FOMC tries to offset undue stress on the monetary system and influence the economy by affecting the cost and availability of credit.

The time is just before noon on the Tuesday before Thanksgiving Day. The place is the eight-floor trading room of the Federal Reserve Bank of New York. The manager of the Federal Reserve System's Open Market Account has made his decision. He tells his second in command to buy about $500 million in U.S. Treasury bills for immediate delivery.

The decision made, the officer in charge turns to the ten officers and securities traders who sit before telephone consoles linking them to more than 40 primary dealers in U.S. government securities. "We're going in to ask for offerings of all bills for cash," he says. Each person is quickly assigned two to four dealers to call.

Eileen, a New York Federal Reserve trader, presses a button on her telephone console, sounding a buzzer at the corresponding console of a government securities dealer.

"Jack," Eileen says, "we are looking for offerings of all bills for cash delivery."

Jack replies, "I'll be back in a minute." The salespeople of his firm quickly contact customers to see if they wish to make offerings. Jack consults the partner in charge about how aggressive he should be in offering the firm's own holdings.

Ten minutes later Jack calls back. "Eileen, I can offer you for cash $5 million of January 5 bills to yield 5.85 percent—$10 million of January 26 bills at 5.90—$20 million of March 23 bills at 6.05—and $30 million of May 30 bills at 6.14."

Eileen says, "Can I have those offerings firm for a few minutes?"

"Sure."

Within minutes, the "go-around" is completed. The traders have recorded the offerings obtained from their calls on special preprinted slips. The officer in charge arrays the individual dealer offerings. A tally shows that dealers have offered $1.8 billion of bills for cash sale—that is, with delivery and payment that very day.

"Jack, we'll take the $5 million of January 5 bills at 5.85 and the $30 million of May 30 bills at 6.14 both for cash; no thanks on the others," Eileen says.

Forty-five minutes after the initial decision, the calls have been completed and $523 million Treasury bills purchased. Only the paper work remains. The traders write up tickets, which provide the basic authority for the Fed's government bond department to receive and pay for the specific Treasury bills bought. The banks that handle the dealers' deliveries—the clearing banks—will authorize deductions of the securities from the book entry list of their holdings at the Federal Reserve. In return, they will receive credit to the reserve accounts the banks maintain at the New York Reserve Bank.

The Federal Reserve credits to the dealers' banks immediately adds over $500 million to the reserves of the U.S. banking system.

The Federal Reserve's market entry sparks hurried consultations at dealer firms and many commercial banks throughout the country. Could the Federal Reserve have been trying to push down the interest rate on federal funds—interbank loans usually made for one business day—to encourage a more rapid growth of money and credit in the country? Or was it merely supplying reserves to the banks to meet the public's normal demands for cash and credit around Thanksgiving?

Adapted from Paul Meek, *Open Market Operations* (Federal Reserve Bank of New York, 1978), pp. 1–2. Used with permission.

3.3.4 Significance of FOMC Actions

Of the three tools of monetary policy discussed, open-market operations are the most powerful. They have a direct, continuous, and powerful impact on the reserve funds available to banks, and through them an influence on the whole banking system. The impact is direct since there is no intermediary who might blunt or delay the influence of buying and selling Treasury securities. The impact is continuous because OMO are continuous, touching the market every business day when the market is open. OMO are powerful because of the large dollar magnitudes.

Discount rate changes have informational content, but because most banks do not borrow from the Fed very often, and no bank does so continuously, the impact is certainly not continuous. Changes in reserve requirements are powerful, but so powerful that the tool is seldom used.

3.3.5 Changes in Money Supply on Interest Rates

Liquidity effect. The fall (rise) in the rate of interest caused by an increase (decrease) in the supply of money balances.

If the Fed's actions cause the money supply to increase, nominal interest rates should decline because of a *liquidity effect*. A **liquidity effect** simply means that individuals and businesses in total have excess liquidity, or money, in savings and checking accounts compared to investments in interest-bearing securities. To restore the relationship between their cash balances and income-earning investments, these individuals and businesses purchase more securities. Because a fixed supply of securities exists at that time, the increased demand for securities causes security prices to rise. Increasing prices for securities cause their interest rates, or yields, to fall. Illustration 3.3 discusses the reason for the inverse relationship between prices and interest rates.

ILLUSTRATION 3.3

Buying pressure on interest rates

A government security is selling for $1000 and pays a fixed interest amount of $100 per year. This payment translates to a 10 percent return: $100 ÷ $1000 = 0.10 or 10 percent. More investors want to own this security. To buy the security, investors bid up its price (similar to an auction). The final price is $1200. Since the security only pays $100 interest, the yield falls to 8.3 percent ($100 ÷ $1200 = 0.083).

If the Fed does not create enough money to satisfy a higher demand for money, investors generate their own liquidity by selling some of their securities. Such action results in an increased supply of securities, and this in turn causes a price decline for securities. The final result is an increase in interest rates, or yields, to attract other investors to buy the securities. Illustration 3.4 discusses how selling pressures affect interest rates.

ILLUSTRATION 3.4

Selling pressure on interest rates

A debt security issued by a corporation is selling for $1000 to yield 10 percent to the investors: It pays $100 interest. Some investors decide that they no longer want to hold this security and try to sell their holdings to other investors. Since the potential new buyers have a choice of from whom to buy, the current security holders offer to lower the price to sell the securities. The price settles at $800 per security, offering the new investors a yield of 12.5 percent ($100 ÷ $800 = 0.125).

1. Discuss the broad goals of Federal Reserve activities.
2. Define monetary policy, fractional reserve banking, excess reserves, free reserves, and federal funds rate.
3. How is money created?
4. Explain how the Fed uses the discount rate to carry out monetary policy.
5. Explain how the Fed's open-market operations affect the reserves of commercial banks, the level of interest rates, and the money supply in the hands of the public.
6. Explain how changes in buying and selling pressures of securities affect interest rates.

3.4 FED WATCHING

What do the Fed's activities mean to the economy and businesses? Although the Fed does not dictate the level of interest rates, its activities move interest rates in one direction or the other. When the Fed's policy is to discourage lending, it raises interest rates at the source of the money supply—the banks. These higher rates ripple throughout the economy at every level. The couple trying to buy their first home cannot obtain a mortgage. A small business owner cannot obtain the funding to expand business operations. Large corporations order smaller quantities of raw materials, such as steel, lumber, and concrete, employ fewer people, and defer payment to the last moment to conserve their existing funds. In the securities industry, debt securities with interest rates lower than other competitive rates decline in market value. Also, the prices of equity securities often decline in reaction to higher interest rates. All these consequences result simply from the Fed's setting and implementing its monetary policy.

However, management of the nation's economic affairs is excruciatingly difficult. The Fed, like all central banks, has a conflict about whether it should target money supply or interest rates.[11] Over the past 40 years, the Fed has targeted both money supply and interest rates, or used a combination of them. However, only by chance is the Fed able to satisfy both interest rate and money supply targets. Illustration 3.5 explains the Fed's dilemma.[12]

ILLUSTRATION 3.5

The Fed's dilemma

When interest rates are falling, credit for both firms and individuals is easier to obtain and when interest rates are rising, credit is more difficult or tighter. The idea that high interest rates mean money is tight has dire consequences. The essence of the problem is the *Fed's conceptual failure to work out the difference between money and credit.*

[11]Monetarists, such as Milton Friedman, argue that a money supply rule should be followed by the Fed for monetary policy. The monetarist view is that there is a rate of growth in the money supply which, if maintained in the long run, leads to a zero rate of inflation. The economy would also grow at this stable rate and eliminate the temptation of financing federal government deficits by monetizing the debt at excessive rates.

[12]In mid-1993, Alan Greenspan, Fed Chairman, informed Congress that money supply was an unreliable indicator of economic growth. Greenspan indicated that real interest rates, as opposed to money supply, would be more important in Fed policy decisions.

Imagine that the economy is starting out on an upswing in business activity. Demand for credit tends to increase, which also tends to cause a rise in interest rates. The Fed observes the increase in interest rates, and in accordance with its procedures, the open-market desk in New York buys Treasury bills and bonds, adding cash to the system. This action increases the available cash in banks and ultimately increases the money supply as banks make more loans. Increased money supply leads to more economic activity, which eventually pushes once again up against the limits of available loanable funds. Hence, interest rates rise once again. The Fed desk sees rates starting once again to go over the target. The person on the desk buys more securities and puts out more cash and the process continues with economic activity increasing again.

Eventually an inflationary boom develops. The person on the Fed desk in New York continues to buy securities in an attempt to stop interest rates from rising. At some point there is a crisis. Interest rates become so high that businesses consider it too costly to borrow to continue expanding. Inflationary expectations dominate the financial markets, which causes the economic boom to burst.

At that stage, there is little demand for money. The person on the desk in New York, who by now has been given a much higher operating target for interest rates by the FOMC, starts selling securities. This action pulls money out of the banking system. The hope is to moderate the collapse of interest rates and the accompanying decline in the demand for both business and consumer credit. The more the Fed desk sells securities, the more it exaggerates the downturn in business. Unfortunately, the Fed desk is pulling money growth down at the very time businesses and individuals are looking for cash.

Look at Table 3.2. It indicates the close attention that financial markets pay to interest rates and Fed actions. Whenever U.S. Treasury bills yield at least 15 percent less than they did 15 months earlier, the stock market has always risen in the following 12 months—*no exceptions!*[13] The rise has been at least 10 percent. The average gain is about 24 percent.

The October 1987 stock market collapse is an example of how financial markets respond to interest rate fears. Interest rates in most of the industrialized countries were at ten-year lows. The decline in purchasing power of the U.S. dollar against the Japanese yen and the German mark raised fears that foreign governments' finance ministers would pressure the Fed to raise interest rates to stem the dollar's decline.[14] Higher interest rates would make it more expensive for firms to borrow money, which in turn would reduce their ability to generate cash from their business operations. Investors translated

[13]Ignore any following consecutive months where the T-bill yield is 15 percent less than it was 15 months earlier.

[14]The appendix to this chapter explains the purchasing power linkage between currencies and interest rates around the world.

TABLE 3-2

INTEREST RATES DOWN AND STOCK PRICES UP

Date	Average 90-Day T-bill Rate	Change from 15 Months Prior	S&P Industrial Stock Index	The Index 1 Year Later	% Gain
February 1958	1.56%	−48.3%	44.0	58.3	32.5
July 1960	2.40	−19.7	59.3	69.2	16.7
June 1967	3.48	−24.7	98.6	109.2	10.4
December 1970	4.80	−32.6	98.7	109.7	11.1
December 1974	7.17	−18.3	80.2	100.9	25.8
June 1980	7.23	−23.1	128.8	148.7	15.5
July 1982	11.58	−16.8	122.6	187.4	52.9
January 1985	7.01	−19.0	191.6	230.4	20.2
January 1991	6.30	−17.0	382.8	493.4	28.9
				Average	23.8

The S&P Industrial Stock Index is a stock price index of 400 publicly traded industrial companies.

these expected lower cash flows into lower stock prices for the firms.[15] The following Financial Reality discussion provides another example of global influence on interest rates. Hence, it is necessary to observe both foreign and domestic investors' sensitivity to interest rates.

Comprehension Check

1. What is the significance of targeting interest rates instead of money supply in implementing monetary policy?
2. How does inflation affect interest rates, lending by financial institutions, and investment by corporations?
3. How does the existence of a foreign economy affect domestic interest rates?

3.5 THE NEXT STEP

This chapter concludes Part I of the text. To many of you, the material in these first three chapters is a review of sorts. However, because it has been a semester or two since you studied accounting and economics, these chapters should refresh your memory and provide you with a stronger foundation for analyzing finance. Part II of the text builds on this foundation. Specifically, the next two chapters examine the determinants of value: time value of money and risk-return trade-off concepts. These concepts are critical to understanding finance. Interest rates are central to time value of money discussion. So whenever we use an interest rate in time value of money calculations, we will explicitly assume that it is a nominal rate that incorporates the several factors discussed in this chapter.

[15]We examine the issue of stock valuation in Chapter 9.

THE ROUTINE BOARD MEETING

When Fed Chairman Volcker lost a committee vote, the world financial markets narrowly avoided a financial crisis.

February 24, 1986 was a nearly disastrous day for monetary policy. The board met in a regular morning session to consider requests by eight district Federal Reserve Banks for a discount rate cut to 7 percent from $7\frac{1}{2}$ percent. Chairman Volcker started the meeting by recommending that any board action on the discount rate cut requests be delayed until a Fed discount rate cut could be coordinated with similar actions by Japan and Germany. Such a coordinated move was needed, Volcker explained, to minimize the negative effect of a Fed discount rate cut on the dollar. However, Volcker cautioned that Germany remained reluctant to reduce its discount rate and, although Japan was more willing to cooperate, it wanted to delay the move.

Expecting prompt approval, Volcker asked whether there was any discussion of his recommendation for a delay in the discount rate cut. Vice Chairman Martin immediately challenged the chairman. "I think we should discuss this issue," Martin asserted. There ensued an extended discussion of whether the discount rate should be cut immediately or delayed, as favored by the chairman.

With a final admonition that he, as their chairman, urged a delay, Volcker called for the formal vote. The jarring results were as expected; four board members in favor of an immediate discount rate cut, three (including Volcker) against.

The seeds of doom had been sown by earlier events. First, there had been growing antagonism between the Fed chairman and Vice Chairman Martin, who could not hide his ambition to become Fed chairman. As a long-time associate of President Reagan, Martin had a direct, inside political track to the White House. Nor was there any love lost between Volcker and Governor Seger, who intensely disliked Volcker for his secrecy in arriving at policy decisions.

A second event that helped set the stage for the fateful February meeting was the early February 1986 swearing in of two new Reagan appointees, Governors Johnson and Angell. Their appointments were highly politicized.

The afternoon of February 24, 1986 turned out to be at least as eventful as the morning. Governor Angell saw the opening for a workable compromise. He set up an appointment with the chairman after lunch. Vice Chairman Martin, who happened to be walking by the chairman's office at the same time that Angell was arriving, joined in the meeting with the chairman. A compromise on a delayed discount rate cut was discussed. A second board meeting on the proposed discount rate cut would be held later that afternoon.

Just 45 minutes before the impending afternoon announcement on February 24, the board, in its unusual second meeting, switched its vote to favor a delay in the discount rate cut. Thus a potential international financial crisis triggered by Volcker's almost certain resignation was narrowly averted. A surprise resignation by the highly respected U.S. central bank head would almost certainly have triggered a free-fall in the U.S. dollar in the foreign exchange markets. Such a dollar crisis would most likely have been accompanied by fears of renewed inflation and a loss of confidence in the Reagan administration. This, in turn, would almost certainly have triggered a pullback of private foreign investors desperately needed to help finance excessive U.S. budget deficits, resulting in upward pressures on U.S. longer-term interest rates.

On March 7, just 12 days later, the Fed, in a coordinated move with Japan and Germany, lowered the discount rate to 7 percent. In all likelihood, this high point in international financial crisis was averted because Volcker's trusted German and Japanese central banking friends acted primarily out of a common human motivation, to get a good friend out of an embarrassing jam.

Adapted from David M. Jones, *Politics of Money: The Fed Under Alan Greenspan* (New York: New York Institute of Finance, 1991), pp. 97–102. Used by permission of the publisher, New York Institute of Finance, a division of Simon & Schuster, New York.

SUMMARY ▼▼▼▼▼▼▼▼▼▼▼▼

THE ECONOMIC SYSTEM

- The market economy system forms the basis for the financial market system.
- The economic system allows for the exchange of goods or services and capital between its participants: the business sector, the government sector, and the household sector.
- Production opportunities allow an individual to increase wealth.
- The financial system allows money flows from savers to borrowers. Securities, representing indebtedness of borrowers, flow from borrowers to savers.
- Financial markets allow participants in the economic system to separate their investment decision from their consumption decision. These markets also allow participants to borrow against future cash flows to satisfy current consumption needs.
- Participants should invest in all projects offering returns in excess of the market interest rate. Doing so results in increased wealth.

STRUCTURE OF INTEREST RATES

- Interest rates reflect the time value of money and risk.
- Quoted interest rates are called nominal interest rates. These rates consist of the real rate of interest + expected inflation premium + risk premium.
- The real rate of interest + expected inflation premium represents the pure time value of money, and is called the risk-free rate—the rate on a short-term government security.
- The risk premium adjusts the risk-free rate for default risk, reinvestment risk, market risk, and currency risk.

FEDERAL RESERVE SYSTEM

- Nominal interest rates are critically influenced by a nation's money supply, which is controlled by the Federal Reserve Bank (Fed).
- The Fed uses monetary policy to provide money and credit for orderly economic growth and stable prices.
- Monetary policy can be either tight or loose. Restrictive monetary policy pushes interest rates higher in an effort to fight inflation. A policy of monetary ease attempts to provide a boost to the economy.
- Monetary policy is carried out in the Federal Reserve System through setting reserve requirements for banks, changing the borrowing rate (discount rate) the Fed charges banks to borrow from it, and buying or selling federal government securities to inject or reduce liquidity in the money system.
- The Fed creates money by creating checking accounts. Fractional reserve requirements mean that only about $0.10 of each $1 deposited in a bank must be kept in bank (or Fed) vaults. The remaining $0.90 can be loaned to businesses and individuals. Thus, for each $1 deposit, $9 in new loans can be created. These new loans represent the change in the money supply.
- An increase in the money supply depresses nominal interest rates because of a liquidity effect. If money is in short supply, nominal interest rates increase as participants bid up the price of money.

The Economic System

Business sector
Debt security
Deficit (borrowing) units
Economic system
Equity security
Financial system
Fiscal policy
Household sector
Interest rate
Investment goods
Monetary policy
Production opportunities
Rate of return
Surplus (saving) units
Time preference rate

Structure of Interest Rates

Credit
Currency risk
Default risk (credit risk)
Expected inflation premium
Inflation
Market risk
Nominal interest rates
Purchasing power risk
Pure time value of money
Real interest rates
Reinvestment risk (interest rate risk)
Risk aversion
Risk-free rate

Federal Reserve System

Discount rate
Excess reserves
Federal funds rate
Federal Reserve Bank (Fed)
Fractional reserve banking system
Free reserves
Liquidity effect
Money supply
Open-market operations (OMO)
Reserve requirements

- The Fed targets both money supply and interest rates in its attempt to conduct monetary policy. These targets often result in erratic changes in interest rates and greatly influence capital markets.
- Interest rates are not determined in isolation. Global influences affect all economies' prices and interest rates.

FURGER READING ▼▼▼▼▼▼▼▼▼▼▼

Carnes, W. Stansbury, and Stephen D. Slifer, *The Atlas of Economic Indicators,* New York: HarperCollins Publishers, Inc., 1991. An excellent book for understanding the investment impact of daily economic information.

Maisel, Sherman J., *Managing the Dollar,* New York: W.W. Norton & Company, Inc., 1973. A book written by a former governor of the Federal Reserve Bank describes monetary policy, how such policy is made, what the policy expects to accomplish, and why the policy often fails.

Newton, Maxwell, *The Fed: Inside the Federal Reserve, The Secret Power Center that Controls the American Economy,* New York: Times Books, 1983. It provides an excellent discussion of the importance of the Federal Reserve System to financial markets, inflation, and the economy.

Rueff, Jacques, *The Age of Inflation,* Chicago, IL: Henry Regnery Company, 1964. An excellent book about the ravages of inflation on world economies.

SELF-TEST PROBLEMS ▼▼▼▼▼▼▼▼▼▼▼

ST3-1. Use the following data to calculate the real rate of return for years 2 through 4.

Year	Nominal Return	Price Index	Real Return
1		100	
2	10%	105	?
3	6	110	?
4	15	115	?

ST3-2. If the real interest rate is 3 percent and the expected inflation premium is 5 percent, what should be the nominal interest rate on U.S. Treasury bills?

ST3-3. If reported data on commercial bank reserves were as shown in the following table, what would be the amount of excess reserves and free reserves for the U.S. banking system for the dates shown? What interpretation should be given to the Federal Reserve's monetary policy based on your calculations?

Daily Average in $Millions	May 14	April 15
Total reserves of member banks	$61,010	$60,110
Required reserves	61,220	60,000
Borrowing at Federal Reserve banks	220	50

ST3-4. A deposit of $10,000 is made in a bank. What is the maximum expansion of deposits in the banking system if the Federal Reserve has set reserve requirements at 15 percent? What must happen if the maximum expansion of the initial $10,000 deposit is to occur?

PROBLEMS ▼▼▼▼▼▼▼▼▼▼▼▼

THE ECONOMIC SYSTEM

3-1. What is the financial goal of the various participants in the economic system? How is the goal achieved by these participants?

3-2. Distinguish between fiscal policy and monetary policy.

3-3. When a dog is given bones to chew on, it often buries some of them to have another day.

  a. What economic principle is the dog exhibiting?
  b. Assume the dog was given ten bones of equal size. Draw a graph depicting the dog's possible consumption patterns.
  c. Do investment opportunities exist for the dog? Explain.

3-4. If investment opportunities exist in the previous problem, would the dog's present and future consumption pattern change? Explain.

3-5. Carlos is offered four equally risky investments:

Project	Cost	Return in 1 Year
A	$10	$11
B	15	18
C	16	19
D	20	23

What is each project's percentage return (rate of return)? How does he decide which project(s) to choose?

3-6. Refer to Problem 3-5. Assume that the market rate of interest is 12 percent. Rank the investments from most profitable to least profitable.

  a. Which project(s) does Carlos choose? Why?
  b. Does his choice change if he has only $30 in his pocket? Explain.

3-7. Refer to Problems 3-5 and 3-6.

  a. What is the *maximum* amount that Carlos can consume this period if he undertakes investments B, C, and D in Problem 3-5? The market rate of interest is 12 percent.
  b. How much can Carlos consume next period if he invests in projects B, C, and D this period and he maximizes his current period consumption?
  c. What is his maximum consumption this period if he does not invest in any projects?
  d. How much can Carlos consume next period if he does not invest in any project(s) this period and he does not consume any of the $30 this period?
  e. Is Carlos better or worse off by investing in projects? Explain.

3-8. Assume that Ann's investment opportunities consist of the following possibilities. Each project has a life of one year. The market interest rate is 10 percent.

Project	Investment Outlay	Rate of Return
A	$1 million	8%
B	1 million	20
C	2 million	4
D	3 million	30

a. Which projects should be undertaken and why?
b. If Ann invests in the projects selected in part (a), how much is the present value of her investments?
c. How much do the projects she selects in part (a) increase her overall wealth?

3-9. A recent graduate has an income of $20,000 this year and expects to earn $22,000 next year. If the opportunity cost of money (that is, market interest rate) is 8 percent, what is the most he can consume this year? Next year? (*Hint:* Find current or future values of income.)

3-10. Complete the following table using the information in Problem 3-9.

Consumption	
Today	Next Period
$ 0	
5,000	
10,000	
20,000	
30,000	
40,000	
40,370	
50,000	

3-11. Ms. Nealon, president of her own company, has an income of $75,000 this year and expects to earn $110,000 next year. She plans to consume $63,000 this year and $125,000 next year. Determine the market rate of interest.

3-12. An investment in ball bearings for satellites costs $4 million and is expected to return $4.32 million at the end of one year. If the market interest rate (that is, opportunity rate) for this investment is 10 percent, is this a good investment to undertake? Explain.

3-13. Frank landed a new job at Michigan Micro Brewery. To impress people, he wants to buy a new $48,000 Mercedes immediately. He also plans to spend $3000 on a new wardrobe. His salary this year is $60,000; next year it will be $63,000. Other required expenditures this year amount to $40,000. How much will he be able to spend next year if the market rate of interest is 7 percent?

3-14. Sandra is interested in maximizing current consumption. Her income at the *Mesa Tribune* this year is $22,000. Next year she will earn $25,300. She has three investment opportunities available.

Investment	Cost	Return Next Period
1	$ 500	$ 540
2	1000	1100
3	1200	1800

The market interest rate is 10 percent.

a. What is the maximum amount that she can consume in the current period?

b. How much will she borrow in the current period to support her consumption?

c. How much can she consume next period?

STRUCTURE OF INTEREST RATES

3-15. Is it possible for the nominal interest rate to increase while the real interest rate decreases? Explain.

3-16. Use the following data to calculate the real rate of return for years 2 through 5.

Year	Nominal Return	Price Index	Real Return
1		100	
2	8%	105	?
3	9	110	?
4	11	115	?
5	12	125	?

3-17. a. If the real interest rate is 3 percent and the expected inflation premium is 6 percent, what should be the nominal interest rate on U.S. Treasury notes?

b. If the real interest rate is 2 percent and the expected inflation premium is 7 percent, what should be the nominal interest rate on U.S. Treasury notes?

c. If the real interest rate is 3 percent and the expected inflation premium is 8 percent, what should be the annual nominal rate on U.S. Treasury bills?

d. If the real interest rate is 6 percent and the expected inflation rate is 24 percent, what should be the nominal interest rate on a country's government notes?

e. If the nominal interest rate on U.S. Treasury notes is 7 percent and the expected inflation premium is 4 percent, what is the current real interest rate?

f. If the nominal interest rate on U.S. Treasury bonds is 8.25 percent and the expected inflation premium is 4.5 percent, what is the current real interest rate?

3-18. a. If the real interest rate is 3 percent and the expected inflation premium is 8 percent, what should be the annual *approximate* nominal interest rate on U.S. Treasury bills? (See footnote 5 for the approximation formula.)

b. If the nominal interest rate on medium-quality corporate bonds is 11 percent, the expected inflation premium is 3 percent, and the corporate bond risk premium is 4 percent, what is the *approximate* real interest rate on these bonds? (See footnote 5 for the approximation formula.)

3-19.   a. What are two basic goals of the Federal Reserve System?
        b. Explain how the actions of the Federal Reserve may be counterproductive in achieving these basic goals at a given time.

3-20.   The Federal Reserve has three formal tools of monetary policy: open-market operations, discount rate changes, and changes in reserve requirements. Which of these tools is the most powerful and why?

3-21.   A reserve deficiency in the banking system automatically leads to a deposit contraction, whereas the existence of excess reserves does not guarantee an expansion of deposits. Why is this the case? Discuss the implications of the different behavior for the implementation of monetary policy.

3-22.   a. If an initial deposit of $10,000 is made in a bank that is part of a fractional reserve banking system, what will be the maximum expansion of deposits in the banking system if the Federal Reserve has set reserve requirements at 12 percent?
        b. What must happen if maximum expansion of the initial deposit is to occur?

3-23.   The commercial banking system has $19 billion in reserves and $200 billion in demand deposits outstanding. The reserve requirement is 10 percent. Answer the following questions.

        a. Is the banking system in equilibrium? Explain.
        b. How much borrowing from the Federal Reserve will enable the banking system to be in equilibrium? What are the effects of this transaction on deposits outstanding and the size of the money supply?
        c. If the banking system can return to a position of equilibrium by selling bonds to the public, what amount of bonds should it sell? What would be the effect on the money supply?

3-24.   How much money is created after three transactions for an initial deposit of $2000 (the first transaction) if the reserve requirement is 8 percent? How much money will be created beyond the initial $2000 deposit?

3-25.   If the treasurer of General Motors sold $10 million of U.S. Treasury bills through a government bond dealer that were purchased by the Federal Reserve System, what would be the immediate effect on:

        a. The money supply in the United States?
        b. The reserve position of the U.S. banking system?
        c. What would be the ultimate effect on the U.S. money supply if the reserve requirement for commercial banks is 12 percent and full expansion of bank reserves is assumed? Why wouldn't this occur immediately?

3-26.   a. What will be the effect on commercial bank reserves and the money supply if the Federal Reserve sells $30 million of U.S. Treasury securities? Reserve requirements for banks are 10 percent.
        b. What difference, if any, would it make if the Fed's securities were purchased by individual investors instead of by commercial banks for the banks' investment portfolios?

3-27.   As the result of the Federal Reserve Bank of New York carrying out the Open Market Committee's directives, if the Fed sells $500 million of U.S. Treasury bills, what will be the effect on the reserve position of the U.S. commercial banking system? Banks' reserve requirements are 11 percent currently. What would be the ultimate effect on the money supply of such an action?

3-28. a. If reported data on commercial bank reserves were as shown in the following table, what would be the amount of excess reserves and free reserves for the U.S. banking system for the dates shown?

Daily Average in $Millions	March 3	February 3
Total reserves of member banks	$60,535	$60,114
Required reserves	59,220	59,164
Borrowing at Federal Reserve banks	210	313

b. What interpretation should be given to the Federal Reserve's monetary policy based on your calculations for part (a)?

3-29. a. If reported data on commercial bank reserves were as shown in the following table, what would be the amount of excess reserves and free reserves for the U.S. banking system for the dates shown?

Daily Average in $Millions	December 3	November 4
Total reserves of member banks	$ 65,010	$ 65,110
Required reserves	65,320	65,030
Borrowing at Federal Reserve banks	230	75

b. What interpretation should be given to the Federal Reserve's monetary policy based on your calculations for part (a)?

FED WATCHING

3-30. a. Based on Table 3.2, what would be the minimum change you might expect next year in the overall level of common stock prices if the yield on U.S. Treasury bills is at least 15 percent lower today compared with 15 months ago?

b. How do you explain this possibility?

LIBRARY ASSIGNMENTS

3-31. By studying the *Federal Reserve Bulletin, Survey of Current Business, The Wall Street Journal,* or some other economic reports in your library, summarize in a one-page report the level and changes in interest rates and the money supply during the past year. Include in your summary the actions the Federal Reserve has taken to affect the level of interest rates and the money supply. Comment on why you think the Fed is taking these actions and how corporations may be affected.

3-32. What are the current borrowing rates for short-term business loans, as reported in the Money Rates column in Section C of *The Wall Street Journal?* What interest rates are commercial banks paying for negotiable certificates of deposit? Comment on the current difference between short-term interest rates in the United States and overseas.

3-33. Use either Section C of *The Wall Street Journal* or the *Federal Reserve Bulletin* to compare the current federal funds rate and the discount rate with the rates prevailing one year ago. What does your comparison tell you about the actions taken by the Federal Reserve and the Fed's view of prospects for inflation?

3-34. a. Briefly explain how the interest rate may be viewed as a device to allocate funds.
   b. Why is the market rate of interest important to individual investors? What is the relationship between wealth and the market rate of interest when investments are riskless?
   c. How do financial markets enhance an individual's opportunities for present and future consumption?
   d. Craig has the following risk-free opportunities in which to invest $5000:

   • an account at his credit union paying 6.5 percent in one year.
   • a loan to Howard, who promises to pay back $5450 at the end of one year.
   • the purchase of a Packard Company security which returns $5425 (including the original investment).

   The market rate for risk-free investments is 4 percent. Which investment will increase Craig's wealth the most? How much will Craig's wealth increase by selecting that investment?

   e. Craig is also considering buying a used car this week. How can he buy a car costing $5200 and still undertake the investment selected in part (d)?
   f. If inflation is 3 percent, what are the real interest rates for each investment opportunity stated in part (d)?
   g. Describe how monetary policy impacts on aggregate demand for funds.
   h. Give an example of an action by each of the following that will change the amount of reserves held by commercial banks:

   • Craig and other individuals
   • the Federal Reserve
   • the U.S. Treasury

   i. What are open-market operations? Describe their nature and purpose. Indicate the effect of open-market operations on market interest rates.

ANSWERS TO SELF-TEST PROBLEMS ▼▼▼▼▼▼▼▼▼▼▼▼

ST3-1.	Year	Nominal Return	Price Index	Real Return
	1		100	
	2	10%	105	4.76%
	3	6	110	1.18
	4	15	115	10.00

Use Equation 3.3 to solve for the real rates:

Year 1: $r_R = [(1 + 0.10) \div (1 + 0.05)] - 1 = 0.0476$ or 4.76 percent

Year 2: $r_R = [(1 + 0.06) \div (1 + 0.0476)] - 1 = 0.0118$ or 1.18 percent

Year 3: $r_R = [(1 + 0.15) \div (1 + 0.04545)] - 1 = 0.10$ or 10 percent

ST3-2. $r_N = (1 + 0.03) \times (1 + 0.05) - 1 = 0.0815$ or 8.15%

ST3-3.

Daily Average in $Millions	May 14	April 15
Total reserves of member banks	$61,010	$60,110
Required reserves	61,220	60,000
Excess reserves	($ 210)	$ 110
Borrowing at Federal Reserve banks	220	50
Free reserves	($ 430)	$ 60

Since no free reserves exist in the banking system on May 14 (and actually are negative) and have decreased over the four-week period, the Fed appears to be pursuing a tight monetary policy. Such action is confirmed by the fact that borrowing by commercial banks at regional Federal Reserve banks has increased significantly over this period. Thus, one would expect interest rates to be rising, which could dampen economic activity.

ST3-4. $10,000 \div 0.15 = $66,667$ maximum increase in deposits.

Banks must be willing to loan all their excess reserves. All money loaned must be redeposited into the banking system. Potential borrowers must be willing to commit themselves for loans. The Federal Reserve leaves reserve requirements unchanged.

Appendix: Purchasing Power Parity and Interest Rate Parity

This appendix discusses the importance of interest rates and inflation to international financial decisions. We examine *purchasing power parity, spot* and *forward exchange rates,* and *interest rate parity.*

3A.1 PURCHASING POWER PARITY

Purchasing power parity describes the relationship of the exchange rate between two countries and the relative level of prices of goods and services in each economy. As an example, the price per pound of copper in the United States is $0.80 ($P_{us}$), whereas in Chile it is 328 pesos (P_{chile}). Let the current, or spot, exchange rate between the two countries, in terms of Chilian pesos per U.S. dollars, be $E_{chile/us}$. If we can buy 410 pesos with $1, then $E = 410$. This exchange rate must be related to the price of copper in the two countries as:

> Price in Chile = Price in United States × exchange rate
> $$P_{chile} = P_{us} \times E_{chile/us} \tag{3.5}$$
>
> $$= \$0.80 \times 410$$
> $$= 328 \text{ pesos}$$

Equation 3.5 is the formal relationship of **purchasing power parity, PPP.** With PPP, money has the same purchasing power regardless of the currency in which it is held.

Purchasing power parity. A principle stating that comparable goods should sell for equivalent prices regardless of the currency used to price the goods.

If inflation is greater in Chile, the exchange rate automatically adjusts. For instance, assume Chile has inflation of 20 percent and inflation in the United States is 0 percent. Then the price in Chile should adjust to 393.6 pesos: $P_{chile} = 328 \times (1 + 0.20) = 393.6$. Since there is no inflation in the United States, $P_{us} = \$0.80$. For equal purchasing power to exist, the new exchange rate is 492 pesos per U.S. dollar: 393.6 pesos ÷ \$0.80 = 492.

If the Fed follows a monetary policy that increases the prices of goods in the United States relative to Chile, P_{us} will rise while P_{chile} will remain stable. The exchange rate between the two currencies, from the U.S. perspective, will decline. As a result of Fed policy, the value of the U.S. dollar in international markets declines. It is more expensive for Americans to purchase goods from Chile. However, now it is cheaper for Chilian buyers to purchase U.S. goods. The net result is that U.S. exporters gain sales and profits and U.S. importers lose.

Thus, if the monetary policy of one country is expansionary compared with that of another country, and the first country experiences more inflation than the other, then the exchange rate between the two countries *must* adjust to satisfy PPP. If exchange rates do not adjust, then PPP may not hold. Unless it is profitable to transport goods from one country to the other for sale, no profit opportunity exists. The lower purchase price of the foreign country plus the transportation costs approximate the purchase price in the domestic country.

 ## 3A.2 SPOT AND FORWARD EXCHANGE RATES

Spot exchange rate. The rate at which one currency can be converted into another, or the price of one currency in terms of another. For example, if the price of the German mark were \$0.25 per mark, it would require \$0.25 to purchase one mark or four marks to purchase \$1.

Forward exchange rate. Foreign exchange bought (or sold) at a given time and at a stipulated current or "spot" price, but payable at a future date. By buying or selling forward exchange, importers and exporters can protect themselves against the risks of fluctuations in the current exchange market.

When a company or an individual buys goods from another country, they usually need to pay for those goods in the currency of the selling country. They need to be able to convert their home currency into the foreign currency. All conversions of one currency into another involve trading in the foreign exchange market. In this market, banks are some of the largest dealers in foreign currency.

The price the purchaser pays for buying a foreign currency, say, Chilian pesos, with U.S. dollars is the peso-dollar exchange rate. The exchange rate tells us how many pesos we can buy with one U.S. dollar. Table 3.3 is an example of prices of foreign exchange quoted on a daily basis in *The Wall Street Journal*. The exchange rate represents the closing **spot exchange rate.** On April 8, 1994, the Chilian peso/dollar exchange rate, on a *dollar basis*, was 414.08 pesos per dollar. Conversely, we can look at the peso-dollar relationship in *dollar equivalents*: one peso was worth \$0.002415 on April 8. If we purchased pesos on this date, we would make a *spot transaction* at the time of purchase.

For Britain, the table shows three additional lines labeled *30-, 90-,* and *120-day forward*. The 30-day **forward exchange rate** is the rate quoted that day for exchanges taking place 30 days in the future. In other words, the forward rate allows a person or business to lock in a known exchange rate in 30 days. The result is reduced uncertainty about exchange rates and thereby reduced uncertainty about future costs and profits. Given that the 30-day pound-dollar forward rate is higher than the spot rate, the pound is trading at a *forward premium*. When the forward rate is lower than the spot rate, the pound is trading at a *forward discount*.

 ## 3A.3 INTEREST RATE PARITY

When we discussed purchasing power parity, we mentioned inflation as a factor that can cause prices to differ between countries. Let's now explore the relationship between interest rates, inflation, and currency exchange rates to derive interest rate parity. Assume that the Fed is following a monetary policy that businesses expect will result in high inflation relative to other countries. Instead of investing funds in domestic pro-

TABLE 3-3

CURRENCY TRADING

EXCHANGE RATES
Friday, April 8, 1994

The New York foreign exchange selling rates below apply to trading among banks in amounts of $1 million and more, as quoted at 3 p.m. Eastern time by Bankers Trust Co., Dow Jones Telerate Inc. and other sources. Retail transactions provide fewer units of foreign currency per dollar.

Country	U.S. $ equiv.		Currency per U.S. $	
	Fri.	Thurs.	Fri.	Thurs.
Argentina (Peso)	1.01	1.01	.99	.99
Australia (Dollar)	.7272	.7179	1.3751	1.3930
Austria (Schilling)	.08307	.08283	12.04	12.07
Bahrain (Dinar)	2.6522	2.6522	.3771	.3771
Belgium (Franc)	.02835	.02827	35.27	35.37
Brazil (Cruzeiro real) .	.0010277	.0010277	973.00	973.01
Britain (Pound)	1.4775	1.4730	.6768	.6789
30-Day Forward	1.4757	1.4713	.6776	.6797
90-Day Forward	1.4727	1.4683	.6790	.6811
180-Day Forward	1.4694	1.4650	.6805	.6826
Canada (Dollar) ....,	.7229	.7232	1.3833	1.3828
30-Day Forward	.7218	.7222	1.3854	1.3847
90-Day Forward	.7199	.7201	1.3891	1.3886
180-Day Forward	.7174	.7175	1.3940	1.3938
Czech. Rep. (Koruna)				
Commercial rate	.0335627	.0335965	29.7950	29.7650
Chile (Peso)	.002415	.002415	414.08	414.08
China (Renminbi)	.114986	.114986	8.6967	8.6967
Colombia (Peso)	.001218	.001218	820.78	820.78
Denmark (Krone)	.1492	.1488	6.7014	6.7210
Ecuador (Sucre)				
Floating rate	.000478	.000478	2090.00	2090.04
Finland (Markka)	.18154	.18129	5.5085	5.5160
France (Franc)	.17054	.17011	5.8636	5.8785
30-Day Forward	.17018	.16976	5.8761	5.8906
90-Day Forward	.16962	.16920	5.8955	5.9103
180-Day Forward	.16906	.16865	5.9151	5.9293
Germany (Mark)	.5843	.5826	1.7115	1.7165
30-Day Forward	.5832	.5815	1.7146	1.7196
90-Day Forward	.5817	.5800	1.7190	1.7242
180-Day Forward	.5804	.5788	1.7230	1.7278
Greece (Drachma)	.003975	.003967	251.60	252.05
Hong Kong (Dollar) ...	.12941	.12941	7.7275	7.7275
Hungary (Forint)	.0096395	.0096469	103.7400	103.6600
India (Rupee)	.03212	.03212	31.13	31.13
Indonesia (Rupiah)	.0004640	.0004640	2155.00	2155.03
Ireland (Punt)	1.4242	1.4200	.7021	.7042
Israel (Shekel)	.3372	.3372	2.9655	2.9655

jects, businesses and investors place their funds abroad in competitive markets where they expect to earn a fair return adjusted for inflation.

If market participants compare nominal interest rates for similar risky securities in two countries, they expect that any differences are largely attributable to one of two factors: differences exist either in expected real interest rates or in expected inflation. If governments do not restrict companies and individuals from moving funds from country to country, the expected real interest rate in each country should be equal for comparable risky investments. Thus, any differences in nominal interest rates in different countries should be purely a reflection of differences in expected inflation rates in those countries. Let's assume that government restrictions on monetary transfers are inconsequential. The following example illustrates interest rate parity.

Bessembinder International, Inc. has $100,000 in U.S. currency to invest for one year. If the company's treasurer invests the funds in the United States, the company will receive a 6 percent nominal interest rate. At the end of a year the investment would be worth $106,000. A similar risky investment in Japan offers a 7 percent return. However, the treasurer must convert the $100,000 into yen. The dollar basis spot yen-dollar exchange rate is 105.27. Thus, $100,000 become ¥10,527,000. At the end of one year, the company would have ¥11,263,890 (= ¥10,527,000 × 1.07), which the treasurer would want to convert to dollars. The problem is that if the treasurer waits to see what the actual spot exchange rate between yen and dollars is at the end of one year, the company bears the risk of fluctuations in the exchange rate between the time it invests in yen and the time it converts yen back to U.S. dollars.

An attractive alternative for the treasurer of Bessembinder is to contract for a known rate of exchange when the firm initially makes the foreign investment. The treasurer does this through the forward exchange market by contracting for a known forward exchange rate in one year. The treasurer is *hedging the currency or exchange rate risk*. **Hedging** means to take action to reduce or eliminate risk exposure. What forward exchange rate must prevail for the same amount of dollars to result from the investment in Japan as would result from the investment in the United States? There would be $106,000 at the end of a year if the treasurer invests in the United States. The treasurer knows there would be ¥11,263,890 at the end of a year if the funds are invested in Japan. The treasurer needs to determine the forward exchange rate that allows him to convert yen into exactly $106,000. The forward exchange rate formula is:

$$\frac{\text{Amount of yen}}{\text{Amount of dollars}} = \text{Number of yen per \$1} \qquad (3.6)$$

$$\frac{\text{¥11,263,890}}{\$106,000} = 106.26 \text{ yen per \$1}$$

Because of the U.S. interest rate of 6 percent, the Japanese interest rate of 7 percent, and the spot yen-dollar exchange rate of 105.27, any one-year forward exchange rate other than 106.26 gives an advantage to either the Japanese or the American investment. For example, assume that the one-year forward exchange rate is ¥110 per $1. Then ¥11,263,890 converts to $102,399 (= ¥11,263,890 ÷ ¥110), which is equivalent to earning about 2.4 percent investing $100,000 in the United States (= ([$102,399 ÷ $100,000]−1) × 100). If the one-year forward exchange rate is ¥103 per $1, then ¥11,263,890 converts to $109,358 (= ¥11,263,890 ÷ ¥103) in the United States, which is a 9.4 percent return. The treasurer would rather see the yen appreciate to 103 than see it depreciate to 110.

What rate should prevail for the treasurer to be indifferent between investing in the United States and investing in Japan, that is, for equilibrium to exist? Equilibrium exists in the foreign exchange market if the relationship between spot and forward exchange rate markets in the two countries behave according to **interest rate parity,** defined as:

Forward exchange rate of ¥/$

$$= \frac{\begin{array}{c}(\text{Spot exchange rate between yen and dollars})\\ \times (1 + \text{nominal interest rate in Japan})\end{array}}{1 + \text{nominal interest rate in U.S.}} \qquad (3.7)$$

$$= 105.27 \times 1.07 \div 1.06$$
$$= 106.26$$

Let's check the exchange rate calculated using Equation 3.7. If one year from now the treasurer of Bessembinder International wants to convert ¥11,263,890 to dollars, the dollar equivalent will be $106,003 (= ¥11,263,890 ÷ ¥106.26). Given the original investment of $100,000, the return is 6 percent (= $106,003 ÷ $100,000), the same return earned by investing in the United States. Thus, the expression in Equation 3.7 reveals a basic equilibrium relationship between current nominal interest rates, the spot exchange rate, and the forward exchange rate. Interest rate parity is an important relationship governing markets in foreign exchange around the world.

3A-1. The price of an espresso at a café on the Champs Elysees in Paris is 15 francs. Melissa has just come from the nearby American Express office, having cashed a few AMEX traveler's checks at the rate of francs for U.S. dollars of 5.422. What is the cost of the espresso in dollars?

3A-2. Peggy sees a beautiful camera in a Heidelberg shop which could replace the one she dropped into the Rhine River the night before. The shop operator offers to sell her the camera for U.S. $238. The list price in the shop is 412 German marks. She has the dollars in her money belt but notices the posted exchange rate at the bank next door is 1.6352 marks per $1. Should she buy the camera with dollars or exchange dollars for marks at the bank and then buy the camera? Assume there is no service charge for exchanging money.

3A-3. The price of a Honda Civic in Japan is ¥1,552,800. The same car costs $12,000 in the United States. If purchasing power parity exists between the two countries, what is the exchange rate between yen and dollars?

3A-4. Economists are forecasting the inflation rate to be 2 percent in Japan and 4 percent in the United States over the coming year. The current exchange rate is ¥1 = $0.00773 (that is, 1 yen = 0.773 cents). Assume that purchasing power parity exists.

   a. What is the expected spot exchange rate in one year? State it in terms of dollars for yen.

   b. If you wait one year to buy the Honda Civic in Problem 3A-3, what is the price of the car in yen and in dollars?

   c. What is the new exchange rate expected to be next year as a result of inflation?

3A-5. a. What does *trading at a forward discount* mean when discussing foreign currencies?

   b. What might cause a *forward discount*?

   c. Are any foreign currencies trading at a forward discount to the U.S. dollar in Table 3.3? Use the columns labeled *currency per US$*.

   d. Using Table 3.3, indicate whether each of the following currencies has strengthened or weakened against the U.S. dollar over the two days shown.

British pound
Canadian dollar
German mark
Hong Kong dollar
Irish punt
Israeli shekel

3A-6. a. State the equation for interest rate parity in terms of U.S. dollars and Swiss francs.

   b. The current Swiss franc-dollar exchange rate is 1.4823 francs per dollar. The risk-free interest rate in Switzerland is 5 percent, whereas it is 4 percent in the United States. What is the expected future exchange rate between the two countries in one year?

   c. Is the Swiss franc trading at a forward premium or a forward discount to the U.S. dollar? Explain.

Video Case 3

How The Fed Does Business

from *Business World*

This video describes one part of the nation's financial market system, the Federal Reserve Bank. The Federal Reserve System was created in 1913 to be the nation's central bank. The Fed's most important responsibility is controlling the nation's monetary policy by setting the Federal Funds rate – the interest rate charged to member banks – and managing the money supply. The Fed carries out a number of other functions as the nation's banker, such as clearing checks, managing government debt offerings, and publishing economic information in the *Federal Reserve Bulletin.*

The Fed is a semi-independent government agency. A seven-member board of governors oversees the Fed's activities. The president appoints the members of the board of governors, and the appointments are approved by the United States Senate. Members of the board of governors, along with the presidents of the 12 Federal Reserve Banks, comprise the Federal Open Market Committee. This group influences economic growth through interest rates and the money supply by buying and selling government securities on the open market, thereby the committee's name. Selling government bonds takes money out of the economy, tends to increase interest rates, and so slows down economic growth. Buying back government securities releases money into the economy, lowers interest rates, and so stimulates economic growth. The Fed also influences economic conditions by changing the interest rate at which it lends funds to member banks. Banks pass increased interest rates on to their customers, which reduces demand for loans and curbs expansion plans. The same effect occurs if the Fed raises the reserve requirement of member banks. The reserve requirement stipulates the portion of deposits that must be kept in the banks. Higher reserve requirements imply less money to lend, higher rates, and slower expansion.

Why would the Fed, or any other governmental agency, want to reduce economic expansion? This is the issue addressed in the video. As the video clip dramatically documents, the Fed is a lightening rod for criticism. Politicians see the Fed as the cause of recessions and, possibly more importantly, of their not being reelected. But the Fed has an important and difficult assignment. It is charged with finding a balance between economic growth and inflation. As the video makes clear, politicians want economic growth. New jobs and higher incomes make constituents happy, and help reelection campaigns. But if economic growth accelerates too quickly prices rise, resulting in inflation. If wages rise as fast as or faster than prices, then inflation is not a problem. However, many groups have no price adjustments built into their incomes. For example, many retirees live on fixed incomes. As prices rise they see their purchasing power diminish and find it increasingly difficult to meet their basic needs of housing, food, medical care, and transportation. Inflation places a severe tax on people living on fixed incomes.

Study Questions

1. The video shows that some people, often politicians, want more control over the Fed and its policies. Respond to this suggestion by explaining why the Fed should remain independent. As you answer, think of the incentives of incumbent politicians regarding economic policy.

2. At one point the video clip mentions that the Fed must sometimes administer discipline to the economy. What type of 'discipline' do you think the commentator means? Discipline usually implies exerting self-control, as in foregoing some thing or some activity. What sort of self-control does the Fed impose on the economy and for what end?

CHAPTER 4

The Time Value of Money

Although in "Hamlet" Shakespeare cautioned, "Neither a borrower nor a lender be," using and providing credit is a way of life in today's economy. Just as the goods or services that individuals or firms buy or sell involve a price, the extension of credit has a price attached to it. This price is the interest paid or earned. Consumers shop for the best price on a particular item of merchandise, and so too should they comparison shop for credit—whether borrowing or lending. But comparing prices for credit can be confusing.

In business as well as with an individual's transactions, a borrower receives a sum of money in return for a promise to repay certain sums of money in the future. The common characteristic of these two types of transactions is that the *time value of money* (the interest factor) is at play. The timing of the returns on the investment has an important effect on the worth of the investment (asset), and the timing of debt repayments has an effect on the value of the commitment (liability).

Most businesspeople and investors are acutely aware of the importance of time as it is associated with money, and they invest and borrow only after carefully analyzing the relative values of the cash outflows and inflows. This analysis requires an understanding of compound interest, annuities, and present and future value concepts to value the cash flows.

Examples of business applications involving time value of money are valuing receivables and payables that carry either a lower than market interest rate or no stated interest rate; valuing long-term lease agreements; evaluating alternative investments; determining the necessary contributions to a fund to retire debt; and measuring periodic payments on long-term purchase contracts. Our objective in this chapter is not to discuss exhaustively this list of applications. Rather, we examine the fundamental principle of finance that underlies each application: *Money has a time value represented by the interest cost.* Later chapters use time value concepts to value bonds and stocks, determine the worth of a firm, and calculate whether an investment opportunity contributes to improving shareholder wealth.

When you have studied this chapter, you should:

- Be able to calculate both the future and present values of cash flows.
- Understand the difference between ordinary annuities, annuities due, and perpetuities.
- Know how to measure time value amounts when cash flows occur either annually or more frequently.
- Know the difference between simple and compound interest, and derivations of each of them.

We begin by discussing simple interest. This discussion provides a base for examining the more complex issue of compound interest, which is the underlying theme of this chapter.

 ## 4.1 SIMPLE INTEREST

Time deposit. Bank accounts and other deposits that earn a higher interest than savings accounts but which must be left on deposit for a specified period of time (their maturity).

Principal. The face (or par) value of a loan that must be repaid at maturity.

Simple interest. Interest computed by multiplying the original principal by the percent of interest by the time period involved. It is paid when the loan matures.

The first experience most people have with interest is a *time deposit* in a bank. A **time deposit** is money held in the bank account of a person or firm for which the bank can require advance notice of withdrawal. Calculations of interest involve three elements: the *principal* amount, an *interest rate*, and the length of *time*. **Principal,** the amount borrowed, is the basis for all simple interest charges. The lender expresses the *interest rate* as a percentage of the principal; it can also be shown as decimals (0.14 instead of 14 percent). The *time* involved determines the total amount the borrower will pay on the loan. Time may be less than, equal to, or more than one year. The distinction is important because the *interest rate is usually expressed annually.* A 12 percent loan means a charge of 12 percent per year, or per annum.

The basic concept underlying **simple interest** is that the borrower pays interest only on the loan principal for the length of time the loan is outstanding. An excellent way to understand how to calculate simple interest is to reduce it to the formula:

$$\text{Interest} = \text{Principal} \times \text{interest rate} \times \text{time} \tag{4.1}$$
$$I = P \times r \times t$$

It is necessary to state r and t consistently. That is, if the interest rate r is an annual rate, then state time t in years; if the rate is a monthly rate, then state time in months. To figure the total amount of repayment for simple interest, we add the principal to the total interest due. (See Illustration 4.1.) Expressed as a formula, the total payment is:

$$\begin{aligned}\text{Total payment} &= \text{Principal} + (\text{principal} \times \text{interest rate} \times \text{time}) \\ &= \text{Principal} \times (1 + \text{interest rate} \times \text{time}) \\ &= P \times (1 + r \times t)\end{aligned} \tag{4.2}$$

ILLUSTRATION 4.1

Calculation of simple interest

Lasorda Printing Company wants to purchase a photocopy machine costing $10,000. The manufacturer agrees to the company's request that payment be made in one year if Lasorda agrees to pay 14 percent simple interest on the outstanding balance. The interest cost would be $1400, payable in one year along with the $10,000 purchase price.

$$\text{Interest} = \text{Principal} \times \text{interest rate} \times \text{time}$$
$$= \$10{,}000 \times 0.14 \times 1 \text{ year}$$
$$= \$1400$$

$$\text{Total payment} = \text{Principal} \times (1 + \text{interest rate} \times \text{time})$$
$$= \$10{,}000 \times (1 + 0.14 \times 1 \text{ year})$$
$$= \$11{,}400$$

What is the interest cost if Lasorda Printing negotiates a two-year deal? Interest for the first year is $1400, so the balance after one year is $11,400 (assuming no payments have been made). The next question is whether interest for the second year will be computed on only the original $10,000 or on $11,400.

Under the simple interest method, the seller calculates interest for the second year using the $10,000 principal amount owed by Lasorda Printing. The calculation for simple interest for two years is:

$$\text{Interest} = \text{Principal} \times \text{interest rate} \times \text{time}$$
$$= \$10{,}000 \times 0.14 \times 2 \text{ years}$$
$$= \$2800$$

The total amount repaid under the simple interest method is the summation of the principal amount of $10,000 plus total interest due of $2800, or using Equation 4.2:

$$\text{Total payment} = \text{Principal} \times (1 + \text{interest rate} \times \text{time})$$
$$= \$10{,}000 \times (1 + 0.14 \times 2)$$
$$= \$12{,}800$$

Interest does not always apply for periods of one year or more. For less than a year, the time factor is a fraction. Since *time* = 1 represents one full year, the days or months are proportions of 1. What if the photocopy manufacturer in Illustration 4.1 is willing to carry the debt only for 90 days? A $10,000 debt with annual simple interest of 14 percent requires a total payment of $10,350.

$$\text{Total payment} = \text{Principal} \times (1 + \text{interest rate} \times \text{time})$$
$$= P \times (1 + r \times t)$$
$$= \$10{,}000 \times (1 + 0.14 \times 90 \div 360)$$
$$= \$10{,}350$$

The annual interest rate is still 14 percent, but it is necessary to express the interest rate for a period less than one year. An annual interest rate of 14 percent is the same as 3.5 percent over 90 days: $14\% \times 90 \div 360$.

If the loan is for 15 months at simple interest, the repayment amount is $11,750. The time variable is 1.25, or $15 \div 12$.

$$\text{Total payment} = \text{Principal} \times (1 + \text{interest rate} \times \text{time})$$
$$= P \times (1 + r \times t)$$
$$= \$10{,}000 \times (1 + 0.14 \times 1.25)$$
$$= \$11{,}750$$

Is there anything wrong with simple interest? Yes—it does not conform to the finance principle about the time value of money. *Simple interest calculations do not calculate interest on interest.* The remaining interest methods we discuss in this chapter—

THE VALUE OF TIME VALUE OF MONEY CONCEPTS

by Pegi Carey, Assistant Vice President, Manager Resource and Support Group, First Interstate Bank of Arizona

The concept that money has a value associated with time is certainly one that every business student should master. When I recall my first introduction to the subject, the word *panic* comes to mind. It was confusing at first. However, I could relate many instances in which I had been aware of the time value of money, such as when I borrowed money to pay for my car. When I multiplied the monthly payment by the number of months I was going to pay, the result was an astounding price. I was going to pay dearly for the use of the bank's money for the time it took to pay back that loan. Study and repetition of the subject eliminated any confusion and ultimately compounding and discounting have become second nature to me. In my banking career I use these tools, compounding and discounting, extensively and with ease.

In everyday life the practical applications associated with the time value of money are fairly significant. For instance, in banking, bank customers are confronted with decisions involving interest rates when seeking to borrow money for a home or a car or for any other purpose. They "shop" interest rates and loan terms in order to borrow efficiently. They want to pay as little interest as possible. They also "shop" rates when comparing investment vehicles. They seek to make informed choices about whether they should invest in certificates of deposit, mutual funds, government bonds, municipal bonds, stocks, or money-market funds. The choices offered the typical bank customer have greatly expanded in the last several years. More and more investment choices are being offered to customers by financial institutions. The typical bank customer is more informed today than ever before and is making more sophisticated choices about investing and borrowing. And there is a lot at stake in making the right financial choice. In planning for retirement, owning a home, buying a car, and educating yourself and your children, the time value of money has a major impact.

There is a lot at stake for banks as well. Financial institutions today are faced with an increasingly competitive environment. To retain customers and attract new ones, the bank must develop lending products and investment products that meet the needs of increasingly sophisticated bank customers while maintaining profitability. The tools associated with the time value of money are used extensively in evaluating the profitability of products, their competitiveness and marketability. The business practitioner uses the tools presented in this chapter so often that the concept of the time value of money ultimately becomes intuitive. Business decisions are made daily using these tools.

Lending decisions typically involve evaluating the creditworthiness of the borrower. This may be a fairly straightforward exercise when dealing with an individual but it becomes more complicated when a commercial enterprise is involved. Often bankers are delving into all financial aspects of a business to determine the best answer to their business customers' specific borrowing needs. This may involve valuing the business using discounted cash flow analysis, a classic use of discounting.

What happens when the bank needs to expand its own capabilities to serve its customers better? When large capital acquisitions are considered, one of the financial analyses included in the business case for the acquisition is a net present value analysis of the asset's costs versus benefits, another classic time value of money application.

Good luck in making the tools at hand your own. Whenever you set out to learn something new, make as many mistakes as quickly as possible in order to learn as much as you can in a short period of time. Your time and money will be well spent!

compound interest, add-on interest, and *bank discount interest*—differ from simple interest as to when, how, and on what balance interest is paid.

Comprehension Check

1. How is simple interest calculated when there is one payment involved? How is the total principal plus interest amount determined?
2. What is the major weakness of the simple interest method?

4.2 COMPOUND INTEREST

If we invest money, wouldn't we like both our interest income and original principal to earn interest instead of just the principal amount as under the simple interest method? A technique known as *compounding* allows interest to earn interest. **Compounding** is the process of calculating interest on interest. Thus, compounding accurately reflects the true opportunity cost of funds over time. **Compound interest** is simple interest applied over and over to a sum that is increased by the simple interest each time it is earned. Investments paying compound interest are more valuable because they pay interest on interest; that is, they recognize the time value of money.

> **Compounding.** Process by which a given amount is adjusted at interest to yield a future value. Compounding is the opposite of *discounting.*

> **Compound interest.** Interest computed on a principal sum and also on all the interest earned by that principal sum as of a given date.

We will calculate time value of money from two different perspectives: *future value* and *present value.* Our discussion relies primarily on the use of formulas. We use time value tables sparingly. Keystrokes applicable for most simple financial calculators are shown in the margin. The notation is similar to that found on these calculators: PV is present value, FV is future value, PMT is equal payments per period, %i is interest rate percent per period, N is the number of periods, and CPT is compute. For example, to find the future value of $500 three years from now, when interest is compounded annually at 6.5 percent, use the following keystrokes: clear calculator, $500, PV, 6.5, %i, 3, N, CPT, FV. The answer is $603.97.

4.2.1 Future Value with Compounding

The concept of future value with compounding is straightforward. A $100 deposit earning 5 percent interest is worth $105 at the end of the first year. During the entire second year, the $105 balance in the account earns 5 percent interest, or $5.25 ($= 0.05 \times \$105$). Interest earns interest. Thus, at the end of the second year, the account balance is $110.25. Verify that the balance is $115.76 at the end of the third year.[1]

Let's consider the concept of compound interest in a more general form, as it helps us reduce the calculation of interest on interest to an important formula. If the interest rate in decimal form is r, then the value of a deposit at the end of the first period is its future value, FV_1:

> Value next period = Value this period × (1 + interest rate)
>
> $$FV_1 = PV_0 \times (1 + r)$$
> (4.3)

[1]Solution: $1.05 \times \$110.25 = \$115.76$

where PV_0 is the present value (that is, today's value) of FV_1. If FV_1 is compounded for another period,

$$FV_2 = FV_1 \times (1 + r) \qquad (4.4)$$

Alternatively, substitute the right-hand side of Equation 4.4 for FV_1 in Equation 4.4. The result is:

$$\begin{aligned} FV_2 &= FV_1 \times (1 + r) \\ &= PV_0 \times (1 + r) \times (1 + r) \end{aligned} \qquad (4.5)$$

In either case, FV_2 is the value of the initial deposit at the end of the second period. The compounding process can repeat for any number of periods. Rather than write this long expression, the terms can be collected into a simpler general statement:

$$FV_n = PV_0 \times (1 + r)^n \qquad (4.6)$$

where n is the number of periods that money earns interest and FV_n is the future amount at the end of the nth period. Equation 4.6 is the **future value formula.** See Illustration 4.2 for its application.

Future value formula. The value of $(1 + r)^n$, where r is the interest rate and n is the number of time periods.

The time diagram for future value depicts the cash flows as follows:

	Present				Future
Period	0	1	2	. . .	n
Amount	PV_0				

$$\begin{aligned} & PV_0 \times (1 + r) \\ & = FV_1 \end{aligned}$$

$$\begin{aligned} & PV_0 \times (1 + r)^2 \\ & = FV_1 \times (1 + r) \\ & = FV_2 \end{aligned}$$

$$\begin{aligned} & PV_0 \times (1 + r)^n \\ & = FV_n \end{aligned}$$

ILLUSTRATION 4.2

Calculator
Clear
100
PV
5
%i
3
N
CPT
FV
Ans.: 115.76

Future value with compound interest

Ms. Bishop invests $100 for three years at 5 percent annual compound interest.

	Present			Future
Period	0	1	2	3
Amount	$100	$100(1.05) = $105	$100(1.05)^2 = $110.25	$100(1.05)^3 = $115.76

The deposit grows to $105 at the end of the first year. Five percent of $105 added to $105 equals $110.25. This balance is the value of the deposit at the end of the second year. Five percent of $110.25 is $5.51. Thus, the deposit is $115.76 at the end of the third year.

We get the same result using Equation 4.6:

$$\begin{aligned} FV_n &= PV_0 \times (1 + r)^n \\ FV_4 &= \$100 \times (1 + 0.05)^3 \\ &= \$100 \times 1.1576 \\ &= \$115.76 \end{aligned}$$

> First, multiply 1.05 by itself three times, which equals 1.1576. Multiply 1.1576 by the original principal of $100 to get $115.76. This amount is the value of $100 compounded once a year, for three years, at 5 percent.

Table 4.1 is an example of *future value table factors* of compound sums of $1. Tables such as this are commonly used to find future values instead of using Equation 4.6, as long as the interest rate and the number of periods are within the table. In this example, we find the solution to Illustration 4.2 using the table as follows.

- Read down the column labeled *Period* until row 3 is reached. This row represents year 3.
- Read across the top row to the 5% column.
- Find the table value where the 5% column and the 3-year row intersect: 1.1576. This number is commonly called the *future value interest factor* for $r\%$ and n periods, or $FVIF_{r\%, \, n \, periods}$. In this problem, $FVIF_{5\%, \, 3 \, periods}$ represents the value of $1 compounded at 5 percent per year for three years.
- Multiply $100 by the $FVIF_{5\%, \, 3 \, years}$ of 1.1576: $100 \times 1.1576 = 115.76. The result is the value of $100 compounded at 5 percent interest per year for three years.

Note in the table that $FVIF_{r\%, \, n \, periods}$ is always greater than 1. As the interest rate increases, $FVIF_{r\%, \, n \, periods}$ increases. And as the number of periods increases, $FVIF_{r\%, \, n \, periods}$ also increases. Let's look at the 10% column: 1.10 is $1 compounded at 10 percent for one period; 1.21 is $1 compounded at 10 percent for two periods; and so on. If we compare the 10% column with the 9% column, we see that the numbers in the 10% column are larger. The reason is because compounding at 10 percent provides more interest than does compounding at 9 percent.

To extend the illustration, Figure 4.1 depicts different profiles for $1 earning either simple or compound interest at different rates over different periods. We can see that compound interest leads to much greater wealth. Simple interest causes the original investment to increase in a linear fashion. Compound interest causes the investment to grow exponentially. Compound interest is the primary criterion for most interest calculations in finance. Andrew Tobias provides an interesting perspective on the importance of compound interest in the Financial Reality reading on page 112.

4.2.2 Present Value with Compounding

The value of cash flows available in the future has a value at the present time. We need to determine this value, called the *present value,* to help us make decisions among various alternative investments. The process of finding the present value of future cash flows is called **discounting.** The terms in the future value compound interest formula (Equation 4.6) can be algebraically rearranged so that the equation appears as:

$$\text{Present value} = \text{Future value in period } n \div (1 + \text{interest rate})^n$$

$$PV_0 = \frac{FV_n}{(1 + r)^n} \tag{4.7}$$

Equation 4.7 is the *discounting formula,* or **present value formula.** The equation gives the present value (PV_0) of future cash (FV_n) received in period n, discounted at interest rate r.

Discounting. Process by which a given amount is adjusted at interest to yield a present value. Discounting is the opposite of *compounding.*

Present value formula. A formula showing how the current price of an asset is related to its expected future cash flows, through the use of a rate of interest. The formula is $1/(1 + r)^n$ where r is an interest rate and n is time periods.

TABLE 4-1

COMPOUND SUM OF $1 RECEIVED AT END OF PERIOD: $(1 + r)^n$

Period	1%	2%	3%	4%	5%	6%	7%	8%	9%	10%	12%	14%	15%	16%	18%	20%	24%	28%	32%	36%
1	1.0100	1.0200	1.0300	1.0400	1.0500	1.0600	1.0700	1.0800	1.0900	1.1000	1.1200	1.1400	1.1500	1.1600	1.1800	1.2000	1.2400	1.2800	1.3200	1.3600
2	1.0201	1.0404	1.0609	1.0816	1.1025	1.1236	1.1449	1.1664	1.1881	1.2100	1.2544	1.2996	1.3225	1.3456	1.3924	1.4400	1.5376	1.6384	1.7424	1.8496
3	1.0303	1.0612	1.0927	1.1249	1.1576	1.1910	1.2250	1.2597	1.2950	1.3310	1.4049	1.4815	1.5209	1.5609	1.6430	1.7280	1.9066	2.0972	2.3000	2.5155
4	1.0406	1.0824	1.1255	1.1699	1.2155	1.2625	1.3108	1.3605	1.4116	1.4641	1.5735	1.6890	1.7490	1.8106	1.9388	2.0736	2.3642	2.6844	3.0360	3.4210
5	1.0510	1.1041	1.1593	1.2167	1.2763	1.3382	1.4026	1.4693	1.5386	1.6105	1.7623	1.9254	2.0114	2.1003	2.2878	2.4883	2.9316	3.4360	4.0075	4.6526
6	1.0615	1.1262	1.1941	1.2653	1.3401	1.4185	1.5007	1.5869	1.6771	1.7716	1.9738	2.1950	2.3131	2.4364	2.6996	2.9860	3.6352	4.3980	5.2899	6.3275
7	1.0721	1.1487	1.2299	1.3159	1.4071	1.5036	1.6058	1.7138	1.8280	1.9487	2.2107	2.5023	2.6600	2.8262	3.1855	3.5832	4.5077	5.6295	6.9826	8.6054
8	1.0829	1.1717	1.2668	1.3686	1.4775	1.5938	1.7182	1.8509	1.9926	2.1436	2.4760	2.8526	3.0590	3.2784	3.7589	4.2998	5.5895	7.2058	9.2170	11.703
9	1.0937	1.1951	1.3048	1.4233	1.5513	1.6895	1.8385	1.9990	2.1719	2.3579	2.7731	3.2519	3.5179	3.8030	4.4355	5.1598	6.9310	9.2234	12.166	15.916
10	1.1046	1.2190	1.3439	1.4802	1.6289	1.7908	1.9672	2.1589	2.3674	2.5937	3.1058	3.7072	4.0456	4.4114	5.2338	6.1917	8.5944	11.806	16.060	21.647
11	1.1157	1.2434	1.3842	1.5395	1.7103	1.8983	2.1049	2.3316	2.5804	2.8531	3.4785	4.2262	4.6524	5.1173	6.1759	7.4301	10.657	15.112	21.199	29.439
12	1.1268	1.2682	1.4258	1.6010	1.7959	2.0122	2.2522	2.5182	2.8127	3.1384	3.8960	4.8179	5.3503	5.9360	7.2876	8.9161	13.215	19.343	27.983	40.037
13	1.1381	1.2936	1.4685	1.6651	1.8856	2.1329	2.4096	2.7196	3.0658	3.4523	4.3635	5.4924	6.1528	6.8858	8.5994	10.699	16.386	24.759	36.937	54.451
14	1.1495	1.3195	1.5126	1.7317	1.9799	2.2609	2.5785	2.9372	3.3417	3.7975	4.8871	6.2613	7.0757	7.9675	10.147	12.839	20.319	31.691	48.757	74.053
15	1.1610	1.3459	1.5580	1.8009	2.0789	2.3966	2.7590	3.1722	3.6425	4.1772	5.4736	7.1379	8.1371	9.2655	11.974	15.407	25.196	40.565	64.359	100.71
16	1.1726	1.3728	1.6047	1.8730	2.1829	2.5404	2.9522	3.4259	3.9703	4.5950	6.1304	8.1372	9.3576	10.748	14.129	18.488	31.243	51.923	84.954	136.97
17	1.1843	1.4002	1.6528	1.9479	2.2920	2.6928	3.1588	3.7000	4.3276	5.0545	6.8660	9.2765	10.761	12.467	16.672	22.186	38.741	66.461	112.14	186.28
18	1.1961	1.4282	1.7024	2.0258	2.4066	2.8543	3.3799	3.9960	4.7171	5.5599	7.6900	10.575	12.375	14.463	19.673	26.623	48.039	85.071	148.02	253.34
19	1.2081	1.4568	1.7535	2.1068	2.5270	3.0256	3.6165	4.3157	5.1417	6.1159	8.6128	12.056	14.232	16.777	23.214	31.948	59.568	108.89	195.39	344.54
20	1.2202	1.4859	1.8061	2.1911	2.6533	3.2071	3.8697	4.6610	5.6044	6.7275	9.6463	13.743	16.367	19.461	27.393	38.338	73.864	139.38	257.92	468.57
21	1.2324	1.5157	1.8603	2.2788	2.7860	3.3996	4.1406	5.0338	6.1088	7.4002	10.804	15.668	18.822	22.574	32.323	46.005	91.592	178.41	340.45	637.26
22	1.2447	1.5460	1.9161	2.3699	2.9253	3.6035	4.4304	5.4365	6.6586	8.1403	12.100	17.861	21.645	26.186	38.142	55.206	113.57	228.36	449.39	866.87
23	1.2572	1.5769	1.9736	2.4647	3.0715	3.8197	4.7405	5.8715	7.2579	8.9543	13.552	20.362	24.891	30.376	45.008	66.247	140.83	292.30	593.20	1178.7
24	1.2697	1.6084	2.0328	2.5633	3.2251	4.0489	5.0724	6.3412	7.9111	9.8497	15.179	23.212	28.625	35.236	53.109	79.497	174.63	374.14	783.02	1602.9
25	1.2824	1.6406	2.0938	2.6658	3.3864	4.2919	5.4274	6.8485	8.6231	10.835	17.000	26.462	32.919	40.874	62.669	95.396	216.54	478.90	1033.6	2180.1
26	1.2953	1.6734	2.1566	2.7725	3.5557	4.5494	5.8074	7.3964	9.3992	11.918	19.040	30.167	37.857	47.414	73.949	114.48	268.51	613.00	1364.3	2964.9
27	1.3082	1.7069	2.2213	2.8834	3.7335	4.8223	6.2139	7.9881	10.245	13.110	21.325	34.390	43.535	55.000	87.260	137.37	332.95	784.63	1800.9	4032.2
28	1.3213	1.7410	2.2879	2.9987	3.9201	5.1117	6.6488	8.6271	11.167	14.421	23.883	39.204	50.065	63.800	102.96	164.84	412.86	1004.3	2377.2	5483.9
29	1.3345	1.7758	2.3566	3.1187	4.1161	5.4184	7.1143	9.3173	12.172	15.863	26.750	44.693	57.575	74.009	121.50	197.81	511.95	1285.6	3137.9	7458.1
30	1.3478	1.8114	2.4273	3.2434	4.3219	5.7435	7.6123	10.063	13.268	17.449	29.960	50.950	66.212	85.850	143.37	237.38	634.82	1645.5	4142.1	10143.
40	1.4889	2.2080	3.2620	4.8010	7.0400	10.286	14.974	21.725	31.409	45.259	93.051	188.88	267.86	378.72	750.38	1469.8	5455.9	19427.	66521.	*
50	1.6446	2.6916	4.3839	7.1067	11.467	18.420	29.457	46.902	74.358	117.39	289.00	700.23	1083.7	1670.7	3927.4	9100.4	46890.	*	*	*
60	1.8167	3.2810	5.8916	10.520	18.679	32.988	57.946	101.26	176.03	304.48	897.60	2595.9	4384.0	7370.2	20555.	56348.	*	*	*	*

*FVIF > 99,999.

FIGURE 4.1

FUTURE VALUE OF $1, SIMPLE INTEREST VERSUS COMPOUND INTEREST

There is a significant advantage to compound interest as the interest rate increases. A $1 investment earning 5 percent grows to $2 in 20 years using simple interest and is worth $2.65 using compound interest. At an interest rate of 20 percent, $1 is worth $5 after 20 years using simple interest but is worth $38.33 using compound interest.

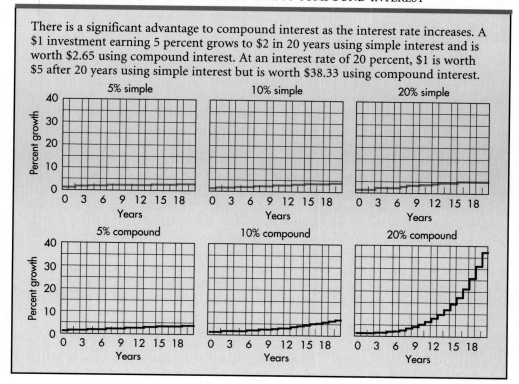

Equation 4.7 shows that present value is the opposite of future value. In Illustration 4.2, the $110.25 expected at the end of the second year has a present value of $100 when discounted at 5 percent interest. Or $100 today has a future value of $110.25 when interest is compounded at 5 percent for two periods. Prove this answer using Equation 4.6.[2]

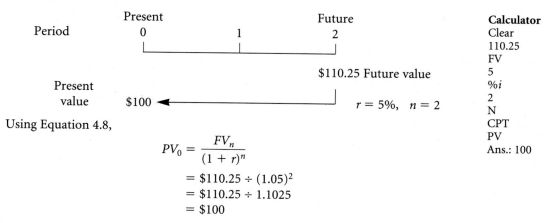

Using Equation 4.8,

$$PV_0 = \frac{FV_n}{(1 + r)^n}$$

$$= \$110.25 \div (1.05)^2$$
$$= \$110.25 \div 1.1025$$
$$= \$100$$

Illustration 4.3 shows how to find the present value of multiple cash flows.

[2]Solution: $FV_2 = \$100 \times (1 + 0.05)^2 = \$110.25$

YOUR OWN BEST INTEREST

Andrew Tobias has written several lucid books on investing. In this excerpt from "Your Own Best Interest," he explains the marvels of compound interest.

If you could be any financial concept in the world, which one would you be? Inflation? Hedging? Disintermediating? (Sorry; Rich is an adjective, not a concept. You've got to pick a concept.) If you were smart, you'd pick compound interest. It never fails to dazzle.

Today, for example, I bought $200,000 worth of zero-coupon municipal bonds. Zero coupon means they pay no interest. Municipal means I pay no taxes. (Why taxes should be a consideration at all when no interest is paid I shall explain momentarily.) All these bonds offer is the promise that on January 1, 2014, they will be redeemed at full face value: $1000. I bought 200 such little promises.

Now, even a fine-arts major knows that $1000 well into the next century is worth something less than $1000 in cash today. (A bird in the hand, and all that.) But how much less?

I called my broker, a man of surpassing charm and experience, who does things the old-fashioned way. "Buy me two hundred of these New Hampshire zeros of 2014," I said. I love to talk like that. "At what price?" he asked, his quill pen at the ready. "They're quoted two and five eights," I told him. "What do you mean?" he asked. "I mean they're quoted two and five-eights," I explained. "What do you *mean*?" he asked.

When a bond is quoted at par (100), that means it's selling for 100 cents on the dollar—its full $1000 face value. When it's quoted at 55, that means it is sell-ing for 55 cents on the dollar. Eventually, it will be redeemed at full face value—$1000—but right now, if you tried to get rid of it, $550 is all you would get. And when a bond is quoted at two and five eights, that means it is selling for two and five-eights cents on the dollar, or $26.25 a bond. Not a lot of money.

"I mean," I said, "that each bond costs twenty-six dollars and twenty-five cents." "That can't be right," said my broker. "It must be two sixty-two fifty." The old decimal-point trick. Not $26.25—$262.50.

"Hunh-unh," I explained again, "twenty-six twenty-five." "You mean," he said, "that for every twenty-six dollars you pay now, you get a thousand dollars in thirty-one years?" "Now you've got it," I said. "Wait," he said, "that can't be right." But it is. And I bought them—$200,000 worth for $5300. It is the so-called magic of compound interest. It aston-ished us as children; it astonishes us today.

I called to tell a young investment banker friend about these bonds. He holds two Harvard degrees and earned a bonus last year of $73,000. Money is his busi-ness. I asked how much he thought it would take to build up $200,000 in after-tax money by 2014.

"You want me to figure it out for you or just guess?" he said. "Just guess," I said. "Three thousand a year?" "No, fifty-three hundred once." "That can't be right," he said, reaching for his calculator. "What rate of return is that?"

"Twelve percent a year, compounded." "It is!" he said, a moment later, marveling at the cherry-cough-syrup display of his pocket calculator.

Used with permission of Andrew Tobias. Originally appeared in *Playboy*, 30, no. 3 (March 1983), pp. 119, 160-162.

ILLUSTRATION 4.3

Present value with compound interest

Ms. Bishop invests $1000 today in an investment that pays her $100 each year for the next three years. At the end of the third year, she receives her initial $1000. If the interest rate is 5 percent, the present value of this investment is $1136.16.

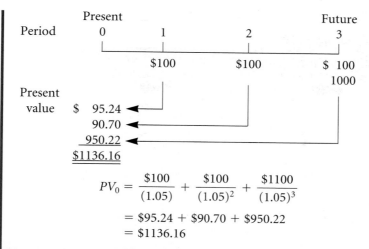

$$PV_0 = \frac{\$100}{(1.05)} + \frac{\$100}{(1.05)^2} + \frac{\$1100}{(1.05)^3}$$

$$= \$95.24 + \$90.70 + \$950.22$$

$$= \$1136.16$$

The receipt of $1136.16 today is equivalent to receiving $100 at the end of each of the next two years and $1100 at the end of the third year. The present value of the cash inflows exceeds the initial cash outflow of $1000 by $136.16.

Figure 4.2 shows the present value profile of a single payment of $1 received at the end of each year n, where $n = 1, 2, \ldots, 10$, for different interest rates. As interest rates increase, the present value of the $1 decreases. As the receipt of the $1 becomes more distant, the present value of the future $1 decreases if the interest rate exceeds 0 percent.

Table 4.2 provides figures, called *discount factors* for r percent and n periods, or $PVIF_{r\%, \, n \text{ periods}}$, for the present value of $1 received in future periods, given different interest rates. These **discount factors** are the result of solving Equation 4.7 for different interest rates, r, and different time periods, n, where $FV_n = 1$. For example, the discount factor for $n = 15$ and $r = 20$ percent is 0.0649, which equals $PVIF_{20\%, \, 15 \text{ years}}$ in Table 4.2.

> **Discount factor.** Present value of $1 received at a stated future date.

$$PV_0 = \frac{FV_n}{(1 + r)^n}$$

$$= 1 \div (1 + 0.20)^{15}$$

$$= 1 \div 15.407$$

$$= 0.0649$$

Notice in the table how quickly $1 received in the future loses value when translated into current (today's) dollars. All $PVIF_{r\%, \, n \text{ periods}}$ are less than 1 and decline quickly as either the interest rate increases or the number of periods increase. For example, $1 received 15 years from now is only worth 6.5 cents today if we can earn 20 percent interest on our investment. Or think of this example in the context of high inflation in some country. If inflation is 20 percent annually, $1 of purchasing power 15 years from now buys as much as 6.5 cents buys today. To reverse the process, an investment of 6.5 cents today, which earns compound interest of 20 percent, grows to $1 in 15 years. Similarly, $1 received 25 years from today is only worth 9.23 cents today if we can earn 10 percent on our investments over this 25-year time period.

4.2.3 Compounding and Intraperiod Flows

Cash flows may occur more frequently than at the end of each period. If cash receipts are offered every six months, for example, instead of once a year, the annual cash

FIGURE 4.2

PRESENT VALUE PROFILE OF $1

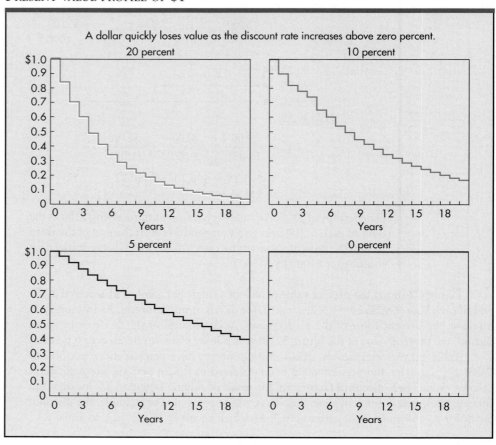

Annual percentage rate (APR). The rate per period times the number of periods per year.

Effective annual rate (EAR). The true interest rate that is paid on a loan.

amount is split in half. If payments are quarterly, the calculation divides the annual cash amount by 4. We need a method of calculating interest in these cases of *intraperiod flows.* A method often used by lenders is called the *annual percentage rate (APR).* **APR** is defined as the *rate for the period × the number of compounding periods per year.* For example, if a lender states interest as 1.5 percent compounded monthly, then the APR is 1.5 percent × 12 months, or 18 percent annually.

However, to put different interest rates and frequencies of cash receipts or payments on a comparable basis, we determine the *effective annual rate.* The **effective annual rate (EAR)** is the annual interest rate which produces the same dollar amount of interest per year as the periodic nominal, or stated, interest rate r compounded m periods per year.

The EAR differs from the APR quoted by many lenders. The formula for calculating the EAR is:

$$EAR = (1 + r/m)^m - 1 \qquad (4.8)$$

If the nominal annual interest rate r is 6 percent and compounding occurs annually ($m = 1$), then both the APR and the EAR are 6 percent:

APR: 0.06 annually × 1 compounding period = 0.06 or 6 percent

EAR: $(1 + 0.06/1)^1 - 1 = 0.06$ or 6 percent

TABLE 4-2

PRESENT VALUE OF $1 RECEIVED AT THE END OF PERIOD: $1/(1 + r)^n$

Period	1%	3%	5%	6%	7%	8%	9%	10%	11%	12%	13%	14%	15%	16%	17%	18%	19%	20%	24%	28%
1	.9901	.9709	.9524	.9434	.9346	.9259	.9174	.9091	.9009	.8929	.8850	.8772	.8696	.8621	.8547	.8475	.8403	.8333	.8065	.7813
2	.9803	.9426	.9070	.8900	.8734	.8573	.8417	.8264	.8116	.7972	.7831	.7695	.7561	.7432	.7305	.7182	.7062	.6944	.6504	.6104
3	.9706	.9151	.8638	.8396	.8163	.7938	.7722	.7513	.7312	.7118	.6931	.6750	.6575	.6407	.6244	.6086	.5934	.5787	.5245	.4768
4	.9610	.8885	.8227	.7921	.7629	.7350	.7084	.6830	.6587	.6355	.6133	.5921	.5718	.5523	.5337	.5158	.4987	.4823	.4230	.3725
5	.9515	.8626	.7835	.7473	.7130	.6806	.6499	.6209	.5935	.5674	.5428	.5194	.4972	.4761	.4561	.4371	.4190	.4019	.3411	.2910
6	.9420	.8375	.7462	.7050	.6663	.6302	.5963	.5645	.5346	.5066	.4803	.4556	.4323	.4104	.3898	.3704	.3521	.3349	.2751	.2274
7	.9327	.8131	.7107	.6651	.6227	.5835	.5470	.5132	.4817	.4523	.4251	.3996	.3759	.3538	.3332	.3139	.2959	.2791	.2218	.1776
8	.9235	.7894	.6768	.6274	.5820	.5403	.5019	.4665	.4339	.4039	.3762	.3506	.3269	.3050	.2848	.2660	.2487	.2326	.1789	.1388
9	.9143	.7664	.6446	.5919	.5439	.5002	.4604	.4241	.3909	.3606	.3329	.3075	.2843	.2630	.2434	.2255	.2090	.1938	.1443	.1084
10	.9053	.7441	.6139	.5584	.5083	.4632	.4224	.3855	.3522	.3220	.2946	.2697	.2472	.2267	.2080	.1911	.1756	.1615	.1164	.0847
11	.8963	.7224	.5847	.5268	.4751	.4289	.3875	.3505	.3173	.2875	.2607	.2366	.2149	.1954	.1778	.1619	.1476	.1346	.0938	.0662
12	.8874	.7014	.5568	.4970	.4440	.3971	.3555	.3186	.2858	.2567	.2307	.2076	.1869	.1685	.1520	.1372	.1240	.1122	.0757	.0517
13	.8787	.6810	.5303	.4688	.4150	.3677	.3262	.2897	.2575	.2292	.2042	.1821	.1625	.1452	.1299	.1163	.1042	.0935	.0610	.0404
14	.8700	.6611	.5051	.4423	.3878	.3405	.2992	.2633	.2320	.2046	.1807	.1597	.1413	.1252	.1110	.0985	.0876	.0779	.0492	.0316
15	.8613	.6419	.4810	.4173	.3624	.3152	.2745	.2394	.2090	.1827	.1599	.1401	.1229	.1079	.0949	.0835	.0736	.0649	.0397	.0247
16	.8528	.6232	.4581	.3936	.3387	.2919	.2519	.2176	.1883	.1631	.1415	.1229	.1069	.0930	.0811	.0708	.0618	.0541	.0320	.0193
17	.8444	.6050	.4363	.3714	.3166	.2703	.2311	.1978	.1696	.1456	.1252	.1078	.0929	.0802	.0693	.0600	.0520	.0451	.0258	.0150
18	.8360	.5874	.4155	.3503	.2959	.2502	.2120	.1799	.1528	.1300	.1108	.0946	.0808	.0691	.0592	.0508	.0437	.0376	.0208	.0118
19	.8277	.5703	.3957	.3305	.2765	.2317	.1945	.1635	.1377	.1161	.0981	.0829	.0703	.0596	.0506	.0431	.0367	.0313	.0168	.0092
20	.8195	.5537	.3769	.3118	.2584	.2145	.1784	.1486	.1240	.1037	.0868	.0728	.0611	.0514	.0433	.0365	.0308	.0261	.0135	.0072
25	.7798	.4776	.2953	.2330	.1842	.1460	.1160	.0923	.0736	.0588	.0471	.0378	.0304	.0245	.0197	.0160	.0129	.0105	.0046	.0021
30	.7419	.4120	.2314	.1741	.1314	.0994	.0754	.0573	.0437	.0334	.0256	.0196	.0151	.0116	.0090	.0070	.0054	.0042	.0016	.0006
40	.6717	.3066	.1420	.0972	.0668	.0460	.0318	.0221	.0154	.0107	.0075	.0053	.0037	.0026	.0019	.0013	.0010	.0007	.0002	.0001
50	.6080	.2281	.0872	.0543	.0339	.0213	.0134	.0085	.0054	.0035	.0022	.0014	.0009	.0006	.0004	.0003	.0002	.0001	*	*
60	.5504	.1697	.0535	.0303	.0173	.0099	.0057	.0033	.0019	.0011	.0007	.0004	.0002	.0001	.0001	*	*	*	*	*

*The factor is zero to four decimal places.

Intraperiod interest rate.
The annual interest rate divided by the number of compounding periods within one year.

If compounding occurs semiannually ($m = 2$), then we divide 6 percent by 2: $r/m = 0.06 \div 2 = 0.03$, or 3 percent interest paid each six months. We call the 3 percent rate (r/m) the **intraperiod interest rate.** So an investment that earns interest at 3 percent each six months has an APR of 6 percent but an EAR of 6.09 percent for the year:

APR: 0.03 each 6 months $\times$ 2 compounding periods = 0.06 or 6 percent

EAR: $(1 + 0.06/2)^2 - 1 = 0.0609$ or 6.09 percent

The EAR result is simply the future value factor for an interest rate of 3 percent for two periods from Table 4.1: $FVIF_{3\%, 2 \text{ years}}$. The APR of 6 percent understates the true interest rate of 6.09 percent. *Thus, an annual interest rate of 6.09 percent compounded annually results in the same amount of interest as an annual nominal interest rate of 6 percent compounded semiannually:*

$$EAR = (1 + 0.0609)^1 - 1 = 0.0609 \text{ or } 6.09 \text{ percent}$$

$$EAR = (1 + 0.06/2)^2 - 1 = 0.0609 \text{ or } 6.09 \text{ percent}$$

Illustration 4.4 provides more examples for calculating EAR.

ILLUSTRATION 4.4

Compounding with intraperiod interest rates

A stated annual percentage rate (r) of 5 percent has a six-month intraperiod rate (r/m) of 2.5 percent: $5\% \div 2 = 2.5\%$. However, the EAR for a semiannual nominal rate of 2.5 percent is 5.0625 percent.

$$
\begin{aligned}
EAR &= (1 + r/m)^m - 1 \\
&= (1 + 0.025)^2 - 1 \\
&= 0.050625
\end{aligned}
$$

The exponent 2 represents two periods of compounding.

For a quarterly payment, divide the stated nominal annual rate by 4, since there are four payments, to get the intraperiod quarterly rate of 1.25 percent: $r/m = 5\% \div 4 = 1.25\%$. The EAR is 5.0945 percent: $(1 + 0.0125)^4 - 1$, where the exponent 4 signifies four periods of compounding.

Calculating monthly payments requires dividing the stated annual rate by 12. The intraperiod monthly rate is 0.4167 percent: $r/m = 5\% \div 12 = 0.4167\%$. The EAR is 5.117 percent: $(1 + 0.004167)^{12} - 1$, where compounding is for 12 periods.

Check that the intraperiod monthly rate (r/m) of 1 percent compounds to an EAR of 12.6825 percent.[3] The interpretation is that a loan costing 1 percent per month has a true annual cost, EAR, of 12.6825 percent. The APR of 12 percent (1% monthly $\times$ 12) understates the true interest rate.

Calculator
Clear
1
PV
3
%i
2
N
CPT
FV
−1
Ans.: 0.0609

Calculator
Clear
1
PV
2.5
%i
2
N
CPT
FV
−1
Ans.: 0.050625

As shown in Illustration 4.4, more frequent compounding results in a higher EAR. The EAR for a 5 percent rate goes from 5.0625 percent for semiannual (six-month) compounding to 5.117 percent for monthly compounding. *The EAR increases because more frequent compounding means that interest is received earlier. Money has a time value!*

We can also see this phenomenon in Illustration 4.5. However, let's assume we know the EAR. We need to find the intraperiod nominal rate r/m to discount the cash flows. Using a little algebra, we can rearrange Equation 4.8 to derive:

[3]Solution: $(1 + 0.01)^{12} - 1 = 0.126825$ or 12.6825 percent

$$r/m = (1 + \text{EAR})^{1/m} - 1 \tag{4.9}$$

where the exponent $1/m$ means to take the mth root of $(1 + \text{EAR})$. If there are three periods, $m = 3$, and $1/3$ means to take the cube root of $1 + \text{EAR}$.

ILLUSTRATION 4.5

Compounding semiannual receipts

Ms. Bishop receives annual cash flows of $100, payable semiannually, plus $1000 at the end of year 3. Thus, she receives $50 each six months and $1000 on the last payment date. If the EAR is 5 percent, the intraperiod (semiannual) nominal rate r/m is 2.4695 percent and the APR is 4.939 percent.

$$
\begin{aligned}
r/m &= (1 + \text{EAR})^{1/m} - 1 \\
&= (1 + 0.05)^{1/2} - 1 \\
&= 0.024695
\end{aligned}
$$

$$
\begin{aligned}
\text{APR} &= r/m \times 2 \text{ periods} \\
&= 0.024695 \times 2 \\
&= 0.04939
\end{aligned}
$$

The present value of these semiannual flows is $1139.53.

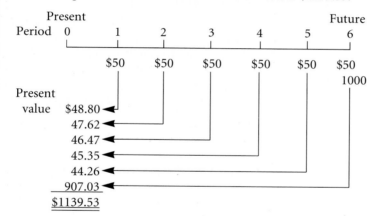

$$
\begin{aligned}
PV_0 &= \frac{\$50}{(1.024695)} + \frac{\$50}{(1.024695)^2} + \frac{\$50}{(1.024695)^3} + \frac{\$50}{(1.024695)^4} \\
&\quad + \frac{\$50}{(1.024695)^5} + \frac{\$1050}{(1.024695)^6} \\
&= \$48.80 + \$47.62 + \$46.47 + \$45.35 + \$44.26 + \$907.03 \\
&= \$1139.53
\end{aligned}
$$

Calculator
Clear
50
PMT
1000
FV
2.4695
%i
6
N
CPT
PV
Ans.: 1139.53

Cash flows received semiannually increase the value of the security by $3.37 as compared to the case of receiving cash flows annually in Illustration 4.3: $1139.53 here versus $1136.16 earlier.

To provide practice with time value concepts, let's solve the preceding problem by first finding the future value of each cash flow at the end of year 3 (that is, at the end of period 6 since compounding occurs each six months). Next, discount this lump-sum amount to the present.

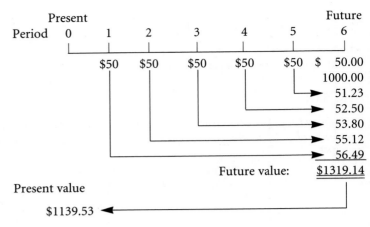

Present value

$1139.53

Calculator
Clear
50
PMT
2.4695
%i
6
N
CPT
FV
+1000
Ans.: 1319.14

STEP 1:

$$FV_6 = \$50 \times (1.024695)^5 + \$50 \times (1.024695)^4$$
$$+ \$50 \times (1.024695)^3 + \$50 \times (1.024695)^2$$
$$+ \$50 \times (1.024695)^1 + \$1050$$

$$= \$56.49 + \$55.12 + \$53.80 + \$52.50 + \$51.23 + \$1050$$
$$= \$1319.14$$

The first $50 payment compounds through five periods: from the end of period 1 to the end of period 2, then from the end of period 2 to the end of period 3, and so on. In similar fashion, the $50 payment received at the end of period 2 compounds through four periods. The exponents in the FV_6 equation in Step 1 represent the number of compounding periods for each cash flow amount.

STEP 2:

$$PV_0 = \frac{FV_6}{(1 + r)^6}$$

$$= \frac{\$1319.14}{(1.024695)^6}$$

$$= \$1139.52$$

We get the same result, except for a rounding error, by discounting the cash flows to find the present value.

Calculator
Clear
1319.14
FV
2.4695
%i
6
N
CPT
PV
Ans.: 1139.53

4.2.4 Compounding and Ordinary Annuity Cash Flows

Illustration 4.5 provides a base for studying *ordinary annuity cash flows*. The definition of an **ordinary annuity** is defined as the receipt (or disbursement) of a constant cash flow amount over a specified period with each cash flow occurring at the end of each interest period. The cash flow stream is:

Ordinary annuity. A stream of cash flows of equal amount occurring at the end of each period for a specified number of periods.

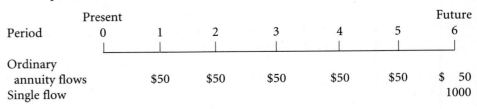

	Present						Future
Period	0	1	2	3	4	5	6
Ordinary annuity flows		$50	$50	$50	$50	$50	$ 50
Single flow							1000

where the \$50 amounts each period represent the annuity flows. The mathematical equation for present value used in Illustration 4.5,

$$PV_0 = \frac{\$50}{(1.024695)} + \frac{\$50}{(1.024695)^2} + \frac{\$50}{(1.024695)^3} + \frac{\$50}{(1.024695)^4}$$
$$+ \frac{\$50}{(1.024695)^5} + \frac{\$1050}{(1.024695)^6}$$
$$= \$1139.53$$

can be written more compactly as:

$$PV_0 = \text{Interest} \times \frac{1 - \dfrac{1}{(1+r)^n}}{r} + \frac{\text{principal}}{(1+r)^n}$$

$$= \$50 \times \frac{1 - \dfrac{1}{(1.024695)^6}}{0.024695} + \frac{\$1000}{(1.024695)^6} \qquad (4.10)$$

$$= \$50 \times 5.51375 + \$1000 \times 0.86384$$
$$= \$275.69 + \$863.84$$
$$= \$1139.53$$

Calculator
Clear
1
PMT
2.4695
%*i*
6
N
CPT
PV
Ans.: 5.51375

The number 5.51375 in the preceding problem represents the *present value ordinary annuity factor* for 2.4695 percent, for six periods. We frequently refer to it as $\text{PVIFA}_{r\%, n \text{ periods}}$. Mathematically, the **present value annuity factor** is given by Equation 4.11.

$$\text{PVIFA}_{r\%, \, n \text{ periods}} \text{ of } \$1 = \frac{1 - \dfrac{1}{(1+r)^n}}{r} \qquad (4.11)$$

Present value annuity factor (PVIFA). The sum of the present value of \$1 amounts, using the present value formula, which occurs in periods 1, 2, . . . , *n*.

We can think of Equation 4.11 as equaling the sum of present value factors. For instance, in Equation 4.10, the $\text{PVIFA}_{2.4695\%, \, 6 \text{ periods}}$ of 5.51375 could be calculated as follows:

$$\frac{1}{(1+r)} + \frac{1}{(1+r)^2} + \frac{1}{(1+r)^3} + \frac{1}{(1+r)^4} + \frac{1}{(1+r)^5} + \frac{1}{(1+r)^6} \qquad (4.12)$$

$$= \frac{1}{1.024695} + \frac{1}{1.024695^2} + \frac{1}{1.024695^3} + \frac{1}{1.024695^4} + \frac{1}{1.024695^5} + \frac{1}{1.024695^6}$$

$$= 0.97590 + 0.95238 + 0.92943 + 0.90703 + 0.88517 + 0.86384$$
$$= 5.51375$$

The advantage of Equation 4.11 is that it shortens the number of calculations required. A comparable expression exists for compounding ordinary annuity cash flows to a future value. The formula for this expression, called the *future value ordinary annuity factor* for *r* percent, *n* periods, or $\text{FVIFA}_{r\%, \, n \text{ periods}}$, is:

$$\text{FVIFA}_{r\%, \, n \text{ periods}} = \frac{(1+r)^n - 1}{r} \qquad (4.13)$$

Future value annuity factor (FVIFA). The sum of the future value of \$1 amounts, using the future value formula, which occurs in periods 1, 2, . . . , *n*.

The **future value ordinary annuity factor,** $\text{FVIFA}_{r\%, \, n \text{ periods}}$, is the sum of the future value factors over *n* periods where the interest rate is *r* per period.

Tables 4.3 and 4.4 show present value and future value ordinary annuity factors, respectively. People frequently use these tables in place of the mathematical expressions, Equations 4.11 and 4.13, because it is easier to take the value from the table than it is to go through the mathematics.[4] However, we must use either of these formulas or a financial calculator whenever the tables do not contain the desired interest rate.

Let's use Illustration 4.5 to show how $FVIFA_{r\%,\ n\ periods}$ is obtained. The value for FV_6 of $1319.14 in Step 1 of the illustration can be found using either the equation for future value of an annuity

Calculator
Clear
50
PMT
2.4695
%i
6
N
CPT
FV
+1000
Ans.: 1319.14

$$FV_6 = \text{Interest} \times \frac{(1 + r)^n - 1}{r} + \text{principal} \qquad (4.14)$$

$$= \$50 \times \frac{(1.024695)^6 - 1}{0.024695} + \$1000$$

$$= \$50 \times 6.38285 + \$1000$$
$$= \$319.14 + \$1000$$
$$= \$1319.14$$

or using Table 4.3,

$$FV_6 = \text{Interest} \times FVIFA_{r\%,\ n\ periods} + \text{principal}$$

$$= \$50 \times FVIFA_{2.4695\%,\ 6\ periods} + \$1000$$

$$= \$50 \times 6.38285 + \$1000$$
$$= \$1319.14$$

We can think of $FVIFA_{2.4695\%,\ 6\ periods} = 6.38285$ as the summation of several $1 cash flows received in different consecutive periods, which are compounded to a known terminal date:

Calculator
Clear
1
PMT
2.4695
%i
6
N
CPT
FV
Ans.: 6.38285

	Present					Future	
Period	0	1	2	3	4	5	6

Ordinary annuity flows	$1	$1	$1	$1	$1	$1

$\times (1 + r)^0$

$\times (1 + r)^1$

$\times (1 + r)^2$

$\times (1 + r)^3$

$\times (1 + r)^4$

$\times (1 + r)^5$

| Compounding factors | | 1.12972 | 1.10250 | 1.07593 | 1.05000 | 1.02470 | 1 | Sum of factors = 6.38285 |

[4] By using algebra, we can rewrite Equation 4.11 as

$$\frac{(1 + r)^n - 1}{r(1 + r)^n}$$

This equation shows that the $PVIFA_{r\%,\ n\ periods}$ is the discounted value of the $FVIFA_{r\%,\ n\ periods}$.

TABLE 4-3

ORDINARY FUTURE VALUE ANNUITY FACTORS: $[(1 + r)^n - 1]/r$

Number of Periods	1%	2%	3%	4%	5%	6%	7%	8%	9%	10%	12%	14%	15%	16%	18%	20%	24%	28%	32%	36%
1	1.0000	1.0000	1.0000	1.0000	1.0000	1.0000	1.0000	1.0000	1.0000	1.0000	1.0000	1.0000	1.0000	1.0000	1.0000	1.0000	1.0000	1.0000	1.0000	1.0000
2	2.0100	2.0200	2.0300	2.0400	2.0500	2.0600	2.0700	2.0800	2.0900	2.1000	2.1200	2.1400	2.1500	2.1600	2.1800	2.2000	2.2400	2.2800	2.3200	2.3600
3	3.0301	3.0604	3.0909	3.1216	3.1525	3.1836	3.2149	3.2464	3.2781	3.3100	3.3744	3.4396	3.4725	3.5056	3.5724	3.6400	3.7776	3.9184	4.0624	4.2096
4	4.0604	4.1216	4.1836	4.2465	4.3101	4.3746	4.4399	4.5061	4.5731	4.6410	4.7793	4.9211	4.9934	5.0665	5.2154	5.3680	5.6842	6.0156	6.3624	6.7251
5	5.1010	5.2040	5.3091	5.4163	5.5256	5.6371	5.7507	5.8666	5.9847	6.1051	6.3528	6.6101	6.7424	6.8771	7.1542	7.4416	8.0484	8.6999	9.3983	10.146
6	6.1520	6.3081	6.4684	6.6330	6.8019	6.9753	7.1533	7.3359	7.5233	7.7156	8.1152	8.5355	8.7537	8.9775	9.4420	9.9299	10.980	12.136	13.406	14.799
7	7.2135	7.4343	7.6625	7.8983	8.1420	8.3938	8.6540	8.9228	9.2004	9.4872	10.089	10.730	11.067	11.414	12.142	12.916	14.615	16.534	18.696	21.126
8	8.2857	8.5830	8.8923	9.2142	9.5491	9.8975	10.260	10.637	11.028	11.436	12.300	13.233	13.727	14.240	15.327	16.499	19.123	22.163	25.678	29.732
9	9.3685	9.7546	10.159	10.583	11.027	11.491	11.978	12.488	13.021	13.579	14.776	16.085	16.786	17.519	19.086	20.799	24.712	29.369	34.895	41.435
10	10.462	10.950	11.464	12.006	12.578	13.181	13.816	14.487	15.192	15.937	17.549	19.337	20.304	21.321	23.521	25.959	31.643	38.593	47.062	57.352
11	11.567	12.169	12.808	13.486	14.207	14.972	15.784	16.645	17.560	18.531	20.655	23.045	24.349	25.733	28.755	32.150	40.238	50.396	63.122	78.998
12	12.683	13.412	14.192	15.025	15.917	16.870	17.888	18.977	20.141	21.384	24.133	27.271	29.002	30.850	34.931	39.581	50.895	65.510	84.320	108.44
13	13.809	14.680	15.618	16.627	17.713	18.882	20.141	21.495	22.953	24.523	28.029	32.089	34.352	36.786	42.219	48.497	64.110	84.853	112.30	148.47
14	14.947	15.974	17.086	18.292	19.599	21.015	22.550	24.215	26.019	27.975	32.393	37.581	40.505	43.672	50.818	59.196	80.496	109.61	149.24	202.93
15	16.097	17.293	18.599	20.024	21.579	23.276	25.129	27.152	29.361	31.772	37.280	43.842	47.580	51.660	60.965	72.035	100.82	141.30	198.00	276.98
16	17.258	18.639	20.157	21.825	23.657	25.673	27.888	30.324	33.003	35.950	42.753	50.980	55.717	60.925	72.939	87.442	126.01	181.87	262.36	377.69
17	18.430	20.012	21.762	23.698	25.840	28.213	30.840	33.750	36.974	40.545	48.884	59.118	65.075	71.673	87.068	105.93	157.25	233.79	347.31	514.66
18	19.615	21.412	23.414	25.645	28.132	30.906	33.999	37.450	41.301	45.599	55.750	68.394	75.836	84.141	103.74	128.12	195.99	300.25	459.45	700.94
19	20.811	22.841	25.117	27.671	30.539	33.760	37.379	41.446	46.018	51.159	63.440	78.969	88.212	98.603	123.41	154.74	244.03	385.32	607.47	954.28
20	22.019	24.297	26.870	29.778	33.066	36.786	40.995	45.762	51.160	57.275	72.052	91.025	102.44	115.38	146.63	186.69	303.60	494.21	802.86	1298.8
21	23.239	25.783	28.676	31.969	35.719	39.993	44.865	50.423	56.765	64.002	81.699	104.77	118.81	134.84	174.02	225.03	377.46	633.59	1060.8	1767.4
22	24.472	27.299	30.537	34.248	38.505	43.392	49.006	55.457	62.873	71.403	92.503	120.44	137.63	157.41	206.34	271.03	469.06	812.00	1401.2	2404.7
23	25.716	28.845	32.453	36.618	41.430	46.996	53.436	60.893	69.532	79.543	104.60	138.30	159.28	183.60	244.49	326.24	582.63	1040.4	1850.6	3271.3
24	26.973	30.422	34.426	39.083	44.502	50.816	58.177	66.765	76.790	88.497	118.16	158.66	184.17	213.98	289.49	392.48	723.46	1332.7	2443.8	4450.0
25	28.243	32.030	36.459	41.646	47.727	54.865	63.249	73.106	84.701	96.347	133.33	181.87	212.79	249.21	342.60	471.98	898.09	1706.8	3226.8	6053.0
26	29.526	33.671	38.553	44.312	51.113	59.156	68.676	79.954	93.324	109.18	150.33	208.33	245.71	290.09	405.27	567.38	1114.6	2185.7	4260.4	8233.1
27	30.821	35.344	40.709	47.084	54.669	63.706	74.484	87.351	102.72	121.10	169.37	238.49	283.57	337.50	479.22	681.85	1383.1	2798.7	5624.8	11198.0
28	32.129	37.051	42.931	49.968	58.403	68.528	80.698	95.339	112.97	134.21	190.70	272.88	327.10	392.50	566.48	819.22	1716.1	3583.3	7425.7	15230.3
29	33.450	38.792	45.219	52.966	62.323	73.640	87.347	103.97	124.14	148.63	214.58	312.09	377.17	456.30	669.45	984.07	2129.0	4587.7	9802.9	20714.2
30	34.785	40.568	47.575	56.085	66.439	79.058	94.461	113.28	136.31	164.49	241.33	356.78	434.75	530.31	790.95	1181.9	2640.9	5873.2	12941.	28172.3
40	48.886	60.402	75.401	95.026	120.80	154.76	199.64	259.06	337.88	442.59	767.09	1342.0	1779.1	2360.8	4163.2	7343.9	22729.	69377.	★	★
50	64.463	84.579	112.80	152.67	209.34	290.34	406.53	573.77	815.08	1163.9	2400.0	4994.5	7217.7	10436.	21813.	45497.	★	★	★	★
60	81.670	114.05	163.05	237.99	353.58	533.13	813.52	1253.2	1944.8	3034.8	7471.6	18535.	29220.	46058.	★	★	★	★	★	★

*FVIFA > 99,999

TABLE 4-4

ORDINARY PRESENT VALUE ANNUITY FACTORS: $[1 - 1/(1+r)^n]/r$

Number of Periods	1%	3%	5%	6%	7%	8%	9%	10%	11%	12%	13%	14%	15%	16%	17%	18%	19%	20%	24%
1	0.9901	0.9709	0.9524	0.9434	0.9346	0.9259	0.9174	0.9091	0.9009	0.8929	0.8850	0.8772	0.8696	0.8621	0.8547	0.8475	0.8403	0.8333	0.8065
2	1.9704	1.9135	1.8594	1.8334	1.8080	1.7833	1.7591	1.7355	1.7125	1.6901	1.6681	1.6467	1.6257	1.6052	1.5852	1.5656	1.5465	1.5278	1.4568
3	2.9410	2.8286	2.7232	2.6730	2.6243	2.5771	2.5313	2.4869	2.4437	2.4018	2.3612	2.3216	2.2832	2.2459	2.2096	2.1743	2.1399	2.1065	1.9813
4	3.9020	3.7171	3.5460	3.4651	3.3872	3.3121	3.2397	3.1699	3.1024	3.0373	2.9745	2.9137	2.8550	2.7982	2.7432	2.6901	2.6386	2.5887	2.4043
5	4.8534	4.5797	4.3295	4.2124	4.1002	3.9927	3.8897	3.7908	3.6959	3.6048	3.5172	3.4331	3.3522	3.2743	3.1993	3.1272	3.0578	2.9906	2.7454
6	5.7955	5.4172	5.0757	4.9173	4.7665	4.6229	4.4859	4.3553	4.2305	4.1114	3.9975	3.8887	3.7845	3.6847	3.5892	3.4976	3.4098	3.3255	3.0205
7	6.7282	6.2303	5.7864	5.5824	5.3893	5.2064	5.0330	4.8684	4.7122	4.5638	4.4226	4.2883	4.1604	4.0386	3.9224	3.8115	3.7057	3.6046	3.2423
8	7.6517	7.0197	6.4632	6.2098	5.9713	5.7466	5.5348	5.3349	5.1461	4.9676	4.7988	4.6389	4.4873	4.3436	4.2072	4.0776	3.9544	3.8372	3.4212
9	8.5660	7.7861	7.1078	6.8017	6.5152	6.2469	5.9952	5.7590	5.5370	5.3282	5.1317	4.9464	4.7716	4.6065	4.4506	4.3030	4.1633	4.0310	3.5655
10	9.4713	8.5302	7.7217	7.3601	7.0236	6.7101	6.4177	6.1446	5.8892	5.6502	5.4262	5.2161	5.0188	4.8332	4.6586	4.4941	4.3389	4.1925	3.6819
11	10.3676	9.2526	8.3064	7.8869	7.4987	7.1390	6.8052	6.4951	6.2065	5.9377	5.6869	5.4527	5.2337	5.0286	4.8364	4.6560	4.4865	4.3271	3.7757
12	11.2551	9.9540	8.8633	8.3838	7.9427	7.5361	7.1607	6.8137	6.4924	6.1944	5.9176	5.6603	5.4206	5.1971	4.9884	4.7932	4.6105	4.4392	3.8514
13	12.1337	10.6350	9.3936	8.8527	8.3577	7.9038	7.4869	7.1034	6.7499	6.4235	6.1218	5.8424	5.5831	5.3423	5.1183	4.9095	4.7147	4.5327	3.9124
14	13.0037	11.2961	9.8986	9.2950	8.7455	8.2442	7.7862	7.3667	6.9819	6.6282	6.3025	6.0021	5.7245	5.4675	5.2293	5.0081	4.8023	4.6106	3.9616
15	13.8651	11.9379	10.3797	9.7122	9.1079	8.5595	8.0607	7.6061	7.1909	6.8109	6.4624	6.1422	5.8474	5.5755	5.3242	5.0916	4.8759	4.6755	4.0013
16	14.7179	12.5611	10.8378	10.1059	9.4466	8.8514	8.3126	7.8237	7.3792	6.9740	6.6039	6.2651	5.9542	5.6685	5.4053	5.1624	4.9377	4.7296	4.0333
17	15.5623	13.1661	11.2741	10.4773	9.7632	9.1216	8.5436	8.0216	7.5488	7.1196	6.7291	6.3729	6.0472	5.7487	5.4746	5.2223	4.9697	4.7746	4.0591
18	16.3983	13.7535	11.6896	10.8276	10.0591	9.3719	8.7556	8.2014	7.7016	7.2497	6.8399	6.4674	6.1280	5.8178	5.5339	5.2732	5.0333	4.8122	4.0799
19	17.2260	14.3238	12.0853	11.1581	10.3356	9.6036	8.9501	8.3649	7.8393	7.3658	6.9380	6.5504	6.1982	5.8775	5.5845	5.3162	5.0700	4.8435	4.0967
20	18.0456	14.8775	12.4622	11.4699	10.5940	9.8181	9.1285	8.5136	7.9633	7.4694	7.0248	6.6231	6.2593	5.9288	5.6278	5.3527	5.1009	4.8696	4.1103
25	22.0232	17.4131	14.0939	12.7834	11.6536	10.6748	9.8226	9.0770	8.4217	7.8431	7.3300	6.8729	6.4641	6.0971	5.7662	5.4669	5.1951	4.9476	4.1474
30	25.8077	19.6004	15.3725	13.7648	12.4090	11.2578	10.2737	9.4269	8.6938	8.0552	7.4957	7.0027	6.5660	6.1772	5.8294	5.5168	5.2347	4.9789	4.1601
40	32.8347	23.1148	17.1591	15.0463	13.3317	11.9246	10.7574	9.7791	8.9511	8.2438	7.6344	7.1050	6.6418	6.2335	5.8713	5.5482	5.2582	4.9966	4.1659
50	39.1961	25.7298	18.2559	15.7619	13.8007	12.2335	10.9617	9.9148	9.0417	8.3045	7.6752	7.1327	6.6605	6.2463	5.8801	5.5541	5.2623	4.9995	4.1666
60	44.9550	27.6756	18.9293	16.1614	14.0392	12.3766	11.0480	9.9672	9.0692	8.3240	7.6873	7.1401	6.6651	6.2492	5.8819	5.5553	5.2630	4.9999	4.1667

The $1 at the end of period 1 compounds from the end of period 1 to the end of period 2, then from the end of period 2 to the end of period 3, and so on, until the process reaches the end of period 6. The total number of compoundings for period 1's $1 is five and its value at the end of period 6 is $1 × 1.12972 = $1.12972. The $1 flow at the end of period 2 compounds through four periods to reach the end of period 6. Its compounded value at this point is $1.10250. Similar compounding exercises happen for each of the cash flows. Summation of the individual compounding factors is 6.38285, indicating that six $1 annual cash flows are worth $6.38 when money earns interest at 2.4695 percent each compounding period.

4.2.5 Compounding and Annuity Due Cash Flows

We call the annuity flows in the previous section ordinary annuities because cash flows occur at the end of each interest period. Another type of annuity is the **annuity due**, in which cash flows occur at the *beginning* of each interest period. Think of an annuity due as an ordinary annuity in advance one period. Figure 4.3 illustrates the difference between an ordinary annuity and an annuity due. An example of an annuity due is monthly rent to lease an apartment. Payment is made at the beginning of the month in advance of actually using the premises.

The equation for the **present value of an annuity due** at r percent for n periods, $PVIFAD_{r\%,\ n\ periods}$, is:

$$PVIFAD_{r\%,\ n\ periods} = \frac{1 - \dfrac{1}{(1 + r)^n}}{r} \times (1 + r) \qquad (4.15)$$

whereas the equation for the **future value of an annuity due** at r percent for n periods, $FVIFAD_{r\%,\ n\ periods}$, is:

$$FVIFAD_{r\%,\ n\ periods} = \frac{(1 + r)^n - 1}{r} \times (1 + r) \qquad (4.16)$$

These annuity due Equations 4.15 and 4.16 are the ordinary annuity Equations 4.11 and 4.13, respectively, multiplied by $(1 + r)$. The result is that $PVIFAD_{r\%,n\ periods}$ and

Annuity due. A series of equal cash payments occurring at the beginning of each period with equal amounts of time between each payment.

Present value of an annuity due. The value today of a series of constant cash flows for a known number of periods, with the cash flows occurring at the beginning of each period.

Future value of an annuity due. The value at a known future date of a series of constant cash flows for a known number of periods, with the cash flows occurring at the beginning of each period.

FIGURE 4.3

ORDINARY ANNUITY VERSUS ANNUITY DUE

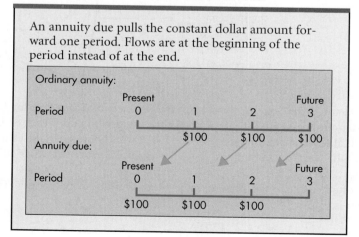

An annuity due pulls the constant dollar amount forward one period. Flows are at the beginning of the period instead of at the end.

Ordinary annuity:

Period	Present 0	1	2	Future 3
		$100	$100	$100

Annuity due:

Period	Present 0	1	2	Future 3
	$100	$100	$100	

$FVIFAD_{r\%, n \text{ periods}}$ are the *ordinary annuity cash flows* simply advanced one period and called *annuity due cash flows*.

If we assume the cash flows in Illustration 4.5 occur at the beginning of each period instead of at the end, the present value of the cash flows is the illustration's answer multiplied by (1 + interest rate): $1139.53 × (1.024695) = $1167.67. We can prove this answer by solving the problem for the following cash flows, which are Illustration 4.5's ordinary annuity cash flows pulled forward one period.

	Present						Future
Period	0	1	2	3	4	5	6
Annuity due flows	$50	$50	$50	$50	$50	$ 50	
Single flow						1000	

Calculator
Clear
50
PMT
1000
FV
2.4695
%i
5
N
CPT
PV
+50
Ans.: 1167.67

$$PV_0 = \text{Interest} + \text{Interest} \times \frac{1 - \dfrac{1}{(1 + r)^n}}{r} + \frac{\text{principal}}{(1 + r)^n}$$

$$= \$50 + \$50 \times \frac{1 - \dfrac{1}{(1.024695)^5}}{0.024695} + \frac{\$1000}{(1.024695)^5}$$

$$= \$50 + \$50 \times 4.64991 + \$1000 \times 0.88517$$

$$= \$50 + \$232.50 + \$885.17$$

$$= \$1167.67$$

4.2.6 Compounding and Perpetuities

Perpetuity. An investment offering a level stream of cash flows with no maturity date.

A special type of annuity is one in which cash flows occur forever; this type of annuity is called a **perpetuity**. The Canadian Pacific Limited, a large diversified Canadian company, issued a security several years ago which promises to pay a constant interest amount forever. The security, a perpetuity, has no maturity date. Since perpetual flows have no terminal point, it makes no sense to discuss the future value of a perpetuity, other than to say that it is a very large amount. For instance, substituting an interest rate of 5 percent ($r = 0.05$) and 100 years ($n = 100$) into the future value ordinary annuity formula (Equation 4.13) and solving for $FVIFA_{5\%, 100 \text{ years}}$, results in a factor of 2610.03.

Calculator
Clear
1
PMT
5
%i
100
N
CPT
FV
Ans.: 2610.03

$$FVIFA_{5\%, 100 \text{ years}} = \frac{(1 + r)^n - 1}{r}$$

$$= \frac{(1.05)^{100} - 1}{0.05}$$

$$= 2610.03$$

The factor 2610.03 means that $1 invested at the end of each year for 100 years (a total of $100) grows to $2610.03 at the end of the hundredth year if each $1 investment compounds at 5 percent annually. And since 100 years is not forever, the value $2610.03 understates the worth of the infinite flow. For example, prove that after 200 years the $FVIFA_{5\%, 200 \text{ years}}$ is 345,831.62.

We often calculate the present value of an annuity in perpetuity. The present value factor is:

$$PVIFA_{r\%, \infty} = 1 \div r \tag{4.17}$$

Multiplying the constant dollar amount to be received in perpetuity by Equation 4.17 gives the present value of the future cash flows. For example, if we and our heirs are to receive $10 per year in perpetuity, the value today of this perpetual future stream of cash is $200, if the interest rate is 5 percent.

$$\text{Present value of perpetuity} = \text{Constant amount} \times \text{PVIFA}_{5\%,\infty}$$
$$= \text{Constant amount} \times (1 \div r) \qquad (4.17)$$
$$= \$10 \div 0.05$$
$$= \$200$$

4.2.7 Working Time Value Problems

To demonstrate basic time value of money concepts in this chapter, we have worked with a given number of periods and rate of interest. In this section we shall look at some different but related problems. Our purpose here is to demonstrate that if we know the values of any three of the four variables in the time value problems—*present value, future value, interest rate,* and *number of periods*—we can determine the value of the fourth variable.

FINDING THE NUMBER OF PERIODS. Assume that Frances needs $25,000 for a down payment on a house in the future. At the present time she has only $11,580. How many years will it take her to accumulate $25,000 if $11,580 is invested at 8 percent interest compounded annually?

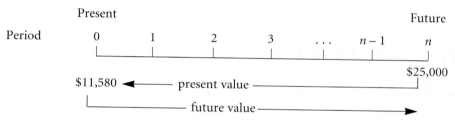

Since both the amounts for present value ($11,580) and future value ($25,000) are known, we can approach the problem from the viewpoint of either present value or future value. We work forward to find the future value of $25,000 and backward to find the present value of $11,580. Let's solve the problem from the future value perspective using Equation 4.6.

$$FV_n = PV_0 \times (1 + r)^n$$
$$\$25,000 = \$11,580 \times (1 + 0.08)^n$$
$$(1.08)^n = \$25,000 \div \$11,580$$
$$(1.08)^n = 2.1589$$

Alternatively,

$$FV_n = PV_0 \times \text{FVIF}_{r\%,n \text{ periods}}$$
$$\$25,000 = \$11,580 \times \text{FVIF}_{8\%,n \text{ periods}}$$
$$\text{FVIF}_{8\%,n \text{ periods}} = 2.1589$$

The unknown variable is the number of periods, n. Using Table 4.1 and reading down the 8 percent column, we find that $\text{FVIF}_{8\%, n \text{ periods}} = 2.1589$ corresponds to ten years. Now, use the present value Equation 4.7 to prove that you can solve this problem from the present value perspective. You should find $\text{PVIF}_{8\%, n \text{ periods}} = 0.4632$, which corresponds to ten years from the present value table, Table 4.2.

FINDING THE COMPOUND INTEREST RATE. The treasurer of Gault Screening, Inc. wants an investment of $5645 (the present value amount) to appreciate to $10,000 (the future value amount) in six years, where interest is compounded annually. What interest rate must this investment earn?

While the problem can be approached as either a present value or a future value problem, we present the solution in terms of present value only. In either case, we are trying to find the interest rate r in Equation 4.7, reproduced here. We can verify the answer using future value.

$$PV_0 = FV_n \div (1 + r)^n$$

$$\$5645 = \$10,000 \div (1 + r)^6$$

$$\frac{1}{(1 + r)^6} = \frac{\$5645}{\$10,000}$$

$$\frac{1}{(1 + r)^6} = 0.5645$$

Using the present value table (Table 4.2) and reading across the sixth period, we find that 0.5645 corresponds to a compound interest rate of 10 percent; that is, $PVIF_{10\%, 6 \text{ periods}} = 0.5645$. Thus, if $5645 is invested at 10 percent annual compound interest, it accumulates to $10,000 at the end of the sixth year.

Calculator
Clear
5645
PV
10,000
FV
6
N
CPT
%i
Ans.: 10

FINDING $FVIFA_{R\%, N \text{ PERIODS}}$. Gary needs to accumulate enough lump-sum funds to retire $30,525 (the future value amount) of student loans at some point in the future. How many year-end deposits of $5000, the first to take place one year from now, are necessary to accumulate to $30,525 if the interest rate is 10 percent compounded annually?

Notice that $30,525 represents the future value of n $5000 year-end cash flows, earning interest at 10 percent compounded annually.

$$FV_0 = \text{Annual amount} \times \frac{(1 + r)^n - 1}{r}$$

$$\$30,525 = \$5000 \times \frac{(1.10)^n - 1}{0.10}$$

Calculator
Clear
−5000
PMT
30,525
FV
10
%i
CPT
N
Ans.: 5

$$\frac{\$30,525}{\$5000} = \frac{(1.10)^n - 1}{0.10}$$

$$6.105 = \frac{(1.10)^n - 1}{0.10}$$

The unknown variable is n, the number of compounding periods. The right-hand expression $((1.10)^n - 1) \div 0.10$ represents the $FVIFA_{10\%, \, n \, periods}$. Consulting the future value interest table for an annuity, Table 4.3, and reading down the 10 percent column, we find that the number of periods corresponding to $FVIFA_{10\%, \, n \, periods} = 6.105$ is five years. Thus, five annual deposits of $5000 are necessary if Gary is to have $30,525 available to pay off the loan.

AMORTIZING A LOAN. A budget analyst for Aztar Holding, Inc. has been asked to construct an amortization table for a $10 million loan. The loan costs 9 percent and matures in four years. Payments are made at the end of each year. The first task is to calculate the annual payment. The analyst uses the present value of an annuity equation to determine the annual payment of $3,086,686.62:

$$\text{Present value} = \text{Annual payment} \times PVIFA_{9\%, \, 4 \, years}$$

$$\$10,000,000 = \text{Annual payment} \times 3.23972$$
$$\text{Annual payment} = \$10,000,000 \div 3.23972$$
$$= \$3,086,686.62$$

The annual payment consists of both interest payable on the loan and a reduction of the $10 million principal amount. The allocation of the annual payment amount into interest and principal components is shown in the following table. The analyst calculates interest by multiplying the beginning balance by 9 percent; in year 1, $10,000,000 \times 9\% = \$900,000$. Thus, the principal reduction is $3,086,686.62 - \$900,000 = \$2,186,686.62$. The process continues for each year. At the end of the fourth year, the loan balance is zero.

Year	Beginning Balance	Annual Payment	Interest at 9% of Beginning Balance	Principal Reduction	Loan Outstanding at the End of the Period
1	$10,000,000.00	$3,086,686.62	$900,000.00	$2,186,686.62	$7,813,313.38
2	7,813,313.38	3,086,686.62	703,198.20	2,383,488.42	5,429,824.96
3	5,429,824.96	3,086,686.62	488,684.25	2,598,002.37	2,831,822.59
4	2,831,822.59	3,086,686.62	254,864.03	2,831,822.59	0.00

Comprehension Check

1. How does compound interest differ from simple interest? Explain how the process of compounding affects the interest earned on a bank deposit.
2. What is the effect on the future value of a deposit if:
   a. the number of periods increases?
   b. the interest rate increases?
3. Explain the meaning of the present value of a future cash receipt.

4. What is the relationship between the future value of a dollar and the present value of a dollar using Equations 4.6 and 4.7?

5. Would you prefer to have the bank compound interest on a deposit quarterly rather than annually? Why?

6. How do you calculate the effective annual rate for a cash flow stream? Your answer should include discussion of intraperiod flows.

7. What is an ordinary annuity cash stream? How does an ordinary annuity differ from an annuity due? How does a perpetuity differ from an ordinary annuity?

4.3 ADD-ON INTEREST

Add-on interest. Interest calculated on the amount of funds to be lent and added to loaned amount to determine loan's face value.

A popular interest technique used by banks is the *add-on interest* method. The **add-on interest** method calculates interest on the full amount of the original principal and then adds the interest amount to the original principal. Payments are determined by dividing principal plus interest by the total number of payments to be made.

$$\text{Equal payment amount} = \frac{\text{Principal} + \text{interest charges over the life of the loan}}{\text{Total number of payments}} \tag{4.18}$$

Either simple add-on interest or compound add-on interest can be used.

4.3.1 Simple Add-on Interest

If the lender uses simple interest, the add-on formula for calculating the equal payment amount is:

$$\text{Equal payment amount} = \frac{\text{Principal} \times (1 + \text{interest rate} \times \text{time})}{\text{Total number of payments}} \tag{4.19}$$

The numerator is the simple interest Equation 4.2 divided by the total number of payments. (See Illustration 4.6.)

ILLUSTRATION 4.6

Simple add-on interest

Seth borrows $10,000 from the NYC Bank at a nominal interest rate of 10 percent. The loan's terms require repayment in equal installments at the end of each month over a period of five years. The bank uses simple interest to calculate the equal monthly payment, or installment payment, of $250.

	Present						Future
Month	0	1	2	3	4	59	60

Borrows $10,000
Repays $250 $250 $250 $250 $250 $250

Equal payment amount

$$= \text{Principal} \times \frac{(1 + \text{interest rate} \times \text{time})}{\text{Total number of payments}}$$
$$= \$10,000 \times (1 + 0.10 \times 5) \div (12 \text{ months} \times 5 \text{ years})$$
$$= \$250$$

4.3.2 Compound Add-on Interest

Under compound add-on interest, we calculate equal installment payments as:

$$\text{Equal payment amount} = \frac{\text{Principal} \times (1 + r/m)^{nm}}{\text{Total number of payments}} \qquad (4.20)$$

The intraperiod rate is r/m; it is the annual nominal rate r divided by the number of compounding periods m within the year. The superscript nm is the total number of payments: the years of the loan, n, times the number of compounding periods, m, within each year. (See Illustration 4.7.)

ILLUSTRATION 4.7

Compound add-on interest

Assume the same facts as in the preceding illustration except that the NYC Bank uses monthly compound add-on interest for Seth's loan; that is, the amount borrowed is $10,000 for five years at 10 percent interest with monthly payments. If the bank uses compound add-on interest, the monthly payment is $274.22.

	Present				Future		Calculator
Month	0	1	2	59	60		Clear
				...			10,000
Borrows	$10,000						PV
							0.83333
Repays	$274.22	$274.22	$274.22	$274.22	$274.22		%i
							60
							N
							CPT
							FV

$$\text{Equal payment amount} = \frac{\text{Principal} \times (1 + r/m)^{nm}}{\text{Total number of payments}}$$

$$= \frac{\$10,000 \times (1 + 0.10/12)^{5 \times 12}}{60}$$

$$= \$274.22$$

Ans.: 16453.06

$$\frac{16453.06}{60} = 274.22$$

Compound add-on interest results in a higher monthly payment than required by simple add-on interest because interest is paid on interest.

4.3.3 Add-on EAR

We find the EAR for either a simple or compound add-on loan in two steps. First, solve Equation 4.21 for r/m, the intraperiod rate. We will know the values for *principal* and *equal payment amount*. Table 4.3 can be used to approximate r/m; alternatively, a financial calculator which solves for the interest rate can be used.

$$\text{Principal} = \text{Equal payment amount} \times \text{PVIFA}_{r\%/m,\ nm\ \text{periods}} \qquad (4.21)$$
$$= \text{Equal payment amount} \times ((1 - (1 + r/m)^{-mn}) \div r/m)$$

Next, annualize r/m to calculate the EAR:

$$\text{EAR} = (1 + r/m)^m - 1 \qquad (4.22)$$

Illustration 4.8 calculates the EAR for both simple and compound add-on interest.

ILLUSTRATION 4.8

Add-on interest and EAR

In Illustration 4.6, Seth borrowed $10,000 from the NYC Bank with terms requiring simple add-on interest at 10 percent annually and equal monthly installment payments of $250 for five years. To find the EAR of this loan it is necessary to solve the following equation for the monthly interest rate, r/m, where $m = 12$ and $n = 5$:

$$\text{Principal} = \text{Equal payment amount} \times \text{PVIFA}_{r\%/m,\ nm\ \text{periods}}$$

$$\$10{,}000 = \$250 \times ((1 - (1 + r/m)^{-60}) \div (r/m))$$

Using either a *trial-and-error approach* (that is, iteratively substitute different values for r/m in the equation) or a financial calculator that solves for the interest rate, we find that r/m is 0.014395. Thus, the EAR is 18.71 percent.

$$\begin{aligned} \text{EAR} &= (1 + r/m)^m - 1 \\ &= (1 + 0.014395)^{12} - 1 \\ &= 0.18709 \text{ or } 18.71 \text{ percent} \end{aligned}$$

If Seth's loan uses compound add-on interest (Illustration 4.7), the monthly payment is $274.22. The cost of this loan is 1.804 percent monthly. Again, we can solve for 1.804 percent using either a trial-and-error approach or a financial calculator:

$$\text{Principal} = \text{Equal payment amount} \times \text{PVIFA}_{r\%/m,\ nm\ \text{periods}}$$

$$\$10{,}000 = \$274.22 \times ((1 - (1 + r/m)^{-60}) \div (r/m))$$
$$r/m = 0.018044 \text{ or } 1.8 \text{ percent}$$

In this case, the loan's EAR is 23.93 percent.

$$\begin{aligned} \text{EAR} &= (1 + r/m)^m - 1 \\ &= (1.018044)^{12} - 1 \\ &= 0.2394 \text{ or } 23.94 \text{ percent} \end{aligned}$$

Calculator
Clear
10,000
PV
250
PMT
60
N
CPT
%i
Ans.: 1.4395

Calculator
Clear
1
PV
1.4395
%i
12
N
CPT
FV
−1
Ans.: 0.1871

Calculator
Clear
10,000
PV
274.22
PMT
60
N
CPT
%i
Ans.: 1.8044

Calculator
Clear
1
PV
1.8044
%i
12
N
CPT
FV
−1
Ans.: 0.2394

It is interesting to note that the amount borrowed (principal) does not have any effect on the EAR. Also note that the EAR is higher if we use the compound interest method rather than the simple interest method. The term to maturity, n, of the loan also has an impact on the EAR. This influence results because the length of the loan affects the number of equal installment payments and hence the intraperiod rate r/m.

In general, if equal installments are obtained using the *simple* add-on rate method, then the longer the length of the loan, the smaller the EAR. If the lender computes installment payments using the compound add-on method, then the longer the length of the loan, the greater the EAR. The reason for the difference is that simple interest does not compute interest on interest whereas compound interest does. (See Illustration 4.9.)

ILLUSTRATION 4.9

Simple add-on interest once more

Let's recompute the EAR for Illustration 4.6 assuming Seth borrows $10,000 at 10 percent for one year instead of five years. Monthly payments are still required. Using simple add-on interest, his monthly payment is $916.67, whereas it was $250 earlier.

Equal payment amount

$$= \frac{\text{Principal} \times (1 + \text{interest rate} \times \text{time})}{\text{Total number of payments}}$$

$$= \$10,000 \times (1 + 0.10 \times 1) \div 12$$
$$= \$916.67$$

The monthly interest rate r/m is 0.014977 or 1.4977 percent.

$$\text{Principal} = \text{Equal payment amount} \times \text{PVIFA}_{r\%/m,\ nm \text{ periods}}$$

$$\$10,000 = \$916.67 \times [(1 - (1 + r/m)^{-12}] \div (r/m)$$
$$r/m = 0.014977$$

which results in an EAR of 19.53 percent:

$$\text{EAR} = (1 + r/m)^m - 1$$
$$= (1.014977)^{12} - 1$$
$$= 0.1953 \text{ or } 19.53 \text{ percent}$$

The EAR is higher for this one-year loan with simple add-on interest than for the five-year loan (18.71 percent) in Illustration 4.8 because of the shorter term.

Calculator
Clear
10,000
PV
916.67
PMT
12
N
CPT
%i
Ans.: 1.4977

Calculator
Clear
1
PV
1.4977
%i
12
N
CPT
FV
−1
Ans.: 0.1953

Comprehension Check

1. Describe how to calculate add-on interest. Does simple add-on interest differ from compound add-on interest? If so, how?

2. How do you calculate the effective annual rate (EAR) when add-on interest is used?

3. Why does the add-on method result in an equal or higher EAR than the nominal rate shown in the simple interest method?

4. Why does the amount borrowed not have any effect on the EAR?

4.4 BANK DISCOUNT METHOD

Short-term business loans commonly use the *bank discount method* to compute interest. Under the **bank discount rate method,** the lender calculates interest on the amount to be paid back and the borrower receives the difference between the amount to be paid back and the interest amount. Interest is paid at the time of receiving the loan.

Bank discount rate method. Interest calculated on the face amount of the loan. Lender deducts the interest in advance.

The computation of the bank discount is exactly the same as the computation of simple interest in Equation 4.1 except that we base the calculation on the amount to be paid rather than the present value. The bank discount formula is:

$$\text{Bank discount} = \text{Principal} \times \text{interest rate} \times \text{time} \qquad \textbf{(4.23)}$$

Since the proceeds, or present value of the loan, is the difference between the *principal* and the *bank discount,* we can say:

$$\text{Present value} = \text{Principal} - \text{bank discount}$$
$$= \text{Principal} - (\text{principal} \times \text{interest rate} \times \text{time}) \quad \textbf{(4.24)}$$
$$= \text{Principal} \times (1 - \text{interest rate} \times \text{time})$$

However, because the borrower has use of less than the amount borrowed, the effective cost of the loan exceeds the interest rate used in Equation 4.24. Illustration 4.10 calculates the effective cost of the loan.

ILLUSTRATION 4.10

Bank discount rate method

Morris Industries borrows $1 million for one year from Norwest Bank, which discounts the loan at 6 percent. What is the bank discount amount and how much money does Morris Industries receive?

$$\text{Bank discount} = \text{Principal} \times \text{interest rate} \times \text{time}$$
$$= \$1,000,000 \times 0.06 \times 1.0$$
$$= \$60,000$$

Thus, Norwest Bank keeps $60,000 of the $1 million loan. Since the proceeds to the company are the difference between the *principal* and the *bank discount,* Morris Industries receives $1,000,000 − $60,000 = $940,000. The effective cost of the loan is 6.38 percent.

$$FV_1 = PV_0 \times (1 + r)^1$$
$$\$1,000,000 = \$940,000 \times (1 + r)^1$$
$$r = (\$1,000,000 \div \$940,000) - 1$$
$$= 0.0638 \text{ or } 6.38 \text{ percent}$$

In the preceding example, Morris Industries receives only $940,000 of the $1 million loan. Suppose Morris actually needs $1,000,000; that is, the present value amount in Equation 4.24 must be $1 million. How much would the company need to borrow if Norwest Bank discounts the loan at 6 percent? Solving Equation 4.24 for *principal* results in a formula which allows us to find the answer: $1,063,830.

$$\text{Principal} = \text{Present value} \div (1 - (\text{interest rate} \times \text{time})) \qquad \textbf{(4.25)}$$

$$= \$1,000,000 \div (1 - (0.06 \times 1))$$
$$= \$1,063,830$$

Let's check this answer. Since Norwest Bank discounts the loan at 6 percent, it keeps 6 percent or $63,830 of the principal amount: $1,063,830 × 0.06 = $63,830. Thus, borrowing $1,063,830 provides Morris Industries with $1 million to invest.

▶ *Comprehension Check*

1. How does the bank discount method differ from the other interest calculation methods?
2. Describe how to calculate the present value of a loan using the bank discount method.

SIMPLE INTEREST

- Money has a time value, represented by the interest cost.
- The interest cost is the price, or rent, of money.
- Interest calculations involve three elements: principal, interest rate, and time period.
- Simple interest computes interest cost on the original principal, or the amount of principal still owed. Under simple interest, interest does not earn interest—this is the weakness of simple interest.

COMPOUND INTEREST

- Compound interest computes interest on interest. Compound interest is simple interest applied over and over to a sum, which is increased by simple interest each time it is earned.
- Future value finds the worth of all cash flows to be received in the future at some known future date.
- Present value finds the worth of all future cash flows today.
- The effective annual rate (EAR) is the annual interest rate, which produces the same amount of interest per year as the nominal, or stated, interest rate compounded m times per year.
- The intraperiod interest rate is the nominal rate divided by the number of compounding periods in one year.
- Ordinary annuity is the receipt (or disbursement) of a constant cash amount over a specified period with each cash flow occurring at the end of each interest period.
- Annuity due advances the cash flows of an ordinary annuity to the beginning of each interest rate period.
- Perpetuity is an ordinary annuity with no maturity date.

ADD-ON INTEREST

- Add-on interest adds the interest amount to the principal amount.
- Payments are determined by dividing principal plus interest by the total number of payments.
- Add-on interest results in an effective higher interest rate than the nominal rate.

BANK DISCOUNT METHOD

- Bank discount method calculates interest on the principal (amount borrowed), but the lender receives the difference between the principal amount and the interest amount.
- The effective rate of interest calculated by this method is relatively high because the lender pays interest on funds not received.

FURTHER READING ▼▼▼▼▼▼▼▼▼▼▼

Cissell, Robert, and Helen Cissell, *Mathematics of Finance,* 4th ed., Boston: Houghton Mifflin Company, 1973. An excellent book about financial mathematics.

Thomsett, Michael C., *The Mathematics of Investing: A Complete Reference,* New York: Wiley, 1989. This book is a primer on the mathematics of finance.

SELF-TEST PROBLEMS ▼▼▼▼▼▼▼▼▼▼▼

ST4-1. Your uncle has just given you a gift of $1000 but specifies that you must save the money for four years. There are four banks in the community, each of which pays interest at a stated annual rate of 6 percent on four-year savings certificates. What would be the effective annual rate of interest on your savings account in each of the four banks?

    a. City Bank compounds interest annually.

    b. First Western Bank compounds interest semiannually.

    c. Union Bank compounds interest quarterly.

    d. Citizens Bank compounds interest daily (360-day year).

ST4-2. a. Upon graduation, Mike decided to establish an individual retirement account (IRA). What would be the value of the IRA in 35 years if he contributes $1800 annually at the end of each year for the next 35 years? Each contribution earns 7 percent annually.

    b. What would be the value of Mike's IRA if he made annual contributions at the beginning of each year instead of at the end of each year?

ST4-3. Mr. Wynn has just won the state lottery and has the option of receiving $500,000 in 14 years or a check today for $150,000. If he can invest at 8 percent, which option should he choose, assuming he doesn't need the money now for consumption?

PROBLEMS ▼▼▼▼▼▼▼▼▼▼▼

SIMPLE INTEREST

4-1. Assume that any deposit in a bank account earns 6 percent simple interest.

    a. If you deposit $10,000, how much will you have in one year?

    b. If you deposit $10,000, how much will you have in two years if you do not withdraw anything in the first year?

    c. If you need $15,000 in one year, how much must be invested in the account today?

    d. If you do not need the $15,000 for five years, how much must be invested in the account today?

4-2. Trish gets $63.75 every six months from an investment which pays 4.25 percent simple interest annually. How much money does she have invested (that is, what is the principal amount)?

4-3. Grand Valley Bank pays 4.5 percent simple interest per annum on savings accounts and credits interest quarterly on March 31, June 30, September 30, and December 31. Money deposited by the tenth of the month earns interest for the entire month. Linda opens an account with a deposit of $250 on January 8. How much interest will the bank pay on March 31?

4-4. Simple interest paid on a loan of $500 for four months is $12.50. What is the simple interest rate?

4-5. Your favorite uncle has provided you a three-year certificate of deposit that pays 7 percent simple interest annually. You receive a check from the bank every six months for $420. What is the principal amount of the certificate of deposit?

4-6. Gary loans Adam $300 for a weekend trip to Las Vegas. Adam agrees to pay Gary $320 in one month. What is the annual simple interest rate Gary is receiving?

4-7. a. What is the amount of simple interest due in one year on a loan of $14,000 if the interest rate is 8.5 percent?
b. What is the amount of simple interest due if the $14,000 loan has two years to maturity at a rate of 8.5 percent?

COMPOUND INTEREST

4-8. Assume that any deposit in a bank account pays 6 percent compound interest.
a. If you deposit $10,000, how much will you have in one year?
b. If you deposit $10,000, how much will you have in two years if you do not withdraw anything in the first year?
c. If you need $15,000 in one year, how much must be invested in the account today?
d. If you do not need the $15,000 for five years, how much must be invested in the account today?

4-9. Use either Equation 4.6, 4.7, 4.11, 4.13, or 4.17 to answer the following questions.
a. Calculate the discount factor for an interest rate of 15 percent and a holding period of seven years.
b. If you receive $139 two years from today and you are told that its present value is $123.71, what is the discount rate?
c. If the eight-year discount factor is 0.2848, what is the discount rate?
d. What is the future value factor for a cash flow to be received in nine years, where the interest rate is 12 percent?
e. The interest rate to discount a cash flow to be received in perpetuity is 9 percent. What discount factor should you use to find the present value of the cash flows?
f. Assume that you invest $1000 at the end of each of the next nine years at an interest rate of 13 percent. What is the discount factor for finding the present value of the cash flows? How much is the present value of the nine annual $1000 investments? How much money will you have at the end of nine years?
g. A company is offering to pay you $1600 at the end of eight years if you invest $488 with it today. What is the annual compound rate of return?
h. What is the present value factor for an investment made today which matures in 20 years and earns interest at 15 percent compounded annually?
i. A recent advertisement stated: "Pay us $200 a year for 20 years and we will pay you $200 a year thereafter in perpetuity." Assume that the opportunity cost of money is 6 percent and that each payment is at the end of the year.

What is the factor you use to determine the present value of your $200 payments? What is the present value of your payments?

j. In part (i), what is the factor you use to find the future value of your $200 payments? What is the future value of your payments?

k. In part (i), what factor do you use to determine the present value of your receipts? What is the present value of the receipts?

4-10. Use either Table 4.1, 4.2, 4.3, or 4.4 to answer the following questions.

a. What is the present value of $1 to be received seven years from now? You can earn 15 percent on your investments.

b. If you are to receive $139 two years from today and you are told its present value is $123.71, what is the discount factor? Can you determine the discount rate from the table? If yes, how?

c. If the eight-year discount factor is 0.2848, what is the discount rate?

d. What is the future value factor for a cash flow to be received in nine years, where the interest rate is 12 percent?

e. The interest rate to discount a cash flow to be received in perpetuity is 9 percent. What is the discount factor to use to find the present value of the cash flows?

f. Assume that you invest $1000 at the end of each of the next nine years at an interest rate of 13 percent. What is the discount factor for finding the present value of the cash flows? What is the future value of an annuity factor for these flows?

g. A company is offering to pay you $1600 at the end of eight years if you invest $488 with it today. What is the table value to use to solve this problem? What is the annual compound rate of return?

h. What is the table value to use to find the value of an investment today that matures in 20 years and earns interest at 15 percent compounded annually?

4-11. a. Using the appropriate future value formula, what is the amount of Penny's certificate of deposit if a single deposit of $2000 is allowed to earn 7 percent interest compounded annually for 14 years?

b. How much interest does Penny earn on her deposit in part (a)?

4-12. George borrows $1500 to be repaid in five years with 10 percent interest compounded annually. The lender agrees to allow the loan to be repaid at the end of any year with no prepayment penalty.

a. What would be George's payment if the loan is repaid at the end of the first year?

b. What would be his payment if the loan is repaid at the end of the third year?

c. What would be his payment if the loan is repaid when due at the end of the fifth year?

d. Under what circumstances would it be desirable for George to repay the loan before its maturity of five years?

4-13. Just before graduation, Gerald has an interview with a prospective employer. His first question is, "What are the retirement benefits?" Assuming it will be 45 years until Gerald is eligible for retirement, what is the present value of $10,000 of his retirement benefits if the risk-free rate of return is 6 percent?

4-14. What sum of money to be received in three years is equally preferable to $15,000 received today? The interest rate is 6 percent.

a. Solve using the formula approach.

b. How much is the table factor?

4-15. The market rate of interest for risk-free assets is 8 percent. Stuart promises to pay you $2400 in one year in exchange for $2250 now. How much is the promise worth to you? Solve using both the present value and the future value equations. Would you take the offer? Why?

4-16. Leah has promised to pay you $1200 one year from now. With interest at 8 percent, what is the worth of this promise today?

4-17. For each of the following parts, calculate the effective annual rate:

	Stated Rate	Number of Times Compounded	Effective Rate
a.	5%	semiannually	?
b.	11	quarterly	?
c.	16	daily (360 days)	?

4-18. Suppose the effective annual rate on a loan is 8 percent. If you make monthly payments, what is the stated or nominal interest rate?

4-19. A local bank is offering an account that has an effective annual interest rate of 12.75 percent. If the bank is using daily compounding, what is the stated or nominal interest rate? Assume that there are 360 days in a year.

4-20. A local bank is offering an effective annual rate of interest of 9 percent, based on monthly compounding. If you deposit $600 today, how much will you have in (a) two years? (b) 2.5 years?

4-21. The following values are taken from present value (PV) and future value (FV) tables. Prove that these numbers are correct using the appropriate present and future value equations.

		Table Values	
		7%, 3 Periods	3%, 9 Periods
a.	PV of $1	0.8163	0.7664
b.	FV of $1	1.2250	1.3048
c.	PV of an annuity of $1	2.6243	7.7861
d.	FV of an annuity of $1	3.2149	10.1590

4-22. The payments on a $250,000 life insurance policy are $2000 annually for 30 years. Assume that payments are made at the end of each year. The insurance company earns 5 percent on investments.

a. What is the present value of the annual premium payments?

b. What is the present value of the $250,000 face amount of the policy if it is paid in year 30?

c. What is the future value of the $2000 annual payments?

d. What is the future value of the $250,000 face amount of the policy in year 30?

e. If payments were made at the beginning of each year, how would your answer to part (a) change?

4-23. Duncan wants to deposit $300 in his savings account at the end of every three months (that is, each quarter). The bank is offering an effective annual rate of

8 percent, using quarterly compounding. What will be his balance in two years assuming that his first deposit occurs at the end of the first quarter?

4-24. Cybil is about to retire and has the option of receiving an immediate lump sum of $175,000 or equal amounts over a ten-year period. She can earn 8 percent on her money. How much is the annual amount? Solve using the annuity equation. Check your annuity factor against the table value.

4-25. Mr. Wynn has $226,925 to invest. His financial advisor tells him that he can purchase an annuity for this amount which will pay him $25,000 a year for 25 years. If he purchases the annuity today, the first payment will be received one year from now. What interest rate will he earn on this investment? Use the present value annuity table to solve this problem.

4-26. An investment offers an expected dollar return of $800 each year for years 1 through 5, and $1200 each year for years 6 through 9. If you can earn 12 percent in the financial market on investments as risky as this one, what is the present value (worth) of the investment? Cash flows occur at the end of each year.

4-27. Is an investment costing $1,234,200, with expected returns of $300,000 per year for six years, acceptable? The interest rate is 10 percent.

4-28. How much can you borrow if you promise to make annual payments of $450 for five years and pay 9 percent interest? Derive the table factor using the formula and then use the factor to solve the problem.

4-29. Robert earns 6 percent compounded annually on his savings account.
   a. What will be the account's balance in five years if he makes annual deposits of $2000 at the end of each year?
   b. How much will he have in the account at the end of five years if deposits are made at the beginning of each year?

4-30. Susan wishes to draw five equal annual receipts from her $65,000 savings account at the end of each year and have $25,000 remaining at the end of the final withdrawal. Assuming the fund earns 7 percent per year, how much can she withdraw each period?

4-31. Steve's parents established a college trust fund for him. Now that he is starting college, the balance of the fund is $20,000 and earns 5 percent interest annually. He wishes to make equal lump-sum withdrawals at the end of each of the next four years so that the balance is $0 at the end of year 4. How much should be each withdrawal?

4-32. Glenda intends to deposit $2000 at the end of each year into her individual retirement account (IRA) for 40 years. The annual deposits are tax deferred until she is ready to retire and withdraw the money at age 67.
   a. If Glenda deposits the money into a bank savings plan which pays 7 percent annually, what will be the value of her IRA at age 67?
   b. If she invests her IRA money in a common stock mutual fund which grows at a rate of 10 percent annually, what will be the value of her IRA at age 67?
   c. If Glenda makes her annual IRA deposit at the beginning of each year for 40 years instead of at the end of the year, what will be the value of her IRA at maturity if she earns 7 percent compounded annually or she earns 10 percent compounded annually?

4-33. Your uncle owns an investment that returns $195 per year in perpetuity. He paid $1000 for this investment. What interest rate is he earning?

4-34. A government-sponsored agency has issued bonds that pay annual interest of $425 in perpetuity. The original selling price of the bonds was $5000. The market rate of interest today for government agency bonds is 7.25 percent.

   a. What was the interest rate when these bonds were first issued?
   b. What is today's market price of these bonds?

ADD-ON INTEREST

4-35. Peggy borrowed $3000 from the First State Bank with the loan to be repaid in equal installments at the end of each month for three years. The nominal interest rate is 12 percent and the bank uses simple add-on interest to calculate the installment payments. How much is Peggy's monthly payment?

4-36. Herb borrowed $3000 from the Arizona Credit Union with the loan to be repaid in equal installments at the end of each month for three years. The credit union uses the add-on method to calculate the installments. The nominal interest rate is 12 percent and the credit union uses monthly compounding to calculate interest. How much is Herb's monthly payment?

4-37. Describe how to calculate the effective annual rate for:

   a. A simple add-on loan.
   b. A compound add-on loan.

BANK DISCOUNT METHOD

4-38. Royal Shoe Company negotiated a one-year loan with the First State Bank of Mountain Grove for $600,000 to cover short-term needs. The bank discounts the loan at 8 percent.

   a. What is the amount of the bank discount?
   b. How much money does Royal Shoe receive to use during the year?
   c. If Royal Shoe really needs the full $600,000 loan in cash, how much should the company borrow from the bank?

4-39. Tri-City Trust Company loaned $2 million to Monrovia Industries for one year under an arrangement where the loan's 7.5 percent interest is discounted.

   a. What is the amount of the bank discount?
   b. How much money does Monrovia Industries receive to use during the year?
   c. If Monrovia Industries really needs the full $2 million loan in cash, how much should the company borrow from the bank?

COMPREHENSIVE PROBLEMS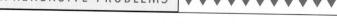

4-40. Suppose it is late May 1996. You are planning some personal finances and decide to deposit $2000 into a savings account on July 1, 1996. You have a choice between receiving 8 percent simple interest or 6 percent compound interest.

   a. If the bank pays simple interest annually, how much will you have in your account on July 1, 1999?
   b. If the bank pays 6 percent compound interest annually, how much will you have in your account on July 1, 1999?
   c. If the bank pays 6 percent, but compounds quarterly, how much will you have in your account on July 1, 1999?

d. You plan to deposit four payments of $500 each on July 1 of 1996, 1997, 1998, and 1999. How much will your account balance be on July 1, 1999, based on 6 percent annual compounding?

e. If you deposit four equal payments in your account on July 1 of 1996, 1997, 1998, and 1999, how large will each of these payments have to be for you to obtain the same ending balance as calculated in part (b)?

4-41. Suppose that it is July 1, 1996. After much deliberation, you determine that you need $2000 on July 1, 1999.

a. How much must you deposit in your bank on July 1, 1996 to have a balance of $2000 on January 1, 1999? The bank compounds interest at an 8 percent rate annually.

b. If you decide to make equal deposits to the bank in part (a) on each July 1 from 1996 through 1999 to accumulate the $2000, how large must each payment be?

c. Your mother is considering whether she should make the four payments calculated in part (b), give you a lump sum of $1500 on July 1, 1996, or give you nothing. Which alternative is best for you?

d. If you take the $1500 offered in part (c) on July 1, 1996, and this is the only funds you have available to deposit, what interest rate, compounded annually, must the deposit earn to have the necessary $2000 on January 1, 1999?

e. If you can deposit $400 each July 1 from 1996 through 1999, but you still need $2000 on July 1, 1999, what interest rate must you earn to achieve your goal if compounding is monthly?

f. If your mother doesn't help you reach your $2000 goal, your uncle is willing to give you $800 on July 1, 1996, on the condition that you get a part-time job and make six additional payments of equal amounts each six months thereafter. How large must your semiannual deposits be if all of this money earns 8 percent compounded semiannually?

g. What is the bank's effective annual interest rate in part (f)?

4-42. As part of a merger agreement between a regional telephone company and a television cable company, the telephone company agreed to employ the chief executive officer (CEO) of the cable company for a period of ten years. Part of the compensation agreement included a retirement package for the CEO amounting to $90,000 at the beginning of each year for a period of 20 years to start after the ten-year employment period. In the event that the CEO did not live to receive the retirement benefits, the $90,000 annual payments would be made to the CEO's heirs.

To fund this retirement program, the telephone company's chief financial officer (CFO) desired to make equal payments at the beginning of each year during the ten-year employment period so that no additional company investments would be necessary after the first ten contributions. The CFO assumed for planning purposes that the first ten years' payments would earn at a rate of 8 percent compounded annually, while the annual earning rate on the retirement fund would be 9 percent once the retirement payments began. Based on these assumptions, how much will the telephone company's annual contributions have to be to provide this retirement benefit? (*Hint:* Think of this problem as made up of the present value of one annuity due and the future value of another annuity due.)

ST4-1. The effective annual rate is calculated by the equation:

$$EAR = (1 + r/m)^m - 1$$

City Bank: $(1 + 0.06/1)^1 - 1 = 0.06$ or 6 percent

First Western Bank: $(1 + 0.06/2)^2 - 1 = 0.0609$ or 6.09 percent

Union Bank: $(1 + 0.06/4)^4 - 1 = 0.06136$ or 6.136 percent

Citizens Bank: $(1 + 0.06/360)^{360} - 1 = 0.06183$ or 6.183 percent

ST4-2.

    a. Solve using the future value of an annuity:

$$\text{Future value} = \text{Annual amount} \times \frac{(1 + r)^n - 1}{r}$$

$$= \$1800 \times \frac{(1 + 0.07)^{35} - 1}{0.07}$$

$$= \$1800 \times 138.2369$$

$$= \$248,826$$

    b. An annuity due compounds the cash flows from one period earlier. Thus, by investing at the beginning of each period, the value of the IRA would be:

$$\$248,826 \times 1.07 = \$266,244$$

ST4-3. Find the present value of a future amount of $500,000:

$$\text{Present value} = \frac{\text{Future value}}{(1 + r)^n}$$

$$= \frac{\$500,000}{(1 + 0.08)^{14}}$$

$$= \$170,231$$

Mr. Wynn would be better off receiving $500,000 at the end of 14 years. It is worth $20,231 more than the current payout of $150,000.

Video Case 4

Family Financial Planning:
An Application Of Present Value Techniques

from *Business World,* February 5, 1989

Chapter 4 introduces the techniques for computing *future values* and *present values.* These techniques not only are important for understanding much of the rest of the text, but also in everyday life. Family financial planning requires calculating the amount to invest or save to attain a desired future amount. In this video clip the Quilici family learns that they must begin a strict savings plan to prepare for retirement and their children's college education. The financial planner tells the Quilicis that their children's college expenses will be approximately $32,000 when their first child starts college. How much must the Quilicis invest per year to have enough in the bank in 13 years to completely finance both children's education?

We need to make some assumptions to get started. Assume savings earn 10 percent per year, that the children will overlap two years at college, that college expenses increase 8 percent per year, and that once the first child begins college no more deposits are made to the college fund. We begin to answer this question by computing how much the Quilicis need 13 years from today to finance their children's college education, and then we compute how much they must invest each year to accumulate that amount. Suppose the children will be in school in years 13 through 18 (the oldest attends in years 13, 14, 15, and 16, and the youngest attends in years 15, 16, 17, and 18). If the expense is $32,000 in year 13 and increases 8 percent each year, then the costs are shown in the table.

Year	Cost Per Child	Cost for Both
13	$32,000	$32,000
14	$34,560	$34,560
15	$37,324	$74,648
16	$40,310	$80,620
17	$43,535	$43,535
18	$47,018	$47,018

How much money must be available immediately before the first college payment? It is the amount that will pay the first bill ($32,000) and leave enough principal so, with interest earned, the remaining five payments can be made. The amount needed, $X, is $32,000 plus the present value of the remaining five payments discounted at 10 percent. (*Answer:* $244,611.21)

How large must the annual deposits be to accumulate $244,611.21 in 13 years? If the first deposit is made one year from today, the annuity must grow to $244,611.21 in 13 years at 10 percent, or

$$\text{Future value annuity} = \text{Annual deposit} \times \text{FVIFA}_{(10\%, \ 13 \text{ years})}$$

$$\$244,611.21 = \text{Annual deposit} \times 24.522$$
$$\text{Annual deposit} = \$ 9,975.17$$

So the Quilicis need to save about $10,000 per year to finance their children's college education.

Study Questions

1. Can you explain how the annual college expenses for years 14 to 18 were computed?

2. How would the annual deposit amount change if the Quilicis had only seven years to save?

3. How would the annual deposit amount change if the Quilicis only earned 8 percent on their savings?

Risk, Return, and the CAPM

A key principle in finance is the trade-off between expected return and risk. People often use the words *expected return* and *risk* in financial discussions, and most people have an intuitive understanding of their meanings. However, how can we define expected return and risk? Expected return is similar to an average return. Risk has different meanings, however, depending on the context of the discussion. We relate risk to individual stock returns (*standard deviation*), to investment choices in terms of an effective collection of securities (*portfolio*) either for financial management or for the single investor, and in terms of the market as a whole (*beta*). However we view risk, from a financial perspective it is the price an investor pays to seek the exceptional returns that are *potentially* available in financial markets, regardless of the location of these markets in the world. Risk is all that matters in pricing (valuing) assets as long as relevant information is fully available in the markets in which assets trade.[1]

The theoretical *capital asset pricing model*, or simply *CAPM* (pronounced *cap M*), plays an important role in evaluating individual assets in terms of their effect on the risk and expected return of an entire group of assets. CAPM is widely embraced by practitioners in the investment world.

When you have completed this chapter, you should understand:

- Why consideration of risk is important.
- How to calculate the standard deviation as a measure of risk.
- What the term *risk aversion* means in finance.
- The role of diversification in the investment process.
- Fundamentals of the CAPM and how its risk measure, called beta, can be useful to investors and managers.
- Some limitations of beta.

---

[1]In this chapter, we use the words *asset, stock,* and *security* interchangeably.

5.1 EVALUATING RISK

Uncertainty, rather than loss, is the essential characteristic of risk in making an investment. An investment can be risky even if it has no likelihood of loss. For example, suppose an investment has two possible results: a 10 percent gain or a 20 percent gain. Even though the investor will not suffer a loss, the investment is risky because the outcome is uncertain.

When most people consider risky situations, they sometimes think of two possible results. The flip of a coin comes up heads or tails. Exceeding the speed limit results in either getting caught or getting away. In investing, the situation is different because the range of possible results is unlimited. An investor may lose her or his entire investment, gain a large amount, or realize a result between these two extremes.

In financial markets, it is not enough to calculate only the chance of losing money. We need a measure of risk that encompasses the full range of potential results. To understand how to measure risk, it is necessary to first understand *expected return.*

5.1.1 Expected Return

> **Expected return.** The weighted average of all possible outcomes, where the weights are the probabilities that each outcome will occur. It is the expected value or mean of a probability distribution.

Expected return is not the return we hope for, nor is it the return that occurs most frequently; rather it is similar to average return. More precisely, **expected return** is a weighted average return of all possible returns, both positive and negative. The weights represent the chance associated with the occurrence of each possible return. In calculating expected return, a return that is less likely carries less weight than a return that is more likely to happen with a given investment. (See Illustration 5.1.)

ILLUSTRATION 5.1

Calculating returns

An investment has the following possible returns and associated probabilities of each outcome happening:

Outcome	Possible Return	Probability of Outcome
#1	0.30	0.20
#2	0.20	0.30
#3	0.10	0.50
		1.00

The most likely return is 10 percent, since it has the highest probability of happening. The least likely outcome is 30 percent. The *average return* is 20 percent:

$$\text{Average return} = \frac{\text{Outcome \#1} + \text{outcome \#2} + \text{outcome \#3}}{\text{Number of outcomes}}$$

$$= \frac{0.30 + 0.20 + 0.10}{3}$$

$$= 0.20 \text{ or } 20 \text{ percent}$$

The expected return is 17 percent. We calculate it by multiplying each possible return by its likelihood of occurring:

Expected return

$$
\begin{aligned}
&= \text{Outcome \#1} \times \text{probability of outcome \#1} \\
&\quad + \text{outcome \#2} \times \text{probability of outcome \#2} \\
&\quad + \text{outcome \#3} \times \text{probability of outcome \#3} \\
&= 0.30 \times 0.20 + 0.20 \times 0.30 + 0.10 \times 0.50 \\
&= 0.06 + 0.06 + 0.05 \\
&= 0.17 \text{ or } 17 \text{ percent}
\end{aligned}
$$

Notice that the expected return does not equal any of the possible returns. Such an outcome is common.

5.1.2 Measuring Risk

We alluded to risk as being uncertainty. However, think of **risk** as the variability of possible returns. When there are only a few possible results, we can define risk by looking at the possible *range* of results, as in Illustration 5.2. **Range** is the difference between the highest outcome and the lowest outcome.

Risk. Quantitative measurement of an outcome, such as a gain or loss; the chance of an outcoming occurring.

Range. A crude measure of dispersion defined as the difference between the highest value and the lowest value in a data set.

ILLUSTRATION 5.2

The range of outcomes

Mike Berry is considering investing in the common stock of either Bankston Corporation or Thomas Limited. He believes that only two possible outcomes exist for each security, and each outcome has a 50-50 chance of occurring. By investing in Bankston Corporation, he realizes either a 40 percent gain or a 10 percent loss. An investment in Thomas Limited results in either a 60 percent gain or a 30 percent loss. Based on these possible results and their associated probabilities, the expected return is 15 percent for both securities.

Security	Possible Outcome #1		Probability of Outcome #1		Possible Outcome #2		Probability of Outcome #2		Expected Return
Bankston	0.40	×	0.50	+	(−0.10)	×	0.50	=	0.15
Thomas	0.60	×	0.50	+	(−0.30)	×	0.50	=	0.15

However, Thomas Limited is riskier because its range of possible returns (60 percent to −30 percent) is greater than the range of possible returns for Bankston Corporation (40 percent to −10 percent).

When many possible results exist a comparison of ranges is unwieldy, if not impossible. Fortunately, a common statistical measure, called the *standard deviation,* exists for this situation. It provides a simple mathematical description of how much variability exists in a group of numbers. We define standard deviation later, but for now think of it as follows. If returns are constant period after period, the standard deviation is zero. If the range of returns is very wide, the standard deviation is large.

Figure 5.1 illustrates the idea. We have collected several months of returns for the securities Synerdyne Corporation and Express Air, Inc. Based on these historical data, the expected return of 9 percent is the same for each security. However, Express Air

FIGURE 5.1

<small>PLOT OF MONTHLY RETURNS</small>

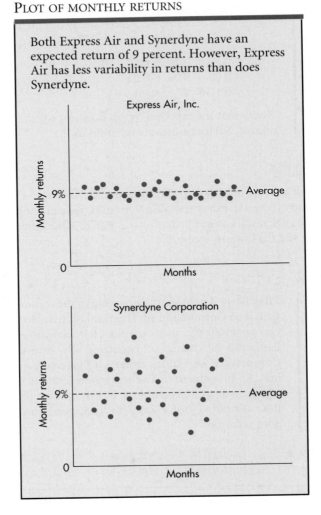

Both Express Air and Synerdyne have an expected return of 9 percent. However, Express Air has less variability in returns than does Synerdyne.

Express Air, Inc.

Monthly returns

9% - - - - - - - - - - - - - - - - - - Average

0   Months

Synerdyne Corporation

Monthly returns

9% - - - - - - - - - - - - - - - - - - Average

0   Months

clearly has less variability in returns than does Synerdyne. Calculation of the standard deviation of returns for each security provides a specific measure of the variability of each security's performance. The calculation provides an expression of the degree of risk about each security's average return. To state it differently, the standard deviation provides an estimate of how much divergence exists between actual return and expected return.

Figure 5.2 shows a different way to express risk. Suppose we record the returns on the Synerdyne security over many periods and plot the frequency of returns for different ranges of returns. We might record historical monthly returns for five years and plot how many of the 60 observations are between 0 and 1 percent, 1 percent and 2 percent, 0 and –1 percent, and so on. The result would probably have a pattern similar to that in the upper graph in Figure 5.2.

Two conclusions are apparent from this analysis.

- The figure shows the dispersion of returns for the investment. For a different investment, the pattern might look similar, but the amount of dispersion could be different, as shown in the lower distributions in Figure 5.2.

FIGURE 5.2

PROBABILITY DISTRIBUTION OF RETURNS

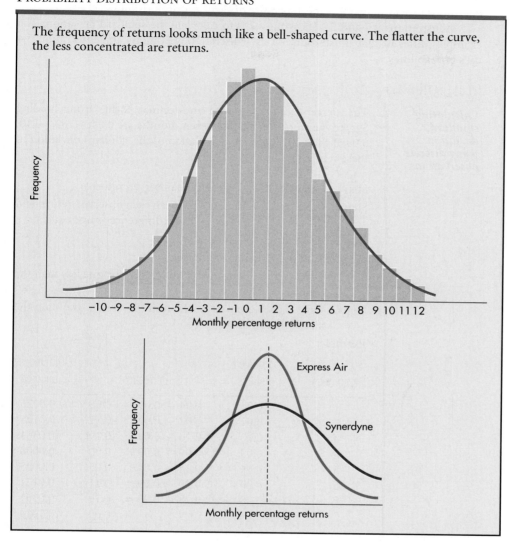

The frequency of returns looks much like a bell-shaped curve. The flatter the curve, the less concentrated are returns.

- The pattern derived from plotting the frequency of returns probably looks like a bell-shaped curve.

5.1.3 Calculating the Standard Deviation

Let's see how to calculate the standard deviation and relate it to this bell-shaped pattern, which statisticians call the *normal distribution*. If we assume that returns follow this bell curve, then the **standard deviation** is a single number that describes the riskiness of returns for a particular security. The standard deviation is represented by a single point on the curve, which we will show you later. The two bell curves in the lower part of Figure 5.2 have the same center, which says that their expected returns are equal. The Synerdyne security, however, has much greater dispersion (a larger range) than does the

Standard deviation. A statistic used to measure dispersion about an expected value. A high (low) standard deviation is associated with high (low) risk. It is the square root of the variance.

Express Air security. This means that returns for Synerdyne are more variable, or less certain, and therefore riskier. How much riskier is Synerdyne? The respective standard deviations provide a mathematical measure of each security's riskiness.

Illustrations 5.3 and 5.4 show the steps to calculate the standard deviation. The examples differ in that Illustration 5.3 uses discrete observations and Illustration 5.4 uses probabilities.

ILLUSTRATION 5.3

Calculating standard deviation using discrete observations

The percent returns, stated in decimal form, from holding Synerdyne stock for the past seven months are 0.04, −0.02, −0.10, 0.09, 0.14, 0.20, and 0.28. Calculation of the standard deviation of these returns follows several steps.

Step 1: Calculate the average of the observed returns.

Step 2: Calculate the difference between each observed return and the average. The sum of these differences must equal 0.

Step 3: Square each difference.

Step 4: Sum the squared differences.

Step 5: Divide the sum of squared differences by one less than the number of observations.

Step 6: Take the square root of the result in Step 5 to obtain the standard deviation.

Example:

Observation	Observed Returns	Differences	Differences Squared
1	0.04	0.04 − 0.09 = −0.05	0.0025
2	−0.02	−0.02 − 0.09 = −0.11	0.0121
3	−0.10	−0.10 − 0.09 = −0.19	0.0361
4	0.09	0.09 − 0.09 = 0.00	0.0000
5	0.14	0.14 − 0.09 = 0.05	0.0025
6	0.20	0.20 − 0.09 = 0.11	0.0121
7	0.28	0.28 − 0.09 = 0.19	0.0361
	0.63	0.00	0.1014

Average = 0.63 ÷ 7 = 0.09

Standard deviation = $(0.1014 \div 6)^{1/2} = 0.13$

ILLUSTRATION 5.4

Calculating standard deviation using a probability distribution

A study of several months of stock return data for Express Air, Inc. reveals the following pattern, where the probabilities must sum to 1.

Occurrence	1	2	3	4	5	6	7
Possible return	−0.10	−0.02	0.04	0.09	0.14	0.20	0.28
Probability of return	0.05	0.10	0.20	0.30	0.20	0.10	0.05

The steps to calculate the standard deviation are:

Step 1: Calculate the expected return of the possible occurrences.

Step 2: Calculate the difference between each possible occurrence and the expected return.

Step 3: Square each difference and multiply it by the associated probability.

Step 4: Sum the product of the squared differences times their probabilities.

Step 5: Take the square root of the result in Step 4 to obtain the standard deviation.

Example:

Expected return

= Possible return #1 × probability of return #1
+ possible return #2 × probability of return #2
+ possible return #3 × probability of return #3
+ possible return #4 × probability of return #4
+ possible return #5 × probability of return #5
+ possible return #6 × probability of return #6
+ possible return #7 × probability of return #7

= −0.10 × 0.05 + (-0.02) × 0.10 + 0.04 × 0.20 + 0.09 × 0.30
+ 0.14 × 0.20 + 0.20 × 0.10 + 0.28 × 0.05
= 0.09 or 9 percent

Standard deviation

= [(Possible return #1 − expected return)^2 × probability of return #1
+ (possible return #2 − expected return)^2 × probability of return #2
+ (possible return #3 − expected return)^2 × probability of return #3
+ (possible return #4 − expected return)^2 × probability of return #4
+ (possible return #5 − expected return)^2 × probability of return #5
+ (possible return #6 − expected return)^2 × probability of return #6
+ (possible return #7 − expected return)^2 × probability of return #7]$^{1/2}$

= [(-0.10 − 0.09)^2 × 0.05 + (-0.02 − 0.09)^2 × 0.10
+ (0.04 − 0.09)^2 × 0.20 + (0.09 − 0.09)^2 × 0.30
+ (0.14 − 0.09)^2 × 0.20 + (0.20 − 0.09)^2 × 0.10
+ (0.28 − 0.09)^2 × 0.05]$^{1/2}$

= 0.084 or 8.4 percent

The standard deviation is important for two reasons.

- It compares the riskiness of different alternatives. The higher the standard deviation, the greater is the risk.
- It measures risk in relation to expected return.[2] A standard deviation of 2.5 and an expected return of 1.25 means that two units of risk are present for each unit of expected return.

5.1.4 Historical Risk and Return of U.S. Financial Markets

Once we know the expected return and the standard deviation, we have an important insight into the behavior of financial markets. For example, Table 5.1 summarizes realized returns and risk for different securities in the United States for the period 1926–1993.

The numbers in Table 5.1 reveal that over the 67-year period from 1926 to 1993, the simple arithmetic average for nominal returns on common stocks, as measured by the Standard & Poor's 500 Stock Index (S&P 500), is 12.3 percent. The **S&P 500 index** is a weighted stock price index for 500 large American companies. Risk, as measured by the standard deviation, is 20.5 percent. If we assume that investment returns follow a normal distribution, approximately 67 percent of all returns fall within one standard deviation of the expected return; 95 percent fall within two standard deviations; and 99.7 percent fall within three standard deviations. We can calculate ranges for annual returns for the S&P 500 index in the table using the following equation:

$$\text{Range} = \text{Nominal average annual return} \pm Z \times \text{standard deviation} \quad (5.1)$$

where Z represents the number of standard deviations desired. Thus,

- 67 percent of the time, returns are in the range:

$$12.3\% \pm 1 \times 20.5\% = -8.2 \text{ to } 32.8\%$$

- 95 percent of the time, returns are in the range:

$$12.3\% \pm 2 \times 20.5\% = -28.7 \text{ to } 53.3\%$$

- 99.7 percent of the time, returns are in the range:

$$12.3\% \pm 3 \times 20.5\% = -49.2 \text{ to } 73.8\%$$

From Table 5.1, the *risk-to-return ratio* (called the *coefficient of variation* in statistics) for common stocks is $20.5 \div 12.3 \approx 1.7$. This ratio indicates that significant risk accompanies the return. Each unit of return has 1.7 units of risk. Small company stocks are even riskier than the S&P 500 index. Their risk-to-return ratio is $34.8 \div 17.6 \approx 2.0$. The historical risk of common stocks is roughly 2.4 times as large as the risk associated with long-term government and corporate bonds ($20.5 \div 8.4 \approx 2.4$). Historical risk of common stocks is almost six times as large as the risk of U.S. Treasury bills, called T-bills, ($20.5 \div 3.3 \approx 6.2$).

The **risk premium** in Table 5.1 is the difference between returns on the various securities compared to the 3.7 percent arithmetic mean return on risk-free T-bills. T-bills are risk free because the probability of the government defaulting is minimal, zero for all practical purposes, and because these securities have short maturities, reinvestment risk is minimal. Thus, the return an investor earns investing in T-bills is compensation for pure time value of money, discussed in Chapter 3.

[2]The calculation of standard deviation assumes a normal bell-shaped probability distribution curve. Thus, expected return and average return are equal. These two returns can differ if a nonnormal distribution is assumed, as shown earlier in Illustration 5.1.

TABLE 5-1

ANNUAL RATES OF RETURN AND RISK: 1926–1993

Series	Geometric mean	Arithmetic mean	Standard deviation	Distribution
Large company stocks	10.3%	12.3%	20.5%	
Small company stocks	12.4	17.6	34.8	
Long-term corporate bonds	5.6	5.9	8.4	
Long-term government bonds	5.0	5.4	8.7	
Intermediate-term government bonds	5.3	5.4	5.6	
U.S. Treasury bills	3.7	3.7	3.3	
Inflation	3.1	3.2	4.6	

−90%   0%   90%

The 8.6 percent risk premium for common stocks is the 12.3 percent annual return for common stocks less the 3.7 percent T-bill return. This 8.6 percent risk premium is the additional annual average return that investors receive for assuming risk of common stock ownership as opposed to investing in risk-free T-bills. Frequently, investors use the historical risk premium to help them forecast the expected return on total common stock returns. They add the historical 8.6 risk premium to the current T-bill yield. Similar calculations provide forecasts of expected returns for the other securities. For instance, if T-bills currently yield 5.25 percent, the forecast of nominal annual returns for common stocks is 13.75 percent (= 5.25 + 8.50). For small company stocks, the forecast would be 19.15 percent (= 5.25 + 13.90).

Comprehension Check

1. What does the expected return on an investment mean? Why is the expected return not the most likely return?
2. Risk is defined as variability. What is variability and how can we measure it?
3. Describe how to calculate the standard deviation using either discrete observations or probability distributions.

4. When are average return and expected return equal?

5. Use the data in Table 5.1. How is the risk of various securities measured? Which class of securities is most risky? Which is least risky? Explain the reasons for these differences in risk.

6. Define the risk premium on common stocks. Why are U.S. Treasury bills used as the basis for calculating risk premiums?

 ## 5.2 RISK AVERSION

We suspect that most people prefer certainty to uncertainty in managing their finances. If so, then they dislike risk. When faced with two investments that have the same expected return, they choose the investment with the lower risk. They exhibit **risk aversion,** as shown in Illustration 5.5.

Risk aversion. Riskiness matters and is disliked.

ILLUSTRATION 5.5

Risk aversion at work

The pension fund manager of Textile Supplies, Inc. is considering investing in stock of either Southwest Public Utility Company or Calcutex Limited, each costing $100 per share. The only possible outcome of Southwest Public Utility is an $80 gain. Alternatively, we can think of the outcome as an 80 percent return on investment with a 100 percent chance of occurring.

Calcutex has two possible results:

- A 20 percent chance of no dollar gain (a zero percent return on investment)—it will still be worth $100 at the end of the period.
- An 80 percent chance of a $100 gain (a 100 percent return)—the investment doubles in value.

Calcutex's expected return is 80 percent:

Expected return

$$= \text{Possible outcome \#1} \times \text{probability of outcome \#1}$$
$$+ \text{possible outcome \#2} \times \text{probability of outcome \#2}$$
$$= 0\% \times 0.20 + 100\% \times 0.80$$
$$= 80\%$$

Which investment should the pension fund manager choose? Although the expected return of both investments is the same, if the treasurer is like many people, the choice will be Southwest Public Utility.

Why do many people choose the stock of Southwest Public Utility? The reason is that its return is certain, but the expected return from Calcutex Limited is uncertain. So Calcutex is risky. Many people are often unwilling to assume the risk associated with higher possible returns.

Investors who choose the investment in Southwest Public Utility demonstrate risk aversion; they choose the investment with lower risk when faced with two investments with the same expected return. By choosing Southwest Public Utility, investors decide that the expected return for Calcutex is not high enough to pay for its risk. What expected profit must Calcutex offer to entice an investor to select it? Is an 80 percent chance of a $150 gain large enough? If not, will an 80 percent chance of a $200 gain intrigue the investor? As expected return increases, a reluctant investor will eventually choose Calcutex because the higher expected return will justify the higher risk. The point at which the investor switches to Calcutex may differ from the point at which other investors switch. The amount of the possible gain that influences risk taking depends on individual preference for expected return, given the risk.

Is everyone risk averse? The financial news seems to reveal many examples of investors making risk-seeking choices. However, the most common situation for risk seeking occurs when small amounts of money are at risk with the potential, however small, for very high returns. A state lottery is a prime example. The risk of losing $1 is extremely high and the expected return is negative. Yet millions of people buy lottery tickets. The perceived value of a large gain, no matter how unlikely, overwhelms the cost of a losing ticket.

Despite occasional risk-seeking behavior, most people are risk averse. However, as we have discussed, people are not equally risk averse. Some people keep their money only in insured bank savings accounts or T-bills. Other people invest in very risky securities. It is clear from Table 5.1 that if we take on risk we are rewarded, at least over reasonably long periods. By accepting the risks of common stock ownership, we earn a higher return than an investor who seeks the safety of T-bills.

Is a high-return, high-risk investment better than a low-return, low-risk investment? The answer is not a simple yes or no. We must consider alternative risk-return trade-offs. Illustration 5.6 shows how the principle works.

ILLUSTRATION 5.6

Risk versus expected return

As depicted in the graph below, security 1 (S_1) has higher expected return than either security 2 (S_2) or security 3 (S_3), as well as equal or lower risk, as measured by the standard deviation. Thus, S_1 dominates both S_2 and S_3. It is irrational for us to select either S_2 or S_3 over S_1. We gain nothing by selecting S_2. Similarly, although securities S_2 and S_3 have equal expected returns, S_2 has lower risk. Thus, S_2 dominates S_3.

Security S_1 has both higher expected return and higher risk than investment S_4. The choice between S_1 and S_4 is inconclusive. The decision depends on individual judgment of the trade-off between risk and return.

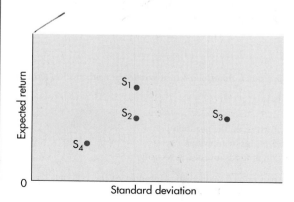

> ## Comprehension Check

1. Explain how risk aversion applies to investment selection.
2. How do you account for the success of state lotteries to raise revenue for government when the risk of losing the $1 spent for a ticket is extremely high and the expected return is negative?
3. "It's a mistake for people to invest their hard-earned money in stocks when they could avoid the risk of losing their money by keeping it in federally insured bank savings accounts." Evaluate this statement.

5.3 DIVERSIFYING TO REDUCE RISK

Earlier in Illustration 5.2, an investor was offered the securities Bankston Company and Thomas Limited, each with the same expected return of 15 percent. The investment choice between the two was simple; select the security with less risk. What happens if the person invests an equal amount of money in both securities? The investor will be forming a portfolio of the two securities. The expected portfolio return of investing in both Bankston and Thomas is still 15 percent because each security has an expected return of 15 percent. This return does not change, even if proportions invested in each security are other than 50-50 as used in the illustration.

Most securities do not offer equal expected returns. When a portfolio includes securities with different expected returns, we calculate the **expected portfolio return** by weighting the expected return of each security by the proportion of funds distributed to each security, and then summing across all the securities:[3]

Expected portfolio return. The weighted arithmetic average of all possible outcomes for the portfolio, where the weights are the probabilities that each outcome will occur.

Expected portfolio return

$$= \text{(Expected return for security \#1)} \times \text{(proportion of funds invested in security \#1)}$$

$$+ \text{(expected return for security \#2)} \times \text{(proportion of funds invested in security \#2)} \quad \text{(5.2)}$$

$$+ \ldots + \text{(expected return for security } N) \times \text{(proportion of funds invested in security } N)$$

The sum of the proportions invested in each security is 1.0.

Why bother to combine securities in a portfolio? Wouldn't our wealth improve more by investing all our investable funds in the security with the highest expected

---

[3]Often the expression for portfolio return is stated in mathematical terms as:

$$R_p = \sum_{i=1}^{N} R_i W_i$$

where

R_p = expected return on the portfolio
R_i = expected return for security i
W_i = proportion of funds invested in security i

$\sum_{i=1}^{N}$ means to sum the mathematical product of the expected return and proportion of funds invested for each security i across all N securities.

return? Not necessarily. Higher expected return is associated with higher risk. There is no guarantee that the security with the highest expected return will realize the expected return. The actual return can be higher or lower, and possibly negative. By forming securities into a portfolio, we reduce risk. The next two sections examine how to calculate the risk of the portfolio under different assumptions about the relatedness of the securities to each other. First, we assume that all securities are *independent* of each other; second, we assume that *dependencies* exist among all the securities.

5.3.1 Diversification with Independent Securities

The risk of the portfolio is not normally a simple weighted average of the risks of the individual securities. The portfolio's risk is a simple weighted average if the price changes for each security are independent of price changes of every other security in the portfolio. Thus, **independence** means **zero correlation** (or no relationship) exists between securities. Although such an occurrence is most unlikely, for simplicity we will assume that it is the case here. Then we define **portfolio risk** — the standard deviation of the portfolio—as:[4]

Standard deviation of portfolio

$$= [(\text{Standard deviation of security \#1})^2 \times (\text{proportion invested in security \#1})^2$$

$$+ (\text{standard deviation of security \#2})^2 \times (\text{proportion invested in security \#2})^2 \quad (5.3)$$

$$+ \ldots + (\text{standard deviation of security } N)^2 \times (\text{proportion invested in security } N)^2]^{1/2}$$

Illustration 5.7 applies Equations 5.2 and 5.3. Remember, we are assuming that no correlation exists between the securities; that is, the securities are independent of each other. We relax this assumption later.

ILLUSTRATION 5.7

Risk reduction using independent securities

Financial securities of National Vision Limited (NVL) and Interactive Technology Limited (ITL) offer the following possible returns:

Outcome	Return of NVL	Probability of Return	Return of ITL	Probability of Return
1	0.40	0.55	0.40	0.55
2	−0.10	0.45	−0.10	0.45

[4]Stated as a mathematical formula, the portfolio standard deviation is defined as:

$$\sigma_p = [\Sigma_{i=1}^{N} \sigma_i^2 \ W_i^2]^{1/2}$$

where

σ_i = standard deviation of returns for security i

W_i = the proportion of funds invested in security i

N = number of securities in the portfolio

In words, the expression says that the portfolio standard deviation is the sum of the products of the squared standard deviations times the squared proportions for each security, and then the square root of the summation is taken.

The expected return for the NVL security is 17.5 percent.

Expected return for NVL

$$= \text{(Possible outcome \#1)} \times \text{(probability of outcome \#1)}$$
$$+ \text{(possible outcome \#2)} \times \text{(probability of outcome \#2)}$$

$$= 0.40 \times 0.55 + (-0.10) \times 0.45$$
$$= 0.175 \text{ or } 17.5 \text{ percent}$$

The preceding calculation also represents the expected return for the ITL security, since its probability distribution is the same as the distribution for security NVL.

The expected return for a portfolio with equal proportions invested in each security is also 17.5 percent.

Expected portfolio return

$$= \text{(Expected return for NVL)} \times \text{(proportion invested in NVL)}$$

$$+ \text{(expected return for ITL)} \times \text{(proportion invested in ITL)}$$

$$= 0.175 \times 0.50 + 0.175 \times 0.50$$
$$= 0.175 \text{ or } 17.5 \text{ percent}$$

The calculation of portfolio risk uses Equation 5.3. First, we calculate the standard deviation of each security. The calculation for security NVL is as follows:

Standard deviation for NVL

$$= [\text{(Possible outcome \#1} - \text{expected return)}^2 \times \text{(probability of outcome \#1)}$$

$$+ \text{(possible outcome \#2} - \text{expected return)}^2 \times \text{(probability of outcome \#2)}]^{1/2}$$

$$= [(0.40 - 0.175)^2 \times 0.55 + (-0.10 - 0.175)^2 \times 0.45]^{1/2}$$
$$= 0.249 \text{ or } 24.9 \text{ percent}$$

Since security ITL has the same probability distribution as security NVL, it also has the same standard deviation.

Next, substitute the standard deviation and the proportion invested in each security into Equation 5.3 to calculate the portfolio's standard deviation:

Standard deviation of portfolio

$$= [\text{(Standard deviation of NVL)}^2 \times \text{(proportion invested in NVL)}^2$$

$$+ \text{(standard deviation of ITL)}^2 \times \text{(proportion invested in ITL)}^2]^{1/2}$$

$$= [(0.249)^2 \times (0.50)^2 + (0.249)^2 \times (0.50)^2]^{1/2}$$
$$= 0.176 \text{ or } 17.6 \text{ percent}$$

If the portfolio consists only of either the NVL security or the ITL security, the portfolio risk is 24.9 percent, as shown by the calculated standard deviation for the individual security. However, the combination of securities NVL and ITL in the portfolio lowers risk to 17.6 percent without changing the expected return.

How is it possible that the combination of two securities with the same probability distributions can lower risk? Illustration 5.8 shows how by looking at Illustration 5.7 from a different perspective.

ILLUSTRATION 5.8

Another look at diversification

In the last illustration, securities NVL and ITL both offer a possible return of 40 percent, with a 55 percent probability, and a possible return of −10 percent, with a 45 percent probability. The expected return is 17.5 percent.

Expected return for either NVL or ITL

$$= \text{(Possible outcome \#1)} \times \text{(probability of outcome \#1)}$$
$$+ \text{(possible outcome \#2)} \times \text{(probability of outcome \#2)}$$

$$= 0.40 \times 0.55 + (-0.10) \times 0.45$$
$$= 0.175 \text{ or } 17.5 \text{ percent}$$

Several combinations of returns for these two securities are possible:

- *Both securities gain 40 percent.* The joint probability of this happening is $0.55 \times 0.55 = 0.3025$.
- *Both securities lose 10 percent.* The joint probability of this happening is $0.45 \times 0.45 = 0.2025$.
- *The NVL security gains 40 percent and the ITL security loses 10 percent.* The joint probability of this happening is $0.55 \times 0.45 = 0.2475$.
- *The NVL security loses 10 percent and the ITL security gains 40 percent.* The joint probability of this happening is $0.45 \times 0.55 = 0.2475$.

The expected return of a portfolio containing both NVL and ITL, with equal amounts invested in each security, is still 17.5 percent.

Expected portfolio return

$$= [(40\% \text{ return for NVL}) \times \text{(proportion invested in NVL)}$$
$$+ (40\% \text{ return for ITL}) \times \text{(proportion invested in ITC)}]$$
$$\times \text{(probability of both securities earning 40\%)}$$

$$+ [(-10\% \text{ return for NVL}) \times \text{(proportion invested in NVL)}$$
$$+ (-10\% \text{ return for ITL}) \times \text{(proportion invested in ITL)}]$$
$$\times \text{(probability of both securities earning } -10\%)$$

$$+ [(40\% \text{ return for NVL}) \times \text{(proportion invested in NVL)}$$
$$+ (-10\% \text{ return for ITL}) \times \text{(proportion invested in ITL)}]$$
$$\times \text{(probability of NVL earning 40\% and ITL earning } -10\%)$$

+ [(−10% return for NVL) × (proportion invested in NVL)
+ (40% return for ITL) × (proportion invested in ITL)]
× (probability of NVL earning −10% and ITL earning 40%)

= [(0.40 × 0.50) + (0.40 × 0.50)] × 0.3025
  + [(−0.10 × 0.50) + (−0.10 × 0.50)] × 0.2025
  + [(0.40 × 0.50) + (−0.10 × 0.50)] × 0.2475
  + [(−0.10 × 0.50) + (0.40 × 0.50)] × 0.2475
= 0.121 − 0.02025 + 0.037125 + 0.037125
= 0.175

The following graphs show the difference between a one-security portfolio consisting of either NVL or ITL and a two-security portfolio consisting of both NVL and ITL. This example indicates diversification at work!

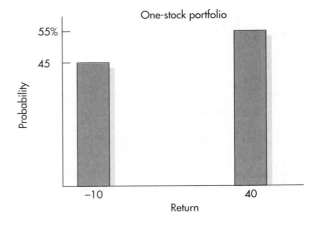

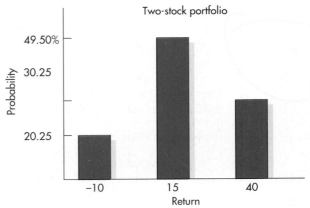

The risk of losing 10 percent has declined from 45 percent for a one-security portfolio to 20.25 percent for a two-security portfolio (the joint probability). Note that the chance of a 40 percent gain is also reduced from 55 percent for a one-security portfolio to 30.25 percent for a two-security portfolio.

5.3.2 Diversification with Dependent Securities

The preceding illustrations explain the effects of diversification when all the securities are independent. At the other extreme is the case when all securities in the portfolio are perfectly and positively correlated with each other. When one security's return changes, the returns of all other securities in the portfolio change by the same amount. These securities exhibit total dependency. No risk reduction occurs by combining these securities in a portfolio. However, most pairs of securities are neither independent nor totally dependent. Instead, securities exhibit some correlation but less than perfect correlation. For these securities, we can reduce risk by combining them into a portfolio.

Whenever **dependency,** or correlation, exists among the securities, it is necessary to adjust the formula for the standard deviation of a portfolio, given earlier by Equation 5.3. The new formula seems rather complex, but as we will show in Illustration 5.9, it is not difficult to use. For a two-security portfolio, the formula is:[5]

> Standard deviation of portfolio
>
> = [(Standard deviation of security #1)² × (proportion invested in security #1)²
>
> + (standard deviation of security #2)² × (proportion invested in security #2)² **(5.4)**
>
> + 2 × (standard deviation of security #1) × (standard deviation of security #2)
> × (proportion invested in security #1) × (proportion invested in security #2)
> × (correlation between returns of security #1 and security #2)]^{1/2}

The first two expressions on the right-hand side of Equation 5.4 are the *weighted variances* for securities #1 and #2, respectively. **Variance** is the standard deviation squared. The third expression is the *weighted covariance*. **Covariance** considers the interaction risk of the securities; the degree to which securities move together. Multiplying the respective variance and covariances by the squared proportions invested in each security weights the variance and covariance terms. Illustration 5.9 shows how to calculate portfolio return and risk for two securities that are highly correlated.

Dependency. The degree of association, or correlation, between two variables. Dependency is low for small levels of correlation and high for high levels of correlation.

Variance. A statistic that measures dispersion about the expected value. A high (low) variance is associated with high (low) risk. It is the standard deviation squared.

Covariance. A statistical term used to reflect the extent to which two variables move together. A positive value means that on average, they move in the same direction. The covariance depends not only on the correlation between the two variables but also the standard deviations of each variable.

ILLUSTRATION 5.9

Diversification when dependency exists

Securities NVL and ITL both offer a possible return of 40 percent with a 55 percent probability, and a possible return of -10 percent with a 45 percent probability. The correlation coefficient between the securities is 0.75. Think of the correlation coefficient measure as follows. If correlation is 1.0, then the securities move up and down in perfect harmony. A correlation coefficient of 0.75 means that the securities move together 75 percent of the time.

[5]The mathematical expression for the *N*-security portfolio's standard deviation is:

$$\sigma_p = [\textstyle\sum_{i=1}^{N} \sigma_i^2 \, W_i^2 + \sum_{i=1}^{N} \sum_{j=1}^{N} \rho_{ij}\, \sigma_i \, \sigma_j \, W_i \, W_j]^{1/2}$$

σ is the standard deviation of returns. W is the proportion of funds invested in a security. Subscripts i and j represent securities i and j, respectively, and ρ_{ij} is the correlation between security i and security j.

The expected return of each security is 17.5 percent. The calculation for the NVL security is as follows:

Expected return for NVL

$$= \text{(Possible outcome \#1)} \times \text{(probability of outcome \#1)} \\ + \text{(possible outcome \#2)} \times \text{(probability of outcome \#2)}$$

$$= 0.40 \times 0.55 + (-0.10) \times 0.45$$
$$= 0.175 \text{ or } 17.5 \text{ percent}$$

Since the ITL security has the same probability distribution, its expected return is also 17.5 percent.

The expected return for a portfolio with equal amounts invested in each security is *still* 17.5 percent since *correlation does not affect the expected return of the portfolio*. The portfolio return is a weighted average of the expected security returns:

Expected portfolio return

$$= \text{(Expected return for NVL)} \times \text{(proportion invested in NVL)} \\ + \text{(expected return for ITL)} \times \text{(proportion invested ITL)}$$

$$= 0.175 \times 0.50 + 0.175 \times 0.50$$
$$= 0.175 \text{ or } 17.5 \text{ percent}$$

To calculate portfolio risk, we apply Equation 5.4. However, we must first calculate the standard deviation of each security. The standard deviation for the NVL security is 24.9 percent.

Standard deviation of NVL

$$= [\text{(Possible outcome \#1} - \text{expected return)}^2 \times \text{probability of outcome \#1}$$

$$+ \text{(possible outcome \#2} - \text{expected return)}^2 \times \text{probability of outcome \#2]}^{1/2}$$

$$= [(0.40 - 0.175)^2 \times 0.55 + (-0.10 - 0.175)^2 \times 0.45]^{1/2}$$
$$= 0.249 \text{ or } 24.9 \text{ percent}$$

Since the ITL security has the same probability distribution as the NVL security, its standard deviation is also 24.9 percent. Note that any correlation between the securities does not affect the individual standard deviations.

Next we substitute the standard deviations of each security, the proportion of funds invested in each, and the correlation coefficient showing the relationship between the two securities into Equation 5.4, shown again in the following equation. The portfolio standard deviation is 23.3 percent.

Standard deviation of portfolio

$$= [\text{(Standard deviation of NVL)}^2 \times \text{(proportion invested in NVL)}^2$$

$$+ \text{(standard deviation of ITL)}^2 \times \text{(proportion invested in ITL)}^2$$

$\qquad$ + 2 × (standard deviation of NVL) × (standard deviation of ITL) × (proportion invested in NVL) × (proportion invested in ITL) × (correlation between returns of NVL and ITL)$]^{1/2}$

$$= [(0.249)^2 \times (0.50)^2 + (0.249)^2 \times (0.50)^2$$
$$+ 2 \times 0.249 \times 0.249 \times 0.50 \times 0.50 \times 0.75]^{1/2}$$

$$= 0.233 \text{ or } 23.3 \text{ percent}$$

For this example, the two-security portfolio has lower risk than the one-security portfolio, but the same expected return.

The preceding illustration shows that risk reduction is possible by forming securities into a portfolio when less than perfect positive correlation (that is, less than +1.0) exists between securities. The lower the correlation coefficient, the more we can reduce risk. The largest risk reduction occurs when correlation between securities is perfectly negative (−1.0).

For example, suppose the two securities NVL and ITL in Illustration 5.9 are perfectly and positively correlated; that is, correlation is +1.0. Under this circumstance, the portfolio standard deviation is 24.9 percent, as calculated earlier in Illustration 5.9.

Standard deviation of portfolio

$$= [(\text{Standard deviation of NVL})^2 \times (\text{proportion invested in NVL})^2$$

$$+ (\text{standard deviation of ITL})^2 \times (\text{proportion invested in ITL})^2$$

$$+ 2 \times (\text{standard deviation of NVL}) \times (\text{standard deviation of ITL})$$
$$\times (\text{proportion invested in NVL}) \times (\text{proportion invested in ITL})$$
$$\times (\text{correlation between returns of NVL and ITL})]^{1/2}$$

$$= [(0.249)^2 \times (0.50)^2 + (0.249)^2 \times (0.50)^2$$
$$+ 2 \times 0.249 \times 0.249 \times 0.50 \times 0.50 \times 1]^{1/2}$$

$$= 0.249 \text{ or } 24.9 \text{ percent}$$

In this case, the portfolio standard deviation is the same as each security's. Thus, *diversification with perfectly and positively correlated securities results in no risk reduction at all.*

Now, suppose that the two securities NVL and ITL are perfectly and negatively correlated with each other; correlation is −1.0. The portfolio's standard deviation is zero; the portfolio is riskless.

Standard deviation of portfolio

$$= [(\text{Standard deviation of NVL})^2 \times (\text{proportion invested in NVL})^2$$

$$+ (\text{standard deviation of ITL})^2 \times (\text{proportion invested in ITL})^2$$

$$+ 2 \times (\text{standard deviation of NVL}) \times (\text{standard deviation of ITL})$$
$$\times (\text{proportion invested in NVL}) \times (\text{proportion invested in ITL})$$
$$\times (\text{correlation between returns of NVL and ITL})]^{1/2}$$

$$= [(0.249)^2 \times (0.50)^2 + (0.249)^2 \times (0.50)^2$$
$$+ 2 \times 0.249 \times 0.249 \times 0.50 \times 0.50 \times (-1)]^{1/2}$$

$$= 0.00 \text{ or } 0 \text{ percent}$$

Perfect negative correlation does not always eliminate all risk, as shown in Illustration 5.10, using securities issued by Promus Corporation and Nextel Communications.

ILLUSTRATION 5.10

Effect of correlation on diversification

Securities for Promus Corporation and Nextel Communications offer expected returns of 8 and 10 percent, respectively. The standard deviation of the returns for Promus is 6 percent, whereas it is 9 percent for Nextel. An investment of 30 percent of our funds in Promus and 70 percent in Nextel results in an expected portfolio return of 9.4 percent.

Expected portfolio return

= (Expected return for Promus) × (proportion invested in Promus) + (expected return for Nextel) × (proportion invested in Nextel)

= 0.08 × 0.30 + 0.10 × 0.70
= 0.094 or 9.4 percent

Let's look at the risk of the portfolio under three different assumptions about the correlation that exists between the two securities: +1.0, -1.0, and +0.4. If the correlation is +1.0, the portfolio's standard deviation is 8.1 percent.

Standard deviation of portfolio

= [(Standard deviation of Promus)^2 × (proportion invested in Promus)^2

+ (standard deviation of Nextel)^2 × (proportion invested in Nextel)^2

+ 2 × (standard deviation of Promus) × (standard deviation of Nextel) × (proportion invested in Promus) × (proportion invested in Nextel) × (correlation between returns of Promus and Nextel)]$^{1/2}$

= [(0.06)^2 × (0.30)^2 + (0.09)^2 × (0.70)^2 + 2 × 0.06 × 0.09 × 0.30 × 0.70 × 1]$^{1/2}$

= 0.081 or 8.1 percent

If the correlation is -1.0, the standard deviation of the portfolio is 4.5 percent. The portfolio's standard deviation is 7.21 percent if the correlation between the securities is +0.4. Try to derive these answers.[6]

Figure 5.3 graphs the effects of different degrees of correlation between the returns of Promus and Nextel in a portfolio, as examined in Illustration 5.10. When correlation is perfectly positive (+1.0) between the securities, portfolio risk is a simple weighted average of the standard deviations of the individual securities (point A). Less than perfect positive correlation offers better risk reduction; that is, diversification as at point B. Negative correlation among the securities offers even better diversification. Point C is an extreme case; the securities are perfectly negatively correlated.

[6]Standard deviation when correlation is −1

= [(0.06)^2 × (0.30)^2 + (0.09)^2 × (0.70)^2 + 2 × 0.06 × 0.09 × 0.30 × 0.70 × (−1)]$^{1/2}$
= 0.0449 or 4.5 percent

FIGURE 5.3

EFFECT OF CORRELATION ON DIVERSIFICATION

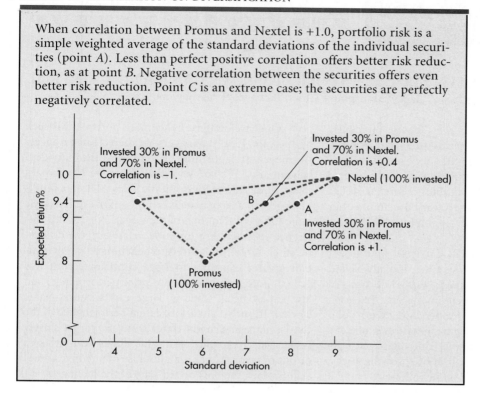

When correlation between Promus and Nextel is +1.0, portfolio risk is a simple weighted average of the standard deviations of the individual securities (point *A*). Less than perfect positive correlation offers better risk reduction, as at point *B*. Negative correlation between the securities offers even better risk reduction. Point *C* is an extreme case; the securities are perfectly negatively correlated.

We can eliminate portfolio risk entirely if the correlation between the Promus and Nextel securities is −1.0 *and* we construct the portfolio using the following proportions: 60 percent invested in the Promus security and 40 percent invested in the Nextel security.[7] The portfolio return becomes 8.8 percent and risk becomes 0 percent. Verify these answers.

If the portfolio expands to a third security, Sierra Computer Company, we need to *add* the following expressions to the standard deviation of the portfolio formula (Equation 5.4) before taking the square root:

> (Standard deviation of Sierra)^2 × (proportion invested in Sierra)^2
>
> + 2 × (standard deviation of Promus) × (standard deviation of Sierra) × (proportion invested in Promus) × (proportion invested in Sierra) × (correlation between returns of Promus and Sierra)
>
> + 2 × (standard deviation of Nextel) × (standard deviation of Sierra) × (proportion invested in Nextel) × (proportion invested in Sierra) × (correlation between returns of Nextel and Sierra)

(5.5)

---

[7]When correlation is −1.0, the proportion to invest in the Promus security, denoted W_{Promus}, to entirely eliminate risk is $W_{Promus} = \sigma_{Nextel} \div (\sigma_{Promus} + \sigma_{Nextel})$. σ_{Promus} and σ_{Nextel} are the standard deviations for returns for securities Promus and Nextel, respectively. The proportion to invest in the Nextel security is $1 - W_{Promus}$.

Executive Commentary

EXECUTIVE COMMENTARY: PORTFOLIO RISK ANALYSIS AND CONTROL

by Jeffery V. Bailey, Managing Partner, Richards & Tierney, Inc.

My firm, Richards & Tierney, focuses on identifying and controlling risk in the domestic equity portfolios of pension funds and other tax-exempt institutional investors. Many of the risk control concepts with which we deal are applicable to foreign stocks and domestic bonds. However, we have found that our resources are most effectively employed in domestic stocks.

When a company, such as Digital Equipment Corporation, hires our services, we initially spend considerable time reviewing the investment process of the pension fund's investment managers. For each manager, we design a specific benchmark portfolio that exhibits the persistent elements of the manager's investment style. For example, one manager may select primarily small capitalization growth stocks. This manager's portfolio is quite different from a portfolio composed of S&P 500 companies. The benchmark that we build for this manager includes the stocks of small companies with considerable growth potential. Furthermore, it will incorporate specific security selection criteria applied by the manager. That is, to reflect the manager's investment process, we might exclude all companies with equity values greater than $200 million and limit the benchmark's holdings in any one industry to 15 percent of the portfolio. We make every effort to involve the manager in constructing the benchmark, as only the manager can provide the subtle insights required to accurately capture her or his investment style.

If properly designed, the benchmark represents a neutral risk position for the manager. The portfolio manager's objective is to exceed the benchmark's performance. A comparison of the manager's actual portfolio performance relative to that of the benchmark provides a risk-adjusted measure of the manager's investment skill. We update the benchmark quarterly and periodically check it for consistency with the manager's investment style.

Once we design a benchmark portfolio for each of a pension fund's managers, we then create an aggregate benchmark portfolio by combining the individual benchmarks. We compare this aggregate benchmark to the fund's target for domestic stocks. Often a fund's managers in aggregate will exhibit an investment style quite different than that of the target. We call this difference *style bias*. For example, relative to the domestic stock target the aggregate benchmark might contain greater exposure to large companies with low growth potential, poor recent price performance, and low equity betas (that is, large capitalization value stocks). In such a situation, actual performance of the fund's managers might differ from the target simply because large capitalization value stocks were either in or out of favor, rather than because of any investment skill (or lack thereof) on the part of the managers.

We can control this style bias by creating a separate portfolio whose holdings are determined by the difference between the domestic target and the aggregate benchmark. In the previous example, the risk-control portfolio would emphasize small capitalization growth stocks while deemphasizing large capitalization value stocks. Correctly constructed, this portfolio will minimize style bias; in aggregate the managers' performance relative to the domestic stock target will be affected only by how well they perform against their benchmarks.

The final service that we provide to our clients is to analyze their managers' actual performances against their respective benchmarks. This analysis provides insights into which managers have been successful and why. When we conduct the analysis at the aggregate level, we focus on the investment program's success in exceeding the domestic stock target return and the ability of our risk-control portfolio to minimize style bias. We highlight problems, which in turn may suggest ways to improve portfolio risk control.

TABLE 5-2

NUMBER OF VARIANCES AND COVARIANCES IN A PORTFOLIO

Securities	Variance Expressions	Covariance Expressions
1	1	0
2	2	1
3	3	3
4	4	6
5	5	10
6	6	15
10	10	45
100	100	4,950
1,000	1,000	499,500

Adding a fourth security to the portfolio adds another weighted variance term and three more weighted covariance terms. The weighted variance term is for the fourth security. The weighted covariance terms represent how the fourth security interacts with the Promus security, with the Nextel security, and with the Sierra security. Table 5.2 shows the number of new variance and covariance expressions to add to the two-security portfolio formula as the size of the portfolio increases. We need a computer to solve for the portfolio's standard deviation once just a few securities are added to the portfolio.

Comprehension Check

1. How is portfolio return calculated?
2. How is portfolio risk measured?
3. What is the formula for the portfolio standard deviation when no correlation exists among the securities?
4. Why can a portfolio made up of two securities reduce risk even if both securities have the same standard deviation of returns?
5. What condition is necessary for a portfolio of two (or more) securities to reduce the risk of investing?
6. How is the portfolio's standard deviation calculated when dependency (correlation) exists among the securities?

5.4 THE CAPITAL ASSET PRICING MODEL

As Table 5.2 summarizes, the addition of more securities to a portfolio results in a proliferation of the number of calculations needed to determine risk. Fortunately, a model exists which greatly simplifies the problem. The model is called the capital asset pricing model, or CAPM.

The CAPM uses a benchmark portfolio for calculating correlation. This benchmark portfolio is defined theoretically as a market-value-weighted portfolio of *all* pos-

Market portfolio. An imaginary portfolio that includes all risky assets in proportion to their market value.

Efficient frontier. The frontier is the boundary line marking off the best risk-and-return combinations available to the investor.

Efficient investment. An investment offering the best expected return for a given risk, or the lowest risk for a given expected return.

Capital market line (CML). The relationship between risk and return in well-diversified portfolios.

sible risky investments. So, instead of finding the correlation between security returns for, say, Promus and Nextel, we find the correlation of each of these securities with the benchmark portfolio, called the **market portfolio.** In addition to using a market portfolio, the CAPM incorporates a risk-free asset (it has zero variance and zero covariance). A government Treasury bond represents the risk-free asset. The risk-free asset provides investors a small but positive return, r_f, for the time value of money.

Together, the CAPM uses the risk-free asset and the market portfolio in combination to represent the most efficient trade-off between risk and expected return, as illustrated in Figure 5.4. The curve *EF* is similar to the bowed curve segment *Promus-B-Nextel* in Figure 5.3. Only this time the curve *EF* consists of *all* assets formed into hundreds of different portfolios using different weighting combinations for the assets. For a moment, ignore the line *CML* in Figure 5.4. Then, the curve segment *EF* is the *efficient frontier*. The **efficient frontier** is the best risk-return combinations of all efficient portfolios or investments. An **efficient investment** has either more return than any other investment in its risk class or less risk than any other security with the same return. The efficient frontier of the opportunity set dominates all other investments in the opportunity set. In one portfolio the weight, or proportion, of funds invested in stock of Promus may be 1 percent, while in another portfolio this security may represent 6 percent of the value of the portfolio. These two different portfolios may be points *K* and *L* in Figure 5.4.

If lending and borrowing are permissible at the risk-free rate r_f, then the efficient frontier becomes the line denoted *CML*, which stands for *capital market line*. The **capital market line** represents the most efficient trade-off between risk and expected return for portfolios of assets. It says the expected return on an efficient portfolio, $E(r_p)$, is a linear function of its standard deviation, σ_p:

$$CML = r_f + \frac{(r_m - r_f)}{\sigma_m} \sigma_p \qquad (5.6)$$

FIGURE 5.4

CAPITAL MARKET LINE

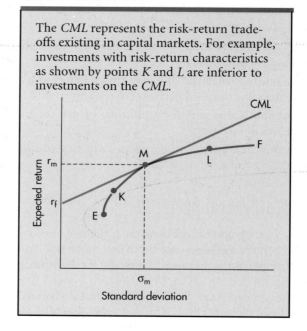

The *CML* represents the risk-return trade-offs existing in capital markets. For example, investments with risk-return characteristics as shown by points *K* and *L* are inferior to investments on the *CML*.

where $(r_m - r_f)/\sigma_m$ is the slope of the CML. We refer to the point M in Figure 5.4 as the market portfolio with return r_m and standard deviation σ_m. In practice, we usually represent the market portfolio M by a popular stock average, such as the S&P 500 index. The market portfolio represents the ultimate diversification.

Since the CML holds only for efficient portfolios, it does not describe the relationship between the rates of return on individual assets (or inefficient portfolios) and their standard deviations. A relationship for an individual asset that is similar to, and theoretically derived from, the CML is the CAPM, or as it is frequently called, the security market line (SML). We define it as:

$$E(r_i) = r_f + \beta_i \, [E(r_m) - r_f] \tag{5.7}$$

The advantage of this precise relationship is that risk (called *beta*, β_i) is the only asset-specific forecast that must be made in the CAPM to estimate a security's expected return, $E(r_i)$. Both the risk-free rate r_f and the expected market return $E(r_m)$ are forecasts that are the same from asset to asset. Once we know r_f and $E(r_m)$, we can forecast returns for every asset in the portfolio if we know each asset's beta. However, the task still before us is to define beta in the context of the CAPM.

5.4.1 Risk and the CAPM

Two types of risk influence individual assets:

- *Diversifiable* risk (also called *specific* or *unsystematic risk*).
- *Market* risk (also called *nondiversifiable* or *systematic risk*).

Remember that risk represents the variability of returns, both below and above the expected return. Diversification increases the chance that realized returns will be closer to expected returns. Therefore, diversification reduces the chance of the occurrence of both extreme negative and positive results. On the other hand, failure to diversify does not lead to higher expected return; it simply puts investors at more risk.

Diversifiable risk is risk specific to a particular security. It arises from events about the security and how these events affect investors' perceptions of the security's outlook and value. Examples include the unexpected death of the company's president, gold discovered on the company's property, or the recall of defective products sold by the company. Diversifiable risk is unexpected, unpredictable. The financial market does not reward investors with high return for having diversifiable risk in their portfolios.

Diversifiable risk. The amount of risk that can be eliminated through proper diversification.

Research shows that a small amount of diversification reduces most of the diversifiable risk. Table 5.3 suggests that investors realize the major benefits of diversification as the portfolio size increases to about 10 to 20 securities. Beyond this size, further diversification results in minor risk reduction. Of course, for diversification to be effective, the portfolio's securities must not all respond to every market influence in the same way. For example, a portfolio consisting of ten airline stocks is poorly diversified because the securities are highly correlated. Each airline stock has some unique characteristics and influences, but there are very strong influences such as energy costs on airline stocks as a group. Airline stocks tend to move together. Effective diversification requires the securities in the portfolio to have reasonably low correlation with each other.

Risk that cannot be diversified is called **market risk.** We associate market risk with movements in the overall market and the economy in total. Socioeconomic and political events that affect the returns of all assets cause market risk. For example, an outburst of inflation may affect different companies in different ways, but it affects all

Market risk. The variability of investment returns that cannot be eliminated through diversification. Also called nondiversifiable risk or systematic risk.

TABLE 5-3

PORTFOLIO SIZE AND RISK REDUCTION

Number of Stocks in Portfolio	Average Standard Deviation of Annual Portfolio Returns	Ratio of Portfolio Standard Deviation to Standard Deviation of a Single Stock
1	49.24%	1.00
2	37.36	0.76
4	29.69	0.60
6	26.64	0.54
8	24.98	0.51
10	23.93	0.49
20	21.68	0.44
30	20.87	0.42
40	20.46	0.42
50	20.20	0.41
100	19.69	0.40
200	19.42	0.39
300	19.34	0.39
400	19.29	0.39
500	19.27	0.39
1000	19.21	0.39

These figures are from Table 1 in Meir Statman, "How Many Stocks Make a Diversified Portfolio?" Journal of Financial and Quantitative Analysis *(September 1987), pp. 353–364.*

companies to some extent. Or consider this example. A public utility company relying on coal-fired generators may be relatively immune to rising oil prices; thus, its market risk may be lower than that of the market as a whole. Market risk, then, is an estimate of how the expected returns from an asset or portfolio will move relative to the returns from the market portfolio. If individual securities either exaggerate or understate the stock market's moves, then they carry varying degrees of market risk. Market risk varies from security to security and from industry to industry.

Figure 5.5 depicts diversification and risk. The horizontal axis shows the number of securities included in the portfolio. The vertical axis shows the standard deviation of returns across the entire group of securities, or portfolio risk. The curved line shows the amount of risk for different portfolio sizes. Risk declines to some minimum level as the number of securities in the portfolio increases. This minimum level represents market risk. As the lower diagram shows, a portfolio of high-quality stocks (such as General Electric, Coca-Cola, J.P. Morgan, and AT&T) has less market risk than does a portfolio of lower-quality stocks (such as U.S. Surgical, Dell Computer, and CML Group).

However, no matter how many securities we include in a portfolio, we cannot eliminate market risk. We can reduce it by investing in high-quality securities. We can diversify across international financial markets to lower the market risk. However, we cannot eliminate market risk unless we get out of the market altogether.

FIGURE 5.5

DIVERSIFIABLE AND MARKET RISKS

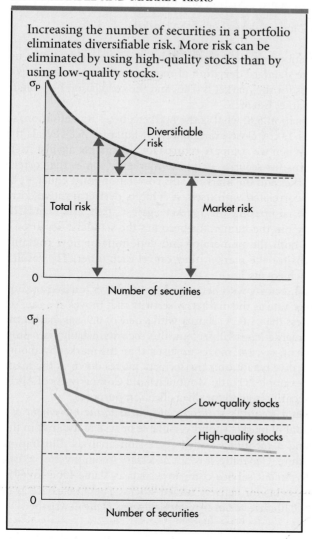

Increasing the number of securities in a portfolio eliminates diversifiable risk. More risk can be eliminated by using high-quality stocks than by using low-quality stocks.

5.4.2 Measuring Market Risk

Most securities respond differently to movements of the financial market and have different levels of market risk. How can we measure this risk? The CAPM provides a simple and convenient estimate of market risk called *beta*, β. The formal definition of **beta** for security *i* is:[8]

Beta. A measure of a security's nondiversifiable risk; shows the relationship between an individual security's performance and the performance of a market index.

---

[8]The mathematical expression for stock *i*'s beta, $β_i$, is:

$$β_i = \frac{ρ_{im}σ_i}{σ_m}$$

where

$ρ_{i,m}$ = Correlation between security *i* and the market, *m*
$σ_i$ = Standard deviation of returns for security *i*
$σ_m$ = Standard deviation of returns for the market

$$\beta_i = \text{(Correlation between the returns for security } i \text{ and the market)}$$

$$\times \text{ (standard deviation of returns for security } i\text{)} \qquad (5.8)$$

$$\div \text{ (standard deviation of the market)}$$

Although the equation may look formidable, it is relatively easy to use. Prove that $\beta = 0.87$ where the standard deviation of returns for the security is 0.60, the standard deviation of returns for the market is 0.45, and the correlation between returns for the security and the market is 0.65.[9]

Based on Equation 5.8, what is the market's beta? By definition, the beta of the market portfolio is 1.0. A close examination of Equation 5.8 reveals that the market beta must be 1.0. When we compare returns for the market against itself, the correlation between returns for security i and the market becomes the correlation between returns for the market and the market. This correlation must equal +1 because whenever something is correlated with itself, it exhibits perfect positive correlation of +1. Also, since we are comparing the market against itself, the standard deviation of returns for security i in the numerator becomes the standard deviation of returns for the market. Since both the numerator and denominator now contain the standard deviation of returns for the market, they cancel each other. The result is the market portfolio beta, which equals 1.

An individual security with beta equal to 1.0 moves, on average, up and down at the same percentage rate as the market. A security that moves at a rate slower than the market has a beta less than 1.0. A security with a beta of 0.9 lags market moves by about 10 percent. If the market rises 10 percent, this security usually rises only 9 percent. A security with a beta of, say, 1.4, moves up faster than the market by about 40 percent. A security with a negative beta means the security moves down as the market moves up, and vice versa. An example is Battle Mountain Gold Company. As of April 1994, its beta was –0.7. Such a security is good for diversification purposes.

Beta measures a security's sensitivity of returns to the movement of the market. It measures the amount of market (nondiversifiable or systematic) risk in the security. We calculate beta using a technique called regression analysis. Illustration 5.11 briefly explains the procedure. Generally, it is not necessary for an investor to calculate a security's beta. An investment service company, such as Value Line Investment Services, regularly publishes betas for actively traded stocks. These betas are available at most metropolitan public libraries or in *Investor's Business Daily* newspaper.

ILLUSTRATION 5.11

Calculating beta

Regression analysis is a mathematical procedure based on the *least-squares method,* which is discussed in most introductory quantitative business analysis courses. The graph shows the results of applying the technique. The technique fits a straight line to the relationship that exists between the scatter diagram for returns on security i (r_i) and returns on a proxy for the market portfolio (r_m), say, the S&P 500 index. This straight line minimizes the sum of the squared deviations between the observed data and the fitted line.

[9]Solution: $\beta = 0.65 \times 0.60 \div 0.45 = 0.87$

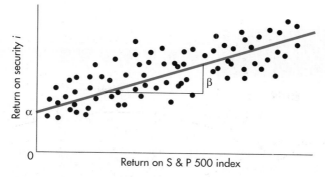

The regression equation for the straight line is:

$$r_i = \alpha_i + \beta_i\, r_m + \epsilon_i.$$

We cannot observe the intercept α and the slope of the line β. Rather we observe the past returns r_i on security i and the returns on the market r_m and estimate α and β. Most elementary statistics books develop the equations to compute α and β.[10] ϵ is an error term with expected value of zero.

The Financial Reality reading on page 172 discusses how a very successful money manager selects stocks using the CAPM's beta calculation technique outlined in Illustration 5.11.

5.4.3 Portfolio Beta

The beta of an individual security does not represent its total riskiness, as already discussed. A *security's beta* is the *amount of market risk the security contributes to a diversified portfolio.* As each security has a beta, so does each portfolio. However, a *portfolio beta* is the riskiness of the total portfolio in relation to the market. The portfolio beta defines the riskiness of the portfolio, and it is portfolio risk that determines the return investors expect to earn. Formally, **portfolio beta,** β_p, is calculated as follows:

> **Portfolio beta.** An index representing the undiversifiable risk of a group of stocks formed into a portfolio.

Portfolio beta
= Beta of security #1 × proportion of funds in security #1
+ beta of security #2 × proportion of funds in security #2
+ beta of security #3 × proportion of funds in security #3   (5.9)
+ . . .
+ beta of security N × proportion of funds in security N

The betas of the individual securities are weighted by their individual market values as a proportion of the total market value of the portfolio, as shown in Illustration 5.12.

---

[10]Statistical tests check if α and β are different from zero. A measure called the *coefficient of determination* is the goodness of fit of the line to the data. It measures the explained proportion of the total variation in the stock's returns and can take any value between 0 and 1. The closer the coefficient of determination is to 1, the better the line fits the data. The coefficient of determination is the square of the correlation coefficient. For instance, in footnote 8, the correlation coefficient between security i and the market m is denoted $\rho_{i,m}$. If the correlation coefficient is 0.7, then the coefficient of determination is 0.49. The regression line explains 49 percent of the variation in the data.

AN ALPHA-BETA MAN

Risk versus reward analysis is the basis for successful investing. Many approaches exist to pick stocks to invest in. Louis Nevellier relies on capital asset pricing theory, or as the article refers to it, modern portfolio theory.

Navellier's $150-a-year *OTC Insight* letter, published monthly, has a remarkable record. And he's doing it all with modern portfolio theory (MPT), the rigorously quantitative, academically approved investment technique that scared Wall Street when it burst out of the business schools in the 1970s but more recently has been greeted with resounding yawns.

OTC Insight's performance is a matter of public record, because since 1985 it has been one of about 100 such advisory services monitored by the *Hulbert Financial Digest,* arbiter of the investment letter industry. Navellier concentrates on relatively obscure over-the-counter stocks.

The operating assumption of the *OTC Insight* is that the stock market is not completely efficient—it does not discount information so quickly that it cannot be outguessed.

Every month Navellier's computer begins by inspecting a database containing 1000 over-the-counter stocks. For each one, it crunches out a "beta" and an "alpha." Beta in MPT-speak is the extent to which a stock's fluctuation is related to the movement of the market. A beta of 2 would mean that a stock goes up (or down) twice as much as the average. Alpha represents the stock's propensity to move independently of the market.

Navellier's computer calculates betas and alphas over a 12-month period; this has proved more sensitive to market movements than the five years usually favored in academe. The computer works out each stock's mean monthly rate of return. Additionally, it computes the variance for the mean monthly return, a statistical measure that helps tell how likely the return is to occur.

Got that? Now, the crucial step: The computer divides each stock's alpha by its monthly variance of return. This gives a reward/risk ratio—the market-independent gain per unit of volatility. The computer then lists the top 98 stocks in order of reward/risk. This constitutes the *OTC Insight Buy List*—those stocks for which the reward potential is highest relative to the risk involved.

For the *OTC Insight* model portfolio, Navellier uses only the top 20 or so buy list stocks. At this stage, he doesn't hesitate to contaminate the process by inserting his own eyeball. "I like stocks with strong earnings growth, in low-risk industries, preferably dominating their market niches," he says.

Navellier and his partner are now investigating the extension of his system to listed stocks. "But to be very frank with you," says Navellier, "the stock market is much more efficient in listed stocks. There's no way we are going to get the same returns."

Adapted from Peter Brimelow, "An Alpha-Beta Man," *Forbes,* October 6, 1986, pp. 62, 64.
Reprinted by permission of FORBES magazine ©, FORBES, Inc.

ILLUSTRATION 5.12

Portfolio beta | The treasurer of Eastman Paper Company purchased five securities to include in a portfolio. Each security's beta and the proportion that each security represents of the portfolio's market value are as follows:

	Beta	Weight
Security A	1.5	0.10
Security B	0.6	0.30
Security C	0.9	0.20
Security D	2.0	0.15
Security E	−0.3	0.25
		1.00

The portfolio beta is 0.735.

Portfolio beta

$$
\begin{aligned}
&= \text{Beta of security } A \times \text{proportion of funds in security } A \\
&\quad + \text{beta of security } B \times \text{proportion of funds in security } B \\
&\quad + \text{beta of security } C \times \text{proportion of funds in security } C \\
&\quad + \text{beta of security } D \times \text{proportion of funds in security } D \\
&\quad + \text{beta of security } E \times \text{proportion of funds in security } E \\
&= 1.5 \times 0.10 + 0.6 \times 0.30 + 0.9 \times 0.20 + 2.0 \times 0.15 \\
&\quad + (-0.3) \times 0.25 \\
&= 0.735
\end{aligned}
$$

A portfolio beta has another important usage. It allows us to compare the performance of different investors. One investor can achieve higher returns—and incur higher risk—than another investor, but that does not mean the first investor is a superior investor. Beta adjusts returns for the amount of risk involved. This adjustment makes portfolio comparisons possible, as shown in Illustration 5.13. Beta-risk adjustment is an important tool used by professionals such as pension fund administrators who must evaluate prospective investment managers on the basis of past performance.

ILLUSTRATION 5.13

Comparing portfolio returns

Jack Treynor developed an index to rate **mutual fund** performance.[11] He reasoned that investors should diversify away all diversifiable risk, leaving beta as the appropriate market risk measure. The top-ranked mutual fund is then the fund providing the highest return per unit of risk taken.

The **Treynor index** is defined as:

$$
\frac{\text{(Average return on the portfolio)} - \text{(average risk-free interest rate)}}{\text{Beta of the portfolio}}
$$

EXAMPLE:

	Average Portfolio Return	Portfolio Beta
Portfolio 1	0.15	1.5
Portfolio 2	0.10	0.5

Average risk-free rate = 0.04

Mutual fund. An investment company that issues redeemable shares (sometimes called units) to the public and invests the proceeds in a portfolio of securities.

Treynor index. A measure of reward per unit of risk. It indicates the rate of return on the market index required to make the expected rate of return on a portfolio equal to the risk-free rate.

[11]Jack Treynor, "How to Rate Management of Investment Funds," *Harvard Business Review* (January–February 1965), pp. 63–75.

For portfolio 1, the Treynor index is 0.073:

$$\frac{0.15 - 0.04}{1.5} = 0.073$$

Portfolio 2 has a Treynor index of 0.12:

$$\frac{0.10 - 0.04}{0.5} = 0.12$$

The second portfolio provides superior return relative to market (nondiversifiable) risk.

Comprehension Check

1. Distinguish between diversifiable risk and market risk. What other terms may be used for each of these types of risk?
2. Why can an investor not eliminate market risk from a portfolio?
3. About how many securities do you need to achieve the major benefits of diversification?
4. Why would a portfolio consisting of 20 public utility stocks not provide an investor with an effectively diversified portfolio of common stocks?
5. What are the benefits of investing in a diversified portfolio of securities rather than simply selecting a single good security and sticking with it? What does a person give up when investing in a diversified portfolio?
6. Why is the beta of the market defined as 1.0?
7. How is the beta of a portfolio created?
8. How is the Treynor index calculated?

5.5 SOME CAUTIONS ABOUT BETA

The calculation of beta (shown in Illustration 5.11) compares the historical behavior of returns of the security with the historical behavior of returns of the market over many periods. The result of the calculation reveals an *average* relationship between the security's returns and the market's returns. The important word is *average*. No security follows the market perfectly all the time. In calculating beta for, say, Texaco Company's stock, β_{Texaco}, we only get an average relationship between Texaco's stock and the market; a tendency, not a rule. Even if we could predict the action of the market, β_{Texaco} is neither a reliable nor an accurate predictor of Texaco's stock action. *The reason is that market risk is too small a part of the total variability in the returns of an individual security.* Diversifiable risk is much more significant than market risk. The riskiness of an individual security is best described by its standard deviation of returns.

To use beta to predict the future is an uncertain proposition. Research shows that the calculated beta, using historical data, is a poor predictor of a stock's future beta. Table 5.4 provides evidence of the instability of beta for most of the stocks included in the **Dow Jones Industrial Average,** a popular gauge of stock market performance.

If we look up beta values provided by different investment services companies, we are likely to find that the quoted values differ from one investment services company to

Dow Jones Industrial Average. A price index of 30 listed stocks. The price of the stocks is added and divided by a number that adjusts for stock splits. An example of a stock split is when a share selling for $90 is split into two shares selling for $45 each.

TABLE 5-4

INSTABILITY OF β VALUES OVER TIME

Name	1986	1988	1990	1992
Alcoa	1.13	1.59	1.20	1.44
AT&T	1.19	1.43	1.33	0.87
Bethlehem Steel	1.74	2.02	1.19	2.06
Boeing	1.13	1.45	1.88	0.93
Caterpillar	1.30	1.56	1.25	1.47
Chevron	0.97	1.56	0.73	0.36
Coca Cola	1.63	1.63	1.69	1.06
Disney	1.73	1.50	1.64	1.41
Du Pont	1.38	1.58	1.35	1.09
Kodak	1.08	1.52	1.33	0.72
Exxon	1.03	1.66	0.63	0.25
General Electric	1.42	1.79	1.51	1.00
General Motors	0.94	1.43	1.39	1.79
Goodyear	1.15	1.40	1.08	1.55
IBM	0.90	1.39	1.09	0.90
International Paper	1.14	1.99	1.09	1.36
McDonalds	1.29	1.50	1.51	1.01
Merck	1.40	1.58	1.42	0.89
3M	1.14	1.63	1.16	0.65
J.P. Morgan	1.39	1.50	1.40	1.07
Procter & Gamble	1.26	1.26	1.59	1.08
Sears	1.69	1.54	1.36	1.00
Texaco	0.89	0.82	0.57	0.49
Union Carbide	1.05	1.93	1.16	1.73
United Technologies	1.39	1.35	1.20	1.07
Westinghouse	1.48	1.70	1.40	1.20

The betas are calculated using the model discussed in Illustration 5.11. Five years of monthly returns were used for each security. The S&P 500 index represented the market return.

another for the same stock. For example, Table 5.5 shows different betas for popular stocks trading in October 1993. The betas for the same company differ because the investment services companies who publish *Value Line Investment Survey* and *Daily Graphs* use different methods to calculate them. Still other organizations use different techniques to calculate beta. Some organizations use only past price changes to form estimates, while others smooth these past estimates. Some organizations use weekly data, while others use monthly data. Some organizations use the S&P 500 stock index as a proxy for the market, while others use the **New York Stock Exchange Composite Index.** Other differences may also exist. Thus, it is hardly surprising that the beta estimates differ from one source to another.[12]

New York Stock Exchange Composite Index. Value-weighted price index based on all stocks traded on the New York Stock Exchange. Value-weighted means the market value of the firm's equity, relative to the aggregate equity market value of all firms traded on the exchange.

---

[12]Frank K. Reilly and David J. Wright, "A Comparison of Published Betas," *Journal of Portfolio Management* (Spring 1988), pp. 64–69, suggest that the different interval measure (weekly versus monthly) is the primary reason for different beta estimates. It seems that shorter intervals lead to understated betas for small-sized firms and overstated betas for large-size firms.

TABLE 5-5

BETAS—OH HOW THEY VARY

Name	Value Line	Daily Graphs
Advanced Micro Devices	1.60	2.04
Amgen	1.30	0.49
A. G. Edwards	1.65	2.08
Gap	1.40	1.12
Omnicare	1.10	0.77
Schwab, Charles	1.80	2.41
Sterling Software	1.40	1.81
Teradyne	1.25	2.55
Thor Industries	0.75	0.66
U.S. Surgical	1.30	1.26
Wausau Paper	1.00	1.33

The beta values were published within two weeks of each other in March 1994 by Value Line Investment Services and by Daily Graphs, Inc.

A security's beta measures the risk contribution of the security to a well-diversified portfolio, the riskiness for which investors are to be rewarded. Historical evidence confirms that high-beta securities (hence high-beta portfolios) do yield higher returns, but there are some warnings.[13]

- *Actual stock returns are not proportional to* β. High-beta stocks do not achieve returns as high as we might expect. This means that the additional risk is only partially rewarded. Fortunately, the discrepancy is not large.
- *Risk cuts two ways.* High-beta portfolios achieve high returns over time, but in the short run they simply exaggerate the market trend. When the trend is positive, high-risk investors are richly rewarded, but when the market turns down, they are correspondingly punished.
- *β may fail to work.* Sometimes low-beta stocks are leaders in strong uptrending, or *bull,* markets, and sometimes high-beta stocks perform better in declining, or *bear,* markets. These phenomena can occur when major shifts in investors' perceptions of different types of stocks take place. Growth in firms' income may be in vogue during one period, while stability and strong balance sheets are fashionable in another period.

There is another warning about beta. In recent years, beta has come under attack as a useful measure of risk. Two professors from the University of Chicago, Eugene Fama, who helped make beta popular, and Kenneth French, conclude that beta is the wrong measure of risk.[14] If beta is an inappropriate predictor of risk, then perhaps risk is not related to returns in the way financial theorists have predicted for about three decades. Does this

[13]Some statistical problems exist in measuring beta. However, such a discussion is beyond the scope of this book.

[14]Eugene F. Fama and Kenneth R. French, "The Cross Section of Expected Stock Returns," *Journal of Finance* (June 1992), pp. 427–465.

mean that the capital asset pricing model is the wrong model? These findings are highly controversial and scholars are hard at work trying to prove Fama and French wrong.

 **Comprehension Check**

1. Comment on the stability of betas for individual stocks over time. Why might betas calculated by different investment advisory services be different for the same stock?

2. How can individual stock betas and portfolio betas be useful to investors?

3. What are some of the limitations of beta analysis for investors?

5.6 THE NEXT STEP

We've come to the end of Part II of the text. The time value of money concepts and the risk-return principles discussed in this part lay an important foundation for our discussion in Part III, the valuation of securities. The daily price quotes for stocks and bonds, as shown in newspapers and reported on radio and television, are based on investors' forecasts of future cash flows discounted to the current time. The aggregation of value of a firm's bonds and stocks held by investors represents a proxy of the company's value. We will see in the next several chapters how this value differs from the value accountants show in financial statements, as we reviewed in Chapter 2.

SUMMARY

EVALUATING RISK

- An investment is risky if the outcome is uncertain.
- Risk is the variability of possible returns, usually measured by the standard deviation of returns.
- Expected return is a weighted average of all possible returns, where the weights are the chance the outcome occurs. Expected return can differ from average return.
- Securities with greater risk offer investors larger risk premiums.

RISK AVERSION

- Most people are risk averse; they prefer less risk to more risk. For a given expected return, they seek the investment with the lowest risk.

DIVERSIFYING TO REDUCE RISK

- Forming securities into portfolios provides the investor with risk reduction, regardless if the securities are correlated (dependent) or not with each other.
- Portfolio risk is the standard deviation of returns for the portfolio.
- Perfectly correlated securities allow no risk reduction by forming the securities into a portfolio. The largest risk reduction occurs when correlation between securities is negative.

THE CAPITAL ASSET PRICING MODEL

- The capital asset pricing model simplifies pricing of assets. Instead of finding the correlations between each pair of securities, each security is assumed to be correlated with a market portfolio which includes all risky assets.
- Two types of risk influence securities: diversifiable risk and market risk. Diversifiable risk can be eliminated in a portfolio. Market risk is nondiversifiable risk associated with the market and the economy in total.
- Market risk is measured by beta in the capital asset pricing model.
- Portfolio risk is the risk of a portfolio. In a well-diversified portfolio, portfolio risk is market risk. In a less well-diversified portfolio, portfolio risk consists of market risk and some diversifiable risk not eliminated.
- A portfolio with about 20 securities representing different business sectors eliminates practically all the diversifiable risk.
- A security with a beta of 1.0 is as risky as the market; a security with a beta above 1.0 means the security is riskier than the market; a security with a beta below 1.0 means the security is less risky than the market.
- Individual security betas change over time.
- A portfolio's beta is simply a weighted average of the betas of securities in the portfolio. The portfolio beta measures the riskiness of the total portfolio in relation to the market.

SOME CAUTIONS ABOUT BETA

- Beta shows the average relationship a company's historical stock returns exhibit with the market's historical stock returns.
- Beta is unstable over time and has some limitations. Actual stock returns are not proportional to beta. Beta may fail to work. Generally high-beta stocks are leaders in a bull market, but sometimes low-beta stocks are the leaders, and vice versa in a bear market.
- There is concern that beta is an inappropriate measure of risk.

FURTHER READING ▼▼▼▼▼▼▼▼▼▼▼

Harrington, Diana R., *Modern Portfolio Theory & the Capital Asset Pricing Model: A User's Guide*, Englewood Cliffs, NJ: Prentice Hall, Inc., 1983. An excellent book designed for the practitioner dealing with portfolio analysis from either the investment or corporate perspective.

Peters, Edgar E., *Chaos and Order in the Capital Markets*, New York: John Wiley & Sons, Inc., 1991. This book questions perceived theory of risk and return.

Valentine, Jerome L., and Edmund A. Mennis, *Quantitative Techniques for Financial Analysis*, 2nd ed., Homewood, IL: Richard D. Irwin, Inc., 1980. This book is about practical applications of quantitative tools to the techniques of professional financial analysis and portfolio management.

SELF-TEST PROBLEMS ▼▼▼▼▼▼▼▼▼▼▼

ST5-1. Consider an investment which has the following probability distribution of returns, given different economic conditions:

Economic Conditions	Probability	Return Rate
Boom times	0.25	40%
Normal times	0.40	20
Recession times	0.30	0
Depression times	0.05	−20

a. Calculate the expected return on this investment.
b. Calculate the standard deviation of returns.

ST5-2. If Helen purchases the following four securities, what is the beta of her portfolio? What does the portfolio beta suggest about her attitude toward investment in securities?

Security	Beta	Amount
KAT	1.6	$25,000
LRK	1.2	20,000
NMX	0.9	30,000
SPS	1.1	25,000

ST5-3. Bryan received information about two mutual funds. In studying the past performance of each fund, he discovered the following information:

Mutual Fund	Return	Beta
Growth Prospects Fund	23%	1.8
Fundamentals Fund	11	1.0

The average risk-free rate is 3 percent.
a. Calculate the Treynor index for each fund.
b. Which fund provides the superior return to risk?

PROBLEMS ▼▼▼▼▼▼▼▼▼▼▼▼

EVALUATING RISK

5-1. Carol is considering an investment with payoffs dependent on what happens to the economy. She thinks the following scenarios are representative of what could happen. What is the expected return for this investment?

State of Economy	Probability	Return
Recession	0.15	-20%
Recovery	0.15	10
Normal	0.50	16
Boom	0.20	30

5-2. Ward is evaluating a proposed investment for his company. He estimates that if there is a recession, the return on the investment will be a loss of 10 percent, if the industry booms the investment will return 40 percent, and if business is normal the return will be 20 percent. The respective probabilities of these results occurring are 20 percent, 25 percent, and 55 percent. Calculate the expected return on the proposed investment.

5-3. Calculate the standard deviation of the following cash flows.

Possible Outcome	Value	Probability
1	$100	0.25
2	500	0.50
3	700	0.25

5-4. Gary is considering an investment which has the following probability distribution of returns for different economic conditions:

Economic Conditions	Probability	Return
Boom times	0.20	30%
Normal	0.30	10
Recession	0.40	0
Depression	0.10	−15

a. Calculate the expected return for this investment.
b. Calculate the standard deviation of returns.

5-5. Calculate the expected return on the market, the variance of returns on the market, and the standard deviation of the returns on the market.

Year	S&P 500
1	−0.75%
2	1.73
3	1.73
4	−3.27
5	−3.46
6	4.97

5-6. A Wall Street economist estimates the likelihood of future states of the economy and corresponding stock market returns as follows:

State	Probability	Market Return
Recession	0.10	−0.14
No growth	0.20	0.10
Slow growth	0.45	0.20
High growth	0.25	0.28

Calculate the expected return, the variance, and the standard deviation.

5-7. Based on analysis of past performance, an analyst estimates the possible prices for Santa Fe Pottery Company's common stock as follows:

Probability	Price
0.10	$ 8
0.10	12
0.35	20
0.30	25
0.15	35

    a. Calculate the expected value of the stock price.

    b. Calculate the standard deviation of the stock price.

5-8. a. GM offers a possible return of either 4 percent or 16 percent with each outcome as equally probable. Calculate the expected rate of return, variance, and standard deviation.

    b. GE offers possible returns of 5 percent, 7 percent, 9 percent, or 11 percent with each outcome being equally probable. Calculate the expected rate of return, variance, and standard deviation.

    c. Given the facts developed in parts (a) and (b), do you have sufficient information on which to base a choice between GM and GE?

    d. Is there enough information to make a choice if the correlation of GM with the market portfolio is -0.40 and the correlation of GE with the market portfolio is 0.60?

5-9. The average return for a large common stock portfolio over the years has been 14.2 percent and the standard deviation of returns for the portfolio has been 34 percent.

    a. What is the risk-to-reward ratio for this portfolio? Compare your answer with the risk-to-reward ratio for the S&P 500 index given in Table 5.1 and comment on the difference.

    b. If a friend of yours is extremely risk averse, would you advise her to invest in the common stock portfolio? Why?

5-10. Given the common stock portfolio described in Problem 5-9, what is its historical risk premium if the return on U.S. Treasury bills is 3.5 percent?

RISK AVERSION

5-11. How should the probable attitude toward investment risk of each of the following persons be categorized?

    a. A retired person living on social security payments.

    b. A college graduate, five years after graduation employed in a career position.

    c. A person buying a lottery ticket at the supermarket.

    d. A division manager making investment decisions for the company's manufacturing plant.

DIVERSIFYING TO REDUCE RISK

5-12. Ms. Morrissey has $10,000 invested with 30 percent of it invested in Hall Printing Company and 70 percent invested in Simon Communications, Inc. The expected return on Hall stock is 15 percent, whereas the stock of Simon has an expected return of 9 percent.

a. What is the expected dollar return on her portfolio?

b. What is the expected percentage rate of return on her portfolio?

5-13. Chuck Myler's securities portfolio has the following market values and expected returns:

Security	Market Value	Expected Return
Allied Signal	$ 6,500	12%
Disney	8,600	16
Intel	10,100	18
Pepsi	7,400	15
Syntex	3,800	14

a. What is the expected dollar return for the portfolio?

b. What is the expected percentage rate of return for the portfolio?

5-14. Each time that America East Airline stock sees a 1 percent jump in rate of return, Dial Food Company sees a 0.5 percent increase. What does this indicate to you about the correlation between the two stocks?

5-15. a. What is the difference between variance and covariance?

b. How many variances and covariances are in 1, 2, 3, 10, 100, and 1000 securities portfolios?

5-16. Mitch wants to build a portfolio with equal dollar amounts invested in two stocks which have the following characteristics:

	Stock A	Stock B
Expected return	0.10	0.15
Standard deviation	0.20	0.35

Compute the expected return and variance of the portfolio under each of the following assumptions about the correlations between returns of stocks A and B:

$$\text{Correlation} = 1$$
$$\text{Correlation} = 0$$
$$\text{Correlation} = -1$$

5-17. The treasurer of Busch Limited is considering investing 60 percent of the company's surplus funds in stock A and the balance in stock B. The standard deviation of return on A is 8 percent and on B it is 16 percent. Calculate the variance of the portfolio returns assuming the following correlations between the stocks: 1.0, 0.5, and 0.

5-18. A prominent Shearson stockbroker believes there is a 40 percent chance that Stanford Company stock will decline by 10 percent and a 60 percent chance that it will increase by 20 percent. Correspondingly, the stock of Berkeley Incorporated has a 30 percent chance of a 10 percent decline and a 70 percent chance of a 20 percent rise. The correlation between the two stocks is 0.80. Calculate the expected return, the variance, and the standard deviation for each stock. What is the covariance between the stock returns?

5-19. Two securities have the following characteristics:

Security	A	B
Expected return	0.15	0.10
Standard deviation	0.09	0.12

The correlation coefficient of security A with security B is –1.0. Calculate the expected returns and standard deviations of each of the following portfolios of the two securities. Plot the securities and the portfolios consisting of the securities on a graph with expected return and standard deviation on the axes.

	Investment in Security	
	A	B
Portfolio 1	2.0	−1.0
Portfolio 2	0.5	0.5
Portfolio 3	0.3	0.7
Portfolio 4	−0.5	1.5

5-20. The expected returns on securities are estimated as follows:

State	Probability	Security A	Security B
1	0.25	−0.20	0.15
2	0.30	0.10	0.12
3	0.25	0.16	0.08
4	0.20	0.25	−0.18

a. What is the expected return for each security?
b. Calculate the variance for each security.
c. If equal amounts are invested in each security, what is the expected return on the portfolio?
d. What is the variance of the portfolio return if the correlation between the securities is 0.9?

5-21. Common stocks that Mr. Garrett is considering investing in have the following characteristics:

Company	Expected Return	Standard Deviation
CML	6%	10%
Flex	15	12
Max	20	14

The correlations of all possible pairs are:
CML and Flex = −0.9; CML and Max = 0.0; Flex and Max = 0.5

a. Calculate the expected return of a portfolio with equal amounts invested in each security.

b. Calculate the standard deviation of the portfolio.

5-22. The expected stock returns for companies A, B, C, and D are 20 percent, 10 percent, 12 percent, and 9 percent, respectively.

a. If equal amounts are invested in each security, prove that the portfolio's expected return is 12.75 percent.

b. Calculate the variance of the portfolio. The correlations and variances of each stock are as follows:

Correlations	A	B	C	D
B	0.40			
C	0.50	0.20		
D	−0.10	−0.15	−0.05	
Variances	0.05	0.18	0.03	0.12

5-23. Securities A, B, and C have the following possible returns for different states of the world:

		% Rates of Return on Stocks		
State	Probability	A	B	C
1	0.20	12%	8%	1%
2	0.25	9	6	4
3	0.30	5	3	5
4	0.15	−1	2	6
5	0.10	−6	1	11

The covariance between securities is: A and B = 11.772; A and C = −13.980; and B and C = −5.680.

a. Calculate the expected return for each security.

b. Calculate the variance of each security.

c. Calculate the correlation between each pair of securities. (*Hint:* Correlation between security i and security j is defined as [covariance of returns between the two securities] ÷ [standard deviation of i × standard deviation of j]).

5-24. Contrarian Corporation's stock has possible returns of 0 percent and 40 percent with equal probability—its standard deviation is 20 percent. Optimistic Company's possible returns are 20 percent and 10 percent with equal probability—its standard deviation is 5 percent. If the returns for the two securities are perfectly negatively correlated, can a risk-free portfolio be constructed using just these two securities? (*Hint:* See footnote 7.) If so, what proportion of funds should be invested in each security?

THE CAPITAL ASSET PRICING MODEL

5-25. In January of this past year, Edwards & Lynch Brokerage Inc. reported the following betas:

Company	Beta
IBM	0.95
Bally	1.40
Cigna	1.00
British Telecom	0.60

a. What is the interpretation of these betas?
b. Is the expected return of British Telecom less than that of IBM?
c. Cigna's beta equals the beta of the market portfolio. Thus, if you want to mimic market returns all you need do is buy stock in Cigna. Is this statement correct?
d. Suppose you picked up a ten-year-old report issued by Edwards & Lynch Brokerage. Would the betas of the companies be the same as reported previously? Why or why not?

5-26. The beta of Ramtec Corporation is 1.5. If the rate of return on the market goes from 15 percent to 5 percent, what would you expect to happen to the rate of return on the firm? Explain.

5-27. The beta of a diversified portfolio is 1.4. If the rate of return on the market goes from 10 percent to 5 percent, what would you expect to happen to the rate of return on the portfolio? Explain.

5-28. The beta of a diversified portfolio is 1.2. The rate of return on the market goes from 7 percent to 12 percent.

a. What would you expect to happen to the rate of return on the portfolio? Explain.
b. What would you expect to happen to the prices of the individual securities in the portfolio given the changes that occurred in the market rate of return?

5-29. Janice has just received an inheritance of $100,000. After spending $19,000 on a new car, she invested the remainder in equal dollar amounts in the following stocks:

Security	Beta	Security	Beta
AET	0.9	LLY	1.0
CSR	0.8	MYG	0.9
DIS	1.2	MCD	1.1
EMR	1.1	PPG	1.2

a. Calculate the beta for Janice's portfolio.
b. Comment on Janice's apparent attitude toward investment risk.

5-30. If Eileen purchases the following five securities, what is the beta of her portfolio? What does the portfolio's beta suggest about her attitude toward investment in common stocks?

Security	Beta	Weight
INTC	2.0	0.30
KCS	1.6	0.15
MRY	1.5	0.20
MICA	1.8	0.20
WMT	1.4	0.15

5-31. The following information is given for three common stocks Jerry plans to purchase for a portfolio.

	NVP	GE	MD
Expected return	13%	15%	20%
Security's beta	0.80	1.00	1.40
Risk-free rate	5%	5%	5%

    a. What is the portfolio's expected return if an equal amount is invested in each security?

    b. What is the portfolio's Treynor index?

5-32. The AJI Money Management Company manages an equity fund consisting of five stocks with the following market values and betas:

Stock	Market Value	Beta
ATG	$100,000	1.10
TGW	50,000	1.20
GWG	75,000	0.75
WGW	125,000	0.80
CFD	150,000	1.40

The risk-free rate is 6 percent and the expected return on the market is 13 percent.

    a. Calculate the portfolio's beta.

    b. Calculate the Treynor portfolio performance index. Assume that each security is appropriately valued (that is, no security is overvalued or undervalued).

5-33. Harvey has received information about two mutual funds. In studying the mutual funds' performance, he discovers the following information:

Mutual Fund	Average Portfolio Return	Portfolio Beta
Aggressive	0.18	1.9
Moderate	0.12	1.0

The risk-free rate is 3.5 percent.

    a. Calculate the Treynor index for each fund.

    b. Comment on which fund provides the superior return relative to market risk.

    c. If limited to these two funds, which would Harvey likely choose for investment?

5-34. Calculate the Treynor index for each of the following three mutual funds. Rank the funds for desirability based on their returns relative to market risk. Assume the average risk-free rate to be 4 percent.

Mutual Fund	Average Portfolio Return	Portfolio Beta
Fidelity	14.9%	0.87
Janus	36.8	1.26
Vanguard	16.2	0.65

5-35. What should an investor be concerned about when using beta analysis in stock selection and development of portfolios?

5-36. When you look up a stock's beta value, why does that beta differ depending on which investment service you use?

DISCLOSURE ASSIGNMENTS

5-37. Use the *Disclosure* database to answer the following questions pertaining to Nike, Inc. and Reebok International Ltd.

   a. What is the range of five-year growth in earnings as provided by *Zacks Earnings Estimates*? Which firm has greater risk associated with the estimates? Explain.

   b. Using quarterly data, calculate each firm's standard deviation for net income. Which firm has greater variability in its income?

LIBRARY ASSIGNMENTS

5-38. Select three stock mutual funds with growth objectives from Morningstar's *Mutual Fund Values* or Wiesenberger's *Investment Companies*. Calculate the Treynor index for each mutual fund and rank the funds according to investment desirability. Base the risk-free rate on the current yield for U.S. Treasury bills found in *The Wall Street Journal* or the financial section of a daily newspaper.

5-39. Use the financial services reports provided by Moody's Investors Service, Standard & Poor's Corporation, or Value Line Investment Services to form a $100,000 portfolio containing at least 12 different common stocks. Calculate the beta of your portfolio based on data given in the advisory services. Track your portfolio's performance over a two-month period. Compare the portfolio's percentage return (including dividends and stock price changes) in relation to the changes in S&P 500 index over the two months. How do you explain the difference, if any, in your portfolio's performance and the S&P index?

COMPREHENSIVE PROBLEM ▼▼▼▼▼▼▼▼▼▼▼▼

5-40. As a bank trust officer, Ms. Carey has been assigned to manage the proceeds of an $800,000 trust for a 20-year-old college student, established as a result of the death of her last living parent. The student needs $20,000 annually for the next two years to complete her bachelor's degree, after which she plans to enter the job market. Once she graduates, the objective of the trust is to provide long-term growth of principal with income to supplement her earnings. None of the principal can be withdrawn for five years. After five years, all the funds can be withdrawn. Given the following information about the economy and investment alternatives, answer the following questions.

State of the Economy	Probability	T-bills	Market Portfolio	Gate Co.	Central Utility
				Possible Returns on Investments	
Depression	0.05	4%	–12%	–15%	3%
Recession	0.15	4	3	–6	6
Steady	0.60	4	10	12	8
Low growth	0.15	4	12	15	9
High growth	0.05	4	16	24	10
Estimated beta		0.0	1.0	1.2	0.9
Correlations: T-bills		1.00			
Market		0.00	1.00		
Gate		0.00	0.95	1.00	
Central		0.00	0.99	0.98	1.00

The market portfolio used by the bank is a mutual fund which is similar in composition to the S&P 500 stock index.

a. Calculate the expected return for each investment.
b. Calculate each investment's standard deviation of returns.
c. Calculate each investment's risk-to-reward ratio (coefficient of variation).
d. What would be the portfolio's beta and expected return if equal proportions were invested in each of the four securities?
e. What would be the portfolio's beta and expected return if 60 percent of the funds were invested in Gate Company and 40 percent in Central Utility?
f. For the portfolios constructed in parts (d) and (e), what are their expected Treynor indexes? Which portfolio offers the superior risk-return trade-off?
g. For the portfolio with the superior risk-return trade-off in part (f), what is its standard deviation?
h. As the trust officer, which portfolio would you create at the present time? Explain your decision.

ANSWERS TO SELF-TEST PROBLEMS ▼▼▼▼▼▼▼▼▼▼▼▼

ST5-1.

a.

Economic Conditions	Probability		Return Rate		Product
Boom times	0.25	×	0.40	=	0.10
Normal times	0.40	×	0.20	=	0.08
Recession times	0.30	×	0.00	=	0.00
Depression times	0.05	×	–0.20	=	–0.01
Expected return					0.17

b.

Economic conditions	(Return Rate − Expected Return)^2 × Probability
Boom times	$(0.40 - 0.17)^2 \times 0.25 = 0.013225$
Normal times	$(0.20 - 0.17)^2 \times 0.40 = 0.000360$
Recession times	$(0.00 - 0.17)^2 \times 0.30 = 0.008670$
Depression times	$(-0.20 - 0.17)^2 \times 0.05 = \underline{0.006845}$
Variance	$\underline{0.029100}$

Standard deviation $= (0.0291)^{1/2} = 0.171$ or 17.1 percent

ST5-2.

Security	Beta × Proportion
KAT	$1.6 \times 0.25 = 0.400$
LRK	$1.2 \times 0.20 = 0.240$
NMX	$0.9 \times 0.30 = 0.270$
SPS	$1.1 \times 0.25 = \underline{0.275}$
Portfolio beta	$\underline{1.185}$

The portfolio beta of about 1.2 suggests that Helen has a tolerance for risk that is greater than the stock market. Presumably she wants a higher rate of return on her portfolio than the market earns.

ST5-3.

a. Treynor index =

$$\frac{\text{Average portfolio return} - \text{average risk-free rate}}{\text{Portfolio beta}}$$

$$\text{Growth Prospects Fund} = \frac{0.23 - 0.03}{1.8} = 0.111$$

$$\text{Fundamentals Fund} = \frac{0.11 - 0.03}{1.0} = 0.080$$

b. The Growth Prospects Fund provides a superior return relative to nondiversifiable (market) risk.

CHAPTER 6

Financial Markets

On any day, *The Wall Street Journal* carries announcements of new security issues of corporations and governments totaling billions of dollars. On the same day, thousands of businesses and individuals contact their local banks about new loans. These events have one feature in common—they are attempts to raise funds for expenditures. Retailers need funds for inventories before they receive the cash from sales and receivables. Governments spend funds for social programs and to build infrastructure before receiving full tax payments from businesses and individuals. Farmers need funds for fertilizer and seed before they get cash for their crops. Financial institutions make it possible for some businesses, governments, and consumers to spend their expected income before they receive it and for others to earn money on funds that they want to hold for future expenditures. These transactions link the real world of goods and services with the financial world of money and credit, commonly called the financial markets.

There is no central market for economic capital, that is, the plant and equipment and inventory produced. But there is a group of financial markets for the monetary instruments that represent either title to or claims to economic capital and to the other resources owned by government, business, and individuals. We divide these markets into *money markets* and *capital markets,* and further divide money and capital markets into *primary markets* and *secondary markets.* The **money market** provides for quick and dependable transfer of claims with maturities of less than one year. Longer-term claims are transferred in **capital markets.** If the claims are newly created, they exchange in **primary markets.** Already outstanding claims trade from old to new owners in **secondary markets** without generating new funds or creating new obligations.

Important participants in the financial system are financial intermediaries (financial institutions) responsible for moving funds from savings pools into the primary markets. These intermediaries provide centralized markets for users and savers of funds. Relying on portfolio diversification strategies, intermediaries make borrowing, selling stock, and investing easier and less costly.

Money market. A market for securities with less than one year to maturity. Typical securities are Treasury bills, repurchase agreements, and negotiable certificates of deposit.

Capital market. A market for securities with maturities beyond one year.

Primary market. The market in which the initial sale of securities occurs.

Secondary market. Securities markets that handle transactions in existing securities. Often contrasted with *primary market.*

After you have studied this chapter, you should have a better understanding of:

- The major types of financial intermediaries and how they function in the financial market.
- The role of investment bankers.
- The use of shelf registrations, rights offerings, and private placements to raise funds.
- The distinction between the various secondary markets.

6.1 FINANCIAL INTERMEDIATION

Financial intermediaries responsible for transferring funds from savers to users are mentioned in the financial columns of the newspapers and are briefly described in Table 6.1. Essentially, these intermediaries buy and sell rights to future payments. For instance, if you open a savings account at Home Savings of America, you give it a current payment in exchange for its promise to make a payment to you in the future. Home Savings then turns around and uses your payment to make a loan to someone. Thus, financial intermediaries obtain funds by issuing their own financial securities to investors and then invest the cash received in securities issued by borrowers.

The largest intermediaries are banks and insurance companies. Table 6.2 lists the world's ten largest banks and insurance companies as of 1992. Many of the firms listed operate internationally. These intermediaries established foreign offices to serve their homeland clients who were aggressively acquiring companies and building production facilities around the world. The international integration of financial intermediaries is apparent by the ease by which funds of corporations and large investors in one country are transferred to borrowers in other countries. Dollars, Deutsche marks, yen, sterling, or other currencies deposited in a bank almost anywhere in the world are usually transferred via a computerized system called CHIPS (Clearing House Interbank Payments System) to a bank in London and then on from London to a bank in some other country for lending to customers in that country.

The process of **financial intermediation,** which means receiving money from savers and transferring it to borrowers and sellers of equity, results in two important benefits for the financial system. First, consider the difficulty and expense individual borrowers and lenders have matching each other's needs. Financial institutions reduce transaction and monitoring costs by providing centralized markets for borrowers and lenders of all types. Because a financial intermediary specializes in "buying and selling" money, it is able to realize economies of scale not available to most borrowers or individual investors. These economies result from the volume of money the intermediary buys and sells.

Financial intermediaries lower monitoring costs because they can develop information on organizations needing funds more efficiently than individual investors can. If several investors who lent money to one borrower each had to incur their own costs watching the borrower directly, it would be far more costly than if an intermediary performed this service for multiple clients. The intermediary can also reduce the problem of unreliable information by using specialized resources, such as computerized databases.

A second benefit of intermediation is that the process overcomes any barriers arising from the incompatibility of the financial needs and objectives of borrowers and lenders. The lender is looking for **liquidity,** that is, safety and an ability to redeem the investment quickly and at low cost. Often the borrower cannot promise liquidity. Financial institutions reconcile these different needs by offering suppliers of funds

Financial intermediation. The process of wholesaling or retailing funds between lenders and borrowers by financial intermediaries.

Liquidity. A characteristic of a security that refers to its risk, both credit risk and market risk, and its marketability. High liquidity requires low risk and high marketability.

TABLE 6-1

Major Types of Financial Intermediaries

Commercial banks

Businesses chartered by either the Comptroller of the Currency or a state agency. These banks receive deposits and make loans. *Example:* Chemical Bank.

Saving and loan associations (S&L)

Businesses chartered by federal and state agencies that receive savings deposits and checkable deposits. They use the funds primarily to make mortgage loans. *Example:* Home Savings of America.

Mutual savings banks

Similar to savings and loan associations, but only chartered by a state agency. They accept deposits and make mortgage loans. *Example:* Green Point Savings Bank.

Credit unions

Small cooperative institutions often organized in a place of work or by a labor union. They take deposits and make consumer loans. *Example:* Arizona State Employees Credit Union.

Mutual funds

Businesses that obtain funds by selling shares and using the proceeds to buy a portfolio of securities. In the case of money-market mutual funds, shareholders can write checks against the value of their shares. *Example:* Fidelity Investment Trust.

Life insurance companies

Businesses that insure people against the financial result of death, receiving their funds in the form of periodic payments (premiums). The companies invest most of their funds in long-term corporate bonds and commercial mortgages. *Example:* The Travelers Insurance Company.

Property and casualty insurance companies

Businesses that receive premiums from individuals and companies to insure them against burglary, fire, negligence lawsuits, auto collision, and other losses. They invest primarily in low-risk debt and equity securities. *Example:* State Farm Insurance Company.

Pension plans

Plans whose inflow of money comes from working people building monetary reserves for their retirement years. Investment of most funds is in long-term corporate bonds and stocks. *Example:* CalPERS.

Real estate investment trusts (REITs)

Investment organizations that hold properties, cash, and sometimes mortgages. REITs issue equity securities that trade on major stock exchanges. *Example:* DeBartolo Realty Corporation.

TABLE 6-2

WORLD'S LARGEST BANKS AND INSURANCE COMPANIES

Rank 1992	Rank 1991	Name (Country)	Assets (U.S. $Million)
BANKS:			
1	1	Dai-Ichi Kangyo Bank (Japan)	$473,276
2	3	Sumitomo Bank (Japan)	453,274
3	2	Sakura Bank (Japan)	446,448
4	5	Fuji Bank (Japan)	443,833
5	4	Sanwa Bank (Japan)	437,294
6	6	Mitsubishi Bank (Japan)	425,019
7	9	Credit Lyonnais (France)	350,870
8	11	Norinchukin Bank (Japan)	326,899
9	7	Industrial Bank of Japan (Japan)	321,188
10	10	Deutsche Bank (Germany)	305,002
INSURANCE COMPANIES:			
1	1	Nippon Life (Japan)	$236,380
2	2	Prudential Insurance (U.S.)	199,625
3	3	Zenkyoren (Japan)	167,555
4	4	Dai-Ichi Mutual (Japan)	164,856
5	5	Sumitomo Life (Japan)	144,398
6	6	Allianz Group (Germany)	128,114
7	8	Union des Assurances de Paris (France)	123,736
8	–	AXA (France)	120,068
9	7	Metropolitan Life (U.S.)	118,178
10	10	Meiji Mutual Life (Japan)	99,386

Note the relative absence of U.S. companies. The six largest banks are Japanese companies and not one U.S. bank is listed. Two U.S. companies made the insurance list, which is also dominated by Japanese companies.

Source: The Wall Street Journal, *September 24, 1993, p. R26–27.*

safety and liquidity, and by turning around and using the funds for loans and investments with varying degrees of risk and liquidity. Intermediaries can give their cash suppliers long-term contracts and lend to borrowers on short-term contracts, or vice versa. For example, Home Savings of America buys a security that promises to pay $100 for each of the next three years. Based on these expected cash flows, Home Savings can issue three securities with maturities of one year, two years, and three years.[1] The ability of intermediaries to change the maturities on securities makes financial markets more attractive to both borrowers and investors than if a loan were between the borrower and the investor directly, bypassing the intermediation process.

[1]The process is actually complex. Mathematicians and statisticians determine the default risk associated with the security bought by the intermediary. The securities issued by the intermediary promise lower payoffs than the payments the intermediary receives.

The secret in being able to match different types of contracts lies in the structure of financial intermediaries. These institutions consist of two large diversified portfolios of financial contracts—their sources of funds (that is, their liabilities) and their assets. The intermediary's success depends upon the overall performance of these portfolios, which are shaped by individual contracts. However, the performance of the portfolios is much more dependable and predictable than that of individual contracts.

The portfolios have the statistical advantage of large numbers. This means that the average loss rates and the average liquidity requirements can be predicted with considerable accuracy even when the prospects for individual contracts are uncertain. For example, a bank's asset portfolio may consist of mortgages, car loans, and government-guaranteed loans to a broad cross section of borrowers. Such a portfolio is better diversified than most individuals could easily achieve by their own efforts. The risks to each investor are much lower than they would be if he or she had to lend directly to individual borrowers. As a result, the security issued by the intermediary provides a higher degree of liquidity to the investor than does a similar commitment to a single security of a corporate borrower.

  Comprehension Check

1. Define each of the following financial intermediaries and include in your definition the primary sources and uses of funds for each: commercial banks, savings and loan associations, mutual savings banks, credit unions, mutual funds, life insurance companies, property and casualty insurance companies, private pension funds, and real estate investment trusts.

2. Define financial intermediation.

3. Discuss the benefits provided by financial intermediaries.

6.2 THE MONEY AND CAPITAL MARKETS

We noted how financial intermediaries assist in the process of bringing savers and borrowers together to reallocate funds. There cannot, however, be a single pool of funds up for competitive bids. There must be separate markets for short-term funds and long-term funds. Some borrowers can only obtain short-term loans until they establish their credit worthiness; other borrowers are well known and can borrow long term. The subject of finance broadly classifies these submarkets into either the money market or the capital market, respectively. These two markets are closely linked with the money market acting as the central mechanism of the financial system. The money market provides a major link between monetary authorities, such as the U.S. Federal Reserve Bank and the German Bundesbank, and the financial system. The money market absorbs the day-to-day pressures of monetary adjustments that cannot be handled by the normal financing channels.

6.2.1 The Money Market

The money market is not easy to identify. It consists of the set of markets for financial instruments that is normally used by financial institutions, businesses, and individuals to adjust their cash positions. The instruments used may vary from time to time, and the nature and structure of the markets may change. In the United States and other countries with highly developed secondary markets, many types of government or private securities may be traded as money-market instruments. In less well-developed countries, money-market transactions may be confined to trades among banks and with the central bank or monetary authorities.

The most active money market outside of the United States is the *Eurodollar market*. The **Eurodollar market** is a network of financial centers around the world that provides much of the innovation in international banking and finance. The prefix *Euro-* indicates that the markets exist principally in Europe; however, the markets do cover transactions in other parts of the world. London is the largest Eurodollar market with Paris a distant second. The Cayman Islands and the Bahamas have become major Eurodollar markets primarily because of tax advantages.

A major difference between the Eurodollar market and domestic money markets is that the Eurodollar market operates free from government regulations and control. It has the tacit approval of all major governments of the world. The absence of government controls allows the Eurodollar market to provide special services to businesses, such as:

- Lower costs on loans and deposits
- Immediate and complimentary response to liquidity needs
- Reduction in political risk due to future changes in existing regulations.

However, the lack of government controls means that more default risk exists in the Eurodollar market than in the domestic market. More risk means higher expected returns to investors.

Money-market instruments must meet all the requirements for easy secondary trading and, in addition, must carry very little market and default risks. Compared to capital-market securities, money-market securities offer lower return, lower risk, and shorter maturities. Marketability and liquidity of money-market securities are comparable to capital-market securities. Table 6.3 summarizes the major money-market instruments. Each of the securities is a relatively safe investment. A U.S. Treasury bill is the safest; commercial paper is the least safe.

THE MONEY MARKET AS A SOURCE OF FUNDS. Access to the money market as a source of new funds is limited to a relatively small number of large, well-established borrowers, such as the U.S. Treasury, government agencies, and many large well-known financial and business organizations such as First Chicago Corporation and Union Carbide Company. These borrowers use money-market securities as an alternative to other sources of funds when flexibility is needed or when they reduce borrowing costs. Money-market securities are most attractive to borrowers when they are less expensive than longer-term funds or when the issuer does not want to get locked into high long-term interest rates.

THE MONEY MARKET AS AN INVESTMENT. An investor's access to the market is limited only by the large denominations involved. Anyone with enough money can buy money-market securities. However, we can classify potential buyers into two types. The first group includes anyone who holds or manages cash. They are willing and happy to invest their cash balances if their conditions can be met: assurance of access to the funds when they need them, and rates that are high enough to cover transactions costs. These buyers are important because they control a source of funds that would otherwise not be available.

Money-market mutual funds (MMMFs), such as Merrill Lynch Ready Cash Fund, provide a concrete illustration of the role of the money market in activating idle

> **Eurodollar market.** A market for dollar-denominated deposits outside the United States.

TABLE 6-3

PRINCIPAL MONEY-MARKET INSTRUMENTS

Instrument	Borrower	Term to Maturity and Denominations	Interest Payment
Treasury bills (T-bills)	Federal government	91- and 182-day bills sold weekly; 52-week bills sold monthly; denominations of $10,000 to $1 million or more	Discounted; interest exempt from state income taxes
Federal funds	Commercial banks temporarily short of reserves borrow from banks with excess reserves	Overnight to 3 days; denominations of $1 million or more	Interest paid at maturity
Federal agency notes	Various agencies	6 months to 10 years; denominations of $10,000 and up	Usually discounted
Commercial paper (unsecured note)	Large companies with high credit ratings	Up to 270 days; denominations of $25,000 to $1 million or more	Discounted or interest bearing
Negotiable certificates of deposit (receipts for time deposits)	Commercial banks	14 days and over; denominations of $100,000 or more	Usually interest bearing; paid at maturity
Eurodollar deposits (dollar time deposits at overseas banks)	London and other non-U.S. branches of banks	Overnight to 1 year; denominations for $1 million or more	Interest bearing; paid at maturity
Bankers' acceptances (negotiable bills accepted by banks and sold to investors)	Commercial banks	Up to 6 months; denominations of $25,000 to $1 million	Discounted
Repurchase agreements or repos (sale of government securities with an agreement to repurchase them)	U.S. government securities dealers	Overnight to 180 days; denominations of $100,000 and up	Interest paid at maturity in the form of a higher repurchase price

(Continued)

TABLE 6-3 (CONTINUED)

PRINCIPAL MONEY-MARKET INSTRUMENTS

Instrument	Borrower	Term to Maturity and Denominations	Interest Payment
Money-market mutual funds (invested in the money-market securities)	Investment companies such as Merrill Lynch	No maturity date; minimum deposits as low as $500	Interest earned daily by the fund

money balances of this first group. MMMFs appeared on the scene when the cost of money became high enough to justify the expense of trying to reach holders of small amounts of idle balances. By serving as intermediaries between the money market and cash managers of businesses and individuals who would not otherwise have access to the market, MMMFs add to the effectiveness of the money market in mobilizing idle balances.

The second group of investors of money-market instruments includes banks, financial institutions, governments, corporations, and anyone else who uses money-market instruments as part of an investment portfolio to achieve the desired mix of liquidity and yield. These investors provide the regular demand for money-market instruments and absorb the newly issued instruments as part of the turnover of their portfolios as their money-market investments mature.

6.2.2 The Capital Market

Capital markets are for the issuing and trading of securities with maturities in excess of one year; generally, the securities issued by governments and businesses. The bulk of capital-market activity occurs in secondary markets, with the most active and best known being the New York Stock Exchange (NYSE) located in New York City. Later in this chapter, we will describe how the NYSE functions. Figure 6.1 summarizes the allocation of the world's secondary capital markets as of June 1991 between debt and equity, and by country. The equity market was about $9.5 trillion and the debt market was approximately $12 trillion.

A less well-known capital market to most people is the **Eurocapital market.** It consists of three distinct submarkets of *Eurocurrency loans, Eurobonds,* and *Euroequity.* **Eurocurrency loans** from commercial banks are loans denominated in a currency other than that of the country in which the bank is located. (For example, U.S. Sprint borrows Italian lira from a Swiss bank.) **Eurobonds** are bonds offered for sale in a country or countries other than the one in whose currency the bonds are denominated. (For example, the Spanish firm Telephona España sells bonds denominated in peseta to investors in Germany.) **Euroequity** is an equity interest of a company that is sold in a country or countries other than the one in whose currency the equity shares are denominated. (For example, the British firm BAT Industries sells equity denominated in sterling to investors in France.) Eurocapital securities with long maturities, such as bonds or stocks, typically sell in more than one country simultaneously.

Eurocapital market. An international market for debt and equity securities.

Eurocurrency loans. Loans by commercial banks denominated in currencies other than the currency of the country in which the bank resides.

Eurobond. An international debt instrument denominated in a currency different from the currency of the country in which it is sold.

Euroequity. An ownership financial instrument denominated in a currency different from the currency of the country in which it is sold.

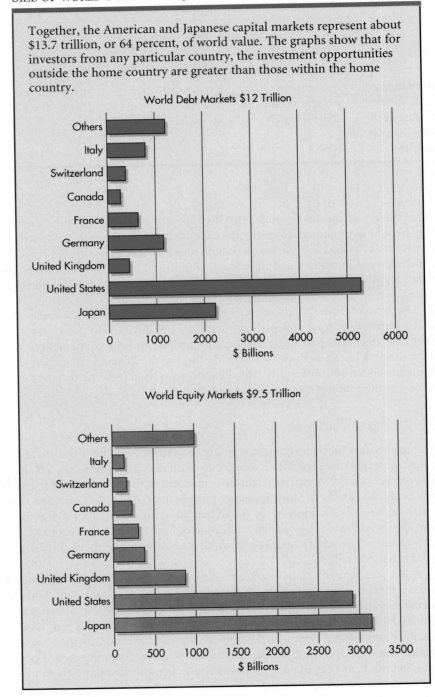

FIGURE 6.1
SIZE OF WORLD DEBT AND EQUITY MARKETS AS OF JUNE 1991

Together, the American and Japanese capital markets represent about $13.7 trillion, or 64 percent, of world value. The graphs show that for investors from any particular country, the investment opportunities outside the home country are greater than those within the home country.

1. Distinguish between money markets and capital markets.
2. Define the following money-market securities: Treasury bills, federal funds, federal agencies' debt instruments, commercial paper, negotiable certificates of deposit, Eurodollars, banker's acceptance, repurchase agreement, money-market mutual funds.
3. Describe the Eurocapital market. Define its three submarkets.

6.3 THE PRIMARY MARKETS

When corporations, governments, or individuals short of funds raise capital by issuing new securities, these securities initially sell in primary markets. Examples of primary market transactions include a sale of U.S. Treasury bonds by the federal government to investors, a new mortgage loan from Countrywide Mortgage Company issued on a home, and new stock sold by Lotus Development Corporation to financial institutions and the public. In developed primary markets, the borrower does not have to find a lender or investor directly; there are many kinds of go-betweens to bring primary issuers and investors together. Typically, corporations in need of funds use *investment bankers* as the go-between to help them raise new capital in primary markets. Other alternatives to raise new capital are *shelf registrations, rights offerings,* and *private placements.*

6.3.1 Transactions Through Investment Bankers

A business usually requires large amounts of funds to support growth opportunities. Often the fund requirements are beyond the business's capacity to save in any reasonable period. The financial market permits the firm to raise needed funds by selling securities in primary markets. However, many financial managers undertake an offering of securities only once in their lifetime, if ever. To help sell securities to investors, the firm hires the services of investment bankers, who are financial services companies familiar with the financial markets (see Table 6.4). Functions performed by investment bankers include *investigative, risk bearing,* and *selling.*

INVESTIGATIVE FUNCTION. The investment banker is the *originating house.* It serves as an informational link between the capital markets, the company issuing securities, and other investment bankers who may join to form an *underwriting group* or *syndicate.* Important responsibilities of the investment banker include drawing up mandatory provisions (known as *covenants*) of the security issue and ensuring the securities to be issued comply with state and federal regulations.[2] The covenants are to protect investors but they must not be so restrictive that the firm issuing the securities has too little flexibility.

The investment banker and the firm must agree on a price for the securities. The pricing decision begins with the investment banker's expert estimate of what the primary market will pay for the securities, given the proposed features of the offering. The investment banker considers the current market prices of *seasoned* (that is, existing)

---

[2]Securities market regulation, under the Securities and Exchange Commission, had the laudable objective of assuring full disclosure of material information concerning the condition and operations of corporations whose securities are offered to the public. However, the rules and regulations, particularly those applying to new issues of securities, add significantly to the costs of financing in public markets in the United States. These costs have helped to divert a large volume of financing of both U.S. and foreign corporations away from U.S. capital markets and into the Euromarkets, where regulatory constraints are less stringent.

TABLE 6-4

THE WORLD'S LEADING INVESTMENT BANKERS

Rank 1993	Name	Volume ($ Billions)	Number of Issues	Rank 1992
1	Merrill Lynch	$155.4	908	1
2	Goldman Sachs	123.2	626	2
3	Lehman Brothers	99.7	612	3
4	First Boston	94.3	470	4
5	Kidder Peabody	83.6	288	5
6	Salomon Brothers	79.3	439	6
7	Morgan Stanley	66.2	379	7
8	Bear Stearns	40.3	192	8
9	Numura Securities	28.7	89	11
10	Donaldson, Lufkin & Jenrette	27.5	162	13
	Industry totals	$1153.1	7275	

These rankings are based on underwriting activity of worldwide debt and equity offerings for the first nine months of 1992 and 1993. Full credit for the issue is given to the originating house, or lead manager. The lead manager is the investment bank with primary responsibility for the issue.

Source: Investment Dealers Digest, *October 11, 1993, p. 32.*

securities of similar quality and similar features trading in the secondary market. Since seasoned securities have some market history, the investment banker usually wants to price the new issue a little lower to help it sell. However, the firm wants to get as much for the securities as possible. If the price is set too high, the securities are difficult to sell.

RISK-BEARING FUNCTION. The investment banker can either leave the risk associated with the security offering with the firm issuing the securities or assume the risk and relieve the issuer of the uncertainty. By assuming the risk, the investment banker acts as a *principal* and agrees to *underwrite* the issue. **Underwriting** is the process whereby the investment banker buys all the securities for resale at a preestablished price. Such an arrangement is a *firm-commitment offering.* An alternative arrangement is a *best-efforts offering.* In this latter case, the investment banker acts as an *agent* and the risk associated with the sale of the security issue remains with the issuer. There is a fixed selling price, but the amount of the securities that will sell at that price is uncertain.

When the investment banker or syndicate agrees to underwrite the issue, each agrees to deliver a check to the issuer for the price paid by the public investors less an amount called the *spread.* The **spread** is the fee paid to the investment banker for selling the issue. It must cover all costs of investigating, risk bearing, and selling the issue if the investment banker is to realize a profit.

SELLING FUNCTION. The securities sell through the sales divisions of the underwriting syndicate and selected retail brokerage houses. The selling effort begins before the offering date. An announcement of the forthcoming offering alerts prospective investors. The formal announcement is via a *prospectus,* which is filed with the Securities and Exchange Commission (SEC) and made available to interested investors. The **prospectus** sets forth the basic facts about the company and states the use of the funds; it is the only means of legal solicitation. Initially, the prospectus is a *red herring* because it is not known when the SEC will permit the sale of the securities. Figure 6.2 shows the front

Underwriting. A guarantee by investment banking firms to an issuing corporation that a definable sum of money will be paid on a specified date for the issue of stocks or bonds.

Spread. In underwriting, the difference between the price that the underwriter pays the company for the new securities and the price at which the securities are sold to the public or are privately placed.

Prospectus. A legal document provided to potential investors in a new securities issue detailing all pertinent facts concerning the securities to be offered.

FIGURE 6.2

PETsMART's RED HERRING

SUBJECT TO COMPLETION, DATED JUNE 4, 1993

PROSPECTUS
, 1993

7,200,000 Shares

Common Stock

Of the 7,200,000 shares of Common Stock offered, 5,748,494 shares are being offered by the Company and 1,451,506 shares are being offered by the Selling Stockholders. See "Principal and Selling Stockholders." The Company will not receive any proceeds from the sale of shares by the Selling Stockholders.

Of such 7,200,000 shares, 5,760,000 shares are being offered hereby in the United States and Canada by the U.S. Underwriters and 1,440,000 shares are being offered in a concurrent offering outside of the United States and Canada by the International Managers, subject to transfers between the U.S. Underwriters and the International Managers. The initial public offering price and the aggregate underwriting discount per share will be identical for both offerings.

Prior to this offering, there has been no public market for the Common Stock. It is currently estimated that the initial public offering price will be between $15.50 and $17.50 per share. See "Underwriting" for a discussion of the factors considered in determining the initial public offering price. The Common Stock has been approved for quotation on the NASDAQ National Market System under the symbol "PETM", subject to official notice of issuance.

See "Certain Investment Considerations" for information that should be considered by prospective investors.

THESE SECURITIES HAVE NOT BEEN APPROVED OR DISAPPROVED BY THE SECURITIES AND EXCHANGE COMMISSION OR ANY STATE SECURITIES COMMISSION NOR HAS THE SECURITIES AND EXCHANGE COMMISSION OR ANY STATE SECURITIES COMMISSION PASSED UPON THE ACCURACY OR ADEQUACY OF THIS PROSPECTUS. ANY REPRESENTATION TO THE CONTRARY IS A CRIMINAL OFFENSE.

	Price to the Public	Underwriting Discounts and Commissions(1)	Proceeds to the Company(2)	Proceeds to Selling Stockholders
Per Share	$	$	$	$
Total (3)	$	$	$	$

(1) The Company and the Selling Stockholders have agreed to indemnify the U.S. Underwriters and the International Managers against certain liabilities, including liabilities under the Securities Act of 1933, as amended. See "Underwriting."

(2) Before deducting expenses estimated at $810,000, payable by the Company.

(3) The Company has granted the Underwriters a 30-day option to purchase up to 1,080,000 additional shares of Common Stock, on the same terms and conditions as set forth above, solely to cover over-allotments, if any. If such option is exercised in full, the total Price to the Public, Underwriting Discounts and Commissions and Proceeds to the Company will be $, $ and $, respectively. See "Underwriting."

The shares of Common Stock are being offered by the several Underwriters when, as and if delivered to and accepted by the Underwriters and subject to various prior conditions, including their right to reject orders in whole or in part. It is expected that delivery of the shares will be made in New York, New York, on or about July   , 1993.

Donaldson, Lufkin & Jenrette
Securities Corporation

Alex. Brown & Sons
Incorporated

Montgomery Securities

▼▼▼▼▼▼▼▼▼▼▼▼▼

STUDY THAT RED HERRING

A prospectus is a legal document that must be issued by a firm making a public offering of securities. Ignore this document at your own peril!

Consider the red herring of Lezak Group. It discloses many interesting items. It was prepared by an investment banker who is a market maker in the securities of six of the companies that Mr. Lezak, the CEO of Lezak Group, is associated. Mr. Lezak is also a significant brokerage customer of the underwriter. Legal counsel to the company in this offering is counsel to the underwriter (but not for this offering). The prospectus further informs you:

. . . the funds to be raised are not at all allocated; in the company does not know what business it will engage in; has no plan of operations; owns no assets; and investors will entrust their funds to management on whose judgment they must depend with no information whatsoever about management's intentions.

The prospectus lists 19 "extremely high risk factors" that an investor should note. An important risk listed is that the stock issue is a blind-pool offering.

This means the prospective investors are told nothing, promised nothing, and assured only that management doesn't have any idea of what it will do with the money from the offering.

Another risk factor states that the firm is totally dependent on the CEO. However, the very next risk factor informs you that the firm has "no employment agreement with the chief executive officer." While many investors balked at taking a plunge into the blind-pool offering, many others thought nothing of the risk. Adventuresome investors contributed $440,000 for 9.7 million shares. That works out to 4.5 cents a share, on average. Mr. Lezak got 5 million shares for just $5010. The cash from that sale was the only asset owned by the Lezak Group. Four years later the stock traded over the counter for between 3 and 6 cents.

A prospectus like this may seem like a joke, but it isn't. The Securities and Exchange Commission can order the seller to send a prospectus to a buyer. However, it can't force the buyer to read it.

Adapted from Alan Abelson, "Up & Down Wall Street," *Barron's,* June 13, 1983, p. 41. Used with permission of Dow Jones, 1983. Reprinted by permission of *Barron's* © 1983 Dow Jones & Company, Inc. All Rights Reserved Worldwide.

page of a red herring issued by PETsMART Company, a warehouse retailer of pet foods and supplies. Notice that the red herring has warnings across the top and down the left margin, and excludes information about the price of the securities and specific dates. The above Financial Reality reading suggests that prospective investors should carefully read the red herring.

Only a few days, or even a few hours, before the sale of the initial public offering (IPO) is there final agreement on the price and the spread. The late signing of the agreement permits the investment banker to consider any last-minute changes in capital-market conditions. The firm receives the check for the sale of the securities on the *settlement date.* This date is within a specified number of days after the public offering date.

As shown on the front page of the offical prospectus for PETsMART Company, in Figure 6.3A, the spread is the "underwriting discount" of $8.64 million—the fee

FIGURE 6.3A
PETsMART's PROSPECTUS

PROSPECTUS
July 22, 1993

7,200,000 Shares

Common Stock

Of the 7,200,000 shares of Common Stock offered, 6,445,688 shares are being offered by the Company and 754,312 shares are being offered by the Selling Stockholders. See "Principal and Selling Stockholders." The Company will not receive any proceeds from the sale of shares by the Selling Stockholders.

Of such 7,200,000 shares, 5,760,000 shares are being offered hereby in the United States and Canada by the U.S. Underwriters and 1,440,000 shares are being offered in a concurrent offering outside of the United States and Canada by the International Managers, subject to transfers between the U.S. Underwriters and the International Managers. The initial public offering price and the aggregate underwriting discount per share are identical for both offerings.

Prior to this offering, there has been no public market for the Common Stock. See "Underwriting" for a discussion of the factors considered in determining the initial public offering price. The Common Stock has been approved for quotation on the NASDAQ National Market System under the symbol "PETM."

See "Certain Investment Considerations" for information that should be considered by prospective investors.

THESE SECURITIES HAVE NOT BEEN APPROVED OR DISAPPROVED BY THE SECURITIES AND EXCHANGE COMMISSION OR ANY STATE SECURITIES COMMISSION NOR HAS THE SECURITIES AND EXCHANGE COMMISSION OR ANY STATE SECURITIES COMMISSION PASSED UPON THE ACCURACY OR ADEQUACY OF THIS PROSPECTUS. ANY REPRESENTATION TO THE CONTRARY IS A CRIMINAL OFFENSE.

	Price to the Public	Underwriting Discounts and Commissions(1)	Proceeds to the Company(2)	Proceeds to Selling Stockholders
Per Share	$18.00	$1.20	$16.80	$16.80
Total (3)	$129,600,000	$8,640,000	$108,287,558	$12,672,442

(1) *The Company and the Selling Stockholders have agreed to indemnify the U.S. Underwriters and the International Managers against certain liabilities, including liabilities under the Securities Act of 1933, as amended. See "Underwriting."*

(2) *Before deducting expenses estimated at $810,000, payable by the Company.*

(3) *The Company has granted the Underwriters a 30-day option to purchase up to 1,080,000 additional shares of Common Stock, on the same terms and conditions as set forth above, solely to cover over-allotments, if any. If such option is exercised in full, the total Price to the Public, Underwriting Discounts and Commissions and Proceeds to the Company will be $149,040,000, $9,936,000 and $126,431,558, respectively. See "Underwriting."*

The shares of Common Stock are being offered by the several Underwriters when, as and if delivered to and accepted by the Underwriters and subject to various prior conditions, including their right to reject orders in whole or in part. It is expected that delivery of the shares will be made in New York, New York, on or about July 29, 1993.

Donaldson, Lufkin & Jenrette
Securities Corporation

Alex. Brown & Sons
Incorporated

Montgomery Securities

FIGURE 6.3B
PETsMART's PROSPECTUS (CONTINUED)

No dealer, salesperson or other person has been authorized to give any information or to make any representations not contained in this Prospectus, and, if given or made, such information or presentations must not be relied upon as having been authorized by the Company, any Selling Stockholder or the U.S. Underwriters. This Prospectus does not constitute an offer to sell or a solicitation of an offer to buy to any person or by anyone in any jurisdiction in which such offer or solicitation would be unlawful or to any person to whom it is unlawful. Neither the delivery of this Prospectus nor any sale made hereunder shall, under any circumstances, create any implication that there has been no change in the affairs of the Company or that the information contained herein is correct as of any time subsequent to the date hereof.

TABLE OF CONTENTS

Until August 16, 1993 (25 days after the date hereof), all dealers effecting transactions in the Common Stock, whether or not participating in this distribution, may be required to deliver a Prospectus. This delivery requirement is in addition to the obligation of dealers to deliver a Prospectus when acting as Underwriters and with respect to their unsold allotments or subscriptions.

7,200,000 Shares

Common Stock

PROSPECTUS

Donaldson, Lufkin & Jenrette
Securities Corporation

Alex. Brown & Sons
Incorporated

Montgomery Securities

July 22, 1993

NONFINANCIAL COSTS OF AN IPO

Going public is attractive to closely held firms because it provides nonrefundable funds that can be used for expansion, research and development, or some other pressing need facing the company. But it also presents problems that are frequently overlooked.

Going public brought tiny Dynatrend, Inc. $1.9 million for product development. Ronald Massa, the founder and chief executive officer, could have raised the money from a venture capitalist. But this meant giving up control of the company, something he didn't want to do.

Massa had mixed feelings about going public. It meant he had to change his management style with the result that he became less friendly with his employees. Public companies are judged by Wall Street standards that he disagrees with, but which he is forced to try and meet.

A New York investment banker says that going public puts owners "through an emotional wringer." Information that used to be just his business now must be disclosed to the public.

Being public costs Dynatrend about $100,000 a year. There are costs for a transfer agent, legal, auditing, investment banking, financial public relations, printing, and mailing costs. And time is spent talking to brokers, analysts, and investors looking for information.

Massa says that investors like to see earnings rise each quarter. Everyone judges the company by the stock price, which can change for reasons having nothing to do with the company's performance. That influences his decisions. He says a quarter-to-quarter emphasis results in him manipulating the company and not managing it.

Adapted from "Small Business," *The Wall Street Journal*, November 15, 1982, p. 31.
Reprinted by permission of *The Wall Street Journal*, © Dow Jones & Company, Inc.
All Rights Reserved Worldwide.

earned by the investment bankers.[3] However, as the above Financial Reality article reveals, not all costs are of a monetary nature. The back page of the prospectus, shown in Figure 6.3B, provides an index of the information contained in the document. It indicates that a fairly complete history of the firm is revealed in the prospectus.[4]

The corporation issuing the securities pays all underwriting costs of the issue, which allows investors to buy the stock free of any commissions or other charges. In general, the initial offering of stock is the only time a fixed price exists for the stock. The investment bankers support the price temporarily. Shortly after an issue's initial public sale, any price stabilization by the underwriter ceases. Share price is then set according to supply and demand in the secondary market.

The public becomes aware of the sale of securities after the fact in an announcement called a *tombstone* (see Figure 6.4). It shows the company name, the underwriters,

---

[3]Costs associated with issuing securities vary significantly. The costs are a function of size of the issue and whether it is a firm-commitment offer or a best-efforts offer. Best-efforts offers are more expensive for two reasons. They are more often associated with speculative firms and, therefore, the success of the offering is riskier. And best-efforts offers usually involve a smaller issure size than firm-commitment offers. Larger issues realize monetary cost economies of scale.

[4]This information is also revealed in the red herring.

FIGURE 6.4

A TOMBSTONE AND ITS INTERPRETATION

This announcement is under no circumstances to be construed as an offer to sell or as a solicitation of an offer to buy any of these securities. The offering is made only by the Prospectus.

March 10, 1994

7,446,250 Shares

Gaylord Entertainment Company

Class A Common Stock

Price $26 Per Share

Copies of the Prospectus may be obtained in any State or jurisdiction in which this announcement is circulated from only such of the undersigned or other dealers or brokers as may lawfully offer these securities in such State or jurisdiction.

5,957,000 Shares

The above shares were underwritten by the following group of U.S. Underwriters.

Merrill Lynch & Co.

CS First Boston	**Morgan Stanley & Co.** Incorporated	**PaineWebber Incorporated**
Prudential Securities Incorporated	**UBS Securities Inc.**	**S.G. Warburg & Co. Inc.**
J. C. Bradford & Co.	**Equitable Securities Corporation**	**Gerard Klauer Mattison & Co., Inc.**
J. J. B. Hilliard, W. L. Lyons, Inc.	**Josephthal Lyon & Ross** Incorporated	**Legg Mason Wood Walker** Incorporated
Morgan Keegan & Company, Inc.	**The Seidler Companies** Incorporated	**Wheat First Butcher & Singer** CAPITAL MARKETS

1,489,250 Shares

The above shares were underwritten by the following group of International Underwriters.

Merrill Lynch International Limited

CS First Boston	**Daewoo Securities (Europe) Limited**	**Dresdner Bank** Aktiengesellschaft
Nomura International	**UBS Limited**	**S.G. Warburg Securities**

and some information about the issue. This nonsales-oriented announcement must contain no exaggeration, elaboration, or solicitation.

6.3.2 Alternatives to Investment Bankers

If a firm is making an initial issue of securities to the public, it uses an investment banker because of its specialized knowledge. However, once firms mature they may find that they can raise funds through *shelf registrations, rights offerings,* and *private placements.* Let's now discuss these methods.

SHELF REGISTRATIONS. In 1982, the SEC changed the practice of negotiated agreements between firms and investment bankers. SEC Rule 415 allows large firms to register securities with the SEC and sell them piecemeal during a two-year period. Securities sold this way are called **shelf registrations** because in effect they are "on the shelf" and can be taken down and sold on short notice (as short as one day) whenever it suits the issuing firm. In early December 1993, Commonwealth Edison Company registered $1 billion of debt securities as a shelf offering. Typically, firms use shelf registrations for the sale of debt rather than equity securities.

> **Shelf registration.**
> Securities and Exchange Commission Rule 415, which allows a company to register all securities it plans to issue over the following two years. The company then files short statements when it wishes to sell any part of these securities during the period.

At the original shelf registration filing with the SEC, the firm does not designate an investment banker as the official underwriter. The firm hires an underwriter when the shares are taken down from the shelf. Some people worry that the speed with which the firm wants the shares to be issued from the shelf may prevent underwriters from providing adequate *due diligence,* that is, adequate analysis of risk associated with the securities and ensuring the completeness of the registration statement.

A chief advantage of shelf registration is that the fixed cost of registration is distributed over a series of issuances, which results in lower overall transaction cost. Another advantage is that competitive bidding between investment bankers is aggressive, which in turn results in lower fees paid by the issuer to the investment banker. For instance, Morgan Stanley, an investment banking company, netted about $400,000 on one deal that would have netted about $3 million before Rule 415. The Financial Reality article on page 209 discusses how Time Warner Inc. threatened to take its business to more accommodating investment bankers if the bankers did not waive their contractual rights.

RIGHTS OFFERING. A company can bypass investment bankers and issue new equity securities directly to existing shareholders through a *preemptive rights offering.* **Preemptive rights** are certificates issued by the corporation to the existing shareholders that specify the conditions under which the shareholders may purchase shares of the new equity issue. The rights grant current shareholders an option, not an obligation, to buy some proportion of new shares issued at a *price below market value* before the general public has a chance to buy them. One right is distributed for each share the shareholder owns. The company may stipulate the number of rights necessary for the purchase of one or more shares of the new stock. For example, four rights may enable a shareholder to buy one share. By exercising the rights, shareholders can maintain their respective ownership percentages of the company's common stock. Figure 6.5 outlines the key dates associated with a rights offering.

> **Preemptive right.** A provision in the corporate charter or in state law that allows the existing stockholders to purchase additional shares of stock before they are offered for sale to the public. This allows existing stockholders to maintain their proportionate ownership in the firm.

The *ex-rights date* is the day when the old stock begins trading in the market without the subscription privilege, or rights. Buyers are no longer entitled to receive rights to subscribe for shares. The share price decreases by the value of the right to which it is no longer entitled. Rights are exercisable before a final expiration date. The length of the subscription period during which rights are exercisable is typically from two to four

PRIVATE PLACEMENTS FOR THE SMALL FIRM

by David G. Bonagura, Partner-in-Charge of Entrepreneurial Services of the Long Island Office of Ernst & Young

A new product or service may exist only in an entrepreneur's mind or on blueprints. A private placement offers an avenue to financing when bankers prove reluctant to lend without a record of profitability. The entrepreneur should not be concerned whether the financing is in the form of debt or equity. Assuring an infusion of cash for facilities, equipment, payroll, and working capital is of paramount importance. Successful rounds of private financing may help grow a business to a point at which the entrepreneur can successfully offer stock to the general public, an event that may handsomely reward early investors if the company has done well and the public is eager to snap up shares.

Private financing is highly customized; many aspects of a deal can be negotiated after an investor has expressed interest. Entrepreneurs and investors may seem fairly far apart at first, but deals are limited only by the creativity of the parties involved. For example, a Washington, DC-area high-tech startup, stymied by bankers' loan turndowns, teamed up with a real estate developer that had space to spare in a new project. In exchange for locating in the building and an option to purchase stock, the developer provided financial backing.

Private placements can be completed in a matter of days, but the entrepreneur must be prepared to devote considerable time and energy to the search for financing. Prior to the search, the entrepreneur and his or her advisers should prepare a document known as a private placement memorandum for circulation to potential investors. There is no legal requirement for this document, but similar to a detailed business plan, it presents the company's case to those who do not personally know the entrepreneur. The memorandum should contain information on how the capital will be used, include business forecasts, and disclose risks to potential investors. Preparation of a memo-

randum is a valuable exercise in its own right; it helps entrepreneurs take stock of their business and consider the future in some detail. At a later date, the document may serve as the centerpiece of the registration statement for an initial public stock offering.

Attorneys and accountants can often introduce the entrepreneur to potential investors. Professional business brokers can locate investors and arrange deals for a fee. Even the commercial banker who holds the mortgage on an entrepreneur's house can be a source of leads. However, the relationship between the entrepreneur and investor must click on the personal level. The entrepreneur must be sure there is a commonality of interest and goals and a shared vision of the future. Entrepreneurs should take their time to get to know potential investors—away from the office.

The Securities and Exchange Commission and the securities departments of the individual states recognize that a minimum of regulations helps smaller companies quickly raise the capital they need. Private equity placements are "exempt" financing because the entrepreneur does not have to file registration documents that would precede a public stock sale. The entrepreneur simply completes a form, which provides general information about the company and the stock the company plans to issue, the costs associated with the financing, and the uses planned for the proceeds. Entrepreneurs should be aware that federal antifraud and civil liability statutes remain in force.

With knowledge and persistence, entrepreneurs can strategically use private capital to add value to their company and make it more attractive to future investors. Entrepreneurs should constantly build their network of potential investors. It does not hurt to get to know potential investors long before they are needed.

TIME WARNER MUSCLES ITS UNDERWRITERS

Wall Street investment bankers don't usually let themselves get pushed around by the corporate clients. But that's exactly what Time Warner did to Salomon Inc. and Lazard Freres & Co.

Salomon and Lazard Freres were left with millions of dollars in paper losses on Time Warner notes after they bowed to the demands of Time Warner.

The bankers got hurt when Time Warner, eager to take advantage of plunging interest rates, unloaded its latest batch of $1 billion in 30-year bonds authorized by a shelf registration. The problem: Wall Street underwriters led by Salomon were still trying to find buyers for Time Warner's last $1 billion offering of a week earlier.

The new bonds hammered the price of Time Warner notes held by Salomon, Lazard, and their customers. What made matters worse is that Salomon, as lead manager, had the legal right to delay the Time Warner bond sale by three days. Time Warner made it clear that if Salomon didn't waive its legal right, Salomon's entire relationship with Time Warner could be in jeopardy. And that could deprive Salomon of its chance for big fees on future sales of securities and corporate assets for Time Warner. Bond market watchers say the episode shows the ability of corporate giants such as Time Warner to play big Wall Street firms off against each other.

Before the advent of shelf registrations, big corporations would plan their entire program of bond sales in advance with a small circle of underwriters. Now the companies can fire off bond sales at a moment's notice, moving quickly to take advantage of market conditions and letting big Wall Street firms bid for the bonds.

Wall Street firms don't want to alienate big issuers because the bond sales carry sizable fees. On the $1 billion Time Warner bonds, the fee was $10 million.

Adapted from Randall Smith and Thomas T. Vogel, Jr., "Time Warner Muscles Its Underwriters," *The Wall Street Journal*, January 28, 1993, pp. C1, C12. Reprinted by permission of *The Wall Street Journal*, © 1993 Dow Jones & Company, Inc. All Rights Reserved Worldwide.

weeks. Figure 6.5 identifies this period as the *stock trades ex-rights period.* Shareholders can sell the rights in secondary markets if they do not want to exercise them.[5]

The issuing firm may engage an investment banker to stand by to purchase shares not subscribed on an underwritten basis. The investment banker would then sell the unsubscribed shares to other investors. The *standby agreement* calls for the issuing firm to pay a standby fee to the investment banker.

From the perspective of the corporation and management, there are benefits to using a rights offering to raise new financing. By offering the stock to existing shareholders, who are presumably happy with the present firm management, the likelihood

---

[5]The theoretical value of a right is:

$$\frac{\text{Price of old stock with rights} - \text{price of new stock}}{\text{Number of rights for one share} + 1}$$

For example, a company permits its stockholders to subscribe to one new share of stock at $45 for each four shares of that stock currently owned. The stock is trading at $55 per share. The theoretical value of a right is $2: ($55 − $45) ÷ (4 + 1). The actual value may deviate from the theoretical value because of transactions costs and speculation.

FIGURE 6.5

Key rights offering dates

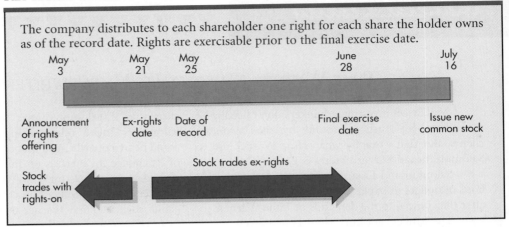

The company distributes to each shareholder one right for each share the holder owns as of the record date. Rights are exercisable prior to the final exercise date.

| May 3 | May 21 | May 25 | June 28 | July 16 |

Announcement of rights offering

Ex-rights date

Date of record

Final exercise date

Issue new common stock

Stock trades ex-rights

Stock trades with rights-on

of successfully raising the amount of new funds is increased. Furthermore, the underwriting costs of a rights offering, compared to a public offering of new stock, are substantially lower. Hence, it is normally in the firm's best interest to issue stock to a friendly, receptive audience while at the same time save the underwriting costs. However, companies in the United States tend to rely on rights offerings to raise additional equity capital to a lesser extent than foreign companies.[6]

PRIVATE PLACEMENT. An organization issuing securities can also bypass investment bankers by placing an entire issue of new securities directly with investors.[7] This process is called **private placement.**[8] The Prudential Corporation Finance Group has a portfolio of about $20 billion of loans privately placed with it.[9] As a rule of thumb, private placements are about 25 to 50 percent less costly than using an investment banker. The savings may result from two sources. First, if investment bankers are not used, the investment banking fee is saved. Second, privately placed securities are exempt from the costly SEC registration requirement of issuing a prospectus.

Private placements allow the issuer and investor to negotiate specialized contract terms. The terms may be either less or more restrictive to the firm than a public offering. For example, the issuer of debt securities may be able to convince investors to allow the firm to forgo any repayments of the loan for several years. Such a deferral is difficult to achieve with a public offering. On the other hand, an investor may require a higher rate of return for a private placement of securities.

Private placement. A securities issue offering made to institutional investors. The securities are not registered with the Securities and Exchange Commission.

---

[6]A review of *The Wall Street Journal* for December 14, 1993 indicated that rights for only two firms traded on the previous day: Latin American Discovery Fund and D&N Financial.

[7]Sometimes companies use an investment banker to locate investors to purchase the securities from the company. The banker receives a fee for this service.

[8]Private placements are prevalent in most countries. However, Japan had virtually no private placement activity of foreign stocks. Moreover, for a company listed on the Tokyo Stock Exchange, no private placement of shares is allowed unless the value of the placement is less than 1 million yen and the number of investors the securities are placed with is less than 50.

[9]The source of this information is *The Corporate Finance Sourcebook, 1993* (New Providence, NJ: National Register Publishing), p. 388.

1. Define: investment banker, underwriter, spread.
2. What does the term *syndicate* mean when applied to investment banking?
3. Describe the three essential functions performed by investment bankers in issuing new securities in the primary market.
4. Discuss the dilemma faced by the investment banker in pricing an issue of new securities.
5. What is the difference for a corporation which is selling its common stock to the public for the first time if the investment banker underwrites the issue or sells the stock on a best-efforts basis?
6. Define shelf registration (SEC Rule 415). What are the advantages and disadvantages of shelf registrations?
7. Describe the rights offering process.
8. What is a private placement and why would a firm choose this type of financing?

6.4 THE SECONDARY MARKETS

Earlier discussion mentioned that secondary market transactions have no effect on the original issuers of securities: Issuers do not receive additional cash from trades in secondary markets. However, well-functioning secondary markets make it possible for investors to convert claims issued by primary borrowers into cash or other securities on a moment's notice. This feature frees investors from the need to wait for financial contracts to mature before they can recover their funds, thereby increasing their willingness to invest in financial assets. Secondary markets also serve as sensitive indicators for borrowing and lending decisions in primary markets and for pricing new loans and securities.

Secondary markets range from informal groups of traders who deal with each other by telephone, making verbal agreements that are later confirmed in writing, to highly organized markets where brokers meet each other face to face. In either case, an investor places an order to buy or sell a specific security, say, Long Island Power and Lighting Company, with a broker or a dealer. A broker acts as the investor's agent but does not take title to the security. Brokers execute trades with other brokers for a commission. A dealer buys a security from one investor and resells it to another investor or another dealer. The dealer's profit (or loss) is the difference between the price he or she pays and the price at which he or she sells. The dealer bears the risk of price changes while owning the security. The primary service of both brokers and dealers is to bring buyers and sellers together.

In the secondary markets the migration of securities brokers and dealers to other countries from their home markets has been stimulated by the rapid growth of cross-border investing by individuals and institutions such as mutual funds, insurance companies, and pension funds. In Japan, for example, governmental authorities attempted until the late 1970s to control the direction and volume of financial flows into and out of Japan. The relaxation of Japanese capital controls on international transactions in the late 1970s was followed by an outpouring of Japanese investment funds into the securities of other countries. Japanese securities dealers established large operations in New York and London and other major capital markets to buy and sell foreign securities for their Japanese clients. As another step in the liberalization of its financial system, Japan

FIGURE 6.6

THE SECONDARY MARKETS

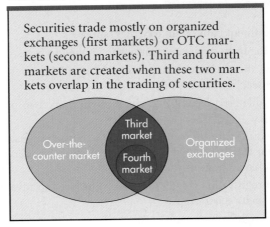

Securities trade mostly on organized exchanges (first markets) or OTC markets (second markets). Third and fourth markets are created when these two markets overlap in the trading of securities.

granted European and North American banks and securities firms greater access to the Tokyo market, to buy Japanese securities for foreign investors and to sell foreign securities to Japanese investors.

We can think of secondary markets as consisting of four submarkets: *organized stock exchanges, over-the-counter (OTC) markets, third market,* and *fourth market.* Figure 6.6 shows the relationship between these markets.

6.4.1 Organized Stock Exchanges

Corporations like Blockbuster Entertainment Corporation and Xerox Corporation list their equity securities for trading on a *stock exchange (first market).* The two national U.S. stock exchanges are the New York Stock Exchange (NYSE) and the American Stock Exchange. There are five regional U.S. exchanges: Boston Stock Exchange, Cincinnati Stock Exchange, Midwest Stock Exchange, Pacific Stock Exchange, and Philadelphia Stock Exchange. The operation of stock exchanges in other parts of the world is similar in nature to U.S. exchanges.

The **stock exchange** centralizes trading in one location, the floor of the exchange (see Figure 6.7). Public buy and sell orders for stocks of companies are conducted on the floor at *trading posts* by participants yelling out prices. A **trading post** is the location at which various stocks or groups of stocks are traded on the floor of the exchange. Each company's stock trades at only one post so that trading can be tracked and kept orderly. At each trading post is a *specialist.* A **specialist** is a dealer assigned to the stocks trading at the post; he or she has the responsibility of ensuring that each listed stock experiences an "orderly succession of prices."[10] If the demand for Xerox stock equals the supply of Xerox stock at a given price, the shares trade. If there is more stock for sale than buyers are willing to buy, the specialist can buy the excess stock using her or his own capital. The specialist will mark up the price of the stock and, hopefully, later sell it for a profit. If prices move down, the specialist may have to sell the stock at a loss.

Stock exchange. A physical location where securities trade like at an auction. Securities are always bought by the highest bidders and sold by the lowest offerers.

Trading post. Place on the exchange floor where a company's stock trades.

Specialist. Brokers to the brokers.

[10]Tokyo's stock exchange operates without specialists. The *saitori* who keep the records of the bid and asked prices for the stocks traded at their posts work for stock exchange member firms. But they do not in fact buy and sell, and they have no obligations to maintain a market—indeed, quite the contrary. If the best bid they have is 10 percent below the closing price of the day before, they are required not to open the stock at all.

FIGURE 6.7

ORDER FLOW FOR A NYSE LISTED SECURITY

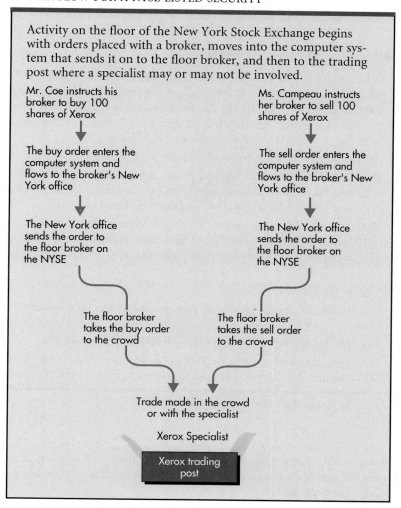

Activity on the floor of the New York Stock Exchange begins with orders placed with a broker, moves into the computer system that sends it on to the floor broker, and then to the trading post where a specialist may or may not be involved.

Mr. Coe instructs his broker to buy 100 shares of Xerox

The buy order enters the computer system and flows to the broker's New York office

The New York office sends the order to the floor broker on the NYSE

The floor broker takes the buy order to the crowd

Ms. Campeau instructs her broker to sell 100 shares of Xerox

The sell order enters the computer system and flows to the broker's New York office

The New York office sends the order to the floor broker on the NYSE

The floor broker takes the sell order to the crowd

Trade made in the crowd or with the specialist

Xerox Specialist

Xerox trading post

However, not all trades at the post go through the specialist. Many trades occur between two floor brokers who show up at a post at the same time. When floor brokers are unable to execute a trade, the trade goes through the specialist. In 1993, specialists participated in about 20 percent of all trades on the NYSE.[11]

Firms that list their securities on an exchange receive a number of benefits. Their shares are more marketable due to greater awareness of the firm by investors and public confidence in standards for trading enforced by the stock exchange. The increased marketability makes it easier for the firm to raise equity funds from both individuals and institutions. However, public listing incurs significant reporting costs for issuing 10-Ks, annual reports, and other documents required by regulatory agencies.

Table 6.5 summarizes the criteria for both listing and possible delisting of a security on the NYSE.[12] Requirements for listing on other stock exchanges, both in the

[11]*New York Stock Exchange Fact Book, 1993.*

[12]An alternative set of listing standards exists for companies organized outside the United States that meet the normal size and earnings yardsticks for NYSE listing.

TABLE 6-5

NYSE Listing and Delisting Requirements

Initial Listing Requirements:

1. Either (a) the pretax income for the most recent year must be at least $2.5 million and the pretax income over each of the preceding two years must be at least $2 million, or (b) the pretax income over the most recent three years must be at least $6.5 million in total with a minimum of $4.5 million in the most recent year. All three years must be profitable.

2. Net tangible assets must be worth at least $18 million.

3. There must be at least 1.1 million shares outstanding that are publicly held, and these shares must have an aggregate market value of at least $18 million. (This amount is subject to periodic adjustment based on market conditions.)

4. There must be either (a) at least 2000 stockholders who each own a minimum of 100 shares, or (b) at least 2200 stockholders with the monthly trading volume averaging at least 100,000 shares over the most recent six months.

Conditions for Possible Delisting:

1. The number of stockholders with each owning at least 100 shares falls below 1200.

2. The number of shares that are publicly held falls below 600,000.

3. The aggregate market value of publicly held shares falls below $5 million. (This amount is subject to periodic adjustment based on market conditions.)

Adapted from the New York Stock Exchange Fact Book, 1993.

United States and abroad, are less rigorous. Generally, the NYSE requires all the criteria to be met for an initial listing. Any subsequent violation of a requirement risks possible expulsion from the exchange.

One of the most significant developments in equity markets that began in the 1980s was the growing trend toward the trading of common stocks across political borders. For instance, the common stock of Texas Instruments Corp. trades on the London and Tokyo exchanges and in Switzerland on the Zurich, Geneva, and Basel stock exchanges. London's International Stock Exchange displays prices for over 600 overseas securities.

It is clear that one reason companies seek a foreign listing relates to lowering the cost of financing. Corporations confined to a single financial market may feel constrained in various ways. For example, a company such as Philip Morris, Inc., which has global operations, may have such substantial demands for capital that it must tap several financial markets simultaneously. A presence in a number of markets can increase the size of any given issue and enhance the flexibility for raising funds. As another example, issuing stock in other markets can help raise the name recognition of a company with potentially beneficial effects on sales and profits. Also, having a presence in various world stock markets may serve strategic interests. By broadening the shareholder base, the company may be better able to resist takeover pressure from another company and, in turn, may be able to undertake foreign mergers and acquisitions more easily.

▼▼▼▼▼▼▼▼▼▼▼▼▼▼

THIRD-MARKET TRADING CROWDS EXCHANGES

The third market is coming on strong in competition with stock exchanges for trading business. And one big third-market player is speeding the growth by paying brokers to funnel their customers' orders through his system.

The third market is off-exchange trading in stocks that are listed on exchanges. The growth in trade and share volume in the third market is a serious concern for executives at the New York Stock Exchange, which still dominates the activity in its own listings but lately has lost business to others, including regional exchanges.

In 1989, the third market became the third-largest trading arena for New York Stock Exchange listed stocks, behind the Big Board itself and the Midwest Stock Exchange in Chicago.

What's especially frustrating, regional exchange executives say, is that the third market plays by different rules. "We are being forced to play full-contact football in tennis whites," says Caroline B. Austin, president of the Midwest specialist firm Dempsey & Co. "We must abide by the rules of the exchangele competing in a relatively deregulated environment."

Nothing can be more deregulated than paying brokers for their business. That's what Bernard L. Madoff Investment Securities, a New York firm, is doing. Mr. Madoff gives brokers a rebate of one cent a share on orders of 3000 shares or less.

A 500-share order would cost a broker about 80 cents to trade on the Midwest exchange. That order can earn the broker $5 when traded with Mr. Madoff.

Mr. Madoff can make money even with rebates by rapidly turning over those transactions at slightly better prices elsewhere, often on the very exchanges he competes with. "We have more efficient, faster execution than any exchange, and absolutely at a competitive price," says Mr. Madoff.Mr. Madoff.

Mr. Madoff won't talk about his customers. But people close to the situation say they include many brokers that specialize in small investor orders: Alex. Brown & Sons Inc.; A.G. Edwards & Sons Inc. and Charles Schwab & Co., among others.

Mr. Madoff says the exchanges feel threatened by automated trading systems, which are proving to be faster and cheaper than the specialists who handle trading on the exchange floor.

Of course, there are disadvantages to overseas listings, not the least of which are disclosure requirements and investor relations. Differences in the quantity of information, the frequency of disclosure, and accounting procedures all pose burdens in both financial and managerial terms. When a company decides to seek a foreign listing, investor relations can be a delicate issue because of cultural differences and may demand particular attention. A variety of other barriers such as foreign exchange controls, limitations on domestic ownership of foreign securities, and different tax rules can present problems.

6.4.2 The Over-the-Counter Market

Thousands of security dealers linked by a computerized network comprise the **over-the-counter (OTC) market** (second market). The OTC market is a *negotiated market* in con-

> **Over-the-counter (OTC) market.** Secondary markets conducted by dealers who supply buy-sell quotes on the securities in which they deal. If the securities are listed on an organized exchange, the market is called the *third market*.

trast to the auction markets of the organized exchanges. Individual dealers, actually the brokerage firms they work for, declare themselves "market makers" in an OTC-listed stock. These brokerages buy the stock directly from the seller, mark it up, and sell it to someone else. OTC dealers do not have an obligation to make a fair and orderly market. And unlike exchanges, which operate within fixed trading hours, OTC market hours are not fixed. Securities continue to trade in the OTC market even if an exchange halts trading.

The OTC market consists of two classes of securities. One class is for relatively inactive securities that normally trade in regional brokerage offices. The second class is for actively traded OTC securities. These securities trade on the National Association of Securities Dealers' Automated Quotation System (NASDAQ) or on the National Market System (NMS). NASDAQ and NMS are computer-based quotation systems.

NASDAQ is the largest market in the world as measured by the number of companies listed, the second largest based on dollar volume of equity trading, and the third largest in terms of number of shares traded.[13] NASDAQ International is a U.K.-based version of the U.S. NASDAQ system. Its purpose is to provide transatlantic securities markets for U.S. stocks.

6.4.3 The Third Market

Third market. Over-the-counter trading of securities that are listed on organized exchanges.

The **third market** refers to the trading of any *exchange-listed* security in the over-the-counter (OTC) market by firms that are not members of an exchange. The transaction bypasses an organized exchange, such as the NYSE. Weeden and Co., for example, is a large brokerage firm that operates in the third market. It maintains inventories of about 300 securities and competes with the specialists on the floor of the exchange who deal in these issues. The company finances its inventory of securities with loans payable on demand from commercial banks. Since Weeden's inventories average four to five times its equity capital, an unexpected change in the market price of the securities it holds could cause a decline in the value of its inventory that would substantially lower or even destroy the value of Weeden's stockholders' equity. The Financial Reality article on the previous page discusses the emerging prominence of the third market and how it is affecting securities trading on organized exchanges.

6.4.4 The Fourth Market

Fourth market. Direct trading of securities between institutions without the service of dealers or brokers.

The **fourth market** is an electronic trading system for securities. Buyers and sellers in this market deal directly with each other to trade securities without the aid of brokers. Several NYSE member firms, such as Morgan Stanley, Salomon Brothers, and Bear, Stearns and Company, and institutional investors, such as pension funds and mutual funds, are participants.

Much of the trading in the fourth market is done through computerized systems called *Instinet Crossing Network, Portfolio System for Institutional Investors,* and *Single Price Auction Network.* For instance, Morgan Stanley may enter the price per share that it is willing to pay for Microsoft Corporation stock. TIAA-CREF, a large pension fund, may enter the price per share it is willing to accept to sell Microsoft stock. These systems automatically record any transaction and set up the paperwork for its completion without revealing the identity of the transacting parties to each other. Electronic trading systems represent an important step in the continuing development of secondary markets for trading securities without an exchange floor.

[13] *1993 NASDAQ Fact Book & Company Directory,* p. 4.

1. Why is a secondary market an important part of the financial system?
2. Describe how the first, second, third, and fourth secondary markets differ from each other.
3. Why would a U.S. company's management apply to have its common stock listed on a major exchange such as the NYSE? Why would management want to list the company's stock on a foreign exchange?

6.5 THE NEXT STEP

The overview of financial markets in this chapter lays important groundwork for later discussion of trading and valuing of bonds (Chapters 7 and 8) and stocks (Chapter 9), and the concept of efficient capital markets (Chapter 10). An understanding of bonds and stocks and how they are valued in relatively efficient markets is critical for comprehending how a firm's value is determined, as we will discuss in Part IV of the text. The value of the firm equals the value of its outstanding debt and equity securities exchanged in financial markets. The time value of money concepts and risk-return principles discussed in Chapters 4 and 5 provide the necessary valuation tools.

SUMMARY ▼▼▼▼▼▼▼▼▼▼▼

INTRODUCTION

- Markets are differentiated as to money markets and capital markets. Securities with maturities of one year or less trade in money markets. Securities with maturities of more than one year trade in capital markets.
- Primary markets are markets for the sale of new securities.
- Secondary markets are markets for the sale of securities subsequent to their initial sale.

FINANCIAL INTERMEDIATION

- Financial intermediaries are specialists in bringing together investors and net fund users without direct contact between these parties. These intermediaries lower transaction costs associated with securities, lower monitoring costs of lenders who oversee the borrowers, vary the maturities of securities, allow securities to be divided, and lower the risk of investing.
- Financial intermediaries issue their own securities to investors and then use the funds obtained to buy securities of other issuers.

THE MONEY AND CAPITAL MARKETS

- Money markets are referred to as near-money markets since money and close substitutes are exchanged in this market. These securities offer lower return, lower risk, and shorter maturities than capital-market securities.
- The capital market consists of long-term debt and equity securities. These markets are both national and international in scope.

KEY TERMS

Introduction

Capital markets
Money market
Primary market
Secondary market

Financial Intermediation

Financial intermediation
Liquidity

The Money and Capital Markets

Eurobonds
Eurocapital market
Eurocurrency loans
Eurodollar market
Euroequity

- The Eurodollar market is a network of world financial centers to transfer funds from surplus units to deficit units. The Eurodollar market is less regulated than domestic money markets.
- The Eurocapital market has three submarkets: Eurocurrency loans, Eurobonds, and Euroequity. The distinctive feature of these markets is that the securities are denominated in a currency other than that of the country in which the issuer of the security is located.

THE PRIMARY MARKETS

- Investment bankers play an important role in issuing new securities in primary markets. These bankers are financial services organizations specializing in transferring funds from those who wish to invest to those who need the funds. Their role in issuing securities includes three functions: investigative, risk bearing, and selling.
- Investment bankers can either assume the risk of selling the securities by underwriting the sale of the securities (firm-commitment offering) or leave the risk with the issuer (best-efforts offering).
- Alternate means of issuing new securities are shelf registrations, rights offerings, and private placements.

THE SECONDARY MARKETS

- Secondary markets consist of organized stock exchanges (first markets), over-the-counter market (second markets), third market, and fourth market.
- First markets are auction markets. The other markets are negotiated markets. The third market is the trading of exchange listed securities in the OTC (or second) market. The fourth market is an electronic trading system in which participants deal directly with each other without the aid of brokers.

FURTHER READING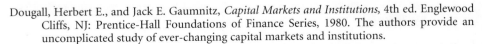

Dougall, Herbert E., and Jack E. Gaumnitz, *Capital Markets and Institutions,* 4th ed. Englewood Cliffs, NJ: Prentice-Hall Foundations of Finance Series, 1980. The authors provide an uncomplicated study of ever-changing capital markets and institutions.

Hayes, Samuel L., III and Philip M. Hubbard, *Investment Banking: A Tale of Three Cities.* Boston, MA: Harvard Business School Press, 1990. This excellent book provides unique insight into the business of investment banking in the international arena.

O'Connor, Dennis, "For Best Underwriting, Pick Right Issues to Negotiate," *Corporate Cashflow* (February 1993), pp. 24–25. This article provides a practitioner's view of issuing stocks.

Zayachek, Jon, *Jon Z's Primer.* Upper Montclair, NJ: X-Rho Enterprises, Inc., 1988. This book provides a concise, readable guide about money markets.

SELF-TEST PROBLEMS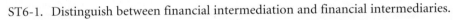

ST6-1. Distinguish between financial intermediation and financial intermediaries.

ST6-2. What is the difference between money-market mutual funds (MMMFs) and other money-market instruments? How have investors been benefited by the development of MMMFs?

ST6-3. Since trading on the New York Stock Exchange (NYSE) and the over-the-counter (OTC) markets do not provide new capital to business corporations and governments, how can the NYSE and the OTC markets be justified as part of the system of financial markets?

PROBLEMS ▼▼▼▼▼▼▼▼▼▼▼▼

FINANCIAL INTERMEDIATION

6-1. When are the services of a financial intermediary required? Who uses financial intermediaries? Why?

6-2. There are many different types of financial intermediaries. How do they differ and what do they have in common?

6-3. Financial intermediaries provide useful roles in financial markets. What are they?

6-4. Financial intermediaries are often quite profitable businesses. Can you provide an argument that justifies high profits?

THE MONEY AND CAPITAL MARKETS

6-5. Distinguish between the money market and the capital market.

6-6. What ties the money market to the capital market? Why can capital markets be considered more important than money markets?

6-7. What are Eurodollars? Why do Eurodollar deposits typically pay higher returns than deposits in the United States?

6-8. Defend the stock market as a financial institution of real social and economic value.

THE PRIMARY MARKETS

6-9. What role do investment bankers play in the capital markets? Are investment bankers brokers, dealers, both brokers and dealers, or neither of these?

6-10. a. Why might a corporation decide to use the services of an investment banker to sell an issue of its common stock on an underwritten basis?
b. Why might a corporation decide to have an investment banker sell an issue of its common stock on a best-efforts basis?

6-11. Figure 6.3 in the chapter indicates that the investment bankers Donaldson Lufkin & Jenrette Securities Corporation were hired by PETsMART, Inc. to sell common stock of the firm to the public. Within the prospectus there is mention that the initial offering price of $18 "has been determined by negotiations between the Company, the Selling Stockholders and the Representative of the Underwriters."
a. Who are the "Selling Stockholders"?
b. What factors do you think were considered in determining the $18 price?

6-12. Why should an investor interested in buying a new security issue pay close attention to the red herring?

6-13. Describe the difference between shelf registrations, rights offerings, and private placements.

6-14. Why should stockholders sell their rights to a new security issue if they do not wish to exercise the rights and make an additional investment in the corporation?

THE SECONDARY MARKETS

6-15. Indicate if the following transactions taking place in financial markets are examples of primary or secondary market transactions. If the transaction is in the secondary market, indicate whether it occurs in the first, second, third, or fourth market.

a. Ms. Jewell instructs her broker to buy U.S. government bonds issued seven years ago with a remaining maturity of three years. (The bonds had an original maturity of ten years.) The broker executes the order in the OTC market.

b. Mr. Ifflander buys through his broker some newly issued Apple Computer common stock.

c. An insurance company buys a new issue of bonds sold by the State of Arizona through Merrill Lynch brokerage.

d. Mr. Griggs withdraws $10,000 from his passbook savings account and uses the money to purchase General Motors stock, which is listed on the New York Stock Exchange. The broker fulfilled the transaction by buying the stock in the OTC market.

e. Wesley Mutual Fund sells 100,000 shares of Apple Computer common stock to another mutual fund using the Instinet Crossing Network.

f. Ms. Bender instructs her broker to trade 100 shares of General Motors stock (listed on the New York Stock Exchange). The broker transacts through the Pacific Stock Exchange.

LIBRARY PROBLEM

6-16. Write a one-page report comparing the amount of new equity securities issued in two foreign markets of your choice. Your report should include both private placements and initial public offerings.

COMPREHENSIVE PROBLEM ▼▼▼▼▼▼▼▼▼▼▼

6-17. As a registered sales representative for a New York Stock Exchange firm, you have been asked to address a group of undergraduate students about the financial markets. In background preparation for your remarks, you outline the answers to the following questions.

a. What is the role of financial intermediaries?

b. What are the main types of financial intermediaries?

c. What benefits for the financial system do financial intermediaries provide?

d. What is the distinction between the money and capital markets?

e. What is the distinction between primary and secondary securities markets?

f. How do investment bankers facilitate the operation of the primary security market?

g. What alternatives to the use of an investment banker does a firm have in selling its securities?

h. How do the secondary securities markets work to the advantage of both users and savers of funds?

i. What submarkets make up the secondary securities markets?

ANSWERS TO SELF-TEST PROBLEMS ▼▼▼▼▼▼▼▼▼▼▼▼

ST6-1. Financial intermediation is the process of receiving money from savers and transferring it to users through the creation of debt and equity contracts. Financial intermediaries are the numerous classes of financial institutions such as banks, insurance companies, mutual investment funds, and pension funds that carry out the process of financial intermediation. These institutions provide two important benefits for the financial system through intermediation. First, by taking advantage of economies of scale, the financial institutions are able to reduce transaction and monitoring costs by providing central markets for savers and users of funds. Second, financial intermediaries create a variety of financial instruments to meet the saving and investment needs of various types of savers and users.

ST6-2. Money-market mutual funds (MMMFs) receive cash from small businesses or individuals who do not have sufficient money to invest in a diversified portfolio of regular money-market instruments which have minimum denominations ranging from $10,000 to $100,000 or more. MMMFs are organized by investment bankers and other money managers to pool the short-term funds of small investors for the purchase of large-denomination money-market instruments such as Treasury bills, commercial paper, negotiable certificates of deposit, and bankers' acceptances. Thus, small investors have access to a portfolio of money-market investments with a minimum of from $500 to $1000. Thus, MMMFs have benefited small investors by giving them greater access to a variety of short-term investments other than passbook savings accounts in banks and savings and loan institutions.

ST6-3. It is true that transactions on the New York Stock Exchange and other stock exchanges constitute trading in the secondary market (with sellers not being the original issuers of the securities traded). However, if no secondary securities markets existed, such as organized exchanges or over-the-counter markets, the liquidity of corporate and government securities would be greatly impaired. This would make it difficult for investors who purchased the corporate or governmental securities at the time of their original issue to find buyers at some future date. In the case of bonds, this would mean that original purchasers might be locked into holding the debt until its maturity even though the purchaser needed funds for some other purpose. Since common stocks have no maturity date, investors in common stocks would have even less liquidity unless they undertook an expensive and tedious process of seeking out interested buyers. By providing an after market for securities, organized secondary markets such as the stock exchanges facilitate raising capital by corporations and governments.

Video Case 6

Trading Stocks the Old-Fashioned Way

The New York Stock Exchange (NYSE) traces its origin back to the Buttonwood Agreement made on May 17, 1772. Since then it has become the world's leading stock exchange and, as the video commentator says, "a world symbol of capitalism." In this video the method of trading on the NYSE is compared to the computer-based screen trading common in other stock markets. On the NYSE trading is done the old-fashioned way—between two people on the exchange floor. The exchange floor provides a single, central location for trading. Centralized trading concentrates buyers, sellers, and pertinent information, thereby enhancing both price setting and liquidity.

In the NYSE's system, when investors want to buy or sell stock, they call their stockbrokers who relay the orders to floor brokers who make the trade sometimes in an open outcry auction, and earn a commission for doing so. If the trade is a limit order, that is, an order to sell or buy when a specified price is reached, the order is given to the specialist in that stock and recorded in his or her limit order book. As the stock reaches new price levels, the specialist completes the pending limit orders and shares the commission with the floor trader. Specialists are unique to the NYSE. Besides maintaining the limit order book, they act as dealers in certain stocks and are required to maintain an orderly market in those stocks. That means buying and selling from their own accounts to even out temporary imbalances in sell or buy orders, which in volatile markets can expose the specialist to great risk.

Computer-based markets, such as the NAS-DAQ market, link many geographically separated market makers via computer screen. These screens show the current price at which dealers will sell (the *asked* price) or buy (the *bid* price) a given share of stock. Unlike the NYSE where a single specialist serves a firm (or a few firms), on the NASDAQ there can be many (sometimes over 30) market makers for a single company's stock. When an order is placed, the stockbroker looks through available quotations and contacts the dealer with the best price and completes the trade. A significant difference between these two markets—NYSE and NASDAQ—involves how participants are compensated. Dealers in the NASDAQ market earn money through the bid-asked spread, not via straight commissions as on the NYSE. Competition between many market makers should, in theory, narrow the spread between the bid and asked prices. Whether or not that occurs is the topic of considerable discussion (see "Investors Beware! The hanky-panky behind NASDAQ volatility," by Gretchen Morgenson, *Forbes,* August 16,1993). Despite having multiple market makers, the bid-asked spreads on the NASDAQ tend to be much wider than on the NYSE. The video points out a final difference between the two markets. In the NASDAQ market, market makers will not always accept the risk required to carry out market stabilization efforts. This was evident during the market crash of 1987, when many NASDAQ stocks simply did not trade. The dealers did not answer their phones.

Study Questions

1. A criticism of the NASDAQ system is that when markets fall there is no single person to restore or maintain an orderly market. Can you explain why, with multiple market makers, not one of them has an incentive to accept this responsibility?

2. One of the most important concepts in finance is *market efficiency,* or the extent to which information is reflected in stock prices. Do you think that a centralized exchange or a computer-linked trading system would set prices more efficiently? Explain why.

CHAPTER 7

Fixed-Income Securities

In the financial world, there are two kinds of securities: debt and equity, commonly called bonds and stocks, respectively. They are often mentioned in the same breath, but they are very different kinds of investment. Stocks get most of the press. The ups and downs of the stock market—not bond prices—are highlighted on the nightly news. But the bond market in terms of dollar volume traded is many times larger than the stock market. When we buy the stock of Walt Disney Inc., we gain equity in the company and become part owners. When we buy Disney's bonds, we own debt and become creditors because we have loaned money to the company.

Over the last few decades there has been a dramatic shift away from the use of equity to finance corporations in the United States. Many of the strongest firms used to operate with little or no debt. In recent years a great many companies, including some of the biggest and strongest, have dramatically increased their debt levels. For example, in 1984 the proportions of long-term debt funds used by General Electric Company and General Motors Corporation to finance their assets were 6 percent and 10 percent, respectively. Starting 1993, these respective figures were 46 and 84 percent, about eight-fold increases.

Why the significant substitution of debt for equity financing by U.S. companies? There is no simple answer to the question. Financial commentators offer several explanations. We will discuss two of the more important reasons—taxes and financial innovation.[1] The current tax code provides an advantage to corporations that use debt financing. And financial innovation has blurred the distinction between debt and equity securities.

We will see why debt investors must understand their legal rights stated in the *indenture*, a contract between investors and the issuer of the security. We will examine

---

[1] Financial economists conclude that debt remains a puzzle even after decades of research. Agency costs, corporate control, information transmission, and optimal allocation of property rights are also suggested as reasons for issuing debt. An examination of these reasons is beyond the scope of this book.

Fixed-income securities. Debt and preferred stock securities that make fixed dollar payments to investors over their lives.

rating systems for assessing the default risk of debt securities. Furthermore, we will explain how to read price quotations for these securities as published in *The Wall Street Journal* or other daily business newspapers. Finally, we will discuss a security called *preferred stock*. Although preferred stock is not formally a debt security, it possesses enough debt characteristics that people often group it with debt and collectively call both securities *fixed-income securities*. **Fixed-income securities** are marketable financial instruments that offer fixed payments monthly, quarterly, semiannually, or annually.

When you have completed this chapter, you should understand:

- What a debt security is and why it has priority for cash distributions over stocks.
- What an indenture is and how to identify the characteristics of different types of debt securities.
- What tax advantage debt securities have over stocks.
- The process for rating the default risk of fixed-income securities.
- How the financial press reports prices and yields for debt securities.
- How the government and municipal debt markets function.
- Why preferred stock is a fixed-income security.

 ## 7.1 WHAT IS DEBT?

Historically, most of the controversy in defining debt focused on *closely held companies*. Investors in these relatively small and often family-controlled businesses usually want to treat most of their investment as debt. As debt investors they have a better chance of recouping at least part of their investment if the business encounters financial difficulty. The reason is because debt investors have legal priority over both preferred and common stock investors in any cash distributions to investors by the company.

The 1969 Tax Act provides four factors which the Internal Revenue Service (IRS) used to distinguish debt from equity for tax purposes. To be called debt, the financial instrument must have the following features: an unconditional promise to pay interest income and principal, a fixed maturity date, pay a fair market rate of interest, and debt investors must not hold a significant equity ownership interest. If these features exist, the IRS allows the security to be called a debt instrument, and interest paid to debt investors is allowed as a tax-deductible expense to the business.

Bill (T-bill). Short-term (one year or less) security issued by the U.S. Treasury. T-bill is issued at a discount and pays no coupon.

Note. Medium-term (one to ten years) security. Note holder receives coupon payments.

Bond. Long-term (over ten years) security that pays a specified sum (called the principal) either at a future date or periodically over the length of a loan, during which time a fixed rate of interest may be paid on certain dates.

Debenture. A debt obligation not secured by specific property but backed by the general credit of the issuing company.

Mortgage bond. A bond secured with a lien on real property.

7.1.1 The Different Forms of Debt

Newspaper announcements and articles about debt can be hard to understand if you are not familiar with some features and terminology. Given that a security satisfies the legal definition of debt, the financial instrument is either a *bill, note,* or *bond*. **Bills** mature in one year or less, **notes** in one to ten years, and **bonds** in over ten years. Often debt securities are called *debentures,* which has a simple meaning. **Debenture** refers to any bond which is backed only by the good credit of the organization issuing it. As a debenture buyer, you rely on the issuer's full faith and credit as your only assurance of being paid the interest and principal on your loan. When issued by reliable institutions, debentures are usually safe investments.

Secured bonds have specific titles attached to them, such as *mortgage bond, equipment trust certificate,* and *collateral trust bond*. **Mortgage bonds** are collateralized with specific corporate assets, such as buildings. Some of the company's property backs each issue. Occasionally a firm issues mortgage bonds in series. Some issues may be *subordinated,* or *junior* (lower in priority), compared to higher-priority *senior* issues. Most mortgage bonds have a *call provision.* A **call provision** allows the issuer to redeem the security before the maturity date at a given price.

Equipment trust certificates (**ETC**) and collateralized trust bonds are other secured financing alternatives. ETCs are a form of mortgage bonds issued frequently by airlines, railroads, and shipping companies to finance the purchase of "rolling stock" assets such as railroad freight cars, airplanes, or ocean-going oil tankers. These assets secure the loan. The certificate gives bondholders first right to the airplane, railroad car, or ship in the event that the interest and principal are not paid. To protect investors from having their investment retired before maturity, ETCs do not have a call feature.

Collateral trust bonds are similar to mortgage bonds except that they are backed by securities of another company. An independent party, called a *trustee,* keeps the securities to protect their safety. If the issuer defaults in the payment of principal or interest or in the performance of some other provision of the loan contract, lenders can seize the securities securing the bonds and sell them to pay off the debt obligation.

Remember, buying a bond makes you a money lender to the organization; you are a creditor. In case of default, senior bondholders receive funds before junior bondholders and general creditors.[2] In late 1992, the creditors of Continental Airlines received less than full return of their principal. The unsecured creditors got about 5.5 cents on each dollar they were owed by the carrier, much less than the secured creditors received. Because of the greater default risk confronting subordinated bond investors, they should earn higher yields than secured bonds. However, in reality, large firms issuing subordinated bonds often have strong financial positions and their subordinated bonds may carry a lower yield than secured bonds of less financially sound firms.

Table 7.1 summarizes several other types of debt instruments that have been issued in the past few years. The list is by no means all-inclusive, but it does suggest the extent to which management is willing to go to design debt securities to appeal to various market segments based on different investors' needs.

7.1.2 The Indenture

Accompanying a debt security is an *indenture.* The **indenture** is a legal contract setting forth the *covenants*—the provisions and conditions—the firm must follow for the debt securities sold to investors. The indenture usually includes the following information.

- *Name of the issuer,* or borrower.
- *Par (face) value,* or *principal,* is the amount the issuer agrees to pay when the security matures. The par value remains constant over its life and usually equals $1000.
- *Maturity date* is the date of the final payment. Some debt securities have a *call provision,* which allows the issuer to retire the security before its maturity date.
- *Trustee,* usually a large bank or trust company, handles the administrative procedure for making interest payments for the issuer. It is also charged to see that the issuer follows the terms of the security.
- *Coupon rate* is the percentage interest amount of the par value paid each year. The rate usually remains constant over the life of the bond.

---

[2]If the firm files for bankruptcy, some other creditors have a priority over debtholders. For instance, employees have a right to some unpaid wages and governments have a right to unpaid taxes.

Call provision. A feature that allows the issuer to repurchase outstanding bonds at a given price from the holders after a given date.

Equipment trust certificate (**ETC**). A bond issued to pay for new equipment; secured by a lien on the purchased equipment.

Collateral trust bond. A bond secured by pledges of stocks and bonds.

Indenture. A contract specifying the legal requirements between the bond issuer and the bondholders.

TABLE 7-1

CREATIVE DEBT FINANCING AND THE FIRMS OFFERING THEM

> **Zero-coupon security.** A note or bond that earns no annual interest payments. The difference between the purchase price and the par value at maturity represents interest to the holder.

- *Extendable notes* give the issuer the right to change the rate from time to time and give the holder the right to be repaid the principal whenever the value is changed. They have been offered by Federated Department Stores, Inc.
- *Limited period, interest build-up bonds* in which interest accumulates through the third year and thereafter is paid semiannually have been offered by Caterpillar Corporation.
- *Three-year, zero-coupon notes* with a one-year option to acquire a second zero-coupon note have been offered by Citicorp. A **zero-coupon security** (or **zero**) is usually a debenture that sells at a deep discount from its principal amount (par value) and pays no cash interest. At the zero's maturity date, the investor receives all the accrued interest plus the original investment, which together add up to the security's par value.
- *Subordinated put bonds,* which give the holder the right to sell the bond back to the issuer at face value to protect against an increase in interest rates, have been offered by Associates Corporation of North America.
- *Debt securities with "poison put options,"* which allow debtholders to recoup any losses if the firm is taken over, have been offered to clients by the investment banking firm Merrill Lynch.
- *Floating-rate debt securities that convert to fixed-rate debt* when interest rates fall below a benchmark level have been offered by ITT.
- *Certificates of automobile receivables (CARS),* which are backed by car loans, have been offered by GMAC, a subsidiary of General Motors Company.
- *Liquid yield option notes (LYONS),* which are zero-coupon debt securities with options to sell the securities after a fixed period at a specified yield that rises over time, have been offered by Waste Management International.

- *Payment dates* are the dates for paying interest.
- *Type of security* refers to either *bearer bonds* or *registered bonds.* **Bearer bonds** are not registered and have a series of coupons physically attached to them. The bondholder clips each coupon and presents it to a bank or brokerage house for collection. **Registered bonds** usually have no coupons attached. The corporation or its trustee keeps a record of the security owner and sends the interest payment automatically to the registered owner.[3]
- *Conversion feature* allows the holders to exchange their certificates for a specified number of shares of common stock in the corporation.[4]

> **Bearer bond.** A bond issued without a record of the owner's name. Payment is made to whoever holds the bond.
>
> **Registered bond.** A bond issued with a record name of the owner. Payment is made directly to the registered owner of the bond.
>
> **Covenants.** Restrictions placed on the borrower requiring specific standards be met, as verified by the trustee.

Several *covenants* are set forth in the indenture. **Covenants** are specific contracts between the lenders and the borrower. The normal covenants require the firm to maintain property in good working condition, carry property and liability insurance, and restrict the sale of assets, the types of investments, the amount of debt, and the payment

[3]The Tax Act of 1986 prohibits the issuance of new bearer bonds.

[4]Conversion is attractive to investors because it permits them seniority as creditors as well as the advantage of potential price appreciation in the common stock at the same time. The conversion feature usually allows the corporation to issue the debt security with a lower interest rate than is necessary for other debt securities.

FINE-PRINT FOLLIES

The debt indenture is intended to protect all parties by setting forth in legal terms what can and cannot be done. Can one of the parties change the rules after the fact? That's exactly what the trustees did. The lesson for investors: Read the fine print!

Bond indentures spell out the terms of the bond and the obligations of the issuer. It's the job of the bondholders' trustee to enforce the terms of the indenture and protect the interests of the bondholders.

First Trust National Association was trustee for subordinated discount debentures issued by Community Newspapers in 1987. The debt was intended to be subordinated to other debts.

In 1988, Community Newspapers decided to float a second bond series. These bonds were intended to be senior to the debentures. But when the lawyers started to draft the indenture for the new debt, they discovered what Community Newspapers euphemistically calls a "scrivener's error."

The "error" relates to an "antilayering" clause included in the 1987 indenture for the debentures.

The clause protects bondholders, preventing the borrower from adding more senior debt without the holders' permission. The error apparently gave debenture holders more seniority than they were meant to have.

Legal counsel to Community Newspapers convinced First Trust to allow a supplement to the covenants of the debenture. The purpose was to get rid of the antilayering clause. First Trust agreed. This allowed the new, more senior debt issue to be sold. Suddenly, other debt that had been junior only to bank debt found itself moved down in the priority list.

The change became important in February 1991 when Community Newspapers found it necessary to file for Chapter 11 bankruptcy protection. Then on April 1, 1991 First Trust changed its mind about the antilayering clause. It now claimed that the supplement was invalid.

Community Newspapers asked the U.S. Bankruptcy Court judge to allow the supplement.

Adapted from James Lyons, "Fine-print Follies," *FORBES*, October 28, 1991, p. 56. Reprinted by permission of FORBES magazine. © Forbes Inc., 1991.

of cash dividends to equity investors. Failure of the firm and the debt's trustee to follow the covenants can result in a lawsuit, as the above Financial Reality article discusses happened to Community Newspapers.

 Comprehension Check

1. Describe the difference between bills, notes, and bonds.
2. Describe mortgage bonds, equipment trust certificates, collateral trust bonds, and subordinated bonds.
3. What is the purpose of an indenture? What are covenants?
4. Define: par value, maturity date, trustee, coupon rate, call provision, bearer bond, registered bond, and conversion feature.

7.2 ADVANTAGES OF DEBT

Much of the increase in corporate indebtedness that took place during the 1980s was the result of financial innovations which had tax implications. These innovations reduce the difference between the investment characteristics of debt and equity. Corporations are able to issue securities that function very much like equity but are treated as debt for tax purposes.

7.2.1 Tax Motive for Issuing Debt

The desire of firms to issue debt securities instead of equity is largely motivated by the income tax code. Interest payments for debt securities are tax-deductible business expenses to the issuing corporation. Dividend payments associated with stocks are not tax-deductible expenses to the company. Illustration 7.1 shows the significant advantage debt has over equity with respect to lowering the total amount of taxes paid.

ILLUSTRATION 7.1

Multiple taxation of dividends—or why debt financing reduces cash outflows

Conway Corporation and Burnette Limited are equal in all aspects (markets, technology, risk) except for the securities they have issued. Conway has issued both equity and debt securities, with debt securities requiring a $6600 interest payment each year. Burnette has issued only equity securities. The IRS taxes income earned by each corporation at 34 percent. Both firms distribute all net income to equity investors as cash dividends, and these dividends are taxed at 28 percent.

TAXED ONCE

Both companies earn before-tax income of $10,000. Their net incomes are calculated as follows.

	Conway	Burnette
Earnings before interest and taxes	$10,000	$10,000
Interest expense	6,600	0
Earnings before taxes	$ 3,400	$10,000
Income taxes (34%)	1,156	3,400
Net income paid as dividends	$ 2,244	$ 6,600

Conway pays income taxes of $1156, whereas Burnette pays $3400 in income taxes. Dividends are paid out of after-tax dollars. Thus, dividends are taxed by the IRS before the firms pay them to their investors.

TAXED TWICE

When investors receive cash flows from the companies, either as interest income or dividends, they pay tax at the personal income tax rate of 28 percent.

| | Investors in: | |
	Conway	Burnette
Dividend income	$2244	$6600
Interest income	6600	0
Total income	$8844	$6600
Income taxes (28%)	2476	1848
After-tax income	$6368	$4752

RECAP

The effective cumulative tax rates on the original $10,000 income before taxes for each firm is about 36 percent for Conway and 52 percent for Burnette. Thus, a definite tax advantage exists for using debt financing.

	Conway	Burnette
Taxes paid at the company level	$1156	$3400
Taxes paid at the investor level	2476	1848
Total taxes paid	$3632	$5248
Effective tax rate on $10,000 earnings before interest and taxes	36.32%	52.48%

7.2.2 Erosion of Covenants

Some corporate issuers have engaged in innovative financing schemes that hurt debt investors. The classic illustrations of this sort of behavior occur when organizations called *buyout specialists* are able to find ways to make large payments to themselves without paying off the debtholders. **Buyout specialists** raise funds through debt financing to buy the outstanding equity of public companies. Once these specialists control the company, they retire all the equity formerly outstanding to outsiders and take the firm private. The private firm is financed with a tremendous amount of debt, and very little new equity from the buyout specialists. In other cases, management simply ignores the terms of the indenture, or claims there is no violation of any covenants. Illustration 7.2 provides some examples.

Buyout specialists.
Organizations that use borrowed funds to buy public firms and privatize them.

ILLUSTRATION 7.2

Bypassing the covenants

• Drexel Burnham Lambert, a former investment banking company and buyout specialist, controlled more than 50 percent of the equity in a company called Rexene. The remaining 50 percent was owned by investors solicited by Drexel. About six months before announcing that Rexene had serious financial difficulties, Drexel had Rexene make a $7 per share payment to equityholders—Drexel and its solicited investors. This payment exceeded the original equity investment.

- The buyout specialist firm Kohlberg Kravis Roberts (KKR) managed to return to the equity investors in the buyout of Beatrice Company all of their original investment. However, many debt investors found themselves holding securities of a financially distressed company called the E-II Corporation.
- KKR refinanced a leveraged buyout of Storer Communications and paid itself and other equity investors $1 billion. The unfortunate debt investors of the new SCI Communications were left with debt securities selling for only a fraction of their par values.
- May Department Stores and Houston Lighting & Power Company retired high-coupon debt before the first call date allowed by the indenture. The companies offered to pay premium prices to bondholders who voluntarily tendered, while simultaneously announcing that any bonds not tendered voluntarily would be "cash called" at a lower price. Even though the debt covenants forbade the companies from issuing lower-coupon debt to retire higher-coupon debt, the firms ignored this fact and claimed any recent new low-cost debt financing was not the source of funds to retire the called debt.

Comprehension Check

1. Describe the tax advantage associated with debt securities.
2. How did buyout specialists circumvent the indenture?

7.3 RATING DEBT SECURITIES

Four major firms rate default risk of debt securities: Moody's Investors Service, Standard & Poor's Corporation, Fitch Investors Service, and Duff & Phelps, Inc. Standard & Poor's and Moody's are the largest rating firms. Before selling a debt issue, the issuing company may pay a rating firm from $1000 to $50,000 to rate the debt.

7.3.1 Rating Categories

Investment-grade rating. Bond ratings *BBB* (by S&P) or *Baa* (by Moody's) or above.

Junk bonds. Bonds rated below investment grade—rated *BB* (by S&P) or *Ba* (by Moody's) or below.

Table 7.2 provides definitions of bond ratings by Moody's and Standard & Poor's (S&P). The top four categories (*BBB* or *Baa* and above) are **investment-grade ratings.** This term means that the bonds have a minimal level of default risk and a high chance of full payment. For many regulated financial institutions (for example, insurance companies), only investment-grade bonds can be used as collateral for the institution's liabilities.

The market values of investment-grade bonds vary almost entirely in response to changes in the general level of interest rates in the economy. Bonds with ratings below the top four rating grades are lower-grade bonds that entail greater default risk. These bonds are the often-called **junk bonds,** or speculative bonds.

In general, the higher a bond's rating, the lower its interest rate will tend to be. Issuers of higher-rated bonds do not need to offer high interest rates because their credibility attracts investors. But issuers of lower-rated bonds offer higher rates to induce investors to take the potentially greater risk. Over the past few years the difference in

TABLE 7-2

BOND RATING CATEGORIES

Inv grade det

	Very High Quality		High Quality		Speculative		Very Poor	
Standard & Poor's	AAA	AA	A	BBB	BB	B	CCC	D
Moody's	Aaa	Aa	A	Baa	Ba	B	Caa	C

S&P adjusts these ratings with + or – signs. For example, A+ is the strongest A rating. Moody's adjusts using a 1, 2, or 3 designation—1 is the strongest.

Moody's	S&P	
Aaa	AAA	Capacity to pay interest and principal is extremely strong.
Aa	AA	Very strong capacity to pay interest and principal.
A	A	Strong capacity to pay interest and principal, although more susceptible to adverse effects of changes in circumstances and economic conditions.
Baa	BBB	Adequate capacity to pay interest and principal. Adverse economic conditions or changing circumstances are more likely to lead to a weakened capacity to pay interest and principal.
Ba through Ca	BB CC	Predominantly speculative with respect to capacity to pay interest and repay principal according to terms of the obligation.
C	C	Bonds on which no interest is being paid.
D	D	Bonds in default on interest and principal payments.

Source: Standard & Poor's Bond Guide _and_ Moody's Bond Guide.

yield between _AAA_ and _AA_ grades has averaged about 25 _basis points,_ or a quarter of 1 percent. (A **basis point** is one one-hundredth of 1 percent.) The yield difference between _AAA_ and _BBB_ grades is usually more than 100 basis points.

> **Basis point.** One hundredth of a percentage point. Used to express changes in interest rates.

7.3.2 Factors Influencing Ratings

Various states have what are called _prudent-man investment laws_ as eligibility standards for investments of savings banks, trust companies, insurance companies, and other fiduciaries. Since investors and regulators place great reliance on rating services, it is difficult to sell unrated debt securities to the public.

The rating agencies do not reveal exactly how they assign ratings. However, they do indicate the major factors that are evaluated. S&P bases its ratings, in varying degrees, on the following factors.

- The likelihood of default capacity.
- The willingness of the issuer to make timely payments of interest and repayment of principal under the terms of the agreement.
- The nature and provisions of the debt agreement.
- The protection afforded by, and relative position of, the debt issue in the event of bankruptcy, reorganization, or other arrangement under the laws of bankruptcy and other laws affecting creditors' rights.

TABLE 7-3							
RATING CHANGES OF BONDS							
	1987	1988	1989	1990	1991	1992	1993
Upgrades	188	261	306	200	220	262	263
Downgrades	285	386	417	766	695	492	279
Total	473	647	723	966	915	754	542

The figures for 1993 are for January through September.
Source: Various issues of Standard & Poor's Credit Week.

All public debt ratings are monitored on an ongoing basis by S&P specialists. S&P generally conducts a formal written rating review of larger issuers at least annually. As a result of the surveillance process, it may become apparent that changing conditions require reconsideration of a debt rating, which can have important consequences to both the issuer and investors.

- Rating downgrades mean higher financing costs for the issuer; rating upgrades mean less expensive financing.
- Rating downgrades mean losses in market value to the holder of the bond; rating upgrades mean appreciation in value.

In recent years, rating agencies have given advance notice of possible changes in ratings. S&P signals the likelihood of a rating change through its publication *Credit Watch*. The summary given in Table 7.3 indicates that debt rating downgrades dominate any upgrades. The Financial Reality reading on page 233 discusses a model that Shell Canada uses to maintain an investment-grade bond rating.

Comprehension Check

1. Distinguish between investment-grade bonds and junk bonds. Why might an investor choose to purchase one category of these bonds instead of the other?
2. Outline the factors considered by the rating agencies when they determine the rating to assign a particular bond issue.
3. What is the process Shell Canada follows to maintain an investment-grade debt rating?

Bid price. The price at which a dealer offers to buy a security.

7.4 CORPORATE BONDS

Corporate bonds trade primarily among bond dealers, institutional investors, investment banking firms, and wealthy individual investors. Bond trading takes place in the over-the-counter (OTC) market, the American Stock Exchange (AMEX), and the New York Stock Exchange (NYSE).

OTC-traded bonds may have large spreads between the price dealers are willing to pay, the **bid price,** and the price dealers are willing to sell, the **asked price.** The *asked price* minus the *bid price* is the *spread* and represents the dealer's profit. Most bonds

Asked price. The lowest price at which a dealer offers to sell securities— the sell side of the bid-asked spread.

THE RATINGS GAME

For most companies, getting and keeping an investment-grade rating in the United States is crucial. Rating agencies like the way Shell Canada communicates with them. Indeed, the Calgary-based company's relationship with raters is cited as a model. Here is chief financial officer Glenn Darou's common-sense strategy for getting and preserving an investment-grade rating.

1. *No surprises.* Whenever there's a significant structural change in the company or an event that may affect future earnings and cash flow, Darou offers to discuss the matter with the agencies—before the press release. Since a rating agency typically takes a long-term view of a company, it is not likely to have a knee-jerk reaction to normal ups and downs. "But major surprises that suggest fundamental changes will cause them to pause," Darou warns.

2. *Tell all.* "Treat the agencies as insiders," Darou advises. For example, before Shell Canada announced the sale of its coal business in early June, Darou's staff informed the rating agencies. They also disclosed the purchase price, a figure that was not publicly available.

3. *Provide a comprehensive package—in advance.* About a week before a meeting with raters, Darou sends along a complete report with all the company's business assumptions, including price projections for oil, gas and sulfur; forecasts for economic growth, inflation, and interest rates; a detailed five-year plan for earnings, cash for operations, and financings; and, for each division, five-year strategies and a discussion of strengths and vulnerabilities together with the company's response to them.

4. *Bring key executives.* CFO Darou always attends rating reviews with his treasurer and a key operating executive.

5. *Allow adequate time for a routine meeting.* "Three hours is good, four hours is better," in Darou's assessment. For companies meeting with agencies for the first time, be aware that the process can take one or two days.

6. *Follow up immediately.* If rating analysts ask questions that cannot be answered at the meeting, get the information—fast—and pass it on without delay.

7. *Maintain a dialogue.* This should include a regularly scheduled annual review. If Darou suspects difficult times ahead that could threaten the company's credit rating, he calls or meets with the agencies more frequently than usual.

Source: Ida Picker, "The Ratings Game," *Institutional Investor* (August 1991), p. 77.
This copyrighted material is reprinted with permission from Institutional Investor, Inc.,
488 Madison Avenue, New York, NY 10022.

trading on the major exchanges have narrow spreads. However, as Illustration 7.3 shows, the spread can be large. Although the illustration is about U.S. Treasury zero-coupon bonds, similar price disparities can exist for corporate bonds.

ILLUSTRATION 7.3

OTC bond quote disparities

On Friday, April 5, 1991 and Monday morning, April 8, 1991, the editor of *Personal Finance* newsletter asked several dealers for bid-asked quotes on Treasury zero-coupon bonds that expire February 15, 2019. The editor said he wanted to invest $5000, equivalent to about 45 bonds, depending on their price.

The quotes the editor received were as follows. *The Wall Street Journal (WSJ)* quoted price is for transactions of $1 million or more.

Dealer	Bid	Asked	Spread	Commission
Associated Investors	$107.77	$109.25	$1.48	$50
Bidwell & Co.	102.60	109.70	5.10	50
Fidelity Brokerage	102.85	109.96	7.11	0
Gruntal & Co.	109.88	113.88	4.00	0
Ladenburg, Thalmann	105.27	112.04	6.77	0
Merrill Lynch	105.28	109.45	4.17	0
Paine Webber (Boston)	104.12	112.04	7.92	0
Paine Webber (Vienna, VA)	109.10	112.26	3.16	0
WSJ, April 5, 1991, price	105.00	105.60	0.60	

7.4.1 Keeping Tabs on Corporate Bonds

Many daily newspapers, such as *The Wall Street Journal*, report bond transactions that occur on the NYSE and AMEX. Although not stated in the newspapers, the par value of these bonds is $1000. Table 7.4 shows information about NYSE bonds traded April 20, 1994. *Volume* of $35,960,000 is the par value of bonds traded on this date. This number differs from the actual market value of the bonds traded, since bond prices vary from par value. The dollar volume reported is a small fraction—1 to 12 percent—of all the bonds traded on that day because most bonds trade in the OTC market or directly among market makers (brokerage houses) for institutional investors. Fred Zuckerman, treasurer of RJR Nabisco Holdings Corporation, which lists its debt on the NYSE, says: "You're not legally obligated to list your bonds, but you are morally obligated to. Institutional investors can take care of themselves but you owe a lot more to the individual investors."[5] Unfortunately, this view is not shared widely by many corporations.

Issues traded lists the number of different bonds sold on April 20 and on the previous trading day. *Advances* shows the number of bonds that traded at a price higher than on the previous day. *Declines* represents the number of bonds that traded at a price below the price of the previous trading day. *Unchanged* indicates the number of bonds with no price changes from the previous day. *New highs* lists the number of bonds trading at all-time highs. *New lows* shows the number of bonds trading at all-time lows. The *Dow Jones Bond Averages* are straight arithmetic summaries and averages of the prices of 20 selected utility and industrial bonds.

The highlighted Navistar Company *(Navstr)* bond has a coupon rate of 9 percent and the bond matures in the year 2004. This is shown by the coding *9s04*. The bond promises to pay the bearer $90 a year (that is, 9% × $1000 par value) until it matures. The *s* appearing after the interest rate is not a meaningful symbol. It is used simply to separate the interest rate figures from the following figures. Usually *s* appears when the interest rate does not include a fraction and may be confused with the numbers following (see, for example, its exclusion in the quote for Harris 7 3/4 01). The *Cur Yld* column shows that the current yield is 9.2 percent, which is more than the 9 percent coupon rate.

[5]See Leslie Scism, "Big Board Fights to Revive Bond Market," *The Wall Street Journal*, May 27, 1993, p. C1.

TABLE 7-4

NEW YORK STOCK EXCHANGE BONDS

NEW YORK EXCHANGE BONDS

Quotations as of 4 p.m. Eastern Time
Wednesday, April 20, 1994

Volume $35,960,000

	Domestic Wed.	Domestic Tue.	All Issues Wed.	All Issues Tue.
Issues traded	352	393	360	398
Advances	106	115	107	116
Declines	162	209	168	213
Unchanged	84	69	85	69
New highs	1	0	1	0
New lows	86	100	91	103

SALES SINCE JANUARY 1
(000 omitted)

1994	1993	1992
$2,578,365	$3,533,852	$4,243,408

Dow Jones Bond Averages

—1993— High	—1993— Low	—1994— High	—1994— Low		—1994— Close	—1994— Chg.	—1994— %Yld	—1993— Close	—1993— Chg.
109.77	103.49	105.61	98.49	20 Bonds	98.49	−0.10	7.33	107.00	+0.16
105.59	102.30	103.43	96.25	10 Utilities	96.30	+0.05	7.65	104.06	−0.07
114.51	104.58	107.93	100.68	10 Industrials	100.68	−0.25	7.02	109.95	+0.39

CORPORATION BONDS
Volume, $35,720,000

Bonds	Cur Yld	Vol	Close	Net Chg.
AMR 9s16	9.2	315	98⅛	− ⅜
Actava 9½98	10.5	6	90⅛	− ⅞
AirbF 6¾01	cv	45	101½	+ ½
AlskAr 6⅞14	cv	77	80½	...
AlskAr zr06	...	6	38¾	+ ¾
AlldC zr97	...	10	81	− ¼
AlldC zr03	...	5	48	+ ½
AlldC zr09	...	150	30	...
AlegCp 6½14	cv	30	99	− 1
AlgLud 02	cv	13	107	− 4
Allwst 7¼14	cv	30	88	− 1
AmBrnd 8½03	8.2	23	103½	...
AmHme 6⅞97	6.8	18	101	...
AmStor 01	cv	20	118	...
ATT 4¾98	5.1	107	93¼	− ½
ATT 4⅜96	4.5	90	96¼	− ⅛
ATT 4⅜99	4.8	5	90¼	+ ¼
ATT 6s00	6.3	97	95½	...
ATT 8⅝31	8.3	74	103⅝	...
ATT 7⅛02	7.1	438	99⅞	+ ⅛
ATT 8⅛22	8.1	375	100¾	+ ¾
ATT 8⅛24	8.1	187	99⅞	...
ATT 6¾04	7.1	102	95	...
Amsco 2002	cv	10	81	− 6
AnnTaylr 8¾00	9.2	257	95½	− 1⅛
Arml 8.7s95	8.7	3	100¼	...
Arml 8½01	8.9	10	96	+ ⅞
Arml 13½94	13.5	20	100	− ¾
AshO 6¾14	cv	30	99½	− ¼
Atchn 4s95r	4.1	5	98⅛	− ⅜
ARch 10⅜95	9.9	30	105¼	− ½
AubrnHl 12⅜20f	...	25	135	+ ¼
AutDt zr12	...	210	38½	− 1⅜
Avnet 6s12	cv	15	99½	− 1½
Bally 10s06f	cv	31	95	− 1½
BkNY 7½01	cv	3	146½	+ 1½
Barnt 8½99	8.1	50	104⅞	− ⅜
Barnet 8½07	8.3	1	103	...
BellPa 7½13	7.8	52	96	...
BellsoT 8¼32	8.1	53	102	+ 1⅛
BellsoT 7⅞32	8.1	52	97⅛	+ ¼
BellsoT 6½00	6.6	52	98	...
Bellso 6¼03	6.8	7	92½	− ¼
BellsoT 6⅜04	6.9	55	93	+ ⅛
BellsoT 7½33	8.1	75	92¾	− ¼
Bellso 5⅞09	6.9	10	84⅝	− ⅜
Bellso 6¾33	7.9	3	85⅛	+ ⅛
BstBuy 8⅝00	9.1	377	95	...
BethSt 9s00	8.9	51	100¾	− ¼
BethSt 8.45s05	8.8	13	95½	...
BethSt 8⅜01	8.6	60	97	− ¼
Bevrly 7⅝03	cv	20	102¾	+ 1½
Boeing 8⅜96	8.0	85	104¾	...
BoisC 7s16	cv	51	88	− 1½
BoltBer 6s12	cv	70	77	− 5
Bordn 8⅜16	8.8	99	95	− 2⅜
BorgWS 9⅛03	9.6	25	95	+ 1
BwnFer 6¼12	cv	93	91¾	− ¾
CATS zr2006-11	...	10	39½	− ⅞
CIGNA 8.2s10	cv	60	102	− ½
CarnCr 4½97	cv	3	139	...
Champ 6½11	cv	48	97¾	− ¼
CPoM 7¼12	7.8	10	93¼	+ ¼
ChvrnC 9¾17	8.7	10	112¼	+ ¼
Chvrn 9⅜16	8.6	12	109¼	...
Chiquta 10½04	10.5	50	100⅜	...
ChckFul 7s12	cv	10	97	− 1
ChryF 12¾99	10.4	32	122¾	...
Chryslr 13s97	12.2	230	106¼	+ ⅛
Chryslr 9.6s94	9.5	32	101⅛	...
Chryslr 10.95s17	9.5	182	114⅞	...
Chryslr 10.4s99	9.6	51	108¾	+ ¼
ClrkOil 9½04	9.4	47	101⅜	− ⅜
Clmt zrD02	...	10	40	− ⅛
ClevEl 9¼09	9.2	5	101	− ⅛
ClevEl 8⅜11	8.9	26	93⅞	− ⅛
ClevEl 8⅜12	8.7	10	95⅞	− ⅜
Coastl 11¾06	10.6	23	111	− ¾
Coeur 7s02	cv	80	118	− 7
ColeWld zr13	...	1	25	+ 1
vjColuG 9s94f	...	37	115¼	+ ¼
vjColuG 9s93f	...	10	119	...
CmwE 8s03	8.0	5	100⅛	...
CmwE 8⅛07J	8.1	5	99¾	− ¼
CmwE 8¼07	8.2	20	100½	− ¼
CompUSA 9½00	10.5	144	90¼	+ ⅛
ConrPer 6¾01	cv	16	85	− ¼
ConrPer 6½02	cv	328	85	− 2
Consec 8⅛03	8.6	76	94⅞	− 1⅛
ConNG 7¼15	cv	58	102¼	+ ¾
CnPw 6⅞98	7.0	5	98⅛	+ ⅜
CnPw 7½01	7.5	1	100	+ ¾
DataGn 01	cv	50	83½	− 5½
Datpnt 8⅞06	cv	25	77½	− ½
DetEd 6.4s98	6.4	7	100½	+ 2
Dole 7s03	7.6	75	92	− ¼
Dole 6¾00	7.1	5	95¼	...
duPnt dc6s01	6.4	742	94	+ 1⅜
EMC 4¼01	cv	5	104½	− 6½
Eckerd 9¼04	10.1	841	91¼	+ ¼
EBP 6¾06	cv	15	72¼	− 1¼
EnqStr 10⅜02	9.9	50	105⅜	...
EnqStr zr97	...	8	75	...
Enron 10¾98	10.2	7	105½	+ 1
EthAln 8¾01	9.1	65	96½	+ 1¼
Exxon 8¼94	8.2	20	101 3/32	− 5/16
F&M 11½03	12.5	251	92	− 1½
FabrCtr 6¼02	cv	22	81	− 1
FairCp 13⅛06	13.3	12	98½	+ 1¼
Fidcst 6s12	cv	38	88	− 1
Frpt dc6.55s01	cv	90	88½	− ⅞
FremntGn zr13	...	14	33	− ¾
GMA dc6s11	7.7	128	78	...
GMA zr12	...	4	217½	+ ½
GMA zr15	...	52	174	+ ⅛
GMA 8¼16	8.5	521	96¾	...
GPA Del 8¾98	10.7	55	82	...
GEICap 7⅞06	7.6	1	103⅜	+ ⅜
GHost 11½02	11.8	76	97¾	+ ½
GnSgnl 5¾02	cv	20	101	− 2
Gene 10⅜03	12.1	82	85⅝	− 1⅛
GaGlf 15s00	14.0	36	107	− ⅜
GaPw 10s16J	9.7	14	103	...
Grancre 6½03	6.6	46	98	− 1¼
GrnTrFn 10¼02	9.1	25	112½	− 1⅜
Gulfrd 6s12	cv	10	96¾	+ 1¾
Hallb zr06	...	10	48¾	− ⅛
Hallwd na13½09	...	22	89½	− ½
Hallw na13½09C	...	1	89	− 1
Hallwd 7s00	11.1	4	63⅛	+ ⅞
Harris 7¾01	7.8	5	99⅛	− ⅞
Hlttrst 8¾05	9.5	25	92	...
HeclMn zr04	...	19	44¾	+ ¼
HomeDp 4½97	cv	35	112	− 2½
HostM 10⅛99	10.1	10	100½	− 2
HostM 9⅛00	9.3	25	97⅞	...
HostM 9⅞01	10.1	37	97⅞	+ ⅞
HostM 10⅞01	10.9	175	99¾	...
HostM 11¼05	11.3	30	100	− ⅜
HostM 11s07	11.0	20	99⅞	− ⅛
HudFd 8s06	cv	10	102⅝	...
ICN 12⅞98	12.8	51	100⅝	+ ⅜
IMC Fer 6¼01	cv	40	90	...
IllBel 7⅝06	7.6	26	100	+ ⅝
Intlgc 11.99s96f	...	10	100⅛	+ ¼
IBM 9s98	8.7	45	103	− ¼
IBM 8⅜19	8.4	252	99⅞	− ⅛
IBM 6⅜97	6.4	261	99	+ ¼
IBM 7¼02	7.4	249	97⅜	...
IBM 6⅜00	6.7	75	95	...
IBM 7½13	8.1	806	93	+ ⅜
IntShip 9s03	9.6	50	93¾	...
IntTch 9⅜96	9.7	2	97⅛	...
Jamswy 8s05	cv	2	19	...
K mart 8⅜17	8.4	10	100	+ ¼
KaufB 10⅜99	10.1	65	102½	− 1½
KaufB 9⅜03	9.9	385	94½	− ¼
Kolmrg 8¾09	cv	180	98	...
Kroger 9s99	8.9	73	100¾	− 1⅞
Kroger 6⅜99	cv	31	128	− 5
LehmnBr 8¾02	8.3	10	105⅝	+ 1⅞
Leucadia 5¼03	...	1	96	...
Litton 12⅝05	11.5	1	109¾	...
LomasFn 9s03	9.9	1	91	...
LglsLt 7.3s99	7.3	5	100	...
LglsLt 8.9s19	9.4	147	94⅞	+ ⅝
MACOM 9¼06	cv	15	95	− ½
MGM Grd 11¾99	10.8	1	108⅞	...
MGM Grd 12s02	10.7	20	112⅝	+ 3¾
MarO 8½00	8.5	50	100½	...
MarO 8.5s06	8.5	17	100¼	+ 1
MarO 9¾99	9.3	226	105⅜	...
MrtM d7s11	7.7	7	90½	− 5½
Masco 5¼12	cv	40	87¾	− 1¾
Mascotch 03	cv	2	83	− 2½
Maxus 8½08	9.3	10	91	+ 1
vjMcCro 7½s94f	...	14	18½	...
vjMcCro 7½94nf	...	12	22	− 1
McDnlDg 8⅝97	8.3	35	104⅜	...
McDnlDg 9¼02	8.7	78	105¾	+ ½
McDnlDg 9¾12	8.9	165	109	...
Mead 6¾12	cv	6	98	...
Medplx 11¾02	11.1	50	106⅛	− ½
MerLyGlbl 98	...	32	102	− ¼
MKT 5½33f	...	10	54	...
Mobil 8⅝94	8.6	45	100⅜	− ¾
Mobil 8⅜01	7.9	10	106⅜	− ¼
Moran 8¾08f	cv	15	80	...
Motrla zr09	...	60	76¼	− 4
NBD 7¼04	7.3	15	99	− ⅝
NJBTl 7¼11	7.6	17	95	+ ⅜
NJBTl 7⅜12	7.7	5	96	− 1⅝
NtEdu 6½11	cv	15	70½	+ ½
NMed 12⅛95	11.5	5	105⅞	+ 25/32
Navstr 9s04	**9.2**	**15**	**98**	**− 1**
NETelTel 7⅜07	7.6	45	96½	+ 1⅜
NETelTel 6¼03	6.8	5	92	− 1
NETelTel 6⅞23	8.1	7	85	...
NYTel 4⅝04	5.8	15	80⅛	+ ⅛
NYTel 7½09	7.7	30	97¼	− ¼
NYTel 7¾06	7.8	10	99½	− ⅛
NYTel 7⅜11	7.8	5	94	...
NYTel 7⅞17	8.1	7	97	− 1
NYTel 7⅝23	8.2	110	93	− ⅛
NYTel 6½00	7.1	15	92	− 5½
NYTel 7s25	8.1	10	86⅜	+ ½
NYTel 5¼98	5.6	5	94	+ 1
NYTel 5⅝03	6.5	35	87¼	...
NYTel 7¼24	8.1	39	89½	...
Novacr 5½2000	cv	75	91½	− ½
NuevE 12½02	11.8	50	105⅞	+ 1
OccIP 9⅝99	9.2	10	104¾	− ¼
OccIP 9¼19	8.7	40	106¾	− ½
OccIP 10⅛01	9.2	20	109½	+ ¼
OffDep zr07	...	20	70	...
OhBIT 7⅞13	8.0	10	99	− ⅛
OldRep 5¾02	cv	10	103	− 5
Oryx 7½14	cv	150	90	− 1
OutbM 7s02	cv	18	102	+ 1
OwnIll 10¼99	10.2	45	100⅞	+ ⅞
OwIll 11s03	10.4	55	106¼	+ ¾
OwnIll 10½02	10.4	50	100½	+ ⅝
OwnIll 10s02	10.1	808	98¾	+ 1⅝
OwnIll 9¾04	10.1	50	96½	+ ⅞
OwnIll 9.95s04	10.0	5	99½	− 3½
PhilEl 6⅛97	6.3	37	98	+ 1
PhilEl 7¾23	8.3	9	93⅞	− ⅛
PhilEl 7¼24	8.2	8	88½	+ 1
PacTT 7.8s07	7.9	10	99¼	...
PacTT 7¼08	7.6	2	95⅝	...
PacTT 7⅝09	7.8	30	97¾	− ⅛
PacBell 7¼02	7.3	161	99	− ¾
PacBell 7½33	8.1	154	92¾	+ ¾
PacBell 6¼05	6.9	19	91⅛	+ ¼
PacBell 7⅛26	7.8	27	90⅞	+ ⅝
PacBell 6⅞23	7.9	10	87¼	− ⅛
ParCm 7s03A	8.0	70	87½	...
ParCm 7s03B	8.1	10	86½	...
Paten 8¼12	cv	12	80½	+ 1
PaylCsh 9⅛03	9.8	115	93	− 1
PennTr 9⅝05	9.8	15	98½	− ⅜
Pennzl 6½03	5.6	25	115½	+ ¼
Pennzl 4¾03	5.2	10	91½	+ ½
PeryDr 8½10	cv	7	91½	− ½
Petrie 8s10	cv	50	114¼	...
Pier1 6⅞02	cv	124	95½	− 1½
PionFn 8s00	cv	56	104⅞	+ ⅜
PotEl 7s18	cv	13	98	− 1
Primark 8¾00	9.1	10	96⅝	+ ½
PSEG 6⅞97	6.8	10	101	+ 1
PSEG 7½23	8.1	15	92¼	+ 1
RJR Nb 10½98	10.2	124	103¼	− ⅛
RJR Nb 8.3s99	8.9	460	93	− ¼
RJR Nb 13½01	12.6	595	107⅛	− ⅛
RJR Nb zrcld	...	503	107 3/16	+ 3/32
RJR Nb 8¾04	10.0	454	87¾	− ⅛
RJR Nb 8⅝02	9.8	352	88¼	...
RJR Nb 7⅝03	9.2	203	82⅞	+ ⅞
Telxon 7½12		20	90	...
VLSI 7s12		24	96	+ 1½
WstwdOne 6¾11		10	64½	− ½
RJR Nb 8s00	8.9	264	90	− 1
RJR Nb 8¾05	10.1	255	86¼	− ⅜
RJR Nb 9¼13	10.6	305	87¼	...
Rallys 9⅞00	10.9	266	90¾	− ⅛
RalsP 9½16	9.0	68	105⅛	...
RalsP 9s96	8.7	26	103⅜	− ⅜
vjRapA 12s99f	...	7	⅜	+ ⅛
RelGrp 9s00	9.9	196	90¾	+ ⅜
RelGrp 9¾03	10.6	242	91¾	+ 1¼
Revl 10⅞10	11.7	94	92¾	− ⅛
Revl 9½99	10.5	334	90⅜	+ ¼
RiteA zr06	cv	64	43⅝	− ¼
Rivrwdlnt 11¼02	10.4	5	107¾	...
Rohr 7s12	cv	59	74	+ ½
Rotorx 5s96	cv	3	90	...
Rowan 11⅞01	11.1	58	107	− 1
Safwy 10s01	9.6	50	104½	+ ⅞
Safwy 9.65s04	9.5	186	101⅞	+ ¼
Safwy 9.35s99	9.2	1146	101¾	+ 1⅛
Safwy 9.3s07	9.3	30	100	− 2
Safwy 9⅞07	9.7	5	102	− 1⅛
Sears 9½99	8.8	19	107½	− 1¾
Sequa 10½98	10.2	7	103⅜	...
Sequa 9⅝99	9.6	35	100	+ 1
Sequa 8¾01	9.3	120	94	− 4
SvcMer 9s04	9.8	728	92	− ½
SvcMer 8⅜01	9.1	27	92	− 1
ShellO 7¼02	7.3	9	99⅛	+ ⅛
Showboat 9¼08	10.3	72	89¾	− ¾
SoCnBel 8¼17	8.3	5	100	− 1
SouBell 4¾00	5.4	10	88	− ½
SouBell 4⅜03	5.4	15	80¾	− ¾
SouBell 8⅛17	8.2	70	99	− ¼
SouBell 8½29	8.6	50	98¾	− 2⅝
SoCG 6⅞02	6.9	5	99	...
SoCG 6½97	6.5	25	100	− 3
StdPac 10½00	10.8	666	97½	− ⅝
StrlSft 5¾03	cv	13	115	− 1
StoneCn 11½99	12.0	273	96	+ ¼
StoneCn 11⅞98	11.8	86	100¾	+ ⅜
StoneCn 6¾07	cv	157	69	− ½
StoneCn 10¾02	11.7	663	91¾	...
StoneCn 10¾97	11.1	292	97⅛	− ¼
StoneCn 11s99	11.6	2	94⅞	+ ⅛
StrTch 8s15	cv	207	98	− 3
SwBell 7⅝23	7.9	15	96½	+ ½
SwBell 7s15	7.7	10	91½	+ 1
Teledy 7s99	7.2	15	97¼	...
Teledy 10s04A	9.8	30	102	+ ¼
Teledy 10s04C	9.8	10	101¾	− ⅛
TennGas 9s97	8.8	10	102¾	− ¼
TennGas dc6s11	7.8	75	77¼	+ ⅛
Tenneco 7⅞02	7.8	3	100½	+ ½
Tesor dc12¾01	12.8	25	100	...
Tesor 13s00	12.9	45	101	+ 1
Texco 9s99D	8.3	15	108	+ 1¾
Texco 8.65s98	8.1	15	106½	− 2¼
Texfi 11¼97	cv	6	103	− ⅛
TmeWar 8¾17	9.1	65	96½	+ ¼
TmeWar zr02	...	72	91⅛	+ ⅛
TmeWar 7.45s98	7.5	264	98¾	+ ¼
TmeWar 9⅛13	9.3	409	98	+ 1
TmeWar 7.95s00	8.1	366	98⅛	− ½
TmeWar 9.15s23	9.6	695	95⅛	+ ¼
TmeWar 8¾15	cv	885	101¼	− ⅞
TmeWar zr13	...	357	35¾	− ⅝
TolEd 7½02	8.2	5	91⅞	− ⅛
Toll 9½03	10.0	7	95⅛	− 1⅞
TollCp 4¾04	cv	11	80	− 6
Trimas 5s03	cv	3	123½	− ½
TucEP 8⅛01	8.3	20	97½	− ½
Tyco 10⅛02	10.9	249	93	− ¼
UJer 7¾97	7.7	2	101	− 1½
US West zr11	...	10	29½	...
USAir 12⅞00	15.6	2830	82¾	− 3⅞
USLICO 8s11	cv	21	98	...
USX 5¾01	cv	53	84	...
USX 7s17	cv	11	86	− 2
USX zr05	cv	25	42⅛	− ¼
UBk 7.35s01	7.9	5	93	− 3⅝
Unisy na15s97	...	185	112	...
Valhi zr07	...	7	35	...
Vencor 6s02	cv	95	99	− 3
WMS 5¾02	cv	5	103	...
WasteM zr12	...	1	34¼	...
Waban 6½02	cv	1	92	...
Watrhse 03	cv	10	84	− 3
Wendys 7s06	cv	22	150	− 1
WstCNA 7¼15	cv	53	94	...
WstDig 9s14	cv	194	102	− 4
Wstvco 12⅛12	11.2	27	108	− 2⅞

NASDAQ

Convertible Debentures

Wednesday, April 20, 1994

Issue	Vol.	Close	Net Chg.
Bindly 6½10	17	89¾	− ¾
BoxEngy 8¼02	25	114½	− 1
CalMicr 03	60	89½	− 2
Commnet 6¾09	50	91	− 1
CmpPd 9½97	10	103½	+ ¾
Daka 03	4	106½	− 2
DixYrn 7s12	50	78	+ 2½
DrgEmp 7¾14	35	77	− 1
EagleH cv01	51	93	− 1
Hechng 5½12	43	80	− ⅜
IntgHlth 6s03	15	118	...
Jacobsn 6¾11	66	79	− 2
LAGear 7¾02	100	79	+ 1
LTX 13½11	70	94	− 5
MrshSup 7s03	5	93½	...
MedVsn db	100	35	− 6
Microp 6s12	50	59	− 1½
MidlBk 8¼10	23	99½	− 1
PrceCo 5½12	50	85¼	− 1¾
PrceCo 6¾01	300	96½	− 2
Proffitt cv03	20	73½	...
RPM zr12	200	37½	− ¾
SCI Sy 5⅝12	34	89	− 2
Sanifll 7½06	26	98	+ 1¼
Seagte 6¾12	300	85½	− ½
Synetic 7s01	25	88	− 3¼

Source: The Wall Street Journal, *April 21, 1994, p. C16.*

We calculate the yield by dividing the annual coupon interest amount of $90 by the closing price of the bond listed under the *Close* column. We must multiply the closing price of 98 by 10 to obtain the true closing price of $980 (= 98 × 10). The newspaper simply quotes bond prices as a percent of par value. Thus, the calculation of current yield is $90 ÷ $980 = 0.0918, or 9.2 percent. The *Vol* column says that $15,000 worth of face value Navistar 9s04 bonds traded on April 20. The last column labeled *Net Chg.* informs us that the closing price was down 1 percent of par value over the previous trading day, or down $10 (= $1000 × 0.01). The New England Telephone (NETel 6⅞23) rows below this one shows three dots (. . .) in the net change column. This coding informs us that the April 20 closing price was the same as the previous trading day.

Bonds trade on an accrued interest basis. This means that the buyer of the bond pays to the seller, in addition to the price of the bond, a sum representing the interest that the original owner has earned since the last interest payment. Normally, interest is paid on a bond every six months. If 30 days have passed since the last interest payment, the buyer pays 30 days of accrued interest. In the preceding example of the Navistar bond, accrued interest would amount to 9% × $1000 × 30 days ÷ 360 days, or a $7.50 additional payment.

7.4.2 Convertibles and Yankees

Convertible bond. Bond that can be converted into common stock of the issuing corporation at the discretion of the holder.

Yankee bond. A foreign bond denominated in U.S. dollars.

Table 7.4 also includes convertible bonds, as shown by the letters *cv* under the *Cur Yld* column. A **convertible bond** is a corporate bond that allows the holder to exchange it at any time for a fixed number of shares of common stock of the firm. The issuance of convertible bonds by a company avoids the immediate issuance of common stock at a current market price that a firm's managers may believe to be below the stock's long-run economic value.

A class of bonds exists within the United States referred to as foreign bonds or **Yankee bonds.** Foreign governments, corporations, and municipalities issue these instruments for U.S. dollars. The bonds pay interest and trade normally. In most cases, these debt securities are comparable in the eyes of market participants to highly rated U.S. bonds.

► *Comprehension Check*

1. Distinguish between dealers' bid and asked prices for corporate bonds.
2. Are you able to read and understand the NYSE bond tables published in *The Wall Street Journal?*
3. Define current yield.
4. What does it mean that "bonds trade on an accrued interest basis"?
5. Define convertible bonds and Yankee bonds.

7.5 GOVERNMENT AND AGENCY DEBT SECURITIES

The U.S. Treasury and a variety of federal agencies issue bills, notes, or bonds. Treasury securities are the safest of all debt instruments. The full taxing power of the U.S. government supports them. Several federal agency issues do not carry this same backing. Nevertheless, agency securities are low-risk, high-quality investments. *The Wall Street Journal* reports activity in the primary and secondary markets for Treasury securities in its daily "Credit Markets" article. Figure 7.1 is an example. Besides providing a comparison of yields, the article discusses economic factors affecting the credit markets.

7.5.1 The Government Bond Market

The federal government sells U.S. Treasury securities in the primary market, known as the government bond market, when it needs funds (see Figure 7.2). The buyers are pri-

FIGURE 7.1
WSJ "CREDIT MARKETS" ARTICLE

CREDIT MARKETS

Treasury Prices Push Upward as Bond Market Continues to Recover From Plunge Early in Week

By THOMAS D. LAURICELLA
And JACQUELINE DOHERTY
Special to THE WALL STREET JOURNAL

NEW YORK — Prices of U.S. Treasury notes and bonds rallied yesterday as the market continued to recover from the sell-off early in the week.

Traders stressed there was no news behind the upward push. Instead, they described it as a bear-market technical rally. Most of the buying was deemed short-covering, during which traders scramble to buy back securities they sold, betting that prices would fall.

More importantly, players said, so far this month there has been an absence of the capitulation selling that overwhelmed the bond market in February and March. At that time, the market was blindsided by waves of hedge selling, especially as investors frantically dumped mortgage-backed and municipal securities. Dealers noted that in yesterday's rally, the best performing sector of the market was the part hardest hit by hedge selling — Treasurys maturing in five to 10 years.

Long Bond Rises

The price of the 10-year note rose more than ⅜ point, or more than $3.75 for a bond with a $1,000 face value, to 91 27/32. The yield, which moves in the opposite direction of price, dropped to 7.02% from 7.09% on Tuesday. The benchmark 30-year Treasury bond rose more than ½ point to 87 3/32 to yield 7.31%, down from 7.37%.

"The positions most vulnerable to abrupt market declines have already been sold off," said William V. Sullivan Jr., senior vice president at Dean Witter Reynolds. "Those coconuts have already been shaken out of the tree."

In the wake of Monday's tightening by the Federal Reserve, there is also a greater degree of comfort that the Fed really intends to squash inflationary pressures, contended Mickey Levy, chief financial economist at NationsBanc Capital Markets. "The market feels like the Fed is

Reflecting the slightly less negative tone, the market was able to weather stronger-than-expected economic news when the Commerce Department reported that housing starts jumped 12% during March following an 8% drop in February. Prices dipped in response to the report, but selling didn't last for long.

Bond investors often react negatively to news of economic strength because they fear that it will lead to inflation, which reduces the value of investments with a fixed rate of return.

"We did see some willingness to sell in the wake of the housing-starts data, but the market held its ground," said Mr. Sullivan of Dean Witter.

The Treasury announced yesterday that it will sell $17 billion of two-year notes and $11 billion of five-year notes next week. The offering sizes were in line with expectations. In when-issued trading, the two-year note was yielding 5.73% yesterday while the five-year note was yielding 6.67%.

Traders now have turned their attention to the Philadelphia Federal Reserve's Business Outlook Survey scheduled to be released this morning. Earlier this year, strong readings on the Philadelphia Fed's inflation index helped trigger a significant downdraft in Treasurys.

Corporate & Junk Bonds

Yields range from 4.30% in 1996 to 6.15% in 2013 and 2014. Both Moody's Investors Service and Standard & Poor's have rated the bonds double-A.

The offering is sold, Goldman Sachs said.

Mortgage & Asset-Backed Securities

Mortgage securities were quietly firmer but lagged Treasurys.

Mortgage securities have performed better than governments many times since rates began to rise, and that's unusual, traders point out. Normally, investors avoid buying bonds when rates rise, and they particularly avoid bonds whose effective maturities can change when rates do, such as mortgages.

But yesterday's underperformance and generally slow trade could be just what the market needs to bring buyers in, says Joseph Hu, director of mortgage research at Oppenheimer & Co. Right now, though, most investors aren't willing to take the plunge.

Meanwhile, Ginnie Mae 8s for May delivery were up 6/32 at 99 23/32; Freddie Mac Gold 8s for May were up 7/32 at 100 3/32; Fannie Mae 8s for May were up 7/32 at 99 30/32, and the Treasury 5 7/8% 10-year note was up 13/32 at 91 28/32.

Additionally, Chrysler Corp. priced its second auto-loan, asset-backed deal of the year yesterday. It's a five-part offering totaling $1.5 billion. The largest part totaled $424.7 million of total-rate-of-return notes that were priced to yield 43 basis points over the Treasury's three-year note. The notes have a 2.9 year average life. Bear, Stearns & Co. was lead underwriter.

Treasury Plans to Raise $13 Billion in Offering Of 2-Year, 5-Year Notes

By a WALL STREET JOURNAL *Staff Reporter*

WASHINGTON—The Treasury plans to raise slightly more than $13 billion in fresh cash next week with the sale of $17 billion of two-year notes and $11 billion of five-year notes.

The balance of the proceeds will be used to redeem $14.84 billion in maturing notes.

The two-year notes will be dated May 2, and will mature April 30, 1996. The five-year notes will be dated May 2, and will mature April 30, 1999.

The Federal Reserve holds $1.56 billion of the maturing securities for its own account. The Fed also holds $1.39 billion of maturing securities as agent for foreign and international monetary authorities.

Tenders for the two-year notes are available in minimum denominations of $5,000. Noncompetitive tenders for the two-year notes must be received by noon EDT next Tuesday at the Treasury or at Federal Reserve banks or branches. Competitive tenders for the two-year notes must be

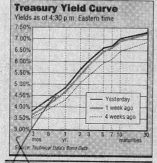

Treasury Yield Curve
Yields as of 4:30 p.m. Eastern time

(Yesterday, 1 week ago, 4 weeks ago)

Source: Technical Data's Bond Data

YIELD COMPARISONS

Based on Merrill Lynch Bond Indexes, priced as of midafternoon Eastern time.

	4/20	4/19	52 Week High	Low
Corp.-Govt. Master	6.86%	6.90%	6.90%	5.19%
Treasury 1-10yr	6.13	6.18	6.18	4.23
10+ yr	7.53	7.58	7.63	6.01
Agencies 1-10yr	6.71	6.72	6.78	5.03
10+ yr	7.75	7.77	7.77	6.40
Corporate				
1-10 yr High Qlty	7.14	7.16	7.16	5.32
Med Qlty	7.47	7.49	7.49	5.76
10+ yr High Qlty	8.03	8.06	8.06	6.93
Med Qlty	8.46	8.49	8.49	7.29
Yankee bonds(1)	7.69	7.71	7.71	6.27
Current-coupon mortgages(2)				
GNMA 8.00%	8.15	8.16	8.37	6.07
FNMA 8.00%	8.05	8.09	8.24	6.10
FHLMC8.00%	8.07	8.11	8.25	6.10
High-yield corporates	10.53	10.49	10.53	9.25
New tax-exempts				
7-12-yr G.O. (AA)	5.72	5.81	5.97	4.56
12-22-yr G.O. (AA)	6.13	6.20	6.69	4.91
22+yr revenue (A)	6.46	6.53	6.71	5.30

Note: High quality rated AAA-AA; medium quality A-BBB/Baa; high yield, BB/Ba-C.
(1) Dollar-denominated, SEC-registered bonds of foreign issuers sold in the U.S. (2) Reflects the 52-week high and low of mortgage-backed securities indexes rather than the individual securities.

Short-Term Interest Rates
(Weekly averages)

Federal Funds
3-Month Commercial Paper
3-Month Treasury Bills

(1993 — 1994: O N D J F M A; 2.8% to 4.2%)

Source: Federal Reserve Bank of New York

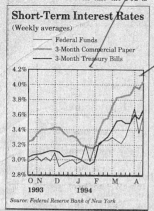

Source: The Wall Street Journal, *April 21, 1994, p. C19.*

FIGURE 7.2

TREASURY MARKET

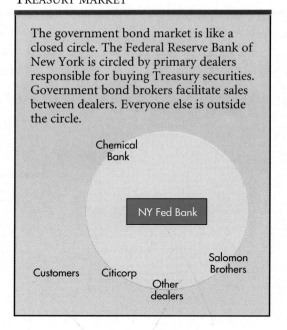

The government bond market is like a closed circle. The Federal Reserve Bank of New York is circled by primary dealers responsible for buying Treasury securities. Government bond brokers facilitate sales between dealers. Everyone else is outside the circle.

Chemical Bank

NY Fed Bank

Salomon Brothers

Customers   Citicorp

Other dealers

mary dealers appointed by the Fed to maintain liquid markets in all government and agency securities. Included in this group are Citicorp, Chemical Bank, and Salomon Brothers. They must bid on all U.S. Treasury auctions, both for their own accounts and for the accounts of customers. These dealers must report their securities positions and trading volumes daily to the New York Fed, as well as how they financed their securities positions.

Government bond brokers ask for bids or offers from the primary dealers and arrange for primary dealers to trade between themselves. These brokers allow dealers to maintain anonymity from each other and prevent one dealer from taking advantage of an unfavorable bond inventory position of another dealer. Everyone else is outside of the dealer-broker network and is a customer. It does not matter if the customer is a very large institution, such as the World Bank or the Japanese Postal Retirement System, or if the customer is a small commercial bank or an individual investor. The nearby Financial Reality article discusses how the firm of Salomon Brothers corrupted the system. Some senior executives of Salomon lost their positions because of the scandal.

A bank or securities broker can act as our agent if we wish to purchase U.S. Treasury securities in the secondary market. This market is very liquid; however, significant bid-asked price spreads can exist from broker to broker. We can reduce this risk of price variation by purchasing government debt securities directly from the U.S. Treasury through the Federal Reserve System's Treasury Direct program. Illustration 7.4 outlines the process.

ILLUSTRATION 7.4

Direct purchase of U.S. Treasury securities

The federal government's Treasury Direct system makes buying U.S. Treasury bills, notes, and bonds as easy as a phone call. To open a Treasury Direct account, the investor contacts one of the 12 Federal Reserve district banks or any of the Fed's branch banks

▼▼▼▼▼▼▼▼▼▼▼▼▼▼

THE REAL SALOMON SCANDAL

Salomon Brothers is a primary dealer for U.S. Treasury securities. In 1991 it was revealed that Salomon was rigging the Treasury market.

The most worrisome aspect of the affair is the gross incompetence of regulatory overseers at the U.S. Federal Reserve. Though it clearly had regulatory oversight in the matter, the Fed failed to notice that Salomon Brothers had been rigging bids under its nose in Treasury debt auctions for months and maybe even years.

What Salomon did is really quite simple to understand: It bought more Treasury bills, bonds, and notes at auctions than the law allows—and it did so literally under the wide-open eyes of Federal Reserve regulators in New York as well as of Treasury Department higher-ups in Washington.

Over the years, the Fed has worked out arrangements to buy and sell Treasury debt with some 40 banks and Wall Street investment firms it calls "primary dealers," the most important of which is Salomon Brothers. So when the Fed gets a call from the Treasury to sell debt, it calls up these 40 primary dealers and tells them to put in writing, on specially prepared forms, how much each is prepared to buy, and at what price. These are known as the "bids," and each primary dealer has to make sure it gets its bid into the Fed by 1 p.m. on the day of the auction.

A primary dealer can submit bids for its own account as well as for the accounts of customers. But its customers have to be identified by name. To prevent anyone from cornering the market, Fed regulations stipulate that no bidder—be it a primary dealer or a customer—can bid for more than 35 percent of the auction.

That's the law Salomon violated; when it wrote up its bids and submitted them to the Fed, it claimed to be acting not only for itself but for customers that apparently didn't know Salomon was claiming to act in their name. In this way, Salomon wound up holding more than the 35 percent limit. Salomon lied.

Apparently, no attempt was made at any time—even on a sporadic, random basis—to see if the names on each list were real entities, let alone whether the customers had instructed the primary dealers to submit bids in their behalf.

Adapted from Christopher Byon, "The Real Salomon Scandal," *New York,* September 2, 1991, pp. 16-17. Used with permission of Christopher Byon.

located in major cities nationwide. Under this system, a single master account registers all the investor's Treasury holdings. Account options include automatic reinvestment when securities mature, direct deposit of interest payments to the investor's specified bank account, and the ability to make additional purchases of new Treasury securities. Transactions are fast and commission-free. Let's examine the process.

Ms. Santos wants to invest $30,000 in newly issued 26-week Treasury bills. The U.S. Treasury offers these T-bills for sale every Monday. At her bank, she fills out a form for submitting a noncompetitive bid to buy T-bills, stipulating that she wants three bills. Every bill has a par value of $10,000, so she includes a bank cashier's check for $30,000 to open her Treasury Direct account.

Across the country, institutional investors want to buy T-bills at Monday's auction. If they plan to buy at least $500,000 worth, they are entitled to participate in the auction as competitive bidders. As competitive bidders, their bids state how much less than $10,000 they are willing to pay for each T-bill. Because T-bills pay no interest, investors earn what substitutes for interest by purchasing the bills for less than face value.

All bids, competitive and noncompetitive, received by the Federal Reserve before the Monday 1 p.m. deadline are forwarded to the U.S. Treasury Department in Washington. The Treasury accepts bids beginning with those closest to the $10,000 par value until its quota is filled. The Treasury announces that its cutoff point is, say, $9600 per bill. Then the Treasury takes the average accepted bid and informs all noncompetitive bidders, like Ms. Santos, that this average, say $9675, is their price for the T-bills. Thus, $29,025 (= $9675 × 3 T-bills) is taken from her account. She can have the difference refunded to her or leave it in the account.

Six months later, when her T-bills come due, she receives a check for $30,000 from the Treasury. The difference of $975 between what she receives and what she paid is her interest income, which is subject to federal income taxes but not state and local income taxes.

7.5.2 Keeping Tabs on Government Bonds

The third section of *The Wall Street Journal* reports trading on the secondary market for U.S. Treasury securities on a daily basis. Table 7.5 shows some of the information for trades made on November 4, 1993. The prices quoted are for **round lots,** which for Treasuries means multiples of $1 million. Prices for $1000 multiples, or **odd lots** in this case, are somewhat higher to buy and lower to sell. The manner of reporting quotes on transactions is slightly different from that described earlier for corporate bonds.

The first three columns describe the bond or note. *Rate* means coupon rate based on $1000 par value. *Maturity Mo/Yr* stands for the month and year of maturity. If the security has two maturity dates, such as *05-10*, the bond matures in the year 2010 but can be called by the Treasury as early as year 2005. Thus, if market interest rates drop below the *05-10* bond's coupon rate, the U.S. Treasury may redeem the security in the year 2005. The letter *n* following the year indicates that the security is a note. All other issues are bonds. The risk to investors of having the bond called are discussed in the Financial Reality article on page 242.

Treasury issues trade over-the-counter, in thousands of private, one-on-one telephone transactions. Prices are quoted as *bid* and *asked*. It is impossible to determine the exact prices of the last transactions. The best information available for these issues is the highest price dealers were asking to sell the security (the *asked*) and the lowest price dealers were willing to pay (the *bid*) at midafternoon of the trading day.

The price quote is a percentage of $1000 par value, with the number after the colon representing thirty-seconds. For example, an asked price of 137:08 for the 13³/₈ August bonds maturing in year 2001 means that on April 20, 1994 dealers were willing to sell the bond for 137:08, or $1372.50 [= (137 + 8/32) × 10]. Dealers would buy it for 137:04, or $1371.25 [= (137 + 4/32) × 10]. The spread represents the dealer markup. Since this bond's market price exceeds its $1000 par value, the bond trades at a **premium.** If the price of the security is below par value, it trades at a **discount.** The second

Round lot. A unit of trading of a security.

Odd lot. The quantity of securities that is less than the established unit for trading.

Premium. The amount by which a bond (or preferred stock) sells above its par value. The security trades at a premium when the coupon rate is above the market rate of interest.

Discount. The amount by which a bond (or preferred stock) sells below its par value. The security trades at a discount when the coupon rate is lower than the market rate of interest.

TABLE 7-5

Treasury Bonds and Notes

TREASURY BONDS, NOTES & BILLS

Wednesday, April 20, 1994

Representative Over-the-Counter quotations based on transactions of $1 nillion or more.

Treasury bond, note and bill quotes are as of mid-afternoon. Colons in id-and-asked quotes represent 32nds; 101:01 means 101 1/32. Net changes in 2nds. n-Treasury note. Treasury bill quotes in hundredths, quoted on terms of rate of discount. Days to maturity calculated from settlement date. All ields are to maturity and based on the asked quote. Latest 13-week and 26-week ills are boldfaced. For bonds callable prior to maturity, yields are computed to he earliest call date for issues quoted above par and to the maturity date for issues elow par. *-When issued.

Source: Federal Reserve Bank of New York.

U.S. Treasury strips as of 3 p.m. Eastern time, also based on transactions f $1 million or more. Colons in bid-and-asked quotes represent 32nds; 101:01 neans 101 1/32. Net changes in 32nds. Yields calculated on the asked quotaion. ci-stripped coupon interest. bp-Treasury bond, stripped principal. np-Treaury note, stripped principal. For bonds callable prior to maturity, yields are omputed to the earliest call date for issues quoted above par and to the naturity date for issues below par.

Source: Bear, Stearns & Co. via Street Software Technology Inc.

GOVT. BONDS & NOTES

Rate	Maturity Mo/Yr	Bid	Asked	Chg.	Ask Yld.
3/8	Apr 94n	100:00	100:02	− 1	2.48
	May 94n	100:06	100:08	....	2.97
1/2	May 94n	100:11	100:13	− 1	2.97
1/8	May 94n	100:19	100:21	....	2.63
1/8	May 94n	100:05	100:07	....	3.02
	Jun 94n	100:07	100:09	....	3.46
1/2	Jun 94n	100:28	100:30	− 1	3.46
	Jul 94n	100:30	101:00	....	3.58
1/4	Jul 94n	100:02	100:04	....	3.76
7/8	Aug 94n	100:28	100:30	....	3.84
5/8	Aug 94n	101:13	101:15	....	3.88
3/4	Aug 94	101:14	101:16	....	3.91
5/8	Aug 94n	102:21	102:23	− 1	3.87
1/4	Aug 94n	100:01	100:03	....	3.96
	Sep 94n	99:29	99:31	+ 1	4.06
1/2	Sep 94n	101:27	101:29	....	4.07
1/2	Oct 94n	102:12	102:14	....	4.32
1/4	Oct 94n	99:29	99:31	....	4.31
	Nov 94n	100:26	100:28	....	4.41
1/4	Nov 94n	102:01	102:03	....	4.45
1/8	Nov 94	103:02	103:04	− 1	4.45
5/8	Nov 94n	103:28	103:30	− 1	4.48
5/8	Nov 94n	100:01	100:03	....	4.47
5/8	Dec 94n	99:31	100:01	+ 1	4.58
5/8	Dec 94n	101:31	102:01	+ 1	4.61
5/8	Jan 95n	102:24	102:26	....	4.68
1/4	Jan 95n	99:19	99:21	....	4.71
3	Feb 95	98:25	99:25	− 2	3.27
1/2	Feb 95n	100:16	100:18	....	4.79
3/4	Feb 95n	102:09	102:11	....	4.80
1/2	Feb 95	104:15	104:17	− 1	4.79
1/4	Feb 95n	105:02	105:04	− 2	4.79
3 7/8	Feb 95n	99:05	99:07	....	4.82
3 7/8	Mar 95n	99:01	99:03	+ 1	4.87
3/8	Apr 95n	103:05	103:07	+ 1	4.97
3 7/8	Apr 95n	98:27	98:29	+ 1	4.99
7/8	May 95n	100:26	100:28	+ 1	5.02
1/2	May 95n	103:16	103:18	+ 1	5.02
3/8	May 95	105:15	105:17	+ 1	4.97
1/4	May 95n	106:12	106:14	....	4.96
5/8	May 95	107:25	107:29	....	4.91
4 1/8	May 95n	98:31	99:01	+ 1	5.03
4 1/8	Jun 95n	98:26	98:28	....	5.11
7/8	Jul 95n	104:11	104:13	+ 2	5.14
4 1/4	Jul 95n	98:26	98:28	+ 1	5.17
4 5/8	Aug 95n	99:06	99:08	....	5.22
8 1/2	Aug 95n	104:02	104:04	+ 1	5.22
1/2	Aug 95n	106:19	106:21	....	5.21
3 7/8	Aug 95n	98:06	98:08	+ 1	5.23
3 7/8	Sep 95n	98:01	98:03	+ 1	5.27
8 5/8	Oct 95n	104:17	104:19	+ 1	5.36
3 7/8	Oct 95n	97:26	97:28	+ 1	5.35
5 1/8	Nov 95n	99:18	99:20	+ 1	5.38
8 1/2	Nov 95n	104:17	104:19	+ 1	5.40
9 1/2	Nov 95n	106:02	106:04	+ 1	5.37
1/2	Nov 95	109:00	109:04	+ 1	5.34
4 1/4	Nov 95n	98:06	98:08	+ 1	5.40
4 1/4	Dec 95n	98:00	98:02	+ 2	5.46
9 1/4	Jan 96n	105:31	106:01	− 1	5.55
4	Jan 96n	97:12	97:14	+ 1	5.53
7 1/2	Jan 96n	103:06	103:08	+ 1	5.56
4 5/8	Feb 96n	98:09	98:11	+ 1	5.60
7 7/8	Feb 96n	103:27	103:29	+ 1	5.59
8 7/8	Feb 96n	105:18	105:20	+ 1	5.58
4 5/8	Feb 96n	98:09	98:11	+ 1	5.58
7 1/2	Feb 96n	103:07	103:09	+ 1	5.62
5 1/8	Mar 96n	99:02	99:04	+ 2	5.61
7 3/4	Mar 96n	103:24	103:26	+ 1	5.65
9 3/8	Apr 96n	106:25	106:27	+ 1	5.67
7 5/8	Apr 96n	103:19	103:21	+ 2	5.69
4 1/4	May 96n	97:05	97:07	+ 2	5.70

Rate	Maturity Mo/Yr	Bid	Asked	Chg.	Ask Yld.
8	Aug 99n	105:28	105:30	+ 7	6.66
6	Oct 99n	96:25	96:27	+ 5	6.70
7 7/8	Nov 99n	105:12	105:14	+ 8	6.69
6 3/8	Jan 00n	98:09	98:11	+ 6	6.73
7 7/8	Feb 95-00	102:02	102:06	− 4	5.11
8 1/2	Feb 00n	108:13	108:15	+ 8	6.72
5 1/2	Apr 00n	94:03	94:05	+ 7	6.70
8 7/8	May 00n	110:18	110:20	+ 6	6.71
8 3/8	Aug 95-00	103:12	103:16	− 1	5.59
8 3/4	Aug 00n	110:01	110:03	+ 8	6.76
8 1/2	Nov 00n	108:27	108:29	+ 6	6.80
7 3/4	Feb 01n	104:27	104:29	+ 6	6.84
11 3/4	Feb 01	126:22	126:26	+ 8	6.78
8	May 01n	106:05	106:07	+ 8	6.87
13 1/8	May 01	135:01	135:05	+ 10	6.78
7 7/8	Aug 01n	105:13	105:15	+ 8	6.91
8	Aug 96-01	103:29	104:01	+ 3	6.11
13 3/8	Aug 01	137:04	137:08	+ 6	6.82
7 1/2	Nov 01n	103:06	103:08	+ 7	6.94
15 3/4	Nov 01	151:31	152:03	+ 8	6.82
14 1/4	Feb 02	143:30	144:02	+ 5	6.87
7 1/2	May 02n	103:00	103:02	+ 3	7.00
6 3/8	Aug 02n	95:31	96:01	+ 7	7.01
11 5/8	Nov 02	129:13	129:17	+ 9	6.99
6 1/4	Feb 03n	94:23	94:25	+ 7	7.05
10 3/4	Feb 03	124:00	124:04	+ 7	7.03
10 3/4	May 03	124:11	124:15	+ 7	7.05
5 3/4	Aug 03n	91:00	91:02	+ 7	7.08
11 1/8	Aug 03	127:09	127:13	+ 10	7.06
11 7/8	Nov 03	132:22	132:26	+ 8	7.09
5 7/8	Feb 04n	91:26	91:28	+ 10	7.03
12 3/8	May 04	137:11	137:15	+ 8	7.10
13 3/4	Aug 04	147:27	147:31	+ 11	7.11
11 5/8	Nov 04	132:24	132:28	+ 11	7.14
8 1/4	May 00-05	105:29	106:01	+ 5	7.01
12	May 05	136:08	136:12	+ 10	7.18
10 3/4	Aug 05	127:05	127:09	+ 11	7.19
9 3/8	Feb 06	117:01	117:05	+ 13	7.20
7 5/8	Feb 02-07	101:28	102:00	+ 8	7.28
7 7/8	Nov 02-07	103:19	103:23	+ 7	7.28
8 3/8	Aug 03-08	106:31	107:03	+ 8	7.31
8 3/4	Nov 03-08	109:26	109:30	+ 9	7.29
9 1/8	May 04-09	112:27	112:31	+ 13	7.28
10 3/8	Nov 04-09	122:12	122:16	+ 10	7.28
11 3/4	Feb 05-10	133:05	133:09	+ 10	7.26
10	May 05-10	120:15	120:19	+ 12	7.26
12 3/4	Nov 05-10	142:06	142:10	+ 12	7.28
13 7/8	May 06-11	152:02	152:06	+ 6	7.30
14	Nov 06-11	154:18	154:22	+ 15	7.28
10 3/8	Nov 07-12	125:12	125:16	+ 13	7.37
12	Aug 08-13	140:12	140:16	+ 14	7.37
13 1/4	May 09-14	152:28	153:00	+ 16	7.37
12 1/2	Aug 09-14	146:16	146:20	+ 11	7.37
11 3/4	Nov 09-14	140:04	140:08	+ 13	7.36
11 1/4	Feb 15	139:25	139:27	+ 18	7.45
10 5/8	Aug 15	133:14	133:16	+ 18	7.46
9 7/8	Nov 15	125:12	125:14	+ 12	7.48
9 1/4	Feb 16	118:27	118:29	+ 16	7.48
7 1/4	May 16	97:18	97:20	+ 14	7.47
7 1/2	Nov 16	100:04	100:06	+ 15	7.48
8 3/4	May 17	113:21	113:23	+ 16	7.49
8 7/8	Aug 17	115:02	115:04	+ 15	7.49
9 1/8	May 18	118:01	118:03	+ 16	7.49
9	Nov 18	116:23	116:25	+ 17	7.50
8 7/8	Feb 19	115:11	115:13	+ 16	7.50
8 1/8	Aug 19	106:31	107:01	+ 15	7.50
8 1/2	Feb 20	111:10	111:12	+ 17	7.50
8 3/4	May 20	114:07	114:09	+ 16	7.50
8 3/4	Aug 20	114:10	114:12	+ 17	7.49
7 7/8	Feb 21	104:10	104:12	+ 15	7.49
8 1/8	May 21	107:09	107:11	+ 15	7.49

Mat.	Type	Bid	Asked	C
Aug 01	np	60:06	60:10	-
Nov 01	ci	58:31	59:04	-
Nov 01	np	58:31	59:04	-
Feb 02	ci	57:26	57:30	-
May 02	ci	56:25	56:29	-
May 02	np	56:28	57:00	-
Aug 02	ci	55:18	55:22	-
Aug 02	np	55:25	55:29	-
Nov 02	ci	54:15	54:19	-
Feb 03	ci	53:13	53:17	-
Feb 03	np	53:26	53:30	-
May 03	ci	52:11	52:15	-
Aug 03	ci	51:10	51:14	-
Aug 03	np	51:27	52:00	-
Nov 03	ci	50:11	50:16	
Feb 04	ci	49:10	49:14	
Feb 04	np	48:29	49:01	
May 04	ci	48:10	48:15	
Aug 04	ci	47:09	47:14	
Nov 04	ci	46:09	46:13	
Nov 04	bp	46:14	46:19	
Feb 05	ci	45:09	45:13	
May 05	ci	44:12	44:17	
May 05	bp	44:21	44:26	
Aug 05	ci	43:14	43:19	
Aug 05	bp	43:26	43:31	
Nov 05	ci	42:20	42:25	
Feb 06	ci	41:25	41:30	
Feb 06	bp	42:14	42:19	
May 06	ci	40:30	41:03	
Aug 06	ci	40:04	40:09	
Nov 06	ci	39:10	39:15	
Feb 07	ci	38:17	38:22	
May 07	ci	37:25	37:30	
Aug 07	ci	37:01	37:06	
Nov 07	ci	36:10	36:14	
Feb 08	ci	35:17	35:22	
May 08	ci	34:26	34:31	
Aug 08	ci	34:04	34:09	
Nov 08	ci	33:16	33:21	
Feb 09	ci	32:26	32:31	
May 09	ci	32:06	32:10	
Aug 09	ci	31:17	31:21	
Nov 09	ci	30:29	31:01	
Nov 09	bp	30:31	31:04	
Feb 10	ci	30:07	30:11	
May 10	ci	29:19	29:24	
Aug 10	ci	29:00	29:04	
Nov 10	ci	28:14	28:18	
Feb 11	ci	27:26	27:31	
May 11	ci	27:10	27:14	
Aug 11	ci	26:24	26:28	
Nov 11	ci	26:08	26:12	
Feb 12	ci	25:22	25:27	
May 12	ci	25:07	25:12	
Aug 12	ci	24:24	24:28	
Nov 12	ci	24:09	24:13	
Feb 13	ci	23:25	23:29	
May 13	ci	23:10	23:15	
Aug 13	ci	22:29	23:01	
Nov 13	ci	22:14	22:19	
Feb 14	ci	22:01	22:05	
May 14	ci	21:20	21:24	
Aug 14	ci	21:06	21:10	
Nov 14	ci	20:27	20:31	
Feb 15	ci	20:14	20:18	
Feb 15	bp	20:18	20:22	
May 15	ci	20:02	20:06	
Aug 15	ci	19:22	19:26	
Aug 15	bp	19:26	19:30	
Nov 15	ci	19:10	19:14	
Nov 15	bp	19:14	19:18	
Feb 16	ci	18:30	19:02	
Feb 16	bp	19:02	19:06	
May 16	ci	18:19	18:23	
May 16	bp	19:00	19:04	
Aug 16	ci	18:07	18:11	
Nov 16	ci	17:29	18:01	
Nov 16	bp	18:07	18:11	
Feb 17	ci	17:18	17:22	
May 17	ci	17:07	17:11	
May 17	bp	17:11	17:15	
Aug 17	ci	16:29	17:01	
Aug 17	bp	17:01	17:04	
Nov 17	ci	16:19	16:23	
Feb 18	ci	16:10	16:14	
May 18	ci	16:00	16:04	
May 18	bp	16:02	16:06	
Aug 18	ci	15:22	15:26	
Nov 18	ci	15:13	15:17	
Nov 18	bp	15:15	15:19	
Feb 19	ci	15:03	15:07	
Feb 19	bp	15:07	15:11	
May 19	ci	14:26	14:30	

Source: The Wall Street Journal, *April 21, 1994, p. C16.*

Reprinted by permission of The Wall Street Journal, © *1994 Dow Jones & Company, Inc. All Rights Reserved Worldwide.*

to last column, *Chg.*, is the change in bid price, expressed in thirty-seconds, from the previous day. The August 2001 bond increased $1.875 (= 6/32 × 10) in price from the previous day's closing price.

Yield to maturity. Percentage figure reflecting the effective yield on a bond, based on the difference between its purchase and redemption prices, and any returns received by the bondholder in the interim.

The last column, *Ask Yld.*, is the yield to maturity using the asked price. It is not the current yield as shown for corporate bonds. For the August 2001 bond, the **yield to maturity** means that if you bought the security on April 20, 1994, reinvested all cash flows received from the bond at the yield to maturity rate, and held it until maturity, you would receive a total annual return of 6.82 percent. The total annual return includes both interest income and price change of the bond. Because the August 2001 bond is selling at a premium, and since the U.S. Treasury only pays the par value at maturity, the price of the bond will decrease as the maturity date approaches. We examine bond valuation and related issues in the next chapter.

7.5.3 Keeping Tabs on Federal Agency Securities

The securities of federal agencies are underwritten by syndicates of investment bankers. A syndicate buys the new issue, sets a coupon rate, receives a sales commission, and retails the issue at par to investors. Some of these bonds are actually issued by *government-sponsored* enterprises. These agencies were originally owned by the U.S. Treasury but are now publicly owned. The government does not guarantee repayment of the sponsored agencies, although the bonds are issued under the Treasury's supervision. Other agency bond issuers are actually federal agencies whose debts are U.S. government guaranteed.

Table 7.6 shows the status of U.S. government agency securities. Nonguaranteed agency securities normally offer higher returns than guaranteed agency securities because of potential default risk. However, it is difficult to imagine that the federal government would allow any of the federal agencies to default on their securities.

There is an active secondary market for agency securities, making it easy to buy and sell these securities. *The Wall Street Journal* reports the quotes daily for major agency securities under the title "Government Agency & Similar Issues." Table 7.7 is an example of daily quotes for November 4, 1993. The columns read much the same as for the Treasury securities in Table 7.5.

 Comprehension Check

1. What are the responsibilities of a primary dealer in the federal government bond market?
2. How did Salomon Brothers circumvent the auction rules for buying Treasury securities?
3. What is the purpose of the Treasury Direct system and how does it work?
4. Why are Treasury bond calls bad news for investors?
5. What are some differences between government-sponsored agencies and federal agencies?
6. Can you read the *The Wall Street Journal*'s price quotes for Treasury and agency securities?

7.6 MUNICIPAL BONDS

The two principal types of municipal securities (called *munis*) are **general obligation (GO) bonds** and revenue bonds. GOs provide funds for capital improvements. The taxing power of the town, city, county, or state government authority that issues them backs the bonds. Most city, county, and school district bonds are secured by a pledge of unlimited property taxes.

Revenue bonds depend on the cash flows from the specific project they finance. For example, projects such as water systems, turnpikes, and port authorities, all of which may be funded by revenue bonds, levy fees, as toll charges for their use. The risk of owning a revenue bond is that not enough revenue may be generated to meet interest and principal payments. The risk is real. In recent years, the states of California, Massachusetts, New Jersey, Oklahoma, and Texas, and the cities of Detroit, New Orleans, Philadelphia, and Washington have all faced severe budget shortfalls.

Municipal bonds sell in five-bond units, with the par value of each unit being $5000. Once the bond offering is made in the primary market, the bonds are free to trade in the secondary market. For municipal bonds this market is entirely OTC. Quotes are on a *yield-to-bid* basis. An example illustrates this principle. A municipal bond with a 6 percent coupon, maturing in ten years, may show 6.50 bid and 6.40 asked.

General obligation bond (GO). A municipal bond for which the coupon and maturity payments are backed by the "full faith and credit" of the issuing municipality.

Revenue bond. A municipal bond for which the coupon and maturity payments are paid from revenues from a specific revenue-generating project, such as a toll road.

TABLE 7-6

FEDERAL STATUS OF AGENCY SECURITIES

Agency	Full Faith and Credit of the U.S. Government	Authority to Borrow from the Federal Treasury
Farm Credit System	No	No
Farm Credit Financial Assistance Corporation (FACO)	Yes	Yes
Farmers Home Administration (FmHA)	Yes	Yes. Secretary of Agriculture has authority to issue notes to the U.S. Treasury.
Federal Financing Bank (FFB)	Yes	Yes. FFB can require the Treasury to purchase up to $5 billion of its obligations.
Federal Home Loan Banks (FHLB)	No	Yes. The Treasury is authorized to purchase up to $4 billion of FHLB securities.
Federal Home Loan Mortage Corporation (FHLMC or Freddie Mac)	No	Yes. The Treasury may purchase up to $2.25 billion of FHLMC securities.
Federal National Mortgage Association (FNMA or Fannie Mae)	No	Yes. At FNMA request the Treasury may purchase $2.25 billion of FNMA securities.
Financing Corporation (FICO)	No	No
General Services Administration (GSA)	Yes	No
Government National Mortgage Association (GNMA or Ginnie Mae)	Yes	Yes
Maritime Administration bonds issued after 1972	Yes	Yes
Resolution Funding Corporation (REFCORP)	No	Yes. The Treasury is the ultimate source of funds to the extent not obtainable from other sources.
Small Business Administration (SBA)	Yes	No
Student Loan Marketing Association (Sallie Mae)	No	Yes. At its discretion, the Treasury may purchase $1 billion of the obligations.
Tennessee Valley Authority (TVA)	No	Yes, up to $150 million.
United States Postal Service	Guarantee may be extended if Postal Service requests it and Treasury determines this to be in the public interest.	Yes. The Postal Service may require the Treasury to purchase up to $2 billion of its obligations.
Washington Metropolitan Area Transit Authority	Yes	No

TABLE 7-7

GOVERNMENT AGENCY & SIMILAR ISSUES

GOVERNMENT AGENCY & SIMILAR ISSUES

Thursday, November 4, 1993

Over-the-counter mid-afternoon quotations based on large transactions, usually $1 million or more. Colons in bid-and-asked quotes represent 32nds; 101:01 means 101 1/32.

All yields are calculated to maturity, and based on the asked quote. * – Callable issue, maturity date shown. For issues callable prior to maturity, yields are computed to the earliest call date for issues quoted above par, or 100, and to the maturity date for issues below par.

Source: Bear, Stearns & Co. via Street Software Technology Inc.

[Table of Government Agency & Similar Issues quotations — FNMA Issues, Federal Home Loan Bank, Student Loan Marketing, Federal Farm Credit Bank, World Bank Bonds, Financing Corporation, Inter-Amer. Devel. Bank, GNMA Mtge. Issues, Tennessee Valley Authority, Farm Credit Fin. Asst. Corp., Resolution Funding Corp., Federal Land Bank — columns: Rate, Mat., Bid, Asked, Yld.]

Source: The Wall Street Journal, *April 21, 1994, p. C16.*

Reprinted by permission of The Wall Street Journal, © 1994 Dow Jones & Company, Inc. All Rights Reserved Worldwide.

The dealer will buy the security at a price to yield the dealer 6.5 percent to maturity and will sell the security at a price to yield the investor 6.4 percent to maturity.

In recent years, a new municipal security called a *mini-muni* has been issued. A **mini-muni,** or **mini,** is a municipal bond that sells in denominations as small as $500 and is usually a zero-coupon bond. It is targeted to small investors. There is no active secondary market for minis. If an investor wants to sell the mini before the maturity date, the issuer will frequently buy the bond back with a small penalty assessed against the investor.

Mini-muni. Municipal bond with a par value of less than $1000.

7.6.1 Tax-Equivalent Yields

The main appeal of municipal bonds lies in the federal tax-exempt status of their interest payments; this feature is most attractive to investors in high marginal income tax brackets. In some cases, the interest income is exempt from state income taxes. However, any gains or losses because of realized price differences are taxed at the federal and state levels. Some states do not allow an income tax exemption for the state's own municipal bonds, as Table 7.8 shows. The table also shows those states that exempt the income of municipal bonds issued by other states from income taxes within their states.

The 1992 election of Bill Clinton as president of the United States resulted in millions of dollars being invested in municipal securities because of the fear of higher individual income tax rates. As Illustration 7.5 describes, a tax-free yield of 7 percent is equivalent to a taxable yield of 12.96 percent for an investor in a combined federal-state-local marginal income tax bracket of 46 percent. If the investor is in a higher tax bracket, the taxable yield must be even higher to be equivalent to the 7 percent yield. We calculate the equivalent taxable yield using the formula:

$$\text{Taxable yield} = \frac{\text{(Tax-exempt yield)}}{\text{(1 - tax bracket)}} \tag{7.1}$$

where the tax bracket includes the investor's federal, state, and local marginal income tax rates.

ILLUSTRATION 7.5

Equivalent taxable yield of a muni

Alex's marginal income tax rates are 36 percent federal, 8 percent state, and 2 percent local. A tax-exempt yield of 7 percent on a municipal security is equivalent to a taxable yield of 12.96 percent:

$$\text{Taxable yield} = \frac{0.07}{1 - 0.36 - 0.08 - 0.02} = 0.1296$$

Therefore, he is indifferent between a taxable yield of 12.96 percent and a tax-exempt yield of 7.00 percent for securities of similar risk.

TABLE 7-8

INCOME TAX STATUS OF MUNICIPAL BONDS

States whose own municipal bonds are not tax exempt by the state's own income tax policy: Illinois, Iowa, Kansas, Oklahoma, and Wisconsin.

States that allow tax-exempt status for municipal bonds from other states: Alaska, Florida, Indiana, Nebraska, Nevada, New Mexico, South Dakota, Texas, Utah, Vermont, and Wyoming.

7.6.2 Keeping Tabs on Munis

Prices of most municipal bonds are not quoted in the daily press. They can be obtained by calling municipal bond dealers. *The Wall Street Journal* publishes a daily representative list of actively traded munis under the heading "Tax-Exempt Bonds." And each Friday, *The Wall Street Journal* publishes a "Municipal Bond Index" prepared by Merrill Lynch, the country's largest brokerage company. The report shows the latest yields on a variety of municipal bond groups.

Table 7.9 on page 248 shows examples of both reports. The "500 Municipal Bond Index" indicates that during the week, the average yield of municipal bonds fell 28 basis points from 6.68 percent (not shown) to 6.40 percent (shown). The table shows that the average yield of revenue bonds (6.38 percent) is higher than the yield of general obligation bonds (6.23 percent). The yield difference exists because revenue bonds are less securely backed and involve somewhat more risk. Generally the prices of municipal bonds are quoted in terms of the yield to maturity rather than in percentage of face value, as with other bonds.

Comprehension Check

1. What is the difference between the two principal types of municipal securities (munis)?
2. What is a mini-muni?
3. Demonstrate how the equivalent yield is calculated on a municipal bond which pays tax-exempt interest.
4. Look at Table 7.9 and explain why the two Orlando-Orange Co Fla bonds, with coupons of 5.125 and 5.250, respectively, do not sell for the same price.

7.7 PREFERRED STOCK

A security that is neither pure debt nor pure equity is **preferred stock.** For example:

- Some preferred stock has a maturity date like a debt security. Most preferred stock has no maturity date like a common stock, which we examine in Chapter 9.
- Most preferred stock has a fixed cash income amount like a debt security. Some preferred stock has an adjustable cash income amount.
- Preferred stock is similar to common stock in that the holder of it cannot force the firm into bankruptcy.

An example of a preferred stock with a fixed life is **money-market preferred stock (MMPS).** The stock's life may be as short as seven weeks. An issuer sells MMPS in $100,000 denominations to large corporate investors using a process called a *Dutch auction.* In a **Dutch auction,** the issuer announces the range of percentage yields it is willing to pay. Investors tender bids within that range. The issuer ranks the bids, starting at the lowest yield and works its way up until it has the *clearing yield,* the lowest yield which fills all submitted bids. The clearing yield becomes the yield for all tendered bids. The advantage of the auction is that it allows the marketplace to set the yield within the range, thereby minimizing the risk of either underpricing or overpricing the issue.

An example of a preferred stock with a variable cash dividend is an **adjustable-rate preferred stock (ARPS).** The cash dividend varies from quarter to quarter accord-

Preferred stock. Shares of stock that receive priority over common stock at a fixed rate in the distribution of dividends, or in the distribution of assets if the company is liquidated.

Money-market preferred stock (MMPS). Preferred stock with a short life that trades in the money market.

Dutch auction. A process where investors submit bids for securities. The issuer ranks the bids from high to low and sequentially selects those bids that are most advantageous to the issuer.

Adjustable-rate preferred stock (ARPS). A capital-market security that periodically adjusts the dividend amount in the direction of interest rate movements.

TABLE 7-9

MUNICIPAL BOND REPORTS

Municipal Bond Index
Merrill Lynch 500
Week ended April 12, 1994

The following index is based on yields that about 500 major issuers, mainly of investment grade, would pay on new long-term tax-exempt securities. The securities are presumed to be issued at par; general obligation bonds have a 20-year maturity and revenue bonds a 30-year maturity. The index, prepared by Merrill Lynch, Pierce, Fenner & Smith Inc., is calculated using yields on major outstanding bonds in the market. Yields are obtained from an internal source.

—500 MUNICIPAL BOND INDEX—
6.40 −0.28

—REVENUE BONDS—
Sub-Index 6.38 −0.30

	4-12	Change In Week
—25-YEAR REVENUE BONDS—		
AAA-Guaranteed ...	6.34	− 0.34
Airport	6.95	− 0.29
Power	6.34	− 0.25
Hospital	6.37	− 0.29
Housing-Single Family	6.61	− 0.30
Housing-Multi Family	6.80	− 0.28
Miscellaneous	n/a	....
Pollution Control/Ind. Dev.	6.25	− 0.28
Transportation	6.31	− 0.27
Water	6.41	− 0.28
Advance Refunded .	5.54	− 0.34
—20-YEAR GENERAL OBLIGATIONS—		
Sub-Index 6.23 −0.22		
Cities	6.38	− 0.21
Counties	6.39	− 0.22
States	6.02	− 0.31
Other Districts	n/a	....

The transportation category excludes airports; other districts include school and special districts.

TAX-EXEMPT BONDS

Representative prices for several active tax-exempt revenue and refunding bonds, based on institutional trades. Changes rounded to the nearest one-eighth. Yield is to maturity. n-New. Source: The Bond Buyer.

ISSUE	COUPON	MAT	PRICE	CHG	BID YLD	ISSUE	COUPON	MAT	PRICE	CHG	BID YLD
Anne Arundel Md Ser94	6.000	04-01-24	94½	− ⅛	6.41	NYC Muni Water Fin	5.500	06-15-23	89¼	− 1	6.31
Brazos River Auth	5.600	12-01-17	90⅛	− ½	6.41	NYC Muni Wtr Fin Auth	5.500	06-15-19	88⅜	− ¾	6.44
Calif Health Fac	5.550	08-15-25	86⅝	− 1	6.55	NYS Dorm Auth Mt Sinai	5.000	07-01-21	83¼	− ½	6.28
Calif Hlth Fac	5.000	07-01-14	84⅞	− ¾	6.33	NYS Med Care Agncy	5.375	02-15-25	86⅜	− ⅞	6.39
Chgo Gen Airpt Rev	5.000	01-01-18	83⅛	− ⅝	6.38	NYS Med Care Facil	5.250	08-15-14	88⅛	− ¾	6.27
Conn Hlth & Ed Facs	5.000	07-01-23	82⅜	− ⅜	6.33	NYS Power Auth Ser C	5.250	01-01-18	87	− ½	6.30
Dade Co Fla Wtr & Swr	5.000	10-01-13	85⅞	− ⅜	6.25	Ohio Tpke Comm	5.750	02-15-24	91⅞	− ¼	6.36
Dekalb Wtr & Swr	5.250	10-01-23	84⅛	− ⅜	6.39	Orl Utl Comm Subo	5.000	10-01-20	83⅞	+ ⅛	6.24
Fla BdEdPub EdCap	5.250	06-01-23	85⅜	− 1	6.35	Orlando-Orange co Fla	5.125	07-01-20	84⅞	− ½	6.30
Fla Mun Pwr Agy Ser93	5.100	10-01-25	83⅛	− ½	6.34	Orlando-Orange Co Fla	5.250	07-01-19	86⅝	− ½	6.30
Florida St Bd Ed	5.125	06-01-22	84¼	− ¾	6.33	Reedy Creed Fla	5.000	10-01-14	85⅞	− ¼	6.22
Fulton Co Sch Dist Ga	5.625	01-01-21	91⅞	− ⅜	6.25	Reedy Creek Fla	5.000	10-01-19	83¾	− ⅜	6.27
Harris Co Tex	5.375	08-15-20	87⅞	− ⅜	6.36	S.F. Cal. Sewr Ref Rev	5.375	10-01-22	87⅛	− ⅞	6.36
Harris Co Tex	5.500	08-15-21	88¾	− ½	6.37	Salem Co Pol Ctrl	5.450	02-01-32	85⅝	− ½	6.48
Hawaii Dept Budgt&Fin	5.450	11-01-23	86½	− ½	6.48	Salt Riv Pol Ariz	5.000	01-01-16	84⅞	− ⅜	6.29
Hawaii Hsng Fin & Dev	6.000	07-01-20	92⅜	− ½	6.55	San Ant Tex El Gas	5.000	02-01-14	84⅞	− ½	6.33
LA Comm Redev Ag	5.600	12-01-28	89⅛	− ¾	6.38	Seattle Wash Swr SerZ	5.500	01-01-33	86¼	− ¼	6.47
Lehigh Co Pa. Ind Dvl	5.500	02-15-27	88⅜	− ¼	6.34	TBTA NY	5.000	01-01-24	81¾	− 1⅛	6.36
Mo Hlth & Ed Facs	5.250	05-15-21	84¾	− ⅜	6.48	Valdez Al Marine Term	5.650	12-01-28	87½	− ¼	6.57
NYC Lcl Govt Asst Cp	5.500	04-01-18	88⅞	− 1	6.40	Washn Metro TA	5.250	07-01-14	88⅛	− ⅜	6.28

Source: The Wall Street Journal, *April 15, 1994, pp. C6 and C21.*

Reprinted by permission of The Wall Street Journal, *© 1994 Dow Jones & Company, Inc. All Rights Reserved Worldwide.*

TABLE 7-10

TYPES OF PREFERRED STOCK

Type of stock	Characteristics
Cumulative	Investor claims previously deferred dividends before common stock can share in profits.
Noncumulative	Investor cannot claim previously deferred dividends before common stock can share in profits.
Participating	Investor can receive extra dividends beyond fixed amounts.
Convertible	Investor can exchange shares for common stock.
Prior	Investor claims seniority over other preferred and common stocks in payment of dividends or in distribution of assets if the firm goes out of business.
Callable	Investor receives premium price if stock is redeemed within a specified number of years after issuance, otherwise, only par value is received if the company retires it later.

ing to market interest rates. The varying cash dividend rate reduces the price fluctuations of the preferred stock. If market interest rates increase, an increase in the dividend stabilizes the price of the preferred stock, and vice versa.

We classify preferred stock as either *cumulative* or *noncumulative* with each class having any combination of the following distinctive features: *participating, convertible, prior,* and *callable*. If all features are present, it is likely the case that the firm is desperate for cash and management finds it necessary to offer all these features to entice investors to buy the stock. Table 7.10 summarizes the classes and features.

If preferred shareholders do not receive their dividends, they cannot force the firm into bankruptcy like debtholders can if they fail to receive their cash interest and principal payments. Owners of preferred stock usually do not have voting rights. However, when preferred cash dividends are in default, preferred shareholders may have the right to elect a portion of the board of directors of the firm. In case the firm is liquidated, preferred shareholders must receive the par value of the preferred stock before common shareholders receive anything.[6]

Rating agencies, such as Standard & Poor's, rate preferred stock one level below its nearest debt issue. The reason is that debt is senior to preferred stock for cash flow distributions to investors. If a corporation's most junior debt is rated *AA*, the firm's preferred stock likely receives an *A* rating.

► **Comprehension Check**

1. Why is preferred stock called a hybrid security?
2. Define MMPs and ARPS.
3. Describe the two classes of preferred stock and the features that can be associated with either class.

[6]See the appendix to this chapter for a discussion of why the primary purchasers of preferred stock are other corporations and not individuals.

MANAGING FIXED-INCOME PORTFOLIOS

by Frank J. Fabozzi, Ph.D., Editor of *The Journal of Portfolio Management* and Adjunct Professor of Finance, Yale University

The fixed-income market includes Treasury and agency securities, corporate bonds, mortgage-backed securities, municipal bonds, foreign bonds, and preferred stock. Prior to the early 1980s, the fixed-income market was comprised mainly of "plain vanilla" bonds with simple structures—a fixed coupon rate, a stated maturity date, and an option for the issuer to call the bond prior to the maturity date. Today, the fixed-income market has securities that are much more complicated and, as a result, offer a wide range of risk-return patterns that appeal to investors with different investment objectives.

The investment objective will vary by type of financial institution. For pension funds the investment objective is to generate sufficient cash flow so to satisfy its obligations. The investment objective of life insurance companies is to earn a higher return on the insurance premium that it invests than the interest rate it has guaranteed policyholders. For depository institutions like banks and thrifts (S&Ls), the investment objective is to earn a return on invested funds that is higher than the cost of acquiring those funds. For the institutions I have cited, the investment objectives are essentially dictated by the nature of their liabilities. For investment companies (mutual funds), the investment objectives can vary widely.

Policy guidelines to satisfy the investment objectives must be established by the board of directors of an institution or by a client. This involves specifying the acceptable risks that the portfolio manager may expose the portfolio. Regulatory constraints must be considered in establishing an investment policy. For example, there are usually restrictions on the types of fixed-income securities that a regulated financial institution may invest.

A portfolio strategy that is consistent with the objectives and policy guidelines of the client or institution must be selected. These strategies can be classified as either active strategies or passive strategies. Essential to all active strategies is expectations about the factors that are expected to influence the performance of a fixed-income security. For example, with active fixed-income portfolios this may involve forecasts of future interest rates, future interest rate volatility, or future differences in yields between the various sectors of the fixed income market. Active portfolio strategies involving foreign bonds will require forecasts of future exchange rates. Passive strategies involve minimal expectational input. A popular type of passive strategy is indexing. The objective of an indexing strategy is to replicate the performance of a predetermined index. While indexing has been employed extensively in the management of common stock portfolios, the use of indexing for managing fixed-income portfolios is a relatively new practice. Between these extremes of active and passive strategies have sprung strategies that have elements of both.

The selection of a portfolio strategy depends on the client or portfolio manager's view of the pricing efficiency of the market and the nature of the liabilities to be satisfied. Pricing efficiency refers to a market in which prices at all times fully reflect all available information that is relevant to the valuation of securities so that active strategies will not consistently produce superior returns after adjusting for risk and transaction costs. If an investor believes a market is price efficient, an indexing strategy should be pursued. There is no reason for each sector within the fixed-income market to have the same degree of price efficiency. For example, it appears that the Treasury sector is efficient while the other sectors have pockets of inefficiency.

Once a portfolio strategy is selected, the portfolio manager must select the specific securities to include in the portfolio. This requires an evaluation of individual securities. In an active strategy, security selection means identifying mispriced securities. The characteristics of a specific fixed-income security must be carefully examined to determine how these characteristics will influence the performance of the security.

SUMMARY ▼▼▼▼▼▼▼▼▼▼

What Is Debt?

- There has been a significant increase in the use of debt financing by corporations in the last few decades.
- The growth in debt is largely because of tax advantages debt enjoys and financial innovation which has blurred the distinction between debt and equity.
- Debt represents a financial security with the following characteristics: an unconditional promise to pay, a fixed maturity date, pays a market rate of interest, and is not held by investors with significant equity ownership. There are exceptions to these features.
- Debt is classified as either a bond or a debenture. A bond is secured with collateral, whereas a debenture has no collateral and is a promissory note.
- Accompanying a debt security is a document called an indenture. It states the covenants the issuer must follow.

Advantages of Debt

- A firm pays interest out of before-tax income, whereas it pays dividends out of after-tax income. The result is double taxation of dividends, once at the corporate level and once at the investor level.
- The issuance of creative debt securities has eroded the priority of debt over equity.

Rating Debt Securities

- The default risk of debt securities is rated by independent companies. However, these ratings are not guarantees of the financial strength of the issuer.
- Several factors influence a debt security's rating, including the likelihood of default, the willingness of the issuer to make time payments, and the protection afforded borrowers.

Corporate Bonds

- Most bonds trade in the over-the-counter market.
- Bonds trading on major exchanges have narrower bid-asked spreads.
- Convertible bonds allow the investor to exchange the bond for common stock of the issuing company.

Government and Agency Debt Securities

- The initial sale of U.S. government bonds is conducted by the New York Federal Reserve Bank. The bank sells to primary dealers. Brokers arrange trades between dealers and customers.
- The Treasury Direct system allows individuals to buy Treasury securities directly from the Fed.
- Debt securities issued by the federal government are exempt from state and local income taxes, but not from federal income taxes.
- Investors can buy a wide range of federal agency securities. The government guarantees issues of the Farm Credit System Financial Assistance Corporation, Farmers Home Administration, Federal Financing Bank, General Services

▼

General obligations bonds
(GOs)
Mini-muni (mini)
Revenue bonds

Preferred stock
Adjustable-rate preferred
stock (ARPS)
Money-market preferred
stock (MMPS)

Administration, GNMA, Maritime Administration bonds, Small Business Administration, and the Washington Metro Area Transit Authority.

MUNICIPAL BONDS

- Municipal securities are classified as either general obligation bonds or revenue bonds. General obligation bonds depend on the taxing power of the authority for repayment. Revenue bonds depend on the cash flows of specific projects they finance.
- Many debt securities issued by municipalities are not taxed at the state level and are exempt from federal taxes.

PREFERRED STOCK

- Preferred stock has characteristics of both debt and equity securities. Debt has priority over preferred stock which, in turn, has priority over common stock.

FURTHER READING ▼▼▼▼▼▼▼▼▼▼

Bruck, Connie, *The Predator's Ball: The Junk Bond Raiders and the Man Who Staked Them*. New York: Simon and Schuster, 1988. This entertaining book provides insight into the use of debt for corporate buyouts.

Lehman, Michael B, *The Dow Jones-Irwin Guide to Using the Wall Street Journal*, 3rd ed. Homewood, IL: Business One Irwin, 1990. The author shows how to read *The Wall Street Journal*.

Shoven, John B., and Joel Waldfogel, eds., *Debt, Taxes, and Corporate Restructuring*. Washington, DC: The Brookings Institution, 1990. The articles in this book discuss the relationship between debt, taxes, and corporate restructuring in simple language.

SELF-TEST PROBLEMS ▼▼▼▼▼▼▼▼▼▼

ST7-1. Corktop, Inc. is considering selling $10 million of bonds at par to finance a factory expansion. The bonds would pay an interest rate of 9 percent and mature in 15 years. At present Corktop has no debt securities outstanding. What is the expected net income for Corktop if the forecast for earnings before interest and taxes is $8 million and the corporate tax rate is 34 percent?

ST7-2. Comtrex Corporation and Domoco, Inc. both had earnings before interest and taxes last year of $80,000. These firms are essentially the same except as to how they have financed their long-term needs. Comtrex has issued both debt and equity securities. Interest on the debt securities is $30,000 annually. Domoco has used only equity securities. The income tax rate on taxable income for both corporations is 35 percent. Both businesses pay all net income to their equity investors as cash dividends. Investors are taxed on dividends and interest at 31 percent.

   a. Calculate the income taxes paid by the corporation and its debt and equity investors in both cases. How much in after-tax income will each set of investors have after all income taxes are paid?

   b. How much is paid in total taxes and what is the effective cumulative tax rate for investors in each of these corporations on the original $80,000 of operating income?

c. How do you account for the difference in total taxes paid and after-tax investors' income between these two cases?

PROBLEMS ▼▼▼▼▼▼▼▼▼▼▼▼

WHAT IS DEBT?

7-1. a. List the factors which the Internal Revenue Service (IRS) considers when distinguishing debt from equity.

b. Why is the IRS concerned about the difference between debt and equity?

7-2. Distinguish between bonds and debentures.

7-3. Explain why bond indentures place restrictions on the following actions of borrowers:

a. Selling company assets.
b. Paying dividends to shareholders.
c. Issuing additional senior debt.

7-4. Given the characteristics of bearer and registered bonds, speculate as to what reasons might have prompted Congress to require all new bonds be issued as registered bonds.

7-5. What are the advantages for investors of corporate bonds which have a conversion feature? What are the disadvantages, if any?

ADVANTAGES OF DEBT

7-6. Railings, Inc. is considering selling $10 million of bonds at par to finance a factory expansion. The bonds would pay an annual interest rate of 11 percent and mature in ten years. At present Railings has no debt securities outstanding. Assume Railings sells the bonds and forecasts next year's earnings before interest and taxes (EBIT) to be $8 million. What would be the firm's net income (earnings after taxes) next year if the firm's marginal corporate tax rate is 34 percent?

7-7. Assume Railings, Inc. situation is the same as in Problem 7-6 except that management is considering financing the new factory through the sale of $10 million of common stock. Given the same forecast for earnings before interest and taxes, what would be the firm's net income next year?

7-8. Given the calculations for Railings, Inc. in Problems 7-6 and 7-7, if Railings's board of directors paid out all net income to common stockholders as cash dividends, what would be the total taxes paid by investors and the corporation if the stockholders' marginal income tax rate is 31 percent? Calculate taxes (a) when the new factory is financed with debt, and (b) with the sale of common stock. How do you explain the fact that total taxes are higher when the corporation finances its expansion with common stock instead of debt?

7-9. Johnson, Inc. and Roberts Corporation are essentially the same except for how they have financed their long-term needs. Johnson has issued both debt and equity securities. Interest on the debt securities is $18,000 annually. Roberts has used only equity securities. The income tax rate on taxable income for both corporations is 35 percent. Both businesses pay all net income to their equity investors as cash dividends. Investors are taxed on dividends and interest at a rate of 31 percent. Both corporations had earnings before interest and taxes last year of $50,000.

a. Calculate the income taxes paid by the corporation and its debt and equity investors in both cases. How much in after-tax income will each set of investors have after all income taxes are paid?

b. How much is paid in total taxes and what is the effective cumulative tax rate for investors in each of these corporations on the original $50,000 of corporate operating income?

c. How do you account for the difference in total taxes paid and after-tax investors' income between these two cases?

7-10. Explain how buyout specialists are able to take over corporations, make large payments of cash to themselves without paying off the debtholders, and end up with the companies having large amounts of debt and relatively little equity.

RATING DEBT SECURITIES

7-11. What is the purpose of having debt securities rated by firms such as Moody's Investors Service and Standard & Poor's?

7-12. If a debt rating service such as Duff & Phelps gives a company's bonded debt a high investment-grade rating, does this imply that the investor can expect little change in the debt's market price over its life? Explain your answer.

7-13. Based on the Financial Reality article on page 233, what guidelines can be helpful to a corporation in receiving and keeping an investment-grade rating for the company's fixed-income securities besides simply having a strong financial position?

CORPORATE BONDS

7-14. A Mobile Corporation debenture listed on the New York Stock Exchange is shown as follows:

Bonds	Cur. Yld.	Vol.	Close	Net Chg.
Mobile 8½ s01	8.0	166	106 1/8	+1/4

Explain each of the items.

7-15. A Citicorp bond listed on the New York Stock Exchange is shown as follows:

Bonds	Cur. Yld.	Vol.	Close	Net Chg.
Citicp 8.45s07	8.2	10	103 1/8	−5/8

Explain each of the items.

7-16. A Safeway Corporation debenture listed on the New York Stock Exchange is shown as follows:

Bonds	Cur. Yld.	Vol.	Close	Net Chg.
Safwy 9.35s99	8.9	4	105 1/2	. . .

Explain each of the items.

7-17. Distinguish between the functions of dealers and brokers in the U.S. government securities market.

7-18. a. After reviewing the Financial Reality reading on page 239, summarize what Salomon Brothers did in 1991 that created a financial scandal.
b. According to the writer of the article, what was the *real* Salomon scandal?

7-19. What is the purpose of the Treasury Direct system as part of the U.S. Treasury securities market?

7-20. What is the income tax treatment of the interest income on U.S. Treasury securities?

7-21. What is the difference in reporting of U.S. Treasury bonds and notes in the financial press such as *The Wall Street Journal* compared with quotations on corporate bonds?

7-22. The following listing was found in *The Wall Street Journal's* "Treasury Bonds and Notes" section. Explain what each item means.

Rate	Maturity	Bid	Asked	Chg.	Ask Yld.
4¼	1999–09 May	86.4	87.4	+.12	6.25

7-23. A recent article in *The Wall Street Journal,* describing an issue of FNMA (Fannie Mae) securities with a 10 percent coupon, noted that FNMA issues were subject to New York state and city income taxes whereas federal agency issues were not. (As an aside, both issues are subject to the federal income tax.) For investors with a combined marginal New York state and city income tax rate of 10 percent, how much difference would this make? The observed difference was less than one-fourth of 1 percent. Why could this be?

MUNICIPAL BONDS

7-24. Distinguish between a general obligation municipal bond and a revenue bond.

7-25. What risk is there to buying municipal bonds?

7-26. Consider a tax-exempt municipal bond yielding 6 percent. What is the equivalent before-tax yield on a taxable bond if the investor's marginal tax bracket is 10 percent? 28 percent? 33 percent?

7-27. A firm with a 34 percent marginal tax rate can buy a short-term, tax-exempt obligation with a yield of 5.2 percent. What equivalent yield does it need for a fully taxable obligation?

PREFERRED STOCK

7-28. What are the characteristics that make preferred stock a hybrid security?

7-29. Based on Table 7.10, what types of preferred stock would probably appeal to the following classes of investors? (Choose more than one type or feature if appropriate.)
a. Retired individual investor depending on dividend and interest payments for current income.
b. Individual investor interested in the possibility of appreciation in stock price as well as current dividend income.
c. Corporate treasurer investing excess funds for a year or more.

7-30. Explain why rating agencies, such as Standard & Poor's, usually rate a corporation's preferred stock one level below its nearest debt issue.

LIBRARY ASSIGNMENTS

7-31. By checking a current issue of *The Wall Street Journal* or the financial section of a daily newspaper which reports corporate bond transactions, what was the general direction of bonds' price changes that day? What effect did these price changes have on the yield of fixed-income securities to investors? Check the news reports for that day or the "Credit Markets" column in the third section of *The Wall Street Journal* and report the possible explanations for the general trend of price changes.

7-32. From the corporate bond quotation section in *The Wall Street Journal, Investor's Business Daily,* or some other newspaper listing bond quotations, find the difference in reporting the quotation for a convertible bond versus a corporate bond without a conversion feature. Why do you think this difference in reporting exists?

COMPREHENSIVE PROBLEM ▼▼▼▼▼▼▼▼▼▼▼▼

7-33. The Arizona Baseball Organization, Inc. (ABO) is a newly formed, taxable corporation looking to raise $250 million to build a new baseball stadium in the hope of attracting a major league team to Phoenix. The owners of ABO are willing to invest $10 million of their own money and believe the balance of $240 million should come from debt financing. They are considering a number of sources for this money.

    a. What are some important features that must exist with the debt for it to be legally classified as debt and not as equity?

    b. Some potential lenders have suggested that they are willing to lend a portion of the $240 million if ABO issues mortgage bonds. Other lenders are willing to accept debentures if the interest rate is attractive and a call protection exists. What is the distinction between these two different groups of lenders? Why do you think the debenture lenders want call protection?

    c. If you are a potential investor in the debentures, what sort of covenants (other than call protection) do you want stated in the indenture? Do your requirements change if you are a mortgage bond lender? Discuss.

    d. What are the tax implications to the firm from issuing debt as opposed to equity?

    e. Another potential group of investors in the debentures has asked for ABO to have the debentures rated by an independent agency. Who might ABO approach to do this? What sort of rating do you think the debentures would receive?

    f. Do you think ABO could issue either convertible debt or preferred stock to help finance the stadium construction? Would there be any advantage to using these types of securities?

    g. Would there be any advantage to the owners of ABO to convince the city of Phoenix to issue bonds with the proceeds used to help finance the stadium?

Appendix: Bond Yields versus Preferred Stock Yields

Preferred stock is attractive to investors who seek a fixed-income security where relatively little chance exists that the corporation will suspend dividend payments. Because the contract between the issuer of preferred shares and the investor is weaker than the contract between the issuer of debt and the investor, preferred stock should offer a higher yield than debt. The weaker position of the preferred stock is based on the fact that debt investors have priority to claims if the firm is beset with financial difficulty. Not paying interest and principal to these debtholders can result in bankruptcy for the firm. No such chance exists if the cash dividend paid to preferred shareholders lapses. Thus, preferred stock has greater exposure to default risk.

Risk-return principles state that preferred stock should offer a higher return because of its higher risk. However, typical data indicate that preferred stock investors do not receive a higher yield. Table 7A.1 shows that average annual yields on *Aa*-grade corporate bonds exceed average annual yields on comparably graded preferred shares by over 100 basis points. Why the inconsistency?

Tax laws and demand for preferred stock by other corporations appear to be the reason for the difference in yields. First, as noted earlier, interest paid on debt securities is a tax-deductible expense in the calculation of net income of the issuing firm. Dividends on preferred stock are not a tax-deductible expense for the corporation. For example, if we assume a marginal corporate income tax rate of 34 percent, the after-tax yield for the 1993 bonds in Table 7A.1 is 5.12 percent (= $7.75 \times [1 - 0.34]$) versus the existing after-tax yield of the preferreds of 6.48 percent. The nondeductibility of preferred stock dividends makes preferred stock financing more costly than debt financing for tax-paying companies. Therefore, from the perspective of firms needing long-term funds, they have an incentive to issue debt rather than preferred shares.

Utility companies are the largest issuers of preferred stock. Government regulatory agencies permit utilities to recover preferred cash dividends paid to investors through the rates they charge customers for utility services. However, utilities cannot recover common stock dividends through rates charged to customers. Because there is a limit to the amount of preferred dividends allowable in the rate base that a utility uses to charge its customers, preferred stock often represents only 10 to 15 percent of a utility company's financing.

However, another federal tax law provides incentive for one corporation to buy dividend-paying preferred or common stock of another corporation. The tax law results in a lower tax rate on any dividend income earned by a company investing in another corporation's stock. The corporate tax rate on dividend income is lower than the tax rate individual investors pay because taxable companies exclude 70 percent of dividend income in calculating their taxable income.[7] The tax exclusion for dividends does not apply to any interest income received by taxable corporations that invest in the debt of other corporations. As a result, firms such as insurance companies would rather buy high-grade preferred stocks than high-grade bonds. The demand for quality preferred shares causes their prices to increase, thereby reducing the yield of preferred stock below that of similar risky bonds as shown in Table 7A.1. Since the risk of holding high-grade preferred stocks is not materially greater than for high-grade bonds, the legal weakness in the preferred stock

---

[7]The tax exclusion is not available to individual investors. Thus, dividends are taxable to individual investors and the yield on preferred stock is actually lower than debt of the same default risk.

AVERAGE YIELDS: CORPORATE Aa BONDS VERSUS PREFERRED
STOCK YIELDS BEFORE TAXES

	Aa-grade Bonds	High-grade Preferreds	Spread
1993*	7.75%	6.48%	1.27
1992	8.46	7.05	1.41
1991	9.05	7.87	1.18
1990	9.56	8.28	1.28
1989	9.46	7.82	1.64
1988	9.94	8.17	1.77
1987	9.68	7.94	1.74
1986	9.46	8.13	1.33
1985	11.82	9.41	2.41
1984	13.31	10.21	3.10
1983	12.42	10.05	2.37

*The 1993 figures are averages for January through June.
Source: Moody's Industrial Manual (1993), pgs. A44 and A50.

contract is not viewed as a significant problem for many corporate investors. Illustration 7A.1 highlights the tax advantage corporations enjoy over individual investors.

ILLUSTRATION 7A.1

Tax advantage of dividends over interest income to taxable firms

Preferred stock of Baxter Company is selling at its par value of $100 and pays an 8 percent dividend. Collins Company has a marginal income tax rate of 34 percent, but it can exclude 70 percent of any dividend income it receives from taxable income. If Collins Company purchases preferred stock issued by Baxter Company, the after-tax yield on the preferred stock is 7.18 percent.

After-tax yield

$$= \frac{\text{Dividend} - \text{dividend} \times (1 - \text{exclusion rate}) \times \text{tax rate}}{\text{Beginning price of preferred share}}$$

$$= \frac{\$8 - \$8 \times (1 - 0.70) \times 0.34}{\$100}$$

$$= .0718 \text{ or } 7.18 \text{ percent}$$

Without the dividend tax exclusion, the yield would be 5.28 percent. Verify this result.[8]

If Collins buys debt issued by Baxter and not Baxter's preferred stock, the debt must yield 10.88 percent before tax to yield a comparable after-tax return of 7.18 percent earned on the preferred stock.

[8]Solution: $8 \times (1 - 0.34) \div \$100 = 0.0528$ or 5.28 percent.

$$\text{Before-tax bond yield} = \frac{\text{After-tax yield on preferred stock}}{(1 - \text{tax rate})}$$

$$= \frac{0.0718}{1 - 0.34}$$

$$= 0.1088 \text{ or } 10.88 \text{ percent}$$

ANSWERS TO SELF-TEST PROBLEMS ▼▼▼▼▼▼▼▼▼▼▼▼

ST7-1.

EBIT	$8,000,000
Interest expense	900,000
Earnings before taxes	$7,100,000
Income taxes (34%)	2,414,000
Net income	$4,686,000

ST7-2.

a.

	Comtrex	Domoco
EBIT	$80,000	$80,000
Interest expense	30,000	0
Earnings before taxes	$50,000	$80,000
Income taxes (35%)	17,500	28,000
Net income	$32,500	$52,000

Investors in:	Comtrex	Domoco
Dividend income	$32,500	$52,000
Interest income	30,000	0
Total income	$62,500	$52,000
Income taxes (31%)	19,375	16,120
Investors' after-tax income	$43,125	$35,880

b. Effective cumulative tax rates

	Comtrex	Domoco
Taxes paid at the corporate level	$17,500	$28,000
Taxes paid at the investor level	19,375	16,120
Total taxes paid	$36,875	$44,120
Effective tax rate on $80,000 operating income	46.09%	55.15%

c. The difference existing in taxes at the corporate level is because Comtrex's interest paid to debtholders is a tax-deductible business expense. The difference is $10,500: $30,000 interest × 35 percent tax rate.

At the investor level, Comtrex investors pay $3255 more in taxes because they receive $10,500 more cash flow from the corporation than do investors of Domoco: $10,500 × 31 percent tax rate.

The net cash flow advantage to investors in Comtrex is $7245 (= $10,500 − $3255), which is the overall taxes saved ($44,120 − $36,875).

Video Case 7

Bond-Rating Agencies:
Using Financial Analysis To Forecast
The Riskiness Of Bonds

from *Business World*, June 23, 1991

Chapter 18 will introduce the topic of financial analysis. An important use of financial analysis is the evaluation of investments. Bond-rating agencies such as Moody's and Standard and Poor's apply these techniques when evaluating the riskiness of corporate and municipal bonds. Using past financial data and forecasts of economic trends, these agencies give borrowers a letter rating such as *AA* (double A) or *BBB* (triple B), which indicates the overall quality of the bond being rated. The higher the rating (*AAA* is the highest), the more certain the rating agency is that the interest and principal payments of a bond will be paid in a timely manner. Bond ratings matter. For example, a lower bond rating translates into higher interest payments. If a rating is too low, the issuer may find it difficult to sell its bonds.

The video clip describes some of the factors that Moody's and Standard and Poor's take into account when assigning or revising a city's bond rating. For any analysis the information required depends on the question being asked. In the case of rating a municipal bond, the question is how easily can the city issuing the bond repay the loan. If repayment is certain, then you assign the bond a high rating (*AAA* or *AA*), but if there are situations that might threaten repayment, a lower rating is assigned. Cities and states differ from firms because they raise money through taxation, not selling goods. Analysts need to examine the tax base to determine the revenue stream or the stability of the tax revenues. The tax revenues of states that rely on just a sales tax or just an income tax may be affected differently during economic downturns than states using both types of taxing mechanisms. Other debt outstanding, such as previously issued bonds, also

affect a city or state's ability to service its debt. Sometimes bonds are repaid from receipts from a particular activity or facility. In some states, toll roads repay highway construction bonds. Such facility-specific repayment requires that a thorough examination of the demand and usage of that facility must be completed. For example, Denver, Colorado, is building a new airport, DIA (Denver International Airport). When Standard and Poor's rates the bonds used to finance the airport's construction, it analyzes the airlines that have secured gates and landing rights at the airport, the health of those carriers, the growth of passenger traffic through Denver, and the use of Denver as a hub by certain companies.

How much do the bond ratings assigned to a city or state government matter? Here is an example. When the bond-rating agencies threatened to lower the rating on bonds about to be issued by the State of California from *AAA* to *AA*, the state treasurer estimated that it would cost the State of California (actually, the taxpayers of California) an extra $8 million per year in higher interest expense over the 25-year life of the bonds (*The New York Times*, December 14, 1991).

Study Question

1. A number of states have passed spending or revenue limitation laws. The most famous is California's Proposition 13. These laws often require voters to approve any tax increases or spending plans. How do you think such rules affect the riskiness of bonds issued by those states? In turn, how would you modify your bond-quality rating following passage of such bills?

CHAPTER 8

Valuation of Fixed-Income Securities

In late December 1993, an AT&T bond was selling for $947.50. How was this value determined? We will see that the bond's value comes from three sources. The first source is the interest income. The second source arises from the difference between the bond's purchase price and its ultimate sale or redemption price. The third source is from reinvesting interest income, thereby earning interest on interest.

The key component in valuing each of these sources is the interest rate, which represents the cost of money to the borrower and the return to the lender. When AT&T originally issued the bond, investors received a competitive return, or market interest rate, with other financial instruments of similar risk. However, once issued, any change in market rates can make the bond more or less attractive to investors. If the bond pays more interest than is available elsewhere for comparable risk, investors willingly pay more to own the fixed-income security. However, if the bond pays less interest than can be earned for comparable risk, investors pay less for the instrument. Consequently, interest rates and prices of fixed-income securities fluctuate like two sides of a see saw. When interest rates decline, the value of an existing fixed-income security goes up; when interest rates increase, the value of this security falls.

The magnitude of the bond's price change is affected by the security's maturity, coupon rate, and the general perception of the level of future interest rates, as captured by a *yield curve*. A technique called *duration analysis* can measure the increasing or decreasing price, or volatility, of the security as a result of interest rate changes.

When you have completed this chapter, you should understand:

- Several different return measures associated with bonds.
- The interpretation of yield curves.
- The behavior of prices of bonds to changing interest rates and maturities.
- Duration analysis and how it can be used to measure the sensitivity of bond prices to changing interest rates.
- The valuation of convertible debt and preferred stock.

8.1 WHAT ARE THE RETURN MEASURES FOR BOND PRICES?

There are several measures that may determine a bond's return, or yield. These are coupon rate, current yield, holding-period rate of return, and yield to maturity. Making decisions on which measure to apply in the valuation process is central to the valuation process. The previously mentioned AT&T bond, listed in *The Wall Street Journal* as ATT 4³/₈99, closed at 94³/₄ on December 22, 1993.

- *Coupon rate* of 4³/₈ percent is the fixed rate of interest printed on the bond certificate and cannot be changed once the bond is issued.

- *Current yield* is an annual cash flow measure based on the current market price of the bond. The definition of **current yield** is:

$$\text{Current yield} = \frac{\text{Annual dollar amount of coupon interest}}{\text{Bond's current market price}} \quad (8.1)$$

$$= \frac{\$43.75}{\$947.50}$$

$$= 0.046 \text{ or } 4.6 \text{ percent}$$

A bond's current yield may be exactly the same as its coupon rate, or it may be more or less. Usually it differs from the coupon rate. Notice in Equation 8.1 that if the bond rises in price, its current yield falls. And if the bond falls in price, its current yield rises.

- *Holding-period rate of return* can be calculated for any period of time, for example, one month, one quarter, one year, or longer. Let's assume that you bought the AT&T bond for $980 (or 98 in terms of the newspaper quote) one year ago and have received the annual interest payment of $43.75. Since the bond is currently selling for $947.50, you have an unrealized loss of $980 − $947.50 = $32.50. The formula to calculate the **holding-period rate of return** is:

Holding-period rate of return. Rate of return earned from holding an asset during a given time period.

$$\text{Holding-period rate of return}$$
$$= \frac{\text{Coupon interest amount + change in price of the bond}}{\text{Beginning price of bond}} \quad (8.2)$$

$$= \frac{\$43.75 - \$32.50}{\$980}$$

$$= 0.0115 \text{ or } 1.15 \text{ percent}$$

- *Yield to maturity (YTM)* is a term often used in conjunction with a bond investment. In more general usage, YTM is called the *internal rate of return (IRR)*. The **yield to maturity** is the interest rate earned by holding the security until its maturity date and reinvesting all cash flows received prior to maturity at the IRR. For the AT&T bond, we know the bond's current market value (B_0) is $947.50. We also know the expected interest payment (I_t) to be received every six months is $21.875 (= 4³/₈% × $1000 ÷ 2) and the principal amount (P_n) of $1000 is to be paid at maturity in year 1999, or 12 periods from our assumed purchase date of December 1993. The YTM equation is:

Yield to maturity (YTM). The interest rate that makes the present value of a bond's interest and principal equal to its current price.

$$B_0 = \frac{I_1}{(1 + r)} + \frac{I_2}{(1 + r)^2} + \cdots + \frac{I_n + P_n}{(1 + r)^n} \quad (8.3)$$

$$\$947.50 = \frac{\$21.875}{(1 + r)} + \frac{\$21.875}{(1 + r)^2} + \cdots + \frac{\$21.875 + \$1000}{(1 + r)^{12}}$$

The unknown variable is r, the YTM. Using a financial calculator, we find the YTM to be 2.705 percent per six months, or 5.58 percent annualized: $(1 + 0.02705)^2 - 1$. (Appendix 8A discusses interpolation as an alternate method to calculate YTM.)

Calculator
Clear
21.875
PMT
1000
FV
947.50
PV
12
N
CPT
% i
Ans.: 2.705

- *Approximate yield to maturity (AYTM)* provides a good estimate of the YTM when we do not have a financial calculator available. The formula is:[1]

$$AYTM = \frac{\text{Amount of interest per period} + \dfrac{(\text{Face value} - \text{bond price})}{\text{Periods until maturity}}}{\dfrac{\text{Face value} + 2 \times \text{bond price}}{3}} \tag{8.4}$$

$$= \frac{\$21.875 + (\$1000 - \$947.50)/12}{\dfrac{\$1000 + 2 \times \$947.50}{3}}$$

$$= 0.0272 \text{ or } 2.72 \text{ percent every 6 months}$$

Figure 8.1 shows how *current yield, YTM,* and *coupon rate* interact with the market price of the ATT 4³/₈99 bond. The *holding-period rate of return* depends on both beginning and ending prices, and this cannot be shown in the graph.

▶ **Comprehension Check**

1. Define coupon rate, current yield, holding-period return, and yield to maturity (internal rate of return).
2. Explain how the approximate yield to maturity equation works.

8.2 HOW RETURN MEASURES INTERACT WITH THE BOND PRICE

Let's explore key relationships that exist between a bond's market interest rate (r), its maturity (n), and its price (B_0). To understand these relationships, we use the present value model:

$$B_0 = \frac{I_1}{(1 + r)} + \frac{I_2}{(1 + r)^2} + \cdots + \frac{I_n + P_n}{(1 + r)^n} \tag{8.5}$$

where I_t and P_n represent interest coupon payments in period t and principal payment at the maturity of the bond, respectively. If the bond is callable, then P represents the call price and the subscript n is the expected call period. Five bond theorems succinctly state the relationship between coupon payments, market rates, maturity, and price.[2]

Theorem 1: A bond's price moves inversely with its market interest rate, or yield.

[1]See Ricardo J. Rodriquez, "The Quadratic Approximation to the Yield to Maturity," *Journal of Financial Education* (Fall 1988), pp. 19–25.

[2]The theorems were derived by Burton G. Malkiel in "Expectations, Bond Prices, and the Term Structure of Interest Rates," *Quarterly Journal of Economics* (May 1962), pp. 1–26.

FIGURE 8.1

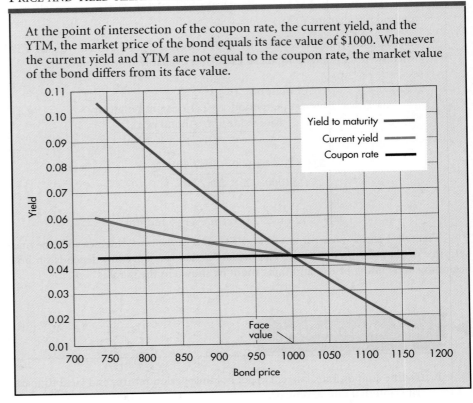

At the point of intersection of the coupon rate, the current yield, and the YTM, the market price of the bond equals its face value of $1000. Whenever the current yield and YTM are not equal to the coupon rate, the market value of the bond differs from its face value.

Theorem 2: The longer the bond's maturity, the greater its price change for a change in its market interest rate.

Theorem 3: Price changes at an increasing rate as time to maturity decreases.

Theorem 4: For a given maturity, a decrease in a bond's market interest rate results in a price increase that is larger than a price decrease resulting from an equal increase in market yields.

Theorem 5: For a given change in a bond's market interest rate, a bond with a higher coupon rate has a lower percentage price change than does a bond with a lower coupon rate.

The following sections examine these theorems. Instead of using the AT&T bond, we illustrate the theorems with hypothetical bonds that have different market interest rates and maturities.

8.2.1 Theorem 1: Bond Prices Vary Inversely with Yields

If we hold the coupon (I) and principal (P) amounts constant in Equation 8.5 but let the market interest rate (r) change, the price of the bond (B) changes inversely to the interest rate. As market rates increase, bond prices decline, and vice versa. (See Illustration 8.1.)

ILLUSTRATION 8.1

Market rates go one direction, prices the other

Three situations can exist: the coupon rate equals the market rate; the coupon rate is less than the market rate; or the coupon rate exceeds the market rate. For each case in this illustration, the bond has a face value of \$1000 and an 8 percent coupon rate.

A. COUPON RATE (8%) = MARKET RATE (8%)

When the coupon rate equals the market rate, the market value of the bond equals its \$1000 face value. The current yield equals the coupon and market rates of 8 percent (= \$80 ÷ \$1000).

$$B_0 = \frac{\$80}{1.08} + \frac{\$80}{(1.08)^2} + \frac{\$80}{(1.08)^3} + \frac{\$80}{(1.08)^4} + \frac{\$80 + \$1000}{(1.08)^5}$$

$$= \$74.07 + \$68.59 + \$63.51 + \$58.80 + \$735.03$$
$$= \$1000$$

B. COUPON RATE (8%) < MARKET RATE (9%)

Suppose the bond's market interest rate increases by 100 basis points (1 percent) for all time periods. Thus, the discount rate for each period increases from 8 percent to 9 percent. The new market value of the bond is \$961.09. The higher market rate means that the present value of each cash flow is smaller, which results in the bond selling at a discount (less than face value). The current yield is 8.32 percent (= \$80 ÷ \$961.09).

$$B_0 = \frac{\$80}{1.09} + \frac{\$80}{(1.09)^2} + \frac{\$80}{(1.09)^3} + \frac{\$80}{(1.09)^4} + \frac{\$80 + \$1000}{(1.09)^5}$$

$$= \$73.39 + \$67.33 + \$61.77 + \$56.67 + \$701.93$$
$$= \$961.09$$

C. COUPON RATE (8%) > MARKET RATE (7%)

Now suppose the bond's market interest rate falls 100 basis points, from 8 percent to 7 percent. The bond's new value is \$1041.01, which is greater than its face value of \$1000. Thus, the bond sells at a premium and has a current yield of 7.68 percent (= \$80 ÷ \$1041.01).

$$B_0 = \frac{\$80}{1.07} + \frac{\$80}{(1.07)^2} + \frac{\$80}{(1.07)^3} + \frac{\$80}{(1.07)^4} + \frac{\$80 + \$1000}{(1.07)^5}$$

$$= \$74.77 + \$69.88 + \$65.30 + \$61.03 + \$770.03$$
$$= \$1041.01$$

The following table summarizes this process.

	Value of Bond When:		
Coupon Rate	8%	8%	8%
Market Rate	7%	8%	9%

Bond with 5 years to maturity:			
Price	$1041.01	$1000.00	$961.09
% price change relative to case where coupon rate = market rate	+4.10%		−3.89%
Current yield	7.68%	8.00%	8.32%

Figure 8.2 graphs the illustration's results. A bond with a fixed coupon rate loses value relative to its face value when the market rate increases over the coupon rate. Why the loss in value? It is because investors can earn 9 percent on other assets with risk comparable to this bond's risk. However, since the bond only offers a fixed coupon rate of 8 percent, investors will not pay $1000 for it if they want to earn the market yield of 9 percent. The price of the bond *must* decline (sell at a discount) to boost the return to the 9 percent market level.

When the market interest rate is less than the coupon rate, the bond sells for more than its face value (at a premium). If market participants consider a 7 percent market

FIGURE 8.2

PRICES MOVE INVERSELY TO MARKET RATES

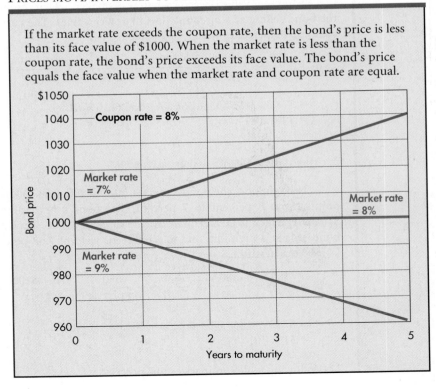

If the market rate exceeds the coupon rate, then the bond's price is less than its face value of $1000. When the market rate is less than the coupon rate, the bond's price exceeds its face value. The bond's price equals the face value when the market rate and coupon rate are equal.

.turn to be adequate for the risk exposure, they will pay more than the $1000 face value of the bond. Paying more results in a market yield less than the coupon rate.

8.2.2 Theorem 2: The Longer the Maturity, the Greater the Price Change

Consider two fixed-rate coupon bonds of equal risk and both having face values of $1000. One bond matures in five years and the other in three years. As Figure 8.2 shows, when each bond's coupon rate equals the market rate, each bond sells for its face value of $1000. Different maturities do not affect the value of the bonds when their coupon and market rates are equal.

However, when the coupon rate does not equal the market rate, the bond's market value is affected by time remaining until maturity. Again, Figure 8.2 captures the relationship under two different scenarios for market rates. When the coupon rate is less than the 9 percent market rate, a shortening of the bond's maturity from five years to three years results in an increase in the market value of the bond from about $960 to about $975. If the coupon rate exceeds the 7 percent market rate, a shortening of the bond's maturity from five years to three years causes the market value of the bond to fall from about $1040 to about $1026. Illustration 8.2 works through the calculations for the three-year bond. (Calculations for the five-year bond are given in Illustration 8.1.)

ILLUSTRATION 8.2

When bond maturity changes

Suppose the maturity of the bond in Illustration 8.1 is three years instead of five years. Let's examine situations in which the coupon rate equals the market rate, the coupon rate is less than the market rate, and the coupon rate exceeds the market rate. As before, the bond has a face value of $1000 and a coupon rate of 8 percent.

A. Coupon rate (8%) = market rate (8%)

The value of the bond at an 8 percent market interest rate with three years to maturity is $1000. The current yield, coupon, and market rates are equal to 8 percent (= $80 ÷ $1000).

$$B_0 = \frac{\$80}{1.08} + \frac{\$80}{(1.08)^2} + \frac{\$80 + \$1000}{(1.08)^3}$$

$$= \$74.07 + \$68.59 + \$857.34$$
$$= \$1000$$

B. Coupon rate (8%) < market rate (9%)

If the bond's market interest rate increases 100 basis points, the bond's value is $974.68. The current yield is 8.21 percent (= $80 ÷ $974.68), which exceeds the coupon rate.

$$B_0 = \frac{\$80}{1.09} + \frac{\$80}{(1.09)^2} + \frac{\$80 + \$1000}{(1.09)^3}$$

$$= \$73.39 + \$67.33 + \$833.96$$
$$= \$974.68$$

C. COUPON RATE (8%) > MARKET RATE (7%)

If the bond's market interest rate falls 100 basis points to 7 percent, the value of the 8 percent coupon bond is $1026.25. The current yield is 7.80 percent (= $80 ÷ $1026.25), which is less than the coupon rate.

$$B_0 = \frac{\$80}{1.07} + \frac{\$80}{(1.07)^2} + \frac{\$80 + \$1000}{(1.07)^3}$$

$$= \$74.77 + \$69.88 + \$881.60$$

$$= \$1026.25$$

The following table summarizes this process.

		Value of Bond When:		
Coupon Rate		8%	8%	8%
Market Rate		7%	8%	9%
Bond with 5 years to maturity: (Illustration 8.1)				
Market price		$1041.01	$1000.00	$961.09
% price change relative to case where coupon rate = market rate		+4.10%		−3.89%
Current yield		7.68%	8.00%	8.32%
Bond with 3 years to maturity:				
Market price		$1026.25	$1000.00	$974.68
% price change relative to case where coupon rate = market rate		+2.63%		−2.53%
Current yield		7.80%	8.00%	8.21%

The summary table in Illustration 8.2 reveals that price changes for longer-maturity bonds are greater than price changes for shorter-maturity bonds. For instance, when the market interest rate increases 100 basis points, the three-year maturity bond declines 2.53 percent in value (= 1 − $974.68 ÷ $1000), whereas the five-year maturity bond loses 3.89 percent in value (= 1 − $968.09 ÷ $1000). A decline in market interest rates of 100 basis points results in the three-year maturity bond appreciating 2.63 percent ($1026.25 ÷ $1000 − 1), whereas the five-year bond increases 4.10 percent ($1041.01 ÷ $1000 − 1).

8.2.3 Theorem 3: Price Changes at an Increasing Rate as Maturity Decreases

Figure 8.3 indicates how a bond's value changes as maturity changes. Values plotted in this figure use the bond valuation model of Equation 8.5 (shown earlier) to calculate prices with maturity (n) declining from five years to one year.

FIGURE 8.3

VALUES CHANGE BY DIMINISHING AMOUNTS

Maturity has no effect on bond value when the coupon rate equals the market rate. If the market rate is less than the coupon rate, the bond loses value from one period to the next at an accelerating rate as maturity shortens. If the market rate is greater than the coupon rate, the bond gains value at an accelerating rate as maturity shortens. At maturity, the bond's value is its face value.

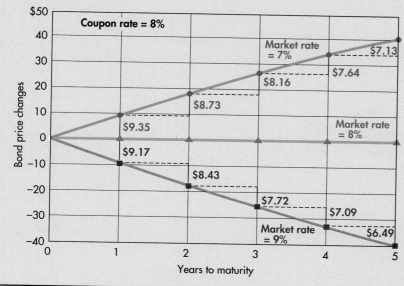

$$B_0 = \frac{I_1}{(1 + r)} + \frac{I_2}{(1 + r)^2} + \cdots + \frac{I_n + P_n}{(1 + r)^n}$$

$$= \frac{\$80}{(1 + r)} + \frac{\$80}{(1 + r)^2} + \cdots + \frac{\$80 + \$1000}{(1 + r)^n}$$

The coupon rate is 8 percent and the face value is $1000. The upper curve in Figure 8.3 assumes a market interest rate of 7 percent, whereas the lower curve uses a market interest rate of 9 percent. You might want to see if you can calculate the bond price changes by substituting into the preceding equation and solving for different maturities.[3]

The graph shows that bond value increases by larger increments from period to period as maturity shortens *if* the market rate exceeds the coupon rate. If the market rate is *less* than the coupon rate, the bond's value decreases in larger increments from period to period as maturity shortens.

8.2.4 Theorem 4: Unequal Gains and Losses

Figure 8.4 displays the same bond information calculated for Figure 8.3 but in a slightly different form. Instead of showing the increments or decrements as maturity decreases,

[3]For example: $80 PVIFA$_{9\%, 2 \text{ years}}$ + $1000 PVIF $_{9\%, 2 \text{ years}}$ = $982.41
 $80 PVIFA$_{9\%, 3 \text{ years}}$ + $1000 PVIF $_{9\%, 3 \text{ years}}$ = 974.69
Change in value $ 7.72

FIGURE 8.4
CAPITAL GAINS AND LOSSES

Maturity has no effect on bond value, and thus gains or losses, when the coupon rate equals the market rate. If the market rate is less than the coupon rate, the bond's capital *gains*—the price minus the face value of $1000—become smaller as maturity shortens. If the market rate is greater than the coupon rate, the bond's capital *losses* become smaller as maturity shortens.

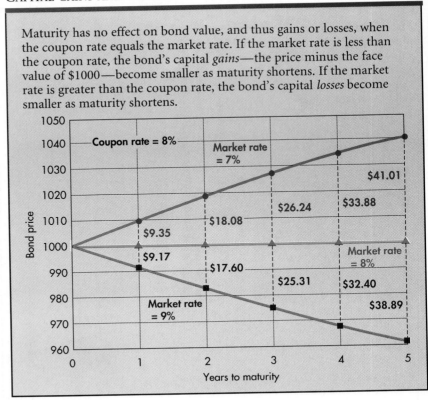

Capital gain. Increase in value of a security over its original cost.

Capital loss. Decrease in value of a security from its original cost.

the graph reveals *capital gains* and *capital losses* relative to the bond's face value. A **capital gain** is the difference between a security's purchase price and its higher selling price. A **capital loss** is the difference between a security's purchase price and its lower selling price.

What's the interpretation of the graph? When the bond (Figure 8.4) is selling for its face value of $1000, the current yield, market interest rate, and coupon rate are all equal to 8 percent. If the bond's market interest rate increases 100 basis points from 8 percent to 9 percent, its market value declines across all maturities. If the bond has four years until maturity, the capital loss is $32.40 (= $1000 – $967.60). With one year until maturity, the capital loss is only $9.17 (= $1000 – $990.93). Now assume that market interest rates decline from 8 percent to 7 percent. The bond appreciates in price across all maturities. For a four-year maturity, the increase is $33.88 (= $1033.88 – $1000). When maturity is one year, the bond's value increases only $9.35 (= $1009.35 – $1000). The capital gains for these two different maturities are $33.88 and $9.35, respectively.

For a given maturity, a bond's value increases more for a decrease in market interest rates than does a bond's value decrease for a similar increase in market interest rates. For example, in year 5 the gain is $41.01, whereas the loss is $38.89. Also note that as maturity increases, both capital gains and capital losses increase, but the dollar advantage of the capital gain over the capital loss widens. In year 1 the difference is $0.18 (= $9.35 – $9.17); by year 5 the difference is $2.12 (= $41.01 – $38.89).

8.2.5 Theorem 5: Market Interest Rates Have Less Effect on Higher Coupon Bonds

Three bonds, each with five years until maturity, are held in a portfolio. The first bond has a coupon rate of 0 percent, the second bond has a coupon rate of 4 percent, and the last bond has a coupon rate of 8 percent. Table 8.1 summarizes the price of each bond for market interest rates ranging from 0 to 6 percent. Check your understanding of bond prices by using Equation 8.5 (or a financial calculator) to calculate the values in the table. The results reveal that when market interest rates change, bonds with higher coupon rates are subject to less change in value than are lower-coupon bonds, assuming all else remains constant.

 Comprehension Check

1. Outline the five bond price theorems.

2. What will be the market value of a bond when its coupon rate is the same as the market rate of interest?

3. What will be the change in the market value of a bond when:
   a. Market interest rates rise?
   b. Market interest rates fall?
   c. How do you explain the price changes in (a) and (b)?

4. Explain what will happen to the market value of a bond that has the same coupon rate as the bond's market interest rate as it approaches maturity.

5. Explain how the market value of a bond will vary when the time to maturity declines and market interest rates remain either above or below the coupon rate on the bond.

TABLE 8-1

BOND PRICES FOR DIFFERENT COUPONS AND MARKET INTEREST RATES

Market Rate	0% Coupon	%Δ	4% Coupon	%Δ	8% Coupon	%Δ
0%	$1000.00		$1200.00		$1400.00	
1	951.47	−4.85%	1145.60	−4.53%	1339.74	−4.30%
2	905.73	−4.81	1094.27	−4.48	1282.81	−4.25
3	862.61	−4.76	1045.80	−4.43	1228.99	−4.20
4	821.93	−4.72	1000.00	−4.38	1178.07	−4.14
5	783.53	−4.67	956.71	−4.33	1129.88	−4.09
6	747.26	−4.63	915.75	−4.28	1084.25	−4.04

%Δ for a 0 percent coupon bond, with a market rate of 2 percent, is calculated as: [($905.73 ÷ $951.47) − 1] × 100 = −4.81 percent. The other percent changes are calculated similarly. Each bond has a five-year maturity and a face value of $1000.

FIGURE 8.5

YIELD CURVES

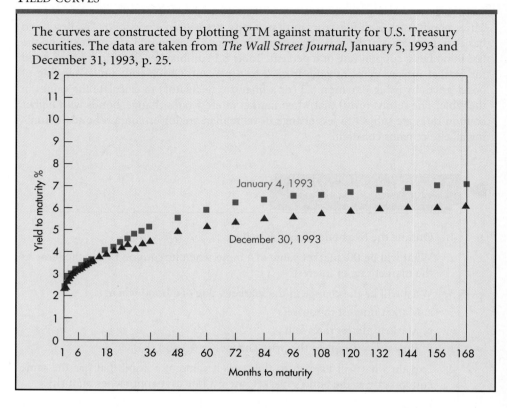

The curves are constructed by plotting YTM against maturity for U.S. Treasury securities. The data are taken from *The Wall Street Journal*, January 5, 1993 and December 31, 1993, p. 25.

▲▼ 8.3 EFFECT OF CHANGING YIELD CURVES ON BOND PRICES

Analysis of the bond theorems in the previous section assumes that market interest rates are equal for all future time periods. Although such an assumption is unrealistic, it does not affect the results captured by the bond theorems. Typically, interest rates on securities with longer maturities are higher than rates on short-term securities. We refer to such an interest rate pattern as an upward sloping *yield curve,* or *term structure of interest rates*. But sometimes, long-term rates are lower than short-term rates; in this case, the yield curve is described as downward sloping or inverted.

> **Term structure of interest rates.** The relationship between yield and time to maturity of a debt security.

The **term structure of interest rates** compares the relationship between YTMs of comparable risky bonds and maturities at a particular point in time.[4] It is necessary to consider bonds of similar default risk, such as all U.S. Treasury securities. Otherwise, the YTMs also capture different default risk premiums, and this makes it difficult to understand whether the level of future expected interest rates is because of expected inflation effects or expected default effects.

Figure 8.5 depicts graphs of yield curves for January 4, 1993 and December 30, 1993. The maturity of U.S. Treasury securities is shown on the horizontal axis; their

---

[4]Appendix 8B discusses prevalent theories about the term structure of interest rates.

YTMs appear on the vertical axis. Graphing each bond's maturity against its YTM results in a series of points. The graph encompasses a range, from bonds that are close to maturity to bonds with several years remaining before maturity. A **yield curve** is the pattern of plotted points. In this example, both yield curves are upward sloping, but flatten out beyond 96 months.

Yield curve. A pictorial representation of the term structure of interest rates.

The term structure of interest rates is important because it contains information about the market's forecasts of future inflation and interest rates as well as about its perception of risk. For example, Figure 8.5 shows that from January 1993 to the end of December 1993, long-term interest rates fell relative to short-term rates. To some extent, this may have reflected beliefs that inflation would be lower in the future, that the federal government's deficit reduction would reduce future short-term real interest rates, or that risks associated with long-term investments may have diminished. If properly understood, this information can help investors.

We will be exploring interest rate theories of the term structure in Appendix 8B, following this chapter. Essentially this refers to theories explaining the shape of the yield curves, as we see in Figure 8.5. The Financial Reality article on page 274 gives us a real-world look into the complex interaction of policy, interest rates, and the term structure of bond yields. In the following discussion, we will see how to determine bond value when yield curves are either upward sloping or downward sloping.

8.3.1 An Upward Sloping Yield Curve and Bond Prices

With an upward sloping yield curve, market participants expect future one-period interest rates (**forward rates**) to be higher than the current period's interest rate. Illustration 8.3 is an example of how changing forward rates affect the price of the bond.

Forward rates. Future interest rates implied by currently available spot interest rates.

ILLUSTRATION 8.3

Bond value with an upward sloping yield curve

An economist with Prudential Securities forecasts market interest rates to be 6 percent next year, 7 for the second year, and 11 percent for the third year. Based on this interest rate forecast, a bond analyst estimates the value of a Connor Periphal, Inc. bond, with an 8 percent coupon rate and three years to maturity, to be $1003.85:

$$B_0 = \frac{\$80}{1.06} + \frac{\$80}{(1.06)(1.07)} + \frac{\$80 + \$1000}{(1.06)(1.07)(1.11)}$$

$$= \$75.47 + \$70.53 + \$857.85$$
$$= \$1003.85$$

What have we done? Consider the cash flows in Illustration 8.3 as three separate investments:

- A *one-year investment* that pays $80 at the end of year 1. The market interest rate is 6 percent.

Period   0   1

rate = 6%

$80

Value = $75.47

Calculator
Clear
80
FV
75.47
PV
1
N
CPT
% i
Ans.: 6

SHORTEN TREASURIES' MATURITIES?

Upon assuming office in January 1993, the Clinton administration set to work on a proposal to shorten the maturity of U.S. Treasury debt. The Senate Budget Committee Chairman Jim Sasser included the concept in his budget resolution.

The proposals to shorten the maturity of Treasury debt ignore the realities of interest rate movements over time. The theoretical basis for them is questionable. The administration says that the Treasury Department would save billions in interest costs because it would issue new debt at current 3 percent short-term interest rates versus the nearly 7 percent long-term Treasury bond rate.

The expectations theory of the interest rate term structure looks at the yield curve of U.S. Treasuries itself as an interest rate forecasting tool. The theory argues that an investor can measure market expectations of higher or lower future short-term rates by examining the present differences between rates at various maturities. It also argues that all interest rates, for the entire maturity spectrum, tend to average out to short-term rates over long periods of time. Expectations theory currently indicates that much higher interest rates are coming soon—for example, one-year Treasury notes would trade at 5.5 percent (currently 3.25 percent) within two years. But market expectations are not pure. Empirical evidence suggests that there are premiums in the term structure on interest rates.

Many investors have specific investment horizons. They try to match assets with liabilities by structuring holding of Treasuries to discharge future liabilities at lowest cost. These investors demonstrate the preferred habitat theory of the term structure. They will move away from their maturity preferences, but only if they are paid a premium.

None of the variations in term structure theory perfectly forecasts interest rates. But the term structure does forecast trends in interest rates well, and it does capture the consensus expectations in the marketplace. It's naive to believe that government manipulation of the yield curve can permanently overpower market forces.

The Clinton proposal must be examined in the context of rollover risk that governments assume when issuing debt. The shorter the average maturity of debt outstanding, the greater the rollover risk to the issuer.

Italy has the highest rollover risk of the industrialized countries. Its debt is nearly all short term. Italy consistently experiences higher interest rates, a weaker currency and a higher inflation rate than the other highly industrialized countries.

Germany has the lowest rollover risk; most of its debt is long term. The United States is in the middle. Do Senator Sasser and the Clinton administration want our country to emulate a "hard currency" policy like Germany or a "soft" one like Italy? As a global investor, which country's bonds would you buy?

The risk to a debt-issuing government is the mirror image of the risk that debtholders assume when they buy that government's bonds. Think of the financial market as a single global investor who continually places more and more funds at risk in U.S. Treasury bonds and notes. He presumes that there is no default risk. But the investor still faces the risk of reinvesting both coupons and principal.

If rollover risk to an issuing government equals reinvestment risk to the investor, then the Clinton administration should now lengthen the average life of Treasury debt, not shorten it. That's precisely what private market players are doing as they "lock in" rates that are very low by historical standards.

- A *two-year investment* that pays $80 at the end of year 2. The investment earns market rates of 6 percent the first year and 7 percent the second year.

Calculator
Clear
80
FV
70.53
PV
2
N
CPT
% i
Ans.: 6.49

$$\text{Period} \qquad 0 \qquad\qquad 1 \qquad\qquad 2$$
$$\boxed{\quad \text{rate} = 6\% \ \mid\ \text{rate} = 7\% \ \mid}$$
$$\$80$$

Value = $70.53

- A *three-year investment* that pays $1080 at the end of year 3. The investment earns market rates of 6 percent the first year, 7 percent the second year, and 11 percent the third year.

Calculator
Clear
1080
FV
857.85
PV
3
N
CPT
% i
Ans.: 7.9786

$$\text{Period} \qquad 0 \qquad\quad 1 \qquad\qquad 2 \qquad\qquad 3$$
$$\boxed{\quad \text{rate} = 6\% \ \mid\ \text{rate} = 7\% \ \mid\ \text{rate} = 11\% \ \mid}$$
$$\$1080$$

Value = $857.85

What is the YTM for each of these investments? The one-year YTM is the 6 percent market rate for the first year. We calculate the two- and three-year YTMs using the *geometric average*. The **geometric average** is an annualized holding-period return and is defined mathematically as:

$$YTM_n = [(1 + r_1)(1 + r_2) \ldots (1 + r_n)]^{1/n} - 1 \qquad (8.6)$$

where

$$YTM_n = \text{Yield to maturity for } n \text{ periods}$$
$$r_t = \text{Forward rate for period } t$$
$$n = \text{Number of periods}$$

Geometric average. The *n*th root of the product of *n* observations.

The two-year YTM is $(1.06 \times 1.07)^{1/2} - 1 = 0.064988$, or about 6.5 percent. The three-year YTM is $(1.06 \times 1.07 \times 1.11)^{1/3} - 1 = 0.079786$, or about 8.0 percent. The more distant and higher forward rates cause the YTM curve to slope upwards, as shown in Figure 8.6.

FIGURE 8.6

UPWARD SLOPING YIELD CURVE

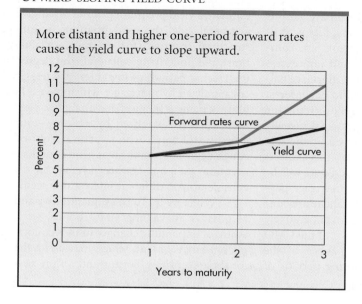

More distant and higher one-period forward rates cause the yield curve to slope upward.

CMOs AND THEIR PRICING

by Anand K. Bhattacharya, Ph.D., Managing Director, Fixed-Income Strategies,
Financial Strategies Group, Prudential Securities, Inc.

You may have never heard of CMOs, which stands for collateralized mortgage obligations, but they play a significant role in fixed-income portfolios of banks, insurance companies, mutual funds, pension funds, and investment management firms. The "run of the mill" CMO bond is backed by securitized mortgages on residential and commercial mortgages. CMOs are like corporate bonds in that they have higher yields than U.S. Treasury bonds. While corporate bonds pay interest semiannually, most recent CMO bonds pay interest on a monthly basis. The rating of a corporate bond is mainly determined by the default risk associated with the bond. However, the default risk of most CMO bonds is negligible as they are collaterized by high-grade mortgage-backed securities (MBS). Nonetheless, CMO bonds have other risks, such as the risk of early payment of principal (callability) and, hence, the risk of uncertain maturity.

One of my responsibilities is to evaluate CMOs for our clients and determine relative value among various sectors of the CMO market. Using MBS, Prudential Securities carves the cash flows into tradeable CMO bonds, called tranches, which have various maturities, volatilities, and levels of callability protection. An individual's mortgage payments are composed of interest, regular principal, and any excess payments to be applied to pay down the mortgage balance. This combined cash flow is used to pay interest to all the CMO classes. Any excess cash flows retire the CMO bonds by paying down the principal, usually sequentially to the first tranche, followed by the second tranche, and so on. Investors of the shortest tranche know that the maturity of the bond will be shorter than the actual pattern of the mortgage payments while the buyers of the longest tranche are confident of having funds invested for a comparatively long period of time. The actual paydown of the CMO bonds depends on the prepayment pattern of the mortgages in the collateral pool. During periods of high interest rates, the economic incentive to refinance mortgages is not high, although due to relocation and other demographic factors some of the homeowners may repay their mortgage. Alternatively, during periods of low interest rates, the economic incentive to refinance the mortage and repay the principal is high.

The pricing of CMOs is more of an art than a science, mainly because of the diversity of collateral types and CMO structures. However, for pricing of these bonds, we rely heavily on computer models, which help us to understand the underlying pool of mortgages, the forecasted principal repayment patterns under various interest rate environments, and the various risk premia. Most CMOs are priced off the U.S. treasury yield curve. In order to determine which part of the curve to use, we calculate the average life of the bond, which is the time-weighted period over which principal (not interest) is returned. For example, if a CMO bond has a five-year average life, we use the five-year treasury yield as our benchmark. However, because a CMO bond has additional risk, we estimate a yield premium prior to pricing the bond. As a general rule, the yield premium is influenced by structural features (for example, callability protection), the underlying collateral, and degree of liquidity. During periods of low interest rates, CMO bonds collateralized by mortgages which have a high probability of being refinanced have a higher-yield premium than deals collateralized by new low-coupon mortgages. CMO bonds with structural features providing a high degree of prepayment protection have a smaller premium than bonds whose average life can fluctuate considerably in different interest rate scenarios.

While we try to be as quantitative and analytical as possible in valuing CMO bonds, we have to be aware of impending changes in the economic and regulatory environment, which may affect the premium for these securities. For instance, if the government is considering regulation which would lower the capital requirement that banks need to hold against a particular type of CMO bond, we would expect the premium to be less as demand for such securities is likely to increase in the future. We would also use these opportunities to point out to our clients the relative value in these securities if the premiums have not become smaller. Similarly, if our economists forecast a reduction in interest rates, either due to the effect of reduced inflation or fiscal policy, we would increase the risk premium for CMO bonds collateralized by high-coupon securities, as these mortgages would most likely be repaid in the near future.

If we substitute these two- and three-year YTMs as the discount rates in Illustration 8.3, we also obtain $1003.85 as the bond's price:

$$B_0 = \frac{\$80}{1.06} + \frac{\$80}{(1.064988)^2} + \frac{\$80 + \$1000}{(1.079786)^3}$$

$$= \$75.47 + \$70.53 + \$857.85$$
$$= \$1003.85$$

Thus, the value of the bond is the same whether we discount the cash flows using the product of single-period yields (Illustration 8.3) or YTM rates. The YTM rates are the geometric averages of the forward rates.

8.3.2 A Downward Sloping Yield Curve and Bond Prices

A downward sloping yield curve is also a possibility, as shown in Figure 8.7. If market participants expect forward rates to be lower than the current period's interest rate, then the more distant and lower forward rates cause the yield curve to slope downward. Illustration 8.4 provides an example of bond valuation in a downward sloping yield curve environment.

ILLUSTRATION 8.4

Bond value with a downward sloping yield curve

Let's reverse the interest rates in the previous illustration so that forward rates for years 1, 2, and 3 are 11, 7, and 6 percent, respectively. The value of the Connor Periphal bond in this case is $997.28.

$$B_0 = \frac{\$80}{1.11} + \frac{\$80}{(1.11)(1.07)} + \frac{\$80 + \$1000}{(1.11)(1.07)(1.06)}$$

$$= \$72.07 + \$67.36 + \$857.85$$
$$= \$997.28$$

FIGURE 8.7
DOWNWARD SLOPING YIELD CURVE

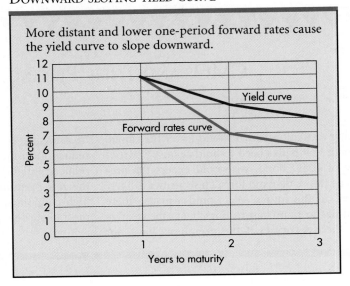

More distant and lower one-period forward rates cause the yield curve to slope downward.

Yield curve

Forward rates curve

Percent

Years to maturity

Test your understanding of the geometric average by using Equation 8.6 to calculate one-, two-, and three-year YTMs. If you use these YTMs to discount the cash flows, you should get a value of $997.28.[5]

Comprehension Check

1. Define term structure of interest rates.
2. What is the meaning of the yield curve for investors and borrowers?
3. What are the characteristics of an upward sloping yield curve? What conditions would cause an upward sloping yield curve, and how would you interpret such a curve?
4. What are the characteristics of an inverted yield curve? What could cause an inverted yield curve, and how would you interpret this curve?
5. How can an upward or downward sloping yield curve be used to find the value of a bond?

8.4 DURATION ANALYSIS AND PRICE COMPARISON

Our illustrations about valuing bonds indicate that their prices are volatile; they are influenced by their coupon rates, maturities, and market interest rates. Without a quantitative method, it is difficult to compare bonds that have different maturities, coupons, and market interest rates. Fortunately, such a method exists; it is called *duration* and is used extensively by knowledgeable investors and managers of institutional bond portfolios.

[5]Solution: $B_0 = \dfrac{\$80}{1.11} + \dfrac{\$80}{(1.0898)^2} + \dfrac{\$80 + \$1000}{(1.07979)^3} = \$997.28$

8.4.1 What Is Duration?

Duration is the amount of time in a fixed-income security's life that potential price changes, as rates go down or up, will be about equally offset by changes in the amount of interest-on-interest the security earns. The longer a bond investor must wait to recoup the initial investment, the longer is the bond's duration, and thereby its risk. Mathematically, duration is a weighted average of the life of the bond, or simply, its average life. Each year is weighted according to the proportionate contribution of its cash flow to the total present value of the bond. The duration equation is:

> **Duration.** A number that summarizes the various factors affecting a bond's price sensitivity to changes in interest rates.

$$\text{Duration} = \frac{\begin{aligned} &= (\text{Present value of payment \#1} \times 1 \\ &= + \text{ present value of payment \#2} \times 2 \\ &= + \cdots \\ &+ \text{ present value of payment \#}n \times n) \end{aligned}}{\text{Total present value of all payments}} \qquad (8.7)$$

$$= \frac{1}{B_0} (PV_1 \times 1 + PV_2 \times 2 + \cdots + PV_n \times n)$$

where

$B_0 =$ Total present value of all payments (Equation 8.3)

$PV_t =$ Present value of cash flow in period t

$n =$ Maturity period of the bond

As Equation 8.7 shows, each cash flow (PV_t) is weighted by the period (t) in which it occurs. (See Illustration 8.5.)

ILLUSTRATION 8.5

Calculating duration

The value of a five-year bond with both coupon and market interest rates of 8 percent is $1000.

$$B_0 = \frac{\$80}{1.08} + \frac{\$80}{(1.08)^2} + \frac{\$80}{(1.08)^3} + \frac{\$80}{(1.08)^4} + \frac{\$80 + \$1000}{(1.08)^5}$$

$$= \underset{PV_1}{\$74.07} + \underset{PV_2}{\$68.59} + \underset{PV_3}{\$63.51} + \underset{PV_4}{\$58.80} + \underset{PV_5}{\$735.02}$$

$$= \$1000$$

This bond's duration is 4.31 years.

Duration

$$= \frac{1}{B_0} (PV_1 \times 1 + PV_2 \times 2 + \cdots + PV_5 \times 5)$$

$$= \frac{1}{\$1000} (\$74.07 \times 1 + \$68.59 \times 2 + \$63.51 \times 3$$
$$+ \$58.80 \times 4 + \$735.02 \times 5)$$

$$= \frac{\$4312.13}{\$1000}$$

$$= 4.31 \text{ years}$$

In effect, the duration number readjusts the maturity date of five years to account for the receipt of coupon interest payments and interest on interest. If the bond's *only* cash flow is $1000 (for example) in year 5, its duration is five years. Prove this yourself.[6]

8.4.2 Factors Affecting Duration

A bond's duration varies with changes in maturity, market interest rate, coupon rate, and payment frequency.

- *Maturity.* As the maturity of a bond increases, duration increases. For instance, the durations of two zero-coupon bonds with maturities of two and three years are 2 and 3, respectively. (See footnote 6 for proof of this claim.)
- *Yield.* As the YTM of a bond increases, duration decreases because higher yield means higher cash flows.
- *Coupon rate.* A lower coupon rate results in lower interest cash flows than does a higher coupon rate, thereby increasing the bond's duration.
- *Payment frequency.* Duration decreases as the frequency of coupon payments increases because more frequent payments result in faster recoupment of the investment.

Figure 8.8 summarizes graphically several of these influences.

8.4.3 Uses of Duration

Why, you might ask, do you need to worry about duration at all? Why not just concentrate on the bond's maturity date? The maturity date, after all, tells you when the repayment of principal will eliminate all risk. If it's a 20-year $1000 bond, you get your $1000 back in 20 years, after which your risk of losing money is zero. The trouble is, by using maturity alone, you are saying a 20-year bond is a 20-year bond is a 20-year bond, whether it is a U.S. Treasury issue or a junk bond. Common sense tells you that this cannot be the case. These securities do not behave the same way even if they have the same maturity. Some measure other than maturity must differentiate bonds in the eyes of the investors. That is where duration comes into the picture.

Duration can be used to predict how much specific bonds will go up or down in price if interest rates (r) change, that is, to predict interest rate risk of bonds. To calculate the approximate change of a bond's price (ΔB) to a change in market interest rates (Δr), we can use the equation:

$$\Delta B = \frac{-\text{Duration} \times \Delta r}{(1 + r)} \qquad (8.8)$$

A negative sign is placed before the duration number because interest rate changes and bond prices move in directions opposite to each other (recall Theorem 1). An increase in r (that is, $\Delta r > 0$) results in a decrease in ΔB. A decrease in r (that is, $\Delta r < 0$) results in ΔB increasing, since a rule of algebra states that "a minus times a minus equals a plus."

Equation 8.8 indicates that the longer the duration of a bond, the greater the change in value produced by a change in the market interest rate. If you believe that

[6]Solution: $B_0 = \$1000 \div (1.08)^5 = \$680.58$

$$\text{Duration} = \frac{1}{\$680.58} \times (\$680.58 \times 5) = 5 \text{ years}$$

FIGURE 8.8

FACTORS INFLUENCING DURATION

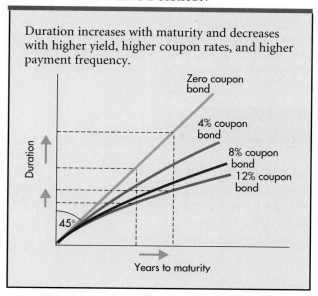

Duration increases with maturity and decreases with higher yield, higher coupon rates, and higher payment frequency.

market interest rates will fall, you want a bond with a long duration, perhaps ten years or more. As interest rates decline, value of a long-term bond increases more than value of a short-term bond (recall Theorem 2). If you expect market rates to rise, you keep duration short, perhaps less than five years. Again, according to Theorem 2, value of the short-term bond declines less than the long-term bond. (See Illustration 8.6.)

ILLUSTRATION 8.6

Price sensitivity

In Illustration 8.5, we found that duration for the 8 percent coupon bond was 4.31 years when the market discount rate r is 8 percent. The approximate influence on the bond's price of an interest rate increase of 100 basis points is $(-4.31 \div 1.08) \times 1\% = -3.99\%$. The summary in Illustration 8.1 shows that this bond actually depreciates 3.89 percent when interest rates increase 100 basis points. If r decreases 100 basis points to 7 percent, $\Delta B = (-4.31 \div 1.08) \times (-1\%) = +3.99\%$. Illustration 8.3 shows an increase of 4.1 percent in value for a decrease of 100 basis points.

Thus, bond price changes calculated by Equation 8.8 provide a reasonably good approximation of actual bond price changes. Note, however, that Equation 8.8 does not adhere to Theorem 4, which states that capital gains exceed capital losses. The duration approach assumes capital gains and capital losses are equal in absolute terms.

Since duration is a measure of a bond's price sensitivity to changes in interest rates, investors and bond portfolio managers use it to rank fixed-income securities according to their interest rate risk. For example, by comparing two bonds of different default risk, different coupon rates, and different maturities, the portfolio manager may find that the lower-coupon, lower-maturity bond has a longer duration. Thus, it is the riskier bond.[7]

In summary, duration is not perfect, but simply one more tool for making wise fixed-income investments. Understanding duration can make buying bonds safer and more rewarding. Duration is equivalent to what stock market investors try to estimate with beta. The two concepts differ in that a stock's beta, as discussed in Chapter 5, is based on past performance, while duration is based on what is expected to happen in the future.

Comprehension Check

1. When analyzing bonds, what is duration and why is it useful?
2. Explain why a high-coupon bond has a shorter duration than a low-coupon bond when each has the same maturity date and the same default risk.
3. What factors affect duration?
4. How is duration used by investment managers?

8.5. CONVERTIBLE BONDS

We can think of the discussion to this point as pertaining to a *straight bond*. Another type of bond is a *convertible bond*. It is a debt security that can be exchanged for another type of financial security, usually the common stock of the company issuing the convertible. A **convertible bond** includes a *fixed-income claim* and a *conversion option* issued by the firm to the bondholder to purchase the common stock of the company. The value of the convertible bond is equal to the sum of its value as a straight bond and the value of the conversion option attached to it:

> **Convertible bond.** A bond that pays fixed interest payments and has a specified maturity, just like an ordinary bond, but differs in that it can be exchanged for a specified number of shares of common stock.

$$\text{Convertible bond price} = \text{Straight bond value} + \text{value of option to convert} \tag{8.9}$$

The **straight bond value** is the price the bond would sell for if it could not be converted into common stock. This value depends on the coupon rate, the maturity length, and the bond's market interest rate.

> **Straight bond value.** That component of a callable bond that acts like an ordinary bond.

Figure 8.9 graphs the price of a convertible bond. When a company's stock price rises, the value of the convertible bond rises almost as much, since it can be converted literally into the higher-priced shares of stock. If the stock price drops, the convertible bond's value can also decline significantly if the risk of default is high. However, as long as the bond continues to pay coupon interest, bond investors still receive a steady stream of income, like they do with any bond.

The *conversion ratio* indicates the number of common shares received when the investor converts the bond to common stock. A convertible bond's exchange feature may be stated in terms of the conversion price per share of common stock. The *conversion price* is equal to the convertible bond's face value divided by the conversion ratio. The conversion price is usually fixed about 15 percent above the market price of the common stock at the time the bond is issued.

---

[7]Probably the most important use of duration is as a tool for managing interest rate risk, that is, reducing uncertainty. By adjusting the duration of a bond or a portfolio of bonds, managers of fixed-income securities can protect or enhance portfolio value. However, this topic is beyond the scope of this book.

FIGURE 8.9

PRICE OF A CONVERTIBLE BOND

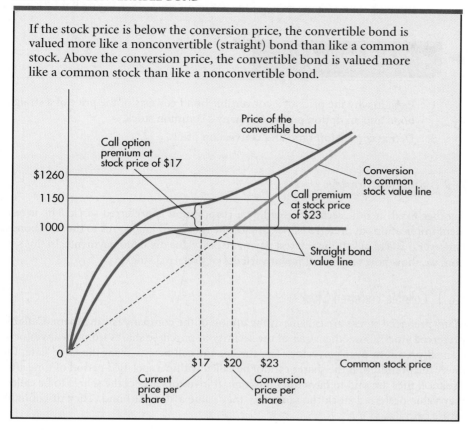

If the stock price is below the conversion price, the convertible bond is valued more like a nonconvertible (straight) bond than like a common stock. Above the conversion price, the convertible bond is valued more like a common stock than like a nonconvertible bond.

The conversion option usually lasts as long as the maturity of the bond. Investors are willing to pay a premium for the conversion option because they feel that the underlying common stock price will appreciate in value beyond the conversion price before the bond matures. In exchange for the conversion option, convertible bondholders typically receive lower coupon interest rates than they would receive on nonconvertible debt issues of similar risk. Also, the bond indenture usually subordinates the claims of convertible bondholders to those of other bondholders in the same firm in case of liquidation or reorganization of the corporation. (See Illustration 8.7.)

ILLUSTRATION 8.7

Value of a convertible bond

Amac, Inc. issued a $1000 face value bond which was convertible into 50 shares of its common stock. When the stock trades at $20, the bond's conversion price, the bond's minimum value, is $1000 (= 50 shares × $20 per share). At a stock price of $23, the minimum value of the convertible bond is $1150 (= 50 shares × $23 per share). When the common stock trades below the $20 conversion price, the minimum value of the convertible bond is the value of the straight bond. If risk of default is high, the straight bond loses value quickly because its value no longer depends on the underlying value of the common stock. (See Figure 8.9.)

Comprehension Check

1. Explain why the price of a convertible bond consists of the price of a straight bond and an option on the company's common stock.
2. Define conversion ratio and conversion price.

8.6. PREFERRED STOCK

Another fixed-income security issued by a corporation is preferred stock. The investment implications of preferred stock are for the most part analogous to those of bonds. However, instead of valuing interest payments, we value dividend payments. In this section, we show how to value different varieties of preferred stock.

8.6.1 Callable Preferred Stock

Callable preferred stock. Preferential stock that can be retired by the issuer; unlike common stock, may not have infinite life.

Many preferred stocks are callable at the option of the company issuing them. **Callable preferred stock** allows the issuer of the security to purchase shares from the investor at a small premium over par value. The further the call date is from the issue date, the lower the premium. If the shares cannot be called within a specified period of time after issuance, they are said to have *call protection*. If investors expect the shares to be called, they value preferred stock the same way they value a straight bond. They discount all future cash flows:

$$
\begin{aligned}
\text{Price} = \ & \text{Present value of dividend in period 1} \\
& + \text{present value of dividend in period 2} \\
& + \cdots \\
& + \text{present value of dividend in period } n \\
& + \text{present value of call price in period } n
\end{aligned}
\tag{8.10}
$$

$$
P_0 = \frac{D_1}{(1 + r_c)} + \frac{D_2}{(1 + r_c)^2} + \cdots + \frac{D_n + P_c}{(1 + r_c)^n}
$$

where

$$
\begin{aligned}
P_0 &= \text{Current price} \\
D_t &= \text{Dividend in period } t, \text{ where } t = 1, 2, \ldots, n \\
n &= \text{Number of periods until call} \\
P_c &= \text{Call price} \\
r_c &= \text{Yield to call date}
\end{aligned}
$$

There is a significant difference between preferred stock and bonds, and it relates to the fact that the maturity date n, or call date, of preferred stock is unknown. Investors must estimate when the shares may be called. Generally speaking, a company is expected to call its preferred shares if the current yield on similar preferred shares is substantially below the coupon rate being paid by the company. (See Illustration 8.8.)

ILLUSTRATION 8.8

Pricing a preferred share	The preferred stock of Midwest Public Utilities Company has a dividend of $2 per year, which is 20 percent of the stock's $10 par value. An analyst at Merrill Lynch expects the stock to be called in three years at a price of $15. Given the perceived risk of the preferred stock, she thinks the appropriate market rate is 12 percent. Her estimated value for the preferred stock is $15.48:

$$P_0 = \frac{\$2}{(1.12)} + \frac{\$2}{(1.12)^2} + \frac{\$2 + \$15}{(1.12)^3}$$

$$= \$1.79 + 1.59 + 12.10$$

$$= \$15.48$$

If the market interest rate should increase 200 basis points to 14 percent, her forecasted price is $14.77. Verify this answer.[8]

8.6.2 Perpetuities, or Noncallable Preferred Stock

A preferred share that is noncallable may be thought of as a *perpetual stream of dividends* accruing to the shareholder. (See Illustration 8.9.) This type of preferred stock is known as a **perpetuity** security. To define such an item, we rewrite Equation 8.10 as:

$$P_0 = \frac{D_1}{(1 + r)} + \frac{D_2}{(1 + r)^2} + \cdots + \frac{D_\infty}{(1 + r)^\infty} \tag{8.11}$$

> **Perpetuity.** An investment that promises an infinite stream of equal payments.

where ∞ means infinity and r is the annual market rate of return to the preferred shareholder. If the cash dividend amount is constant, $D_1 = D_2 = \cdots = D_\infty$ and Equation 8.11 simplifies mathematically to

$$P_0 = \frac{D_1}{r} \tag{8.12}$$

ILLUSTRATION 8.9

Value of preferred stock with perpetual dividends	Using the numbers in Illustration 8.10, the value of the Midwest Public Utilities preferred stock with no call feature is $16.67. It is found by dividing *next* period's $2 dividend by the 12 percent market rate.

$$P_0 = \frac{\$2}{0.12} = \$16.67$$

8.6.3 Floating-Rate Preferreds

Normally, preferred cash dividends are a fixed percentage of a stock's par value. In this case, the price of the preferred stock changes when long-term interest rates change. If interest rates increase, the price of preferred shares declines, and vice versa. The influ-

---

[8]Solution: $P_0 = \dfrac{\$2}{(1.14)} + \dfrac{\$2}{(1.14)^2} + \dfrac{\$2 + \$15}{(1.14)^3} = \$14.77$

ence of interest rates on preferred stock prices is the same as on bond prices. Thus, a preferred stock investor is subject to interest rate risk.

A type of preferred stock that helps insulate the investor from interest rate risk is called a **floating-rate preferred,** and has been issued by Citicorp, the largest U.S. bank. Dividends for this security go up and down with the general level of interest rates. Usually there are limits on the maximum and minimum dividends that can be paid.

From the perspective of management of a company, it is widely believed that fixed-rate securities are preferable to floating-rate securities because the variability of *earnings available to common shareholders (EAC)* is reduced. Accountants define EAC as after-tax net income minus preferred dividends paid. The variability of earnings is reduced only if the gains and losses taking place on the firm's balance sheet are ignored. For instance, if the preferred dividend rate is fixed, the market value of the preferred stock changes inversely to changes in market rates, as shown earlier in Illustration 8.8. On the other hand, if dividend rates float along with current market rates, the market value of the preferred stock is fixed. This point is shown in Illustration 8.10.

> **Floating-rate preferreds.** A preferential security whose dividend adjusts periodically to track changing interest rates.

ILLUSTRATION 8.10

Floating preferreds

A preferred stock with par value of $10 has its dividend rate fixed at 10 percent of par. The market rate for this stock is 8 percent. The value of the stock, using Equation 8.11, is $12.50.

$$P_0 = \frac{0.10 \times \$10}{0.08} = \$12.50$$

Now suppose the market rate increases 40 basis points, or 5 percent from its current level. The new discount rate is 8.4 percent ($= 0.08 \times 1.05$). Discounting the fixed dividend stream at 8.4 percent causes the preferred stock's price to fall to $11.90.

$$P_0 = \frac{0.10 \times \$10}{0.08 \times 1.05} = \$11.90$$

On the other hand, if the dividend is a floating dividend that adjusts automatically for any change in the market rate, the value of the stock remains at $12.50.

$$P_0 = \frac{0.10 \times 1.05 \times \$10}{0.08 \times 1.05} = \$12.50$$

The price is preserved because the numerator grows at the same rate as the denominator.

Illustration 8.10 highlights an interesting point. Assume accountants are required (which they are not) to adjust the preferred stock on the issuing firm's balance sheet to its market value at the end of each year. A decrease in value would be recorded as a gain on the income statement; an increase in value would result in a loss on the income statement.[9] It would soon become apparent to both investors and managers that the cost of fixed-rate financing to a firm is really floating, and the cost of floating-rate financing is really fixed in terms of the effect on market value.

---

[9]If the market value declines, the accounting entry would be a debit to the preferred stock account on the balance sheet and a credit to an income statement account, such as "change in value of preferred stock." The reverse entry would be made for an increase in the market value of the preferred stock.

1. How is the valuation of a share of callable preferred stock similar to that of a bond? How does the valuation process for a callable preferred stock differ from that for a bond?
2. How is the market price of a noncallable preferred stock determined?
3. What are the advantages to an investor of buying floating-rate preferred stock instead of regular fixed-rate preferred stock?
4. Why might a corporation's management choose to sell floating-rate preferred stock?

SUMMARY ▼▼▼▼▼▼▼▼▼▼▼

WHAT ARE THE RETURN MEASURES FOR BOND PRICES?

- There are several rates associated with bonds: coupon rate, current yield, holding-period rate of return, and yield to maturity.
- The coupon rate represents the percent of par value promised as annual interest to investors.
- The current yield states the dollar interest amount as a proportion of the current bond price. This yield is not the true yield of the bond.
- Investors often use the holding-period rate of return, although this method is seriously deficient in that it fails to incorporate the time value of money.
- The yield to maturity is the true yield on the bond only if interest receipts are reinvested at the internal rate of return and the bond is held until its maturity date.

HOW RETURN MEASURES INTERACT WITH BOND PRICES

Analysis of interest rates and bond prices reveals five bond theorems.
1. Bond prices move inversely to changes in market interest rates.
2. Longer-maturity bond prices are affected more by changing interest rates than are shorter-maturity bond prices.
3. Bond prices change at an increasing rate as time to maturity decreases.
4. Capital gains exceed capital losses for an absolute change in interest rates.
5. Bonds with high coupon rates are less affected by changing interest rates than are bonds with low coupon rates.

EFFECT OF CHANGING YIELD CURVES ON BOND PRICES

- A plot of YTMs of bonds with constant default risk against maturity periods results in a yield curve, or a plot of the term structure of interest rates.
- The yield curve can be flat, upward sloping, downward sloping, or humped. The curve provides investors with information about financial market participants' expectations of future interest rates.

KEY TERMS ▼

What Are the Return Measures For Bond Prices?

Holding-period return
Yield to maturity (YTM)

How Return Measures Interact with Bond Prices

Capital gain
Capital loss

Effect of Changing Yield Curves on Bond Prices

Forward rates
Geometric average
Term structure of interest rates
Yield curve

- Changing yield curves have no effect on the mechanics of bond valuation other than the fact that the rate used to discount the cash flows is not constant from period to period.

DURATION ANALYSIS AND PRICE COMPARISON

- Duration is a technique that measures the price sensitivity of a bond to change in maturity, yield, coupon level, and coupon frequency.
- Analysis of duration allows investors to compare the risk of different bonds.

CONVERTIBLE BONDS

- A convertible bond consists of a straight bond claim and an option to convert the bond to common stock of the company. The straight bond is the price the bond sells for if it cannot be converted into common stock.
- The conversion option is attractive because the investor may exchange the bond for common stock if the firm's common stock appreciates and exceeds the conversion value.
- As long as the bond does not default, there is limited downside risk, since the buyer will continue to receive coupon payments and can redeem principal at maturity.

PREFERRED STOCK

- Preferred stock is a fixed-income security. If the stock has a call feature, it is valued like a bond. If no call feature exists, the preferred stock is valued as a perpetuity security offering a fixed return.
- The security is subject to the same risks associated with debt.
- In an effort to minimize interest rate risk for investors, some firms issue floating-rate preferreds. The issuer of these securities adjusts stated interest rates periodically to reflect market interest rates.

FURTHER READING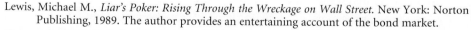

Lewis, Michael M., *Liar's Poker: Rising Through the Wreckage on Wall Street*. New York: Norton Publishing, 1989. The author provides an entertaining account of the bond market.

Sherwood, Hugh C., *How to Invest in Bonds*. New York: Walker and Company, 1983. This book provides both the average investor and the novice with a basic working knowledge of different kinds of bonds, bond funds, and bond markets.

Thau, Annette, *The Bond Book*. Chicago, IL: Probus Publishing Company, 1992. This practical book assumes little or no knowledge of bond investment.

SELF-TEST PROBLEMS

ST8-1. Using the approximation formula, calculate the yield to maturity for a $1000 face value bond maturing in five years. Its coupon rate is 9 percent and it currently sells for $1040.

ST8-2. a. Compute the duration of a 9 percent coupon bond with three years to maturity when the $1000 face value bond is selling at par.

b. Without doing further calculations, does duration increase, decrease, or remain the same if the bond in part (a) has five years to maturity rather than three? Explain your answer.

PROBLEMS ▼▼▼▼▼▼▼▼▼▼▼▼▼▼

WHAT ARE THE RETURN MEASURES FOR BOND PRICES?

8-1. Claire's broker tells her that the price of a $1000 par value 8 3/8 17 Kmart bond is $1040.

a. What is the coupon rate on this bond issue and when does it mature? How much annual interest will be paid by Kmart on each bond?

b. What is the current yield on this bond?

8-2. Ross bought a $1000 par value Kmart 8 3/8 17 bond for $1040. Calculate his holding-period rate of return if:

a. The bond is sold one year after purchase for $1060.

b. The bond is sold three years after purchase for $980.

c. The bond is sold six months after purchase for $1020.

8-3. Assume that Glenn expects the annual price (that is, value) of a bond that pays $70 interest annually to be as follows:

	Year		
0	1	2	3
$960	$970	$985	$1000

a. Calculate the current yield for each year.

b. Compute the one-year holding-period return on the bond for each of the periods represented in the data.

c. Repeat the exercise for two-year holding-period returns: periods 0 to 2 and 1 to 3.

8-4. If a $1000 par value bond with a coupon rate of 10 percent has a current market price of $1200 and matures in five years, calculate the yield to maturity of this bond.

8-5. If a $1000 par value bond with a coupon rate of 10 percent has a current market price of $900 and matures in five years, calculate the yield to maturity of this bond.

8-6. A corporate bond carrying a B rating by Moody's currently sells for $955, has a 12 percent coupon and $1000 par value, pays interest annually, and has 15 years to maturity. Using the approximation formula, estimate the yield to maturity for this bond.

8-7. Using the approximation formula, calculate the yield to maturity for a $1000 par value bond maturing in ten years having a coupon rate of 11 percent selling for $1075.

8-8. Linda can buy a $5000 par value tax-free municipal bond maturing in 15 years with a coupon rate of 5 percent. It currently sells for $4700. What is the approximate yield to maturity of this bond?

8-9. A $1000 par value, six-year bond sells at $920. It has a coupon rate of 8 percent. Calculate the yield to maturity using both the approximation formula and a financial calculator.

How Return Measures Interact With Bond Prices

8-10. The treasurer of Micron Corporation purchased 100 bonds three years ago at their aggregate par value of $100,000. The current market value of these bonds is $90,000. What are some reasons why the value of these bonds has declined?

8-11. Assume that Herb paid $875 for a $1000 face value, 5 percent coupon bond that will mature in one year.

    a. What is the coupon rate of the bond?
    b. How much is the annual interest payment?
    c. Is the bond's current yield lower than, equal to, or higher than the coupon rate? Is the bond's yield to maturity lower than, equal to, or higher than the coupon rate? Explain how you can tell.
    d. What is the bond's current yield? What is its yield to maturity? Use both the internal rate of return method and the approximation approach.
    e. What does the bond's current yield indicate? What does the yield to maturity indicate?

8-12. What is the current market value of a bond that has four years remaining to maturity, a par value of $1000, a coupon rate of 6 percent, and a market interest rate of 9 percent? Interest is paid annually.

8-13. A five-year bond and a thirty-year bond both pay $60 interest each year and have $1000 maturity values.

    a. What is the value of each bond for the following interest rates: 4 percent, 8 percent, 12 percent, 16 percent, and 20 percent? Graph your results with bond value on the vertical axis and interest rates on the horizontal axis.
    b. Can you tell from your graph where the values of the two bonds are equal?
    c. According to your graph, which bond is more sensitive to fluctuations in interest rates?

8-14. a. A bond with a maturity in 25 years has a face value of $1000 and a coupon rate of 5 percent. What is the price of the bond if the market interest rate is 4 percent? 6 percent? 8 percent? Why does the value of the bond change?
    b. A bond has one year until maturity. Its face value is $1000 and the coupon rate is 5 percent. What is the price of this bond if the market interest rate is 4 percent? 6 percent? 8 percent?
    c. Which bond is riskier with respect to changes in interest rates? Why?

Effect of Changing Yield Curves on Bond Prices

8-15. A bond analyst at Morgan Stanley Group observes one-year, two-year, and three-year bonds with yields to maturity of 8 percent, 9 percent, and 10 percent, respectively. What is the market's expectation of the geometric mean yield to maturity for:

    a. A one-year bond one year in the future (that is, a bond held over period 2)?
    b. A two-year bond one year in the future (that is, a bond held over periods 2 and 3)?

8-16. Investors require a premium to lend for longer periods. The premium increases 100 basis points per year. Without the premium, current yields to maturity for one-year, two-year, and three-year bonds are currently 7 percent, 8 percent, and 9 percent, respectively.

    a. What is the expected one-year rate one year from now?

    b. What is the expected one-year rate two years from now?

DURATION ANALYSIS AND PRICE COMPARISON

8-17. Why must the duration of a coupon-bearing bond always be less than the time to its maturity date?

8-18. Rank order the following bonds in terms of duration. Explain the rationale behind your ratings. You do not have to actually calculate each bond's duration. Logical reasoning will suffice.

Bond	Term to Maturity	Coupon Rate	Yield to Maturity
1	30 years	10%	10%
2	30	0	10
3	30	10	7
4	5	10	10

8-19. a. Compute the duration of an 8 percent coupon bond with three years to maturity when the $1000 par-value bond is selling at par. Interest payments are annual.

    b. Without doing further calculations, does duration increase, decrease, or remain the same if the bond has six years to maturity rather than three? Explain your answer.

8-20. Lotus Templates, Inc. needs to make payments of $2000 one year from now and $3000 two years from now to a creditor. The company's treasurer can invest in tax-free securities with a yield to maturity of 8 percent.

    a. Compute the duration of the company's liability to the creditor.

    b. Suppose market rates change to 9 percent. Use the duration amount you computed in part (a) to approximate the percentage change in the present value of the liability.

    c. Check your answer to part (b) by discounting the cash flows at 9 percent.

8-21. Consider a bond with a 3.5-year duration. If its yield to maturity increases from 8 percent to 8.3 percent, what is the expected percentage change in the price of the bond?

8-22. An investor buys two zero-coupon bonds. One matures in one year paying $200. Its current price is $113.86. The other bond matures in two years paying $2200. Its current price is $1886.14.

    a. What is the yield of each bond?

    b. What is the duration of each bond?

    c. Calculate the weighted average yield for the two-bond portfolio.

    d. What is the yield to maturity of the two-bond portfolio? (*Hint:* Combine the cash flows.)

    e. What is the duration of the two-bond portfolio? (*Hint:* Combine the cash flows.)

8-23. Scottsdale Aircraft has issued a 5 percent convertible bond due in 15 years. The conversion price is $49 and the bond is callable at 103. The market price of the convertible is 92 percent of face value and the price of the common is $44.50. Assume that the value of the bond in the absence of a conversion feature is about 60 percent of face value.

   a. What is the conversion ratio of the bond?
   b. If the conversion ratio were 52, what would be the conversion price?
   c. What is the conversion value?
   d. At what stock price is the conversion value equal to the straight bond value?
   e. Can the market price be less than the conversion price?
   f. How much is the convertible holder paying for the option to buy one share of common stock?
   g. By how much does the common stock have to rise by the bond's maturity date to justify conversion?
   h. When should Scottsdale call the bond?

8-24. The BASF Company had $20 million (face value) of convertible bonds outstanding last year. Each bond has the following features:

Face value per bond	$1000
Conversion price	$40
Current call price	104 percent of face value
Current trading price	120 percent of face value
Maturity	10 years
Current stock price	$45 per share
Coupon interest rate	8 percent of face value

   a. What is the bond's conversion value?
   b. Explain why the bond is selling above conversion value.
   c. Should management call the bond? What happens to the bond's price if it does so? Why?

8-25. Morrisey, Inc. has a 10 percent subordinated convertible bond outstanding, maturing in eight years. The bond's face value is $1000. It currently sells for $990. The bond is convertible into 15 shares of common stock. The company's common stock currently sells for $50 per share.

   a. What is the bond's conversion value?
   b. What is the bond's conversion premium?

PREFERRED STOCK

8-26. Johnston Corporation has a preferred stock outstanding with no call provision. The issue has par value of $100 and pays an annual dividend of $8 per share. Preferred stocks with similar risk are currently selling to provide investors with an annual rate of return of 12.5 percent.

   a. What should be the market value of Johnston's preferred stock per share?
   b. If you purchase this stock at the price calculated in part (a), how much would you gain or lose per share if the required return rate for similar preferred stocks declined to 10 percent?

8-27. The preferred stock of Seaver Company is discounted in the market at 12 percent. The stock has a dividend rate of 8 percent of its $125 par value.

a. What is the market price per share? Assume no call feature exists.

b. If a call price of $130 exists, is this security likely to be called in the near future? Explain.

c. If the market rate drops to 7 percent is call more likely? Why?

8-28. The 8 percent preferred stock of Amel Corporation is expected to sell for $25 in two years. Its par value is $20. What would be the return if it can be purchased for $20.25 today?

8-29. The Cornell Value Company has preferred stock outstanding which pays a $3 annual dividend.

a. If the stock initially sold at its $100 par value, what is the yield to investors who bought the original issue?

b. If preferred stocks of equal risk are yielding 6 percent, what should be the value of Cornell's preferred stock?

LIBRARY ASSIGNMENT

8-30. Based on data from a recent issue of *The Wall Street Journal,* construct a yield curve consisting of Treasury bond and note yields. Select one Treasury issue from each of the following periods to maturity: 6 months, 1 year, 3 years, 5 years, 10 years, 15 years, 20 years, and 30 years. Copy down the quotation for these bonds exactly as it appears in *The Wall Street Journal.* Use the reported yield for each quotation to graph your yield curve, putting term to maturity on the horizontal axis and yield to maturity on the vertical axis. Briefly discuss the general shape of your yield curve. What is your interpretation of this curve?

COMPREHENSIVE PROBLEM

8-31. A bank trust officer needs to select fixed-income securities to include in a portfolio for a client. As an analyst for the trust department, you are asked to provide the following information. (Each question is independent of the others.)

a. What is the current yield and the yield to maturity of an AT&T bond with a coupon rate of 7.125 percent which matures in eight years? The bond recently traded for 107 percent of its face value on the New York Stock Exchange. Assume that interest is paid annually.

b. What should be the market price of a $1000 par value Safeway bond trading on the New York Stock Exchange which has a 10 percent coupon rate, matures in seven years, and the required market rate currently is 8 percent? Assume interest is paid annually.

c. What is meant by the term *bond duration?* Calculate the duration of a 9 percent coupon bond with four years to maturity when the bond is selling at its par value of $1000.

d. Morgan Stanley Co. has a preferred stock outstanding which pays an annual dividend of $2.34 per share. The stock is callable at the company's option in three years at $25. Investors require a market return to the call date of 8.5 percent. What is the market price of the preferred stock?

e. What is the yield on an issue of GM's preferred stock, which has an annual dividend of $2.28 per share and trades on the New York Stock Exchange for $27.75? This stock does not have a call feature attached to it.

Appendix 8A: How To Interpolate

Without the use of a financial calculator, we can find the YTM of a bond through a trial-and-error hunt involving iteration and interpolation. *Iteration* is the process of using different interest rates in the denominator of the present value equation until a rate that discounts the cash flows so that they approximately equal the market value of the bond is obtained. After that point, we use a technique called *interpolation* to calculate the YTM. Illustration 8A.1 shows the procedure.

ILLUSTRATION 8A.1

An exercise in interpolating

A bond with a coupon rate of 7 percent and a face value of $1000 matures in three years. The bond currently sells for $1100. What is the YTM? We find YTM by solving the following present value equation for the market rate of interest, r:

$$\$1100 = \frac{\$70}{(1 + r)} + \frac{\$70}{(1 + r)^2} + \frac{\$70 + \$1000}{(1 + r)^3}$$

The annual $70 coupon payment represents 7 percent of the $1000 principal amount. By discounting the right-hand side (RHS) of the preceding equation at 7 percent, we obtain $1000.[10] Whenever the discount rate r equals the coupon rate, the value of the bond equals the principal amount of $1000.

However, since the left-hand side (LHS) equals $1100, a discount rate of 7 percent is too high. On the other hand, the discount rate is more than 0 percent because with $r = 0$, the RHS of the equation equals the sum of the amounts in the numerators: $1210. Thus, the YTM is somewhere between 0 and 7 percent.

Figure 8A.1 plots the problem. The horizontal line at $1100 is the value of the LHS of the equation. The downward sloping line is an approximation of values for different interest rates, r, of the RHS of the equation. When $r = 0$ percent, the RHS line equals $1210. When $r = 7$ percent, the RHS line equals $1000. We are interested in the value of r on the interest rate axis which corresponds to the point where the RHS line intersects the LHS line. The value of r is the internal rate of return (IRR), or YTM.[11]

We need to select a rate between 0 percent and 7 percent and use it to solve the RHS of the preceding equation. Let's try 4 percent. The result is a discounted value of $1083.26.

[10]Solution: $70 PVIFA$_{7\%, \text{3 years}}$ + $1000 PVIF $_{7\%, \text{3 years}}$ = $1000

[11]Actually, the RHS line should not be linear. You may recall from Chapter 4 that the present value of $1 does not change in a fixed increment as either the interest rate changes or the time period changes. As interest rates and time periods increase, the present value of $1 becomes smaller. Thus, the line should bow slightly downward like a saucer.

$$\frac{\$70}{(1.04)} + \frac{\$70}{(1.04)^2} + \frac{\$70 + \$1000}{(1.04)^3}$$

$$= \$67.31 + \$64.72 + \$951.23$$
$$= \$1083.26$$

Because the answer is less than $1100, we must decrease the discount rate. We can visually check this in Figure 8A.1: $1083.26 lies below the horizontal $1100 line.

Discounting the cash flows at 3 percent results in a value of $1113.14.

$$\frac{\$70}{(1.03)} + \frac{\$70}{(1.03)^2} + \frac{\$70 + \$1000}{(1.03)^3}$$

$$= \$67.96 + \$65.98 + \$979.20$$
$$= \$1113.14$$

A 3 percent discount rate is too low, since $1113.14 exceeds the market value of $1100. Again, Figure 8A.1 shows us why: $1113.14 lies above the $1100 line. Therefore, the YTM is between 3 and 4 percent. Interpolating between the 3 and 4 percent interest rates (which cause the computed value to be above and below the $1100 value, respectively) will determine the YTM. This calculation requires some elementary algebra.

Step 1: Find the dollar difference in value of the bond when cash flows are discounted at 3 percent and 4 percent.

3%	$1113.14
4%	1083.26
Δ1%	$ 29.88

Step 2: Find the difference between the value of the bond when it is discounted at 3 percent and the market value.

Value at 3%	$1113.14
Market value	1100.00
Difference	$ 13.14

Step 3: Solve for YTM using the following equation, where 3 percent is the lower interest rate in Step 1, $29.88 is the dollar difference calculated in Step 1, 1 percent is the difference in interest rates that equates to the dollar difference of $29.88, and $13.14 is the dollar difference calculated in Step 2.

$$\text{YTM} = 3\% + \frac{1\% \times \$13.14}{\$29.88}$$

$$= 3\% + 0.440\%$$
$$= 3.440\%$$

The answer in Step 3 represents the yield that is realized if the bond is purchased for $1100 and held for three years until it matures; that is, 3.4 percent is the YTM. The actual YTM, as solved by a financial calculator, is 3.435 percent.

Calculator
Clear
1000
PV
70
PMT
1000
FV
3
N
CPT
% i
Ans.: 3.435

FIGURE 8A.1
PLOT TO ESTIMATE YTM

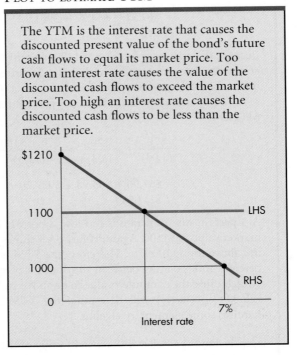

The YTM is the interest rate that causes the discounted present value of the bond's future cash flows to equal its market price. Too low an interest rate causes the value of the discounted cash flows to exceed the market price. Too high an interest rate causes the discounted cash flows to be less than the market price.

Appendix 8B: Interest Rate Theories of the Term Structure

A number of theories on the term structure of interest rates attempt to explain the relationship between short-term and long-term interest rates. Three of the most popular theories are the *pure expectations theory,* the *liquidity preference theory,* and the *market segmentation theory.* Figure 8B.1 depicts the shapes of the yield curve that each of these interest rate theories suggests. The major forces creating the actual term structure include the borrowing practices of governments, open-market operations of central banks, investment behavior of financial institutions, and borrowing practices of businesses. The net result of these forces is a term structure which can assume any shape.

8B.1 PURE EXPECTATIONS THEORY

The simplest theory of the term structure is known as the pure expectations theory. According to this theory, the shape of the yield curve is determined by expectations about future changes in short-term interest rates. The expected return earned by holding long-term and short-term bonds over the same period of time should be the same.

PROFILE OF INTEREST RATE THEORIES

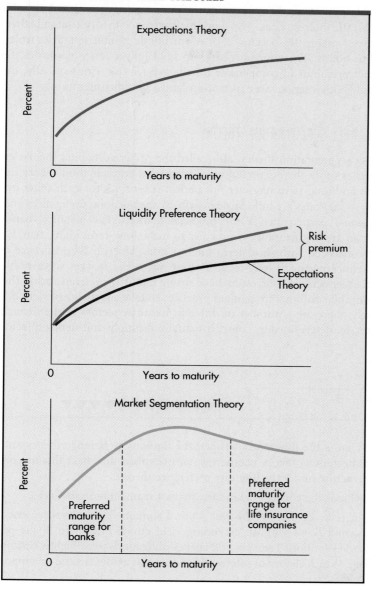

In particular, the term structure slopes upward when short rates are expected to rise, and it slopes downward when short rates are expected to fall. To see why, suppose the future short-term rates are expected to rise. If the yield curve were flat, investors could make more money by rolling over short-term bills than by holding long-term bonds. To eliminate this profit opportunity, the long-term bond rate must be greater than the current short-term rate. In this case, the yield curve must slope upward. The theory holds that the long-term rate is a (geometric) average of the current interest rate and expected forward rates. Illustrations 8.3 and 8.4 are examples of this theory.

8B.2 LIQUIDITY PREFERENCE THEORY

The liquidity preference theory extends the pure expectations theory by adding a risk premium to the interest rates. The liquidity preference theory contends that investors prefer shorter maturities because short-term bonds exhibit less price volatility than longer-term bonds. To induce investors to hold longer-term maturities, firms must offer a yield premium to compensate for the greater risk. Consequently, the forward rates include both interest rate expectations and a liquidity premium.

8B.3 MARKET SEGMENTATION THEORY

The market segmentation theory, also called the preferred habitat theory, emphasizes market niches more than expectations. The market segmentation theory implies that short-term and long-term rates are not perfect substitutes for each other in investors' portfolios, so that rates are influenced heavily by the portfolio preferences and rigidities of institutional participants in the financial markets. For instance, banks are less inclined than are life insurance companies to make long-term loans. Banks, therefore, are more concerned with short-term interest rates, whereas life insurance companies are more concerned with long-term interest rates. The market segmentation theory assumes that lenders and borrowers have strong maturity preferences and they will not depart from their habitual investment practices to take advantage of yield differentials. Accordingly, there are a number of different maturity sectors in the financial market where rates are determined by compartmentalized supply-and-demand factors.

APPENDIX 8B PROBLEMS ▼▼▼▼▼▼▼▼▼▼▼

8B-1. What is the difference between the liquidity preference theory and the pure expectations theory of interest rates? Explain the effect this has on the term structure under the liquidity preference theory.

8B-2. What is the concept behind the market segmentation theory?

8B-3. An issue of *The Wall Street Journal* contained an advertisement for a tax-exempt bond with an ascending yield curve. Elsewhere in the paper, yield curves for both Treasury and agency obligations were slightly downward sloping. Which theory of interest rates does this evidence tend to support? Why?

ANSWERS TO SELF-TEST PROBLEMS ▼▼▼▼▼▼▼▼▼▼▼

ST8-1.

$$AYTM = \frac{\text{Amount of interest per period} + \dfrac{(\text{Face value} - \text{bond price})}{\text{Periods until maturity}}}{\dfrac{\text{Face value} + 2 \times \text{bond price}}{3}}$$

$$= \frac{\$90 + (\$1000 - \$1040)/5}{\dfrac{\$1000 + 2 \times \$1040}{3}}$$

$$= \$82 \div \$1026.67$$

$$= 0.07987 \text{ or } 8.0 \text{ percent}$$

ST8-2. a.

$$\text{Duration} = \frac{\dfrac{\$90 \times 1}{1.09} + \dfrac{\$90 \times 2}{(1.09)^2} + \dfrac{(\$90 + \$1000) \times 3}{(1.09)^3}}{\$1000}$$

$$= \frac{\$82.57 + \$151.50 + \$2525.04}{\$1000}$$

$$= 2.76 \text{ years}$$

b. Duration increases for a given bond as its maturity lengthens.

Video Case 8

Long-Term Interest Rates

from *Business World,* March 29, 1992

New job creation, home buying, home construction—indeed, the general well-being of our economy—depend on the level of long-term interest rates. This video describes how long-term interest rates influence decisions to make investments in corporate plant and equipment. Without such investment in capital equipment, corporations generate few new jobs. Home construction is also sensitive to interest rate increases. As mortgage rates rise, fewer families can afford to buy newer or larger homes and home construction wanes, which affects the producers of a vast array of materials—lumber, wire, concrete, plumbing fixtures, and furnishings. As home construction activity falls, many other businesses also feel the pain.

The video also discusses factors that influence the level of long-term interest rates. Investing in a long-term bond requires making judgments about the future. For corporate bonds, investors must consider the prospects of the issuing company and its industry. For government bonds, commentator Stephen Aug suggests concern about future growth of the budget deficit may be an important factor. As economist Howe of the Federal Reserve Bank points out, long-term rates, on both corporate and government bonds, depend largely on the perceived riskiness of bonds and the return investors can earn on alternative investments. Why invest in bonds if you can earn more elsewhere? Such an attitude among investors forces the coupon rate of bonds up to attract buyers. Rates must rise until investments of similar risk promise similar returns.

What risk exists from owning government bonds? Long-term government bonds are the safest possible long-term investments a person can make. There is no risk about getting the promised interest payments and principal repayment. So where is the risk? One risk is inflation. If you buy a 30-year bond with a 7 percent coupon rate for $1,000 you will receive interest payments of $70 each year for 30 years, and a final repayment of principal 30 years from today. Suppose though that the 7 percent rate assumed that inflation would be about 3 percent per year. If inflation accelerates to 5 percent, you will find your purchasing power fall; that is, prices will rise faster than anticipated so the $70 interest payments will buy fewer and fewer items. At the bond's maturity the $1,000 principal may buy only $800 or $900 of goods and services at today's prices. Once you invest in a bond, you receive a fixed dollar amount of interest and principal, so if inflation picks up you lose.

Does buying bonds with a high coupon rate alleviate this problem? We need to consider two situations. With low market interest rates, bonds with high coupon rates have high prices. Investors see such bonds as attractive, bid up the price so they earn no bonus. If rates are high and a bond is issued with a high coupon rate, you will pay a price close to par (usually $1,000). But as rates drop, the issuing company may try and call the bond away from you. The company realizes that it can save money by repaying high-coupon rate debt with issues of low-coupon bonds. In most cases, a high-coupon bond, if it is callable, is called if interest rates fall. The prospect of savings is too great for companies to pass up. As the chief financial officer of Pacific Gas & Electric mentioned, that company has called in $500 million of bonds with interest expense savings of $25 million!

Study Questions

1. Besides the inflation risk that holders of long-term government bonds face, there is another risk. Suppose you buy a 30-year bond and sell it before maturity. What risk might you face in that situation?

2. If a company calls its high-coupon bonds, is that good or bad for bondholders?

CHAPTER 9

Common Stock and Its Valuation

When you buy common stock in IBM Corporation, or any other company, you become a part owner or common shareholder. You immediately own a part, no matter how small, of every building, piece of office furniture, machinery—whatever IBM owns. As a shareholder, you stand to profit when IBM profits. You are also legally entitled to a voice in major policy decisions, such as whether to issue additional stock, sell the company to outside buyers, or change the board of directors. The general rule is that each share has the same voting power, so the more shares you own, the greater your power.

Indeed, common stock is quite different from bonds. Buying common stock in a company makes you a part owner; buying a company's bonds simply makes you a creditor of the company. As a shareholder you expect to collect dividends on that stock and share in the company's profits. As a bondholder you expect only to earn a fixed return on that investment in the form of interest payments. Another important difference between stocks and bonds relates to valuation. If a company is successful, as a shareholder you can hope to make a substantial profit because the value, or price, of the stock should go up. As a bondholder you enjoy no such hope. Market price appreciation for a company's bonds is usually limited, regardless of how successful the company may be, although price changes sparked by interest rate fluctuations have often been quite dramatic.

When you have completed this chapter, you should understand:

- The basic features of common stock.
- How to read and interpret stock market reports and how stock transactions occur.
- The valuation process for common stock.
- The controversy surrounding dividend policy and stock valuation.

9.1 DISTINGUISHING FEATURES OF COMMON STOCKS

There are five principal features associated with common stock ownership. *Voting rights* provide common stock investors the right to vote on corporate matters. *Dividend receipts* provide the common shareholder a proportion of the profits earned by the company. *Limited liability* protects the shareholders against obligations incurred by the company. *Liquidation rights* provide the shareholder with cash amounts from the company once all debts are paid. *Preemptive rights* allow existing shareholders to maintain their proportional stock ownership.

9.1.1 Voting Rights

Common shareholders are usually entitled to one vote per share. It is not unusual for companies to issue multiple classes of common stock. The nearby Financial Reality article discusses several prominent features of different classes of stock issued in the United States. Some classes of stock may be voting and others nonvoting. If a business is not managed in the best interests of the *voting* shareholders, they can exercise control by electing a new board of directors or by opposing resolutions at shareholders' meetings. Shareholders who cannot attend meetings may participate in voting matters by **proxy,** which is a legal transfer to another party of a shareholder's right to vote (see Figure 9.1).

Proxy. A document that a stockholder gives to another party for the purpose of voting the shares.

9.1.2 Dividend Receipts

A firm distributes its profits to its shareholders through dividends. Cash is the most common method of paying dividends. Alternative approaches, however, are available. Growing firms that want to conserve cash frequently pay a stock dividend. Firms with excess cash use another approach: they repurchase some of the outstanding shares. Portland Brewing, Inc. pays a novel dividend. Each of the company's 600 shareholders receives a card worth a free pint of ale at the firm's brewery. The liquid dividends are paid daily. Unfortunately they're neither cumulative nor retroactive.

The *Dividend Record,* a publication of Standard & Poor's Corporation (S&P), provides statistical information about dividends and dividend payment policies of publicly held corporations. Table 9.1 shows typical information published by S&P for Chevron Corporation. The quarterly dividend amount is $0.825 per common share. The table sets forth essential dates for cash and stock distributions of the company in the current year, as well as its total payments in the preceding year. The number 168751, called the CUSIP number, is an identifier (like your social security number is an identifier).

All firms follow a standard procedure in their actual payment of cash dividends. Table 9.2 shows the key dates. The **declaration date** is the day the firm's board of directors declare the regular quarterly dividend of, say, $0.25 per share, payable on June 15 to holders of record on May 9. The firm pays the dividend to all shareholders registered on the company's books on the **holder-of-record date** as owners of specified numbers of company shares. The **ex-dividend date** is the fourth business day before the record date. *Ex-dividend* means, literally, without dividend. The *ex-date,* as this is called, is a deadline that determines who receives the dividend and allows brokers enough time to notify the company concerning the new shareholders. Up to (but not including) the fourth business day before the record date, the firm pays the dividend to the old owner. A new shareholder must purchase the stock before the ex-date to receive the dividend. The last date in the dividend table is the **payment date,** which indicates when payment is to be made to shareholders.

Declaration date. The date the firm's directors issue a statement declaring a dividend. The dividend becomes a legally binding obligation of the corporation.

Holder-of-record date. The date as of which all shareholders listed in a company's records are noted to receive the declared cash or stock dividend when it is paid.

Ex-dividend date. Date when ownership of the security is without the right to a dividend about to be paid by a firm.

Payment date. Date company actually mails out dividend checks to stockholders.

DIFFERENT CLASSES OF COMMON STOCK

Assaulting Fort Knox would be easier than trying to take over Smucker, the jewel among jam makers. Think of J.M. Smucker Co., the venerable maker of jams and jellies, as a closely guarded honey pot. Lest the controlling family be disturbed in its highly successful reign, the management has set up dragon's teeth defenses of a staggered board, cumulative voting, supervoting power, and supermajority proxy rules.

The food industry has been in the throes of consolidation, with few companies feeling safe from takeover. But thanks to the carefully drawn fine print in the corporate charter, control of about 27 percent of outstanding shares gives the Smucker family as much as 55 percent of the vote.

Recently, the Smuckers issued a new class of nonvoting common. The Smuckers told shareholders that the objective was to give the family more flexibility in estate planning and acquisition strategy without having its "relative voting power reduced."

The mechanism: a split that gave holders one share of the nonvoting B for each share of the redesignated A voting stock owned. The move enables older members to sell stock "while maintaining their influence in the company."

The Smuckers have made it plain that the new nonvoting stock does more than "just increase their liquidity for estate planning purposes." The family wants its company to remain independent and wants no bankers or outsiders telling it what to do. Smucker has grown mainly from within, and the modest acquisitions that have helped expand the product line have all been for cash.

Curious thing. The nonvoting B stock, though equal in every respect except for the franchise, has been trading at a discount of $4 to $5 a share below the A stock.

Shares among other Big Board-listed companies with dual classes of stock also tend to act in eccentric ways—sometimes trading at parity, sometimes even putting a premium on the nonvoting stock (see table).

The incentives for nonfamily members are to sell what is really a notional vote on the A stock and put the premium into a larger number of B shares.

The arithmetic: 100 shares of A sold at 35 buys (not counting commissions) 112 shares of B—same earnings, same dividends, same liquidation rights. Since the B has been moving up, holders who have taken this route have so far shown good profits.

Company	Vote	No/Low Vote	
Alberto-Culver	24-3/8 B	21-1/4 A	B stock 1 vote, A 1/10th; insiders=46%
Crawford & Co.	27-1/4 B	25-1/2 A	B stock 1 vote, A none; insiders=59%
Laidlow Inc.	8-3/4 A	8-3/4 B	A stock 1 vote, B none; insiders=47%
Playboy Enterprises	7-1/4 A	8-1/8 B	A stock 1 vote, B none; insiders=71%
Sequa	49 A	58 B	A stock 1 vote, B higher dividend; insiders=49%
J.M. Smucker	34-7/8 A	31 B	A stock 10 votes, B none; insiders=55%

Adapted from Richard Phalon, "Closely Guarded Honey Pot," *Forbes,* November 25, 1991, pp. 48–49. Reprinted by permission of FORBES magazine. © Forbes, Inc. 1991.

A firm pays a **stock dividend** by issuing additional shares to shareholders instead of cash. If the share distribution is 25 percent or more, firms are required to account for this as a **stock split** rather than as a stock dividend.[1] (The difference affects the account-

Stock dividend. A dividend paid in securities rather than cash.

Stock split. The division of a corporation's outstanding shares into a larger number of shares.

[1]The economic impact on the firm is the same whether a stock dividend or a stock split is done.

FIGURE 9.1

PROXY VOTING FOR MERRILL LYNCH & CO., INC.

SEE VOTING INSTRUCTION NO. 2 ON REVERSE *

Charles Schwab

P.O. BOX 976
NEW YORK, NY 10274-0976
THIS ADDRESS TO BE USED
FOR PROXY MATERIAL ONLY

MERRILL LYNCH & CO., INC.
ANNUAL MEETING OF SHAREHOLDERS AS OF 02/23
TO BE HELD ON 04/19/94
CUSIP 590188108

28264 43-079

DIRECTORS RECOMMEND: A VOTE FOR ELECTION OF THE FOLLOWING DIRECTORS
1- 1-WILLIAM O. BOURKE,2-STEPHEN L. HAMMERMAN,3-AULANA L. PETERS,
4-JOHN J. PHELAN, JR.,5-CHARLES A. SANDERS

AND A VOTE FOR PROPOSAL(S) 2, AND AGAINST PROPOSAL(S) 3
2 - APPROVAL OF PERFORMANCE GOALS GOVERNING, AND ELIGIBILITY REQUIREMENTS FOR, CERTAIN ANNUAL BONUSES AND GRANTS OF RETRICTED SHARES AND UNITS

NOTE THE BOARD OF DIRECTORS RECOMMENDS A VOTE "AGAINST" STOCKHOLDER PROPOSAL (3)

3 - INSTITUTE CUMULATIVE VOTING

NOTE SUCH OTHER BUSINESS AS MAY PROPERLY COME BEFORE THE MEETING OR ANY ADJOURNMENT THEREOF

NOTE TIME OF MEETING: 10:30 A.M. EDT

DETACH HERE DETACH HERE

28264 ACCOUNT NO: ME 35400 CUSIP: 590188108 P16442

PLEASE MARK BOXES LIKE THIS: [X] *********200** 164 04/19/94

ELECTION OF DIRECTORS:
(PRINTED ABOVE)
PLEASE X ONLY
ONE BOX

[ ] FOR ALL NOMINEES

[ ] WITHHOLD ALL NOMINEES

[ ] PLACE AN "X" IN THIS BOX TO WITHHOLD AUTHORITY TO VOTE FOR ANY INDIVIDUAL NOMINEE AND WRITE THAT NOMINEES' NUMBER FROM THE LIST ABOVE ON THE LINE BELOW.

PROPOSALS: (PRINTED ABOVE)

	FOR	AGAINST	ABSTAIN
02.	[ ]	[ ]	[ ]
3 .	[ ]	[ ]	[ ]

CNTL: 4061941088 375809945608 102

SIGNATURE DATE / /

SIGNATURE IF HELD JOINTLY DATE / /

[ ] PLEASE "X" HERE IF YOU PLAN TO ATTEND THE MEETING AND VOTE YOUR SHARES

IN ORDER TO **EXPEDITE** PROCESSING OF YOUR VOTE PLEASE ENSURE THAT THE **BARCODE** ABOVE APPEARS IN THE WINDOW IN THE BACK OF THE ENVELOPE.

PX1102

TABLE 9-1

DIVIDEND INFORMATION

Divd $	Declared	Ex-Date	Stk Record	CUSIP Payable
CHEVRON CORP				168751
□ COM p$3 (I)				107
Rate 0.825Q Pd '92 3.30	'91 3.25			
0.825	Jan 29	Feb 4	Feb 10	Mar 10
0.825	Apr 29	May 5	May 11	Jun 10
0.825	Jul 29	Aug 4	Aug 10	Sep 10
0.825	Oct 28	Nov 3	Nov 9	Dec 10

Source: Standard & Poor's Dividend Record, 1993.

ing procedure.) The key dates shown in Table 9.2 for a cash dividend also apply to a stock dividend. A stock dividend increases each shareholder's shares proportionally, and it should leave the aggregate market value of a company's equity unchanged. However, the stock dividend may convey new information that can affect the market's assessment of stock value. For instance, stock dividends are usually associated with growth companies. If management declares a stock dividend instead of a cash dividend, investors may perceive the company as conserving cash to fund wealth-enhancing investments. Management often uses a stock dividend or a stock split to reduce the price of a share to within a more popular trading range. This action may signal to investors

TABLE 9-2

KEY DIVIDEND PAYMENT DATES

1		2	3		4
□		□	□		□

1. Declaration date:

   The date the board of directors meets and declares a dividend issuing a statement similar to the following: On October 19 the directors of Precision Company met and declared the regular quarterly dividend of 25 cents per share, payable to holders of record on November 15, payment to be made on December 10.

2. Ex-dividend date:

   This is the date on which the right to receive the dividend no longer accompanies the stock. It is four business days prior to the holder-of-record date. In this case, it is November 11, assuming all intervening days are working days.

3. Holder-of-record date:

   On November 15, the company makes up a list of shareholders as of that date. These are the investors who will receive the declared dividend.

4. Payment date:

   The date on which dividend checks are actually mailed to holders of record.

that management expects the company's share price, in the absence of the stock dividend or split, to move above the top of the customary trading range.[2]

If the stock dividend conveys no new information, the economic condition of the firm does not change. Hence, a stock dividend reduces the market price of each remaining outstanding share to maintain total value of the firm's equity. Illustration 9.1 shows what should happen to the stock price and how the stock dividend is accounted for by the company.

ILLUSTRATION 9.1

Stock dividend paid

Currently, Dagny Taggert Industries has 1 million shares outstanding with a par value of $3. These shares sell for $20 per share. Thus, the market value of Taggert's equity is $20 million. Management declares a 10 percent stock dividend. The number of shares now outstanding is 1.1 million, although the total market value of the equity does not change. The new stock price is $20 million ÷ 1.1 million shares = $18.19.

The accounting is as follows. The fair market value of the stock dividend is $2 million: $20 per share × 100,000 shares. Accountants reduce retained earnings by this amount. The stock dividend does not affect the par value of the stock. So the accountant adds $300,000 (= $3 × 100,000 shares) to *shares issued at par* and $1.7 million ($17 × 100,000 shares) to *capital contributed in excess of par value*. The company's overall net worth does not change.[3]

	Before	After
Shares issued at par	$ 3,000,000	$ 3,300,000
Capital contributed in excess of par value	2,000,000	3,700,000
Retained earnings	8,000,000	6,000,000
Total net worth	$13,000,000	$13,000,000

An alternate way for a company to return cash to its shareholders is to buy its own stock from the shareholders. The firm conducts stock repurchases as either an *open-market purchase* or a *tender offer purchase*. In either case, stock repurchase represents a liquidating dividend to an investor willing to sell the stock to the company. In an **open-market purchase,** the firm purchases its shares through normal financial market channels at the existing market price. Market participants do not know that the firm is buying shares. A **tender offer** is a public offer by the firm to all stockholders to purchase from them a specified number of shares at a specified price that is above the current market price. The tender offer generally lasts from a few days to a few weeks.

In either case, management uses a stock repurchase approach when the firm has excess cash resources and good investment opportunities appear to be limited. Instead of investing in marginal projects, managers might decide the purchase of the company's own outstanding stock is an excellent investment, particularly if they believe the stock

Open-market purchase. Purchase of shares on the exchanges or in the over-the-counter market without any public announcement.

Tender offer. A publicly announced offer to buy the stock of a firm directly from its shareholders.

---

[2]There is evidence that investors react favorably to news of stock splits. See Guy Charest, "Split Information, Stock Returns and Market Efficiency—I," *Journal of Financial Economics* 6 (June–September 1978), pp. 265–296.

[3]A stock split alters the par value of the shares but does not involve any transfer of balances between the various shareholders' equity accounts.

is undervalued. Other reasons include elimination of small shareholdings, increase in the firm's financial leverage *(debt-equity ratio)*, consolidation of control within the firm by reducing the number of shareholders, and increase in earnings per share *(net income ÷ shares outstanding)*. Management seldom cancels any acquired shares; instead the shares are kept as **treasury stock** and may be reissued later.

Treasury stock. Common stock that has been repurchased by the company that originally issued it.

Advantages of stock repurchase programs include:

- Payment goes to someone who wants it because each stockholder can decide whether or not to sell.

- Repurchases often have favorable tax implications. Suppose, for example, an investor bought the stock for $20 a share, the price is now $30 a share, and the investor's marginal tax rate is 40 percent. If the company buys back that share for $30, the tax authorities tax the investor only on the $10 gain. The after-tax cash flow to the investor is $26: $30 − $10 gain × 0.40 tax. If the firm distributes $30 in dividends instead, the entire $30 is taxed. The investor's after-tax cash flow is $18: $30 × (1 − 0.40).

- The repurchase in lieu of cash dividends should result in a higher price for the remaining shares. For instance, assume the economic value of a firm, which has no debt financing, is $10 million and there are 5 million shares outstanding. Thus, the value of each share is $2. If the firm buys 1 million of its own shares, there are now 4 million shares outstanding. However, the economic value of the firm has not changed since the same productive assets are still in place producing products and services. But because the number of shares outstanding has decreased, the price per share is now $2.50. For shareholders not selling shares, the $0.50 price appreciation per share escapes tax until the shares are sold.

9.1.3 Limited Liability

Common shareholders have limited liability. No claims can be made upon them for the company's liabilities in the event of bankruptcy, unless the shares were issued for less than par value or no par value was stated on the stock certificate. If these situations exist, the recipient shareholders in most states in the United States are automatically liable to the corporation's creditors for the unpaid liabilities. Otherwise, the par value of a common stock, unlike the par value of a bond or preferred stock, has no significant economic value.

9.1.4 Liquidation Rights

When a company liquidates its assets, common shareholders have the right to receive their pro rata share of the proceeds after all debts have been paid. Common shareholders' dividend and liquidation rights are subordinate to the rights of debtholders and preferred stockholders. If a declared common stock cash dividend remains unpaid at the liquidation decision, it can only be paid once liquidation proceeds satisfy debt interest and principal, and preferred stock cash dividend obligations. Unlike fixed-income securities, common stock promises neither a fixed periodic return nor a return of principal.

9.1.5 Preemptive Rights

In the event the company issues new common shares, existing shareholders often possess *preemptive rights*. As we discussed in Chapter 6, preemptive rights give the current shareholders the opportunity to subscribe to a new share issue before new investors.

9.1.6 Foreign Practices

Rights attached to common stock can vary widely from country to country. Stock ownership in some countries does not entitle shareholders to all the rights they get in the United States. In some countries investors can only vote a small percentage of common shares, no matter how many shares they own; 51 percent ownership may not insure control; directors may be able to delegate all management power to one outsider; and sometimes dividend decisions are outside of the control of the board of directors. For example, some German companies have a two-tiered board of directors system. Social representatives—including labor—sit on one board while active, professional managers sit on another. Volkswagen Corporation includes social representatives from the federal government, the state government, labor, and public shareholders. Whatever influence flows directly from government is countered in the Volkswagen system by the influence of labor representatives, stockholder representatives, and professional managers.

Comprehension Check

1. What rights do the owners of a corporation's common stock have?
2. Explain the cash-dividend payment process by defining the declaration, holder of record, ex-dividend, and payment dates.
3. What is a stock dividend and why might a corporation's management choose to make such a payment? What economic benefit results for the corporation's shareholders?
4. Why might a stock repurchase program be undertaken by a corporation's management and what are its advantages?
5. How does the concept of limited liability protect common stockholders?
6. How do shareholder rights differ in other countries from U.S. practices?

9.2 READING THE STOCK TABLES AND PLACING AN ORDER

You've likely noticed the stock listings in the newspaper but quickly passed over them. At first glance, these listings look like an endless sea of numbers. This impression has more to do with the volume of listings and the use of small type than with the complexity of the information. And once you get beyond the sea of numbers, how do you buy and sell stocks? This section examines how to understand the tables and provides some insight into how to place an order.

9.2.1 Keeping Tabs on Stocks

Stock quotations represent a large portion of the financial pages. Figure 9.2 on page 310 shows a sample of NYSE quotations for April 20, 1994. The table provides daily information on share prices, yields, and trading volume of both preferred and common stocks of many companies that trade on the exchange. Prices are in dollars and a dollar fraction. The fractions are in eighths, or "eighths of a point." Every eighth of a dollar has a value of 12.5 cents. The figure also provides some "explanatory notes."

Interpretation of the information in the table is straightforward. Assume you have an interest in Avon Products, the cosmetic company. It is shown in the table as

AvonPdts in the second column under the heading *Stock*.[4] The company's symbol on the NYSE is *AVP*, as indicated in the column labeled *Sym*. The two columns to the left of the company's name labeled *52 Weeks/Hi Lo* show the price range of the stock over the preceding 52 weeks. At some point in the previous 12 months, Avon's stock traded as high as $61 1/4 per share and as low as $47 5/8 per share. On April 20, 1994, the stock closed the day at a price of $58 3/4, as shown under the *Close* column. The $-1/8$ entry under the *Net Chg* column means the stock closed $0.125 cents lower than the previous day's close. During the day the stock sold as high as $59 1/8 and as low as $58 1/2, as shown under columns *Hi* and *Lo,* respectively. The *Vol 100s* column indicates that 270,100 shares traded on April 20.

The figure under the *Div* column estimates the company's annual dividend to be $1.80 per share. The dividend amount represents the most recent quarterly payment to shareholders multiplied by 4 to obtain an annual dividend. The dividend yield, shown under the column *Yld %*, is found by dividing the dividend amount by the closing stock price: $1.80 ÷ $58.75 = .031 or 3.1 percent. Yield is one calculation used by investors to compare different companies.

The remaining item, listed under column *PE,* is the price-earnings ratio. The *PE ratio* measures the relationship between the current price of the stock and the company's annual earnings per share *(EPS)*. PE is the current price of the stock divided by the EPS. The latter figure is not shown in the table but is available from other investment sources. Based on Avon's closing price of $48.25 and its PE of 15, EPS must be $3.22 (= $48.25 ÷ 15). The price-earnings ratio helps investors judge how expensive or inexpensive a stock's price is relative to its reported earnings. A PE of 15 means 15 years of constant earnings of $3.22 are necessary to repay the investment if you buy the stock at a price of $48.25 (ignoring the time value of money). In general, "out-of-favor" companies have low price-earnings ratios and popular companies have high ratios. Growth prospects of the firm greatly affect its PE ratio.

Usually, companies smaller than those listed on the NYSE trade on either the American Stock Exchange (AMEX) or over the counter. *The Wall Street Journal's* AMEX report, called "American Stock Exchange Composite Transactions," is identical in form to "NYSE Composite Transactions." Over-the-counter (OTC) stocks, generally issued by even smaller or newer companies than those traded on the AMEX, do not trade at an exchange. For OTC stocks, brokers have established a market using a computerized network referred to as NASDAQ (National Association of Securities Dealers Automated Quotations).

We can follow the OTC market in *The Wall Street Journal* in the "NASDAQ National Market Issues," a section that lists the most actively traded OTC stocks. The listing is similar to the New York and American Exchange listings. The remainder of the OTC stocks is listed with last traded price under "NASDAQ Small-Cap Issues" (see Figure 9.3). About every six months, a committee of the National Association of Securities Dealers meets to determine what revisions are necessary in each of these NASDAQ listings. Some stocks are downgraded because of lack of trading volume, whereas others are promoted to the higher prestige category.

Foreign shares listed in the United States trade as **American depository receipts (ADRs).** There are about 700 foreign companies currently trading as ADRs. Examples of prominent companies include the Honda Motor Company Ltd., Sony Corporation, Telefonos de Mexico, S.A. de C.V., British Telecommunications plc, and Glaxo Holdings plc. An ADR is a negotiable receipt issued by an American banking institution, such as Morgan Guaranty Trust or Citibank, in lieu of the underlying shares it holds

American depository receipt (ADR). Receipts issued by banks representing ownership of a foreign company's common stock. The shares of the foreign companies are held in trust.

[4]If the company name is followed by the letters *pf,* this means the listing is for a preferred stock.

FIGURE 9.2

THE WALL STREET JOURNAL'S NYSE STOCK TABLES

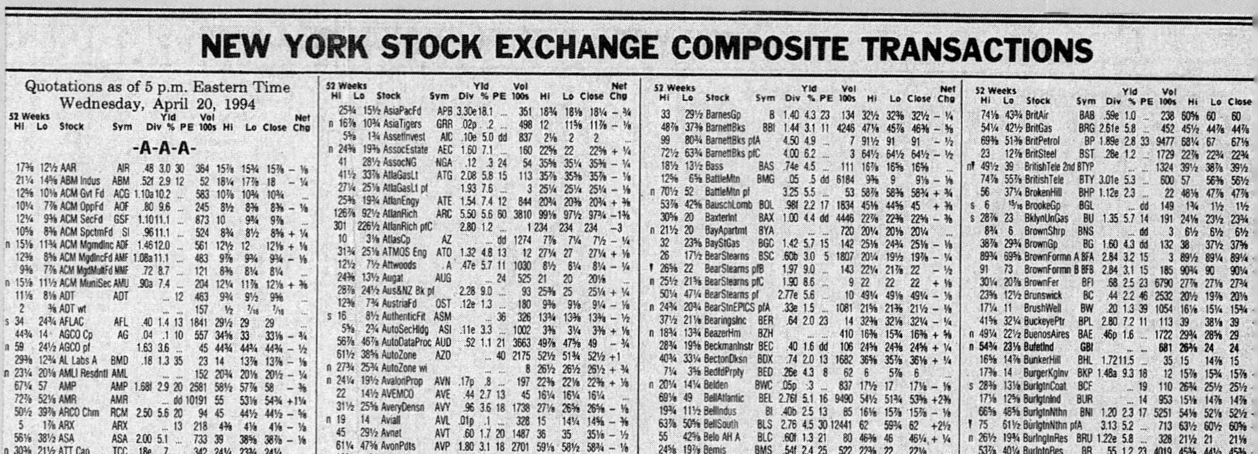

NEW YORK STOCK EXCHANGE COMPOSITE TRANSACTIONS

Quotations as of 5 p.m. Eastern Time
Wednesday, April 20, 1994

Source: *The Wall Street Journal*, April 21, 1994, p. C3. Reprinted by permission of *The Wall Street Journal*, © 1994 Dow Jones & Company, Inc. All Rights Reserved Worldwide.

in custody outside the United States. The bank acts as an intermediary between the foreign company's stock transfer agent and the U.S. investor. A buyer of an ADR is entitled to the same dividends and gains or losses accruing to a shareholder purchasing shares on an exchange in the home country of the company. ADRs are denominated in dollars, so price quotes reflect the latest currency exchange rates.

Sponsored ADR. ADR issued by a single depository institution.

Unsponsored ADR. ADR issued by more than one depository institution.

ADRs are either *sponsored* or *unsponsored*. For a **sponsored ADR** the foreign issuer agrees to comply with all SEC reporting requirements and signs a contract with a single despository bank. Such ADRs trade on the exchanges and NASDAQ. **Unsponsored ADRs,** by contrast, usually have more than one bank acting as depository. In general, these ADRs trade on the so-called *pink sheets*—a thinly traded segment of the over-the-

EXPLANATORY NOTES

The following explanations apply to New York and American exchange listed issues and the Nasdaq Stock Market. NYSE and Amex prices are composite quotations that include trades on the Chicago, Pacific, Philadelphia, Boston and Cincinnati exchanges and reported by the National Association of Securities Dealers.

Boldfaced quotations highlight those issues whose price changed by 5% or more if their previous closing price was $2 or higher.

Underlined quotations are those stocks with large changes in volume, per exchange, compared with the issue's average trading volume. The calculation includes common stocks of $5 a share or more with an average volume over 65 trading days of at least 5,000 shares. The underlined quotations are for the 40 largest volume percentage leaders on the NYSE and the Nasdaq National Market. It includes the 20 largest volume percentage gainers on the Amex.

The 52-week high and low columns show the highest and lowest price of the issue during the preceding 52 weeks plus the current week, but not the latest trading day. These ranges are adjusted to reflect stock payouts of 1% or more, and cash dividends or other distributions of 10% or more.

Dividend/Distribution rates, unless noted, are annual disbursements based on the last monthly, quarterly, semiannual, or annual declaration. Special or extra dividends or distributions, including return of capital, special situations or payments not designated as regular are identified by footnotes.

Yield is defined as the dividends or other distributions paid by a company on its securities, expressed as a percentage of price.

The P/E ratio is determined by dividing the closing market price by the company's primary per-share earnings for the most recent four quarters. Charges and other adjustments usually are excluded when they qualify as extraordinary items under generally accepted accounting rules.

Sales figures are the unofficial daily total of shares traded, quoted in hundreds (two zeros omitted).

Exchange ticker symbols are shown for all New York and American exchange common stocks, and Dow Jones News/Retrieval symbols are listed for Class A and Class B shares listed on both markets. Nasdaq symbols are listed for all Nasdaq NMS issues. A more detailed explanation of Nasdaq ticker symbols appears with the NMS listings.

FOOTNOTES: ▲-New 52-week high. ▼-New 52-week low. a-Extra dividend or extras in addition to the regular dividend. b-Indicates annual rate of the cash dividend and that a stock dividend was paid. c-Liquidating dividend. cc-P/E ratio is 100 or more. dd-Loss in the most recent four quarters. e-Indicates a dividend was declared in the preceding 12 months, but that there isn't a regular dividend rate. Amount shown may have been adjusted to reflect stock split, spinoff or other distribution. f-Annual rate, increased on latest declaration. g-Indicates the dividend and earnings are expressed in Canadian money. The stock trades in U.S. dollars. No yield or P/E ratio is shown. gg-Special sales condition; no regular way trading. h-Temporary exemption from Nasdaq requirements. i-Indicates amount declared or paid after a stock dividend or split. j-Indicates dividend was paid this year, and that at the last dividend meeting a dividend was omitted or deferred. k-Indicates dividend declared this year on cumulative issues with dividends in arrears. m-Annual rate, reduced on latest declaration. n -Newly issued in the past 52 weeks. The high-low range begins with the start of trading and doesn't cover the entire period. p-Initial dividend. pf-Preferred. pp-Holder owes installment(s) of purchase price. pr-Preference. r-Indicates a cash dividend declared in the preceding 12 months, plus a stock dividend. rt-Rights. s-Stock split or stock dividend amounting to 10% or more in the past 52 weeks. The high-low price is adjusted from the old stock. Dividend calculations begin with the date the split was paid or the stock dividend occurred. t-Paid in stock in the preceding 12 months, estimated cash value on ex-dividend or ex-distribution date, except some Nasdaq listings where payments are in stock. un-Units. v-Trading halted on primary market. vj-In bankruptcy or receivership or being reorganized under the Bankruptcy Code, or securities assumed by such companies. wd-When distributed. wi-When issued. wt-Warrants. ww-With warrants. x-Ex-dividend, ex-distribution, ex-rights or without warrants. z-Sales in full, not in 100s.

counter market. Although the bank registers the ADR with the SEC, less financial information is usually available for an unsponsored ADR than for a sponsored ADR.

9.2.2 Buying and Selling Stocks

It's easy to place an order for common stock if you have an account with a brokerage house. Illustration 9.2 provides a narrative of the process between an investor and a broker at Charles A. Schwab, a large discount brokerage firm. The payment for any trade must occur by the *settlement date,* which for most transactions is the fifth business day after the transaction date.

FIGURE 9.3

NASDAQ SMALL-CAP ISSUES

NASDAQ SMALL-CAP ISSUES

Issue	Div	Vol 100s	Last	Chg
A&A Fd g		308	1½	+ ⅛
ACR		440	½	− 1/32
ACTV		401	5¾	...
ADM Tr		22	11/32	− 1/32
AFP		27	9/16	− 1/16
AGBag		237	1 5/16	− 1/32
AGP &Co		288	1 3/16	...
APA		34	3¾	− ½
ASA Int		5	1 1/16	...
ATC Env		913	9⅜	− ⅞
ATC wt B		60	3	− 1
ATC EnC		50	1½	+ ¼
ATC Inc		50	11/32	+ 1/16
Abatix		51	2 3/16	+ 1/16
AberRs		28	3	− ⅛
AcrnVn		474	2	− ⅜
AcresGm		160	8½	− ¼
AcreG wt		12	3 9/32	+ 5/32
AcreG un		26	9¾	− ⅛
ActnPr		10	1⅝	+ 1/32
ActnP wt		25	3/16	...
Activisn		155	7	...
Actrade		211	2⅛	− ⅛
AdapSol		702	5¼	+ ½
AdapSl wt		273	2¼	+ ¼
Admar		507	1⅞	...
AdvCre		390	1 9/16	− 1/16
AdvDp wt		412	¾	+ 5/16
AdvEnv		637	¾	− 1/16
AdvEn wt		344	1/32	...
AdvMam		555	7½	...
AMam wt		150	4¼	− ⅛
AdvMat		266	2	− 3/16
AdvSurg		878	3⅜	...
AdvSu wt		15	⅞	...
AdvanLfe		74	13/32	− 1/32
AdvntTc		376	31/32	...
Aerial		242	3¾	− ⅛
Aerial wt		109	1⅛	+ ⅛
AgesHlt		515	1⅝	− ½
AgesHl wt		105	⅝	+ ¼
AirTrn	.01e	30	1 3/16	+ ⅛
AirInt		1473	¼	− 1/16
AirInt pf	.18r	297	2¼	− 3/32
Ajay		1940	3/16	− 3/32
AladnKn		218	6⅝	− ⅜
Alamar		10	1½	− ⅜
Alanco		325	3⅞	− ⅛
AlskAplo		322	⅞	− 3/16
Alcde pf		2	2¼	...
AllACm		127	9½	+ ¼
AllPrd un		27	8⅞	− ¼
AllQt wt		118	⅝	+ ⅛
AllQuote		40	3⅜	...
AlnEnt		375	5¾	− 1/16
AlnE wtA		698	1⅜	− 3/16
AlnE wtB		240	1 3/16	...
AldCAdv		446	4 1/16	+ 1/16
AlphHsp		87	12¾	− ¼
AlphH wt		405	3⅛	− ⅝
AlpnGme		94	3¾	...
Alpnet		90	13/32	...
AlterSal		221	13/16	− ⅛
Ambanc	.84	10	32	...
Amdur wt		25	¼	− 1/16
vjAWAirl		1155	2 13/16	...
AmBiom		756	1 11/16	+ 1/16
ABsCpt		1686	1¼	− ⅛
AmCasn		317	21/32	...

Issue	Div	Vol 100s	Last	Chg
Caretnd		272	2⅛	− ¼
CaroF pf	1.88	8	26¾	...
CaroFt pf		54	25¼	+ ¼
CascBcp		152	13¾	...
Cavco		17	16	− 1¾
CecoEnv		40	2 13/16	− ⅛
CedarGp		265	3 13/16	− 1/16
Cedarl	.40	23	4½	...
CelebEnt		28	3⅜	− ⅛
CelEnt wt		1272	6¾	+ ⅞
CelEnt pf		215	13¼	+ ¾
Cellex		256	½	...
Cellex un		209	5⅞	...
Celltch s		129	4½	+ ⅛
CellCm		1967	39¼	+ 1½
CelTel		17	7/16	− 5/16
Celox		38	1¼	+ ⅛
Centcre		760	1½	+ 3/16
CtrlVA	.56	2	14½	+ 1
CntMne		280	3 9/16	− ⅛
Cerprbe	.03e	134	6½	...
Certron		3	1 1/16	...
Chalint		10	2⅝	+ ⅛
ChmpSp h		1380	⅛	− ⅛
Chantal		590	2	+ ¼
CharEnt s		145	1⅜	+ 1/16
ChkExp s		25	1 1/16	− 1/32
ChkEx wt		38	4⅝	− 1⅛
Chefint s		22	1¾	...
Chemex		42	1	+ 3/16
Cherokee		185	3	− ¼
Chrk wtB		2	⅛	...
Chrk wtC		4	⅛	...
ChestH s		197	9/16	− 1/16
ChldBrd		82	3½	− ¼
Chinl wtA		20	¼	+ 1/16
Chinaln s		661	3 19/32	− 11/32
ChromCS		33	2⅞	...
ChrchllD	.50e	8	43½	− 2½
ChchTc s		3881	1 3/16	− 3/16
CtzFBk pf	2.19	15	24⅜	− ⅜
CtzSec		4	4¼	+ ⅜
CtyLTr		3	⅝	...
Classics		191	6⅛	− ⅜
CstFncl s		1		...
CodeCm		686	2½	...
Codenol		15	1⅛	...
ColCm pf		65	½	− 1/16
ColoMED		1	1	...
ComCent		123	1 9/16	...
CmCen wt		58	2	+ ¾
CmndCr		2644	7/16	+ 1/32
ComndAr		45	4¾	...
CmclPr		265	1⅛	− ⅛
Compartr		1475	1/16	...
Complnk		59	4¾	...
CmpMed		1489	13/32	...
CmMd wt		408	5/32	− 1/16
CptConc		688	2	− ⅛
CptMkt		1051	6¾	− 1/32
CptM wtA		90	1⅜	− ¼
CptMk wtB		119	1⅛	− ⅛
CmpTel		10	3¼	− ⅜
ComstBk	.26	9	7½	...
Comtrx		30	13/16	− 1/16
ConcTch		201	6 11/16	+ 1/16
CnqAr wt		3	5/16	− 3/16
CnqAir		1386	1¼	− 1/16
ConsSv pf	1.52	4	31¼	+ ¼
ConHCre		8	¾	− ⅛

Issue	Div	Vol 100s	Last	Chg
FstEnter		73	13/16	− 3/32
FtFdBcp	.60	2	21	...
FFnBcp	.50r	2	18	− ¼
FtIndp	.05e	50	11½	− ¼
FtLesprt	.30e	5	16½	− 1⅝
FtNtFlm		233	⅝	− 1/16
FStdVen		40	55/64	+ 1/32
FUtdSv	.32e	24	14¾	+ ¾
FFFn pfA	1.75	2		...
FlaGam		67	7	...
FlaWest		10130	5⅜	− 1⅛
FocusEn		103	3 1/16	− 5/16
Focus wt		346	13/16	...
Fonar		1372	1½	− ⅛
FoodIntg		23	4⅞	...
FoodIn wt		80	⅞	...
ForeInd		510	2 5/16	+ ¼
Forum		60	7½	− ¼
FountP		512	5/32	...
Foxmor		118	2 13/64	− 3/64
FrkBncp		10	3½	+ ¼
FrankOp		16	6¼	+ 1
FrnkOp wt		80	1 25/32	− 3/32
FrnkOp un		10	7⅜	...
FrJuice		375	3⅜	− ¼
FrntNat		109	4	...
FrtNt wt		100	13/16	+ 3/16
FrntNt pf	1.20	27	10	− ½
FuelTch		20	10½	...
FullHse		1516	4 15/16	+ ⅛
FullHs wt		358	1 7/16	− 1/16
FutMed		137	23/32	− 1/32
GB Fds		10	7¾	− ⅜
GFS Bcp		2	13	+ ⅝
GTEC 56pf	.90	3	11⅝	+ ⅜
GTEC 5pf	1.00	8	12½	+ ½
GameFn		342	5½	− ⅜
GamngCp		1143	10	...
Gamng wt		109	3 15/16	− 1/16
Gamng un		7	11¾	− ½
GarmGph		100	3¼	...
GnPrcl		3	5	+ ⅜
Gentnr		85	1 1/16	+ 1/16
GeoWste		1	⅝	+ 1/16
Gerant s		12	1¼	...
GlbCasn		294	3¼	+ ⅜
GlbRsc		47	6	− 2
GlbSpill		226	2 1/16	+ 1/16
Globlink		208	10½	− ⅛
Glblnk wt		40	2¼	− ¼
GoldRs		83	8½	...
GldStd		13	2¼	...
GldEg wt		8	⅞	− ⅛
GldQual		1066	11/16	− 1/16
GoldTrl s		29	1 1/16	+ 1/16
GoodT wt		10	¼	...
GoodTm		216	1 5/16	− ⅛
GrcHlth		14	2½	...
GrcHlt wt		10	½	− 1/32
GrndToy		99	7⅜	+ ⅜
GrntSt	.60c	22	⅝	...
GrayCm	.08a	5	13⅛	+ ⅛
GtARc pf		31	2	...
GrnDan		4	4½	...
GrnstRs		38	1⅝	+ ¼
GrnstR		16	19/32	...
GrntrSf h		130	13/32	− 1/32
GManning		17	2 3/16	− 5/16
GMann wt		69	¾	...
GMann un		22	7	+ 1¼

Issue	Div	Vol 100s	Last	Chg
KSB Bc	.10e	5	12½	− ¼
KnCtyL	1.36	8	47	...
KellyRus		26	4½	...
KdyWils		55	1⅞	− ¼
Kinert un		459	5⅜	+ ⅜
Kineret		836	3¾	...
Kinert wt		2246	61/64	+ 5/32
KooKR		546	6⅝	+ ⅛
Krantor		501	4⅞	...
L Rex		50		...
LDB		52	4	+ ⅛
LF Bcp	.30e	10	16	− ¼
LSB SC	.68	16	34½	+ 1¾
LaTeko		295	1⅞	+ ⅛
LaMan wt		100	½	+ ⅛
LakeAriel	.12e	2	14	...
Lambert		1294	½	− ⅞
Lamonts		5	2	+ ⅜
LarDav		116	4⅞	...
LasVEnt		680	1 9/16	− 1/16
LasVE wtA		236	1⅜	...
LasVMal		657	4⅜	+ ⅛
LVMal wt		144	⅞	+ 1/16
LasrMd s		42	1 1/16	− 1/16
LsrSght		100	5⅜	− ⅛
Lasrtch		532	17/32	− 1/32
LsrVide		1041	4⅛	+ ⅛
LsrV wtA		90	1½	+ ¼
LsrVis		350	6⅛	...
LsrVs wt		30	1 5/16	+ 1/16
LatexRs		440	1⅛	− ⅛
Latex wt		142	½	+ 5/16
LaurlCa s	.32	1	22½	...
LeakX		217	3¾	− ⅜
Leak X wt		456	3⅜	+ ⅜
Leggons		75	1⅝	− ⅛
Legon wt		105	5/32	...
LeisMkt		140	1⅛	+ 1/16
LetchInd	.40	1	22¼	+ ¾
Letch wt		3	4	+ 1
LibNBk	.47e	49	4¼	+ ¼
Licon		2411	21/32	− 1/32
LfeMed		34	6	...
LfMd wtA		21	2⅜	...
Lifecell		76	4½	+ ¼
Lifeway		3	2⅛	+ ⅛
Lifschlt		150	9/32	+ 1/32
LightSav		155	2⅝	− ¼
LincSnk		5	3¾	...
Linium		1843	9/16	+ 5/64
LiveEn pf	.50	4	7 9/16	− 5/16
LneStar		880	3 11/16	− 3/16
LouG 5pf	1.25	15	17½	...
LouG pf	1.86	4	25½	...
LucileFr		169	3½	...
Lucile wt		35	1¼	− ⅜
LukMed		69	2⅜	...
LuthMed		219	3⅛	− ⅛
Luxcel		897	15/32	− 3/32
Luxcl wt		2	¼	...
Luxcel wt		62	¼	− ½
M-SysFD		12	6⅝	− ⅜
MHMey un		17	7	...
MBF		1280	1 13/32	...
MCM Cp		4	2	...
MLX		20	5¾	− ⅜
MPTV s		41	3⅛	− ¼
MacG Sp		350	9/16	+ 1/16
MacInd h		145	3/16	+ 1/16
MacroCh		451	1⅜	− 1/16

Issue	Div	Vol 100s	Last	Chg
Omnicp h		1886	9/16	− 1/16
OnGrdSy		694	5¾	− ⅛
OnGrd wt		15	2⅛	− 1/16
OpthImg		83	1⅝	− 1/16
Opticm		19	3⅜	− ⅛
Optima		49	3 15/64	− 17/64
Orbitron		160	2⅞	− ¼
Orgnk un		120	6	− ¼
Orthlog		554	6½	+ ½
OryxTc		32	3¼	...
OutTake		45	11/32	− 1/32
OxboroM		1	1⅝	− 13/64
Oxigene		50	6¼	...
Oxign wt		155	2⅝	...
PHC Inc		499	6⅛	− 3/16
PHC wt		10	1 1/32	+ 1/32
PHC un		62	7 5/16	+ 9/32
PacTec		92	1¼	...
PceOstr		27	1 9/16	− 3/16
PacAnim		184	5¼	...
PcRimEn		383	3¾	+ ¾
PacR wt		53	¾	...
PacSen		105	2½	− 1/16
PackRs s		98	6¼	...
PackRs wt		36	1⅛	...
PlmSSB	.12	46	7¼	− 1¼
PalmrMd		816	3	+ ⅜
PalMd wt		29	1	...
Panthen s		1532	13/32	− 1/16
Parcisn		1	1⅛	+ 1/16
ParMtg h		460	7/16	− 1/32
ParPet		322	4⅜	...
ParlTch		405	1 1/16	− 1/32
ParkMed		5	2⅞	+ 7/32
Parlux		95	4½	...
PartchHd		68	1	− ⅛
PartOil		431	1 1/16	− 7/16
PatPtr pf	.80	36	10¼	+ ¼
PatnPr		15	5 1/16	− 3/16
Paulson		28	31/32	− 1/32
PearceSy		35	1 13/16	+ 5/16
PenG pf	2.25	2	25	− ⅛
Penult wt		54	1⅞	+ ¼
Penultm		94	3⅝	...
Perfdta		105	1 1/16	+ 1/64
PermFix		38	3½	− ⅜
PerSep un		295	25⅜	− 1⅜
PersCpt		448	25/32	+ 3/32
PerDia		115	1⅜	...
PetPrd		66	5¼	− ⅛
PetroUn		203	1 5/32	− 7/32
Petroln B	.08e	180	10¼	− ¼
PtHel nv	.04	3	9¾	− 1¼
Petromt		2	6⅛	+ 9/64
PhrP wtA		10	2¾	...
PhrP wtB		28	1¼	+ ⅛
PhrP wtC		51	2	...
Phrmhse		26	3⅞	+ 1/16
PhnxA wt		30	1	+ 1/32
PhnxA		62	3¾	+ 5/16
Phonetel		562	2⅛	− ⅛
Photcm		112	1⅞	...
PhyInM1	1.57t	6	16¾	− ½
PinBG	1.08	6	31½	− 1½
PizzaInn		291	3 7/16	...
PlntT		190	7/32	− 1/16
PlntT wtB		40	1/32	...
PlasThrm		96	2⅞	− ⅛
Plastgn		55	⅝	...
PochFdl		1	10½	...

Issue	Div	Vol 100s	Last	Chg
StratCp		134	6	− ½
StrtCp wt		241	1⅝	− 13/64
StrngSv s	.30	19	17	− 1
StrctIns		10	1¾	...
SubBnc		265	1¾	+ ⅛
SubBn wt		52	⅞	...
Sunport		1322	33/64	− 1/32
SupVsn		1	4½	+ 1
SupVs un		153	6⅛	...
Suprmail		455	3⅝	...
Swank		6	1	...
Symb wtA		10	⅞	− ⅛
Symbl un		478	6	+ ⅜
Symetr		176	6	− 1
Synthe		57	2	− 1/16
TEL		532	1 13/16	− 3/16
TEL Off	.60e	80	1⅜	...
THT		31	1¼	+ ⅛
TJ Sys s		245	4⅞	+ ⅛
TJ Sys wt		580	5/32	...
TJ Sys pf	1.00	36	9¾	− ⅛
TM Cent		123	3	− ⅛
TMBR Sh		1	5⅛	+ ¼
TNC		72	2½	+ 1/64
TNC wt		80	¾	− 1/16
TSS wt		320	1/32	...
TSS s		715	9/32	+ 1/32
TSS un		20	13/16	− 1/16
TVG Tch		1034	2 7/16	− 1/16
Taseko		420	13⅜	...
TaylrDv		10	3¼	+ ½
Tecngn s		4	⅛	...
TchRsh		384	2 3/32	+ 1/16
TelMed		7	7	+ ½
TelMd wt		6	4¼	− ⅜
TelegCm		11	5⅜	+ ½
TelC wtB		15		...
TelePad		11	7	− ½
TelPd wtA		65	3	− ⅛
TelPd wtB		28	⅞	− ¼
TelPd un		96	11¾	+ ⅛
Telepanel		20	5¼	+ ⅛
Telescan		1089	6¼	− 1
Teletek		3833	3½	+ 1/16
Tellus		172	15/32	− 1/32
Teltron		616	13/32	+ 1/32
Terano		17	2	...
Tescrp		100	1½	...
TexStar		5	3⅜	+ 23/64
ThrdFn	.25e	131	17⅝	− ⅜
3 CI		5	2⅜	− ⅛
3Net Sy		33	1⅜	...
TitleWve		3	1¾	+ ¼
Topro		125	3⅜	...
Topro wt		94	1	+ ⅜
TotalRs		425	1	− 1/16
TchApd s		474	2¼	...
TchA wtB		7	2	...
TowrTch		140	5⅛	− ¼
TracrPt		243	1 11/16	− 3/16
TA Wst un		z20	720	+ 30
Transcor		170	3¾	+ ⅛
TwldH wt		318	1⅛	...
Tubbys		980	13/32	+ 1/32
Turbochef		230	6	− ¼
TurfPar	.10	15	10½	− ¼
21Inc		11	[illegible]	+ 1 25/64
Tyrex		4	9/32	+ 1/32
UFP Tch		448	3⅞	− 3/16
US LAN		34	3⅛	...

Source: *The Wall Street Journal*, April 21, 1994, p. C8. Reprinted by permission of *The Wall Street Journal*, © 1994 Dow Jones & Company, Inc. All Rights Reserved Worldwide.

ILLUSTRATION 9.2

A typical trade at Schwab

Schwab:

Good morning, this is Bill. Can I have your account number and name, please?

Customer:

My account number is 9876-5432. My name is John Doe.

Schwab:

How can I help you today, Mr. Doe?

Customer:

I'd like a quote on XYZ, please.

Schwab:

XYZ is 29³/₄ bid, 30 ask.

Customer:

Good. I'd like to buy 100 shares.

Schwab:

Very good, Mr. Doe. Will this be at the market, or a limit order?

Customer:

At the market, please.

Schwab:

Let me verify that for you. Your order is to buy 100 shares of XYZ at the market. The asking price is 30. Is that correct?

Customer:

Yes, that's right.

Schwab:

Good, I'm entering your order now, and if you'd like to hold on, I'll see if I can get an instant confirmation for you.

Customer:

Great.

Schwab:

Yes, Mr. Doe. There it is. You've just bought 100 shares of XYZ at 30. Is there anything else I can do for you?

Customer:

Not today, thanks.

Schwab:

Thank you, Mr. Doe.

From Schwab Investor Handbook, 1990. *Used with permission of Charles A. Schwab, Inc.*

In the illustration, the customer places an order to buy *at the market,* which means to buy the stock at the best available price. The sample transaction also mentions a *limit order;* this is one of various types of orders that can be taken. Table 9.3 defines market and limit orders, along with several other types of orders.

Stop-loss orders may be used to limit losses in a declining market or to protect gains if the stock's price has risen above the investor's cost. Such a technique provides a disciplined approach when stock prices are falling. However, the stop-loss order does not guarantee that the investor's stock will be sold at a stated price. When the stop-loss order price has been reached in a declining market, the investor's order becomes a market order which could be executed significantly below the last transaction if prices are falling rapidly.

Although not mentioned in Illustration 9.2's conversation between the customer and the broker, the customer pays a commission—both when buying and when selling. As Table 9.4 shows, the commission varies considerably from one brokerage firm to another. It is necessary to include the commission in calculating the return on investing in stock. Failure to include the commission results in an overstated return. For example, if the investor buys 200 shares of a stock for $25 per share, the cheapest commission cost shown in Table 9.4 is $44. If the investor sells the stock two years later for $30 per share, a second commission fee is incurred. Let's assume this commission

TABLE 9-3

TYPES OF ORDERS

Orders

PRINCIPAL KINDS OF ORDERS:

Market order	Immediate execution at best available price
Limit order	Minimum (sell) or maximum (buy) price acceptable for a trade to occur
Stop-loss order	Immediate trade if the specified price is reached
Stop-limit order	Activates a limit order if a specified price is reached

PERIOD FOR WHICH AN ORDER IS EXECUTABLE:

Good till canceled	Executable until filled or canceled
Day	Executable only during the day the order is placed
Fill or kill	Cancel if not immediately executed

ORDERS FOR MORE THAN ONE ROUND LOT:

All or nothing	Execute as a block
If not specified	May be executed in blocks as small as one round lot

charge is $50. The investor's annual return on this investment is about 8.6 percent, using the future value model of Chapter 4.

$$\text{Future value} = \text{Present value} \times (1 + \text{rate of return})^n \qquad (9.1)$$

$$\$30 \times 200 - \$50 = (\$25 \times 200 + \$44) \times (1 + r)^2$$
$$\$5950 = \$5044 \times (1 + r)^2$$
$$\$5950 \div \$5044 = (1 + r)^2$$
$$r = 0.0861 \text{ or } 8.6 \text{ percent}$$

TABLE 9-4

COMPARISON OF BROKERAGE FEES

Shares	Fidelity Spartan Brokerage	Merrill Lynch	Smith Barney Shearson	Charles Schwab
200 @ $25	$ 44	$130	$137	$ 89
500 @ $30	59	293	316	127
1000 @ $25	84	428	487	155
1000 @ $50	104	599	668	210

Many firms offer additional discounts or rebates for active traders, with the amount linked to the trading activity. Minimum investments may be required.

Without commissions, the overstated annual return is about 9.5 percent. Verify this result.[5]

Illustration 9.3 highlights another problem that is not present in the conversation between the customer and the broker in Illustration 9.2. When we invest in foreign stocks, it is necessary to state the return in our home currency because each government allows its currency to fluctuate against other countries' currencies. Fluctuating currencies introduce *exchange rate risk* when comparing returns on investments in different countries, as we discussed in Chapter 3. For example, if Gabelli Investment Company invests in a Japanese company's stock, it could see any yen profits turn into dollar losses if the U.S. dollar appreciates against the yen. When Gabelli liquidates the yen investment and converts the funds to U.S. dollars, each yen buys fewer U.S. dollars. The following illustration highlights the issue.

ILLUSTRATION 9.3

International investing: Total return from Mazda stock

Gabelli Investment Company bought 1000 shares of Mazda stock listed on the Tokyo Stock Exchange at ¥400 per share about six months ago. The price per share is now ¥473 and Gabelli wants to sell and reinvest the proceeds in the United States. While owning the stock, Gabelli received a dividend of ¥16 per share. The *annualized* return from holding Mazda stock is about 49.5 percent (assume both prices include commission charges).

$$\text{Future value} = \text{Present value} \times (1 + \text{rate of return})^n$$

$$(¥473 + ¥16) \times 1000 = (¥400 \times 1000) \times (1 + r)^{0.5}$$
$$¥489,000 = ¥400,000 \times (1 + r)^{0.5}$$
$$(1 + r)^{0.5} = ¥489,000 \div ¥400,000$$
$$r = 0.4945 \text{ or } 49.5 \text{ percent}$$

Gabelli has 1000 shares $\times$ (¥473 + ¥16) = ¥489,000 to reinvest in the United States. The Japanese investment made a ¥89,000 profit.

When Gabelli originally exchanged U.S. dollars for yen to buy Mazda stock, the exchange rate was 120 yen per U.S. dollar. Thus, it required Gabelli to convert $3333 (= ¥400,000 ÷ 120) to ¥400,000 to buy the 1000 shares. Now when Gabelli wants to sell the Mazda stock, the exchange rate is 130 yen per dollar. The yen has been devalued against the dollar. The proceeds of ¥489,000 convert to $3762 (= ¥489,000 ÷ 130). Gabelli's annualized return, in terms of U.S. dollars, is 27.4 percent.

$$\text{Future value} = \text{Present value} \times (1 + \text{rate of return})^n$$

$$\$3762 = \$3333 \times (1 + r)^{0.5}$$
$$(1 + r)^{0.5} = \$3762 \div \$3333$$
$$r = 0.274 \text{ or } 27.4 \text{ percent}$$

The devaluation of the yen has eroded 2210 basis points of Gabelli's annualized return when it converts the funds to U.S. dollars: 49.5 percent in yen versus 27.4 percent in dollars.

Another option for stock purchases is *margin buying,* in which the customer may be able to buy the stock on credit by putting up 50 percent of the purchase price. The

[5]Solution: $30 \times 200 = \$25 \times 200 \times (1 + r)^2$. Solve for r to get 9.54 percent.

balance comes from the broker as an interest-bearing loan. The broker holds the stock as collateral for the loan. The Federal Reserve Board regulates the percentage amount that an investor can borrow from the broker. This amount is called the *margin requirement*. Since 1974, the margin requirement (amount of borrowed funds) has remained steady at 50 percent, when the Fed lowered the rate from 65 percent.

 Comprehension Check

1. Interpret the information for AbbotLab in Figure 9.2.
2. Define PE, yield, hi, and lo.
3. Describe the different kinds of stock orders.

 ## 9.3 COMMON STOCK VALUATION

Common stock valuation follows the same basic approach used to value fixed-income securities. However, instead of receiving an interest amount or a fixed preferred dividend, common shareholders participate in the firm's profits through receipt of common dividends and, hopefully, price appreciation of the stock. Investors expect that profits not paid as dividends but instead retained in the business will increase future earnings and dividends. Because much of the expected flow of cash comes in the form of dividends far into the future, the interest rate risk of common stocks is conceptually equivalent to that of long-term fixed-income securities such as U.S. Treasury and corporate bonds.

The nearby Financial Reality reading excerpts a classic article by John Burr Williams about the economic logic for using dividends to value common stocks. He provides the rationale for understanding the importance of dividends to common stock valuation. We will elaborate on Williams's conceptual foundation of value by forming models for the various dividend patterns shown in Figure 9.4 and illustrate how they work, explaining value for nondividend-paying growth stocks, discussing price volatility and what it means to the investor, and, finally, revisiting the issue of dividends versus earnings problem raised by Williams.

9.3.1 Valuation of a Nonconstant Dividend Stream

Our valuation models define a security's *intrinsic value* as opposed to its actual value. **Intrinsic value** is the value the security "ought" to have as judged by an investor, that is, its underlying fundamental value. Discrepancies between current market value and intrinsic value are often the basis for investors' decisions to buy or sell the security. In principle, discounting a stock's future dividend stream and future expected market value should yield its intrinsic value. If the future expected dividend stream of a stock is nonconstant, the intrinsic value of the stock is given by the equation:

Intrinsic value. The "real" value that a stock "should" have, based on fundamental factors affecting value.

> Intrinsic value = Present value of dividends in period 1
> + present value of dividends in period 2
> + present value of dividends in period 3
> + · · ·
> + present value of dividends in period n
> + present value of expected stock price in period n

EVALUATION BY THE RULE OF PRESENT WORTH

Let us define the investment value of a stock as the present value of all the dividends to paid upon it. The purchase of a stock represents the exchange of present goods for future goods—dividends in this case being the claim on future goods. To appraise the investment value, then, it is necessary to estimate the future payments.

Most people will object at once to the foregoing formula for stocks by saying that it should use the present worth of future *earnings,* not future *dividends.* But should not earnings and dividends both give the same answer under the implicit assumptions of our critics? If earnings not paid out in dividends are all successfully reinvested at compound interest for the benefit of the stockholder, as the critics imply, then these earnings should produce dividends later; if not, then they are money lost. Furthermore, if these reinvested earnings will produce dividends, then our formula will take account of them when it takes account of all future dividends; but if they will not, then our formula will rightly refrain from including them in any discounted annuity of benefits.

Earnings are only a means to an end, and the means should not be mistaken for the end. Therefore, we must say that a stock derives its value from dividends, not its earnings. In short, a stock is worth only *what you can get out of it.* Even so spoke the old farmer to his son:

A cow for her milk,
A hen for her eggs,
And a stock, by heck
For her dividends.
An orchard for fruit,
Bees for their honey,
And stock, besides,
For their dividends.

The old man knew where milk and honey came from, but he made no such mistake as to tell his son to buy a cow for her cud or bees for their buzz.

In saying that dividends, not earnings, determine value, we seem to be reversing the usual rule that is drilled into every beginner's head when he starts to trade in the market, namely, that earnings, not dividends, make prices. The apparent contradiction is easily explained, however, for we are discussing permanent investment, not speculative trading, and dividends for years to come, not income for the moment only. Of course it is true that low earnings together with a high dividend for the time being should be looked at askance, but likewise it is true that these low earnings mean low dividends *in the long run.* On analysis, therefore, it will be seen that no contradiction really exists between our formula using dividends and the common perception regarding earnings.

How to estimate the future dividends for use in our formula is, of course, the difficulty.

Adapted from John Burr Williams, *The Theory of Investment Value* (Cambridge, MA: Elsevier, 1938), pp. 542–543. Used by permission of Elsevier Science Publishers B.V.

$$P_0 = \frac{D_1}{(1 + r)} + \frac{D_2}{(1 + r)^2} + \frac{D_3}{(1 + r)^3} + \cdots + \frac{D_n + P_n}{(1 + r)^n} \qquad (9.2)$$

where

P_0 = Present intrinsic value of a share

D_t = Expected dividend per share for period t

r = Required market rate

P_n = Expected intrinsic share price in period n

FIGURE 9.4

DIFFERENT DIVIDEND PATTERNS

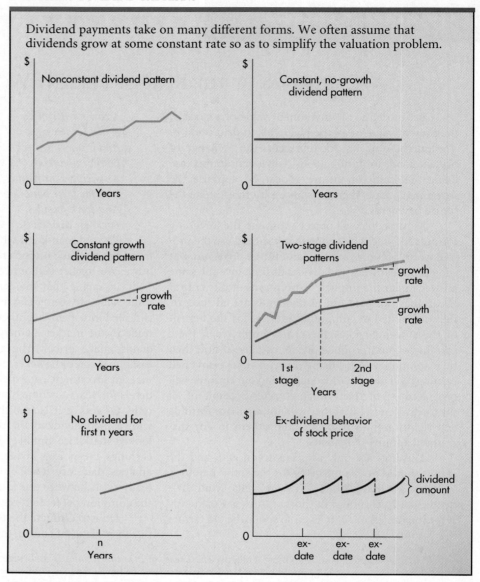

Dividend payments take on many different forms. We often assume that dividends grow at some constant rate so as to simplify the valuation problem.

The expected price in period n, P_n, is the discounted value of future dividends in period $n + 1$ and thereafter. (See Illustration 9.4.) We call Equation 9.2 the *nonconstant dividend model*.

ILLUSTRATION 9.4

Calculating the intrinsic stock price of a nonconstant dividend stream

Stan Weinstein, a market forecaster, expects dividends for Hurst Transmission Company to start at $1 next year and increase $0.50 each year. His forecast for the stock price at the end of year 4 is $15. The appropriate market rate of return is 12 percent. Discounting the expected cash flows at 12 percent results in an intrinsic price of $14.63.

$$P_0 = \frac{D_1}{(1+r)} + \frac{D_2}{(1+r)^2} + \frac{D_3}{(1+r)^3} + \frac{D_4 + P_4}{(1+r)^4}$$

$$= \frac{\$1.00}{(1.12)} + \frac{\$1.50}{(1.12)^2} + \frac{\$2.00}{(1.12)^3} + \frac{\$2.50 + \$15}{(1.12)^4}$$

$$= \$0.89 + \$1.20 + \$1.42 + \$1.59 + \$9.53$$

$$= \$14.63$$

The expected stock price of $15 in year 4, P_4, is based on the equation:

$$P_4 = \frac{D_5}{(1+r)} + \frac{D_6}{(1+r)^2} + \frac{D_7}{(1+r)^3} + \cdots + \frac{D_t + P_t}{(1+r)^t}$$

where the dividends in years 5, 6, 7, . . . , t must be estimated, as must the stock price in year t, P_t. Thus, P_4 is the value of all *future* cash flows beginning in year 5 that are discounted to the end of year 4.

9.3.2 Valuation of a Constant, No-Growth Perpetual Dividend Stream

If all the dividends in Equation 9.2 were constant, then $D_1 = D_2 = \cdots = D_n$. Now suppose we expect the dividends to remain constant in perpetuity. Then from Chapter 4, the stock valuation model for a perpetuity becomes:

$$\text{Intrinsic value} = \frac{\text{Expected dividend next period}}{\text{Required market rate}}$$

$$P_0 = \frac{D_1}{r} \tag{9.3}$$

The intrinsic value of the stock is *next* period's expected dividend (D_1) capitalized at the market rate r. Equation 9.3 represents the *constant, no-growth perpetual dividend model.* (See Illustration 9.5.)

ILLUSTRATION 9.5

Intrinsic value of constant dividends in perpetuity

Instead of having the dividend in Illustration 9.4 increase each year, assume it stays constant at $1 per share in perpetuity. The value of receiving $1 forever, discounted at 12 percent, is $8.33.

$$P_0 = \frac{\$1}{0.12}$$

$$= \$8.33$$

This constant dividend stream is not worth as much since investors are expected to receive lower cash flows.

9.3.3 Valuation of a Constant Growth Dividend Stream in Perpetuity

Let's suppose the dividends are not constant each period. Instead, we forecast dividends to start out at an amount D_1 and allow them to grow g percent per year (that is, year 2's dividend is $D_1 \times (1 + g)$; year 3's dividend is $D_1 \times (1 + g)^2$; and so on). The stock valuation model of Equation 9.3 becomes:

$$\text{Intrinsic value} = \frac{\text{Expected dividend next period}}{\text{Required market rate} - \text{expected growth rate for dividends}}$$

$$P_0 = \frac{D_1}{r - g} \qquad (9.4)$$

We call this model the *constant growth dividend model*.[6] (See Illustration 9.6.)

Equation 9.4 shows the mathematical significance of growth to the valuation process. By subtracting growth from the market rate, the denominator becomes smaller. Dividing a smaller denominator into the dividend causes the intrinsic value to increase. The economic logic for a higher intrinsic value is that firms with good growth prospects should be more profitable than firms with lesser growth prospects. We examine this issue in greater detail in Chapter 11.

ILLUSTRATION 9.6

Common stock value with constant dividend growth

A research analyst for A.G. Edwards brokerage firm expects JSB Financial Company's dividend next year to be $1. Thereafter, he forecasts dividends to increase 8 percent per year in perpetuity. The market discount rate is 12 percent. Based on these assumptions, the analyst concludes that the intrinsic value of the stock is $25 per share.

$$P_0 = \frac{\$1}{0.12 - 0.08}$$

$$= \$25$$

If the expected growth rate in dividends is 5 percent instead of 8 percent, the analyst's estimate of intrinsic value is $14.29. On the other hand, if the growth rate is 11 percent, the intrinsic value is $100. Prove these answers.[7] What is the intrinsic value if growth is 15 percent? (We will give you the answer shortly.)

Equation 9.4 and Illustration 9.6 highlight two important factors.

- The estimate for the current intrinsic value of the stock, P_0, is very sensitive to the difference between the required market rate and the expected growth rate for dividends, $r - g$.
- The required *market rate r must exceed the growth rate g*, otherwise the stock has negative value, which is impossible. Thus, a constant growth rate of 15 percent in Illustration 9.6 is not possible, given a market rate of 12 percent.

9.3.4 Valuation of a Two-Stage Dividend Growth Stream

A variation of the constant growth dividend model (Equation 9.4) applies to firms with different expected growth stages in their development. For example, you may forecast

---

[6]This model is often referred to as the Gordon model. For its development, see Myron J. Gordon, "Dividends, Earnings, and Stock Prices," *Review of Economics and Statistics* (May 1959).

[7]Solution: $\$1 \div (0.12 - 0.05) = \$14.29$; $\$1 \div (0.12 - 0.11) = \$100$.

dividends in the early high-growth period to grow at different rates, whereas you expect later dividends to grow at a lower, constant rate. For the first stage, you must find the present value of each year's expected dividend by discounting each dividend to the present time. You can use the constant growth dividend model to calculate the second-stage stream of dividends. You must then discount the intrinsic value of the second stream of dividends to the present time. Illustration 9.7 shows the process.

ILLUSTRATION 9.7

Intrinsic value of two-stage growth stock

A stock analyst at Montgomery Securities, Inc. expects JSB Financial Company's dividend to be $1 next year and then increase $0.10 per year for each of the next three years. Starting in year 5, she forecasts dividends to grow 5 percent per year in perpetuity. The required market rate is 12 percent.

The value of the dividend stream for the first four years is:

$$\frac{D_1}{(1+r)} + \frac{D_2}{(1+r)^2} + \frac{D_3}{(1+r)^3} + \frac{D_4}{(1+r)^4}$$

$$= \frac{\$1}{1.12} + \frac{\$1.10}{(1.12)^2} + \frac{\$1.20}{(1.12)^3} + \frac{\$1.30}{(1.12)^4}$$

$$= \$0.89 + \$0.88 + \$0.85 + \$0.83$$

$$= \$3.45$$

The value of the dividend in year 5 is $1.365 (= $1.30 dividend in year 4 × 1.05). The dividend grows thereafter at a constant rate of 5 percent per year. As of the end of year 4, the value of the future dividend stream starting in year 5, called P_4, is worth $19.50.

$$P_4 = \frac{D_5}{r - g}$$

$$= \frac{\$1.30 \times (1.05)}{0.12 - 0.05}$$

$$= \$19.50$$

The $19.50 represents the expected sale value of the stock at the end of year 4. But what is it worth today? By discounting $19.50 for four years, its value today is $12.39.

$$\frac{\$19.50}{(1.12)^4}$$

$$= \$12.39$$

The analyst's estimate of intrinsic value of the multigrowth stream, P_0, is $3.45 + $12.39 = $15.84.

By comparing Illustrations 9.5 through 9.7, it is apparent that the determination of intrinsic value can be elusive, since it changes significantly with the assumptions. However, the illustrations do indicate that a firm with better growth prospects has higher intrinsic value. A higher intrinsic value makes economic sense because investors believe good growth prospects are more profitable than lesser growth prospects.

9.3.5 Valuation of a Nondividend-Paying Growth Stock

The fact that a firm may not currently pay a dividend is no real impediment to applying a dividend model to valuation. For example, in the New York Stock Exchange stock tables (Figure 9.2), the closing price for AutoZone is $52.50, yet the company pays no dividend, as the *Div* column shows. Expected future dividends are the basis for value in the stock. For the nonconstant dividend stream model (Equation 9.2), we substitute for dividends in the appropriate future periods. It is not necessary for all periods to show a dividend.

As another example, assume in Illustration 9.5 that the analyst expects the company to not pay dividends during the first four years. After that period, the analyst forecasts the firm to pay a constant dividend of $1 in perpetuity. If the market discount rate is 12 percent, the current intrinsic value of the cash flows is $5.29 rather than $8.33. We calculate this value as follows. The expected price of the stock at the end of year 4 is $8.33, which is solved using the no-growth perpetuity dividend model of Equation 9.3.

$$P_4 = D_5 \div r$$
$$= \$1 \div 0.12$$
$$= \$8.33$$

Next, discount P_4 for four years:

$$P_0 = P_4 \div (1 + r)^4$$
$$= \$8.33 \div (1.12)^4$$
$$= \$5.29$$

Now assume that the dividend in the preceding example starts out in year 5 at $1 but then is expected to grow at a constant rate of 2 percent thereafter. Based on the constant growth dividend model (Equation 9.4), the stock should have a price of $10 at the end of year 4.

$$P_4 = \$1 \div (0.12 - 0.02) = \$10$$

The value of P_4 today is $10 \div (1.12)^4 = \$6.36$. Thus, if investors expect dividends to grow 2 percent per year in perpetuity, the stock price should immediately increase in value from $5.29 to $6.36.

9.3.6 Ex-Dividend Behavior of Stock Price

Since the value of stock is greatly dependent on the expected dividends, what happens to stock price on the ex-dividend date? Theoretically, the price of the stock should drop by the amount of the dividend because the new owner will not receive the dividend. However, evidence indicates that the price decline is less than the dividend amount for reasons not fully understood. (See Illustration 9.8.)

ILLUSTRATION 9.8

Ex-dividend behavior of stock price

Suppose stock market participants value the stock of Alcan Instruments, Inc. according to the no-growth dividend model of Equation 9.3. The expected annual dividend payment is $2 and the required market rate is 20 percent. The value of the stock is $10.

$$P_0 = \$2 \div 0.20 = \$10$$

As the year goes by, the stock price rises in anticipation of the next dividend payment. Just before the ex-dividend day, the price should be $12.

$$P_1 = \$2 + (\$2 \div 0.20) = \$12$$

On the ex-dividend day, the price should drop by the amount of the dividend and finish the day at $10.

An investor who purchases the stock on the day before the ex-dividend date and sells it on the ex-dividend date should pay $12 and receive $10 from the sale of the stock plus $2 dividend as the owner of the stock at the time the stock goes ex-dividend. The investor realizes neither a gain nor a loss—if we ignore commissions and taxes (which we should not do).

9.3.7 Are Stock Prices Too Volatile for the Models?

Whether actual stock prices reflect intrinsic value as determined by the valuation models discussed in this chapter is a difficult question. In a 1984 Louis Harris poll of top executives from over 600 companies, only about 33 percent thought the stock market fairly valued their company's stock. About 60 percent of the executives said the market undervalued their shares. The managers are skeptical of a valuation process that depends on stock analysts' prophecies about a very uncertain future. Corporate managers believe that if they cannot figure out what is going to happen, how can stock analysts and investors? Moreover, managers contend that value is sensitive to different assumptions about the economy, the competitive dynamics of the industry, and the company's strategic position. While these concerns are valid, evidence indicates that the stock market takes whatever information is available and incorporates its view of the company's future prospects in the stock price. The stock price is the clearest measure of shareholders' expectations about the company's performance.

The critical assumption of the constant growth dividend model is that the dividend next period, D_1, will grow in perpetuity at the rate g. If g is large, then the estimate for the current intrinsic value, P_0, is most likely unrealistic. No firm can continually grow at a large growth rate. The life-cycle concept indicates that people go through different phases of growth, maturity, and decline. Firms also go through these phases. Thus, investors should use the constant growth model with caution, always questioning the assumptions about dividends and growth.

As investors revise their estimates of future dividends, stock prices should reflect these revisions. Many investors and academicians feel that stock prices are much more volatile than dividend valuation models predict. An important disruptive factor contributing to volatility is the rate of inflation, which may not have a parallel impact on both the required market rate r and the growth rate g in the valuation models. For example, during the late 1960s, unexpected changes in inflation were quickly reflected in higher required market rates but had little (if any) impact on growth rate expectations. Growth in profits and dividends finally occurred in the early 1970s. The result of the lag between the market discount rate and the growth rate was a negative impact on stock prices; that is, the differential between r and g became larger in the 1960s, which depressed stock prices.

COMMON STOCK VALUATION ISSUES

by Alan R. Wilson, Managing Director, Talon Asset Management, Inc.

Our firm invests in public companies with the mind set of a private investor purchasing a minority interest in a business. Prior to any concern with valuation questions, our first step in the investment process is to identify attractive businesses. Our preference is always for the better business, not mediocrity at an attractive valuation. Purchase candidates should possess a current or expected profile substantially superior, by quantitative and qualitative measures, to both broad market and industry averages. Companies that fail to achieve a double-digit return on shareholders' invested equity, without excessive leverage, or to attain attractive profit margins, do not deserve our capital. Where the company sustains a high return on equity, we prefer that net income be reinvested in the business rather than distributed as dividends.

Our search for value may be defined by earnings potential, dividend growth, or balance sheet assets. Like most investors, we prefer the dynamics of growth. The question is what price or price-earnings ratio to pay for that growth. Occasionally, the answer is suggested by private transactions in that industry. We find that a ratio of price to cash flow is usually more discerning than a reported price-earnings ratio. But there are no absolutes; private transactions reflect the same economic and interest rate environments that influence the stock market.

Technology has permanently altered the valuation process. Computer databases alone allow us to monitor every line item or ratio for roughly 12,000 domestic companies. How we screen these data is limited only by our creativity. Our standard analytical format captures on one computer screen a company

profile with 106 statistical measures grouped under ten categories; additional screens provide quarterly changes in all measures going back ten years. These screens provide the dynamics of a business based on history. The challenge is to model a company, developing forecasts for the firm's earnings and stock price, among others. Because the stock market so efficiently discounts consensus expectations, we focus on a company's profile and earning power at least nine months from today. Our internal expectations are then judged against those of influential Wall Street analysts. Companies that exceed earnings expectations are, in our opinion, the most likely to experience advancing stock prices.

Numbers alone will never answer all of the critical questions, particularly regarding the quality of management. We consider a direct dialogue with management a prerequisite to purchasing stock. Management's depth, motivation, equity ownership, corporate culture, and ability to fulfill key functions are reflected in valuations. Well-managed companies ultimately reward shareholders.

We take exception to many analysts' indiscriminate reliance on relative valuations to project the price-earnings ratio paid on future earnings. The logic assumes that any public company historically trades in a fairly predictable relationship to the overall market price-earnings ratio. If a company has superior characteristics, then we are willing to pay an appropriate premium to the market price-earnings ratio. We certainly are less willing to pay a premium when we consider the market to be overextended and the market price-earnings ratio unjustified.

9.3.8 Dividends versus Earnings

In the Financial Reality article on page 317, John Burr Williams states that "earnings are only a means to an end, and the means should not be mistaken for the end." His point is that many people claim that the firm's earnings stream is more important than the dividend stream for valuing common stock. But think about this for a moment in the context of the constant dividend model, where the dividend does not grow:

$$\text{Intrinsic value} = \frac{\text{Expected dividend next period}}{\text{Required market rate}}$$

$$P_0 = D_1 \div r$$

(9.5)

If we assume that a firm pays out all expected earnings (E_1) as dividends (D_1), then $E_1 = D_1$, and

$$\text{Intrinsic value} = \frac{\text{Expected dividend next period}}{\text{Required market rate}} = \frac{D_1}{r}$$

$$= \frac{\text{Expected earnings next period}}{\text{Required market rate}} = \frac{E_1}{r}$$

(9.6)

If the firm retains some earnings and reinvests them in the business, hopefully both future earnings and dividends will grow; that is, $g > 0$. Let's go to an extreme position and assume that management retains all earnings and promises never to pay a dividend (and investors believe this to be true). Then the constant dividend growth model says the stock has zero value because next period's dividend and all dividends thereafter are zero, ($D_1 = 0$):

$$\text{Intrinsic value} = \frac{\text{Expected dividend next period}}{\text{Required market rate} - \text{growth rate}}$$

$$P_0 = \frac{D_1}{r - g}$$

$$= \frac{0}{r - g}$$

$$= 0$$

(9.7)

However, if earnings replace dividends in the numerator, now the stock apparently has value because expected future earnings are positive ($E_1 > 0$):

$$\text{Intrinsic value} = \frac{\text{Expected earnings next period}}{\text{Required market rate} - \text{growth rate}}$$

$$P_0 = \frac{E_1}{r - g} > 0$$

(9.8)

This cannot be! Investors have been told that they will never receive a dividend, and they believe it to be true. Thus, the stock's value *must* be zero. Any cash outflow to buy the stock will *never* be recouped. Hence, no investor will ever want to own the stock if he or she believes dividends will never be paid.

Now, suppose management promises to set the **dividend payout ratio** to k percent; that is, k percent of earnings are paid as dividends. The earnings valuation equation becomes:

Dividend payout ratio. The proportion of earnings paid out in dividends.

$$\text{Intrinsic value}$$

$$= \frac{\text{Dividend payout ratio} \times \text{expected earnings next period}}{\text{Required market rate} - \text{expected growth in dividends}}$$

$$P_0 = \frac{k \times E_1}{r - g}$$

(9.9)

But this equation is the constant growth dividend model because *dividend payout ratio × expected earnings next period* is next period's expected dividend: $k \times E_1 = D_1$.

Comprehension Check

1. In principle, what process should yield the intrinsic value of a corporation's stock?
2. State the formula for determining the intrinsic value of a share of stock when future dividend payments are expected to remain constant. For what type of stock might this analysis be useful?
3. What formula might be used for determining the intrinsic value of a share of common stock when future dividends are expected to increase at a constant growth rate? What conditions are necessary to use this formula?
4. When dividend growth rates are expected to vary in future years, how can a common stock's intrinsic value be calculated using the constant growth dividend model?
5. Comment on the importance of future earnings versus future dividends as a factor in determining the investment value of common stocks.

9.4 VALUATION AND DIVIDEND POLICY

We showed that common stock valuation is based on discounting the future expected dividend stream. But the issue is more complex than this, as summarized in the nearby Financial Reality reading. The question is: Are investors indifferent between receiving a dividend today and foregoing the dividend to realize future price appreciation in the common stock price? In practice, a firm's board of directors has considerable latitude regarding when, and how much, cash flows generated by the firm are paid out in the form of dividends or retained in the business. Thus, the dividend policy of a firm seems as though it may be relevant to the valuation of the firm. Conflicting points of view exist on this issue.

An investment banker who was present at the roundtable discussion excerpted in the Financial Reality reading said, "If you want to find out whether the institutions want dividends, for God's sake, go and . . . ask them!" He did ask and the replies were "yes, yes, yes."

9.4.1 The View That Dividends Do Not Matter

Theory developed by economists Miller and Modigliani suggests that a company's stock market value is relatively insensitive to its choice of dividend policy.[8] How can that be? If it is a mature company, shareholders rightly expect the company to pay out a high percentage of its earnings and not go off on a (probably) wasteful diversification scheme.[9] Keeping the money, or paying it out to shareholders, should be a major concern for management. But the dividend-irrelevance theory fails to address that issue.

---

[8]M. H. Miller and F. Modigliani, "Dividend Policy, Growth and the Valuation of Shares," *Journal of Business,* 34 (October 1961), pp. 411–433.

[9]Ben Ball, Jr. studied the 50 largest mature, publicly held U.S. companies for the 1970–1984 period to discover how much a five-year investment in each would enrich the long-term shareholder. He found that many companies' profits simply never found their way to shareholders, either as dividends or as higher stock value over time. For more than half of the companies, including Coca-Cola, Procter & Gamble, and American Express, a large portion of retained earnings simply disappeared into money-losing investments. See "Mysterious Disappearance of Retained Earnings," *Harvard Business Review* (July–August 1987), pp. 56–63.

TAX POLICY AND DIVIDENDS

Some academicians argue that the theory of finance, combined with the tax laws, suggest that low dividends benefit investors. Other academicians argue that high dividends benefit some investors, while others say dividends don't matter. The following excerpt is by Joel Stern.

I'd like to point out that the major reason why people like Fischer Black believe they don't know the answer to the question of the appropriate dividend policy is this: The evidence that has been accumulated in the academic community by serious researchers—by people that we have a lot of respect for, who are on the faculties of the premiere business schools—almost without exception, these academics find that there is no evidence to suggest that investors at the margin, where prices are set, have any preference for dividends over capital gains. This supports the point of view that the price-setting, marginal investor is "dividend-neu-

tral," which means that a dollar of dividends gained is equal to a dollar of capital gains returned, while being indifferent how that return was divided between dividends and price appreciation. There is a second point of view that has been expressed recently in research, which shows that investors who receive dividends cannot undo the harmful tax consequences of receiving that dividend. And as a result, the market is actually "dividend averse," marking down prices of shares that pay cash dividends, so that the pretax returns that investors earn are high enough such that, posttax, the returns are what they would have been had the company not paid cash dividends in the first place. But there is no creditable evidence that I am aware of—none that has been accepted by the academic finance community—that shows that investors prefer dividends over capital gains.

Source: Donald H. Chew, Jr., ed., "Do Dividends Matter? A Discussion of Corporate Dividend Policy," *Six Roundtable Discussions of Corporate Finance with Joel Stern* (New York: Quorum Books, 1986), pp. 67–101.

Figure 9.5 illustrates the residual dividend policy decision process. According to this view, dividend policy is a passive rather than an active decision. For each period, a company pays out as dividends whatever earnings are left over after satisfying needed investments in such things as plant and equipment. Management treats dividend policy as a *residual cash flow* policy. The theory fails to address how a company reinvests its cash flows. No sensible manager would make such an assumption. It's as if the head of a company's Asian division asked for a blank check without telling corporate officers what the division's investment plans would be.

The residual dividend policy approach conveniently assumes that the investment policy of the company is known and fixed. Further, the theory assumes that the chief executive officer (CEO) is not tempted to buy a jet or expand a corporate empire, thereby creating a principal-agent problem of management investing in low-return projects. No matter how talented or foolish the CEO may be, the theory asks us to believe that (taxes aside) a dollar left inside the company, with little or no control over how it is utilized, is as valuable to investors as one outside. The idea is that if dividends are paid, shareholders are that much richer but the firm is that much poorer, thereby reducing the value of the shareholders' common stock.

FIGURE 9.5

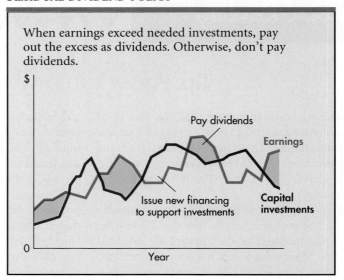

FIGURE 9.5

RESIDUAL DIVIDEND POLICY

9.4.2 The View That Dividends Seem To Matter

From a practical standpoint, companies seem to behave as though the dividend decision does matter. At an industry level, dividend payout ratios remain reasonably stable over time within industry groups (see Table 9.5). In 1992, 1300 New York Stock Exchange firms paid out estimated cash dividends of $124 billion, up from $102 billion just two years earlier. These results suggest that neither management nor investors view dividends as residual, or left over from the investment decision. Indeed, it is common to find rapidly growing companies with cash needs greater than internally generated funds. Nevertheless, many of these companies pay small dividends, at times having to borrow money to do so. Also many companies, such as electric utilities, have relatively high cash dividend payout ratios and sell new issues of common stock from time to time instead of lowering the dividend payout.

The Financial Reality reading on page 330 underscores management's awareness of shareholder concern about dividends. The CEO of Delta Air Lines wrote shareholders in an effort to calm their fears about the future of the company. Most firms make every attempt to pay cash dividends regularly and are reluctant to reduce the dividend amount or miss a dividend payment. Many firms proudly point to their excellent dividend record. Table 9.6 is a sample listing of firms with long-term continuous dividend payments.

9.4.3 Economic Reasons Why Dividends Matter

Miller and Modigliani's world is a stylized environment in which financial markets fully reflect all relevant information in share prices. However, shareholders do not have access to all information relating to the company's future cash flows and risk. Corporate managers are better informed about the firm's cash flow expectation than are participants in the financial market. Theories that support the importance of dividends are labeled *informational signaling* and *agency considerations*.

TABLE 9-5

INDUSTRY DIVIDEND PAYOUT RATIOS

	Five-Year Averages		Ten-Year Average
	1983–87	1988–92	1983–92
Special construction	49.8%	40.1%	44.9%
Food and kindred products	38.2	38.6	38.4
Textile mills	38.6	30.6	34.6
Paper and allied products	54.3	52.7	53.4
Publishing and printing	27.7	23.6	25.5
Chemical and allied products	77.5	79.2	78.4
Primary metal products	56.9	68.1	63.6
Miscellaneous manufacturing	32.8	37.6	35.3
Electrical, gas services	92.0	81.1	86.4
Nondurables wholesale	31.4	29.1	30.2
Apparel stores	26.8	39.6	33.3
Commercial banks	56.6	63.3	60.3
Credit services	36.6	28.2	31.8
Health services	24.9	36.2	30.3
Engineering, accounting	47.2	42.5	44.7
Average	46.1%	46.0%	46.1%

Dividends as a proportion of earnings have remained reasonably stable over the decade for these industries. Computed from the 1993 Compustat Tape.

First, let's describe informational signaling. A company usually sets a target for the dividend payout ratio (*dividends ÷ profits*) and changes this target infrequently. Usually, the stock market reacts favorably to announced dividend increases and adversely to announced dividend decreases. Because management is reluctant to cut the dividend rate, any dividend decrease signals a substantial worsening of the company's future operating cash flow prospects. A dividend increase signals an improvement in the minimum sustainable level of operating cash flows. Thus, **informational signaling** means that any change in the dividend payout ratio signals a corresponding change in management's assessment of the company's future operating cash flows. For example, in February 1989, General Motors raised its annual dividend 20 percent. The chairman of GM said the increase was to send a message to shareholders that GM's fundamental earning power had increased. On the announcement, GM stock increased about 5 percent—a gain of over $1.3 billion in market value.

Because dividend changes convey information, Miller and Modigliani's dividend policy of only paying out the residual cash flow after satisfying investment needs on a year-by-year basis does not appear to be in the shareholders' best interest. Such a policy leads to a dividend level and a payout ratio that fluctuates wildly, depending on the yearly availability of attractive investment projects. Investors seem to suggest that a company should manage its dividend policy so that dividend changes are orderly and consistent with changes in its earnings prospects.

Agency considerations complete the pro-dividend argument. Dividend policy

Informational signaling. An increase in the dividend signals positive information; a decrease signals negative information.

RESPONSE TO PROTEST OVER A DIVIDEND CUT

DELTA AIR LINES, INC.

Hartsfield Atlanta International Airport
Atlanta, Georgia 30320

September 1, 1983

Dear Stockholder:

As you have undoubtedly learned, Delta Air Lines has lowered its dividend for the current quarter from 25¢ to 15¢ per share. I hope you will agree with me that this was a prudent and wise step which will redound to the future benefit of the Company and its stockholders, but I wanted to explain to you some of the major factors which figured in our Board of Directors' decision.

First, we are proud of our dividend record. This is the thirty-fifth consecutive year that the Company has paid a dividend. This is by far the longest and most consistent dividend payment record in the United states air transport industry. (A number of other large U.S. airlines have not paid dividends for years or have done so only sporadically.) Currently, Delta is one of only two large U.S. air carriers paying a dividend. Moreover, Delta has increased its rate of payout every year since 1976 to and through 1982. The quarterly dividend rate of 25¢ per share (established at the times the stock split in December of 1981) was maintained during the one loss quarter experienced in fiscal 1982, and during the loss quarters experienced during fiscal 1983.

Second, now that fiscal year 1983 as a whole has developed into a loss after thirty-five consecutive years of profits, it seemed to the Board of Directors that it would be prudent to lower the dividend rate for the current quarter. While Delta's cash flow posture and its overall financial situation remain good and strong, the Company does have major capital commitments for modern, efficient aircraft and other properties, and has increased debt to a significant level in connection with these commitments. The conservation of $4 million in cash for the quarter therefore appeared to be a wise course of action.

Third, I also want you to know that in view of the reduction in dividend rate for this quarter, Delta's directors voluntarily lowered their retainers, and all officers of the Company voluntarily reduced their salaries for the period September 1, 1983 through the end of the new fiscal year, June 30, 1984.

A number of the problems which have plagued our industry in the recent past, particularly uneconomic, discount fare pricing, seem to be resolving themselves, and some reasonably favorable trends seem to be developing. In the meantime, your Company has taken significant steps to reduce its expenses and capital requirements during the next five years. We are hopeful that these various factors combined will result in a sufficient level of profitability during those years to permit the Board to consider raising the dividend rate once again in the future.

I trust that the foregoing is helpful to you in understanding why the dividend rate was reduced.

David C. Garrett, Jr.
President &
Chief Executive Officer

may be important for helping resolve agency problems between managers and shareholders. A company that finances its investments through internally generated funds deals with its shareholders infrequently—usually only when it sends out annual reports and dividend checks. If the risk to the firm of a takeover is minimal, pressures from outside investors are insignificant.

However, dividend payments serve as an effective way for managers to tell share-

CONSECUTIVE YEARS OF INCREASING DIVIDEND PAYMENTS

Name of Company	Number of Years
Winn-Dixie Stores, Inc.	49
Ohio Casualty Corporation	47
FPL Group, Inc.	46
Texas Utilities Company	46
Central & South West Corporation	42
Aon Corporation	41
The Dun & Bradstreet Corporation	41
SCANA Corporation	41
Tambrands, Incorporation	41
Torchmark Corporation	41
American Home Products Corporation	40
AMP, Incorporation	40
Florida Progress Company	40
Harland (John H.) Company	40
Household International	40
Warner-Lambert Company	40
Diebold, Incorporation	39
Procter & Gamble Company	39
Southern California Water Company	39

About 360 companies have increased their dividends for at least ten consecutive years. For at least 31 consecutive years, 56 firms have increased their dividends.
Source: Moody's Dividend Achievers, Moody's Investors Service, Inc., 1993.

holders about any uncertainty of the firm's future cash flows. As the proportion of earnings paid as dividends increases, the likelihood that management will have to go outside the firm to obtain funds to finance investments increases. Outside financing means higher transactions costs for the firm because managers face the scrutiny of investment bankers, the SEC, and potential new investors. Most likely, nonpublic information will also be furnished by the firm in its prospectus. Thus, the financial markets will force managers to conduct business in a manner that withstands close scrutiny, thereby reducing any agency problems.

Other practical considerations also can affect dividend decisions without directly affecting the value of the firm. The most prevalent considerations are institutional restrictions, debt covenants, statutory law, and tax law.

INSTITUTIONAL CONSTRAINTS. Certain institutions are prohibited, either by law or by policy, from investing in common stocks of companies that do not have a history of regular dividend payments. Other investors, such as many trust and endowment funds, can only spend dividend income as a matter of policy. These investors have a preference for some minimum level of regular dividend income.

DEBT COVENANTS. Lenders view the equity investment of the firm as their protection in the event of bankruptcy. Hence, lenders often require restrictive debt covenants forbidding any dividends to be paid from earnings accumulated prior to the loan date. The covenants may also prohibit dividends to be paid until debt is reduced to a specified level.

STATE LAWS. **Various state laws prohibit the paying of dividends from capital contributed to the firm. Here the definition of** *capital* **is the par value of the common stock, and in some cases it also includes the** *paid-in surplus,* **the amount the firm received over the stock's par value. Laws prohibit dividends to be paid when the company is insolvent or when the payment of dividends would lead to insolvency, which means the firm is not able to pay its liabilities.**

IRS IMPUTED DIVIDENDS. **The Internal Revenue Service (IRS) has the power to establish minimum dividend amounts. If the IRS considers a firm's retained earnings to be higher than needed for any legitimate business reason, the IRS can impose a tax on excess accumulated profits. The rationale is that the firm is avoiding paying dividends which are taxed in the hands of the recipients. The IRS seldom uses this power and when it does closely-held family businesses are usually involved.**

 Comprehension Check

1. Summarize the main points of a residual dividend policy.
2. How do corporate managers indicate that they believe dividend policy is important?
3. How do the concepts of signaling and agency theory relate to the importance of dividends in the stock valuation process?
4. Summarize the several other factors which can influence dividend policy.

SUMMARY ▼▼▼▼▼▼▼▼▼▼▼▼

DISTINGUISHING FEATURES OF COMMON STOCKS

- Several features distinguish common stock from other securities:

    First, holders of common stock have the right to vote on corporate matters.

    Second, shareholders as residual owners of the firm, can only receive distributions from the firm (that is, dividends, either in cash or stock) if the board of directors declares dividends payable.

    Third, common shareholders have limited liability.

    Fourth, common shareholders participate in proceeds from the liquidation of the firm if a surplus exists after all other claimants have been paid.

    Finally, stockholders have preemptive rights. If new shares are issued, old shareholders have the right to maintain their current proportional ownership.

READING THE STOCK TABLES AND PLACING AN ORDER

- Most newspapers print daily information about individual stocks and stock activity in general. Depending on which market the securities trade, the information may include the prior day's trading volume, high and low prices, yields, and price-earnings ratios. This information allows the investor to see how particular stock prices changed.

- Assuming the investor has an account with a brokerage firm, it is easy to buy and sell stocks in the United States. Within seconds of phoning the broker, the transaction is usually complete.
- Several different kinds of orders can be used: market order, limit order, stop-loss order, and stop-limit order. These orders can have different maturities: good till canceled, day, and fill or kill.
- It may be possible to buy stock on margin, with the investor borrowing half the purchase cost from the broker.
- Each stock transaction incurs a transactions cost. These costs vary significantly from broker to broker.

COMMON STOCK VALUATION

- The theoretical principle for a common stock valuation is the determination of present value of all future cash dividends expected to be received by the common shareholder. Valuation of common stock uses time value of money concepts examined in Chapter 4.
- Usually, the valuation models assume either a future dividend stream growing at a constant rate or at a nonconstant rate for some period followed by constant growth thereafter.
- On the ex-dividend date the price of the stock should decline by the dividend amount.
- Small changes in either r or g can significantly change the stock price.

VALUATION AND DIVIDEND POLICY

- Whenever earnings are used in the valuation process, they are proxying for dividends.
- Conflicting views exist about the importance of dividend policy to the value of the firm.
- "The dividends-don't-matter view" considers dividends as a residual. If funds are left over after funding capital expenditures, then pay the remainder as a dividend. The approach makes for a volatile dividend pattern.
- "The dividends-seem-to-matter view" takes the position that investors want to receive stable dividends each year.
- Informational signaling and agency considerations support the position that dividends are important. In both cases, the financial markets receive information about the firm through any dividend changes.
- Other reasons supporting "dividends matter" are institutional constraints, debt covenants, state laws, and IRS's power to tax retained earnings.

KEY TERMS

▼

Common Stock Valuation

Intrinsic value

Valuation and Dividend Policy

Informational signaling

FURTHER READING ▼▼▼▼▼▼▼▼▼▼

Engel, Louis, and Brendan Boyd, *How to Buy Stocks,* 7th ed. New York: Bantam Books, Inc., 1987. Market novices will find this book a useful source for how Wall Street works.

Rappaport, Alfred, "Stock Market Signals to Managers," *Harvard Business Review* (November–December 1987), pp. 57–62. This article explains the importance of stock price as a measure of corporate performance.

SELF-TEST PROBLEMS ▼▼▼▼▼▼▼▼▼▼▼

ST-1. The exchange rate between the United States and Canada was $0.80/C$1 at the beginning of the year and $0.88/C$1 at the end of the year. Over the year, the stock of Maple Leaf Corporation, a Canadian firm, increased by 15 percent on the Toronto Stock Exchange. What was the net return to a U.S. investor who bought this Canadian stock at the beginning of the year and sold at the end of the year, bringing proceeds back to the United States? Disregard commission charges.

ST-2. Zero Corporation paid a cash dividend of $2 per share on its common stock last year. The corporation's earnings and dividends are expected to grow at an annual rate of 8 percent indefinitely. The required rate of return on investments with the same level of risk as Zero Corporation is 14 percent.

  a. What is the intrinsic value of Zero's common stock?
  b. If the stock currently is selling for $30 per share, as an investment advisor what would be your recommendation to your clients? Explain your answer.

ST-3. Amgene, Inc., a biotech firm, paid a dividend of $1 per share last year. A stock analyst at Merrill Lynch expects this dividend to grow at a rate of 5 percent for the next three years after which the analyst expects dividends to grow at a rate of 10 percent annually for the foreseeable future. The required rate of return on this security is 15 percent. Calculate the intrinsic value of Amgene's common stock.

PROBLEMS ▼▼▼▼▼▼▼▼▼▼▼

DISTINGUISHING FEATURES OF COMMON STOCKS

9-1. Why might a corporation wish to issue more than one class of common stock?

9-2. With respect to the payment of corporate dividends, distinguish between declaration date, ex-dividend date, and date of record.

9-3. The directors of Marriott Corporation declared a cash dividend of $0.07 per share of common stock on Thursday, June 3. The dividend was payable on Monday, July 19 to stockholders of record on Friday, July 2.

  a. What was the ex-dividend date of this cash dividend?
  b. If you wished to receive this cash dividend, what would be the last possible day you could buy the stock on the New York Stock Exchange?

9-4. What is the rationale behind the practice of paying a stock dividend?

9-5. If a share of stock that originally sold for $100 per share falls to $50 per share as the result of a 2-for-1 split or 100 percent stock dividend, what is the stock's one-period rate of return during the time period before and the one after this change occurred?

9-6. If an investor buys a share of stock for $100 per share and the stock pays a 50 percent stock dividend, what is the adjusted cost on which the investor should calculate her or his taxable gain when the stock is sold?

9-7. Over the past decade, Transcontinental, Inc. has achieved average annual growth in dividends of approximately 7 percent. Directors are about to declare a dividend 8 percent higher than that paid last year. This level is consistent with expectations contained in recent press comment.

However, Transcontinental has an opportunity to invest in a project which promises a discounted cash flow return considerably above its cost of funds. The project will produce no significant cash flows for the first three years. The only internal funds available are those which would otherwise be used for a dividend. Undertaking the project means paying no dividend this year. The president believes that shareholders deserve some reward and suggests that if the cash dividend is not paid this year the company should issue a stock dividend to shareholders.

Advise the president on the major theoretical and practical factors to be considered before arriving at a decision concerning undertaking the project or paying a dividend. Comment on the president's suggestion for rewarding shareholders with a stock dividend.

READING THE STOCK TABLES AND PLACING AN ORDER

9-8. The following information is taken from the New York Stock Exchange stock table for transactions occurring January 10, 1994:

$47\frac{7}{8}$ 36 Disney DIS .25 .5 40 31775 $47\frac{7}{8}$ $46\frac{1}{4}$ $47\frac{3}{4}$ $+1\frac{1}{4}$

a. What is the closing price of Walt Disney Corporation's common stock on January 10, 1994?
b. What was the price range of Disney's common stock over the past 52 weeks?
c. How many shares of Disney common stock traded on January 10?
d. What is the NYSE trading symbol for Walt Disney's common stock?
e. What is Disney's annual cash dividend based on its latest quarterly payment? What is the dividend yield?
f. What was the high and low price range for Disney's stock on January 10? What was the net change in the stock from the previous day's closing price?
g. What is the PE (price-earnings) ratio for Disney stock based on its closing price and the latest year's reported earnings per share? If the average PE for the stock market as a whole was 18, how would you interpret Disney's PE?

9-9. The current quotation for KCS Energy's common stock on the New York Stock Exchange is $24\frac{3}{4}$ bid, 25 asked.

a. Assume that you have researched KCS Energy's common stock and wish to buy 200 shares. If you place a market order for the stock through your Merrill Lynch broker, what is the total amount you will pay including commissions? Determine the brokerage fee from Table 9.4.
b. If you own 200 shares of KCS Energy common stock and wish to sell them at the market through Charles Schwab, what will be the net proceeds credited to your account after the commission? Determine the brokerage fee from Table 9.4.

9-10. a. Carol is interested in purchasing a corporation's common stock but believes the price might go lower in the next few days. What type of order might she place with her broker?

b. If Carol owned a stock which had risen considerably in price and she wanted to protect her gain without immediately selling the stock, what type of order might she place with her broker?

c. If Helen were a portfolio manager for an insurance company and wanted to sell some holdings of Apple Computer stock at a specified price, what type of order would she place?

9-11. Assume the exchange rate between the United States and Canada is $0.89/C$1 at the beginning of the year and $0.80/C$1 at the end of the year. Over this one-year period, the Canadian equity market increased by 12 percent.

a. What is the net return to a U.S. investor in the Canadian equity market over this one-year period?

b. What return would the U.S. investor have earned if the exchange rate at the end of the year was $0.95/C$1?

9-12. One year ago, Leah took $1000 of her savings and bought common stock of a German company. The exchange rate at the time of the purchase was 1.60 Deutsche marks (DM) per $1. This allowed her to purchase stock worth DM1600. Her investment has resulted in a 10 percent annual rate of return, stated in Deutsche marks. Today, the exchange rate closed at 1.82 marks per $1. Calculate her rate of return in U.S. dollars.

9-13. Mike Sherman plans to invest in Jag, Ltd., a British corporation that is currently selling for £50 per share. Mike has $110,000 to invest at the current exchange rate of $1.85/£1.

a. How many shares can Mike purchase?

b. What is his return in U.S. dollars if the price of Jag, Ltd. at the end of the year is £60 and the exchange rate at that time is $1.75/£1?

COMMON STOCK VALUATION

9-14. Why would an investor, concerned primarily with capital gains, estimate a stock's current market price on the basis of expected future dividends?

9-15. An investment banker is trying to determine the intrinsic price of a stock that has never traded before. The company has been in business for 40 years. During this time, it has maintained a constant dividend payout ratio and has enjoyed an annual growth rate in earnings of 10 percent. What information does he need to estimate the price of the stock? Explain.

9-16. Last year, four different companies each had earnings per share of $4 and dividends of $1. The required rate of return is 12 percent on the common stock of each company. The first company is a declining firm with a −5 percent growth rate. The second company is a no-growth firm. The third company has a normal growth of 5 percent. The fourth company is expecting three years of supernormal 20 percent growth, which is to be followed by constant annual growth of 5 percent. Find the intrinsic stock value of each company.

9-17. A firm's common stock paid a dividend of $1.50 last year. Earnings, dividends, and stock price are expected to grow at an annual rate of 5 percent indefinitely. The required rate of return for an investment with this amount of risk is 9 percent.

a. What is the intrinsic value of the stock?

b. The stock is selling for $36. Is it a good buy? Why?

9-18. A firm's stock sells currently for $40 a share. This year, the firm earned $4 a share and paid a $3 dividend. What is the rate at which earnings, dividends, and stock price must grow if investors seek a 10 percent rate of return on this stock?

9-19. A share of common stock is expected to pay a $3 dividend next year. Any investor of this stock expects a return of 15 percent.

a. If the estimated price of the stock at the end of the year is forecasted to be $54, what is the current intrinsic value of the stock?

b. The $3 dividend is expected to grow annually in perpetuity at a constant rate and the required market rate is 15 percent. Based on your answer to part (a), what is the growth rate in dividends?

9-20. Hewlett Inc. has just paid a dividend of $0.20 per share. The market expects this dividend to grow constantly in each future year at the rate of 6 percent per annum. The required market rate for Hewlett's stock is 8 percent.

As soon as the dividend was paid, however, the board of Hewlett Inc. decided to finance a new project by retaining the next three annual dividend payments. The project is seen by the market to be of the same riskiness as the existing projects and it is expected that the dividend paid at the end of the fourth year from now will be $0.25 per share and will grow at the rate of 7 percent annually from then on.

You hold 1000 shares in Hewlett Inc. and your personal circumstances require that you receive at least $200 each year from this investment.

a. Assuming there is an active market in Hewlett Inc.'s shares, and that the market uses a dividend valuation model, show how the market value of its shares has been affected by the board's decision.

b. Show how you can still achieve your desired consumption pattern in the first three years while improving your expected dividend stream from then on.

9-21. The sale value of Jordan Air Company is expected to be $22 million at the end of five years. Until then the common shareholders expect to receive a constant dividend of $3 per share. Wall Street investment bankers believe that after five years, the dividend will likely grow at an annual rate of 3 percent in perpetuity. Investors require a 14 percent return on investment in this firm. There are 800,000 shares of stock outstanding.

a. What is the current market value per share of Jordan Air if liquidation is expected in five years?

b. What is the current market value per share if liquidation is not anticipated?

c. Should the firm plan to liquidate? Explain.

9-22. A common stock currently pays $2 in dividends. The dividend is expected to grow at 6 percent for the first three years and at 4 percent thereafter. The market required rate of return is 10 percent. What is the stock's value?

9-23. Pacific Ltd. is an all-equity financed firm (that is, it does not use any debt financing). Its before-tax income of $12 million is expected to grow at a 15 percent rate for the next five years. The dividend payout ratio is 30 percent. The corporate tax rate is 34 percent and is expected to remain constant. Investors require a 12 percent return.

a. Before-tax income is forecasted to grow at 9 percent per year. What is the expected value of the firm after the period of supernormal growth, that is, at the end of period 5?

b. If after the supernormal growth period there is zero growth in before-tax income, what is the value at the end of period 5?

9-24. The Kaufman Company is currently growing much faster than the economy. Expected growth of the company is 11 percent for the next three years; then it is expected to settle down to a constant 4 percent growth rate thereafter. The dividend last year was $1.75. Investors required a rate of return on stocks of similar risk of 11 percent.

a. What is the present value of dividends paid during the supernormal growth period?

b. How much is the first dividend paid at the end of the first year after the supernormal growth period is over?

c. What is the expected price of Kaufman stock at the end of the supernormal growth period?

d. What is the present price of the common stock?

e. Compare the expected price of the stock at the end of the supernormal growth period with the current price. What is the compound annual growth rate?

f. Suppose you want to hold the stock for one year. What do you expect the selling price to be one year hence?

9-25. George McGarity is thinking about buying stock in HydroMex, a Mexican utility company. HydroMex recently paid a dividend of 100 pesos per share; that is, $D_0 = 100$ pesos. He expects the dividend to grow indefinitely at 12 percent per year. However, because inflation in Mexico is expected to be higher than in the United States, he forecasts the peso to depreciate against the dollar at a rate of 3 percent per year. The current exchange rate is 15 pesos per U.S. dollar. This ratio will change as the peso depreciates.

a. Mr. McGarity wants a 25 percent rate of return, including exchange rate risk. What is the maximum price in dollars that he should pay for the stock?

b. Suppose the peso is expected to appreciate rather than depreciate against the dollar at the rate of 2 percent per year. Assume all other facts are unchanged. Now how much is the maximum price that he should pay for the stock?

9-26. The common stock of a firm currently sells at $40 per share. Management declares a dividend of $2 per share to all those holding the stock at the end of next month.

a. What should happen to the stock price and when should it happen?

b. If the company declares a 10 percent stock dividend in place of the cash dividend, what should happen to the price of the stock?

9-27. Five years ago, an investor bought shares of Brass Fixtures, Inc. at $8 per share. The stock is now selling for $12 a share. A $0.50 per share dividend is expected in the near future.

a. When the stock trades ex-dividend, what price change should the investor expect?

b. If a 5 percent stock dividend is declared in place of the $0.50 cash dividend, what price effect should the investor expect?

9-28. Explain how the earnings and dividends approaches to stock valuation are equivalent.

VALUATION AND DIVIDEND POLICY

9-29. If the dividend decision is truly irrelevant to the economic value of a firm, are dividend discount models of any use in estimating the intrinsic value of a firm's stock? Explain.

9-30. Mason Manufacturing Corporation's management follows a residual cash flow policy for payment of cash dividends. The financial officer has prepared three investment budgets for next year amounting to $15 million, $24 million, and $28 million depending on the final analysis of projects and available funding. The firm's forecast for cash flow from profitable operations next year is $22 million.

　　a. Calculate the amount of cash dividends that would be paid to common stockholders next year under each budget assuming that long-term funds are provided entirely by common stockholders' equity.

　　b. Calculate the amount of cash dividends that would be paid to common stockholders each year under each budget assuming that 30 percent of long-term funds are provided by debt financing.

9-31. Rhone Rapids, Inc. has the following record of earnings per share over the past seven years. Year 1 is the earliest year.

Year	Earnings Per Share
1	$4.40
2	4.80
3	3.00
4	−0.60
5	1.90
6	5.40
7	6.00

　　a. Calculate the annual dividend each year if the firm has a dividend policy of a constant payout ratio of 50 percent when earnings are positive and no cash dividend when there is a loss.

　　b. Calculate the annual dividend each year if the firm has a dividend policy of paying $1 per share whenever this will result in a dividend payout of 50 percent or less. Cash dividends will be increased in increments of $0.50 per share for those years when the $1 regular dividend plus the extra payment does not exceed 50 percent of current earnings per share.

　　c. Comment on the advantages and disadvantages of each dividend policy.

9-32. The chairperson of the board of Maple, Inc. announced that the company will change its dividend policy from paying a target proportion of earnings per share. Instead, dividends will be paid out as a residual; that is, any cash flows left over after the firm has undertaken all profitable investments will be paid out to shareholders.

What are the possible effects of increased variability of future dividends on the value of the firm?

9-33. How does management use dividends as a signaling device? To the extent that dividends are a signaling device, how are dividend changes related to stock prices?

9-34. In late July 1993, the new chairman of the board of International Business Machines (IBM) announced a loss from operations for the second quarter, a special pretax charge of almost $9 billion to reduce employees, factories, office space, and other physical assets, and a cut in the quarterly dividend from $0.54 a share to $0.25. The announcement came at a press conference on Tuesday, July 27, 1993, and was reported in the financial press on July 28. This was the second cash dividend reduction for IBM in 1993.

   a. What do you think was the initial reaction of investors to IBM's announcement? Explain your answer.

   b. Check the price movement of IBM's common stock in late July, 1993 using a source in the library. What was the actual reaction of investor to IBM's July 27 announcement? How do you explain this reaction?

9-35. About nine years ago John Galt Ltd., a large established firm, stopped paying dividends because of its poor financial performance and mounting losses. After considerable reorganization and investment, the firm is now an efficient, profitable, and soundly managed company.

Management is considering recommencing the payment of dividends. However, when initially discussed at the board meeting there was no agreement on the merits of reintroducing dividend payments. Three main views were expressed:

• A stable dividend policy should be introduced as soon as possible.

• Dividends are irrelevant to shareholders.

• Dividends should be paid only when the firm has no investment opportunities promising returns equal to or greater than that required by shareholders. This situation is unlikely to arise for several years.

What are the main points which should be considered when deciding upon dividend policy? Comment on the three main views expressed by Galt's board.

DISCLOSURE ASSIGNMENTS

9-36. Use the *Disclosure* database to answer the following questions for both Nike, Inc. and Reebok International Limited.

   a. Which stock has the largest market value for its equity?

   b. What is the price-earnings ratio for each firm? Which firm is more highly valued in the market on this basis?

   c. What is the dividend yield of each stock?

   d. What is the expected growth rate for each stock?

   e. Estimate the cost of equity for each stock using the dividend growth model. Which firm has a lower cost of equity? Why?

   f. How much is the dividend payout for each firm? Which firm retains more of its profits? Does the firm that retains more of its profits have a higher growth rate and a lower equity cost?

LIBRARY ASSIGNMENTS

9-37. Based on reports in the financial section of your daily newspaper, *The Wall Street Journal,* or weekly news magazines, write a one-page commentary of your evaluation of the present attitude of investors toward investing in common stocks. Include in your commentary a summary of the most recent 30-day trend of common stock prices on the New York Stock Exchange.

9-38. By studying current newspapers, news magazines, or investment advisory services found in the library, quote at least three stock market analysts' opinions about the current level of stock prices. Include at least one view which is contrary to the others you report. Based on your study, what is your opinion of the current level of common stock prices? What would be your recommendation to a person who has just received a $100,000 inheritance about starting now to buy common stocks for an investment portfolio?

9-39. By studying newspaper articles found in your library, find three companies that reduced or eliminated their cash dividends in the past year. What was the initial reaction of the stock market to these dividend cuts? How do you explain the market's reaction?

COMPREHENSIVE PROBLEM ▼▼▼▼▼▼▼▼▼▼▼

9-40. Jon Hunter, an analyst for a regional investment banking firm, is researching a number of questions relating to the common stock of Andrew's Corporation.

a. The directors of Andrew's Corporation declared a quarterly cash dividend of $0.25 per share on the common stock on Thursday, October 13. The dividend was payable on Wednesday, November 9, to stockholders of record on Friday, October 28. What was the ex-dividend date of this cash dividend?

b. If customers of the brokerage firm wished to be sure of receiving this cash dividend, what would be the last possible day they could buy the stock on the NYSE?

c. Andrew's Corporation paid $1 per share cash dividend during the most recent year. If Jon believes dividends will grow at a rate of 10 percent annually into the foreseeable future, what is the intrinsic value of Andrew's common stock in one year if investors require a return of 16 percent on this investment?

d. Given the $1 per share cash dividend paid in the recent period, assume that dividends will grow $0.10 per year for the next two years and then will grow at a rate of 15 percent indefinitely. If the required rate of return on the stock is 16 percent, what is the stock's current intrinsic value?

e. Assume that the current market price of Andrew's common stock is $104 per share. Management believes there would be more investor interest in the stock if it were trading at a lower price to enable stockholders to purchase 100-share lots for a lower capital investment. If Andrew's board of directors declared a 2-for-1 split with the approval of stockholders, what would you expect the market price of the common stock to be after the split? What would be the gain for present stockholders of such an action?

f. If at the time the board of directors declared the 2-for-1 split in part (e) it also announced an increase in cash dividends and a new-product development, what would you expect to happen to the market price of the common stock? Why?

ST9-1. If $100 U.S. were converted to Canadian currency, it would amount to C$125. With a 15 percent increase the value is C$143.75 by year end. At a rate of $0.88/C$1, the C$143.75 would be worth $126.50 U.S. Thus, the $100 investment would have earned 26.5 percent.

ST9-2. a. Intrinsic stock value

$$= \frac{\text{Expected dividend next period}}{\text{Required market rate} - \text{expected growth rate}}$$

$$= (\$2 \times 1.08) \div (0.14 - 0.08)$$
$$= \$36$$

b. Since your estimate of the intrinsic value of the stock is $36 and the market price is $30, you would recommend purchase of the stock to those clients who were willing to accept the level of risk for a stock with a required market rate of 14 percent. For those clients who were more risk averse, this stock might not be appropriate even though it apparently is selling below its intrinsic value.

ST9-3. The present value of the dividend stream for the first three years is:

$$\frac{\$1.05}{1.15} + \frac{\$1.1025}{1.3225} + \frac{\$1.1576}{1.5209}$$

$$= \$0.91 + \$0.83 + \$0.76$$
$$= \$2.50$$

The dividend in year 4 is $1.273 (= $1.1576 dividend in year 3 × 1.10). The dividend grows at a constant rate of 10 percent from then on. At the end of year 3, the value of the future dividend stream is:

$$P_3 = D_4 \div (r - g)$$

$$= \$1.273 \div (0.15 - 0.10)$$
$$= \$25.46$$

Discount $25.46 for three years at 15 percent:

$$\$25.46 \div (1.15)^3 = \$16.74$$

Thus, the intrinsic value of the stock is:

$$P_0 = \$2.50 + \$16.74$$
$$= \$19.24$$

Video Case 9

R&D Investing: How Wall Street Values It

from *Business World,* May 20, 1990

This video discusses investment in research and development (R&D). Firms must make R&D investments to maintain their long-term competitiveness. As new products appear on the market, consumers shift to these products for increased convenience, newer style, or better technology. Firms introduce new products to keep up with the competition; otherwise they are left behind.

Companies in the United States lag firms in other industrialized countries in the percent of GNP (gross national product) dedicated to research and development. The video suggests that this may be due to managers worrying about investors' reactions to announcements of increases in R&D spending. Such concerns are real. The stock of Merck, the large drug company, fell dramatically both times it announced large increases in R&D spending. Economists cite such negative stock price reactions to R&D expenditures announcements as evidence of a myopic, short-sighted stock market more concerned with short-run profits than the long-run viability of firms. But if R&D investments are necessary to stay competitive, why do investors react negatively to increases in these expenditures? Is such a response by investors rational? As the chapter explains, investors set today's stock price by discounting a company's anticipated future cash flows (dividends and capital gains) at a rate that reflects the risk of the stock. A negative stock price reaction to an announcement of increased R&D spending could mean many things: Investors see the stock as riskier; investors think the expenditures will prevent future dividend increases so they reduce future cash flows; or, a sudden increase in R&D may signal current research is not generating marketable products and that cash flows will be lower than anticipated.

If this investor behavior is rational, then managers are correct in their reluctance to increase R&D budgets, but reducing R&D investments will eventually make companies less competitive. This is a serious problem. Corporate managers want to maximize shareholder wealth, so they do not want their company's stock price to fall. However, reduced R&D investment reduces a company's ability to compete. Is there a solution to this conflict?

A number of solutions has been tried. For example, tax incentives reduce the cost, and thereby the financial risk, of undertaking risky research investments. Joining forces with government laboratories helps businesses reduce the risk of particularly uncertain research projects. In a number of cases, companies have separated the risk of R&D from other (presumably less risky) operations by establishing separate R&D partnerships (master limited partnerships—MLPs). By placing the more risky portions of the business into a separate business entity, investors can choose how much risk they are willing to bear. Those wanting a safe investment may invest in the relatively safe part of the company, while investors looking for higher potential returns who are willing to bear the commensurate risk, can do so by investing in the R&D partnerships.

Study Questions

1. One of the interesting aspects of this video is focusing on Merck and investors' reactions to its R&D announcement. In fact, research shows that for most companies there is *not* a negative stock price reaction to R&D expenditure increases. Do you trust the result from a large sample or a sample of size one (that is, Merck)? Explain.

2. Do you think R&D MLPs entirely solve the R&D risk problem? Consider top-secret projects that would be difficult or impossible to explain to potential investors.

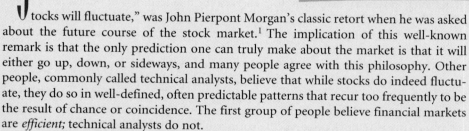

CHAPTER 10

Efficiency of Financial Markets

"**S**tocks will fluctuate," was John Pierpont Morgan's classic retort when he was asked about the future course of the stock market.[1] The implication of this well-known remark is that the only prediction one can truly make about the market is that it will either go up, down, or sideways, and many people agree with this philosophy. Other people, commonly called technical analysts, believe that while stocks do indeed fluctuate, they do so in well-defined, often predictable patterns that recur too frequently to be the result of chance or coincidence. The first group of people believe financial markets are *efficient*; technical analysts do not.

Although the precise definition of an **efficient market** is mathematically complex, its basic meaning is simple: all known information relevant to a stock, a bond, or some other financial security is continually incorporated into its price. If people believe inflation is rising, the price of a McDonald's bond will fall so that an investor purchasing it at its new, lower price will expect the same after-inflation return on each dollar invested as he or she would have expected at the previous price and previous inflation outlook. Similarly, the price of McDonald's common stock in an efficient market takes into account everything investors currently know about the company and its earnings prospects, the scope of the fast-food industry, and the general state of the economy now and in the future. Thus, a security's market price reflects its intrinsic value.

If the valuation of a financial security is to mean anything at all, it must be bought and sold in a market that is relatively efficient, or competitive. In efficient markets, management can assess the market's evaluation of its decisions by looking at the company's stock price. Shareholders suffer a loss in wealth if a decision causes the stock price to decline. A decision the market views as good for the company results in an

Efficient market. Market condition which prices alway fully reflect all ava able information. Adjustment to nev information is virt ally instantaneous.

---

[1] John Pierpont Morgan was a wealthy investment banker. His father, of the same name, started the investment banking company J.P. Morgan & Company.

increased stock price, that is, enhanced shareholder wealth. If the stock price does not immediately capture information about the decision, then the market is inefficient; the stock price fails to reflect the security's intrinsic value.

After you have studied this chapter, you should have a basic understanding of:

- How a competitive financial market works to achieve efficiency.
- Variations in efficient market theory.
- Evidence for and against market efficiency.
- How technical analysts gauge financial markets.

10.1 A COMPETITIVE MARKET SYSTEM

Much evidence indicates that capital markets in the United States and many other developed countries are efficient—not *perfectly* efficient but highly efficient. The Financial Reality article on page 346 suggests that the Japanese market is not one of the more efficient markets.

Let's consider why financial markets might be reasonably efficient.[2] Consider the case of fans at a sports event as they approach the turnstiles to enter the stadium. Figure 10.1 represents this hypothetical situation. The objective of most fans is to enter the stadium as quickly as possible. However, if the situation is similar to that depicted on the left side of Figure 10.1, fans will spend unequal amounts of time in line. Fan 2 will obviously pick turnstile B since there is only one other fan in line, compared with four fans in line at both turnstiles A and C.

However, if the right side of Figure 10.1 depicts the situation, it likely does not matter which line the four fans approaching the turnstiles choose. Although turnstile B has only two fans in its line, fans 2 and 3 will go to it. Fans 1 and 4 are probably indifferent to which line they choose. Fan 1 can choose either turnstile A or B, and the odds are there will be four fans ahead of fan 1. Similarly, fan 4 can choose either turnstile B or C and expect to spend the same amount of time in line.

What is the difference between the left side of Figure 10.1, where fans can easily identify a specific turnstile to minimize the wait, and the right side of Figure 10.1 where the waiting time is approximately the same, regardless of which line is chosen? The answer is there are more fans, *more competitors,* in the second situation. As long as there is a sufficient number of competitors, the waiting times to pass through any individual turnstile are likely to be about equal.

The substitution of investors and securities markets for fans and turnstiles allows us to draw an analogy to financial markets. The objective of investors is to maximize their return for a given level of risk. If investors find a security that is underpriced, they quickly rush to buy it, just as the fans rushed to turnstile B. In the process of bidding for the underpriced security, investors will drive up the security's price, thus reducing its return to a normal level. Those investors who are talented enough to *consistently* identify underpriced securities, and alert enough to buy before the rest of the crowd bids up the price, will be the market's superior performers.

Hence, as long as there are enough active competitors, it is unlikely that a security will remain either underpriced or overpriced for long. In such a competitive environment, it is difficult for an investor to consistently achieve superior performance. Most

---

[2]The following example is adapted from Russell J. Fuller and James L. Farrell, Jr., *Modern Investments and Security Analysis* (New York: McGraw-Hill, Inc., 1987), pp. 97–98.

UNEQUAL EQUITIES

The Tokyo Stock Exchange deserves its speculative reputation. Share prices of many companies are out of line with their fundamental value.

Japanese investors do not use any theory to value a share. Without a standard, it is difficult to say when a stock is fairly priced. This stems in part from the preponderance of stable shareholders and a corresponding lack of professional fund managers.

Stable shareholders are not people but companies referred to as *keiretsu*, a group arranged in order. The top six stable shareholders own 25 percent of all listed shares in Japan. This concentration of ownership makes the stock market illiquid. So long as the company and stable shareholders trust each other, the stable shareholders remain silent and infrequently sell their shares. Their voting rights are entrusted to management.

The United States and the United Kingdom have fund managers who have developed investment theories. There are no such people in Japan.

Faced with an illiquid stock market lacking a consistent method of valuing shares, Japanese brokers need a basis for recommending stocks that can appeal to investors and thus generate business. This problem is solved through the use of market themes, which are usually related to the improvement of a company's business. For stockbrokers, the best themes are those that are easy to understand and will take several years to bear fruit.

Investors will have less reason, therefore, to concern themselves with short-term corporate performance.

Themes make life easy for brokers. They can recommend shares without worrying how much the shares are really "worth." They merely have to find a plausible story to support their recommendations. There must be some underlying logic, though, since Japanese investors place great store in the shares of companies with improving fundamentals. The difficulty lies in working out how much to pay.

The four largest investment houses use a top-down approach in creating a theme. After a careful review of the economy, a picture of the future is created. All of Japan's large brokerage houses operate large research organizations to help them do this.

There are two ways in which Japanese shares defy fundamentals. The first is the distribution of price-earnings ratios (PERs) by industry sector. Companies with a good outlook ought to have higher PERs than companies with a poor outlook. Often the opposite is the case: the poorest industries have the highest PERs. The second is the share-price record of industries over a long period of time. An investor would have made as much investing in mines and fisheries as in Japan's much-vaunted electrical companies. Share prices have gone up regardless of earnings.

securities will be correctly priced, thereby offering normal returns for their given risk levels. This is the essence of market efficiency.

Before we leave our analogy, let us emphasize that investors must be able to do more than simply count the number of "fans" in each line. The securities markets are complex—there are potentially millions of able competitors in the securities markets, including thousands of well-educated, well-trained, and highly motivated individuals whose roles are to identify potentially mispriced securities. Thus, at least as a first approximation, we should consider securities markets efficient, despite their complex-

FIGURE 10.1

COMPETITION AT THE TURNSTILES

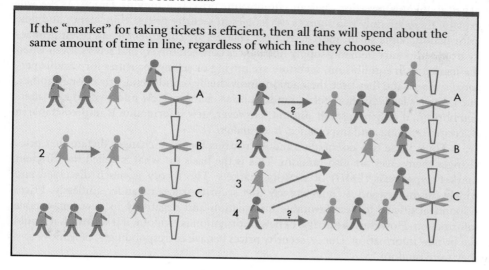

If the "market" for taking tickets is efficient, then all fans will spend about the same amount of time in line, regardless of which line they choose.

ity. This conclusion is supported by much empirical evidence, but perhaps securities markets are not as efficient as was once believed to be the case, as we will discuss later.

 Comprehension Check

1. Describe an efficient market.

10.2 THE EFFICIENT MARKET HYPOTHESIS

Because there are frequent movements in daily security prices, you may find it hard to accept that the financial market is efficient, or stated differently, that it is a system in equilibrium. The financial market often fails to give the impression that prices move in an orderly, purposeful way. The stock market crash of October 1987 left this impression in just about everyone's mind. The preceding Financial Reality reading reinforces this impression, at least as it pertains to the Japanese stock market. Still, when you realize that the arrival of new information constantly disturbs equilibrium, you also realize that there is a mechanism in place that pulls the system back into equilibrium. Financial markets have the power to self-adjust.

Consider the almost unlimited supply of news reports on national and international economies. Add to these economic events all the developments in various industries, such as new research findings or advanced technology, as well as new information that applies to particular companies. For example, *The Wall Street Journal* reported: "News that gross domestic product rose a sluggish 1.8 percent . . . damped investors' appetite for stocks early in the day. But signs that interest rates were headed down sparked a turnaround in the market later in the day."[3] You get a clear impression that an equilibrium price is a moving target that is usually gone by the time you get there.

---

[3]"Stocks Climb; Bonds Are Up; Dollar Mixed," *The Wall Street Journal*, April 30, 1993, p. C1.

10.2.1 Reasons for Price Changes

What about this assertion that an equilibrium price is a moving target? As we will explain, there are only two sources of changes in security prices: coincidence and new information. Some small, short-term price changes are coincidental and result primarily from temporary demand-supply imbalances between buyers and sellers. Even when the market is in equilibrium, investors are buying or selling securities for various personal reasons, and they time their actions individually or independently of one another. Such activity leads to short-term, random price changes. New information also alters equilibrium, if only by a small amount. However, new information is unpredictable in its content, timing, and importance. It is *random.*

Thus, these two essentially random reasons for price changes dictate that price changes themselves are also random. This is the basis for what is called the **efficient market hypothesis (EMH)** of security markets. The theory is much discussed and widely misunderstood. It does *not* say that security prices meander aimlessly. Prices respond positively to new favorable information and negatively to new unfavorable information. However, the *arrival* of new information is random; if it were not, it would not be new information. Hence, security prices behave correspondingly; they move as if they were random.[4]

Efficient market hypothesis (EMH). The concept that competition in the financial markets alerts investors to information so that prices adjust almost instantaneously to new information.

10.2.2 Degrees of Market Efficiency

Competition in financial markets keeps security prices moving toward their equilibrium values. How rapidly, accurately, and smoothly the process occurs determines how efficient the market is. As mentioned at the outset of this chapter, an efficient market is one in which buyers and sellers react to cause securities prices to reflect fully and instantaneously what is knowable about the future of companies.[5] Additionally, in an efficient market, the expected returns of all securities are proportional to their riskiness. The efficient market theory holds that you cannot consistently find securities that beat the market.

Financial professionals and academicians who support the EMH view it in terms of the level of information that must be considered. They define efficient markets in three different forms according to how security prices reflect the information available:

- *Weak-form efficiency:* Historical information is of no value for pricing securities.
- *Semistrong-form efficiency:* Publicly available information is of no value for pricing securities.
- *Strong-form efficiency:* All information, whether publicly available or not, is irrelevant for pricing securities.

Let's use Figure 10.2 to illustrate the different forms of market efficiency. Think of the outer circle as a perimeter wall that encloses *all* available information—both public and private, and current and historic. The second largest circle partitions the information so that it includes only historic and new information made public. This circle

---

[4]If you believe that security markets are random, your optimal investment strategy is not to try to "beat the market," that is, finding a security that achieves returns favorably disproportionate to its amount of risk. For that you need exceptional luck. EMH believers advocate an investment strategy known as *indexation.* This means that you invest in a portfolio of securities that mimics the financial market; your strategy is indexed to the market. (For example, a mutual fund can track the S&P 500 index). An indexed portfolio tries to track the market as a whole, not to beat it.

[5]Actually, the current price will not always be perfectly correct, but it will be what mathematicians call an unbiased estimate of true value. If the price is wrong, it is just as likely to be too high as too low.

FIGURE 10.2
SUBSETS OF MARKET EFFICIENCY

If security prices are strong-form efficient, then they are also semistrong-form and weak-form efficient. The reverse direction does not necessarily hold. Securities that are weak-form efficient may be semistrong-form efficient, but not necessarily, and most likely are not strong-form efficient. Similarly, securities that are semistrong-form efficient may be strong-form efficient, but not likely.

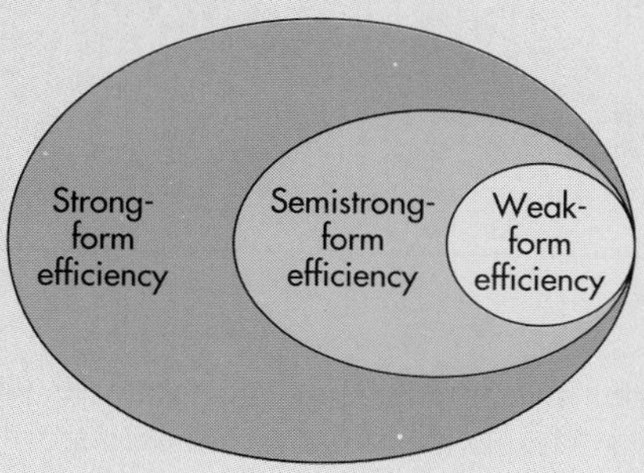

Strong-form efficiency

Semistrong-form efficiency

Weak-form efficiency

does not enclose private information known only by a select number of people. The smallest circle partitions the information set further. Enclosed in this circle is just public historical information.

10.2.3 Weak-Form Efficiency

In a **weak-form efficient** market, security prices discount all publicly available information as soon as it becomes available. You cannot enhance your ability to select securities by knowing the history of successive prices and the results of analyzing historical prices in all possible ways. Stated directly, you cannot develop profitable trading rules. If you are interested in L.A. Gear stock, for example, in a weak-form efficient market you cannot use, say, the past year of daily closing stock prices or returns for the company to derive a mathematical model or chart pattern to earn returns beyond what you would ordinarily earn given the risk of L.A. Gear's common stock. Later in this chapter we examine technical analysis, which approaches security markets as being weak-form inefficient. Technical analysts believe that their trading rules, based on historical information, can beat the market.

10.2.4 Semistrong-Form Efficiency

In a **semistrong-form efficient** market, current security prices fully reflect all public knowledge about the companies issuing the securities. Examples of this information include dividend announcements, stock splits, management firings, investment advisory data, and mergers between companies. Efforts to acquire and analyze this knowl-

Weak-form efficiency. Market condition in which current prices reflect all information that is contained in the historical sequence of prices.

Semistrong-form efficiency. Market condition in which current prices not only reflect all informational content of historical prices but also reflect all publicly available knowledge about the firm under study.

FIGURE 10.3

PRICE ADJUSTMENT PATTERNS

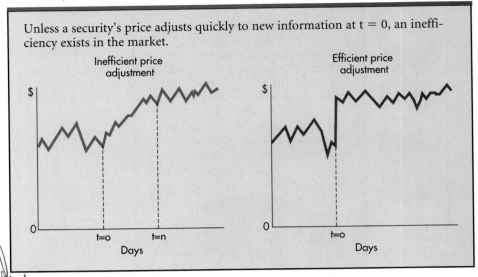

Unless a security's price adjusts quickly to new information at t = 0, an inefficiency exists in the market.

edge cannot produce superior investment results. For example, you cannot expect to earn a superior rate of return by analyzing a company's annual report or acting on announcements of dividend changes or stock splits. All this information is publicly available.

Figure 10.3 illustrates the price adjustment patterns that might occur in efficient and inefficient markets. The left side shows that in an inefficient market, the security price appears to move randomly before the announcement of new information at time $t = 0$. Upon the news becoming publicly available, investors react to the information, causing the security price to increase nonrandomly for several periods. The price reaches a new equilibrium level at day $t = n$. In contrast, in an efficient market the security price reacts *immediately* to the new information, as shown on the right side. After the adjustment, the price again changes randomly.

10.2.5 Strong-Form Efficiency

Strong-form efficiency. Market condition in which no information that is available, be it public or private, can be used to earn superior investment returns consistently.

Insider trading. Process of trading in a company's stock to profit from information that is not available to the public.

Strong-form market efficiency asserts that not even investors with privileged "inside" information can make use of it to secure superior investment results. **Insider trading** refers to trading on any information apt to have a material effect on the price of a bond or stock before such information is publicly available to investors. As is clear by the number of insider trading scandals in the past several years, strong-form market efficiency does not exist. Illustration 10.1 provides examples of how broadly courts interpret insider trading.

ILLUSTRATION 10.1

Insider trading

- Vincent Chiarella worked as a proofreader for a printing company hired to print documents that offeror companies had to file with the Securities and Exchange Commission (SEC) before making an offer to buy another company. Documents Chiarella read did not mention the name of the target company.

However, through research he identified the company. Chiarella bought stock of the target firm and made a profit of about $30,000. The SEC brought criminal charges against him. The court ruled that Chiarella was "not guilty" because he determined the identity of the target company himself.

- A judge convicted R. Foster Winans of tipping and trading on inside information. Winans wrote the "Heard on the Street" column in *The Wall Street Journal*. He made about $31,000 for leaking prepublished information contained in his articles to several of his investor friends. The stories often contained information about public companies and the views certain securities analysts had about the investment potential of these firms.

- A director of Cady, Roberts & Co., a public corporation, learned at a board of directors meeting that the board was going to reduce the company's dividend rate. The director excused himself from the meeting and phoned his broker to sell his shares in the company. The broker then used the information to sell Cady, Roberts stock held by his other customers. The SEC held both the director and broker guilty of trading on insider information.

Comprehension Check

1. Why are there such frequent and rapid changes in stock market prices if the market is always in a state of equilibrium?
2. Discuss the three degrees of market efficiency.

10.3 IMPLICATIONS OF THE EFFICIENT MARKET HYPOTHESIS

The EMH has startling and controversial implications. It is controversial because it runs counter to most people's instincts and traditional ideas about investing. For example, in its strong form, the EMH contends that not even investors with inside information about the company can earn excess profits trading in the company's securities. The theoretical reason insiders cannot profit from private information is because other investors watch the investing activity of insiders and quickly adjust prices of the company's securities by buying or selling them in the financial markets. However, is theory enough to convince us that this happens in reality? No. Securities markets are not strong-form efficient. However, to a large extent these markets are semistrong-form and thereby weak-form efficient; most public information is quickly impounded in security prices.

Semistrong-form efficient markets suggest that no one can consistently beat the market. Today's price for any security is the best available estimate of that security's intrinsic value. Thus, all securities are neither overvalued nor undervalued (as far as each investor can tell). Thus, the implication is that the collective judgment of a competitive, efficient market is accurate enough to make individual security analysis pointless.

The primary products of investment houses are information and analysis. They try to use both quick access to information and analytical skills to identify overvalued or undervalued securities and exploit any profit opportunities. Thousands of highly trained security analysts with large staffs, state-of-the-art communications and computing equipment, and large budgets devote their professional lives to this exercise. If the securities markets are efficient, however, it is an exercise in futility. In an efficient market, security analysis does not give you an edge over other investors. In theory, you cannot beat an efficient market.[6]

Here is a paradox. According to theory, analysis of securities makes financial markets efficient, but analysis is useless in an efficient market. If everyone recognizes the market's efficiency and stops analyzing securities, the market would soon stop being efficient because information about the firm would cease being published. Security analysis is necessary, but—and this is the crucial point—as long as plenty of other people are performing the necessary analysis there is no need for the investor to do it. Most investors, in effect, can take a free ride on the analytical efforts of others. Informed investors have little, if any, advantages over uninformed investors. Search costs for finding market imperfections are only worth it to the large institutional investors. Everyone else should take the price and not waste time looking for returns off the security market line (a concept we discussed in Chapter 5).

What is true for security selection also applies to *market timing*. **Market timing** refers to the decision to purchase a security just before it is likely to increase in value and sell the security just before it is likely to decrease in value. The timing decision assumes that the price of a security follows some pattern and you can accurately forecast the change in prices. In an efficient market, the current price of a security is the best estimate of its intrinsic value. New developments and information determine the market's future. Because developments are random, so is the market.

Figure 10.4 illustrates the possible rewards from the timing of buying and selling decisions. A study done for T. Rowe Price Associates, Inc. calculated the average annual rates of return for market timing versus a *buy-and-hold strategy*. **A buy-and-hold strategy** means to invest and hold the securities through the investor's predetermined investment horizon period. The T. Price Rowe study transferred funds between common stocks and Treasury bills according to the following rules. Invest in stocks when the bull market starts, and invest in Treasury bills when the bear market starts. The results show that the market timer must be correct at least 70 percent of the time to do as well as "buying and holding." Less accurate forecasts result in returns inferior to the conservative buy-and-hold strategy. However, Nobel Prize winner William Sharpe disagrees, as discussed in the Financial Reality reading on page 354. Sharpe, who did much to develop the theory of efficient markets, now sells his services to "beat the market" via market timing.

The efficient market theory has important implications for managerial finance. Much of the early finance and management accounting literature perceived the firm's financing and investment decisions as exclusively the subjects of managers' preference and approval. The decision process of investors was considered a totally unrelated issue. The efficient market theory recognizes that the decisions of the firm cannot be undertaken without paramount regard for the decisions of its investors, the suppliers of capital.

The securities market is the interface between the company's managers and its investors, and the market's pricing efficiency is an important element in achieving effective communication between the two groups. Some principal decision areas of the firm affected directly by market efficiency are the timing of new securities issues, the type of security issued, the maturity of securities, and project investment decisions.

Market timing. Strategy of varying the proportion of certain types of securities in a portfolio depending on where the investor views the market to be at a particular time.

Buy-and-hold strategy. Investment strategy of buying securities and holding them for a period of time. Opposite of trading in an attempt to sell at each market high and buy at each market low.

---

[6]The documented performance of mutual fund managers supports the notion that markets are relatively efficient. On average, these managers are unable to consistently "beat the market." However, notable exceptions exist. One in particular that stands out is the performance of Peter Lynch, who used to manage the Fidelity Magellan Fund. During the period from 1977 to 1989, Lynch achieved a total return of 2541 percent—about five times the gains of the Standard & Poor's index of 500 stocks. No other fund came close.

FIGURE 10.4
MARKET TIMING VERSUS BUY AND HOLD

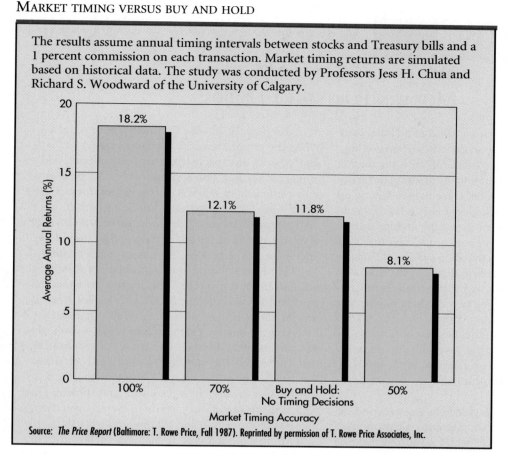

The results assume annual timing intervals between stocks and Treasury bills and a 1 percent commission on each transaction. Market timing returns are simulated based on historical data. The study was conducted by Professors Jess H. Chua and Richard S. Woodward of the University of Calgary.

Source: *The Price Report* (Baltimore: T. Rowe Price, Fall 1987). Reprinted by permission of T. Rowe Price Associates, Inc.

TIMING OF NEW SECURITIES ISSUES. The traditional presumption of market inefficiency implies that new issues of capital should be timed to coincide with the right conditions. This kind of concern makes little sense if the market is an efficient price setter. Even if current prices are historically low, market efficiency implies that they are at their correct level, and that it is illusory to assume that they must be due for a recovery. The best estimate of a future share price is the current share price.

TYPE OF SECURITY ISSUED. A by-product of market inefficiency is the belief by some managers that it is possible to endow a security with certain characteristics that make it cheaper to issue than alternatives. Convertible bonds, for example, allegedly combine some of the advantages of debt and equity without incurring the corresponding disadvantages. The rationale for issuing convertible debt is that by introducing an equity element into a debt instrument it is possible to reduce the coupon rate the firm pays investors. If markets are efficient, the error of this argument is that the security market trades in claims to future cash flow streams. Market efficiency requires a consistency in the pricing of claims regardless of their form. The price per unit of risk is the same for all securities and there can be no intrinsically superior security.

THE MATURITY OF CAPITAL. Can a company benefit from choosing one maturity over another for its debt securities? It is beneficial for a company to issue debt with a six-year life, if it requires the funds for six years. Matching the maturity of the funds with needs

MODERN PORTFOLIO TIMING

William Sharpe won one-third of a Nobel Prize in 1990 for work building on the efficient market theory that says no one can consistently beat the market because stocks are always rationally priced. The theory isn't popular just with Nobel Prize judges. Giving up on trying to beat the market, investors are flocking to index funds that eschew stock picking and instead try to duplicate the broad market in a single portfolio.

Sharpe's business is based on a slight divergence from his basic theory. He says that, yes, the market is efficient, but efficient in a way that permits some participants to beat it. All they have to do is buy heavily when other investors are too poor to bid. The market is still "efficient" because the other investors, who may be out of work, are acting rationally in dumping stocks. The ones with deep pockets profit. In short, Sharpe has gone from being an efficient market advocate to a market timer.

His market timing is guided by an exotic indicator he calls the "relative risk premium." This number represents the additional expected reward for bearing risk. His formula calculates the number based on cumulative returns (net of inflation) for stocks, bonds, and bills held by U.S. investors. He won't say much more about the calculations except that the returns go back to 1946, with more weight on recent years.

He pegs the relative risk premium norm at 100. When the premium is 120, investors will get 120 percent of normal expected returns for incurring additional risk; at that point, presumably, Sharpe clients with a stomach for risk will shift to riskier stocks, since risk and reward go together according to the efficient market hypothesis. At 80, investors get only 80 percent of expected returns for taking risk; so they should buy safer securities or get out of the stock market entirely.

How does Sharpe square this black box with his belief in efficient markets? "This is not a story that the market is screwed up," he declares. "This is a story of how investors behave when their wealth changes. Say I tell you the relative risk premium is 120—you'll get 120 percent of the normal expected reward for bearing risk. If that was the only thing I told you, you'd say, 'Let's buy stocks.' But what if I also told you the reason for that is we're in a recession, and someone in your family is out of work. If you're average, you'll say, 'I guess these are offsetting. I'll stay with what I've got.' In fact, that's what has to happen in an efficient market. The risk premium has to adjust to where the average investor doesn't want to do anything. If the average investor wants to buy stocks, that means more people want to buy than sell, and that can't physically take place."

Adapted from Marcia R. Berss, "Modern Portfolio Timing," *Forbes,* December 24, 1990, pp. 76–78. Reprinted by permission of FORBES magazine. © Forbes, Inc. 1990.

avoids the transaction costs of issuing a series of shorter-term bonds or the inconvenience and costs of retiring bonds with longer maturities. If the security market is efficient, choosing the maturity for a bond that does not match the maturity of the investment on the grounds that the interest rate is lower is misguided. If long-term rates, for instance, happen to be higher than short-term rates, this does not make them more expensive. The long-term rate should be higher if it correctly reflects an expectation of a future rise in short-term rates. Issuing a short-term bond to secure a lower coupon rate might appear to be beneficial in the short term. Although when the time comes to replace it, if expectations are fulfilled, short-term rates will have risen to a level such that the average cost over the period will be no less than that of the longer, apparently more expensive bond. Unnecessary transactions costs will have been incurred in the process.

EMT AND OFFERING BOOZE TO PERENNIAL DRUNKS

by Louis Lowenstein, Simon H. Rifkind Professor of Finance and Law, Columbia University and former president of Supermarkets General Corporation

In the 1980s some things went right on Wall Street but much went wrong, and what went wrong has caused a lot of pain. Scholars played an important role in the debacle, providing ingenious free-market theories to justify some of the worse excesses. Let me discuss how efficient market theory (EMT) contributed to the damage. EMT rests on several quite controversial assumptions, the most striking of which is the terribly convenient but circular assumption that mispriced stocks cannot long exist because if they did, "smart money" investors or arbitrageurs would already have eliminated them. Like some computer virus, EMT, the notion of "trusting prices," has spread far beyond its origins as a scholarly study of the trading market. It has contaminated issues and analyses in Wall Street but also in executive offices on Main Street.

We know that the traders and other professionals on Wall Street by and large lack the temperament to invest money on a rational long-term basis. Long-term investment requires not only analytic skills but also the confidence to make what are necessarily lonely, no-help-from-the-pundits judgments about a handful of stocks. EMT posits that we should assume that stock market valuations reflect everything there is to know about business realities and prospects, and that *they will only change as new information appears.* It is discouraging to see scholars dignify, with complex algebraic formulas and computer runoffs, the notion that it is foolish to argue with market values.

I doubt there is any substitute for studying annual reports as the reknowned investor Warren Buffett does. But it is odd, is it not, that not one EMT theorist has seen fit to study Buffett? Since he began managing money independently 35 years ago, during strong markets and weak, he has produced average annual rates of return of over 27 percent. For 35 years he has been steadily mining the imperfect prices that EMT says do not exist. The idea seems to be that if we believe pitchers are now so "efficient" that no one can hit .300, we should study large numbers of average hitters, rather than a star who has systematically studied the pitchers and the elements of hitting. And best of all, Buffet is willing to impart his knowledge. EMT believers explain Buffet's results as 35 lucky flips of a coin in a row.

A remarkable application of EMT goes by the acronym CAPM. This capital asset pricing model, in substance, creates for stocks a measuring stick of risk and then calculates the trade-off between risk and expected returns. Starting from the appealing principle of no-free-lunch, it states that not only is risk measurable but that the expected payoffs, the rewards, are commensurate. Increase your risk, as CAPM measures it, and your rewards will grow apace. CAPM has insinuated itself into the language and framework of finance so thoroughly that terms such as *risk-adjusted* and the *beta* of a stock are widely used, usually with little comprehension of what a mischievous model underlies them.

CAPM confuses the past with the future and the long term with the short term. It stubbornly refuses to acknowledge that in the typical business, there is no quantifiable risk but only immeasurable uncertainty. The beta of Capital Cities/ABC is 1.0, the same as that of the market index, but what could we possibly learn from that? The company owns a variety of media properties, including newspapers and the ABC network. Do we really believe that a computer, this remembrance of stock prices past, can tell us that a business with an emerging technology and in a changing regulatory environment will be no more or less risky over the next decade than the market as a whole? Think for a moment about Homestake Mining, an extremely unattractive company, but somehow one that has an extremely low beta of 0.20. It is said, therefore, to be only 20 percent as "risky" as the market generally. Homestake lost money the last three years, and its record over the longer haul is not much better. Still its beta says that it is far less risky than an Exxon or a strong public utility.

But EMT and CAPM go still further. They say that the beta measures not just the risk but the expected returns as well. With EMT and CAPM, if you want better than average results, buy a bunch of super risky, high beta stocks, such as the new issue of the latest trendy restaurant chain or biotech startup. Encouraging money managers to substitute betas for careful research and analysis is like offering Jack Daniels to an alcoholic. It is far too tempting. The crime is that it has succeeded so well.

INVESTMENT DECISIONS. Historically, the investment decision process in a firm assumed that management needed to consider the total portfolio of the firm's investments in order to assess the relevant risk of any new investment. The implication was that a project could fall into one risk category if undertaken by Company A and into another risk category if undertaken by Company B, depending on the relative composition of the companies' other investments. Efficient market theory recognizes that the risk class of a project depends exclusively on its relationship with the *market* portfolio of assets, not the *firm's* portfolio. Hence, the investment's risk class is the same regardless which firm undertakes it.

 Comprehension Check

1. What are the implications of the theory of efficient markets for investors in common stocks?
2. What is market timing? Under what circumstances may market timing be helpful to investors? Under what circumstances may market timing be detrimental to investors?
3. What are the principal decision areas of managerial finance affected by efficient markets?

 ## 10.4 EVIDENCE FOR AND AGAINST MARKET EFFICIENCY

Tests of market efficiency have changed how academicians and many market professionals view financial markets and practice their trade. Much evidence collected over the past several years supports the idea that financial markets are efficient, as defined by either weak-form or semistrong-form efficiency. Table 10.1 summarizes several events that support the idea of market efficiency. For each event, the market quickly incorporated any new information into the stock price.

The markets are not entirely efficient. Certain persistent exceptions to market efficiency, called **market anomalies,** exist. The following discussion examines some of these anomalies.

Market anomalies. Situations in which the efficient market hypothesis is not supported.

SIZE EFFECT. Firms with a low total market value of common stock (that is, price × shares outstanding) produce returns above those warranted by efficient markets. Empirical evidence shows that small firms with large *abnormal returns* (returns more than expected risk-adjusted returns) can outperform the market.[7] These small firms either pay no dividend or have a high dividend yield, have low prices, and have low price-earnings ratios.

PRICE-EARNING (PE) EFFECT. Stocks that sell at low PE ratios outperform high PE stocks. A size effect may be a factor for explaining this anomaly. The idea behind buying low PE stocks to beat the market is that these stocks may be unwanted now. However, if these firms have strong finances, high yields, and good earnings records, these stocks almost always do well eventually.

 JANUARY EFFECT. On average, stocks produce an excess return in January (see Figure 10.5). One suggested explanation is tax-loss selling. Investors sell stocks in December to

---

[7]The smallest 20 percent of firms, in terms of equity value, traded on the New York Stock Exchange are classified as small firms.

TABLE 10-1

SOME EVENTS SUPPORTING MARKET EFFICIENCY

The market quickly incorporates information revealed by the following events into security prices:

- Earnings announcements by firms.
- Dividend announcements by firms.
- Accounting change announcements for depreciation methods, mergers, inventory valuation techniques, research and development costs.
- Macroeconomic data announcements for changes in the Federal Reserve discount rate, the money supply, the level of the consumer price index, and changes in monetary and fiscal policy.
- Announcements about purchase or sale of securities.

Studies have also found:

- Newly issued annual reports contain little new information.
- Stock prices exhibit very small relationships between successive price changes.
- Most buy-and-hold strategies outperform trading rules for timing trades of common stocks.
- Mutual fund managers do not consistently outperform the market.

FIGURE 10.5

SEASONALITY IN STOCK RETURNS

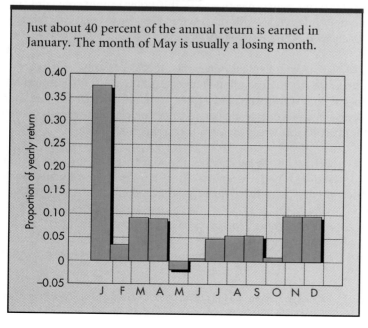

Just about 40 percent of the annual return is earned in January. The month of May is usually a losing month.

FIGURE 10.6
RETURNS BY DAY OF THE WEEK

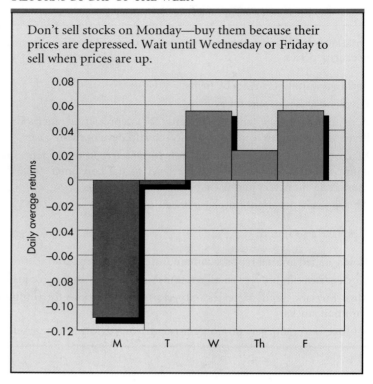

Don't sell stocks on Monday—buy them because their prices are depressed. Wait until Wednesday or Friday to sell when prices are up.

realize tax losses. In January demand is high for stocks as investors start a new tax year. However, a January effect for stocks exists in Australia where the tax year ends in July—not in December! The evidence gathered to this point cannot solve the January mystery.[8] The mystery intertwines with other anomalies. On average, the January return is higher for smaller firms and lower stock prices.

DAY-OF-THE-WEEK EFFECT. Evidence suggests that significant differences occur in expected returns for stocks depending on the day of the week. On average, Monday is a poor day to sell, but Wednesday and Friday are good days to sell (see Figure 10.6). Whether the average percentage change in prices on these three days is economically significant is questionable when we include commission costs.

QUARTERLY EARNINGS EFFECT. A lag exists in the adjustment of stock prices to the information in corporations' quarterly reports. Short-term price movements soon change in the same direction that announced quarterly earnings change.

Timeliness. Indicator used by Value Line Investment Services to signify the potential price changes in stocks.

VALUE LINE EFFECT. *The Value Line Investment Survey* is the largest and best-known investment advisory service in the country. Value Line ranks about 1700 publicly traded stocks from 1 (best) to 5 (worst) as to **timeliness**—probable relative price performance

[8]The book by Robert A. Haugen and Josef Lakonishok, *The Incredible January Effect* (Homewood, IL: Dow Jones-Irwin, 1988) is recommended for anyone seeking some entertaining reading.

within the next 12 months. Value Line updates the timeliness ranks weekly. Actual performance of securities follows Value Line's timeliness groups closely. Stocks in rank 1 perform much better than stocks in the other ranks. Stocks in ranks 4 and 5 perform the worst. Figure 10.7 is an advertisement for the service that depicts the performance record of the various timeliness groups.

REVERSAL EFFECT. The top-performing stocks in one week or month tend to fare poorly in the following period. The worst performers often follow up with good performance.

BRILOFF EFFECT. Abraham Briloff is a respected critic of financial accounting reporting standards. Using publicly available information, he analyzes accounting method choices and corporate disclosures of a firm. *Barron's* newspaper publishes his studies. The studies reveal that management uses the flexibility inherent in generally accepted accounting principles (GAAP) to smooth earnings over time, recognize revenues early and costs late. On average, there is about an 8 percent decline in a firm's stock price on the day *Barron's* publishes Briloff's analysis.

BENJAMIN GRAHAM APPROACH. Evidence shows that investors can generate superior risk-adjusted returns following rules set forth by Benjamin Graham, who is known as the father of modern security analysis.[9] Table 10.2 states the rules. Graham's investment strategy requires diversifying across prominent, conservatively financed, and consistently profitable companies the stock market considers undervalued. You earn profits when the markets eventually recognize these undervalued situations.

The stock market crash of October 19, 1987, referred to as Black Monday, is not an anomaly in the normal sense. However, Black Monday caused many people to question the efficiency of financial markets. The Dow Jones Industrial Average declined by 508 points, the largest single-day change in history. The decline was not unique to the U.S. stock market. Every major stock market in the world suffered a decline. Figure 10.8 shows the movements in the Dow Jones Industrial Average leading up to Black Monday.

How can a market in which the value of stocks drop 23 percent in one day be efficient? Efficient market theory cannot explain the October 1987 crash. Suppose rational investors set prices on the basis of all available information. Then it does not make sense that IBM stock is worth $135 per share on Friday, October 16, 1987, and worth only $102 on the following Monday. IBM did not dispose of any productive assets, employees, customers, patents, or products over the weekend!

Explanations for Black Monday include overvaluation of stock prices before the crash, overreaction to economic news, mechanical breakdown of the computer system handling transactions, and speculative buying frenzy in the months before the crash (see the Financial Reality article on page 362). Another explanation states that the market lost all rationality to a "herd instinct." Investors started to sell because other investors sold. The reason for selling was not a change in any stock market fundamentals.[10] There is likely some truth to each of these factors. However, these explanations are not consistent with the competitive market assumption of the efficient market theory.

Findings of anomalies have indisputably damaged the reputation of the market, but in practice few, if any, of the surviving anomalies offer realistic prospects of supe-

---

[9]See the study by Henry R. Oppenheimer and Gary G. Schlarbaum, "Investing with Ben Graham: An Ex Ante Test of the Efficient Market Hypothesis," *Journal of Financial and Quantitative Analysis* (September 1981), pp. 341–360.

[10]This study was conducted by Yale University economist Robert Shiller. It was reported in *Business Week*, February 22, 1988.

FIGURE 10.7
VALUE LINE'S TIMELINESS RANKINGS

The Value Line Experience:
AN UNPARALLELED
RECORD OF STOCK PROFIT

Ranked No.1 by Hulbert for long-term performance. 804% total returns, 1980-1993. The Hulbert Financial Digest Annual Issue, August 1993.

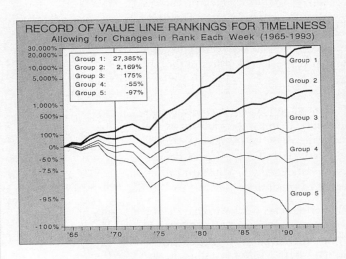

RECORD OF VALUE LINE RANKINGS FOR TIMELINESS
Allowing for Changes in Rank Each Week (1965-1993)

Group 1:	27,385%
Group 2:	2,169%
Group 3:	175%
Group 4:	-55%
Group 5:	-97%

Based on Timeliness™

This chart compares the Value Line rankings from 1965-1993. Not every stock has always performed in accordance with its rank, but it is a fact that stocks ranked 1 and 2 for Timeliness™ have, as groups, outperformed stocks ranked 3, 4 or 5 as groups year after year.* Number 3 ranked stocks have generally performed in line with the market averages. And, as anticipated, Number 4 and 5 ranked stocks have performed far below average. Past performance, of course, is no guarantee of future results, but the record speaks for itself.

* Past Performance Record, allowing for weekly changes in rank.

TIMELY STOCKS
Stocks Ranked 1 (Highest) for Performance in the Next 12 Months.

Every week, Value Line lists the 100 stocks currently ranked Number 1 for (Timeliness™): best year ahead performance.

In addition to NYSE issues, Value Line also ranks ASE and Over-The-Counter stocks.

Recent price per share is provided for comparison.

Stocks are ranked for relative long-term Safety™ from 1 (most safe) to 5 (least safe).

A stock's Beta is its relative sensitivity to market fluctuation (NYSE average =1.00)

Page No.	Stock Name		Recent Price	Safety Rank	Beta	Current P/E Ratio	Est'd Yield	Industry Group	Industry Rank
773	ADC Telecom.	(OTC)	38	3	0.95	30.2	NIL	Telecom. Equipment	10
2046	ADVANTA Corp. 'A'	(OTC)	41	4	1.75	21.7	0.5%	Financial Services	4
499	Airgas Inc.		42	4	1.20	38.2	NIL	Chemical (Specialty)	63
114	Allen Group		23	3	1.35	19.7	0.7%	Auto Parts (Replacement)	3
1220	Amer. Barrick Res.		27	3	0.35	31.0	0.3%	Gold/Silver Mining	25
1079	Amer. Power Conv.	(OTC)	22	4	1.70	39.3	NIL	Computer & Peripherals	75
1834	Anadarko Petroleum		45	3	0.95	32.8	0.7%	Petroleum (Producing)	14
1060	Analog Devices		21	3	1.40	18.8	NIL	Semiconductor	1
774	Andrew Corp.	(OTC)	38	3	0.95	22.0	NIL	Telecom. Equipment	10
1061	Applied Materials	(OTC)	29	3	1.65	20.3	NIL	Semiconductor	1
1023	Arrow Electronics		35	3	1.35	12.8	NIL	Electronics	23
1186	Bear Stearns		22	3	1.60	6.3	2.7%	Securities Brokerage	2
1666	Best Buy Co.		57	4	1.25	30.0	NIL	Retail (Special Lines)	65
796	Big B, Inc.	(OTC)	13	3	0.70	16.7	0.9%	Drugstore	39
1668	Blockbuster Entertain.		29	4	1.20	25.7	0.3%	Retail (Special Lines)	65
555	Bombardier Inc. 'B'	(TSE)	17	3	1.00	13.8	1.2%	Aerospace/Defense	36
1306	Briggs & Stratton		86	3	0.95	16.9	2.0%	Machinery	44
294	Brinker Int'l		40	3	1.30	32.5	NIL	Restaurant	26
265	Builders Transport	(OTC)	14	4	1.00	24.1	NIL	Trucking/Transp. Leasing	22
2052	CUC Int'l		36	3	1.35	47.4	NIL	Financial Services	4
208	Cardinal Distribution	(OTC)	46	3	1.15	25.6	0.2%	Medical Supplies	67
2013	Citicorp		37	3	1.35	9.7	NIL	Bank	11
136	Coherent, Inc.	(OTC)	15	3	0.80	16.5	NIL	Precision Instrument	43
2119	Computer Associates		33	3	1.60	18.9	0.4%	Computer Software & Svcs	46
1032	Core Inds.		12	3	1.10	12.4	2.0%	Electronics	23
1632	Dollar General Corp.	(OTC)	25	3	1.20	21.9	0.7%	Retail Store	71
1091	EMC Corp.		34	4	1.30	24.6	NIL	Computer & Peripherals	75
1759	Electronic Arts	(OTC)	40	3	1.85	44.4	NIL	Recreation	24
331	Equifax, Inc.		25	2	1.10	18.7	2.4%	Industrial Services	38
116	Federal-Mogul		25	3	1.00	22.3	1.9%	Auto Parts (Replacement)	3
1681	Fingerhut Cos.		27	3	1.45	17.1	0.6%	Retail (Special Lines)	65
2020	First Interstate Bancorp		62	3	1.60	9.0	3.2%	Bank	11
1007	Franklin Electric	(OTC)	34	3	0.70	13.8	0.6%	Electrical Equipment	72
2058	Green Tree		58	4	1.65	17.4	0.7%	Financial Services	4
1763	Harley-Davidson		43	3	1.60	21.5	0.6%	Recreation	24

(Reduced from 8-1/2 x 11 page)

Estimated Price to Earnings ratio is based on past 6 months' earnings plus estimated future 6 months' earnings.

Estimated Yield is based on estimated dividends for the next 12 months.

Each stock is grouped in one of 98 industry categories.

Industry Rank is based on the overall Timeliness™ ranks for all stocks in the industry.

Value Line's 28 year record of performance suggests that if an investor were to buy and hold ten or more stocks ranked 1 or 2 in eight or more industries, and give no further thought to his portfolio, the probabilities are high that he would beat the market year-in and year-out.

Value Line Publishing, Inc., 711 3rd Avenue, New York, NY 10017-4064

TABLE 10-2

GRAHAM'S STOCK SELECTION CRITERIA

REWARDS:

- An earnings-to-price yield (inverted PE ratio) of at least twice the Aaa bond yield. If Aaa bonds yield 10 percent, EPS should equal at least 20 percent of the stock's price (PE of 5 or less).
- A PE no higher than 40 percent of its five-year high.
- A dividend yield of two-thirds of the Aaa yield.
- A stock price below two-thirds of tangible book value per share.
- A stock price less than two-thirds of net quick liquidation value—current assets less total debt.

RISKS:

- Total debt less than tangible book value.
- Current ratio of 2 or more.
- Total debt no greater than twice the net liquidation value.
- Compound ten-year annual earnings growth of at least 7 percent.
- Two or fewer annual earnings declines of 5 percent or more in the preceding ten years.

FIGURE 10.8
THE DOW'S RETREAT

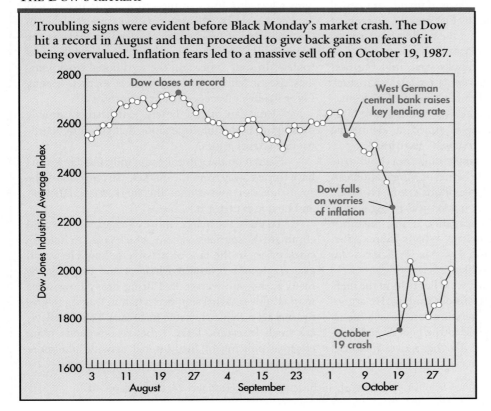

Troubling signs were evident before Black Monday's market crash. The Dow hit a record in August and then proceeded to give back gains on fears of it being overvalued. Inflation fears led to a massive sell off on October 19, 1987.

DANGEROUSLY INEFFICIENT

How could an efficient market lose one-third of its value in a single month—as the world's stock exchanges did in October 1987? Here is one professor's answer.

Strange that so many academics still cling to the illusion that the stock market is an efficient pricing mechanism. If the stock market were truly efficient, it would never have reached 2700 on the Dow in the summer of 1987, nor would it have crashed to 1750 little more than a month later. To argue that this was efficient pricing would be to argue that the corporate world lost one-third of its real value in a single month. Clearly this is an unsustainable view.

Despite piles of research from academics and government regulatory agencies, there is still no clear consensus on what triggered Black Monday. But it happened and could happen again, without reasonable cause, says Avner Arbel, professor of finance at Cornell University. Arbel isn't lulled by the market's subsequent recovery. He is convinced that the crash is but a symptom of dangerous inefficiency in the stock market.

For decades the textbooks have told business students that the stock market is rational, that stock prices accurately reflect all publicly available information. This efficient market they say is the basis of hundreds of investment strategies aimed at identifying both "undervalued and overvalued" securities.

But the theory certainly does not hold true today, says Arbel. No single kernel of information can account for the market's precipitous crash. To Arbel, this indicates that the stock market was riding a wave of speculative buying. In academic terms, the stock market had become inefficient. What's more, Arbel warns that unless the causes of this inefficiency are corrected, another crash is likely.

Arbel thinks he knows what lies behind the inefficient and volatile pricing: insider trading. He argues that today's stock market gyrations are largely fueled by information not available to the general public—especially takeover rumors. The big moves in stocks have mostly been in takeover situations and the like,

and here, Arbel says, the mass of investors are at an enormous disadvantage vis-à-vis the deal makers, big traders, and institutions.

With investing increasingly dominated by institutions, Arbel has reached the radical conclusion that there are really two stock markets in the United States, each running on a different pool of information. The first market we all know about. It consists of the traditional stock exchanges, where prices are based on information provided by news accounts, brokerage analysts, and disclosure documents filed with the Securities and Exchange Commission.

More sinister is a second market, or what Arbel calls the "shadow market." Here the stock prices of companies involved in mergers and restructuring are determined away from the market, be it in a company's boardroom or in the offices of its investment banker. Generally, this information isn't available to the public on a timely basis. Instead, it remains the preserve of a few big institutions and professional traders. In time, prices on the traditional stock markets rise or fall to meet the shadow market, leaving savvy shadow players clutching fat profits.

"How can pricing be efficient if stocks double overnight because of discussions that go on in boardrooms?" Arbel gripes.

Soured on the game, he says individual investors have turned away from the market. "In an odd way the small investor knows that the market is inefficient, and he doesn't trust it."

To make the market more efficient, Arbel would eliminate the specialist system, which failed to hold up stock prices in the face of massive selling. He would also create one centralized market and one government agency to oversee it. During heavy downward market moves, Arbel supports a halt in trading to give the market a chance to catch its breath. To help alleviate small investors' fears, Arbel recommends more effective policing of institutional activity and more timely public disclosure of merger negotiations.

Adapted from Matthew Schifrin, "Dangerously Inefficient," *Forbes,* December 24, 1990, pp. 60–61. Reprinted by permission of FORBES magazine. © Forbes Inc. 1990.

rior performance for the ordinary investor. The practical issue at stake for investors and managers, however, is not whether the market is efficient or inefficient, but *how* efficient. The market's overall efficiency rating had been exceptionally high until the October 1987 crash. The issue is not whether the crash makes the market inefficient but whether it reduces its efficiency to a level that has significant economic consequences.

Comprehension Check

1. What types of research studies have supported the efficient market theory?
2. What anomalies suggest limitations to the efficient market?
3. What explanations are there for the Black Monday stock market crash on October 19, 1987? Would you expect this occurrence from an efficient capital market?

10.5 TECHNICAL ANALYSIS

Weak-form efficiency hypothesizes that current security prices reflect all information that is contained in the historical sequence of prices. Thus, it is futile to analyze past prices and their patterns, that is, if you believe markets are weak-form efficient. Technical analysts do not believe the markets are efficient. And since the stock market crash of October 1987, studies supporting technical analysis have appeared in reputable finance and economics journals. Table 10.3 summarizes some conclusions of recent studies. Based on this evidence, it would appear shortsighted to summarily dismiss technical analysis as an exercise in "reading tea leaves," as many people suggest.

10.5.1 What Is Technical Analysis?

Psychological and emotional factors are important in financial markets. If investors move from optimism to pessimism, then the market falls, as in the case of the October 1987 crash. Advocates of efficient markets treat market movements as random (unpredictable) events that cannot be measured. Investors known as technical analysts ignore the concept of market efficiency. They study and try to quantify the psychological and emotional characteristics of investors that affect the movement of market prices. For technicians, the financial market becomes the center for studying various behavioral investment patterns. Market technicians do not care whether the personal motivation of investors is rational or irrational. Technicians only care about measuring investors' motivations by the price movement of securities.

The technician's investment approach is that financial markets follow patterns. These patterns change because of investors' attitudes to a variety of economic, monetary, political, and psychological forces. The technical analyst can be compared to a doctor who specializes in cardiology. The doctor graphs the changing behavior of the heart and from it can tell what has happened. From the information in the graph, the doctor notes problems that have existed and concludes that they may well recur. The doctor can determine the strength or weakness from past performance, evaluate new information, and then judge future prospects.

The technician, too, believes in trends. The art of technical analysis is to identify changing patterns early and to maintain an investment posture until a reversal of that pattern happens. Technical analysts consider the study of intrinsic value a waste of time and money. They believe that the only important factor to study is the action of the

TABLE 10-3

ACADEMICIANS IN SUPPORT OF TECHNICAL ANALYSIS

"We tested two of the simplest and most popular trading rules—moving averages and trading range break. . . . Our results are consistent with technical trading rules having predictive power."

William Brock, Josef Lakonishok, and Blake LeBaron, "Simple Technical Trading Rules and Stochastic Properties of Stock Returns," *Journal of Finance,* XLVII, no. 5 (December 1992), 1731–1764.

"Filters used in the CRISMA trading system are based squarely upon the findings of academic studies. The bottom line, of course, is that the apparent success of CRISMA trading system suggests that the market may not be as efficient as many scholars would like to believe."

Stephen W. Pruitt and Richard E. White, "The CRISMA Trading System: Who Says Technical Analysis Can't Beat the Market?" *Journal of Portfolio Management* (Summer 1988), 55–58.

"These trading systems are not a way to get rich quickly as many users hope, but they are not totally worthless as many academics believe."

Louis P. Lukac and B. Wade Brorsen, "A Comprehensive Test of Futures Market Disequilibrium," *The Financial Review,* 25, no. 4 (November 1990), 593–622.

"Moving average rules capture information."

Salih N. Neftci, "Naive Trading Rules in Financial Markets and Weiner-Kolmogorov Prediction Theory: A Study of Technical Analysis," *Journal of Business,* 64, no. 4 (1990), 549–571.

---

market itself. The market's reaction provides clues to the future because it reflects the collective mind and mood of the participants. In effect, the technician tries to follow and predict the psychological actions of many buyers and sellers in the marketplace.

Among other newspapers, the financial pages of *The Wall Street Journal* and *Barron's* report the market action of the previous day or week (see Figure 10.9). The technician watches the market action to find unusual opportunities and get a feel for the market.

10.5.2 Types of Technical Indicators

A bewildering variety of analytical methods and tools exists under the umbrella of technical analysis. Most of these involve the analysis of price and volume patterns, either separately or together. Their description could fill many books. However, we separate technical analysis into three areas: *sentiment indicators, market structure indicators,* and *monetary indicators.*

Sentiment indicators.
Factors that attempt to measure the buying and selling pyschology of investors.

Table 10.4 describes some sentiment indicators. **Sentiment indicators** record the actions of particular groups of market participants. The logic behind the use of these indicators is that different groups of investors are consistent in their actions at major market turning points. For example, technicians consider top management of companies and specialists on the New York Stock Exchange to be people with important pri-

FIGURE 10.9

BARRON'S STOCK MARKET STATISTICS

The market laboratory has a wealth of information about different segments of the market. Much of these data provide technicians a snapshot of the market's psychology and emotions.

BARRON'S MARKET LABORATORY

STOCKS

DJ HALF-HOURLY AVERAGES

The Dow Jones Averages current divisors are, respectively: 0.42025523, 0.56637223, 1.8964991 and 2.1776801.

Dow Jones 30 Industrial Average

Daily	Apr18	19	20	21	22
Open	3661.17	3620.12	3637.08	3622.50	3662.95
10:00	3667.12	3622.80	3629.34	3607.93	3656.11
10:30	3642.73	3638.86	3620.12	3607.03	3662.95
11:00	3626.07	3634.10	3598.11	3611.79	3659.98
11:30	3625.18	3629.34	3604.06	3622.80	3648.38
12:00	3632.91	3628.15	3603.76	3616.85	3651.65
12:30	3628.75	3621.01	3592.76	3617.44	3643.92
1:00	3625.77	3613.58	3583.24	3627.26	3651.06
1:30	3619.53	3590.08	3584.73	3634.10	3652.84
2:00	3623.10	3594.24	3580.86	3636.48	3652.24
2:30	3619.53	3606.44	3571.34	3632.61	3656.11
3:00	3625.48	3627.56	3594.24	3645.70	3659.09
3:30	3625.18	3626.96	3585.62	3644.81	3650.46
Close	**3620.42**	**3619.82**	**3598.71**	**3652.54**	**3648.68**
High (t)	3679.61	3670.39	3662.66	3673.96	3690.32
Low (t)	3593.35	3567.18	3546.65	3582.94	3621.01
High (a)	3668.01	3642.13	3646.00	3652.84	3664.14
Low (a)	3613.58	3582.94	3570.15	3599.30	3640.64
Change	−41.05	−.60	−21.11	+53.83	−3.86

Theoretical range (t): High 3690.32 Low 3546.65
Actual range (a): High 3668.01 Low 3570.15

Dow Jones 20 Transportation Average

Open	1608.04	1582.22	1561.25	1556.18	1587.74
10:00	1608.70	1579.57	1566.77	1560.37	1586.41
10:30	1600.10	1577.14	1562.58	1561.69	1590.83
11:00	1595.02	1575.38	1555.96	1561.03	1592.37
11:30	1595.68	1571.63	1552.65	1559.05	1587.52
12:00	1597.89	1568.98	1554.63	1559.93	1588.40
12:30	1595.02	1569.42	1548.01	1560.92	1587.52
1:00	1590.39	1565.67	1544.04	1565.45	1590.16
1:30	1588.84	1555.51	1548.45	1573.39	1591.49
2:00	1586.63	1555.07	1547.35	1573.39	1589.50
2:30	1585.31	1559.71	1543.82	1571.63	1591.27
3:00	1585.09	1566.11	1546.24	1574.94	1593.48
3:30	1585.31	1564.34	1544.70	1577.58	1590.16
Close	**1585.31**	**1556.84**	**1546.02**	**1583.54**	**1595.02**
High (t)	1613.56	1587.74	1572.07	1591.49	1606.94
Low (t)	1576.48	1546.24	1530.80	1547.57	1574.05
High (a)	1610.03	1584.87	1569.42	1583.76	1595.24
Low (a)	1582.44	1553.75	1540.51	1546.47	1582.88
Change	−24.94	−28.47	−10.82	+37.52	+11.48

Theoretical range (t): High 1613.56 Low 1530.80
Actual range (a): High 1610.03 Low 1540.51

Dow Jones 15 Utilities Average

Open	194.17	193.98	195.76	200.44	201.23
10:00	194.90	194.37	197.40	200.50	200.57
10:30	193.84	195.03	196.74	200.63	200.17
11:00	193.05	195.16	196.35	201.03	200.24
11:30	192.92	194.90	196.88	201.56	198.92
12:00	193.78	194.57	196.81	201.49	199.64
12:30	193.58	194.90	196.74	201.49	199.18
1:00	193.38	194.90	197.01	201.82	199.38
1:30	193.51	194.31	197.14	202.15	199.31
2:00	193.84	194.37	198.13	202.28	198.85
2:30	193.51	194.83	197.80	201.75	199.38
3:00	193.98	195.62	199.18	202.21	199.18
3:30	194.57	195.82	198.92	202.08	198.92
Close	**194.11**	**195.56**	**199.64**	**201.16**	**199.25**
High (t)	195.89	197.21	200.50	203.53	202.87
Low (t)	192.33	193.12	195.16	199.18	197.54
High (a)	195.03	196.28	199.64	202.54	201.36
Low (a)	192.59	193.84	195.62	199.58	198.52
Change	−.13	+1.45	+4.08	+1.52	−1.91

Theoretical range (t): High 203.53 Low 192.33
Actual range (a): High 202.54 Low 192.59

Dow Jones 65 Composite Average

Open	1293.87	1279.06	1278.42	1278.37	1295.07
10:00	1295.82	1279.23	1280.03	1276.70	1292.83
10:30	1287.95	1282.27	1276.36	1276.99	1294.96
11:00	1282.73	1281.01	1270.04	1278.08	1294.84
11:30	1282.61	1278.88	1270.79	1279.97	1290.19
12:00	1285.43	1277.68	1271.19	1279.17	1291.68
12:30	1283.71	1276.70	1267.29	1279.54	1289.56
1:00	1281.75	1274.29	1264.65	1282.90	1291.80
1:30	1280.26	1266.54	1266.20	1286.58	1292.43
2:00	1280.66	1267.35	1266.03	1287.15	1291.40
2:30	1279.34	1271.31	1262.98	1285.48	1293.06
3:00	1280.84	1277.74	1269.24	1289.27	1294.04
3:30	1281.35	1277.33	1266.94	1289.68	1291.28
Close	**1280.03**	**1273.78**	**1270.45**	**1291.91**	**1292.49**
High (t)	1300.35	1293.00	1290.31	1300.18	1306.78
Low (t)	1270.96	1258.74	1252.54	1267.40	1280.20
High (a)	1295.99	1283.13	1282.39	1292.03	1295.70
Low (a)	1278.20	1264.82	1262.81	1270.56	1288.70
Change	−14.52	−6.25	−3.33	+21.46	+ .58

Theoretical range (t): High 1306.78 Low 1252.54
Actual range (a): High 1295.99 Low 1262.81

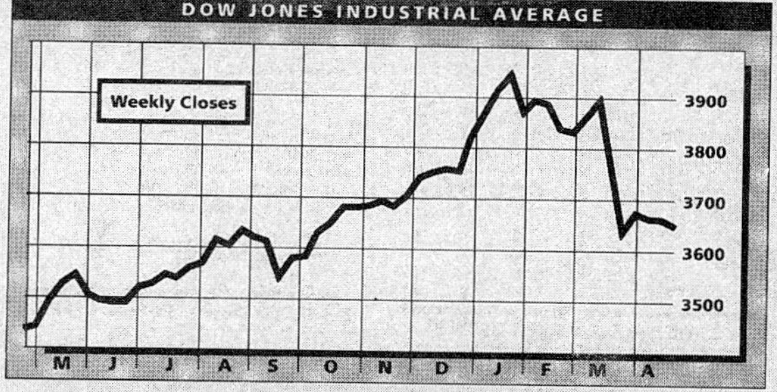
DOW JONES INDUSTRIAL AVERAGE
Weekly Closes
3900
3800
3700
3600
3500
M J J A S O N D J F M A

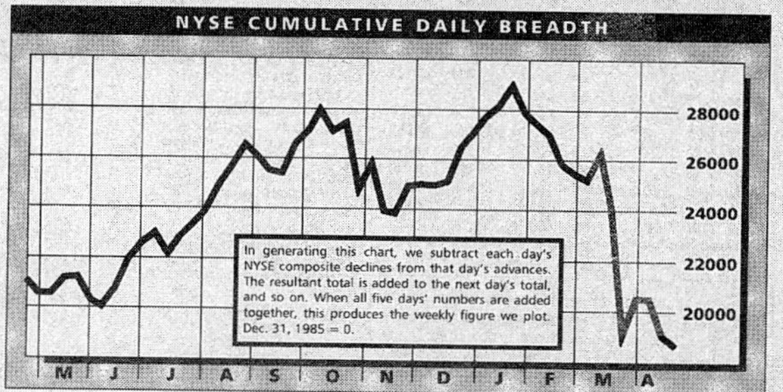
NYSE CUMULATIVE DAILY BREADTH
28000
26000
24000
22000
20000
In generating this chart, we subtract each day's NYSE composite declines from that day's advances. The resultant total is added to the next day's total, and so on. When all five days' numbers are added together, this produces the weekly figure we plot. Dec. 31, 1985 = 0.
M J J A S O N D J F M A

THE WEEK IN STOCKS

MAJOR INDEXES

12-Month High	12-Month Low		Weekly High	Weekly Low	Friday Close	Friday Chg.	Weekly %Chg.	12-Month Chg.	12-Month %Chg.	Change From 12/31	Change From 12/31 %Chg.
Dow Jones Averages											
3978.36	3398.37	**30 Indus**	3652.54	3598.71	3648.68	(12.79)	(.35)	234.91	6.88	(105.41)	(2.81)
1862.29	1485.43	**20 Transp**	1595.02	1546.02	1595.02	(15.23)	(.95)	(23.00)	(1.42)	(167.30)	(9.49)
256.46	192.99	**15 Utilities**	201.16	194.11	199.25	5.01	2.58	(39.61)	(16.58)	(30.05)	(13.11)
1447.06	1265.81	**65 Comp**	1292.49	1270.45	1292.49	(2.06)	(.16)	7.10	.55	(88.54)	(6.41)
456.27	410.71	**Equity Mkt.**	425.41	418.81	424.38	1.63	.39	9.88	2.38	(17.81)	(4.03)
New York Stock Exchange											
267.71	239.91	**Comp**	248.18	244.46	247.95	.29	.12	6.10	2.52	(11.13)	(4.30)
327.93	287.83	**Indus**	303.37	298.30	303.37	(.27)	(.09)	14.20	4.91	(11.89)	(3.77)
246.95	204.27	**Utilities**	216.79	208.25	214.36	5.70	2.73	(10.74)	(4.77)	(15.56)	(6.77)
285.03	228.71	**Transp**	248.32	240.19	248.32	(2.72)	(1.08)	12.04	5.10	(22.16)	(8.19)
233.33	200.75	**Finan**	209.02	207.57	208.21	(1.79)	(.85)	(3.63)	(1.71)	(8.61)	(3.97)
American Stock Exchange											
487.89	415.64	**Amex Index**	434.00	427.60	433.31	(4.98)	(1.14)	14.58	3.48	(43.84)	(9.19)
398.86	349.58	**MajorMkt**	369.93	362.72	367.92	2.09	.57	17.34	4.95	(11.49)	(3.03)
Standard & Poor's Indexes											
446.67	401.90	**100 Index**	414.05	406.94	412.35	1.04	.25	7.91	1.96	(17.11)	(3.98)
482.00	433.54	**500 Index**	448.73	441.96	447.63	1.45	.32	10.60	2.43	(18.82)	(4.03)
560.59	496.48	**Indus**	519.09	510.05	519.09	1.08	.21	20.13	4.03	(21.10)	(3.91)
453.63	365.11	**Transp**	389.36	378.22	389.36	(4.52)	(1.15)	1.90	.49	(36.24)	(8.52)
189.49	153.30	**Utilities**	164.31	156.50	161.31	4.81	3.07	(8.31)	(4.90)	(11.27)	(6.53)
48.40	41.39	**Finan**	44.05	43.60	43.60	(.52)	(1.18)	.11	.25	(.67)	(1.51)
184.79	156.62	**MidCap**	170.33	166.41	170.33	(1.16)	(.68)	11.41	7.18	(9.05)	(5.05)
Nasdaq Stock Market											
803.93	645.87	**Comp**	722.56	705.52	722.56	(5.41)	(.74)	64.15	9.74	(54.24)	(6.98)
418.45	327.28	**100 Index**	369.08	355.38	369.08	2.79	.76	35.42	10.62	(29.20)	(7.33)
851.80	660.17	**Indus**	758.42	735.44	751.71	(15.55)	(2.03)	79.32	11.80	(54.13)	(6.72)
956.91	824.99	**Insur**	881.13	858.96	880.48	(3.75)	(.42)	21.39	2.49	(40.11)	(4.36)
725.65	578.79	**Banks**	682.32	677.37	682.32	(.39)	(.06)	58.62	9.40	(7.11)	(1.03)
205.94	137.12	**Telecom**	153.09	150.44	152.68	.02	.01	15.22	11.07	(32.34)	(17.48)
356.61	285.44	**NNM Comp**	320.24	312.50	320.24	(2.25)	(.70)	29.13	10.01	(23.37)	(6.80)
342.72	263.79	**NNM Indus**	304.77	295.46	302.26	(6.15)	(1.99)	33.51	12.47	(20.50)	(6.35)
Russell Indexes											
258.31	231.31	**1000**	240.36	236.70	239.91	.68	.28	6.36	2.72	(10.79)	(4.30)
271.08	219.48	**2000**	248.40	242.14	246.55	(3.60)	(1.44)	23.86	10.71	(12.03)	(4.65)
278.44	247.43	**3000**	258.74	254.85	258.41	.31	.12	8.48	3.39	(11.72)	(4.34)
251.44	223.94	**Value**	235.63	233.30	235.04	(.95)	(.40)	8.11	3.57	(7.50)	(3.09)
222.33	199.81	**Growth**	204.99	200.74	204.74	2.04	1.01	3.75	1.87	(11.96)	(5.52)
258.10	224.14	**MidCap**	238.98	235.36	238.95	(2.14)	(.89)	11.73	5.16	(11.37)	(4.54)
Others											
476.75	398.57	**Value Line-a**	441.80	435.84	441.77	(3.41)	(.77)	38.99	9.68	(14.11)	(3.10)
305.87	268.81	**Value Line-g**	281.41	277.43	281.05	(2.58)	(.91)	9.31	3.43	(14.23)	(4.82)
4804.31	4249.46	**Wilshire 5000**	4454.13	4387.80	4453.77	1.17	.03	161.82	3.77	(204.06)	(4.38)
353.82	285.35	**Wilshire SC**	322.66	313.94	320.04	(4.66)	(1.44)	29.65	10.21	(17.01)	(5.05)

a-Arithmetic Index. g-Geometric Index.

TRADING DIARY

Supplied by Quotron, "QCHA" is the average percentage movement for all exchange listed stocks each day on an unweighted basis.

Market Advance/Decline Volumes

Daily	Apr 18	19	20	21	22
NY Up	74,485	103,587	116,473	276,490	145,026
NY Off	175,976	186,663	215,639	74,554	125,489
% (QCHA)	−.77	−.65	−.66	+.87	+.33
Amex Up	3,168	4,129	3,766	7,717	9,898
Amex Off	8,186	10,227	9,747	3,282	4,165
% (QACH)	−1.01	−.88	−.69	+.46	+.22
NASD Up	60,149	87,247	83,267	224,738	180,582
NASD Off	157,083	204,154	209,539	82,083	100,807

Market Advance/Decline Totals

Week ended last Friday compared to previous Friday

Weekly Comp.	NYSE	AMEX	Nasdaq
Total Issues	2,938	977	5,207
Advances	1,031	280	1,676
Declines	1,563	535	2,720
Unchanged	344	162	811
New Highs	39	20	141
New Lows	476	144	619

NYSE Common

Daily	Apr 18	19	20	21	22
Issues Traded	2,362	2,360	2,364	2,362	2,359
Advances	554	633	659	1,339	1,068
Declines	1,383	1,249	1,231	582	795
Unchanged	425	478	474	441	496

NYSE Composite Daily Breadth

Daily	Apr 18	19	20	21	22
Issues Traded	2,800	2,804	2,802	2,789	2,784
Advances	631	749	835	1,573	1,282
Declines	1,645	1,491	1,417	704	930
Unchanged	524	564	550	512	572
New Highs	14	11	6	12	18
New Lows	180	218	168	95	77
Blocks	6,145	7,668	8,606	8,952	6,639
Total (000)	321,108	385,171	426,920	446,873	352,457

AMEX Composite

Daily	Apr 18	19	20	21	22
Issues Traded	836	825	821	809	816
Advances	174	203	202	364	307
Declines	426	414	395	242	268
Unchanged	236	208	224	203	241
New Highs	11	3	3	4	6
New Lows	44	74	49	39	26
Blocks	221	285	289	229	N.A.
Total (000)	16,503	20,464	18,552	16,614	20,200

Nasdaq

Daily	Apr 18	19	20	21	22
Issues Traded	4,977	4,980	4,985	4,987	4,990
Advances	1,199	1,179	1,150	1,844	1,695
Declines	1,935	2,036	2,046	1,219	1,394
Unchanged	1,843	1,765	1,789	1,924	1,901
New Highs	43	32	35	28	40
New Lows	149	238	251	155	118
Blocks	4,367	6,257	6,319	6,781	6,310
Total (000)	246,576	328,193	335,340	341,226	319,543

DOW JONES ADVANCES/DECLINES

Dow Jones 30 Industrial Average

Daily	Apr 18	19	20	21	22	Wkly
Advances	5	14	9	22	15	11
Declines	21	15	19	7	14	16
Unchanged	4	1	2	1	1	3

Dow Jones 20 Transportation Average

Daily	Apr 18	19	20	21	22	Wkly
Advances	1	1	6	17	11	7
Declines	17	18	12	1	6	12
Unchanged	2	1	2	2	3	1

Dow Jones 15 Utility Average

Daily	Apr 18	19	20	21	22	Wkly
Advances	5	11	14	11	4	12
Declines	6	3	0	4	10	2
Unchanged	4	1	1	0	1	1

Dow Jones 65 Composite Average

Daily	Apr 18	19	20	21	22	Wkly
Advances	11	26	29	50	30	30
Declines	44	36	31	12	30	30
Unchanged	10	3	5	3	5	5

TABLE 10-4

SENTIMENT INDICATORS

Members' short index. Each week the NYSE publishes data that break down the total round-lot short sales into those made by stock exchange members and those made by nonmembers. Technicians consider the ratio of members' short sales to the total short sales (smoothed by a ten-week moving average) to forecast market movements.

Public specialists' ratio. The ratio measures the round-lot short selling done by the public against the NYSE specialists on the floor of the exchange. It pits the smart money (specialists) against one of the least informed groups (public).

Short interest ratio. This statistic is available around the end of the month and reports the number of shares sold short on the NYSE. Other exchanges publish similar data. Many shares sold short suggests a bearish attitude, and vice versa. However, some investors interpret a high short-interest ratio as optimistic because short sellers must cover their short positions by buying shares.

Insider trading. Stockholders who hold more than 5 percent of the total voting stock of a company and corporate officers or other employees who have access to important corporate information must file any purchases or sales within ten days with the Securities and Exchange Commission. On average, these insiders are correct in their trading decisions. Large insider purchases usually precede increases in the stock price, and vice versa.

Advisory services. *Investors' Intelligence* compiles data on the opinions of publishers of market letters. You might expect this group to be knowledgeable investors who recommend buying equities at market bottoms and selling them at market tops. The evidence suggests just the opposite. Technicians use the index as a contrarian indicator.

Mutual funds. Investment Company Institute publishes data monthly on mutual funds. Mutual funds hold a certain amount of liquid assets. The cash position is expressed as a percentage of the total value of mutual funds' portfolios. A low cash ratio says that funds are fully invested and little buying power exists. A high cash ratio says that much buying power exists.

Margin debt. Money borrowed from brokers and bankers using securities as collateral is margin debt. Investors use the money for the purchase of securities. At the beginning of a typical stock market cycle, margin debt is relatively low. As prices rise, the margin traders become more confident and wish to take maximum advantage of an advancing market. They buy more stock by using additional margin debt.

Contrary opinion. Most investors are wrong at major market turning points. Since the news media normally reflect majority opinion, then reports, cover stories, network news items, and other public sources are useful for measuring market sentiment. When there is too much optimism, you sell stocks, and vice versa.

Confidence index. This index is a ratio of the average yield on ten corporate bonds with a S&P's rating of AA+ divided by the average yield on ten corporate bonds with an average rating of BBB+. The ratio is always below 1 because the high-grade bonds offer lower promised yields to maturity. When the index approaches 1, the signal is bullish.

CBOE put/call ratio. Owning a call option is like owning the common stock. Owning a put option is like selling the common stock short. The put/call indicator is a five-day average of the ratio of the number of put options sold on the Chicago Board Options Exchange (CBOE) to the number of call options sold. A high ratio suggests pessimism about the market.

vate information. Thus, if these people are buying they must know something that other people do not know. This signals that it is time to buy stocks. If management and specialists are selling stocks, technicians conclude that the market is near its top and it is time to sell securities.

Conversely, mutual funds and investment advisory services as a group are consistently bullish at market tops and bearish at market bottoms. Technicians consider the actions of mutual funds and investment advisors to be indicators upon which to form a *contrary* predictory opinion.

Table 10.5 summarizes some major **market structure indicators.** For example, indicators such as stock market volume and breadth, Dow Jones industrial average, and stocks reaching new highs or new lows measure the underlying market structure to test the health of bull and bear markets. In the past, these patterns may seem to have preceded upward or downward price movements. Once these movements are underway, they tend to continue. As a trend begins to shift, a pattern or series of patterns forecasting the change in direction will show up. Technicians believe that the patterns reveal predictive information about supply and demand forces underlying all stock price movements.

In the stock market, money drives both the domestic and international markets. Since monetary conditions exert great influence on stock prices, technical analysts monitor *monetary indicators* of the markets. Indeed, the **monetary indicators**—primarily the trend in interest rates and Federal Reserve policy—are dominant factors in determining the major direction for the stock market. Falling interest rates reduce the competition on stocks from other investments and stocks begin to look more attractive. Also, when interest rates fall, it costs companies less to borrow. Less expensive borrowing reduces interest expense for many firms and increases their profitability. Higher profits make firms more attractive as investments. Table 10.6 summarizes three key monetary indicators.

> **Market structure indicators.** Factors that measure actions of the market in terms of highs and lows, breadth, volume, and strength.
>
> **Monetary indicators.** Factors that signal monetary changes in the economy which influence stock prices.

10.5.3 Charts for Technical Analysis

Technical analysts have developed an arsenal of charts to illustrate and support the predictions recommended by their indicators. Figure 10.10 identifies the primary types of charts used for technical analysis.

The **bar chart** shows the daily price range, closing price, and daily volume. A line chart connects the daily closing stock prices. A *moving average line,* the average stock price for the past 50 days, and a relative strength line often supplement the basic format of the bar and line charts. The moving average line smoothes out the price series so that a more stable pattern emerges. The *relative strength line* plots the ratio of the company's stock price to that of a stock market index, such as the S&P 500 average. If the ratio increases, the company's stock is doing better than the market.

The **point and figure chart** is another way to diagram stock movements. This chart has no time dimension and volume is not charted. The vertical axis measures the stock price. To construct the chart, you must determine a threshold level of price movement. One dollar per share is the typical threshold. Every time the stock moves past a whole number level, you record a mark. If the price moves upward, you enter an X. A downward price movement calls for an O. As the price rises, you stack Xs on top of each other for each $1 change in price. When the price direction changes, you enter an O in the next column. You add Os below for each $1 the stock price falls.

Technicians base charting on the premise that stock prices follow patterns. Technicians believe that stock prices behave as if they have momentum. They expect momentum to carry the price in its current direction until some new force causes price

> **Bar chart.** A graph of a period's high, low, and closing prices. The price range is a vertical bar. The close is a short horizontal bar.
>
> **Point and figure chart.** A charting device that records every price change of a certain minimum amount, rather than every price change.

TABLE 10-5

MARKET STRUCTURE INDICATORS

Stock market indices. The Dow indices (Industrial, Transportation, and Utility), the S&P 500, and Value Line Index reflect market activity. The Dow Theory is one of the oldest methods used to determine the major trend in the stock market. To signal a bear trend, both the Dow Jones Industrial Average and the Dow Jones Transportation Average must drop below their respective lows of previous secondary reactions. To signal a bull trend, both averages must rise above their respective highs of previous upward secondary reactions.

Market volume. If the market is rising and volume is heavy, most investors are optimistic. An increase in stock prices on light volume is unconvincing. The same is true with a decrease in prices.

New highs and new lows. This indicator supposedly measures continued upward (new highs) or downward (new lows) strength in the stock market. The steady weakening in the number of new highs is a signal of a weakening in the market's overall trend. The market is about to turn in direction.

Relative strength. The extent to which a security performs compared to the market as a whole or its particular industry measures relative strength. You calculate relative strength as: (security's price) ÷ (price index of the market, or industry). A rising relative strength ratio implies the stock is outperforming the market. Now is the time to buy the stock because technicians believe relative strength persists over time.

Wall $treet Week Index. This index is the creation of the PBS television program, *Wall $treet Week*. The moderator announces the index every Friday near the beginning of the program. The opinions of ten prominent technical analysts make up the index. When the net difference between bullish and bearish analysts is +5 or higher, prospects are for higher prices within six months. The index signals a bear market when the net difference between analysts' opinions is −5 or lower.

Market breadth. This indicator measures the number of stocks advancing, declining, or remaining unchanged at the end of the trading day. In a strong market, advancing stocks outnumber decliners two to one or more. Technicians calculate breadth by adding each day's advances and declines to their respective previous day's totals. The direction of the cumulative series suggests the broad market trend.

Tick and trin. These are measures of buying and selling pressure. An *up tick* is when a stock trades at a price higher than its previous trade. A trade at a lower price is a *down tick*. The cumulative number of ticks for all stocks traded on the NYSE provides a sense of the direction of the market at a point in time. *Trin* compares the advancing and declining stocks to the advancing and declining volumes: (number of issues advancing in price ÷ number of issues declining in price) ÷ (total up volume ÷ total down volume). A *trin* < 1 suggests buying demand; *trin* > 1 suggests selling pressure.

to change direction. Technicians believe also that volume goes with the trend. In a major uptrend, volume increases as the price rises. When volume contracts as prices rise, the forecast is for an imminent decline because the rally is apparently beginning to starve for want of anxious buyers. Conversely, if prices continue to fall as volume declines, the forecast is for a rally in the near future. This opinion supposes that those who wanted to sell have done so already and all holders left have strong positive convictions about that stock's future.

TABLE 10-6

MONETARY INDICATORS

Prime rate indicator. This indicator is the short-term interest rate that banks charge their least risky business customers. Any decline below 8 percent is a bullish signal.

Fed indicator. An increase in either the discount rate or reserve requirements is bearish. Technicians consider two, or more, successive cuts in either the discount rate or reserve requirement a bullish signal.

Installment debt indicator. The Federal Reserve issues the monthly total of consumer installment debt report around midmonth for the month ended about six weeks earlier. For example, data for September come out about mid-November. Technicians read a buy signal when the year-to-year change (measured each month) is falling and drops under 9 percent. The reverse situation provides a signal to sell.

The discussion in this table is based on the book by Martin Zweig, a highly successful technician, Martin Zweig's Winning on Wall Street *(New York: Warner Books, Inc., 1986).*

Comprehension Check

1. Describe the three areas of technical market indicators. Give examples of each.
2. In technical charting, what is the reason for using moving averages of stock prices rather than simply charting day-to-day stock price movements?
3. What are the basic premises for charting stock price movements?

10.6 SOME CAUTIONS ABOUT EMH AND TECHNICAL ANALYSIS

It is the *perception of future value* rather than current and past fact that influences most heavily the value of a security. With that in mind, we must expect prices to reflect the ever changing beliefs of all investors. In reality, price movements usually reflect an overreaction to news, good or bad. Also, if enough investors feel a company's common stock is a good buy at $27 per share, it will become a good buy if that level is reached. The orders to purchase *will* cause a rise in the value of the stock independent of any basic changes in the fortunes of the company.

The stock market is full of self-fulfilling prophecies. The free-market ideal that supply and demand for securities govern the market's price behavior does not contradict the notion of intrinsic value. It simply explains why security prices swing from one side of intrinsic value to the other. However, the swing in security prices also leads many people toward technical analysis. Technical analysts, like security analysts, recognize that patterns and fads are rampant in the market. Technicians, however, do not relate these patterns and fads to intrinsic value. If patterns send security prices swinging far above or below intrinsic value, then why bother to analyze value? Analyze patterns instead! So, the security analyst looks at demand for IBM products, while the technician looks at demand for IBM stock.

Some technical approaches that appear plausible may not be profitable. They may work under some conditions but can cause significant losses under others. Often there is little margin for error. The signals are either right or wrong. If the signal, or our interpretation of it, is wrong, we lose money.

FIGURE 10.10

PRICING PATTERNS: EXAMPLES OF TECHNICAL ANALYSIS CHARTS

Technicians believe that chart patterns foretell the direction of the stock being charted. Nontechnicians believe that interpreting charts is like reading tea leaves in a teacup—you see what you want to see.

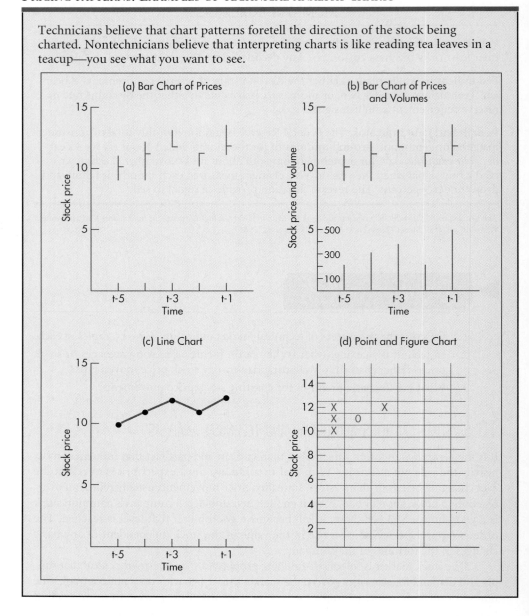

A pure technician ignores the underlying fundamentals of a security and considers financial markets to be weak-form inefficient. Serious shortcomings of technical analysis include the following.

- All data used in technical analysis are historical. It ignores future events.
- False signals frequently occur. A chart may show a sudden, deep decline, which is a signal to sell. The decline may be the result of one large trade at a lower-than-market price. The value of the stock may bounce back quickly.

- Technical indicators are mechanical and subject to errors, breakdowns, and misinterpretation.

Perhaps the main cautionary point about technical analysis has to do with whether the markets are efficient or inefficient. Whatever view you may hold about the efficient market debate, it is beyond dispute that the efficiency concept is central to fundamental policies of investment practice and corporate financial management. It follows that if market efficiency is at any time discredited by recent market history, the implications may be far-reaching.

Comprehension Check

1. What are the disadvantages of technical analysis?

10.7 THE NEXT STEP

This chapter brings Part III of the book to a close. The concepts we have examined about the valuation of bonds (Chapter 8), stocks (Chapter 9), and efficiency of markets (Chapter 10) provide the basis for valuation of the firm, which we will study in Part IV. We will see that the value of the firm equals the value of its issued bonds and the value of its issued stock. As we have mentioned before, the value of the firm is not the accountant's value reflected in the firm's balance sheet. The value of the firm is an economic value derived from discounting the future cash flows expected to be received by security holders.

We will also see in Part IV that the firm's value is affected by the proportion of its debt-to-equity financing. Too much debt relative to equity lowers firm value, as does too little debt relative to equity. This result suggests an optimal debt-to-equity financing relationship exists. We will find that the firm's financing is important for determining its cutoff rate for accepting investments. Shareholder wealth is diminished if investments earn less than the cutoff rate. On the other hand, accepting investments earning higher than the cutoff rate contributes to shareholder wealth.

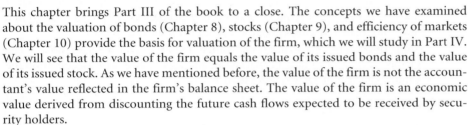

SUMMARY ▼▼▼▼▼▼▼▼▼▼▼▼

A COMPETITIVE MARKET SYSTEM

- Competition among investors to buy or sell securities is critical for making markets efficient.

THE EFFICIENT MARKET HYPOTHESIS

- In competitive markets each investor has access to all information necessary to determine intrinsic value of each security. This information is generated randomly, thereby causing prices to change randomly as investors incorporate the information into their analysis of intrinsic stock value.
- Efficient markets reflect fully and instantaneously what is knowable about a security in its price.

KEY TERMS
▼

A Competitive Market System

Market efficiency

The Efficient Market Hypothesis

Efficient market hypothesis
 (EMH)
Semistrong-form efficiency
Strong-form efficiency
Weak-form efficiency

- Expected return for each security is proportional to its risk and investors cannot consistently earn more than the appropriate risk-adjusted rate of return for the security.
- In reality markets are not fully efficient. Thus, researchers identify an event's impact on returns as being weak-form efficient, semistrong-form efficient, or strong-form efficient.

IMPLICATIONS FOR THE EFFICIENT MARKET HYPOTHESIS

- In an efficient market detailed security analysis is futile, as is market timing.
- Corporate finance managers should not concern themselves with either the timing of new securities issues or the types of securities issued. Nor should managers view that the risk of an investment varies from firm to firm. The market determines the appropriate risk.
- Managers should match the maturity of funds with the duration of the investment need.

EVIDENCE FOR AND AGAINST MARKET EFFICIENCY

- Literally hundreds of studies over the past several years support the efficient market theory. The overall conclusion is that financial markets in the United States are relatively efficient, although some inefficiencies exist.
- Some persistent anomalies exist which puzzle financial economists. The October 1987 stock market crash caused many people to seriously question the validity of the efficiency market theory.

TECHNICAL ANALYSIS

- The randomness in stock price movement leads many investors to use technical analysis in an effort to uncover some sort of order existing in price changes.
- Technicians ignore the concept of market efficiency and try to capture the psychological and emotional characteristics of investors.
- Technicians use a large assortment of indicators in their attempt to uncover patterns. These indicators fall into one of three groups: sentiment indicators, market structure indicators, and monetary indicators.

SOME CAUTIONS ABOUT EMH AND TECHNICAL ANALYSIS

- Price movements for securities usually reflect an overreaction to news. Prices swing from one side of their intrinsic value to the other.
- Technical analysis ignores much relevant information and concentrates solely on patterns generated from historical data.

FURTHER READING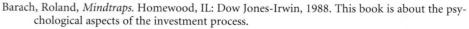

Barach, Roland, *Mindtraps.* Homewood, IL: Dow Jones-Irwin, 1988. This book is about the psychological aspects of the investment process.

Bernstein, Peter L., *Capital Ideas: The Improbable Origins of Modern Wall Street.* New York: The Free Press, 1992. This book provides an entertaining account of how the modern finance revolution grew.

Fogler, H. Russell, *Analyzing the Stock Market: Statistical Evidence and Methodology,* 2nd edition. Columbus, OH: Grid Publishing, Inc., 1978. This short book provides a readable mathematical discussion of the stock market.

Malkiel, Burton G., A *Random Walk Down Wall Street,* 2nd ed. New York: W. W. Norton & Company, 1981. The author describes the operations of the stock market and the methods used by professional investors.

Stoken, Dick A., *Strategic Investment Timing in the 90's.* Chicago, IL: Probus Publishing Company, 1990. The book was honored as the best investment book by the Stock Trader's Almanac.

SELF-TEST PROBLEMS ▼▼▼▼▼▼▼▼▼▼▼

ST10-1. Comment on this observation: If the stock market is efficient and investors cannot expect to earn high returns on their stocks, why invest in the stock market?

ST10-2. How do investors who practice technical analysis assess psychological and emotional factors in financial markets?

PROBLEMS ▼▼▼▼▼▼▼▼▼▼▼

A COMPETITIVE MARKET SYSTEM

10-1. Investors have widely diverse opinions about the future direction of the economy and earnings forecasts for various industries and companies. How is it possible for all these investors to arrive at an equilibrium price for any particular security?

10-2. Studies conclude that stock prices follow a random walk. Does this mean that stock markets operate in an irrational manner? Discuss.

THE EFFICIENT MARKET HYPOTHESIS

10-3. Describe the efficient market hypothesis and discuss its different forms.

10-4. Security markets may not be perfectly efficient. What is the rationale for expecting them to be highly efficient?

IMPLICATIONS OF THE EFFICIENT MARKET HYPOTHESIS

10-5. The efficient market hypothesis implies that you cannot earn returns in excess of market risk-adjusted levels. Yet in order for markets to be efficient, investors must be able to force prices back into equilibrium. If they earn profits in doing so, is this fact inconsistent with market efficiency?

10-6. In a perfectly efficient market no investor can consistently earn a profit. Is this statement true? Discuss.

10-7. Discuss the relevance of the efficient market hypothesis for the internal financial management of companies whose stock is publicly traded in the secondary market.

10-8. The net present value of a financial investment should be zero if markets are efficient. Discuss.

10-9. What is the role of financial analysts if security markets are highly efficient?

10-10. Suppose an article in a leading academic finance journal states that the best researchers conclude that the stock market is 95 percent efficient. Based on this news, most Wall Street investment firms have decided to retire all their portfolio managers and securities analysts. Security selection would be done randomly. What is wrong with this action?

10-11. Does the efficient market hypothesis encourage or discourage small investors from investing?

10-12. If the stock market is weak-form efficient, what do security prices reflect?

EVIDENCE FOR AND AGAINST MARKET EFFICIENCY

10-13. Discuss whether the following events violate the weak form of the efficient market hypothesis.

a. Mr. Weston has studied the historical price changes of common stock of several companies. As a result of his analysis, he has been able to beat the S&P 500 stock index over the past four years.

b. A study covering 15 years indicates that the historical correlation of price changes of the Carlsbad Company is 0.8 using a one-quarter lag. In other words, the change in price today is highly correlated with price change one quarter earlier.

c. Ms. Lorie has developed a trading rule which allows her to beat the S&P 500 return by 6 percent per year. Returns are risk adjusted and include all transactions costs.

10-14. What is the January effect in stock prices? Can you devise a simple strategy to take advantage of the January effect?

10-15. Discuss whether the following conditions are consistent with semistrong-form market efficiency.

a. The Berry Company has developed a computer model for selecting undervalued stocks. Testing the model on historical data shows that investors could have earned 7 percent more than the S&P 500 index, after adjusting for all transactions costs.

b. Elaine Arzac's investment strategy is to concentrate on stocks with low PE ratios and good earnings prospects. Over the past 20 years, the results of this strategy are very impressive. After adjusting for transactions costs, Elaine has beaten the S&P 500 by at least 9 percent per year.

10-16. Is the hypothesis of a semistrong-form efficient financial market contradicted in each of the following situations?

a. You are able to earn a consistent 4 percent risk-adjusted profit above normal market returns. Your investment strategy depends on analyzing historical stock prices using a computer program you wrote.

b. Your friend discovers that the cube root of any given stock price multiplied by the day of the week provides an indication of the direction in price movement with a probability of 65 percent.

c. The Securities and Exchange Commission filed suit against Texas Gulf and Sulphur Company in 1965. The suit alleged that some employees earned high profits on buying the company's stock before the general public knew about a large mineral deposit discovery.

10-17. Suppose today is your first day as a new security analyst. At lunch you argue strongly for the strong form of the efficient market hypothesis. Your supervisor looks at you oddly. What troubles the supervisor?

10-18. a. Explain the reasons why new equity issues are more common when share prices are high than when share prices are low.
   b. To what extent can the reasons given be considered inconsistent with the efficient markets hypothesis?

10-19. State Company has 2 million shares outstanding and West Company has 6 million shares outstanding.

On day 1: The market value per share is $2 for State and $3 for West.

On day 2: The management of West decide at a private meeting to make a cash takeover bid for State at a price of $3 per share. The takeover will produce large operating savings with a present value of $3.2 million.

On day 4: West publicly announces an unconditional offer to purchase all shares of State at a price of $3 per share with settlement on day 15. Details of the large savings are not announced and are not public knowledge.

On day 10: West announces details of the savings which will be derived from the takeover.

Ignoring tax and the time value of money between days 1 and 15, and assuming the details given are the only factors having an impact on the share price of State and West, determine for parts (a) and (b) the day 2, day 4, and day 10 share prices of State and West if the market is (i) semistrong-form efficient and (ii) strong-form efficient.

   a. The purchase consideration is cash.
   b. The purchase consideration, decided upon on day 2 and publicly announced on day 4, is one newly issued share of West for each share of State.

10-20. The efficient market hypothesis teaches us the following lessons:

Random selection of securities is as good as any other method. Therefore, just throw darts at the newspaper listing of stocks.

A buy-and-hold investment strategy is as good as any other. It is not necessary to follow and keep up with the economic fundamentals of the companies in which you own securities.

   a. Explain what the term *efficient market hypothesis* means to you. Describe the categories of tests relating to the model and their significance for the validity of the model.
   b. Examine the validity of the statements for (i) an investment manager of a large pension fund and (ii) a small private investor.

TECHNICAL ANALYSIS

10-21. Technical analysis is based on stock prices moving in repetitive patterns. What would you have to believe about the timing of the receipt of information by financial market participants in order to believe in the existence of such patterns?

10-22. Discuss the differences between technical and fundamental security analysis. Fundamental analysis seeks to determine the intrinsic value of the stock.

10-23. What are the implications of the three forms of market efficiency for technical and fundamental (intrinsic value) analysis?

10-24. Following are several test results from studies of technical trading systems. For each test result, identify the primary research error committed and comment as to why the error is applicable to the study.

a. Portfolio management using a filter rule (that is, buying a stock after it has appreciated in price by x percent, holding it until its price has depreciated by x percent, then selling the stock) outperforms a broad stock market index when the filter is very small (that is, when x is small).

b. An investment system estimated over the 1970 to 1980 time period indicates that the system outperformed a broad stock market index in the latter half of that period.

c. A portfolio composed of stocks of highly cyclical industrial companies outperforms a broad stock market index.

d. Buying and selling U.S. stocks based on a measure of liberal and conservative voting patterns in Great Britain produces returns that outperform a broad U.S. stock market index.

e. The price performance of a portfolio of initial public offering high-technology stocks outperforms a broad stock market index.

10-25. What is the New York Stock Exchange (NYSE) short-interest ratio? How is it used by technicians?

10-26. As a sentiment indicator, discuss the role of insider trading in technical analysis.

10-27. What is the confidence index? Explain the interpretation of a bullish signal in it.

LIBRARY ASSIGNMENTS

10-28. Watch the PBS television program called *Wall $treet Week,* which airs on Friday evenings, for two consecutive weeks. Report the status of the *Wall $treet Week Index* over this period. How would you interpret the index? Did the comments of the analysts appearing on the program those two weeks concur with the index?

10-29. Based on daily reports in the financial press, such as *The Wall Street Journal,* plot the number of new highs and new lows in the prices of New York Stock Exchange listed stocks for fifteen trading days. Prepare a short summary of your analysis regarding possible direction of the stock market.

10-30. Measure the current breadth of the stock market using the daily closing advances and declines on the New York Stock Exchange for fifteen trading days. Graph the breadth statistics (cumulative daily advances – cumulative daily declines) over this period and interpret the results.

COMPREHENSIVE PROBLEM ▼▼▼▼▼▼▼▼▼▼▼

10-31. a. What is the difference in the view of the security prices between investors who believe that financial markets are efficient and those who believe in technical analysis?

b. Define the three degrees of market efficiency identified by supporters of the efficient market hypothesis.

c. What is insider trading and what implications does it have for strong-form market efficiency?

d. If a major pharmaceutical firm announces quarterly earnings lower than had been expected by security analysts and investors, what do you expect would happen to the firm's common stock price that day?

e. A manufacturing firm is considering borrowing money to finance a major expansion of production facilities. Management estimates that sufficient funds will be generated to pay for the expansion over a five-year period. The company has the choice of obtaining the funds with one-year notes, currently costing 6 percent interest, or five-year bonds with an interest rate of 8 percent. The notes would have to be refinanced each year. Explain which alternative you would recommend.

    f. Was the stock market crash on Monday, October 19, 1987, consistent with the efficient market theory? How do you explain the sharp drop in stock prices on that Black Monday?

    g. Technical analysis includes a wide variety of approaches to stock valuation, selection, and timing. Briefly describe three types of technical indicators.

ANSWERS TO SELF-TEST PROBLEMS ▼▼▼▼▼▼▼▼▼▼▼▼

ST10-1. Markets are not fully efficient under all conditions. Therefore, investors should be concerned about the degree of efficiency as applied to certain events for particular stocks.

The observation disregards the fact that different securities will have different degrees of risk. The expected return for a security is proportional to its risk. Thus, while investors cannot expect to earn consistently more than the appropriate risk-adjusted rate of return, investors can select securities with a greater degree of risk and expect to earn a greater return to compensate for this additional risk.

ST10-2. Technical analysts believe that financial markets follow patterns that are affected by investors' attitudes because of a variety of psychological, economic, and political forces. Technicians measure the patterns of investors' attitudes by graphing or charting stock prices and the volume of transactions. Whether the personal motivation of investors is rational or irrational is immaterial to market technicians. They only care about measuring investors' motivations by the price movement of securities. Technicians believe that stock prices move in identifiable trends and the art of technical analysis is to identify changing patterns early for evidence of price movements, which would suggest a particular stock should be bought or sold to benefit from future price changes.

Video Case 10

Who Needs Experts?

from *20/20*, November 27, 1992

To attract investors, investments with higher risk must promise to pay higher returns. The risk of an investment depends on several factors—the uncertainty of future cash distributions and the return on other investments, that is, opportunity costs. Historically, bank deposits have paid 4 percent to 5 percent per year with only slight risk. Stocks are riskier so have returned about 10 percent to 12 percent per year, on average, but with a great deal of variation from year to year. Investors demand a higher return from stocks because of this variation. Investors can reduce risk by diversifying their investment portfolio.

Earning 10 percent to 12 percent does not seem like a very high return. We have all heard about people who have made a fortune in the stock market; that is, they have earned a return far in excess of the average market return. As this video describes, however, hiring experts does not necessarily assure you will beat the stock market. Professor Burton Malkiel, of Princeton University, is one of the country's foremost experts on the stock market and the author of *A Random Walk Down Wall Street.* He describes why Wall Street experts are no more likely than you or I, or a monkey throwing darts at the stock table, to pick a good stock. His explanation goes something like this. Stock prices change based on news about a company's or an industry's prospects. Good news sees prices rise, and vice versa. Since news is unpredictable, so are stock prices. The idea of a random walk comes from trying to predict the direction a drunken man will move next. You cannot tell, so the direction of each step is random, and therefore unpredictable based on previous directions the man has moved. If the random-walk theory is correct, then a randomly selected set of stocks will, on average, perform as well as any other set, including those selected by high-paid investment professionals.

The evidence discussed in this video supports the validity of the random-walk theory. On average (that can be translated as "over many analysts and a long period of time") the recommendations of expert stock analysts perform no better than the S&P 500 stock index. Investing in the S&P 500 is what is known as a "no brainer" on Wall Street. It is so simple it does not require any brain activity whatsoever. We can invest in the S&P 500, or other market index portfolios, by buying index mutual funds. These mutual funds usually have the lowest management fees of all mutual funds, which translates into additional savings. Alternatively, you can design your own portfolio by throwing darts to select stocks. You do not even need a monkey to do it, you can do it yourself and the result, over time, is as effective as implementing brokers' recommendations.

Study Questions

1. If the random-walk theory is correct, how can you explain investment managers like Peter Lynch, who consistently outperformed the stock market while managing the Magellen Fund?

2. Some investors, known as technicians or chartists, make their investment decision solely by examining the past price and volume information of stocks. Is this approach feasible under the random-walk theory of stock price movements?

3. Do you think that other markets have prices that follow a random walk? If prices do not follow a random walk, it suggests that someone knows the direction that prices will move. If so, what actions would that person take, and how would that affect prices?

CHAPTER 11

Creating Shareholder Value

"Two years ago, Sears was the nation's largest retailer. It's now number three. Its share price today is less than it was in 1986. In my opinion the reputation of the Sears Board of Directors also has fallen, due largely to its lack of energy and interest in making management accountable to shareholders. Make no mistake, a board's value translates into stock price." So wrote Robert Monks, a Sears shareholder, urging all Sears shareholders to vote for proposals he had placed on the agenda for the next shareholders' meeting.[1] Robert Monk was actively soliciting votes to force Sears's management and board of directors to focus on creating shareholder value.

While many corporate executives talk about shareholder value in their annual reports and speeches, most have not made it part of their everyday business decisions. It is easier to state the objective than it is to fulfill it in practice. Companies take different approaches to increasing shareholder value. For example, the 1984 annual report of Coca-Cola states that "to increase shareholder value over time is the objective driving this enterprise." The next page of the report mentions that to accomplish this objective "growth in annual earnings per share and increased return on equity are still the names of the game." In contrast, Georgia-Pacific Corporation says the way to provide superior return to its shareholders is to focus on creating shareholder value through the generation of *free cash flow*, which is cash flow from operations less normal investments (see Figure 11.1). The 1984 annual report of Hillenbrand Industries takes a similar position. It explains that shareholder value "is created when a company generates free cash flow in excess of the shareholders' investment in the business."

The point is that although each company states that its objective is to increase shareholder value, Coca-Cola attempts to accomplish the objective by emphasizing accounting indicators, whereas Georgia-Pacific and Hillenbrand emphasize cash flow. The accounting approach is fraught with problems. Accounting numbers are fairly elas-

[1]See the proxy solicitation by Robert Monk in *The Wall Street Journal*, May 8, 1992, p. A13.

FIGURE 11.1
THE ONLY YARDSTICK THAT COUNTS

THE ONLY YARDSTICK THAT COUNTS.

Much has been written about various ways
to measure corporate performance. But over the years, the
odds-on favorite would have to be earnings.

We think that a focus on earnings misses
a much more relevant factor.

Free cash flow.

And once again, we expect ours to remain strong.
Extremely strong. In fact, in a year when business has certainly
not been booming, our free cash flow will run close to
$1 billion. And we expect that number to average substantially
more in the coming years.

And the point?

Cash, not earnings, has put us on the fast track to debt reduction.
In fact, between cash from operations and the sales of
certain non-strategic assets, we're well ahead of schedule. Which
means we're adding economic value to the company
more quickly than many thought we could.

To be sure, there are as many opinions on the subject
of how best to judge value as there are people to pen them.
But we think we'll stick with cash. It sure works for us.

And we think it works for our shareholders.

Georgia-Pacific

tic, since management has much flexibility in how it wants to record transactions.[2] Cash flow, however, is the basis for valuing assets. Our discussion of valuing debt and equity securities in Chapters 8 and 9, respectively, showed this important point.

Our purpose in this chapter is to make the transition from the broader discussion of financial markets and the valuation of securities to the valuation of the firm. When you have completed this chapter, you should understand:

- How the firm's value is affected by the exchange of values between it and its customers and suppliers.
- The agency problem, or the series of conflicts that exist in the value-exchange system.
- How the interaction between the firm's investment opportunities and market rates affect the value of the firm.
- What causes a firm's value to increase, decline, or remain constant.
- How to calculate the value of the firm.

11.1 THE CORPORATE VALUE-EXCHANGE SYSTEM

A modern corporation is an interrelated set of contracts among several different groups: customers, employees, governments, investors, and vendors. Each group willingly enters into a contract with the expectation of receiving something of value from the arrangement. The exchange of values between the firm and the various parties can be summarized as follows. Suppliers provide inputs (values) to the firm, which are processed by the firm into products and services and ultimately supplied to customers in exchange for money. The firm uses the funds received from customers to help support its operations and satisfy obligations to suppliers: wages and benefits to employees in exchange for productive labor, technical skills, or management; payments to vendors for quality materials or services; interest and principal payments to creditors for use of their funds; taxes to governments; and dividends to shareholders.

The following Financial Reality article outlines how Cooper Industries, a firm with over $6 billion in sales, views its value-exchange system. The last sentence of the reading ends by stating that the key objective of the value-exchange system is to enhance shareholder wealth. This objective is not easy to meet. In reality, conflicts among various participants of the value-exchange system impede satisfying the shareholder-wealth-maximization objective.

The source of the conflict between consumers and the firm is rooted in whether the consumer can rely on the firm to fulfill its obligations in terms of providing adequate products or services now and in the future. The reputation of the firm, which translates into economic value for shareholders, is the issue at stake. A firm with a low reputation faces extreme difficulty in encouraging consumers to buy its products. For example, American Express lost more than two million cardholders in the early 1990s because management failed to understand that consumers preferred value to prestige. Consumers wanted "plastic" that could be used anywhere, not just in fine restaurants

---

[2]You may recall from your accounting classes that several different ways exist to record sales (percent of completion, installment, or point of sale). Each method results in different revenues for the period. Differences in recording costs also exist. Does the firm use straight-line depreciation or some accelerated method? Should bad debt expense be, say, 3 percent or 4 percent of sales? Should inventory be recorded using first-in, first-out or last-in, first-out methods? These are only a sample of the many alternatives available to management.

BEST VALUE DELIVERED

Cooper Industries is in the business of creating value for its customers and shareholders. Management asserts that customers buy Cooper's products and shareholders invest in the company because they judge Cooper to provide value.

What constitutes value?

The word is elusive. It defies easy definition. The problem is that most efforts at definition make it seem very abstract or highly subjective, while to most customers, value is something much simpler. However hard to articulate, they know it when they see it.

Economists have attempted to quantify value by talking of "units of satisfaction" or "utils." While this may be helpful to economists, it is of little help to a manufacturer competing in the real world for a customer's order. The one clear message that emerges is that the customers are not just the ultimate judges of value, they are the only judges who count. The customers we know don't sit down and calculate the units of satisfaction they expect from a product, but they do look for value—and they either find it, or they don't. When they don't, we lose a customer.

In any case, the fact that something is hard to define doesn't mean it isn't quite real and very important.

Value comes in many forms. For some buyers, value simply means the lowest price; for them, that's the end of the discussion. Others will settle for nothing less than the highest quality, never mind the cost. Those are the extremes. More typically, price and quality are just two of the elements of value.

Customers also assign value to such criteria as design, performance, durability, delivery, safety and service or to less tangible factors, such as a manufacturer's reputation, or the comfort level that comes with doing business with one company with an established reputation rather than another. Since value reflects what something is worth to the customer *as seen through the customer's eyes*, success in manufacturing is determined by the ability to look outward to the marketplace. That's how manufacturers create value—by attending closely to the needs of their customers. An inward concentration on costs, organization, management, and facilities is also necessary—but only to the extent it adds or creates value for the customer.

There are, indeed, examples in which the sole determinant of value is cost or selling price. But they rarely involve manufactured products. They are more likely to be about commodities, such as copper, which have a world price that moves up or down depending on supply or demand. The copper one buys will be of a prescribed standard quality, no matter where it was mined, by whom, or how. Only when it passes through the hands of a fabricator and value is added does the raw material emerge as a unique and distinguishable product.

At Cooper, we are in the business of making products that deliver value. We add value to commodities by manufacturing thousands of useful and necessary products. Our challenge is to make them so different that our customers, for one reason or another, consider them to be of greater value than those available elsewhere. Our goal is to provide consistently the best value delivered.

We believe that a constant focus on providing value to our customers is the key to improved earnings and, consequently, to meeting our other objective of providing shareholders with a superior return on their investment.

Source: Cooper Industries 1991 Annual Report, pp. 13–15. Used by permission.

and upscale retail stores. Consumer unrest was considered a major reason for significant decline in the stock price of American Express during this period.

Labor and vendor conflicts can cause serious problems for the firm. Lost production due to employee strikes or vendors' unwillingness to ship materials may result in lost customers because of unavailability of product. If the problems are well publicized, customers may also boycott the firm in sympathy with the employees or vendors.

Investor conflicts may arise if some investors perceive the firm to be less socially responsible than they would like. These investors are known to sell their securities because a company operates in a racially troubled country, because a firm manufactures war materials, or because it is a heavy industrial polluter. Johnson & Johnson Company created a dilemma for socially responsible investors. J&J has long been recognized as a business committed to its employees and communities. It was one of the first corporations to endorse the rights of individuals diagnosed with the AIDS virus. The company receives praise for its child-care programs, sick-care services, and flextime for employees. However, Johnson & Johnson is the fifth largest corporate user of animals in testing.[3] Can socially conscientious investors adversely affect the value of Johnson & Johnson's stock price? Unlikely, but the firm's management dislikes negative publicity.

Comprehension Check

1. Describe the corporate value-exchange system.

11.2 PRINCIPAL-AGENT PROBLEMS

An aspect of the corporation's value-exchange system that is of great interest to the study of finance is the principal-agent problem that exists between shareholders and management. A survey of finance officers in the largest British companies found that maximization of shareholders' wealth is neither the only goal of management nor is it the most important. The results summarized in Table 11.1 show that maximization of stock price (that is, shareholder wealth) ranks fourth. An earlier study in the United States found similar results.[4]

A much-debated reason that maximization of shareholder wealth may not be of top priority with many managers is because a *separation of ownership from management* exists in most publicly traded firms. Separation of ownership from management means that responsibility for administering companies is conferred to professional managers (agents). These managers effectively control the firm by their decisions, even though shareholders (principals) are the legal owners. Since the ownership of shares in large firms is often diffused, most individual shareholders have neither influence on, nor interest in, corporate governance issues such as the election of board members. Therefore, boards are largely responsive to management. Management, in turn, can ignore shareholders and run companies as it sees fit.

For example, the annual shareholder meeting is not an open forum for discussion. With the permission of the U.S. Securities and Exchange Commission (SEC), the firm places curbs on proposals made from the floor. In particular, unless a shareholder

[3]The source of this information is John C. Harrington, *Investing with Your Conscience* (New York: John Wiley & Sons, Inc., 1992), p. 122.

[4]See the article by J. W. Petty, D. F. Scott, and M. M. Bird, "The Capital Expenditure Decision-Making Process of Large Corporations," *The Engineering Economist* (Spring 1975), pp. 159–172.

TABLE 11-1	

IMPORTANCE OF FINANCIAL OBJECTIVES

Rank	Objective
1	Maximize percentage return on assets
2	Maximize earnings or earnings per share
3	Target share of the market
4	Maximize stock price
5	Target growth rate in earnings per share

Source: R. H. Pike, "Owner-Manager Conflict and the Role of the Payback Method," Accounting and Business Research (Winter 1985), pp. 47–51.

owns at least $1000 of the company's stock and has held it for at least one year, the shareholder is unable to file a resolution, no matter how much merit it might have, unless the issue relates to executive compensation.

There is much discussion in both practitioner and academic journals arguing that a number of factors exist to induce managers to act in the best interests of shareholders. These factors are derived from an assumption that the more unfavorable the expected consequences to the manager who decreases the wealth of shareholders, the less likely the manager will act against the interests of shareholders. The primary factors that are expected to induce management to align its interest with shareholders are:

- Management holds a relatively large ownership position.
- Management compensation is tied to shareholder return performance.
- Management faces loss of its position if the firm is taken over by another firm.
- Management faces a competitive labor market for its skills.

11.2.1 Ownership Position by Management

We would expect that managers with more stock ownership in the company would identify more closely with the shareholders' economic interests. However, a survey of *Fortune* 500 firms found that most chief executive officers do not have significant equity positions in their firms.[5] Even when managers own shares in their company, their perspective on risk may differ from that of shareholders. Managers, like most people, act in their own self-interest.

11.2.2 Compensation and Shareholder Return

A direct means of linking top management's interests with those of shareholders is to base management compensation, and particularly the incentive portion, on market returns realized by shareholders. In many cases, this linkage is accomplished by issuing the executives *stock options* on the company's common stock. These options have an expiration date sometime in the future, as determined by the board of directors.

---

[5]M. McComas, "Atop the *Fortune* 500: A Survey of the CEOs," *Fortune,* 113 (April 28, 1986), 26–31. *Fortune* 500 refers to the 500 largest manufacturing companies included in the annual financial survey by *Fortune* magazine.

THIS YEAR'S MODEL

Don't like the salary? Just change the formula.

For several years, the formula for determining a chief executive's bonus has been simple: As profits or stock prices rise, so does the bonus. But times are changing. Corporations are patching together innovative systems that take into account everything from quality improvement to buying and selling assets. The upshot: Executive pay can soar even when the company does poorly.

Chief executive bonuses typically are drawn from a pool made up of a percentage of net income that exceeds a certain return on equity; say 5 percent of the net that exceeds an 8 percent return on equity. But if net income falls, so does the bonus pool. Unless, that is, a company changes its absolute performance standards to relative ones. When companies compare performance with a group of competitors, the chief executive of the best-performing company would get a pay raise—even if every company in the group is doing poorly. Companies in troubled industries are especially likely to turn to this method.

Some companies are using flexible measures to compensate chief executives. Unlike the traditional fixed formulas, the flexible ones aren't spelled out in the corporate proxies, so it is harder to tell what the chief executive is being paid for. Among the objectives: divesting underperforming business units, synchronizing technology at diverse factories, laying off people, and restructuring money-losing operations.

Some companies are turning to a relatively new "sum of the awards" approach. Under the traditional formula, a CEO's entire bonus depends on a target return on equity or investment of the company. Using the new method, perhaps only 50 percent of the CEO's bonus would be based on return on equity or return on investment. Another 25 percent would be based on comparisons with competitors and a final 25 percent on successful restructuring of a troubled division. The percentages set by the board of directors can differ depending on a company's situation.

The concept of stock options is that if the company does well, the executives can exercise their options. This means the executives can convert the options to common stock of the company by paying a price that is well below the market value of the shares. The executives receive immediate reward. If the company does not do well, the options lose their value and the executives are not rewarded. Although stock option compensation sounds like a good way to reward executives, stock options can encourage management to optimize performance in the short run before the options expire while ignoring the long run.

Rather than link incentive compensation directly to the market returns earned by shareholders, most *Fortune* 500 companies tie annual bonuses and long-term performance plans to internal financial goals, such as accounting earnings, accounting return on equity, or how the company compares to its competitors (see the above Financial Reality reading). Unfortunately, these criteria often conflict with how the financial market values common stock. If incentives are largely based on factors not determined by the market, such as accounting earnings, management might be motivated to pursue strategies shareholders view as unsound. In such a situation, what is economically irrational from the shareholder viewpoint may be perfectly rational for the executive.

11.2.3 Threat of Takeover

If managers are significantly exploiting shareholders, such action should be reflected automatically in a lower stock price of a publicly traded firm and, thereby, lower shareholder wealth. A lower price, relative to what it might be with more efficient management, offers an attractive takeover opportunity for another company, which usually replaces incumbent management. The threat of an unsolicited takeover and the possible loss of executive jobs is supposed to act as a constraint on corporate managers who might choose to pursue personal goals at the expense of shareholders.

In 1988, Coniston Partners initiated a shareholder revolt at Gillette, Inc. to force a sale of the business. Coniston had no complaint whatever with the excellent progress of Gillette, other than it thought Gillette management was not promoting the company vigorously enough in the financial markets. Coniston thought the company could be sold for more than its then trading price.[6]

In recent years, management has shown great ingenuity in escaping the clutches of unwanted suitors. Table 11.2 outlines the major defenses to thwart a takeover.

Possibly one of the greatest abuses of executive power in this antitakeover defense process is the changing of corporate bylaws to deprive or delay the transfer of control to an acquiring raider. The aim of the defensive bylaws changes is to retain present management's clout in the firm past the time it legally has a controlling interest. For instance, the elimination of *cumulative voting* in favor of *majority voting* can greatly diminish your voting power as a shareholder. Under **cumulative voting** you can allocate all your votes to just one candidate, thereby possibly helping to elect at least one member of the board of directors who is sympathetic to your concerns. Suppose there are four directors to be elected and you own 200 shares. Thus, you have a total of 800 votes: 4 directors × 200 shares. Under cumulative voting, you can cast all 800 votes for your favorite candidate. The alternative voting system is called *majority voting*. Under **majority voting,** you can cast a maximum of 200 shares for any one candidate.

Gulf Oil management, in defending its position against a takeover lead by T. Boone Pickens, convinced shareholders to approve a switch of its state of incorporation to Delaware which did not require cumulative voting. Gulf's stock price at the time was about $40 per share. Only the persistence of T. Boone Pickens enabled stockholders to eventually sell their Gulf stock to a white knight at a price near its true worth of $80 per share.

Other bylaws changes often used include the elimination of preemptive rights, the requirement that board of directors vacancies be filled by remaining directors, and an increased percentage of votes needed to call a shareholder meeting or approve a merger. The clear intent is to vest control in incumbent management. Significant costs can be incurred in pursuing antitakeover measures. As the Financial Reality article on page 388 explains, a long-term employee and shareholder of a company lost most of his retirement savings as management tried to defend against an unwanted suitor.

11.2.4 Labor Market for Executives

Another often stated remedy for aligning management's interests with those of shareholders is the executive job market. Managerial labor markets are an essential mecha-

Cumulative voting. A voting system in which a shareholder may cast votes equal to the number of shares owned times the number of directors to be elected. The votes may be cast for only one director.

Majority voting. A voting system in which the number of votes a shareholder may cast for any director may not exceed the number of shares owned.

[6]See Louis Lowenstein and Ira M. Millstein, "The American Corporation and the Institutional Investor: Are There Lessons from Abroad?" *Columbia Business and Law Review* (1988), pp. 744–745.

TABLE 11-2

ANTITAKEOVER DEFENSES

Poison Pill. This technique triggers actions that make the target financially unattractive or by giving target shareholders rights to demand conversion into securities of the bidder on terms attractive to the target company but not to the bidder.

White Knight. Sometimes a company cannot resist a takeover attempt alone and resorts to offering itself to another company (the *white knight*) that it considers more suitable.

Shark Repellent. The directors amend the certificate of incorporation to permit additional defense measures if they feel they have sufficient votes to do so. For example, they might try an amendment requiring a supermajority ratification of any merger proposal, say, 75 percent.

Golden Parachute. Senior managers worried about losing their jobs as a result of a takeover contrive *golden parachutes* for themselves. The parachutes consist of lucrative bailout measures such as large severance pay or stock allowances in case of a takeover.

Dual Class Recapitalization. Management has the company distribute a second class of common stock that possesses superior voting rights (for example, 15 votes per share). The new shares can only be sold to the company. Over time, management's voting power increases as shareholders sell their shares.

Employee Stock Ownership Plan (ESOP). Management has the company purchase a large block of common stock (or voting preferred stock) in the secondary market and sells it to a company-sponsored ESOP. Management votes the ESOP's shares until they are distributed to employees, which typically takes place over several years.

Staggered Election of Directors. The company's board of directors is divided into three equal classes. Only one class stands for reelection each year. A hostile raider cannot obtain control through a single proxy contest.

Pac-Man Defense. The company under attack makes a counterbid for the common stock of the acquirer.

Standstill Agreement. Target company gets the prospective acquirer to agree, during the term of the agreement, (1) not to increase its share holdings above a specified percentage and, usually, (2) to vote its shares with management. The potential acquirer is often given a significant monetary amount, called *greenmail*, to agree to the agreement.

Leveraged Capitalization. The company borrows a large sum of money and distributes the loan proceeds, along with any other excess cash, to its shareholders as dividends. The additional debt on the company's balance sheet is designed to make it more difficult for a takeover raider to fund the acquisition with borrowed funds.

Litigation. The company files suit against the bidder alleging violation of state takeover statute(s), antitrust laws, securities laws, or other laws or regulations.

Share Repurchases or Sales. The company uses excess cash or borrows cash to repurchase a large number of its shares in the secondary market. Alternatively, the company repurchases shares from the takeover raider with any premium over fair market value representing greenmail. As a third alternative, the company sells shares to a "friendly" third party.

▼▼▼▼▼▼▼▼▼▼▼▼▼

ESOP's Fable, an Unhappy One

Just before Halloween, the stockholders of the Harcourt Brace Jovanovich publishing company received in the mail a 264-page book explaining the ins and outs of a proposed merger between HBJ and General Cinema Corporation. I own 9839.55 shares, the rewards of working for HBJ for 26 years. As a member of the employee stock ownership plan, I never had control of those shares. I could not sell them when they were at $18, the high three years ago, unless I quit my job and thus gained control of the stock. Now General Cinema has bought them for 75 cents a share—payable not in cash but in chits convertible to GCC stock. The stockholders voted in favor of this offer at a special meeting on Saturday. HBJ advised a yes vote from the stockholders, saying 75 cents a share was about as much as we were going to get.

This was the second time around on the deal. The first time, this spring, GCC offered to pay HBJ bondholders certain fractional proportions, ranging from 32 to 91 cents on the dollar and give stockholders $1.30 a share. But the bondholders wanted more and scotched the deal. My nest egg, once worth $177,000, has just been marked down to about $6000.

Now, at least, it's under my control: On May 7, HBJ sold the magazine I edited for them, *Michigan Farmer,* and its ten other state farm magazines to Capital Cities/ABC, Inc. The new owner wanted the titles but not all the personnel, so HBJ terminated about 50 people, including me.

The chief culprit is William Jovanovich, now retired. In 1987, as chairman of the board of the company that has had his name on it since 1955, he led an ego-driven charge to keep it there. On May 18 that year, HBJ had received a letter from Robert Maxwell offering to buy HBJ for $44 a share in cash. I had 3000 shares then, so for me this deal was worth $132,000. Stockholders never got to vote on that. Mr. Jovanovich and the board turned the offer down.

The board opposed an alternate plan, the HBJ Recapitalization. Without stockholder vote, it declared a dividend of $40 a share in cash, plus one share of HBJ preferred stock, a new class worth $12 a share. Suddenly I was to get $52 for each of my 3000 shares, a deal now worth $156,000 for my retirement account. This was all done with borrowed money. Faced with buying a company with $1.6 billion in new debt, Mr. Maxwell bought Macmillan instead. HBJ had fended off the raider—but it was left hopelessly crippled. Employees were in a quandary. We could keep our jobs, and work to pay off this monstrous debt, or quit and cash in. The dividend was paid to ESOP members in new stock, bumping my numbers from 3000 shares to nearly 10,000. I liked my job, so I stayed. For a while, the stock went up, and my retirement account grew to a value of $177,111.90 before the precipitous slide began. But soon the unraveling began.

nism for motivating managers to function in the best interests of shareholders, since managers compete for positions both within and outside of the firm. The increasing number of executive recruiting firms and the length of the "Who's News" column in *The Wall Street Journal* (see Figure 11.2) are evidence that the managerial labor market is very active. What is less apparent is how the financial market evaluates managers. Within the firm, performance evaluation and incentive plans are the mechanisms for

FIGURE 11.2
"WHO'S NEWS"

The daily news indicates that the executive labor market is very active.

WHO'S NEWS

Tambrands Names as President, CEO Fogarty of Colgate-Palmolive U.S. Unit

By SUEIN L. HWANG
Staff Reporter of THE WALL STREET JOURNAL

Tambrands Inc., struggling with shrinking market share and a perceived lack of direction, named Edward T. Fogarty, head of **Colgate-Palmolive** Co.'s U.S. unit, as its president and chief executive officer, ending a search that lasted nearly a year.

Colgate appointed Lois Juliber, its 45-year-old chief technological officer, to succeed Mr. Fogarty, whose appointment at Tambrands is effective May 31. The move makes Ms. Juliber the highest-ranking woman in the giant consumer-products company's history and puts her in line to possibly succeed Reuben Mark, Colgate's 55-year-old chairman and chief executive.

Edward T. Fogarty

As president of the unit, Ms. Juliber, like Mr. Fogarty, will have responsibility for Colgate's consumer-products businesses in the U.S. and Canada.

The changes come at a crucial time for both Colgate and Tambrands.

Long Vacancies

Mr. Fogarty, 57, is assuming two posts that have been vacant since last summer, when Martin F.C. Emmett was abruptly ousted as chief executive by the board and President and Chief Operating Officer Charles J. Chapman was demoted. At the time, the tampon maker was roiled by charges that Mr. Emmett spent company money lavishly and had questionable dealings with outside consultants who were also his friends. Mr. Emmett has denied any impropriety.

The White Plains, N.Y., maker of Tampax tampons hasn't regained market share lost during Mr. Emmett's regime, and its share price, which traded as high as $70 in 1992, has been in a steady decline. Tambrands stock closed yesterday at $36.875, up $1.125 or 3.1%, in New York Stock Exchange composite trading.

Wall Street's rather mild reaction to Mr. Fogarty's appointment indicates growing concern about the company's outlook. Tambrands' first-quarter earnings were nearly flat at $22 million, or 58 cents a share, compared with the year-earlier $21.9 million, or 56 cents a share. Excluding the effect of an accounting charge taken in 1993, operating profit fell 32%. Sales fell 10% to $139.2 million from $154.3 million.

Analysts worry about new competition from **Kimberly-Clark** Corp., which recently launched a new tampon with a curved applicator.

Still, hiring Mr. Fogarty is something of a coup for Tambrands. As the months wore on, industry executives say numerous candidates turned the job down, leading Tambrands to eventually switch executive-search firms early this year.

Doing 'the Search Right'

A Tambrands spokesman said the board simply "wanted to do the search right. The search lasted as long as it took to find the right candidate."

Tambrands * Chairman Howard B. Wentz Jr., who is also a Colgate board member, first contacted Mr. Mark about the possibility of hiring Mr. Fogarty. Tambrands' board approved Mr. Fogarty's appointment at a meeting Monday night, and Mr. Fogarty announced his move to his staff yesterday morning.

While they were surprised by his departure, Colgate executives say Mr. Fogarty was unlikely to succeed Mr. Mark, who shows no interest in retiring anytime soon. Mr. Fogarty couldn't be reached for comment.

When Mr. Fogarty, who had worked for New York-based Colgate in the 1960s and early 1970s, returned to Colgate in 1989, he was viewed by many as a possible heir-apparent to Mr. Mark. Analysts say that Colgate's U.S. business performed reasonably well for the first few years of his tenure, but by the end of 1993, Colgate's U.S. unit was suffering in a number of categories from market-share erosion, which company executives have blamed on overly aggressive cost-cutting that stifled new-product activity.

Colgate, with about $7 billion in annual sales, is in the midst of an offensive to increase ad spending and accelerate new-product activity. Colgate's stock rose 25 cents, or 0.4%, to $58.25 in Big Board trading yesterday.

Mr. Fogarty brings an extensive marketing background, which his CEO predecessor at Tambrands lacked. In the mid-1970s, he was a vice president

Lois Juliber

and general manager of the predecessor to **Playtex Products** Inc., with responsibilities for marketing tampons there.

Outside director Mr. Wentz, who also serves as chairman of **Esstar** Inc. of New Haven, Conn., will continue as chairman of Tambrands.

* * *

SOUTHWESTERN PUBLIC SERVICE Co. (Amarillo, Texas) — C. Coney Burgess, 56 years old, was elected to the board of this utility company, increasing the number of members to 12. Mr. Burgess is chairman of **Herring Bancorp** of Vernon, Texas, and owns agricultural operations in the Texas Panhandle.

Wells-Gardner Names New Chief, Chairman, Posts 1st-Period Loss

By a WALL STREET JOURNAL Staff Reporter

CHICAGO — **Wells-Gardner Electronics** Corp. named Anthony Spier chairman and chief executive officer, effective immediately.

Mr. Spier, 50 years old, is former president and CEO of Oce-Bruning Inc., Itasca, Ill., an engineering-graphics company. He has been a Wells-Gardner director since 1990.

Mr. Spier succeeds Frank Myers, 64, who indicated he didn't wish to stand for re-election as a director or as chairman and CEO. Mr. Myers, who cited health reasons for his decision, joined the company as president in June 1989 and was named to the top post in April 1990.

Wells-Gardner, a maker of video monitors, also reported a widened first-quarter net loss of $1.3 million, or 33 cents a share, reflecting a $762,000 special charge for management reorganization. In the year-earlier quarter, the company had a loss of $236,000, or six cents a share. Sales slid 23% to $7.6 million from $9.9 million.

Management attributed the results to a decline in the market for coin-operated video-arcade games. Sales of video monitors to arcade-game customers fell 40%.

* * *

BANKAMERICA Corp. (San Francisco) — Joseph Bauman, head of business development for Citibank's derivatives business and chairman of the International Swaps and Derivatives Association, will join this bank as head of its U.S. financial engineering and risk management group, a newly created position. He will report to Robert D. McKnew, head of U.S. Capital Markets, and be based in San Francisco. The appointment of Mr. Bauman, 44 years old, reflects Bank of America's continued expansion of its derivatives business. Mr. Bauman had been with **Citicorp's** Citibank unit since 1992. Prior to that, he was a senior executive in global derivatives at **Chemical Banking** Corp. Mr. Bauman will have to resign as head of the ISDA trade group as a result of changing employers.

BORDEN Inc. (Columbus, Ohio) — Robert P. Magrann was named to the new position of senior vice president, sales, for Borden's North American foods division. He had been executive vice president of E.J. Brach Corp. Borden produces packaged foods, consumer products, packaging and industrial products.

BURLINGTON INDUSTRIES Inc. (Greensboro, N.C.) — John G. Medlin Jr. was elected a director of this textile company, expanding board membership to 10. Mr. Medlin, 60 years old, is chairman of **Wachovia** Corp., a banking company based jointly in Winston-Salem, N.C., and Atlanta.

CITICORP (New York) — This bank holding company named Michael Ricciardi, 38 years old, co-head of fixed income in the U.S. In this newly created position, Mr. Ricciardi will be responsible for developing Citicorp Securities Inc.'s investor base and jointly managing its fixed-income business. Mr. Ricciardi was most recently managing director of fixed-income sales at General Electric Co.'s Kidder, Peabody & Co. subsidiary.

FARR Co. (El Segundo, Calif.) — H.J. Meany was named chairman, president and chief executive officer. Mr. Meany, 71 years old, succeeds Charles R. Wofford, 61, who resigned to pursue other interests, the company said. Mr. Meany has been a Farr director since 1976, and Mr. Wofford joined Farr in 1991 from **Texas Instruments** Inc. Farr makes filters for particulate, liquid and gaseous filtration systems.

NETWORK GENERAL Corp. (Menlo Park, Calif.) — Charles J. Abbe, 53 years old, senior vice president for electronics at Raychem Corp., was elected a director of this software company, expanding board membership to seven.

THIOKOL Corp. (Ogden, Utah) — Richard L. Corbin was named senior vice president and chief financial officer, effective May 15. Mr. Corbin, 48 years old, succeeds James R. Wilson, 53, who was named president and chief executive last October. Mr. Corbin had served as chief financial officer and vice president, administration, for **General Dynamics** Corp.'s space systems division in San Diego. Thiokol makes solid-propulsion systems, ordinance and composite products for the space and defense industries.

WCT COMMUNICATIONS Inc. (Santa Barbara, Calif.) — Donald H. Sledge was named president of this long-distance telecommunications company, and will also hold the newly created position of chief operating officer. Mr. Sledge, 53 years old, assumes the president's position from Richard Frockt, 49, who remains chairman and chief executive. Mr. Sledge most recently served as interim head of operations of New T&T, a new telephone company in Hong Kong, and has held several other positions in various telecommunications concerns.

OLD AMERICA STORES Inc. (Howe, Texas) — The company said its president and chief executive officer, C. Wayne Brush, 54 years old, told it that he intends to step down from both posts when his employment agreement expires on Jan. 31, 1995. The home-decorating and arts and crafts retailer said Mr. Brush, the company's founder, will help hire and train a successor.

GTE Corp. (Stamford, Conn.) — Jeffrey S. Rubin, 50 years old, was named to the new position of senior vice president, corporate planning and development, at the telecommunications company.

ZENITH ELECTRONICS Corp. (Glenview, Ill.) — Ilene S. Gordon, vice president-operations for Tenneco Inc., was named a director of this maker of consumer electronic products. Ms. Gordon, 40 years old, succeeds G. Ralph Guthrie, retired chairman of Urban Investment & Development Co., who died last July.

monitoring managerial performance. The unresolved issue is whether these measures are reliably linked to the market price of the company's stock.

 Comprehension Check

1. Why is there a separation of control between management and ownership of large investor-owned corporations?
2. List the factors that may encourage corporate management to act in the interests of shareholders.
3. How have corporate top managements acted to prevent unsolicited (and unwanted) takeover attempts in recent years?
4. How can common stockholders possibly benefit from takeover attempts? What are possible disadvantages for shareholders of takeover attempts?

 ## 11.3 HOW IS SHAREHOLDER VALUE CREATED?

Economic returns. Payments to a firm in excess of the economic costs, including normal profit.

Efforts to increase shareholder value can be hampered by conflicts within the firm's value-exchange system. Nevertheless, maximization of shareholder wealth is still the most appropriate objective management *should* pursue. Managerial finance is grounded on the premise that managers should be evaluated by the **economic returns** they generate for shareholders: *dividends* plus *share price appreciation*. As managers consider alternative business strategies, those strategies expected to develop the greatest sustainable competitive advantage are those that also create the greatest value for the firm and its shareholders.

Shareholders, both current and prospective, analyze information about the firm, including its successes, failures, and conflicts. Because financial markets in the United States and other economically developed nations are relatively efficient in processing information, we can think of the market value of the firm as equaling the market value of its financial securities issued to investors. Suppose the market value of debt and equity is $3 million and $10 million, respectively. Then the value of the firm is $13 million:

$$\begin{aligned}
\text{Market value of the firm} \\
= \text{Market value of debt} + \text{market value of equity} \quad \text{(11.1)} \\
V = B + S \\
= \$3,000,000 + \$10,000,000 \\
= \$13,000,000
\end{aligned}$$

The equation shows that managers can increase shareholder wealth (equity) either by increasing the value of the firm or by decreasing the value of the debt with firm value staying constant. The second strategy results in value being transferred from debt investors to equity investors, which raises a conflict between creditors and shareholders.

The reality of the financial market is that all managers and companies are essentially in the business of allocating scarce funds to their most promising uses. To increase their company's stock price, managers must perform better than other competitors seeking investors' funds. The company must earn rates of return on investments that exceed the return offered by other companies of equal risk. If managers allocate resources efficiently, value is added to the funds placed at their disposal and the market value of the firm and its equity increase. If managers misallocate resources, the company's market value is less than the value a more competent management team could realize.

FIGURE 11.3

ECONOMIC MODEL OF VALUE

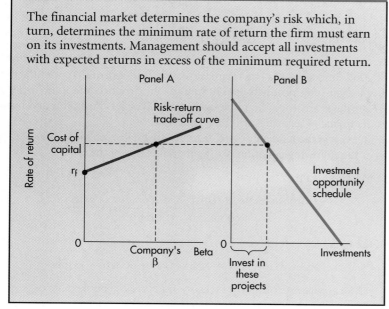

The financial market determines the company's risk which, in turn, determines the minimum rate of return the firm must earn on its investments. Management should accept all investments with expected returns in excess of the minimum required return.

unlevered firm 100% equity

11.3.1 Interaction of the Investment Opportunity Schedule and the Cost of Capital

The allocation of scarce resources should work as follows. A firm's management ranks proposed investment projects according to their prospective rates of return, as depicted in Figure 11.3, Panel B, by the *investment opportunity schedule*. The downward-sloping **investment opportunity schedule** indicates that the most attractive investment opportunities are taken first and the least attractive ones last, if at all.

We can conceptualize the minimum required rate of return management should accept for creating value in the company by relating the investment opportunity schedule to risk-return concepts studied in Chapter 5. Panel (a) of Figure 11.3 helps illustrate the relationship. Let's assume that we have determined the firm's risk to be as shown in panel (a). We will address how we determined this risk level in Chapter 14; it is not critical to the present discussion. At the company's risk level in panel (a), we draw a vertical line that intersects the upward sloping risk-return trade-off curve. At the point of intersection, we draw a horizontal line to intersect the rate of return axis. The intersection at the axis represents the firm's minimum required market rate of return, that is, its *cost of capital,* a topic we will discuss extensively in the next chapter. The firm's **cost of capital** is equal to the minimum percentage return investors expect to earn by buying a portfolio of stocks and bonds of other companies of similar risk.

By extending the horizontal line into panel (b) in Figure 11.3, we find where it intersects the firm's investment opportunity schedule. Let's assume that the investments in the firm's portfolio are of risk equal to that of the firm.[7] Only investments offering returns greater than or equal to the market rate of return (cost of capital) should be undertaken.

Investment opportunity schedule. A graph of the firm's investment projects ranked in order of their rates of return.

Cost of capital. Minimum market rate of return on new investments required to maintain the value of the firm.

[7]We relax this assumption in Chapter 14.

Managers should reject projects providing returns less than the cost of capital because the company's investors can do better with other investments. Management measures the amount of funds needed to undertake the investments on the investment axis.

11.3.2 Distribution of Value in the Financial Market

Essentially, the financial markets distribute economic value created by the firm's production of goods and services. The financial securities of a firm that manufactures and sells quality, sought-after products gain in value as the firm becomes more profitable. A firm whose products are not as highly sought after will be less profitable and have lower cash flows. Its financial securities will lose value.

We can express the tendency of value to flow from low- to high-return companies by looking at the following equation for the market value of the firm:

$$\text{Market value of the firm} = \frac{\text{Corporate rate of return} \times \text{book value of assets}}{\text{Required market rate}} \quad (11.2)$$

We define the variables as follows:

$$\text{Market value of the firm} = \text{Market value of debt} + \text{equity}$$

$$\text{Corporate rate of return} = \text{Economic profit} \div \text{book value of assets invested}$$

$$\text{Book value of assets} = \text{Accounting value of the firm, recorded at initial cost}$$

$$\text{Required market rate} = \text{Market determined rate (based on risk and diversification concepts discussed in Chapter 5)}$$

Theoretically, both expressions for the value of the firm, Equations 11.1 and 11.2, result in the same market value of the firm. Equation 11.2 states that the relationship between the rate of return a company earns and the market return investors require is what determines whether the company's market value is at a premium or at a discount to the book value of assets invested in the business.[8] If the corporate rate of return exceeds the required market rate, market value of the firm exceeds the book value of the assets used in the firm. (See Illustration 11.1.)

ILLUSTRATION 11.1

Value eroded; value created

Warren Buffett, chairman of Berkshire Hathaway, concluded in the company's 1984 annual report that if a company's rate of return does not at least equal that available to investors in the financial markets (adjusted for risk), the money should be distributed to shareholders. Otherwise, he says, the company might be invested to earn 8 percent when shareholders could on their own buy stocks with an average annual return of, say, 10 percent. The dollar that a

---

[8]Equation 11.2 is conceptually similar to the common stock model for perpetual cash flows discussed in Chapter 9:

$$P_0 = \frac{\text{Cash flows}}{\text{Required market rate}} = \frac{D_1}{r}$$

company keeps won't be worth a dollar in the market price of its shares unless it can produce a return of 10 percent on that dollar. Dollars invested at 8 percent will soon be marked down in market price and the shareholders will have suffered a loss of $0.20 per $1.

Market value of the firm

$$= \frac{\text{Corporate rate of return} \times \text{book value of assets}}{\text{Required market rate}}$$

$$= \frac{8\% \times \$1}{10\%}$$

$$= \$0.80 \text{ per } \$1 \text{ of assets}$$

If the firm is able to earn 15 percent on investments when investors require 10 percent, management's actions create value. For every dollar of invested assets, $1.50 appears in the stock market's valuation of the firm:

Market value of the firm

$$= \frac{\text{Corporate rate of return} \times \text{book value of assets}}{\text{Required market rate}}$$

$$= \frac{15\% \times \$1}{10\%}$$

$$= \$1.50 \text{ per } \$1 \text{ of assets}$$

The moral is this: *If management is to create value, it must identify investments that promise expected returns in excess of the required market rate.* Failure to invest in such projects leads to erosion of firm value which, in turn, means erosion in value of either the firm's debt or equity, or both.

11.3.3 Change in Economic Value

Let's use our earlier formula (Equation 11.1) for market value of the firm to discuss changes in that value. The formula shows that the firm's market value is the sum of its market values of equity *(S)* and debt *(B)*. Change in the firm's value, ΔV, can be viewed from the perspective of change in market value of any financial securities issued by the company. We can express the relationship as:

> Change in the firm's value
> $$= \text{Change in value of debt} + \text{change in value of equity} \qquad (11.3)$$
> $$\Delta V = \Delta B + \Delta S$$

Alternatively, we can express any change in value as investing in a new project, ΔI:

$$\text{Change in firm's value} = \Delta I \begin{cases} > & \text{Value increases} \\ & \text{No change in value} \\ < & \text{Value decreases} \end{cases} \qquad (11.4)$$

or

$$\Delta V = \Delta B + \Delta S = \Delta I \begin{cases} > & \text{Value increases} \\ & \text{No change in value} \\ < & \text{Value decreases} \end{cases} \qquad (11.5)$$

Equation 11.5 shows that in the financial market, the contribution of new projects to a firm's value is reflected in the market values of the firm's debt and equity securities. Since the firm only promises debtholders a fixed return on their funds, most of the changing value of the firm is reflected in the changing value of the equity, ΔS. As we will discuss in Chapters 12 and 13, any risk of debt default can change the value of debt, ΔB.

For a new investment (ΔI) to enhance firm value, it is necessary for the expected change in value of the company (ΔV), as a result of undertaking a new investment, to exceed the cost of the new investment: $\Delta V - \Delta I > 0$. Or stated differently, $\Delta V/\Delta I > 1$. The firm's value increases:

- If net operating cash flows can be made to grow without tying up any more funds.
- If funds can be diverted or liquidated from business activities that do not provide adequate returns.
- If new funds can be invested in projects that earn more, in a time value of money framework, than the market cost of funds.

When the new investment neither contributes to an increase in shareholder wealth nor erodes such value, then $\Delta V/\Delta I = 1$. The new investment earns simply the cost of financing it; that is, the corporate rate of return equals the required market rate. Management erodes shareholder value if as a result of the investment, $\Delta V/\Delta I < 1$. The new investment fails to earn the minimum required return. Erosion of value happens when:

- Management passes over new investments likely to earn more than the required market rate.
- Management invests funds in projects that earn less than the required market rate.
- Management retains existing assets that earn less than the required market rate.

The change in shareholder value is also dependent upon whether management pursues a short-term or long-term investment strategy. Maximizing shareholder value often requires commitments for resources that may adversely affect short-run cash flows but contribute significantly to long-run cash flows. For instance, Merck & Company, Inc. spends about 11 percent of each sales dollar on research and development. Merck's R&D expenditures amount to over $1 billion annually. It can be years before successful products emerge from any R&D efforts. However, Merck must fund such large R&D expenditures if it is to retain its leadership position in the pharmaceutical industry. Other examples of long-term value-maximizing approaches faced by management may require product, market, or labor relations strategies that lead to higher expenses in the short run but superior-quality products, higher market share, improved employee productivity, and higher operating cash flow in the long run.

The financial market's pricing of common stock suggests that management should resist actions that boost only short-term profits. The results reported in Table 11.3 suggest that financial markets take a long-term perspective of five years or more to price common stock of firms. We calculate the **long-term value index (LVI)** as:[9]

Long-term value index (LVI). The proportion of the stock price that is based on cash flows expected to be received after the first five years.

[9]Alfred Rappaport developed the index. He discusses it in "Don't Sell Stock Market Horizons Short," *The Wall Street Journal*, June 27, 1983, p. 28. He assumes that the growth rate in dividends equals the market rate of return.

TABLE 11-3

LONG-TERM VALUE INDEX

Company	Recent Stock Price	Sum of Dividends for Next 5 Years	LVI
General Motors	$ 60.00	$ 4.00	93.3*
Exxon	66.75	14.75	77.9
Ford Motor	64.63	8.00	87.6
IBM	52.75	5.00	90.5
Mobil	80.88	17.00	79.0
General Electric	109.13	14.40	86.8
Texaco	66.88	16.00	94.8
AT&T	54.25	6.60	87.9
Du Pont	54.50	8.80	83.9
Chrysler	58.63	4.00	93.2
Chevron	89.00	18.50	79.2
Philip Morris	58.13	13.00	77.6
Amoco	53.00	11.00	79.2
United Technologies	70.63	9.00	87.3
Occidental Petroleum	18.38	5.00	72.8
Procter & Gamble	58.25	6.20	89.4
Atlantic Richfield	102.63	27.50	73.2
Boeing	47.75	5.00	89.5
Tenneco	56.88	8.00	85.9

*$[1 - (\$4/\$60)] \times 100 = 93.3$

Dividend data taken from Value Line Investors Survey, *February 11, 1994. Prices are taken from* The Wall Street Journal, *February 17, 1994.*

$$LVI = \left(1 - \frac{\text{Sum of dividends for next 5 years}}{\text{Current stock price}}\right) \times 100 \qquad \textbf{(11.6)}$$

LVI provides an estimate of investors' confidence in the ability of management to create a sustainable long-term competitive advantage in its business. For instance, as of February 1994, the market was saying that only about 7 percent of the value of General Motors common stock was attributable to dividends over the next five years. Cash flows expected to occur beyond five years contribute about 93 percent of the stock's value.

▶ *Comprehension Check*

1. What is the purpose of a company's investment opportunity schedule? What does the schedule give as the minimum acceptable rate of return?
2. Explain how the formula for the market value of a firm (Equation 11.2) can result in an increase or decrease in investors' wealth.
3. Under what conditions does the value of a firm increase?

4. Based on Table 11.3, comment on the relative importance of short-term and long-term investment values.

 ## 11.4 FINDING SHAREHOLDER VALUE IN THE BUSINESS ENVIRONMENT

Let's examine the creation of shareholder wealth more explicitly. Ownership of the company means ownership of the *net assets* (assets less liabilities) currently held by the company. Shareholders own any residual future cash returns which may arise either from use or sale of these net assets. The size and timing of any future cash returns are dependent upon the present and future investment decisions of management. At one extreme management could decide to sell all the firm's currently held assets and, after paying off all debtholders, give an immediate and final cash return (liquidating dividend) to shareholders. A more likely management investment policy is to replace and perhaps expand currently held assets at future points in time. This strategy is likely to result in shareholders receiving a continuing and perhaps increasing series of cash returns from ownership. The former policy yields a minimum value of the shares of a company as the current salable value of its currently held net assets. The latter policy yields the share value of a company at a point in time as the market value of the future cash returns to shareholders.

It is the ongoing strategy that interests us. First, we will explain the underlying basics of firm valuation by valuing a no-growth firm. Next, we will add more complex features to the problem.

11.4.1 Valuation of a No-Growth, All-Equity Financed Firm

The simplest valuation case is a firm without any growth prospects and financed entirely with equity.[10] Such a firm is also called an **unlevered firm.** We define a **no-growth firm** to include the following features.

- No investment opportunities exist that allow the firm to increase its market value and profitability.[11]

- Management makes necessary investments to replace assets used up so that the new investments simply maintain current profitability and assets levels.

- Any operating cash flows remaining after making necessary investments are paid as dividends to shareholders.

The existing cash operating profit of an unlevered, no-growth company determines its value. We obtain this value by capitalizing, or dividing, the constant after-tax perpetual cash operating profit at a market rate of return that compensates shareholders for bearing business risk.[12] The formula for **value of an unlevered firm** is:

Unlevered firm. A firm financed entirely with equity financing.

No-growth firm. Firm whose investment opportunities simply earn the required market rate.

Value of unlevered firm. Value of a firm that is financed entirely with equity.

---

[10]The basis for much of the discussion on firm valuation is two articles by Franco Modigliani and Merton Miller. Although they were much criticized at the time, their theory is now accepted doctrine. For further information, see Franco Modigliani and Merton H. Miller, "The Cost of Capital, Corporation Finance and the Theory of Investment," *American Economic Review,* 48 (June 1958), 261–297, and "Corporate Income Taxes and the Cost of Capital: A Correction," *American Economic Review,* 53 (June 1963), 433–443.

[11]You can think of this feature in terms of our earlier discussion in this chapter where we stated $\Delta V/\Delta I = 1$; that is, change in value of the firm divided by new investment equals 1. The investment earns the minimum required rate of return and no more.

[12]Think of *cash operating profit* as cash accounting profit as opposed to accrual accounting profit. *Accrual accounting* records revenues and expenses when management considers the transaction to be complete, whether or not money has been exchanged at the time of the transaction. *Cash accounting* requires an exchange of money before management considers the transaction completed.

Value of unlevered firm

$$= \frac{\text{Constant cash operating profit} \times (1 - \text{tax rate})}{\text{Market rate that compensates for business risk}} \qquad (11.7)$$

$$V^u = \frac{COP \times (1 - \tau)}{r_u}$$

Business risk is the only risk affecting potential returns to shareholders of an unlevered firm. **Business risk,** also called *operating risk,* represents the uncertainty surrounding expected cash operating profit (COP). The following factors lead to high business risk:

> **Business risk.** The risk associated with the returns generated by a firm's assets as if the firm were financed entirely by equity. Risk associated with debt financing is ignored.

- *The relationship between the firm's performance and the economy is high.* General Motors' profitability increases when the economy grows and falls when the economy slows.

- *The firm has a small market share in a competitive industry.* Digital Equipment Corporation has a market share in the personal computer industry of less than 1 percent. With such a small market share, Digital cannot dictate direction for the personal computer industry.

- *The firm is small relative to its major competitors.* Microbreweries, like San Francisco's Anchor Brewing, own less than 1 percent of the market. In 1993, Philip Morris's Miller Brewing introduced an all-barley Reserve Amber Ale to compete against the microbreweries.

- *The firm is not very well diversified.* It depends on one or two products for its income. American Power Conversion was founded in 1981 to make solar power products. The products flopped and the company nearly went out of business. However, American Power Conversion was able to become a profitable company by manufacturing backup power supply products for personal computers and minicomputers.

- *The firm's cost structure has significant fixed operating costs.* Public utilities, such as Long Island Lighting, have massive investment in plant and equipment with the result that much of its costs are fixed. Long Island Lighting must depend on a friendly New York state government regulatory agency to grant utility price increases to offset rising costs.

Shareholders incorporate their assessment of these business risk factors into the market discount rate r_u of Equation 11.7. Illustration 11.2 outlines the procedure for capitalizing the cash operating profit to value an unlevered company.

ILLUSTRATION 11.2

Valuation of a no-growth unlevered firm

Let's suppose that Ethridge Publishing Company's cash operating profit is $2000 and its income tax rate is 28 percent. Management has financed investment in assets solely by issuing 1000 shares; it has not used debt. Shareholders of this unlevered company require a market rate of return (r_u) of 10 percent to compensate them for business risk.

Below is a partial income statement of expected cash earnings (or profit) based on cash and not accrual accounting.

Cash operating profit	
before interest and taxes (COP)	$2000
Interest expense	0
Cash earnings before taxes	$2000
Income taxes (28%)	560
Cash earnings after taxes	$1440
Number of shares outstanding	1000
Cash earnings per share ($1440/1000)	$ 1.44

Based on this information, the value of Ethridge Publishing is $14,400, computed as follows:[13]

$$V^u = \frac{COP \times (1 - \tau)}{r_u}$$

$$= \frac{\$2000 \times (1 - 0.28)}{0.10}$$

$$= \frac{\$1440}{0.10}$$

$$= \$14,400$$

With no debt financing, all of the company's $14,400 value belongs to its common shareholders. The stock price is $14.40 per share (= $14,400 ÷ 1000 shares) and cash earnings per share are $1.44. The firm's stock sells at a price-earnings (PE) ratio of 10 (= $14.40 ÷ $1.44). Stated differently, Ethridge Publishing stock sells for ten times expected cash earnings because each common share is worth $14.40. The firm does not have a $14.40 share price because it sells for ten times cash earnings.

11.4.2 Tax Benefit of Debt Financing

Suppose our no-growth, unlevered firm decides to change. Its managers wish to retire some equity and replace it with debt. Neither the assets of the firm nor the earning power of those assets change. The interest expense associated with debt financing is a tax-deductible expense to the business. For every $1 of interest cost incurred by the company, the government subsidizes the firm $1 × τ, where τ is the tax rate. This subsidy occurs because the tax statutes issued by the government allow interest expense as a deduction in computing taxable income. Thus, the company's after-tax interest cost is $1 × (1 − τ) per $1 of interest incurred. Alternatively, if the company finances with common stock and pays a dividend to shareholders, the government does not pay any part of the dividend. Hence, it is more expensive for management to finance the company with equity alone than with debt.

The value of the income tax saved by using some debt in place of some equity adds value to common share price. The additional value is the present value of the government

---

[13]Because the firm is unlevered, COP × (1 − τ) equals *cash earnings after taxes*. This relationship does not hold if the firm finances with both debt and equity, as you will see shortly.

"subsidy." Only the shareholders receive value from the subsidy because debt investors receive a fixed amount—their interest income. Illustration 11.3 shows the effects of debt financing. It causes earnings per share to increase.

ILLUSTRATION 11.3

Cash earnings with debt financing

Let's use the same information for Ethridge Publishing Company as in Illustration 11.2, but now assume that management replaces $7200 of financing, one half the equity ($14,400 ÷ 2) with debt, which costs 8 percent before taxes. Management uses the $7200 proceeds from debt financing to buy back 500 common shares at $14.40 each, the share price we calculated in Illustration 11.2.

	With No Debt	With $7200 Debt
Cash operating profit		
before interest and taxes	$2000	$2000.00
Interest expense ($7200 × 8%)	0	576.00
Cash earnings before taxes	$2000	$1424.00
Income taxes (28%)	560	398.72
Cash earnings after taxes	$1440	$1025.28
Number of shares outstanding	1000	500
Cash earnings per share: $1440/1000	$1.44	
$1025.28/500		$ 2.05

Cash _operating_ profit after taxes—not cash earnings after taxes—for the levered firm is:

Cash earnings after taxes	$1025.28
+ Interest expense × (1 − τ) = $576 × (1 − 0.28)	414.72
= Cash operating profit after taxes	$1440.00

Cash _operating profit after taxes (COPAT)_ for the levered firm equals the _cash earnings after taxes (CEAT)_ for the unlevered firm. Since the unlevered firm has no debt, by definition, its CEAT is synonymous with its COPAT. The distinction between COPAT and CEAT for the levered firm is that COPAT excludes the debt's interest cost, whereas CEAT includes it.

The preceding result should not come as a surprise. If some debt simply replaces some equity in the financing of the company's assets, neither the assets nor the earning power of the assets are affected. Therefore, _cash operating profit after taxes_ for the levered and unlevered firms must be the same, which is the case if you compare Illustrations 11.2 and 11.3.

We mentioned earlier that the government effectively subsidizes a firm $1 × τ per $1 of interest cost incurred when the firm uses debt financing. The amount of interest expense "paid" by the government increases the firm's market value of equity. Debt investors receive no part of the income tax savings because they are only promised a fixed payment (for example, 8 percent coupon rate). The cash flow saving to the firm is the difference in income taxes paid if management does not use debt to finance the firm versus the income taxes paid when management uses debt, that is, $1 \times \tau$ per $1 of interest. From Illustration 11.3:

Income taxes when no debt is issued	$560.00
Income taxes when debt is issued	398.72
Income tax saving	$161.28

Alternatively,

$$\text{Income tax savings} = \text{Interest expense} \times \text{income tax rate} \qquad (11.8)$$

$$= \$576 \times 0.28$$
$$= \$161.28$$

Notice in Illustration 11.3 that the levered firm could earn as little as $576 *cash operating profit before taxes* and still be able to pay the interest amount. In the absence of debt, with cash operating profit of $576, the firm would pay $161.28 in income taxes ($576 \times 0.28$). Thus, the risk associated with saving income taxes is the same risk of meeting the interest payment. Accordingly, the debt's market borrowing rate (r_d) of 8 percent is appropriate for discounting the income tax savings to a present value of $2016.

$$\text{Present value of tax savings} = \frac{\text{Tax savings}}{r_d} \qquad (11.9)$$

$$= \frac{\$161.28}{0.08}$$

$$= \$2016$$

The specific meaning of the present value of tax savings, $2016, is as follows. A firm in the 28 percent income tax bracket, which incurs interest expense of $576 each year in perpetuity, is actually only paying $414.72 [$= \$576 \times (1 - 0.28)$] of this amount annually. The government "pays" the balance of $161.28 ($= \$576 \times 0.28$). The value of the annual government subsidy of $161.28 received in perpetuity is $2016, as shown by Equation 11.9.

11.4.3 Valuation of a Debt and Equity Financed Firm

How does the tax subsidy affect firm and shareholder values? Very simply; it increases both of them. The logic is as follows. The capitalized value of cash operating profit after taxes is the same whether or not debt is used; that is,

$$\frac{\text{COP} \times (1 - \tau)}{r_u} = \$14,400$$

which, as shown earlier, is the value of the unlevered firm. We find the value of the levered firm (V^L) by adding the present value of the tax savings (PVTS) to the capitalized cash operating profit after tax value:

$$V^L = \frac{\text{COP} \times (1 - \tau)}{r_u} + \text{PVTS} \qquad (11.10)$$

$$= \$14,400 + \$2016$$
$$= \$16,416$$

Stated differently, the value of the levered firm equals the value of the unlevered firm ($V^u = \text{COP} \times (1 - \tau) \div r_u$) plus the present value of the tax savings associated with debt financing:

$$V^L = V^u + \text{PVTS} \tag{11.11}$$

Alternatively, the value of the levered firm is:

$$\begin{aligned} V^L &= \text{Market value of debt} + \text{market value of equity} \\ &= B + S \end{aligned} \tag{11.12}$$

Recall from Chapter 8 that we calculated the market value of debt by discounting its future cash flows. To simplify the discussion, assume that all debt issued by the firm has no maturity date (similar to the consols issued by Canadian Pacific in Chapter 7). If the required market rate of interest for the debt is 8 percent, which equals its coupon rate, the company's market value of outstanding debt (B) is $7200:

$$\begin{aligned} B &= \frac{\text{Coupon rate} \times \text{par value of debt}}{\text{Market rate of interest}} \\ &= \frac{0.08 \times \$7200}{0.08} \\ &= \$7200 \end{aligned} \tag{11.13}$$

(*Question:* What is the debt's value if the market interest rate is 7 percent and the coupon rate is 9 percent?[14])

We can calculate the equity value to be $9216 by rearranging Equation 11.12 as the value of the levered firm minus the value of the debt:

$$\begin{aligned} S &= V^L - B \\ &= \$16,416 - \$7200 \\ &= \$9216 \end{aligned} \tag{11.14}$$

In our example, only 500 common shares remain outstanding after issuing debt. Thus, the stock price per share should be $18.43 (= $9216 ÷ 500 shares). The stock price increases from $14.40 for the unlevered situation to $18.43 for the levered case. Or look at the stock price from this perspective. Without debt financing, the stock price is $14.40. The use of debt financing results in a tax subsidy of $2016, or $4.03 per share (= $2016 ÷ 500 shares). Adding the tax subsidy of $4.03 to the old stock price of $14 results in the new stock price of $18.43.

The price-earnings (PE) ratio for the levered firm is approximately nine times:

$$\begin{aligned} \text{PE} &= \frac{\text{Price per share}}{\text{Earnings per share}} \\ &= \frac{\$18.43 \quad \text{(from the preceding paragraph)}}{\$2.05 \quad \text{(from Illustration 11.3)}} \\ &= 8.99 \end{aligned} \tag{11.15}$$

Without the use of debt financing, the PE ratio was ten times ($14.40 stock price ÷ $1.44 earnings per share, as given in Illustration 11.2). Thus, based on the PE ratio, which is usually shown on the financial pages of the newspaper, this company's common stock

[14]Solution: $7200 × (0.09 ÷ 0.07) = $9257.14. Chapter 8 discussed that if the coupon rate equals the market rate, then the par value of the debt equals the market value of the debt. The debt's market value exceeds its par value if the coupon rate exceeds the market rate. Finally, the debt's market value is less than its par value if the coupon rate is less than the market rate.

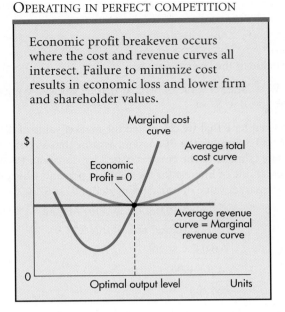

FIGURE 11.4

OPERATING IN PERFECT COMPETITION

Economic profit breakeven occurs where the cost and revenue curves all intersect. Failure to minimize cost results in economic loss and lower firm and shareholder values.

appears to be worth less under debt financing than as an all-equity financed firm. Such a result is absurd. Cash operating profit of the firm has not changed and both price per share and total firm value increase. If management uses debt financing, this result suggests that the PE ratio is seriously deficient as a valuation tool.

11.4.4 Valuation of Growth Opportunities

To this point, we have based our discussion of creating shareholder value on two restrictive assumptions: Cash operating profit stays at a constant level in perpetuity; and cash operating profit results in the firm's investments earning only the market rates required by investors. We will now relax the restrictions and show how investment in growth opportunities, which have expected returns in excess of the minimum required market return, increase both firm and shareholder values.

In our context, no growth means that the ratio of the change in value of the firm to the change in the firm's investment (assets) equals 1, $\Delta V/\Delta I = 1$. Incremental investments add no value beyond their cost to either the firm or the equity when they only earn the minimum required return. Your microeconomics course labeled this type of environment *perfect competition*. As shown in Figure 11.4, in **perfect competition** firms break even in an economic setting; they do not earn any economic profit.[15]

If management can find a way to influence the price of the product or service, then the firm may be able to earn economic profit. For example, economic profit is present if the firm's investors require a return of 9 percent yet investments earn 15 percent. We call such an environment *imperfect competition*. In **imperfect competition** management's objective is to maximize economic profit, not to minimize cost. Management

Perfect competition. A theoretical state that occurs in markets in which a large number of firms sell an identical product; there are many buyers; there are no restrictions on entry; firms have no advantage over potential new entrants; and all firms and buyers are fully informed about the prices of each and every firm.

Imperfect competition. A market type in which a large number of firms compete with one another by making similar but slightly different products; there is asymmetrical information — not all firms know what other firms are doing.

[15]Firms make accounting profits, however.

FIGURE 11.5

OPERATING IN IMPERFECT COMPETITION

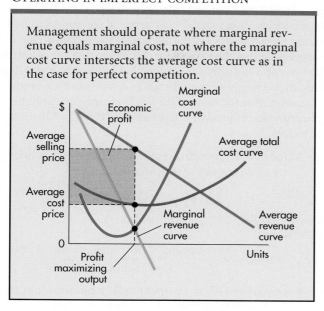

Management should operate where marginal revenue equals marginal cost, not where the marginal cost curve intersects the average cost curve as in the case for perfect competition.

accomplishes the objective by operating the firm where marginal revenue equals marginal cost (see Figure 11.5).

Several reasons can account for the presence of economic profit.

- *Financing barriers to entry make it costly for new firms to enter the industry.* To start a new airplane manufacturing company to compete against Boeing or McDonnell Douglas costs a few billion dollars.

- *Legal barriers in the form of regulation keep some firms out of the industry.* Intel's patented microprocessors make it difficult for other firms to compete against it on a large scale. Intel successfully litigates most patent infringement suits.

- *Firm-specific competitive advantage factors exist for the firm.* The competitive edge may result from superior product differentiation, high research and development expenditures, and patent or trademark protection. Coca-Cola's patented formula and trademarked name Coke™ have made Coke the world's most recognized brand. Over the period 1981 through 1993, management enriched total shareholder value by $50 billion.[16]

For firms operating in imperfect competition, investors attempt to estimate the length of time each firm can continue to earn superior returns on new investment. Unless the company benefits from extremely restrictive barriers to entry in its markets, other firms will enter the product market in an effort to also earn economic profit. Increased competition eventually results in erosion of the high returns. Competition may become so aggressive that some firms in the industry must exit the market. When only the stronger firms remain in the industry, economic profit levels usually have reached levels lower than existed before the fierce competition.

[16]See John Huey, "The World's Best Brand," *Fortune,* May 31, 1993, pp. 44–54.

Apple Computer is an example of the struggle. Apple's management tries very hard to improve the company's market position and profitability in the personal computer industry. However, Apple's profit growth has been slowed considerably by Microsoft's Windows™ software, which allows DOS-based personal computers to look and handle more like Apple computers. In early 1993, John Sculley, then chairperson of Apple, proposed to IBM management that the two companies merge to form one strong competitive company. IBM was also struggling at the time but ignored Sculley's suggestion.

We can easily allow for growth circumstances in the valuation model. Simply add an expression to accommodate the value of the firm's growth opportunities. We call this expression the **present value of growth opportunities (PVGO)**. The restated equation for value of the firm is:[17]

$$V^L = \text{Value of unlevered firm} + \text{present value of tax savings} \\ + \text{present value of growth opportunities}$$

$$= \frac{COP \times (1 - \tau)}{r_u} + PVTS + PVGO \qquad \textbf{(11.16)}$$

where we define PVGO as:

$$PVGO = \frac{\text{Investment} \times (\text{investment's rate of return})}{\text{Required market return}} \qquad \textbf{(11.17)}$$

For simplicity, we state PVGO as a perpetuity. The numerator of the equation is equivalent to annual cash operating profit after taxes expected to be realized from investing in growth projects with perpetual life. We capitalize this forecasted profit at the market's required return, given in the denominator. In Chapters 14 and 15 we will examine how to determine if investments are of the PVGO type.

Illustration 11.4 shows how to apply the valuation models for PVGO investments. The process is an extension of our previous discussion.

ILLUSTRATION 11.4

Present value of growth opportunities

Earlier in Section 11.4.3, we found the value of the no-growth levered Ethridge Publishing Company to be $16,416 (see Equation 11.10).

$$V^L = S + B \qquad \text{or} \qquad V^L = \frac{COP \times (1 - \tau)}{r_u} + PVTS$$

$$= \$9216 + \$7200 \qquad\qquad = \$14,400 + \$2016$$
$$= \$16,416 \qquad\qquad\qquad = \$16,416$$

Investments that have the potential to earn economic profit result in higher value for both the firm and the equity. The firm's value becomes

$$V^L = \$16,416 + PVGO$$

Suppose Ethridge Publishing invests $1000 in new equipment today and expects a 15 percent return on the PVGO investment each year in perpetuity. If the minimum required market rate of return is 8.772 percent for the equipment, the value contributed to firm value is $1710.

[17]The discussion also applies to the all-equity financed firm; in this case PVTS = 0.

Present value of growth opportunities (PVGO). Projects available to a firm that have an expected return in excess of the firm's required market return.

$$PVGO = \frac{\text{Investment} \times (\text{investment's rate of return})}{\text{Required market rate}}$$

$$= \frac{\$1000 \times 0.15}{0.08772}$$

$$= \frac{\$150}{0.08772}$$

$$= \$1710$$

The $150 in the numerator of the equation reflects the *investment's annual cash operating profit after taxes (IACOPAT)*. The present value of receiving these annual cash operating profits in perpetuity is $150 ÷ 0.08772 = $1710. After this investment, the value of Ethridge Publishing is $16,416 + $1710 = $18,126.

The following table summarizes the effect of different growth opportunities (some of them negative) along several dimensions. Column *A* is the problem we have just solved. Column *B* shows results when the new investment's rate of return equals the market required rate (MRR) of 8.772 percent. In this case, IACOPAT = $87.72 and PVGO = $1000. The PVGO simply equals the $1000 investment. Thus, the value of the firm increases by only $1000. This situation is the no-growth scenario discussed earlier in the chapter. Column *C* shows that when the firm fails to earn the MRR of 8.772 percent on new investments, then IACOPAT and PVGO are both negative and the firm loses value.

DIFFERENT SCENARIOS FOR A $1000 INVESTMENT

	A	B	C
MRR	8.772%	8.772%	8.772%
Investment return	15.000%	8.772%	−11.228%
IACOPAT	$150	$87.72	−$112.28
PVGO	$1,710	$1,000	−$1,280
V^L	$18,126	$17,416	$15,136

IACOPAT = Investment × investment's rate of return
PVGO = IACOPAT ÷ MRR = IACOPAT ÷ 0.08872
V^L = $16,416 + PVGO

Figure 11.6 aids in the explanation of the results in Illustration 11.4. A company's value is higher if expected PVGOs are positive. But any present value growth opportunity is dependent on the length of time that it takes the company to progress from a state of earning economic profit to a fully competitive equilibrium; that is, until PVGO = 0.

In theory, the contribution of PVGO to firm and shareholder values grows smaller with each passing year, unless the firm invests in new growth projects that earn economic profit. As management makes new investments and the investments realize

FIGURE 11.6
CONTRIBUTION OF PVGOs

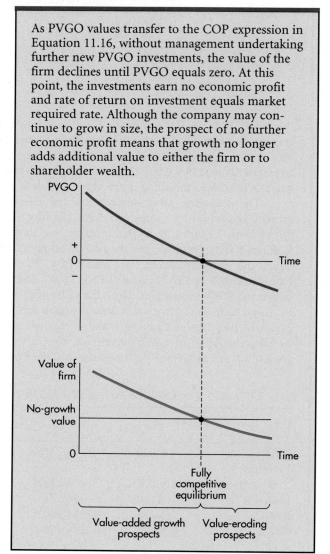

As PVGO values transfer to the COP expression in Equation 11.16, without management undertaking further new PVGO investments, the value of the firm declines until PVGO equals zero. At this point, the investments earn no economic profit and rate of return on investment equals market required rate. Although the company may continue to grow in size, the prospect of no further economic profit means that growth no longer adds additional value to either the firm or to shareholder wealth.

their forecasted potentials, economic value flows from present value of growth opportunities into cash operating profit in Equation 11.16:

$$V^L = \frac{\text{COP} \times (1 - \tau)}{r_u} + \text{PVTS} + \text{PVGO} \qquad (11.16)$$

PVGO becomes COP, which in turn earns the required market rate of return r_u but no excess return. That is to say, as PVGOs lose their economic profit, these projects move from an imperfect market environment of positive economic profit to a perfect market environment of zero economic profit.

1. How is the value of an unlevered firm calculated?
2. Under what conditions would a firm operate with a high degree of business risk? How could management reduce such a firm's business risk?
3. When a firm uses debt to finance part of its operations, what effect does this have on the firm's cash operating profit after taxes? What are the benefits of debt financing for the firm's shareholders?
4. How is the value determined for a firm that is financed with both debt and equity?
5. What conditions may limit a firm from earning economic profit indefinitely on its investments?
6. How may profitable growth opportunities be included in the valuation model of the firm?

SUMMARY ▼▼▼▼▼▼▼▼▼▼▼

THE CORPORATE VALUE-EXCHANGE SYSTEM

- A corporation is an interrelated set of contracts among customers, employees, governments, investors, and vendors.
- Service values flow from the firm to the customer.
- Monetary amounts and customer and brand loyalty are the primary values flowing from customers to the firm.
- The supplier-firm value-exchange system consists of employees being fairly compensated in exchange for providing productive labor and skills to the firm, and investors earning a fair return given the risk of the firm.
- Any conflicts within the value-exchange system can result in lower value of both the firm and shareholder wealth.

PRINCIPAL-AGENT PROBLEMS

- Principal-agent problems exist in that shareholder wealth maximization is not the primary objective of management.
- Theory suggests that managers act in the best interests of shareholders because of management's ownership position, compensation tied to performance, takeover threats, and the competitive labor market.

HOW IS SHAREHOLDER VALUE CREATED?

- The investment opportunity schedule and the market rate of return schedule interact to determine investments expected to increase firm value.
- The value of the firm declines if management invests in projects earning less than the market rate of return.
- The long-term value index suggests that the financial market prices common stock on the basis of long-term cash flow potential of the firm.

- A no-growth firm is one that invests in new plant and equipment to simply maintain current operating levels. Any cash flows remaining are paid as dividends to shareholders.

- Current after-tax cash operating profit, COP $\times (1 - \tau)$, is capitalized at a rate that compensates shareholders for bearing business risk, r_u.

- Financing the company with debt provides a tax benefit that increases both the value of the firm and shareholder wealth. This benefit is called the *present value tax savings (PVTS)*.

- Growth opportunities mean the firm can earn more than its minimum required market rate of return.

- Firms operating in perfect competition do not have growth opportunities since no firm is strong enough, or has a differentiated product, to command premium prices.

- Firms in imperfect competition can earn economic profit as a result of growth opportunities not available to other firms.

- The present value of growth opportunities is the economic profit capitalized by the market return:

$$PVGO = \frac{\text{Investment} \times \text{investment's rate of return}}{\text{Required market rate}}$$

- PVGO increase both the value of the firm and shareholder wealth, since debtholders receive a fixed return.

FURTHER READING ▼▼▼▼▼▼▼▼▼▼▼▼

Lowenstein, Louis, *Sense and Nonsense in Corporate Finance*. Reading, MA: Addison-Wesley Publishing Company, Inc., 1991. The author, a former executive, provides a thought provoking discussion about financial theory.

Porter, Michael E., *Competitive Strategy: Techniques for Analyzing Industries and Competitors*. New York: The Free Press, 1980, and *Competitive Advantage: Creating and Sustaining Superior Performance*. New York: The Free Press, 1985. These two books provide much insight into factors affecting the long-term value of a firm.

Rappaport, Alfred, *Creating Shareholder Value: The New Standard for Business Performance*. New York: The Free Press, 1986. This book is widely acclaimed by practitioners.

SELF-TEST PROBLEMS ▼▼▼▼▼▼▼▼▼▼▼

ST11-1. What is the market value of a corporation that has 2 million shares of common stock traded over the counter at $13 per share? Its debt is valued at $10 million.

ST11-2. Calculate the market value of a firm which earns 15 percent in perpetuity on its $80 million investment in assets, stated at book value. Investors require a return of 10 percent and there is no growth. Comment on the job that management is doing for the shareholders.

ST11-3. The future expected cash flow from operations of the Ridefast Company are $44,000 in perpetuity. The current liquidation value of the firm is estimated to be $400,000. If investors require a 13 percent return, should Ridefast continue operations?

<table>
<tr><td>**PROBLEMS**</td><td>▼▼▼▼▼▼▼▼▼▼▼▼</td></tr>
</table>

PRINCIPAL-AGENT PROBLEMS

11-1. a. It can be argued that economic profit maximization for the firm and wealth maximization for the owners are equivalent objectives. Discuss this issue. Identify your assumptions.

   b. Discuss an alternative to the corporate objective of maximizing share value.

11-2. Discuss examples of potential conflicts of interest between managers and shareholders. Why do managers generally work hard to make the firm successful?

11-3. As merger and takeover activity has increased in recent years, the issue of corporate ownership versus control has become more controversial. Discuss the principal-agent problem as it relates to shareholder-management relations. Why is there a potential conflict between the two groups? What steps can be taken to mitigate this problem?

11-4. The stated objective of commercial businesses is often taken to be the maximization of firm and equity valuation. Comment on the extent to which this objective is realistic and explain why management must be concerned with firm valuation. How can financial management techniques assist in meeting actual corporate objectives?

HOW IS SHAREHOLDER VALUE CREATED?

11-5. What is the market value of a corporation which has its 5 million shares of common stock listed on the American Stock Exchange and its bonds traded over the counter? The stock currently sells for $6 per share and the total value of the debt is $8 million.

11-6. Calculate the value of a public company. The asset value, as shown on the balance sheet, is $10 million. The firm has $5 million of debt, which is equal to its market value. There are 150,000 shares of common stock outstanding with a current market value of $75 per share.

11-7. The GRT Corporation's common stock and bonds are traded on the New York Stock Exchange. The most recent balance sheet for GRT records the bonds at $60 million, whereas equity has a value of $240 million. There are 10 million shares of the company outstanding with a current market value of $56 per share. GRT's bonds have a par value of $1000 but are currently trading for 85 percent of par. Calculate the market value of GRT.

11-8. Royal Players, Inc. has 50 million shares of common stock outstanding, with a book value of $900 million. The market price per share is $44. Bonds are shown on the balance sheet at $400 million. The noncallable bonds, which mature in 12 years, have a coupon rate of 10 percent with interest payable annually. The current market interest rate for similar risky debt is 9 percent. What is the market value of the company?

11-9. Use the following equation to answer the questions:

Market value of the firm

$$= \frac{\text{Corporate rate of return} \times \text{book value of assets}}{\text{Required market rate}}$$

    a. If investors increase the required market rate, what happens to the value of the firm, assuming all else remains constant?

    b. If the market value of the firm declines and the value of assets remain unchanged, what is the relationship between *corporate rate of return* and the *required market rate?*

    c. Management purchases some new assets that earn the *corporate rate of return.* However, the market value of the firm declines. Why?

11-10. Calculate the market value of a firm that earns 14 percent on its assets, which have a book value of $144 million. The required rate of return by investors is 12 percent. Comment on the job that management is doing for its shareholders.

11-11. Warman Limited has assets with a book value of $18 million on which management is currently earning a 15 percent return. Due to increasing concern over prospects for Warman's industry, investors have raised their rate of return expectations from 12 percent to 16 percent. Calculate the new market value of Warman given this change. What is the net change in Warman's value? Why did it occur?

11-12. Maui Sunset, Inc.'s assets have a book value of $1.6 million. Management is able to earn a return of 20 percent on these assets. Because of a large increase in tourism and increased foreign investment in the area, investors have changed their rate of return expectation from 15 percent to 10 percent. Calculate the new market value of Maui Sunset. What is the net change in Maui Sunset's market value as a result of investors revising their rate?

11-13. Healthmax, Inc. is valued by the market at $30 million. The firm's accounting records indicate that assets are recorded at a value of $10 million. Investors require a market rate of 25 percent.

    a. What is the corporate rate of return that is necessary to maintain the firm's value at $10 million?

    b. What is the value of the firm if the assets earn a 60 percent rate of return? Does the value of the firm increase or decrease? Why?

    c. At what point will loss of value occur?

11-14. Investment bankers believe the investors require a 12 percent market return to invest in Journal Press Corporation. For every $1 invested in assets of the firm, what is the contribution to the market value of the company if the corporate rate of return is 4 percent? 8 percent? 12 percent? 16 percent? 20 percent? Which corporate rates of return result in value being created, destroyed, or unchanged?

11-15. The management of Landstar Partners estimates that investors require a return of 15 percent to invest in the partnership. For each $1 invested in projects by the firm, what is the contribution to the value of the partnership if the rate of return on assets is 9 percent? 12 percent? 15 percent? 18 percent? 21 percent? Which rates of return on partnership assets result in value being created, destroyed, or unchanged?

11-16. When a firm uses a market rate of return that is too low for evaluating investment decisions, how is the firm's objective of value maximization affected?

11-17. In past years, Aerosouth Commuter Airline has earned 10 percent on its assets, which have a book value of $6 million. However, in the last recession Aerosouth's return fell to 2 percent on assets and has remained there as the economy started to improve. This airline is privately owned so there is no market value for its common stock. Investors of publicly owned commuter airlines have expected a rate of return of 12 percent. Estimate the value of Aerosouth before and after the recession. Comment on the company's condition.

11-18. Annual operating cash flows for Turborun Tracks, Inc. are expected to be $4.2 million. Management believes that the firm's required rate of return on investment is 12 percent. Calculate the value of the firm by capitalizing its operating cash flows. If management is correct, what will happen to the value of the firm if new investments are made that return 14 percent?

11-19. The value of a firm is given by capitalizing operating cash flow at an appropriate market rate of return; for example, $20 ÷ 0.10 = $200. Suppose management considers a new investment that requires an initial outlay of $100. The project is very risky and management estimates that if it is taken, the firm's market rate of return will increase to 0.20. Calculate the minimum required rate of return from the new project so that the value of the firm after the investment equals its preinvestment value plus the initial outlay for the investment.

11-20. Calculate the market value of Jayne Limited. It is expected to generate cash flow from operations of $3.8 million in perpetuity. Investors require an annual return of 19 percent.

11-21. What is the market value of Renner Company if investors require a 16 percent return? They believe the firm can earn annual cash flow from operations of $67 million.

11-22. How much in annual cash flows must McWilliams Company generate to maintain its market value of $100 million if management believes that investors require an 18 percent return?

11-23. The market value of Thomas II Mutual Fund is $45 million. If its annual cash flows are $3 million, what is the rate of return that investors require?

11-24. The future expected cash flow from operations for Packard Company is $35,000 in perpetuity. The liquidating value is estimated to be $200,000. If investors require a 15 percent return on their investment, should Packard continue operations?

FINDING SHAREHOLDER VALUE IN THE BUSINESS ENVIRONMENT

11-25. What is the value of an unlevered firm where annual cash flow from operations is expected to remain constant at $430,000? The tax rate is zero. Owners of the firm require an 11 percent return for their exposure to business risk.

11-26. Calculate the value of an unlevered firm which has expected cash flow from operations of $120,000 annually. Cash flows are expected to remain constant for the foreseeable future. The firm's tax rate is 40 percent. Owners expect a rate of return on their investment of 9 percent to compensate them for the business risk.

11-27. What is the value of an all-equity firm where management expects no growth in cash earnings of $200,000 annually? The firm's owners expect a return of 14 percent on their investment. The tax rate for the business is 36 percent.

11-28. How much does the annual interest of $225,000 on a long-term loan actually cost a firm that is operating profitably? Assume the firm's marginal income tax rate is 36 percent.

11-29. If a corporation borrows money on a perpetual basis, which results in interest payments of $800,000 annually, what is the present value of the firm's income tax savings if the market rate on this debt is 12 percent? The firm's marginal tax rate is 28 percent.

11-30. A firm's management wants to substitute $100,000 of perpetual debt with an annual coupon interest rate of 9.5 percent for an equal amount of equity. The market rate for the debt will also be 9.5 percent. Presently, the firm is unleveraged. How much will the value of the firm be increased or decreased if business operations continue unchanged? The firm's tax rate is 36 percent.

11-31. a. What is the market value of a firm's perpetual debt which has a par value of $10.5 million? The debt's coupon rate is 9 percent and investors require a 12 percent return.
 b. What possible explanations are there for the present market value of the firm's debt?

11-32. Compute the value of the interest tax shield generated by the following debt issues. The marginal corporate tax rate is 34 percent and the market rate of interest is 8 percent.
 a. A $1000, one-year loan at 9 percent.
 b. A five-year balloon note of $1000 at 9 percent, with interest payable annually.
 c. A $1000 perpetuity at 9 percent.

11-33. Logic, Inc. is an unlevered firm with an expected net operating income of $10,000 per year. No growth in operating cash flow is expected. Shareholders require a 12 percent return on their investment. The tax rate is zero.
 a. Calculate the value of the firm.
 b. If the firm issues $25,000 of 7 percent perpetual bonds at face value, and retires $25,000 worth of stock with the proceeds, what is the value of the firm's equity?
 c. Now assume that the tax rate is 34 percent. Recalculate parts (a) and (b). Also calculate the value of the levered firm. You need to adjust operating income to an after-tax basis.

11-34. The book and market values for iTech Corporation are as follows:

Book value:	Net working capital	$ 30	Debt	$ 40
	Long-term assets	70	Equity	60
	Totals	$100		$100
Market value:	Net working capital	$ 30	Debt	$ 40
	Long-term assets	150	Equity	140
	Totals	$180		$180

The firm expects no growth. The $40 debt is permanent (that is, perpetual). The debt's coupon rate is 7 percent, which equals the required market rate. The tax rate is 34 percent.
 a. How much does the tax shield from debt contribute to the value of the firm?
 b. What happens to the value of the firm if Congress passes a law that eliminates the tax deductibility of interest? What is the new value?

11-35. Prime Box Company is an unlevered firm valued at $500,000. It has no growth prospects and there are 5000 shares outstanding. Investors require a 14 percent return on the stock and the firm's tax rate is 34 percent.

   a. How much is the firm's before-tax cash flow from operations?
   b. If the firm issues $200,000 of 8 percent debt at par and retires stock with the proceeds, what is the new value of the firm?
   c. What is the new value of the equity in part (b)?
   d. How much is the price per share before and after the debt swap?
   e. What is the price-earnings ratio before and after the debt swap?

11-36. The unlevered value of MacPower Corporation is $2 million. Operating cash flows are constant. The firm's marginal tax rate is 34 percent. Management is considering retiring some equity by issuing $600,000 of perpetual debt with a coupon rate of 9 percent.

   a. What is the firm's value after issuing the debt, if the required market rate for the debt is also 9 percent? What is the value of the equity?
   b. What is the value of the debt, the equity, and the firm if the required market rate for the debt is 8 percent? 10 percent?

11-37. Phoenix Enterprise, Inc. is an all-equity firm with a current market value of $80 million. This value reflects a required rate of return of 20 percent on its common stock. One million common shares are outstanding. Management of Phoenix has decided to undertake a project costing $6 million. The project's expected after-tax cash flow is $8 million at the end of the first year. (*Note:* The cash flows are not in perpetuity.) The required return on the nonrisk-changing investment is 20 percent.

   a. What is the value of Phoenix's shares after publicly announcing the decision to accept the investment, assuming the financial markets are efficient? The project will be financed with internally generated cash.
   b. What should be the new share price if the investment is financed by issuing 75,000 new shares?
   c. Suppose the level of interest rates increases and, consequently, the rate of return required on Phoenix's shares increases to 25 percent. What will be the value of each of Phoenix's shares if the project is financed with 75,000 new shares?

11-38. FastMicro, Inc. has a current market value of $2 million. The firm's present cash flow from operations is $200,000 annually. Management is considering investing in a new project which costs $1 million. This project is less risky than the existing projects and the discount rate for the firm would be reduced by 2 percentage points should management decide to make the investment.

   a. Find the minimum required rate of return that should be attached to the new project.
   b. Suppose the project's rate of return is larger by 9 percent in comparison to the minimum rate of return you calculate in part (a); that is, multiply your answer by 1.09 and then subtract 1. Calculate the value of the new project. What is the new value of the firm? (*Hint:* Add the current value of the firm to the value of the new project.)

11-39. Assume that two firms exist which differ only by how they are financed. The constant operating cash flows for both firms are equal. The unlevered firm is financed by 3 million shares of common stock with a market price per share of $10. The market discount rate for the unlevered firm is 15 percent. The levered firm has 2 million shares of stock and $10 million in long-term debt with an interest rate of 10 percent. The corporate tax rate is 40 percent.

a. Calculate the value of each firm. (*Hint:* First calculate the unlevered firm's value and use your answer to value the levered firm.)
b. Calculate the cash flow from operations (before taxes and interest payments) for each firm.
c. How much is the net income for each firm? How much is each firm's earnings per share?

11-40. Two firms are identical except for how they are financed. One firm uses debt in its financing, whereas the other firm does not. At a tax rate of 34 percent and a discount rate of 10 percent, the value of the unlevered firm is $660, assuming the firm has no-growth opportunities.

a. What is the amount of constant operating cash flow that is capitalized?
b. If the tax rate increases from 34 percent to 46 percent, what is the value of the unlevered firm?
c. If the levered firm is financed with $100 debt, what is the value of the firm before and after the tax rate change?

11-41. A company currently has no debt financing. The market value of each of its 5 million outstanding shares is $25. The new management of the company is convinced that debt financing increases the aggregate market value of the company's outstanding securities by the present value of the corporate tax shield on interest payments. In other words, they believe that $V^L = V^u + \tau B$. Cash flow from operations before taxes is expected to be constant at $35 million. The corporate tax rate is 30 percent.

Management is considering a tender offer at $25 per share to repurchase 2.4 million of its own shares. The tender offer will be financed by issuing (at par) $60 million in 9 percent perpetual debentures.

a. What is the current value of the firm?
b. What is the required return on the company's stock?
c. How much is the tax shield on the debt?
d. If management is correct in believing that $V^L = V^u + PVTS\, B$, what is the likely market value per common share once the firm replaces some shares with debt financing?

DISCLOSURE ASSIGNMENT

11-42. Use the *Disclosure* database to answer the following questions for Nike, Inc. and Reebok International Limited.

a. What is the market value of each firm? You will need to make an assumption as to the value of their respective outstanding debt amounts.
b. If the return for business risk is 10 percent, what is the unlevered value of each firm?
c. Which firm takes greater advantage of the debt tax shield to improve shareholder value? What proportion is each firm's tax shield of its total value?
d. Use Equation 11.2 to estimate the market rate of return required by investors for each firm.

LIBRARY ASSIGNMENTS

11-43. Update Table 11.3 using the latest information available from Value Line Investment Services. Has the market's view changed much since February 1994?

11-44. An organization called CalPERS has been very active during the past few years monitoring actions of corporate executives performing below expectations. Based on a library search, write a short report outlining CalPERS's strategy to force management to improve returns to shareholders.

COMPREHENSIVE PROBLEM ▼▼▼▼▼▼▼▼▼▼▼▼

11-45. a. Increasing or maximizing share value is frequently expressed as the goal of corporate managements. What are some alternatives to this objective?

b. The separation of ownership and management in today's publicly owned corporations results in potential conflicts of interests between managers and shareholders. What factors induce management to align its interest with shareholders?

c. Takeover and merger activity has increased in recent years. This activity has increased the possible conflict between corporate management and owners. Discuss the principal-agent problem as it relates to shareholder-management relations. Why is there a potential conflict between the two groups? How can this conflict be reduced?

d. Why is the maximization of shareholder wealth the most appropriate objective for management to pursue?

e. Calculate the value of a publicly owned corporation. Its asset value, as shown on the balance sheet, is $98 million. The firm has $26 million of debt, which is equal to its market value. There are 5 million shares of common stock outstanding with a current market value of $33 per share.

f. Use the following equation to answer the questions:

Market value of the firm

$$= \frac{\text{Corporate rate of return} \times \text{book value of assets}}{\text{Required market rate}}$$

i. If investors increase the rate of return they require, what happens to the value of the firm, assuming all else remains constant?

ii. If the market value of the firm declines and the value of assets remains unchanged, what is the relationship between the corporate required rate of return and the required market rate of return?

iii. Management purchases new assets which earn the corporate rate of return. However, the market value of the firm declines. Why?

g. Using the equation in part (f), calculate the market value of a firm that earns 18 percent on its assets and has a book value of $100 million. Investors require a return of 12 percent. Comment on the job that management is doing in creating value for the firm's shareholders.

h. Jason Corporation, which has assets with a book value of $30 million, currently earns 10 percent. Due to increased concern over prospects for Jason's industry, investors have raised their required return from 10 percent to 15 percent. Calculate the new market value of the firm given this change. What is the net change in Jason's value? Why did it occur?

i. When a firm uses a rate of return that is too low for evaluating investments, how is the firm's objective of value maximization affected?

j. Calculate the market value of a firm that is expected to generate cash flow from operations of $5.6 million in perpetuity. Assume that investors require an annual return of 14 percent.

k. If the market value of a firm is $60 million and its annual cash flow from operations is $9 million, what is the rate of return investors require?

l. Zeron, Inc. issues $10 million of perpetual debt at a 9 percent annual interest rate. Its corporate income tax rate is 36 percent. How much is the annual income tax savings brought about by this borrowing? What is the present value of this savings?

m. Using the debt and tax rate for Zeron, Inc. in part (l), what is the value of Zeron if the cash operating profit before taxes is $4.2 million? The required rate of return for the unlevered operating cash flows is 12 percent.

n. A new corporate investment of $10 million has an expected rate of return of 14 percent. If the firm's required rate of return is 11 percent, what is the present value of the firm's growth opportunity if the project has a perpetual life expectancy?

ANSWERS TO SELF-TEST PROBLEMS ▼▼▼▼▼▼▼▼▼▼▼▼

ST11-1. Value of firm = Value of debt + value of equity

$$= \$10,000,000 + \$13 \times 2,000,000$$
$$= \$36,000,000$$

ST11-2. Value of firm

$$= \frac{\text{Corporate rate of return} \times \text{book value of assets}}{\text{Required market rate}}$$

$$= \frac{0.15 \times \$80,000,000}{0.10}$$

$$= \$120,000,000$$

Since the rate of return earned by the company is greater than the investors' required return, management is increasing common shareholders' wealth and acting in their best interests.

ST11-3. Value of firm

$$= \frac{\text{Corporate rate of return} \times \text{book value of assets}}{\text{Required market rate}}$$

$$= \frac{\text{Expected perpetual cash flows}}{\text{Required market rate}}$$

$$= \$44,000 \div 0.13$$
$$= \$338,462$$

Based on financial considerations, since the liquidation value exceeds the going-concern value by a considerable margin, the firm should discontinue operations, liquidate the assets, and distribute the proceeds to the owners.

Video Case 11

Southwest Air and Trans World Airlines: Creating Shareholder Value in an Ailing Industry

This Week with David Brinkley, July 18, 1993

Corporate managers have only one duty: Use the funds invested by the company's shareholders in the most profitable way possible. This rule is called *the shareholder wealth-maximization rule.* To satisfy this objective, the manager must identify and pursue profitable projects, control costs, and constantly be aware of opportunities as well as competitors' actions. This video describes how two airlines are trying to create wealth for their shareholders.

The airline industry is going through difficult times. Industry losses for the past $3^1/_2$ years are greater than the cumulative profits for the previous 60 years, and in 1992 the three largest U.S. airlines, American, United, and Delta, lost a total of $3.6 billion! There are, however, a few bright spots. Southwest Air has been consistently profitable, earning a profit of $104 million in 1992, and TWA's new chairperson has high hopes for that firm. This video discusses how these airlines plan to create shareholder wealth as other airlines struggle.

Companies typically compete in terms of price or quality. George Will, the interviewer, suggested that Southwest prospers because it pays low wages, so it can compete on price. But Mr. Kelleher disagrees, stating that Southwest's wages are as high or higher than its competitors. He claims that Southwest makes money because it gives customers a low price with on-time arrivals and departures, and little waiting. Southwest charges a low price by using its planes more efficiently than other airlines. Southwest leaves on time, lands at less expensive airports, prepares the plane for its next flight in about 15 minutes, then takes off for the next destination. By flying each plane more per day, the cost of the plane is spread over more passengers, so the flight cost is lower for each passenger. Southwest accomplishes its quick turnaround by having no food service and by having open seating. Open seating saves time and simplifies ticket sales.

While this approach works well on Southwest's short routes of usually about an hour of flying time, it might not work as well for longer flights. William Howard, the chairperson of TWA, describes how that company plans to find a profitable niche flying longer routes. Rather than provide low-cost, no-frills service, TWA plans to provide "comfort-class" service. Mr. Howard says customers want good service, good food, more leg room, and timely arrivals and departures. By providing precisely that type of service, TWA will differentiate itself from other carriers and capture enough of the market to earn a profit. Without differentiation, customers see air travel as a commodity, so they shop solely on the basis of price. If price alone determines demand, then companies will slash price to attract customers. If price wars break out, prices will drop so far that no company can earn a profit. Since every company must match the lowest price or risk losing its customers, every company loses. By differentiating itself from commodity service providers, TWA hopes to avoid fighting price wars, maintain its profit margins, and increase the wealth of its shareholders.

Study Questions

1. Do you think TWA's strategy will be successful? If you were the CEO of a competitor and saw that TWA was doing well, what would your response be? What does that imply about TWA's likelihood for success?

2. Investors price securities according to systematic risk. Which of the strategies described in the video is likely to have the greater systematic risk? Explain what system-wide factors influence the strategy you choose.

CHAPTER 12

The Cost of Capital

"**W**e would be much more modernized and therefore more competitive had the cost been lower."[1] James Geier, chief executive officer of Cincinnati Milacron, was expressing his concern that the high cost of financing has been one factor leading to the demise of many firms in the U.S. machine tool industry. Ken Olsen, former president of Digital Equipment Corporation, and Carl Ledbetter, former president of Control Data's abandoned supercomputer project, each claimed that if their company's financing costs had been lower, then their respective companies would have been more profitable.[2] These executives are saying that a firm's cost of funds, commonly called *cost of capital*, affects creation of shareholder value.

The cost of capital is made up of the return that both debt and equity investors expect to receive by investing in a firm's financial securities. In general, investors will demand a return equal to the return they could receive on an alternative set of cash flows carrying the same risk. Implicit in this statement is the fact that cost of capital is determined by the current market prices investors place on securities in their pursuit of risk-adjusted returns. Historical prices, including prices existing at the date the securities were originally issued, do not matter in calculating cost of capital. The cost of capital that results from investors' demands is, in turn, the minimum rate managers must receive on the firm's investments if they are to serve the investors' best interests.

Most corporate finance officers estimate the cost of capital by determining how much debt a firm can support and, by implication, how much equity capital must be invested. Then the yield to be paid on the debt and the required rate of return demanded by shareholders on the equity can be combined for an estimate of cost of capital. Cost of capital is conceptually straightforward. As a practical matter, the num-

---

[1]Joseph Morone and Albert Paulson, "Cost of Capital: The Managerial Perspective," *California Management Review* (Summer 1991), p. 15.

[2]See Peter Dunn, "DEC's Olsen: Capital Cost Hurting," *Electronic News*, March 29, 1989, p. 1, and Louis S. Richman, "How Capital Costs Cripple America," *Fortune*, August 4, 1989, p. 50.

bers that actually can be used in the cost of capital calculation are necessarily approximate. The financial manager must make simplifying assumptions, looking backward in order to speculate about the future.

This chapter will examine how to calculate the cost of capital. When you have completed this chapter, you should understand:

- How to calculate the cost of debt and the cost of preferred stock.
- How to calculate the cost of equity financing.
- How to combine the costs of different forms of financing into a weighted average cost of capital, or WACC.
- How the weighted average cost of capital and firm value are related.

To help us explain the concepts and calculations used in this chapter, we will once again follow the progress of Ethridge Publishing, Inc., the company we introduced in Chapter 11.

12.1 THE COST OF DEBT

In a world free of both taxes and risk, corporations could finance any and all investments through borrowing, provided that those investments were sure to return more than the interest rate demanded by lenders. In the real world, of course, taxes complicate the picture, and it is impossible to predict with absolute certainty that all required payments to creditors will be made on time. However, creditors are willing to bear a certain level of risk if the return is adequate. The return they demand is the *cost of debt* to the firm.

The **cost of debt** is the yield to maturity (YTM) to be realized by investors of the company's debt in the current market. Chapter 8 provided extensive discussion of how to calculate YTM; we will rely on that basic calculation and not repeat the steps. In this discussion, we will focus on adjusting the YTM for taxes, a necessary step because debt interest payments are tax-deductible expenses to the issuing firm. The firm's after-tax cost of debt is:

Cost of debt. Yield to maturity of the instrument.

$$\text{After-tax cost of debt} = \text{YTM} \times (1 - \text{tax rate})$$
$$= r_d \times (1 - \tau) \tag{12.1}$$

For example, if Ethridge Publishing's income tax rate is 28 percent and the bond's YTM is 8 percent, the cost of debt to the corporation is 5.76 percent: $8\% \times (1 - 0.28)$. It does not matter if the bond was originally issued to yield the investor, say, 9 percent. If Ethridge Publishing had to issue similar debt today, it would cost 5.76 percent after taxes. In the current market, Ethridge Publishing would pay debt investors 8 percent but would effectively reclaim 2.24 percentage points of interest payments on its tax return ($= 8.00\% - 5.76\%$).

Some people may question the use of the YTM in the cost of debt formula. Why not use the coupon rate stated on the bond instead? Isn't this the amount of interest expense actually incurred by the firm? Yes, the coupon amount is the interest expense incurred by the firm, but investors bid the price of the bond either up or down depending on market rates they can earn in alternative investments of equal risk. We saw this phenomenon in Chapter 8. *Investors will earn the market interest rate, given the risk of the security, regardless of the stated coupon rate.* This fact is critical to understanding the cost of capital for all securities. It underscores our earlier point that the return to the investor is the cost to the firm.

1. State the equation to calculate the cost of debt.
2. Explain why the market value of debt is used to calculate the cost of debt.

12.2 THE COST OF PREFERRED STOCK

Cost of preferred stock.
Preferred stock dividend divided by the market price of the stock.

If a firm issues preferred stock to help finance its assets, the cost is the market rate required by investors who buy the security. Since most preferred stock has a fixed dividend amount, investors bid the price up or down to earn the market rate, similar to how they price debt in the financial markets. Thus, the **cost of preferred stock** is its dividend yield:

$$\text{Cost of preferred stock} = \text{Dividend} \div \text{market price of preferred stock} \quad (12.2)$$

If the firm's preferred stock pays a dividend of $3 per share, and shares sell for $24 each, the firm's cost of preferred stock is its dividend yield of 12.5 percent: $3 ÷ $24. Unlike debt interest, the preferred stock dividend is not a tax-deductible expense to the firm. Thus, we do not make any tax adjustment to the dividend yield.

1. Explain why market value is used to calculate the cost of preferred stock.
2. State the equation to calculate the cost of preferred stock.

12.3 THE COST OF EQUITY

Cost of equity. Market rate of return required by investors to hold the company's common stock.

Like debt and preferred stock investors, common stock investors also require an appropriate market rate of return. Equity investors determine this market rate, or **cost of equity,** by bidding the price of the company's shares up or down until the share price reflects the rate of return participants willingly accept. But calculation of the cost of equity is more complicated than are the calculations for either the cost of debt or the cost of preferred stock because equity is not a fixed-income security. A number of methods exist to calculate the cost of equity. The predominant methods are the *dividend growth model,* the *security market line,* and the *inverted price-earnings ratio.*

12.3.1 The Cost of Equity Using the Dividend Growth Model

When we used the dividend growth model (DGM) in Chapter 9 to value common stock, we assumed that we knew the appropriate market rate. Now let's turn the problem around. Suppose we know the stock price but not the required market rate. We need to rearrange the DGM so that it is clear that the required market rate (cost of equity) is determined by the expected dividend next period, the current price of the stock, and the expected growth rate for dividends. For instance, the DGM is:

$$\text{Stock price} = \frac{\text{Expect dividend next year}}{\text{Required market rate} - \text{expected growth rate for dividends}} \quad (12.3)$$

which, when rearranged, becomes:

Required market rate

$$= \frac{\text{Expected dividend next year}}{\text{Stock price}} + \text{expected growth rate for dividends}$$

$= \text{Dividend yield} + \text{expected growth rate for dividends}$ (12.4)

$$r_e = \frac{D_1}{P_0} + g$$

Calculation of the dividend yield, D_1/P_0, is usually straightforward. It is next year's expected dividend divided by the current common stock price. A good estimate of next year's dividend is this year's dividend, possibly increased a little to reflect any change in the dividend that has occurred in recent years. But how is growth, g, estimated?

A popular approach used to calculate g is to calculate the historical growth rate of dividends using the future value model. For example, assume that Ethridge Publishing, Inc. paid a dividend of $0.267 per share in year 1 (the earliest year) and paid $0.533 in year 10 (the latest year):

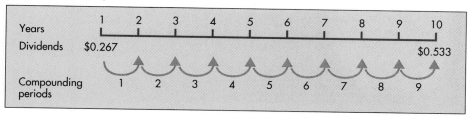

We find the annual compound growth rate in dividends by solving the future value equation:

$$\text{Future value} = \text{Past value} \times (1 + \text{growth rate})^{n-1} \quad (12.5)$$

$$\$0.533 = \$0.267 \times (1 + \text{growth rate})^9$$

$$(1 + \text{growth rate})^9 = \frac{\$0.533}{\$0.267} = 2$$

$$(1 + \text{growth rate}) = (2)^{1/9}$$

Growth rate $= 0.08$ or 8 percent

The exponent n in Equation 12.5 is the number of years (10); $n-1$ represents the number of compounding periods (9). The calculation assumes that past growth is representative of future growth.[3]

A second approach to estimating growth is to learn what growth rates various securities analysts at brokerage houses project for the stock. Figure 12.1 is a sample from *Nelson's 1994 Directory of Investment Research*. In addition to other useful information, this directory provides the names of analysts who follow publicly traded stocks. We can check the reports these analysts issue to obtain different growth rates for a given firm, or we can

---

[3]When the table for the present value of $1 is available, an easy approximation of the growth rate between two periods of time is found by dividing the dividend for the earlier period by the dividend for the later period. Use the result as a present value interest factor to enter the present value table for the elapsed number of years and read up to the nearest whole percentage point. In the example given, enter the table for nine periods and read across the row until you find 0.500 (= $0.267 ÷ $0.533), or a value close to it. From the table, the growth rate is 8 percent.

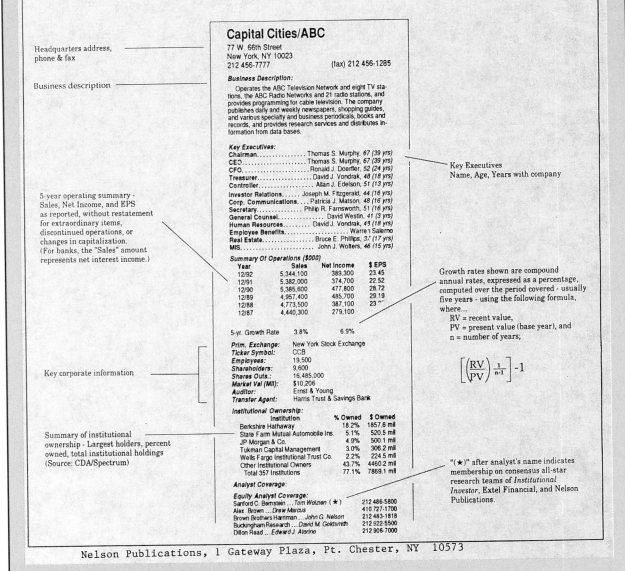

Nelson's 1994 Directory of Investment Research,

Section 6 - Company Profiles/Analyst Coverage:

In-depth corporate profiles of over 12,500 publicly-owned companies worldwide. Key executives, telephone number, five-year operations summary, key investment characteristics.... Plus the names and phone numbers of all security analysts who follow each company. Volume I includes over 6,000 companies whose principal equity trading market is in the United States; Volume II covers 6,500 companies traded outside the U.S., in 40 countries on six continents.

Headquarters address, phone & fax

Business description

5-year operating summary -
Sales, Net Income, and EPS
as reported, without restatement
for extraordinary items,
discontinued operations, or
changes in capitalization.
(For banks, the "Sales" amount
represents net interest income.)

Key corporate information

Summary of institutional
ownership - Largest holders, percent
owned, total institutional holdings
(Source: CDA/Spectrum)

Capital Cities/ABC

77 W. 66th Street
New York, NY 10023
212 456-7777   (fax) 212 456-1285

Business Description:
Operates the ABC Television Network and eight TV stations, the ABC Radio Networks and 21 radio stations, and provides programming for cable television. The company publishes daily and weekly newspapers, shopping guides, and various specialty and business periodicals, books and records, and provides research services and distributes information from data bases.

Key Executives:
Chairman	Thomas S. Murphy, *67 (39 yrs)*
CEO	Thomas S. Murphy, *67 (39 yrs)*
CFO	Ronald J. Doerfler, *52 (24 yrs)*
Treasurer	David J. Vondrak, *48 (18 yrs)*
Controller	Allan J. Edelson, *51 (13 yrs)*
Investor Relations	Joseph M. Fitzgerald, *44 (16 yrs)*
Corp. Communications	Patricia J. Matson, *48 (16 yrs)*
Secretary	Philip R. Farnsworth, *51 (16 yrs)*
General Counsel	David Westin, *41 (3 yrs)*
Human Resources	David J. Vondrak, *43 (18 yrs)*
Employee Benefits	Warren Salerno
Real Estate	Bruce E. Phillips, *37 (17 yrs)*
MIS	John J. Wolters, *46 (15 yrs)*

Key Executives
Name, Age, Years with company

Summary Of Operations ($000)
Year	Sales	Net Income	$ EPS
12/92	5,344,100	389,300	23.45
12/91	5,382,000	374,700	22.52
12/90	5,385,600	477,800	28.72
12/89	4,957,400	485,700	29.19
12/88	4,773,500	387,100	23 ^
12/87	4,440,300	279,100	
5-yr. Growth Rate	3.8%	6.9%	

Growth rates shown are compound annual rates, expressed as a percentage, computed over the period covered - usually five years - using the following formula, where...
RV = recent value,
PV = present value (base year), and
n = number of years;

$$\left[\left(\frac{RV}{PV}\right)^{\frac{1}{n-1}}\right]-1$$

Prim. Exchange:	New York Stock Exchange
Ticker Symbol:	CCB
Employees:	19,500
Shareholders:	9,600
Shares Outs.:	16,485,000
Market Val (Mil):	$10,206
Auditor:	Ernst & Young
Transfer Agent:	Harris Trust & Savings Bank

Institutional Ownership:
Institution	% Owned	$ Owned
Berkshire Hathaway	18.2%	1857.6 mil
State Farm Mutual Automobile Ins.	5.1%	520.5 mil
JP Morgan & Co.	4.9%	500.1 mil
Tukman Capital Management	3.0%	306.2 mil
Wells Fargo Institutional Trust Co.	2.2%	224.5 mil
Other Institutional Owners	43.7%	4460.2 mil
Total 357 Institutions	77.1%	7869.1 mil

"(★)" after analyst's name indicates membership on consensus all-star research teams of *Institutional Investor*, Extel Financial, and Nelson Publications.

Analyst Coverage:

Equity Analyst Coverage:
Sanford C. Bernstein ... *Tom Wolzien* (★)	212 486-5800
Alex. Brown ... *Drew Marcus*	410 727-1700
Brown Brothers Harriman ... *John G. Nelson*	212 483-1818
Buckingham Research ... *David M. Goldsmith*	212 922-5500
Dillon Read ... *Edward J. Atorino*	212 906-7000

Nelson Publications, 1 Gateway Plaza, Pt. Chester, NY 10573

speak to them directly. Once all the estimated growth rates are collected, we can compute an average value and let it represent expected sustainable growth. If much variability exists among the estimates, the result will be a large range for the estimated cost of equity.

A third approach to estimating growth is to use the firm's sustainable growth rate, which we can approximate as:

Sustainable growth

$$= (1 - \text{dividend payout ratio}) \times (\text{return on beginning equity}) \qquad \textbf{(12.6)}$$

The calculation for the dividend payout ratio is dividends per share ÷ earnings per share and **return on beginning equity** is net income ÷ beginning of period equity.[4] Much evidence exists to indicate that the use of sustainable growth as a proxy for *g* is appropriate. Illustration 12.1 provides an application of the technique. In Chapter 14, we will discuss how management of well-run mature firms use the concept of sustainable growth to help set realistic financial targets and make long-term investments.

> **Return on beginning equity.** An accounting profitability measure, which divides profits by beginning equity shown on the balance sheet.

ILLUSTRATION 12.1

Estimating the cost of equity using the DGM

Several security analysts hold a consensus view that Ethridge Publishing, Inc. will pay an expected dividend of $0.576 per share next year. Analysts expect the dividend to grow 8 percent each year into the foreseeable future. Currently the stock price is $18.43.

The dividend yield of the stock is $0.576 ÷ $18.43 = 0.03125, or 3.125 percent. Given that the growth rate is estimated to be 8 percent, the firm's cost of equity is 11.125 percent.

$$\text{Cost of equity} = \text{Dividend yield} + \text{growth}$$
$$= 0.03125 + 0.08$$
$$= 0.11125$$

Suppose the $0.576 dividend per share represents 28 percent of earnings per share. Thus, earnings per share are $0.576 ÷ 0.28 = $2.06. If 500 shares are outstanding, net income of the firm is $2.06 × 500 = $1030. If the firm's beginning equity value is $7410, *return on beginning equity* is $1030 ÷ $7410 = 0.139 or 13.9 percent.[5] Sustainable growth is 10 percent:

Sustainable growth
$$= (1 - \text{dividend payout rate}) \times \text{return on beginning equity}$$
$$= (1 - 0.28) \times 0.139$$
$$= 0.10 \text{ or } 10 \text{ percent}$$

Adding sustainable growth of 10 percent to the dividend yield of 3.125 percent results in a cost of equity of 13.125 percent.

The two approaches yield different answers because of disagreement over the expected growth rate. Which estimate is correct? Probably neither; however, the required cost of equity may be in the 11 to 13 percent range.

[4]Return on equity is frequently calculated as profits ÷ ending equity. The sustainable growth Equation 12.6 uses beginning equity to calculate return on equity.

[5]*Return on beginning equity* is an accounting measure of profitability; shareholders require a market rate.

The DGM (see Equation 12.3) reveals that the expected growth of dividends and common stock value are closely related. Increased dividends lead to higher stock price, and vice versa. However, there is *no relation* between growth and the cost of equity if the expected growth is *properly* reflected in the current share price. Illustration 12.2 demonstrates the apparent paradox of this statement using two different firms, both with the same cost of equity.

ILLUSTRATION 12.2

Growth and market returns to equity

Assume that the common stock of Jewell, Inc. and Nealon, Inc. are valued according to the dividend growth model of Equation 12.3:

$$\text{Stock price} = \frac{\text{Expect dividend next period}}{\text{Required market rate} - \text{expected growth rate for dividends}}$$

Both firms have initial expected dividends of $2 per share for period 1, and both firms have market rates for equity of 12 percent. Jewell expects a constant growth rate of 4 percent, whereas Nealon expects a constant growth rate of 8 percent. Each firm's share value is:

$$\text{Jewell } P_0 = \$2 \div (0.12 - 0.04) = \$25$$

$$\text{Nealon } P_0 = \$2 \div (0.12 - 0.08) = \$50$$

Market participants value Nealon, Inc. more highly because it has a higher growth rate.

At the end of one year, the values of the two securities are:

$$\text{Jewell } P_0 = \$2 \times 1.04 \div (0.12 - 0.04) = \$26$$

$$\text{Nealon } P_0 = \$2 \times 1.08 \div (0.12 - 0.08) = \$54$$

Nealon, Inc. has appreciated more in value than Jewell, Inc., but the total market return for each security (their respective equity cost) is still 12 percent! That is,

$$\text{Market return} = \frac{\text{Ending price} - \text{beginning price} + \text{dividend}}{\text{Beginning price}}$$

$$\text{Jewell total return} = (\$26 - \$25 + \$2) \div \$25 = 0.12$$

$$\text{Nealon total return} = (\$54 - \$50 + \$2) \div \$50 = 0.12$$

The reason the returns in Illustration 12.2 are the same is that share price reflects all anticipated growth. Thus, when the financial market anticipates the growth, higher-growth securities do not offer higher returns. It is only if the financial market does not anticipate high growth that higher-growth firms produce higher returns for their shareholders in excess of what they require.

12.3.2 The Cost of Equity Using the SML

A major limitation of deriving the cost of equity from the dividend growth model is that it offers no insight into the source of variation in market rates among different securi-

FIGURE 12.2

RISK-REWARD TRADE-OFF AND THE COST OF EQUITY

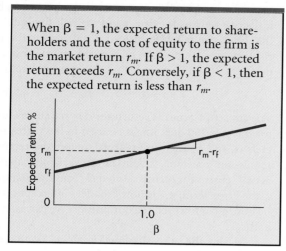

When $\beta = 1$, the expected return to shareholders and the cost of equity to the firm is the market return r_m. If $\beta > 1$, the expected return exceeds r_m. Conversely, if $\beta < 1$, then the expected return is less than r_m.

ties. Conceptually, the appropriate market rate for a security is the sum of an interest rate on some safe investment plus a risk premium that is positively related to the risk of the stock. Capital asset pricing theory, discussed in Chapter 5, directs us to use the security market line (SML) for calculating the cost of equity:

Cost of equity

= Risk-free rate + beta $\times$ (expected market return − risk-free rate)   (12.7)

$$r_e = r_f + \beta \times (r_m - r_f)$$

Figure 12.2 shows Equation 12.7 graphically.

Although many theoretical arguments can be made in support of the SML, when it comes to plugging in the real numbers it can be a problem to implement. Should we use a Treasury bill or a Treasury bond to represent the risk-free rate? What stock index should we use to act as a proxy for the market return? Does β really capture the risk we need to be concerned with? Our discussion in Chapter 5 raised some concerns about β.

These issues are not inconsequential. Treasury bonds are likely a better choice than Treasury bills for the risk-free rate because the longer maturity of bonds better approximates the life of investments in the firm. The difference in yields between T-bills and T-bonds can be considerable, particularly if future expectations about future interest rates are very different than current short-term rates. And do we use already published betas or calculate our own? If we use published betas, whose do we use—Value Line's, Merrill Lynch's, or some other company's? The problem is that published betas differ from one source to another. If we calculate β, what do we use as the market return? Different market proxies can result in different β values.

However, let's assume that we can resolve any concerns about applying the SML for calculating cost of equity. Illustration 12.3 outlines the general procedure to use.

ILLUSTRATION 12.3

Cost of equity from a β perspective

Calculating beta requires the use of a statistical technique called *regression analysis*. We regress the daily differences between historical stock returns for firm i and the risk-free rate, $r_{it} - r_{ft}$, against the difference between historical returns for the market and the risk-free rate (that is, the market risk premium), $r_{mt} - r_{ft}$. Returns on the S&P 500 stock index represent market returns.

$$r_{it} - r_{ft} = \alpha_i + \beta_i \times (r_{mt} - r_{ft}) + \epsilon_{it}$$

The subscript t means return for day t. Returns for r_{it}, r_{ft}, and r_{mt} for the past 250 days might be used in the regression. The parameters α_i and β_i are outputs from solving the regression. Since the regression does not explain all the variability that exists between actual returns for security i on day t and the market return on day t, the error term, ϵ_{it}, is nonzero. The intercept term, α_i, may also be nonzero. However, for our purpose we can safely ignore both α_i and ϵ_{it}.

Using the preceding methodology, assume we find that the beta for Ethridge Publishing is 0.36765. Suppose the risk-free rate r_f is 8 percent and the risk premium for common stocks, $r_m - r_f$ is 8.5 percent. Substituting these values into the equation for the SML results in Ethridge Publishing's cost of equity, r_e, being 0.11125, or 11.125 percent:

$$r_e = r_f + \beta \times (r_m - r_f)$$
$$= 0.08 + 0.36765 \times 0.085$$
$$= 0.11125$$

This return is the same as we calculated using the dividend growth model in Illustration 12.1.

In reality, the DGM and the SML provide different answers for r_e. The reason is because it is difficult to know whether the inputs to the models are correct; we don't operate in a world with perfect knowledge.[6] The nearby Financial Reality reading discusses how difficult practitioners find it to calculate the cost of equity. The article makes reference to several different approaches and concludes that calculating "the cost of equity is an art, not a science."

The management of Thermo Electron Corporation believes that there is much "art" associated with equity costs. Many years ago, its chief executive officer decided to drive the ownership of Thermo stock into the hands of individuals and institutions that were both interested in understanding Thermo's businesses and intent on investing for the long term. Management accomplished the task by keeping in almost daily contact with many of its stockholders to inform them of not only favorable but also unfavorable developments and to clearly articulate its strategy. By attracting investors who view management's forecasts as credible, Thermo management felt it was able to undertake longer-horizon projects.

One class of investors Thermo pursued was Europeans. They are typically more long-term oriented than Americans. Moreover, most Europeans pay no capital gains tax

[6]Theoretically, we can prove that the SML model provides the same answer as the dividend growth model if the cost of debt equals the risk-free rate ($r_d = r_f$) or the beta for debt is zero.

WHAT DOES EQUITY FINANCING REALLY COST?

Corporate America has a disdain for equity financing. The chief financial officer of Gannett Co. expresses a commonly held view about equity. "We borrow as cheaply as we can, and we pay it back rather rapidly. With equity, you've always got it out there, and you've got to cover it with earnings."

At first blush it may appear that issuing stock rather than bonds might appear to be a cheap way to raise money. The only perceived cost to the new shares is any dividends paid. The average dividend payment in the Standard & Poor's 500 stock index is 3.4 percent. That is lower than the cost of debt, even after the tax deductibility of interest.

But equity financing is more expensive than debt. How much more is the question debated among experts. The managing director of Prudential Securities, Inc. says, "We give clients three answers, and it doesn't matter which one they use as long as they understand the implications."

Those who view the dividend payout as the cost of equity point out that when stock is issued, new shareholders have a claim on both the current dividend and any future dividends, which likely will grow in amount. For instance, suppose Stupendous Corp. stock sells for $25 a share and has a $1 per share dividend. That's a 4 percent yield. Dividends are expected to grow at 10 percent a year into the future. That translates into a cost of equity of 14 percent.

Some companies do not pay any dividend, but their cost of equity is not zero. When a firm sells stock, there may not be any out-of-pocket dividend costs, but more people now have a stake in the company. The new shareholders have an equal claim to the earnings as possessed by old shareholders. To keep the stock price from falling, management must create additional earnings each year with the new shareholders' money. The rate that the company must earn on the new money is its "cost of equity."

Some managers determine the cost of equity using the so-called capital asset pricing model (CAPM). The CAPM is based on the idea that the greater the risk in holding a stock the greater the return—dividends + appreciation—investors must receive. If the required return is not received, then investors will dump the stock until the stock offers return in line with expected return-risk trade-off. Because all shareholders suffer if the stock price falls, the real cost of capital is the expected return. If the company can't meet the stock market's expectations, prices will fall.

The CAPM states that the required return depends on interest rates, the risk of owning stocks in general, and the risk of owning a specific company's stock. The calculation begins with the long-term, risk-free rate of return on a U.S. government bond. No one buys a stock if they think that the total return will be less than that of a Treasury bond.

To this figure is added the risk premium. The premium varies, depending on factors related to inflation outlook, recession, and investor sentiment toward stocks. Historically this premium runs 4 percent to 7 percent a year. This premium is the amount in excess of the risk-free rate that investors want to entice them into the market. This risk premium is adjusted for the risk of owning a specific stock. The risk adjustment is called beta. It measures the stock's volatility compared with the rest of the market. A beta of 1 means that a stock's price moves in tandem with the overall market. A beta of 2 means it moves twice as much as the market. To obtain the cost of equity, multiply the market risk premium by beta and add the result to the risk-free rate.

Whichever method is used to calculate the cost of equity, they're all based to some degree on numbers that can only be guessed at. John Lonski, senior economist for Moody's Investors Service, Inc., says, "Determining the cost of equity is an art, not a science."

Adapted from Jeffrey M. Laderman, "What Does Equity Financing Really Cost?" *Business Week*, December 7, 1988, pp. 146–147. Reprinted by permission, copyright © 1988 by McGraw-Hill, Inc.

long-term oriented than Americans. Moreover, most Europeans pay no capital gains tax on the appreciation of equities, thereby making Thermo's nondividend-paying shares of particular interest.

12.3.3 The Effect of Debt on the Cost of Equity

Financial risk. Variability in the earnings stream of a company that results from the use of debt.

Default risk premium. The chance that interest or principal on a debt security will not be paid on a payment date and in the promised amount.

If Ethridge Publishing finances entirely with common stock, assets equal equity. The only risk facing the shareholders is business risk, and the unlevered cost of equity is 10 percent.[7] But since management uses some debt to help finance the assets, this action exposes shareholders to *financial risk*. **Financial risk** exists whenever lenders require a firm to meet fixed finance payments on a security, such as debt interest. With debt financing, the levered return shareholders expect is 11.125 percent, as calculated in Illustration 12.3. The cost of equity is higher than when no debt is used because shareholders require higher returns given their greater exposure to business and financial risks.

Shareholders in Ethridge Publishing require a *default risk premium (DRP)* to offset the risk of default if the firm does not pay its debt obligations. This **default risk premium** is the difference between the cost of equity for the levered firm (r_e^l) and the cost of equity for the unlevered firm (r_e^u):

$$\text{Default risk premium} = \text{Levered equity return} - \text{unlevered equity return}$$
$$\text{DRP} = r_e^l - r_e^u \tag{12.8}$$
$$= 0.11125 - 0.10$$
$$= 0.01125$$

Shareholders require that their rate of return be increased 1.125 percentage points for a default risk premium.

An alternate way to calculate the cost of equity, which explicitly captures the DRP, is to use the following equation:

$$\text{Cost of equity} = \text{Unlevered equity return} + (1 - \text{tax rate})$$
$$\times (\text{unlevered equity return} - \text{cost of debt})$$
$$\times \frac{\text{market value of debt}}{\text{market value of equity}} \tag{12.9}$$
$$r_e^l = r_e^u + (1 - \tau) \times (r_e^u - r_d) \times B/S$$

If Ethridge Publishing does not use debt financing, shareholders require a 10 percent return; that is, $r_e^u = 0.10$. However, as we discussed in the last chapter, Ethridge Publishing does use $7200 of debt financing, the debt's YTM (r_d) is 0.08, and the market value debt-to-equity ratio (B/S) is $7200/$9216. The tax rate, τ, is 28 percent. Substituting these values into Equation 12.9 results in a cost of equity of 11.125 percent:

$$r_e^l = r_e^u + (1 - \tau) \times (r_e^u - r_d) \times B/S$$
$$= 0.10 + (1 - 0.28) \times (0.10 - 0.08) \times \$7200/\$9216$$
$$= 0.11125$$

---

[7]This rate could be derived using the SML. Ethridge Publishing's beta would be 0.235, which is less than the current beta because the equity would be exposed to less risk if debt financing is not used.

Although the cost is the same as the one we calculated using DGM in Illustration 12.3, in the real world the two models would result in different numbers. In a perfect world, the two models would always give the same answer. However, our information is always imperfect. Because we do not know future cash flows with certainty, we must estimate values for the variables, and this leads to unknown errors creeping into the analysis.

If the firm is all-equity financed (or unlevered), the ratio of debt to equity (B/S) equals zero and $r_e^l = r_e^u = 0.10$, which is the appropriate rate of return shareholders expect to earn for business risk. However, when management uses debt financing, shareholders calculate the default risk premium of 1.125 percent as the after-tax difference in cost between the unlevered cost of equity and the cost of debt times the market valued debt-equity ratio: $(1 - \tau) \times (r_e^u - r_d) \times B/S$. Figure 12.3 graphs the effect debt has on the cost of equity.

12.3.4 The Cost of Equity and the PE Ratio

Business magazines and practitioners often refer to the cost of equity as the firm's inverted price-earnings (PE) ratio:

$$\text{Cost of equity} = 1 \div \text{PE ratio} \qquad (12.10)$$

For instance, if Ethridge Publishing, Inc.'s PE ratio is 8, then its cost of equity is 12.5 percent ($= [1 \div 8] \times 100$). If the PE ratio is 20, then the cost of equity is 5 percent.

Any cost of equity calculation based on the PE ratio is suspect. The PE approach assumes that management undertakes only maintenance-type projects that result in neither appreciation nor depreciation in shareholder value. The board of directors authorizes payment of all cash flows remaining after making these value maintenance investments as dividends to shareholders. It is fair to say that such assumptions are inappropriate for about all firms. Illustration 12.4 explains the faulty logic some people use to justify the inverted PE ratio as the cost of equity.

FIGURE 12.3

COST OF EQUITY

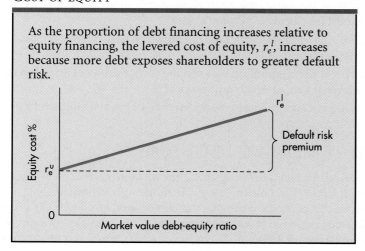

As the proportion of debt financing increases relative to equity financing, the levered cost of equity, r_e^l, increases because more debt exposes shareholders to greater default risk.

ILLUSTRATION 12.4

Misguided use of the PE ratio

We can derive a firm's price-earnings ratio from the dividend growth model by dividing both sides of the model by next period's earnings:

$$\frac{P_0}{E_1} = \frac{D_1/E_1}{r_e - g}$$

P_0/E_1 is the price-earnings ratio (PE ratio) using expected earnings next year. The numerator on the right-hand side of the equation is the expected dividend payout ratio next period (D_1/E_1). The denominator is simply the difference between the required market rate and expected growth rate for dividends.

Now let's rearrange the preceding equation to state it in terms of r_e, the cost of equity:

$$r_e = \frac{D_1/E_1}{P_0/E_1} + g$$

$$= \frac{\text{Dividend payout ratio}}{\text{PE ratio}} + g$$

For the cost of equity to equal the inverted PE ratio (1/PE), the dividend payout ratio must equal 1. In other words, all earnings must be paid as dividends. If this is the case, then $g = 0$ because the firm has no earnings to reinvest in value-enhancing projects.

Comprehension Check

1. How is the dividend growth model used to determine the cost of equity?
2. What approaches can be used to estimate the growth rate in the dividend growth model?
3. Explain how it is possible for stocks with similar growth rates to have different values but the same expected returns.
4. Why is the use of the SML conceptually superior to the dividend growth model for calculating cost of equity?
5. Describe problems with implementing the SML approach for calculating the cost of equity.
6. What is the relationship between the cost of equity of an unlevered firm and a levered firm of equal business risk?
7. When is it appropriate to use the inverted PE ratio to estimate the cost of equity?

12.4 THE WEIGHTED AVERAGE COST OF CAPITAL

We have been discussing how to calculate the separate costs of debt, preferred stock, and common stock. If a company were able to use only debt financing, an impossible occurrence, its cost of capital is the after-tax cost of debt, $r_d \times (1 - \tau)$. If a company uses neither debt nor preferred stock financing, which is a possible but infrequent occurrence, the firm's cost of capital is the unlevered equity return required by the common shareholders, r_e^u. The most common practice is to use a combination of debt and equity

THE ROLE OF COST OF CAPITAL

by A. James Ifflander, Ph.D., Principal, Ifflander & Associates Consulting

I previously taught the beginning corporate finance class some years ago. Students always wanted to know the practical application of the topic. A frequent question was, "What is the cost of capital used for?" Today much of my livelihood entails teaching the basic concepts that are related to the cost of capital to lawyers, judges, and others in the legal environment. I am a financial consultant who testifies in court in support of my opinion of a firm's cost of capital. Many times the only point of dispute between the parties is the cost of capital. In these court cases the cost of capital is the discount rate used to value the cash flows generated by the company's assets.

These assets can be quite varied. I have valued coal and gold mines, aluminum smelting facilities, paper and pulp mills, telecommunications companies including local, long-distance, and cellular companies, railroads, electric utilities, and natural gas pipelines, among others. As you can well imagine these all involve different problems and quite different answers. But the basic techniques are similar. In fact, you might be surprised to see a report prepared for the court and submitted as evidence that includes the formulas, methods, and even a basic discussion of each of the financial models that corresponds very closely to the materials you study in this chapter. Very often these court decisions discuss terms, such as beta, the risk-free rate, the risk premium, and the expected growth rate. More than one judge has commented on the need for a degree in finance to understand the testimony of the assorted experts.

Let me give some examples of the testimony that may be given in court. In a recent case the capital asset pricing model (CAPM) and the dividend growth model (DGM) were utilized by the experts for each side in the dispute. In this case, the CAPM gave much higher answers than the DGM. A large part of the tes-timony revolved around which model gave the better answer. In my opinion, the CAPM's answer was inferior because the risk premium and the beta were incorrectly calculated by the opposing expert. The case also involved discussions of the proper weights to use for the debt and equity costs. In fact, the experts disagreed over whether to use a company-specific debt-to-equity mix or a financing mix that was closer to the industry average.

The cost of capital is also examined at length in many government agencies. For instance, your electric bill to a certain extent is based on calculations of the cost of capital. A utility's approved customer rates are based on factoring in their cost of capital. And don't be surprised if new health-care regulations yet to be issued by the Clinton administration include required examinations of the cost of capital for a wide range of medical-related industries. How else could we tell if these industries are earning an abnormal profit, as claimed by the Clinton administration?

Investment bankers concerned with the valuation of companies for merger or other corporate purposes also calculate the cost of capital. I have seen presentations to the board of directors of various companies where the cost of capital and all the inputs such as beta and the dividend growth rate are clearly stated to facilitate discussion.

Hopefully, I've convinced you that the cost of capital is one of the most crucial calculations that affects all of us in some way. It is widely used, discussed, and criticized in many different situations. It affects your electric and telephone bills. It is discussed by government officials and top managers of almost every company. Numerous court cases have examined various aspects of the cost of capital. Finally, millions of dollars are invested based on somebody's opinion of the cost of capital.

financing, and possibly preferred stock. In the latter case, we need to combine the costs of the different forms of financing to calculate an overall cost. Such a cost is called the firm's *weighted average cost of capital.*

12.4.1 Calculating the Weighted Average Cost of Capital

To calculate Ethridge Publishing's weighted average cost of capital, we must first calculate the proportion that the market value of the firm's debt is to the total market value of the firm (W_d), the proportion that the market value of the firm's preferred stock is to the total market value of the firm (W_p), and the proportion that the market value of the firm's equity is to the total market value of the firm (W_e). The market value of the firm is the summation of the market values for its debt (B), preferred stock (P), and common stock (S). For Ethridge Publishing, $B = \$7200$, $P = \$0$, and $S = \$9216$, as calculated in Chapter 11.

$$W_d = \frac{\text{Market value of debt}}{\text{Market value of the firm}}$$

$$= \frac{B}{B + P + S}$$

$$= \frac{\$7200}{\$7200 + \$0 + \$9216}$$

$$= 0.4386$$

(12.11)

$$W_p = \frac{\text{Market value of preferred stock}}{\text{Market value of the firm}}$$

$$= \frac{P}{B + P + S}$$

$$= \frac{\$0}{\$7200 + \$0 + \$9216}$$

$$= 0.0$$

(12.12)

$$W_e = \frac{\text{Market value of equity}}{\text{Market value of the firm}}$$

$$= \frac{S}{B + P + S}$$

$$= \frac{\$9216}{\$7200 + \$0 + \$9216}$$

$$= 0.5614$$

(12.13)

The proportions W_d, W_p, and W_e must sum to 1 (= 0.4386 + 0.0 + 0.5614) to indicate that all financing is considered in the calculation of the weighted average cost of capital. Multiplying these proportions by their respective after-tax costs and summing the results provides the firm's **weighted average cost of capital (WACC)**:

Weighted average cost of capital (WACC). The minimum rate of return that is acceptable on new nonrisk-changing investments in order to maintain the value of the firm.

$$\begin{aligned} \text{WACC} = {}& \text{After-tax cost of debt} \times \text{weight for debt} \\ & + \text{cost of preferred stock} \times \text{weight for preferred stock} \\ & + \text{cost of equity} \times \text{weight for equity} \\ = {}& r_d \times (1 - \tau) \times W_d + r_p \times W_p + r_e \times W_e \end{aligned}$$

(12.14)

Since debt interest is tax deductible, we adjust the cost of debt for taxes. Neither preferred stock nor common stock enjoy the same tax treatment. To calculate the WACC, we simply substitute the appropriate values into Equation 12.14. In practice, the difficult part is determining these values.

Let's continue with Ethridge Publishing to show how to apply Equation 12.14. Previously, we found that: $r_d = 0.08$, $\tau = 0.28$, and $r_e = 0.11125$. Ethridge does not use any preferred stock financing; thus, $r_p = W_p = 0$. Equations 12.11 through 12.13 show the weights to use. After making the necessary substitutions, we find that the WACC is 8.772 percent:

$$WACC = r_d \times (1 - \tau) \times W_d + r_p \times W_p + r_e \times W_e$$
$$= 0.08 \times (1 - 0.28) \times 0.4386 + 0 \times 0 + 0.11125 \times 0.5614$$
$$= 0.08772$$

Look at this WACC equation and consider how Ethridge Publishing should react to the increase in the corporate income tax rate enacted by the Clinton administration in 1993.[8] We should see Ethridge Publishing making greater use of debt because the government will now pay an even larger portion of each $1 of interest expense. The effect is to lower the after-tax cost of debt, and thereby the WACC, assuming that other factors affecting the cost of debt do not change.

12.4.2 Advantage of Debt Financing

A firm's cost of debt is *always* less than its cost of equity.[9] The reasons are twofold. First, debtholders are exposed to less risk than shareholders. Debtholders are the first investors (or are supposed to be) to receive cash distributions from the firm. Shareholders are last in priority to receive any cash distributions. Second, debt interest is a tax-deductible expense, thereby lowering its cost to the firm. Dividend payments are not tax-deductible expenses. Hence, the use of debt financing lowers the firm's WACC.

According to the WACC equation, as the firm finances with more debt and less equity, the WACC declines. The continually declining WACC curve in Figure 12.4 shows this phenomenon.

However, a continually falling WACC does not exist in the real world. A firm cannot be 100 percent debt financed. Lenders will not lend funds unless the owners of the firm have some of their own money (that is, equity) invested. Also, the Internal Revenue Service (IRS) has the authority to classify debt as equity if the firm uses too much debt financing, as we discussed in Chapter 7. The IRS views abnormally high amounts of debt as attempts by management to take extraordinary advantage of the tax deductibility of interest payments. And we can see the government's point. Higher interest deductions mean lower tax payments and less revenue for Uncle Sam. These factors, along with others discussed shortly, cause the cost of capital to increase beyond some level of prudent debt financing, as shown by the saucer-shaped curve for WACC in Figure 12.4.

Figure 12.4 suggests that there is an *optimal capital structure* for minimizing WACC. We will discuss some of the factors that management must consider in Section 12.6. First, let's examine the relationship that exists between firm value and WACC.

---

[8]Without the feature of tax deductibility of interest, the value of the firm is independent of its capital structure. As more debt is used, the cost of equity capital increases, which offsets any advantage of debt with the result that the WACC remains constant.

[9]We ignore preferred stock for this discussion. Few firms other than public utilities issue it. We could include it without changing our conclusions.

FIGURE 12.4

WEIGHTED AVERAGE COST OF CAPITAL

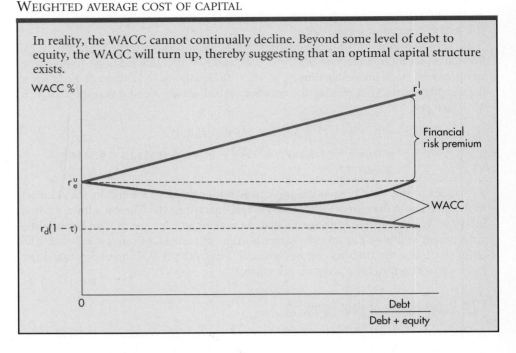

In reality, the WACC cannot continually decline. Beyond some level of debt to equity, the WACC will turn up, thereby suggesting that an optimal capital structure exists.

Once you understand the link between firm value and WACC, the concept of optimal capital structure should be easier.

Comprehension Check

1. How is the weighted average cost of capital calculated?
2. Why is the calculation of the cost of debt treated differently from the cost of equity when calculating the weighted average cost of capital?
3. Explain why the weighted average cost of capital is lowered for a firm that uses debt to replace some of the equity in its capital structure.
4. What practical limitations prevent a firm from being 100 percent debt financed?

 12.5 THE RELATIONSHIP BETWEEN FIRM VALUE AND WACC

At the beginning of this chapter, we heard a few laments from business executives about the high cost of capital and the hardships it has caused for their firms. They believed that if capital costs were lower, then their firms would have been more competitive and valued more highly in the financial markets. We briefly discussed this relationship in Chapter 11, but now let's formally tie together the concepts of valuation and cost of capital. We will continue to use Ethridge Publishing as our example. Table 12.1 summarizes important information about the company discussed in Chapter 11.

TABLE 12-1

PERTINENT INFORMATION ABOUT ETHRIDGE PUBLISHING, INC.

Cash operating profits before taxes (COP)	$2,000
Debt financing	$7,200
Interest rate on debt financing	8%
Interest expense (8% × $7200)	$576
Income tax rate (τ)	28%
Return to shareholders for business risk (r_e^u)	10%
Present value of tax shield provided by interest	
= Debt financing × tax rate	$2,016

Value of the firm

$$= \frac{COP \times (1 - \tau)}{r_e^u} + \text{present value of tax shield}$$

$$= \frac{\$2000 \times (1 - 0.28)}{0.10} + \$2016 \qquad \$16,416$$

The $16,416 value of Ethridge Publishing (in Table 12.1) uses Equation 11.10 from Chapter 11. We can derive the same value using Ethridge Publishing's WACC of 8.772 percent. WACC replaces r_e^u in the equation for the value of the firm and we drop the expression for the present value of the interest tax shield. The valuation equation that uses the firm's WACC is:

$$V^L = \frac{\text{Cash operating profits after taxes}}{\text{Weighted average cost of capital}} \qquad (12.15)$$

$$= \frac{\$2000 \times (1 - 0.28)}{0.08772}$$

$$= \$16,416$$

The WACC rate incorporates the tax shield provided by debt financing. It is important to realize that, although we get the same value for Ethridge Publishing using either Equation 12.15 or

$$V^L = \frac{COP \times (1 - \tau)}{r_e^u} + \text{present value of the tax shield}$$

in Table 12.1, there is an important conceptual difference. The difference is this: *A firm derives its WACC from the value of the firm; the firm's value is not derived from its WACC.*

Consider the issue from the following perspective. The investors of a publicly traded company often number in the thousands. Most of these investors do not know each other, and generally investors in a company's stock are not investors in its bonds. When these investors buy and sell the firm's debt and equity securities, they do so in the expectation of earning a return that satisfies them for the amount of risk they are exposed to by owning these securities. Any buying and selling activity determines market prices for the securities. If the financial markets are efficient, then the securities prices and thereby their returns are satisfactory to the participants.

Given that investors do not buy the firm's debt and equity securities in the same proportion that the firm has issued them (although they could), the return that these investors seek is not the firm's WACC—because WACC is dependent on the proportions of debt to equity in the financing mix. Rather, investors demand the market-determined rates for the individual securities. Or think of the issue from another perspective. When we calculated the firm's WACC, we used costs and weights based on market values for all securities issued by the firm. Thus, we had to know the market valuations investors put on the securities before we could calculate the WACC. And the firm's value equals the market value of its debt plus the market value of its equity.

What is the significance of the WACC? *It is the minimum return that new investments with risk characteristics similar to the firm's present portfolio of assets should earn.* Illustration 12.5 elaborates on why the WACC represents the minimum return.

ILLUSTRATION 12.5

Firm value and the WACC

The current financial status of Ethridge Publishing is reflected in its balance sheet, as stated in market values. Management is considering investing $1000 in a new project to be financed in the same proportions as its market-based balance sheet.

Balance Sheet Stated in Market Values

				Financing Proportion	Costs
Assets	$16,416	Debt	$ 7,200	43.86%	8.000%
		Equity	9,216	56.14	11.125
			$16,416	100.00%	8.772%*

*WACC = 0.08 × (1 − 0.28) × 0.4386 + 0.11125 × 0.5614 = 0.08772

Project earns the WACC

Management believes the project will earn its WACC. Thus, the incremental amount of value that this investment should add to the value of the firm is $1000: $1000 investment × 8.772% expected return ÷ 8.772% WACC. By financing the investment in its market-valued balance sheet proportions, management will use $438.60 debt and $561.40 equity. The amount of cash operating profit before taxes (COP) that must be earned each year is $121.83. At this level of COP, debt investors earn their 8 percent and shareholders earn their 11.125 percent.

Cash operating profit before taxes	$121.83
Interest (8% × $438.60)	35.09
Cash profit before taxes	$ 86.74
Taxes (28%)	24.29
Cash profit after taxes	$ 62.45

Debtholders would receive $35.09, which represents an 8 percent return on their $438.60 investment. The $561.40 investment by shareholders would earn 11.125 percent: $62.45 ÷ $561.40 = 0.11125. The project's total return would be 8.772 percent; the after-tax cash operating profit divided by the initial investment: $121.83 × (1 − 0.28) ÷ $1000 = 0.08772 or 8.772 percent.

By earning the WACC, the project would increase the value of the firm from $16,416 to $17,416. The $1000 difference is the the amount of the investment. Since the investment only earns its WACC, there is no value created beyond $1000.

Project's contribution to firm value

$$= \frac{\text{Cash operating profit after taxes from the project}}{\text{Required rate for business risk}}$$

$$+ \text{ present value of tax shield from debt financing}$$

$$= \frac{\$121.83 \times (1 - 0.28) + 0.28 \times \$438.60}{0.10}$$

$$= \$877.18 + \$122.81$$

$$= \$1000 \text{ (rounded)}$$

PROJECT EARNS LESS THAN THE WACC

Although the project is expected to earn 8.772 percent, what happens if it doesn't? Suppose the $1000 project only earns $100 cash operating profit before taxes? The project's total return would be 7.2 percent: $100 × (1 − 0.28) ÷ $1000. The debtholders would still receive $35.09 as interest payment, thereby earning their 8 percent. The shareholders who put up $561.40 as their share of the $1000 investment would only realize $46.74.

Cash operating profit before taxes	$100.00
Interest (8% × $438.60)	35.09
Cash profit before taxes	$ 64.91
Taxes (28%)	18.17
Cash profit after taxes	$ 46.74

The return to shareholders would be $46.74 ÷ $561.40 = 0.08326 or about 2.8 percentage points below what they require: 11.125% − 8.326%.

By only earning $100 of cash operating profit before taxes, the contribution of this $1000 project to the value of the firm would be $842.81.

Project's contribution to firm value

$$= \frac{\text{Cash operating profit after taxes from the project}}{\text{Required rate for business risk}}$$

$$+ \text{ present value of tax shield from debt financing}$$

$$= \frac{\$100 \times (1 - 0.28)}{0.10} + 0.28 \times \$438.60$$

$$= \$720 + \$122.81$$

$$= \$842.81$$

Thus, shareholders lose $157.19 of value ($1000 cost − $842.81 value) because the investment fails to earn the WACC.

PROJECT EARNS MORE THAN THE WACC

Suppose the project unexpectedly earns cash operating profit before taxes of $150. Value of the firm, and thereby shareholder value, should increase by $202.81 in excess of the project's $1000 cost. The total return in this case is 10.8 percent, about 2 percentage points greater than the firm's WACC. Can you derive these amounts?[10]

It is apparent from this illustration that cost of capital affects whether an investment makes any contribution to shareholder wealth. If management can lower cost of capital, projects become more valuable since they contribute value beyond their cost. This issue is at the heart of the point the executives quoted in our introduction were making. The remaining question to consider is *how much* debt to use.

 ## 12.6 AN OPTIMAL CAPITAL STRUCTURE

How much debt minimizes the firm's WACC? It is difficult to say exactly, although theory provides us with an understanding of important factors to consider: *agency costs, tax benefits,* and *financial distress costs.* Debtholders, shareholders, and managers often have conflicting objectives, as we discussed in Chapter 11. Let's briefly examine the conflicts as they pertain to capital structure.

12.6.1 Debtholder-Shareholder Conflicts

Why may debtholders and shareholders have different incentives? Debtholders are interested in safeguards for the firm's solvency to ensure repayment of funds they lent the firm. Shareholders invest in the firm with the understanding that getting an increased return on their equity investment requires taking risks; more risks than debt investors take. If the firm undertakes risky projects, shareholders reap most of the benefits from a successful project, while debt investors are paid a fixed return. On the other hand, if the project becomes unprofitable, debt investors may incur a portion of the loss due to the limited liability of the shareholders. Think of this situation as shareholders turning over their ownership interest in the firm to the debtholders. Such events occur whenever firms are unable to repay their creditors.

In an effort to prevent investment abuses by management, debt investors impose agency costs on the firm through the bond indenture, which restricts management's actions. For example, the indenture may place a ceiling on the dollar amount and a restriction on the type of new investment by the firm, the amount of total debt the firm can issue, or the amount of cash dividends the firm can pay common shareholders.

12.6.2 Management-Shareholder Conflicts

The conflict between management and shareholders arises because management does not always act in the best interest of shareholders. For most publicly traded firms, management's personal investment in the company's debt and equity financing is small. So

---

[10]Solutions: Value of project = [$150 × (1 − 0.28)] ÷ 0.10 + 0.28 × $438.60 = $1202.81; total return = [$150 × (1 − 0.28)] ÷ $1000 = 0.108 or 10.8 percent.

instead of acting as investors, managers act as *agents* for investors. As agents their responsibility is to operate the firm to satisfy objectives of investors. However, many people hold the view that management's primary objective is to increase its compensation, its perquisites (such as lavish offices and company airplanes), and the size of the firm to provide executives with more status in the business community.

In an attempt to minimize such problems, shareholders incur *agency costs* to monitor management. Monitoring activities can range from something as simple as hiring certified public accountants to audit the company's financial statements to the more difficult task of determining whether management should be removed.

12.6.3 Trade-off of Agency Costs

Theory suggests that the smaller the proportion of the firm's equity financing owned by management, the larger the incentive for management to act in its own self-interest. By replacing some of the firm's equity with debt, management's proportionate equity ownership increases. The beneficial result should be a better alignment of management and shareholders' objectives. However, greater use of debt to align the interest of management and shareholders puts debt investors at more risk. Thus, debt agency costs increase. Figure 12.5 graphs the problem.

12.6.4 Bankruptcy Costs Are Important

The trade-off of agency costs between debt and equity investors suggests that an optimal capital structure exists. However, the reality of an optimal capital structure is more

FIGURE 12.5

AGENCY COSTS AND CAPITAL STRUCTURE

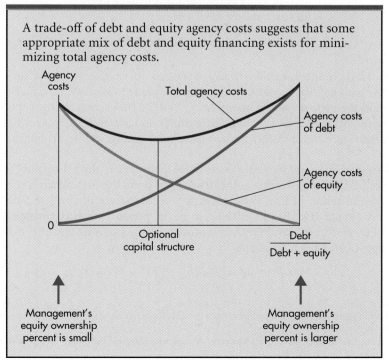

complex. There is a trade-off between the present value tax saving of borrowing and the cost of financial distress or bankruptcy.[11] Bankruptcy costs can amount to millions of dollars in legal and administrative fees. For instance, one estimate of direct costs associated with the 1990 Allied Stores/Federated Department Stores bankruptcy proceedings was $60 million annually until completion of the bankruptcy.[12] Accountants and attorneys were the largest recipients of these funds. Beyond the legal and administrative costs are indirect costs associated with business operations. The operations can be disrupted with the possible loss of customers and skilled employees.

However, a firm's bankruptcy does not have the same consequences for its investors as it does for its managers and employees. Investors can diversify their investment portfolios. They are concerned only with market risk of their investments; that is, the β risk. In contrast, managers, employees, and vendors are concerned with a larger risk. Managers and employees have so much of their investment in time and human capital tied up in the firm. They cannot diversify their efforts across other firms. Unless the firm represents a major portion of the vendor's business, a vendor is exposed to less risk than managers and employees. However, managers, employees, and vendors, in varying degrees, all concern themselves with the **total risk** of the firm defined as *diversifiable risk* plus *market risk*. Managers must balance the tax benefit of debt interest against their dual concern of financial distress costs and agency costs.

Total risk. Diversifiable risk plus nondiversifiable risk.

Figure 12.6 illustrates factors contributing to an optimal capital structure from the perspective of maximizing the firm's value. Value of the levered firm in the figure consists of several components:

Value of the firm with debt
= Value of the firm without debt
+ present value of growth opportunities
+ present value of the tax savings using debt
− present value of the costs of financial distress
− present value of agency costs

$$V^L = \frac{COP \times (1 - \tau)}{r_u} + PVGO + PVTS - PVFD - PVAC$$

(12.16)

Equation 12.16 is the valuation model discussed in Chapter 11 (and included in Table 12.1) with new expressions included for the *present value of financial distress costs (PVFD)* and the *present value of agency costs (PVAC)*. These costs are the expected discounted amounts incurred in avoiding bankruptcy and in minimizing agency problems between managers and investors and, at least theoretically, lead to an optimal capital structure.

The optimal capital structure exists at the point where the debt-equity financing mix maximizes the market value of the firm; at this point the firm minimizes its cost of capital. Maximization of firm value (Max V^L) occurs where the present value of the interest tax savings (PVTS) minus the sum of the present values of financial distress costs (PVFD) and agency costs (PVAC) is most positive, assuming the other expressions in Equation 12.16 remain constant:

$$\text{Max } V^L = \text{Max } \{PVTS - PVFD - PVAC, 0\}$$

(12.17)

---

[11]Part of agency costs of debt are *bankruptcy costs*. However, we separate bankruptcy costs to simplify the discussion.

[12]Louis Lowenstein, *Sense and Nonsense in Corporate Finance* (Reading, MA: Addison-Wesley Publishing Company, 1991), p. 44.

FIGURE 12.6

THEORETICAL OPTIMAL CAPITAL STRUCTURE

Optimal capital structure occurs at the point where the value of the firm is
maximized. At this point, WACC is minimized. Management must trade
off benefits realized from the interest tax shield against financial distress
and agency costs.

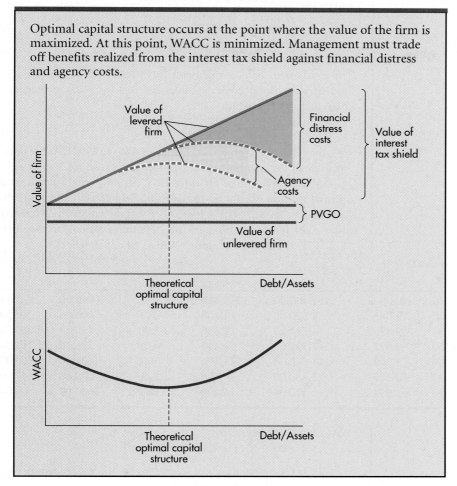

If management's choice of capital structure results in PVTS – PVAD – PVAC being negative, then that capital structure should be rejected. A better one can be found for
increasing value of the firm.

Illustration 12.6 provides a stylized example to show the tradeoff of various costs
which result in maximization of firm value and minimization of WACC. In reality, it is
extremely difficult to be as precise. For clarity, we assume that the present value of
growth opportunities is zero.

ILLUSTRATION 12.6

*Maximize
value of the
firm*

Assume that Ethridge Publishing is all-equity financed with a market value of $14,400. Management is considering issuing debt at
par to repurchase common stock. The corporate income tax rate is
28 percent. An investment banker advises management that the

present value of financial distress costs (PVFD) and the present value of agency costs (PVAC) can be estimated by the following equations:[13]

$$PVFD = 0.0001 \times (\text{debt financing})^2$$

$$PVAC = (PVFD)^{1/2}$$

The investment banker calculates the estimated value of the levered firm, in the presence of financial distress costs and agency costs, using the equation:

$$V^L = V^u + PVTS - PVFD - PVAC$$

V^u is the value of the unlevered firm ($14,400) and PVTS is the present value of the interest tax saving, both discussed in Chapter 11.

Value of the firm for different debt amounts follows. The optimal amount of debt for maximizing firm value is about $1250. At this debt level, PVTS − PVFD − PVAC is larger than for any other debt level, resulting in the maximum value for the firm ($14,581.25) and the minimum WACC (9.876 percent).

Debt	WACC	V^L	=	V^u	+	PVTS	−	PVFD	−	PVAC
$ 0	10.000%	$14,400.00		$14,400		$ 0		$ 0.00		$ 0.00
1000	9.883	14,570.00		14,400		280		100.00		10.00
1250	9.876	14,581.25		14,400		350		156.25		12.50
1500	9.877	14,580.00		14,400		420		225.00		15.00
2000	9.904	14,540.00		14,400		560		400.00		20.00
4000	10.375	13,880.00		14,400		1120		1600.00		40.00
6000	11.594	12,420.00		14,400		1680		3600.00		60.00

$$WACC = \text{Cash operating profit after taxes} \div V^L$$
$$= \$2000 \times (1 - 0.28) \div V^L$$

$$V^u = \text{Cash operating profit after taxes} \div \text{unlevered equity cost}$$
$$= \$2000 \times (1 - 0.28) \div 0.10$$
$$= \$14,400$$

$$PVTS = \text{Tax rate} \times \text{debt financing}$$
$$= 0.28 \times \text{debt financing}$$

Comprehension Check

1. Why is there a conflict between management and investors, and between debtholders and shareholders? How do these conflicts get resolved?
2. What factors affect the determination of a firm's optimal capital structure?
3. What is the interpretation of maximizing the value of the firm model, shown as Equation 12.17?

[13]These costs have been simplified greatly and are much more difficult to estimate than we assume in this illustration.

SUMMARY ▼▼▼▼▼▼▼▼▼▼▼

THE COST OF DEBT

- The firm's cost of debt is its yield to maturity adjusted for corporate income taxes.

THE COST OF PREFERRED STOCK

- The firm's cost of preferred stock is its market dividend yield.

THE COST OF EQUITY

- Analysts often use the dividend growth model, restated in terms of the required market return, to estimate the cost of equity.
- An accurate forecast of cost of equity depends on estimating the expected growth rate for dividends. The sustainable growth model and security analysts' forecasts are the primary means of estimating the growth component.
- Estimating the cost of equity from the dividend growth model fails to offer insight into the source of different cost-of-equity rates among firms.
- The SML model has a strong theoretical base for estimating cost of equity, but in practice it may be difficult to implement.
- A firm financed entirely with equity compensates shareholders for business risk. When the firm uses debt financing, it incurs financial risk (default risk).
- Financial risk causes the return expected by shareholders to increase.
- The inverted PE ratio provides a poor estimate of the cost of equity for all but the exceptional cases of no growth in the firm and all earnings are paid as dividends.

THE WEIGHTED AVERAGE COST OF CAPITAL

- Weighted average cost of capital (WACC) sums the weighted after-tax costs for debt, preferred stock, and equity.
- Weights are based on market values for each type of financing used.
- WACC represents the minimum required return the firm must earn for non-risk-changing investments.
- Debt financing lowers the WACC (at least up to some point). Lower WACC means higher value for the firm. However, it is not feasible for a firm to be 100 percent debt financed.

THE RELATIONSHIP BETWEEN FIRM VALUE AND WACC

- A firm derives its WACC from the value of the firm, not the other way around.
- Projects earning more than the WACC improve shareholder value and the value of the firm.
- Projects earning less than the WACC cause the value of the firm and shareholder value to decline.

AN OPTIMAL CAPITAL STRUCTURE

- Conflicts between debt investors, shareholders, and management set the stage for agency costs.

The Cost of Debt

Cost of debt

The Cost of Preferred Stock

Cost of preferred stock

The Cost of Equity

Cost of equity
Default risk premium
Financial risk
Return on beginning equity

The Weighted Average Cost of Capital

Weighted average cost of capital

An Optimal Capital Structure

Total risk

- The trade-off of agency costs for debt against agency costs for equity suggest that an optimal mix of debt and equity financing exists for maximizing the value of the firm.
- The optimal capital structure is also affected by the trade-off of tax savings and financial distress costs.

FURTHER READING ▼▼▼▼▼▼▼▼▼▼▼▼

Kester, W. Carl, and Timothy A. Luehrman, "The Myth of Japan's Low Cost Capital," *Harvard Business Review* (May–June 1992), pp. 130–138. This article discusses differences between cost of capital for U.S. and Japanese firms.

Lewellen, Wilbur G. *The Cost of Capital.* Dubuque, IA: Kendall/Hunt Publishing Company, 1976. This book clearly reveals an integrated view of the corporate financing decision, the cost of capital, and value of the firm.

SELF-TEST PROBLEMS ▼▼▼▼▼▼▼▼▼▼▼▼

ST12-1. Use the internal rate of return (IRR) model of Chapter 8 to calculate the cost of debt for Matrix Limited's outstanding bonds. The bonds mature in 15 years, have a coupon rate of 9 percent, pay interest annually, and have a maturity value of $1000. The bonds have a current market price of $923.94. Matrix's income tax rate is at 34 percent.

ST12-2. Several years ago, General Motors sold preferred stock for $30 per share. The annual dividend is $1.98. If the current market price of this preferred stock is $26\frac{3}{8} per share, what is the cost of this preferred stock to GM?

ST12-3. Photon Graphics Corporation's current stock price is $19.50, as quoted on the American Stock Exchange. Last year's dividend was $0.60. Dividends have grown 10 percent annually and are expected to continue to grow at this rate for the foreseeable future. What is Photon's cost of common stock?

PROBLEMS ▼▼▼▼▼▼▼▼▼▼▼▼

THE COST OF DEBT

12-1. Assuming a corporate tax rate of 34 percent, what is the cost of debt to the company if it can issue additional bonds at the same market rate currently earned on its 25-year, 10 percent bonds which sell for $1511.34 each? The bonds have a maturity value of $1000 and pay interest annually. (*Hint:* Use the IRR model of Chapter 8.)

12-2. Calculate the cost of a new issue of bonded debt for Starter Corp. The new bonds are expected to have the same market rate as a currently outstanding bond issue that matures in ten years for $1000, has a coupon rate of 7 percent, and pays interest annually. The old bonds currently sell for $871.26. The company's tax rate is 25 percent. (*Hint:* Use the IRR model of Chapter 8 to solve the problem.)

12-3. If the debt of Jorge's, Inc. has an A rating by Standard & Poor's rating service and A-rated bonds currently yield 9.5 percent, what is the after-tax cost of debt if Jorge's marginal tax rate is 39 percent?

12-4. What is the after-tax cost of debt for Starpoint Corporation if its borrowing cost is 11 percent and the firm's tax rate is 30 percent?

The Cost of Preferred Stock

12-5. Morgan Stanley has an issue of preferred stock outstanding that pays an annual dividend of $2.22 per share. The current market price of the stock is $27.75. What is the company's cost of capital for preferred stock?

12-6. RJR Nabisco Limited has an issue of preferred stock outstanding that pays a dividend of $0.84. If the current market price of the stock is $7.75, what is the current cost of this preferred stock?

12-7. Is the preferred stock issued by Morgan Stanley (Problem 12-5) more or less risky than the preferred stock issued by RJR Nabisco (Problem 12-6)? Why?

The Cost of Equity

12-8. A stock has a current market price of $27.50 and is expected to grow at a constant rate of 4 percent in perpetuity. The *current* dividend is $2.25. What is the required market rate that justifies this price? State any necessary assumptions.

12-9. Common dividends paid by Dime Department Store are expected to grow at a rate of 6 percent in perpetuity. Dividends are *currently* $2.10 per share on stock traded at $35. Calculate Dime's expected equity return.

12-10. The stock of ISG is selling for $34.50 per share. The firm is expected to pay a dividend of $2.50 per share next year and experience long-term growth of 6 percent. What is the firm's cost of equity?

12-11. Charlotte Luggage Company is planning to pay its initial common stock dividend next year. Total earnings this year are expected to be $400,000. The common stock of the company is currently trading at $7.25 per share and there are 200,000 shares outstanding. The company anticipates long-run growth of 8 percent each year. If investors want a return of at least 12 percent, what is the minimum dividend payout amount the firm should make?

12-12. The Southern Steel Company expects earnings per share of $3 next year. Its retention ratio averages about 60 percent annually. If the expected dividend yield over the next year is 10 percent, and the growth rate in dividends is 5 percent, what is the cost of equity?

12-13. The cost of equity financing decreases as a firm employs more leverage. Is this statement correct? Discuss.

12-14. a. Determine the cost of equity capital for McEnroe Tennis Corporation. The company has a debt-to-equity ratio of 0.4, a 34 percent tax rate, a cost of debt of 12 percent, and an unlevered cost of equity of 15 percent.

b. If the debt-to-equity ratio rose to 0.8 with no change in the cost of debt, what would be the cost of equity?

12-15. Assume that the risk-free rate of interest is 7 percent, the expected return on the market portfolio is 13 percent, and the betas for five companies are as follows: Firm 1 = 0.25; Firm 2 = 0.75; Firm 3 = 1.0; Firm 4 = 1.45; Firm 5 = 2.25.

a. Calculate the cost of equity for each firm.
b. Explain the relationship between beta and the cost of equity.

12-16. Calculate Quadra, Inc.'s cost of equity using the capital asset pricing model approach. The company's beta is 2.0, the risk-free rate is 6 percent, and the average return on the market is 12 percent.

12-17. The market return for Zisson Corporation is 18 percent, whereas the risk-free rate and the market portfolio yield are 6 percent and 12 percent, respectively. What is the value for Zisson's beta?

12-18. Renner Company's equity beta is 1.2. The dividend growth model suggests a cost of equity of 15 percent. If the cost of equity derived by the security market line and the dividend growth model are equal, and the return on the market portfolio is 14 percent, what is the risk-free rate?

THE WEIGHTED AVERAGE COST OF CAPITAL

12-19. MAG Computers is financed by 40 percent debt and 60 percent equity. There are 10,000 outstanding common shares valued at $30 each. Equityholders require a 16 percent return and debtholders require a 10 percent return. The tax rate is 34 percent. What is its weighted average cost of capital?

12-20. The management of Exclusive Designers has reason to believe that its current financing of 50 percent debt and 50 percent equity is optimal in a valuation sense. The firm pays 8 percent interest on its debt and estimates an equity cost of 14 percent. The company's tax rate is 34 percent. What is the weighted average cost of capital?

12-21. The Costello Company's debt-equity ratio is 0.6 using market values. Debt requires a 10 percent return, whereas equity requires a 17 percent return. The market value of common stock is $8 million. Calculate Costello's weighted average cost of capital assuming no change in the current financing mix and no sale of additional common stock. The tax rate is 34 percent.

12-22. Calculate the weighted average cost of capital for the Dryden Corporation using the following data. Market values represent value per bond and value per common and preferred share.

	Accounting Value	Market Value
Bonds, 9% coupon, $1000 par	$ 4,500,000	$1000
Preferred stock, 7%, $100 par	1,500,000	90
Common stock, 100,000 shares	1,000,000	65
Retained earnings	2,500,000	

Common stock dividends are expected to be $400,000 this year and grow at 5 percent per year. The firm's tax rate is 34 percent.

12-23. Calculate the weighted average cost of capital for a firm with the following financing:

- Debt: 40,000 bonds, par $1000, 8 percent interest in perpetuity
- Preferred stock: 250,000 shares, par $100, 10 percent interest
- Common equity: $75 million

The tax rate is 34 percent, the cost of equity is 15 percent, the market rate for debt is 10 percent, and the market rate for preferred stock is 12 percent.

12-24. The total assets of LEMA Company are expected to increase by $15 million during the next year. The firm's financing consists of the following amounts:

Debt, 9% coupon bonds, $1000 par	$ 7,000,000
Preferred stock, 12% coupon, $100 par	3,000,000
Common stock, $1 par	1,000,000
Retained earnings	9,000,000
Total financing	$20,000,000

Bonds with a 10 percent coupon can be sold at par and 12 percent preferred stock can be sold at a 10 percent discount from par. The risk-free rate is 6 percent and the return on the market is 13 percent. The beta for the common stock of LEMA is 1.4. The expansion is not expected to affect the beta. The corporate tax rate is 34 percent.

Compute the firm's weighted average cost of capital. The firm's target weights are the current accounting (that is, book) weights.

12-25. The Sale Co. is soon to be incorporated. Its promoters are considering five different possible capital structures for the new company. An analysis of comparable companies with equivalent business risks has been undertaken. This analysis shows that if the before-tax cost of debt is a constant 10 percent, regardless of the capital structure, then the cost of equity capital will be as follows:

Debt-Total Capital	Cost of Equity
0%	20.00%
20	21.25
40	23.33
50	25.00
60	27.50

The preceding predictions for the equity cost of capital also assume that the earnings of the Sale Co. will be taxed at a rate of 40 percent and that the debt interest is an allowable expense for tax purposes. The promoters expect that the company will generate a steady annual earnings stream of $12.6 million, before the payment of debt interest and taxes, for the foreseeable future.

a. Calculate the effective after-tax weighted average cost of capital for each of the five possible capital structures, assuming that the before-tax annual cost of debt will be a constant 10 percent, regardless of the capital structure chosen.

b. Discuss the possible consequences to a company of having a capital structure containing a high leverage ratio.

THE RELATIONSHIP BETWEEN FIRM VALUE AND WACC

12-26. Assume that two firms exist which differ only by how they are financed. The constant operating cash flows for both firms are equal. The unlevered firm is financed by 3 million shares of common stock with a market price per share of $10. The market discount rate for the unlevered firm is 15 percent. The levered firm has 2 million shares of stock and $10 million in long-term debt with an interest rate of 10 percent. The corporate tax rate is 40 percent.

a. Calculate the value of the firm. (*Hint:* First calculate the unlevered firm's value and use your answer to value the levered firm.)

b. Calculate the operating cash flows (before taxes and interest payments) for each firm.

c. How much is the net income for each firm?

d. Calculate the cost of equity and the weighted average cost of capital for each firm.

e. Prove that your cost of capital figures in part (d) are correct by using them to capitalize each firm's after-tax operating cash flow to derive the firm's respective market value found in part (a).

12-27. Two firms are identical except for how they are financed. One firm uses debt in its financing, whereas the other firm does not. At a tax rate of 34 percent and a discount rate of 10 percent, the value of the unlevered firm is $660.

a. How much is the amount of constant cash flow from operations for the unlevered firm?

b. If the tax rate increases from 34 percent to 46 percent, what is the value of the unlevered firm?

c. If the levered firm is financed with $100 debt, and the balance with equity, how much is the value of the firm before and after the tax rate change?

d. How much is the levered firm's cost of capital before and after the tax rate increase?

12-28. A company currently has no debt financing. The market value of each of its 5 million outstanding shares is $25. The new management of the company is convinced that debt financing increases the aggregate market value of the company's outstanding securities by the present value of the corporate tax shield on interest payments. In other words, management believes that $V^L = V^u + PVTS$. Operating earnings before taxes are expected to be constant at $35 million. The corporate tax rate is 30 percent.

Management is considering repurchasing 2.4 million of its own shares at $25 per share. The repurchased shares will be financed by issuing (at par) $60 million in 9 percent perpetual debentures.

a. What is the value of the firm before it issues debt?

b. What rate does the market require on the unlevered shares?

c. How much is the tax shield if $60 million of debt is issued?

d. If management is correct in believing that $V^L = V^u + PVTS$, what is the expected market value of equity on a per share basis once the firm replaces some equity with debt financing?

e. What is the market return required by the company's shareholders?

f. What is the firm's cost of capital if it issues debt and retires some equity?

12-29. Refer to the data in Problem 12-28. As an alternate strategy, management is considering a leveraged buyout. An offer would be made to purchase all of the 5 million outstanding shares at $30 per share. The purchase price of $150 million would be financed as follows. A temporary loan of $105 million would be obtained from banks and insurance companies. In addition, management would invest $45 million of its own funds. Once all the company's shares were purchased, management would recapitalize the firm. Recapitalization would be done by borrowing $105 million and repurchasing for $105 million 70 percent of the shares (3.5 million of the 5 million shares) just acquired by management. Thus, 1.5 million shares would be left outstanding and owned by management.

a. What is the required rate of return to shareholders?

b. How much is the weighted average cost of capital?

12-30. The Rolf Company is all-equity financed. It has 750,000 shares outstanding with a market value of $10 each. The company earns an average of $2.5 million in annual operating cash flows before interest and taxes. Every year all earnings are paid out as dividends. Management is considering issuing (at par) $3 million in 15 percent perpetual debt to repurchase stock at $10 per share. The corporate tax rate is 30 percent.

a. How much is the cost of equity if no debt is issued?

b. If the firm issues debt to retire equity, how much is the value of the firm?

c. If the firm issues debt to retire equity, how much is the firm's cost of capital?

An Optimal Capital Structure

12-31. Given that interest payments are tax deductible for a corporation while dividend payments are not, should companies finance all of their assets with debt?

12-32. Management of Mesa, Inc. is contemplating a leveraged buyout whereby it would acquire 100 percent of the 500,000 outstanding common shares of the all-equity financed firm. All shares are currently owned by one investor. The purchase price would be equal to the current fair market value of $30 per share.

Management has a limited amount of cash it can commit to the purchase. Thus, management plans to recapitalize. Mesa would repurchase a portion of the shares initially acquired by management and issue debt to investors to finance the purchase. A possible consequence of indebtedness is the likelihood the firm will become bankrupt. Management's analysis suggests that different levels of debt would be associated with the following likelihood of bankruptcy costs:

Level of Debt	Likelihood of Bankruptcy	Present Value of Bankruptcy Costs If They Occur
$0 million	0.0000	$0.000 million
3 million	0.0537	2.795 million
6 million	0.1518	3.953 million
9 million	0.2789	4.841 million
12 million	0.4293	5.590 million
15 million	0.6000	6.250 million

The market value of interest tax shield is equal to τB—tax rate $\times$ market value of debt. Mesa's tax rate is 30 percent of taxable income.

a. If management wants to maximize the gain derived from the buyout, how much debt should it use? (*Hint:* Determine the expected present value bankruptcy costs and then apply the model Max $\{\tau B - $ present value of bankruptcy costs$\}$).

b. What would the respective market values of debt and equity be? (*Hint:* First, find the value of the unlevered firm before the buyout. This value equals V^u. Next, find the value of the levered firm: $V^L = V^u + \tau B - $ PVFD. Finally, use the equation $V^L = $ Value of debt $+$ value of equity.)

12-33. A new firm forecasts $900,000 in constant operating income before taxes. The chief financial officer is considering four separate alternatives for financing the firm's required investments:

- 100 percent equity ($4 million in shares of stock)
- $3 million in stock and $1 million of 7 percent bonds
- $2 million in stock and $2 million of 7 percent bonds
- $1 million in stock and $3 million of 7 percent bonds

The corporate tax rate is 34 percent. For each alternative, calculate the value of the firm and the weighted average cost of capital. The capitalization rate for the unlevered firm is 12 percent. The bonds are issued at par.

DISCLOSURE ASSIGNMENTS

12-34. Use the *Disclosure* database to obtain the following information for Nike, Inc. and Reebok International Limited.

- Latest closing stock price
- Zack's earnings estimates for the expected growth rate in earnings per share over the next five years
- Annual dividend
- Dividend payout ratio

Use this information in the dividend growth model to estimate each firm's cost of equity.

LIBRARY ASSIGNMENT

12-35. Select a company whose name begins with the first letter of your last name, and whose common stock trades on the New York Stock Exchange.

a. If the firm has publicly traded debt, what is its current internal rate of return (yield to maturity)?
b. If the firm issues preferred stock, what is the market cost of the stock?
c. Calculate the firm's cost of equity using both the dividend growth model and the security market line model. Use the yield of a 30-year Treasury bond as a proxy for the risk-free rate. Assume that the annualized yield for the Standard & Poor's 500 stock index is representative of the return on the market portfolio. Estimate the growth rate for the dividend growth model using the past ten-year growth in dividends per share. If the stock pays no dividends, then use the ten-year growth rate in earnings per share.

COMPREHENSIVE PROBLEM ▼▼▼▼▼▼▼▼▼▼▼▼

12-36. The capital structure of Xebys Corporation is shown below. It reflects management's desired proportions of debt and equity financing.

Debt, 8% coupon bonds, $1000 par	$10,000,000
Preferred stock, 7% coupon, $50 par	5,000,000
Common stock, $1 par	1,000,000
Retained earnings	34,000,000
Total	$50,000,000

New $1000 par-value bonds may be sold at par with a 9 percent coupon. New $25 par-value preferred stock may be sold at par with a dividend of $2.10. Cash dividends on the firm's common stock have grown at a rate of 12 percent, which is expected to continue. Next year's expected common stock dividend is

$0.90. The company's common stock, with a beta of 1.2, sells over the counter for $18 per share. The risk-free rate is 5 percent and the market portfolio yields 15 percent. The company's tax rate is 34 percent.

a. Calculate the cost of debt for Xebys Corporation.
b. Calculate the cost of the company's preferred stock.
c. Calculate the company's cost of equity using both the dividend growth model and the security market line.
d. How much is the weighted average cost of capital?
e. What is the minimum expected rate of return for new investments by Xebys, assuming that the new projects do not change the overall risk of the company?

ANSWERS TO SELF-TEST PROBLEMS ▼▼▼▼▼▼▼▼▼▼▼▼

ST12-1. By trial and error, or using a financial calculator, the discount rate is 10 percent:

$$\$90 \times \text{PVIFA}_{10\%, \ 15 \text{ years}} + \$1000 \times \text{PVIF}_{10\%, \ 15 \text{ years}}$$

$$= \$90 \times 7.60607 + \$1000 \times 0.23939$$
$$= \$684.55 + \$239.39$$
$$= \$923.94$$

The after-tax cost of the debt is $0.10 \times (1 - 0.34) = 0.066$ or 6.6 percent.

ST12-2.

$$\text{Cost of preferred stock} = \frac{\text{Dividend}}{\text{Market price of stock}}$$

$$= \$1.98 \div \$26.375$$
$$= 0.0751 \text{ or } 7.51 \text{ percent}$$

ST12-3. Use the dividend growth model to calculate the equity cost.

$$\text{Cost of equity} = \frac{\text{Dividend next period}}{\text{Current stock price}} + \text{expected growth}$$

$$= \frac{\$0.60 \times (1 + 0.10)}{\$19.50} + 0.10$$

$$= 0.1338 \text{ or } 13.38 \text{ percent}$$

Video Case 12

RJR Nabisco Bondholder Lawsuits: An Example Of Leverage Related Agency Problems

from *Business World,* November 20, 1988

Financing the firm with debt creates both benefits and costs for shareholders. The advantages of debt financing include the tax deductibility of interest payments and some potentially valuable changes in managerial incentives. The disadvantages of debt include costs associated with an increased probability of financial distress or bankruptcy, and the costs of satisfying bond covenants. The *optimal* capital structure adds debt until the advantages and disadvantages just offset one another. Increasing debt beyond this optimal point causes the value of the firm to decrease. The accompanying video clip provides a real-world example of how leverage increases affect securityholders.

The video clip describes how the announcement of the RJR management buyout proposal sparked the wrath of a number of investors who own RJR Nabisco bonds. To complete the management buyout RJR had to borrow an enormous amount of money—possibly $12 to $16 billion—to repurchase all the firm's outstanding common stock and take the firm private. By adding this new debt to the company's existing debt, the risk of the older bonds increased dramatically. As risk increased, prices fell. After the announcement RJR bondholders suddenly owned bonds worth 20 percent less than they were the day before! For Metropolitan Life Insurance Company this meant a $40 million loss of value of its investment in RJR bonds.

When MetLife purchased the RJR Nabisco bonds, it accepted a coupon rate appropriate for the risk of the company as it was organized at that time. With additional debt the probability of the company defaulting on its interest payments increases. The interest on the new debt drains cash out of the firm, reducing the safety buffer that holders of the older bonds included in their estimate of their bonds' risk. As you

know from earlier chapters, as risk increases security prices fall. Bondholders have a contractual agreement to accept a fixed interest payment or coupon rate. This coupon rate was determined when there was no suspicion that a leveraged buyout might occur. The announcement of the buyout suddenly increased the risk of the bonds, but bondholders are stuck with the agreed upon coupon rate—a coupon rate that does not reflect the new risk of the firm. Interestingly, while bondholders lost, shareholders gained. The new debt financed a bid to purchase RJR's common shares at a price well above the share price prior to the announcement. This demonstrates that the interests of bondholders and shareholders differ, and at times actually conflict, adding yet another dimension to corporate decision making.

Study Questions

1. How can a transaction that harms RJR's bondholders be good for shareholders? How do shareholders benefit at the expense of bondholders? What can bondholders do to protect themselves from being taken advantage of?

2. Why do you think that bondholders are often forgotten in corporate decisions?

3. The conflict of interest between bondholders and shareholders exists on several levels. For example, consider the risk of the investments that the company makes. Bondholders want projects that assure payment of the interest and principal on their bonds. What does this imply about bondholders preference toward risky versus safe investments? On the other hand, common shareholders get nothing until senior securityholders are paid. Thus, they are interested in large payouts. What does this imply about their preference toward risk?

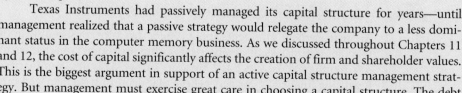

CHAPTER 13

Capital Structure Management

Texas Instruments, Inc. (TI) is in the semiconductor memory business. Based on internal studies in the late 1980s, management concluded that if it did not reduce TI's cost of capital, the company would never regain its ability to be a world-class computer memory manufacturer. TI management concluded that the cost of capital of the U.S. semiconductor industry was roughly 75 percent higher than that of its Japanese counterpart. Such a large difference in cost of funds put the American firm at a clear and direct disadvantage in a business where success is in large measure determined by ability and willingness to invest. To overcome this disadvantage and regain its leadership in this capital-intensive business, TI management decided to pursue a more active role in managing its capital structure so as "to stimulate access to a low cost of capital environment."[1]

TI entered into a series of joint ventures in an effort to lower its cost of capital. Partners included the Italian government, Acer of Taiwan, and Kobe Steel of Japan, among others. The partners contributed millions of dollars, low-cost loans, tax incentives, and infrastructure improvements; TI contributed technical know-how and management expertise.

Texas Instruments had passively managed its capital structure for years—until management realized that a passive strategy would relegate the company to a less dominant status in the computer memory business. As we discussed throughout Chapters 11 and 12, the cost of capital significantly affects the creation of firm and shareholder values. This is the biggest argument in support of an active capital structure management strategy. But management must exercise great care in choosing a capital structure. The debt versus equity choice is difficult because the factors involved are complex and the impact of each on firm and equity value is not obvious. Any advantage of additional debt must be balanced against any additional costs. Neither the advantages nor the costs lend them-

---

[1]Joseph Morone and Albert Paulson, "Cost of Capital: The Managerial Perspective," *California Management Review* (Summer 1991), p. 15.

TABLE 13-1

FINANCING POLICIES AND PRACTICES

Does your firm believe that there is a functional relationship between its capital costs and the amount of debt which it utilizes in its financial structure?

Yes responses: 92%

Does your firm believe that the use of an excessive amount of debt will eventually result in an increase in the yield (cost) of debt faced by your company?

Yes responses: 97%

Does your firm believe that the use of an excessive amount of debt will eventually result in the market price of your common stock being adversely affected?

Yes responses: 90%

Does your firm believe that there is some maximum amount of debt financing that should not be surpassed? (That is, does your firm subscribe to the concept of a corporate debt capacity?)

Yes responses: 87%

Source: D. F. Scott and D. J. Johnson, "Financing Policies and Practices in Large Corporations," Financial Management *(Summer 1982), pp. 51–59.*

selves to precise measurement. In the end, the choice of capital structure requires expert judgment on the part of the chief financial officer and the firm's investment bankers.

This chapter examines some practical ways to manage the complex capital structure problem. When you have completed this chapter, you should understand:

- How the firm's ability to service debt, use tax shields, attain a desired bond rating, and manage subsidiaries affects the capital structure decision.
- How to measure business risk and financial risk using accounting data.
- How firms alter their capital structures over time to more desired debt levels.

13.1 PRACTICAL ISSUES ABOUT CAPITAL STRUCTURE

Are management's thoughts about capital structure consistent with the theoretical idea that an optimal debt-equity relationship exists, as we discussed in Chapter 12? Apparently so, as suggested by one survey's results, summarized in Table 13.1. Practicing financial managers believe that debt must be managed carefully. Otherwise, they feel that financing costs will increase too much, and the result will be that value of the firm's securities will decline.

The nearby Financial Reality articles illustrate how debt helped focus management of Goodyear Tire & Rubber Company in its pursuit of improving shareholder value. On the other hand, too much debt financing led to the destruction of Harcourt Brace Jovanovich, Inc.

Some of the principal factors influencing management's decision about capital structure include the following:

DEBT FOCUSES THE MIND

Jimmy Goldsmith is not beloved at Goodyear Tire, but his thwarted raid of 1986 had some beneficial results.

Mark 1990 as the Year of the Blowout for Goodyear Tire & Rubber Co. It took its first annual loss since 1932. But 1990 was also the year that Goodyear began to put the rubber to the road. As a result, the company's future looks brighter than it has in years.

Goodyear's problems crystallized in 1986, when Sir James Goldsmith threatened to take over the company. To buy him off, Goodyear added $2.6 billion to its long-term debt, ransomed the raider's 12.5 million shares and bought back another 40 percent of its stock, reducing the total to near its current $58 million.

Goodyear's $3.3 billion in long-term debt remains a millstone. Debt service is over $300 million a year, equal to over $3 on every one of the tires Goodyear makes.

Say this for debt: It does focus the managerial mind on efficiency. During 1988 through 1990, Goodyear sold many of its nontire businesses and consolidated operations, modernized factories, and cut jobs—saving an estimated $250 million a year. It has grown more market sensitive at its 6300 outlets.

Also during 1988–1990, Goodyear invested $1.4 billion to upgrade its production facilities and switch almost exclusively to radial-tire production. The company has always been considered the low-cost producer but has improved on that.

In January 1990, after dropping two points of market share because of untimely price increases, Goodyear stopped trying to sell its tires at premium prices over competing brands. It cut prices on most tires by around $15 a tire. Result: Goodyear has recovered that lost market share, to about 28 percent of the North American business.

- Ability to service debt.
- Ability to use tax-shield benefits.
- Desired bond rating category.
- Use of foreign and finance subsidiaries.

We will examine each of these factors in turn.

13.1.1 Ability to Service Debt

The most direct and relevant measure of risk inherent in a leveraged capital structure is the projection of a firm's future cash flows and resources available to meet future cash requirements. A shortage of cash available to service debt is the most adverse possibility for any company. Thus, management must have:

- A strategy for selling future securities when the firm needs access to new financing.

DEBT MISMANAGED

Men such as Bruce Wasserstein, who with his partner, Joseph Perella, made hundreds of millions of dollars buying, selling and restructuring businesses through their investment-banking firm, Wasserstein Perella & Co.

In September 1987, during an appearance before a House Energy and Commerce subcommittee, Wasserstein discussed corporate debt and the unique abilities of sophisticated financial advisers to determine which companies were capable of carrying large amounts of debt.

He cited as an example Harcourt Brace Jovanovich Inc., a book publishing company that had expanded into other areas, including the Sea World theme parks and insurance.

In May 1987, British media mogul Robert Maxwell sought to buy Harcourt for about $2 billion, or $44 a share. To fend off the bid, Harcourt took on $2 billion in debt and distributed cash to stockholders.

Wasserstein approved of the move. "The shareholders have every reason to be ecstatic over what happened at Harcourt, because the offer that came in for the company was at something in the mid-$40, and the total value of the package shareholders received was something over $60 a share. We are confident that Harcourt will do very well, and that is reflected in the marketplace today."

Notwithstanding the sophisticated financial advice that Harcourt received, the company was unable to meet the interest payments on a staggering $2.5 billion debt without selling off properties, closing some operations, and laying off employees.

For 1987, the year it took on the new debt, Harcourt reported net income of $83.4 million. In 1988, the year after, the company lost $53.5 million. In 1989, Harcourt reported net income of $12.4 million. But that was due to the sale of its theme parks for $1.1 billion. Without the sale of assets, Harcourt would have lost $242.2 million on its operations.

As for the company's stock, in 1986—the year before the money industry moved in—it traded at a high of $104 a share. In late November 1991, it traded at 62.5 cents per share.

Ever since the restructuring that Wasserstein oversaw, Harcourt had been losing money, selling assets, scrambling to make ends meet. The company became a division of General Cinema Corp. in a $1.5 billion buyout. Harcourt disappeared as an independent company.

There is no mistaking the cause of Harcourt's demise: excessive debt made possible by a tax code that provides for a nearly unlimited interest deduction.

Source: *America: What Went Wrong?* Copyright 1992 by Donald L. Barlett and James B. Steele. Reprinted with permission of Andrews and McMeel. All rights reserved.

- A plan for cutting dividends if cash flows decline too much and financial difficulty looms over the firm.
- A strategy for debt service in a worst-case economic scenario—in the worst set of economic conditions that is likely to occur.

Cash inadequacy. Insufficient cash to meet current obligations.

Management's principal focus for the firm should be on minimizing the risk of **cash inadequacy**—the probability of running out of cash. The financial officer must have a detailed cash budget (a topic discussed in Chapter 17) completed to identify cash inflows and outflows and establish their timing. Table 13.2 indicates several ways

TABLE 13-2

MOBILIZATION OF RESOURCES

Resources	Available for Use Within:		
	One Quarter	One Year	Three Years
1. Uncommitted reserves			
Instant reserves:			
Surplus cash	$1,500		
Unused line of credit	2,000		
Negotiable reserves:			
Additional bank loans	1,200		
Issue of long-term debt		$4,000	
Issue of stock:			
Preferred stock		1,000	
Common stock		3,000	
2. Reduction of planned outflows			
Volume related:			
Change in production schedule	600		
Scale related:			
Marketing program		500	
R&D budget		200	
Administrative overhead		600	
Capital expenditures		2,000	
Value related:			
Dividend payments		200	
3. Liquidation of assets			
Sale of assets:			
Land and real estate		3,000	
Equipment		700	
Accounts receivable		600	
Inventory		400	
Sale of business units			$7,000
Total financial resources available	$5,300 ⇒	5,300	
		$21,500 ⇒	21,500
			$28,500

Source: Based on Gordon Donaldson, Strategy for Financial Mobility *(Boston: Division of Research, Harvard Graduate School of Business Administration, 1969), p. 72.*

management can mobilize financial resources if a liquidity problem arises. The choices vary from using excess cash or unused lines of credit established with a bank; cutting production, dividends, or marketing activities; and selling assets. Associated with each activity is an estimate of the length of time it would take to mobilize the funds.

There are two measures of debt-servicing capacity often used by external analysts; the *fixed-charge coverage (FCC)* ratio and the *interest coverage ratio*. The **fixed-charge coverage ratio** is an index of earnings available to pay interest, various fixed expenses

Fixed-charge coverage ratio. A risk ratio to measure the level of earnings available per dollar of interest, fixed charges, and principal payments. Does not reflect the true cash flows available to meet the obligations.

management considers essential (such as rent and lease payments), debt principal payments, and preferred dividends. The formula is:

Fixed charge coverage

$$= \frac{\text{Earnings before interest, taxes and fixed charges}}{\text{Interest} + \text{fixed charges} + \dfrac{\text{principal repayment} + \text{preferred dividends}}{(1 - \tau)}} \quad (13.1)$$

The larger the value of the index, the more *income* there is supposedly to pay the amounts included in the ratio.

Because debt principal payments and dividends are not tax-deductible expenses, it is necessary to divide them by 1 – tax rate (τ). A company pays debt principal and dividends out of after-tax dollars. For instance, assume that Westinghouse Corporation must make a $10 million principal payment. How much must earnings before taxes be if management uses the total net income amount as the source of funds to pay the principal amount? If the tax rate is 35 percent, management needs $15,384,615 income before taxes to pay $10,000,000 after taxes: $10,000,000 ÷ (1 – 0.35) = $15,384,615. We can verify that this amount is correct as follows: earnings before taxes ($15,384,615) – taxes (35% × $15,384,615) = net income ($10,000,000).

The **interest coverage ratio** is an index of earnings available to pay debt interest. Its definition is:

Interest coverage ratio. Measures the amount of earnings before interest and taxes available to pay interest. Its shortcoming is that earnings are not cash flow.

$$\text{Interest coverage} = \frac{\text{Earnings before interest and taxes}}{\text{Interest}} \quad (13.2)$$

We can derive this ratio from the FCC ratio by assuming that fixed charges, principal payments, and preferred dividends are zero.

Management and financial analysts use rules of thumb to assess the FCC and interest coverage risk. The interpretation of higher ratios is less risk. Illustration 13.1 shows calculations for both ratios.

ILLUSTRATION 13.1

Debt coverage ratios

Healey Manufacturing Company reports earnings before interest and taxes (EBIT) of $21 million. Included in the calculation of the EBIT balance is $5 million deducted for operating expenses (for example, operating lease payments) that management considers fixed and necessary to pay. Based on the firm's debt level, it incurs $2 million interest expense and $7 million in principal payment. The income tax rate is 30 percent.

The fixed-charge coverage ratio is 1.53:

Fixed charge coverage

$$= \frac{\text{Earnings before interest, taxes and fixed charges}}{\text{Interest} + \text{fixed charges} + \dfrac{\text{principal payment}}{(1 - \tau)}}$$

$$= \frac{\$21,000,000 + \$5,000,000}{\$2,000,000 + \$5,000,000 + \dfrac{\$7,000,000}{1 - 0.30}}$$

$$= 1.53$$

> The interpretation of an FCC ratio of 1.53 is that the firm has $1.53 of *earnings* before interest, taxes, and operating fixed charges to pay for every $1 of interest, fixed operating charges, and principal due.
>
> By ignoring the fixed charges and principal payments, the interest coverage ratio is $21 million ÷ $2 million = 10.5. The interpretation is similar to that for the FCC: $10.50 of earnings are available to pay for every $1 of interest.

Management and analysts use both the fixed-charge coverage ratio and the interest coverage ratio to evaluate the impact of different capital structures under different projected business scenarios. They then compare the calculated values for these ratios with benchmarks that reflect the company's desired credit rating. For example, if the firm's FCC ratio is 1.1 but the norm for firms with the same amount of risk is 2.5, then lenders may either refuse to lend or require a much higher interest rate to compensate for higher financial risk. *A problem with both of these ratios is that earnings are not cash flows. Debt obligations are paid with cash—not with earnings.* Thus, these coverage ratios misstate the true ability of the firm to meet its obligations.

13.1.2 Ability to Use Tax Benefits

A firm's taxable income is affected not only by the tax deductibility of interest, but also by other tax savings, such as the noncash charge for depreciation and tax loss from prior years, which reduce tax payments. These tax benefits represent savings as long as sufficient earnings exist or are expected to exist. When the current year's income is not large enough to allow the firm to take a tax deduction for all of its expenses, the tax law permits any unrecovered tax deductions (such as interest and depreciation) to be *carried back* to the three previous periods or *carried forward* for up to 15 future years.

For example, if Columbia Manufacturing Company has tax benefits totaling $1 million and income before considering these benefits of only $850,000, then the company cannot use $150,000 of the tax benefits this year. Columbia can recompute its taxable income in the earliest (third) prior year using the $150,000 as a tax deduction. The *carrybacks* allow the firm to claim a tax refund for taxes paid in previous years, since carrying back the deductions lowers income in the previous years. If no, or insufficient, taxable income exists in the third prior year, then the taxable income for two years ago is recomputed, and the same is done for one year ago if necessary.

If there are still unused tax deductions, the firm carries any excess deductions forward into future years to reduce taxable income. These tax *carryforwards* are also called **tax-loss carryovers.** The Financial Reality reading on page 460 outlines the importance of the carryovers to some firms. The essential point is that the firm can use tax-loss carryovers to reduce future tax payments. By reducing future cash outflows, the firm has more cash available to invest in growth opportunities to return the company to profitability.

Tax-loss carryovers. Taxable losses carried forward into future years to offset tax liability of those years.

If agency costs of debt and equity are immaterial, a company that currently pays no taxes (such as a bankrupt company) and does not expect to in the near future should not incur additional debt. Added debt increases the default risk with no additional interest tax benefit. If a company does not currently generate taxable income but expects to in the future, then management must consider whether to finance with additional debt. The added debt is beneficial only if the expected present value of the interest tax saving (PVTS) exceeds the expected present value of financial distress costs (PVFD) and the present value of agency costs (PVAC), as we discussed in Chapter 12. In other words, it is necessary for PVTS > (PVFD + PVAC).

WHERE LOSSES ARE ASSETS

If a company suffering from poor profitability can be put back on a profitable trend, its tax-loss carryforward is like money in the bank.

Gone are the days when raiders captured companies for their tax-loss carryforwards. The 1986 tax act changed that by substantially limiting the use of the shelters when 50 percent or more of a company's stock changes hands. But carryforwards, a.k.a. net operating losses, still have value to companies that are not changing hands. Such corporations are sheltered from federal income tax until the loss carryforward is fully absorbed. Every dollar of past losses thus saves 34 cents in future taxes.

Chrysler and MCI Communications used carryforwards to get back on their feet. So have plenty of smaller companies. Fedders Corp., the air-conditioner manufacturer, ran into trouble, and by 1985 the company had stockpiled $139 million in carryforwards and the stock languished at around $4. But, a few years before, the company had begun a restructuring that included the elimination of the central air-conditioning line and the aggressive marketing of its room air conditioners. Today Fedders' tax losses are used up, but the stock has nearly quadrupled since 1985.

Other companies have used their tax credits by acquiring new profit-making businesses. An example includes Chicago Pacific. It emerged from bankruptcy in 1984 after disposing of all its railroad assets. The company had $135 million in loss carryforwards but no operating businesses. A string of acquisitions, including the Hoover vacuum cleaner line in 1985, turned the company into a consumer products manufacturer. Chicago Pacific's shares climbed seventeen-fold between 1984 and 1988, when Maytag bought the company.

Adapted from Christopher Palmeri, "Where Losses Are Assets," *Forbes,* August 7, 1989, pp. 154–155. Reprinted by permission of FORBES magazine. © Forbes Inc., 1989.

13.1.3 Desired Bond Rating

A company that forecasts substantial investments to expand its product line or undertake a massive national advertising campaign, for example, wants access to the financial markets on acceptable terms. To do so, it must have adequate credit strength, as measured by independent bond rating companies, such as Standard & Poor's or Moody's, which we examined in Chapter 7. An adequate bond rating is, in practice, a very important factor in a company's choice of capital structure. The distinction between investment-grade ratings (S&P's *BBB* rating or better) and speculative-grade ratings (below *BBB*) is important because of restrictions placed on certain classes of institutional investors. For instance, the U.S. comptroller of the currency allows commercial banks to invest only in investment-grade bonds. Various state laws impose minimum bond ratings (such as single *A*) and other standards that debt obligations must meet to qualify as legal investments for savings banks, trust companies, public pension funds, and insurance companies.

The issuance of high-rated bonds by a company also reduces the likelihood that creditors might impose restrictive covenants that could seriously impair the company's operating and financial flexibility. All in all, experience suggests that a single-*A* rating is a worthy rating target because it ensures reasonably good access to the financial markets. However, managers must consider two factors in their decisions to set a bond-rating goal:

- The degree of risk of future financial distress the firm is willing to bear.
- The degree of future access to the financial markets the firm would like to achieve.

In reaching a judgment about the most appropriate rating, rating agencies apply a large number of criteria. While no all-purpose rating formula exists, the values of certain key credit statistics for comparable companies whose debt carries the target debt rating offer useful guidance. Table 13.3 shows how values of three key credit statistics vary across the six highest rating categories assigned by Standard & Poor's. The higher the firm's senior debt rating, the progressively better are *interest coverage, funds from operations relative to total debt,* and *total debt to all financing used to capitalize the firm.* These three elements represent measures of a company's ability to continue to service its debt on a current basis.

13.1.4 Financing Through Subsidiaries

Firms often have many different subsidiaries. Management establishes most subsidaries as separate business units because their products are distinctive from other products of the company. However, two types of subsidiaries that can affect the capital structure decision are foreign subsidiaries and finance subsidiaries.

FOREIGN SUBSIDIARIES. Firms with foreign subsidiaries must decide how to finance them. The parent company's worldwide capital structure dominates the subsidiary's capital structure. A subsidiary maintains a separate capital structure from the parent only if there is a reason management might allow the subsidiary to default with no recourse to corporate resources. If legal or ethical obligations exist to prevent default by a subsidiary, then the subsidiary does not have an independent capital structure. The subsidiary's true capital structure is equal to that of the whole enterprise. Thus, the parent company's worldwide capital structure dominates the foreign subsidiary's capital structure.

TABLE 13-3

MEDIAN RATIO VALUES BY RATING CATEGORY, 1990–1992

Rating Category	AAA	AA	A	BBB	BB	B
Pretax interest coverage (×)	17.7	7.6	4.1	2.5	1.5	0.9
Funds from operations to total debt (%)	120.1	65.3	37.0	26.3	15.5	9.8
Total debt/capitalization (%)	21.9	32.7	40.3	48.8	66.2	71.5

Firms with *AAA* ratings have more than twice as much interest coverage as *AA*-rated companies, about three times as much funds from operations relative to total debt as single-*A* companies, and use much less debt, as a proportion of total financing, to finance investments then all other rating categories.

Source: Standard & Poor's CreditStats, October 27, 1993, p. 12.

The firm typically finances its foreign subsidiary with a high proportion of debt. The parent company's equity investment in the subsidiary is generally small. The subsidiary usually obtains the debt financing from local sources. The reasons are several.

- Local funds are not subject to losses because of currency devaluations.
- Debt repayment is easier because there are no currency exchange costs or restrictions.
- Local financial institutions are happy when borrowing is done locally (although other businesses needing funds may not be happy if borrowing costs increase).
- The political risk of investing in countries where the threat of expropriation of foreign assets is significant is reduced. If the host government takes over the subsidiary, the parent corporation's loss of investment is relatively minimal because it invested very little equity.
- In countries with miminal threat of expropriation of assets, the parent company may still use much debt, but if it guarantees the subsidiary's debts, then host-country lenders usually provide loans to the subsidiary at favorable rates.

Finance subsidiary. A separate legal entity owned by the parent corporation that specializes in financing the company's sales.

FINANCE SUBSIDIARY. Where credit is important to a firm's marketing efforts, it is not unusual for the firm to form its own *finance subsidiary*. Generally, the **finance subsidiary's** sole purpose is to buy the accounts receivable of the parent company. The subsidiary pays for the receivables by borrowing from banks or issuing commercial paper in the money market. A prominent finance subsidiary is General Motors' General Motors Acceptance Corporation, or GMAC. It finances GM's auto and truck sales.

The parent company is usually able to improve the total company's (parent plus subsidiary) debt capacity by establishing a finance subsidiary. This happens because lenders base the incremental debt capacity of the subsidiary on the highly marketable accounts receivable rather than on the standard cash operating profit (discussed in Chapter 12). Illustration 13.2 demonstrates how a financial subsidiary increases the firm's debt capacity.

ILLUSTRATION 13.2

How a finance sub works

Suppose the expected sales volume of Arneson Marketing Limited is unable to generate enough earnings before interest to take advantage of any additional interest tax savings. To overcome this problem, management of Arneson establishes a finance subsidiary to buy its receivables. Arneson finances the subsidiary entirely with 8 percent debt.[2] Management expects the receivables to be collected every three months.

The subsidiary relies on the collection of the receivables to repay principal and interest to lenders. Arneson must sell the receivables to the subsidiary at a discount large enough to provide cash operating profit to the subsidiary to be able to meet payments to the lenders. Since the receivables have an average life of three months and the effective annual interest rate is 8 percent, a 2 percent discount on the sale of the receivables to the subsidiary is necessary (one quarter of the annual rate).[3]

[2]Normally the parent company has a small equity investment in the subsidiary.

[3]As we examined in Chapter 4, the correct quarterly rate is $(1 + 0.08)^{1/4} - 1 = 0.0194$, or 1.94 percent. The use of 2 percent is satisfactory for explaining the concept.

During the year the parent company expects credit sales of $107.1 million. The subsidiary buys the receivables for $107.1 ÷ 1.02, or $105 million, which represents a $2.1 million discount. At any one time, about $26.25 million of receivables (at cost) will be uncollected: ($105 million ÷ 12 months) × 3 months outstanding. Thus, the subsidiary requires $26.25 million of debt to support its operations. The annual interest expense is 8% × $26.25 million = $2.1 million. With discount income of $2.1 million (the difference between what the sub collects and what it pays for the receivables) and interest expense of $2.1 million, the subsidiary reports no taxable income.

For Arneson the net effect of this arrangement is the addition of $26.25 million of debt capacity and realization of the attendant interest tax savings.

Comprehension Check

1. Based on Table 13.1, discuss practicing managers' views on whether there is an optimal capital structure for business firms.
2. Briefly list the four basic considerations involved in choosing a firm's capital structure.
3. Explain how federal income tax law helps corporations that borrow money, even for those firms which have operating losses and are not able to benefit from the tax deductibility of interest payments in the current accounting period.
4. What is the general relationship between the ratings on a corporation's debt and the firm's interest cost?
5. How can foreign and finance subsidiaries affect the firm's capital structure?

13.2 BUSINESS RISK VERSUS FINANCIAL RISK

Underlying capital structure decisions about the firm's ability to service debt, to use all its tax benefits, to obtain its desired bond ratings, or to use foreign or finance subsidiaries is the issue of *business risk* versus *financial risk*. We introduced both of these risks in Chapters 11 and 12, but they take on even more meaning here. Recall that a firm's business risk arises from investment in plant and equipment and technology to make its products and from the markets in which it sells the finished products. Financial risk arises from how management finances the firm.

Most firms with high business risk fall into at least one of the following categories:[4]

- *Products that require costly repairs.* Customer demand drops for a product when consumers feel the product cannot be serviced if the firm encounters financial difficulty. Caterpillar Inc. has an excellent worldwide reputation for its heavy equipment. A long and violent labor strike against Caterpillar in 1992

[4]See Sheridan Titman, "The Effect of Capital Structure on a Firm's Liquidation Decision," *Journal of Financial Economics,* 13 (1984), 137–151.

caused the firm to lose market share to a Japanese manufacturer, thereby increasing its business risk.

- *Goods or services whose quality is difficult to determine before buying.* The concern is that firms in financial difficulty will reduce quality in an effort to conserve funds. Consumers levied this criticism against the U.S. automotive manufacturers during the 1980s. With increasing costs and lagging sales because of Japanese competition, the quality of American-made cars declined as the Big 3 U.S. auto companies tried to improve profits. Business risk increased as consumers purchased more foreign-made cars and trucks.
- *Products that have significant switching costs.* If customers must encounter large costs to switch suppliers (for example, mainframe computer suppliers), they will buy from the financially strong company.

Management usually tries to trade off business risk against financial risk. A company operating in an industry with low business risk can support greater financial leverage. On the other hand, a firm operating in an industry with high business risk generally takes on lower financial risk. Debt ratios summarized in Table 13.4 suggest that capital structure choices by management differ across industries. Why do you suppose broadcasting and health care drugs are so different? Broadcasting's exposure to business risk is much less. A few dominant firms control the broadcasting industry. Neither the broadcasting industry's technology nor exposure to government regulation is as risky as in the drug industry. A health care firm developing a new drug may find that it takes five or more years to develop the drug, only to have the Federal Drug Administration deny the firm the right to sell it in the United States. Thus, to offset high business risk, health care drug firms reduce their exposure to financial risk.

TABLE 13-4

MEDIAN INDUSTRY DEBT-TO-TOTAL CAPITAL RATIOS IN 1992

Aerospace/defense	38%
Aluminum	27
Beverages, alcoholic	32
Broadcasting, media	69
Chemicals, diversified	28
Entertainment	20
Foods	31
Hardware and tools	51
Health care drugs	12
Medical products and supplies	32
Oil and gas drilling	20
Pollution control	41
Publishing, newspapers	32
Retail stores general merchandise	46
Steel producers	64
Telecommunications, long distance	33

Source: Standard & Poor's Analyst's Handbook Official Series, *1993 Annual Edition.*

Management attempts to quantify business and financial risks. Two popular techniques for this process are analysis of *trading on the equity* and *degree of leverage*. These techniques evaluate whether the firm can realize *favorable, neutral,* or *unfavorable financial leverage.* **Favorable financial leverage** results if the firm's assets earn more on the use of debt than the debt's after-tax cost. **Unfavorable financial leverage** means the firm's assets earn less on the use of debt funds than their after-tax cost. **Neutral financial leverage** is the result of the assets simply earning the after-tax cost of debt.

13.2.1 Trading on the Equity

No creditor is willing to put up loan funds without the safety provided by the owners' equity capital. Thus, management **trades on the equity; that is, a given amount of** equity capital contributed by shareholders acts as a base against which to borrow debt funds. The two ratios used to analyze trading on the equity are *return on equity* and *return on assets.* **Return on equity** is the return shareholders earn on their investment— the firm's equity financing:

$$\text{Return on equity} = \frac{\text{Net income}}{\text{Equity}} \qquad (13.3)$$

Return on assets measures the accounting profitability, or earning power, of the assets used by the company in its business. Its formula is:

$$\text{Return on assets} = \frac{\text{Earnings before interest and taxes} \times (1 - \text{tax rate})}{\text{Assets}}$$
$$= \frac{\text{Net income} + \text{interest} \times (1 - \text{tax rate})}{\text{Assets}} \qquad (13.4)$$

We must measure return on assets (ROA) before any deductions for interest cost, since we want to calculate the earning power of the assets.[5] For instance, consider the firm's balance sheet and income statement in Figure 13.1. Interest expense in the income statement is the financing cost for the debt appearing in the balance sheet. Because ROA seeks to determine the earning power of the assets, it is necessary to exclude interest expense in the calculation. Unlike cost of sales and operating expenses, which result from the production, advertising, and administration of the firm's products, interest expense arises from using debt financing.

If management decides to finance the assets entirely with equity capital, the interest cost would be zero but the ability of the assets to produce the firm's products would not be affected. Although we discussed in the last chapter that interest expense provides a tax saving that adds value to both the firm and shareholders' wealth, *interest expense does not affect the earning power of the assets.* We work through the consequences of trading on the equity in Illustration 13.3. *An important assumption of trading on the equity analysis is that asset size remains constant while management looks at different debt and equity financing combinations.*

[5]Many managers, accountants, and academicians incorrectly calculate ROA as:

$$\text{ROA} = \frac{\text{Net income}}{\text{Assets}}$$

This definition mixes earning power of the assets with the financing of the assets and understates the actual return on assets.

Favorable financial leverage. Positive effects of debt financing on shareholders' claims on earnings.

Unfavorable financial leverage. Negative effects of debt financing on shareholders' claims on earnings.

Neutral financial leverage. Debt financing has no effect on shareholders' claims on earnings.

Trades on the equity. The use of debt to increase the expected return on equity.

Return on equity. An accounting-based ratio showing the return on the book value of equity.

Return on assets. An accounting-based ratio showing the profitability of the book value of assets.

FIGURE 13.1

A FIRM'S FINANCIAL STATEMENTS

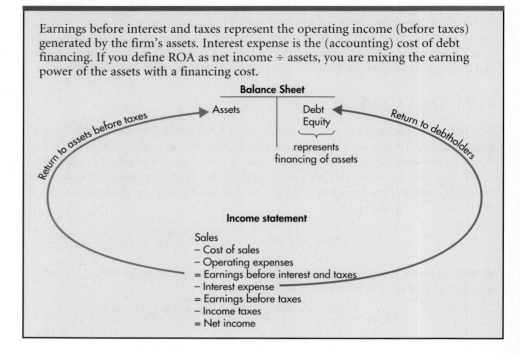

Earnings before interest and taxes represent the operating income (before taxes) generated by the firm's assets. Interest expense is the (accounting) cost of debt financing. If you define ROA as net income ÷ assets, you are mixing the earning power of the assets with a financing cost.

ILLUSTRATION 13.3

Trading on the equity

Two companies with identical assets and *accounting* earnings before interest expense and taxes (EBIT) are financed differently. Levered Company finances 40 percent of its assets with debt; Unlevered Company does not use debt.

	Company	
	Levered	Unlevered
Assets	$1000.0	$1000.0
Debt (8% interest)	$ 400.0	$ 0.0
Equity	600.0	1000.0
Total	$1000.0	$1000.0

FAVORABLE FINANCIAL LEVERAGE CASE:

EBIT	$ 200.0	$ 200.0
Interest (8%)	32.0	0.0
Earnings before taxes	$ 168.0	$ 200.0
Taxes (30%)	50.4	60.0
Net income	$ 117.6	$ 140.0

Return on assets

$$= \frac{\text{Net income} + \text{interest} \times (1 - \tau)}{\text{Assets}}$$

$$\frac{\$117.6 + \$32(1 - 0.30)}{\$1000} \quad 14.0\%$$

$$\frac{\$140.0}{\$1000} \qquad\qquad 14.0\%$$

Return on equity

$$= \frac{\text{Net income}}{\text{Equity}}$$

$$\$117.6 \div \$600 \qquad 19.6\%$$

$$\$140.0 \div \$1000 \qquad\qquad 14.0\%$$

Return on assets is 14 percent for both firms. The return on equity is higher for Levered Company than it is for Unlevered Company. The reason is because the assets of Levered Company earn more (14 percent) for the use of debt than its after-tax cost ($5.6\% = 8\% \times [1 - 0.30]$). For Unlevered Company, the return on assets always equals the return on equity because management does not use debt financing.

NEUTRAL FINANCIAL LEVERAGE CASE:

	Company	
	Levered	Unlevered
EBIT*	$80.0	$80.0
Interest (8%)	32.0	0.0
Earnings before taxes	$48.0	$80.0
Taxes (30%)	14.4	24.0
Net income	$33.6	$56.0

*EBIT has decreased relative to the first situation. The assets generate less operating income than in the favorable case.

Return on assets

$$= \frac{\text{Net income} + \text{interest} \times (1 - \tau)}{\text{Assets}}$$

$$\frac{\$33.6 + \$32.0(1 - 0.30)}{\$1000} \quad 5.6\%$$

$$\frac{\$56.0}{\$1000} \qquad\qquad 5.6\%$$

Return on equity

$$= \frac{\text{Net income}}{\text{Equity}}$$

$$\$33.6 \div \$600 \qquad 5.6\%$$

$$\$56.0 \div \$1000 \qquad\qquad 5.6\%$$

Return on assets equals the return on equity for both companies. We should expect this result for Unlevered Company, since it does not use debt. However, for Levered Company return on assets and return on equity are equal. The reason is that the firm's assets earn the same return (5.6 percent) from the use of debt as the after-tax cost of debt. The equal returns neutralize financial leverage.

UNFAVORABLE FINANCIAL LEVERAGE CASE:

| | Company | |
	Levered	Unlevered
EBIT*	$60.0	$60.0
Interest (8%)	32.0	0.0
Earnings before taxes	$28.0	$60.0
Taxes (30%)	8.4	18.0
Net income	$19.6	$42.0

*EBIT is decreased again because assets continue to generate less operating profit.

Return on assets

$$= \frac{\text{Net income} + \text{interest} \times (1 - \tau)}{\text{Assets}}$$

$$\frac{\$19.6 + 32.0(1 - 0.30)}{\$1000} \qquad 4.2\%$$

$$\frac{\$42.0}{\$1000} \qquad\qquad 4.2\%$$

Return on equity

$$= \frac{\text{Net income}}{\text{Equity}}$$

$$\$19.6 \div \$600 \qquad 3.3\%$$

$$\$42.0 \div \$1000 \qquad\qquad 4.2\%$$

These results show leverage to be a double-edged sword. When return on assets (4.2 percent) is below the after-tax cost of debt (5.6 percent), Levered Company's return on equity is less than that of Unlevered Company. Levered Company experiences unfavorable financial leverage.

What have we just learned? Different debt and equity financing mixes result in different accounting results. If the firm's assets can earn more on the use of debt funds than their after-tax cost, then profitability increases as a result of favorable financial

FIGURE 13.2

EBIT-PROFITABILITY ANALYSIS

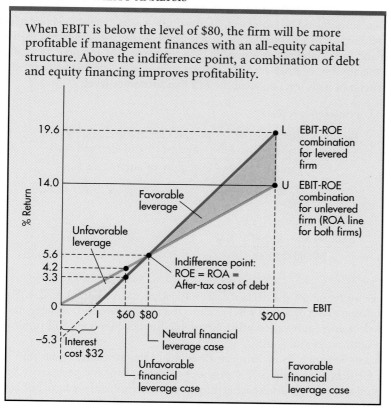

When EBIT is below the level of $80, the firm will be more profitable if management finances with an all-equity capital structure. Above the indifference point, a combination of debt and equity financing improves profitability.

leverage. Of course, the reverse situation could also occur.[6] Figure 13.2 plots the different scenarios of Illustration 13.3. The graph shows the trade-off between EBIT and return on equity (ROE) and return on assets (ROA) for an all-equity financing alternative versus a capital structure including both debt and equity financing.

In Figure 13.2, the line *OU* represents the different EBIT-ROE combinations for the illustration's unlevered firm. This line also represents the ROAs for both firms because changes in the capital structure do not affect the earning power of the assets. Possibly you noticed the constant earning power of assets in Illustration 13.3. Both firms have equal ROAs for each scenario. The line *IL* in the figure represents the

---

[6]A comparison of the correct calculation (Equation 13.4) and the incorrect calculation (see footnote 5) for ROA shows a significant error exists when you use the wrong equation. For our two firms, the error is $32.0 \times (1 - 0.30) \div \$1000 = 0.022$ or 2.2 percent, which is the difference between the following two ROA columns.

	Incorrect ROA	Correct ROA
Favorable leverage	$117.6 \div \$1000 = 11.8\%$	14.0%
Neutral leverage	$33.6 \div \$1000 = 3.4\%$	5.6%
Unfavorable leverage	$19.6 \div \$1000 = 2.0\%$	4.2%

EBIT-ROE combinations when management uses debt financing. The line intercepts the EBIT-axis at the (before-tax) level of interest costs ($32) incurred. When interest cost exceeds the level of EBIT, then ROE is negative.

Where lines *IL* and *OU* intersect, ROA = ROE = after-tax interest rate of debt. We call the intersection the *indifference point,* the point at which assets earn only the cost of financing and financial leverage is neutral between some debt and no debt at all. We can calculate the amount of EBIT for which management is indifferent between alternative capital structures. This level is called the **EBIT indifference level:**

EBIT indifference level. The level of earnings before interest and taxes to which management is indifferent between financing alternatives.

$$\text{EBIT indifference level}$$

$$= \frac{\text{Equity of alternative \#1} \times \text{interest cost of alternative \#2} - \text{equity of alternative \#2} \times \text{interest cost of alternative \#1}}{\text{Equity of alternative \#1} - \text{equity of alternative \#2}} \quad (13.5)$$

$$= \frac{E_1 \times I_2 - E_2 \times I_1}{E_1 - E_2}$$

$$= \frac{\$600 \times \$0 - \$1000 \times \$32}{\$600 - \$1000}$$

$$= \$80$$

The answer we found for the neutral case in Illustration 13.3 and plotted in Figure 13.2 is the *indifference level* of $80. If EBIT is expected to be above $80, management should chose the debt and equity alternative. Favorable financial leverage will result in higher return on both assets and equity.

What if the firm is considering an all-equity capital structure versus some different scenarios for debt? Illustration 13.4 provides an example of the necessary calculations. You will find some subtle differences compared to the problem we have just solved.

ILLUSTRATION 13.4

EBIT indifference level for capital structure

Financial data for three different capital structures under consideration by managers at Deguzman Enterprises are as follows:

| | | Possible Capital Structures | |
	#1	#2	#3
Debt	$ 0	$ 300	$ 600
Equity	1000	700	400
Assets	$1000	$1000	$1000
Interest (9%)		$ 27	
Interest (10%)			$ 60

Management is indifferent between capital structures #1 and #2 when earnings before interest and taxes (EBIT) are $90.

EBIT indifference level

$$= \frac{\text{Equity of alternative \#1} \times \text{interest cost of alternative \#2} - \text{equity of alternative \#2} \times \text{interest cost of alternative \#1}}{\text{Equity of alternative \#1} - \text{equity of alternative \#2}}$$

$$= \frac{E_1 \times I_2 - E_2 \times I_1}{E_1 - E_2}$$

$$= \frac{\$700 \times \$0 - \$1000 \times \$27}{\$700 - \$1000}$$

$$= \$90$$

Similar calculations provide EBIT of $100 as the indifference level between capital structures #1 and #3. The EBIT indifference level between capital structures #2 and #3 is $104. Can you derive these answers?[7]

Let's calculate ROA and ROE for an EBIT level of $104. You can do similar calculations for the other levels. (See the capital structure comparisons following these calculations.)

$$\text{ROA} = \frac{\text{Net income} + \text{interest} \times (1 - \tau)}{\text{Assets}}$$

$$\text{ROA \#2} = \frac{\$53.9 + \$27.0 \times (1 - 0.30)}{\$100} = 0.0728 \text{ or } 7.28\%$$

$$\text{ROA \#3} = \frac{\$30.8 + \$60.0 \times (1 - 0.30)}{\$100} = 0.0728 \text{ or } 7.28\%$$

$$\text{ROE} = \text{Net income} \div \text{equity}$$

$$\text{ROE \#2} = \$53.9 \div \$700 = 0.077 \text{ or } 7.7\%$$

$$\text{ROE \#3} = \$30.8 \div \$400 = 0.077 \text{ or } 7.7\%$$

Capital Structure Comparisons

	#1 vs. #2		#1 vs. #3		#2 vs. #3	
EBIT	$ 90.0	$ 90.0	$ 100.0	$100.0	$ 104.0	$104.0
Interest	0.0	27.0	0.0	60.0	27.0	60.0
Earnings before tax	$ 90.0	$ 63.0	$ 100.0	$ 40.0	$ 77.0	$ 44.0
Taxes (30%)	27.0	18.9	30.0	12.0	23.1	13.2
Net income	$ 63.0	$ 44.1	$ 70.0	$ 28.0	$ 53.9	$ 30.8
Debt	$ 0.0	$300.0	$ 0.0	$600.0	$300.0	$600.0
Equity	1000.0	700.0	1000.0	400.0	700.0	400.0
ROA	6.3%	6.3%	7.0%	7.0%	7.28%	7.28%
ROE	6.3%	6.3%	7.0%	7.0%	7.70%	7.70%
After-tax debt cost	6.3%	6.3%	7.0%	7.0%	6.30%	7.00%

Notice that when a capital structure with debt (either #2 or #3) is compared against an all-equity capital structure (#1), ROA = ROE = after-tax debt cost at the level of EBIT for which management is indifferent between the capital structures. This

[7]Solutions: EBIT indifference level for #1 and #3 = ($1000 × $60 − $400 × $0)/($1000 − $400) = $100; EBIT indifference level for #2 and #3 = ($700 × $60 − $400 × $27)/($700 − $400) = $104.

relationship does not hold when two capital structures both using debt are compared (#2 versus #3). The reason is that capital structures #2 and #3 have different interest rates for debt. If interest rates for both capital structures were 9 percent, the EBIT indifference level would be $90, and ROA = ROE = after-tax debt cost = 6.3%. Again, see if you can get this result.[8]

Let's return to our assumption of different interest rates for the debt. We can verify that if EBIT exceeds $104, then capital structure #3 is better. For example, if EBIT is $150, ROE #2 is 12.30 percent, ROE #3 is 15.75 percent, and ROA for both capital structures is 10.5 percent. Therefore, if EBIT exceeds the EBIT indifference amount of $104, then management should use capital structure #3, which makes greater use of debt.

What financing mix should management use if EBIT is less than $90? Any EBIT amount less than $90 will do to show the concept, but let's choose $80. You should be able to calculate the following amounts for ROA, ROE, and after-tax cost of debt:

Capital Structure	ROA	ROE	After-tax Cost of Debt
#1—no debt	5.6%	5.6%	—
#2—$300 debt	5.6%	3.7%	6.3%
#3—$600 debt	5.6%	1.4%	7.0%

We see that the firm should not use debt if EBIT is less than $90. Debt financing causes ROE < ROA < after-tax cost of debt. Unfavorable financial leverage has resulted; the assets earn less than the after-tax cost of debt.

Finally, what capital structure should management use if EBIT is greater than $90 but less than $104? Suppose EBIT is $95. At this level of EBIT, we calculate the following amounts for ROA, ROE, and after-tax cost of debt for different capital structures:

Capital Structure	ROA	ROE	After-tax Cost of Debt
#1—no debt	6.65%	6.65%	—
#2—$300 debt	6.65%	6.80%	6.3%
#3—$600 debt	6.65%	6.13%	7.0%

The results indicate that capital structure #2 is the best choice. Its ROE exceeds the ROEs for the other two capital structures and ROE > ROA > after-tax cost of debt.

[8]Solutions: EBIT indifference level = ($700 × $54 − $400 × $27)/($700 − $400) = $90; ROE = ($90 − $54) × (1 − 0.30)/$400 = 0.063; cost of debt = 0.09 × (1 − 0.30) = 0.063; ROA = $90 × (1 − 0.30)/$1000 = 0.063.

Figure 13.3 graphs the three capital structure choices examined in Illustration 13.4. Management wants to follow the thick curve, which represents the best ROE-EBIT combinations. The decision should be as follows:

Level of EBIT	Capital Structure Choice
EBIT < $90	#1—$1000 equity; no debt
EBIT = $90	Indifferent between #1 and #2
$90 < EBIT < $104	#2—$300 debt; $700 equity
EBIT = $104	Indifferent between #2 and #3
EBIT > $104	#3—$600 debt; $400 equity

As Illustrations 13.3 and 13.4 show, ROE usually differs from ROA. Why? Because debt financing results in default risk, which is not present with an all-equity capital structure. If the firm defaults on any debt payments, shareholders could lose their entire investment. Therefore, with debt financing shareholders expect ROE > ROA > after-tax cost of debt. Equation 13.6 is an alternative way to define ROE to show the relationship that exists between return on equity, return on assets, and the after-tax cost of debt as the mix of debt and equity in the capital structure changes.

FIGURE 13.3
CHOICE AMONG DIFFERENT CAPITAL STRUCTURES

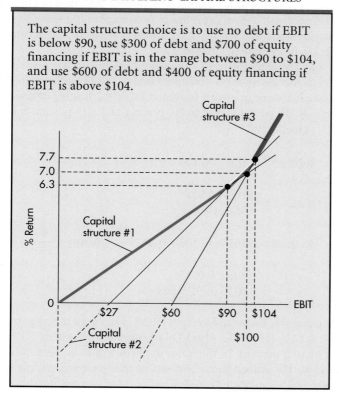

The capital structure choice is to use no debt if EBIT is below $90, use $300 of debt and $700 of equity financing if EBIT is in the range between $90 to $104, and use $600 of debt and $400 of equity financing if EBIT is above $104.

$$Return on equity$$

$$= \text{Return on assets}$$

$$+ (\text{return on assets} - \text{after-tax cost of debt}) \; \frac{\text{debt}}{\text{equity}} \qquad (13.6)$$

$$\text{ROE} = \text{ROA} + [\text{ROA} - i(1 - \tau)] \; \frac{\text{debt}}{\text{equity}}$$

Let's substitute values from Illustration 13.4 into Equation 13.6 to calculate ROE for each capital structure for the case of EBIT = \$150, or \$105 after taxes.

$$\text{ROE \#2} = 0.105 + [0.105 - 0.09 \times (1 - 0.30)] \; \frac{\$300}{\$700}$$

$$= 0.105 + 0.018$$
$$= 0.123 \text{ or } 12.3 \text{ percent}$$

$$\text{ROE \#3} = 0.105 + [0.105 - 0.10 \times (1 - 0.30)] \; \frac{\$600}{\$400}$$

$$= 0.105 + 0.0525$$
$$= 0.1575 \text{ or } 15.75 \text{ percent}$$

Without the use of financial leverage (Case #1), shareholders only require a 10.5 percent return, which is the return on assets number. Shareholders require a higher debt default risk premium (5.25 percent) under capital structure #3 than they require under capital structure #2 (1.8 percent). This risk premium is conceptually similar to our definition of default risk premium in Chapter 12. However, here we use accounting data as opposed to market-based data in Chapter 12.

Let's look at a slightly different situation but maintain the assumption that the earning power of the assets stays constant; that is, ROA still equals 10.5 percent. Suppose interest rates were to return to their 1981–1982 heights of about 22 percent. For our example, ROEs would shrink to 8.4 percent and 3.15 percent for capital structures #2 and #3, respectively.

$$\text{ROE \#2} = 0.105 + [0.105 - 0.22 \times (1 - 0.30)] \; \frac{\$300}{\$700}$$

$$= 0.105 - 0.021$$
$$= 0.084 \text{ or } 8.4 \text{ percent}$$

$$\text{ROE \#3} = 0.105 + [0.105 - 0.22 \times (1 - 0.30)] \; \frac{\$600}{\$400}$$

$$= 0.105 - 0.0735$$
$$= 0.0315 \text{ or } 3.15 \text{ percent}$$

The result is unfavorable financial leverage—ROA is less than the after-tax interest cost of 15.4 percent: $0.22 \times (1 - 0.30)$. Also ROE of either 8.4 percent or 3.15 percent is less than the ROA of 10.5 percent. In this case, the firm would be better off without debt financing. *Thus, as the interest-rate environment changes, management should be prepared to alter the firm's capital structure in an effort to protect profitability.* However, this task is harder than it sounds, as we will discuss later in this chapter.

13.2.2 Degree of Leverage

An alternative approach managers use to assess the trade-off between debt and equity financing is to measure the volatility of net income available for shareholders. This volatility is affected by the *degree of financial leverage* and the *degree of operating leverage*. **Degree of financial leverage (DFL)** calculates the change in net income for a given change in earnings before interest and taxes:

$$DFL = \frac{\%\Delta \text{ Net income}}{\%\Delta \text{ Earnings before interest and taxes}} \qquad (13.7)$$

Degree of financial leverage (DFL). The percentage change in net income for a given change in earnings before interest and taxes.

where %Δ means percentage change. Recall our income statement in Figure 13.3. It shows that to proceed from EBIT to net income we must deduct interest expense and income taxes. Thus, DFL measures the significance of after-tax interest expense on profit.

An alternative calculation for DFL, which provides the same result, is:

$$DFL = \frac{\text{Earnings before interest and taxes}}{\text{Earnings before interest and taxes} - \text{interest}} \qquad (13.8)$$

This formula shows that interest expense is the cause of financial leverage, as measured by DFL. If the firm is unlevered, interest expense in the denominator of Equation 13.8 is zero with the result that the DFL = 1 because the numerator equals the denominator. As the firm adds debt to its capital structure, the DFL increases above 1. Thus, 1 is the minimum value for DFL and indicates an all-equity financed firm with no financial risk.

Regardless of whether management uses debt financing, the firm still faces business risk. We can analyze business risk in terms of the volatility of numbers contained in a firm's income statement. We call this volatility the **degree of operating leverage (DOL)** and define it as:

$$DOL = \frac{\%\Delta \text{ Earnings before interest and taxes}}{\%\Delta \text{Sales}} \qquad (13.9)$$

Degree of operating leverage (DOL). The percentage change in earnings before interest and taxes for a given change in sales.

Again, an alternate definition provides the same result, but gives insight into what causes operating leverage:

$$DOL = \frac{\text{Sales} - \text{variable operating costs}}{\text{Sales} - \text{variable operating costs} - \text{fixed operating costs}} \qquad (13.10)$$

Notice that the only difference between the numerator and the denominator of Equation 13.10 is the *fixed operating costs*. Fixed operating costs are expenses for items that do not change as sales volume changes. Examples include the salary of administrative employees, property taxes, and depreciation for plant and equipment. If a firm has no fixed operating costs—an unlikely situation—then DOL = 1. In this case, as long as revenues from sales exceed the variable operating costs incurred in manufacturing and selling the products, the firm will always show a profit. However, as management adds fixed operating costs to business operations, the firm's profit declines and it becomes possible for total costs—variable plus fixed—to exceed sales and the firm to report a loss. On the other hand, it is also possible for the firm to greatly expand its output and profits with the addition of fixed costs. The firm may be able to realize economies of scale with these fixed costs and generate a significantly higher amount of output. In either case, the inclusion of fixed costs exposes the firm's profits to operating risk. As management adds fixed costs, DOL increases above 1 signifying higher operating leverage, that is, business risk.

Illustration 13.5 reveals the problem of putting financial risk on top of business risk. Although both the unlevered and levered firms have equal business risk, as indicated by the degree of operating leverage, the levered firm is in a riskier situation because of its financial risk.

When both DFL and DOL are present, the resulting *degree of total leverage* captures both business risk and financial risk from an accounting perspective. We define the **degree of total leverage (DTL)** as:

Degree of total leverage (DTL). The percentage change in net income for a given change in sales.

$$DTL = \frac{Sales - variable\ operating\ costs}{Sales - variable\ operating\ costs - fixed\ costs - interest} \qquad (13.11)$$

which can be restated as:

$$DTL = DFL \times DOL \qquad (13.12)$$

Thus, DTL is not a simple addition of the separate risks; rather it is multiplicative. An alternative definition of DTL is:

$$DTL = \%\Delta\ Net\ income \div \%\Delta\ Sales \qquad (13.13)$$

ILLUSTRATION 13.5
*Total risk =
business risk ×
financial risk*

	Unlevered Firm			Levered Firm		
	Present	Expected	%Δ	Present	Expected	%Δ
Sales	$1000	$1200	20.00%	$1000	$1200	20.00%
Costs:						
Variable (60%)	$ 600	$ 720		$ 600	$ 720	
Fixed	100	100		100	100	
Total	$ 700	$ 820		$ 700	$ 820	
EBIT	$ 300	$ 380	26.67	$ 300	$ 380	26.67
Interest	0	0		50	50	
EBT	$ 300	$ 380		$ 250	$ 330	
Taxes (30%)	90	114		75	99	
Net income	$ 210	$ 266	26.67	$ 175	$ 231	32.00

DOL = %ΔEBIT ÷ %ΔSales
  = 26.67 ÷ 20.00   1.33   1.33

DFL = %ΔNet income ÷ %ΔEBIT
  = 26.67 ÷ 26.67   1.00

  = 32.00 ÷ 26.67   1.20

DTL = %ΔNet income ÷ %ΔSales
  = 26.67 ÷ 20.00   1.33

  = 32.00 ÷ 20.00   1.60

When we use the alternative formulas, we use the present (base) period to calculate business and financial risk.

$$DOL = \frac{Sales - variable\ operating\ costs}{Sales - variable\ operating\ costs - fixed\ costs}$$

$$= \frac{\$1000 - \$600}{\$1000 - \$600 - \$100} \qquad 1.33 \qquad 1.33$$

$$DFL = \frac{EBIT}{EBIT - interest}$$

$$= \frac{\$300}{\$300 - \$0} \qquad\qquad 1.00$$

$$= \frac{\$300}{\$300 - \$50} \qquad\qquad\qquad\qquad 1.20$$

$$DTL = DOL \times DFL$$
$$= 1.33 \times 1.00 \qquad\qquad 1.33$$
$$= 1.33 \times 1.20 \qquad\qquad\qquad\qquad 1.60$$

Comprehension Check

1. Distinguish between favorable, unfavorable, and neutral financial leverage.
2. Explain the correct calculation of return on assets, or ROA, for a levered firm. Why is this calculation different from the ROA calculation for an unlevered firm?
3. What is the significance of the financing indifference point?
4. How can you calculate the influence of debt financing on a firm's return on equity?
5. Define: the degree of financial leverage (DFL); the degree of operating leverage (DOL); the degree of total leverage (DTL).

13.3 EFFECTING CHANGES IN CAPITAL STRUCTURE

The firm's investment in plant and equipment and technology, and its type of industry and the markets it has chosen to serve, determine its level of business risk. It is costly and difficult to change factors affecting business risk. However, it is relatively easy for a firm to modify its financial risk to change total risk. We will consider changing financial risk for two types of firms: a financially healthy firm and a financially distressed firm.

13.3.1 Capital Structure Changes in a Healthy Firm

Suppose management of a financially healthy firm decides that the desired capital structure for the firm differs significantly from the current capital structure. What should management do? It can decide on one of two general strategies: slow adjustment or quick adjustment.

Management can slowly alter the capital structure over several years by adjusting the future financing mix. For example, suppose the target capital structure of DeGroot Electrical Components, Inc. consists of 30 percent debt and 70 percent equity, whereas the current capital structure is 65 percent debt and 35 percent equity. Management can change the overleveraged condition by financing with, say, 10 percent debt and 90 percent equity whenever it needs funds until its debt ratio reaches 30 percent. However, this tactic means that the capital structure continues to be above target proportions for as long as it takes the company to correct the condition.

A number of strategies are available to alter the capital structure more quickly, say, within one month to a year. However, the firm usually incurs significant transaction costs with these alternatives.

- *Exchange offer.* Current debt investors can be offered shares of common stock to replace some of their debt.
- *Debt repurchase program.* The firm may buy its own debt in the financial markets and retire it.
- *Debt defeasance.* The firm may transfer debt from its balance sheet to a trustee. In this instance, the firm is still obligated for the debt but it does not appear on the balance sheet. This is called *off-balance sheet debt.* (See the nearby Financial Reality reading.)
- *Sale-leaseback agreement.* The firm may sell assets and lease them back under an operating lease agreement. Management uses proceeds from the sale of assets to retire debt.[9]
- *Private placement.* Equity securities may be placed with private investors. The securities do not have to be registered with the U.S. Securities and Exchange Commission.
- *Sale of subsidiary.* All or part of a subsidiary may be taken public. Management then uses proceeds from the stock issue to pay down the debt.

Is a slow adjustment to the targeted capital structure better than a quick approach? If a company's capital structure deviates from its target debt-equity proportions to the extent that it is one or more categories away from its bond-rating objective, an exchange offer or some other type of transaction designed to effect an immediate change in capital structure is probably justified. If the company is less than one category away from its bond-rating objective, then changing the firm's dividend payout ratio may be more appropriate. Increasing the amount of profits paid as dividends results in less earnings for the firm to retain. The effect is that equity on the balance sheet will not increase as much with the result that the debt-to-equity ratio increases.

13.3.2 Capital Structure Changes in a Distressed Firm

When financial distress sets in, it typically does so over an extended period. Any financial deterioration eventually reveals itself in the company's published balance sheet and income statement. It is possible to build predictive models to detect the onset of financial distress. These models use a variety of financial ratios to detect the significant deterioration in profitability and liquidity and the significant increase in financial leverage that typically signal bankruptcy. The Financial Reality reading on page 480 discusses the popular Z-score bankruptcy prediction model.

Arthur Andersen, the public accounting firm, uses the Z-score model when auditing firms. Many credit analysts use similar models when evaluating credit applicants. The Z-score model, or variants of it, has been applied in Australia, Brazil, Canada, England, France, Germany, Ireland, Japan, the Netherlands, and the United States to

---

[9]From an accounting perspective, operating leases show neither the asset value nor the associated liability on the balance sheet. If the asset is leased under a financial (capital) lease, then both the asset value and the associated liability appear on the balance sheet.

REDUCE LEVERAGE AND INCREASE PROFITS

In 1983, the Financial Accounting Standards Board decided to permit companies to consider their fixed-rate known maturity debt to be extinguished for financial reporting purposes even though the debt is not extinguished. The transaction is called *insubstance defeasance of debt.*

Defeasance of debt can be an attractive way for companies with low coupon debt outstanding to boost earnings and improve their debt-equity ratio. Indeed, Standard & Poor's disregards any debt issue defeased, and its related interest and escrowed assets, when computing financial ratios for debt-rating purposes.

The company irrevocably segregates assets with a third party. The third party invests them in direct obligations of the U.S. government, U.S. government guaranteed obligations, or securities backed by U.S. government obligations as collateral under which the interest and principal payments on the collateral generally flow immediately to the holder of the security.

The investment and the interest on it are then used to satisfy scheduled debt payments of principal and interest on the outstanding debt. The outstanding debt has a lower coupon yield than the segregated assets, so less funds must be set aside to satisfy the outstanding lower coupon debt obligation than would be required if management just retired the debt. If management is virtually assured that no further funds will need to be transferred to the third party, the firm can account for the transaction as an extinguishment of debt. The firm can then take any difference between the face value of the outstanding debt and the funds set aside as a gain, to be reported in the income statement. For tax purposes, the company continues to deduct interest expense but also pays tax on the income from trust securities. The gain from defeasance is not taxed until the debt actually matures.

Defeased debt must be disclosed in the annual report's footnotes through a description of the transaction as long as the debt is outstanding.

With defeasance, the firm gives up present liquidity to enhance profitability and lower perceived financial risk as measured by the debt-equity ratio.

George W. Gallinger and P. Basil Healey, *Liquidity Analysis and Management* (Reading, MA: Addison-Wesley, 1991), pp. 135–138. ©1991 by Addison-Wesley Publishing Company, Inc. Reprinted by permission of the publisher.

---

measure the likelihood of bankruptcy by firms. Although considerable variation exists among the scores of the different countries, in all cases financially distressed firms have much lower Z-scores than nondistressed firms. For each country, the overall average Z-score of firms that subsequently fail is below the critical Z-score value of 1.8.[10]

A company that finds itself in financial distress has four basic alternatives.

- It can seek to sell some of its assets in order to raise cash to pay its lenders.
- It can ask its lenders to renegotiate the terms of their loans or to exchange voluntarily some portion of their debt holdings for equity instruments of the distressed company.

---

[10]Edward I. Altman, "The Success of Business Failure Prediction Models: An International Survey," Occasional Paper, No. 5, Salomon Brothers Center for the Study of Financial Institutions, Graduate School of Business Administration, New York University, 1983.

Financial Reality

PREDICTING BANKRUPTCY

The detection of company operating and financial difficulties is a subject susceptible to financial ratio analysis. The following discussion briefly reviews a quantitative model for predicting corporate bankruptcies.

Several years ago, Edward Altman developed a model for predicting corporate bankruptcy. His model was the forerunner of many studies for predicting corporate bankruptcy.

After careful consideration of the nature of the problem, Altman chose a multiple discriminant analysis (MDA) model as the appropriate statistical technique.

MDA is a technique used to classify an observation into one of several *a priori* groupings dependent upon the observation's individual characteristics. MDA has the advantage of considering an entire profile of characteristics common to the relevant firms, as well as the interaction of these properties. The best combination of variables Altman tested for his MDA model follows at the end of this reading.

Altman found the model to have high predictive ability. One year before bankruptcy, it correctly predicted 95 percent of the firms that went bankrupt. Two years before bankruptcy, 72 percent of the firms were predicted correctly. The model predicted 36 percent of the firms correctly up to five years before ultimate bankruptcy.

Application of the model requires calculating the indicated ratios for a firm and substituting them into the equation. Each ratio is multiplied by its coefficient, shown in the model. Results are then summed to get the overall index, frequently referred to as the *Z-score*.

Firms with Z-scores greater than 2.99 fall into the nonbankrupt sector, while those with a Z below 1.81 are considered bankrupt. The area between 1.81 and 2.99 is a gray area and requires more analysis.

Subsequent authors were critical of this methodology. However, variations of it are used by many firms today.

Z-score = 0.012 × [working capital ÷ total assets] + 0.014 × [retained earnings ÷ total assets] + 0.033 × [EBIT ÷ total assets] + 0.006 × [market value equity ÷ book value of total debt] + 0.999 × [sales ÷ total assets]

The model is from Edward I. Altman, "Financial Ratios, Discriminant Analysis and the Prediction of Corporate Bankruptcy," *Journal of Finance* (September 1968), pp. 589–609.

Bankruptcy. A legal proceeding to decide whether to liquidate or reorganize a company and the administration thereof.

Reorganization. A legal process in which all financial claims against the company are settled to reflect the firm's intrinsic value. The firm continues its operations.

- It may seek a merger with a company that is strong financially.
- If the company's situation is acute and the first three alternatives are unavailable or unworkable, the company may have to seek bankruptcy protection from its creditors under the provisions of the U.S. bankruptcy code.

The first three alternatives are reasonably straightforward. But bankruptcy is more complex.

WHAT IS BANKRUPTCY? **Bankruptcy** is a judicial process through which debtors can obtain relief from their indebtedness. It gives debtors a fresh start, but it also provides for equal treatment of various creditors. There are two basic forms of bankruptcy: *reorganization* and *liquidation*. **Reorganization,** as governed by Chapter 11 of the U.S.

bankruptcy code, restrains the creditors while the debtor works out a plan to settle its debt obligations, usually for less than 100 cents on the dollar. The debtor's business continues to operate under the supervision of the bankruptcy trustee. Under a **liquidation**, as governed by Chapter 7 of the U.S. bankruptcy code, the bankruptcy court liquidates the debtor's business in an orderly manner and distributes the proceeds to creditors according to a strict order of priority. Shareholders receive any residual proceeds.

Liquidation. The termination of the firm. Assets are sold and the proceeds are paid to creditors. Any monies remaining after paying creditors are distributed to shareholders.

REORGANIZATION OR LIQUIDATION? A company that seeks protection from its creditors under the bankruptcy laws must choose between reorganization and liquidation. If the company's creditors believe that the value of the payments they will realize if the bankruptcy court liquidates the company exceeds the present value of the payments they could expect to receive in the future if the company is reorganized, they will seek to have the company liquidated. If the bankruptcy court liquidates the company under Chapter 7 of the U.S. bankruptcy code, the legal rules observed in the distribution of proceeds normally leaves nothing for shareholders. Consequently, shareholders usually prefer a reorganization under Chapter 11 to a liquidation under Chapter 7. However, a reorganization can be mutually beneficial to stockholders and creditors if the company's difficulties are only temporary. For example, new management might be able to revitalize the business by correcting the excesses of prior management and by operating the business more efficiently.

Certain types of businesses are more difficult to reorganize than others. For example, a company in a high-technology industry that is dependent on a few critical employees for its competitive edge, or a company in heavy equipment manufacturing that is dependent on a network of independent dealers for distributing its products may cease to be viable if its key personnel and distributors leave. On the other hand, a retailing company competes more on price than on technical superiority and its sales do not require a specialized distribution network. Such a firm is more likely to emerge from reorganization successfully.

When Congress adopted the Bankruptcy Reform Act of 1978, it expressed concern that liquidations destroy corporate assets and are costly for stockholders, bondholders, employees, suppliers, and customers. Therefore, it changed Chapter 11 to make it significantly easier for managers to obtain protection from creditors and give them more control over reorganizations. The Financial Reality reading on pages 482 and 483 raises serious doubts about the benefit to creditors, employees, and shareholders of the Bankruptcy Reform Act. A popular view is that Chapter 11 serves mainly to protect managers' jobs, not to preserve valuable assets.

▶ *Comprehension Check*

1. When management determines that the firm needs an adjustment in its capital structure, what are the relative merits of a quick adjustment compared with a slow adjustment?
2. What are the alternatives for a company that finds itself in financial distress?
3. What is bankruptcy? Explain the two basic forms of bankruptcy.
4. What factors can influence whether owners, seeking protection from a firm's creditors, will choose reorganization or liquidation?
5. Based on the Financial Reality article on pages 482 and 483, discuss the uses and abuses of Chapter 11 of the federal bankruptcy law.

USES AND ABUSES OF CHAPTER 11

Charles Lamb, an eighteenth-century English essayist, reckoned that all bankrupts should be hanged. Fortunately for Mr. Frank Lorenzo, former chairman of Texas Air, American law is lenient. In 1983 Continental Airlines, which was owned by Texas Air, filed under Chapter 11 of the bankruptcy code. In March 1989 another part of Mr. Lorenzo's empire, Eastern Air Lines, followed suit. Today, Continental is one of America's most profitable airlines. But how can America have a system where going bankrupt does not mean going bust?

The reason is Chapter 11. Many other countries' laws aim to protect creditors rather than debtors: If a company runs into trouble and is unable to reach a deal with its creditors, it has to apply for liquidation. A liquidator is appointed and the company is wound up. American companies can do this as well under Chapter 7 of the bankruptcy code. But they can also file under Chapter 11. Japan and West Germany have similar laws.

Chapter 11 gives a company protection from its creditors until it proposes a reorganization plan. That plan has to be passed by all the creditor committees (secured, unsecured, trade, and so on). If the company's plan is accepted, it can trade again, even if some of its creditors have not been paid in full.

Filing for Chapter 11 is relatively easy. A company is only refused if there is evidence of fraud or if there are no jobs at stake (and thus no reason to give the debtor a second chance). The company can also file before if defaults on any debt. Both Continental and Eastern had enough cash to meet their immediate obligations. Two other big Chapter 11 cases, Manville, an asbestos maker, and A.H. Robbins, a drugs firm, were profitable when they filed. Both took this action because they faced a host of consumer lawsuits— Manville for asbestos, A.H. Robbins for allegedly harmful birth control devices.

Technically a company that has filed under Chapter 11 has a set period—usually 120 days—in which to propose a reorganization plan. But the bank-ruptcy judge can grant extensions. Manville filed in 1982; it emerged only in November 1988. In the interim, a company's hands look tied: It cannot sell an important asset without the court's permission.

On the other hand, Chapter 11 allows a company's managers to stay on. And a company can do anything to survive that the judge decides is in its interests. This can help a great deal, as Mr. Lorenzo demonstrated at Continental. Arguing that the airline could not survive without lower wage costs, he tore up its union contracts, sacked two-thirds of the work force and forced the remaining third to accept 50 percent wage cuts. By offering extremely cheap flights Continental won back customers and paid back its creditors. Mr. Lorenzo emerged with a low-cost, nonunion airline.

Partly because of what Lorenzo did at Continental, Congress has changed the rules to stop companies abrogating labor contracts while in Chapter 11.

America's biggest bankrupt, Texaco, which owned some $35 billion of assets when it filed in 1987, also used Chapter 11 to attack an old foe: Pennzoil, which had just won damages of $10.5 billion because Texaco had "stolen" Getty Oil from under its nose a year earlier. Texaco managed to reduce its damages to $3 billion.

Mr. Lorenzo or Texaco claim that their use of Chapter 11 is defensive, but it doesn't look that way. "What was designed as a shield has become a sword," argued Mr. Marc Hyman of *Business Bankruptcy Report,* a trade magazine. In 1987, 17,500 companies filed under Chapter 11; in 1988 the figure may have topped 20,000. Many of those companies, particularly the largest ones, filed in order to defy their creditors, not to help them.

Is there, then, a case for reforming Chapter 11? There is—and a powerful one. Critics point out, first, that its provisions help big companies more than small ones. In 1987, 69 percent of companies with annual sales of over $100 million survived; only 30

13.4 THE NEXT STEP

This chapter on capital structure management brings to a close Part IV of the book. Chapter 11, the first chapter in Part IV, provided an overview of how to calculate the value of the firm and how shareholder value is created. Chapters 11 and 12 lay the foundation for analyzing investment decisions, which we will examine in Part V. The cost of capital discussion in Chapter 12 provides a managerial perspective to the concept of market rates of return required by debt and equity investors. If the firm undertakes nonrisk-changing investments, the cost of capital is the discount rate management will use to evaluate investments, as we will see in Chapters 14 and 15.

Management's decision on how much debt financing to use (Chapter 13) affects the firm's cost of capital and, thus, the contribution of investments to firm value. Chapter 12 provided an illustration of how a project adds to or subtracts from the preinvestment value of the firm. In the next three chapters you will study investment decisions in greater detail.

The several profitability and debt ratios discussed in this chapter help managers, creditors, and investors evaluate the profitability and default risk of the firm. You will see many of these ratios again in Chapter 18 when we discuss them in conjunction with several other ratios. Our purpose there will be to analyze a firm's financial statements to provide an overall view of how well the firm is doing.

SUMMARY ▼▼▼▼▼▼▼▼▼▼▼

PRACTICAL ISSUES ABOUT CAPITAL STRUCTURE

- Financial managers believe that capital structure is important to the cost of capital and value of the firm.
- The most direct approach to understanding risk associated with debt financing is to evaluate the potential for cash inadequacy. This requires evaluation of sources and uses of cash.
- The fixed-charge coverage and the interest coverage ratios are often used to measure financial risk. Higher ratios mean less risk.
- If a firm cannot generate enough income to take advantage of tax-deductible expenses, managers should consider using less debt.
- A firm's managers often determine the debt-equity mix that leads to a desired bond rating.
- Foreign and finance subsidiaries allow the firm to increase its debt capacity.

BUSINESS RISK VERSUS FINANCIAL RISK

- Business risk is a function of the firm's investment in production and technology and its markets. Business risk increases as production technology becomes more complex and markets become more competitive. Products that require costly repair, are difficult to determine their quality before buying, and have significant switching costs lead to higher business risk.
- Financial risk arises when a firm uses debt financing.
- Financial leverage represents the relationship between the after-tax cost of debt and the return the borrowed funds earn in the business.
- Favorable leverage results when a firm's assets earn more than its after-tax cost of debt. Unfavorable leverage results when the return on assets is less than the after-tax cost of debt.
- The financing indifference point indicates the level of earnings before interest and taxes where two different capital structures result in equal return-on-asset ratios and equal return-on-equity ratios.
- Financial leverage can also be measured by the degree of financial leverage ratio. The ratio shows the impact of interest expense on net income.
- The degree of operating leverage provides an index for business risk. It shows the impact of fixed operating costs on the firm's financial results.
- Total business risk can be measured by multiplying the degree of financial leverage by the degree of operating leverage.

EFFECTING CHANGES IN CAPITAL STRUCTURE

- A firm's mix of debt and equity can be changed quickly or slowly to meet management's desired capital structure.

- Some strategies for changing capital structure include exchange offers, debt repurchase plans, sale-leaseback agreements, private placements, and sale of subsidiaries.
- Financially distressed firms encounter the threat of bankruptcy. The outcome of bankruptcy is either a liquidation of the firm or a reorganization of the debt structure so the firm can survive without a burdensome debt repayment problem.

FURTHER READING ▼▼▼▼▼▼▼▼▼▼▼▼

Friedman, Benjamin M., *The Changing Roles of Debt and Equity in Financing United States Capital Formation.* Chicago: University of Chicago Press, 1982. This book provides broad coverage of the capital structure issue.

Friedman, Benjamin M., *Corporate Capital Structures in the United States.* Chicago: University of Chicago Press, 1985. This is another book providing broad coverage of capital structure issues.

SELF-TEST PROBLEMS ▼▼▼▼▼▼▼▼▼▼▼▼

ST13-1. PCG Manufacturing Company has just reported annual earnings before interest and taxes (EBIT) of $25 million. Included in the calculation of EBIT is $5 million of operating lease payments. Annual interest payments are $8 million and preferred dividend payments are $6.6 million. The firm's income tax rate is 34 percent.

   a. Calculate the interest coverage ratio.

   b. Calculate the fixed-charge coverage ratio.

ST13-2. a. Calculate the return on equity and return on assets for the two corporations whose partial financial statements follow.

	Javier Corp.	Crystal Corp.
Assets	$10,000,000	$10,000,000
Debt (10% interest)	$ 0	$ 3,000,000
Equity	10,000,000	7,000,000
Total	$10,000,000	$10,000,000
EBIT	$ 1,500,000	$ 1,500,000
Interest	0	300,000
Earnings before taxes	$ 1,500,000	$ 1,200,000
Taxes (40%)	600,000	480,000
Net income	$ 900,000	$ 720,000

   b. How do you account for the differences, if any, in the return on equity and return on assets for these two corporations?

ST13-3. a. Calculate the degree of operating leverage for a firm that has fixed operating costs of $1,200,000. Variable costs are $5 per unit of production. Sales revenue is $20 per unit. Total sales for the year amount to $4 million. The firm's income tax rate is estimated to be 28 percent. Based on its debt, the firm pays annual interest of $600,000.

b. Based on the information in part (a), calculate the firm's degree of financial leverage at its current level of sales.

c. Based on the information in part (a) or your calculations for parts (a) and (b), what is the firm's degree of total leverage at its current level of sales?

PROBLEMS ▼▼▼▼▼▼▼▼▼▼▼▼

PRACTICAL ISSUES ABOUT CAPITAL STRUCTURE

13-1. Given that interest payments are tax deductible for a corporation whereas dividend payments are not, should companies finance all of their assets with debt?

13-2. Jamison Company had earnings before interest and taxes (EBIT) of $450,000 for the year just ended. No significant fixed charges were included in calculating EBIT. Based on current borrowing, Jamison's annual interest payments are $180,000; no principal payment is due on the debt. The firm's directors have called for a preferred dividend payment of $250,000. The firm's income tax rate is 25 percent.

a. Calculate the interest coverage ratio.
b. Calculate the fixed-charge coverage ratio.

13-3. Flagstaff Tool & Die, Inc. has widely fluctuating sales. The firm has just reported annual earnings before interest and taxes (EBIT) of $6 million. Included in the calculation of EBIT is $2 million of operating lease payments. Annual interest payments are $1.5 million. The firm must make a debt principal payment of $3 million. The firm's income tax rate is 28 percent.

a. Calculate the interest coverage ratio.
b. Calculate the fixed-charge coverage ratio.
c. What conclusions might you draw about this firm from the ratios computed in parts (a) and (b)?

13-4. Surefire Electric Company's management reported earnings before interest and taxes (EBIT) of $37 million for the year just ended. Management also reported that the public utility had interest payments of $10 million and paid principal and preferred dividend payments amounting to $6 million in total. The firm's income tax rate is 35 percent.

a. Calculate the interest coverage ratio.
b. Calculate the fixed-charge coverage ratio.

13-5. Royal Manufacturing Corporation reports earnings before interest and taxes (EBIT) of $24 million. Included in the firm's EBIT balance is $2 million deducted from operating lease payments, which management considers as fixed expenses. Royal's long-term debt provides for the annual payment of $3 million in interest and $4 million in principal. Royal's income tax rate is 35 percent.

a. Calculate the interest coverage ratio.
b. Calculate the fixed-charge coverage ratio.

13-6. Compare the two sets of ratios for Surefire Electric and Royal Manufacturing computed in Problems 13-4 and 13-5. If you were a bondholder of these two corporations, which investment would you consider more secure? Explain your answer.

Use the following data for Problems 13-7 through 13-11.

Renaldo Corporation's earnings before taxes (EBT) and tax liabilities for the years 1985 through 1994 follow. Renaldo's tax rate is 30 percent.

Year	EBT	Tax Liability
1985	$1,000,000	$300,000
1986	1,500,000	450,000
1987	800,000	240,000
1988	500,000	150,000
1989		
1990	700,000	210,000
1991	1,000,000	300,000
1992	1,200,000	360,000
1993	400,000	120,000
1994	200,000	60,000

13-7. Calculate Renaldo's tax liability after considering any tax carryback or carryforward for each year if in 1989 the company had earnings before taxes of $300,000. What would be the total change in taxes for the ten-year period as a result of using carrybacks or carryforwards?

13-8. Calculate Renaldo's tax liability after considering any tax carryback or carryforward for each year if in 1989 the company had an operating loss before taxes of $1.8 million.

13-9. Calculate Renaldo's tax liability after considering any tax carryback or carryforward for each year if in 1989 the company had $0 earnings before taxes.

13-10. Calculate Renaldo's tax liability after considering any tax carryback or carryforward for each year if in 1989 the company had an operating loss before taxes of $4.5 million.

13-11. Calculate Renaldo's tax liability after considering any tax carryback or carryforward for each year if in 1989 the company had an operating loss before taxes of $7.3 million.

13-12. Influtex, Inc., a biotech research and development corporation started ten years ago, has had operating losses since its origin. Today, the firm has a number of products in the development pipeline that management believes have prospects for commercial application at some unknown time in the future. The firm has no long-term debt. When the firm was started, management decided to finance operations with common stock sales to the founders and a small group of private investors.

As an outside consultant, would you advise management to raise financing now through the sale of long-term bonds? Explain your answer so that management, whose expertise is in science and not finance, can easily understand it.

13-13. Based on Table 13.3, what bond rating would you assign the following corporation's bonds?

			Company		
	A	B	C	D	E
Pretax interest coverage (×)	5.10	16.51	1.17	10.95	2.90
Funds from operations to total debt (%)	34.18	135.90	18.53	56.01	22.59
Total debt/capitalization (%)	41.47	17.35	59.87	29.79	52.15

13-14. What reasons would a financial officer give to a firm's board of directors for financing a foreign subsidiary's operations mostly with debt denominated in the currency of the country of the subsidiary?

13-15. Why might a manufacturing corporation establish its own finance subsidiary?

BUSINESS RISK VERSUS FINANCIAL RISK

13-16. a. Based on Table 13.4, rank the following industries according to debt-to-total capital ratios. Show the debt percentages in your answer.

        Hardware and tools
        Aerospace/defense
        Telecommunications, long distance
        Broadcasting, media
        Steel producers
        Foods

    b. How do you account for the difference in these capital structures?

13-17. a. Calculate the return on equity and the return on assets for the companies whose accounting statements follow.

	Company A	Company B
Assets	$4,000,000	$4,000,000
Debt (9% interest)	$ 0	$1,000,000
Equity	4,000,000	3,000,000
Total	$4,000,000	$4,000,000
EBIT	$ 500,000	$ 500,000
Interest	0	90,000
Earnings before taxes	$ 500,000	$ 410,000
Taxes (35%)	175,000	143,500
Net income	$ 325,000	$ 266,500

    b. How do you account for the differences, if any, in the return on equity and return on assets for these two companies?

13-18. a. Calculate the return on equity and the return on assets for the companies whose accounting statements follow.

	Company C	Company D
Assets	$5,000,000	$5,000,000
Debt (10% interest)	$ 0	$2,000,000
Equity	5,000,000	3,000,000
Total	$5,000,000	$5,000,000
EBIT	$ 300,000	$ 300,000
Interest	0	200,000
Earnings before taxes	$ 300,000	$ 100,000
Taxes (30%)	90,000	30,000
Net income	$ 210,000	$ 70,000

b. How do you account for the differences, if any, in the return on equity and return on assets for these two companies?

13-19. a. Calculate the return on equity and the return on assets for the companies whose accounting statements follow.

	Company E	Company F
Assets	$2,000,000	$2,000,000
Debt (7.5% interest)	$ 0	$ 500,000
Equity	2,000,000	1,500,000
Total	$2,000,000	$2,000,000
EBIT	$ 150,000	$ 150,000
Interest	0	37,500
Earnings before taxes	$ 150,000	$ 112,500
Taxes (20%)	30,000	22,500
Net income	$ 120,000	$ 90,000

b. How do you account for the differences, if any, in the return on equity and return on assets for these two companies?

13-20. Following are the simplified balance sheet and income statement for Wal-Mart Stores, Inc. Calculate Wal-Mart's return on equity and return on assets. Is Wal-Mart realizing favorable or unfavorable financial leverage? Dollar amounts are in millions.

Balance Sheet

Current assets	$10,198	Current liabilities	$ 6,754
Net fixed assets	9,792	Long-term debt	5,052
Other assets	575	Equity	8,759
Total	$20,565	Total	$20,565

Income Statement

Total revenues	$55,985
Cost of sales	44,175
Gross income	$11,810
Selling, general and administrative expenses	8,321
Earnings before interest and taxes	$ 3,489
Interest	323
Earnings before taxes	$ 3,166
Taxes	1,171
Net income	$ 1,995

13-21. LaserMicro, Inc. has debt of $40,000 and equity of $60,000. Its debt has an average interest cost of 10 percent before taxes; equity earns a 12 percent return. Given a tax rate of 34 percent, how much is the firm's return on assets.

13-22. Learner Corporation has equity of $70,000 and debt of $30,000. The before tax cost of debt is 9 percent and the return on equity is 10 percent. The firm's income tax rate is 28 percent. Calculate the company's return on assets rate.

13-23. Wyatt Oil Company has assets of $50 million, which are financed 45 percent by debt and 55 percent by equity. The firm currently earns 8 percent on its assets and 12 percent on its equity. The tax rate is 40 percent.

   a. How much is Wyatt's net income?
   b. How much is interest expense? (*Hint:* Use the ROA equation.)

13-24. ATech, Inc. is considering the following alternative financing arrangements:

	Alternative	
	A	B
Market values:		
Bonds (8%)	$200,000	
Common stock	400,000	$600,000
Assets	$600,000	$600,000

Management estimates that earnings before interest and taxes (EBIT) for this year will be $40,000. The company's income tax rate is 34 percent. Assume that the degree of economic risk associated with the sources of funds remains the same for both alternatives.

   a. Calculate return on assets and return on equity under both alternatives and decide which alternative management should select.
   b. If EBIT doubles next year, what happens to return on assets and return on equity?
   c. Calculate the EBIT indifference level for the two financing alternatives. Construct partial income statements and calculate return on assets, return on equity, and the after-tax cost of debt to prove that your EBIT indifference level is correct.

13-25. Rearden Metal, Inc. has assets of $100 million financed with $25 million of debt and $75 million of equity. The debt has an average cost of 9 percent before taxes. Hank Rearden, owner of the business, is considering replacing $30 million of equity financing with $30 million of debt financing. There would be no change in the capabilities of the assets to generate earnings. He expects the average cost of all debt financing to increase to 9.25 percent if the change is made. Earnings before interest and taxes (EBIT) are $20 million and should not change as a result of the new capital structure. The income tax rate is 34 percent.

a. Calculate the current net income, return on assets, and return on equity.
b. Calculate net income, return on assets, and return on equity if Rearden adopts the new capital structure.
c. Compare your answers for parts (a) and (b). Why are return-on-asset numbers unchanged?
d. Does Rearden Metal currently enjoy favorable financial leverage? Will the financial leverage be favorable if the new capital structure is adopted?

13-26. a. Use Equation 13.5 to calculate the EBIT indifference level between the two capital structures in Problem 13-25.
b. Verify your answer to part (a) by calculating return on assets, return on equity, and the after-tax cost of debt for each capital structure when the firm operates at the EBIT indifference level.

13-27. How much is the incremental tax-shield benefit from using additional debt financing in Problem 13-25?

13-28. Rearden Metal in Problem 13-25 earns 13.2 percent return on assets. Its return on equity is 15.62 percent when the debt-equity ratio is 1/3 (that is, $25 million debt ÷ $75 million equity).

a. Use Equation 13.6 to solve for return on equity under each of the following debt-equity ratio cases. The tax rate is 34 percent.

Debt-equity Ratio	% Interest Cost
0.333	9.00%
1.222	9.25
1.500	10.50
2.333	15.00
4.000	20.00
9.000	24.00

b. What is the best capital structure, given these six alternatives?
c. At what debt-equity ratio is financial leverage neutral?
d. At what debt-equity ratio is financial leverage unfavorable? What is the relationship between return on assets, return on equity, and the after-tax cost of debt at this point?

13-29. Supra, Inc. is an unlevered firm earning 14 percent return on assets. What will be the firm's return on equity if the income tax rate is 34 percent, the interest rate on debt financing is 8 percent, and the proportion of debt to equity is either 0.25, 0.667, 1.50, or 4.0?

13-30. Discuss the factors which might influence a firm's managers to increase or decrease the use of interest-bearing debt to finance operations. Build your discussion around the concepts of degree of operating leverage and the degree of financial leverage.

13-31. Over a rather wide range of production, Smythe Company has fixed operating costs of $100,000. Variable costs are $3 per unit of production and the company's product is sold for $7 each. Smythe pays annual interest of $60,000 and incurs an income tax rate of 30 percent.

   a. What is the company's EBIT and net income if 50,000 units are sold annually?
   b. Calculate the degree of operating leverage at the current sales level.
   c. Calculate the degree of financial leverage at the current sales level.
   d. Calculate the degree of total leverage at the current sales level.

13-32. Gitman Limited has fixed operating costs of $480,000, and variable costs are $10 per unit of production. Sales revenue is $19 per unit with total sales for the year amounting to $1,520,000. The firm's income tax rate is 25 percent. The firm pays annual interest of $100,000.

   a. Calculate the firm's degree of operating leverage at the current sales level.
   b. Calculate the firm's degree of financial leverage at the current sales level.
   c. Calculate the firm's degree of total leverage at the current sales level.
   d. Calculate net income for the current year.
   e. If units sold decline 25 percent to 60,000, how much should earnings before interest and taxes decline?
   f. Construct an income statement to prove your answer to part (e).
   g. What advice do you have for management regarding its operating and financing policies?

13-33. The Harper Corporation sold 100,000 units last year at $11 each. Its income statement is shown below.

Sales	$1,100,000
Variable costs	550,000
Contribution margin	$ 550,000
Fixed operating costs	150,000
Earnings before interest and taxes	$ 400,000
Interest expense	50,000
Income before taxes	$ 350,000
Income taxes	119,000
Net income	$ 231,000

   a. Calculate the degree of financial leverage at the current level of sales.
   b. Calculate the degree of operation leverage at the current level of sales.
   c. Determine the degree of total leverage at the current level of sales.

13-34. Harper Corporation's sales manager in Problem 13-33 forecasts sales growth of 12 percent next year over the current sales of $1.1 million. Variable costs are expected to remain at 50 percent of sales and no additional fixed costs or interest expense are expected to be incurred. The tax rate remains at 34 percent.

   a. Calculate the expected income statement for next year.
   b. Calculate the degree of financial leverage, the degree of operating leverage, and the degree of total leverage at next year's forecasted sales level.
   c. Is total risk expected to be more or less than the levels found in Problem 13-33? If risk changes, what is the reason(s)?

13-35. Let's change the assumptions for the analysis in Problem 13-34. Sales are still forecasted to grow 12 percent and variable costs remain at 50 percent of sales. However, fixed operating costs and interest expense should increase $20,000 and $5,000, respectively. The tax rate remains at 34 percent.

    a. Calculate the new income statement.

    b. Calculate the degree of financial leverage, the degree of operating leverage, and the degree of total leverage for the new income statement.

    c. Why are each of the firm's risk components in this problem's analysis expected to increase over the forecast in Problem 13-34?

    d. Using the current year's activity in Problem 13-33 as the base period, calculate the degree of operating leverage, the degree of financial leverage, and the degree of total leverage.

DISCLOSURE ASSIGNMENT

13-36. Use the *Disclosure* database to answer the following questions for Nike, Inc. and Reebok International Limited. Do the calculations for the two most recent years provided by the database.

    a. Calculate the interest coverage ratio for each firm.

    b. How much is the tax shield benefit that each firm enjoys by using debt financing?

    c. Calculate the return on equity, return on assets, and the default risk premium for each firm.

    d. Calculate each firm's degree of operating leverage, degree of financial leverage, and degree of total leverage.

    e. Use the Z-score model in the Financial Reality on page 480 to estimate each firm's bankruptcy score. Is either firm close to bankruptcy?

LIBRARY ASSIGNMENT

13-37. Use the Z-score model discussed in the Financial Reality reading on page 480 to estimate the bankruptcy risk of three firms of your choosing which operate within the same industry. Do the calculations for the latest four years of financial information. You can find the information in the current edition of *Value Line*.

COMPREHENSIVE PROBLEM ▼▼▼▼▼▼▼▼▼▼▼▼

13-38. Smart Manufacturing Corporation's accounting statements for the year just ended follow.

Balance Sheet

Assets	$100,000,000	Debt (10% interest)	$ 40,000,000
		Equity	60,000,000
		Total	$100,000,000

Income Statement

Sales revenue	$150,000,000
Variable operating costs	90,000,000
Fixed operating costs	35,000,000
EBIT	$ 25,000,000
Interest	4,000,000
Earnings before taxes	$ 21,000,000
Taxes (30%)	6,300,000
Net income	$ 14,700,000

a. Calculate the interest coverage ratio and the fixed-charge coverage ratio for Smart Manufacturing. Annual principal payments on debt are $4.2 million.
b. How much is the tax-shield benefit to Smart from its use of long-term debt?
c. Calculate the return on equity and the return on assets for the company.
d. How much is the default risk premium? Compare the return on equity against the return on assets.
e. Calculate the degree of operating leverage, the degree of financial leverage, and the degree of total leverage based on the current sales level.
f. Comment on Smart Manufacturing's capital structure. The company produces industrial goods where demand is highly sensitive to economic conditions. The year just ended was a good one for the company and the industry.

ANSWERS TO SELF-TEST PROBLEMS ▼▼▼▼▼▼▼▼▼▼▼▼

ST13-1. a. $\text{Interest coverage ratio} = \dfrac{\text{Earnings before interest and taxes}}{\text{Interest}}$

$$= \$25,000,000 \div \$8,000,000$$
$$= 3.125 \text{ times}$$

b. Fixed-charge coverage ratio

$$= \frac{\text{Earnings before interest, taxes and fixed charges}}{\text{Interest + fixed charges} + \dfrac{\text{preferred dividends}}{(1 - \text{tax rate})}}$$

$$= \frac{\$25,000,000 + \$5,000,000}{\$8,000,000 + \$5,000,000 + \dfrac{\$6,600,000}{(1 - 0.34)}}$$

$$= 1.30$$

ST13-2. a. Return on equity = Net income ÷ equity

Javier: $900,000 ÷ $10,000,000 = 0.09 or 9 percent

Crystal: $720,000 ÷ $7,000,000 = 0.1029 or 10.29 percent

Return on assets = EBIT $\times$ (1 − tax rate) ÷ assets

Javier: $\$1,500,000 \times (1 - 0.40) \div \$10,000,000$

$\quad = 0.09$ or 9 percent

Crystal: $\$1,500,000 \times (1 - 0.40) \div \$10,000,000$

$\quad = 0.09$ or 9 percent

b. The return on assets is the same for both companies because EBIT, the tax rate, and assets are identical. However, return on equity is greater for Crystal Corp. in view of the favorable employment of debt. The after tax cost of debt is $0.10 \times (1 - 0.40) = 0.06$ or 6 percent, which is less than the return on assets of 9 percent. Thus, leverage works in favor of Crystal's stockholders.

ST13-3. a. Degree of operating leverage (DOL)

$$= \frac{\text{Sales} - \text{variable costs}}{\text{Sales} - \text{variable costs} - \text{fixed costs}}$$

$$= \frac{\$4,000,000 - (\$5 \times 200,000)}{\$4,000,000 - \$1,000,000 - \$1,200,000}$$

$$= 1.667$$

b. Degree of financial leverage (DFL) $= \dfrac{\text{EBIT}}{\text{EBIT} - \text{interest}}$

$$= \frac{\$1,800,000}{\$1,800,000 - \$600,000}$$

$$= 1.50$$

c. Degree of total leverage = DOL $\times$ DFL

$\quad = 1.667 \times 1.50$

$\quad = 2.50$

Video Case 13

Completion Bonds: Making Sure Hollywood Can Finish What It Starts

from *Business World,* March 29, 1992

Bonds are a significant component of the financing used by most companies. Bonds issued with a low-quality rating must offer a correspondingly higher coupon or interest rate. During the 1980s, several billion dollars worth of high-yield bonds, more commonly known as *junk bonds,* were issued. These bonds had ratings of *BB, B, CCC, CC* or lower. They were far from being investment-grade bonds! Because of the risk associated with these bonds, the issuing companies had to offer investors a high return in the form of high promised interest payments. Some junk bonds had coupon rates of 15 percent to 17 percent. For a small, growing company, such high interest payments drain cash that the company could otherwise use for expansion. Thus, if a company must pay very high interest payments, it may elect to not issue the bonds at all, and forego using the funds. The economy suffers if companies pass up good investment opportunities.

This video describes another approach to issuing risky debt: providing a guarantee or insurance. It is hard to think of many industries riskier than the movie business. Big budgets, big egos, and an uncertain public combine to make movie making very risky. To borrow money movie producers need to assure the lender that the film will be completed within (or at least close to) budget. Bonding companies, like those mentioned in the video clip, provide this type of insurance. For movies, completion bonds are particularly important. Unless a movie is completed, it has no value. Unlike raw materials and inventories in many other businesses, a partially filmed movie cannot be sold. Given this all-or-nothing aspect, completion bonds play an important role in film financing.

Study Question

1. The video commentator mentioned that bonding companies do "due diligence" for investors and lenders. Define due diligence and give several examples of where it plays a role in finance.

CHAPTER 14

Capital Budgeting: Decision Process And Models

Next time you are trying to overtake a tractor-trailer rig on an uphill stretch of interstate highway, think of Cummins Engine, Inc. This firm is the number-one maker of the diesel engines that propel these 18-wheelers. By following a sound business strategy and sticking to it, Cummins has seen its stock price more than triple since late 1991. In the late 1970s, Cummins was at a crossroads. Its diesel engine business was stuck in a mature, highly cyclical industry. In 1981, management considered a short-term strategy that would have maximized reported profits, paid large dividends to shareholders, and left little money for reinvestment in the company. Instead of pursuing this strategy, Cummins decided to commit $1 billion for capital expenditures to develop three new engines for small and mid-sized trucks. Management decided that it could create additional value for the firm through a massive investment in new products. The additional value would result from the capitalized cash flows of the new products, a concept we discussed in Chapters 11 and 12.

Thus, *firm value* can be seen as a collection of individual investments in areas such as property, plant, equipment, and research and development to produce salable products that generate cash flows. We call these investments **capital investments.** Some capital investments add to the firm's growth, and others, if unsuccessful, detract from it. The value of an investment lies not in its cost but in its ability to produce positive cash flows in excess of its cost.

Capital investment decisions affect the competitive posture and financial well-being of the firm for many years in the future, as we see in the Cummins Engine story. As one expert has expressed it, "today's capital expenditures make the bed that the company must lie in tomorrow."[1] To make rational decisions today, management must have a vision of what it wants and expects the future to look like.

Capital investments.
Expenditures of a firm for assets, such as plant and equipment.

---

[1]Joel Dean, "Measuring the Productivity of Capital," *Harvard Business Review* (January–February 1954), p. 123.

Managers make decisions about capital investments through a process called *capital budgeting*. This process involves several steps: *proposal generation, project evaluation, project selection, project execution,* and *project postaudit.* We will briefly examine each of these steps, but we will concentrate on two of them in this and the next chapter: project evaluation and project selection. The remaining steps are covered in detail in books about capital budgeting.[2] In this chapter, we will show that not all evaluation and selection techniques are equal—some are more appropriate than others. An exploration of the models for these techniques will prove which are theoretically sound and which are not.[3] The rule of thumb is, once again, the time value of money (TVM). The appropriate models use TVM concepts; the inappropriate models largely ignore TVM concepts.

When you have completed this chapter, you should understand:

- The nature of the capital investment problem.
- Whether accounting profits or cash flows are more important in making investment decisions.
- The models managers use to evaluate capital budgeting projects.
- The significance of the net present value model and certain shortcomings of other capital budgeting models.
- How to evaluate projects whose level of risk is different from the firm's risk.
- The effect of capital rationing on capital budgeting decisions.
- How to analyze the interaction of investment and financing decisions.

14.1 WHAT IS THE CAPITAL INVESTMENT PROBLEM?

Capital budgeting. Process of identifying, evaluating, and implementing approved capital expenditures.

Real assets. Land, buildings, plant and equipment, inventories.

Financial assets. Financial instruments with claims on real assets.

Decisions about investment in projects and products fall within the field of capital budgeting. **Capital budgeting** is the process of identifying, evaluating, and deciding which long-term investments will contribute to shareholder value. Normally investments with a life in excess of one year are subjected to the rigors of capital budgeting. However, any permanent investment in so-called short-term investments such as accounts receivable and inventory also qualify. The art of capital budgeting is making investments that are worth more than they cost.[4] An investment is wealth creating if the present value of all forecasted cash inflows exceed the present value of all forecasted cash outflows.

Since the consequences of a firm's selection of capital investments extend into the future, management may find it is locked into an investment. This situation is particularly true if the investment relates to **real assets,** such as land, buildings, plant, and equipment, as opposed to **financial assets,** such as receivables or securities. Real assets represent, for practical purposes, a permanent investment of resources. Once purchased, real assets rarely can be resold and converted back into cash at anywhere near their original cost. The liquidity and marketability of real assets are low. For instance, in

---

[2]For example, see Neil E. Seitz, *Capital Budgeting and Long-Term Financing Decisions* (Chicago: The Dryden Press, 1990).

[3]Although it is important for management to evaluate investment opportunities correctly, successful investment programs are more dependent on the ability of management to create profitable investment opportunities (that is, PVGO-type projects) that help satisfy consumers' needs than on its investment appraisal ability.

[4]Some investments must be made with no easily definable cash inflows resulting from them. An example is building an employee cafeteria. Employees may be happier, but how much is the benefit compared to the cost? Decisions such as these are made largely for a firm's long-run benefit—it may be easier to hire and keep desirable employees with an attractive environment or good fringe benefits. Our discussion is limited to investments designed to create shareholder wealth.

the early 1990s, Ford Motor Company committed $6 billion to the Mondeo, a mid-size car. This $6 billion decision cannot be reversed easily.

The basic management problem of capital budgeting lies in the search for the optimal quantity, quality, and mix of capital expenditures to achieve a balance of short- and long-range goals of the company. The mix of expenditures is made up of decisions such as funding research and development of new products, investing in existing products in an effort to support or improve their market positions, and maintaining or upgrading existing equipment to improve product quality as the firm strives to implement a total quality management (TQM) strategy.

Balancing the investment mix often requires managers to consider investing overseas. Diversifying corporate assets across several different countries can lead to reduced overall business risk. In this case, we might think of business risk as political risk. For example, managers of the German firm Daimler-Benz AG decided to build an assembly plant for Mercedes Benz in South Carolina. They were aware that cash flows for this project would be affected by future decisions of the U.S. government: trade policies, in particular restraints on German auto imports to the United States; regulations with regard to trade unions in foreign-owned companies in the United States; and taxation, including withholding tax and double-taxation treaties. Although the German company or any other foreign investor may have certain expectations with regard to U.S. government policies, these expectations may prove wrong. Political decisions are often difficult to predict.

The capital budgeting process, then, involves more than the technical evaluation and ranking of capital spending proposals. From an administrative viewpoint, the total process involves the chronological steps of proposal generation, project evaluation, project selection, various stages of project execution, and project postaudit. Figure 14.1 illustrates the typical capital budgeting decision process. The problem is continuous because changes in external and internal factors affect the firm in its business environment.

The Financial Reality reading on page 501 provides empirical evidence that shows how the financial markets react to firms' capital budgeting decisions. However, as we will see, many firms do not have adequate funds available to undertake all desirable projects.

14.1.1 Limited Resources Available

A popular notion in finance is that abundant opportunities and resources await firms that show initiative.[5] The standard finance textbook advocates bottom-up investment planning. Each potential project begins with an initial screening in which management considers the project on its own merits. The project's return must exceed some minimum rate and contribute to the firm's cash flows. For most projects, the minimum rate of return is the firm's weighted average cost of capital. Because evaluation of a project on its own merits is so straightforward, some lower-level managers may believe that if it clears the minimum rate, it has taken a step toward approval.

However, if the minimum rate were the most important criterion, capital markets have to be perfect and money always has to be available at the right price. In other words, no **capital rationing** could exist; management freely could pursue all its financial goals simultaneously and without the conflict created by inadequate funding. Dividend decisions would not influence investment decisions, or vice versa. Pursuit of growth for one product would not restrict growth for another. A target *rate of return for investments*

> **Capital rationing.** A situation in which new investments are limited to less than those economically justifiable.

---

[5]The discussion in this section is based on findings by Gordon Donaldson and Jay W. Lorsch reported in *Decision Making at the Top: The Shaping of Strategic Direction* (Basic Books, Inc., 1983).

FIGURE 14.1
TYPICAL CAPITAL BUDGETING SYSTEM

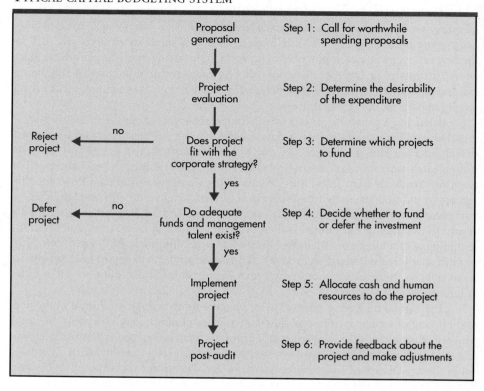

would direct investment opportunities but not restrict them. In sum, management would not have to make hard choices between investors' objectives and their own.

We know this not to be true. Management *does* ration funds and it does so for two possible reasons. First, managers ration funds when they believe the firm cannot obtain financing at favorable market rates. Second, managers ration funds in order to cope with capital constraints. What do we mean by *capital constraints*? To what extent do these constraints exist among firms? A British study concludes that:[6]

- The problem of low investment for a firm derives primarily from a shortage of demand for funds; there is a poor choice of investments available.
- Management usually imposes the capital constraint; it is not imposed by the financial markets.
- Smaller, less profitable, and high risk-taking firms experience capital constraints more acutely than larger, more profitable, more conservative firms.

In fact, management's primary responsibility is to make just such choices. As indicated by the preceding study, managers feel they must ration funds carefully, even among the various projects that have passed the minimum rate-of-return hurdle. Why? Managers often have a strong desire to avoid dependence on the financial markets, par-

[6]R.H. Pike, "The Capital Budgeting Behaviour and Corporate Characteristics of Capital-Constrained Firms," *Journal of Business Finance and Accounting* (Winter 1983), pp. 663–671.

CORPORATE CAPITAL EXPENDITURE DECISIONS . . .

Do capital budgeting decisions affect the value of the firm or the wealth of its shareholders? Yes, according to an empirical study of stock prices of 658 companies. Statistical analysis of common stock prices around the date that large capital expenditures are publicly announced by management indicates a couple of important findings.

First, the results support the idea that managers reveal information about capital expenditures to the marketplace that is important to the valuation of their firms. Second, these announcements cause stock prices to change in a manner that is consistent with predicted theory.

A sample of industrial firms likely to have positive net present value investment opportunities had the market value of their common stocks increase on announcements of significant capital expenditure increases. And stock prices dropped on announcements of significant decreases in capital expenditures.

On the other hand, the common stock price of a sample of public utility companies appeared to be unaffected by announced capital expenditures. These companies are regulated and thus less likely to earn positive net present values on their investments.

The evidence suggests that investors react to news about corporate capital expenditures. They reassess the market value of the firms making the announcements since they believe that managers seek to maximize the market value of the firm in making capital budgeting decisions.

Adapted from John J. McConnell and Chris J. Muscarella, "Corporate Capital Expenditure Decisions and the Market Value of the Firm," *Journal of Financial Economics* (September 1985), pp. 399–422.

ticularly the equity markets, to fund established products. Experience has taught managers that investors' judgments and expectations are often out of phase with their own judgments, expectations, and needs. If a project does not materialize as quickly as participants in the financial markets think it should, the firm's stock price can be driven down by a wave of investors selling the stock. This experience can make it more difficult for the firm to sell equity in the future. Another reason management may exercise capital rationing is that there may be insufficient managerial and technical talent to take charge of new projects in a time of growth. The Financial Reality reading on page 502 discusses how this problem affected American Express Company in the 1980s.

Instead of believing that unlimited resources exist for investment purposes, some managers often choose to rely on internally generated funds as the primary source of capital for corporate growth. This decision imposes real financial constraints on managers. A firm can be independent from external capital markets only if management succeeds in balancing the flow of funds within the firm. The price of independence from the financial markets is the discipline of self-sustaining growth.

14.1.2 Sustainable Growth

Capital rationing in well-managed firms is conducted under the guiding principle of managing *sustainable growth*. The principle of **sustainable growth** centers on the self-sufficiency of funds to sustain investment growth. It is growth the firm can sustain given

Sustainable growth. Growth the firm can maintain over time given its dividend policy, financing policy, asset management performance, and profitability of sales.

A SPATE OF ACQUISITIONS . . .

Capital rationing is usually considered in terms of the amount of money available for investment purposes. An important factor often overlooked is the amount of managerial talent that is available to manage growth.

American Express Company shocked Wall Street by announcing that its profit for 1983 would decline about 10 percent over the previous year. This broke 35 years of consecutive earnings growth.

Interviews with people at American Express and with analysts who follow the company led to the conclusion that the problem was caused by too many acquisitions in a short period of time. There was insufficient management talent to go around. With management stretched thin, the firm lost control over its ability to properly integrate the businesses. An analyst at Morgan Stanley stated, "There are a lot of portfolio managers out there who would like them to just tend to the store and not buy anything."

Confusion reigns as to whether the various new business can be integrated. Two years ago in public statements, American Express sounded a corporate theme known as "One Enterprise." When the 1983 annual report was issued, "One Enterprise" had disappeared and was replaced by the slogan "Marketing to America and the World." Within American Express, middle-level managers often speak of "One Enterprise" in the kind of embarrassed tones used to refer to a disgraced relative.

An investment banker at Donaldson, Lufkin & Jenrette, Inc. believes it will take American Express three to five years to determine if "there are really any big synergy possibilities among its insurance, securities, international banking and credit-card operations."

Another serious concern is that executives at American Express have a reputation for serious internal politics. The recent acquisitions have intensified the political maneuvering.

Adapted from D. B. Hilder and T. Metz, "A Spate of Acquisitions Puts American Express in a Management Bind," *The Wall Street Journal*, August 15, 1984, pp. 1+. Reprinted by permission of *The Wall Street Journal*, © 1984 Dow Jones & Company, Inc. All Rights Reserved Worldwide.

its dividend, financing, asset policies, and its profitability of sales. We can measure sustainable growth as:[7]

$$
\begin{aligned}
\text{Sustainable growth} \\
&= \text{Retention rate} \times \text{return on beginning equity} \\
&= \text{Retention rate} \times \text{return on sales} \times \text{asset turnover} \times \text{leverage} \\
&= \left(1 - \frac{\text{dividends paid}}{\text{earnings}}\right) \\
&\quad \times \underbrace{\frac{\text{net income}}{\text{sales}}}_{\substack{\text{profitability} \\ \text{of sales}}} \times \underbrace{\frac{\text{sales}}{\text{assets}}}_{\substack{\text{asset} \\ \text{turnover}}} \times \underbrace{\frac{\text{assets}}{\text{beginning equity}}}_{1 + \text{debt/equity}}
\end{aligned}
$$

$$(14.1)$$

[7] We introduced this model in Chapter 9 when we discussed common stock valuation. It is the growth variable in the dividend growth model. An underpinning of the dividend growth model is that the growth in sales, assets, debt, and equity are all equal.

The model focuses on a primary goal of the firm, that is, the target corporate sustainable growth rate in sales and assets (the left-hand side of the equation). This goal is dependent on goals related to:

- Target dividend payout ratio.
- Target profitability of sales.
- Target asset turnover ratio.
- Target debt-to-equity ratio.

By controlling each of these factors, management is able to generate sustainable growth and thereby avoid cash flow problems. (See Illustration 14.1.)

ILLUSTRATION 14.1

Calculating sustainable growth

For the year just finished, Utah Turbo Engines had sales of $10 million and net income of $1.5 million, earning a 15 percent return on sales. Management's policy is to maintain a dividend payout ratio of 70 percent of earnings. The company started the year with equity of $9.375 million.

Janet Parks, the chief financial officer, is wondering what growth rate the firm can sustain without turning to the outside financial markets to support its investment plans. She decides to use the sustainable growth model to provide an answer. To her dismay, the firm's sustainable growth is only 4.8 percent.

Sustainable growth

$$= (1 - \text{dividend payout}) \times \text{return on beginning equity}$$
$$= (1 - 0.70) \times \$1.5 \text{ million} \div \$9.375 \text{ million}$$
$$= 0.30 \times 0.16$$
$$= 0.048 \text{ or } 4.8 \text{ percent}$$

Janet decides that if the firm is to support investments that will allow for a 10 percent growth rate, then dividend payout will need to be cut back. The question is: What should the new payout ratio be?

Sustainable growth

$$= (1 - \text{dividend payout}) \times \text{return on beginning equity}$$
$$0.10 = (1 - \text{dividend payout}) \times 0.16$$
$$(1 - \text{dividend payout}) = 0.10 \div 0.16$$
$$(1 - \text{dividend payout}) = 0.625$$
$$\text{Dividend payout} = 1 - 0.625$$
$$= 0.375 \text{ or } 37.5 \text{ percent}$$

Thus, the dividend payout that allows the firm to sustain a 10 percent growth is 37.5 percent. Because it is considerably below the current payout ratio, she is not sure how to convince management to adopt such a change in the company's dividend policy.

The following Financial Reality reading provides a glimpse of what can go wrong in the planning and evaluation of an investment. Reuter's profitability on the investment, which was lower than expected, lowered the firm's sustainable growth rate and affected its ability to be independent of financial markets.

GARBAGE IN, GARBAGE OUT

Reuter, Inc. lost a bundle with what seemed like a promising recycling idea: It built a costly plant before figuring out who its customers were going to be.

Every few years someone comes up with a swell new idea that's supposed to be a breakthrough in finding new uses for garbage. Reuter, Inc. spent two years and $20 million to build a state-of-the-art waste reprocessing plant. It turns garbage into pellet fuel that cuts emissions that produce acid rain.

In its fourth year of production, the plant sold only 30 percent of its production. The rest of the pellets had to be either stockpiled or simply sent to the landfill at a cost of $50 a ton. Reuter learned that making new garbage products is easier than finding markets for them.

Environmental pressures that got Reuter into the business made it tough for the company to survive. The Minnesota Pollution Control Agency insisted that every potential customer do a test burn before using the pellets. This discouraged many companies from using the product. What's to be learned from this failure? Essentially a marketing lesson. Reuter spent too much time shopping for technology and not enough on market research.

Adapted from Ruth Simon, "Garbage In, Garbage Out," *Forbes,* October 1, 1990, pp. 170–171.
Reprinted by permission of FORBES magazine. © Forbes Inc., 1990.

▶ *Comprehension Check*

1. Define: capital budgeting, real assets, financial assets.
2. What are the advantages and disadvantages of investing in real assets compared with financial assets?
3. Based on the Financial Reality reading on page 501, what is the typical reaction of common stock investors to news of capital budgeting announcements by corporate managements? How do you account for this reaction?
4. What is capital rationing, and why does it occur?
5. Under what conditions is a firm independent of the capital markets when considering its capital budget commitments?
6. Explain the sustainable growth model shown in Equation 14.1.

▲▼▲ 14.2 PROJECT EVALUATION MODELS

In this section, we discuss various models used to evaluate capital expenditures. Our focus is primarily on the *net present value* model; experience has shown that this model is the most theoretically correct of the ones presented. The *internal rate of return* model is a close second in terms of accuracy and usefulness. Other techniques have one or more serious defects, as we will see. First, we need to address the important issue of whether *accounting profit* or *cash flow* is more appropriate to use in the evaluation models.

14.2.1 Accounting Profits or Cash Flows?

In making capital budgeting decisions, management must first determine whether accounting profit or cash flow is more important. **Accounting profit** recognizes revenues and expenses when the firm incurs them, not when the cash flow actually occurs. In addition, accounting methods deduct noncash charges, such as depreciation for plant and equipment, to determine taxable income. Although this accounting practice provides a better picture of the benefits of a particular investment, it ignores the fact that some expenses, such as depreciation, are noncash tax-deductible expenses. The cash outflow occurred when the firm bought the asset, not when the periodic expense for depreciation is created.

Cash flow is the stream of purchasing power provided by an investment and a measure of that investment's productivity. When the firm invests, it gives up some future purchasing power. When an investment provides cash inflow, it creates purchasing power. The future cash flow from an investment is money, generated by the investment, that is available to pay dividends and interest to the company's investors. In capital budgeting analysis, we compute cash flow as though equity capital finances the investment. When a firm uses debt financing to buy an asset, we ignore any interest amount as a cash flow expense item. *Thus, in the computation of cash flow, we ignore the method of financing the investment.*[8] However, we do not ignore the method of financing in the overall scheme; it becomes part of the cost of capital.

Accounting profit. Earnings amount derived from accrual accounting practices that correspond with generally accepted accounting principles.

14.2.2 Net Present Value Model

The time value of money concepts you studied in Chapter 4, and again in Chapters 8 and 9 to value bonds and stocks, are readily transferable to the valuation of capital budgeting decisions. Investment decisions involve an initial payment followed by a stream of cash receipts and cash disbursements in later periods. The time value formula called **net present value (NPV)** is the most theoretically correct model for evaluating the desirability of investment opportunities. We define the model as:

Net present value (NPV). A time value of money technique that nets the present value of cash inflows against the present value of cash outflows.

Net present value

$$= - \text{ Initial investment} + \text{present value of forecasted cash flows}$$

$$\begin{array}{l} > \\ = 0 \\ < \end{array} \left\{ \begin{array}{l} \text{accept project} \\ \text{indifferent to project} \\ \text{reject project} \end{array} \right. \qquad \textbf{(14.2)}$$

$$\text{NPV} = - I + \sum_{t=1}^{n} \text{CF}_t/(1 + r)^t = 0 \begin{array}{l} > \\ \\ < \end{array} \left\{ \begin{array}{l} \text{accept project} \\ \text{indifferent to project} \\ \text{reject project} \end{array} \right.$$

where

$I =$ Initial cash outflow required for the investment

$\text{CF}_t =$ Forecasted after-tax net cash flow arising at the end of year t (the difference between operating cash receipts and operating cash payments)

$r =$ Required risk-adjusted rate of return

$n =$ Economic life of the project in years

$$I = 100 \quad y 1$$
$$t = 1$$
$$n = 10$$
$$r = .1$$
$$-100 + 259.37 / (1 + .1)^{10}$$
$$159.37 / 1.34337$$

[8]The appendix to this chapter relaxes the constraint of ignoring the financing.

CAPITAL BUDGETING DECISIONS, PART I

by William J. Post, Senior Vice President, Arizona Public Service Company

Capital budgeting analysis is particularly important for companies in the electric utility industry. Utilities invest in projects that typically have 30- to 40-year lives and can exceed $500 million to build. These facts are important to note since a utility's customers, that is, its rate payers, typically do not pay any portion of the construction costs for the plant until it is completed and placed in commercial operation. The utility must rely on external financing by issuing bonds, preferred stock, and common stock, and cash generated from operations to meet its immediate financing needs for the new power plant. In some instances, state or federal regulatory agencies, who have jurisdiction over the utility, may allow the project's financing costs to be recovered from customers prior to commercial operation. But this situation is not normal, as these governmental agencies attempt to fulfill their responsibility of ensuring that the utility charges fair, nondiscriminatory rates and renders safe, reliable service to the public on demand.

Once a plant is constructed and placed in commercial operation, the utility can file a rate application with the regulators to recover the costs of the new plant. In determining the new rates, the regulators include a market-based return on the capital investment as well as recovery of associated operating and maintenance expenses. However, several years usually elapse between the completion of construction and the resolution of the rate case hearing. Only then can a utility begin to recover its investment through higher rates.

At Arizona Public Service Company (APS), one of the first steps we take to determine whether or not to build a new power plant is to prepare a load forecast. This forecast predicts future customer growth by analyzing economic and demographic factors, electricity sales, and the peak load (that one hour during the year when the demand for electricity reaches its highest level). This information forms the basis for planning additional power plants to meet customers' future energy needs. Because APS operates in a territory free from substantial direct competition, it has an obligation to serve all customers located in the territory. Therefore, APS must have adequate generation to meet these future needs.

If APS does not have enough generating capacity, then we conduct a capital budgeting analysis to evaluate all possible investment alternatives. These alternatives may include programs to encourage customers to reduce future electricity use, purchase electricity from other utilities, or build a new power plant. Capital budgeting is the tool that aids APS's investment decision.

Many corporations adopt the net present value method for capital budgeting. This method evaluates the merits of an investment by measuring the profits it should generate. In contrast, APS uses the revenue requirements method, which is a standard procedure for capital budgeting in the electric utility industry. The revenue requirements method mirrors the rate-making process used by regulatory agencies in that it calculates the revenue required to earn a return on the investment and recovery of operating and maintenance costs, depreciation, and taxes. The revenue requirement method evaluates an investment by projecting the identified costs over the life of the investment and discounting back to obtain the present value. The decision criterion is to choose the alternative which has the lowest present value revenue requirements, in other words, the least-cost option. The revenue requirements method can be thought of as the revenues required from an investment to provide a minimum acceptable return to investors.

Investors do not like risk. The greater the nondiversifiable risk of an investment, the greater the return expected by investors. Thus, the required rates of return used to discount forecasted cash flows of investment opportunities reflect nondiversifiable market risk. Figure 14.2 shows the risk-return relationships and NPVs of seven projects. Consider the upward sloping line as the minimum rate of return required by the capital market for investing in these projects. The line slopes upward because higher risk means that the market demands higher return.

The NPV rules for project selection are as follows.

- *Accept positive NPVs.* Projects B and E lie above the market risk-return line. Their expected returns are higher than those required for the corresponding risk levels; that is, they have positive NPVs. An investment is only wealth creating if its NPV is positive. It is management's responsibility to locate such projects.
- *Indifferent to zero NPVs.* Projects A, F, and G fall on the market risk-return line. Their expected returns just compensate for their riskiness; that is, they have NPVs of zero. These projects neither add to nor detract from the value of the firm. Firms operating in perfect competition expect these types of investments.
- *Reject negative NPVs.* Projects C and D, which lie below the market risk-return line, have negative NPVs. Adoption of either of these projects would result in reduced value of the firm.

Illustration 14.2 examines the net present value calculation. It shows that you obtain the NPV of a project by following these steps:

Step 1. Discount each period's cash flow at a rate that reflects the cost of financing of equivalent risk on the capital market.

Step 2. Sum the discounted cash flows over the project's life.

Step 3. Deduct the initial investment outlay.

FIGURE 14.2
RISK-RETURN TRADE-OFF FOR PROJECTS

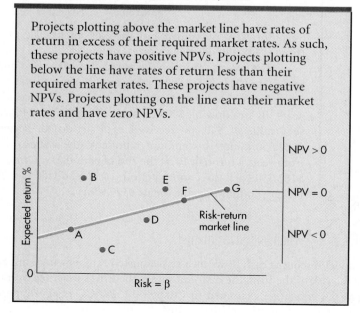

Projects plotting above the market line have rates of return in excess of their required market rates. As such, these projects have positive NPVs. Projects plotting below the line have rates of return less than their required market rates. These projects have negative NPVs. Projects plotting on the line earn their market rates and have zero NPVs.

ILLUSTRATION 14.2

Calculating net present value

Engineers for Wesley Electronics estimate the cost of a new wafer bath machine to be $250,000, fully installed. The machine is expected to result in the following labor and material savings:

		At the End of Year:		
0	1	2	3	4 through 10
$0	$50,000	$80,000	$70,000	$40,000 each period

Wesley's cost of capital for a project with this amount of risk is 12 percent. The NPV of the wafer bath equipment is found by discounting each period's cash flow at 12 percent and subtracting the purchase cost of $250,000.

STEPS 1 AND 2

The present value (PV) of the cash inflows is $288,180.

$$\frac{\$50,000}{(1.12)} + \frac{\$80,000}{(1.12)^2} + \frac{\$70,000}{(1.12)^3} + \$40,000\frac{\left(\frac{1 - (1.12)^{-7}}{0.12}\right)}{(1.12)^3}$$

$$= \$44,643 + \$63,776 + \$49,825 + \$129,936$$
$$= \$288,180$$

STEP 3

Subtract the cost of the wafer bath machine from the PV of the cash inflows to get an NPV of $38,180.

$$NPV = \$288,180 - \$250,000$$
$$= \$38,180$$

Since the NPV is positive, buy the equipment. The project contributes $38,180 of value in excess of its cost.

The last expression in the numerator of the PV equation (see Steps 1 and 2) is the present value, as of the end of year 3, of annuity cash flows for years 4 through 10. This is a period of seven years. By multiplying $40,000 by $(1 - (1.12)^{-7}) \div 0.12$, the present value of $40,000 received each period for seven years is $182,550. Since this amount represents the value of cash flows from years 4 through 10, at the end of period 3, you must discount $182,550 back three more periods (that is, divide the amount by $(1.12)^3$) to find its value today: $129,936.

14.2.3 NPV of Risk-Changing Investments

The NPV model discounts cash flows by a risk-adjusted rate. For investments that do not change the risk of the firm, the discount rate is the firm's weighted average cost of capital (WACC), which we examined in Chapter 12. WACC is appropriate for discounting cash flows of nonrisk-changing investments because such investments are "carbon copies" of the firm's current investments. But how do we evaluate a risk-changing investment? There are three prevalent approaches: *arbitrary adjustment*, the *capital asset pricing model*, and the *certainty-equivalent model*.

ARBITRARY ADJUSTMENT APPROACH. The usual procedure to adjust for risk is to take the firm's WACC and add or subtract percentage points. Add points to adjust for higher risk; subtract points to adjust for lower risk. For example, discount "carbon-copy" projects at the WACC of, say, 12 percent. For investments in related but new fields, add, possibly, 1 to 2 points to the WACC. The risk-adjusted discount rate becomes 13 or 14 percent. If the investment is for an unrelated project, add, say, 4 to 10 points to the WACC. Subtract points for less risky investments.

Managers can be reluctant to reduce the discount rate because it is more conservative to use the higher rate. Either adding or subtracting points to the WACC is an approach to determine risk-adjusted discount rates that change with each particular firm's needs and managers' styles. The risk adjustment is a *fudge factor* based on management's aversion to risk and likely has little relevance to market-determined risk.

CAPM APPROACH. The capital asset pricing model (CAPM), discussed in Chapters 5 and 12, addresses the issue of risk versus expected return directly. The basis of the model is that financial markets are in equilibrium. Thus, only nondiversifiable market risk, as measured by beta (β), is important to investors in pricing risky cash flows. Equation 14.3 represents the risk-reward trade-off.

> Expected market risk-adjusted return
>
> $\quad$ = Risk-free rate + $\beta \times$ (market risk premium)
>
> $r = r_f + \beta\,(r_m - r_f)$
>
> (14.3)

r_m is the average rate of return earned in the market.

For capital budgeting purposes, it is necessary to find the beta of the project. No easy method exists to estimate this beta.[9] However, once you have an estimate for the project's beta, $\beta_{project}$, you substitute it into the CAPM equation,

$$r = r_f + \beta_{project}\,(r_m - r_f)$$

[9]The recommended steps to estimate a project beta are as follows:

Step 1: Identify several publicly traded firms whose businesses are similar to the project under consideration.

Step 2: Obtain estimates of the equity betas (β_{equity}) for these firms. Value Line Investment Services is a prime source.

Step 3: Calculate each firm's asset beta (β_{asset}) as a weighted average of the firm's debt and equity betas. Debt betas, β_{debt}, are not readily available but are typically in the range of 0.0 to 0.4. The debt and equity weights are debt ÷ (debt + equity) and equity ÷ (debt + equity), respectively. The numerators and denominators of the weights use market values for debt and equity.

$$\beta_{asset} = \beta_{debt} \times \frac{debt}{debt + equity} + \beta_{equity} \times \frac{equity}{debt + equity}$$

Step 4: Calculate the average of these asset betas.

Step 5: Take this average beta and adjust it for financial leverage of the firm considering the project. The adjustment is:

$$\beta_{project} = \beta_{asset} \times [1 + (1 - \text{tax rate}) \times debt/equity]$$

The resulting beta is used in Equation 14.3.

Most analysts use historical average values for the risk-free rate (r_f) and the market return (r_m). For the period 1926 to 1993, the arithmetic mean for common stocks, a proxy for r_m, is 12.3 percent. The risk-free rate, using U.S. Treasury bonds, has an arithmetic average of 5.4 percent.[10] Use the risk-adjusted rate in the NPV model to discount the cash flows of the project or use it to compare the project's rate of return as shown in Illustration 14.3.

ILLUSTRATION 14.3

Using CAPM to calculate a risk-adjusted rate

Gary Floyd, a newly appointed financial analyst for Astar Casinos, believes that capital investments should be evaluated using the capital asset pricing model. Based on his best estimates for the risk-free rate and the market premium, he specifies the CAPM as follows:

Project's risk-adjusted rate
= Risk-free rate + beta project × (market risk premium)

$$r = r_f + _{project}\beta \times (r_m - r_f)$$

$$= 0.08 + \beta_{project} \times 0.09$$

Following are risk and return characteristics of projects under examination.

Project	β	Forecasted Return
Security system	0.4	0.12
New game	2.6	0.20

The risk-adjusted return required for the security system project is: $0.08 + 0.4 \times 0.09 = 0.116$ or 11.6 percent. Because the forecasted return exceeds the risk-adjusted return, Gary recommends the company accept the security system proposal. The risk-adjusted return for the new game project is 31.4 percent. (See if you can get this result.[11]) Since the forecasted return is less than 31.4 percent, he recommends that the casino reject this proposal.

Implementation of the CAPM procedure is fairly complex, as you can see from footnote 9. You must be careful using the CAPM because attempts to carry out its theory can be subject to considerable error, as we discussed in Chapters 5 and 12. An equity beta is an incomplete and inadequate risk measure for individual stocks. In addition, a debt beta is even more difficult to measure than is an equity beta. A debt beta has a wide range for its most likely value. Thus, the asset beta is only as good as the debt and equity beta estimates.

CERTAINTY-EQUIVALENT APPROACH. Another approach for finding the NPV of a risk-changing project is the certainty-equivalent model. It asks the question: What is the

---

[10]The source for both of these rates is from R.G. Ibbotson and R.A. Sinquefield, *Stocks, Bonds, Bills and Inflation* (SBBI). Updated in *SBBI 1994 Yearbook* (Chicago: Ibbotson Associates, 1994), p. 31.

[11]Solution: Risk-adjusted return = $0.08 + 2.6 \times 0.09 = 0.314$.

smallest *certain* cash flow in each period that you are willing to accept in place of that period's risky cash flow? Illustration 14.4 outlines the approach. The **certainty-equivalent (CE)** net present value model discounts these *certain* cash flows at the risk-free rate, since risk has been eliminated from the flows.

> CE net present value
>
> $$= - \text{Investment} + \frac{\text{certain cash flow in period 1}}{(1 + \text{risk-free rate})} + \cdots$$
>
> $$+ \frac{\text{certain cash flow in period } n}{(1 + \text{risk-free rate})^n}$$
>
> (14.4)

Certainty-equivalent (CE). A technique used to adjust uncertain cash flows downward to a level that the decision maker is indifferent between the risky unadjusted cash flows and the certain adjusted cash flows.

ILLUSTRATION 14.4

Project selection using certainty equivalents

The president of Trennepohl Financial Services is considering an advertising campaign expected to generate cash flows of $900,000 and $800,000 in the next two years, respectively. The advertising agency has quoted him a cost for the campaign of $700,000. He considers the probability of these forecasted cash flows actually happening to be less than certain, regardless of the advertising agency's claim.

After careful consideration, the president concludes that he is indifferent between the forecasted risky cash flow of $900,000 and a certain cash flow of $600,000 in year 1. For year 2, the president is indifferent to a risky cash flow of $700,000 and a certain cash flow of $300,000. He believes that these certain cash flows will be achieved and instructs his financial analyst to consider the "certain" cash flows as being risk free.

Since there is no risk, the analyst discounts the certain cash flows at 5 percent, the current yield for a two-year Treasury bond, whose maturity matches the duration of the ad campaign. He calculates the certainty-equivalent net present value to be $143,538. Because the result is positive, he advises the president to hire the advertising agency to conduct the campaign.

$$\text{CE NPV} = - \$700,000 + \frac{\$600,000}{(1 + 0.05)} + \frac{\$300,000}{(1 + 0.05)^2}$$

$$= - \$700,000 + \$571,429 + \$272,109$$
$$= \$143,538$$

The certainty-equivalent method is theoretically sound. It should provide the same solution as a risk-adjusted discount model, because it implicitly incorporates management's risk aversion and expected satisfaction into the wealth-creating net present value model. However, to our knowledge few managers use the technique. In practice, it is possible to reach a different conclusion using the certainty-equivalent model than using a risk-adjusted discount model. Different results mean that either the selected certainty equivalents are wrong, the risk-adjusted discount rate is wrong, or both are wrong.

Louis Lowenstein makes an important point about risk-adjusted rates that can get lost in application of the CAPM and certainty equivalents. He says:

In capital budgeting, it is the analysis and the discipline that are valuable, not the close tweaking of the numbers. Companies such as FMC and Coca-Cola recognize this reality by not changing hurdle (discount) rates often. Exxon does so by defining its cost of capital only within a range of one to two percentage points.[12]

14.2.4 Internal Rate of Return

Internal rate of return (IRR). A time value of money technique that finds the interest rate that equates the present value of cash inflows with the present value of cash outflows.

The **internal rate of return (IRR),** or yield, of a project is the rate of return that equates the present value of expected net cash flows with the initial outlay for the investment. In Chapter 8, we called this type of calculation the yield to maturity for a bond.

When you solve for the NPV you know the values for all the variables on the right-hand side of Equation 14.2, reproduced here:

$$NPV = -I + \sum_{t=1}^{n} CF_t / (1 + r)^t$$

The conceptual approach to solving for the IRR in the above equation is as follows:

Step 1. Set the NPV equal to zero so you can state the equation as
$$\sum_{t=1}^{n} CF_t / (1 + r)^t = I.$$

Step 2. Find the discount rate r that causes the discounted cash flows to equal the initial investment, I.

Satisfying Step 2 is essentially a trial-and-error approach without a financial calculator.[13]
The validity of the IRR model rests on three important but unstated assumptions.

Assumption 1. The amount and timing of each future period's cash flow occurs when expected and there are no deviations.

Assumption 2. All future cash flows generated by a project earn the same r in new projects; that is, the reinvestment rate is the IRR.

Assumption 3. The investment lasts for n periods, which is the expected maturity of the new project.

Many people, students and practitioners alike, misunderstand the IRR method by not taking into account the full implications of these rather strict assumptions. It is doubtful that actual cash flows generated by an investment agree with any of these assumptions in the real world. Estimation of future cash flows involves much uncertainty. Both the size and timing of realized cash flows in future periods will likely differ from the forecast. And it is not possible in reality to assume that all cash flows will be reinvested at the IRR rate. Many of the cash flows generated by the investment go to pay suppliers, employees, and interest expense. Some of the cash flows finance new projects. Moreover, it is unlikely the new projects earn the same IRR as the project throwing off the cash flows. Therefore, the true rate earned on the investment will likely not equal its IRR. (See Illustration 14.5.)

[12]Louis Lowenstein, *Sense and Nonsense in Corporate Finance* (Reading, MA: Addison-Wesley Publishing Company, Inc., 1991), p. 137.
[13]Chapter 8, Appendix 8A discusses the use of a trial-and-error technique called interpolation to find the IRR.

ILLUSTRATION 14.5

Calculating internal rate of return

Let's use the data of Illustration 14.2 to calculate the IRR of the wafer bath machine. *Since the NPV of the equipment is positive, the IRR is more than the market cost of capital (12 percent) used to discount the cash flows.* Without the use of a financial calculator, you use a trial-and-error approach.

First, try a rate of 16 percent.

$$\frac{\$50,000}{(1.16)} + \frac{\$80,000}{(1.16)^2} + \frac{\$70,000}{(1.16)^3} + \frac{\$40,000\left(\frac{1 - (1.16)^{-7}}{0.16}\right)}{(1.16)^3}$$

$$- \$250,000$$

$$= \$43,103 + \$59,453 + \$44,846 + \$103,494 - \$250,000$$
$$= \$896$$

Since the cash flows, discounted at 16 percent, are positive, the IRR is higher than 16 percent.

Next, try a 17 percent rate.

$$\frac{\$50,000}{(1.17)} + \frac{\$80,000}{(1.17)^2} + \frac{\$70,000}{(1.17)^3} + \frac{\$40,000\left(\frac{1 - (1.17)^{-7}}{0.17}\right)}{(1.17)^3}$$

$$- \$250,000$$

$$= \$42,735 + \$58,441 + \$43,706 + \$97,961 - \$250,000$$
$$= -\$7,157$$

The discounted value of the cash flows is $-\$7157$. Thus, the IRR is between 16 percent and 17 percent, and closer to 16 percent. Repeated trial-and-error attempts will eventually provide the IRR.

Panel A in Figure 14.3 graphically depicts the relationship between the IRR and the required return *r* for **investment-type cash flows,** defined as an initial negative flow followed by positive flows. A project is acceptable if IRR > *r*. This method of project appraisal usually gives the same decision to accept or reject as NPV. The decision rules are:

- *Accept projects with values of IRR greater than r;* they have positive NPVs.
- *Reject projects with values of IRR less than r;* they have negative NPVs.
- *Be indifferent to projects with values of IRR equal to r;* they have zero NPVs.

If you indiscriminately compare the IRR to the rate required by investors (*r*), problems can arise. Taken together, Figure 14.3, panel B, and Figure 14.4 illustrate this point. In panel B of Figure 14.3, cash flows have positive slopes. These flows are **loan-type cash flows,** in which negative flows follow an initial positive flow. In this case, present value increases with higher discount rates. The reason the present value increases is that future cash outflows decline in value when discounted to the present. Therefore, for loan-type flows you must reverse the previously mentioned accept-reject rules. To apply the decision rules you must know whether the cash flows are of the investment type or of the loan type.

Investment-type cash flows. An initial cash outflow followed by positive cash inflows in future periods.

Loan-type cash flows. An initial cash inflow followed by cash outflows in future periods.

FIGURE 14.3
IRR AND NPV PROFILES

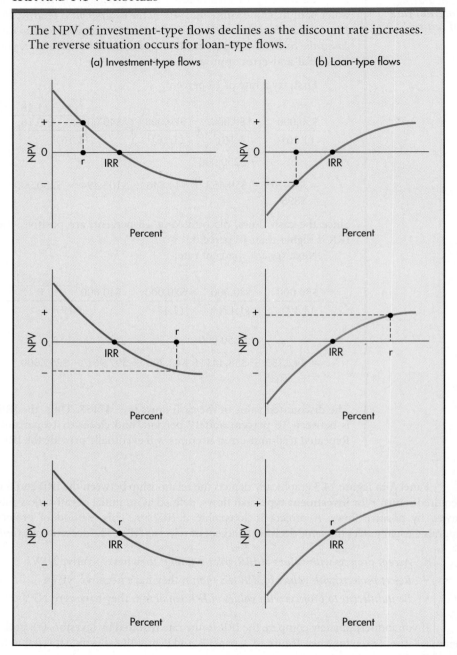

The NPV of investment-type flows declines as the discount rate increases. The reverse situation occurs for loan-type flows.

(a) Investment-type flows

(b) Loan-type flows

Figure 14.4 depicts a different issue. A comparison of the IRR of project N to the firm's weighted average cost of capital (WACC) shows that project N should be accepted. Its IRR exceeds the WACC. Note that this project is a risk-changing project: project N's market risk is greater than the firm's market risk. You need to compare the project's IRR to investors' required rate r^N. When you do, you reject this project because project N's expected return is less than the required rate r^N.

FIGURE 14.4
IRR RELATIVE TO REQUIRED RISK-ADJUSTED RATES

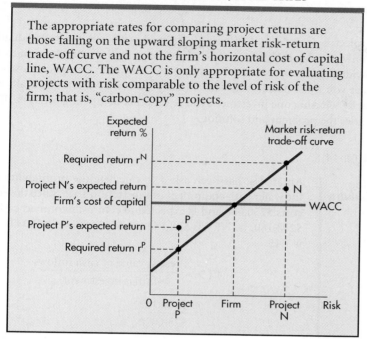

The appropriate rates for comparing project returns are those falling on the upward sloping market risk-return trade-off curve and not the firm's horizontal cost of capital line, WACC. The WACC is only appropriate for evaluating projects with risk comparable to the level of risk of the firm; that is, "carbon-copy" projects.

Project *P* represents the opposite problem. In this case, using the firm's WACC as the cutoff rate, you decide to reject the project. Because project *P*'s risk is less than the firm's risk, the appropriate rate to check the project is r^P. In this case, project *P* offers a return higher than the investors' required risk-adjusted rate. Therefore, you should accept the project.

14.2.5 Profitability Index

Another model that uses time value of money concepts is the *profitability index*. We calculate the **profitability index (PI)** by dividing the present value of the forecasted cash flows by the initial cash outlay. The only difference between the NPV and PI methods is how each method uses the initial investment. The NPV technique deducts the initial outlay from the present value of anticipated cash flows. The PI uses the initial outlay as a divisor:

> **Profitability index (PI).** A discounted cash flow technique that compares the present value of future cash flows to the initial cash outflow.

Profitability index

$$= \frac{\text{Present value of cash inflows}}{\text{Initial investment}} \quad \begin{matrix} > \\ = 1 \\ < \end{matrix} \begin{cases} \text{accept project} \\ \text{indifferent} \\ \text{reject project} \end{cases}$$

(14.5)

$$\text{PI} = \frac{\sum_{t=1}^{n} \text{CF}_t / (1+r)^t}{I} \quad \begin{matrix} > \\ = 1 \\ < \end{matrix} \begin{cases} \text{accept project} \\ \text{indifferent} \\ \text{reject project} \end{cases}$$

By using a little algebra, the profitability index can also be stated as:[14]

$$PI = \frac{NPV}{I} + 1 \qquad (14.6)$$

A project is acceptable if PI exceeds unity. As you can see from Equation 14.6, PI > 1 is only possible if NPV > 0. The PI gives exactly the same decision to accept or reject individual projects as that offered by NPV. However, complications occur with the PI when you must decide between *mutually exclusive projects*. **Mutually exclusive** means that by selecting one investment you reject other competing projects. Illustration 14.6 examines the problem and solution.

Mutually exclusive. Either-or decision; take one project or the other.

ILLUSTRATION 14.6

Calculating the profitability index

An analyst has been asked to calculate the profitability index for the wafer bath equipment of Illustration 14.2. Since the equipment costs $250,000 and is expected to return discounted cash flows of $288,180, its NPV is $38,180 (= $288,180 − $250,000) and its PI is 1.15:

$$PI = \frac{\text{Present value of cash inflows}}{\text{Initial investment}}$$

$$= \frac{\$288,180}{\$250,000}$$

$$= 1.15$$

The chief financial officer has given the analyst information about a competing (mutually exclusive) proposal for a new machine. It has present value of cash inflows of $150,000 and an initial investment of $125,000. Thus, the PI is 1.20 and its NPV is $25,000.

Should the analyst recommend accepting the initial proposal with an NPV of $38,180 and a PI of 1.15? Or is the new proposal with an NPV of $25,000 and a PI of 1.20 better? The correct decision is to select the investment with the higher NPV. *It should increase shareholder value by $13,180 more than the competing project (the difference between the two NPVs).*

14.2.6 Accounting Rate of Return (ARR)

Accounting rate of return. Nondiscounted profitability measure that divides accounting earnings by average investment.

Many managers use *accounting rate of return* as an indicator of performance. The definition of **accounting rate of return** is after-tax accounting profits divided by either gross or net investment. Both accounting profit and investment usually are stated as averages over the expected life of the project.

$$ARR = \frac{\text{Average accounting profits}}{\text{Average investment}} \qquad (14.7)$$

Division by gross as opposed to net investment ignores accumulated depreciation amounts and helps make the comparison among assets at different stages of their lives

---

[14]The numerator of Equation 14.5 can be restated as net present value + investment, which reduces to Equation 14.6.

a simpler process. Gross investment has the supposed advantage of conservatism; the accounting rate of return is a smaller number. The decision rule is that the greater the ARR, the better the investment.

The virtues of the ARR method are simplicity, focus on return, and consistency with the accounting numbers reported to outside investors. However, the critical drawbacks of the ARR method are its concentration on accounting profits and its inability to cope with the size, risk, and time dimension of cash flows. Accounting rate of return depends to some extent on the firm's depreciation policy. The biggest problems surround the fact that the ARR fails to say *whether a project is wealth creating and how much cash flow the project generates for future use.* (See Illustration 14.7.)

ILLUSTRATION 14.7

Calculating accounting rate of return

An analyst for Manhattan Cycle Company has identified the annual *accounting profits* expected to be generated by a new metal lathe as follows:

		Year		
1	2	3	4	Total
$5000	$6000	$4000	$3000	$18,000

The average accounting profit is total profits divided by four years: $18,000 ÷ 4 = $4500. The cost of the lathe is $15,000. The average investment in this new lathe is simply one half its initial cost: $15,000 ÷ 2 = $7500.

The ARR for the lathe is 60 percent.

$$ARR = \frac{\text{Average accounting profits}}{\text{Average investment}}$$

$$= \frac{\$4500}{\$7500}$$

$$= 0.60 \text{ or } 60 \text{ percent}$$

14.2.7 Payback Period

Managers often use a model called the *payback period.* The **payback period** is the length of time required to recover the initial investment. To calculate the payback period, sum the future net cash flows until they turn positive. The period in which cumulative cash flow is positive is the payback period. Illustration 14.8 shows the calculation.

Payback period. A nondiscounted cash flow technique that determines the estimated time it takes to recover the original investment.

ILLUSTRATION 14.8

Calculating payback period

Investments *A* and *B* have projected cash flows as follows.

		Year		
	0	1	2	3
A	−$800	$660	$363	$133
B	−$800	$110	$363	$799

The projects differ significantly in the timing of their cash returns. Project A is better because it derives most of its value from the first year. Project B derives most of its value from the last year.

Payback for each project is:

Project A. $-\$800 + \$660 = -\$140$ not recouped after year 1. Thus, the project needs $\$140 \div \$363 = 0.38$ of year 2's cash flow.

Payback = 1 + 0.38 = 1.38 years.

Project B. $-\$800 + \$110 = -\$690$ not recouped after year 1. $-\$690 + \$363 = -\$327$ not recouped after year 2. Thus, the project needs $\$327 \div \$799 = 0.41$ of year 3's cash flow.

Payback = 2 + 0.41 = 2.41 years.

The payback method involves a subjective establishment of an acceptable cutoff period and totally neglects a project's potential for wealth creation. All cash flows beyond the cutoff point, even though they may be positive and thereby add to wealth creation, are ignored. For example, in the preceding illustration, both projects A and B have an NPV of $200 when discounted at 10 percent. If the cutoff for project acceptance is two years, project B is rejected.

While academicians have almost unanimously denigrated the use of the payback period as misleading and worthless in reaching investment decisions, many practitioners continue to apply it. The main advantage of the payback rule is that it is a simple tool for informing managers how long capital is subject to a time risk factor. Payback assumes that the faster you recoup the investment, the less the risk exposure and the better the investment.

14.2.8 Discounted Payback Period

Discounted payback period. A discounted cash flow technique that calculates the time it takes to recover the original investment.

The **discounted payback period** differs slightly from the payback period. You discount each cash flow and then apply the payback technique. Applying this method results in a longer and more realistic period to recover the investment than does the payback period method. The discounted payback technique is a considerable improvement over payback period in that it considers the riskiness of the project via the discount rate, the rate required by investors. However, discounted payback suffers the same overall shortcomings as does the payback period. Because you ignore cash flows beyond the discounted payback period, it does not allow you to decide whether a project is wealth creating. (See Illustration 14.9.)

ILLUSTRATION 14.9

Calculating discounted payback period

Let's continue the previous illustration. With a required cost of capital of 10 percent, the *discounted* cash flows for investments A and B are:

	Year			
	0	1	2	3
A	$\dfrac{-\$800}{1}$	$\dfrac{\$660}{1.10}$	$\dfrac{\$363}{1.10^2}$	$\dfrac{\$133}{1.10^3}$
	$= -\$800$	$= \$600$	$= \$300$	$= \$100$
B	$\dfrac{-\$800}{1}$	$\dfrac{\$110}{1.10}$	$\dfrac{\$363}{1.10^2}$	$\dfrac{\$799}{1.10^3}$
	$= -\$800$	$= \$100$	$= \$300$	$= \$600$

Discounted payback for each project is:

Project A. $- \$800 + \$600 = - \$200$ not recouped after year 1.
Thus, you need $\$200 \div \$300 = 0.67$ of year 2's cash flow.
Payback $= 1 + 0.67 = 1.67$ years.

Project B. $- \$800 + \$100 = - \$700$ not recouped after year 1.
$- \$700 + \$300 = - \$400$ not recouped after year 2.
Thus, you need $\$400 \div \$600 = 0.67$ of year 3's cash flow.

Payback $= 2 + 0.67 = 2.67$ years.

14.2.9 Comparison of Project Rankings by Different Techniques

The several techniques we have discussed are used in practice to allocate funds for capital expenditures. Surveys indicate that financial managers rely primarily on the IRR method; NPV and payback play significant supporting roles.[15] Although not the first choice of many practitioners, the NPV technique is the most correct technique for evaluating capital expenditures. Consider the information about projects A, B, C, and D given in the top part of Table 14.1. Assume each project is of similar risk and the tax rate is zero. Your task is to rank the attractiveness of the projects.

The lower part of the table shows that the "best" project depends on the technique used. If you choose either payback or discounted payback, project B is better than project D. You reverse this ranking under the ARR criterion. The IRR is indifferent between projects B and D, and the NPV ranking is dependent on the firm's cost-of-capital rate.

The bothersome conclusion to draw from the table is that each model rank orders identical sets of investments differently. However, the time value techniques (IRR, NPV, and discounted payback) preserve the ranking by inspection. Project B is better than project A, and project D is better than project C. The nontime value of money techniques (ARR and payback) fail to rank these pairs in the obvious order. Hence, reject the nontime value of money approaches.

[15]See L. J. Gitman and J. R. Forrester, Jr., "A Survey of Capital Budgeting Techniques Used by Major U.S. Firms," *Financial Management* (Fall 1977), pp. 67–71 and by D. J. Oblak and R. J. Helm, Jr., "Survey and Analysis of Capital Budgeting Methods Used by Multinationals," *Financial Management* (Winter 1980), pp. 37–41.

TABLE 14-1

COMPARISON OF PROJECT RANKINGS

Project	A	B	C	D
Initial cost	$10,000	$10,000	$10,000	$10,000
Cash flow:				
Year 1	$10,000	$10,000	$3,762	$5,762
Year 2		1,100	7,762	5,762
Total	$10,000	$11,100	$11,524	$11,524
Average flow	$10,000	$5,500	$5,762	$5,762
Average depreciation	$10,000	$5,000	$5,000	$ 5,000
Average profit	$0	$550	$762	$762
Average investment	$10,000	$5,000	$5,000	$5,000
Payback (years)	1.00	1.00	1.80	1.74
Rank	1	1	4	3
Discounted payback (6%)	Never	1.58	1.93	1.89
Rank	4	1	3	2
ARR (%)	0.0	11.0	15.2	15.2
Rank	4	3	1	1
IRR (%)	0	10	9	10
Rank	4	1	3	1
NPV (6%)	−$566	413	457	564
Rank	4	3	2	1
NPV (30%)	−$2,308	−$1,657	−$2,513	−$2,158
Rank	3	1	4	2

Project B is better than project A. Project B continues to earn cash flows longer. Project D is more desirable than project C. Although both projects generate the same amount of cash flows, project D does it earlier. The unanswered question: Is project D better than project B?

 Comprehension Check

1. In capital budgeting analysis, what is the distinction between accounting profit and cash flow? Which approach provides a better way to analyze the purchasing power ability of a company?
2. In the analysis of a capital budgeting project, why is cash flow computed as though the investment is financed entirely with equity funds, even though debt financing may be used as well?
3. When you make an investment that does not change the firm's risk profile, what discount rate do you use to calculate the project's NPV?
4. What is the advantage of applying the capital asset pricing model when determining capital budgeting discount rates? What are the practical limitations of this application of CAPM?

5. Define the certainty-equivalent model for finding the net present value of a risk-changing project.

6. How is the IRR calculated and used for project selection? On what assumptions is the IRR based? What problems can arise if you compare the IRR to the firm's cost of capital?

7. What is the profitability index and how is it calculated?

8. How are the accounting rate of return and payback period calculated? What are the drawbacks of these methods?

14.3 THE TIME VALUE MODELS: COMPARING IRR AND NPV

Managers are more inclined to use IRR than NPV. The reason may be simply that they are not aware of problems associated with the IRR calculation. Another reason may be that IRR is simpler to interpret, or so they think, than is NPV. Because they are used to working with percentages, managers may think they understand a project with an IRR of 12 percent better than they understand the same project with an NPV of $12,000. However, NPV directly shows the expected wealth contribution generated by the investment. At the end of this section we will provide a rationale for senior managers to use IRR to evaluate projects recommended by lower-level managers.

When projects are not mutually exclusive and no capital rationing exists, NPV and IRR accept and reject the same projects. However, when projects are mutually exclusive or capital rationing exists, NPV and IRR may rank projects differently. The reason for this is that several problems exist with the IRR calculation: problems of *size, cash flow pattern, nonunique solution,* and *undervaluation of later cash flows.* The superiority of NPV is recognized by Quaker Oats Company. Its 1988 annual report mentions that NPV lets the company "assess the relative desirability of future investment. . . . That way we keep improving our profitability for shareholders."[16]

14.3.1 Size Problem

The size of a project needs to be borne in mind. Suppose there are two mutually exclusive investment projects. The investment requiring a larger initial outlay offers a lower IRR but provides a larger NPV. Because NPV is a direct measure of wealth creation, it is the criterion upon which to base project acceptance or rejection. Illustration 14.10 shows the problem and how to solve it.

ILLUSTRATION 14.10

Size problem with IRR

Project *L* involves a $20,000 initial outlay and offers an IRR of 30 percent. Project *K* involves a $10,000 initial outlay and offers an IRR of 40 percent. The cost of capital is 10 percent. The NPV of project *L* is higher than the NPV of project *K*.

Project	Year 0	1	2	IRR	NPV
L	−$20,000	$15,000	$14,300	30%	$5,455
K	−10,000	5,000	12,600	40%	4,959
L − K	−$10,000	$10,000	$ 1,700	14.8%	$ 496

[16]The Quaker Oats Company, *1988 Annual Report,* p. 5.

The smaller project K has a higher IRR and the larger project L has a higher NPV. Conflicting messages about which project is better occur because IRR ignores the size difference in the initial cash outflow, but NPV does not.

If the company has $20,000 to invest, then it can either select project L or, alternatively, invest $10,000 in project K and $10,000 in a new project P, assuming it exists. Compare the NPVs of the two $20,000 investment schedules and select the higher NPV: project L versus the combination of projects K and P. The new investment P must earn at least a 14.8 percent IRR or a $496 NPV for the combination of project K and project P to be as attractive as project L. You calculate these answers by subtracting project K's cash flows from project L's cash flows and solving for IRR and NPV for the incremental cash flows:

$$\text{NPV} = -\,\$10{,}000 + \frac{\$10{,}000}{1.10} + \frac{\$1700}{(1.10)^2} = \$496$$

$$\text{IRR} = -\,\$10{,}000 + \frac{\$10{,}000}{1.148} + \frac{\$1700}{(1.148)^2} = \$0$$

14.3.2 Cash Flow Pattern Problem

A similar complication occurs with the IRR rule when you must decide between mutually exclusive projects with different cash flow patterns. The critical assumption of IRR is that you reinvest cash flows at the computed IRR. Net present value, on the other hand, reinvests cash flows at the market discount rate. As we discussed in Chapter 11, the investment schedule is downward sloping. It would be most unusual for the schedule to be flat, which would be necessary to justify the reinvestment assumption of the IRR model.[17]

If cash flows are reinvested at rates lower than the IRR, projects that generate cash flows more slowly are better. This is true despite identical IRRs. (See Illustration 14.11.)

ILLUSTRATION 14.11

Different cash flow patterns for mutually exclusive projects and IRR

Projects A and B are both expected to generate total nondiscounted cash flows of $171.60. However, their cash flow patterns differ.

Project	0	1	Year 2	3	4	IRR
A	− $100	$20	$30	$40	$81.60	20%
B	− $100	$5	$10	$138.66	$17.94	20%

Although both projects earn 20 percent and provide the same amount on nondiscounted cash flow, project B is the more attractive investment using NPV, where the reinvestment rate is 10 percent.

[17]The investment schedule ranks projects from high to low according to their internal rates of return. If *all* projects earned the same IRR, the schedule would be horizontal, or flat.

$$\text{NPV}_A = -\$100 + \frac{\$20}{1.1} + \frac{\$30}{1.1^2} + \frac{\$40}{1.1^3} + \frac{\$81.60}{1.1^4}$$

$$= -\$100 + \$18.18 + \$24.49 + \$30.05 + \$55.73$$
$$= \$28.75$$

$$\text{NPV}_B = -\$100 + \frac{\$5}{1.1} + \frac{\$10}{1.1^2} + \frac{\$138.66}{1.1^3} + \frac{\$17.94}{1.1^4}$$

$$= -\$100 + \$4.55 + \$8.26 + \$104.18 + \$12.25$$
$$= \$29.24$$

We make the same decision if we reinvest cash flows each year at 10 percent to calculate a value at the end of year 4. This value is called the **terminal value (TV).**

$$\text{TV}_A = -\$100(1.1)^4 + \$20(1.1)^3 + \$30(1.1)^2 + \$40(1.1) + \$81.60$$
$$= -\$146.41 + \$26.62 + \$36.30 + \$44.00 + \$81.60$$
$$= \$42.11$$

$$\text{TV}_B = -\$100(1.1)^4 + \$5(1.1)^3 + \$10(1.1)^2 + \$138.66(1.1)$$
$$+ \$17.94$$
$$= -\$146.41 + \$6.66 + \$12.10 + \$152.53 + \$17.94$$

$$= \$42.82$$

Terminal value. The value of cash flows compounded forward to some later time at an appropriate interest rate.

The terminal value of project B exceeds the terminal value of project A. The present values for these terminal values are:

Present value of A: $\$42.11 \div (1.1)^4 = \$28.75$

Present value of B: $\$42.82 \div (1.1)^4 = \$29.24$

which are the same NPVs as found previously.

14.3.3 Nonunique Solution Problem

The IRR calculation may provide multiple solutions because the IRR equation is a polynomial equation. There can be as many possible solutions as the number of changes in sign in the *cumulative* cash flows. When several rates satisfy the IRR equation and all rates are mathematically correct, it is difficult to use this method to assess projects. The NPV rule has no such problem. Illustration 14.12 examines the situation, called the *nonunique solution problem.*

ILLUSTRATION 14.12

Multiple IRR solutions

A project expects to generate the following cash flows.

| | Year | | | | |
	0	1	2	3	Total
Cash flows	−$200	$1200	−$2200	$1200	$0
Cumulative cash flows	−$200	$1000	−$1200	$ 0	

Year 1's cumulative cash flow is positive and follows an initial negative cash flow. Cumulative cash flows in years 2 and 3 are negative and positive, respectively. In this case, it is possible that three different IRRs can exist; one for each change of sign in the cumulative cash flows.

A simple summation of the cash flows results in a total of zero, which means that 0 percent is an IRR for the project. However, rates of 100 percent and 200 percent are also IRRs.

$$\text{IRR}_{0\%}: -\$200 + \frac{\$1200}{(1+0)} - \frac{\$2200}{(1+0)^2} + \frac{\$1200}{(1+0)^3} = 0$$

$$-\$200 + \$1200 - \$2200 + \$1200 = 0$$

$$\text{IRR}_{100\%}: -\$200 + \frac{\$1200}{(1+1)} - \frac{\$2200}{(1+1)^2} + \frac{\$1200}{(1+1)^3} = 0$$

$$-\$200 + \$600 - \$550 + \$150 = 0$$

$$\text{IRR}_{200\%}: -\$200 + \frac{\$1200}{(1+2)} - \frac{\$2200}{(1+2)^2} + \frac{\$1200}{(1+2)^3} = 0$$

$$-\$200 + \$400 - \$244.44 + \$44.44 = 0$$

What is the project's true IRR? All rates are correct! The project realizes positive NPVs for rates greater than 100 percent but less than 200 percent. Discount rates greater than 0 percent, but less than 100 percent, and rates greater than 200 percent cause the NPV to be negative. (Check this for yourself by substituting different discount rates into the IRR equation.)

14.3.4 Undervaluation of Later Cash Flows Problem

Internal rate of return undervalues cash flows that occur late in a project's life. When IRR is greater than the cost of capital, the severity of undervaluation increases with project life. This leads to managers ranking projects differently than under the NPV approach. (See Illustration 14.13.)

ILLUSTRATION 14.13

Undervaluation of later cash flows

A project expects to generate the following cash flows. Discounting these cash flows at the project's 15 percent cost of capital results in an NPV of $2.84.

Year			
0	1	2	3
− $20	$10	$10	$10

$$\text{NPV} = -\$20 + \frac{\$10}{1.15} + \frac{\$10}{(1.15)^2} + \frac{\$10}{(1.15)^3}$$

$$= -\$20 + \$8.70 + \$7.56 + \$6.58$$

$$= \$2.84$$

The IRR of these cash flows is 23.4 percent:

$$NPV = -\$20 + \frac{\$10}{1.234} + \frac{\$10}{(1.234)^2} + \frac{\$10}{(1.234)^3}$$

$$= -\$20 + \$8.10 + \$6.57 + \$5.33$$

$$= \$0$$

The period-by-period differences in discounted cash flows when discounted at the cost of capital (15 percent) and the IRR (23.4 percent) are as follows.

	Year				
	0	1	2	3	NPV
NPV at 15%	− $20	$8.70	$7.56	$6.58	$2.84
NPV at 23.4%	− 20	8.10	6.57	5.33	0
Difference	$ 0	$0.60	$0.99	$1.25	$2.84

If the firm's cost of capital is only 10 percent, the difference between the discounted cash flows becomes larger.

	Year				
	0	1	2	3	NPV
NPV at 10%	− $20	$9.09	$8.26	$7.51	$4.86
NPV at 23.4%	− 20	8.10	6.57	5.33	0
Difference	$0	$0.99	$1.69	$2.18	$4.86

These examples show that as the project's cost of capital decreases, the IRR technique undervalues later cash flows even more. Since the cost of capital, and not the IRR, is the minimum rate the firm should earn reinvesting the cash flows, a ranking of investments by IRR can be different from a ranking by NPV. The IRR procedure biases against projects with cash flows occurring in later years. This problem can lead to lack of vision in longer-term planning.

The undervaluation of later cash flows can become an advantage. When middle managers have incentives to overstate the forecasts of cash flows occurring late in a project's life, the IRR technique is helpful for evaluating investments. These later cash flows have greater uncertainty than earlier cash flows. Middle managers perceive upward forecast biases as improving their chances of receiving project funding or career promotion.[18] Senior managers can use the IRR to adjust downward the positively biased cash flow forecasts.

[18]Stephen W. Pruitt and Lawrence J. Gitman report in "Capital Budgeting Forecast Biases: Evidence from the Fortune 500," *Financial Management* 16, no. 1 (Spring 1987), that "profitability inflation improved the chance that a given project would eventually be accepted and implemented by the firm." Project sponsors are often rewarded with higher pay, promotions, and enhanced social status.

Comprehension Check

1. Why may the NPV and IRR approaches rank projects differently? Briefly discuss each of the four problems.
2. Discuss why IRR may be better than NPV for evaluating investment proposals of middle-level managers.

14.4 CAPITAL RATIONING

Funding constraint. A fixed amount of money available for investments aggregating in excess of the amount.

In our overview of the capital budgeting process in Section 14.1.1, we mentioned that most capital expenditure decisions are subject to a **funding constraint.** Often the set of projects with positive NPVs requires more total capital than is available. Some people argue that if a project has a positive NPV, then management should find some way of increasing the funding.[19] However, in the short run, additional funding may not be possible and management must allocate a limited capital budget.

How should managers solve this problem? They should rank projects by their NPVs. The goal is to increase total NPV subject to the funding constraint. Illustration 14.14 shows the NPV solution.[20] It also contrasts NPV with the profitability index and shows why the latter is inappropriate for the task of choosing among projects subject to a budget constraint.

ILLUSTRATION 14.14

Capital rationing

Karsten Golf Manufacturing Company has five projects with equal lives under consideration. The total funding requirement for these investments is $75,000. However, management has only allocated a budget of $30,000. The budget analyst has computed each project's NPV and ranked them from high to low. She has also shown each project's profitability index.

Project	Investment	NPV	PI
A	$22,000	$10,000	1.45
B	20,000	9,400	1.47
C	25,000	9,000	1.36
D	5,000	3,000	1.60
E	3,000	1,200	1.40
Total	$75,000		
Budget	$30,000		

Her task is to recommend the set of projects that will increase value of the firm the most. She prepares an analysis that compares the NPV solution against a PI approach.

[19]Recall in the Financial Reality reading on page 502 that it was not monetary capital that was in short supply, but managerial talent.

[20]Complex problems can be solved using integer and linear programming techniques.

Net Present Value Approach

Management wants to increase total NPV, given the budget constraint. Projects A, D, and E use the total budget of $30,000 (= $22,000 + $5,000 + $3,000) and provide total NPV of $14,200 (= $10,000 + $3,000 + $1,200). Projects C and D also spend the total budget but only provide total NPV of $12,000 (= $9,000 + $3,000). The combination of projects B, D, and E uses $28,000 of the budget and provides total NPV of $13,600 (= $9,400 + $3,000 + $1,200). With this set, the budget's remaining $2,000 would need to yield an NPV of $600 in some unknown investment if the B-D-E combination is to overtake the A-D-E combination.

Profitability Index Approach

The best combination of projects under NPV (A-D-E) has a combined PI of 1.47, which is inferior to the PI of 1.49 for the combination D-B-E.

Project	Investment	NPV	PI
A	$22,000	$10,000	1.45
D	5,000	3,000	1.60
E	3,000	1,200	1.40
Total	$30,000	$14,200	1.47

Project	Investment	NPV	PI
D	$ 5,000	$ 3,000	1.60
B	20,000	9,400	1.47
E	3,000	1,200	1.40
Total	$28,000	$13,600	1.49

Selecting projects on the basis of increasing the PI for the set, subject to the budget constraint, can result in a poor selection decision if it is not done correctly. The project set D-B-E leaves $2,000 of the budget not invested and its NPV is $600 less than the A-D-E set. The $2,000 must be invested to earn at least $600 for projects D, B, E, and the yet unknown $2,000 investment to contribute as much value as the projects chosen using the NPV approach.[21]

Comprehension Check

---

1. When faced with capital rationing, what should be management's objective?

---

[21]The PI gives the same ranking as an NPV approach if the projects are completely divisible. However, few investments possess this quality. Another limitation of PI is that it is only appropriated (if it is at all) when capital rationing is restricted to one period, which is not usually the case. Firms experiencing capital rationing tend to experience it over a number of periods.

SUMMARY ▼▼▼▼▼▼▼▼▼▼▼▼

WHAT IS THE CAPITAL INVESTMENT PROBLEM?

- The capital investment problem looks for value-enhancing projects. Capital budgeting decisions affect the future competitiveness of the firm.

- Several phases are involved in capital budgeting: proposal generation, project evaluation, project selection, project execution, and project postaudit.

- The search for projects is usually in an environment of capital rationing; that is, limited available resources are available to invest in projects.

- Project's cash flows, and not accounting profits, are important to the evaluation process. Value is based on cash flows, not accounting profits.

PROJECT EVALUATION MODELS

- Several models can be used to evaluate proposals. These include: net present value, internal rate of return, profitability index, accounting rate of return, and payback.

- The time value models of NPV and IRR are superior to the other approaches. However, inconsistencies can occur between time value models. We examine the problems and conclude that NPV is the superior technique.

- The NPV decision rule says to accept projects whose NPVs are positive. The IRR rule accepts projects whose rate of return exceeds the cost of capital.

- Risk-changing investments can be analyzed by arbitrary adjustments to the firm's cost of capital, by the capital asset pricing model, or by a certainty-equivalent model. The latter two approaches are superior to any arbitrary approach.

- Accounting rate of return and payback methods are inferior techniques for evaluating capital expenditures. They both ignore the time value of money. Payback also ignores any cash flow occurring after the initial investment is recouped. Discounted payback ignores later cash flows.

- The evaluation techniques can result in different desirability rankings for the same set of projects.

THE TIME VALUE MODELS: COMPARING IRR AND NPV

- NPV and IRR can rank similar projects differently because of the size of the investments, the cash flow patterns of the investments, the multiple (nonunique) solutions, and the undervaluation of a later period's cash flows.

CAPITAL RATIONING

- Capital rationing results from a funding constraint.
- The NPV approach is the superior model to use to allocate capital to projects subject to capital rationing.

FURToHER READING ▼▼▼▼▼▼▼▼▼▼▼▼▼

Donaldson, Gordon, *Managing Corporate Wealth: The Operation of a Comprehensive Financial Goals System.* New York: Praeger Publishers, 1984. This book focuses on the utilization and maximization of corporate wealth from a real world perspective.

Hastie, K. Larry, "One Businessman's View of Capital Budgeting," *Financial Management* (Winter 1974), pp. 36–44. The author provides a business person's perspective on what is important in the capital budgeting process.

SELF-TEST PROBLEMS ▼▼▼▼▼▼▼▼▼▼▼▼▼

ST14-1. Norwood Motors, Inc. has earned 16 percent on equity in recent years. Because of significant investment opportunities, the company's cash dividend payout policy was only 20 percent of earnings. What is the sustainable growth rate that Norwood Motors can achieve based on retaining earnings?

ST14-2. Calculate the net present value for a six-year project that is expected to generate after-tax cash inflows of $30,000 annually. The initial investment is $100,000. Management estimates the firm's required rate of return to be 13 percent and this project will not change the risk of the firm. What is your recommendation on this project?

ST14-3. Calculate the net present value for the following proposed investment project, using the present value tables. Round the table factors to three places of decimals. Assume the firm's cost of capital is 10 percent. The project requires an initial investment of $210,000 and has an estimated salvage value of $0 at the end of its useful life in the fifth year. Annual operating after-tax cash inflows are estimated as follows:

Year:		
1	$50,000
2	60,000
3	70,000
4	50,000
5	40,000

What is your recommendation on this project?

ST14-4. Calculate the internal rate of return on the following project to the nearest whole percentage point. The project will not change the firm's market risk. If the firm's cost of capital is 12 percent, should management accept the project?

Year:		
0	–$75,100
1	40,000
2	30,000
3	20,000
4	10,000

WHAT IS THE CAPITAL INVESTMENT PROBLEM?

14-1. a. Precision Parts, Inc. typically has earned 15 percent on equity in recent years. The board of directors has a policy of paying out 30 percent of earnings in cash dividends. What is the sustainable growth rate Precision Parts can achieve by relying on retained earnings?

   b. What sustainable growth rate can Precision Parts support with retained earnings if return on equity improves to 20 percent and the board of directors decides to retain 80 percent of earnings to take advantage of investment opportunities?

14-2. a. If the management of General Health Foods, Inc. desires to increase sustainable growth to 20 percent annually, what return on equity rate must the corporation earn if 60 percent of earnings are retained?

   b. If the maximum return on equity General Health Foods expects to earn is 20 percent, what is the maximum dividend payout percentage the corporation can pay in cash dividends and still sustain growth of 18 percent annually?

14-3. Calculate the return on equity for a company which has return on sales of 6 percent, asset turnover of 3 times, and leverage of 2.

14-4. What return on sales percentage must a company earn to achieve a return on equity of 30 percent if its asset turnover is 2 times and its leverage is 2.5?

14-5. What asset turnover must a company achieve to produce a return on equity of 24 percent if its return on sales is 4 percent and its leverage ratio is 4?

14-6. What leverage ratio must a company have to produce a return on equity of 18 percent if its return on sales is 6 percent and its asset turnover ratio is 1?

PROJECT EVALUATION MODELS

14-7. Respond to the following statement: "It's all very well telling companies to maximize net present value, but net present value is just an abstract notion. What I tell my managers is that profits are what matters and it's profits that we're going to maximize."

14-8. Calculate the net present value for the following 16-year projects. Assume that the company has a cost of capital of 15 percent. Indicate your recommendation as to the acceptability of each project.

   a. Initial investment is $20,000; after-tax cash inflows are $3000 annually.

   b. Initial investment is $20,000; after-tax cash inflows are $3600 annually.

   c. Initial investment is $18,999; after-tax cash inflows are $3191 annually.

14-9. Calculate the net present value for a five-year project that is expected to generate after-tax cash inflows of $26,000 annually. The initial investment is $80,000. Management estimates the firm's cost of capital is 14 percent and this project will not change the risk of the firm. What is your recommendation on this project?

14-10. Calculate the net present value for the following proposed investment project using the present value tables. Round the table factors to three places of decimals. Assume the firm's cost of capital is 12 percent. The project requires an initial investment of $366,000 and has an estimated after-tax salvage value of $20,000 at the end of its useful life (the sixth year). Annual operating after-tax cash inflows are estimated as follows:

Year 1	$80,000
Year 2	$90,000
Year 3	$90,000
Year 4	$90,000
Year 5	$90,000
Year 6	$80,000 (excludes the salvage value)

What is your recommendation on this project?

14-11. Do any of the project criteria considered in this chapter explicitly allow for differences in risk among projects? How would you suggest handling risk?

14-12. How might the capital budgeting decision be modified to allow for differences in risk between two mutually exclusive projects?

14-13. Management of Francisco Airlines believes that capital projects should be evaluated using the capital asset pricing model (CAPM). The chief financial officer estimates the CAPM as follows:

Required risk-adjusted rate for the project
$$= \text{Risk-free rate} + \beta_{\text{project}} \times (\text{market risk premium})$$
$$= 0.08 + \beta_{\text{project}} \times 0.08$$

The following projects are under examination.

Project	β	Forecasted Return
NIT	0.4	0.12
NAT	2.6	0.20

Evaluate these projects and determine if they are acceptable.

14-14. The financial vice president of Henderson-Cincinnati Company is evaluating the following projects:

Project	β	Forecasted Return
A	0.9	0.075
B	1.2	0.140
C	1.8	0.120

Using the capital asset pricing model, determine whether each investment falls above or below the risk-return trade-off line. The risk-free rate is 0.06 and the market return is 0.13.

14-15. A budget analyst provides the following information about a project:

Year	Expected Cash Flow	Risk-free Rate	Certainty-equivalent Coefficient*
0	−$6000	—	1.00
1	2000	0.05	0.90
2	3000	0.06	0.85
3	3400	0.07	0.80

The certainty-equivalent coefficient is the factor to reduce the uncertain expected cash flow amount to a certain cash flow amount.

Calculate the certainty-equivalent net present value and make a recommendation.

14-16. Salzman Enterprises is evaluating a new piece of equipment which costs $150,000. The vendor of the equipment says it should save Salzman $50,000 per year for each of the next five years. If a $40,000 overhaul is made at the end of the fifth year, savings of $15,000 per year should be expected for years 6 through 8. All amounts are after any tax adjustment.

a. Use net present value to decide if the company should buy the equipment. The appropriate discount rate is 14 percent.
b. Management decides to use the certainty-equivalent approach to see if the same decision would be made as part (a) indicates. The risk-free rate is 5 percent. Management's carefully debated certainty-equivalent cash flows are as follows:

($000)

Year	Cash Flow	Year	Cash Flow
0	−$150	5	$10
1	40	5	−50
2	40	6	10
3	35	7	5
4	20	8	0

c. Which solution is correct? Discuss.

14-17. Which project evaluation criteria implicitly assumes that the rate of return can be earned on reinvested funds? How significant is this assumption?

14-18. Calculate the internal rate of return on this seven-year project. The initial investment is $100,000. Annual operating cash flows after taxes are estimated to be $20,542 over the life of the project. If the firm's cost of capital is 9 percent, what is your recommendation on this project?

14-19. The cash flows associated with an investment are as follows. The project will not change the firm's market risk. Calculate the internal rate of return on this project to the nearest whole percentage point. If the firm's cost of capital is 10 percent, what is your recommendation on this project?

Time Period	Cash Flow
0	−$650,700
1	300,000
2	200,000
3	200,000
4	100,000
5	100,000

14-20. Calculate the profitability index for Problem 14-19. Discount the cash flows at the cost of capital of 10 percent.

14-21. A proposed project requires an initial investment of $500,000. The present value of its cash inflows, discounted at the required rate of 12 percent, is $600,000. Calculate the profitability index on this investment. If the project is not mutually exclusive with other investments, what is your recommendation?

14-22. Management is recommending three projects to the board of directors. The after-tax cash flow for each project follows. The appropriate rate to discount each cash flow is 12 percent.

		Projects	
Year	#1	#2	#3
0	−$20,000	−$60,000	−$36,000
1	5,600	12,000	13,000
2	6,000	20,000	13,000
3	8,000	24,000	13,000
4	8,000	32,000	13,000

a. Rank the projects on the basis of their profitability indices.

b. If the firm has only $60,000 to invest, which project(s) should it undertake?

14-23. As a consultant, what comments would you offer the management of a corporation that uses the accounting rate of return method as the primary criterion for evaluating projects?

14-24. Management gives you the following information about a proposed project:

Time Period	Investment	Accounting Profits
0	$70,000	
1		$12,000
2		8,000
3		5,000
4		5,000
5		5,000

a. Calculate the accounting rate of return.
b. What drawbacks are there to using this calculation to determine investment desirability?
c. What is your recommendation for investment in this project?

14-25. The estimated cash flows for a project are:

Time Period	Cash Flows
0	−$40,000
1	20,000
2	15,000
3	10,000
4	5,000

a. Calculate the payback period for the project.
b. What is a significant shortcoming of payback?

14-26. a. Calculate the discounted payback period for Problem 14-25. The discount rate is 8 percent. Use table values and round the factors to three decimal places.
b. "A discounted payback measure overcomes the shortcomings of the payback measure." Discuss this statement.

14-27. Magma Mines plans to invest in a new machine. The projected cash flows follow. Determine both the payback period and the discounted payback period. The firm's cost of capital for an investment of this type is 15 percent.

Year	Expected Cash Flows
Present	−$20,000
1	−8,000
2–6	6,000
7–15	12,000

14-28. Management is evaluating two mutually exclusive investments with the following cash flows:

	Investments	
Year	#1	#2
0	−$10,000	$10,000
1	3,500	−3,500
2	3,500	−3,500
3	3,500	−3,500
4	3,500	−3,500

a. What is the net present value of each investment for discount rates of 0 percent, 5 percent, 10 percent, and 20 percent?
b. Calculate the profitability index for each investment for each discount rate.

c. Based on your answers to parts (a) and (b), which is the better investment? What is your decision based on?

d. The cash flows for the two investments are distinguishable as *investment-type flows* and *loan-type flows*. Which investment exhibits loan-type flows?

14-29. A nonrisk-changing investment has a ten-year life and costs $50,000. Management expects the investment to generate accounting income of $8000 annually during its life. The investment will use straight-line depreciation over its life. The income tax rate is 30 percent and the firm's costs of capital is 12 percent.

a. Evaluate the project's acceptability using accounting rate of return.

b. Should the project be accepted using a net present value approach? Assume depreciation is the only noncash amount included in determining accounting profit.

c. What is the project's internal rate of return? How does it compare with the accounting rate of return?

14-30. a. Calculate the payback period for a project having an initial investment of $50,000 with annual operating cash flows of $8850 for ten years.

b. Calculate the internal rate of return for this project.

14-31. Each of the following projects is independent of the other and will not change the firm's risk. The market cost of capital is 12 percent after taxes. The tax rate on taxable income is 40 percent. (*Note:* This problem differs from Table 14.1 by the fact that taxes are included.)

		Projects		
	A	B	C	D
Initial Investment:	$80,000	$80,000	$80,000	$80,000
After-tax cash inflows:				
Period 1	$80,000	$60,000	$40,000	$28,750
Period 2		40,000	35,000	28,750
Period 3			20,000	28,750
Period 4			20,000	28,750
Annual depreciation	$80,000	$40,000	$20,000	$20,000

Calculate and rank each project by:

a. Payback period
b. Discounted payback period
c. Accounting rate of return
d. Net present value
e. Internal rate of return

Round your discount factors to three decimal places.

THE TIME VALUE MODELS: COMPARING IRR AND NPV

14-32. Querap Corporation has two mutually exclusive projects of similar risk under review. The cash flows associated with these projects follow. The firm's cost of capital is 12 percent.

Project	Period 0	Period 1	Period 2
B	−$91,075	$65,445	$65,445
C	−50,000	22,500	50,000

a. Calculate the net present value and internal rate of return for each project.

b. Which project would you recommend? Support your decision using incremental analysis of the differences in cash flows between the two projects.

14-33. Ifflander Consulting is evaluating the following two mutually exclusive investments.

	Investments #1	Investments #2
Original investment	$240,000	$180,000
Annual cash flows	80,000	62,000
Useful life	6 years	6 years
Discount rate	16%	16%
Net present value (14%)	$54,800	$48,470
Profitability index	1.23	1.27
Internal rate of return	24%	26%

Ms. Ifflander sees that there is a conflict in the ranking of the two investments. Help her select the correct project. Show your supporting calculations of the incremental difference in the cash flows of the two projects.

14-34. Anand Bhattacharya, Inc. is examining mutually exclusive projects Alpha and Beta.

	Year	Alpha	Beta
Cash outflow	0	−$70,000	−$70,000
Cash inflows	1	10,000	50,000
	2	20,000	40,000
	3	30,000	20,000
	4	45,000	10,000
	5	60,000	10,000
Net present value		$32,219	$29,252
Profitability index		1.46	1.42
Internal rate of return		27.2%	37.6%

Management expects to be able to reinvest cash flows from the investments at 20 percent. Find the terminal values of cash inflows for Alpha and Beta using the 20 percent reinvestment rate. Which project should be selected on this basis?

14-35. Bugel Enterprises has an after-tax cost of capital of 14 percent. Management is evaluating the following projects:

		Cash flows:	
Year	Project 1		Project 2
0	−$5,000.00		−$ 5,000.00
1	1,931.45		
2	1,931.45		
3	1,931.45		
4	1,931.45		10,368.00
Net present value	$627.69		$1,138.69
Internal rate of return	20%		20%

a. Show that project #1 has a terminal value of $10,368 when its cash flows are reinvested at 20 percent, its internal rate of return.
b. Calculate the terminal value for each project using a reinvestment rate of 14 percent.
c. Calculate the present value of each project's terminal value in part (b) using a 14 percent discount rate.

14-36. Brothers, Inc.'s management is considering two mutually exclusive projects. The firm's market cost of capital is 10 percent. The expected cash flows associated with each project follow.

Project	0	1	Period 2	3	4
A	−$90,000	$33,457	$33,457	$33,457	$33,457
B	−$105,000	$20,000	$30,000	$50,000	$61,000

a. Calculate the net present value of each project.
b. Calculate the internal rate of return of each project.
c. Based on your evaluation, which project would you recommend for investment?
d. How might your recommendation change if the firm's cost of capital were different? Use discount rates of 0 percent and 15 percent to evaluate the projects.

14-37. Flagstaff Industries is evaluating an investment which requires a present cash outflow of $200,000. The investment should generate cash inflows of $80,000 each year for its six-year life.

a. Flagstaff's required rate of return is 16 percent. Determine the net present value of the investment.
b. Compute the net present value at discount rates ranging from 0 percent to 40 percent, at 5 percent increments. Graph the results by showing the net present values on the vertical axis and the discount rates on the horizontal axis. Join the points with a smooth curve.
c. Based on your graph, what is the approximate internal rate of return for the project?

14-38. A project expects to generate the following cash flows:

Year	Cash Flows
0	−$ 600
1	3600
2	−6600
3	3600

a. Verify that the internal rates of return for this series of cash flows are 0 percent, 100 percent, and 200 percent.

b. How should management decide whether to adopt this project?

CAPITAL RATIONING

14-39. The Globe Company is considering a number of investments. Unfortunately, its capital budget is limited to $600.

Project	Cash Outflow	Net Present Value
A	$100	$22
B	100	20
C	150	14
D	200	42
E	200	38
F	200	50

a. Which projects should be selected?

b. If projects D and F are mutually exclusive, which projects should management select?

14-40. Johnson Company has the following eight projects under consideration for inclusion in the firm's capital budget. The projects are ranked according to their net present values based on the firm's cost of capital of 10 percent. Management estimates all projects to have equal lives.

Project	Investment	NPV
A	$80,000	$28,000
B	50,000	18,000
C	25,000	16,000
D	20,000	15,000
E	5,000	7,000
F	4,000	3,000
G	10,000	2,000
H	35,000	−1,200

a. If management is not operating under capital rationing conditions, which combination of projects would you recommend for investment?

b. If management estimates that $90,000 will be available to finance its capital budget, which combination of projects would you recommend for investment? No combination of projects will change the firm's risk.

14-41. Use *The Index to The Wall Street Journal,* the *Business Periodicals Index,* or some other information source to find a story where the emphasis is on the cash flows associated with an investment decision rather than on the calculation of net income.

COMPREHENSIVE PROBLEM ▼▼▼▼▼▼▼▼▼▼▼▼

14-42. a. Perfection Baking, Inc. has earned 18 percent on equity for the past several years. The company's policy is to pay 10 percent of earnings in cash dividends. What sustainable growth rate should Perfection be able to maintain?

b. If the maximum return on equity that Perfection Baking expects to earn is 20 percent, what is the maximum dividend payout percentage the company can pay in cash dividends and still sustain growth of 16 percent?

c. In making capital budgeting decisions, explain why cash flows should be analyzed rather than accounting profits.

d. Define the net present value model for analyzing capital investment projects. What are the decision rules for project selection under this model?

e. Using the present value tables, calculate the net present value for the following proposed investment. Round the table factors to three places of decimals. Assume the cost of capital is 11 percent. The project requires an initial investment of $140,000 and has an estimated after-tax salvage value of $25,000 at the end of its useful life (the third year). Annual operating after-tax cash inflows are estimated to be: $50,000 in year 1, $70,000 in year 2, and $40,000 in year 3 (excludes salvage value). What is your recommendation on this project?

f. To the nearest whole percentage point, calculate the internal rate of return for the company's project, as detailed in part (e).

g. Calculate the payback period for the investment outlined in part (e).

h. When projects are not mutually exclusive and no capital rationing exists, NPV and IRR accept and reject the same projects. However, when projects are mutually exclusive or when capital rationing exists, NPV and IRR may rank projects differently. What are the reasons for difference in rankings? Which approach gives consistently better results?

i. Given the following schedule of proposed projects for Perfection Baking, what would be the size of the company's capital budget for the coming year if unlimited funds were available?

Project	Investment	NPV
Alpha	$74,000	$30,000
Chi	50,000	26,000
Kappa	40,000	20,000
Sigma	25,000	12,000
Psi	10,000	9,000
Beta	15,000	6,000
Gamma	9,000	5,000
Omega	18,000	− 1,000

j. If Perfection's capital budgeting decisions are limited by capital rationing, which projects should be selected if the budget for next year is $125,000?

Appendix: Interaction of Investment and Financing Decisions

Standard capital budgeting analysis typically involves discounting cash flows back to the present using an appropriate discount rate, which is often the weighted average cost of capital. This approach is appropriate if a new project is a "carbon copy" in that any financing side effects are the type that the firm has encountered before. The side effects are benefits or costs incurred in the actual financing of the investment.

Projects with different risks are likely to possess different side effects, thereby leading to different financial structures for each project. For example, the Italian government contributed $700 million in cash, tax incentives, low-interest loans, and infrastructure improvements to entice Texas Instruments (TI) to build a plant in Italy. These features are specific to the Italian project and do not apply to other projects of TI. The side effects lowered TI's cost of capital for this investment.

Adjusted present value (APV). A divide-and-conquer approach for evaluating financing cash flows separate from operating cash flows.

A technique called *adjusted present value* is the approach to use to evaluate such investments. **Adjusted present value (APV)** analyzes operating and financing cash flows separately. The procedure is as follows.

- Assume the firm is all-equity financed and discount the cash flows at the firm's (unlevered) cost of equity.[22] The result represents the project's NPV, ignoring side effects created by the financing.
- Next, determine the present value of the side effects.
- Last, add or subtract the NPV of the side effects to get APV.

$$\text{APV} = \text{NPV of project if all-equity financed}$$
$$+ \text{ present value of side effects} \atop \text{of financing decisions caused by} \atop \text{new project acceptance} \tag{14A.1}$$

Note that Equation 14A.1 is conceptually similar to our valuation of the firm equation in Chapter 12:

$$\text{Value of firm} = \frac{\text{After-tax cash flow from operations}}{\text{Unlevered cost of equity rate}}$$
$$+ \text{ present value of tax shield} \tag{14A.2}$$

Illustrations 14A.1 and 14A.2 show how the APV model works. We add the present value of the side effects to the NPV of the operating cash flows. *Only accept projects with positive APVs.*

---

[22]This discount rate represents the nondiversifiable business risk of the company and is defined in Chapter 12 as r_e^u.

ILLUSTRATION 14A.1

Calculating adjusted present value

A project has an NPV of $100 when an analyst discounts its cash flows at the firm's unlevered cost of equity. The project is marginally acceptable because its NPV is low. However, management expects the project to enhance the debt capacity of the company. It will allow the firm to increase debt by $10,000. The bank requires amortization of a 9 percent loan over five years. The firm's tax rate is 30 percent.

The analyst determines the value of the tax shield of the interest payments (that is, the side effect) as follows.

Year	Beginning Balance	Annual Payment	Interest	Principal	Ending Balance
1	$10,000.00	$2,570.92	$900.00	$1,670.92	$8,329.08
2	8,329.08	2,570.92	749.62	1,821.30	6,507.78
3	6,507.78	2,570.92	585.70	1,985.22	4,522.56
4	4,522.56	2,570.92	407.03	2,163.89	2,358.67
5	2,358.67	2,570.95*	212.28	2,358.67	0.00

*Adjusts for small rounding error in calculations.

The present value of the interest tax shield is about $701.

Present value of interest tax shield

= Tax rate × (present value of interest payments)

$$= 0.3 \left[\frac{\$900}{1.09} + \frac{\$749.62}{(1.09)^2} + \frac{\$585.70}{(1.09)^3} + \frac{\$407.03}{(1.09)^4} + \frac{\$212.28}{(1.09)^5} \right]$$

= $700.57

The APV of the project is $100 + $700.57 = $800.57. The side effect removes any doubt about the worthiness of the project.

ILLUSTRATION 14A.2

Value of side-effects

Example 1: A project has an NPV of $100 million. The government decides that the project is socially and environmentally worthy and offers a tax-free grant of $10 million. The grant is a special financing arrangement that adds to the value of the project. The adjusted present value is $100 million + $10 million = $110 million.

Example 2: A project has an NPV of $15 million. However, management must raise capital to finance the project, incurring costs of $2 million. The costs relate entirely to the financing decision. The adjusted net present value is $15 million − $2 million = $13 million.

14A-1. The chief financial officer is considering a project which costs $1.5 million. The project's base-case net present value is $0. What is the project's adjusted present value in each following case? Treat each case independently unless instructed otherwise.

    a. By investing in the project, management will need to raise $600,000 by a common stock issue. Issue costs are 14 percent of the net proceeds of $600,000.

    b. Investing in the project results in a $600,000 increase in debt capacity for the firm. The present value of interest tax shields on the debt is $80,000.

    c. If the firm undertakes the investment, it issues equity (as in part a) and borrows debt (as in part b).

14A-2. A project is expected to last one year. The initial investment is $2000 with an expected cash inflow one year later of $2200. The cost of capital is 15 percent. The firm's borrowing rate is 12 percent and the tax shield per dollar of interest is 30 percent. Round your answers to the nearest dollar.

    a. Calculate the project's base-case net present value.

    b. What is the adjusted present value if the firm borrows 25 percent of the required investment?

14A-3. Cameron Industries has the opportunity to invest $2 million now and expects after-tax returns of $1.2 million one year from now and $1.4 million two years from now. The cost of capital for an all-equity financed firm with similar risk as the risk of the project is 11 percent. Cameron's target debt-asset ratio for an investment of this type is 40 percent, which allows the company to borrow at 7 percent. The tax rate is 30 percent. The debt would be repaid according to an amortization schedule. Calculate the adjusted present value.

ANSWERS TO SELF-TEST PROBLEMS ▼▼▼▼▼▼▼▼▼▼▼

ST14-1. Sustainable growth = Retention rate × return on equity
$$= 0.80 \times 0.16$$
$$= 0.128 \text{ or } 12.8 \text{ percent}$$

ST14-2. NPV $= -\$100,000 + \$30,000 \times \dfrac{1 - (1 + 0.13)^{-6}}{0.13}$

$$= -\$100,000 + \$30,000 \times 3.99755$$
$$= \$197,927$$

Accept the project.

ST14-3.

Period	Cash Flow	×	PVIF 10%	=	Present Value
0	−$210,000		1.000		−$210,000
1	50,000		0.909		45,450
2	60,000		0.826		49,560
3	70,000		0.751		52,570
4	50,000		0.683		34,150
5	40,000		0.621		24,840
					−$ 3,430

Based on a negative NPV, reject the project.

ST14-4.

Period	Cash Flow	PVIF 16%	Present Value
0	−$75,100	1.000	−$75,100
1	40,000	0.862	34,480
2	30,000	0.743	22,290
3	20,000	0.641	12,820
4	10,000	0.552	5,520
			$ 10

The IRR is about 16 percent; thus, accept the project.

Video Case 14

Investing In Employee Productivity: An Application Of Capital Budgeting

from *Business World*, October 14, 1990

The capital budgeting problems included in most textbooks involve investments that fit neatly into the net present value (NPV) framework. Unfortunately, in real life managers often face much more complicated situations. This video clip examines such a nontraditional investment—investing in employee morale and commitment. The managers of Fel-Pro, a small manufacturer of gaskets, have decided that making investments in employee morale is good business. Employees receive cash bonuses on special occasions such as marriage, graduation, and birthdays. The firm provides day care for employees' children, a vacation ranch for weekend outings, and profit sharing. Do the standard capital budgeting techniques apply to investments such as this?

To apply NPV analysis, we need to estimate the costs and benefits of the investment. If the program increases employee satisfaction, the firm could benefit in many ways. Lower employee turnover, lower absenteeism, and fewer job-related accidents and illnesses, which translates into lower health insurance claims, all reduce costs and thereby increase profits. If the firm ever comes on hard times, the loyalty built by these programs might allow the firm to ask for help from its employees in the form of lower raises, short unpaid leaves, and so on. As you can see, some of these items can be quantified, but others may be quite difficult to attach a dollar value to (for example, the value of employee loyalty). To estimate the cost of absenteeism and employee turnover, first estimate the costs associated with an employee missing a day of work, and the cost to hire and train a new employee; then estimate how the programs affect absenteeism and turnover.

Program costs are fairly easy to estimate. A problem with cost estimation in programs with volunteer participation is uncertainty about the number of employees that will participate. Once the program is opened to all employees, the firm must either be prepared to make sufficient opportunities available for all interested employees or explain how the resources will be rationed.

Some care must be taken when applying NPV analysis to investments such as this. Since benefits are more difficult to estimate than costs, strict application of NPV analysis may produce results that are biased against acceptance. This is where managerial expertise comes in. Rather than rejecting such projects out of hand, the manager may choose to implement the program and carefully monitor the program's actual benefits and costs. If the program does not generate sufficient benefits to justify its continuation, the manager may elect to abandon it. But the program was given a chance to prove itself and overcome biases in the analysis.

Study Questions

1. Like employee morale, the benefits of adding personal computers to the workplace are difficult to estimate. What benefits arise from providing computers to employees and how might those benefits be estimated?

2. We argue that monitoring the investment after it has been made is important, especially for investments with difficult to measure benefits. Do you think that the same recommendation applies to investments with more easily quantified costs and benefits? Explain the value of postadoption monitoring, and what the firm's options are if the project is either very successful or very unsuccessful.

CHAPTER 15

Capital Budgeting: Identifying Relevant Cash Flows

Who would have thought that the Russians would turn from grizzly bears to teddy bears, thus hurting the U.S. defense industry? That the Iraqis would drive up the price of jet fuel and discourage foreign travel causing great hardship to Trans World Airlines? That gas stations would decide to compete with 7-Eleven's convenience stores? The point is clear: Expected performance of capital expenditures hinges on the behavior of present and prospective competitors, the state of the economy, and the global political environment. However, prior to making a decision to accept and implement a capital expenditure, thoughtful analysis must identify the relevant cash flows associated with the expenditure. Shareholder value can be seriously eroded if management ignores or fails to properly account for expected cash flows during the planning and evaluation stages of a project.

Cash flow identification is commonly acknowledged as the most hazardous aspect of capital budgeting. It is a process that brings together many details and strategic thinking about the firm, the expected economic environment, and political factors. Common sense dictates that unless special circumstances prevail, such as an economic barrier to entry, industry competitors are equally motivated to gravitate toward projects characterized by high economic profits. The end result is highly competitive product markets and less profit potential than would be the case if competition was somehow constrained. Hence, a firm's ease of entry, position in the market, visibility, and pricing strategy are pertinent to the estimation of cash flows.

Capital budgeting investments vary notably in their complexity. Proposals to replace equipment may require little more than an assessment of cost savings per unit, life of the equipment, and its rate of economic obsolescence. Proposals to expand production capacity to increase output of existing products benefit from past experience, order backlog, and anticipated economic and political environments. Projects to enter new areas start from the beginning with market research, a great deal of uncertainty about how competitors will react, and an assessment of the impact of the expenditure on other segments of the business.

Our purpose in this chapter is to examine the cash flow items included in the time value models discussed in the last chapter. We take as a given that the forecasted cash flows have been properly researched and potential threats taken into account. When you have completed this chapter, you should understand:

- The considerations that affect cash flow forecasts.
- Which cash flows are relevant in the capital investment decision.
- How cash flows are calculated, including the initial investment, operating cash flows during the life of the project, and terminal cash flows.

15.1 IDENTIFYING RELEVANT CASH FLOWS

Relevant cash flow. Cash flow that changes as a result of some specific action.

A major part of capital budgeting is the separation of *relevant cash flows* from *irrelevant cash flows*. A **relevant cash flow** is a cash flow that is caused by the course of action. For example, Herman Miller, Inc. has found a way to recycle or reuse nearly all waste left over from its furniture manufacturing process: Fabric scraps are sold to the auto industry to reuse as lining for cars; luggage makers buy Miller's leather trim for attaché cases; stereo manufacturers use vinyl for sound-deadening material; wood scraps help power Miller's own cogeneration facility, thereby cutting the annual gas bill by $450,000. So whenever Miller analyzes a new capital expenditure proposal to produce a new furniture line, the costs for materials must be reduced by the expected savings generated by its recycling program. The recycling program generates a relevant cash flow.

Irrelevant cash flow. Cash flow that does not change as a result of some specific action.

An **irrelevant cash flow** is a cash flow that occurs regardless of whether the proposed action is taken. In our Herman Miller example, the salary of the president is not relevant when evaluating a proposed capital expenditure. The president gets paid regardless of whether the project is adopted or not. In the analysis of an investment, then, an irrelevant cash flow can be ignored. Cash flows that often present difficulty to the analyst in deciding whether they are relevant or not are *sunk costs, indirect costs and benefits, interest expense, tax expense,* and the influence of *inflation.* Let's discuss each in turn.

15.1.1 Sunk Costs

Sunk costs. Cash flow expended in the past.

To get a picture of a proper estimation of the cash outflows and inflows that stem from a particular capital investment, imagine that you are standing at a fork in a road. On one hand, you would make the investment; on the other, you would not. You are concerned only with the future changes in cash flows that result from taking one road rather than another. You must ignore all cash flows that are not affected by the decision, as discussed in Illustration 15.1. Costs representing expenditures that occurred *prior* to the decision for the project under consideration are called **sunk costs.**

ILLUSTRATION 15.1

Relevant and irrelevant costs

During the past year Micro Electronics spent $100,000 for research and development (R&D) of a new computer chip. The R&D efforts have yet to result in a marketable product. Management faces the following decisions:

- Discontinue all efforts on this product.
- Invest $40,000 more, given a high probability that a marketable product will result in a one-year contribution of $55,000 over its variable manufacturing costs.

Engineers working on the project will earn $15,000 during the additional R&D time. If they do not work on this project, they will work on other projects.

The only relevant flows are the future expenditure of $40,000 and the discounted future net revenue of $55,000. As long as $-\$40,000 + \$55,000/(1 + r) > 0$, for a chosen cost of capital rate r, the firm is better off investing the additional $40,000. (Verify that r can be as much as 37.5 percent for the project to be acceptable.)[1]

To show a possible misuse of the data, consider the following *accounting approach* if further investment is made in R&D.

Net revenue		$ 55,000
Costs:		
Past R&D	$100,000	
New R&D	40,000	
Engineers	15,000	155,000
Net loss		$(100,000)

The implication is that the past R&D of $100,000 and the engineering cost of $15,000 are avoidable cash outflows if all R&D efforts cease. But this is not true. If further investment ceases, the accounting loss is $115,000.

Net revenue		$ 0
Costs:		
Past R&D	$100,000	
New R&D	0	
Engineers	15,000	115,000
Net loss		$(115,000)

By not investing, the firm is worse off by $15,000: $55,000 revenue foregone less the $40,000 new R&D expenditure saved. The prior R&D is a sunk cost. It is irrelevant to the analysis because it cannot be recovered. The $15,000 engineer cost is also an irrelevant cost, since it will be incurred regardless of what happens. As mentioned, if the engineers do not work on this project, they will work on other projects.

15.1.2 Joint Costs and Benefits

Joint costs and benefits are those costs and benefits shared by more than a single activity. For example, assume that Compaq Computer Corp. is considering manufacturing a new notebook computer that will share an assembly line with an established desktop computer. It can be difficult to determine how much of the joint costs should be allocated to the new product. Checking the sensitivity of the allocation decision is useful. For instance, the new notebook computer may have a positive net present value if 30 percent of the indirect joint costs, such as supervision and plant overhead for utilities and property taxes, of the assembly line are allocated to it. However, allocation of 35 percent of the indirect joint costs may result in a negative net present value and rejection of the proposed new product.

---

[1]Solution: ($55,000 ÷ $40,000) − 1 = 0.375.

CAPITAL BUDGETING DECISIONS, PART II

by William J. Post, Senior Vice President, Arizona Public Service Company

In the last chapter, I discussed some background about the capital budgeting environment for a public utility. Here I want to discuss a major project undertaken by APS that utilized the revenue requirements method; it was the construction of Palo Verde Nuclear Generating Station (Palo Verde). During the 1970s, projected energy demands for Arizona and the southwestern region were growing dramatically based on historical population growth. This anticipated customer growth translated to increases in both electricity sales and peak load. The company's load forecast showed that additional generating facilities needed to be built to serve these customers. APS considered its alternatives and evaluated the size, fuel type, and location of a future power plant. Gas and oil-fired fuel plants were not given serious consideration because APS felt that gas and oil would be in short supply for power plant use in the future. Coal and nuclear fuels were the only alternatives considered.

Coal-fueled power was a viable alternative but due to concern over APS's already large investment in coal plants, and the rapidly escalating costs and siting problems associated with environmental regulation, it was not selected. The economics of the revenue requirement analysis as well as environmental regulations favored the installation of nuclear-fueled electricity generation. Based on numerous load forecasts, revenue requirements analyses, and independent studies, management made the decision to build Palo Verde for $2.784 billion.

Once the decision to build the nuclear generating station was made, the company continually monitored the Palo Verde expenditures to analyze any variances from the original budget. Unfortunately, many unforeseen cost increases increased the cost of Palo Verde to $5.877 billion. Three primary factors caused the budget overrun: regulatory and safety issues repre-

sented 67 percent of the cost increases; issues or events external to the project, 19 percent; and design/scope changes, 14 percent.

In the first category, several major industry events occurred that affected all areas of the Palo Verde project. These events included the creation of the Nuclear Regulatory Commission (NRC) from the Atomic Energy Commission (AEC), the 1975 Browns Ferry nuclear plant fire, and the 1979 accident at Three Mile Island Nuclear Station. The AEC originally had a dual purpose of regulation and the promotion of nuclear power. However, with the creation of NRC, its sole purpose as a regulatory agency was to implement new and more comprehensive regulations as well as reinterpret existing regulations. This new regulatory environment, coupled with the increase in quality assurance and quality-control requirements stemming from the nuclear plant incidents, increased the complexity of constructing and operating a nuclear power plant. These complexities translated into increased costs.

The second category, externally imposed conditions, consisted of factors such as inflation, shortages of experienced labor, vendor-initiated changes, and severe weather conditions. The third category, design/scope changes, consisted of changes or refinements in the scope of the project including actions to improve the plant's operability, reliability, and maintainability.

As a regulated utility, APS's load forecasts, investment decisions, capital expenditures, and construction schedules were constantly scrutinized to ensure that our decision to build the plant and the manner in which the plant was constructed was fiscally sound. After years of prudence evaluations and rate case hearings, the Palo Verde Nuclear Generating Station was put into the rate base and APS's customers began paying for the new plant.

Or consider this example. By producing the new notebook computer, Compaq's sales of desktop PCs are expected to decline because of lack of production capacity to produce both the notebook and the desktop PC. Thus, forecasted cash flows for the notebook should be reduced by lost sales on desktop PCs. Or consider yet another example. Compaq has adequate production capacity to produce both desktop PCs and notebooks on the assembly line. However, if sales of desktop PCs decline because of a shift in consumer preferences to the lightweight notebooks, then no adjustment should be made to reduce revenues from the notebook line. The erosion in desktop Compaq PCs will happen regardless of whether the company introduces a notebook line. If consumers do not buy from Compaq, they will buy from IBM, Toshiba, or some other source.

The important thing to remember is that, at some point, management must decide on an appropriate allocation. A fine line between accepting or rejecting a project may hinge on a very uncertain assumption. Failure to allocate any joint costs or benefits results in a misstatement of the product's contribution to shareholder value.

15.1.3 Interest Expense

Interest expense, as we know, represents the cost of borrowed money. However, *we do not include interest expense as part of the cash flow amount in time value models.* This rule applies even if management finances the new project entirely with debt.[2] The cost of capital used in the net present value model (or as the standard to evaluate an internal rate of return result) incorporates the firm's financing costs for both debt and equity. A positive net present value (or an internal rate of return that exceeds the cost of capital) indicates that the investment earns more than its costs, including its financing costs for debt and equity capital.

15.1.4 Income Taxes

When evaluating capital investment proposals, managers must include the effect of income taxes on the cash flows. Often an accept-reject decision hinges on tax implications. Certainly the payment of taxes reduces the percent return and the amount of funds available to shareholders. On the other hand, governments often create income tax laws to provide added incentive for firms to make business decisions in the best interest of the economy. For instance, Puerto Rico enticed many pharmaceutical firms to build facilities on the island in exchange for attractive tax benefits. Many businesses today are still uncertain of the ramifications of the tax policies of the Clinton administration. There was general uncertainty when Clinton was elected; some economists blamed the lack of robustness in the economic recovery in 1993 on the fact that businesspeople were not sure of what tax policy would eventually be proposed by the Clinton administration. As such, companies deferred many capital expenditures until some of the uncertainty was resolved.

15.1.5 Inflation

Cash flow estimates for capital expenditures extend over several periods. Thus, managers must consider expected future *inflation* from year to year in cash flow analysis.

---

[2]There are exceptions to this rule. As we discussed in Chapter 14, there may be additional financing costs or benefits as a result of the project. We can use the adjusted present value model to analyze these cases.

Inflation forecasts can be difficult, since rates of inflation vary markedly over time. In the late 1940s and again in the late 1970s the inflation rate, as measured by the consumer price index, was over 14 percent. During other times since 1940, inflation has been under 2 percent annually. Usually inflation is somewhere between these two extremes.

The issue in corporate finance is how to incorporate inflation into cash flow analysis. The recommended approach is to state both the cost of capital and expected cash flows used in the net present value model in nominal terms; that is, include any inflation premium in them both. There should be no need to adjust the cost of capital for the effects of inflation. A cost of capital calculated using financial market information and market values for the firm's debt and equity already incorporates future inflation projections. Financial markets analyze information constantly, including inflation trends, to determine appropriate market prices and returns for financial securities.

Adjusting cash flows of a project to include effects of inflation requires a forecast of expected inflation rates. Input from various economists in academia, business, and government and inflation studies published by business newspapers and magazines such as *The Wall Street Journal, Fortune, Forbes,* and *Business Week* are primary sources of information. Major banks, insurance companies, and the federal government also conduct intensive studies that offer opinions about inflation and where interest rates are headed.

Some cash flows for a proposal are not adjusted for inflation. For example, you determine annual depreciation expense using the original cost of the asset and depreciation tax rules in effect at the time of the investment. In other cases, the effect of inflation lags behind cash flows. For example, a proposed new product's acceptance by consumers is largely dependent on a stable price. Because buyers are price sensitive, any price increases could cause sales demand to falter. Thus, management may forego price increases until later in the product's life cycle.

Comprehension Check

1. What is the distinction between a relevant cash flow and an irrelevant cash flow?
2. Define sunk costs. What role should they play in the capital investment decision?
3. Why exclude interest cost in estimating cash flows?
4. How may inflation be taken into account in capital investment analysis?

15.2 CALCULATING CASH FLOWS

We can separate the information required to develop investment proposals into three categories: (1) data dealing with the *initial cash outlay;* (2) data dealing with *annual operating cash flows;* (3) data dealing with *terminal nonoperating cash flows.* The collection and organization of this information, while perhaps tedious, is crucial to the capital budgeting decision. In explaining each of these important cash flow categories, we first lay out a model and discuss its elements. We then use an illustration to show how to apply the model.

15.2.1 Initial Cash Outlay

The total initial cash outlay for a capital investment project can consist of several items. In addition to the purchase price of the item under consideration, there may be tax cash inflows or outflows, more or less investment in other assets because of the decision, and so on. Equation 15.1 indicates those items that need to be considered as part of the initial investment:

$$
\begin{array}{ll}
- \text{ Installed cash cost of the asset} \\
+ \text{ Investment tax credit} \\
\pm \text{ Net working capital to support the project} \\
- \text{ Incremental after-tax cash expenses incurred} \\
+ \text{ Salvage value of the old asset} \\
\pm \text{ Tax adjustment on the salvage value} \\
= \text{ Initial cash outlay}
\end{array} \qquad (15.1)
$$

A minus sign denotes a cash outflow; a plus sign means a cash inflow. Depending on the circumstances, some items can be either inflows or outflows. Let's discuss each item.

- **Installed cash cost** of the investment is the purchase price plus freight, installation, and any other charges (such as removal or razing of the old asset) associated directly with the new expenditure.
- **Investment tax credit (ITC)** is a tax break sometimes allowed to firms for certain types of new investment in an effort to stimulate the economy. No ITC currently exists in the U.S. income tax code for new investment.[3]
- **Net working capital (NWC)** is the incremental investment in current assets less the incremental short-term noninterest financing of accounts payable and accrued wages that changes spontaneously as production changes.[4] As the firm buys more materials and labor, it generally finances them with interest-free loans provided by suppliers and employees. Suppliers may be paid every ten days, whereas employees are paid every two weeks. The project's NWC component is usually a cash outflow because of increased investment in accounts receivable and inventory. However, it is possible for a new investment to allow NWC investment to decline, and in this case NWC is a cash inflow. The following illustrations are typical scenarios of what to look for in determining net working capital requirements.

  1. Because of the lag between expenses and revenues, the company may have to maintain larger cash balances to pay wages, buy supplies, conduct training programs, or to formulate and implement sales programs. Financing of suppliers or independent sales outlets may be necessary.

  2. Greater sales volume, which may result from plant capacity expansion, is likely to result in more resources tied up in accounts receivable. Slower-paying accounts may also be granted credit to expand sales. Greater sales

Installed cash cost. Cash expenditure to buy, install, and make operative the item proposed by the capital budgeting proposal.

Investment tax credit (ITC). A tax deduction, approved by the federal income tax statutes, allowed corporations investing in equipment. Politicians approve it and repeal it depending on what they think is good for the economy.

Net working capital (NWC). As it applies to capital expenditures, it is defined as current assets less noninterest-bearing current liabilities that change as a result of a capital budgeting decision.

[3]ITC has a history of coming and going: January 1962, 7 percent credit instituted; October 1966, credit suspended; March 1967, 7 percent credit reinstated; April 1969, credit eliminated; April 1971, 7 percent credit reinstated; January 1975, credit increased to 10 percent; January 1986, credit eliminated. We include ITC in our model because you may see it again in the near future.

[4]*Net working capital* is defined normally as current assets minus current liabilities. We exclude interest-bearing short-term financing from current liabilities because such financing becomes part of the determination of the cost of capital, as we discussed in Chapter 12.

FIGURE 15.1

TAX IMPLICATIONS OF DISPOSAL OF ASSET

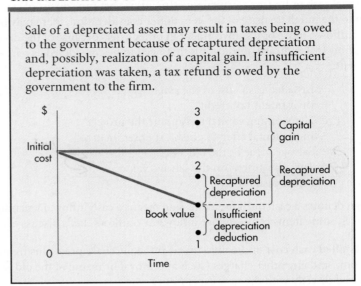

Sale of a depreciated asset may result in taxes being owed to the government because of recaptured depreciation and, possibly, realization of a capital gain. If insufficient depreciation was taken, a tax refund is owed by the government to the firm.

volume or an increased variety of products may lead to more resources invested in inventory.

3. Higher prepaid expenses for items such as advertising, insurance premiums, or rent may absorb current funds if a new project is adopted.

- **Incremental expense cash flows** associated with the investment are cash outflows that are expenses. They do not become part of the depreciable asset amount. The expense is adjusted to an after-tax basis. Examples include training, advertising, and legal expenses associated with the start-up.

- **Salvage (resale) value** of an old asset is the value the firm can receive today by either selling the old asset in a used equipment market or the value allowed on a trade-in for a new asset.

- **Salvage value's tax adjustment** is the tax cash flow calculated on the difference between the old asset's current book value, the value shown on the accounting books, and its current salvage, or resale, value. This adjustment can be positive (cash inflow) or negative (cash outflow). The government allows corporations to write off (depreciate) a portion of their plant and equipment each year to represent the wear and tear and loss of value of the fixed assets. If the *net book value* of the asset (its first cost less accumulated depreciation) differs from the asset's salvage value, then an income-tax adjustment is necessary. Either too much depreciation was taken or not enough. Figure 15.1 helps us visualize the problem.

- When value received for the old asset exceeds its book value, the firm must *recapture depreciation* taken on the old asset. This situation is shown as *point 2* in Figure 15.1. In retrospect, the firm deducted too much depreciation for the old asset. The **recaptured depreciation** is the amount the asset's salvage value exceeds its book value if salvage value is less than original cost. The higher depreciation deductions in past years resulted in lower past taxable income; the government received lower income tax receipts. The firm corrects the problem by remitting the following amount to the government:

Incremental expense cash flow. Additional cash outflows for expenses that result from accepting a capital budgeting project.

Salvage value. The resale value of an asset.

Salvage value tax adjustment. The calculation of income taxes on an asset that is sold for either more or less than its depreciated book value.

Recaptured depreciation. The difference between the selling price of a depreciable asset and its net book value, up to the original cost of the asset.

$$(\text{Salvage value}_{\text{old asset}} - \text{book value}_{\text{old asset}}) \times \text{income tax rate} \qquad (15.2)$$

If book value exceeds salvage value (shown as *point 1* in Figure 15.1), the firm took too little depreciation. In effect, the government owes the company an income tax refund. Past taxable income was higher than it should have been because the depreciation expense was too low. The refund is:

$$(\text{Book value}_{\text{old asset}} - \text{salvage value}_{\text{old asset}}) \times \text{income tax rate} \qquad (15.3)$$

The firm collects the "refund" by adjusting its quarterly income tax payment to the Internal Revenue Service.

When value received for the old asset exceeds its original cost (*point 3* in Figure 15.1), it is necessary to recapture all depreciation taken on the asset and pay income tax on this amount:

$$(\text{Initial cost}_{\text{old asset}} - \text{book value}_{\text{old asset}}) \times \text{income tax rate} \qquad (15.4)$$

The company must also pay a *capital gains tax*. A **capital gains tax** is based on the difference between the resale value of the old asset and its original cost:

$$(\text{Salvage value}_{\text{old asset}} - \text{initial cost}_{\text{old asset}}) \times \text{capital gains tax rate} \qquad (15.5)$$

Currently, the capital gains tax rate equals the income tax rate. However, in the past the capital gains rate has been less than the tax rate.

Illustration 15.2 provides an example of the initial cash outlay calculations. The asset is sold for less than its accounting book value, resulting in a cash inflow for taxes.

Capital gains tax. Tax on the excess of proceeds over cost from the sale of capital asset as defined by the Internal Revenue Code. The Tax Reform Act of 1986 made the capital gains tax rate the same as the tax on other income.

ILLUSTRATION 15.2

Calculating initial investment

Management of Newhart Industries is considering a new punch press with a depreciable life of five years and an installed cost of $25,000. Cash expenses of $4000 would be incurred with the acquisition. The purchase would allow the firm to dispose of an old press for $5000. The current book value of the old press is $6000. It has three more years of depreciable life, but it could be used for five years. In the last two years the firm would incur no depreciation expense. Because of additional production and sales, net working capital would increase $3000 due to higher inventory and accounts receivable investments. The tax rate is 30 percent.

Based on these expected cash flows, the initial cash outflow is $25,500.

− Installed cash cost of the punch press	$(25,000)
+ Investment tax credit	0
− Net working capital to support the project	(3,000)
− Incremental after-tax cash expenses:	
$4000 × (1 − 0.30)	(2,800)
+ Salvage value of the old asset	5,000
+ Tax adjustment on the salvage value:	
($6000 book value − $5000 salvage value) × 0.30	300
= Initial cash outlay	$(25,500)

If the government offers an investment tax credit, the cash outflow is reduced.

15.2.2 Annual Operating Cash Flows

Future expected **annual operating cash flows** of the investment are the incremental operating revenues and costs resulting from the investment. You calculate these cash flows as follows:

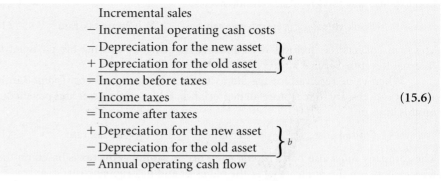

$$
\begin{array}{l}
\text{Incremental sales} \\
- \text{Incremental operating cash costs} \\
\left.\begin{array}{l}
- \text{Depreciation for the new asset} \\
+ \text{Depreciation for the old asset}
\end{array}\right\} a \\
= \text{Income before taxes} \\
- \text{Income taxes} \\
\hline
= \text{Income after taxes} \\
\left.\begin{array}{l}
+ \text{Depreciation for the new asset} \\
- \text{Depreciation for the old asset}
\end{array}\right\} b \\
= \text{Annual operating cash flow}
\end{array}
\qquad (15.6)
$$

The additions and subtractions for depreciation (*a* and *b*) convert the noncash depreciation expense into a cash tax shield.

Alternatively, you can calculate the operating cash flows as:

$$
\begin{array}{l}
\text{Incremental sales} \times (1 - \tau) \\
- \text{Incremental operating cash costs} \times (1 - \tau) \\
+ \text{Depreciation for the new asset} \times \tau \\
- \text{Depreciation for the old asset} \times \tau \\
\hline
= \text{Annual operating cash flow}
\end{array}
\qquad (15.7)
$$

The depreciation tax shield is more clearly seen in Equation 15.7 than in Equation 15.6. Depreciation $\times \tau$ is the amount of depreciation converted into a cash flow tax shield.

Interpretation of Equations 15.6 and 15.7 are straightforward.

- **Incremental sales** are the additional sales receipts resulting from adopting the project.
- **Incremental operating cash costs** include material, labor, and overhead incurred as a result of adopting the project. Excluded are expenses for depreciation, income taxes, and interest.
- Depreciation is not a cash flow item. However, as already mentioned, depreciation offers a cash tax shield. By disposing of an asset that is not fully depreciated, the firm gives up future depreciation tax shields. Thus, you subtract the old depreciation amount times the tax rate. The new asset provides new depreciation tax shields. Hence, you add the new tax shield amount.

It is possible for before-tax cash flow in any forecast period to be negative (see Equation 15.6). We will still adjust the cash flow for taxes and reduce the negative cash flow after the tax deduction. Normally, a firm with a negative before-tax income amount shows no tax expense. Because the project is only one part of the firm, we assume that the firm on the whole generates sufficient positive before-tax cash flows to offset any negative before-tax cash flows of one project.

Illustration 15.3 shows calculations for annual operating cash flows. Keep in mind that the problem of estimating the various cash flow items usually is quite complicated. Several assumptions must be made, and some assumptions may prove incorrect with hindsight.

ILLUSTRATION 15.3

Calculating annual operating cash flows

Management of Newhart Industries expects the new punch press (Illustration 15.2) to generate $17,000 annual incremental revenues for the life of the equipment. The projection for variable costs for material and labor is $10,000 annually. The new machine should reduce scrap costs $1000 annually.

The new machine has a useful life of five years.[5] The annual depreciation charge for this machine is $5000, as calculated on a straight-line basis over the life of the asset: $25,000 ÷ 5 = $5000. The old machine has three years of depreciable life, but five years of economic life. The depreciation charge for each of the next three years for the old machine is $2000. The income tax rate is 30 percent and the market cost of capital for the project is 15 percent.

The annual cash flows are:

	Years 1–3	Years 4–5
Incremental sales	$17,000	$17,000
− Incremental operating cash costs		
$10,000 costs − $1000 reduced scrap	(9,000)	(9,000)
− Depreciation for the new asset	(5,000)	(5,000)
+ Depreciation for the old asset	2,000	0
= Income before taxes	$ 5,000	$ 3,000
− Income taxes	1,500	900
= Income after taxes	$ 3,500	$ 2,100
+ Depreciation for the new asset	5,000	5,000
− Depreciation for the old asset	(2,000)	0
= Annual operating cash flow	$ 6,500	$ 7,100

Alternatively, we can calculate the cash flows as:

	Years 1–3
Incremental sales × (1 − τ): $17,000 × 0.7	$11,900
− Incremental operating cash costs × (1 − τ): $9000 × 0.7	(6,300)
+ Depreciation for the new asset × τ: $5000 × 0.3	1,500
− Depreciation for the old asset × τ: $2000 × 0.3	(600)
= Annual operating cash flow	$ 6,500

	Years 4–5
Incremental sales × (1 − τ): $17,000 × 0.7	$11,900
− Incremental operating cash costs × (1− τ): $9000 × 0.7	(6,300)
+ Depreciation for the new asset × τ: $5000 × 0.3	1,500
− Depreciation for the old asset × τ: $2000 × 0.3	0
= Annual operating cash flow	$ 7,100

[5]Currently, tax rules related to depreciation are dictated by the Tax Reform Act of 1986 and its modified ACRS (accelerated cost recovery system, pronounced "acres") provision. Because changes in the tax laws occur frequently, we have not set forth the various requirements of ACRS. Instead, we assume that assets are depreciated on a straight-line basis over the life of the asset. The asset's expected salvage value is not deducted from the initial cost to determine annual depreciation. In practice, it is important to use current tax laws to determine after-tax cash flows for financial decisions.

The NPV of the project, to this point in the analysis, is −$3070, calculated as follows. It appears that Newhart's management should reject the proposed press and keep the old one.

$$NPV = -\$25{,}500 + \frac{\$6500}{(1.15)} + \frac{\$6500}{(1.15)^2} + \frac{\$6500}{(1.15)^3} + \frac{\$7100}{(1.15)^4} + \frac{\$7100}{(1.15)^5}$$

$$= -\$25{,}500 + \$5652 + \$4915 + \$4274 + \$4059 + \$3530$$

$$= -\$25{,}500 + \$22{,}430$$

$$= -\$3070$$

15.2.3 Terminal Cash Flows

Terminal nonoperating cash flows. Cash flow occurring at the end of the investment's life; included are salvage value, taxes on sale of asset, and liquidation of all net working capital associated with the investment.

If you reject the proposal in Illustration 15.3 because of its negative NPV amount, you have made a mistake. You cannot make an informed decision until you consider **terminal nonoperating cash flows,** which are cash flows for net working capital and salvage value of the new asset at the terminal date of the investment. Equation 15.8 sets forth these flows.

$$
\begin{aligned}
&\pm \text{ Net working capital invested to support the new project} \\
&+ \text{ Salvage value of new project} \\
&\pm \text{ Tax adjustment on salvage value of new project} \quad\quad (15.8)\\
&- \text{ Salvage value of old project} \\
&\pm \text{ Tax adjustment on salvage value of old project} \\
&= \text{ Terminal cash flow}
\end{aligned}
$$

Any incremental net working capital investments, made either initially or throughout the life of the investment, are assumed to be recouped at the terminal date of the new investment. This assumption is based on the fact that there is a terminal date for the proposed expenditure. At the terminal date, all aspects of the project are considered completed: The firm sells all remaining inventory, collects all accounts receivable, consumes all prepaid expenses, and pays all suppliers of labor and material.

The possibility of substantial end-of-life salvage value of a new investment often is overlooked in the appraisal of a proposal. The salvage value may include more than resale value of a piece of equipment, and the amount may be negative. For example, Magma Copper, Inc., a mining company, incurs significant restoration costs to return the land to an environmentally safe condition once the mine is exhausted of copper.

An analyst must calculate the tax effects associated with any eventual salvage value of the new investment. The analysis is similar to that undertaken for salvage value of the old equipment when determining the initial cash outlay. Whenever the salvage value of the new equipment differs from its book value at the terminal date, a tax cash flow exists. The cash flow is an inflow if book value exceeds salvage value and an outflow if book value is less than salvage value. (See Illustration 15.4.)

ILLUSTRATION 15.4

Terminal cash flows

Let's continue our examination of Newhart Industries' proposal to buy a punch press by adding terminal nonoperating cash flows to the picture. Illustration 15.2 mentions that the project requires an incremental investment of $3000 for net working capital at time 0. We assume that this NWC investment remains constant throughout the life of the new equipment. At the end of year 5, the firm recovers the $3000 investment—it becomes a cash inflow.

If management believes the new punch press can be sold for $2000 at the end of five years, this amount represents the salvage value, another cash inflow. However, at the end of year 5 the book value of the new equipment is $0. The initial cost of $25,000 was depreciated $5000 per year for five years. Because salvage value exceeds book value ($2000 versus $0), there is a tax outflow of $600, which represents the excess of salvage value over book value times the income tax rate: ($2000 − $0) × 0.30 = $600. The terminal nonoperating cash inflow is $4400.

	Year 5
Recovery of net working capital	$3000
Salvage value of new punch press	2000
Tax adjustment on the salvage value	(600)
Net terminal value cash inflow	$4400

The present value of this cash inflow is $2188: $4400 ÷ $(1.15)^5$.

We can now estimate the NPV of the proposed punch press that we have been discussing in Illustrations 15.2 through 15.4. It is −$822, consisting of the following amounts:

Initial cash outlay	$(25,500)
Present value of operating cash flows	22,430
Present value of terminal cash flow	2,188
Net present value of project	$ (822)

If management is satisfied with all the assumptions that went into the analysis, the proposal to buy the punch press should be rejected. The market value of the company's stock should increase by $822 less than the amount of equity funds used to purchase the asset. For example, suppose the firm's optimal capital structure is 40 percent debt and 60 percent equity. If management accepts the project, the $25,500 outlay would be financed with $10,200 debt and $15,300 equity. Debtholders would receive their expected return. Equity holders, being the residual cash claimants, would realize $822 less than the $15,300 they contributed.

It is possible that different assumptions could lead to a positive NPV and acceptance of the project. Maybe the cost of capital should be, or could be, lower. If the cost of capital is 10 percent, the project's NPV is about $2000, which makes it an acceptable investment. Possibly the terminal salvage value of the new equipment is too low. Is the forecast of incremental revenue too pessimistic? Managers must be satisfied that the assumptions are correct.

 Comprehension Check

1. Outline the variables that may be included in total initial outlay for a capital project.
2. Why should changes in net working capital requirements be included in capital investment analysis?
3. Discuss the role of an old (replaced) asset's salvage value in determining the initial outlay in a new capital project.

4. Describe the components of a firm's operating cash flows arising out of a capital investment project.

5. What are the components of a capital investment project's terminal cash flows?

 ## 15.3 UNEQUAL LIVES PROBLEM

Often equipment replacement decisions result in choosing among alternative projects that fall into different replacement cycles. For example, a machine manufactured by Wyatt Corporation has a useful life of three years, whereas a machine that does the same task from Dagny Company has a useful life of nine years. Three sequential three-year machines from Wyatt would be needed to do the job of one nine-year machine from Dagny.

How do you choose among different alternatives with different economic lives? The logical answer would seem to be to select the asset with the largest NPV. However, if the investment decision is for a project that is *ongoing in nature, for which investment alternatives are mutually exclusive,* and *for which replacement assets are virtually identical to the asset being replaced,* then it is inappropriate to simply choose the asset with the largest NPV amount.

Let's assume the mutually exclusive investment is ongoing and replacement is with an identical asset. There are several ways to choose among competing assets. Two conventional techniques are *common horizon analysis* and *equivalent annual annuity method.*

15.3.1 Common Horizon Analysis

Panel (a) in Figure 15.2 illustrates the choice between the three-year Wyatt machine and the nine-year Dagny machine. The problem is to find a common horizon to compare the two machines. One approach is to assume a salvage value for the Dagny machine at the end of year 3. Another approach is to assume reinvestment in similar Wyatt machines at the end of years 3 and 6, as shown in panel (b). Illustration 15.5 shows the calculations.

ILLUSTRATION 15.5

Reinvest to a common horizon

The Wyatt machine costs $6000 and incurs annual after-tax maintenance costs of $1000. The Dagny machine costs $15,000, but annual after-tax maintenance costs are only $250. The depreciation tax shield for each machine is based on the straight-line method and a tax rate of 30 percent. The annual depreciation tax shield for Wyatt is ($6000 ÷ 3) × 0.30 = $600, whereas the annual depreciation tax shield for Dagny is ($15,000 ÷ 9) × 0.30 = $500. The cost of capital is 12 percent. The incremental sales and costs other than maintenance costs are identical for both machines.

The NPVs of the Wyatt and Dagny machines are −$6961 and −$13,668, respectively. Although the Wyatt machine has the better NPV (it is less negative), it is not necessarily the better choice.

FIGURE 15.2

COMMON HORIZON

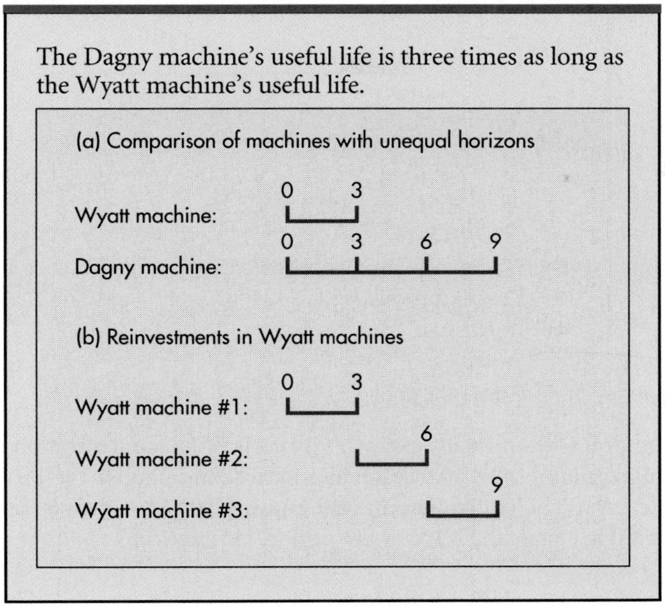

The Dagny machine's useful life is three times as long as
the Wyatt machine's useful life.

(a) Comparison of machines with unequal horizons

Wyatt machine:

$$\begin{array}{cc} 0 & 3 \end{array}$$

Dagny machine:

$$\begin{array}{cccc} 0 & 3 & 6 & 9 \end{array}$$

(b) Reinvestments in Wyatt machines

Wyatt machine #1:

$$\begin{array}{cc} 0 & 3 \end{array}$$

Wyatt machine #2:

$$6$$

Wyatt machine #3:

$$9$$

Wyatt machine:

$$\begin{array}{cccc} 0 & 1 & 2 & 3 \end{array}$$

Investment	−$6000			
Maintenance		−$1000	−$1000	−$1000
Tax shield		600	600	600

$$\text{NPV} = -\$6000 - \$1000 \times \frac{1 - (1 + 0.12)^{-3}}{0.12} + \$600 \times \frac{1 - (1 + 0.12)^{-3}}{0.12}$$

$$= -\$6000 - \$1000 \times 2.4018 + \$600 \times 2.4018$$

$$= -\$6961$$

Dagny machine:

$$\begin{array}{ccccc} 0 & 1 & 2 & 3 & 9 \end{array}$$

Investment	−$15,000			
Maintenance		−$250	−$250	−$250	−$250
Tax shield		500	500	500	500

$$\text{NPV} = -\$15,000 - \$250 \times \frac{1 - (1 + 0.12)^{-9}}{0.12} + \$500 \times \frac{1 - (1 + 0.12)^{-9}}{0.12}$$

$$= -\$15,000 - \$250 \times 5.3282 + \$500 \times 5.3282$$

$$= -\$13,668$$

The next step is to find a common horizon to compare the
two machines. The lowest common number of years is 9. Thus,
there will be three investments in Wyatt machines with cash flows
as indicated previously; investment #1 is at time 0, investment #2 is
at the end of year 3, and investment #3 is at the end of year 6. The

NPV of each investment is −$6961, as calculated earlier. However, the NPV of the three investments as of time 0 is −$15,442.

0	3	6	9
−$6961	−$6961	−$6961	

$$\begin{aligned} NPV &= -\$6961 - \$6961 \times (1 + 0.12)^{-3} - \$6961 \times (1 + 0.12)^{-6} \\ &= -\$6961 - \$6961 \times 0.7118 - \$6961 \times 0.5066 \\ &= -\$6961 - \$4955 - \$3526 \\ &= -\$15{,}442 \end{aligned}$$

The Dagny machine is more cost-effective because it results in a lower cash outflow of $1774 (=$15,442 − $13,668) over the nine-year horizon.

15.3.2 Equivalent Annual Annuity Analysis

Equivalent annual annuity (EAA). An even cash flow that yields the same present value amount as the project's net present value.

Another way to deal with mutually exclusive projects of unequal duration is to find the *equivalent annual annuity (EAA)* of each alternative, and choose the project with the most favorable EAA. The **equivalent annual annuity (EAA)** is defined as the annuity whose present value equals the NPV of the project in question:

$$\begin{aligned} NPV &= EAA \times \frac{1 - (1 + r)^{-n}}{r} \\ &= EAA \times PVIFA_{r\%,\, n \text{ years}} \end{aligned} \qquad (15.8)$$

or rearranging,

$$\begin{aligned} EAA &= \frac{NPV}{\dfrac{1 - (1 + r)^{-n}}{r}} \\ &= NPV \div PVIFA_{r\%,\, n \text{ years}} \end{aligned} \qquad (15.9)$$

The EAA represents the equivalent amount per year incurred by owning the asset over its entire life. Illustration 15.6 applies the EAA technique.

ILLUSTRATION 15.6

Selecting projects using the EAA technique

The Wyatt machine has an NPV of −$6961 (see Illustration 15.5). Divide this amount by the present value annuity factor for 12 percent, 3 years (that is, 2.4018) to obtain an EAA of −$2898.

$$\begin{aligned} EAA &= \frac{NPV}{\dfrac{1 - (1 + r)^{-n}}{r}} \\ &= \frac{-\$6961}{\dfrac{1 - (1 + 0.12)^{-3}}{0.12}} \\ &= -\$6961 \div 2.4018 \\ &= -\$2898 \end{aligned}$$

Similarly, the Dagny machine's EAA is −$2565.

$$EAA = \frac{NPV}{\dfrac{1 - (1 + r)^{-n}}{r}}$$

$$= \frac{-\$13,668}{\frac{1 - (1 + 0.12)^{-9}}{0.12}}$$

$$= -\$13,668 \div 5.3282$$

$$= -\$2565$$

The annual cost advantage of the Dagny machine over the Wyatt machine is $333 (= $2898 − $2565).

Let's compare Wyatt's NPV and EAA numbers.

	0	1	2	3	
					Present values
NPV	−$6000	−$400	−$400	−$400	−$6961
EAA		−$2898	−$2898	−$2898	−$6961

The present values of the two flows are equal:

$$NPV = -\$6000 + \$400 \times \frac{1 - (1 + 0.12)^{-3}}{0.12} = -\$6961$$

$$EAA = -\$2898 \times \frac{1 - (1 + 0.12)^{-3}}{0.12} = -\$6961$$

The EAA technique converts the NPV cash flows into annuity flows that begin one period from time 0.

In Illustration 15.6, we found that the Dagny machine has an annual cost advantage of $333. What is the present value of these cost savings over a nine-year period? Using the present value of an annuity equation, the savings are $1774.

$$NPV = \$333 \times \frac{1 - (1 + 0.12)^{-9}}{0.12}$$

$$= \$333 \times 5.3282$$

$$= \$1774$$

This answer agrees with the savings found using the common horizon approach in Illustration 15.5. Thus, the two methods are equivalent, although the EAA technique usually is simpler to apply.

Comprehension Check

1. If a mutually exclusive investment is not ongoing, how should you evaluate the investment?
2. List the three conditions that must be present for projects to be evaluated by common horizon analysis or the equivalent annual amount technique.
3. Describe how common horizon analysis and the equivalent annual amount technique work.

15.4 APPLICATIONS

In Chapter 14 and up to this point in this chapter, we have formed the necessary foundation for examining capital budgeting proposals. In this section we analyze several situations to provide you with a better operational understanding of capital budgeting.

The situations involve replacement of equipment, sales price of an order, make-or-buy a part, lease-or-buy equipment, and an abandonment decision. For each of the examples, we state the problem, lay out the data, illustrate calculations, and then recommend a decision.

15.4.1 Replacement of Equipment

Management of Eagle Industries is considering replacing a mini-loom used in making cotton thread. The sales pitch of the loom manufacturer is that Eagle's profits will improve, with the ultimate result of a higher stock price for the company. After carefully researching the loom currently in use, the accountant and industrial engineer of Eagle have come up with the following data.

Original cost (2 years ago)	$30,000
Book value (original cost less accumulated depreciation)	$18,000
Remaining useful life	3 years
Salvage value today	$10,000
Estimated salvage value at end of useful life (in 3 years)	$ 2,000
Annual operating costs	$ 8,000

A proposal submitted by the supervisor of Eagle's loom operation for the new mini-loom contains the following data.

Acquisition cost	$27,000
Estimated useful life	3 years
Estimated salvage value at end of useful life	$ 5,000
Annual operating costs	$ 3,000

The finance manager has indicated that the appropriate tax rate and discount rate to analyze the mini-loom proposal are:

Tax rate	30%
Discount rate	10%

Figure 15.3 displays the data on a time line. To analyze the proposed expenditure, *take the perspective that the old loom will be replaced.*

The initial cash outflow for the new loom is $14,600, as shown in the following calculations. The $30,000 purchase cost of the old loom is a sunk cost and irrelevant to the analysis. The old loom's book value of $18,000 is only relevant in that we use it to calculate the tax adjustment on the salvage value of the old loom, and calculate the change in the depreciation tax shield in the next set of calculations.

− Installed cash cost of the new loom	$(27,000)
+ Investment tax credit	0
− Net working capital to support the project	0
− Incremental after-tax cash expenses	0
+ Salvage value of the old loom	10,000
+ Tax adjustment on salvage value of old loom: ($18,000 − $10,000) × 0.30	2,400
= Initial cash outlay	$(14,600)

FIGURE 15.3
TIME LINE FOR ANALYZING A NEW LOOM ($000)

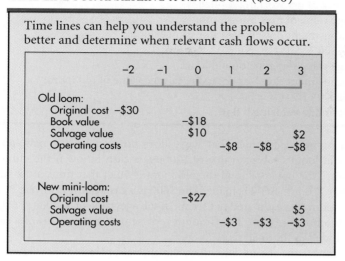

Time lines can help you understand the problem better and determine when relevant cash flows occur.

	−2	−1	0	1	2	3

Old loom:
Original cost −$30
Book value −$18
Salvage value $10 | | | | | | $2
Operating costs | | | | −$8 | −$8 | −$8

New mini-loom:
Original cost −$27
Salvage value | | | | | | $5
Operating costs | | | | −$3 | −$3 | −$3

Annual operating cash flows for years 1 through 3 are $4400.

Incremental sales	$ 0
+ Incremental operating expense savings:	
$8000 for old loom − $3000 for new loom	5,000
− Depreciation for the new loom: $27,000 ÷ 3	(9,000)
+ Depreciation for the old loom: $18,000 ÷ 3	6,000
= Income before taxes	$ 2,000
− Income taxes (30%)	600
= Income after taxes	$ 1,400
+ Depreciation for the new loom	9,000
− Depreciation for the old loom	(6,000)
= Annual operating cash flow	$ 4,400

Alternatively, we can calculate the operating cash flows as:

Incremental sales × (1 − τ)	$ 0
+ Incremental operating cash costs × (1 − τ):	
$5000 × (1 − 0.30)	3,500
+ Depreciation for the new loom × τ: $9000 × 0.30	2,700
− Depreciation for the old loom × τ: $6000 × 0.30	(1,800)
= Annual operating cash flow	$ 4,400

The new mini-loom lowers annual operating costs *before* taxes and depreciation by $5000. The investment saves $8000 in expenses by giving up the old loom but incurs a $3000 cost with the new loom. Depreciation on the new loom is $9000 per year: $27,000 acquisition cost ÷ 3 years. For the old loom, the depreciation is $6000 per year: $30,000 ÷ 5 years. The net depreciation tax shield is $900 cash inflow, the difference in depreciation × tax rate: ($9000 − $6000) × 0.3.

The terminal year nonoperating cash flow (year 3) is $2100.

Recovery of net working capital	$ 0
Salvage value of new mini-loom	5000
Tax adjustment on salvage value of new loom:	
($5000 − $0) × 0.30	(1500)
Salvage value foregone on old loom	(2000)
Tax adjustment saved on foregone salvage value of old loom:	
($2000 − $0) × 0.30	600
Net terminal value cash flow	$2100

For a moment, consider that Eagle does not acquire the new loom. Then in year 3, the old loom's salvage value of $2000 is a cash inflow if the old loom is sold. However, since the book value of the old loom is $0 at that time, a tax adjustment of ($2000 − $0) × 0.3 = $600 is made. The $600 is a cash outflow in year 3. By purchasing the new loom, the estimated net terminal salvage value of $1400 (= $2000 − $600) for the old loom is foregone. This amount represents a lost opportunity cash flow and must be included in the analysis.

By summarizing the initial outlay, the annual operating cash flows, and the terminal cash flow, we conclude that the new loom should not be purchased. Its net present value is −$2080. Buying the new loom should cause the shareholders of Eagle to receive $2080 less value than their contribution.

$$\text{NPV} = -\$14{,}600 + \$4400 \times \frac{1 - (1 + 0.10)^{-3}}{0.10} + \$2100 \times (1 + 0.10)^{-3}$$

$$= -\$14{,}600 + \$4400 \times 2.4869 + \$2100 \times 0.7513$$

$$= -\$14{,}600 + \$10{,}942 + \$1578$$

$$= -\$2080$$

15.4.2 Sales Price of an Order

Trish Chair Company produces a single chair that it regularly sells for $80 per unit. Manufacturing costs are as follows:

Material: 4 units @ $5.00	$20.00
Direct labor: 2 hours @ $8.00	16.00
Variable overhead: 50% of direct labor	8.00
Fixed overhead: 2 hours @ $5.00	10.00
Total manufacturing cost	$54.00

In addition, a cost analysis indicates that variable selling costs are $3 per chair (including a sales commission of 1 percent). Based on normal volume, the fixed selling and administrative costs average $12 per chair. Since the total average cost is $69 (= $54 + $3 + $12), a selling price of $80 generates an $11 per chair profit before taxes. The $11 per chair profit is 13.75 percent of sales, which compares favorably with the company's competitors.

Recently, the company received an offer from a foreign company for 2500 chairs for each of the next three years at a price of $70 per unit. Accepting the order would result in various export duties and special shipping requirements of $5000 per year. No sales commissions would be paid on the order. A high-speed jig saw costing $75,000 would be needed to increase capacity to meet the request. The saw has a useful life of five years. Estimated salvage value after three years would be $5000.

The company's accountant argues against accepting the order. The essence of the argument is that each chair costs $69 to produce. With a $70 sales price, the 2500-unit contract will produce profits of only $2500, even before considering the special costs of $5000 and the new jig saw. What is wrong with this argument?

First, it is necessary to determine the relevant costs. What costs will be avoided if the contract is not accepted?

- The material, labor, and variable overhead costs will not be incurred.
- The fixed factory overhead cost of $10 per chair is an application rate. These fixed costs are present regardless of the contract decision and are not relevant to the decision.
- Variable selling costs would be incurred, but not at $3 per chair. Sales commissions of $0.80 per chair (= 0.01 × $80) are avoided. Thus, the incremental variable selling cost is $2.20 per chair. This amount would be avoided if management refuses the contract.
- Fixed selling and administrative costs are unlikely to change and are irrelevant.
- The company would avoid the $5000 special charges.
- The $75,000 investment for the jig saw would be avoided.

To analyze the project, let's *take the perspective that the order will be accepted.* Thus, the initial cash outlay for the new jig saw is $75,000. The annual operating cash flows are $42,650. Note that the only costs included in getting to this number are those costs which would be avoided if the project is not taken.

Estimated Annual Operating Cash Flows

Revenue ($70 × 2500)		$175,000
Less avoidable costs:		
Material ($20 × 2500)	$50,000	
Labor ($16 × 2500)	40,000	
Variable overhead ($8 × 2500)	20,000	
Variable selling ($2.20 × 2500)	5,500	
Depreciation ($75,000 ÷ 5)	15,000	
Special costs	5,000	135,500
Contribution before taxes		$ 39,500
Taxes (30%)		11,850
Profit		$ 27,650
Add back depreciation		15,000
Annual operating cash flows		$ 42,650

Next we must determine the terminal cash flow. At the end of year 3, the estimated salvage value of the jig saw is $5000. Because the book value of the new jig saw will be $30,000 (= $75,000 original cost − 3 years depreciation of $15,000 per year) at the end of the third year, the government owes the company a "tax refund" of $7500: ($30,000 book value − $5000 salvage value) × 0.30 tax rate. Thus, the total terminal cash inflow is $12,500: $5000 salvage value + $7500 cash refund.

The NPV of the proposal is $40,457.

$$\text{NPV} = -\$75,000 + \$42,650 \times \frac{1 - (1 + 0.10)^{-3}}{0.10} + \$12,500 \times (1 + 0.10)^{-3}$$

$$= -\$75,000 + \$42,650 \times 2.4869 + \$12,500 \times 0.7513$$

$$= -\$75,000 + \$106,066 + \$9,391$$

$$= \$40,457$$

It appears that the order should be accepted. It should contribute $40,457 additional value to shareholders beyond their investment in this project. However, management must ask a critical question: Will the sale of chairs at $70 each have any domino effect on regular customers who have been paying $80? If so, then any revenues lost by having to sell at $70 per unit to regular customers must be factored into the analysis. Because the new customer is in a foreign market, the risk of this effect is probably minimal.

15.4.3 Make-or-Buy Decision

Dana Aerospace requires 10,000 units per year of a metal clip that it uses in manufacturing light aircraft. Management expects its need for the part to remain at this level for the next 20 years. Currently, the company purchases the clip from a reliable outside source at $20 per unit. A Dana engineer proposes that the company make the clip at a cost of $5 per unit for labor and material. A specialized machine costing $2 million would be needed. The expected life of the machine is 20 years. With no expected salvage value at the end of its life.

The engineer's recommendation is based on the following analysis.

10,000 clips × $5/unit material and labor	$ 50,000
10,000 clips × $10/unit depreciation*	100,000
Annual cost	$150,000

*Depreciation per clip is: $2 million ÷ 20 years = $100,000 ÷ 10,000 units = $10.

Purchase cost per clip	$20
Annual production cost per clip: $150,000 ÷ 10,000	15
Saving per clip	$ 5

What do you think of the engineer's analysis?

The analysis is faulty because it fails to consider the time value of money, relevant cash flows, and taxes. Assume the firm's cost of capital is 10 percent and the tax rate is 30 percent. The correct analysis is as follows. *Let's take the position that Dana will decide to make the clip.*

Incremental outflow today:		
Cost of new machine		$2,000,000
Annual incremental inflow for years 1 − 20:		
Current purchase cost of clip: 10,000 × $20		$200,000
Make clip:		
Labor and material: 10,000 × $5	$ 50,000	
Depreciation: $2,000,000 ÷ 20	100,000	150,000
Savings before taxes		$ 50,000
Taxes (30%)		15,000
Savings after taxes		$ 35,000
Add back depreciation		100,000
Cash flow		$135,000

The decision to make the clip has a negative NPV of $850,664. In other words, the value received by shareholders would be $850,664 less than the value of their contribution if Dana makes the clip rather than buys it. *Decision:* Continue to buy the clip.

$$\text{NPV} = -\$2,000,000 + \$135,000 \times \frac{1 - (1 + 0.10)^{-20}}{0.10}$$
$$= -\$2,000,000 + \$135,000 \times 8.5136$$
$$= -\$850,664$$

15.4.4 Lease-or-Buy Decision

Throughout this chapter we have assumed that the firm acquires assets by purchasing them. Leasing an asset is an alternative to outright ownership. A **lease** is a contractual relationship in which the owner of the asset or property (the *lessor*) grants to a firm or person (the *lessee*) the use of the property's services for a specified period of time. Thus, the lessee is able to use the leased asset without assuming ownership. The lessee is effectively borrowing from the lessor, so a lease is a form of debt financing, as we mentioned briefly in Chapter 13.

In general, leases are classified as either *operating leases* or *financial leases*. **Operating leases** are short term and are generally cancelable at the lessee's option prior to the end of the contract period. **Financial (capital) leases** are long term and generally not cancelable by the lessee before the end of the base lease period. Any financial leases that are cancelable require the lessee to reimburse the lessor for any losses occasioned by the cancellation.

In a financial lease transaction, the firm (lessee) only acquires the right to use the asset. The lessor retains both the tax benefits derived from ownership and any claim on the asset's salvage value. Thus, when compared to an outright purchase, leasing for the lessee generally effects the following conditions.

- The immediate need to disburse cash to purchase assets is eliminated.
- The immediate need to disburse cash with periodic lease (rent) payments is substituted.
- A claim on the tax benefits derived from ownership of the asset (that is, the depreciation tax shield and investment tax credits) is foregone.
- A claim against the asset's salvage value at the end of its service life is foregone.
- Incremental differences in operating or other expenses between the leasing and buying alternatives are incurred.

The **net advantage to leasing** equals the purchase cost of the asset minus the present value of incremental after-tax cash flows between the buying and leasing alternatives. The rate to use to discount cash flows associated with lease payments, incremental operating or other expenses, and the lost depreciation tax shield is the after-tax cost of the firm's debt. The rationale for using this rate is that the lease is substituting for secured debt financing to buy the asset. Thus, the rate charged on a secured loan represents the appropriate risk-adjusted discount rate.

You discount any lost salvage value at the required rate of return for the project. This higher rate reflects the greater riskiness of the future salvage value.

As an illustration, assume that Francisco Mining needs a new computer system. The system can be leased for $35,000 annually at the *beginning* of each year for five years. Thus, the cash flows represent an *annuity due*. Francisco's tax rate is 30 percent and the company can borrow money at 11 percent to purchase a computer system. The after-tax cost of debt is 7.7 percent: 11 percent $\times$ (1 − 0.30). The NPV of leasing is −$106,192.

$$\text{NPV} = -\$35,000 \times (1 - 0.30) \times \frac{1 - (1 + 0.077)^{-5}}{0.077} \times (1 + 0.077)$$

$$= -\$24,500 \times 4.0245 \times 1.077$$

$$= -\$106,192$$

Now suppose the price of buying a similar computer system is a cash outflow of $140,000. The computer would be depreciated $28,000 per year: $140,000 ÷ 5 years. A

Lease. A contractual agreement between the owner of an asset (lessor) and the user of the asset (lessee), which calls for the lessee to pay the lessor an established lease payment.

Operating lease. A lease in which the present value of the lease payments is less than 90 percent of the initial cost of the asset; the life of the lease is less than 75 percent of the economic life of the asset; no bargain purchase option exists in the lease; and no transfer of ownership of the lease asset to the user exists.

Financial (capital) lease. A long-term, noncancelable lease that has many characteristics of debt. The lease obligation is shown directly on the balance sheet.

Net advantage to leasing. The difference between the cost to purchase the asset and the present value of lease payments.

salvage value of $1000 is expected at the end of five years. The required rate of return for discounting the salvage value is 12 percent. Using these data, we find the NPV of buying is −$105,797.

$$\begin{aligned} \text{NPV} = &-\text{Purchase price} + \text{present value of depreciation tax shield} \\ &+ \text{present value of salvage value} \\ &- \text{present value of tax adjustment on salvage value} \\ = &-\$140,000 + \$28,000 \times 0.30 \times \frac{1 - (1 + 0.077)^{-5}}{0.077} \\ &+\$1000 \times (1 + 0.12)^{-5} - (\$1000 - \$0) \times 0.30 \times (1 + 0.12)^{-5} \\ = &-\$140,000 + \$8400 \times 4.0245 + \$1000 \times 0.5674 - \$300 \times 0.5674 \\ = &-\$140,000 + \$33,806 + \$567 - \$170 \\ = &-\$140,000 + \$34,203 \\ = &-\$105,797 \end{aligned}$$

The advantage of buying over leasing is $395 (= \$106,192 − \$105,797), which is basically the same as the NPV of the after-tax salvage value, $397 (= \$567 − \$170). In this case, management should determine how likely it is that the salvage value will be realized before deciding that buying is the better decision. If the government offers an investment tax credit (ITC) for buying computers, the buying alternative would be improved, since the ITC is a cash inflow to the owner of the asset.

15.4.5 Abandonment Decision

FTG Steel Company has several plants located throughout the country. Management is considering closing the Grand Rapids plant, which is FTG's oldest and most inefficient facility. The book value of the facility is $12 million, but the estimated salvage value is only $3 million. The latest income statement reflects typical results for the past several years at the Grand Rapids plant.

Most Recent Income Statement: Grand Rapids Plant ($000)

Sales		$21,000
Variable costs:		
Manufacturing	$ 7,000	
Selling	1,000	8,000
Margin before fixed costs		$13,000
Fixed costs:		
Plant:		
Supervision	$4,000	
Property taxes	2,000	
Depreciation	3,000	
Other	5,000	$14,000
Allocated from corporate		6,000 20,000
Before tax loss		$ (7,000)
Taxes (30%)		2,100
Net loss		$ (4,900)

At a recent operations review, one of the corporate officers commented on the latest plant report, noting that the evidence overwhelmingly supports closing the plant. Further, the executive stated, "We cannot continue to subsidize a $4.9 million loss at

Grand Rapids; it is a millstone around our neck. We should have closed it three years ago." Is this conclusion justified?

The results in the income statement are misleading for the decision under consideration. *To infer that company profits will increase by $4.9 million if the plant is closed assumes that all of the costs incurred and allocated to the Grand Rapids plant will be avoided if it is shut down.* Even without additional information, this result can be questioned seriously.

What are the relevant cash flows? The initial cash flow is the after-tax abandonment value of the facility. By closing the facility the company realizes an initial cash inflow of $5.7 million.

	$000
Salvage value	$3000
Tax adjustment on salvage value:	
(Book value − salvage value) × tax rate	
= ($12,000 − $3,000) × 0.30	2700
Initial cash flow	$5700

What are the annual operating cash flows? If the plant is closed, then there is little doubt that the variable costs and the fixed supervision costs would be avoided. The property taxes will be avoided only if the property is sold. There is a temptation to say the same thing about the depreciation figure. However, remember that depreciation represents an allocation of a cash disbursement made in the past and is a sunk cost. The annual tax shield of $900 (= $3000 depreciation × 0.30) provided by the depreciation would be lost by closing the facility. Assume that other fixed plant costs are annual cash outflows that would cease by closing the plant. The final item in the income statement is an allocated share of the costs of operating corporate headquarters. Will corporate costs go down by closing the Grand Rapids plant? Perhaps they will, but before deciding management must conduct a careful analysis. It is doubtful the corporate costs will be eliminated entirely. However, assume that corporate costs do not change. Furthermore, assume that if management continues to operate the facility as it currently does, constant cash flows can be generated for another four years.

The relevant operating cash flows from continued operations of the plant are $2.3 million. Based on this analysis, the plant is contributing cash flow to the company even though accounting income is negative.

		$000
Sales		$ 21,000
Avoidable costs:		
Variable	$8,000	
Supervision	4,000	
Property taxes	2,000	
Depreciation	3,000	
Other	5,000	22,000
Loss before taxes		$ (1,000)
Taxes (30%)		300
After-tax loss		$ (700)
Add back depreciation		3,000
Operating cash flow		$ 2,300

If the cost of capital is 13 percent, a decision to close the facility today has an NPV of $-$1.141 million. Closing the facility today realizes a cash inflow of $5.7 million but gives up future cash inflows of $2.3 million for each of the next four years. The present value of these lost cash flows is greater than the tax-adjusted salvage value of $5.7 million.

$$\text{NPV} = \$5,700,000 - \$2,300,000 \times \frac{1 - (1 + 0.13)^{-4}}{0.13}$$

$$= \$5,700,000 - \$2,300,000 \times 2.9745$$
$$= \$5,700,000 - \$6,841,350$$
$$= - \$1,141,350$$

Is this a good or bad decision? To answer, we need to find NPVs for closing the facility in each of the next four years. Assume that the current salvage value of $3 million declines $1 million each year that management defers closing the facility. The current book value of $12 million declines $3 million (in depreciation) each year. Thus, potential salvage amounts beyond the current time are:

		($000)		
Year	Book Value	Salvage Value	Tax Adjustment	Cash Flow
1	$9000	$2000	$2100	$4100
2	6000	1000	1500	2500
3	3000	0	900	900
4	0	0	0	0

Note:
1. Tax adjustment = (Book value – salvage value) × tax rate
2. Cash flow = Salvage value + tax adjustment.

Operating the facility one more year and then abandoning it results in an NPV of $-$36,000. By deferring the closure one year, management gives up the current abandonment cash inflow of $5.7 million in return for next year's operating cash inflow of $2.3 million and a $4.1 million abandonment value.

$$\text{NPV} = -\$5,700,000 + (\$2,300,000 + \$4,100,000) \times (1 + 0.13)^{-1}$$
$$= -\$5,700,000 + \$6,400,000 \times 0.8850$$
$$= -\$5,700,000 + \$5,664,000$$
$$= -\$36,000$$

Operating the facility for two more years results in an NPV of $94,380.

$$\text{NPV} = -\$5,700,000 + \$2,300,000 \times \frac{1 - (1 + 0.13)^{-2}}{0.13} + \$2,500,000 \times (1 + 0.13)^{-2}$$
$$= -\$5,700,000 + \$2,300,000 \times 1.6681 + \$2,500,000 \times 0.7831$$
$$= -\$5,700,000 + \$3,836,630 + \$1,957,750$$
$$= \$94,380$$

Continuing to operate the facility for three more years has an NPV of $354,550.

$$\text{NPV} = -\$5,700,000 + \$2,300,000 \times \frac{1 - (1 + 0.13)^{-3}}{0.13} + \$900,000 \times (1 + 0.13)^{-3}$$
$$= -\$5,700,000 + \$2,300,000 \times 2.3612 + \$900,000 \times 0.6931$$
$$= -\$5,700,000 + \$5,430,760 + \$623,790$$
$$= \$354,550$$

Operating the facility for four more years and then abandoning it when the salvage value is $0 has an NPV of $1,141,350.

$$NPV = -\$5,700,000 + \$2,300,000 \times \frac{1 - (1 + 0.13)^{-4}}{0.13}$$
$$= -\$5,700,000 + \$2,300,000 \times 2.9745$$
$$= -\$5,700,000 + \$6,841,350$$
$$= \$1,141,350$$

Based on this analysis, the decision should be to continue operating the facility for four more years.

If this were a real-world abandonment decision, the analysis would be more complicated. Some specific real-world issues to consider:

- Do the results in the income statement reflect an optimal operating strategy for the Grand Rapids plant?
- If multiple products and a variety of limited resources exist, then is the plant producing at its best feasible product mix?
- If the product mix can be improved, what are the odds that it can adjust efficiently to the optimum?
- Given that an optimal mix can be achieved, what would be the relevant income?
- Can the plant be modernized? If so, it is doubtful that the cost structure and resource constraints would be as they are now.
- Is it reasonable to assume the annual operating cash flow will remain constant at $2.3 million? Should the cash flow decline over time?
- Are there other costs associated with abandoning the facility, such as cleanup, severance pay for employees, and so on?

Detailed examination of these issues is beyond the scope of our discussion. However, let us mention a real situation that has strong ethical overtones and fits within the last point in the preceding list. Several years ago, Lykes-Youngstown Sheet and Tube Company terminated 5000 employees in the Youngstown, Pennsylvania area without warning. Its action eventually resulted in the loss of over 11,000 associated jobs in the community. Few people would deny that corporations sometimes have a right to move or close, but most would agree that the company has indirect obligations regarding the manner in which they do so, for instance, to warn the community in advance if possible. Here, too, the obligations at stake are indirect. Indirect obligations are difficult to bring into ethical focus.

A strategy that has worked out well for many companies and their employees is to spinoff the problem plant. The plant continues to operate but is no longer a financial burden on the company. The Financial Reality reading on page 572 discusses the issue. FTG management might consider it.

Comprehension Check

1. In the replacement of equipment example, why is the original cost of the equipment ignored in the analysis? Why is salvage value for the old equipment treated as a cash outflow in the terminal cash flow?

2. In the sales price of an order example, why is fixed overhead of $10 per unit excluded from the analysis?

SPIN WHILE YOU CAN

Taxes can have a significant impact on capital budgeting decisions. Spinoffs are just about the only way left to divest assets tax free. Wall Street loves them. The Internal Revenue Service doesn't.

Honeywell, May Department Stores, Quaker Oats, Whitman, and Santa Fe Pacific are among the companies that have distributed assets to their own shareholders. The reason? "Spinoffs are the only remaining way to divest assets tax free," says Scott Greiper, publisher of the *Spinoff Report*, a New York-based newsletter on the subject. Here's why:

In 1986 Congress, reacting to the merger wave, completed the repeal of the so-called general utilities doctrine. Under that doctrine, shareholders could sell the appreciated assets of a corporation at a profit, immediately distribute the proceeds in dividends and owe no corporate tax on the corporate gain. Now the corporation must pay a tax on the gain, and the shareholders must pay again when the company is liquidated.

Spinoffs escaped the 1986 crackdown. The theory here is that the spinoff isn't a sale but more like a reorganization, and the tax code doesn't tax reorganizations. So a parent firm can still divest a business by distributing 100 percent of its stock in it to shareholders. Investors pay tax when selling this stock, of course, but the corporation doesn't get hit as well.

Why do a spinoff? It is an excellent way "to get rid of a piece that just doesn't fit, or even shove a dog out the door," says Lydia Kess, tax expert at New York law firm Davis Polk & Wardwell. An example of the former is the Quaker Oats spinoff of Fisher-Price toys: The stable food company didn't want to be in the volatile toy business.

Another advantage of spinoffs is that the parent can extract a tax-free dividend prior to the spinoff up to the amount of its cost in the business that is spun off. May Department Stores, for example, pulled $263 million out of its discount retailer Venture Stores before divesting it. An alternative to this ploy is to have the parent shift a portion of its unsecured debt to the subsidiary.

Spinoff engineers can get even cleverer. When Affiliated Publications, owner of the *Boston Globe*, owned 47 percent of McCaw Cellular, on which it had a huge profit, it had no way to get rid of McCaw directly without owing $1 billion in tax. Affiliated couldn't spin off McCaw, because the law restricts spinoffs to situations where the parent owns 80 percent or more. So Affiliated spun off the newspaper from Affiliated, then merged the old parent into McCaw in exchange for McCaw stock. Shareholders of Affiliated wound up with stock in the corporation that owned the *Boston Globe* and shares in McCaw—two stocks instead of one—tax free.

Adapted from Laura Saunders, "Spin While You Can," *Forbes*, September 2, 1991, p. 88. Reprinted by permission of FORBES magazine. © Forbes Inc. 1991.

3. The make-or-buy example includes depreciation expense of $100,000. Since depreciation is a noncash flow, shouldn't it be excluded from the analysis?

4. In the lease-versus-buy decision, what are the relevant cash flows? Why are different discount rates used in analyzing the problem?

5. The abandonment decision example iteratively analyzed different abandonment dates. Why?

SUMMARY ▼▼▼▼▼▼▼▼▼▼▼▼

IDENTIFYING RELEVANT CASH FLOWS

- The most critical aspect of capital budgeting analysis is identification of the appropriate assumptions that support the forecasted numbers.
- Competitive factors play a key role in the estimation of cash flows associated with a proposed project. Events in the economic and political environment can be expected and should be looked at in different scenarios.
- Cash flows need to be separated into relevant and irrelevant categories. Only the relevant cash flows affect the outcome of the investment.
- Ignore interest expense in determining cash flows. The cost of capital accounts for the debt cost.
- Income taxes are a part of doing business and must be part of the analysis.
- Cash flows should include expected changes in inflation. The market-determined cost of capital rate will automatically incorporate inflation's effects.

CALCULATING CASH FLOWS

- Three categories of cash flows exist: initial cash outlay, annual operating cash flows, and terminal nonoperating cash flows.
- For each category of cash flow, all relevant cash flows must be identified, including tax adjustments and changes in net working capital investment associated with the decision.
- Although depreciation is a noncash expense, it does provide a tax shield. Any incremental depreciation amount times the tax rate represents a cash flow.

UNEQUAL LIVES PROBLEM

- A problem of choosing among mutually exclusive alternatives, where the economic lives of the alternatives differ and the investment is ongoing, requires the analyst to find a common denominator to make the appropriate selection.
- Common horizon analysis or equivalent annual annuity (EAA) analysis are useful techniques to use in making the decision. EAA is computationally easier than is common horizon analysis.

APPLICATIONS

- The application of TVM concepts to capital expenditure decisions aids in understanding the wealth contribution of investments.
- The analyst must carefully identify all relevant cash flows.

SELF-TEST PROBLEMS ▼▼▼▼▼▼▼▼▼▼▼

ST15-1. Jaffrey Company has spent $50,000 to develop a new product. The research director has just requested an additional $80,000 for the product's development. In addition, the controller estimates that $20,000 in engineering time would be allocated to the project. If the project were abandoned now, the engineers would be used in other work in the company. If the project is successful, management estimates that $30,000 in excess of the variable costs would be received for three years.

a. What are the relevant cash flows in determining whether to continue this project?

b. What would be the return on this project if its relevant cash flows are as you estimate?

ST15-2. United Manufacturing Ltd. is evaluating the purchase of a new machine to replace one presently in use. The following information relates to the disposal of the old machine and purchase of the new machine.

- The original cost of the old machine is $500,000.
- The book value of the old machine is $100,000 and it can be traded in for $150,000 today.
- The cost to remove the old machine is $10,000; it becomes a cost of the new machine and is not tax deductible.
- The new machine costs $800,000.
- Installation costs of the new machine are $25,000.
- Additional working capital requirements are $50,000.
- Straight-line depreciation is used for calculating cash flows.
- The marginal income tax rate is 30 percent.
- The expected useful life of the new machine is ten years.

Calculate the initial cash outlay for this proposed investment.

ST15-3. ACEM, Inc. is evaluating the purchase of equipment, which is expected to generate sales of $170,000 annually for five years. Operating cash costs are estimated at $80,000 annually. Annual depreciation on the equipment will be $40,000. ACEM's income tax rate is 34 percent. What are the expected annual operating cash flows from this investment on an after-tax basis?

ST15-4. In the proposed equipment purchase for ACEM, Inc. in Problem ST15-3, management estimates that the salvage value of the equipment will be $20,000 at the end of its life in year 5. The equipment will require a net increase in working capital of $10,000 at the beginning of its life, which will be recovered at the end of year 5. Assume the annual depreciation will reduce the equipment's book value to zero at the end of year 5. If ACEM's income tax rate is 34 percent, what is the terminal cash flow in year 5?

PROBLEMS ▼▼▼▼▼▼▼▼▼▼▼▼

IDENTIFYING RELEVANT CASH FLOWS

15-1. Arrand Corporation's management must decide whether to discontinue research and development (R&D) activities on a new consumer product or invest $100,000 in it. The firm's R&D director suggests that if the $100,000 is spent there is a high probability that a marketable product will result. The cash flows from this expected product are estimated by R&D personnel to be $125,000 more than its variable manufacturing costs.

Over the past two years, Arrand has already spent $200,000 on this product without success. If the decision is made to pursue the product further, the salaries of R&D personnel on the project will amount to $40,000, which is not included in the $100,000 estimate for new development funds. Should the product be abandoned now, the R&D personnel will be assigned to other activities within the corporation.

As the general manager of Arrand, what is your decision on whether to continue R&D on this new product? Explain your answer.

15-2. As general manager of Arrand Corporation, what would your decision be if you were faced with the same situation as in Problem 15-1 except that the two R&D persons would be released if the project were abandoned? This would save $30,000 of the $40,000 additional R&D salaries. The remaining $10,000 salary expense would continue because one person would be assigned to other duties. Explain your answer.

CALCULATING CASH FLOWS

15-3. The Rayo Corporation's management is evaluating the purchase of a new piece of machinery to replace an old machine. The new machine costs $80,000, including installation costs. The old machine has an estimated salvage value of $5000, which is its book value. Because of greater efficiency of the new machine, raw materials inventories could be reduced by $12,000. The firm's tax rate is 35 percent. No investment tax credit would apply to this investment. What would be Rayo's initial investment in this new piece of machinery?

15-4. Owen Sloan Contracting purchased equipment ten years ago for $1 million and subsequently depreciated it to a book value of $600,000. If the company sells the property for $1.2 million and has a marginal tax rate of 40 percent and a capital gains rate of 25 percent, determine the tax on the recapture of depreciation and the long-term capital gain tax liability if it sells the property.

15-5. Tempe Refinishers has ordinary income before taxes of $150,000, a recapture of depreciation of $30,000, and a $20,000 long-term capital gain. Determine the firm's tax liability if the marginal tax rate is 30 percent and the capital gains rate is one half the marginal rate.

15-6. Visual Systems Corporation is considering the sale of a machine that originally was purchased for $150,000 and has a book value of $75,000. The marginal tax rate is 30 percent, whereas the capital gains rate is 20 percent.

a. Determine the company's tax liability based on selling the machine for $200,000.
b. What is the liability if the machine is sold for $40,000?

15-7. Margotta Technical, Inc. is considering the construction of a new facility. Information relating to the current facility is as follows:

	Book Value	Sale Price
Land	$ 200,000	$5,000,000
Buildings	550,000	(120,000)*
Equipment	1,000,000	750,000

*Cost to demolish old buildings.

Sale prices do not exceed initial cost.

Costs relating to the new facility are as follows:

	Purchase Price	Related Costs	
Land	$4,000,000	$660,000	real estate fees and taxes
Buildings	7,200,000	320,000	taxes and interest during construction are capitalized
Equipment	3,200,000	800,000	installation
Additional working capital	500,000		

For tax purposes, all equipment has a life of five years. Depreciation is on a straight-line basis with a zero salvage value. The company's tax bracket is 34 percent.

a. Determine the net out-of-pocket cost to purchase the new facility.
b. Suppose the new equipment qualifies for a 10 percent investment tax credit (ITC). How does the ITC affect your answer to part (a)?

15-8. Berry Manufacturing has decided to purchase a new machine for its business. The following facts relate to the disposal of the old machine and purchase of the new:

- The original cost of the old machine is $1,000,000.
- The book value of the old machine is $200,000 and it can be traded in for $450,000; it is fully depreciated.
- The cost to remove the old machine is $15,000.
- The new machine costs $1,750,000.
- Installation costs of the new machine are $137,500.
- Additional working capital requirements are $25,000.
- Straight-line depreciation is used for calculating cash flows.
- The marginal income tax rate is 40 percent.
- The expected useful life of the new machine is 20 years.

Calculate the initial cash outlay.

15-9. Johnston, Inc.'s management is considering the purchase of a new fleet of delivery trucks. The new trucks would cost a total of $300,000. The company's maintenance garage would have to increase its inventory of spare parts by $25,000 if the new trucks are acquired. The old delivery trucks could be sold for $60,000. Their current book value is $40,000. Johnston's income tax rate is estimated to be 30 percent. No investment tax credit would apply to this investment. What would be Johnston's initial investment in the new fleet of trucks?

15-10. Rayo Corporation's management estimates that incremental cash flows from operations before taxes, interest, and depreciation amount to $20,000 annually from the new machine referred to in Problem 15-3. The annual incremental depreciation charge for the new machine is $16,000. These cash flows are expected to continue for the five-year life of the machine. The firm's income tax rate is 35 percent. What are the annual operating cash flows from this investment on an after-tax basis?

15-11. Geraldo Company is evaluating the purchase of equipment, which should produce cash flow from operations before taxes, interest, and depreciation of $25,000 annually for three years. Annual depreciation on the equipment will be $20,000. Geraldo's income tax rate is 30 percent. What are the expected operating cash flows from this investment on an after-tax basis?

15-12. Salvage value of the equipment Geraldo is considering in Problem 15-11 is estimated to be $5000 at the end of the third year. At the beginning of this investment's life, about $8000 more working capital will be required to support a higher level of production and sales. This working capital will be recovered at the end of the equipment's life as inventories are reduced and additional accounts receivable are collected. Assuming that the annual depreciation charge in Problem 15-11 reduces the book value of the equipment to zero at the end of the third year, what is the terminal cash flow? Do not include the annual operating cash flow in your calculation.

UNEQUAL LIVES PROBLEM

15-13. Ms. Bosworth is analyzing two computer systems to improve the monitoring of accounts receivable. The systems are mutually exclusive and assumed to be ongoing. So far, her analysis reveals the following, using a cost of capital of 12 percent:

Period	System #1	System #2
0	−$20,000	−$20,000
1	24,000	0
2		0
3		0
4		34,980
NPV	1,429	2,230
IRR	20%	15%
PI	1.07	1.11

a. Based on the preceding analysis for NPV, IRR, and PI, discuss which system is better.
b. Rank the two systems using an appropriate analytical model.
c. If the systems were not ongoing, which one should be selected, and why?

15-14. The Keltner Roofing Company wants to add to its trucking fleet to improve customer service. It has a choice of two models:

• Model 4S4: eight-year life, cost of $26,000, and net cash inflow of $12,000 per year.

• Model 4XS: ten-year life, cost of $38,000, and net cash inflow of $15,000 per year.

Assume that each truck will be replaced at the end of its life by a model with the same cost and future benefits. If the Keltner Company's cost of capital is 18 percent, which is the better model to choose?

15-15. Angela is planning to get into the nursery business. She is considering two plans.

Plan 1: Build a modest greenhouse now and enlarge it later. The construction cost is $300,000. The expected cost of the enlargement at the end of five years is $200,000. Maintenance during the first five years is expected to be $5000 per year.

Plan 2: Build a large greenhouse now at a cost of $400,000. Maintenance is estimated at $8000 per year for the first six years.

Angela's cost of capital is 12 percent.

a. Ignore depreciation and tax effects. What is the net present value of each plan?

b. How much is the equivalent annual amount of each plan? Which plan should she accept?

c. If straight-line depreciation is used over each project's life, and the tax rate is 30 percent, does your decision change?

15-16. Halifax Manufacturing is trying to establish a replacement policy for a lathe; managers forecast the following characteristics:

	0	1	2	3	4
			Year		
Purchase cost	$5000				
Terminal value		$4000	$3600	$3000	$2000
Net operating cash flow		2000	1800	1600	1400

All cash flows are after taxes. The firm's cost of capital for evaluating the lathe is 10 percent.

a. Find the net present values for keeping the lathe one year, two years, three years, and four years.

b. Effectively, each replacement policy represents a rival, mutually exclusive project. What is the optimal replacement period, given that the projects are of different lives, mutually exclusive, and ongoing?

5-17. The Bari Company needs to buy a new machine for its metal stamping operation. The after-tax net cash flows from using the machine are $21,000 per year. The machine could be retained for five years or replaced at any point at a replacement cost of $60,000. The secondhand prices (salvage values) for selling such machines are as follows:

	1	2	3	4	5
			Years Old		
Salvage value	$50,000	$42,500	$37,500	$30,000	$16,000

What is the optimal replacement policy assuming a 10 percent cost of capital? (*Hint:* Calculate EAA for each year.)

15-18. DeGroot Fastners is evaluating two mutually exclusive projects with the following expected cash flows before depreciation but after taxes:

Period	Project #1	Project #2
0	$-$20,000	$-$27,000
1	15,000	12,500
2	16,500	13,875
3		15,401

DeGroot needs the use of this type of asset for at least six years. The company's production engineer expects to be able to replace each asset with a similar asset at the end of its life. He believes the costs and expected future cash flows will be similar for the replacements. Each machine is depreciated straight-line over its life and has zero salvage value. The company's tax rate is 40 percent.

Which asset should be chosen if the company's cost of capital is 12 percent?

APPLICATIONS

15-19. The William Brandt Company considers an investment that falls in the three-year category for straight-line depreciation purposes. However, the manufacturing engineer estimates that the economic life of the investment is ten years. The annual pretax cash flows are $30 before depreciation and the initial investment is $120 plus $40 investment in working capital. The corporate tax rate is 40 percent and the after-tax cost of capital is 10 percent. Should the firm undertake the investment?

15-20. Conti Corporation is considering a new machine that costs $30,000. It has a life of ten years and will be depreciated straight-line to zero salvage value. Use of the machine will result in an increase in sales of $40,000 per year. Concurrently, operating expenses will rise by $32,000 per year. The higher production rate should cause net working capital to increase $5000. Assume that Conti's tax rate is 30 percent. Determine the expected initial cash outlay, the annual operating cash flows, and the terminal cash flow.

15-21. The Contini Company is considering two options. Buy a machine for $100, which induces a pretax cash flow (ignoring depreciation) of $50 during the next four years. The salvage value of the machine at the end of the fourth year is $30. Alternatively, buy the machine and use it for two years and then sell the machine at the end of the second year at an estimated market price of $80. The company cannot repeat the investment. The tax rate is 40 percent and the cost of capital is 11 percent. Annual depreciation is computed using straight-line and assumes a zero salvage value. What is the preferred option?

15-22. The Malone Truck Company is considering opening a new loading dock at a cost of $280,000 for new equipment. The life of the new equipment is seven years. Depreciation will be straight-line using the $280,000 cost. A salvage value of $10,000 is expected at the end of seven years. Gross annual receipts are expected to be $250,000 and the annual costs of the new unit are estimated as follows:

Direct labor costs	$65,000
Fuel	50,000
Electricity	17,000
Direct administrative costs	23,000
Fixed overhead costs	26,000
Pro rata share of general administrative costs	29,000

It is anticipated that the company's net receipts from its other loading docks will decrease by $25,000 annually when the new dock is installed. The corporate tax rate is 30 percent.

a. How much is the initial investment, the terminal cash flow, and the annual operating cash flow for the proposed project?

b. If the cost of capital is 15 percent, is it worthwhile for the company to open the new loading dock?

15-23. Neil Credit, Inc. is considering replacing a machine that has a zero book value but could be sold now for $1000. If this machine is used three more years, its salvage value will be $0. A new machine costing $6000 would have a useful life of three years and a salvage value of $300 at the end of three years. The machine would result in cost savings before taxes and depreciation of $2200 per year. Depreciation would be on a straight-line basis, assuming a zero salvage value. If the tax rate is 40 percent and the firm's cost of capital is 10 percent, should management purchase the new machine?

15-24. Dagny Corporation is evaluating whether to replace a printing press with a newer model, which, owing to more efficient operation, will reduce operating costs from $40,000 to $32,000 per year. Sales are $60,000 annually and are not expected to change. The old press cost $60,000 when purchased nearly five years ago, had an estimated useful life of 15 years, zero salvage value at the end of its useful life and is being depreciated straight-line. At present, its market value is estimated to be $40,000, if sold outright. The new press costs $80,000 and would be depreciated straight-line to a zero salvage value over a ten-year life. However, management expects to be able to sell the new press for $15,000 at the end of ten years. The corporation has a 40 percent marginal tax rate and a cost of capital of 15 percent.

a. Determine the initial investment to acquire the new press assuming the old press is sold at the present time.

b. Calculate the incremental annual operating cash flows resulting from buying the new press.

c. Calculate the terminal cash flow.

d. Calculate the net present value of buying the new press. What should management decide?

15-25. Barkley Mills is considering expanding its production of a new yarn called hoops. The plant is expected to cost $10 million and have a life of five years and no residual value. It will be ready for operation in one year. About $1 million has already been spent on development costs of the product.

The forecast for the new yarn is as follows:

	Year ($ Million)				
	#1	#2	#3	#4	#5
Sales	$12	$14	$14	$14	$14
Costs, including depreciation	10	11	11	11	11
Profit before tax	$ 2	$ 3	$ 3	$ 3	$ 3

The corporate tax rate is 30 percent. Depreciation has been calculated on a straight-line basis. Additional working capital of $0.6 million is required at the beginning of the project.

a. Prepare a statement showing the incremental cash flows of the project relevant to a decision concerning whether or not to proceed with the construction of the new plant.

b. Compute the net present value of the project using a 10 percent discount rate. Should Barkley take on the project?

15-26. Lynx Conveyor Ltd. is considering buying a machine to make bearings. The machine costs $1 million and has a life of five years. Scrap value of the machine at the end of its life is expected to be $200,000. Depreciation will be based on the straight-line method ignoring the scrap value. An investment of $150,000 in working capital will be needed initially. The accountant has prepared the following estimated annual accounting profit for the project.

Bearing sales	$1,400,000
Materials and labor	(800,000)
Depreciation	(200,000)
Fixed overhead allocated	(250,000)
Annual profit before taxes	$ 150,000

The company's discount rate is 10 percent and it pays a marginal income tax rate of 40 percent. What is the net present value of the project?

15-27. Indiana Popcorn Ltd. is planning to introduce a new brand of popcorn. The sales manager expects the new product to have the following annual cash flows before the depreciation tax shield and taxes:

Sales	$400,000
Materials and labor	150,000
Profits	$250,000

The company will need to buy machinery costing $600,000. It will have zero salvage value. Both the economic and depreciable lives of the machine are five years. The firm's cost of capital is 12 percent and its tax rate is 30 percent.

a. What is the net present value of the project?

b. Clearly, there is no certainty that the project will turn out as assumed. Management believes it would be instructive to consider the following scenarios:

• A shortfall in sales to $200,000 per year with an associated reduction in expenses of $50,000.
• An increase in wages and materials costs to $200,000.
• Curtailment of the project in three years, with salvage value of $100,000 for the machine.

Find the impact on net present value of each scenario. Treat each scenario as mutually exclusive.

15-28. James Amgen is considering the acquisition of a machine with an estimated cost of $60,000. The machine would replace an existing machine that has been fully depreciated and has a $0 salvage value. The old machine can still be used for a number of years. However, the old machine has a capacity of producing 10,000 units. The plant engineer expects the new machine to:

- Reduce labor costs $0.90 per unit.
- Reduce net working capital investment $5500.
- Have a salvage value of $5000 after six years.

The accounting department has provided the following income statement showing the profit for the *current* level of production of 10,000 units. Utilities and other expenses shown in the cost of sales are considered fixed expenses.

Sales		$100,000
Cost of sales:		
Labor	$23,000	
Materials	10,000	
Utilities	8,000	
Other	17,000	58,000
Sales expenses		28,000
Depreciation		1,000
Earnings before taxes		$13,000
Taxes (40%)		5,200
Earnings after taxes		$ 7,800

The sales manager indicates that there have been some backorders for the product and that the company could easily increase sales volume 10 percent annually until the capacity volume of 12,100 units per year for the new machine is reached. However, marketing research indicates that the market will only last another six years. Management expects that the total sales expense will be the same with the additional sales volume.

The treasurer's office requires a 15 percent after-tax hurdle rate for projects of this type. The new machine would be depreciated over a five-year life to a zero salvage value for tax purposes using the following depreciation rates for years 1 through 5, respectively: 15 percent, 22 percent, 21 percent, 21 percent, and 21 percent. Note that the machine is expected to last six years.

What is the net present value of this decision? Should management purchase the new machine?

15-29. Five years ago, Riley Bread Company purchased an oven for $60,000. The projected life of the oven was 15 years with zero salvage value. The current book value of the oven is $40,000, whereas the current market value is only $20,000. A new oven is available that has a purchase price of $90,000, including installation costs. The oven has a projected life of 15 years, but can be fully depreciated in five years for tax purposes at the following rates: 15 percent, 22 percent, 21 percent, 21 percent, and 21 percent, for years 1 through 5, respectively. The expected salvage value of the new oven at the end of 15 years is $5000. Mr. Riley expects the new oven to reduce annual operating costs before taxes and depreciation by $14,000. The firm's marginal tax rate is 40 percent. Any capital gains are taxed at 20 percent. Riley's cost of debt is 10 percent and his after-tax cost of capital is 12 percent.

a. Compute the initial and terminal cash outflows for the new oven.
b. Calculate the annual operating cash flows if the new oven is purchased.
c. Calculate the net present value of the investment. Should Riley buy the new oven?

15-30. John Burke, Inc. is considering leasing a machine for eight years at an annual rental of $35,000. The alternative is to purchase the machine for $190,000. Assume a corporate tax rate of 40 percent, an after-tax interest rate of 5 percent, straight-line depreciation, and $0 salvage value. Also assume that no other costs (for example, maintenance, insurance) are affected by the decision to purchase. Should Burke buy or lease the machine?

15-31. Rolland Company is confronted with two mutually exclusive alternatives: Buy a machine which costs $25,000 and has an economic life of ten years; or lease it for $4500 a year. Assume straight-line depreciation, 30 percent corporate income tax rate, no salvage value, and an after-tax interest rate of 6 percent. Should the firm buy or lease the machine?

15-32. Suppose the federal government passed a new law that stipulated that depreciation is not tax deductible. What would be the impact of such a law on the willingness of firms to lease equipment?

15-33. Ainge Basketball Corporation can purchase a machine for $60,000 to make basketballs, financed by a 12 percent bank loan. The machine would be depreciated straight-line over its useful life of three years to a zero salvage value. Annual operating savings of $25,000 before depreciation, interest, and taxes are expected. The firm's after-tax cost of capital is 18 percent and its marginal tax rate is 40 percent.

   a. Calculate the net present value of the machine.
   b. Ainge can lease the machine at an annual rental cost of $21,510, payable at the end of each period. Calculate the net present value of leasing the machine.

LIBRARY ASSIGNMENT

15-34. Using the *Business Periodicals Index* or by examining news stories in publications such as *Business Week, The Wall Street Journal,* or *Fortune,* prepare a one-page summary report on a specific business decision where the identification of relevant cash flows would be critical to evaluating the project. Such a report might involve a merger, discontinuation of a product line or division, or deciding to lease equipment rather than purchase it.

COMPREHENSIVE PROBLEM ▼▼▼▼▼▼▼▼▼▼▼▼

15-35. a. The management of William Brandt Corporation must decide whether to discontinue research and development (R&D) activities on a new industrial product or invest an additional $200,000 in it. Project engineers believe that if the $200,000 is spent there is a high probability of a profitable product being developed. If the product is successfully developed, engineers estimate the present value of after-tax cash flows to be $240,000. Over the past two years, Brandt has already spent $100,000 on this product without success. If the decision is made to pursue the product further, the salaries of R&D personnel on the project will amount to $80,000, which is not included in the $200,000 estimate. If the product is abandoned now, these R&D engineers will be assigned to other activities in the company. Should Brandt continue R&D spending on this project? Explain your answer.

   Use the following information for parts (b) through (f).

The Brandt company is evaluating a machinery investment which falls in the IRS's three-year category for straight-line depreciation purposes. However, engineers estimate the economic life of the asset to be ten years. Salvage value is expected to be $0 at the end of ten years. The forecast for annual pretax operating cash flows before depreciation is $30,000. The machine costs $120,000. The higher output of the machine would require a one-time increase of $40,000 in net working capital at the time the machine is bought. The working capital would be recovered at the end of its economic life. The company's tax rate is 40 percent and its cost of capital is 10 percent. No investment tax credit is available.

 b. What is the initial investment in this project?
 c. What is the project's annual operating cash flow?
 d. What is the investment's terminal cash flow?
 e. What is the expected net present value of this investment?
 f. Should the firm undertake the investment?

ANSWERS TO SELF-TEST PROBLEMS ▼▼▼▼▼▼▼▼▼▼▼▼▼

ST15-1. The only relevant cash flows to consider are those that specifically result from continuing the project. These are the $80,000 additional development cost and the prospective annual contributions of $30,000 for three years. The manager is faced with evaluating the likelihood that the expenditure of $80,000 will result in a marketable product and that the annual discounted $30,000 cash inflows will occur. If the net present value is positive for a chosen cost of capital, then value is added to the firm by investing the $80,000.

The $50,000 already spent on the project is a sunk cost and is irrelevant to the present decision. The $20,000 in engineering time is also irrelevant, since this would be spent on other projects.

The internal rate of return for the project is about 6 percent.

ST15-2.	New machine's cost	+$(800,000)
	Installation costs	+(25,000)
	Cost to remove old machine	+(10,000)
	Working capital increase	+(50,000)
	Salvage value of old machine	150,000
	Tax adjustment:	
	(Salvage value − book value) × tax rate	
	($150,000 − $100,000) × 0.30	+(15,000)
	Initial cash outlay	+$(750,000)

ST15-3.	Incremental sales	$ 170,000
	Incremental costs	+(80,000)
	Depreciation	+(40,000)
	Profit before taxes	$ 50,000
	Taxes (34%)	17,000
	Profit after taxes	$ 33,000
	+ Depreciation	40,000
	Annual operating cash flow	$ 73,000

An alternative approach is:

Incremental sales × (1 − tax rate)
  − Incremental operating costs × (1 − tax rate)
  + Depreciation on new asset × tax rate
  = Annual operating cash flow

$170,000 × 0.66	$112,200
− $80,000 × 0.66	−(52,800)
+ $40,000 × 0.34	13,600
= Annual operating cash flow	$ 73,000

ST15-4.

Salvage value of equipment	$ 20,000
Tax on gain from salvage value	
$20,000 × 0.34	(6,800)
Recovery of net working capital	10,000
Terminal cash inflow	$ 23,200

Video Case 15

Golden Arches In Red Square

from *Primetime*, January 25, 1990

Chapter 15 discusses the importance of identifying the relevant cash flows associated with a proposed investment in order to make a sound financial decision. Estimating cash flows, or any type of forecasting, requires making educated guesses about the future. Some costs need not be estimated at all; we know them with certainty. For example, the cost of machines, equipment, or buildings can be specified to the penny by the manufacturer. Similarly, long-term supply or sales contracts reduce uncertainty about these costs or revenues. But not everything can be contracted for. Inflation, changes in tastes or demand, competitive response, and changes in the political, legal, or tax environment are just a few of the factors that make forecasting cash flows difficult.

Textbook examples often make it appear that identifying a project's relevant cash flows is easy. As this video of McDonald's expansion into Russia shows, in real life estimating cash flows is difficult and fraught with uncertainty and unexpected surprises. The video highlights the opening of the world's largest McDonald's restaurant in Moscow after 14 years and $50 million of investment. In the United States and Canada, opening a McDonald's franchise follows an established formula, so costs can be estimated within a few percent. McDonald's of Canada had no script to follow when it decided to expand into Russia. However, attracted by the enormous Russian market, and running out of expansion opportunities at home, the company persevered.

McDonald's, like most franchises, provides a product of known quality. When traveling you know that you won't get *haute cuisine* at McDonald's, but you also know that you won't get a terrible meal either. In Canada and the United States McDonald's maintains quality by demanding products of a particular quality from suppliers. The quality of some Russian commodities did not satisfy the needs of McDonald's, so the company integrated vertically. That is, they set up their own subsidiaries to supply the restaurant with food. Finding Russian beef had too much fat and was not always available in the quantities needed, the company established its own cattle herds and breeding program. Finding the potatoes too small to make the desired size of french fries, the company brought in seed for the russet potatoes it uses in North America. Then it built a plant to process the food and bake hamburger buns and dessert pies. If foreseen, each of these steps would be a relevant cost in the net present value analysis.

To assure that the Moscow McDonald's embodied the company's trademark of fast, polite service, the company implemented extensive training programs for its Russian employees. Without personal experience of fast-food service, the employees had to learn an entirely new way of working. Fortunately for McDonald's, Russia is full of well-educated, underemployed people, and the wages offered (30¢ per hour) are a bit more than a medical doctor in Russia earns!

A final cash flow consideration for any foreign expansion is how profits will be repatriated (or sent home). McDonald's earns Russian rubles, which cannot leave the country. Therefore, profits can be sent to Canada only by buying Russian products with rubles and selling them for U.S. or Canadian dollars. Just another complexity to add to the analysis!

Study Questions

1. Given the enormous cost of establishing this restaurant, McDonald's may never earn a profit on it. Can you think of reasons that the company, which is obviously very sophisticated, continued this project to completion? What other opportunities might it open up for McDonald's?

2. Do you think McDonald's is shrewd in publicizing how much it cost to get established in Russia? Explain why or why not. Think about potential competitors.

CHAPTER 16

Short-Term Business Investment

"*How to go broke . . . while making a profit.*" This eye-catching title introduced an article in *Business Week* magazine about 40 years ago.[1] The article is old but its message is timely: Manage investments in short-term assets or suffer the consequences. Companies that experience a lag between cash expenditures to produce goods and cash collections from selling goods can have serious cash flow problems. A growing firm must generally produce more units than it sells during a period if it is to have sufficient quantities of inventory on hand for future sales. The cash needed for this higher level of production may well exceed the cash received from the prior period's sales. A cash shortage may develop and, if serious enough, the firm may actually go broke while still showing an accounting profit.

Short-term investment in a firm represents resources committed to cash, accounts receivable, and inventories.[2] Firms invest in cash in order to have funds available to make payments for various business transactions. They should attempt to minimize this investment. Extension of credit to customers is an investment in accounts receivable—it can be an important competitive tool. Nevertheless, granting credit should be done because it is profitable for the company to do so, not because competitors grant credit. Inventories, necessary to satisfy uncertain consumer demand, represent a major investment for manufacturing and wholesale companies. Control of this investment is critical to profitability of the firm.

Just as with long-term investment decisions, managers should solve short-term investment decisions within the framework of the net present value model. However,

---

[1] *Business Week,* April 28, 1956, pp. 46–54.

[2] The firm may also invest in *marketable securities* and *prepaid expenses,* but these items usually represent an immaterial portion of most firms' short-term investments. Marketable securities investments are usually for money-market instruments (see Chapter 6). Prepaid expenses represent cash outflows for services or supplies that will be consumed over a period of time. As the service or supply is consumed, the investment is written off as an expense in the company's income statement.

they seldom do. Instead, managers usually approach short-term investments through analysis of the various current assets using accounting ratios. For example, they compare the ratio of the firm's accounts receivable to sales with competitors' ratios for the same thing or to published industry standards. As we have learned, however, the net present value approach and accounting ratios lead to the same result only by coincidence. As discussed in Chapter 14, the accounting rate of return does not measure an investment's wealth-creation capability. Unfortunately, neither do other accounting-based ratios.

After studying this chapter, you should understand:

- How different models for determining investment in cash, receivables, and inventories operate.
- What methods managers can use to monitor investments in short-term assets to improve financial decisions in their quest to maximize shareholder value.

We will examine the financing of these short-term investments in the next chapter.

 ## 16.1 INVESTMENT IN CASH

Management of cash is the single most important short-term investment activity. To maintain a minimum cash balance that is consistent with a firm's financial goals, managers must have a solid understanding of the *economic value of cash* as well as good information about the business's specific liquidity needs. The **economic value of cash** is simply the cost of retaining money (not lending cash out for someone else to use) or the savings from retaining money (not having to borrow it). In this sense, cash is an investment.

> **Economic value of cash.** The expected return that a firm gives up when it invests in cash rather than in a risk-free security.

Management's primary motive for investing in cash is to have funds available to finance normal transactions, such as payments for supplies and wages. The desired cash balance depends on the size of the firm and the timing of cash inflows and outflows. Some funds may be held for precautionary purposes, as a buffer against the uncertainty of a changing industry and economy. However, most precautionary balances are normally provided by the ability to borrow from a bank.

An important aspect of cash management is the firm's banking system. The firm receives cash, as well as disburses it, through the banking system. In the next several pages, we will describe the banking system and examine models that can be used to determine the optimal cash balance, the one that minimizes the costs associated with holding cash.

16.1.1 An Overview of the Banking System

Major decisions in cash management pertain to the banking system, including bank relations, collections and disbursements, and cash concentration. Bank relations has to do with the design of the firm's banking network, the choice of banks with which the firm will do business, and the particular services the firm will buy from each bank. Small firms may only use a single bank, whereas large corporations may do business with several banks. The banking system is critically important to the firm's collections and disbursements efforts.

> **Float.** Checks in the process of collection.

For many firms, a primary goal of the firm's banking system is to manage *float*. **Float** refers to the length of time that it takes checks, once mailed, to become collected funds. There are three types of float involved in the process. *Mail float* occurs when a customer mails a check and lasts until the firm receives the check. *Processing float* occurs when the firm receives the check; it is the length of time it takes to perform the clerical and accounting tasks and deposit the check in the bank. Once deposited the check incurs *clearing float* (also called *transit* or *Fed float*). This float is the time it takes the customer's check to clear on the customer's bank account through the Federal Reserve System. Figure 16.1 illustrates the types of float and the check-clearing process. Illustration 16.1 provides an example of how to reduce float. Management's strategy is to reduce float associated with collecting accounts receivable (*receipt float*) and increase float associated with paying accounts payable (*disbursement float*).

FIGURE 16.1
FLOAT AND CHECK CLEARING

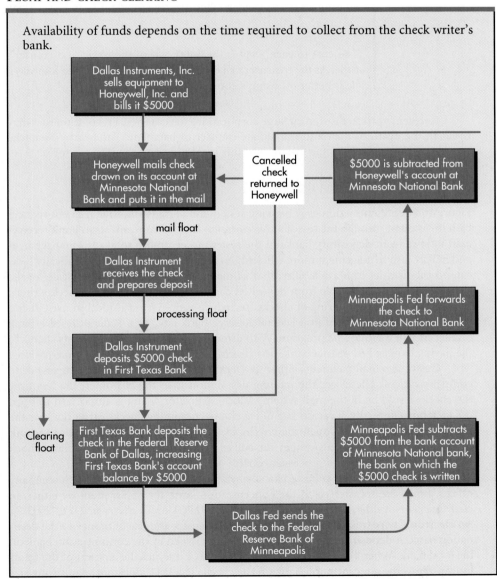

Availability of funds depends on the time required to collect from the check writer's bank.

Dallas Instruments, Inc. sells equipment to Honeywell, Inc. and bills it $5000

Honeywell mails check drawn on its account at Minnesota National Bank and puts it in the mail

mail float

Dallas Instrument receives the check and prepares deposit

processing float

Dallas Instrument deposits $5000 check in First Texas Bank

Clearing float

First Texas Bank deposits the check in the Federal Reserve Bank of Dallas, increasing First Texas Bank's account balance by $5000

Dallas Fed sends the check to the Federal Reserve Bank of Minneapolis

Cancelled check returned to Honeywell

$5000 is subtracted from Honeywell's account at Minnesota National Bank

Minneapolis Fed forwards the check to Minnesota National Bank

Minneapolis Fed subtracts $5000 from the bank account of Minnesota National bank, the bank on which the $5000 check is written

ILLUSTRATION 16.1

The cost of float

Florida Food Company has a contract with Progresso Limited, a grocery chain in the Dominican Republic, to deliver a specified number of cases of canned goods weekly. Progresso is required to make a $1 million payment every Friday morning. The treasurer of Florida Food has two choices: Deposit the check in a Dominican Republic bank, in which case the funds will not be available for investment until four days later; send a courier to pick up the check on Friday morning and return the same day to Miami, in which case, the funds will be available for investment the same day. The cost for the courier's services is $400. The treasurer's opportunity cost of money is 8 percent annually.

By eliminating four days of float, the treasurer can immediately invest the $1 million. The interest earned for four days is $889:

$$\$1,000,000 \times 8\% \times 4 \div 360 = \$889$$

The cost to earn $889 is the $400 cost of the ticket and courier's time. As the treasurer can earn more than $400 over the four days, he is better off using a courier.

In recent years, treasurers of large corporations have started a revolution that may result in the death of float and immediate transfer of payment. The nearby Financial Reality reading provides some insight into this revolution and the impetus for it.

16.1.2 Cash Gathering and Disbursing

Concentration bank. A bank to which a company transfers all excess cash balances daily.

Direct send. The check-clearing process bypasses at least part of the normal Federal Reserve collection system in an effort to accelerate collection of funds.

Lock box. A post office box address to which credit customers mail payments.

Electronic wire transfer. A means of effecting the immediate transfer of funds from one bank account to an account at another bank.

Depository transfer check (DTC). An instrument used to transfer funds between bank accounts of the same firm. No signature is required. The DTC clears through the normal channels, similar to a check.

Figure 16.2 represents a domestic banking system for a large firm. Management reduces cash investment through the use of a *concentration bank*. A **concentration bank** receives cash inflows from depository banks in the system to centralize total cash management and makes cash management more efficient. A computer system will automatically indicate to the firm its cash availability; that is, managers are advised electronically of the actual cash balance available from deposited checks that have cleared on check writers' accounts. For quicker clearing of checks (to reduce Fed float), it is ideal to use either a concentration bank located in a Federal Reserve Bank city (or a Federal Reserve Bank branch city) or a *direct-send* program. With **direct sends,** the company presents checks to the paying bank, a Fed district bank, or a clearinghouse in its area for fast presentations.

Customers mail payments either to a *lock box* (that is, a post office address) or to company offices. The closer the mailing destination is to the customer, the less time the check should be in the mail system. A local depository bank is authorized to open the **lock box** (in reality, a canvas bag of envelopes containing checks earmarked for the bank) several times daily, open the envelopes, record customer information, and put the checks into the clearing system for collection on each customer's account. Lock boxes help reduce mail and processing float.

Once the checks are collected locally, whether by lock box or mailed to company offices, funds are transferred to the concentration bank for deployment by either an *electronic wire transfer,* a *depository transfer check (DTC),* or an *electronic DTC (EDTC).* An **electronic wire transfer** results in immediate transfer and use of money to the destination bank. A **depository transfer check** is a check issued by the concentration bank on the local bank. When the local bank receives the DTC, it writes the amount of the funds to transfer to the concentration bank on the check. The DTC does not require any signature, and collection is through the check-clearing collection system. An **EDTC** differs only in that the funds are transmitted electronically, thereby eliminating the mail float.

Company regional offices often use *zero-balance accounts* for their disbursements. A **zero-balance account (ZBA)** is an account that has a zero balance at the end of the day for all checks presented on the account. The concentration bank funds the ZBA on the day of presentation, not when checks are written.

16.1.3 Estimating Required Cash Balances

How much cash should the treasurer maintain? Several approaches exist for estimating these cash balances. Common techniques include: *ratio projection method; Baumol economic order quantity model;* and *Miller-Orr control limit model.*[3]

[3]See W. J. Baumol, "The Transaction Demand for Cash: An Inventory Theoretical Approach," *Quarterly Journal of Economics* (November 1952), pp. 545–546, and M. H. Miller and D. Orr, "A Model for the Demand for Money by Firms," *Quarterly Journal of Economics* (July 1968), pp. 413–435.

> **Electronic depository transfer check (EDTC).** An electronic version of the DTC. Funds are transferred by wire.
>
> **Zero-balance account (ZBA).** A demand-deposit account that has a zero balance at the end of the day. Checks presented against the account are covered by funds transferred from another account.

FIGURE 16.2

CONCENTRATION BANKING SYSTEM

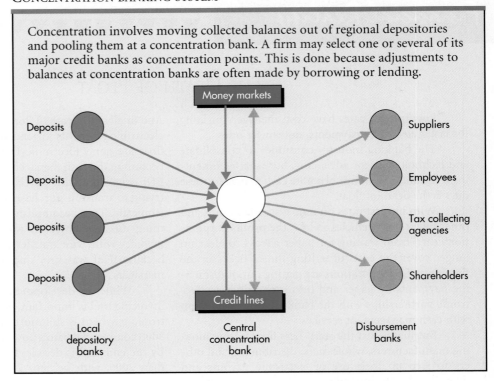

Concentration involves moving collected balances out of regional depositories and pooling them at a concentration bank. A firm may select one or several of its major credit banks as concentration points. This is done because adjustments to balances at concentration banks are often made by borrowing or lending.

Ratio projection method. The historical proportion of cash to sales to estimate the amount of cash that should be held.

RATIO PROJECTION METHOD. The **ratio projection method** assumes a fixed relationship between the cash balance and annual sales. An historical average is often used. For example, a treasury analyst for Eron, Inc. calculates the firm's average cash-to-sales ratio to be 5 percent. Since management forecasts sales of $20 million for the upcoming year, the projected cash balance is 0.05 × $20 million = $1 million. The weakness of this method is that it fails to consider any economies of scale in cash management. There is no reason that cash should increase or decrease in lock step with the level of sales.

Baumol EOQ model. A mathematical model for calculating the optimal cash order size. The model minimizes the total ordering and holding costs.

BAUMOL ECONOMIC ORDER QUANTITY (EOQ) MODEL. The **Baumol EOQ cash model** is consistent with maximizing economic value.[4] EOQ trades off the opportunity *cost of holding* idle cash balances against the *cost of ordering* (securing) cash. The more cash on hand, the less frequent are the transactions to secure cash. However, the larger the cash balance, the larger are holding costs because of foregone opportunities to invest the money in income-producing assets.

Without formal proof, the economic order quantity (that is, optimal) cash balance occurs wherever the holding costs equal the ordering costs. Mathematically, this optimum is given by:

[4]G. W. Gallinger and P. B. Healey, *Liquidity Analysis and Management,* 2nd ed. (Reading, MA: Addison-Wesley, 1991), pp. 499–500, show the EOQ model is a wealth-maximization model. They show also that accounting-based return on investment is not a wealth-creating approach.

Economic order quantity of cash

$$= \sqrt{\frac{2 \times \text{cost per order} \times \text{demand for cash}}{\text{opportunity cost per period}}} \qquad (16.1)$$

The Baumol EOQ model assumes:

- The treasurer knows the demand for cash for the planning period and uses cash at a constant rate.
- There is a fixed-order cost to replenish cash balances and replenishment is instantaneous.
- Cash balances incur an opportunity cost that equals the interest foregone on a risk-free asset.

If the amount of cash the firm gets with each order is the EOQ amount, then the firm's average cash investment is one half this amount:

$$\text{Average cash investment} = \text{EOQ} \div 2 \qquad (16.2)$$

The number of transactions during the period to replenish cash levels to the EOQ level is the total demand for cash for the period (D) divided by the EOQ cash amount:

$$\text{Number of transactions} = D \div \text{EOQ} \qquad (16.3)$$

The total cost of transactions is the dollar cost per transaction (c) times the number of transactions:

$$\text{Cost of transactions} = c \times D \div \text{EOQ} \qquad (16.4)$$

The cost for holding money is the foregone interest income of investing in cash; that is, the opportunity cost (v) times the average investment in cash:

$$\text{Holding cost} = v \times \text{EOQ} \div 2 \qquad (16.5)$$

Figure 16.3 depicts the model, and Illustration 16.2 takes us through the procedure.

ILLUSTRATION 16.2

Application of the Baumol model

The treasurer of Pitney, Inc. expects the demand for cash during the next six months to be $1,537,000. A treasury analyst estimates that it costs $50 for each cash transaction and the company's annual *effective* opportunity cost of funds is 8 percent, or 3.92 percent for six months: $(1.08)^{6/12} - 1 = 0.0392$.

Given these alternatives, the optimal cash replenishment level is $62,617.

Economic order quantity of cash

$$= \sqrt{\frac{2 \times \text{cost per order} \times \text{demand for cash}}{\text{opportunity cost per period}}}$$

$$= \sqrt{2 \times \$50 \times \$1,537,000 \div 0.0392}$$

$$= \$62,617$$

The average cash balance is one half of EOQ, or $31,309 (= $62,617 ÷ 2). There will be 24.5 (= $1,537,000 ÷ $62,617), or actually 25 transactions during the six-month period; about a transaction per week. Ordering costs are 25 × $50 = $1250.

FIGURE 16.3

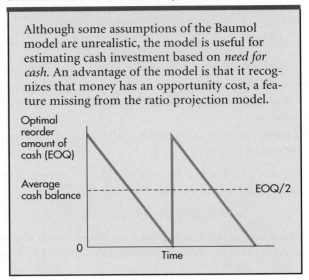

BAUMOL ECONOMIC ORDER QUANTITY CASH MODEL

Although some assumptions of the Baumol model are unrealistic, the model is useful for estimating cash investment based on *need for cash*. An advantage of the model is that it recognizes that money has an opportunity cost, a feature missing from the ratio projection model.

Holding costs are $31,309 \times 0.0392 = \$1227$. Normally, ordering and holding costs are equal at the EOQ level. However, since fractional orders are not possible, ordering costs do not equal holding costs in this example.

Miller-Orr model. A cash management control limit model that allows irregular cash patterns in order to minimize costs of investing in cash.

MILLER-ORR CONTROL LIMIT MODEL. The **Miller-Orr model** incorporates uncertainty into the estimate for investment in cash by allowing the cash balance to fluctuate within upper and lower control limits. The idea is that random fluctuations within the limits are normal. Unless the cash balance exceeds a limit, it is not necessary to transfer cash either to pay down a bank loan (when the upper limit is exceeded) or to borrow from the bank (when the cash balance falls below the lower limit). The control limits are set to minimize fixed costs associated with holding and ordering cash.[5]

Let's examine the model by assuming that its lower limit is a zero balance. The calculation of the upper limit depends on determining the *optimal return cash level* after either a transfer to cash or a transfer from cash, with the offset being to the firm's borrowings from the bank. The optimal return level is:

Optimal return cash level

$$= \sqrt[3]{\frac{3 \times \text{order cost} \times \text{variance of daily cash balance}}{4 \times \text{daily opportunity cost of funds}}} \qquad (16.6)$$

The *upper control limit (UCL)* for the model is three times the optimal return cash level:

[5]The theoretical derivation of the model assumes a portfolio of marketable securities. Very few firms invest in marketable securities for the purpose of using them as a safety stock of funds. Most firms use a line of credit supplied by a bank.

FIGURE 16.4

MILLER-ORR TRANSACTIONAL CASH BALANCE MODEL

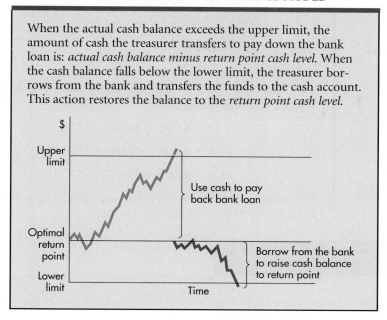

When the actual cash balance exceeds the upper limit, the amount of cash the treasurer transfers to pay down the bank loan is: *actual cash balance minus return point cash level.* When the cash balance falls below the lower limit, the treasurer borrows from the bank and transfers the funds to the cash account. This action restores the balance to the *return point cash level.*

$$\text{UCL} = 3 \times \text{optimal return cash level} \qquad \textbf{(16.7)}$$

and the average cash balance (ACB) is:

$$\text{ACB} = \text{Optimal return cash level} \times 4/3 \qquad \textbf{(16.8)}$$

Figure 16.4 depicts the model. Management only takes action when the cash balance pierces either the upper or lower control limit. When this happens, the difference between the actual cash balance and the optimal return cash level is the amount of cash either transferred to or transferred from the bank.

The minimum cash balance the firm maintains is most likely greater than the zero balance we have assumed. If management or lenders desire the firm to keep a minimum balance above zero, the lower limit becomes the desired minimum balance. We change the vertical orientation of the model without affecting the relationship between the optimal return cash level and the upper limit. The *optimal return cash level,* the *upper limit,* and the *average cash balance* increase by the new lower limit amount. Illustration 16.3 shows an application of the model.

ILLUSTRATION 16.3

Application of the Miller-Orr model

The treasurer has made the following estimates pertaining to managing cash balances: Transaction costs are $75, annual opportunity cost of funds is 11 percent, and variance of daily changes in cash flows is $27,000. Assuming that the minimum cash balance is zero, the treasurer calculates the optimal return cash balance (R) to be $1706, the upper limit (UCL) to be $5118, and the average cash balance (ACB) to be $2275.

$$R = \sqrt[3]{\frac{3 \times \$75 \times \$27{,}000}{4 \times 0.11/360 \text{ days}}} = \$1706$$

$$UCL = 3 \times \$1706 = \$5118$$

$$ACB = \frac{4 \times \$1706}{3} = \$2275$$

If the treasurer wants to maintain a minimum cash balance of $6000, the revised numbers are:

$$R = \$1706 + \$6000 = \$7706$$

$$UCL = \$5118 + \$6000 = \$11{,}118$$

$$ACB = \$2275 + \$6000 = \$8275$$

The treasurer simply adds the minimum cash balance of $6000 to R, UCL, and ACB to get new values.

Comprehension Check

1. Describe the financial manager's major decision areas concerning the banking system.
2. Define the various types of float. What are management's aims in dealing with float?
3. Define concentration bank, zero-balance account (ZBA), lock box system, and cash pooling.
4. What is the Baumol EOQ cash model? What are its advantages and limitations?
5. How does the Miller-Orr cash management model differ from the Baumol model?

 ## 16.2 INVESTMENT IN ACCOUNTS RECEIVABLE

The investment in accounts receivable involves several decisions. Who should receive credit? What should be the credit terms? How much investment in credit should there be? How will the offering of credit affect the firm's cash balances? A decision about credit may involve analyzing the trade-off between holding inventory or holding accounts receivable. Selling on credit may encourage customers to buy, thereby reducing investment in inventory but increasing investment in accounts receivable. However, higher sales may also result in a need for holding more inventories along with more accounts receivable, thereby increasing the investment in both accounts. Careful and thoughtful analysis is needed to ensure that decisions about accounts receivable contribute to shareholder value.

16.2.1 Credit Decision Models

The extension of credit to customers means company policy dictates an investment will be made in accounts receivable. Although the investment is short term, as opposed to the long-term capital budgeting decisions we discussed in Chapters 14 and 15, the granting of credit nevertheless is an investment decision and should be evaluated from the perspective of contributing to increasing shareholder value. The following generalized net present value formulation of a credit model is appropriate for this task:

$$\text{Net present value} = \frac{\text{After-tax cash flow}}{\text{Cost of capital}} - \text{investment} \geq 0$$

$$\text{NPV} = \frac{F \times (1 - \tau)}{r} - I \geq 0$$

(16.9)

The model assumes that the after-tax cash flow resulting from the credit decision, $F \times (1 - \tau)$, is constant and continues in perpetuity. Because cash flow is in perpetuity, we discount it at r instead of $1 + r$.[6] The incremental investment, I, which results from the credit decision, varies depending on whether the decision is for *changing credit terms* or *changing credit standards*.

Credit terms represent the terms of sale between the firm and its customer. For example, present credit terms may be net 15, which means the account is due and payable in full in 15 days. If the company changes the terms to 2/10, n/30, the customer can take a 2 percent cash discount off the purchase price if the account is paid within 10 days, otherwise the account is due for the full amount within 30 days.

Credit standards are totally separate from credit terms. **Credit standards** are essentially company policy based on which customers, or prospective customers, will be able to purchase on credit. Credit standards must not be discriminatory in any legal sense; race, color, religion, and sex cannot be used as variables in any decision about credit.

> **Credit terms.** The payment provisions that are part of a credit arrangement.
>
> **Credit standards.** Criteria used to determine which customers receive credit. Usually encompasses an examination of the customer's credit rating, credit references, outstanding debt, and financial statements.

INVESTMENT RESULTING FROM CHANGING CREDIT TERMS. There is good news and bad news in every credit decision. On the plus side, easing credit by lengthening the credit period should stimulate sales. Accounts receivable balances, in turn, should increase because present customers will take longer to pay and the more attractive credit terms should attract new customers. On the minus side, bad debts likely will increase because the firm will be selling to some customers who are more risky than present customers. Inventory investments likely will increase because of the changing credit policy's stimulus on sales. Increases in operating liabilities, such as accounts payable for materials and accrued wages, will offset some of the additional investment in receivables and inventory.

We consider any increases or decreases in these accounts as a result of the credit decision as the *incremental investment, I.* More formally, we define **incremental investment** as:

> **Incremental investment.** The additional investment the firm will encounter as a result of implementing a new credit policy.

$$\begin{aligned}
I = \ & \text{Incremental investment in accounts receivable} \\
& \quad \text{associated with original sales, stated at cost} \\
& + \text{incremental investment in accounts receivable} \\
& \quad \text{associated with new sales, stated at cost} \\
& + \text{incremental investment in inventories} \\
& - \text{incremental noninterest-bearing financing}
\end{aligned}$$

(16.10)

We calculate the incremental investment in accounts receivable separately for present customers and for prospective customers. In each case, we reduce the investment to a *cost basis* by multiplying the incremental accounts receivable investment by the firm's variable-cost proportion:[7]

---

[6]The use of a perpetuity model should not be new to you. In Chapter 9, we used a perpetuity approach to capitalize the constant stream of dividends associated with common stock.

[7]Note that the incremental investment in accounts receivable is qualified by the words *stated at cost.* Assuming a firm sells a product for more than it costs, the accounts receivable amount shown on the balance sheet consists of cost to make the product and the profit expected to be earned in its sale. Profit is not part of the investment made by the firm. Profit represents a return on investment. Thus, the true investment in accounts receivable is the cost of the product, not its selling price.

$$\text{Incremental accounts receivable investment at cost}$$

$$= \text{Incremental average collection period} \qquad \text{(16.11)}$$

$$\times \text{ sales per day} \times \text{variable-cost ratio}$$

Illustration 16.4 provides an example for analyzing changing credit terms.

ILLUSTRATION 16.4

Analyzing changing credit terms

Management is considering changing the credit terms in the hope of stimulating sales. Presently, the terms are net 15. The proposal is to have new credit terms of 2/10, n/30. Currently, credit sales amount to $2 million. On average, accounts are outstanding 20 days before customers pay. That is, on average, *present* customers pay five days after the current terms of net 15 days. A study forecasts that 70 percent of these customers will take the discount with the remaining 30 percent paying on day 30.

The new credit terms should also attract additional customers who will buy $500,000 of product. Management expects 60 percent of these new sales to be discounted. The forecast is that the remaining 40 percent will pay 45 days after the invoice date.

The higher sales should cause inventory investment to increase $100,000. A higher production level needed to satisfy higher sales projections should result in $75,000 more noninterest-bearing financing from trade payables and accrued wages. The credit manager expects bad debts of $15,000; currently, there are no bad debts. The firm's variable-cost ratio is 55 percent, its tax rate is 30 percent, and its cost of capital is 15 percent.

CALCULATION OF INCREMENTAL INVESTMENT

The expected *average collection period (ACP)* for present customers, as a result of the new credit terms, is 16 days.

(Proportion of customers taking the discount)
    × (ACP of customers discounting)
    + (proportion of customers not taking the discount)
    × (ACP of customers not discounting)

= 0.70 × 10 days + 0.30 × 30 days
= 16 days

The incremental ACP for current customers is −4 days: 16 days forecasted minus 20 days now experienced. Thus, investment in accounts receivable for present customers should decline four days because of the new credit terms.

For new customers, the ACP in accounts receivable is 24 days.

(Proportion of customers taking the discount)
    × (ACP of customers discounting)
    + (proportion of customers not taking the discount)
    × (ACP of customers not discounting)

= 0.60 × 10 days + 0.40 × 45 days
= 24 days

The incremental ACP for new customers is 24, since there are no sales to these customers now.

The incremental investment, as a result of the new credit terms, is $31,111.

$I =$ Variable-cost ratio $\times$ [(incremental ACP to present customers $\times$ sales per day to present customers) + (incremental ACP to new customers $\times$ sales per day to new customers)] + incremental investment in inventory − incremental noninterest-bearing financing

$$= 0.55 \times [- 4 \times \$2,000,000/360 + 24 \times \$500,000/360]$$
$$+ \$100,000 - \$75,000$$
$$= \$31,111$$

CALCULATION OF INCREMENTAL AFTER-TAX CASH FLOW

The incremental operating cash flow of the decision is $123,200:

(New sales $\times$ (1 − variable-cost ratio) − bad debts − cash discounts) $\times$ (1 − tax rate)

$$= (\$500,000 \times (1 - 0.55) - \$15,000 - \$34,000) \times (1 - 0.30)$$
$$= \$123,200$$

Calculation of the $34,000 cash discount amount is as follows:
(Proportion of present customers taking the discount $\times$ sales to present customers $\times$ cash discount rate) + (proportion of new customers taking the discount $\times$ sales to new customers $\times$ cash discount rate)

$$= (0.70 \times \$2,000,000 \times 0.02) + (0.60 \times \$500,000 \times 0.02)$$
$$= \$34,000$$

NET PRESENT VALUE OF THE DECISION

The NPV of the decision to change credit terms is $790,222. If the forecasted cash flows are actually realized, then the value of the firm should increase $790,222 in excess of the $31,111 investment required by the new credit policy.

$$\text{NPV} = \frac{F \times (1 - \tau)}{r} - I$$

$$= \frac{\$123,200}{0.15} - \$31,111$$

$$= \$790,222$$

INVESTMENT RESULTING FROM CHANGING CREDIT STANDARDS. Whenever the credit decision relates to credit standards, we must redefine the incremental investment to exclude the first expression on the right-hand side of Equation 16.10, on page 597. There are two reasons for excluding the first expression. First, *if management relaxes credit standards,* there is no effect on present customers. The looser credit standards will only attract new customers. Second, *if management tightens credit standards,* some present customers will no longer be able to buy on credit. However, the credit manager will tell these customers the news once they have paid off their current outstanding obligation. (See Illustration 16.5.)

ILLUSTRATION 16.5

Analysis of changing credit standards

Management wants to loosen credit standards and expects the new policy to attract an additional $250,000 in sales from new customers. It also expects inventory investment to increase $40,000 and noninterest-bearing liabilities for trade payables and accrued wages to employees to increase $10,000. The credit manager forecasts the average collection period (ACP) for new accounts to be 50 days. None of the accounts will take a cash discount but bad debts should increase $25,000. The cost of capital is 20 percent, the tax rate is 30 percent, and the variable cost ratio is 60 percent.

The expected incremental investment from loosening credit standards is $50,833.

$$\text{Variable-cost ratio} \times \text{incremental ACP} \times \text{sales per day}$$
$$+ \text{ inventory} - \text{liabilities}$$

$$= 0.60 \times 50 \text{ days} \times \$250,000/360 + \$40,000 - \$10,000$$
$$= \$50,833$$

Credit standards should be relaxed because the NPV of this decision is $211,667.

$$\frac{\begin{array}{c}(\text{New sales} \times (1 - \text{variable-cost ratio}) \\ - \text{ bad debts} - \text{cash discounts}) \times (1 - \text{tax rate})\end{array}}{\text{Cost of capital}} - \text{investment}$$

$$= \frac{(\$250,000 \times (1 - 0.60) - \$25,000) \times (1 - 0.3)}{0.20} - \$50,833$$

$$= \$211,667$$

16.2.2 Credit Selection

Today's credit manager does very little credit checking personally. Instead, the credit manager relies on one or more of the following sources: credit reporting agencies, banks, references, and the firm's suppliers. Often the credit manager phones the customer's bank, references, or selected suppliers to check creditworthiness if the order is relatively small. For larger orders, a major source of determining creditworthiness is information provided by credit reporting agencies.

CREDIT REPORTING AGENCIES. There are many business credit agencies operating in the country. The services they offer vary but usually include reference books, ratings, recommendations, and reports. Dun & Bradstreet (D&B), the best known and largest agency, provides all these services and more. Other agencies offer perhaps only one or two of the services.

The rating system used by D&B is a combination of numbers and letters signifying financial strength, as shown in Figure 16.5. Suppose the credit manager for Denver Chemicals receives a $3000 order from a new account, Gorman Manufacturing Co., and finds the account listed in the D&B reference book as 3A3. A 3A3 account shows an estimated financial strength of $1 million to $10 million; the rating could easily absorb an order for $3000 or higher. Figure 16.6 is an example of a credit report for a firm. Note that although Figure 16.6 is a business credit report, there is personal information about the main officers.

C'S OF CREDIT. A popular system used either independently or with a credit agency such as D&B to analyze a credit application is the **five C's of credit:**

- *Character:* willingness to pay.
- *Capacity:* ability to pay.
- *Collateral:* assets available against which to put a lien.
- *Capital:* financial strength of the applicant.
- *Conditions:* economic environment's effect on applicant.

> **Five C's of credit.** An *ad hoc* approach for evaluating credit applicants that looks at the customer's character, capacity, capital, collateral, and conditions.

Three more C's are important when the applicant is a foreigner:

- *Country:* political and economic risk of the country.
- *Culture:* norms for transacting business in a foreign country.
- *Currency:* exchange rate risk.

Information sources for evaluating creditworthiness according to this system include the credit applicant's financial statements, banks, customers, and references. Nevertheless, the scoring system used to measure risk is subjective.

▶ *Comprehension Check*

1. What is the general NPV credit-model formulation?
2. Discuss the factors that influence the firm's decision to change credit terms or credit standards.
3. Why are credit reporting agencies such as Dun & Bradstreet commonly used?
4. Define the C's of credit sometimes used to determine an applicant's creditworthiness.

16.3 INVESTMENT IN INVENTORY

For manufacturers, wholesalers, and retailers, the investment in inventories is significant. And as discussed, a new credit policy can affect inventory investment. If production and delivery of goods are instantaneous, there is no need for inventories, except as a hedge against price changes.[8] In many respects inventories are more sensitive than other assets to general business fluctuations. Large and costly swings in inventory cause just about every business cycle to worsen. In periods of prosperity,

---

[8]Management can use futures or options to help reduce uncertainty about price changes. This topic is beyond the scope of this book.

FIGURE 16.5
DUN & BRADSTREET KEY TO RATINGS

Key to Ratings

ESTIMATED FINANCIAL STRENGTH			COMPOSITE CREDIT APPRAISAL			
			HIGH	GOOD	FAIR	LIMITED
5A	$50,000,000	and over	1	2	3	4
4A	$10,000,000 to	49,999,999	1	2	3	4
3A	1,000,000 to	9,999,999	1	2	3	4
2A	750,000 to	999,999	1	2	3	4
1A	500,000 to	749,999	1	2	3	4
BA	300,000 to	499,999	1	2	3	4
BB	200,000 to	299,999	1	2	3	4
CB	125,000 to	199,999	1	2	3	4
CC	75,000 to	124,999	1	2	3	4
DC	50,000 to	74,999	1	2	3	4
DD	35,000 to	49,999	1	2	3	4
EE	20,000 to	34,999	1	2	3	4
EF	10,000 to	19,999	1	2	3	4
GG	5,000 to	9,999	1	2	3	4
HH	Up to	4,999	1	2	3	4

GENERAL CLASSIFICATION FOR ESTIMATED FINANCIAL STRENGTH AND COMPOSITE CREDIT APPRAISAL

ESTIMATED FINANCIAL STRENGTH			COMPOSITE CREDIT APPRAISAL		
			GOOD	FAIR	LIMITED
1 BR	$125,000	and over	2	3	4
2 BR	$50,000 to	$124,999	2	3	4

EXPLANATION

When the designation "1R" or "2R" appears, followed by a 2, 3 or 4, it is an indication that the Estimated Financial Strength, while not definitely classified, is presumed to be in the range of the ($) figures in the corresponding bracket, and while the Composite Credit Appraisal cannot be judged precisely, it is believed to fall in the general category indicated.

"INV." shown in place of a rating indicates that Dun & Bradstreet is currently conducting an investigation to gather information for a new report. It has no other significance. "FB" (Foreign Branch), indicates that the headquarters of this company is located in a foreign country (including Canada). The written report contains the location of the headquarters.

ABSENCE OF A RATING—THE BLANK SYMBOL

A blank symbol (—) should not be interpreted as indicating that credit should be denied. It simply means that the information available to Dun & Bradstreet does not permit us to classify the company within our rating key and that furher inquiry should be made before reaching a credit decision.

EMPLOYEE RANGE DESIGNATIONS IN REPORTS ON NAMES NOT LISTED IN THE REFERENCE BOOK

Certain businesses do not lend themselves to a Dun & Bradstreet rating and are not listed in the Reference Book. Information on these names, however, continues to be stored and updated in the D&B Business Information File. Reports are available on such businesses and instead of a rating they carry an Employee Range Designation (ER) which is indicative of size in terms of number of employees. No other significance should be attached.

KEY TO EMPLOYEE RANGE DESIGNATIONS

ER 1	1000 or more	Employees
ER 2	500 – 999	Employees
ER 3	100 – 499	Employees
ER 4	50 – 99	Employees
ER 5	20 – 49	Employees
ER 6	10 – 19	Employees
ER 7	15 – 9	Employees
ER 8	1 – 4	Employees
ER N		Not Available

Dun & Bradstreet
Credit Services

D-B a company of
The Dun & Bradstreet Corporation

FIGURE 16.6
DUN & BRADSTREET CREDIT REPORT

 **Dun & Bradstreet Information Services**

Business Information Report

```
                                        SUBSCRIBER:  123-4567L
                                        PREPARED FOR:

                           ANSWERING INQUIRY


DUNS:  00-007-7743              DATE PRINTED                  SUMMARY
GORMAN MANUFACTURING CO. INC.   OCT 30 199-        RATING      3A3
   (SUBSIDIARY OF GORMAN
    HOLDING COMPANIES INC.,     COMMERCIAL PRINTING
    LOS ANGELES, CA)            SIC NO.
                                2752              STARTED      1965
                                                 SALES F      $13,007,229
492 KOLLER ST                                    WORTH F      $2,125,499
AND BRANCH(ES) OR DIVISION(S)                    EMPLOYS      105 (100 HERE)
SAN FRANCISCO CA 94110                           HISTORY      CLEAR
     TEL: 415-555-0000                           FINANCING    SECURED
                                                 FINANCIAL
CHIEF EXECUTIVE: LESLIE SMITH, PRES              CONDITION    FAIR
=====================================================================================
SPECIAL EVENTS
09/11/9-        On Sept 9, 199-, the subject experienced a fire due to an earthquake.
        According to Leslie Smith, President, damages amounted to $35,000, which
        was fully covered by their insurance company.  The business was closed for
        two days while employees settled personal matters due to the earthquake.

03/17/9-        Subject moved from 400 KOLLER ST. to 492 KOLLER ST. on March 11, 199-.

=====================================================================================
                     *  *  *  SUMMARY ANALYSIS  *  *  *
=====================================================================================
RATING SUMMARY . . . .
        The "3A" portion  of the Rating (Estimated Financial Strength) indicates
        that the company has a worth between $1 million and $10 million.  The "3"
        on the right (Composite Credit Appraisal) indicates an overall "fair"
        credit appraisal.  The "fair" credit appraisal was assigned because the
        company's overall payment record shows frequent slowness and because of
        D&B's "fair" assessment of the company's 12/31/9- fiscal financial
        statement.

        Below is an overview of the company's D&B Rating(s) since 1-1-91:
                     RATING                       DATE APPLIED
                     ------                       ------------

                      3A3                          09/11/9-
                      --                           01/01/91
=====================================================================================
   HISTORY
09/11/9-
        LESLIE SMITH, PRES                 KEVIN J. HUNT, SEC-TREAS
        DIRECTOR(S): THE OFFICER(S)
        --------------------------------------------------------------------
        BUSINESS TYPE: Corporation - Profit      DATE INCORPORATED: 05/21/1965
        AUTH SHARES - COMMON: 200                STATE OF INCORP: California
        PAR VALUE - COMMON: No Par Value
        --------------------------------------------------------------------
            Business started May 21, 1965 by Leslie Smith and Kevin J. Hunt.
        100% of capital stock is owned by Parent Company.
            SMITH born 1926. Married. Graduated from the University of
        California, Los Angeles, in June 1947 with a BS degree in Business
        Management. 1947-65 general manager for Raymor Printing Co., San
        Francisco, CA. 1965 formed subject with Kevin J. Hunt.
            HUNT born 1925. Married. Graduated from Northwestern University,
        Evanston, IL. in June 1946. 1946-1965 controller for Raymor Printing Co.,
        San Francisco, CA. 1965 formed subject with Leslie Smith.
            RELATED COMPANIES: Through the financial interest of Gorman Holding
        Company Inc., subject's parent company, the Gorman Manufacturing Co.
        Inc., is related to two other companies:
            1. Smith Lettershop Inc., San Diego, CA; commercial printing,
        started 1972.
            2. Gorman Suppliers Inc., Los Angeles, CA; commercial print, started
        1980.
            Intercompany relations consist of loans.
=====================================================================================
```

when sales are high, firms dispose of inventory readily and quantities on hand may not appear excessive. However, when even a slight downward business fluctuation occurs, many lines of inventory begin to move slowly and excess inventory piles up. Obsolescence of inventory becomes a real possibility. Because of the heavy costs of carrying surplus inventory, management must make an intense effort to determine the appropriate inventory investment. The primary techniques used to accomplish this task include: *economic order quantity (EOQ); materials requirement planning (MRP);* and *just-in-time (JIT)* inventory management.

As we will discuss, an EOQ inventory investment model is reactive. In contrast, a MRP model is proactive. The difference is that EOQ triggers new inventory investment when *past* demand depletes inventory. Forecasts of future demand guide MRP inventory investment. Based on future demand, MRP uses EOQ concepts to determine the economical lot size to order. JIT, on the other hand, tries to make the EOQ amount a single unit. In each case, the goal is to reduce inventory and production costs.

16.3.1 Economic Order Quantity (EOQ)

EOQ model. A mathematical model for calculating the optimal inventory order size; it minimizes the total ordering and holding costs.

The **EOQ model** is the Baumol cash model (discussed earlier) applied to inventory. Demand for cash has been replaced by demand for inventory. The optimal inventory level occurs where costs incurred in ordering inventory equal costs incurred in holding (storing) inventory. The model, shown in Figure 16.7, makes several assumptions:

- Management knows the demand for inventory with certainty.
- The purchase cost per unit does not change.
- There are no discounts for volume purchases.
- Inventory replenishment is instantaneous.[9]

The optimal EOQ (in units) is:

$$EOQ = \sqrt{\frac{2 \times \text{cost per order} \times \text{demand for inventory}}{\text{Holding cost per unit of item per period}}} \qquad (16.12)$$

This results in an average physical inventory investment of EOQ ÷ 2. The average dollar investment is average price per unit × EOQ ÷ 2. (See Illustration 16.6.)

ILLUSTRATION 16.6

EOQ inventory investment

Suppose the annual demand for an item is 1 million units, ordering cost per order is $90, and carrying cost per unit is $0.50. The EOQ is 18,974 units.

$$EOQ = \sqrt{\frac{2 \times \$90 \times 1,000,000}{\$0.50}} = 18,974 \text{ units}$$

The average number of units is EOQ ÷ 2 = 9487 and if each unit costs $3 to buy, the average dollar investment is $28,461 (= $3 × 9487 units). There are 53 orders placed during the year: (1,000,000 ÷ 18,974 = 52.7).

[9]We can relax assumptions of the EOQ model to allow for more realistic applications, such as irregular demand and inventory being received over time instead of all at once. However, the conceptual nature of the model does not change.

FIGURE 16.7
INVENTORY EOQ MODEL

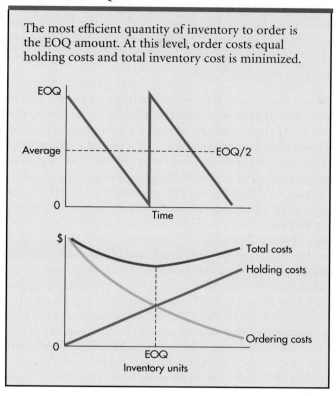

The most efficient quantity of inventory to order is the EOQ amount. At this level, order costs equal holding costs and total inventory cost is minimized.

16.3.2 Materials Requirement Planning (MRP)

MRP is a computer-simulation technique for the inventory investment of each product. At one time, only the large companies with mainframe computers used this approach, but with the ever increasing influence of the personal computer, MRP software is available for small firms to use. The procedure is as follows. When production management finishes a master production schedule, which shows when and how much to produce, an MRP computer program solves for the correct amount of inventory investment.

> **Materials requirement planning (MRP).** A computerized system for determining inventory requirements and when to place orders.

1. The computer program accesses databases for the structured bill of materials (meaning everything needed to make the product), lead times to receive materials, and on-hand and on-order inventory balances.

2. The program breaks down the bill of materials to get parts requirements for each product.

3. The program nets gross requirements against available inventory balances.

4. The program offsets net requirements over lead times and generates a time-phased listing for parts.

5. The projected parts requirements are in turn funneled through their manufacturing routings. This provides a time-phased projection of the loads on the various manufacturing departments resulting from the given time schedule.

6. Production management compares these loads with the capacities of each department to determine whether the master schedule will work. If bottlenecks occur, production managers must revise the master schedule.

7. When the master schedule is satisfactory, the purchasing agent places orders. The agent may use the EOQ model to determine purchase quantities.

16.3.3 Just-in-Time Inventory System

The most dramatic innovation in inventory management in the past decade has been the **just-in-time** inventory system. General Electric Company totally redesigned its dishwasher line to accommodate new production technology, including JIT processes. By switching to one standard tub and frame, GE reduced the number of parts in its 15 models by 25 percent, and reduced product weight by 15 to 25 pounds per unit. The company now uses 850 parts and assemblies to produce these 15 models, down from 5600. When Digital Equipment Corporation implemented a JIT process for manufacturing computer work stations, overall inventory levels fell from 16 weeks to 3 weeks, overall process time declined from 6 weeks to 3 days, and the number of defectives manufactured dropped from 17 percent to 3 percent.

Japanese manufacturers were the first to use JIT in an effort to improve the quality of their products. Rather than have inventory sitting around waiting to be used, a JIT system strives for a zero inventory investment, other than what is in production to satisfy current customer demand. In JIT, authorization to make a part at any fabrication or assembly work station comes from the next work station in the production line. For example, as an assembly work station consumes parts, the supervisor posts a card showing the need for, and the authorization to produce, new parts. All upstream work stations repeat this process, thereby pulling parts through the production system.

Conceptually, JIT treats the EOQ as equal to one unit. JIT pushes inventory investment back on to suppliers. When the firm needs inventory, suppliers deliver it to the company. A JIT system places the burden on suppliers to deliver high-quality parts on time. Any defective goods cause the production line to stop because there is no safety stock inventory. The reliability of delivery times and quality become more important than does price.

16.3.4 Inventory Investment in Foreign Subsidiaries

A major concern of any multinational firm is the level of inventory it must maintain for its foreign operations. Many foreign subsidiaries and branches operate under inflationary economic conditions. When setting inventory levels, management must consider the effects of an increasing price level or currency devaluation.

The foreign country may impose price control regulations on its products during inflationary conditions. Should this happen, a subsidiary would be unable to raise selling prices. Any resulting sales would mean less profit when combined at the level of the parent corporation.

On the other hand, a foreign subsidiary that imports its goods but operates without the restriction of governmental price controls would seek to stockpile inventories in advance of an expected devaluation of the local currency. Any later devaluation effectively would increase the cost of inventory purchases. For example, a 10 percent local currency devaluation requires the firm to pay 10 percent more local currency for the same amount of imported goods. However, any savings realized by purchasing inventory before the devaluation may be minimal. Higher inventory investment means increased carrying, insurance, and financing costs.

1. What information does the EOQ inventory model provide management?
2. How does the MRP model function for materials management?
3. What are the advantages and disadvantages of JIT inventory systems from the point of view both of manufacturers and their parts suppliers?
4. How is inventory investment management complicated when a firm does business and maintains inventories in foreign countries?

16.4 MONITORING SHORT-TERM INVESTMENT

Once management determines the desired level of short-term investment, it must monitor the level. The business environment seldom responds precisely according to the theoretical assumptions used to estimate the short-term investment level. Actual levels and desired levels can deviate significantly from each other. The Miller-Orr model's control limits automatically monitor cash balances.[10] Our discussion in this section examines monitoring accounts receivable and inventories.

16.4.1 Monitoring Accounts Receivable

Monitoring accounts receivable can be complex. Most credit managers try to check the overall status of receivables by analyzing the total balance outstanding. The traditional methods used are the *average collection period (ACP)* and *aging schedules.* A superior technique is the *balance proportions method.* In our discussion of these three methods, we will base all calculations on the following assumptions about customers' payment patterns:

For every $100 of sales in month 1:

$10 is collected in month 1; thus, $90 is outstanding at the end of month 1.
$30 is collected in month 2; thus, $60 is outstanding at the end of month 2.
$40 is collected in month 3; thus, $20 is outstanding at the end of month 3.
$20 is collected in month 4; thus, $0 is outstanding at the end of month 4.

These assumptions allow us to show that the balance proportions method is the best technique.

AVERAGE COLLECTION PERIOD. We compute the **average collection period (ACP)**, or number of days' sales invested in accounts receivable, from balance sheet and income statement information as follows:

> **Average collection period (ACP).** The amount of time accounts receivable are outstanding; used to evaluate the quality of the investment in accounts receivable.

$$\text{Average sales per day} = \frac{\text{Net Sales}}{\text{Days in accounting period}} \qquad (16.13)$$

$$\text{Average collection period} = \frac{\text{Receivables}}{\text{Average sales per day}} \qquad (16.14)$$

---

[10]The Union Tank Car Company has successfully applied the Miller-Orr model. It found that the model lowers both holding and ordering costs associated with cash balances.

PROBLEM RECEIVABLES

by John Burke, Vice President of Credit and Collections, Nestlé USA

Many options are available to deal with an account in financial difficulty. Let's look at a "normal" situation. A customer says, "I can't pay until, say, Monday." In this case, a credit analyst would negotiate the expected payment arrangements, putting a note in the customer's file so that if late payment happened another time, we might raise our level of action, that is, reduce the credit line or hold the order until we received a check.

At the other extreme is the case where we believe the customer will seek bankruptcy court protection. The credit department would immediately send a reclamation wire reclaiming all goods delivered within the previous ten days, as authorized under Bankruptcy Code and Uniform Commercial Code. The theory behind the law is that the company knew at least ten days in advance that it would not be able to pay for the goods. Thus, any merchandise the customer received during that period was under false pretense that the supplier would be paid. The reclamation procedure attempts to ensure that we receive 100 percent of the funds owed us for these specific goods before unsecured creditors without reclamation protection receive anything.

In the case of Southland Corporation, Dallas, Texas, the owner of the 7-11 convenience food stores, we sent a reclamation wire every Friday. Southland had advertised in the newspapers that it was going to file a prepackaged Chapter 11 bankruptcy. This meant that Southland intended to file bankruptcy and a reorganization plan at the same time, calling for 100 percent payment to creditors. I wasn't sure if the court would accept such a filing, so to provide Nestlé with protection as we continued to sell to Southland, we sent a new reclamation wire every Friday.

Another way we can protect ourselves against a customer in financial difficulty who hasn't filed for bankruptcy is to take either a first or second lien on whatever assets might be available. There are instances when I might get other corporations or individuals to guarantee the customer's credit. I stay away from guarantees from insiders because some courts rule that guarantees from an insider expose Nestlé, under certain conditions of bankruptcy preference laws, to refund all monies collected during a one-year period. Without an insider guarantee, the preference period would only be 90 days. The one-year period is a bigger risk to me than an insolvency.

Once a customer files Chapter 11 bankruptcy, Nestlé credit personnel take a very active role serving on creditors' committees. Frequently, we chair or co-chair these committees. This action serves two purposes: (1) it helps give us a direct input on the decisions made in the bankruptcy proceedings; and (2) being on the committee gives us more information for credit purposes.

We don't usually want to force firms into liquidations under Chapter 7 of the Bankruptcy Code. A firm in Chapter 7 has a court-appointed trustee in charge. This trustee gets a percentage of the assets, which means less money will be available for everyone else. Also trustees typically try to claim that money paid to suppliers within the past 90 days represents preference payments and, thus, legally must be refunded to the distressed company. If I don't think the company can be successfully reorganized, I would rather pursue a liquidation under Chapter 11. This procedure has the advantage of no trustee and gives the creditor's committee more influence over its own fate.

I strongly believe in credit associations to track problem accounts. Nestlé is active within the food industry credit association, which has a mechanism, depending on geography and dollar amount of involvement, to get *Fortune* 500 companies, such as Nestlé, to serve on the creditors' committee. The association freely shares historical, factual information. Members can't discuss anything going forward, as a matter of law. However, historical information can mean anything that happens up to the time of sharing the information.

We can express ACP as an *accounts receivable turnover ratio* by dividing it into 360 days, which represents the number of days in the year. The **accounts receivable turnover ratio** represents how often the investment in accounts receivable turns over in a year; a turnover of 4 means that accounts receivable are outstanding 90 days: 360 days in the year ÷ 4 turns = 90 days.

$$\text{Accounts receivable turnover} = \frac{360 \text{ days}}{\text{Average collection period}} \qquad (16.15)$$

> **Accounts receivable turnover ratio.** Method of monitoring trends in customer payments; higher turnover is considered positive.

Knowing the average collection period (or turnover) should help us answer the following question. Considering the credit terms, how promptly are accounts collected? The ACP both suggests the quality of accounts receivable and measures the efficiency of the credit department in collecting these accounts. Some credit managers use a rule of thumb that the average collection period should not exceed 1.5 times the credit period. Illustration 16.7 shows an example of how to calculate the average collection period.

ILLUSTRATION 16.7

Monitoring receivables using ACP

The Bernstein Company has outstanding receivables of $1,620,000 as of the end of June.

Month	1st Quarter Sales	Uncollected	Month	2nd Quarter Sales	Uncollected
January	$ 600,000	$ 120,000	April	$1,800,000	$ 360,000
February	1,200,000	720,000	May	1,200,000	720,000
March	1,800,000	1,620,000	June	600,000	540,000
Total	$3,600,000	$2,460,000	Total	$3,600,000	$1,620,000

Average sales per day for the past 90 days are:[11]

First quarter: $3,600,000 ÷ 90 = $40,000

Second quarter: $3,600,000 ÷ 90 = $40,000

Average collection periods as of the end of March and June are the outstanding receivables divided by the sales per day in each quarter, respectively:

First quarter: $2,460,000 ÷ $40,000 = 61.5 days

Second quarter: $1,620,000 ÷ $40,000 = 40.5 days

Often the average collection period uses sales figures for the past 12 months as a base. Suppose that 12 months' sales ended in March and June are $11,880,000 and $9,720,000, respectively. Thus, sales per day for these respective 12-month periods are:

March: $11,880,000 ÷ 360 days = $33,000

June: $9,720,000 ÷ 360 days = $27,000

[11]For simplicity, we assume that each month has 30 days.

The average collection periods, using these sales-per-day figures, are:

First quarter: $2,460,000 ÷ $33,000 = 74.5 days

Second quarter: $1,620,000 ÷ $27,000 = 60.0 days

The preceding calculations show that *sales per day* influence the average collection period. The example shows the receivable balance at the end of the second quarter is more current than the balance at the end of the first quarter. This conclusion holds whether the ACP uses the past 90 days sales or the past 360 days sales in the calculation.

Sometimes the analyst uses the following variations in computing the average collection period.

- Substitute total credit sales for the total sales figure.
- Use an average receivables figure; for example, add beginning and ending balances and divide by two.
- Compute the average collection period on a monthly basis, if possible. This calculation may allow the credit manager to spot quickly any serious deviations from normal collection patterns. Also, frequent computations keep seasonal variations in sales and receivables from distorting the picture.
- Use the number of business days during the accounting period (say, 250 days for the year instead of 360).

Aging schedule. Process of classifying accounts by the amount of time they have been outstanding. The schedule usually displays the percentage of receivables that are one month old, two months old, and so on.

AGING ACCOUNTS RECEIVABLE. An **aging schedule** shows the proportions of the current outstanding accounts receivable balance arising from sales of previous periods. Credit managers believe that if these proportions change, then collection patterns have changed. The rationale is that as an account ages, the chance of collection decreases.

The conventional way to age the outstanding accounts receivable balance is as follows. Suppose the outstanding receivable balance at the end of June consists of uncollected credit sales made in April, May, and June. The credit manager states the outstanding balances for each of these months as a percentage of the total outstanding balance as of the end of June. It is desirable to have the largest and fastest growing percentage for the most recent sales month (that is, June). (See Illustration 16.8.)

ILLUSTRATION 16.8

Monitoring receivables using an aging schedule

Let's use the data in Illustration 16.7 to calculate an aging schedule. The aging schedule shows the proportion of January's sales still outstanding at the end of March as a proportion of the total outstanding receivable balance. The credit manager makes similar calculations for each month.

Month	1st Quarter Sales	Uncollected	Aging	Month	2nd Quarter Sales	Uncollected	Aging
January	$ 600,000	$ 120,000	4.88%	April	$1,800,000	$ 360,000	22.22%
February	1,200,000	720,000	29.27	May	1,200,000	720,000	44.44
March	1,800,000	1,620,000	65.85	June	600,000	540,000	33.33
Total	$3,600,000	$2,460,000	100.00%	Total	$3,600,000	$1,620,000	99.99%

The aging schedule shows that accounts are more current at the end of the first quarter than they are at the end of the second quarter. We base this conclusion on the higher proportion of outstanding accounts in the third month of each quarter (that is, March and June). About 66 percent of first quarter's outstanding receivables are for the most recent month in the quarter (March). However, only about 33 percent of the second quarter's outstanding receivables are for the most recent month in the quarter (June). The aging schedule provides a different conclusion about the status of receivables than provided by the ACP approach in Illustration 16.7.

BALANCE PROPORTIONS. We calculate **balance proportions** by relating outstanding accounts receivable balances directly to the sales that generate the receivables. The object is to find patterns suggesting whether collections are better or worse without having to be concerned about changing sales patterns.

For example, suppose the accounts receivable balance at the end of June includes uncollected sales from April. Balance proportions relate the outstanding April balance to April's sales, not to the total receivable balance at the end of June. The credit manager makes similar calculations for the other months represented in the June receivable balance. The calculations allow the credit manager to see readily if any shifts are taking place in customer payment patterns. Illustration 16.9 shows how to apply balance proportions.

Balance proportions. An accounts receivable monitoring technique that relates the outstanding balance to the sale that generated the receivable.

ILLUSTRATION 16.9

Balance proportions to monitor receivables

The information to calculate balance proportions is taken from Illustration 16.7.

Month	1st Quarter Sales	Uncollected	Balance %	Month	2nd Quarter Sales	Uncollected	Balance %
January	$ 600,000	$ 120,000	20.0%	April	$1,800,000	$ 360,000	20.0%
February	1,200,000	720,000	60.0	May	1,200,000	720,000	60.0
March	1,800,000	1,620,000	90.0	June	600,000	540,000	90.0
Total	$3,600,000	$2,460,000		Total	$3,600,000	$1,620,000	

We calculate the 20 percent balance proportion for January by dividing the amount of January's sales into the amount for January sales still not collected at the end of March: $120,000 ÷ $600,000 = 0.20 or 20 percent. We calculate the balance proportions for the other months similarly.

The preceding balance proportions show that customers' payment patterns for the second quarter have not changed from customers' first-quarter payment patterns. This conclusion is different from conclusions provided by either the ACP measure or the aging schedule approach.

DIFFERENCES IN MONITORING TECHNIQUES. The three preceding illustrations show that different techniques result in different conclusions about the outstanding receivable balances. The much used ACP and aging schedule approaches do not always agree with each other, as is the case in Illustrations 16.7 and 16.8. Such a result is not unusual. The balance proportion technique provides a correct interpretation of outstanding receivables, as Illustration 16.10 shows.

ILLUSTRATION 16.10

Comparison of monitoring techniques	As mentioned earlier, the assumption underlying Illustrations 16.7, 16.8, and 16.9 is that customers pay according to the following fixed pattern:

For every $100 of Sales in Month 1

$10 is collected in month 1; thus, $90 is outstanding at the end of month 1.
$30 is collected in month 2; thus, $60 is outstanding at the end of month 2.
$40 is collected in month 3; thus, $20 is outstanding at the end of month 3.
$20 is collected in month 4; thus, $0 is outstanding at the end of month 4.

For example, using the second quarter's sales figures we find that:

		Uncollected Balance at the End of:					
Sales in:		April	%	May	%	June	%
April	$1,800,000	$1,620,000	90%	$1,080,000	60%	$ 360,000	20%
May	1,200,000			1,080,000	90	720,000	60
June	600,000					540,000	90
Total uncollected receivables, end of June						$1,620,000	

The $1,620,000 receivable balance outstanding at the end of June is the balance given in Illustrations 16.7, 16.8, and 16.9. Similar calculations result in the March receivable balance. Double check this claim by using the preceding payment patterns to calculate the outstanding receivable balance as of the end of March.[12]

Since the calculations in the illustrations assumed that customers' payment patterns are constant, each monitoring technique should show no change in collection effort from the first quarter to the second quarter. Only the balance proportion technique can reveal this. The ACP and aging schedule approaches are sensitive to the sales pattern. We saw how sensitive the ACP approach, shown in Illustration 16.7, was to the sales averaging period upon which it was computed. However, it is not really the sales

[12]Solution:

		Uncollected Balance at the End of:					
Sales in:		January	%	February	%	March	%
Jan.	$ 600,000	$540,000	90$	$ 360,000	60%	$ 120,000	20%
Feb.	1,200,000			1,080,000	90%	720,000	60%
Mar.	1,800,000					1,620,000	90%
Total uncollected receivables, end of March						$2,460,000	

averaging period that causes problems; rather a changing sales pattern is what can throw things off. If sales are constant from month to month, the ACP and aging schedule methods generate constant average collection periods or aging figures each period. If sales are declining, both ACP and aging schedule techniques seem to indicate that receivables are less current than they really are. Increasing sales result in an opposite conclusion.

The only time that ACP and aging schedules do not emit false signals is when the sales pattern is flat. Because a changing sales pattern does not influence the balance proportions technique, it is the superior technique. (It is important to note that in the real world, sales patterns often fluctuate a great deal.)

16.4.2 Monitoring Inventory

Investment in inventory depends on expected sales, as we discussed previously. The problem of how much inventory to carry is a significant one for management. Overinvestment can result in lost opportunity income, carrying costs, and obsolescence. Lack of inventory can result in lost sales and profits. Two primary means of monitoring inventory are turnover ratios and a technique called the A-B-C method.

INVENTORY TURNOVER. *Inventory turnover* shows how fast inventory is selling. A measure of turnover gives managers an idea of how much inventory investment supports the company's operations. We calculate **inventory turnover** by dividing cost of goods sold by average inventory. Average inventory is the sum of opening and closing inventory balances divided by two. When cost of sales is not available, we use total sales instead. Many times analysts use the end-of-period inventory instead of the average balance.

> **Inventory turnover.** A ratio used to evaluate the number of times average inventory has been sold during the period.

$$\text{Inventory turnover} = \frac{\text{Cost of goods sold}}{\text{Average inventory}} \qquad (16.16)$$

We use Equation 16.17 to calculate the number of days investment in inventory.

$$\text{Days outstanding} = \frac{360 \text{ days}}{\text{Inventory turnover}} \qquad (16.17)$$

ILLUSTRATION 16.11

Monitoring inventory

Let's calculate inventory turnover and days inventory outstanding using financial statement information for Walter Pell, Inc.

	This Year	Last Year	Two Years Ago
Inventories	$ 3,351,367	$ 2,651,760	$2,076,933
Cost of sales	$16,056,856	$12,281,744	
Average inventory	$ 3,001,564	$ 2,364,347	

$$\text{Inventory turnover} = \frac{\text{Cost of goods sold}}{\text{Average inventory}}$$

$$\frac{\$16,056,856}{\$ 3,001,564} \qquad \frac{\$12,281,744}{\$ 2,364,347}$$

$$= 5.35 \qquad\qquad = 5.19$$

$$\text{Days outstanding} = \frac{360 \text{ days}}{\text{Inventory turnover}}$$

$$\frac{360}{5.35} \qquad \frac{360}{5.19}$$

$$= 67.3 \text{ days} \qquad = 69.4 \text{ days}$$

If we use year-end inventories instead of average inventories, inventory turnover is 4.79 for this year and 4.63 for last year. Days outstanding become 75.2 days this year and 77.8 days last year. Verify these numbers.[13]

Usually, a higher inventory turnover rate (or lower days outstanding) suggests better performance. A high turnover may mean that the company can operate with a relatively small investment in inventory, thereby reducing costly inventory carrying costs. A higher ratio also may suggest that inventories are current and salable and contain few unusable items. However, it is possible to overemphasize almost anything. Inventory turnover is no exception. Too much attention to high turnover can lead to inventory shortages and lost sales.

What, then, should the inventory turnover be? The desirable rate depends on the line of business, level of business activity, and method of valuing inventories, as well as on various trends. A study of the inventory turnover rates of similar businesses provides some guidelines that help answer the question.

A problem with comparing one firm to another is that each firm may use a different accounting procedure. For example, Fassell Limited uses *first-in, first-out (FIFO)* as the inventory flow assumption for its products, but comparable Laker Company uses *last-in, first-out (LIFO)*. **FIFO** means that the first inventory bought or produced is the first inventory sold. **LIFO** means that last inventory bought or produced is the first inventory sold. In times of increasing prices, Fassell will show higher inventory value on its balance sheet than Laker. The reason is that under FIFO the most recent and more expensive purchases are still in inventory. Fassell will also show lower cost of sales than will Laker. The reason is that FIFO assumes Fassell sells its earlier and less expensive purchases first.

The solution to how much inventory to carry often is based on some proportion of sales (or cost of sales). This approach is the inverse of the inventory turnover ratio. The problem with this approach is that it ignores any economies of scale the firm should realize.

A-B-C SYSTEM. In many firms, management views inventory investment from the perspective of the **A-B-C system,** which is a simple method of priorization. The idea is that a relatively small proportion of physical units accounts for the largest dollar investment. These units are the A-items. At the other extreme are the C-items, which represent a large percentage of the physical count but a relatively small proportion of the dollar investment. Everything else falls into the B-item group. Figure 16.8 illustrates the A-B-C system.

Management must relate investment in A-items to the production schedule carefully, since these items represent the most expensive parts used in manufacturing the various products. Because the cost of ordering new quantities is considerably less than the cost of holding excess inventory, the purchasing agent places frequent orders. Items

First-in, first-out (FIFO). A method of inventory accounting in which the oldest item in inventory is assumed to be sold first.

Last-in, first-out (LIFO). A method of inventory accounting in which the newest item in inventory is assumed to be sold first.

A-B-C system. An ad hoc technique of monitoring inventory. A-items are high value, whereas C-items are low value with B-items falling between these two extremes.

---

[13]Solutions: Turnovers are $16,046,856 ÷ $3,351,367 = 4.79 and $12,281,744 ÷ $2,651,760 = 4.63; days outstanding are 360 ÷ 4.79 = 75.2 and 360 ÷ 4.63 = 77.8.

in the A-group cause inventory investment to increase rather quickly if management does not closely control ordering.

The C-items are supplies and hardware used in manufacturing the product, for example, screws, washers, and bolts. Management frequently uses a two-bin system for C-items. The purchasing agent places an order when the production process depletes one bin and there is one bin remaining. Literally millions of C-items, like small screws, represent an insignificant investment. Thus, it makes sense to have a simple, inexpensive control system.

Production management frequently uses the economic order quantity model to monitor investment in B-items. The purchasing agent places a new order once inventory level falls to the reorder point.

Comprehension Check

1. Describe the use of turnover ratios for accounts receivable and inventory.
2. What is the relationship between the average collection period and receivable turnover ratio?
3. How is an aging schedule calculated?
4. How are balance proportions for receivables calculated?
5. What weakness does average collection period and aging schedules for checking receivables show? How does the balance proportion approach overcome the problem?
6. Describe how the A-B-C system works. How are the different items of inventory evaluated for investment in this system?

FIGURE 16.8
A-B-C INVENTORY SYSTEM

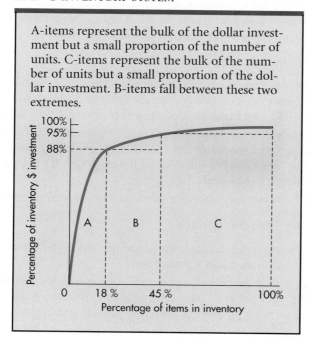

A-items represent the bulk of the dollar investment but a small proportion of the number of units. C-items represent the bulk of the number of units but a small proportion of the dollar investment. B-items fall between these two extremes.

Investment in Cash

Baumol EOQ cash model
Concentration bank
Depository transfer check
    (DTC)
Direct send
Economic value of cash
Electronic depository transfer
    check (EDTC)
Electronic wire transfer
Float
Lock box
Miller-Orr model
Ratio projection method
Zero-balance account (ZBA)

Investment in Accounts Receivable

Credit standards
Credit terms
Five C's of credit
Incremental investment

Investment in Inventory

EOQ model
Just-in-time (JIT) inventory
    system
Materials requirement plan-
    ning (MRP)

Monitoring Short-Term Investment

A-B-C system
Accounts receivable turnover
Aging schedule
Average collection period
    (ACP)
Balance proportions
First-in, first-out (FIFO)
Inventory turnover
Last-in, first-out (LIFO)

SUMMARY ▼▼▼▼▼▼▼▼▼▼▼▼

INVESTMENT IN CASH

- The banking system is important for converting revenues into cash and pay-ing obligations.
- The financial manager uses the banking system to manage float. The objective is to minimize receipt float and maximize disbursement float.
- A concentration banking system uses various tools, such as zero-balance accounts, lock boxes, wire transfers, and depository transfer checks, to reduce float and investment in cash balances.
- The primary motive for investing in cash is to pay for transactions.
- Models used to estimate transaction cash balances include the ratio projection method, the Baumol economic order quantity model, and the Miller-Orr con-trol limit model. The latter two models seek to minimize costs by trading order costs off against holding costs. The ratio projection model does not attempt to minimize cost.
- The Baumol EOQ model ignores uncertainty, whereas the Miller-Orr model incorporates uncertainty into the model.

INVESTMENT IN ACCOUNTS RECEIVABLE

- Credit reporting agencies are a prime source for information about business credit applicants.
- The five C's of credit, character, capacity, collateral, capital, and conditions, are used to evaluate a credit application. Three additional C's, country, cul-ture, and currency, become part of the decision process in international trans-actions.
- A perpetuity NPV model is used to analyze changes in credit policy. The investment component of the model is defined differently for a change in credit terms than it is for a change in credit standards.

INVESTMENT IN INVENTORY

- Inventory investment is significant in nonservice-type companies. Techniques used to control this investment include economic order quantity (EOQ), just-in-time (JIT), and materials requirement planning (MRP) inventory systems.
- The models differ in how they respond to inventory changes. EOQ triggers new inventory investment when past demand depletes inventory. MRP is guided by forecasts of future demand for inventory. JIT attempts to make the EOQ amount a single unit.
- Inventory investment in foreign subsidiaries is affected by currency risk.

MONITORING SHORT-TERM INVESTMENT

- Accounts receivable are monitored using average collection period ratios, aging schedules, or balance proportions.
- Average collection period ratios and aging schedules will be distorted by changing sales patterns. No such problem exists with balance proportions. Thus, as techniques, average collection periods and aging schedules are less effective in understanding receivables balances than are balance proportions.

- Inventory turnover ratios and the A-B-C system help monitor inventory investment.

FURTHER READING ▼▼▼▼▼▼▼▼▼▼▼▼▼

Driscoll, Mary C., *Cash Management: Corporate Strategies for Profit.* New York: John Wiley & Sons, 1983. This is a highly readable book about cash management with actual case studies.

Gallinger, George W., and P. Basil Healey, *Liquidity Analysis and Management.* Reading, MA: Addison-Wesley Publishing Company, 1991. This book provides an in-depth discussion about useful techniques for controlling short-term investment.

SELF-TEST PROBLEMS ▼▼▼▼▼▼▼▼▼▼▼▼▼

ST16-1. Cirrus, Inc. has a total cash need of $800,000 for the coming year. The transaction cost for acquiring cash is $20 and the interest rate is 10 percent. What is the maximum amount of cash the firm should hold? What is the firm's average cash investment balance?

ST16-2. A study by an analyst for Wagner Corporation indicates that the firm's cost of each cash transaction is $20, the opportunity cost of money is 12 percent, and the standard deviation of cash flows is $1000. The corporate treasurer desires a lower cash balance limit of $5000. Compute the optimal return balance for the company, the upper and lower control limits, and the average cash balance. Assume a 360-day year.

ST16-3. Vicki Brothers, Inc. currently has an average collection period of 54 days and annual credit sales of $4 million. Assume a 360-day year to answer the following questions.

a. What is the average amount of accounts receivable on the company's balance sheet?

b. If the variable cost of the firm is 60 percent of sales, what is the average investment in accounts receivable?

c. If the appropriate risk-adjusted opportunity cost of the firm's accounts receivable is 9 percent per annum, what is the opportunity cost of the accounts receivable investment calculated in part (b)? What is the interpretation of how the decision should affect the value of the firm?

ST16-4. Currently, all of Mesa Corporation's sales are on credit with terms of net 30 days. Management is considering a 3 percent cash discount for payment within 10 days. The terms require payment in full in 30 days if the discount is not taken. The firm's current average collection period is 45 days and sales are $4 million. Management expects the new credit policy to result in incremental sales of $400,000, with 80 percent of both old and new sales being discounted. The average collection period of accounts not taking the discount is expected to be 60 days and bad debts are not expected to increase. The firm's variable-cost ratio is 70 percent. Its tax rate is 30 percent and the after-tax opportunity cost rate is 12 percent. Should management adopt the new credit policy?

ST16-5. The Tiki Company has annual demand for 12,000 units of a product that it carries in inventory. The order cost for replenishing this item is $50 regardless of the size of the order. Annual holding costs are $0.40 per unit. What is the economic order quantity for this product? What is the optimal number of orders per year? If the cost of each unit is $13, what is the average dollar investment in inventory if no safety stock is maintained to provide for delays in receiving a new order?

PROBLEMS ▼▼▼▼▼▼▼▼▼▼▼▼

INVESTMENT IN CASH

16-1. In reviewing the company's need to maintain cash balances for normal business transactions, the analyst for Ace Hardware, Inc. has reviewed the historical relationship between the firm's cash balances and sales over a seven-year period. On average, with little variation, the ratio of cash to sales has been 3 percent. The management of Ace forecasts $11 million in sales for the year ahead. Using the ratio projection method, what level of cash should the treasurer provide for next year?

16-2. Make Believe Mail Order, Inc. has average daily cash receipts of $47,000 in the form of personal checks arriving at its headquarters in Athens, Georgia. Based on postmark dates, the company's treasurer estimates that these checks are in the mail an average of 4.5 days. The time required for Make Believe to get the checks to its bank averages two days. Once these payments are deposited in the Athens bank, three days are necessary to clear the checks through the banking system.

a. What is Make Believe's average collection float in days?
b. If Make Believe's short-term borrowing costs are 12 percent annually, how much interest would be saved by reducing the firm's collection float by four days? Assume a 360-day year.
c. What actions might Make Believe take to reduce collection float? What would be the maximum amount the firm should pay for each day's reduction in float?

16-3. General Manufacturing Corporation's credit office in Los Angeles administers the firm's nationwide credit and collection operations. All billing and cash receipts are handled through the Los Angeles office. Cash receipts average $2 million daily. General's financial officer has been approached by a major bank with a proposal to set up a system of regional concentration banks that would reduce General's collection float by an average of five days.

a. If General Manufacturing's cost of capital currently is 11 percent, what would be the annual incremental savings of the proposed concentration banking system over General's present collection operation in Los Angeles? Assume a 360-day year and that the cost of concentration banking is the same as General's present collection operation.
b. What would you expect to be included in the proposed concentration banking system that would reduce the collection float?

16-4. Brunswick Stock Brokers has individual and institutional brokerage accounts located in 43 states from New York to California. Brunswick's home office is in St. Louis, Missouri, with all customer accounting and check disbursements handled from that office. Brunswick uses a St. Louis bank account for all checks mailed to customers, which total $540 million a year. Brunswick's managing partner is considering an arrangement in which checks for customers in different areas of the country would be drawn on banks more distant from the customers' home location than St. Louis. Such a practice would increase Brunswick's disbursement float by two days.

a. If the administrative and service costs of this change would amount to $160,000 annually, what would be your recommendation to Brunswick if the firm's opportunity cost of funds is 10 percent?

b. What would you expect to be included in the proposed check disbursements system for Brunswick?

16-5. A firm has a total cash need of $500,000 for the coming year. The transaction cost for acquiring cash is $25 and the interest rate is 15 percent.

a. Find the maximum amount of cash the firm should hold. Round your answer to the nearest dollar.

b. If the interest rate is 5 percent, what is the maximum amount of cash to hold? Round your answer to the nearest dollar.

16-6. The financial manager of Eaton Industries has decided to use the Baumol model to help her make cash management decisions. She has determined that the total demand for cash over the next year is $172 million; the transactions cost for selling securities is $90 per transaction, including the cost of managerial time, telephone expense, and so on; and the average annual interest rate on marketable securities is 10 percent. She wants all answers rounded to the nearest dollar.

a. What is the economic order quantity of cash?
b. What is the average cash investment?
c. How much are total ordering costs for the period?
d. How much are total holding costs for the period?
e. What happens to the optimal cash amount as ordering costs increase? When opportunity costs decrease?

16-7. The Wesley Corporation expects $2 million in cash outlays during the next year. The outlays are expected to occur uniformly over the year. Management's annual opportunity cost of funds is 10 percent from investments in marketable securities. The cost of each transaction to secure cash is $90, which includes both direct and indirect costs. All cash demands are met by selling marketable securities.

a. Determine the optimal size of a transfer of funds from marketable securities to cash.
b. How much is the average cash balance?
c. How many transfers to cash from marketable securities are needed during the year?
d. What is the total cost associated with the firm's cash requirements?
e. How are the answers to (a) and (b) affected if cost per transaction decreases?

16-8. At the start of a 90-day planning period, the cash manager estimates cash needs of $27,000. The market rate of interest on government securities is 10 percent per annum, and the brokerage commission is a constant $50 per buying-and-selling transaction.

a. Determine the economic order quantity of cash.
b. How much is the average cash balance?
c. If the brokerage cost doubles, how much does the economic order quantity change?

16-9. The treasurer knows that the cost of each cash transaction is $25, the opportu nity cost of money is 15 percent per year, and the standard deviation of dail cash flows is $10,000. The treasurer desires a lower cash balance limit o $100,000. Compute the return point cash balance, the upper control limit, and the average cash balance for the company. Assume 360 days in the year. Round each answer to the nearest dollar.

16-10. Determine the maximum cash balance, the average cash balance, and the optimal return point, using the Miller-Orr model for each of the following situations:

	Variance of Daily Cash Flows	Transaction Cost	Annual Interest Rate
a.	$ 5,000	$90	12%
b.	5,000	90	15
c.	5,000	45	15
d.	50,000	45	15
e.	50,000	45	10
f.	30,000	55	10

16-11. John Morris, a summer intern for Vero Beach Cannery Ltd., performed a study of the company's daily cash flows. He found that the cash flows appeared to be random with an expected value of zero and a standard deviation of $30,000. The cost to buy or sell securities is estimated to be $80. Current money-market rates would enable Vero Beach to earn 8 percent annually on any investments in marketable securities. Assume a 360-day year. Round your answers to the nearest dollar.

a. Using the Miller-Orr model, calculate the return point, the upper limit, and the average cash balance.

b. How much is the lower control limit? What happens to the values calculated in part (a) if the lower limit is set at $200,000?

16-12. The treasurer of Nudder Industries uses the Miller-Orr model to manage the company's cash account. Recently, the chief financial officer asked the treasurer about the sensitivity of the solution for the return point and upper control limit to changes in the transaction cost, the variance of daily net cash flows, and the daily opportunity cost rate. The treasurer is currently using an $80 transaction cost, a $1.5 million daily net cash flow variance, and a 9 percent annual opportunity cost. The company's bank requires a noninterest-earning compensating balance of $0.5 million be maintained.

a. Calculate the optimal return cash level and the upper and lower control limits. Use a 360-day year. Round your answers to the nearest dollar amount.

b. Calculate the answer to part (a) if the transaction cost increases 10 percent to $88.

c. Calculate the answer to part (a) if the cash flow variance increases 10 percent to $1.65 million.

d. Calculate the answer to part (a) if the annual opportunity cost increases 10 percent to 9.9 percent.

e. Calculate the answer to part (a) if parts (b), (c), and (d) happen simultaneously.

f. Discuss the sensitivity of the solution to changes in the variables.

16-13. A firm has collected a sample of 15 cash flows:

Day	Net Cash Flow	Day	Net Cash Flow
1	$ 0	9	$500
2	100	10	−600
3	−200	11	200
4	−300	12	−200
5	100	13	100
6	0	14	−100
7	200	15	−200
8	400		

Management wants to use these amounts to calculate the key variables of the Miller-Orr cash model. The lower limit is assumed to be zero. Order costs are forecasted to be $100. The annual opportunity cost of funds is 12 percent.

Calculate the variance of the preceding cash flows. How much is the optimal return cash level, the upper control limit, the lower control limit, and the average cash balance? Assume a 360-day year and round the answers to the nearest dollar.

16-14. Based on historic data, the cash manager has determined that the standard deviation of daily cash flows is $400,000 with a mean of zero. Interest rates on short-term investments are 6 percent per year (use a 360-day year). Each investment or disinvestment costs the firm $100 in paperwork costs, and so on. The firm's bank requires a minimum cash balance of $500,000; this is the lower control limit.

a. Calculate the optimal return cash level and the upper control limit. Round your answer to the nearest dollar amount.

b. Assume that the firm's initial cash balance is $1 million and that it experiences the following cash flows over the first seven days:

Day	Net Cash Flow
1	−$300,000
2	−400,000
3	500,000
4	−200,000
5	900,000
6	200,000
7	700,000

Using the control limits and return points calculated in part (a), indicate the transactions that would occur for this series of cash flows. Give the amounts of any purchases or sales of short-term investments.

INVESTMENT IN ACCOUNTS RECEIVABLE

16-15. Describe the major weakness with the five C's approach to the credit granting decision.

16-16. Karros Ltd. currently has an average collection period of 48 days and annual credit sales of $3 million. Assume a 360-day year.

  a. What is the average balance in accounts receivable on the balance sheet?
  b. If the variable cost of the firm is 70 percent of sales, what is the average *investment* in accounts receivable? (*Hint:* Interpret *investment* as the actual cost of the products sold and not as cost plus profit as interpreted by accountants.)
  c. If the appropriate risk-adjusted opportunity cost of the firm's accounts receivable is 8 percent per annum, what is the opportunity cost of the investment (from part b) in accounts receivable? What is the interpretation of your answer in terms of value of the firm?

16-17. Currently, all of Harper Company sales are on credit with terms of net 30 days. Management is considering a 2 percent cash discount for payment within 15 days. The terms require payment in full in 30 days if the discount is not taken. The firm's current average collection period (ACP) is 46 days and sales are $1.8 million. Management expects the new credit policy to result in incremental sales of $100,000, with 60 percent of both old and new sales discounted. The ACP of accounts not taking the discount is expected to be 50 days and bad debts are expected to increase $2200. The variable-cost ratio of the firm is 75 percent, its tax rate is 40 percent, and the after-tax opportunity cost rate is 10 percent. Should management adopt the new credit policy?

16-18. The Debbie Software Company is evaluating the company's decision to offer credit to its customers. The initiation of credit terms is expected to increase sales by 50,000 units. The policy is also expected to increase bad debts from 0 percent to 15 percent of sales. Sales are currently 90,000 units at an average price of $60 per unit. The per-unit variable cost amount is $36. If the new policy is adopted, all customers' accounts are expected to be outstanding 20 days. No change is expected in either inventory investment or spontaneous financing. The firm's before-tax opportunity cost of capital is 20 percent.

  a. What is the relevant amount of bad debt to use in analyzing the proposed credit policy change?
  b. Calculate the incremental investment as a result of the new credit policy.
  c. Calculate the net present value of the decision. Should the firm undertake the new credit policy? Why?

16-19. Pittsburgh Industries currently has credit sales of $400 million per year and an average collection period of 50 days. The average selling price of Pittsburgh's product is $70 dollars per unit and the average variable cost is $42. Management is considering relaxing its credit standards. The expectation is that sales will increase 20 percent, the average collection period will change to 55 days, and inventory will increase by $10 million. No change is expected in bad debts. The firm's after-tax opportunity cost of investment in accounts receivable is 12 percent and its tax rate is 40 percent. Use two decimal places in your calculations. Round your answer to the nearest dollar.

  a. Calculate the average collection period for the new accounts.
  b. Calculate the incremental investment as a result of the new credit policy.
  c. Calculate the net present value of the investment, if the new credit policy is implemented.
  d. Should the new credit policy be implemented? Why?
  e. How much in new bad debts (before taxes) can the new policy incur before the decision is made to reject the policy change?

16-20. Michael's Retrofitters, Inc. is considering changing its credit period from net 30 to net 45 days. It is believed that the change will increase credit sales by $250,000. The current credit sales level is $750,000. The company's variable-cost percentage is 70 percent, and the before-tax cost of capital is 20 percent. Currently, the average collection period (ACP) for accounts is 36 days. The new credit policy is expected to result in the ACP for current customers changing to 51 days. New accounts are forecasted to have an ACP of 65 days. Should Michael's change its credit period? Use a 360-day year and round your answers to the nearest dollar.

16-21. Logic, Inc.'s current annual sales are $12,000. Variable costs are $6000 and fixed costs are $1800. Presently, all sales are made for cash. Management is considering the introduction of credit sales with terms of 2/10, n/30. The terms are expected to increase sales by $6000 per year and fixed costs by $60. Inventory should increase $250, but accounts payable and accrued wages should increase $330. Ninety percent of the old customers are forecasted to take the discount and pay on the tenth day. The remaining old customers and all the new customers are not expected to take the discount. They are expected to pay on the fortieth day. The after-tax opportunity cost of funds is 10 percent and the corporate tax rate is 34 percent. No bad debts are expected.

Should management offer credit terms? Round your answer to the nearest dollar.

16-22. Management wants to liberalize the firm's credit standards. It hopes to increase sales from the existing $600,000 to $675,000. The average collection period (ACP) is currently 45 days and is expected to increase to 60 days. The firm's only manufactured product is sold at $2 per unit, has a pretax per-unit variable cost of $1.50, and has a current average total cost per unit of $1.75.

Should the firm liberalize the credit policy if its after-tax cost of capital is 16 percent? The tax rate is 40 percent.

16-23. The Arizona Fruit Company is considering extending credit to some customers with higher risk levels (lower credit rating). These customers can be separated into two classes: A and B. The firm's variable-cost ratio is 85 percent and its tax rate is 34 percent.

	Class A	Class B
Potential sales	$10 million	$30 million
Bad debts as a percentage of sales	5%	12%
After-tax cost of capital of receivables	12%	20%
Average collection period (ACP)	36 days	90 days

What will be cash flows to the firm if credit is extended to each class? What should be the decision?

16-24. Because of recent increases in its outstanding accounts receivable, Swann Corporation is considering tightening credit standards and increasing collection efforts. Sales are $2 million a year, with accounts receivable averaging $250,000. Management expects such a move to cause sales to decline by

$300,000. However, it is believed that the new policy should enable the company to lower the average collection period (ACP) to 36 days from its current level of 45 days. Investigation expenses should drop, but collection expenses should rise. Management estimates that the net effect of investigative and collection expenses is a $10,000 increase in costs. Bad debts are currently 1.5 percent of sales, but the new policy is estimated to cut this to 1 percent. The company's variable-cost ratio is 85 percent.

Management would like to make 25 percent, after taxes, on invested capital. The tax rate is 34 percent. Analyze the policy change. Use a 360-day year. (*Hint:* First, you should calculate the ACP for the accounts which will be lost.)

INVESTMENT IN INVENTORY

16-25. A company buys 30,000 parts per year at a unit price of $10. If it costs $20 to process a purchase order, and interest and storage charges total 20 percent of unit price, what is the approximate economic order quantity?

16-26. The purchase cost of materials employed in the production of office laser printers is $1100 per unit. Warehousing and financing cost of inventory is 15 percent of cost. Suppliers charge a fixed delivery fee of $450 per order and delivery is instantaneous. Given that the firm expects to use 40,000 units of materials per year, what is the economic order quantity?

16-27. The purchasing agent at Kross Machine Company is concerned that his current policy for ordering a certain brand of metal saw blades may be cost-ineffective. The agent purchases 120,000 boxes of saw blades per year at $11.70 per box. The agent believes that he incurs holding costs equal to 20 percent of the firm's average inventory investment. Acquisition costs are $100 per order. What is the optimal order quantity for these saw blades?

16-28. A company experiences annual demand for 2500 units of the single product that it stocks. The replenishment cost for inventory is fixed at $40 regardless of the size of the order. Annual holding costs are $0.80 per unit. What is the optimal number of orders per year?

16-29. The Duncan Company carries a wide assortment of items for its customers. One item is particularly popular. Wishing to keep its inventory under control, management selects this item to initiate its new policy of ordering only the optimal economic order quantity each time. From the following information, help management solve the problem.

Annual demand	160,000 units
Price per unit	$2.00
Carrying costs	$0.10 per unit, or 5% of value
Cost per order	$5.00

Fill in the missing amounts:

Number of orders	1	10	20	40	80	100
Size of order						
Average inventory						
Carrying costs						
Order costs						
Total costs						

Determine the optimal EOQ by inspection and by the use of the EOQ formula.

16-30. The Robie Company is a restaurant supplier that sells a number of products to various restaurants in the area. One of its products is a special meat cutter with a disposable blade. The blades are sold in packages of 12 blades for $20 per package. A sales analyst has determined that the demand for replacement blades is at a constant rate of 2000 packages *per month*. The packages cost Robie Company $10 each from the manufacturer. The ordering cost is $1.20 per order. The annual carrying cost is 10 percent of the purchase cost per unit.

   a. Calculate the economic order quantity. The planning horizon is one year.
   b. Calculate the number of orders per year.
   c. Calculate the total ordering cost of buying blades for the year.
   d. Calculate the total holding cost of carrying blades for the year.

16-31. Analysis establishes the following relations for inventory and storage costs:

   - Orders must be placed in multiples of 100 units.
   - Requirements for the 50-week year are 40,000 units.
   - Carrying cost per unit per year is $0.20.
   - Ordering cost per order is $10.

   a. What is the economic order quantity?
   b. What is the optimal number of orders to be placed during the year?
   c. How much are total ordering costs?
   d. How much are total holding costs?

16-32. Leah Electric Co. produces a line of electric motors with a volume of 50,000 units per year. Currently, it purchases the rotor shaft in quantities of 10,000 units per order. Inventory carrying costs amount to $0.50 per shaft per year and it costs $45 to place an order

   a. Find the EOQ, total ordering costs, and total holding costs.
   b. Determine the yearly savings relative to the firm's current inventory system.

16-33. The Outlook Press, a publisher of travel books, is ready to print a new book about New Zealand. The company must decide how big the first and subsequent printings should be. Management forecasts annual sales of 10,800 copies. Each printing has a setup cost of $1500. The cost of carrying the inventory is estimated at $0.40 per copy per year.

   a. Given these data, what is the optimal size of a printing run for this book?
   b. The company has received a notice that its insurance premium has increased. The effect of higher insurance cost is to increase the carrying cost of inventory to $0.45 per unit. What is the new EOQ amount?

16-34. The Keltner Company uses the EOQ model to determine the optimal order size for its product. You have researched the situation and discovered the following facts:

   - The annual demand for the product is expected to be 200,000 units.
   - The invoice cost of the product is $10 per unit.
   - Purchasing agents are paid $20,000 per year. If they spent their entire time on the purchasing of this product, an agent could do 2000 orders per year. When not working on this product, agents do other essential tasks for the firm.

- A warehouse will be rented exclusively for this product at $0.75 per year per unit of warehouse capacity. The capacity will be equal to the optimal order size.
- The cost of capital is 10 percent.
- The secretarial cost and supplies per order will be $7.60.
- The cost of receiving and processing an order at the warehouse dock is $50.
- Insurance cost of storing inventory is $0.50 per unit of inventory per year.

Determine the optimal order quantity, the number of orders, and the average number of units in inventory.

MONITORING SHORT-TERM INVESTMENT

16-35. Young Inc. finished installing a new computerized billing and monitoring system on June 1. In order to determine the effects of the system on accounts receivable, Young's credit manager has prepared the following aging schedule:

Month	Total Receivables	Current	1 Month Old
May	$ 6.4 million	61.5%	38.5%
June	10.0 million	83.0	17.0
July	16.4 million	86.0	14.0

Credit sales have been (in millions):

March $20   April $12   May $8   June $12   July $20

a. On the basis of the preceding aging schedule, what do you conclude about the value of the new system?
b. Compute the average collection period (ACP) as of May, June, and July. Use the most recent three months' sales for each ACP calculation. What is your assessment of the new system based on ACPs? Round the ACPs to the nearest day. Assume each month has 30 days.
c. Use the aging schedule to complete the following table:

	Sales	May	June	July
April	$12			
May	8			
June	12			
July	20			
Total		$6.400	$10.000	$16.400

d. Use your answer to part (c) to calculate balance proportions. What do you conclude about the new computerized system?

16-36. Given the following data of accounts receivable, calculate the aging schedules and balance proportions for each month from January through May.

Month	Sales	Jan	Feb	Mar	Apr	May
Oct	$ 40	$ 4				
Nov	60	10	$ 6			
Dec	120	60	20	$ 12		
Jan	180	162	92	32	$ 16	
Feb	180		158	84	28	$ 20
Mar	120			100	60	18
Apr	80				70	42
May	60					54
Total		$236	$276	$228	$174	$134

16-37. Ifflander Consulting Services' accounts receivable total $517,000. A break-down of the outstanding accounts on the basis of the month in which the credit sale was made is shown in the following table. Sales for each month are also provided. Assume 30 days in each month.

Month of Credit Sale	Accounts Receivable	Credit Sales
Five months ago	$ 93,500	$225,000
Four months ago	32,600	57,000
Three months ago	81,000	120,000
Two months ago	129,000	290,000
Current month	180,900	275,000
Total	$517,000	$967,000

a. Calculate average collection periods (ACP) using sales for the past 30, 60, 90, 120, and 150 days. Round your sales-per-day answers to the nearest dollar.
b. Calculate the aging schedule.
c. Calculate balance proportions.
d. Discuss whether ACPs, aging schedules, or balance proportions provide the better monitoring tool.

16-38. Mr. Roberts, the credit manager at Terell Manufacturing, has determined from previous experience that 10 percent of a given month's credit sales are collected in the current month, 40 percent are collected in the next month, and 50 percent are collected in the second month following the date of the credit sale. Credit sales were $200,000 in December, $250,000 in January, $120,000 in February, $300,000 in March, and $200,000 in April.

a. What is the level of accounts receivable at Terell Manufacturing in February, March, and April?
b. Calculate the aging schedule for February, March, and April.
c. Calculate average collection periods (ACP) for February, March, and April using the past 30, 60, and 90 days sales per day. Use the following table.

Mon	AR	Sales	For the Last 30 Days Sales Per Day	ACP	For the Last 60 Days Sales Per Day	ACP	For the Last 90 Days Sales Per Day	ACP
Dec		$200						
Jan		250						
Feb	$233	120						
Mar	330	300						
Apr	330	200						

d. Calculate the balance proportions for February, March, and April accounts receivable.

e. Discuss which monitoring technique provides the best answer.

16-39. For a firm with average annual sales of $30 million and trade credit terms of net 30, assume that the credit manager has the following data:

Month	Total Balance	Aging in $Million 0	1	2	3	3 + Months
January	$3.5	$2.2	$0.4	$0.3	$0.3	$0.3
February	4.0	2.8	0.6	0.3	0.2	0.1
March	4.1	2.7	0.8	0.4	0.1	0.1
April	4.6	3.1	0.7	0.5	0.2	0.1

a. Determine the aging schedule for each month.

b. Discuss which month's receivables are the most current and which month's receivables are the least current.

c. Assume actual sales are as follows:

October	$3.6	November	$1.5	December	$2.0
January	$2.5	February	$3.5	March	$3.2
April	$4.0				

Calculate the balance proportions for January, February, March, and April. Ignore any amounts outstanding "3 + months."

16-40. Approximately 20 percent of sales are paid in cash, with the remaining 80 percent sold to established credit customers on a 30-day charge account. Historically, 70 percent of the charge accounts are paid in the month following the sale, with the remaining 30 percent being paid the second month following the sale. Bad debt losses are insignificant. Accounts receivable at the end of April amounted to $4200. Credit sales for the year were as follows:

January	$2000	May	$10,000	September	$21,000
February	2000	June	9,000	October	15,000
March	4000	July	8,000	November	13,000
April	3000	August	14,000	December	18,000

a. Starting with April, calculate the end-of-month accounts receivable balance for the months of April through December.

b. Starting with April, calculate the end-of-month aging schedule for each month, April through December.

c. Starting with April, calculate average collection periods (ACP) for each month, April through December, using 30-, 60-, and 90-day intervals. Assume 30 days in each month.

d. Compare your results for parts (b) and (c) and draw conclusions about why differences exist among them. Which approach is best for analyzing accounts receivable balances?

16-41. What purpose may be served by the use of financial ratios in the management of inventory? What limitations are there on the usefulness of financial ratios in inventory control?

16-42. Hamilton Manufacturing Co. has several different items in its inventory. As shown in the following table, the number of units and cost per item vary widely. You are asked to recommend an A-B-C inventory classification system for these items. Your answer should discuss why you classify the various items into the A, B, and C groups.

Item	Number of Units	Cost Per Unit
1	3600	$ 1.10
2	2000	16.30
3	200	11.90
4	16	200.00
5	800	7.25
6	500	2.50
7	160	87.00
8	3200	3.25
9	1200	1.80
10	6000	0.45
11	1800	32.00
12	130	2.80
13	4400	9.25
14	3600	2.90
15	400	38.75

16-43. The chief financial officer of Columbus Company finds that although the company continues to earn the same net income year after year, the rate of return on stockholders' equity is decreasing. Most of the profits are permitted to remain in the business so that total assets are increasing year by year, but there is very little increase in net income. As the recently hired financial analyst, you are requested to assist the chief financial officer in locating the difficulty and to suggest remedial measures.

Among the data of interest that you find are the following:

	Inventory Dec. 31	Cost of Goods Sold
4 years ago	$257,000	$2,850,000
3 years ago	292,000	2,650,000
2 years ago	365,000	2,800,000
1 year ago	407,000	2,980,000

    a. What conclusions can be reached on the basis of this information only?

    b. What further investigation does it suggest? State exactly how you would proceed.

    c. If your conclusions are confirmed in the additional investigation, what recommendations would you make concerning remedial measures?

16-44. Outline the principal reasons for holding inventory and explain why good inventory management is likely to be one of the most important aspects of overall company management. What other areas of company management is the inventory problem likely to impinge upon?

LIBRARY ASSIGNMENT

16-45. Using the *Business Periodicals Index, The Wall Street Journal Index,* or other sources of business information, select a report of what a specific firm is doing to improve its investment in cash, accounts receivable, or inventories. Prepare a one-page summary of your finding including the specific citation for your information.

COMPREHENSIVE PROBLEMS ▼▼▼▼▼▼▼▼▼▼▼

16-46. The treasurer of Universal Industries is examining various models to aid in cash management decisions. The manager estimates that total demand for cash over the next year is $225 million; the transactions cost for selling securities is $120 per transaction, including the cost of managerial time; and the opportunity cost rate is 8 percent. Use the Baumol model to answer parts (a) through (e). Round all answers to the nearest dollar.

    a. What is the economic order quantity of cash?

    b. What is the average cash balance for part (a)?

    c. How much are total ordering costs for the period?

    d. How much are total holding costs for the period?

    e. What happens to the optimal cash amount when ordering costs increase? What happens when opportunity costs decrease?

    f. The treasurer next turns to the Miller-Orr model. The executive knows that the cost of each cash transaction is $120, the opportunity cost of money is 8 percent per year, and the standard deviation of daily cash flows is $50,000. He is interested in knowing the return point cash balance, the upper control limit, and the average cash balance when the lower limit is a balance of $100,000. Assume 360 days in the year. Round all answers to the nearest dollar.

g. The company currently has annual credit sales of $600 million and an average collection period of 40 days. The average selling price of Universal's product is $350 per unit; the average variable cost is $210 per unit. Management is considering relaxing its credit standards. With easier credit, a financial analyst estimates that sales will increase 25 percent and average collection period (ACP) will rise to 50 days. With this higher level of sales, inventories will have to increase by $8 million. Bad debts would increase by an estimated $3 million annually. The firm's after-tax opportunity cost of investment in accounts receivable is 10 percent. Its tax rate is 35 percent.

- Calculate the ACP for the new accounts.
- Calculate the incremental investment as a result of the new credit policy.
- Calculate the NPV of the credit decision.
- Should the new credit policy be implemented? Why?

16-47. Central Corporation, a competitor of Universal, sells to industrial customers and extends credit for 30 days. Central introduced a new accounts receivable billing and monitoring system this past October 1. Central's credit manager is studying the results of the new system on accounts receivable. The following aging schedule of accounts receivable was prepared:

End of Month	Total Receivables	Current	Over 1 Month
September	$26 million	55%	45%
October	30 million	70	30
November	36 million	80	20

Credit sales were (in millions):

July $30   Aug. $22   Sept. $18   Oct. $22   Nov. $30

a. Based on the preceding aging schedule, what do you conclude about the value of the new system?
b. Compute the average collection period (ACP) as of September, October, and November. Use the most recent three months' sales for each ACP calculation. What is your assessment of the new system based on ACPs? Round the ACPs to the nearest day.
c. Use the aging schedule given in the problem to complete the following table for outstanding balances in accounts receivable:

	Sales	Sept	Oct	Nov
Aug	$22			
Sept	18			
Oct	22			
Nov	30			
Total		$26	$30	$36

d. Use your answer to part (c) to calculate the balance proportions. What do you conclude about the new computerized system?

ST16-1. Economic order quantity of cash

$$= \sqrt{2 \times \text{order cost} \times \text{need} \div \text{interest rate}}$$
$$= \sqrt{2 \times \$20 \times \$800,000 \div 0.10}$$
$$= \$17,889$$

Average cash balance $= \text{EOQ} \div 2$
$$= \$17,899 \div 2$$
$$= \$8945$$

ST16-2. Optimal return cash level

$$= \sqrt[3]{\frac{3 \times \text{order cost} \times \text{variance of daily cash balance}}{4 \times \text{daily opportunity cost of funds}}}$$

$$= \sqrt[3]{\frac{3 \times \$20 \times (\$1000)^2}{4 \times 0.12/360}}$$

$$= \$3557 \text{ without the } \$5000 \text{ minimum balance}$$

Optimal return cash level including the minimum balance
$$= \$3557 + \$5000$$
$$= \$8557$$

UCL $= 3 \times$ optimal return cash level $+$ minimum balance
$$= 3 \times \$3557 + \$5000$$
$$= \$15,671$$

Lower balance $= \$5000$ as stated

ACB $=$ (Optimal return cash level $\times 4/3$) $+$ minimum balance
$$= (\$3557 \times 4/3) + \$5000$$
$$= \$9743$$

ST16-3. a. Average accounts receivable $= \dfrac{\text{Sales} \times \text{average collection period}}{360 \text{ days}}$

$$= \frac{\$4,000,000 \times 54}{360}$$

$$= \$600,000$$

b. Average investment in accounts receivable
$$= \text{Accounts receivable} \times \text{variable-cost ratio}$$
$$= \$600,000 \times 0.60$$
$$= \$360,000$$

c. Dollar opportunity cost $=$ Opportunity rate $\times$ receivable investment
$$= 0.09 \times \$360,000$$
$$= \$32,400$$

The $32,400 represents the minimum dollar return that must be earned on the accounts receivable investment. Earning any amount less than $32,400 will result in a negative NPV for the decision.

ST16-4. Average collection period
$$= \text{Proportion discounting} \times \text{days until discount}$$
$$+ \text{proportion not discounting} \times \text{days until payment}$$
$$= 0.80 \times 10 + 0.20 \times 60$$
$$= 20 \text{ days}$$

Incremental investment
$$= \text{Variable-cost ratio} \times (\text{incremental ACP old accounts})$$
$$\times (\text{sales to old accounts} \div 360)$$
$$+ \text{variable-cost ratio} \times (\text{ACP new accounts}) \times (\text{new sales} \div 360)$$
$$= 0.70 \times (20 - 45) \times \$4,000,000 \div 360 + 0.70 \times 20 \times \$400,000 \div 360$$
$$= -\$194,444 + \$15,556$$
$$= -\$178,888$$

Cash discounts $= \text{Total sales} \times \text{proportion discounting} \times \text{discount rate}$
$$= \$4,400,000 \times 0.80 \times 0.03$$
$$= \$105,600$$

$$\text{NPV} = \frac{(\text{New sales} \times (1 - \text{variable-cost ratio}) - \text{discounts}) \times (1 - \tau)}{\text{Opportunity cost rate}}$$

$$- \text{incremental investment}$$

$$= \frac{(\$400,000 \times (1 - 0.70) - \$105,600) \times (1 - 0.30)}{0.12} - (-\$178,888)$$

$$= \$84,000 + \$178,888$$
$$= \$262,888$$

Accept the proposal since the NPV is positive.

ST16-5. $\text{EOQ} = \sqrt{2 \times \text{order costs} \times \text{demand} \div \text{holding costs}}$
$$= \sqrt{2 \times \$50 \times 12,000 \div \$0.40^{1/2}}$$
$$= 1732 \text{ units}$$

Number of orders $= \text{Demand} \div \text{EOQ}$
$$= 12,000 \div 1732$$
$$= 7$$

Average investment in inventory $= \text{EOQ} \times 1/2 \times \text{unit cost}$
$$= 1732 \times 1/2 \times \$13$$
$$= \$11,258$$

Video Case 16

NCR: *Just-in-Time*

Just-in-time (JIT) inventory and production methods emerged from the total quality management (TQM) movement of the late 1980s. The concept is incredibly simple: reducing inventories of materials and goods-in-process reduces costs and increases profits. As the video states so clearly, inventory has no value until used. Idle inventory, either raw materials waiting to be processed or goods waiting to be sold, generates only costs. It takes space to store them, spoilage or damage may occur, and if technology changes, stored inventory may become obsolete. JIT methods reduce these costs by reducing inventories. In fact, one company, Trane, estimates that adopting the JIT approach allowed it to cut inventories by 75 percent, increase productivity by 40 percent, and decrease its defect rate by 90 percent!

The JIT approach depends on having close links with suppliers. In some cases, companies open up parts of their information system to suppliers. This allows suppliers to monitor material needs and ship materials as needed. By anticipating customer needs, the supplier can assure that JIT processes keep running smoothly. Sometimes this approach is called "pull-through." The manufacturing process's demand for materials pulls the supplies from the supplier, rather than having large inventories being pushed through the system.

JIT methods also require that employees be willing to accept more responsibility. Employees in JIT systems must not only complete manufacturing tasks, but must also order material and parts, complete quality inspections as they work, and provide information about completed items. Therefore, JIT processes are often termed *people driven*. Without employees trained and willing to implement the system, it won't work.

JIT manufacturing makes smaller lots than traditional manufacturing. Smaller lots mean smaller inventories. Smaller lots also mean more machine set-up changes. To be success-ful, JIT manufacturing requires that machine set-up times be reduced. One approach is to make parts interchangeable among a variety of different products. When producing small lots, a company effectively produces on order. Not satisfying an order can mean losing the sale. Therefore, quality inspection must be continual, resulting in high-quality manufacturing and increased customer satisfaction. Manufacturing small lots can expose problems hidden in large-lot manufacturing or large inventories. Large lots hide inexact manufacturing process, since sales of acceptable items can be drawn from the large output. Since sales demands are being met, there is little concern about defect rates. With small-lot processes, every defect matters, so inexact processes are quickly identified and repaired. Small-lot processes also help expose inefficiencies such as waits for materials, queues, or time-consuming equipment set-ups. By exposing such waste, companies can begin to eliminate it.

As competition becomes keener, firms must reassess every aspect of their business to eliminate waste and find cost savings. The total quality movement, and JIT inventory and manufacturing methods are ways that companies can stay competitive.

Study Questions

1. In many operations management models, lost sales due to stockouts justify carrying inventories. Does JIT manufacturing ignore the stockout problem, or is it really a problem? How might you determine whether stockout losses mattered?

2. If employees are asked to do more, that is, to accept more responsibility, what affect will that have on wages and profits? Do you think that asking more of employees works better in some economic environments than in others?

CHAPTER 17

Short-Term Financing

Investment in cash, accounts receivable, and inventories—the primary current assets—must be financed. Should long-term funds supplied by debtholders and equityholders be used, or is short-term or intermediate-term debt financing more appropriate? Financing strategies vary. Duff and Phelps, Inc., a financial services firm, finances all its current assets with current liabilities. U.S. Shoe Corporation, which is more a women's apparel company than a shoe company, finances each $1.60 invested in current assets with $1 of current liabilities and $0.60 of long-term financing. The biotechnology company Genetic Therapy, Inc. only uses $1 of current liabilities for every $14.70 of current assets.

The question of how to finance current assets concerns corporate treasurers and financial managers, and depending on how they respond, the firm's risk of insolvency may be either increased or decreased. All firms that use debt financing, whether it be short term or long term, encounter the risk of not having enough cash available to meet debts that come due. When a firm uses only long-term debt financing, insolvency risk is usually lower because only periodically do the firm's debt payments include principal repayment. Even a small amount of current revenue may be enough to meet interest-only debt service payments. However, insolvency risk is greater with the use of short-term debt. Current revenues must be large enough to meet the firm's debt payments for any interest and principal payments on all debt. If current revenues are not enough, the firm may be able to borrow or sell assets to raise financing. The appropriate amount of short-term financing may hinge on competitors' financial positions and management's willingness to expose the firm to greater insolvency risk. Managers, analysts, and bank loan officers forecast the appropriate level of short-term debt financing using various financial ratios and techniques.

Once you have studied this chapter, you should understand:

- The relationship between the level of investment in short-term assets and the financing of those assets.
- Short-term investment and financing from a *flow of funds approach*.

- Financial liquidity ratios that help determine the appropriate balance between short-term assets and short-term liabilities.
- The importance of a cash budget to a company's overall short-term financial planning.
- Types of bank loans and other sources that are available to finance the firm's short-term needs.

17.1 THE MARGIN OF SAFETY

When the firm's policy is to match the maturities of its assets with the maturity of its liabilities, it uses a **hedging strategy.** In particular, the treasurer finances seasonal variations in *current assets* with *current liabilities* of the same maturity and finances all the nonseasonal current assets and all other assets with long-term debt and equity securities. **Current assets** are those normally expected to flow into cash during an operating cycle. **Current liabilities** are short-term debts requiring the payment of cash on demand or within a year. Think of the nonseasonal current assets as permanent assets, similar to how we consider fixed assets. The nonseasonal current assets are permanent because investments in them are set to remain above a minimum level. For instance, the firm maintains a minimum amount of inventory to help satisfy uncertain customer demand; as long as the firm continues to sell on credit there will always be an investment in accounts receivable. Under the hedging approach, long-term funds should be used to finance all permanent assets. Any short-term borrowings, and subsequent repayments, outside of the permanent amount mirror seasonal swings. At seasonal troughs, short-term borrowings fall to zero. Figure 17.1 illustrates the hedging strategy.

FIGURE 17.1

FINANCING INVESTMENTS USING A HEDGING APPROACH

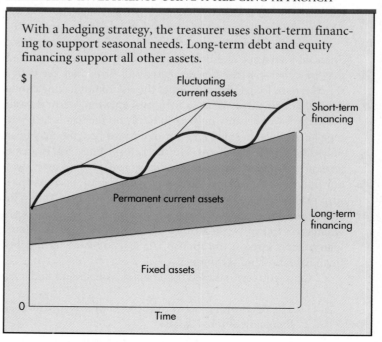

With a hedging strategy, the treasurer uses short-term financing to support seasonal needs. Long-term debt and equity financing support all other assets.

FIGURE 17.2
MARGIN OF SAFETY

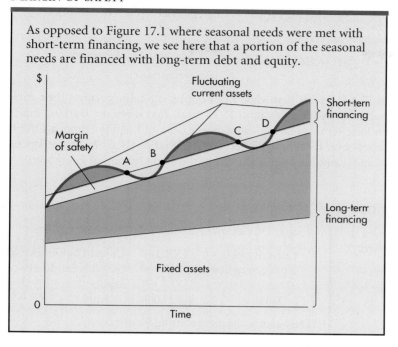

As opposed to Figure 17.1 where seasonal needs were met with short-term financing, we see here that a portion of the seasonal needs are financed with long-term debt and equity.

The situation is really more complicated than Figure 17.1 can show. It is difficult to match cash inflows and outflows precisely. To provide some safety in being able to meet cash obligations, the treasurer can lengthen the maturity schedule of the debt. This task is accomplished by replacing some short-term financing with long-term financing. *In general, there is an inverse relationship between the risk of being unable to pay debt and the debt maturity schedule.* For example, if Lotus Corporation borrows $10 million for two years at 8 percent compounded annually, the annual principal and interest payment is $5,607,692. If the loan matures in five years, the annual principal and interest payment is $2,504,565.[1] Lotus needs to generate about 45 percent less cash flow in each of the next two years for the longer-maturity loan.

As Figure 17.2 illustrates, long-term funds finance a portion of the seasonal needs; this is in contrast to short-term funds financing all seasonal needs in Figure 17.1. Near cyclical troughs (for example, between points *C* and *D*), the firm has excess cash that the treasurer can use to pay back short-term debt that was used to support additional current asset investment during the cyclical peak period (between points *B* and *C*). As the firm approaches point *D*, the treasurer again draws on short-term debt to satisfy cash needs. Any available short-term debt that the treasurer has not used provides a liquidity reserve, or **margin of safety,** to meet uncertain cash needs.

The relationship between current assets and short-term financing that we see in

Margin of safety. The amount long-term financing exceeds permanent asset investment in current and fixed assets.

[1]Solution: Use the equation Present value = Annual amount $\times$ PVIFA$_{r\%,\ n\ years}$. The *present value* is $10 million, *r*% is 8, and *n* is either 2 or 5 depending on which problem you are solving. The unknown variable is the *annual amount.*

Figure 17.2 (or Figure 17.1) is normally discussed in terms of *net working capital*. We define **net working capital** as:

> **Net working capital.** The excess of current assets over current liabilities. Alternatively, the excess of equity and long-term debt over fixed and other non-current assets.

$$\text{Net working capital} = \text{Current assets} - \text{current liabilities} \qquad (17.1)$$

or alternatively as:

$$\text{Net working capital} = \text{Noncurrent debt} + \text{equity} - \text{noncurrent assets} \qquad (17.2)$$

Equation 17.1 indicates that when net working capital is positive, then current assets exceed current liabilities. Equation 17.2 reveals that when net working capital is positive, then long-term financing (noncurrent debt and equity) supports the surplus of current assets over current liabilities. (See Illustration 17.1.) Many lenders use the net working capital amount as an indicator of the firm's margin of safety level.

ILLUSTRATION 17.1

Alternative net working capital definition

Bednar Oil Company has the following balance sheet:

Current assets	$581,100	Current liabilities	$522,000
Noncurrent assets	247,900	Noncurrent debt	45,600
		Equity	261,400
Total	$829,000	Total	$829,000

The balance sheet accounting identity is:

Current assets + noncurrent assets
    = Current liabilities + noncurrent debt + equity

$581,100 + $247,900 = $522,000 + $45,600 + $261,400

where

Noncurrent assets = Fixed assets + other long-term assets

To arrive at the amount of net working capital, subtract noncurrent assets and current liabilities from both sides of the identity. Thus,

Current assets − current liabilities
    = Noncurrent debt + equity − noncurrent assets

Net working capital for Bednar Oil Company is $59,100, the difference between current assets and current liabilities:

$$\$581,000 - \$522,000 = \$59,100$$

The alternative derivation for net working capital is:

Net working capital
    = Noncurrent debt + equity − noncurrent assets
    = $45,600 + $261,400 − $247,900
    = $59,100

This alternative definition shows that Bednar Oil finances the excess of current assets over current liabilities using long-term financing (noncurrent debt and equity). If Bednar Oil increases its net working capital position, then either long-term financing in the form of debt or equity must increase or noncurrent assets must decrease.

The financing policy illustrated in Figure 17.2 is a conservative one; the treasurer uses little short-term debt financing. However, many firms operate less conservatively, possibly using a negative margin of safety, as indicated in Figure 17.3. A negative margin of safety means that the treasurer uses short-term borrowings to finance a portion of permanent current assets (alternative 1) and perhaps some fixed assets (alternative 2). If fixed assets are financed with short-term debt, then current assets are less than current liabilities and net working capital is negative. Even though management's decision to use a negative margin of safety causes the firm's risk of exposure to insolvency to increase, some firms have limited access to the long-term financial markets and must rely heavily on short-term borrowings.

Several factors influence the margin of safety level the firm maintains. Figure 17.4 can help us visualize how the flow of funds through the business influences the use of short-term versus long-term financing. At the top of the diagram, notice that the firm's business operations and capital investments represent both investment (*use of cash:* arrow pointing away from cash) and financing (*source of cash:* arrow pointing to cash). Payments to suppliers for inventory, labor, and plant and equipment require cash. Cash sales, collection of receivables, and the sale of assets generate cash. A firm's receipts and disbursements policies, its efficiency in carrying out these policies, and its reputation with suppliers, employees, and customers are eventually reflected in the firm's cash flow patterns and financial needs. For example, in the introduction we mentioned that for every $14.70 of current assets, Genetic Therapy uses $1 of current liabilities; thus, it uses $13.70 of long-term debt and equity to finance current assets. The reason for so little current liability financing is that Genetic Therapy is still developing products. Until its products generate cash inflows, the company must depend on longer-term financing, which is less demanding in terms of cash outflows (as mentioned earlier in our Lotus example).

FIGURE 17.3
NEGATIVE MARGIN OF SAFETY

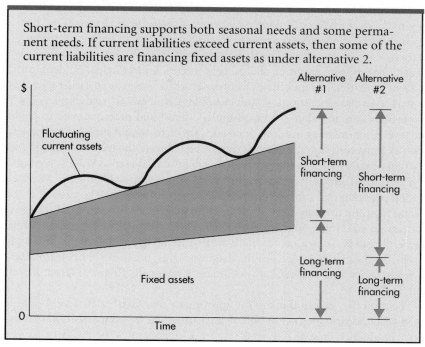

Short-term financing supports both seasonal needs and some permanent needs. If current liabilities exceed current assets, then some of the current liabilities are financing fixed assets as under alternative 2.

FIGURE 17.4

FLOW OF FUNDS THROUGH THE FIRM

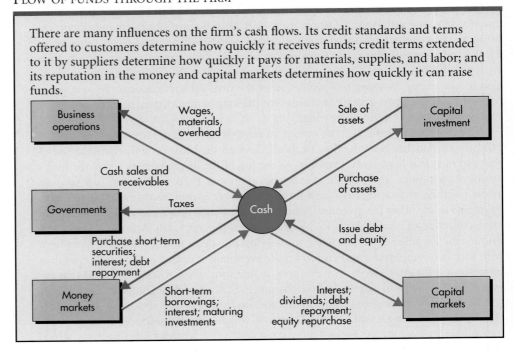

There are many influences on the firm's cash flows. Its credit standards and terms offered to customers determine how quickly it receives funds; credit terms extended to it by suppliers determine how quickly it pays for materials, supplies, and labor; and its reputation in the money and capital markets determines how quickly it can raise funds.

In addition to cash flows associated with business operations and investment in physical assets, the firm both receives cash from and sends cash to the financial markets. Again, the firm's reputation plays an important role. The firm receives cash from the money and capital markets through new issues of financial securities. If the firm is not well perceived by the financial markets, it will have difficulty selling securities, at least at prices that it considers fair. The firm provides cash to the financial markets when it pays cash dividends on common shares, pays interest and principal on debt, purchases short-term securities, or repurchases its own securities issued at an earlier date. Some of these payments are discretionary (for example, dividends to shareholders), whereas other payments are mandatory (for example, interest and principal paid to creditors). As the level of mandatory outflows increases, the firm should make a greater effort to reduce risk in its cash flows. If the risk cannot be reduced, the treasurer should increase the margin of safety level so that more cash will be available to avoid insolvency.

The flow-of-funds diagram (Figure 17.4) also emphasizes how the firm's capital budgeting program and long-term financial structure interact. The cash flows on the left relate typically to short-term investment management in cash, marketable securities, accounts receivable, and inventory. The firm's capital budgeting and financial structure decisions, shown on the right side of the diagram, affect the firm's pool of cash, which appears at the center of the diagram. Thus, the firm's short-term asset decisions relate to its long-run capital investment strategy, its financial structure, and its overall liquidity.

Theoretically, we can think of the appropriate margin of safety level as a trade-off between cost and risk: the cost of borrowing earmarked to reduce cash flow risk versus the actual reduction in cash flow risk. Figure 17.5 illustrates the problem. Long-term

FIGURE 17.5

OPTIMAL MARGIN OF SAFETY

As the treasurer uses more long-term financing, the margin of
safety level improves as noted in Figure 17.2. However, if
long-term funds exceed the cost of short-term funds, then the
financing cost of the margin of safety increases. But a higher
margin of safety level should result in lower risk of having
inadequate funds to meet obligations. Thus, the cost of insolvency risk decreases. The optimal margin of safety level occurs
where the sum for these two costs is minimized.

financing costs usually exceed short-term borrowing costs because investors most often
expect future interest rates to exceed current levels; that is, the yield curve is most often
upward sloping. The difficulty is in quantifying the insolvency risk cost so that the optimal margin of safety level can be calculated. In practice, the treasurer uses the firm's
cash conversion cycle and a *cash budget* to understand the firm's margin of safety needs.
We examine these topics next.

Comprehension Check

1. What is a hedging strategy for financing assets?
2. What information does the alternative definition of net working capital
    (Equation 17.2) provide as opposed to the usual measure (Equation 17.1)?
3. How does the flow-of-funds approach relate to the margin of safety concept?

17.2 THE CASH CONVERSION CYCLE

An understanding of the firm's cash conversion cycle provides the treasurer with an
indication of how much costly financing the firm needs to support its *operating cycle.*

Operating cycle. The period of time between the acquisition of material, labor, and overhead inputs for production and the collection of sales receipts.

Spontaneous financing. Those liabilities such as accounts payable and accrued wages that arise automatically, without negotiation, in the course of doing business.

Cash conversion cycle. The operating cycle less the accounts payable and accrued liabilities deferral period.

Nonspontaneous financing. Financing that has either an explicit or an implicit cost associated with it.

The **operating cycle** is the number of days of investment in both accounts receivable and inventory. We measure the operating cycle as the sum of the *average collection period for receivables* and the *days inventories outstanding,* as we demonstrated in Chapter 16.

Most firms are able to partially self-finance investment in the operating cycle. They are able to purchase materials, supplies, and labor on credit without having to pay any interest cost. We call such interest-free credit **spontaneous financing.** It is shown on a firm's balance sheet as accounts payable and accrued liabilities for wages and other expenses, and it arises naturally from production activities.

The difference between the operating cycle and the spontaneous financing cycle is the **cash conversion cycle.** Alternatively, we can think of the cash conversion cycle as the number of days of *nonspontaneous financing* required to support the operating cycle. **Nonspontaneous financing** is interest-bearing negotiated financing, for example, bank loans and equity financing.[2] We calculate the cash conversion cycle as:

Cash conversion cycle

= Average collection period for receivables + days inventories outstanding

– days accounts payable and accruals outstanding   (17.3)

= Operating cycle – days accounts payable and accruals outstanding

The calculation of the number of days of spontaneous financing for accounts payable and accruals is normally computed as:

Days accounts payable and accruals outstanding

$$= \frac{\text{Accounts payable and accrued liabilities}}{\text{Sales} - \text{earnings before interest and taxes}} \times 360 \qquad (17.4)$$

ILLUSTRATION 17.2

Bednar Oil's cash conversion cycle

Selected financial information for Bednar Oil Company is as follows:

Receivables	$225,600	Accounts payable	$300,612
Inventory	178,265	Accruals	113,003
Other	177,235	Other	108,385
Current assets	$581,100	Current liabilities	$522,000
Noncurrent assets	247,900	Noncurrent debt	45,600
		Equity	261,400
Total	$829,000	Total	$829,000

Sales	$1,042,567
Cost of sales	677,669
Margin	$ 364,898
Selling, general and administrative	344,728
Earnings before interest and taxes	$ 20,170

[2]Although equity financing does not have an interest cost associated with it as does debt, equity does have an opportunity cost. For simplicity in this chapter, we will refer to equity as being part of interest-bearing financing when we discuss the cash conversion cycle.

The average collection period for receivables is:

$$\frac{\text{Accounts receivable}}{\text{Sales}} \times 360$$

$$= \frac{\$225,600}{\$1,042,567} \times 360$$

$$= 77.9 \text{ days}$$

The number of days inventory is outstanding is:

$$\frac{\text{Inventory}}{\text{Cost of sales}} \times 360$$

$$= \frac{\$178,265}{\$677,669} \times 360$$

$$= 94.7 \text{ days}$$

The operating cycle for Bednar Oil is 77.9 + 94.7 = 172.6 days, almost half a year.

The number of days payables and accruals are outstanding is:

$$\frac{\text{Accounts payable and accrued liabilities}}{\text{Sales} - \text{earnings before interest and taxes}} \times 360$$

$$= \frac{\$300,612 + \$113,003}{\$1,042,567 - \$20,170} \times 360$$

$$= 145.6 \text{ days}$$

Bednar Oil's cash conversion cycle is its operating cycle less the payable and accrual cycle: 172.6 – 145.6 = 27 days. The firm needs a little less than one month of negotiated financing to support its operating cycle.

Like the margin of safety level, the cash conversion cycle can be either positive or negative. If it is positive, as in Illustration 17.2 and in Figure 17.6, it measures the number of days of negotiated financing (interest-bearing debt or equity) required to support the operating cycle. If the cash conversion cycle is negative, then the period for outstanding spontaneous financing (accounts payable and accruals) is longer than the operating cycle. Thus, any excess of spontaneous financing over investment in inventory and accounts receivable supports investment in noncurrent assets.

Manufacturing firms have positive cash conversion cycles because of their large investments in accounts receivable and inventory. A service company, such as a hotel or an airline, usually has a small positive, or even a negative, cash conversion cycle because of relatively insignificant inventory investment. Notice that the cash conversion cycle formula does not include the firm's cash balance. The reason is that the cash conversion cycle represents the mismatch, or gap, between receiving cash from customers and paying it to suppliers, employees, and tax agencies.

For some firms it is incorrect to exclude all the cash. Consider the case of Aztar Corporation, a casino hotel operator. In 1992, Aztar had a cash conversion cycle of –24 days, calculated using Equation 17.3. Aztar's spontaneous financing cycle exceeds its operating cycle, thereby leaving the impression that some of the firm's spontaneous financing supports fixed-asset investment. But much of Aztar's cash is really inventory,

FIGURE 17.6

CASH CONVERSION CYCLE

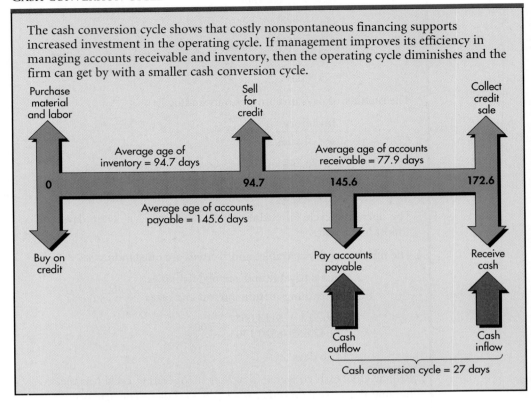

The cash conversion cycle shows that costly nonspontaneous financing supports increased investment in the operating cycle. If management improves its efficiency in managing accounts receivable and inventory, then the operating cycle diminishes and the firm can get by with a smaller cash conversion cycle.

the "product" it transfers to successful gamblers. If we treat *all* of Aztar's cash as inventory (which is inappropriate), then its cash conversion cycle becomes 30 days. Although no longer negative, it is still considerably less than the cash conversion cycle of 114 days for Minnesota Mining & Manufacturing, Inc., a large manufacturing firm.

Management often tries to reduce a positive cash conversion cycle by **stretching accounts payable,** that is, lengthening the number of days before making payment. Stretching may cause the firm to incur two costs. One cost is that the firm's credit reputation may be damaged, if not ruined, if payments are delayed too long. This cost is difficult to quantify. (At a minimum the cost of financing increases, as shown earlier in Figure 17.5.) The second cost arises from missing cash discounts offered by suppliers because invoices are paid after the discount date. Missing cash discounts means that accounts payable is no longer interest-free financing because the firm incurs an expensive opportunity cost, which we call the **annualized cost of a missed discount (ACD):**

Stretching accounts payable. Failing to pay within the prescribed trade credit period.

Annualized cost of a missed discount (ACD). The cost of foregoing cash discounts and paying at some date beyond the discount period.

$$\text{Annualized cost of a missed discount} = \frac{\text{Cash discount \%}}{100 - \text{cash discount \%}} \times \frac{360 \text{ days}}{\substack{\text{number of days payment} \\ \text{made after the discount period}}} \quad (17.5)$$

The equation suggests that the longer the firm waits before paying the invoice, the less is the ACD. Illustration 17.3 shows this to be true.

ILLUSTRATION 17.3

Annualized cost of a missed cash discount

Invoices issued by Kuncans Glass Company display credit terms of 2/10, n/30. The customer can take a 2 percent cash discount if it pays the invoice within 10 days of the invoice date. Otherwise, the customer should pay the invoice 30 days after the invoice date. If the customer pays 45 days after the invoice date, or 35 days after the allowable cash discount period, the annualized cost of missing the cash discount is 21 percent.

Annualized cost of a missed discount

$$= \frac{\text{Cash discount \%}}{100 - \text{cash discount \%}} \times \frac{360 \text{ days}}{\substack{\text{number of days payment} \\ \text{made after the discount period}}}$$

$$= \frac{2\%}{98\%} \times \frac{360 \text{ days}}{35 \text{ days}}$$

$$= 0.2099 \text{ or } 21 \text{ percent}$$

If the customer pays 11 days after the cash discount period (on day 21), the annualized cost of the missed discount is 66.8 percent.

Annualized cost of a missed discount

$$= \frac{2\%}{98\%} \times \frac{360 \text{ days}}{11 \text{ days}}$$

$$= 0.6679 \text{ or } 66.8 \text{ percent}$$

If the customer pays 40 days after the invoice date, the ACD is 24.5 percent. Check this answer.[3]

As the illustration shows, the longer the firm stretches accounts payable, the lower is the ACD. However, repeated delinquent payments may tarnish the firm's reputation. Eventually, suppliers may force the firm to purchase on a cash basis. In this case, the firm suffers a reduction in spontaneous financing and must rely on more negotiated financing. This action results in an increase in the cash conversion cycle and in the cost of financing the company. Other costs can also result, as the Financial Reality reading on page 646 discusses.

 Comprehension Check

1. What is the firm's cash conversion cycle? How does the cash conversion cycle relate to the firm's operating cycle?
2. What is management's aim for the length of its cash conversion cycle?
3. How does stretching of accounts payable affect the cash conversion cycle and what are potential problems from doing so?

[3]Solution: (2% ÷ 98%) × (360 days ÷ 30 days) = 0.245, or 24.5 percent.

FORD TELLS SUPPLIERS IT PLANS TO STRETCH

Stretching payables is a source of short-term financing many companies use when they encounter cash shortage.

In 1982, Ford Motor Co., burdened with heavy spending on new models, looked to its suppliers for a new source of credit. Ford informed its major machine-tool suppliers that it planned to stretch out payments for future supplies over as long as seven years. Ford had been paying within 30 days after delivery.

The new payment plan, which raised considerable controversy among suppliers, was aimed at improving Ford's cash flow. But apparently it also was part of the auto maker's broad strategy to select suppliers for long-term relationships.

The suppliers themselves were strapped for cash because of declining fortunes of the auto industry and most of them had to borrow from outside sources to finance their supplies to Ford. Thus, the price quotes Ford was receiving from suppliers included the projected cost of the money they might have to borrow.

Most of the machine-tool suppliers were small companies and many operated on thin margins. Industry observers said that a great many of them either wouldn't be able to absorb high interest costs or couldn't get any financing from banks.

 ## 17.3 THE CASH BUDGET

If there is a perfect match between a firm's cash receipts and cash disbursements, there is no risk of insolvency and the firm neither needs a margin of safety level nor needs to stretch accounts payable. However, in the real world, synchronized cash flows do not usually exist. Although the cash conversion cycle provides an indication of the financing needs to support operations, it neither determines the risk of the firm being out of cash nor identifies cash needs other than for operations. The treasurer must prepare a *cash budget* to analyze these problems. A **cash budget** is a plan that organizes all cash receipts and disbursements expected to occur according to a given time horizon, such as a week, month, quarter, year, or longer. By figuring cash requirements ahead of time, management is in a better position to:

Cash budget. A schedule of expected cash receipts and disbursements and the borrowing requirements for a given period of time.

- Take advantage of money-saving opportunities, such as buying inventory in economic order quantities and taking cash discounts.
- Make the most efficient use of cash.
- Finance seasonal business needs.
- Develop a sound borrowing program.
- Develop a workable program of debt repayment.
- Plan for the investment of surplus cash.

The groundwork for preparing a cash budget consists of forecasting all cash receipts and cash payments expected during the budget period. The duration of the budget period depends on the nature of the business. Large firms often prepare a cash budget for one year with projections for the next two or three years. Small firms may put together a cash budget for the next quarter, if they do it at all. However, the length of the interval within the budget period is equally important. Should the cash budget be daily, weekly, monthly, or quarterly? For instance, a monthly cash budget, which shows excess cash balances at the end of each month, may mask cash deficiencies within the month. Possibly the firm incurs the majority of its cash outflows in the first two weeks of the month and receives most of its cash inflows during the last two weeks. Thus, the firm may be a borrower during the first half of each month, and then repays the loan during the month's second half. Just looking at a cash budget that shows the cash flow position for the total month ignores intramonth patterns and needs.

In preparing a cash budget, the treasurer must plan carefully for cash sales (including discounts and sales returns and allowances), expected receipts of accounts receivable, and any other expected cash inflows. The same planning must be done for each type of disbursement, whether it relates to payment for dividends, wages, materials, taxes, or new equipment.

If expected cash receipts total more than expected cash payments, the treasurer adds the difference to the expected cash balance existing at the beginning of the period. If cash payments total more than cash receipts, the treasurer subtracts the difference from the beginning expected cash balance. In either case, the result is the expected cash balance at the end of the period. Illustration 17.4 is an example of a monthly cash budget.

ILLUSTRATION 17.4

What are the cash needs?

The treasurer of Matlock Mattress Company needs to prepare a cash budget for June, July, and August. He has the following information available to him.

1. Cash balance for May 31: $15,000. Minimum cash balance required is $5000.

2. Net sales:

Actual:			Forecasted:	
January	$28,000		June	$ 76,800
February	31,500		July	100,000
March	49,500		August	125,000
April	64,000			
May	72,000			

3. All sales are on credit. The credit manager collects 80 percent of accounts receivable in the month following the sale, 10 percent in the second month, 8 percent in the third month, and 2 percent go uncollected.

4. Cost of goods sold: 75 percent of net sales each month. Material purchases are 25 percent of the cost of goods sold. The firm pays for purchases as follows: 75 percent the first month and 25 percent the second month following purchase.

   Direct labor expenses are 50 percent of cost of goods sold. Factory overhead is 25 percent of cost of goods sold. The firm pays both of these expenses in the month it incurs them.

5. The forecast for selling and administrative expenses is $19,000 per month from May to December.

6. In June, the company expects to incur a liability of $120,000 for a new machine to make coiled springs. Equal payments on the machine will start in July and continue for the next three months.

Based on these assumptions, the cash budget for Matlock Mattress shows a need for cash borrowing of over $86,000 at the end of August.

	March	April	May	June	July	August
Net sales	$49,500	$64,000	$72,000	$76,800	$100,000	$125,000
Collections:						
80% first month				$57,600	$ 61,440	$ 80,000
10% second month				6,400	7,200	7,680
8% third month				3,960	5,120	5,760
Total collections				$67,960	$ 73,760	$ 93,440
Disbursements:						
Purchases:						
75% first month				$10,125	$ 10,800	$ 14,062
25% second month				3,000	3,375	3,600
Wages (direct labor)				28,800	37,500	46,875
Factory overhead				14,400	18,750	23,438
Selling and administrative expenses				19,000	19,000	19,000
Capital expenditures					30,000	30,000
Total disbursements				$75,325	$119,425	$136,975
Collections – disbursements				–$ 7,365	–$45,665	–$43,535
+ Beginning cash balance				15,000	7,635	5,000
Ending cash balance with no borrowing				$ 7,635	–$38,030	–$38,535
Borrowing needed to maintain $5000 balance					43,030	43,535
Ending cash balance				$ 7,635	$ 5,000	$ 5,000
Cumulative borrowing					$43,030	$86,565

Calculations for June

Collections on sales:
First month's collections: 80% × $72,000 sales for May = $57,600
Second month's collections: 10% × $64,000 sales for April = $6,400
Third month's collections: 8% × $49,500 sales for March = $3,960

Payments for material purchases:
75% × May's sales = May's cost of sales
25% × May's cost of sales = May's material purchases
75% × May's material purchases = payment in June
25% × May's material purchases = payment in July

$$0.75 \times \$72,000 \times 0.25 \times 0.75 = \$10,125 \text{ payment in June}$$

Wages = 50% × June's cost of sales of $57,600 = $28,800
Factory overhead = 25% × June's cost of sales of $57,600 = $14,400
Selling and administrative = $19,000 per month

Cash budgets help management decide whether it needs short-term or long-term financing. A series of 12 monthly cash budgets shows estimated monthly cash balances for a year. Management compares each of these balances with the cash level desirable for the business. Perhaps the cash balance is ample at the beginning and end of the 12-month period but low at times during the year. Thus, there is a need for short-term funds.

If, however, management develops cash budgets over longer periods and the cash balance is consistently low, the business needs longer-term financing. Intermediate financing is needed if a cash shortage persists for, say, periods lasting from 12 to 36 months. Management needs long-term or permanent financing if the cash shortage persists for a longer period. The firm can obtain long-term funds by issuing bonds or stock through an investment banker, private placement, or a shelf-registration, all techniques we discussed in Chapter 6. For the balance of this chapter, we concentrate primarily on bank borrowing, the major source of short-term and intermediate-term financing.

Comprehension Check

1. What is a cash budget?
2. What advantages does a cash budget provide management that is not provided by analysis of the cash conversion cycle?

17.4 BANK CREDIT

Despite the proliferation of services available to finance ongoing operations, commercial banks remain the fundamental source of short-term and intermediate-term financing for all companies. An important aspect of the bank's lending decision is whether to issue a *secured* or *unsecured* loan. Lending money without requesting the firm to pledge assets as collateral is called an **unsecured loan.** When a banker requires the borrower to pledge an asset as collateral, it is called a **secured loan.** The point at which a loan is determined to be secured is actually a subjective decision that varies from bank to bank and from banker to banker. For instance, if a small company requests $50,000, the banker may grant the loan and not require collateral. Should the same borrower ask for $75,000, the banker might ask for an asset to be pledged as security.

The principal distinction between unsecured and secured short-term borrowing is the existence of a lien. Under the Uniform Commercial Code adopted by all 50 states in the United States, all classes of liens are considered *security interest*, a definition which forms the basis for a security agreement. The presence of the **security interest** means that unsecured creditors cannot look to the value of assets with liens on them as a possible source for eventual repayment. Unsecured creditors can look only to any surplus of value of the secured assets over the value of the liens.

Unsecured loans are generally made when the following conditions exist:

- The borrower is financially strong relative to the amount of money requested.
- The borrower shows a history of stable income.
- The borrower's expenses are not excessive in relation to income.
- The borrower has an excellent history of paying obligations on time.
- The borrower is viewed as being capable, cooperative, and trustworthy.
- The outlook for the borrower's company appears bright.
- The loan will be repaid within the next 12 months.

Unsecured loan. Financing that requires no assets as collateral but allows the lender a general claim against the borrower rather than a lien against specific assets.

Secured loan. Financing that is backed by the pledge of some asset. In liquidation, the secured creditor receives the cash from the sale of the pledged asset to the extent of the loan value.

Security interest. A legal term meaning a lender has a secured interest in an asset. Unsecured lenders cannot look to the secured asset for repayment.

HOW TO SATISFY LENDERS

by Craig F. Sullivan, Treasurer, Aztar Corporation

As the treasurer of a New York Stock Exchange company with annual revenues in excess of half a billion dollars, I have found that the fundamentals involved in obtaining financing have changed little in two decades. What I learned as a young banking officer in the early 1970s on how to evaluate a potential borrower for a loan has served me equally well over the years when, on the other side of the table, I wanted to borrow money to support the company's needs. Whether it be public markets, private placements, lease financing, or commercial bank credit, the lender evaluates a corporate borrower the same way.

When I was an international banker in New York City, I used five "Ps" to evaluate the creditworthiness of prospective borrowers. In one form or another, lenders still use them. As the corporation's borrowing officer, I try to anticipate the lender's queries about these five "Ps." The first "P" is *people*. It encompasses management, business, and industry. Does our management have the ability and the experience? Do we keep our eye on the ball by concentrating on our business? Will the lender be comfortable with the depth and breadth of our management, their age, health, personal habits, and succession plans? Most importantly, does the lender like, respect, and trust us? Can I convince the lender of our integrity and single-minded determination and willingness to meet any loan obligation?

The lender must be educated about our business by providing answers to the following questions: How susceptible is Aztar to economic cycles, seasonality, and competitive pressures? What is the status of relationships with employees and suppliers? Do we pay our bills in a reasonable time frame? Are we constantly in litigation, as either a defendant or plaintiff? What is the current condition and future of our industry? How vulnerable is our industry to inventory obsolescence, new technology, ease of entry, or a change in the regulatory environment? The lender looks at all these factors, both individually and in aggregate, to determine our ability and willingness to repay the loan.

The second "P" is *purpose*. Why does Aztar need or want the funds? The lender must be convinced that the funds will be put to a legal, ethical, and productive use to enhance the value of the company. Aztar may need short-term financing for seasonal needs of the business or long-term funds to buy property, plant and equipment. We may need the financing to replace existing creditors, or existing equity sources, or to expand the business at hand. Whatever the use of the funds, the lender wants to know—and with supporting detail.

The third "P" is *payment*. I must convince the lender that my company has the capacity and ability to generate sufficient cash to pay our present debt as well as the loan being requested. The lender looks to two sources of repayment. If the anticipated funds from the project under consideration don't materialize, is there sufficient cash flow from other operations to pay the contemplated new debt as well? The lender will undertake an in-depth analysis of our company's financial statements. Most important to lenders is a cash flow analysis that is analyzed using a host of fixed-charge coverage ratios. The primary issue with the lender is our past ability to generate operating cash flow to handle obligations and deal with our growth. The lender wants to make sure that the amortization of the proposed loan is consistent with both our cash flow and the type of asset financed. Because the lender is also interested in our future, it expects to see a detailed three- to five-year forecast using best, most likely, and worst-case scenarios, accompanied by a thorough set of logical assumptions for each scenario.

The fourth "P" stands for *protection*. If we are unable to repay, what is the fallback position of the lender? Can the lender secure the loan? Does the collateral have sufficient value and marketability in a liquidation scenario to cover the entire amount of the loan? If the loan is to a subsidiary, is the parent willing to guarantee the loan? Many borrowers feel deserving of the loan simply because it is small compared to the perceived value of the assets used for collateral. However, a lender forecloses on collateral only as a last resort for two principal reasons: (1) Bankruptcy courts today are weighted heavily in favor of the borrower, and (2) the banker neither wants to be in a position of running a business nor disposing of its assets.

The final "P" is *perspective.* How does the lender view the previous four "Ps" and the risks and rewards of lending to my company? Aztar needs to make a strong presentation to convince the lender that the loan will not go bad. In our negotiations, we also have to keep in mind that the lender must make a fair

profit. How much room is there to negotiate on the fees and interest rate? Does Aztar have any operational-type business, such as cash management, investment, or corporate trust services to offer that may be income generators to the lender? All the preceding rewards in aggregate may be summed up from the lender's perspective as its return.

Disparate lending sources may place a different emphasis on each of the "Ps." My job is to understand which of the Ps are most important to each lender. However, even with all the technical sophistication at both the lender's and borrower's disposal today, the relationship that exists between a treasurer and financial sources continues to be an art rather than a science.

If all of these conditions are not met, the banker may be willing to make the loan if acceptable collateral is pledged.

There are at least three benefits to borrowing money on an unsecured basis: (1) The firm's assets are unencumbered; that is, the company is free to sell them, or if desired, pledge them as collateral for future loans. (2) Borrowing on an unsecured basis gives the company more financial freedom. (3) The interest rate for unsecured loans is usually lower than that for collateralized loans. There are a couple of reasons for the lower rates. First, a banker views unsecured loans as being of low risk, for the reasons stated previously. Second, an unsecured loan is less costly for the bank to administer than is a secured loan. However, a banker grants unsecured financing only when the loan officer believes that the general liquidity and overall financial strength of the borrower, relative to the size of the loan, provides ample ability for repayment.

Banks usually assure themselves as to the borrower's financial health by looking at some financial ratios and projections for cash flows and earnings. Then, as an added measure of assurance, the bank satisfies itself by requiring the borrower to agree to several restrictive covenants.

17.4.1 Some Key Financial Indicators

At the outset of the loan analysis, the bank's perspective is built on both objective and subjective analyses of the borrowing company's financial position. These analyses rest on the well-established tenet that permanent asset needs should be financed with permanent capital—our hedging concept discussed earlier. When permanent capital takes the form of long-term debt, the lender wants to find out how healthy the borrower's long-term earning power is. So the bank asks for financial information: historical financial statements (typically five years) as well as a forecast of the company's income statement, balance sheet, and the statement of cash flows for the next year, and maybe beyond. (We examine forecasting in Chapter 19.)

The bank expects the loan's principal and interest to be returned from future operating cash flows. As a proxy for operating cash flows, the bank may use the accounting numbers for earnings before interest and taxes (EBIT). Consequently, the bank wants to learn the extent of business risk; in other words, how much the future EBIT stream could vary. We measured business risk in Chapter 13 as the degree of operating leverage. Another important element is understanding the company's ability to compete within its industry: What are the firm's strengths and weaknesses and what is its overall competitive strategy?

Bankers consider some lines of business inherently risky, and this will also influence their analysis. However, the financial forecast put forward by the cash budget and supporting balance sheets and income statements become the primary basis on which the banker quizzes the company's treasurer to determine the firm's degree of business risk. Bankers also put considerable emphasis on the company's historical earnings record as an indicator of business risk and the ability of operations to generate cash flows. Wide fluctuations in profits (or net losses) usually lead to an assessment of high business risk.

After analyzing cash flows and profits, the company's balance sheet is the next most important financial indicator because the firm's assets are the bank's secondary source of repayment if operating cash flows are not adequate to repay the loan. Therefore, the assessment of balance sheet strength or weakness hinges on the extent to which the banker believes the loan is recoverable if assets must be sold.

Some financial ratios the banker uses to assess the strength of the balance sheet are the *current ratio,* the *quick ratio,* and the *total debt-to-net-worth ratio.* In addition, the banker pays particular attention to the *fixed-charge coverage ratio.* The purpose of the analysis is to gauge the firm's ability to repay the loan.

CURRENT RATIO. The current ratio compares a firm's current assets against its current liabilities. The ratio attempts to measure the assets available to meet all debts due within one year's time. To compute the **current ratio,** we divide current assets by current liabilities:

> **Current ratio.** A measure of liquidity, defined as current assets divided by current liabilities.

$$\text{Current ratio} = \frac{\text{Current assets}}{\text{Current liabilities}} \quad (17.6)$$

Amounts for the numerator and denominator are found in the firm's balance sheet. A popular rule of thumb for the current ratio is 2; the firm should have $2 investment in current assets for every $1 of current liabilities. The idea is that current assets can decline 50 percent in value and still be adequate to pay off current liabilities. Whether a specific ratio is satisfactory depends on the nature of the business and the characteristics of its current assets and liabilities.

QUICK RATIO. Lenders consider the quick ratio, also called the *acid-test ratio,* as a better measure of liquidity than the current ratio. The definition of the **quick ratio** is:

> **Quick ratio (acid-test ratio).** A measure of liquidity, defined as cash, marketable securities, and accounts receivable divided by current liabilities.

$$\begin{aligned}\text{Quick ratio} &= \frac{\text{Quick assets}}{\text{Current liabilities}}\\[1em] &= \frac{\text{Cash + marketable securities + receivables}}{\text{Current liabilities}}\end{aligned} \quad (17.7)$$

Because the quick ratio does not include inventories and prepaid expenses as part of the available assets to pay current obligations, it concentrates on the more liquid assets, such as cash, marketable securities, and accounts receivable, whose values are more certain. Thus, lenders consider the quick ratio to be a more exacting measure of available liquid resources than the current ratio.

The quick ratio helps to answer the question: If all sales revenues should disappear for a year, could the business meet its current debts during that period with readily convertible funds on hand? Practitioners consider a quick ratio of about 1 to be satisfactory, subject to the following conditions:

- The pattern of accounts receivable collections should not lag much behind the schedule for paying current liabilities.
- Accounts receivable collection must remain consistent.

Unless the financial manager feels comfortable about these two qualifications, the rule of thumb is to keep the quick ratio somewhat higher than 1.

TOTAL DEBT-TO-EQUITY RATIO. The definition of **total debt-to-equity ratio** is:

$$\text{Total debt to equity} = \frac{\text{Current liabilities} + \text{long-term debt}}{\text{Shareholders' equity}} \tag{17.8}$$

Total debt-to-equity ratio.
A measure of financial leverage risk, defined as total debt divided by shareholders' equity.

To a banker, a company with a total debt-to-equity ratio of 1 can suffer a 50 percent deterioration in asset value and still repay the liabilities. For example, a firm with total debt of $1 and equity of $1 has total assets of $2 (since debt + equity = assets). A 50 percent decline in the value of the assets still leaves $1 to pay the liabilities.[4] If the total debt ratio is 3, creditors can only tolerate a 25 percent shrinkage in asset value. For example, if debt is $3 and equity is $1, then assets are $4. A 25 percent loss in asset value means a $1 decline (= 25% × $4). The new asset value is $3, which equals the outstanding value of the debt. Moreover, since the size of annual principal and interest payments increase as financial leverage rises, the firm faces a greater chance that operating cash flows will not be able to cover these payments.

FIXED-CHARGE COVERAGE RATIO. We discussed this ratio in Chapter 13. It is an index of earnings available to pay interest, various fixed expenses management considers essential, debt principal payments, and preferred dividends. Its definition is:

$$\text{Fixed-charge coverage} = \frac{\text{Earnings before interest and taxes and fixed charges}}{\text{Interest} + \text{fixed charges} + \dfrac{\text{principal repayment} + \text{preferred dividends}}{(1 - \text{tax rate})}} \tag{17.9}$$

The larger the ratio, the more income there is to supposedly pay the amounts included in the ratio. A ratio of 2.5 says that for every $1 in the denominator, there is $2.50 of earnings before interest and taxes and fixed charges available to pay interest, fixed charges, and the tax-adjusted payments for debt principal and preferred dividends.

The general impression about the current, quick, and fixed-charge coverage ratios is that the higher these ratios are, then the better is the firm's liquidity position, that is,

---

[4]In this example, the value of the equity would become $0; the $1 loss of asset value is offset against equity.

its ability to meet debt payments as they come due. Although this position certainly may be best from the perspective of creditors, who stress prudence and safety, high current and quick ratios also may suggest ineffective short-term investment management. For example, as investments in accounts receivable and inventory increase, all else held constant, then the current and quick ratios also increase. But such increases mean that the firm's operating cycle has lengthened, thereby increasing the cash conversion cycle and necessitating that the firm rely on more interest-bearing financing. Thus, the treasurer must persuade the bankers that low current and quick ratios do not necessarily mean poor liquidity management. Indeed, low values for these ratios may mean highly efficient management of accounts receivable and inventory.

17.4.2 Loan Restrictions

A truism in banking states that the only things the banker really knows about a loan to a customer is the collected balance position and the amount owed to the bank—everything else is conjecture. The banker realizes that any analysis of the firm's financial position is tied heavily to the once-a-year audited financial statements as conducted by an independent certified public accountant and, in the interim, unaudited company-prepared figures. In an effort to reduce the risk of the loan, the banker may ask that it be secured.

Bankers use financial ratios as risk indicators to determine the scope and severity of the restrictions they should place on a potential borrower. The possible types of restrictions include cash flow control, strategy control, asset preservation, a default "trigger," and balance sheet maintenance.

CASH FLOW CONTROL. The first source of restrictions comes directly from an analysis of cash flow. The firm's cash budget may indicate that the company wants to build its assets so rapidly or pay excessive dividends to shareholders such that the banker questions whether future operating cash flows will be sufficient to service the loan. In this case, repayment must come from a refinancing by another creditor or a sale of new common stock. If the bank is confident that the company's earnings record and balance sheet will be strong enough to permit refinancing, it will not seek to control the company's cash flow. However, even when refinancing appears possible, bankers will usually limit dividends and any purchases of the company's own common stock to preserve the company's equity base. Philip Morris Companies Inc. has such a restriction, as revealed in its 1992 annual report.

STRATEGY CONTROL. The bank may try to control the firm's future strategy if it believes that the company's resources are ill-matched with the opportunities and risks present in its competitive environment or when a particular strategy seeks an imprudent amount of debt financing. Resulting loan covenants may prohibit managers from implementing such a strategy, force the firm to reduce the total amount of money invested in a particular product market, or force the company to spread the investment out over a longer time period. To accomplish these safety features, the loan covenants may limit both the firm's capital expenditures (and acquisitions) and its debt-to-equity ratio to some maximum amounts. Wheeling-Pittsburgh Corporation, as part of its reorganization to avoid bankruptcy, agreed to such restrictions.

ASSET PRESERVATION. Because bankers regard assets as the ultimate source of repayment, they do not want to see a significant portion of them sold or pledged to other creditors. So, unless the loan is secured, lenders will write a *negative pledge clause* into the covenants. A negative pledge clause will restrict the sale of fixed assets to forestall disposal for less than their market value or for securities that could prove worthless. If the bank permits the sale of fixed assets, it may require that the firm use the proceeds to reduce the bank loan. In 1991, Supermarkets General Holding Corporation faced this restriction. It had to use all the proceeds received from the sale of a division to retire a bank loan for $155 million and use surplus proceeds to reduce the balance of another loan.

Bankers often place liens against accounts receivable to secure the loan. While lenders make distinctions among industries and individual firms, advances usually amount to 70 to 90 percent of the value of quality receivables. Often an open limit permits the amount of financing to vary as the amount of accounts receivable outstanding grows or declines.

Bankers will also use inventory to secure a loan. They use three basic forms of liens: blanket inventory liens, trust receipts, and warehouse financing. A *blanket inventory loan* results in the banker placing a lien on all inventory held by the firm. If the borrower defaults on the loan, then the lender has the right to seize the inventory. A *trust receipt loan* provides the banker with a claim on specific inventory until full payment of the loan. However, actual possession of the goods remains in the hands of the borrower. The firm can use or sell the goods while conducting its normal business. A *warehouse financing loan* provides the banker with title or ownership of the inventory. Instead of the inventory remaining under the control of the borrower, as with either blanket or trust receipt loans, a disinterested third party takes physical possession of the goods. The third party only releases inventory to the borrower under certain prespecified instructions from the banker. In some instances, the third party stores the inventory in a bonded public warehouse. In a variation called *field warehousing*, there is a clearly defined area on the premises of the borrower over which a bonded warehouse concern takes full charge for the inventory against which the banker extends credits.

THE TRIGGER. One of the most feared aspects of the covenants is the bank's right to call the loan, or trigger a default. The readiness of the trigger depends on the strength of the firm's balance sheet and the potential variability in operating cash flows. If operating activity erodes the value of the company's assets and the equity base, the banker wants the right to call the entire loan for repayment before deterioration advances further. If the company cannot repay the loan, the bank has legal recourse on the assets, usually the accounts receivable and inventory. Thus, the covenants will stipulate the negative pledge clause.

Banks, however, seldom pull the dreaded trigger. Such action usually means bankruptcy for the company, adverse publicity for the bank, and a time-consuming, costly legal proceeding for both parties. In most cases, if the restrictions trigger a default, the loan is not called. Instead, this imminent possibility forces the borrower to return to the bargaining table. The banker then wants a proposal for corrective action. In return for continuing the loan, the bank may boost the interest rate and demand collateral as compensation for the risk. The banker may also rewrite the covenants to give the bank greater protection.

BALANCE SHEET MAINTENANCE. A company can harm its balance sheet either by excessive use of debt or by financing fixed assets with too much short-term debt. These situations can increase the risk of insolvency. To keep the borrower from wantonly employing short-term credit, bankers may impose minimums for the current ratio and net working capital. The bank may also limit the debt-to-equity ratio to a maximum amount or prohibit additional borrowings.

1. What are the characteristics of unsecured business loans? Why are they popular with business firms and commercial banks?
2. Compare the current ratio and the quick ratio as measures of liquidity.
3. What is the purpose of the total debt-to-equity ratio and the fixed-charge coverage ratio?
4. Discuss the significance of loan restrictions.

17.5 TYPES OF BANK LOANS

Intertwined with the banker's analysis of the firm is consideration of the type of loan being sought. The bank classifies business loans into four types: *business cycle loans, net working capital loans, term loans,* and *interim loans.* Each type of loan is geared to meet a different kind of financing need. Both business cycle loans and net working capital loans support the operating cycle, so let's refer to them as *operating loans.* Term loans and interim loans generally are not for operating purposes, although there are exceptions.

17.5.1 Operating Loans

A firm's treasurer may predict that the company requires short-term financing for a specified interval, perhaps three to five months, to support its operating cycle while it is waiting to collect outstanding accounts receivable. To meet needs such as this, **operating loans** are available. In this case the bank may issue a *business cycle loan* to bridge the gap in the operating cycle to increase inventory, to meet payroll, or to assist with marketing and selling the products. Regardless of the need, this type of loan is always paid by the end of the operating cycle. Generally these loans constitute a fairly low risk to the bank because typically the debt is repaid within a short period of time. Thus, the loan is usually unsecured.

It is more likely, however, that the short-term borrowing needs will continue over the cyclical growth pattern of the business and, therefore, a net working capital loan for one year may be more appropriate. A working capital loan recognizes a permanent need for more net working capital. Business cycle loans, by contrast, are designed to meet a temporary need. Although the net working capital loan is usually for one year, the bank may handle the transaction with a series of renewable 90-day notes. At 90-day intervals the bank appraises the firm's credit situation. It could conceivably *call the note,* that is, ask for repayment in full. In practice, the 90-day maturity date is usually only a technicality if the borrower lives up to the bank's expectations. For the bank, the longer repayment period of the net working capital loan creates more risk. However, if the bank considers the risk tolerable, it will issue the loan as unsecured.

Frequently, the bank issues a *line of credit* to meet the firm's net working capital needs. A **line of credit** is an arrangement by which a bank agrees to lend a borrower up to a given amount of money. It is similar to a credit card. For instance, a bank might agree to set up a credit line for a company in the amount of $200,000. The credit line can be established on either an unsecured or a secured basis, and usually is valid for one year. Many times accounts receivable and inventory are used as collateral for a secured credit line. The banker agrees to lend an amount up to, say, 75 percent of the company's accounts receivable and 50 percent of its inventory.

Operating loan. Bank credit used to finance a temporary need for working capital funds.

Line of credit. Prearranged agreement with a lender for short-term borrowings on demand under prespecified terms. There is no legal commitment on the part of the lender to provide the stated credit.

A line of credit arrangement is designed to cut down the paperwork for both the firm and the banker. It is beneficial for companies that have frequent and fluctuating financing needs, for example, businesses that borrow and repay it soon thereafter, but then soon have a need for more money. This type of borrowing activity results in a fair amount of paperwork for both borrower and banker if a line of credit is not used.

Often a credit line works by the company's treasurer simply calling the bank and having money transferred from the credit line to the firm's checking account. Another call can repay all or some portion of the outstanding credit line. Under other circumstances, the bank may require the company to deliver a document to the bank stating the current amount of the accounts receivable and inventory. The banker then gives the firm a percentage of the amount pledged.

Once a year the bank expects the firm to pay off the credit line, or possibly reduce it to some stated amount, for perhaps 30 to 60 days. For instance, Supermarkets General had a working capital loan that allowed up to $210 million. The agreement required Supermarkets General to not use $75 million of the available proceeds for 30 consecutive days. This period of being in compliance with the agreement is called the **annual clean-up period** and it normally occurs following the seasonal sales peak we discussed when we examined Figure 17.2. During the sales peak, the firm reduces inventories; after the sales peak, it collects accounts receivable from customers before the beginning of a new business buildup. The funds collected are used to satisfy the clean-up requirement.

Sometimes a firm discovers that it becomes progressively more difficult to repay debt or satisfy a clean-up period requirement. Such a condition usually occurs for the following reasons.

- The firm is growing, so the current period of relative inactivity is considerably less than for the corresponding period of the previous year.
- The firm is increasing its immediate short-term capital requirements because of some new promotional program or addition to operations.
- The firm is experiencing a reduction in profitability and cash flow that, hopefully, is temporary in nature.

At this point the treasurer may negotiate with the banker to convert the outstanding balance on the line of credit into a term loan.

17.5.2 Term Loans

Terms loans are for a period in excess of one year. Some term loans may be to support net working capital, whereas others may be used to finance the acquisition of a non-current asset, such as equipment, fixtures, or facilities. Term loans are a higher risk to the bank than business cycle and net working capital loans. The reason is that the time frame to repay the bank is longer than that used with the operating-type loans.

In most cases term loans are made only to companies of demonstrated earning power. The soundness of a term loan, therefore, is generally measured by the financial strength of the company and the expected adequacy of future cash flow to retire the loan. As a result, most term loans are made on an unsecured basis. It is sometimes prudent, however, for the banker to require adequate collateral as security for the loan. Foods 4 Less Supermarkets, Inc. was required under a 1991 agreement to pledge common stock of various companies it held ownership in.

Depending on the policies of the bank, term loan agreements can be very broad or quite specific. These agreements can be as simple as a letter signed by the borrower or as complex as a thick document drawn up by the bank's attorney. More frequently it

Annual clean-up period. Period of time the bank wants the borrower to be free of bank credit or to have the balance below some agreed amount. The purpose is to show the bank that the firm does not need the loan as a source of permanent financing.

Term loan. A loan with a maturity greater than one year.

is a standardized form, and the banker simply fills in some or all of the appropriate blanks. The agreement outlines the borrower's obligation—what the firm will and will not do. Sometimes bankers use affirmative or negative covenants to control the borrower further. Affirmative covenants are acts that borrowers agree to perform. Negative covenants restrict businesses from taking certain actions. Usually covenants are based on common sense and are designed to ensure that management does not jeopardize the company's financial health—and the bank's repayment. Occasionally, a banker will suggest covenants that are unrealistic and do not allow the company enough room to maneuver.

One of the important advantages of a term loan is flexibility in adapting it to the special requirements of the borrower. Initially, term loans were in most cases obligations payable according to a fixed schedule (an amortization schedule) over the life of the loan. As the needs of borrowers changed, new types of term credit evolved, such as revolving credits and standby credits, most of which contain an additional feature permitting the borrower to convert the commitment into an amortizing term loan.

Amortizing term loan. A loan with serial payments for principal and interest.

AMORTIZING TERM LOAN. Under an **amortizing term loan,** funds are made available to the borrower immediately, and the obligation is repayable serially over the life of the loan on a monthly, quarterly, semiannual, or annual basis. The serial term loan has been used for financing the purchase of plant, machinery, and equipment; refunding existing long-term debt; funding existing current debt; or acquiring another company.

The periodic payments are computed using time value of money techniques. However, the bank may call the loan if the borrower fails to follow the repayment schedule. Illustration 17.5 provides an example of an amortizing loan.

ILLUSTRATION 17.5

Amortizing a loan

The treasurer of Mendenhall Fabrics Ltd. borrows $10,000 from First Interstate Bank of California to buy a new high-speed cutting machine. The loan officer requires Mendenhall to make semiannual payments over the next two years with the first payment due six months from now. The annual interest rate negotiated with the bank is 12.36 percent, thereby making the semiannual rate 6 percent: $(1 + 0.1236)^{1/2} - 1$. Thus, each semiannual payment is for $2885.91.

$$\text{Value of loan} = \text{Semiannual payment} \times \frac{1 - \left(\frac{1}{(1 + r)^n}\right)}{r}$$

$$\$10,000 = \text{Semiannual payment} \times \frac{1 - \left(\frac{1}{(1 + 0.06)^4}\right)}{0.06}$$

$$\$10,000 = \text{Semiannual payment} \times 3.46511$$

$$\text{Semiannual payment} = \$10,000 \div 3.46511$$
$$= \$2885.91$$

The breakdown of the semiannual payment into its principal and interest components is shown in the following table.

Calculator
Clear
10,000
PV
6
%i
4
N
CPT
PMT
Ans.: 2885.91

Year	Beginning Balance	Semiannual Payment	Interest at 6%	Principal Reduction	Ending Balance
0.5	$10,000.00	$2,885.91	$600.00	$2,285.91	$7,714.09
1.0	7,714.09	2,885.91	462.85	2,423.06	5,291.03
1.5	5,291.03	2,885.91	317.46	2,568.45	2,722.58
2.0	2,722.58	2,885.91	163.33	2,722.58	0.00

Note: Calculate the interest amount for payment 1 by multiplying the beginning balance of $10,000 by the 6% interest rate. Next, subtract the $600 interest amount from the $2885.91 semiannual payment to get the principal reduction of $2285.91. Then subtract this amount from the outstanding loan balance at the beginning of the period to get the loan balance of $7714.09 after six months. Repeat this exercise for all remaining payments.

REVOLVING CREDIT. This type of loan permits the firm to avail itself of funds from time to time up to the maximum amount of the commitment, with the right to repay and reborrow during the life of the credit. Such a loan is commonly referred to as a **revolving loan,** or *revolver*. It is actually a line of credit for a period extending beyond one year (usually for three to five years), for which the borrower is willing to pay a commitment fee based on the daily average unused portion of the credit. Foods 4 Less Supermarkets paid a commitment fee of 0.5 percent on the average daily unused portion of a $70 million revolving loan. Generally, the borrower has the right to terminate the credit at any time by giving the prescribed notice, reduce the credit whenever it is determined that the full amount is no longer necessary, and convert any outstanding amount into a serial term loan.

> **Revolving loan.** Legally assured line of credit with a bank. Interest is charged for both the amount used and the amount not used.

Revolving loans are, as a rule, used to provide seasonal working capital needs, but may also be used for interim construction financing when there is a pronounced seasonal factor in the flow of cash from operations and the firm desires flexibility. In recent years, major companies have established revolving credit agreements for such purposes as assuring a source of funds during a tight money period, supplying a backup to its commercial paper sales, and providing for general and unspecified corporate purposes.

STANDBY CREDIT. Under this arrangement the bank grants the company a commitment for a period which permits it to borrow from time to time, up to the maximum amount available, to the expiration date. **Standby credit** differs from the revolving credit in that there exists no privilege to repay outstanding notes *and* to reborrow. Notes usually mature at the expiration of the standby period, and a commitment fee is charged for the unused portion on the basis of the unused daily balance. The borrower generally has the right to reduce the credit upon furnishing proper notice. Like a revolver, a standby credit grants the borrower the option to convert any outstanding notes and any unused portion of the credit, on or before the expiration of the standby period, into a serial term loan repayable over a period of years.

> **Standby credit.** A term loan that matures at the expiration date of the loan. It cannot be paid down and reused again without being renegotiated.

17.5.3 Interim Loans

Interim loans are less common than the other loan types. With interim loans, the concern of the loan officer is with how the money will be repaid. Unlike the operating loans or the term loans, why the firm requests the money is of less importance to the banker. By definition, with an **interim loan,** the bank is repaid from one of two sources: by another creditor or through additional long-term equity sold by the firm.

As mentioned in an earlier example, a treasurer may use either a revolver or a

> **Interim loan.** A bridge loan until permanent financing is arranged.

standby loan as interim financing for a construction project. The company either sells equity or places long-term notes with institutional investors for permanent financing when the project is completed.

 Comprehension Check

1. Identify the two types of operating loans. How do they differ from each other? How do they differ from term loans?
2. Why may an annual clean-up of unsecured borrowing become more difficult for a firm?
3. Describe the different types of term loans.
4. What is the purpose of an interim loan?

 ## 17.6 THE COST OF THE LOAN

Calculator
Clear
PV
1,000,000
%*i*
8
N
5
CPT
PMT
Ans.: 250,456.45

If the company is successful, the most important point for the treasurer to remember about the cost of the loan is that the interest rate is negotiable. Depending on the amount of money borrowed, negotiating a slightly lower rate can save the firm thousands of dollars. For example, a $1 million term loan with annual payments amortized over five years at 8 percent requires yearly payments of $250,456.45.[5] A similar loan with an interest rate of 7.5 percent has annual payments of $247,164.72. Over the term of the loan, the lower-interest loan saves about $16,459: ($250,456.45 − $247,164.72) × 5. The treasurer must also consider how various loan-related fees affect the effective cost of the loan.

17.6.1 Negotiate Interest Rates

To be a good negotiator, the treasurer needs to understand the factors a banker considers in determining the interest rate to charge a customer. These factors include:

- The bank's cost of funds.
- The perceived risk to the bank.
- The repayment period of the loan.
- The amount of money being borrowed.
- The bank's handling costs (the time and effort it takes a banker to process the loan).
- The average balance on deposit.
- The competition.

BANK'S COST OF FUNDS. The most important factor that determines the interest rate charged to a company is the bank's cost of funds, that is, what the bank has to pay to obtain its supply of money. The difference between the interest a bank pays its depositors and the interest it collects from borrowers has to cover the bank's expenses.

PERCEIVED RISK TO THE BANK. The higher the perceived risk of the company, the higher is

---

[5]Solution: $1,000,000 = Annual payment × PVIFA$_{8\%,\ 5\ years}$. Solve for the annual payment amount.

the interest rate. Banks offer their lowest interest rate to their best customers. While no loan is ever completely risk free, a new loan to a new young company has more risk than a loan to a well-established, financially sound company like McDonalds, Inc.

REPAYMENT PERIOD OF THE LOAN. The further we look into the future, the more uncertainty we see. From a banker's viewpoint, uncertainty is just another word for risk. Since the interest rate charged is a reflection of risk, loans repaid over several years are charged a higher rate than loans that will be repaid in the near future.

AMOUNT OF MONEY BEING BORROWED. Usually borrowing a large amount rather than a small amount of money results in a lower interest rate. It is cheaper for a banker to administer one loan of $500,000 than to handle 20 loans of $25,000 each.

BANK'S HANDLING COSTS. The more paperwork and review the bank needs to do for a loan, the higher the interest rate is. Some collateralized loans, such as those secured by accounts receivable or inventory, require continual monitoring by bank personnel, thus increasing bank expenses. To recoup these costs the bank charges a higher rate.

AVERAGE BALANCE ON DEPOSIT. Bankers care about how much money stays in the bank. The more money there is in the bank, the more loans the banker can make, as we discussed in Chapter 3. And the more loans the bank makes, the more profit it realizes. As part of the loan-negotiating process, the bank may require the firm to maintain a certain balance in a checking account that averages an agreed-on percentage of the loan amount. The common term used for this type of arrangement is **compensating balance.** A compensating balance essentially increases the effective cost of borrowing. The 1992 annual reports for Hershey Food Corporation and Avon Products, Inc. both report insignificant compensating balance requirements. Illustration 17.6 is an example of the additional cost of a compensating balance from a borrower's perspective.

> **Compensating balance.** A bank's requirement that the borrower maintain a minimum noninterest-bearing average balance; used to compensate banks for services; borrower pays interest on these balances.

ILLUSTRATION 17.6

Cost of a compensating balance

Burdick Fans Limited borrows $2 million on a nonamortizing term loan from Penn State Bank. The loan carries an annual interest rate of 8 percent. As part of the credit agreement, Penn State Bank requires the firm to maintain a compensating balance in the form of noninterest-earning demand deposits equal to 15 percent of the loan. Thus, Burdick Fans pays interest on $2 million even though it only uses $1.7 million of the funds.

Interest on $2 million is $160,000 (= 0.08 × $2 million). Because only $1.7 million is available for actual use, the effective borrowing rate is $160,000 ÷ $1,700,000 = 0.09412 or 9.412 percent. Although the stated rate is 8 percent, the compensating balance increases the borrowing rate 141.2 basis points to 9.412 percent.

COMPETITION. The deregulation of banks has made the market more competitive for banks. Banks that provide high-quality service at competitive prices are gaining new accounts. Most of the time, loan officers would rather offer a good customer a lower rate of interest than lose the account to a competitor.

17.6.2 The Effective Interest Cost

Most banks call their lowest rate their prime rate. Over the years, the prime rate has undergone considerable fluctuation. In 1980, it skyrocketed to a high of 21.5 percent. As of August 1994, the prime rate charged by some of the nation's largest banks was 7 ¼ percent. To assist lending officers in deciding which rate to offer a customer, a bank's top management issues interest rate guidelines, such as presented in Table 17.1.

Many banks charge up-front loan fees in addition to the annual interest rate. These fees are commonly called **points,** with 1 point being equal to 1 percent of the loan amount. If the business is charged 1 point on a $200,000 loan, the up-front fee is $2000. Points are a method whereby the bank can increase its income, since the fee is paid at the time the loan is made.

When presented with a proposal, a banker refers to the guidelines in the table and selects an appropriate rate. For example, a lending officer has decided to lend a company $155,000 for 90 days without requiring collateral. The banker would refer to the unsecured category for loans between $100,001 and $250,000. The suggested rate for

Points. An up-front fee where one point is 1 percent of the value of the loan.

TABLE 17-1

INTEREST RATE SCHEDULE GUIDELINES

First City Bank
Prime Rate, March 18, 1994, 6%

BASE RATE	AMOUNT
10.75%	Up to $25,000
10.25	$25,001 to $50,000
9.75	$50,001 to $100,000
9.25	$100,001 to $250,000
8.75	$250,001 to $500,000
8.25	$500,001 to $1,000,000
7.75	Over $1,000,000

LOAN TYPE	SUGGESTED RATE
Unsecured	Base rate + or − 0.25%
Assigned receivables	Base rate + 0.75% to 1.25%
Equipment, fixtures	Base rate + 0.75% to 1.25%
Crops, livestock	Base rate + 0.50% to 1.00%
Inventory, warehouse receipts	Base rate + 1.00% to 1.50%
Marketable securities/bonds	Base rate − 0.25% to + 0.75%
Certificates of deposit	Base rate − 0.75% to + 1.25%
Term loans	Base rate + 1.75% to 2.25%

LOAN MATURITY	SUGGESTED LOAN FEES
Less than 1 year	0.5 to 1.0 points
1 to 3 years	1.0 to 1.5 points
Over 3 years	1.5 to 2.0 points

this type of loan is between 9.00 and 9.50 percent (the base rate of 9.25 percent, plus or minus 0.25 percent). In addition, fees (or points) for the loan would be between $775 and $1550 (= 0.5 to 1 point of $155,000). If the loan was for revolving credit or standby credit, the bank would charge interest at one rate on the amount of the line that is actually borrowed and a lesser rate, or flat fee, on any unused balance. For example, the 1992 annual report for Eastman Kodak mentions that the company has a $3.5 billion revolving credit facility that requires a $6.3 million per year commitment fee if it is unused.

Sometimes a banker will offer some options. Avon Products, Inc.'s 1993 credit agreement gives it the option to base the borrowing rate on LIBOR, certificates of deposit, prime, federal funds or money-market auction rates.[6] Another example is where the bank might offer to make the loan at the bank's prime interest rate plus 1.5 percent with 2 points, or at the bank's prime rate plus 2 percent with 1 point. The company gets to choose the option. Both alternatives result in about the same return for the bank. The lower annual interest rate is simply offset by a higher up-front fee.

Comprehension Check

1. What factors influence the interest rate the banker charges?
2. Why may the effective interest cost of the loan exceed the negotiated rate?

17.7 OTHER SOURCES OF FUNDS

There are several sources for funds besides the types of bank loans discussed here. Some of the more important ones are *factoring, securitization of accounts receivable,* and *leasing.* We provide but a brief overview of each.

17.7.1 Factoring

In secured financing involving accounts receivable as collateral, the borrower maintains ownership of the accounts receivable unless the lender forecloses. An alternative financing method using accounts receivable is called *factoring.* In this situation a company called a **factor** purchases the accounts receivable. Sales to the factor, called **factoring,** may be with or without *recourse,* although they are most often *nonrecourse arrangements.* If the account cannot be collected, the factor absorbs the loss. However, the factor is protected against circumstances that would invalidate the sale, such as defective merchandise.

Factoring is logical when it makes sense for outside parties to assume the responsibility for follow-up and collection. Traditionally, companies factor receivables when factors have better first-hand knowledge of customers and their creditworthiness than do the sellers. As a result, factors can be more effective in converting the accounts receivable into cash. Historically, companies in the textile and apparel industry were the primary companies factoring. Today, companies in many industries avail themselves of factoring as a means of raising funds.

> **Factor.** A company in the business of buying accounts receivable from other businesses at a discount to their face value.
>
> **Factoring.** Selling accounts receivable at a discount to a financial institution. The factor usually bears the risk of collection.

---

[6]LIBOR stands for London InterBank Offered Rate, the rate at which prime banks offer one another deposits in the London market. It is similar in concept to the federal funds rate in the United States.

17.7.2 Securitization of Accounts Receivable

Securitization of accounts receivable. Substitution of tradable financial securities for privately negotiated accounts receivable.

Some large firms such as General Motors Acceptance Corporation, Chrysler, Sperry, and Volvo have adopted **securitization of accounts receivable** as a means of raising funds: the firm sells its accounts receivable to a *grantor trust,* a separate legal entity. The sale of accounts receivable shortens the firm's cash conversion cycle, thereby freeing resources for investment in income-earning activities. The grantor trust purchases the receivables from the company with proceeds it receives from issuing financial securities, called *pass-through certificates,* to investors. The certificates are sold to investors through an underwritten public offering or private placement. The certificates represent fractional undivided interests in one or more pools of receivables. The receivables are usually sold outright to the grantor trust and act as collateral for the securities. The selling company has no obligation with respect to the repayment of certificates.

Collections on receivables are remitted to the trustee of the grantor trust who pays scheduled interest and principal payments to the investors on the same business day of every month at the coupon rate of interest. Typically, any prepayments on the receivables are also paid by the trustee to investors on these payment dates. The aggregate cash flow from the receivables is always equal to or greater than the required payments on the pass-through certificates.

17.7.3 Leases

A lease is a contractual obligation to rent specific property for a specific term at a predetermined rental rate.[7] Why should a company consider a lease instead of borrowing money and buying the asset? Some of the most common reasons leasing has become an acceptable method of acquiring equipment are: cost, cash flow, lease term, additional line of credit, loan restrictions, off-balance sheet financing, and budget limitations. Let's briefly examine each reason.

- *Cost.* A lease may be the least expensive method of funding or acquiring the use of a specific asset. See Chapter 15 for an example of how to analyze a lease.
- *Cash flow.* One of the biggest advantages to leasing equipment is that 100 percent of the cost of the equipment is advanced by the lessor. Lessors do not require any clean-up period or compensating balance as is often required by bank loans.
- *Lease term.* Leases are usually structured to match the useful life of the equipment. A longer lease term (relative to a bank loan) will allow the same monthly cash payment to acquire much more equipment.
- *Additional line of credit.* Sometimes lease obligations are not perceived by lenders as influencing the firm's available debt capacity. Such a claim is doubtful in efficient financial markets.
- *Loan restrictions.* Lessors usually do not require the lessee to maintain minimum financial ratios as banks do.
- *Off-balance sheet financing.* If a lease qualifies as an operating lease, it does not have to be shown on the balance sheet. Some managers believe such balance sheet presentation affords the company greater debt capacity. Again, in an efficient financial market this should not be the case.

---

[7]In Chapter 15 we viewed leases from the perspective of an investment decision. Here we discuss the lease as a financing decision.

- *Budget Limitations.* In many cases leasing provides the most attractive method for staying within the budget while, at the same time, providing the asset required.

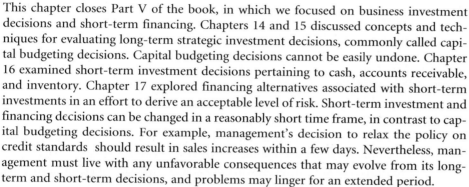

Comprehension Check

1. What is factoring and why is it used?
2. What is meant by securitizing accounts receivable?
3. Discuss several reasons why a firm may use a lease instead of borrowing.

17.8 THE NEXT STEP

This chapter closes Part V of the book, in which we focused on business investment decisions and short-term financing. Chapters 14 and 15 discussed concepts and techniques for evaluating long-term strategic investment decisions, commonly called capital budgeting decisions. Capital budgeting decisions cannot be easily undone. Chapter 16 examined short-term investment decisions pertaining to cash, accounts receivable, and inventory. Chapter 17 explored financing alternatives associated with short-term investments in an effort to derive an acceptable level of risk. Short-term investment and financing decisions can be changed in a reasonably short time frame, in contrast to capital budgeting decisions. For example, management's decision to relax the policy on credit standards should result in sales increases within a few days. Nevertheless, management must live with any unfavorable consequences that may evolve from its long-term and short-term decisions, and problems may linger for an extended period.

The investment and financing decisions affect the firm's financial position and subsequent planning decisions. These are the topics of Part VI. Chapter 18 discusses how to compute and interpret financial ratios for a firm so that you can see the impact of management's investment and financing decisions. The analysis will examine the firm's liquidity position, the effectiveness of assets in generating sales, the risk associated with financing, and the profitability of the assets and return to shareholders. Chapter 19 examines how to build on ratio analysis to derive financial forecasts for the firm. Chapter 19 will also tie together many concepts that we discussed earlier in the book to show that there is a consistent and logical flow to the material. After studying Chapter 19, you should have a better appreciation of the integrative nature of finance as a subject.

SUMMARY

THE MARGIN OF SAFETY

- A hedging strategy matches the maturities of assets and liabilities.
- A positive net working capital amount represents the amount of permanent financing used to finance the excess of current assets over current liabilities.
- Flow-of-funds analysis indicates the cash inflows and outflows within a firm. It highlights the firm's interactions with financial markets, governments, suppliers, investors, customers, and employees.
- Conceptually, the optimal margin of safety level trades off the cost of borrowing to reduce risk of being out of cash against the reduction in liquidity risk by using the funds.

KEY TERMS

The Margin of Safety

Current assets
Current liabilities
Hedging strategy
Margin of safety
Net working capital

THE CASH CONVERSION CYCLE

- The operating cycle is the number of days investment is tied up in accounts receivable and inventory.
- The cash conversion cycle is the shortfall of spontaneous financing in supporting the operating cycle. The shortfall requires costly financing.
- Management often delays payment of accounts payable so as to reduce the cash conversion cycle. If the firm foregoes cash discounts, the annualized cost can be quite expensive and the firm's credit reputation can be tarnished or ruined.

THE CASH BUDGET

- A cash budget identifies when cash receipts and cash disbursements are expected to occur. This budget is important for determining the risk of being out of cash.
- The duration of the budget varies according to the sophistication of the firm. Large firms budget more often and for longer periods of time than smaller firms.

BANK CREDIT

- Secured credit is more expensive than unsecured credit because of higher administrative costs and greater risk to the lender.
- With secured credit, the lender places a lien on specific assets, which provides some protection in the event the borrower is unable to repay the loan.
- Unsecured credit is made only to borrowers with excellent credit history and a strong financial position.
- Management uses the current ratio, quick (acid-test) ratio, total debt-to-equity ratio, and fixed-charge coverage ratio to determine the margin of safety.
- Business characteristics should be more important than some arbitrarily assigned rule for a ratio.
- Accounts receivable and inventory are used as collateral for loans. The lender selects the receivables and inventory acceptable as collateral.
- Depending upon the perceived risk associated with inventory financing, the lender uses different approaches. For low-risk lending, a blanket inventory lien is used. Trust receipts are used for moderate risk with warehouse financing reserved for the most risky inventory lending.

TYPES OF BANK LOANS

- Business cycle loans and working capital loans support operations to bridge the gap between the operating cycle and spontaneous financing.
- Operating loans usually are offered as a line of credit with an annual clean-up period required.
- Term loans are for a period in excess of one year, usually offered as secured loans.
- Revolving credit loans and standby credit loans charge interest for the amount of funds used and a lower rate or fees for the unused portion of the loan.

THE COST OF THE LOAN

- The cost of the loan is influenced by many factors: the cost of money to the bank, the duration of the loan, competitive factors, and the bankers perception of the borrower, among others.

- Compensating balances may be required to be held by the borrower, thereby effectively increasing the cost of the loan.
- Fees are usually charged by the bank as service fees, which effectively increase the cost of the loan.

OTHER SOURCES OF FUNDS

- Factoring, or the sale of accounts receivable, is prevalent in many industries. The sale reduces investment in the operating cycle.
- Securitization of receivables is the sale of receivables to a grantor trust, which then issues securities to investors. The receivables act as collateral for the securities.
- Many influences can cause a treasurer to consider leasing as a means of financing. The cost is usually competitive with banks without the necessity of a clean-up period or minimum ratio requirements.

FURTHER READING ▼▼▼▼▼▼▼▼▼▼▼

MacPhee, William A., *Short-term Business Borrowing: Sources, Terms, and Techniques.* Homewood, IL: Dow Jones-Irwin, 1984. The author, a former banker, discusses how to obtain short-term financing.

Pavel, Christine A., *Securitization: The Analysis and Development of the Loan-Based/Asset-Backed Securities Market.* Chicago, IL: Probus Publishing, 1989. The author discusses a complex subject in a straightforward manner.

SELF-TEST PROBLEMS ▼▼▼▼▼▼▼▼▼▼▼▼

ST17-1. Cheryl's Trinkets, Inc. has asset needs for the coming year as follows:

	$000		
Month	Current Assets	Fixed Assets	Total Assets
January	$100	$200	$300
February	80	200	280
March	60	200	260
April	50	200	250
May	40	200	240
June	90	200	290
July	100	200	300
August	120	200	320
September	90	200	290
October	80	200	280
November	150	200	350
December	170	200	370

a. What is Cheryl's minimum permanent funds requirement based on asset projections for next year?

b. If Cheryl's manager chooses no margin of safety for funding needs, what is the minimum level of long-term financing?

c. Assuming no margin of safety, what is the maximum amount of short-term seasonal financing needed by Cheryl's?

d. Calculate the monthly average long-term funds needed and the monthly average short-term seasonal financing for the year ahead.

e. If Cheryl's manager desires a $15,000 margin of safety, what effect will this have on the calculations in parts (a) through (d)?

f. Would you recommend a margin of safety for Cheryl's? Explain your answer.

ST17-2. Starter Industries has 71 days investment in accounts receivable, 55 days investment in inventory, and 22 days of outstanding accounts payable.

a. Calculate the firm's cash conversion cycle.

b. What actions might management take to reduce the firm's cash conversion cycle? Discuss the positive and negative implications of each action.

ST17-3. What is the annual percentage cost of failing to pay your business account if the terms of sale are 4/10, n/45. You pay bills 45 days from the invoice date. Assume a 360-day year.

ST17-4. The following information is provided by the management of Nelsen Corporation.

Sales:

Actual:			Forecasted:		
	June	$100,000		September	$260,000
	July	140,000		October	280,000
	August	200,000		November	240,000

All sales are on credit. The collection pattern has been 60 percent received the month following the sale and 36 percent the second month following the sale. The remaining 4 percent of sales is uncollected.

The firm's cost of goods sold are 50 percent of sales each month. Purchases are 40 percent of the monthly cost of goods sold and paid for in the month following purchase. Direct labor and factory overhead amount to 60 percent of cost of goods sold. These expenses are paid during the month in which they are incurred. Selling and administrative expenses are estimated at 10 percent of monthly sales and are paid the month they are incurred.

A tax payment is due in September for $40,000. New equipment is scheduled to be purchased in September for $70,000, but paid for in October.

The company's cash balance at the end of August is $35,000. The treasurer desires to maintain a minimum balance of $30,000.

a. Prepare a monthly cash budget for September, October, and November.

b. What is the maximum cash shortage, if any, during this three-month period? When does it occur?

c. What actions could the treasurer take in view of this quarterly cash projection?

ST17-5. McCain Corporation negotiated a $200,000 line of credit with the American National Bank of Maryland. The loan's interest rate is 9.5 percent. McCain agreed to a commitment fee of 0.6 percent on any unused portion of the loan. The bank charged 2 points at the time the loan agreement was signed, based on the maximum amount of the line of credit. McCain immediately drew down $150,000 of the loan. What is the current effective annual rate on the borrowing?

PROBLEMS ▼▼▼▼▼▼▼▼▼▼▼▼▼

THE MARGIN OF SAFETY

17-1. Show-Me Shops, Inc. has asset needs for the coming year as projected in the following table:

Month	Current Assets	Fixed Assets	Total Assets
January	$50,000	$100,000	$150,000
February	40,000	100,000	140,000
March	80,000	100,000	180,000
April	30,000	100,000	130,000
May	40,000	100,000	140,000
June	90,000	100,000	190,000
July	80,000	100,000	180,000
August	70,000	100,000	170,000
September	50,000	100,000	150,000
October	30,000	100,000	130,000
November	60,000	100,000	160,000
December	70,000	100,000	170,000

a. What is Show-Me Shops' minimum permanent funds requirement based on asset projections for next year?

b. If Show-Me's manager chooses no margin of safety for funding needs, what is the minimum level of long-term financing?

c. Assuming no margin of safety, what is the maximum amount of short-term seasonal financing needed by Show-Me?

d. Calculate the monthly average long-term funds needed and the monthly average short-term seasonal financing for the year ahead.

e. If Show-Me's manager desires a $10,000 margin of safety, what effect will this have on the calculations in parts (a) through (d)?

f. Would you recommend a margin of safety for Show-Me? Explain your answer. (*Hint:* What factors should the manager take into account when considering a margin of safety?)

17-2. Renaldo Food Processing has the following expected seasonal monthly funds need. If the firm's bank will lend to Renaldo at a 12 percent annual rate based on monthly needs, what is the firm's estimated interest cost for the year?

Month	Financing Need	Month	Financing Need
January	$800,000	July	$300,000
February	600,000	August	400,000
March	500,000	September	500,000
April	400,000	October	600,000
May	300,000	November	800,000
June	200,000	December	900,000

17-3. Think Snow Ski Shop has the following expected seasonal monthly funds need. If the firm's bank will lend to the ski shop at a 9 percent annual rate based on monthly needs, what is the firm's estimated interest cost for the year?

Month	Financing Need	Month	Financing Need
January	$200,000	July	$ 80,000
February	220,000	August	150,000
March	180,000	September	150,000
April	120,000	October	170,000
May	80,000	November	190,000
June	60,000	December	200,000

17-4. The balance sheet for Sweet Products Company is shown as follows:

Sweet Products Company
Balance Sheet
December 31
($000)

Current Assets:		Current Liabilities:	
Cash	$ 100	Accounts payable	$ 300
Short-term investments	200	Mortgage payable	400
Accounts receivable	720	Taxes payable	200
Inventories	3000	Misc. accrued payables	300
Total	$4020	Total	$1200
Fixed Assets:		Long-term liabilities:	
Plant and equipment	$5000	Mortgage payable	$3000
Less: Accumulated depreciation	3000		
Net fixed assets	$2000	Owners' equity:	
		Common stock	$1000
		Retained earnings	820
		Total	$1800
		Total liabilities	
Total assets	$6020	and net worth	$6020

a. Calculate Sweet Products' current ratio, quick ratio, and net working capital.
b. Based on your calculations, comment on the liquidity of Sweet Products Company. What additional information would be needed before a final judgment could be made on the firm's liquidity?

THE CASH CONVERSION CYCLE

17-5. Star Manufacturing, Inc. has accounts receivable with an average age of 63 days. The average age of Star's inventories is 50 days, and its accounts payable average 36 days.

a. Calculate Star's cash conversion cycle.
b. What actions might Star's management take to reduce the firm's cash conversion cycle? Discuss the positive and negative implications of each alternative for action.

17-6. Mahoney's Market has accounts receivable with an average age of 6 days; inventories have an age of 15 days. Its accounts payable average 28 days outstanding.

    a. Calculate Mahoney's cash conversion cycle.

    b. How do you explain Mahoney's cash conversion cycle?

17-7. Johnson Grocery Stores, Inc. has an average inventory age of 30 days. Johnson's accounts receivable collection period amounts to five days and the firm has spontaneous financing equal to 40 days.

    a. Calculate Johnson's cash conversion cycle.

    b. How do you explain Johnson's cash conversion cycle?

17-8. Xtra Special Books, Inc., a publisher of college textbooks, has accounts receivable from college bookstores of 95 days. Xtra's inventory of books averages 100 days. The publisher's accounts payable and other spontaneous financing sources amount to 50 days.

    a. Calculate Xtra's cash conversion cycle.

    b. What actions might Xtra's management take to reduce the publisher's cash conversion cycle? Discuss the positive and negative implications of each action alternative.

17-9. Joycene Manufacturing, Inc. has accounts receivable with an average age of 65 days, its inventory is 70 days outstanding, and accounts payable average eight days. Joycene sells to trade customers on terms of 2/10, n/30. The company purchases raw materials and component parts from suppliers on terms of 1/20, n/40.

    a. Calculate Joycene's cash conversion cycle.

    b. What actions might Joycene's management take to reduce the firm's cash conversion cycle? Discuss the positive and negative implications of each action.

17-10. Mariposa Manufacturing purchases raw materials using trade credit from its suppliers and pays its accounts promptly in 30 days. The raw materials are processed and finished goods are sold to customers 78 days after raw materials are purchased. Customers typically pay for purchases 60 days from Mariposa's sale date. What is the firm's cash conversion cycle?

17-11. Royal Crown purchases merchandise on trade credit from manufacturers and pays its accounts in 40 days. The merchandise usually is sold to retailers in about 30 days. Royal Crown's customers typically pay their accounts ten days from invoice date to take advantage of cash discounts. What is Royal Crown's cash conversion cycle and how do you interpret your calculation? What questions would you have for Royal Crown's management?

17-12. Jarvis Wholesale Furniture Company purchased $28.5 million of furniture in a year for sale to retail stores. Jarvis's cash conversion cycle is 105 days. Through better credit management and by stretching its payable period slightly, Jarvis's management planned to reduce its cash conversion cycle to 90 days. If Jarvis borrowed from the First State Bank at an annual rate of 9 percent (based on a 360-day year) to finance inventories, how much interest would be saved annually from this reduction in its cash conversion cycle?

17-13. Jackson Stores' annual inventory purchases are $9.8 million. The firm's cost of financing inventories through a commercial finance company is 14 percent annually. Jackson's cash conversion cycle currently is estimated at 94 days. If

Jackson could reduce its average age of inventory by seven days, what would be its annual savings in financing costs? Assume a 360-day year.

17-14. Calculate the percentage cost of failing to pay your business account if the terms of sale were 2/10, n/30. You pay the bill 30 days from the invoice date. Assume a 360-day year.

17-15. What is the percentage cost of foregoing a cash discount under the terms of sale 4/20, n/120 if the account is paid on the last day of the "net" period? Assume a 360-day year.

17-16. Gary's Store, Inc. buys from suppliers on terms of 3/15, n/45. However, Gary has started paying suppliers 60 days from the invoice date for purchases. Assume a 360-day year for the following questions.

   a. What is the percentage cost of foregoing the cash discount under normal trade terms?
   b. What is the percentage cost of foregoing the cash discount by stretching payables by 15 days?

17-17. Jan's Jewelry Store receives credit terms of 2/10, n/40 on purchases from suppliers. Jan also has a line of credit at her commercial bank enabling the firm to borrow at an annual rate of 14 percent to finance short-term needs. Assume a 360-day year.

   a. What are the percentage and dollar costs of foregoing discounts on a $10,000 invoice from suppliers?
   b. Jan wishes to keep good relations with suppliers and therefore is reluctant to stretch payables beyond the "net" due date. When the jewelry store's cash is short, should she borrow from the bank so she can take the cash discount or should she skip the discount and pay on the net date?

17-18. Shiny Rock, Inc. is offered credit terms of 3/10, n/70 by its suppliers but frequently does not have the cash available to take the purchase discount. The firm has a line of credit available from a local bank with an annual interest rate of 15 percent.

   a. What alternatives are available to Shiny Rock's management in dealing with accounts payable?
   b. What is the cost of foregoing the cash discount from suppliers?
   c. What should the firm do when it does not have funds to take advantage of the cash discounts on its invoices?

17-19. Mono Static, Inc. buys supplies in a very tight raw materials market. Typical purchase terms are 3/10, n/30.

   a. What is the percentage cost to Mono Static of failing to take cash discounts on its purchases and paying 30 days from the date of invoice?
   b. What is the percentage cost to Mono Static of stretching its payments to suppliers 15 days beyond the credit period (paying 45 days after the invoice date)?
   c. What factors should Mono Static's management consider in deciding when to pay the firm's accounts payable?

THE CASH BUDGET

17-20. The treasurer of Orion Medical Products Company has assembled the following data to prepare the firm's cash budget for July, August, and September.

   • Cash balance on June 30 is $36,000. Minimum cash balance required is $30,000.

- Net sales:

Actual:			Forecasted:		
	April	$ 80,000		July	$120,000
	May	90,000		August	140,000
	June	100,000		September	150,000

- All sales are on credit. The credit manager collects 50 percent of accounts receivable in the month of sale, 40 percent the month following sale, 8 percent the second month following sale, and 2 percent are uncollected.
- Cost of goods sold: 70 percent of monthly net sales.

  Purchases of raw materials and component parts account for 40 percent of the cost of goods sold. Orion pays for 80 percent of purchases the month of purchase and 20 percent of purchases the month following purchase. Direct labor and factory overhead are 35 percent and 25 percent, respectively, of the cost of goods sold. Orion pays both of these expenses in the monthy incurred.
- Selling and administrative expenses are expected to be $30,000 per month for July through September.
- The company has a tax payment of $12,000 due in September.
- Equipment purchased in June will be paid for in July in the amount of $18,000.

  a. Prepare Orion Medical Products' cash budget for July through September.
  b. What bank loan, if any, will Orion need to finance operations during this period?

17-21. In late December, Samantha Bridges, owner of the Kidz Kloz Shop, was preparing a request for a seasonal line of credit from the First State Bank to cover financing needs for the first half of next year. Ms. Bridges has been a business customer of the bank for the past five years and knew the loan officer would want her estimate of cash needs. Based on past years' results, Bridges estimated sales for the first half of next year as follows:

January	$ 80,000
February	50,000
March	130,000
April	90,000
May	80,000
June	60,000

About one half of the shop's sales are for cash with the remainder on 30-day charge accounts carried by the shop. Bridges screens credit requests carefully. For planning purposes she assumes that credit sales will be collected the month following sale. Customers' accounts receivable on December 31 are estimated at $70,000. In late December, Kidz Kloz Shop had a cash balance of approximately $15,000. Bridges considered this to be a satisfactory minimum amount of cash.

The customary terms under which Kidz Kloz Shop purchased merchandise provided for cash discounts for prompt payment. It had been Bridges's practice to take all cash discounts, which means that merchandise would be paid for in the month following purchase. The cash discounts have already been deducted from the following purchase figures. Therefore, these amounts would be paid the month following purchase.

Estimated purchases of merchandise:

December	$ 80,000
January	100,000
February	50,000
March	20,000
April	30,000
May	50,000
June	50,000

Wages during the first six months of the year are estimated at $10,000 monthly except during March and April when wages would amount to $12,000 each month. This amount covered Ms. Bridges's drawings as proprietor of the shop.

Rent and utility payments have averaged $3,000 monthly and this is expected to remain unchanged during next year. Advertising was scheduled as follows:

December	$5,000
January	2,000
February	1,000
March	3,000
April	2,000
May	1,000
June	1,000

Advertising was paid for in the month following its run. In addition, estimated tax payments of $12,000 are made in the months of March and June. Miscellaneous cash disbursements are estimated at $2,000 monthly covering items ranging from buying trip expenses to charitable contributions.

a. Prepare a cash budget forecast for the first six months of the year based on the data assembled by Ms. Bridges.
b. What is the maximum amount of bank credit required assuming that any cash shortage will have to come from bank loans?
c. When will the maximum amount of funds' shortage occur?
d. When, if at all, during the six-month period, will Kidz Kloz Shop be able to get out of debt to the bank?
e. If you were a bank loan officer, what information would you want in addition to the cash budget forecast before deciding on this request for credit?

17-22. The following data relate to Merced Manufacturing Corporation:

Net Sales:

Actual:	January	$200,000	Forecasted:	April	$260,000
	February	220,000		May	230,000
	March	250,000		June	220,000

All sales are on credit. The collection pattern has been 70 percent received the month following the sale, 20 percent the second month following the sale, and 7 percent in the third month after sale. On average, 3 percent of accounts are uncollected.

The firm's cost of goods sold are 60 percent of sales each month. Purchases are 30 percent of the monthly cost of goods sold. Purchases are paid for the month following purchase.

Direct labor and factory overhead amount to 70 percent of goods sold. These expenses are paid during the month in which they are incurred. Selling and administrative expenses are estimated at 10 percent of monthly sales and are paid the month they are incurred.

The Merced Manufacturing has a tax payment due in June of $40,000. New equipment is scheduled to be purchased in March at a price of $60,000, which will be paid for in April.

The manufacturer's cash balance at the end of March is $50,000. A minimum cash balance of $20,000 is desired by the treasurer.

a. Prepare a monthly cash budget for April, May, and June.
b. What is the maximum cash shortage, if any, during this three-month period? When does it occur?
c. What actions could the treasurer take in view of this quarterly cash projection?

BANK CREDIT

17-23. A simplified balance sheet for Johnson & Johnson is shown below.

Johnson & Johnson
Balance Sheet
December 31

Current Assets:			Current Liabilities:		
Cash	$	595	Accounts payable	$	832
Short-term investments		114	Notes payable		809
Accounts receivable		2,146	Accrued and other		
Inventories		1,856	liabilities		1,396
Other current		872			
Total		$ 5,583	Total		$ 3,037
Fixed Assets:			Long-term Liabilities:		
Plant and equipment, net		$ 4,550	Long-term debt		$ 1,424
Intangible assets		692	Other liabilities		2,047
Other assets		1,388	Equity		5,705
Total assets		$12,213	Total financing		$12,213

Data from Johnson & Johnson's annual report showed:

Earnings before interest and taxes	$11,422
Interest expense	124
Fixed charges	300
Principal payment	275
Effective income tax rate	28%

a. Calculate Johnson & Johnson's current ratio, quick ratio, net working capital, total debt-to-equity ratio, and fixed charge coverage.
b. Based on your calculations, comment on Johnson & Johnson's liquidity. What additional data would be needed before a final judgment is made on the firm's liquidity?

17-24. Maxwell's latest balance sheet reveals the following:

Maxwell, Inc.
Balance Sheet
December 31

Current Assets:		Current Liabilities:	
Cash	$ 1,500	Accounts payable	$15,000
Short-term investments	1,000	Notes payable	12,000
Accounts receivable	12,000	Taxes payable	1,000
Inventories	15,500	Miscellaneous accrued payables	6,000
Total	$30,000	Total	$34,000
Fixed Assets:		Long-term Liabilities:	
Plant and equipment	$19,000		
Less: Accumulated depreciation	4,000	Owners' equity:	
		Common stock	$ 5,000
Net fixed assets	$15,000	Retained earnings	1,000
		Total	$ 6,000
Total assets	$45,000	Total financing	$45,000

a. Calculate Maxwell's current ratio, quick ratio, and net working capital.
b. Based on your calculations, comment on Maxwell's liquidity. What additional data would be needed before a final judgment is made on the firm's liquidity?

17-25. Daybreak, Inc.'s latest balance sheet reveals the following:

Daybreak, Inc.
Balance Sheet
December 31

Current Assets:		Current Liabilities:	
Cash	$ 5,200	Accounts payable	$ 2,800
Short-term investments	4,500	Taxes payable	2,200
Accounts receivable	10,400	Miscellaneous accrued payables	2,900
Inventories	12,900		
Total	$33,000	Total	$ 7,900
Fixed Assets:		Long-term Liabilities:	
Plant and equipment	$28,000	Mortgage payable	$ 6,000
Less: Accumulated depreciation	6,000	Owners' equity:	
		Common stock	$14,000
Net fixed assets	$22,000	Retained earnings	27,100
		Total	$41,100
Total assets	$55,000	Total financing	$55,000

Other information revealed in Daybreak's annual report includes:

Earnings before interest and taxes	$7,500
Interest	480
Fixed charges	600
Principal payments	500
Effective tax rate	35%

a. Calculate Daybreak's current ratio, quick ratio, net working capital, total debt-to-equity ratio, and fixed-charge coverage.

b. Based on your calculations, comment on Daybreak's liquidity. What additional data would be needed before a final judgment is made on the firm's liquidity?

TYPES OF BANK LOANS

17-26. Calculate the equal year-end payment necessary to amortize a loan of $100,000 over ten years with a 9 percent interest rate.

17-27. Calculate the equal annual payment necessary to amortize a loan of $60,000 over six years with an annual interest rate of 12 percent.

17-28. Calculate the equal monthly payment required to amortize a home loan of $100,000 over 15 years with an annual interest rate of 6 percent.

17-29. Riki-Tiki, Inc. has converted a term loan to a serial loan. The loan's balance is $80,000 with an annual interest rate of 7.5 percent. The loan is to be amortized in five annual year-end payments.

a. Calculate the annual payment necessary to amortize this loan.

b. Prepare a loan amortization schedule which shows the amount of interest and principal for each payment.

c. Explain why annual interest charges differ each year.

THE COST OF THE LOAN

17-30. Second State Bank requires a compensating balance on its $800,000 line of credit to Jasper Company. The line carries an annual interest rate of 9 percent, and Jasper must maintain a compensating balance in the form of noninterest-bearing demand deposits equal to 12 percent of the loan. What is the effective interest rate on the line of credit? Assume that Jasper would borrow the full amount of the line of credit for the entire year.

17-31. Payne Golf Equipment has a $3 million line of credit with the Florida Bank which carries an annual interest rate of 8 percent and requires a 20 percent compensating balance. However, the golf company regularly carries a minimum demand deposit of $600,000 at the bank to cover the cost of bank services provided Payne. Assuming that Payne borrows the line of credit up to its limit throughout the year, what is the effective cost of this credit line? (*Hint:* Use the demand deposit to satisfy the compensating balance.)

17-32. National Manufacturing, Inc. has a line of credit with Western National Bank for $1 million, with an annual interest rate of 9 percent. The bank requires a compensating noninterest-earning demand-deposit balance of 10 percent of the loan balance.

a. What is the effective annual interest rate on the line of credit?

b. Explain why the effective annual rate is different than the loan's nominal rate of 9 percent.

17-33. Southwest State Bank has granted a $5 million line of credit to Yuma Fabricating, Inc. The interest rate on the loan is 2 points above the prime rate, which is currently at 6.5 percent. In addition, the bank has imposed a commitment fee of 0.5 point on any unused portion of the loan. Currently, the company has borrowed $3 million under the line of credit. What is the current effective annual rate on the present borrowings?

17-34. Gorman Corporation negotiated a $300,000 line of credit with the Andrew Bank of New York. Gorman agreed to an interest rate of 9 percent and agreed to pay 3 points on the loan, payable at the signing of the loan agreement. There was no standby commitment fee on any portion of the loan balance. Gorman immediately borrowed the maximum amount of the line of credit. What is the current effective annual rate on the loan?

17-35. The treasurer of Raul's Wholesale Limited is considering two alternatives for financing the firm's accounts receivable: a bank line of credit at a nominal rate of 10 percent and a 30 percent compensating balance; a loan from Household Finance Company of up to 80 percent of accounts receivable at a nominal rate of 13 percent of the funds actually advanced.

a. Calculate the annual effective rate of each financing alternative.
b. Which alternative would you recommend to the treasurer? State the assumptions underlying your recommendation.

LIBRARY ASSIGNMENT

17-36. Refer to a recent issue of *The Wall Street Journal, Investor's Business Daily, Barron's, Business Week,* or some other business news publication for information about short-term financing by corporations. Write a one-page summary of the article.

COMPREHENSIVE PROBLEM ▼▼▼▼▼▼▼▼▼▼▼

17-37. United Manufacturing, Inc. has asset needs for the coming year as projected in the following table:

| | $000 | | |
Month	Current Assets	Fixed Assets	Total Assets
January	$200	$300	$500
February	180	300	480
March	160	300	460
April	140	300	440
May	130	300	430
June	110	300	410
July	100	300	400
August	120	300	420
September	150	300	450
October	180	300	480
November	280	300	580
December	260	300	560

a. What is United's minimum permanent funds requirement based on asset projections for next year?
b. If United's manager chooses no margin of safety for funding needs, what is the minimum level of long-term financing? What is the maximum amount of short-term seasonal financing needed by United?
c. Calculate the monthly average long-term funds needed and the monthly average short-term seasonal financing for the year ahead.
d. If United's manager desires a $20,000 margin of safety, what effect will this have on the calculations in parts (a) through (c)?
e. United has accounts receivable with an average age of 47 days. Its inventory is outstanding 38 days and accounts payable average 29 days outstanding. Calculate United's cash conversion cycle. What actions might management take to reduce the cash conversion cycle? What are the positive and negative implications of each action?
f. What is United's annual percentage cost of failing to pay trade accounts to take advantage of the cash discount if its purchase terms are 2/10, n/40? If discounts are not taken, United pays invoices on the net payment date. Assume a 360-day year.
g. United's management provides the following information for a cash budget:

	Sales:				
Actual:	January	$150,000	Forecasted:	April	$120,000
	February	140,000		May	180,000
	March	100,000		June	220,000

All sales are on credit. The collection pattern has been 80 percent received the month following the sale and 18 percent the second month following the sale. The remaining 2 percent are written off as bad debts.

The firm's cost of goods sold is 60 percent of sales each month. Purchases are 50 percent of the monthly cost of goods sold and are paid for in the month following purchase. Direct labor and factory overhead amount to 50 percent of cost of goods sold. These expenses are paid during the month in which they are incurred. Selling and administrative expenses are estimated at 10 percent of monthly sales and are paid the month they are incurred.

United has a tax payment due in June of $50,000. New equipment was purchased in March for $140,000; payment will be made in April.

The treasurer desires a minimum cash balance of $20,000. Currently, the balance is $60,000.

i. Prepare a cash budget for April, May, and June.
ii. What is the maximum cash shortage, if any, during this three-month period? When does it occur?
iii. What actions could the treasurer take in view of this quarterly cash projection?

h. United's balance sheet reveals the following information:

United Manufacturing, Inc.
Balance Sheet
December 31

Current Assets:		Current Liabilities:	
Cash	$ 20,000	Accounts payable	$ 50,000
Short-term		Taxes payable	45,000
investments	15,000	Miscellaneous	
Accounts receivable	90,000	accrued payables	25,000
Inventories	100,000		
Total	$225,000	Total	$120,000
Fixed Assets:		Long-term Liabilities:	
Plant and equipment	$650,000	Mortgage payable	$160,000
Less: Accumulated		Owners' equity:	
depreciation	60,000	Common stock	$200,000
Net fixed assets	$590,000	Retained earnings	335,000
		Total	$535,000
Total assets	$815,000	Total financing	$815,000

Other information revealed in United's annual report includes:

Earnings before interest and taxes	$440,000
Interest	16,000
Fixed charges	120,000
Principal payments	21,000
Effective tax rate	30%

- Calculate United's current ratio, quick ratio, net working capital, total debt-to-equity ratio, and fixed-charge coverage.
- Based on your calculations, comment on United's liquidity. What additional data would be needed before a final judgment is made on the firm's liquidity?

i. Calculate the equal year-end payments necessary to amortize a loan of $60,000 over 12 years with an interest rate of 10 percent.

j. United's financial officer negotiated a $200,000 line of credit with the St. Louis Bancorp. The interest rate on the loan is 8 percent. In addition, the bank imposed a commitment fee of 1 percent on any unused portion of the loan. Currently, the manufacturer has borrowed $80,000 under the credit agreement. What is the effective annual rate on the present borrowing?

k. If the line of credit in part (j) required a compensating balance of 10 percent instead of a commitment fee, what would be the effective interest rate on the loan if the maximum loan is taken?

ANSWERS TO SELF-TEST PROBLEMS ▼▼▼▼▼▼▼▼▼▼▼▼

ST17-1. a. Minimum permanent funds = Lowest level of fixed assets
$$+ \text{ lowest level of current assets}$$
$$= \$200,000 + \$40,000$$
$$= \$240,000$$

b. The minimum level would be the firm's permanent funds need of $240,000.

c. The maximum short-term seasonal financing is the maximum level of assets minus the minimum permanent funds requirement: $370,000 − $240,000 = $130,000.

d. The average monthly long-term funds are the $240,000 of permanent funds. The average monthly short-term seasonal financing needs are the average total assets ($294,167) less the average long-term funds ($240,000), or $54,167.

e. A $15,000 margin of safety would add $15,000 to each of the answers.

f. Factors to consider include:

- The degree of variability of actual monthly funds needs in relation to projections.

- The availability of a short-term credit line from a financial institution to meet unexpected funds needs.

- The higher that market interest rates are, the greater the premium on minimizing financing.

- The manager's attitude toward the risk of being short of funds.

In general, the manager may decide on some minimum margin of safety to trade off between the cost of those funds versus the cost of being caught short of funds.

ST17-2. a. Cash conversion cycle

$$= \text{Average collection period} + \text{days inventory outstanding} - \text{days payable outstanding}$$
$$= 71 + 55 - 22$$
$$= 104 \text{ days}$$

b. Management could:

- Reduce the collection period by offering more attractive cash discounts or by pressing slow accounts for collection. The disadvantage may be lost revenues.

- Reduce inventories, thereby lowering investment. If improved efficiency results, there should be no disadvantages. However, it is possible that lost sales could result because of lack of product availability.

- Lengthen payables to self-finance a greater portion of the operating cycle. Stretching payables could lead to supplier dissatisfaction.

ST17-3. Annualized cost of missed discount

$$= \frac{\text{Discount percentage}}{100 - \text{discount percentage}} \times \frac{360 \text{ days}}{\text{days payment after the discount period}}$$

$$= \frac{4\%}{100\% - 4\%} \times \frac{360}{35}$$

$$= 42.9 \text{ percent}$$

ST17-4. a.

	September	October	November
Monthly sales	$260,000	$280,000	$240,000
Cash receipts:			
First month after sale	$120,000	$156,000	$168,000
Second month after sale	50,400	72,000	93,600
Total cash receipts	$170,400	$228,000	$261,600
Disbursements:			
Purchases	$ 40,000	$ 52,000	$ 56,000
Labor and overhead	78,000	84,000	72,000
Selling and administrative	26,000	28,000	24,000
Tax payments	40,000		
Equipment payment		70,000	
Total disbursements	$184,000	$234,000	$152,000
Collections – disbursements	$–13,600	$ –6,000	$109,600
+ Beginning cash balance	35,000	30,000	30,000
Ending cash balance with no borrowing	$ 21,400	$ 24,000	$139,600
Borrowing needs to maintain $30,000 minimum balance	8,600	6,000	
Debt repayment			14,600
Ending cash balance	$ 30,000	$ 30,000	$125,000
Cumulative borrowings	$ 8,600	$ 14,600	

b. The maximum cash shortage occurs in October, requiring a bank loan of $14,600.

c. Since excess cash will be available after two months, the treasurer could negotiate an operating loan.

ST17-5. Effective cost of loan $= \dfrac{\text{Amount used} \times \text{rate} + \text{unused amount} \times \text{rate}}{\text{Amount used} - \text{points paid}}$

$= \dfrac{\$150,000 \times 0.095 + \$50,000 \times 0.006}{\$150,000 - \$4,000}$

$= 0.09966$ or about 10 percent

Video Case 17

The Campeau Bankruptcy:
The Sudden Deterioration
Of Supplier Accounts Receivables

from *Business World,* January 7, 1990

Understanding and monitoring the flow of resources within the firm is one of management's most important day-to-day tasks. Without cash the company cannot pay employees, suppliers, lenders, or its shareholders. Cash is so important that most firms establish credit lines with banks to assure they will have cash to cover temporary shortfalls. With cash budgets, firms and their lenders can forecast both the timing and amount of the cash need as well as the loan's repayment schedule. However, as this video describes, even the best planning may not be enough to avoid disaster.

At the time of the video, the Campeau retailing empire, which includes the Federated and Allied department store chains, was on the brink of bankruptcy. Campeau's financial problems created serious financial difficulties for many of the small businesses supplying Campeau stores. When one link in the chain of credit sales snaps (or looks like it is about to snap), the effect ripples far down the line. Clothes designers contract with manufacturers to produce their designs, the manufacturers hire labor and buy raw materials to complete the contract. If the designers don't get paid then the lenders, manufacturers, and raw material suppliers also suffer. It is easy to say that the designers should have managed things differently, but could Campeau's suppliers have done anything to protect themselves from these problems? Let's look at their situation and see.

Rumors about cash problems at Campeau stores appeared in the business press in early 1989. In April 1989, Campeau was forced to refinance some of its debt, a sign that the firm was having cash flow problems. On November 14th, 1989, *The Wall Street Journal* reported that Campeau was in the midst of a working capital crisis. Other warnings were given directly to Campeau suppliers by the factoring companies that act as the financing arm of the garment industry. Offsetting the warnings was the fact that the Campeau stores paid their bills on time through the Christmas buying season. The payment history was indicative of financial health. But even if these small firms had been able to determine the severity of Campeau's problems, that may not have been enough to save them.

Because the garment industry sells "dated" goods (fashions are like fruit and vegetables that ripen, spoil, and lose much of their value), it experiences sudden changes in the value of receivables and inventory. This "spoilage" effect puts suppliers over a barrel. If they don't sell at Christmas, they may not have a second chance to sell except at a deep discount. Many suppliers had to try and sell their goods through the Campeau stores, despite the risk of nonpayment. The size of the Campeau chain made it the primary customer of many suppliers, and they suffered the most when Campeau's problems surfaced. This occurs not just in the garment industry. When a customer's sales goes down, it can have an immediate and dramatic effect on suppliers.

Study Questions

1. This video considers the relationship of small suppliers and a dominant customer, but companies must consider the effects of being one of many small customers of a large supplier or distributor. If a business depends on a single large distributor, should it treat that supplier differently than other less important distributors? How might that treatment differ?

2. Apply concepts about diversification from Chapter 5, "Risk, Return and the CAPM," to the problem facing suppliers with a single customer. What does diversification imply about this situation?

CHAPTER 18

Financial Statement Analysis

Financial statement analysis is an information-processing system designed to provide data for people concerned with the economic situation of the firm and predicting its future course. The major groups of users are: (1) investors, for making portfolio decisions; (2) managers, for evaluating the operational and financial efficiency of the firm; (3) lenders, for determining the creditworthiness of the loan applicants; (4) labor unions, for establishing an economic basis for collective bargaining; (5) regulatory agencies, for controlling the activities of companies under their jurisdictions; and (6) researchers, for studying firm and individual behavior.

The ability to analyze and understand financial statements is as much an art form as it is an application of several techniques. The technical side of financial analysis is straightforward. We calculate a variety of common financial ratios to provide insight into the financial condition of a company. The artistic dimension of financial analysis is important because the accounting process relies to a great extent upon the application of judgment, which introduces subjectivity and values. Different, yet valid, views and interpretations of the economic consequences of a specific transaction often exist.

In the past several years, the methods and approaches of financial analysis have come under repeated challenge by people who support the concept of efficient capital markets (studied in Chapter 10). Advocates of efficient markets adhere to theories that security prices already impound all relevant information contained in financial statements; that is, security prices take into account risk, projected earnings, and so on. They claim that any analysis by individuals goes unrewarded by the financial market. Nevertheless, financial statement analysis continues to be important, if for no other reason than to uncover information that aids the market efficiency process.

When you complete this chapter, you should understand some of the principal tools used in financial statement analysis:

- Common-size analysis of financial statements.
- Statement of cash flows.

THE IMPORTANCE OF FINANCIAL ANALYSIS

by Jon Jackson, Manager of Business Support and Development, Hewlett Packard Corporation

In my position with Hewlett Packard's Microwave Instrument Division, I am involved in analyzing many complex and diverse issues. I need to be able to interpret and use financial information. Some issues I've been faced with include the following: How does the volatility of the U.S. dollar in world markets affect our revenues? What is the proper value of a firm that we are considering buying? What is the financial impact of a new global pricing experiment on a multimillion dollar product line? Will new products in R&D contribute to the profits and the growth of the company? Let me expand on some of these issues.

In the global economy in which HP operates, it is clear that fluctuations in world currencies affect the final dollar amount that we receive in payment on a per-unit basis. Even though the same amount of product can be sold, wide swings in currency value can result in lower dollars being returned to the company or, possibly, missed strategic pricing opportunities. In either case, the result is lower return on sales, assets, and equity. For example, as the Japanese yen strengthens against the U.S. dollar, we can offer additional discounts for products sold in Japan, thereby becoming more competitive and improving our market share. Revenues earned in Japan grow, since consumers perceive HP's products as being less expensive. This growth helps increase our sales and profits.

Where feasible, we try to take advantage of the technology and market position held by other firms in markets in which HP competes. We do this through acquisitions and partnering agreements. Both approaches can improve the time it would take HP to bring a product to market acting alone. Acquisitions increase our market share, making us a more dominant player in the market segment. However, before buying the firm, we must carefully analyze it to establish a proper price to pay. A critical factor in this analysis is the amount of cash the firm can generate from operations. We forecast the firm's cash flow generating ability from an in-depth analysis of its financial statements. This analysis also helps us determine if there are any hidden costs that we should know about. We don't want to buy a company and then discover that our newly acquired company has a serious problem that was overlooked in the analysis.

More and more we find it necessary to partner with a third company to either develop a product or to provide products that broaden our product offerings. When we analyze a potential alliance, it becomes critical to estimate the potential partner's ability to deliver quality products on time. One way of estimating this ability is to understand the targeted partner's liquidity: both its ability to generate enough funds, and its access to the appropriate level of funds. If a potential partner is unable to generate a sufficient level of funds to consistently pay its employees and suppliers on time, the result is usually deteriorating product quality as it cuts corners to save cash. Delivery problems escalate because of its inability to produce according to schedule.

Even though Hewlett Packard may be considered an "engineering" company, finance is an essential part of ensuring its ongoing success and profitability. Finance is not just a reporting function but is also involved in providing considerable input into the strategic planning exercise, which helps position the company for the next decade. We do the analysis and "what-if" planning, which hopefully results in increasing value for our shareholders.

Today's business environment provides exciting and challenging career opportunities for people with an understanding of financial concepts.

- Ratios commonly used to measure efficiency, liquidity, leverage, and profitability.

You should also have a better sense of how to interpret the ratios. Throughout our discussion of these various tools, we will use an example set of financial statements to show the calculations. As we go through the process, several natural questions will arise from these practice numbers. We will defer looking for answers to these questions until later in the chapter, when we can suggest specifically what these numbers *may* show in a real-world situation.

 ## 18.1 COMMON-SIZE ANALYSIS AND TRENDS

Common-size analysis. Accounting statements expressed as a percentage of net sales or total assets to aid comparison.

Common-size analysis is a technique that enables us to determine the makeup and patterns of a company's balance sheet and income statement. The analysis can be either *horizontal* (across years) or *vertical* (within a year). In the financial statement, **common-size analysis** reduces absolute numbers to percentages of components at one point in time, or to percentages of change in components over time, thereby revealing possible trends.

18.1.1 Horizontal Analysis

A *balance sheet* shows how a business stands at a given moment in the business year. An *income statement* sums up the results of operations over a period, usually a year. A single balance sheet is like the opening chapters of a book—it presents the initial setting. For example, one balance sheet may show how management has distributed capital to the various accounts, and how much surplus of assets over liabilities exists. A single income statement typically shows the sales volume for a given period, the amount of costs incurred, and the profit after allowing for all costs.

Horizonal analysis. Common-size analysis that compares the same accounts from year to year.

When we arrange several annual balance sheets and income statements in vertical columns we can horizontally compare the annual changes in related items. This comparison, or **horizontal analysis,** of the accounts reveals a pattern that may suggest management's underlying philosophies, policies, and motivations. The annual financial statements are no longer simple snapshots; instead they become important messages of management actions and decisions.

Tables 18.1 and 18.2 show comparative financial statements for three years for our sample firm. The earliest year, the base period, appears as the column on the right. The column labeled "Δ%" shows growth or decline from the base period. For example, the Δ% for receivables in the year 3 balance sheet is $[(\$303,000 \div \$210,000) \times 100] - 100 = 44\%$. Thus, receivables in year 3 increased 44 percent over the base period of year 1, whereas prepaid expenses decreased 38 percent from the base period.

Horizontal analysis of the balance sheet in Table 18.1 reveals significant investment increases in inventories and property and equipment. The 271% for other assets, although a larger figure, is relatively unimportant because the dollar amount of the investment is small. Short-term current liabilities are the chief source of financing for these investments. On the other hand, the decline in the cash balance is noteworthy. Is this decline signaling better cash management or a cash problem?

Horizontal analysis of the income statement, Table 18.2, shows a 3 percent increase in gross sales over the base period, but a 4 percent decline in net sales. The significant increase in sales returns suggests either product quality problems or a liberal sales return policy. We note in Table 18.1 that accounts receivable investment is up 44

TABLE 18-1

HORIZONTAL ANALYSIS OF BALANCE SHEETS OVER A THREE-YEAR PERIOD

Balance Sheets ($000)

	Year 3	Δ%	Year 2	Δ%	Base Year Year 1
Current assets					
Cash	$ 0.3	(97)	$ 13.7	20	$ 11.4
Receivables	303.0	44	293.5	40	210.0
Inventories	262.2	126	272.6	135	116.1
Prepaid expenses	15.6	(38)	19.4	(23)	25.1
Total	$581.1	60	$599.2	65	$362.6
Property and equipment	$323.8	187	$181.7	61	$113.0
Accumulated depreciation	81.1	190	49.8	78	28.0
Net property and equipment	$242.7	186	$131.9	55	$ 85.0
Other assets	5.2	271	11.5	721	1.4
Total assets	$829.0	85	$742.6	65	$449.0
Current liabilities					
Accounts payable	$224.0	317	$185.5	245	$ 53.7
Notes payable	200.1	89	197.3	186	106.0
Taxes payable	31.0	(46)	49.0	(14)	57.0
Accrued expenses	43.9	199	59.6	305	14.7
Portion of LT debt	8.0	74	6.0	30	4.6
Bank overdraft	15.0	∞	0.0	0	0.0
Total	$522.0	121	$497.4	111	$236.0
Long-term liabilities	$ 45.6	262	$ 22.8	81	$ 12.6
Shareholders' equity					
Common stock	$ 60.0	0	$ 60.0	0	$ 60.0
Retained earnings	201.4	43	162.4	16	140.4
Total	$261.4	30	$222.4	11	$200.4
Total debt and equity	$829.0	85	$742.6	65	$449.0

Total assets have shown significant growth over the past two years. Financing has relied heavily on accounts payable.

percent. Why is receivable investment up so much while net sales are down 4 percent? Is collection effort lagging? Also, why is gross profit up 11 percent on a lower sales volume? Does the doubling in interest expense signal too much debt financing? Why are operating and depreciation expenses increasing faster than sales growth? Does the drastic cut in dividends suggest a cash problem? The lower dividend figure supports our concern about the low cash balance we noticed in Table 18.1.

18.1.2 Vertical Analysis

When we analyze the financial statements for one period, we often use *vertical analysis.* **Vertical analysis** is the process of finding the proportion that an item, such as inven-

> **Vertical analysis.**
> Common-size analysis that compares accounts in the income statement to net sales and amounts in the balance sheet to total assets.

TABLE 18-2

HORIZONTAL ANALYSIS OF INCOME STATEMENTS FOR A THREE-YEAR PERIOD

Income Statements ($000)

	Year 3	Δ%	Year 2	Δ%	Base Year Year 1
Gross sales	$1,585.0	3	$1,970.0	27	$1,546.0
Less returns	184.0	114	140.0	63	86.0
Net sales	$1,401.0	(4)	$1,830.0	25	$1,460.0
Cost of sales:					
Beginning inventory	$ 272.6	169	$ 116.1	15	$ 101.3
Purchases	997.6	(11)	1,571.5	40	1,119.8
	$1,270.2	4	$1,687.6	38	$1,221.1
Ending inventory	262.2	126	272.6	135	116.1
Total	$1,008.0	(9)	$1,415.0	28	$1,105.0
Gross profit	$ 393.0	11	$ 415.0	17	$ 355.0
Operating expenses	263.9	27	263.4	26	208.4
Depreciation	31.3	132	21.8	61	13.5
Interest	26.8	121	24.8	105	12.1
Income before taxes	$ 71.0	(41)	$ 105.0	(13)	$ 121.0
Income taxes	31.0	(46)	49.0	(14)	57.0
Net income	$ 40.0	(37)	$ 56.0	(12)	$ 64.0
Dividends	$ 1.0	(97)	$ 34.0	0	$ 34.0

Sales are up slightly from the level of two years ago. However, profits and dividends are lower by a considerable amount.

tory, represents of a total group, such as assets. Table 18.3 shows each asset item as a percentage of total assets. Table 18.4 shows each income statement item as a percentage of net sales.

A vertical analysis of annual balance sheets reveals how the mix of assets and financing is changing over time. In our example, we discover that much of the vertical analysis supports the horizontal balance sheet analysis. Investment in plant and equipment has increased faster than investment in current assets. As a percentage of total assets, net plant and equipment increased about 10 points (18.9 percent to 29.3 percent) and current assets declined about 10 points (80.8 percent to 70.1 percent). The balance sheet shows a significant decline in accounts receivable as a proportion of total assets, even though receivables are 44 percent higher than for the base period (see Table 18.1).

Vertical analysis of liabilities and equity shows a shift from shareholders' equity (44.6 percent to 31.5 percent) to greater reliance on accounts payable (12 percent to 27 percent). We can conclude that management relies heavily on short-term financing to support long-term investment in plant and equipment and to build up inventory.

Vertical analysis of our sample income statement suggests that problems exist. Gross profit has improved about 4 points (24.3 percent to 28.1 percent) while net income has been eroded 1.5 points (4.4 percent to 2.9 percent). Why do increasing

TABLE 18-3

VERTICAL ANALYSIS OF BALANCE SHEETS FOR A THREE-YEAR PERIOD

Balance Sheets ($000)	Year 3	%	Year 2	%	Year 1	%
Current assets						
Cash	$ 0.3	0.0	$ 13.7	1.8	$ 11.4	2.5
Receivables	303.0	36.6	293.5	39.5	210.0	46.8
Inventories	262.2	31.6	272.6	36.7	116.1	25.9
Prepaid expenses	15.6	1.9	19.4	2.6	25.1	5.6
Total	$581.1	70.1	$599.2	80.7	$362.6	80.8
Property and equipment	$323.8	39.1	$181.7	24.5	$113.0	25.2
Accumulated depreciation	81.1	9.8	49.8	6.7	28.0	6.2
Net property and equipment	$242.7	29.3	$131.9	17.8	$ 85.0	18.9
Other assets	5.2	0.6	11.5	1.5	1.4	0.3
Total assets	$829.0	100.0	$742.6	100.0	$449.0	100.0
Current liabilities						
Accounts payable	$224.0	27.0	$185.5	25.0	$ 53.7	12.0
Notes payable	200.1	24.1	197.3	26.6	106.0	23.6
Taxes payable	31.0	3.7	49.0	6.6	57.0	12.7
Accrued expenses	43.9	5.3	59.6	8.0	14.7	3.3
Portion of LT debt	8.0	1.0	6.0	0.8	4.6	1.0
Bank overdraft	15.0	1.8	0.0	0.0	0.0	0.0
Total	$522.0	63.0	$497.4	67.0	$236.0	52.6
Long-term liabilities	$ 45.6	5.5	$ 22.8	3.1	$ 12.6	2.8
Shareholders' equity						
Common stock	$ 60.0	7.2	$ 60.0	8.1	$ 60.0	13.4
Retained earnings	201.4	24.3	162.4	21.8	140.4	31.3
Total	$261.4	31.5	$222.4	29.9	$200.4	44.6
Total debt and equity	$829.0	100.0	$742.6	100.0	$449.0	100.0

Receivables and inventories represent over two-thirds of the total assets, although the proportion for property, plant, and equipment is growing each year. About two-thirds of all financing is short term.

expenses offset the improvement in gross profit? Does management need to control costs better? Is too much debt financing causing unfavorable financial leverage?

Comprehension Check

1. Why is it necessary to analyze a series of balance sheets and income statements across several years?
2. What are common-size financial statements? How can you use them for conducting financial analysis?

TABLE 18-4

VERTICAL ANALYSIS OF INCOME STATEMENTS FOR A THREE-YEAR PERIOD

Income Statements ($000)

	Year 3	%	Year 2	%	Year 1	%
Gross sales	$1,585.0	113.1	$1,970.0	107.7	$1,546.0	105.9
Less returns	184.0	13.1	140.0	7.7	86.0	5.9
Net sales	$1,401.0	100.0	$1,830.0	100.0	$1,460.0	100.0
Cost of sales:						
Beginning inventory	$ 272.6	19.4	$116.1	6.3	$101.3	6.9
Purchases	997.6	71.2	1,571.5	85.9	1,119.8	76.7
	$1,270.2	90.6	$1,687.6	92.2	$1,221.1	83.6
Ending inventory	262.2	18.7	272.6	14.9	116.1	7.9
Total	$1,008.0	71.9	$1,415.0	77.3	$1,105.0	75.7
Gross profit	$ 393.0	28.1	$ 415.0	22.7	$ 355.0	24.3
Operating expenses	263.9	18.8	263.4	14.4	208.4	14.3
Depreciation	31.3	2.3	21.8	1.2	13.5	0.9
Interest	26.8	1.9	24.8	1.4	12.1	0.8
Income before taxes	$71.0	5.1	$ 105.0	5.7	$ 121.0	8.3
Income taxes	31.0	2.2	49.0	2.6	57.0	3.9
Net income	$ 40.0	2.9	$ 56.0	3.1	$ 64.0	4.4

Profitability, as measured by the percentage net income of sales, is steadily declining.

18.2 STATEMENT OF CASH FLOWS

Accrual accounting concepts recognize that it is the economic substance of a transaction that determines the timing of accounting recognition rather than the activity of receipt or payment of cash. However, investors use cash flows and not accrual accounting numbers to value the firm. Many firms report positive net income amounts yet have negative cash income.[1]

The *statement of cash flows (SCF)* is important for understanding the true cash flows of the business. The SCF restates the firm's flow of funds from an accrual accounting basis to a cash accounting basis. As such, it eliminates all noncash revenues and expenses recorded by accrual accounting. Table 18.5 lists the rules to calculate cash flow.

The restatement of financial statements to a cash basis does not suggest that accrual accounting is wrong. Indeed, the purpose of accrual accounting is to show revenues and expenses incurred by the firm, whether paid for or not. However, the cash flow statement shows the true cash inflows and outflows of the firm. We can see how management has employed resources during the period. Where did it get cash from? How did it use cash? Table 18.6 applies the rules of determining the cash flow statement and illustrates the *indirect format* most companies use when they publish the statement:

---

[1]Charter Company, a *Fortune* 100 company in 1983, reported net income in excess of $50 million. Soon after issuing its annual report, the firm filed for bankruptcy. It was unable to generate enough cash to pay its bills.

TABLE 18-5

CONSTRUCTING THE STATEMENT OF CASH FLOWS

Accountants use the following rules to construct the statement of cash flows:
- Revenue accounts are sources of cash.
- Expense accounts are uses of cash.
- Increases in asset accounts are uses of cash.
- Decreases in asset accounts are sources of cash.
- Increases in liability and equity accounts are sources of cash.
- Decreases in liability and equity accounts are uses of cash.

TABLE 18-6

INDIRECT PRESENTATION OF STATEMENT OF CASH FLOWS
FOR A THREE-YEAR PERIOD ($000)

	Year 3	Year 2	Year 1
Net income	$ 40.0	$ 56.0	$ 64.0
+ Depreciation	31.3	21.8	13.5
	$ 71.3	$ 77.8	$ 77.5
− Increase in receivables	−9.5	−83.5	−12.2
− Increase in inventory		−156.5	−5.4
+ Decrease in inventory	10.4		
+ Increase in accounts payable	38.5	131.8	17.0
− Decrease in accrued expenses	−15.7		−7.8
+ Increase in accrued expenses		44.9	
+ Decrease in prepaid expenses	3.8	5.7	4.8
− Decrease in taxes payable	−18.0	−8.0	−8.4
= Net cash flow from operations	$ 80.8	$ 12.2	$ 65.5
− Increase in fixed assets	−$ 142.1	−$ 68.7	−$ 32.0
+ Decrease in other assets	6.3		3.1
− Increase in other assets		10.1	
= Net cash flow from investing	−$ 135.8	−$ 78.8	−$ 28.9
+ Increase in long-term debt	$ 24.8	$ 11.6	$ 13.2
+ Increase in bank debt	15.0		
− Decrease in notes payable			−9.0
+ Increase in notes payable	2.8	91.3	
− Dividends paid	−1.0	−34.0	−34.0
= Net cash flow from financing	$ 41.6	$ 68.9	−$ 29.8
Net cash flow from operations	$ 80.8	$ 12.2	$ 65.5
Net cash flow from investing	−135.8	−78.8	−28.9
Net cash flow from financing	41.6	68.9	−29.8
Decrease in cash account	−$ 13.4		
Increase in cash account		$ 2.3	$ 6.8

Note: + represents a source of cash; − represents a use of cash.

Net cash flow from operations (NCCFO). Shown in the statement of cash flows as cash generated or consumed by the productive activities of a firm over a period of time; represents cash profits.

Net cash flow from investing (NCFFI). Shown in the statement of cash flows as cash generated or reduced from the sales or purchases of investment in long-term securities or plant and equipment.

Net cash flow from financing (NCFFF). Shown in the statement of cash flows as cash generated or reduced from the sales or repurchase of securities used to finance the business or the payment of dividends.

Start with net income and make adjustments to that number to restate it as net cash from operations, or cash profits.

The line **net cash flow from operations (NCFFO)** in Table 18.6 represents cash profits. The lines **net cash flow from investing (NCFFI)** and **net cash flow from financing (NCFFF)** show cash investments and cash financing, respectively. The sum of NCFFO + NCFFI + NCFFF equals the change in the cash account for the year.

Analysis of these three net cash flow subtotals is important. The SCF reveals that the firm has not been self-supporting over the last three years. Investing activities consumed $243,500 (= $135,800 + $78,800 + $28,900) and cash profits supplied only $158,500 (= $80,800 + $12,200 + $65,500), or 65 percent of the investment needs. The firm borrowed and used its cash balances to offset the difference between cash profits and investing activities. Because management cut the dividend to conserve cash, it appears that the firm's borrowing is to the limit.

We can get further insight into the cash flows of the firm if we calculate NCFFO using the *direct format:* Show each income statement item as its cash equivalent. Table 18.7 shows the revised, direct SCF.

The direct SCF method reveals that in year 3 the firm recorded cash profits of $80,800 on cash sales of $1,391,500, which is a 5.8 percent return on sales. The percentages return on sales in the two previous years were 0.7 percent and 4.5 percent, respectively. The improved year 3 cash profit results are due to the much better cash *gross* profits: 31.1 percent in year 3 versus 17.6 percent and 24.5 percent for the two previous years, respectively.

Table 18.8 summarizes the annual differences between accrual gross profit and cash gross profit. For year 1, both the accrual accounting and cash profit margins are about the same: 24.3 percent versus 24.5 percent. However, the large discrepancies in years 2 and 3 suggest that something is wrong. Also, the large increases in both accrual and cash gross margins in year 3 are questionable. It is very unlikely that margins should change this much in such a short time. Is inventory investment purposefully misstated? Is there an accounting error in year 2 that self-corrects in year 3?

Comprehension Check

1. What is the purpose of the statement of cash flows?
2. Summarize the major cash flow categories in this statement.
3. Contrast the direct and indirect presentation formats.

18.3 RATIO ANALYSIS

Common-size analysis and cash flow statements provide some insight to the financial condition of the firm.[2] Financial ratio analysis is the next step in the process. Ratios are among the most widely used tools of financial analysis. They are helpful in providing clues for spotting patterns in the direction of better or poorer performance. However, many times their function is misunderstood and their significance overrated.

We must keep in mind that a financial ratio simply expresses the relationship between one quantity and another. The ratio of $200 to $100 is 2. While the computa-

---

[2]As part of the effort to gather facts and knowledge about the company, we should also analyze the notes to the financial statements. These notes may reveal changes in accounting principles, pending lawsuits, or other factors that do not show on the financial statements.

TABLE 18-7

DIRECT PRESENTATION OF STATEMENT OF CASH FLOWS FOR A THREE-YEAR PERIOD ($000)

	Year 3	%	Year 2	%	Year 1	%
Sales	$1,401.0		$1,830.0		$1,460.0	
− Increase in receivables	−9.5		−83.5		−12.2	
= Cash sales	$1,391.5	100.0	$1,746.5	100.0	$1,447.8	100.0
− Cost of sales	−$1,008.0		−$1,415.0		−$1,105.0	
− Increase in inventory			−156.5		−5.4	
+ Decrease in inventory	+10.4					
+ Increase in accounts payable	+38.5		+131.8		+17.0	
= Cash cost of sales	−$ 959.1	68.9	−$1,439.7	82.4	−$1,093.4	75.5
Cash gross profit	$ 432.4	31.1	$ 306.8	17.6	$ 354.4	24.5
− Operating expenses	−$ 263.9		−$ 263.4		−$ 208.4	
− Decrease in accrued expenses	−15.7				−7.8	
+ Increase in accrued expenses			+44.9			
+ Decrease in prepaid expenses	+3.8		+5.7		+4.8	
= Cash operating expenses	−$ 275.8	19.8	−$ 212.8	12.1	−$ 211.4	14.6
Cash earnings before interest and taxes	$ 156.6	11.3	$ 94.0	5.4	$ 143.0	9.9
− Interest expense	−26.8		−24.8		−12.1	
= Cash income before taxes	$ 129.8	9.3	$ 69.2	4.0	$ 130.9	9.0
− Income tax expense	−31.0		−49.0		−57.0	
− Decrease in taxes payable	−18.0		−8.0		−8.4	
= Net cash flow from operations	$ 80.8	5.8	$ 12.2	0.7	$ 65.5	4.5
− Increase in fixed assets	−$ 142.1		−$ 68.7		−$ 32.0	
+ Decrease in other assets	6.3				3.1	
− Increase in other assets			10.1			
= Net cash flow from investing	−$ 135.8		−$ 78.8		−$ 28.9	
+ Increase in long-term debt	$ 24.8		$ 11.6		$ 13.2	
+ Increase in bank debt	15.0					
− Decrease in notes payable					− 9.0	
+ Increase in notes payable	2.8		91.3			
− Dividends paid	−1.0		−34.0		−34.0	
= Net cash flow from financing	$ 41.6		$ 68.9		−$ 29.8	
Net cash flow from operations	$ 80.8		$ 12.2		$ 65.5	
Net cash flow from investing	−135.8		−78.8		−28.9	
Net cash flow from financing	41.6		68.9		−29.8	
Decrease in cash account	−$ 13.4					
Increase in cash account			$ 2.3		$ 6.8	

Note: + represents a source of cash; − represents a use of cash.

TABLE 18-8

ANALYSIS OF GROSS PROFIT MARGINS

Period	Accrual Accounting	Cash
Year 1	24.3%	24.5%
Year 2	22.7	17.6
Year 3	28.1	31.1

Note: The margins are taken from Tables 18.4 and 18.7.

tion is simple, the interpretation is more complex. *The ratio must express a relationship that has economic significance.* For example, there is a clear, direct, and understandable relationship between the sales price of an item and its cost. The ratio of cost of goods sold to sales is significant. However, there is no economic relationship between freight costs and investment in marketable securities. Hence, a ratio of one to the other in such a case is of no economic significance.

Some important points to keep in mind when doing ratio analysis are:

- *We calculate ratios for specific dates.* If management issues financial statements infrequently, we may not uncover any seasonal characteristics of the business.
- *Financial statements show what has happened in the past.* An important purpose for calculating ratios is to uncover clues to the future so we can prepare for the problems and opportunities that lie ahead. When we use ratios, we must consider our knowledge and judgment about the future.
- *Ratios are not ends in themselves.* They are tools that can help answer some of our financial questions, but we must interpret them with care. For example, it is possible to improve the ratio of operating expenses to sales by reducing costs that act to stimulate sales. However, if the cost reduction results in loss of sales or market share, any profit improvement may have an overall detrimental effect.
- *Businesses are not exactly comparable.* There are different ways of computing and recording some of the items on financial statements. Because the figures for one business may not correspond exactly to those of another firm, good comparisons require reasoned judgment.

How many different ratios are significant? There is considerable difference of opinion on this question. We will discuss a few of the more prevalent ratios, using data for year 3 from Tables 18.1 and 18.2, and compute the ratios. We separate the discussion into the four categories of *efficiency ratios, liquidity ratios, leverage ratios,* and *profitability ratios.*

Efficiency ratios. Measures that portray how quickly assets or liabilities are used. The higher an efficiency ratio, the more efficient management is perceived in utilizing the resources committed to the measured activity.

18.3.1 Efficiency Ratios

Efficiency ratios, also called *activity* or *turnover ratios,* try to measure the effectiveness of management in using a firm's assets. Common efficiency ratios are *accounts receivable turnover* and *inventory turnover.* We discussed these ratios in Chapter 16. Although

O'GLOVE ON RECEIVABLES AND INVENTORY

Thornton O'Glove is the founder and former publisher of one of Wall Street's most highly regarded institutional research publications, the *Quality of Earnings Report.*

Question: Why is accounts receivable analysis so important?

Answer: Conventional accounts receivable analysis involves running a ratio called days sales in accounts receivable. This ratio, which indicates receivable turnover, can illustrate the granting of more liberal credit terms and/or difficulty in obtaining payment from customers.

However, even more importantly, the analysis of sales and accounts receivable may provide a clue as to whether a company is merely shifting inventory from the corporate level to its customers because of a "hard-sell" sales campaign or costly incentives. In such an instance, this type of sales may constitute "borrowing from the future." Within this context, it is important to note that in most instances, a sale is recorded by a company when the goods are shipped to the customer.

Also, there is an added cost to the company in carrying an above-average amount of accounts receivable.

Question: Why is inventory analysis so important?

Answer: Obviously, higher trending inventories in relation to sales can lead to inventory markdowns, write-offs, and so on. In addition, it is important to note that an excess of inventories, time and time again, is a good indicator of future slowdown in production. Within this context, it is important to analyze the components of inventories. If the finished goods segment of inventories is rising much more rapidly than raw materials and/or work-in-process, it is likely that the company has an abundance of finished goods and will have to slow down production. Akin to accounts receivable, bulging inventories are costly to carry.

Source: Thornton L. O'Glove, *Quality of Earnings* (New York: The Free Press, 1987), pp. 107–108.

we can compute an efficiency ratio for any asset, there is not much significance in calculating turnover ratios for cash and intangible assets. Neither of these assets relates directly to operations.

The above Financial Reality reading captures the importance of efficiency measures for accounts receivable and inventory. The person interviewed for this discussion is one of the top financial analysts in the country.

The most significant efficiency ratios are the *average collection period, inventory turnover,* and *investment turnover.*

AVERAGE COLLECTION PERIOD. We calculate the average collection period, or number of days' sales invested in accounts receivable, as:

$$\text{Average sales per day} = \frac{\text{Net credit sales}}{\text{Days in accounting period}} \quad (18.1)$$

$$= \frac{\$1,401,000}{360}$$

$$= \$3891.66$$

$$\text{Average collection period} = \frac{\text{Receivables}}{\text{Average sales per day}} \qquad (18.2)$$

$$= \frac{\$303,000}{\$3891.66}$$

$$= 77.9 \text{ days}$$

The average collection period helps managers and financial analysts decide how prompt customers are in paying their accounts. We can express the average collection period as a turnover ratio by dividing it into 360 days: $360 \div 77.9 = 4.6$. The turnover number indicates how often the receivables investment turns over during the year. A turnover ratio of 12 would mean accounts are collected every 30 days.

INVENTORY TURNOVER. As discussed in Chapter 16, *inventory turnover* shows how fast inventory is selling. It gives managers and analysts an idea of the amount of capital invested in inventory to support the company's operations.

$$\text{Inventory turnover} = \frac{\text{Cost of goods sold}}{\text{Average inventory}} \qquad (18.3)$$

$$= \frac{\$1,008,000}{(\$272,600 + \$262,200)/2}$$

$$= 3.8 \text{ times}$$

Ending inventory often is used in the ratio as opposed to average inventory. Regardless, a high turnover number may mean that the company can operate with a relatively small investment in inventory. If so, inventory carrying costs decline. A high turnover ratio may also suggest that inventories are current and salable and contain few unusable items. However, too much attention to high turnover can lead to inventory shortages and lost sales.

INVESTMENT TURNOVER. An efficiency measure that reflects all of the firm's assets is the *investment turnover ratio*. We calculate **investment turnover** as the ratio of annual net sales to total assets:

Investment turnover. The amount of sales that each $1 of investment generates.

$$\text{Investment turnover} = \frac{\text{Net sales}}{\text{Total assets}} \qquad (18.4)$$

$$= \frac{\$1,401,000}{\$829,000}$$

$$= 1.7 \text{ times}$$

This ratio measures the dollar amount of sales the firm generates for each dollar invested in assets. Ideally, the more sales generated per dollar of assets, the better. However, different accounting procedures and various ages of assets can seriously distort the comparison of this ratio with other firms.

18.3.2 Liquidity Ratios

As we know, *liquidity* can be thought of as a firm's ability to pay its bills as they come due. Measures of liquidity help us answer questions such as the following: Does the firm have enough cash and assets that management can quickly convert to cash? If so, then management is sure of being able to pay debts falling due during the accounting period. We discussed the role of liquidity measures in determining the appropriate level of short-term financing in Chapter 17. Here we limit our discussion of liquidity measures to a brief survey of how to calculate them. We calculate the *current ratio,* the *net working capital amount,* the *quick ratio,* the *defensive interval,* and the *cash conversion cycle.*

CURRENT RATIO. We compute the current ratio from the balance sheet by dividing current assets by current liabilities.

$$\text{Current ratio} = \frac{\text{Current assets}}{\text{Current liabilities}} \qquad (18.5)$$

$$= \frac{\$581,000}{\$522,000}$$

$$= 1.1 \text{ times}$$

As noted in Chapter 17, a popular rule of thumb for the current ratio is 2. Whether a specific number for the ratio is satisfactory depends on the nature of the business and the specific characteristics of its current assets and current liabilities.

If the current ratio is too low, management can easily raise it using the following actions:

- Pay some current debts with cash if the ratio is now greater than 1.
- Finance an increase in current assets with current liabilities if the current ratio is now less than 1.
- Convert noncurrent assets into current assets.
- Increase current assets by getting cash loans or other borrowings that have maturities of more than a year.
- Increase current assets from new equity contributions.

Some of these actions take more time than others to accomplish. The point is that management can improve the current ratio without really improving the liquidity of the firm. The improvement may be more *window dressing* than real substance. **Window dressing** is a general term that describes a variety of techniques, short of fraud, which management can use to make the figures for analysis of the condition of a business appear better or worse than they are. (See Illustration 18.1.)

Window dressing. Making financial statements appear more favorable than they really are.

ILLUSTRATION 18.1

Adjusting the current ratio

Suppose F&C International has current assets of $50,000 and current liabilities of $25,000. Thus, the current ratio is 2. If the firm buys $15,000 of inventory on credit, current assets increase to $65,000 and current liabilities to $40,000. The current ratio drops from 2.0 to 1.6. Suppose that the company, instead of buying more inventory on credit, pays bills amounting to $7000 with cash. This action reduces current assets to $43,000 and current liabilities to $18,000. However, the current ratio increases to 2.4.

NET WORKING CAPITAL. Chapter 17 defined net working capital as either

$$\text{Net working capital} = \text{Current assets} - \text{current liabilities} \qquad (18.6)$$

$$= \$581,100 - \$522,000$$

$$= \$59,100$$

or

$$\text{Net working capital} = \text{Noncurrent debt} + \text{equity} - \text{noncurrent assets} \quad \textbf{(18.7)}$$
$$= \$45,600 + \$261,400 - (\$242,700 + \$5,200)$$
$$= \$59,100$$

Equation 18.7 reveals that permanent financing of $59,100 supports the surplus of current assets over current liabilities, as shown by Equation 18.6. In Chapter 17, we discussed net working capital in terms of management's decision about the margin of safety for determining the appropriate level of short-term financing.

QUICK RATIO. The quick ratio for the firm is:

$$\text{Quick ratio} = \frac{\text{Cash} + \text{marketable securities} + \text{receivables}}{\text{Current liabilities}} \quad \textbf{(18.8)}$$

$$= \frac{\$300 + \$303,000}{\$522,000}$$

$$= 0.6 \text{ times}$$

Many practitioners consider it important to maintain a quick ratio of 1 or better. The idea behind this number is as follows. If all sales revenues should disappear, the business could still meet its current debts with readily convertible funds on hand.

Defensive interval ratio. A measurement of the number of days of normal cash expenditures covered by quick assets.

DEFENSIVE INTERVAL RATIO. The defensive interval ratio differs considerably from the current and quick ratios. The **defensive interval ratio** injects a flow concept into the measurement of liquidity by measuring the number of days the firm can continue to meet its daily cash expenses from its present supply of quick assets. We define it as:

$$\text{Defensive interval ratio} = \frac{\text{Quick assets}}{\text{Daily cash expenses}} \quad \textbf{(18.9)}$$

$$= \frac{\$303,300}{\$3640.8}$$

$$= 83.3 \text{ days}$$

A measure of daily cash expenses is:

Daily cash expenses

$$= \frac{\text{Cash collected from sales} - \text{cash flow from operations}}{360 \text{ days}} \quad \textbf{(18.10)}$$

$$= \frac{\$1,391,500 - \$80,800}{360}$$

$$= \$3640.83$$

Calculate cash collected from sales by converting sales in the income statement from accrual accounting to cash accounting. The equation for cash collected from sales is:

Cash collected from sales

$$= \text{Sales reported in income statement}$$

$$+ \text{decrease in accounts receivable from the previous year} \quad \textbf{(18.11)}$$

or

$$- \text{increase in accounts receivable from the previous year}$$

The *cash flow from operations* number in Equation 18.10 comes directly from the statement of cash flows. This number represents cash profits. The difference between cash collected from sales and cash profits is *cash expenses*. If we divide cash expenses by 360 days, we get *daily cash expenses*.[3]

There is no rule of thumb for the defensive interval ratio as there is for both the current and quick ratios. However, finding that the defensive interval ratio is 82 days this year, compared to, say, 65 days last year, is more appealing than knowing that the current or quick ratios changed from 1.2 to 1.1.

CASH CONVERSION CYCLE. The *cash conversion cycle* is the number of days of negotiated debt and equity financing required to support operations. We define it as:

$$\text{Cash conversion cycle} = \text{Average collection period}$$
$$+ \text{ days inventories outstanding} - \text{days purchases outstanding} \qquad (18.12)$$
$$= 77.9 \text{ days} + 94.7 \text{ days} - 75.1 \text{ days}$$
$$= 97.5 \text{ days}$$

Equation 18.2 showed the calculation for *average collection period*. We calculate days inventories outstanding by dividing 360 days by the number of inventory turns (given in Equation 18.3): $360 \div 3.8 = 94.7$ days. The calculation for *days purchases outstanding* is:

$$\text{Days purchases outstanding} = \frac{\text{Accounts payables} + \text{accruals}}{\text{Daily cash operating expenses}} \qquad (18.13)$$

$$= \frac{\$224{,}000 + \$43{,}900}{\$3566.8}$$

$$= 75.1 \text{ days}$$

Do not include interest-bearing financing (for example, notes or bank loans) in the numerator of Equation 18.13. Only amounts owing for materials, labor, and overhead items (that is, items directly affecting operations) are part of the calculation. We calculate *daily cash operating expenses* of $3566.8 by taking the $3640.8 daily cash expenses (see Equation 18.10) and subtracting daily interest expense of $74 ($26,800 ÷ 360 = $74). It is necessary to exclude interest expense because it is a *financing cost,* not an operating expense.

18.3.3 Leverage Ratios

Leverage comes in two forms: *financial* and *operating*. We hear much about financial leverage in the business press. It concerns debt financing. Operating leverage receives less media attention. It addresses the interaction of sales with variable and fixed operating costs. The discussion of capital structure in Chapter 13 examined the important roles financial and operating leverage play in that decision.

FINANCIAL LEVERAGE. Several different **financial leverage ratios** measure financial leverage. The predominant ones are *long-term debt to equity, total debt to equity, total debt to assets, interest coverage,* and *fixed-charge coverage.* We define each of these ratios next.

> **Financial leverage ratios.**
> Measures that show how the use of debt affects the firm's ability to repay obligations.

[3]A potential problem exists with Equation 18.10. By not paying trade creditors, cash flow from operations increases, which decreases the amount for daily cash expenses. Thus, the defensive interval ratio improves. Clearly, the firm's liquidity does not improve by not paying trade creditors.

$$\text{Long-term debt to equity} = \frac{\text{Long-term debt}}{\text{Shareholders' equity}} \qquad (18.14)$$

$$= \frac{\$45,600}{\$261,400}$$

$$= 0.174 \text{ or } 17.4 \text{ percent}$$

$$\text{Total debt to equity} = \frac{\text{Current liabilities} + \text{long-term debt}}{\text{Shareholders' equity}} \qquad (18.15)$$

$$= \frac{\$522,000 + \$45,600}{\$261,400}$$

$$= 2.171 \text{ or } 217.1 \text{ percent}$$

$$\text{Total debt to assets} = \frac{\text{Current liabilities} + \text{long-term debt}}{\text{Total assets}} \qquad (18.16)$$

$$= \frac{\$522,000 + \$45,600}{\$829,000}$$

$$= 0.685 \text{ or } 68.5 \text{ percent}$$

$$\text{Interest coverage} = \frac{\text{Earnings before interest and taxes}}{\text{Interest expense}} \qquad (18.17)$$

$$= \frac{\$71,000 + \$26,800}{\$26,800}$$

$$= 3.6 \text{ times}$$

Fixed-charge coverage ratio

$$= \frac{\text{Earnings before interest, leases, and taxes}}{\text{Interest} + \text{leases} + \dfrac{\text{principal repayment} + \text{preferred dividend}}{1 - \text{tax rate}}} \qquad (18.18)$$

$$= \frac{\$71,000 + \$26,800 + \$0}{\$26,800 + \$0 + \dfrac{\$0}{1 - 0.437}}$$

$$= 3.6 \text{ times}$$

If the firm had $5000 of operating leases, the fixed-charge coverage ratio would be 3.2 times. If in addition to the operating leases the firm also paid a preferred dividend of $1000, the coverage ratio would be 3.1 times. See if you can get these results.[4] It is necessary to divide the dividend payment in Equation 18.18 by (1 − tax rate) so as to state the dividend amount on a before-tax basis, thereby making it consistent with the expense amounts for interest and leases.

These financial leverage ratios are useful in determining:

- The extent to which debt finances assets.
- The long-term ability of the firm to meet payments to creditors.

[4]Solution: ($71,000 + $26,800 + $5,000) ÷ ($26,800 + $5,000) = 3.23; ($71,000 + 26,800 + $5,000) ÷ ($26,800 + $5000 + [$1000 ÷ (1 − 0.437)] = 3.06.

As the total debt-to-equity ratio approaches 1, or 100 percent, the creditors' interest in the firm's assets approaches the shareholders' interest. Creditors view a higher interest coverage ratio (also called *times interest earned*) better than a lower number. A negative interest coverage number means the firm incurred an operating loss and could not generate profits from operations to meet interest payments. Such a condition does not mean the firm is bankrupt. Management may still be able to pay interest from cash generated from operations or elsewhere in the business, for instance, from the collection of outstanding accounts receivable. It is also important to keep in mind that the ratios do not reflect market values. Accountants record assets, debt, and equity at historical cost. These items are seldom adjusted either up or down to reflect market realities.

OPERATING LEVERAGE. An easy way to consider operating leverage is to divide all operating expenses into fixed and variable classes. Fixed operating expenses do not vary in amount as production levels change. Examples include depreciation and advertising expenses. Variable operating expenses increase or decrease directly with increasing or decreasing production levels. Labor and material used in the manufacture of products are prime examples of variable operating expenses. Many operating expenses have both a fixed and variable component; that is, they are *semivariable* expenses. We must break semivariable expenses into their fixed and variable amounts.

We calculate the dollar **operating breakeven sales level** as:

$$\text{Breakeven sales level} = \frac{\text{Fixed operating expenses}}{1 - \dfrac{\text{Variable costs}}{\text{Net sales}}} \qquad (18.19)$$

$$= \frac{\$295,200}{1 - \dfrac{\$1,008,000}{\$1,401,000}}$$

$$= \$1,052,354$$

> **Operating breakeven sales level.** The point at which the firm's operating revenues equal its operating costs. To compute the breakeven point, costs are divided into fixed and variable components.

Our assumption is that fixed costs include all operating expenses ($263,900) and depreciation ($31,300) shown in Table 18.2. We assume cost of sales is a variable cost. The denominator of the ratio is the *contribution margin proportion*. The **contribution margin proportion** indicates the proportion of each $1 of sales that is available to cover fixed expenses. Figure 18.1 graphs the sales breakeven relationships, both in dollars and units.

> **Contribution margin proportion.** The proportion of each sales dollar left after paying variable costs; ratio of (sales – variable costs) ÷ sales.

Frequently, analysts include the financing cost of interest expense (or $26,800 in our example) as a fixed cost in the numerator of the sales breakeven calculation. The interpretation is the amount of sales required to cover both operating and financing fixed costs. Under this approach, the sales breakeven level increases to $1,147,894. Verify this result.[5]

Note in the graph that if we exclude fixed costs, the company always makes a profit—assuming the selling price exceeds the variable cost price. When we include fixed costs, the firm only makes a profit if sales exceed the breakeven level. Above the breakeven point, profit expands quickly as sales improve because fixed costs remain constant; the business levers the fixed costs into greater profits. However, operating leverage also works in the opposite direction. If output falls short of breakeven units, fixed costs result in greater losses.

---

[5]Solution: $26,800 ÷ 0.28051 = $95,540. Add this amount to the previous breakeven level of $1,052,354.

FIGURE 18.1

SALES BREAKEVEN GRAPH

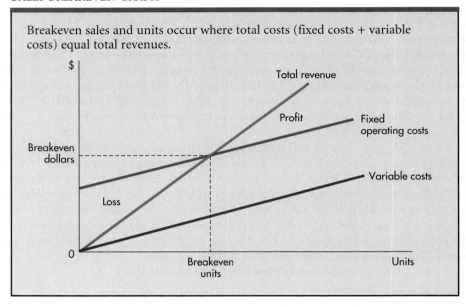

Breakeven sales and units occur where total costs (fixed costs + variable costs) equal total revenues.

18.3.4 Profitability Ratios

The group of ratios called *profitability ratios* tries to answer a key question. Is the company earning as much as it should, considering the amount of money invested? Several ratios help measure a company's success in achieving profitability; the most important profitability ratios are *return on sales, return on assets,* and *return on equity. Sustainable growth* also is significant to profitability.

RETURN ON SALES. Analysts frequently refer to the **return-on-sales** ratio as net profit on sales, or net profit margin. The ratio measures how much of each sales dollar the firm was able to keep, after recording all expenses in the process of doing business. We define it as:

$$\text{Return on sales} = \frac{\text{Net income}}{\text{Sales}} \tag{18.20}$$

$$= \frac{\$40,000}{\$1,401,000}$$

$$= 0.029 \text{ or } 2.9 \text{ percent}$$

The return-on-sales ratio depends mainly on two factors—operating costs and pricing policies. If return on sales declines, is it because management lowered prices in the hope of increasing total sales volume? Or is it because costs are creeping up while prices remain the same?

This ratio is most useful when compared with the numbers for comparable businesses, or when studying trends of a business over several accounting periods.

Comparing the net profit on sales for product groups or territories may also be useful.[6] Such analysis helps us decide which products or areas are profitable.

RETURN ON ASSETS. The *return-on-assets* ratio measures the earning power of assets.[7] Sometimes analysts measure the ratio as earnings before interest and taxes (EBIT) to total assets. We refer to this ratio as **operating return on assets.**

$$\text{Operating return on assets} = \frac{\text{EBIT}}{\text{Total assets}} \qquad (18.21)$$

$$= \frac{\$71,000 + \$26,800}{\$829,000}$$

$$= 0.118 \text{ or } 11.8 \text{ percent}$$

Operating return on assets. A measure of the productivity of assets on a before tax basis; defined as EBIT ÷ assets.

The usual calculation for return on assets is after-tax net income divided by total assets. This calculation is incorrect, as we discussed in Chapter 13. The correct calculation of return on assets is:

$$\text{Return on assets} = \frac{\text{Net income} + \text{interest} (1 - \text{tax rate})}{\text{Total assets}} \qquad (18.22)$$

$$= \frac{\$40,000 + \$26,800(1 - 0.437)}{\$829,000}$$

$$= 0.066 \text{ or } 6.6 \text{ percent}$$

The adjustment of interest $\times$ $(1 - \text{tax rate})$ removes any debt-financing expense included in the calculation of accounting income. Failure to adjust the numerator results in an understatement of the earning power of the assets. Earning power *does not* include financing costs. We compare earning power to the firm's weighted average cost of capital (WACC) to determine if the assets are at least earning the opportunity cost of financing them. Is ROA $\geq$ WACC?

The return-on-assets ratio sometimes uses total *tangible assets* instead of total assets in the denominator. **Tangible assets** are total assets less any *intangible assets* such as patents, goodwill, trademarks, copyrights, and leaseholds. In an ongoing business, intangible assets frequently have a significant but undeterminable value. Until management sells an intangible asset, it is difficult to determine what it might be worth.[8] In some cases, intangible assets have no commercial value except to those who hold them. For instance, to a profitable business up for sale, the company's reputation or goodwill conceivably could represent the potential earning power over several years and actually bring more than the tangible assets themselves. On the other hand, another business might find itself unable to realize anything at all on goodwill. Since the real value of intangible assets is frequently difficult to calculate, intangibles usually receive little consideration in financial statement analysis.

Tangible assets. Physical assets such as plant and equipment.

RETURN ON EQUITY. This measure shows the earning power of the equity invested in the business. We calculate return on equity by dividing net profit by equity.

---

[6]This information is often disclosed by large publicly traded firms in their annual reports.

[7]It may be useful to review Chapter 13's discussion about return on assets and return on equity.

[8]Accounting only records intangible assets that are purchased. Money spent developing goodwill, such as a patent, is expensed because at the time there is no certainty that any goodwill can be obtained.

$$\text{Return on equity} = \frac{\text{Net income}}{\text{Equity}} \qquad (18.23)$$

$$= \frac{\$40,000}{\$261,400}$$

$$= 0.153 \text{ or } 15.3 \text{ percent}$$

Net worth. The ownership interests of common and, perhaps, preferred shareholders in a company; on a balance sheet, equity equals total assets less all liabilities.

The equity, or **net worth,** of the business consists of all outstanding common stock, paid-in (or contributed) surplus, and retained earnings.

Another way to express return on equity is:[9]

$$\text{Return on equity} = \frac{\text{Return}}{\text{on sales}} \times \frac{\text{efficiency in}}{\text{managing assets}} \times \frac{\text{financial}}{\text{leverage}}$$

$$= \frac{\text{Net income}}{\text{Sales}} \times \frac{\text{sales}}{\text{assets}} \times \frac{\text{assets}}{\text{equity}} \qquad (18.24)$$

$$= \frac{\$40,000}{\$1,401,000} \times \frac{\$1,401,000}{\$829,000} \times \frac{\$829,000}{\$261,400}$$

$$= 0.0286 \times 1.69 \times 3.17$$

$$= 0.153 \text{ or } 15.3 \text{ percent}$$

Many analysts refer to Equation 18.24 as the *Du Pont formula,* in honor of the company that first defined it. This formula shows the multifaceted nature of return on equity. Profitability of sales, management's ability to use the assets, and how management finances the firm affect return on equity.

It may not be obvious to you that the ratio assets ÷ equity in Equation 18.24 represents financial leverage. Recall from accounting that assets = liabilities + equity. By substituting liabilities + equity for assets, we can write assets ÷ equity as 1 + debt ÷ equity: 1 + $567,600 ÷ $261,400. Financial leverage is now clearly evident by the debt ÷ equity component: $567,600 ÷ $261,400.

If the firm issues preferred stock, some people treat it as part of the equity and others treat it as a form of debt. Treating preferred stock as equity requires no change to Equations 18.23 and 18.24. However, treating preferred stock as debt requires a different calculation for return on equity. In this case, we must subtract preferred dividends from net income to arrive at **earnings available to common shareholders.** The revised return-on-equity Equation 18.23 is:

Earnings available to common shareholders. Net income less dividends paid to preferred shareholders.

$$\text{Return on equity} = \frac{\text{Earnings available to common shareholders}}{\text{Equity less preferred stock}}$$

$$= \frac{\text{Net income} - \text{preferred dividends}}{\text{Equity less preferred stock}} \qquad (18.25)$$

SUSTAINABLE GROWTH. Sustainable growth is growth the firm can sustain without having to raise external equity financing. Although the sustainable growth measure is not a profitability ratio, it makes sense to discuss it here. Sustainable growth relies on the return-on-equity model. And, as you may recall from Chapter 14, sustainable growth is a guiding criterion used by management in planning capital expenditures.

[9]In Chapter 13, we expressed return on equity as a function of return on assets, the after-tax cost of interest, and the debt-equity ratio. All these different return-on-equity calculations give the same result.

We can define sustainable growth as:

$$\text{Sustainable growth} = \frac{\left(1 - \dfrac{\text{Dividends paid}}{\text{Profits}}\right) \times \text{return on equity}}{1 - \left(1 - \dfrac{\text{Dividends paid}}{\text{Profits}}\right) \times \text{return on equity}} \quad (18.26)$$

$$= \frac{(1 - \$1000/\$40,000) \times 0.153}{1 - (1 - \$1000/\$40,000) \times 0.153}$$

$$= 0.175 \text{ or } 17.5 \text{ percent}$$

where we use end-of-period equity to calculate return on equity.[10]

Sustainable growth is essentially the rate of growth the firm can support without changing its dividend policy and the factors making up the return-on-equity ratio: *return on sales, investment turnover,* and *financial leverage*. The calculation also assumes that the firm does not issue any new common stock.

A firm cannot grow faster than its sustainable growth rate for an extended time. If actual growth, as measured by growth in sales ($[\$1,401,000 \div \$1,830,000] - 1 = -0.234$, or -23.4 percent) or assets ($[\$829,000 \div 742,600] - 1 = 0.116$, or 11.6 percent), were to exceed sustainable growth of 17.5 percent, then management would need to find additional resources to support the firm because operations could not generate enough funds. This condition does not exist in the preceding example. If it did, actions to bring actual growth and sustainable growth into line would be required. Some possible actions would include:

- Cut back sales and production by pruning the less profitable products to improve return on sales and asset investment.
- Encourage more efficiency in operations by a quicker turnover of assets.
- Retain more profits by reducing the dividend payout.

If these actions were not enough, the firm could face a serious liquidity problem and possible bankruptcy.

Comprehension Check

1. How can ratio analysis be useful to the financial analyst? What are the limitations of ratio analysis?
2. Does an increase in the current ratio always result in better protection of the remaining short-term creditors? Why or why not?
3. How does the defensive interval ratio differ from the current and quick ratios?
4. What is the significance of operating leverage?
5. How is the return-on-equity ratio affected when a firm has issued preferred stock?
6. How is a firm's sustainable growth rate defined and what is its significance?

[10]Equation 18.26 differs from Equation 14.1 in Chapter 14 where beginning period equity was used. However, both definitions provide the same answer.

18.4 INTERPRETATION OF THE ANALYSIS

Our earlier analysis of common-size statements, cash flows, and financial ratios raises several questions.

- *Cash.* Is our example firm's low cash balance due to poor cash planning? Or is it because of excessive investment in accounts receivable, inventories, equipment, or buildings?
- *Accounts receivable.* Is the increase because of slower collections or failure to write off uncollectible accounts? Or is it because of a change in sales terms? Or is the increase because of higher unit or dollar volume of sales?
- *Inventories.* Does the fluctuation suggest an unanticipated drop in sales or lack of control over production to meet needs? Or is it the result of poor planning by the purchasing department?
- *Property and equipment.* Why did the company nearly triple its investment in plant and equipment? What specific assets did management purchase? What was the purpose of each purchase? Did the company impair its ability to meet current debts? Did it get adequate long-term capital to finance the assets?
- *Bank overdraft.* Is the overdraft a danger signal suggesting the company is approaching a financial crisis?
- *Accounts payable.* Is the company becoming slow in paying its trade creditors? Is the company losing its cash trade discounts due to inadequate finances?
- *Long-term liabilities.* Do the increases in long-term debt finance all or part of the purchases of equipment?
- *Gross sales.* Why did the sudden increase of dollar sales in year 2 disappear in year 3? Does the change show a decline in sales effort? Was the year 2 sales increase fictitious? Did unit sales suffer a similar decline?
- *Returns and allowances.* Does the doubling of the percentage of returns from year 1 to year 3 mean poor quality, late production, customer ill-will, or, possibly, the falsification of sales? What effect did these increased dollar sales returns have on reducing profit and increasing costs?
- *Gross profit.* Is the jump in the gross profit percentage due to increased efficiency, higher sales prices, or inventory manipulation? Management may have increased inventory valuations to show increased profit.
- *Operating expenses.* Does the dollar and percentage increase of expenses suggest an erosion of managerial control? Which of the expenses have risen in proportion to sales?
- *Net income.* Is the downward trend in the net income amount likely to continue or is the company taking steps to remedy the problem? Is the increase in gross profit percentage explainable in view of the decline in the net income percentage? Is the divergence because of inventory manipulation? If so, a false net income conceals a decline in operating efficiency.

We summarize the several ratios calculated for year 3 in Table 18.9 along with ratios for the two prior years.

18.4.1 Efficiency Ratios

The pronounced lengthening of the collection period from 52 days in year 1 to 78 days in year 3 raises certain questions:

TABLE 18-9

SUMMARY OF RATIOS

	Year 3	Year 2	Year 1
EFFICIENCY RATIOS:			
Average collection period (days)	77.9	57.7	51.8
Inventory turnover (times)	3.8	7.3	10.2
Days inventory outstanding (days)	94.7	49.3	35.3
Investment turnover (times)	1.7	2.5	3.3
LIQUIDITY RATIOS:			
Current ratio (times)	1.1	1.2	1.5
Net working capital ($000)	59.1	101.8	126.6
Quick ratio (times)	0.6	0.6	0.9
Defensive interval (days)	83.3	63.8	57.7
Cash conversion cycle (days)	97.5	56.1	69.3
Days purchases outstanding (days)	75.1	50.9	17.8
LEVERAGE RATIOS:			
Long-term debt to equity (%)	17.4	10.3	6.3
Total debt to equity (%)	217.1	233.9	124.1
Interest coverage (times)	3.6	5.2	11.0
Breakeven sales level ($000)	1052.4	1257.6	912.6
PROFITABILITY RATIOS:			
Gross profit margin (%)	28.1	22.7	24.3
Return on sales (%)	2.9	3.1	4.4
Return on assets, after tax (%)	6.6	9.3	15.6
Return on assets, before tax (%)	11.8	17.5	29.6
Return on equity (%)	15.3	25.2	31.9
Sustainable growth (%)	17.5	11.0	17.6
Actual sales growth (%)	−23.4	25.3	
Actual asset growth (%)	11.6	65.4	

- Is the collection effort competent?
- Is the credit policy lax and inefficient?
- Is credit used as a selling device, with terms extended beyond a normal period and to less creditworthy customers?
- Was the sales record held open beyond the closing date of the balance sheet to window dress the statement? If this occurred, did accounts receivable, sales, and profits increase and inventory decline by the cost of the accelerated sales?
- Was there a change in selling terms?
- Are there extenuating circumstances?

The terms of sale are important to the analysis of accounts receivable. If, for example, credit terms are 2 percent discount when paid in 10 days and net when paid in 30 days (that is, 2/10, n/30), the credit department should collect the bulk of accounts within 30 days. Management can decrease the company's average collection period by shortening the time in which payment is due. However, this action might not be desirable because of its probable adverse affect on sales.

Inventory is another major concern. While there may be reasonable explanations for the decline in inventory turnover from ten times to about four times, such a large decline usually signals trouble. The decline may cause us to be skeptical of the valuation of the inventory. And analysis of gross profit margins supports any skepticism.

By itself, the year 3 gross profit percentage jump to 28.1 percent from either 22.7 percent in year 2 or 24.3 percent in year 1 looks commendable. However, when viewing the gross profit ratio in relation to the reduction in inventory turnover, a logical question arises. Is the five-point increase in gross profit margin because of improved selling efficiency or is it due to unjustified inventory valuation? Five percent of the year 3 net credit sales of $1,401,000 is about $70,000. Thus, a large reduction of inventory value to remove the amount of excess valuation would eliminate almost the entire net income of $71,000 for year 3 and lower the profitability ratios. Any inventory adjustment would also result in a reduction in net working capital and the current ratio.[11] Breakeven sales would increase and interest coverage would decline.

The primary concern of short-term credit grantors is the liquidity of accounts receivable and the control of inventory. Creditors look to the prompt collection of receivables as a principal source of payment for their credit. Firms with excessive inventories may lack enough cash to meet their maturing debts. There is also greater vulnerability to large losses from falling prices or unexpected obsolescence.

18.4.2 Liquidity Ratios

Declines in the current and quick ratios since year 1 require an explanation. Short-term creditors frequently regard these ratios as key liquidity indices. Managers sometimes falsely improve these ratios to support the credit desired. Methods used to give the appearance of an increase in current assets and a decrease in current liabilities include the following. The manager may:

- Inflate the value of inventories.
- Hold sales open beyond the end of the period.
- Close the purchase record before the end of the period.
- Deflate accounts payable by withholding invoices from entry in the accounting records.

Is this last item the reason for the improvement in the defensive interval ratio each year? For example, in year 3 daily cash expenses of $3534 are significantly below the previous year's level of $4662. When the company does not pay its trade creditors, such a result can occur.

The statistics for the cash conversion cycle (CCC) are revealing and support our concerns about receivables, inventories, and short-term creditors. In year 3, the CCC increased 41 days, even though days purchases outstanding increased 25 days as a result

---

[11]The balance sheet figure for inventories reflects the methods by which they are valued (for example, FIFO or LIFO). The amount may also be subject to errors of miscounting, misjudging, computation, and purposeful manipulation.

of delaying payments to trade creditors. The 41-day increase means the firm had to rely on more negotiated financing to support operations. If payments to trade creditors had remained at the year 2 level, the CCC would have increased 65 days in year 3 over the year 2 level. The firm may not be able to secure more negotiated financing. It has a $15,000 bank overdraft (as Table 18.1 revealed) and it cut the dividend from $34,000 to $1000 (as shown in Table 18.2). Thus, it uses trade creditors to provide the necessary financing.

18.4.3 Leverage Ratios

We see additional risk to creditors in the declining pattern in the interest coverage ratio and the (more than) doubling in the debt ratios. The breakeven level for sales, although down from year 2, is up 15 percent over the year 1 level. We must view the recent improvement in breakeven sales with some concern about the gross profit margins. Any overstatement of margins understates the breakeven sales level. For instance, if the true gross profit margin in year 3 is 22.7 percent (the same as in the prior year), then the breakeven sales level increases to $1,300,441. Check this result.[12]

18.4.4 Profitability Ratios

Except for the gross profit margin, the trend of the profitability ratios is down. Return on assets and return on equity are less than one-half of levels attained two years ago. If the pattern continues, the use of debt may result in unfavorable financial leverage.

The sustainable growth figure is favorable for year 3 but unfavorable for year 2 when compared to either growth in sales or growth in assets. The problem is that sustainable growth does not display any pattern around a stable level. It appears that management is not pursuing a stable, well-considered strategy for operating the business.

18.4.5 Overall Assessment

The overall conclusion that emerges from this analysis is that the firm faces financial problems. Liquidity is deteriorating rapidly, creditors may have cut off debt financing, and accounts receivable and inventory are extremely high. The increasing pattern in sales returns suggests that either product quality-control problems exist or salespeople padded sales in year 2. Gross profit margins appear to be misstated and, if so, there may be a serious problem with inventory. Could much of the inventory be obsolete or nonsalable? Is management putting defective returned merchandise back into inventory?[13]

> ### Comprehension Check
>
> 1. Why are so many questions about the example left unanswered?

---

[12]Solution: (Operating expenses of $263.9 + depreciation of $31.3) ÷ 0.227 = $1,300.441.

[13]Miniscribe Corporation, a hard disk manufacturer, followed such a practice until discovered by the independent accountants. Management was propping up earnings illegally.

18.5 INDUSTRY FIGURES

Analysts often compare a firm's results against published industry figures. However, industry data come with a large helping of problems. The data must be used with careful discrimination and judgment. Some of the factors that limit reliability of industry data are:

- Figures are somewhat out of date when published.
- Companies operate under varying conditions because of differences in geographical location and type of marketing systems. Thus, many financial ratios lack direct comparability.
- Accounting methods and principles used by different firms in an industry may vary materially.
- Financial statements used to compile the averages may not all be of the same time frame.
- Companies may vary in size and maturity and, thus, there may be wide differences in scale of operations and staff experience.
- The number of companies represented in the survey may be too few to provide the representative sampling needed for statistical purposes.

Table 18.10 shows the major sources of industry information.

Suppose Kellogg Company operates in the same industry as our sample company and we want to use Kellogg's financial performance as a standard. Thus, we decide to see what Value Line Investment Services (see Figure 18.2) and Standard & Poor's (see Figure 18.3) have to say about Kellogg. However, a close review of Figures 18.2 and 18.3 shows inconsistencies for the same item. For example, Value Line reports that Kellogg had earnings per share of $1.34 in 1986, whereas S&P reports $1.29. Value Line ignores some fac-

---

TABLE 18-10

Major Sources of Industry Financial Information

Dun & Bradstreet. Publishes a survey of different types of retailing, wholesaling, manufacturing, and construction companies. Presented are statistics on the median, upper-quartile, and lower-quartile values for 14 key ratios.

Robert Morris Associates. Members of the association are bank loan and credit officers. The association compiles statistics on the median, upper quartile, and lower quartile for 16 key ratios for over 300 lines of business by firm size.

Investor services. Moody's *Manuals* and *Handbook of Common Stocks*, Standard & Poor's *Industry Survey* and *Analyst's Handbook*, and the *Value Line Investment Survey* provide comparative ratios on companies and industries. (See Figures 18.2 and 18.3 for examples for Kellogg.)

Governmental agencies. The Federal Trade Commission and the Securities and Exchange Commission jointly publish *Quarterly Financial Report for U.S. Manufacturing Corporations.* It contains financial data by firm size and by industry. The Small Business Administration and the U.S. Department of Commerce also issue financial data.

Business periodicals. *Business Week, Forbes,* and *Fortune* magazines provide summary data on a few financial ratios on a regular basis.

FIGURE 18.2

VALUE LINE INVESTMENT SERVICES REPORT FOR KELLOGG

KELLOGG CO. NYSE-K | RECENT PRICE **68** | P/E RATIO **24.3** (Trailing: 26.0 / Median: 15.0) | RELATIVE P/E RATIO **1.60** | DIV'D YLD **2.0%** | VALUE LINE | **1478**

TIMELINESS **1** Highest (Relative Price Performance Next 12 Mos.)

SAFETY **1** Highest (Scale: 1 Highest to 5 Lowest)

BETA .95 (1.00 = Market)

1995-97 PROJECTIONS

	Price	Gain	Ann'l Total Return
High	90	(+30%)	9%
Low	75	(+10%)	5%

Insider Decisions

	O	N	D	J	F	M	A	M	J
to Buy	0	1	1	0	0	1	0	0	0
Options	0	1	1	0	6	2	1	0	2
to Sell	2	0	1	0	1	3	1	2	2

Institutional Decisions

	3Q'91	4Q'91	1Q'92
to Buy	97	123	115
to Sell	101	116	138
Hld's(000)	173194	174261	171146

1976	1977	1978	1979	1980	1981	1982	1983	1984	1985	1986	1987	1988	1989	1990	1991	1992	1993	© VALUE LINE PUB. INC.	95-97
4.54	5.02	5.53	6.04	7.04	7.59	7.74	7.78	10.57	11.88	13.52	15.37	17.69	19.06	21.47	24.06	26.65	29.65	Sales per sh	41.30
.51	.56	.59	.66	.75	.83	.91	.94	1.29	1.44	1.71	2.08	2.52	2.42	2.91	3.45	3.85	4.40	"Cash Flow" per sh	6.25
.43	.45	.48	.53	.61	.67	.73	.75	.85	1.14	1.34	1.60	1.95	1.73	2.08	2.51	2.80	3.20	Earnings per sh A	4.65
.25	.28	.30	.32	.34	.36	.38	.41	.43	.45	.51	.65	.76	.86	.96	1.08	1.20	1.38	Div'ds Decl'd per sh B	2.00
.30	.25	.30	.27	.40	.48	.40	.51	.93	1.00	1.33	1.94	2.19	2.09	1.33	1.39	2.00	2.35	Cap'l Spending per sh	1.50
1.60	1.77	1.95	2.16	2.43	2.65	2.89	3.20	1.98	2.77	3.64	4.91	6.03	6.71	7.88	8.98	10.10	11.55	Book Value per sh C	17.05
304.88	305.56	305.64	305.72	305.73	305.73	305.79	305.97	246.26	246.74	247.12	246.82	245.86	243.75	241.32	240.46	240.00	236.00	Common Shs Outst'g D	230.00
14.2	13.6	11.4	9.0	7.8	8.0	8.7	9.3	9.7	12.2	17.5	18.6	14.4	20.0	16.0	19.5	Bold figures are Value Line estimates		Avg Ann'l P/E Ratio	18.0
1.82	1.78	1.55	1.30	1.04	.97	.96	.79	.90	.99	1.19	1.24	1.20	1.51	1.19	1.24			Relative P/E Ratio	1.40
4.1%	4.6%	5.6%	6.8%	7.1%	6.7%	6.1%	5.8%	5.2%	3.2%	2.2%	2.2%	2.7%	2.5%	2.9%	2.2%			Avg Ann'l Div'd Yield	2.4%

CAPITAL STRUCTURE as of 3/31/92

Total Debt $395.6 mill. Due in 5 Yrs $395.6 mill.
LT Debt $15.0 mill. LT Interest $1.3 mill.
(1% of Cap'l)

Pension Liability None

Pfd Stock None

Common Stock 239,316,407 shs. (99% of Cap'l) as of May 1, 1992

	2367.1	2381.1	2602.4	2930.1	3340.7	3793.0	4348.8	4651.7	5181.4	5786.6	6400	7000	Sales ($mill)	9500
	19.1%	20.0%	20.3%	21.6%	22.2%	21.2%	21.5%	19.4%	21.0%	21.6%	22.0%	22.5%	Operating Margin	23.0%
	55.9	62.8	63.9	75.4	92.7	113.1	139.7	167.6	200.2	222.8	250	275	Depreciation ($mill)	355
	222.1	225.4	254.2	281.1	330.4	395.9	480.4	422.1	502.8	606.0	675	765	Net Profit ($mill)	1070
	45.2%	47.2%	46.6%	46.7%	45.8%	40.5%	38.0%	36.7%	38.3%	38.4%	38.5%	38.5%	Income Tax Rate	38.5%
	9.4%	9.5%	9.8%	9.6%	9.9%	10.4%	11.0%	9.1%	9.7%	10.5%	10.5%	10.9%	Net Profit Margin	11.3%
	256.5	302.4	87.4	173.8	43.2	d51.5	d120.3	d131.1	d68.2	d151.4	185	320	Working Cap'l ($mill)	495
	11.8	18.6	364.1	392.6	264.1	290.4	272.1	371.4	295.6	15.2	315	415	Long-Term Debt ($mill)	580
	884.7	977.9	487.2	683.0	898.4	1211.4	1483.2	1634.4	1901.8	2159.8	2420	2730	Net Worth ($mill)	3925
	25.1%	22.7%	30.0%	28.0%	29.9%	27.4%	28.1%	22.1%	23.5%	27.9%	25.5%	25.5%	% Earned Total Cap'l	25.5%
	25.1%	23.0%	52.2%	41.2%	36.8%	32.7%	32.4%	25.8%	26.4%	28.1%	28.0%	28.0%	% Earned Net Worth	27.5%
	11.9%	10.4%	26.8%	24.9%	22.8%	19.5%	19.8%	13.0%	14.2%	16.1%	16.0%	16.0%	% Retained to Comm Eq	15.5%
	52%	55%	49%	39%	38%	40%	39%	50%	46%	43%	43%	43%	% All Div'ds to Net Prof	43%

CURRENT POSITION ($mill.)

	1990	1991	3/31/92
Cash Assets	100.5	178.0	133.8
Receivables	430.2	420.0	522.1
Inventory (Avg Cst)	359.7	401.1	380.6
Other	151.0	173.9	167.9
Current Assets	1041.4	1173.0	1204.4
Accts Payable	247.1	289.8	287.4
Debt Due	382.6	449.1	380.6
Other	479.9	585.5	587.7
Current Liab.	1109.6	1324.4	1255.7

ANNUAL RATES

of change (per sh)	Past 10 Yrs.	Past 5 Yrs.	Est'd '89-'91 to '95-'97
Sales	12.0%	12.5%	11.5%
"Cash Flow"	14.5%	14.5%	13.5%
Earnings	13.5%	13.5%	14.0%
Dividends	11.0%	16.0%	13.0%
Book Value	12.5%	23.0%	13.5%

QUARTERLY SALES ($ mill.)

Calendar	Mar.31	Jun.30	Sep.30	Dec.31	Full Year
1989	1134	1234	1195	1088	4651.7
1990	1208	1259	1351	1363	5181.4
1991	1421	1415	1506	1445	5786.6
1992	1515	1584	1685	1616	6400
1993	1675	1725	1850	1750	7000

EARNINGS PER SHARE A

Calendar	Mar.31	Jun.30	Sep.30	Dec.31	Full Year
1989	.46	.53	.51	.23	1.73
1990	.40	.57	.67	.44	2.08
1991	.68	.63	.72	.48	2.51
1992	.71	.70	.83	.56	2.80
1993	.80	.80	.95	.65	3.20

QUARTERLY DIVIDENDS PAID B

Calendar	Mar.31	Jun.30	Sep.30	Dec.31	Full Year
1988	.19	.19	.19	.19	.76
1989	.215	.215	.215	.215	.86
1990	.24	.24	.24	.24	.96
1991	.265	.265	.265	.26	1.06
1992	.28	.28	.32		

BUSINESS: Kellogg Company, the world's largest manufacturer of ready-to-eat cereals (38% of U.S. market, 52% of non-U.S. market), also produces frozen foods, dessert items, and other convenience foods. Brand names include: Kellogg's, Frosted Flakes, Rice Krispies, Frosted Mini-Wheats, Special K, Froot Loops, Nutri-Grain, Apple Jacks, All-Bran, Pop-Tarts, Eggo, Mrs. Smith's. Foreign operations accounted for 41% of sales, 36% of net income in 1991. Labor costs: 18% of sales; advertising, 12%. '91 depreciation rate: 5.7%. Estimated plant age: 6 years. Has 17,000 employees, 23,100 stockholders. W.K. Kellogg Foundation controls 34% of common. Chrmn., CEO, & Pres.: Arnold G. Langbo. Inc.: Delaware. Address: Battle Creek, MI 49016. Tel.: 616-961-6122.

Kellogg is continuing to do well around the world. Global unit sales were up 7% in each of the first two quarters of 1992, and the company's market share undoubtedly increased. In an effort to boost demand further, Kellogg increased marketing and promotional spending by 22% in the second quarter, and the results seem to be paying off. Worthwhile sales gains are likely over the remainder of the year, and we look for share earnings for 1992 to be at least $2.80.

Clearly, the greatest potential for strong growth lies abroad. That's not to say the future of the U.S. business is poor —in fact domestic business has been very good so far this year. But markets around the world are growing faster than those here, and they are likely to continue to grow rapidly for many years to come, in large part because the per capita consumption of ready-to-eat cereals is much smaller there than it is in the U.S. Foreign poundage has grown at roughly 8% a year for a number of years, and we expect increases to continue at about the same rate. Kellogg has been selling cereal overseas for more than 60 years, and it is the dominant factor in many markets, with a 50% share of the important European market, and 87% of the smaller Latin American market. In fact, outside North America it is so strong that it outsells its nearest rival by nearly eight to one.

The long-term growth opportunities are outstanding. Working from its strong and well-established base in most parts of the world, Kellogg should be able to increase its sales and earnings for many years to come. It's selling a product that is increasingly recognized for its nutritional value, and the company has the financial and managerial resources to expand rapidly.

This stock carries our top rank for performance in the coming year, and it is also one of the highest quality issues we cover. With a top score for Financial Strength and the Highest rank for Safety, Kellogg is an appropriate holding for conservative, growth-oriented investors. The stock has moved up nicely since our May report, though, and from current levels, near the all-time high, 3- to 5-year total return potential is modest.

Stephen Sanborn *August 21, 1992*

(A) Based on average shares. Excludes non-recurring gains (losses): '82, 2¢; '83, 5¢; '84, (2¢); '86, (5¢); '92, 11¢. Excludes gain from accounting change: '89, 20¢. Next earnings report due late Oct. (B) Next dividend meeting about Oct. 18. Next ex date about Nov. 25. Approx. dividend payment dates: Mar. 15, June 15, Sept. 15, Dec. 15. ■ Div'd reinvestment plan available. (C) Includes intangible assets. In '91 $49.8 mill., 21¢/sh. Includes accumulated currency gain: '91, $14.0 million, 6¢/sh. (D) In millions, adjusted for stock split.

Factual material is obtained from sources believed to be reliable, but the publisher is not responsible for any errors or omissions contained herein. For the confidential use of subscribers. Reprinting, copying, and distribution by permission only. Copyright 1992 by Value Line Publishing, Inc. ® Reg. TM—Value, Inc.

Company's Financial Strength	A++
Stock's Price Stability	90
Price Growth Persistence	95
Earnings Predictability	85

FIGURE 18.3
S&P STOCK REPORT FOR KELLOGG

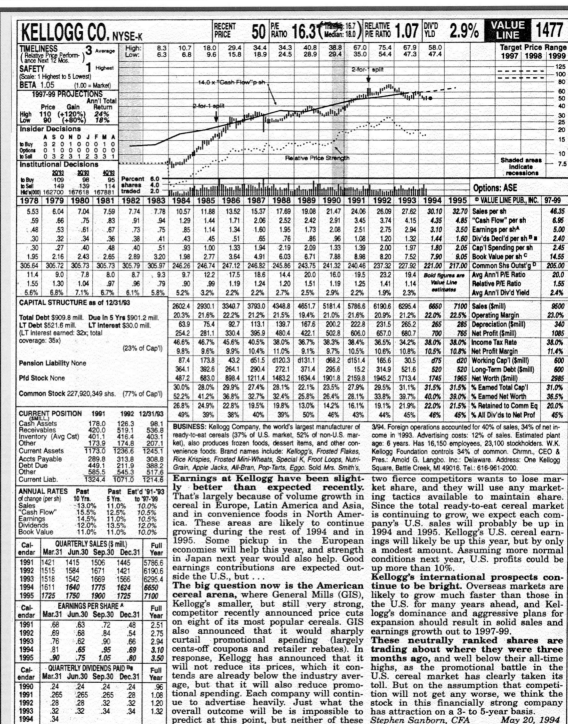

Kellogg Company

Income Data (Million $)

Year Ended Dec. 31	Revs.	Oper. Inc.	% Oper. Inc. of Revs.	Cap. Exp.	Depr.	Int. Exp.	Net Bef. Taxes	Eff. Tax Rate	[2]Net Inc.	% Net Inc. of Revs.	Cash Flow
1992	6,191	1,294	20.9	474	232	33.6	1,070	36.2%	[3]683	11.0	914
1991	5,787	1,251	21.6	334	223	60.7	984	38.4%	606	10.5	829
1990	5,181	1,086	21.0	321	200	84.5	815	38.3%	503	9.7	703
1989	4,652	900	19.3	509	168	72.6	667	36.7%	422	9.1	590
1988	4,349	934	21.5	538	140	60.4	775	38.0%	480	11.0	620
1987	3,793	804	21.2	478	113	48.8	666	40.5%	[3]396	10.4	509
1986	3,341	740	22.2	329	93	49.0	587	45.6%	319	9.5	412
1985	2,930	634	21.6	246	75	52.9	527	46.7%	281	9.6	357
1984	2,602	527	20.3	230	64	18.7	476	47.4%	251	9.6	314
[1]1983	2,381	477	20.0	158	63	7.1	444	45.3%	243	10.2	306

Balance Sheet Data (Million $)

Dec. 31	Cash	Assets	Curr. Liab.	Ratio	Total Assets	% Ret. on Assets	Long Term Debt	Common Equity	Total Cap.	% LT Debt of Cap.	% Ret. on Equity
1992	126	1,237	1,071	1.2	4,015	17.3	315	1,945	2,445	12.9	33.5
1991	178	1,173	1,324	0.9	3,926	15.8	15	2,160	2,514	0.6	29.9
1990	101	1,041	1,110	0.9	3,749	14.2	296	1,902	2,544	11.6	28.6
1989	80	906	1,037	0.9	3,390	12.7	371	1,634	2,295	16.2	27.2
1988	185	1,063	1,184	0.9	3,298	16.1	272	1,483	2,048	13.3	35.7
1987	126	802	853	0.9	2,681	16.6	290	1,211	1,758	16.5	37.5
1986	198	730	686	1.1	2,084	16.7	264	898	1,381	19.1	40.3
1985	128	618	444	1.4	1,726	16.6	393	683	1,270	30.9	48.0
1984	309	752	664	1.1	1,667	17.6	364	487	994	36.6	39.3
1983	249	663	361	1.8	1,467	17.6	19	978	1,097	1.7	26.1

Data as orig. reptd. 1. Refl. merger or acq. 2. Bef. spec. items. 3. Refl. acctg. change.

Business Summary

Kellogg is the world's leading producer of ready-to-eat cereal products, holding 38% of the U.S. market. The company also manufactures and markets a wide variety of other convenience foods, which make up about 20% of its worldwide business. In 1992, international operations (including Canada) accounted for 43% of sales and 34% of net earnings. Products are manufactured in 17 countries and distributed in more than 150 countries. In January 1992, K sold its Fearn International subsidiary (1991 sales of $100 million), a maker of soups and other foodservice products.

Ready-to-eat cereals include Corn Flakes, Rice Krispies, Special K, Frosted Flakes, All-Bran, Corn Pops, Raisin Bran, Bran Flakes, Honey Smacks, Froot Loops, Cocoa Krispies, Apple Jacks, Frosted Mini-Wheats, Nutri-Grain cereals, Bran Buds, Product 19, Cracklin Oat Bran, Crispix, Fruitful Bran, Apple Raisin Crisp, Just Right, Common Sense, Nut & Honey Crunch, Oatbake, Big Mixx, Squares, Heartwise and Mueslix. Principal raw ingredients include corn grits, oats, rice, various fruits, wheat and wheat derivatives. K's primary noncereal products are Eggo frozen waffles and Mrs. Smith's frozen pies, produced by Mrs. Smith's Frozen Foods Co.; Kellogg's Pop-Tarts toaster pastries, produced by Kellogg USA; and Kellogg's

Nutri-Grain Bars, a new product manufactured by Kellogg USA.

The company's U.S. manufacturing facilities include five cereal plants and warehouses, in Battle Creek, Mich., Lancaster, Pa., Memphis, Tenn., Omaha, Neb., and San Leandro, Calif. Manufacturing facilities outside the U.S. are in Australia, Canada, Europe, Japan, Mexico, South Africa, South and Central America and South Korea.

Dividend Data

Dividends have been paid since 1923. A dividend reinvestment plan is available.

Amt. of Divd. $	Date Decl.	Ex-divd. Date	Stock of Record	Payment Date
0.32	Nov. 11	Nov. 24	Dec. 1	Dec. 15'92
0.32	Feb. 10	Feb. 23	Mar. 1	Mar. 15'93
0.32	May 12	May 25	Jun. 1	Jun. 15'93
0.34	Jul. 23	Aug. 26	Sep. 1	Sep. 15'93

Capitalization

Long Term Debt: $320,700,000 (3/93).

Common Stock: 232,234,629 shs. ($0.25 par).
About 34% is owned beneficially by the W. K. Kellogg Foundation Trust; G. Gund owns 8%.
Shareholders of record: 27,438.

Office—One Kellogg Square, P.O. Box 3599, Battle Creek, MI 49016-3599. Tel—(616) 961-2000. Chrmn & CEO—A. G. Langbo. SVP & Secy—R. M. Clark. Treas—J. R. Hinton. Investor Contact—R. E. Loveil. Dirs—C. M. Blias, N. A. Brown, C. W. Elliott, C. X. Gonzalez, G. Gund, W. E. LaMothe, A. G. Langbo, R. G. Mawby, A. McLaughlin, J. R. Munro, D. Rumsfeld, T. P. Smucker, D. D. Wharton. Transfer Agent & Registrar—Harris Trust & Savings Bank, Chicago. Incorporated in Delaware in 1922. Empl—16,551.

Kenneth A. Shea

tors that S&P includes. This type of discrepancy is very common and shows that the profit the company reports depends on who is doing the analysis. For example, S&P accepts the company's accounting for nonrecurring items, but Value Line does not. Value Line removes such items as gains or losses from discounted operations and other special items from the profit calculation. Such a number is more useful for determining the future earning power of a company. Thus, we must make firm-to-firm comparisons very carefully.

> **Comprehension Check**

1. Identify some problems associated with industry financial data.

SUMMARY ▼▼▼▼▼▼▼▼▼▼▼

COMMON-SIZE ANALYSIS AND TRENDS

- Common-size analysis reduces absolute numbers to percentage of assets (balance sheet) or sales (income statement).
- With several years of financial statements, we can conduct vertical and horizontal analysis on the common-size statements to discover trends.

STATEMENT OF CASH FLOWS

- Statement of cash flows converts transactions from accrual accounting to cash accounting.
- Net cash flow from operations is cash profit. By comparing it to net income we can see the impact of noncash revenues and expenses on net income.
- Net cash flow from investing is the cash expenditures made for investment purposes.
- Net cash flow from financing is the actual cash inflow or outflow pertaining to the financing of the company.
- The direct approach reports net cash flow from operations in an income statement format. The indirect approach starts with accounting net income and makes adjustments for noncash items.

RATIO ANALYSIS

- We calculate ratios for data at a point in time. They must be interpreted carefully because variations in how the data were compiled vary from firm to firm.
- Ratios are categorized as efficiency (activity or turnover), liquidity, leverage, or profitability ratios.
- Efficiency ratios include average collection period, inventory turnover, and investment turnover. They measure the dollar amount that investment is able to generate in terms of sales (or maybe cost of sales).
- Liquidity ratios include the current ratio, quick ratio, net working capital, defensive interval ratio, and the cash conversion cycle. Each of these ratios tries to measure the ability of the firm to cover short-term payments.

- Leverage ratios can be separated into financial leverage ratios and operating leverage ratios.

- Financial leverage ratios include long-term debt to equity, total debt to equity, total debt to assets, interest coverage, and fixed-charge coverage. These ratios measure the risk of financing with debt.

- The operating leverage ratio calculates the breakeven level of sales. At the breakeven point, profits are zero.

- Profitability ratios include return on sales, return on assets, and return on equity. Each of these ratios attempts to measure the nondiscounted rate of return earned.

- The sustainable growth measure indicates the rate of growth the firm can sustain without financial difficulty.

- Interpretation of ratios is not clear cut. Much subjectivity enters the analysis.

- Analysis of several ratios can help support a signal emitted by any one ratio.

- Several sources of industry data exist. They must be used with caution. Problems are: The figures can be old; data are usually based on inconsistent accounting practices across firms and nonconstant financial statement dates; large and small firms may be commingled; and too few companies may report, thus distorting industry averages.

FURTHER READING ▼▼▼▼▼▼▼▼▼▼▼▼

Bernstein, Leopold A., *Financial Statement Analysis: Theory, Application, and Interpretation* 4th ed. Homewood, IL: Richard D. Irwin, Inc. This book is the classic text in the field.

Stickney, Clyde P., *Financial Statement Analysis: A Strategic Perspective* 2nd ed. Fort Worth, TX: The Dryden Press, 1993. This book demonstrates financial statement analysis using Coca-Cola and Pepsi.

SELF-TEST PROBLEMS ▼▼▼▼▼▼▼▼▼▼▼▼

ST18-1. Royland Corporation's most recent financial statement summaries follow.

Balance Sheet	This Year	Last Year
Cash	$ 50,000	$ 40,000
Accounts receivable	80,000	60,000
Inventories	180,000	110,000
Plant and equipment	300,000	260,000
Accumulated depreciation	(40,000)	(20,000)
Total	$570,000	$450,000
Accounts payable	$100,000	$150,000
Accrued liabilities	70,000	50,000
Mortgage payable	80,000	
Common stock	130,000	90,000
Retained earnings	190,000	160,000
Total	$570,000	$450,000

Income Statement	This Year
Net sales	$680,000
Cost of goods sold	410,000
Gross profit	$270,000
Operating expenses	190,000
Operating income	$ 80,000
Interest expense	7,000
Profit before taxes	$ 73,000
Taxes	22,000
Net income	$ 51,000

Other data:

- Cash dividends paid this year were $21,000.
- Depreciation is included in cost of goods sold.
- The change in accumulated depreciation account is the depreciation expense for the year.

a. Prepare vertical and horizontal analyses of the balance sheets in good form. Round percentages to one decimal place.
b. Prepare a vertical analysis of Royland's income statement.
c. Prepare the statement of cash flows for Royland using the indirect method. The mortgage balance this year is after Royland made a $10,000 payment.
d. Based on the financial statements prepared in parts (a) and (b), calculate the efficiency ratios, liquidity ratios, leverage ratios, and profitability ratios for Royland Corporation for this year. Where data are available, also calculate ratios for last year. Use a 360-day year. All sales are on credit to business customers. Assume an income tax rate of 30 percent.
e. Comment on the results of your analysis in parts (a) through (d).

PROBLEMS ▼▼▼▼▼▼▼▼▼▼▼▼

COMMON-SIZE ANALYSIS AND TRENDS

18-1. Comparative financial position and operating statements are common tools of analysis and interpretation.

a. Discuss the limitations of single-year statements for purposes of analysis and interpretation. To what extent are these limitations overcome by the use of comparative statements?
b. Comparative balance sheets and comparative income statements that show a firm's financial history for each of the last ten years may be misleading. Discuss the factors or conditions that might contribute to misinterpretations. Include a discussion of the additional information and supplementary data that might be included in or provided with the statements to prevent misinterpretations.

18-2. The following condensed data for Brett Manufacturing Company's financial position are available for two years:

	This Year	Last Year
ASSETS		
Cash	$ 451,500	$ 476,000
Trade receivables	211,200	175,600
Inventories	682,000	640,000
Prepaid expenses	11,000	16,000
Bond sinking fund	120,000	320,000
Long-term investments	176,000	
Land	48,000	48,000
Plant and equipment	673,000	400,000
Accumulated depreciation	(176,000)	(120,000)
Goodwill	3,300	44,400
Total	$2,200,000	$2,000,000
LIABILITIES AND EQUITY		
Accounts payable	$ 310,000	$ 300,000
Income taxes payable	44,000	30,000
Accrued wages	15,400	10,000
Bonds payable	300,000	500,000
Capital stock	1,200,000	1,000,000
Retained earnings	330,600	160,000
Total	$2,200,000	$2,000,000

a. Prepare vertical and horizontal analyses. Round to one decimal place.
b. Evaluate the results in part (a) and pinpoint items that you think need further investigation. Explain what areas warrant further investigation.

18-3. The comparative income statements of the Sussex Manufacturing Company for the past two years are as follows.

	This Year	Last Year
Net sales	$600,000	$500,000
Cost of goods sold	490,000	430,000
Gross margin on sales	$110,000	$ 70,000
Operating expenses	101,000	51,000
Income before taxes	$ 9,000	$ 19,000
Income taxes	2,400	5,000
Net income	$ 6,600	$ 14,000

a. Prepare common-size statements that show the percentage of each item to sales for the two years. Include a column for percent of increase or decrease for this year's amounts from last year's amounts. Round to the nearest one tenth of 1 percent.
b. Is a good trend indicated by your percentage calculations? What areas should be a matter of managerial concern?

18-4. The following data are available for the Docket Company.

	This Year	Last Year
Gross profit percentage	40%	35%
Ending accounts receivable	$150,000	$90,000
Average collection period	60 days	45 days
Income tax rate	50%	40%
Net income as percent of sales	6%	9%
Maximum credit allowed to creditors	60 days	30 days

a. Prepare income statements in comparative form for the two years. Use a 360-day year.
b. Calculate vertical and horizontal common-size income statements. Comment on your results.

STATEMENT OF CASH FLOWS

18-5. Classify each of the items in the following list as an investing (I), financing (F), or operating (O) activity.

	Answer
a. Payment of long-term debt	
b. Purchase of equipment	
c. Issuance of common stock for cash	
d. Sale of marketable short-term equity securities bought three months ago	
e. Cash dividends	
f. Sale of bonds	
g. Purchase of treasury stock	
h. Payment of income taxes payable	
i. Income from operations	
j. Issuance of stock to acquire productive asset	
k. Collection of accounts receivable	
l. Sale of a division of the company	

18-6. Following is the income statement of GWG, Inc.

Sales	$360,000
Cost of sales	228,000
Gross profit	$132,000
Operating expenses	49,200
Income before taxes	$ 82,800
Income taxes	39,600
Net income	$ 43,200

In addition, the following information relating to *changes* in net working capital is presented:

	Increase	Decrease
Cash	$18,000	
Receivables (net)		$3,600
Inventories	25,200	
Accrued expenses		6,000
Accounts payable	4,800	
Income tax payable	1,200	

The company indicates that depreciation expense for the year was $15,600 and that the deferred income tax account credit balance increased $1200.

Determine the cash flow from operations using the indirect approach.

18-7. The income statement and other selected data for the Moyer Company are as follows:

Sales		$19,000
Operating expenses:		
Depreciation	$ 2,300	
Other operating expenses	12,000	14,300
Operating income		$ 4,700
Loss on sale of land		1,500
Income before tax expense		$ 3,200
Tax expense		1,000
Net income		$ 2,200

Supplemental information:

a.	Dividends declared and paid	$ 800
b.	Land was purchased for	3,000
c.	Land was sold for	500
d.	Equipment was purchased for	2,000
e.	Bonds payable were retired for	2,000
f.	Common stock was sold for	1,400
g.	Land was exchanged for common stock	3,000
h.	Increase in accounts receivable	400
i.	Increase in inventories	800
j.	Increase in accounts payable	500
k.	Decrease in income taxes payable	400

Calculate cash flow from operations using the direct approach.

18-8. The Hampton Company's most recent financial statements follow.

	This Year	Last Year
Cash	$ 38,000	$ 60,000
Net receivables	72,000	65,000
Inventory	98,000	85,000
Plant assets	195,000	180,000
Accumulated depreciation	(45,000)	(35,000)
Total	$358,000	$355,000

Accounts payable	$ 85,000	$ 80,000
Accrued liabilities	44,000	61,000
Mortgage payable	11,000	
Common stock	180,000	174,000
Retained earnings	38,000	40,000
Total	$358,000	$355,000

	This Year
Net sales	$145,000
Cost of sales	108,000
Gross profit	$ 37,000
Other expenses	6,000
Profit before taxes	$ 31,000
Tax expense	12,000
Net income	$ 19,000

Other data:

- Dividends paid in cash during this year were $21,000.
- Depreciation is included in cost of sales.
- The change in accumulated depreciation account is the depreciation expense for the year.
- Accrued liabilities related to cost of sales.

   a. Prepare the statement of cash flows using the indirect method.
   b. Comment on the significant items disclosed in the statement of cash flows.

18-9. The income statement and other selected data for the Dagny Transportation Company are as follows:

Net sales	$640,000
Expenses:	
Cost of sales	360,000
Selling and administrative expense	43,000
Other expense	2,000
Income before income tax	$235,000
Income tax	92,000
Net income	$143,000

Other data:

a. Cost of goods sold includes depreciation of $15,000.

b. Selling and administrative expense includes depreciation of $5000.

c. Other expense represents amortization of goodwill, $3000, and amortization of bond premium, $1000.

d. Increase in deferred income taxes (liability account), $4000.

e. Increase in accounts receivable, $27,000.

f. Increase in accounts payable, $15,000.

g. Increase in inventories, $35,000.

h. Decrease in prepaid expenses, $1000.

i. Increase in accrued liabilities, $3000.

j. Decrease in income taxes payable, $10,000.

Calculate cash flows from operating activities on the direct basis.

RATIO ANALYSIS

18-10. a. Of what significance is the current ratio? If this ratio is too low, what may it signify? Can this ratio be too high? Explain.

b. Of what benefit is the defensive interval ratio?

c. In calculating inventory turnover, why is cost of goods sold used as the numerator? As the inventory turnover increases, what increasing risk does the business assume?

18-11. The accompanying financial data were taken from the annual financial statements of Melanie Ltd.

	2 Years Ago	Last Year	This Year
Current assets	$ 450,000	$ 400,000	$ 500,000
Current liabilities	390,000	300,000	340,000
Sales	1,450,000	1,500,000	1,400,000
Cost of goods sold	1,180,000	1,020,000	1,120,000
Inventory	280,000	200,000	250,000
Accounts receivable	120,000	110,000	105,000

a. Based on these data, calculate the following for last year and this year (use a 365-day year):

- Net working capital
- Current ratio
- Quick ratio
- Average accounts receivable turnover
- Average inventory turnover
- Average inventory days outstanding

b. Evaluate the results of your computations in regard to the short-term liquidity of the firm.

18-12. The following data were taken from the financial statements of the Acton Company.

	Year 1	Year 2	Year 3
Sales, cash	$190,000	$200,000	$220,000
Sales, credit	100,000	120,000	130,000
Receivables	25,000	34,000	50,000
Inventory	60,000	70,000	80,000
Cost of goods sold	180,000	190,000	200,000
Accounts payable	70,000	60,000	75,000
Accruals	10,000	8,000	11,000
Cash flow from operations	25,000	30,000	32,000

Answer the following questions using a 360-day year. Carry your answers to two decimal places.

a. What conclusions may be made relative to inventories and receivables? Credit terms are 90 calendar days.

b. How long is the operating cycle each year? What does the operating cycle represent? How is the firm performing on this measure?

c. How long is the cash conversion cycle each year? Comment on the trend. Assume that days purchases outstanding in year 1 are 100 days. (*Hint:* To calculate cash sales in the daily cash operating expense equation, you must define cash sales as total sales ± change in accounts receivable.)

18-13. Indicate the effects of the following transactions on total current assets, total current liabilities, net working capital, and the current ratio. Use + to indicate an increase, − to indicate a decrease, and 0 to indicate no effect. Assume an initial current ratio of more than 1.

	Total Current Assets	Total Current Liabilities	Net Working Capital	Current Ratio
a. Cash is acquired through issuance of additional common stock				
b. Merchandise is sold for cash at a profit				
c. A fixed asset is sold for more than book value and cash is received				
d. Payment is made to trade creditors for previous purchases				
e. A cash dividend is declared and paid				
f. A stock dividend is declared and paid				
g. Cash is obtained through long-term bank loans				
h. A profitable firm increases its fixed assets' accumulated depreciation account				
i. Accrued operating expenses are paid				
j. Ten-year notes are issued to pay off accounts payable				
k. Receivables are collected				

l. Equipment is purchased
    with short-term notes

m. Inventory is purchased
    on credit

n. The estimated taxes
    payable are increased

o. Short-term marketable
    securities are sold
    below cost

18-14. Give the effect of each of the following transactions or events on net working capital, the current ratio, and the quick ratio. Assume a current ratio of 3 and a quick ratio of 1.4 before any of the transactions that follow. Show a + for increase, − for decrease, and 0 for no effect.

	Net Working Capital	Current Ratio	Quick Ratio	Defensive Interval
a. Company pays $5000 short-term notes payable in cash				
b. Company sells equipment for $3000 cash				
c. Company purchases short-term marketable securities for $4000				
d. Company purchases building by issuing common stock, valued at $40,000				
e. Company purchases equipment for $2000 cash				
f. Company pays long-term bond payable, $5000				
g. Company collects $2000 on a long-term note receivable				
h. Company purchases $5000 of inventory for $2000 cash plus long-term note payable of $3000				
i. Company issues short-term note payable and receives $5000 cash				
j. Fire destroys $4000 of inventory (no insurance)				
k. Obsolete inventory of $3000 was found and written off				

l. Accounts payable of
    $10,000 were paid in cash

m. Land with a book value of
    $20,000 is sold for $15,000

n. Inventory of $2000 bought
    on open trade credit

o. Automobile sold for $2000
    at loss of $6000

18-15. The following data were taken from the financial statements of Balston Company. Based on these data, compute the current ratio, the quick ratio, net working capital, and the defensive interval. Discuss the results.

	This Year	Last Year
Cash	$ 30,000	$ 40,000
Short-term investments	10,000	10,000
Trade receivables (net)	60,000	70,000
Notes receivables	6,000	2,000
Inventory	150,000	170,000
Prepaid expenses	4,000	2,000
Total current assets	$260,000	$294,000
Current liabilities	90,000	120,000
Daily cash expenditures	2,500	4,000

18-16. Answer each of the questions in the following unrelated situations.

a. The current ratio of a company is 4 and its quick ratio is 1. If the inventories and prepaid items amount to $450,000, what is the amount of current liabilities?

b. A company had an average inventory last year of $185,000 and its inventory turnover was 4.2. If sales volume and unit cost remain the same this year as last and inventory turnover is 7 this year, what will average inventory have to be during the current year?

c. A company has current assets of $80,000 (of which $30,000 is inventory and prepaid items) and current liabilities of $20,000. What is the current ratio? What is the quick ratio? If the company borrows $10,000 cash from a bank on a 120-day loan, what will be its current ratio? What will be the quick ratio?

d. A company has current assets of $500,000 and current liabilities of $240,000. The board of directors declares a cash dividend of $60,000. What is the current ratio after the declaration but before payment? What is the current ratio after the payment of the dividend?

18-17. Indicate the effect of each of the transactions on the ratios listed. Use + to indicate an increase, − to indicate a decrease, and 0 to indicate no effect. Assume an initial times interest earned of more than 1 and a debt ratio, a debt-to-equity ratio, and a total debt to net worth of less than 1.

	Times Interest Earned	Total Debt to Equity
a. Purchase of buildings financed by mortgage		
b. Purchase of inventory on short-term loan at 1 percent over the prime rate		
c. Declaration and payment of cash dividend		
d. Declaration and payment of stock dividend		
e. Firm increases profits by cutting cost of sales		
f. Appropriation of retained earnings		
g. Sale of common stock		
h. Repayment of long-term bank loan		
i. Conversion of bonds to common stock outstanding		
j. Sale of inventory at greater than cost		

18-18. The Sherwin Company's income statement is as follows:

Net sales	$658
Other income	8
Total revenue	$666
Costs and expenses:	
Costs of products sold	$418
Selling, general and administrative expenses	196
Interest	16
Total costs and expenses	$630
Income before extraordinary items and taxes	$ 36
Income taxes	18
Income before extraordinary items	$ 18
Extraordinary loss	4
Net income	$ 14

a. Compute the times interest earned ratio.
b. Suppose the interest coverage ratio was 5 the year before. Comment on the firm's financial risk as a result of the decline in the coverage ratio.

18-19. Ms. Griggs has asked you to advise her on the long-term debt-paying ability of the Andres Company. She provides you with the following ratios:

	Year 1	Year 2	Year 3
Times interest earned	5.5	6.0	8.2
Debt ratio	40.0%	39.0%	40.0%
Debt to equity	81.0%	81.0%	80.0%

a. Give the implications and the limitations of each item separately. Then state the collective inference one may draw from them about the Andres Company's long-term debt position.

b. What warnings should you offer Ms. Griggs about the limitations of ratio analysis for the purpose stated here?

18-20. The FTG Brewing Company reports the following income statement:

Operating income	$2,989
Costs and expenses:	
Costs of rentals and royalties	$ 543
Cost of sales	314
Selling and administrative	1,424
Total costs and expenses	$2,281
Operating income	$ 708
Other income	27
Interest expense	60
Income before taxes	$ 675
Income taxes	309
Net income	$ 366
Dividends	66
Retained earnings for the year	$ 300

Operating lease payments total $150.

a. Compute the interest coverage ratio.

b. Management wants to expand the coverage ratio to include operating lease payments and dividends. Calculate the revised coverage ratio.

c. Comment on the purpose of the coverage ratios. What is a major shortcoming of coverage ratios?

18-21. The income statement of a retail store for this year follows:

Sales (5000 identical units)		$100,000
Expenses:		
Store rent	$12,500	
Sales agent's commissions	25,000	
Cost of goods sold	60,000	97,500
Profit		$ 2,500

Sales agent's commissions are a constant percentage of sales price. The store lease has five more years to run at the present annual rental. Cost of sales has a $9000 fixed component. Ignore taxes.

a. Compute the breakeven sales dollar and quantity.

b. Compute the sales that would be needed under present conditions to double the amount of net income. (*Hint:* Include the desired income amount as a fixed cost.)

c. Compute the breakeven sales dollars for next year if the company rented additional space for $6500 a year and other operating conditions remained unchanged.

d. What happens to breakeven sales in part (a) if the sale price per unit declines $1.50. Variable costs remain at $76,000 and fixed costs are still $21,500.

18-22. Garrett Company has an operating capacity of 100,000 units per year. Fixed factory overhead is $350,000 per year. Variable manufacturing costs are $20 per unit and variable selling expenses are $4 per unit. Fixed selling and administrative expenses amount to $226,000 annually. The unit sales price is $36.

a. Compute the breakeven point in units and dollars.

b. The company is proposing an addition to the plant that would increase capacity to 250,000 units and increase fixed factory overhead to $452,000 per year. The plant addition will cost $138,000. What *increase* in unit and dollar sales must the company obtain in order to earn a 10 percent return on the additional investment?

18-23. The following are the cost structures of companies Alpha and Beta.

	Alpha	Beta
Fixed costs	$12,000	$10,000
Variable costs (% of sales)	40%	60%

a. What are the breakeven points in sales dollars for each company?

b. What will be the net income at sales of $18,000?

c. What will be the net income at sales of $27,000?

d. Assume that sales can be increased to $30,000. What percentage of accounts receivable does each company have to collect to break even? All sales are made on credit.

18-24. Indicate the effects of the following transactions on net profit, retained earnings, and total stockholders' equity. Use + to indicate an increase, − to indicate a decrease, and 0 to indicate no effect.

	Net Profit	Retained Earnings	Shareholders' Equity
a. A stock dividend is declared and paid			
b. Inventory is purchased on credit			
c. Marketable securities are sold above cost			
d. Accounts receivable are collected			
e. A cash dividend is declared and paid			
f. Treasury stock is purchased and recorded at cost			

g. Treasury stock is sold above cost

h. Common stock is sold

i. A fixed asset is sold for less than book value

j. Bonds are converted into common stock

18-25. Following are the right-hand side of the balance sheets for Winn Company and Barter Company. Each has assets totaling $4 million.

	Winn Company	Barter Company
Current liabilities	$ 300,000	$ 500,000
Long-term debt, 5%	1,500,000	
Common stock ($20 par)	1,600,000	2,800,000
Retained earnings	600,000	700,000
Total	$4,000,000	$4,000,000

For the last two years each company has earned the same income before interest and taxes (EBIT).

	Winn Company	Barter Company
EBIT	$432,000	$432,000
Interest expense	84,000	12,000
Income before taxes	$348,000	$420,000
Income taxes (40%)	139,200	168,000
Net income	$208,800	$252,000

a. Which company is more profitable in terms of return on total assets?

b. Which company is more profitable in terms of return on stockholders' equity?

c. Which company has the greater net income per share of stock (that is, earnings per share)? Why?

d. From the point of view of income, is it advantageous to the stockholders of Winn Company to have the long-term debt outstanding? Why?

18-26. The following data were taken from the published statements of two companies:

	Company A	Company B
Sales	$3,000	$ 9,000
Cost of goods sold	1,900	6,392
Operating expenses	400	1,600
Interest expense	30	108
Income tax	240	300
Current assets	1,000	4,000
Gross fixed assets	5,000	19,000

Accumulated depreciation	2,000	7,000
Long-term investments	400	100
Other assets	600	7,900
Current liabilities	900	2,000
Long-term liabilities	100	1,800
Capital stock ($10 par)	3,000	18,000
Retained earnings	1,000	2,200
Current market value per share	$16.75	$ 1.50

    a. Which company has the best return on assets?

    b. What is each company's return on equity? (Do not use the Du Pont model.)

    c. Now use the Du Pont model to analyze return on equity.

    d. Is Company B's stock a good buy at $1.50 per share?

18-27. The profit margin of Arneson Corporation is 8 percent. Management pays out 40 percent of its net earnings as dividends. The total assets to sales turnover and debt-equity ratios are 60 percent and 50 percent, respectively. Calculate the firm's sustainable growth rate.

18-28. New Mexico Corporation has sales of $1 million, a net profit margin of 5 percent, and total assets of $500,000. Management wants to maintain a debt-to-equity ratio of 0.5 and wants to pay out 60 percent of its earnings in dividends. Assume that the margin and turnover ratios remain unchanged.

    a. The firm has $500,000 of assets. How much is debt financing? How much is equity financing?

    b. What growth rate can be sustained without turning to the outside equity markets?

    c. Suppose management wants to grow at 10 percent a year without selling new equity. If other variables remain unchanged, what portion of earnings can be paid out as dividends?

    d. Management wants to grow at 10 percent a year while paying out 60 percent of earnings in dividends. If other variables remain unchanged, by how much would the company need to increase its total asset turnover ratio?

18-29. Earlier in Chapter 10, we discussed that some people believe that the stock market is efficient with respect to incorporating publicly available information into the stock price. What implication does this statement have for financial statement analysis?

18-30. As loan analyst for the Bayshore Bank, you have been presented the following information.

	Penn Co.	Teller Co.
Cash	$ 85,000	$ 250,000
Receivables	137,000	212,000
Inventories	450,000	460,000
Total current assets	$ 672,000	$ 922,000
Other assets	485,000	627,000
Total assets	$1,157,000	$1,549,000

Current liabilities	$ 250,000	$ 320,000
Long-term liabilities	400,000	500,000
Capital stock and retained earnings	507,000	729,000
Total financing	$1,157,000	$1,549,000
Annual sales	$1,000,000	$1,500,000
Rate of *gross* profit on sales	30%	40%
Cash expenditures	$ 900,000	$1,300,000

Each of these companies has requested a loan of $50,000 for six months with no collateral offered. Your bank has reached its quota for loans of this type and only one of these requests is to be granted.

Which of the two companies, judging by the preceding information, would you recommend as the better risk, and why? Assume that the ending account balances are representative of the entire year. Use a 360-day year. Round the answers to one decimal place.

18-31. The following condensed financial data were taken from the financial statements of Maple Leaf Corporation:

	Year 1	Year 2	Year 3
Current assets	$ 200,000	$ 250,000	$ 270,000
Current liabilities	150,000	180,000	130,000
Quick assets	80,000	90,000	85,000
Accounts receivable	60,000	58,000	64,000
Inventory	120,000	140,000	100,000
Total assets	1,000,000	1,200,000	1,400,000
Cash sales	800,000	780,000	820,000
Credit sales	200,000	280,000	250,000
Cost of goods sold	560,000	600,000	600,000
Spontaneous liabilities	170,000	180,000	150,000
Daily cash expense	4,000	5,000	5,000

Note: Current liabilities represent accounts payable and accruals.

a. Based on the preceding data, calculate the following ratios for each year. Use end-of-period balances, not average balances, for all ratio calculations. Assume interest expenses are insignificant. Use a 360-day year and round answers to two decimal places.

- Current ratio
- Quick ratio
- Receivable turnover
- Average collection period
- Inventory turnover
- Days inventory outstanding
- Defensive interval
- Cash conversion cycle

b. Evaluate the results.

18-32. The following table presents a set of ratios based on financial statement data of Roberts Industries for year 3, year 4, and year 5. Roberts Industries has made no major changes in its product line over this period. Analyze the data to the maximum depth possible and respond to the following questions.

	Year 3	Year 4	Year 5
Rate of return on assets	10.0%	11.0%	12.0%
After-tax profit margin			
adjusted for interest expense	18.0%	16.0%	14.0%
Assets turnover	0.56×	0.69×	0.86×
Percent of sales:			
Cost of goods sold	62.0%	63.0%	65.0%
Selling and administrative	10.0%	10.0%	10.0%
Income tax expense	10.0%	11.0%	11.0%
Turnovers:			
Accounts receivable	2.6×	2.5×	2.4×
Inventory	3.2×	2.8×	2.5×
Fixed asset	0.9×	1.4×	2.6×
Trends (Year 3 = 100):			
Sales	100	102	99
Net income	100	102	99
Capital expenditures	100	90	85
Assets	100	82	64

a. What is the most likely explanation for the decreasing after-tax profit margin?
b. What is the likely explanation for the increasing asset turnovers?

18-33. Some data for Outland Container are as follows:

For Year	Sales	Capital Expenditures
5	$2,999.4	$174.8
6	3,173.2	124.8
7	3,453.2	128.0

End of Year	Gross Fixed Assets	Net Fixed Assets
4	$3,795.0	$1,730.8
5	3,923.3	1,745.2
6	3,704.3	1,552.4
7	3,703.5	1,488.1

a. Calculate the fixed-asset turnover for years 5, 6, and 7 using average net fixed assets in the denominator.
b. Calculate the fixed-asset turnover for years 5, 6, and 7 using average gross fixed assets in the denominator.
c. The trends in the fixed-asset turnovers computed in parts (a) and (b) are the same, but the rate of increase for the fixed-asset turnover based on net

fixed assets is more rapid than that for the fixed-asset turnover based on gross fixed assets. What is the explanation for these differing rates of increase?

d. What factors seem to explain the changes in fixed-asset turnover?

18-34. The following financial information is for Bott Company.

	Year 1	Year 2	Year 3
Rate of return on assets	10.0%	9.6%	9.2%
After-tax profit margin			
adjusted for interest	6.0%	6.1%	6.1%
Total assets turnover	1.7×	1.6×	1.5×
Percent of sales:			
Cost of goods sold	62.5%	62.3%	62.6%
Selling expenses	10.3%	10.2%	10.4%
Interest expense	1.5%	2.0%	2.5%
Turnover:			
Accounts receivable	4.3×	4.3×	4.2×
Inventory	3.2×	3.4×	3.6×
Plant assets	0.8×	0.7×	0.6×
Return on common equity	14.0%	14.2%	14.5%
Capital structure leverage	1.6	1.8	2.1
Current ratio	1.4	1.3	1.2
Quick ratio	1.0	0.9	1.0
Long-term debt ratio	27.2%	33.8%	43.3%
Total debt ratio	37.5%	44.4%	52.4%
Interest coverage ratio	6.7	5.1	4.1

a. What is the likely explanation for the decreasing rate of return on assets?
b. What is the likely explanation for the increasing rate of return on common shareholders' equity?
c. What is the likely explanation for the behavior of current and quick ratios?

18-35. Taylor Ltd. recently had a fire in its building and lost all its inventory. Management must determine the inventory loss for the insurance company. Since the firm did not have perpetual inventory records, the insurance company has suggested that it might accept an estimate using a gross margin test. The beginning inventory, as determined from the last financial statement, was $10,000. Purchase invoices indicate purchases of $100,000. Credit and cash sales during the period were $120,000. Last year, the gross margin for the firm was 40 perecent, which was also the industry average.

a. Based on these data, estimate the inventory loss.
b. If the industry average gross margin were 50 percent, why might the insurance company be leery of the estimated loss?

18-36. Selected information for the Three Bells Ltd. is as follows:

	This Year	1 Year Ago	2 Years Ago
SUMMARY OF OPERATIONS			
Net sales	$1,002,100	$980,500	$900,000
Cost of goods sold	520,500	514,762	477,000
Selling, general and administrative expenses	170,200	167,665	155,700
Nonoperating expenses	9,192	8,860	6,500
Interest expense	14,620	12,100	11,250
Earnings before income taxes	287,588	277,113	249,550
Provision for income taxes	116,473	113,616	105,560
Net earnings	171,115	163,497	143,990
FINANCIAL INFORMATION			
Working capital	$ 190,400	$189,000	$180,000
Fixed assets	302,500	281,000	173,000
Total assets	839,000	770,000	765,000
Total debt	433,000	400,500	423,000
Shareholders' equity	406,000	369,500	342,000
Effective tax rate	40.5%	41.0%	42.3%

a. Compute the following ratios for each year:

- Return on sales
- Total asset turnover
- Return on equity
- Du Pont return on equity
- Return on assets

b. Discuss your findings in part (a).

18-37. The following information is for Saucer Inc.

	Year 1	Year 2	Year 3
Rate of return on assets	8.0%	8.2%	8.1%
Return on sales	5.1%	5.4%	5.7%
Asset turnover	1.6×	1.5×	1.4×
Percent of sales:			
Cost of goods sold	59.8%	59.3%	58.9%
Selling and administrative	31.7%	31.7%	31.6%
Income tax expense	3.4%	3.6%	3.8%
Accounts receivable turnover	8.2×	8.1×	8.2×
Inventory turnover	4.9×	5.0×	4.9×
Fixed-asset turnover	2.8×	2.6×	2.4×
Trend (Year 1 = 100):			
Sales	100	120	144
Net income	100	133	182
Capital expenditures	100	122	152

a. What is the most likely explanation for the increasing return-on-sales percentage over the three years? Answer the question by constructing partial income statements with sales in year 1 of $100.

b. Effective tax rate is defined as income tax expense ÷ profit before taxes. How has the income tax burden changed over the three years?

c. What is the apparent reason for the decreasing assets turnover?

18-38. The Costner Company had maintained its records in a safe place for many years. However, a fire has destroyed them just before its fiscal year end, leaving only the following information:

Inventory	$40,000
Common stock, no par	50,000
Net assets (total assets − liabilities)	110,000
Current ratio	2.25
Inventory turnover	14.4×
Accounts receivable turnover	24.0×
Gross profit	20.0%
Ratio of debt (all current) to equity	0.5:1

Additional balance sheet accounts must be computed. There were no prepaid expenses or accumulated depreciation at fiscal year end. Prepare a balance sheet in good form.

18-39. It is Sunday and you have just opened your briefcase in order to work with Stealth Manufacturing Company's latest balance sheet. To your dismay you discover that the computer printouts that your assistant stuffed into your briefcase contained only the following sketchy information:

a. Accounts receivable and inventory were the same at the end of the year as at the beginning.

b. Net income, $1300.

c. Time interest earned is 5 (assume no income taxes). The company has outstanding 5 percent bonds issued at par.

d. Net income to sales, 10 percent. Gross margin ratio, 30 percent. Inventory turnover, 5.

e. Accounts receivable turnover, 5.

f. Sales to net working capital, 4. Current ratio, 1.5.

g. Quick ratio, 1.0.

h. Plant and equipment is one-third depreciated.

i. Equity at the beginning of the year was $2350.

Given the information available, complete the latest balance sheet. Also, determine the amount of dividends paid on the common stock during the year.

Cash	
Accounts receivable	
Inventory	
Prepaid expenses	
Plant and equipment (net)	$6,000
Total assets	$_____

Current liabilities
Bonds payable
Stockholders' equity
Total liabilities and equity $_____

18-40. a. Calculate the firm's sustainable growth rate from its latest financial statements:

Financial Statements

Cash	$10,000	Accounts payable	$ 5,000
Inventory	15,000	Bonds payable	30,000
Net equipment	60,000	Capital stock	30,000
		Retained earnings	20,000
Total	$85,000	Total	$85,000

Sales	$30,000
Cost of sales	8,000
Gross profit	$22,000
Selling and administrative expenses	11,000
Earnings before interest and taxes	$11,000
Interest (10%) on debt	3,500
Earnings before taxes	$ 7,500
Taxes	2,625
Net income	$ 4,875
Dividends	1,950
Retained earnings	$ 2,925

b. What is the interpretation of the sustainable growth number calculated in part (a)?

INDUSTRY FIGURES

18-41. Revenue and expense data for AJI Plastics, and for the plastics industry as a whole, are as follows:

	AJI Plastics	Industry
Sales	$462,000	100.3%
Sales returns	4,500	0.3
Cost of goods sold	330,000	67.1
Selling expenses	43,000	10.1
General expenses	32,000	7.9
Other income	1,800	0.4
Other expense	7,000	1.3
Income tax	22,000	5.5

Convert the dollar figures for AJI Plastics into percentages based on net sales. Compare these with the industry average, and comment on your findings.

DISCLOSURE ASSIGNMENT

18-42. Use the *Disclosure* database to obtain information for Nike, Inc. and Reebok International Limited. Perform detailed financial analysis for each firm for the periods provided in the database. Look for trends, strengths, and weaknesses.

18-43. Obtain a copy of a corporation's annual report by writing to the company's director of investor relations or by requesting an annual report from a stockbroker's office in your area. Calculate the financial ratios for the most recent two years and prepare a written report on your findings.

COMPREHENSIVE PROBLEM ▼▼▼▼▼▼▼▼▼▼▼

18-44. The following condensed data from Eastern Manufacturing Corporation's financial position are available for the past two years.

	This Year	Last Year
ASSETS		
Cash and cash equivalents	$ 645	$ 739
Accounts receivable	1,243	1,216
Inventories	921	1,054
Prepaid expenses	451	625
Total current assets	$3,260	$3,634
Long-term investments	$ 750	$ 825
Plant and equipment	$2,600	$2,322
Less: Accumulated depreciation	678	518
Plant and equipment, net	$1,922	$1,804
Goodwill and other intangibles	$ 330	$ 380
Total	$6,262	$6,643
LIABILITIES AND EQUITY		
Accounts payable	$ 585	$ 555
Miscellaneous accrued payables	496	865
Short-term debt	500	200
Current portion of long-term debt	200	300
Total current liabilities	$1,781	$1,920
Long-term debt	$1,023	$1,251
Common stock	$1,100	$1,000
Retained earnings	2,358	2,472
Total equity	$3,458	$3,472
Total	$6,262	$6,643

a. Prepare vertical and horizontal analyses of the balance sheet. Round percentages to one decimal place.
b. Evaluate the results in part (a) and discuss the items that need further investigation.
c. Comparative income statements for Eastern Manufacturing Corporation for the past two years are as follows.

Year Ended December 31	This Year	Last Year
Net sales	$4,000	$4,500
Cost of goods sold*	2,700	2,800
Gross profit	$1,300	$1,700
Operating expenses	1,000	1,000
Operating income	$ 300	$ 700
Interest	150	160
Income before taxes	$ 150	$ 540
Income taxes	48	170
Net income	$ 102	$ 370
*Includes depreciation	$ 160	$ 150
Cash dividends paid	$ 216	250

Prepare common-size statements that show the percentage of each income statement item to sales for the two years. Include a column for the percentage of increase or decrease for this year's amounts from last year's amounts. Round percentages to one decimal place.

d. Based on your calculations in part (c), evaluate the performance of the company this year. What areas should be of concern to management?

e. Based on the financial data given, prepare a statement of cash flows for this year using the indirect presentation method.

f. Comment on the significant items disclosed in the statement of cash flows.

g. Based on the financial statements provided, calculate the efficiency ratios, liquidity ratios, leverage ratios, and profitability ratios for this year. Where data are available, also calculate the ratios for last year. Use a 360-day year. Assume an income tax rate of 32 percent. The firm has no lease payments but has $200 annually of principal repayments due on its long-term debt. Calculate sustainable growth based on last year's results in view of sharp reduction in profitability this year.

Briefly comment on the results of your ratio calculations.

ANSWERS TO SELF-TEST PROBLEMS ▼▼▼▼▼▼▼▼▼▼▼▼▼

ST18-1. a.

Balance Sheet	This Year	%	Last Year	%	%Δ
Cash	$ 50,000	8.8	$ 40,000	8.9	25.0
Accounts receivable	80,000	14.0	60,000	13.3	33.3
Inventories	180,000	31.6	110,000	24.4	63.6
Total current assets	$310,000	54.4	$210,000	46.6	47.6
Plant and equipment	$300,000	52.6	$260,000	57.8	15.4
Accumulated depreciation	(40,000)	(7.0)	(20,000)	(4.4)	100.0
Net plant and equipment	$260,000	45.6	$240,000	53.4	8.3
Total assets	$570,000	100.0	$450,000	100.0	26.7

Accounts payable	$100,000	17.5	$150,000	33.3	(33.3)
Accrued liabilities	70,000	12.3	50,000	11.1	40.0
Total current liabilities	$170,000	29.8	$200,000	44.4	(15.0)
Mortgage payable	$ 80,000	14.0			n.a.
Common stock	$130,000	22.8	$ 90,000	20.0	44.4
Retained earnings	190,000	33.3	160,000	35.6	18.8
Total equity	$320,000	56.2	$250,000	55.6	28.0
Total liabilities and equity	$570,000	100.0	$450,000	100.0	26.7

b.

Income Statement	This Year	%
Net sales	$680,000	100.0
Cost of goods sold	410,000	60.3
Gross profit	$270,000	39.7
Operating expenses	190,000	28.0
Operating income	$ 80,000	11.7
Interest expense	7,000	1.0
Profit before taxes	$ 73,000	10.7
Taxes	22,000	3.2
Net income	$ 51,000	7.5

c.

Statement of Cash Flows	This Year
OPERATING ACTIVITIES:	
Net income	$ 51,000
Adjustments:	
Depreciation	20,000
Increase in accounts receivable	(20,000)
Increase in inventories	(70,000)
Decrease in accounts payable	(50,000)
Increase in accrued liabilities	20,000
Net cash outflow from operating activities	$(49,000)
INVESTING ACTIVITIES:	
Increase in plant and equipment	$(40,000)
FINANCING ACTIVITIES:	
Increase in mortgage payable	$ 90,000
Mortgage payment	(10,000)
Increase in common stock	40,000
Dividends paid	(21,000)
Net cash inflow from financing activities	$ 99,000
Net increase in cash	$ 10,000
Beginning cash	40,000
Ending cash	$ 50,000

d.

EFFICIENCY RATIOS:

$$\text{Average collection period} = \frac{\text{Accounts receivable}}{\text{Net credit sales/days in accounting period}}$$

$$= \frac{\$80,000}{\$680,000/360}$$

$$= 42.4 \text{ days this year}$$

$$\text{Inventory turnover} = \frac{\text{Cost of goods sold}}{\text{Average inventory}}$$

$$= \frac{\$410,000}{(\$180,000 + \$110,000)/2}$$

$$= 2.83 \text{ times this year}$$

$$\text{Investment turnover} = \frac{\text{Net sales}}{\text{Total assets}}$$

$$= \frac{\$680,000}{\$570,000}$$

$$= 1.19 \text{ times this year}$$

LIQUIDITY RATIOS:

$$\text{Current ratio} = \frac{\text{Current assets}}{\text{Current liabilities}}$$

$$= \frac{\$310,000}{\$170,000}$$

$$= 1.82 \text{ this year (last year} = 1.05)$$

$$\text{Net working capital} = \text{Current assets} - \text{current liabilities}$$

$$= \$310,000 - \$170,000$$

$$= \$140,000 \text{ this year (last year} = \$10,000)$$

$$\text{Quick ratio} = \frac{\text{Cash} + \text{marketable securities} + \text{receivables}}{\text{Current liabilities}}$$

$$= \frac{\$50,000 + \$80,000}{\$170,000}$$

$$= 0.76 \text{ times this year (last year} = 0.50 \text{ times)}$$

$$\text{Defensive interval ratio} = \frac{\text{Quick assets}}{\text{Daily cash expenses}}$$

$$= \frac{\$130,000}{(\$680,000 - \$20,000 - (-\$49,000))/360}$$

$$= 66 \text{ days}$$

Note:

Daily cash operating expenses

$$= \frac{\text{Sales} - \text{increase in receivables} - \text{cash flow from operations}}{360 \text{ days}}$$

LEVERAGE RATIOS:

$$\text{Long-term debt to equity} = \frac{\text{Long-term debt}}{\text{Shareholders' equity}}$$

$$= \frac{\$80,000}{\$320,000}$$

$$= 0.25 \text{ or } 25 \text{ percent this year}$$
(last year = 0 percent)

$$\text{Total debt to equity} = \frac{\text{Current liabilities} + \text{long-term debt}}{\text{Shareholders' equity}}$$

$$= \frac{\$170,000 + \$80,000}{\$320,000}$$

$$= 0.781 \text{ or } 78.1 \text{ percent this year (last year} = 80 \text{ percent)}$$

$$\text{Total debt to assets} = \frac{\text{Current liabilities} + \text{long-term debt}}{\text{Total assets}}$$

$$= \frac{\$170,000 + \$80,000}{\$570,000}$$

$$= 0.439 \text{ or } 43.9 \text{ percent this year (last year} = 44.4 \text{ percent)}$$

$$\text{Interest coverage} = \frac{\text{Earnings before interest and taxes}}{\text{Interest expense}}$$

$$= \frac{\$80,000}{\$7,000}$$

$$= 11.4 \text{ times this year}$$

$$\text{Coverage ratio} = \frac{\text{Earnings before interest, leases, and taxes}}{\text{Interest} + \text{leases} + \dfrac{\text{principal payments}}{1 - \text{tax rate}}}$$

$$= \frac{\$80,000}{\$7,000 + \$10,000/(1 - 0.30)}$$

$$= 3.8 \text{ times this year}$$

PROFITABILITY RATIOS:

$$\text{Return on sales} = \frac{\text{Net income}}{\text{Sales}}$$

$$= \frac{\$51,000}{\$680,000}$$

$$= 0.075 \text{ or } 7.5 \text{ percent this year}$$

$$\text{Operating return on assets} = \frac{\text{EBIT}}{\text{Total assets}}$$

$$= \frac{\$80,000}{\$570,000}$$

$$= 0.140 \text{ or } 14 \text{ percent this year}$$

$$\text{Return on assets} = \frac{\text{Net income} + \text{interest}(1 - \text{tax rate})}{\text{Total assets}}$$

$$= \frac{\$51,000 + \$7,000(1 - 0.30)}{\$570,000}$$

$$= 0.098 \text{ or } 9.8 \text{ percent this year}$$

$$\text{Return on equity} = \frac{\text{Net income}}{\text{Equity}}$$

$$= \frac{\$51,000}{\$320,000}$$

$$= 0.159 \text{ or } 15.9 \text{ percent this year}$$

$$\text{Return on equity} = \frac{\text{Net income}}{\text{Sales}} \times \frac{\text{sales}}{\text{assets}} \times \frac{\text{assets}}{\text{equity}}$$

$$= \frac{\$51,000}{\$680,000} \times \frac{\$680,000}{\$570,000} \times \frac{\$570,000}{\$320,000}$$

$$= 0.075 \times 1.193 \times 1.781$$
$$= 0.159 \text{ or } 15.9 \text{ percent}$$

Sustainable growth

$$= \frac{\left(1 - \dfrac{\text{Dividends paid}}{\text{Profits}}\right) \times \text{return on equity}}{1 - \left(1 - \dfrac{\text{Dividends paid}}{\text{Profits}}\right) \times \text{return on equity}} \qquad (18.26)$$

$$= \frac{\left(1 - \dfrac{\$21,000}{\$51,000}\right) \times 0.159}{1 - (1 - \dfrac{\$21,000}{\$51,000}) \times 0.159}$$

$$= \frac{0.09353}{0.90647}$$

$$= 0.103 \text{ or } 10.3 \text{ percent}$$

e. The horizontal analysis of Royland's balance sheets reveals a significant increase in total assets (+27 percent) and a large increase in current assets (+48 percent). Inventories increased sharply in dollar amount and as a percentage of assets. Whether the company is gearing up for an expected increase in sales or whether inventory is piling up unsold needs to be considered by management. This year's inventory turnover of 2.8 times could be compared with turnover for previous years.

As measured by the current ratio, the quick ratio, and net working capital, the company's liquidity improved this year. Although the quick ratio is below 1:1, the company does not seem to be in financial difficulty assuming that inventory can be sold and receivables can be collected.

A study of the statement of cash flows for this year reveals a net cash outflow from operating activities due mainly to the increase in inventories and the decrease in accounts payable. Profits and cash generated from depreciation charges resulted in cash inflows. Financing from a $90,000 mortgage taken out this year switched short-term debt to long-term debt. This financing contributed to the improvement in the company's liquidity. Also the company sold additional common stock this year and increased retained earnings by paying out less in cash dividends than the year's net income.

The quality of the company's accounts receivable could be judged by comparing the 42-day collection period with the terms of sale and with collection periods for earlier years.

Company debt appears to be under control based on interest and total coverage ratios. Debt ratios reveal only about 44 percent of total assets are financed with debt, leaving a substantial equity base for the firm.

The Du Pont ROE formula figures could be compared with results for earlier years. The return on equity of almost 16 percent should be compared with prior years and with industry figures. However, this return rate appears to be high enough to attract equity investors, since more stock was sold during the year (although we do not know at what price the stock was sold for and how many shares were issued).

The company can sustain growth in sales of just over 10 percent annually as long as the firm's return on sales, dividend policy, leverage policy, and asset management do not change. Unless the actual growth rate equals the sustainable growth rate, the profit margin, dividend payout ratio, debt-to-equity ratio, or total assets-to-sales ratio must change or the company will have to sell more common stock to support operations.

Overall, Royland appears to have had a good year. Analysis of the company's income statement for last year and of the trend of financial ratios for past years would help the analyst. Also helpful would be a comparison of this company's results with industry figures.

CHAPTER 19

Financial Planning

inancial planning establishes guidelines for change. At a minimum, it entails identification of targets for performance, assessment of any differential between the firm's current position and its target status, and the outlining of steps designed to close the gap between actual and target values within a moving time frame. Key planning policy variables include the kind of business that management elects to operate, the amount of debt that management either chooses to employ or must employ, and the cash flows that management decides to return to shareholders as dividends. These policy variables combine with management quality to influence profitability and internal growth. For any financial planning exercise, we should keep in mind the ultimate objective in business: *maximization of firm value* or *shareholder wealth.*

In recent years there has been a notable change in the thrust of financial planning. The emphasis during the 1980s was on growth. The decade of the 1990s places greater stress on profitability and the need to correct past investment mistakes. The principal output of any financial planning process is a set of estimated, or *pro forma,* financial statements for each business strategy under consideration. Management reviews alternative strategies and selects the most workable one. It is important to appreciate that this process is one of judgment on the part of the firm's managers. It is not some sort of mathematical optimizing routine that ultimately determines which course of action the firm will follow.

Our coverage of financial planning in this chapter provides a synthesis of several chapters. The process of financial planning requires:

- Forecasts of the economic environment, including potential effects of governmental and Federal Reserve Board actions on inflation and interest rates (Chapter 3).
- Decision making regarding capital expenditures necessary to meet business objectives (Chapters 14 and 15).
- Estimation of financing needs (Chapter 13).

- Determination of net working capital investments to support business plans (Chapters 16 and 17).
- Analysis of projected results (Chapter 18).

All this activity is directed toward maximizing firm value and shareholder wealth (Chapters 11 and 12). Discussion about debt and equity securities (Chapters 7, 8, and 9) and the efficiency of financial markets in which these securities trade (Chapter 10) are not discussed explicitly in this chapter, although these concepts underlie financial planning. Thus, once you have completed this chapter, you should have a better understanding of how several of the important topics discussed in this book integrate with each other.

19.1 NONCONTROLLABLE AND CONTROLLABLE EFFECTS ON FINANCIAL PLANNING

Planning problems differ from case to case. For the majority of firms it is difficult to trace any strict relationship between the environment and the firm's own experience. The financial planning process requires a firm's managers to understand both noncontrollable and controllable aspects of its environment; they must be able to formulate policies to meet financial objectives conditioned by this environment.

The environment of a company is the pattern of all the external conditions and influences—both domestic and international—that affect its life and development. The globalization of competition, the increased dominance of multinational corporations, the emergence of new international power brokers, and relationships between private and public sectors of the economy are all important factors. It is important to distinguish between those parts of the economic environment that management is powerless to control and those parts over which it can exert some influence and may be able to change.

19.1.1 Factors Management Cannot Control

Managers of individual firms can do little, if anything, to alter government policy. The debate in 1993 about the North American Free Trade Agreement (NAFTA) between Canada, Mexico, and the United States was hotly argued by businesses and labor unions alike. Some people argued that NAFTA was necessary, if only to combat Europe's and Asia's developing trade blocks. Others argued that NAFTA was the commercial equivalent to Star Wars in that it sounded like a good idea but was actually cost inefficient and self-destructive for workers in both the United States and Mexico. In the end, NAFTA passed, with some people pleased and others disappointed. Political events are part of why managers may feel that there is no point in forecasting, say, the total output of the economy.

However, it is essential for management to attempt to understand changes in government policy in order to gauge the future cyclical movements in the economy that such policies influence.[1] Even though a firm's managers cannot control government action or what happens in the economy, management can often trace valuable links between the economy at large and the individual firm or business units within the firm. For example, in examining a company's sales and expenses over the past decade, a plan-

---

[1]Consultants such as John Naisbitt and Patricia Aburdene, authors of the best-selling book *Megatrends 2000,* make their living by studying these trends. The book is published by William Morrow and Company, Inc., 1990.

ning analyst may find that a pronounced cyclical profit pattern emerges in nearly every case. The firm's peaks and troughs for profits may be separated by intervals that correspond to those in the business cycle for the entire economy. We can see this relationship in Figure 19.1.

Within the economy, cyclical movements or fluctuations take place for different industries at different times. For example, the capital goods industries, including a firm like Cincinnati-Milacron Company, make equipment other firms use in their production processes. Demand for Cincinnati-Milacron's equipment is dependent on the prospects of other firms in the economy. In general, an upturn in company orders and, in turn, cash flow leads to an increase in investment spending about one year later. Such analysis suggests that the business cycle of capital goods producers lags behind other industries within the economy. Knowing this relationship allows management to find the firm's place in the sequence of the general economic cycle.

19.1.2 What Factors Can Management Control?

Firm managers should be able to list a number of factors in the operating environment over which they can exercise some control. Marketing is an obvious example. The design of the product and its promotion, its differentiation from other products, and its selling price are all management decisions. Marketing forecasts will depend to a certain extent upon corresponding forecasts made for the economy.

All sales and cost forecasts ought to be made in the prices likely to exist throughout the forecast period. Thus, the forecaster must pay considerable attention to the possibility of inflation in the economy in order to obtain important knowledge of likely cost and price movements. As another example, business will likely be affected by tax changes, which in turn affect profitability. Any changes in corporate tax rates and rules is of considerable importance to shareholders. Whether or not the firm will be able to pass on tax increases to its customers ought to be considered within the forecast.

Other issues of particular importance are social security taxes and national health insurance. The number of people of retirement age is increasing faster than the

FIGURE 19.1

FIRM PERFORMANCE AND BUSINESS FLUCTUATIONS

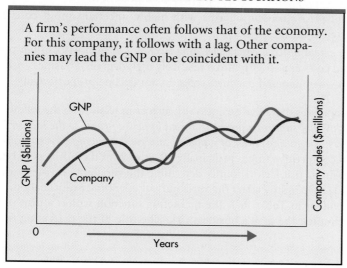

A firm's performance often follows that of the economy. For this company, it follows with a lag. Other companies may lead the GNP or be coincident with it.

population as a whole. Over the next decade the working population will have to support a larger proportion of dependents either as old-age pensioners or as young people receiving education. These demographic changes have important implications for tax and health policies. The incidence of tax changes will affect different firms in various ways. More labor-intensive firms will have to face the prospect of a larger burden of increasing social security taxes and health costs than firms that are more capital intensive.

 Comprehension Check

1. Since managers cannot control the economic environment, why should they attempt to understand it?

 ## 19.2 PLANNING GOALS

An understanding of the environment leads to the establishment of planning goals based on the strengths and weaknesses of the company. Identifying a firm's business (competitive) risk is a key consideration in assessing these strengths and weaknesses. An understanding of business risk can help identify *strategic issues* facing the company. Porter's *competitive-forces framework* is particularly useful for assessing a firm's business risk along several strategic dimensions.[2] These dimensions are:

- *Demand variability.*The more stable the demand for a firm's products, the lower its business risk if other factors remain constant.
- *Sales price variability.* Firms whose products sell in highly volatile industries face more business risk than similar firms in other industries whose selling prices are more stable.
- *Ability to adjust selling prices according to changes in input prices.* Some firms are better able to raise their own selling prices when input costs rise. Others operate in markets where a price much higher than competitors' prices would be unacceptable. The greater the ability to adjust selling prices, the lower the degree of busines risk if other factors remain constant. This factor becomes increasingly important during periods of inflation.
- *Input price variability.* Firms with highly uncertain input costs face a high degree of business risk.
- *The extent of fixed costs (operating leverage).* A firm with a high percentage of fixed costs exposes itself to a relatively high degree of business risk. The risk is that when demand declines, costs do not decline proportionally.

Porter analyzes these five business risk factors in relation to the following competitive forces: *threat of substitute products; threat of new entrants to the industry; bargaining power of buyers; bargaining power of suppliers;* and *rivalry among existing firms.* Table 19.1 shows which competitive forces principally affect each of the business risk factors. The first three business risk factors jointly determine the variability of sales growth. All the business risk factors jointly affect the variability of operating profit margin.

As is evident in Table 19.1, the marketing function within a firm plays a major part in determining the firm's business risk. The role of the marketing function is to

[2]Michael E. Porter, *Competitive Advantage* (New York: The Free Press, 1985).

TABLE 19-1

COMPETITIVE FORCES ON BUSINESS RISK FACTORS

Business Risk Factor	Principally Affected By
Demand variability	Threat of substitute products Threat of new entrants
Sales price variability	Bargaining power of buyers Rivalry among existing firms
Ability to adjust prices	Bargaining power of buyers
Input price variability	Bargaining power of suppliers
Operating leverage	Bargaining power of suppliers Rivalry among existing firms

profitably bring about the sale of products and services within target markets for the purpose of achieving the firm's goals. The price component of marketing strategy is perhaps the single most important consideration to that strategy. Price directly influences demand and supply, profitability, consumer perception, and regulatory response. (See the Financial Reality reading on page 748.)

Once management understands the competitive forces affecting business risks, it must address the following questions.

- What should be considered a reasonable level of revenue growth?
- How will the company finance its operation and expansion needs?
- What return on equity should the company achieve?

Based on answers to these questions, management can then develop other financial measurements, such as expected level of profits and earnings per share, and stock price targets for each of the next few years. This approach clearly implies that revenue growth, a strong cash flow position, and return on equity determine the other financial criteria for success. The basic arguments for using the goals related to growth, cash flow, and return on equity are that growth ensures the basis for longevity, cash flow provides the means to fund the growth, and return on equity provides a means to measure the investors' return.

Once management derives the firm's overall financial targets, then the rest of the organization can establish objectives that are consistent with the strategic goals of the firm (see Figure 19.2). But, just as important, once management defines and quantifies the strategic goals of the firm, these goals become the basis for establishing financial criteria for the specific capital expenditure projects that will be undertaken during the period covered by the plan.

19.2.1 Growth Goal

Perhaps the best way to explain how to establish a growth plan is first to explain how not to establish one. Management should not set a goal of, say, 15 percent growth per year without identifying the growth of each segment of the market. A growth goal should not be set without knowing the physical constraints of the company's capacity to absorb that growth (plant capacity, funding capabilities). Also, a growth goal should not be set without knowing the company's capacity to execute the growth; that is, management must identify the company's strengths, including personnel strengths, that it needs to achieve the goal.

What information does management need to establish a growth goal? Very simply, management needs a comprehensive study of the marketplace that reflects historical, current, and projected growth patterns. Management should review the historical performance of (at least) technological developments, cultural developments, and real growth versus inflationary growth.

TECHNOLOGICAL DEVELOPMENTS. These are among the most far-reaching, quickly unfolding factors that affect firms. They include scientific discoveries, the impact of related product development, and the process of computerization and automation. Industries once considered safe from obsolescence because of their stable technologies or because of the huge capital investment necessary to enter have become vulnerable to new processes or to cross-industry competition, as well as increasing international competition. To cite two examples: (1) Advances in xerography were a key to Xerox's

FIGURE 19.2

FINANCIAL GOALS WITHIN THE ORGANIZATION

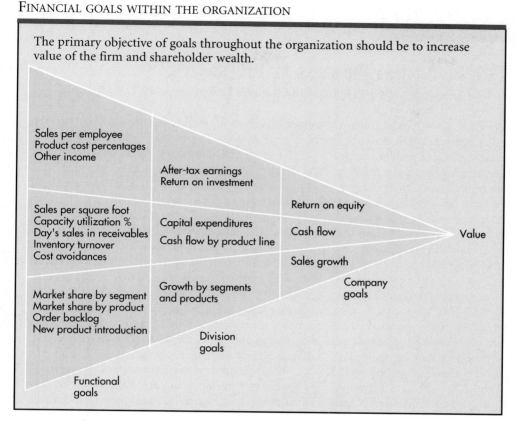

The primary objective of goals throughout the organization should be to increase value of the firm and shareholder wealth.

Sales per employee
Product cost percentages
Other income

After-tax earnings
Return on investment

Return on equity

Sales per square foot
Capacity utilization %
Day's sales in receivables
Inventory turnover
Cost avoidances

Capital expenditures
Cash flow by product line

Cash flow

Value

Sales growth

Market share by segment
Market share by product
Order backlog
New product introduction

Growth by segments
and products

Company
goals

Division
goals

Functional
goals

success but caused major difficulties for carbon paper manufacturers. (2) The development of small computer memory chips changed the nature of competition in the computer industry, seriously weakening IBM's dominance in the industry. Science and technology give the impetus to change not only in capital investment decisions but in all the other aspects of business activity as well.

CULTURAL DEVELOPMENTS. These include such forces as the quest for work-place equality by women and minority groups, the changing patterns of work and leisure, changing demographic patterns, and the urbanization of fully industrialized countries. The tremendously large number of women who have entered the labor market in the past two decades has created or greatly expanded the demand for a wide range of products and services. Businesses that correctly anticipated or quickly reacted to this social change have profited by offering such products and services as convenience foods, microwave ovens, and children's day-care centers for two-career families. Also, the 1980s' "baby boomlet"—children of baby boomers—has created a demographic change and opened markets for more child-centered products and services.

REAL VERSUS INFLATIONARY GROWTH. Normally, the planning analyst compiles information from various sources, analyzes the information, and then draws conclusions. Based on these conclusions, management determines its capabilities for relating to the market. Next management decides what its opportunities are and how it will approach those

THE PLANNING PROCESS AT PETsMART

Donald S. Spear, Sr. Vice President, Strategic Planning and Business Development, PETsMART, Inc.

PETsMART's mission is to be the dominant retailer of pet food, supplies, and services in each of its markets. Formalized strategic planning and budgeting are the means of focusing employees on the mission statement. In September of each year, the executive committee asks for input from department heads and field managers to develop the company's strategic goals and priorities for the coming year. Being a young company, our primary goal is growth via opening new stores and acquiring other pet retailers, such as the PETZAZZ chain in Ohio. But our goal of growth must be profitable growth that is expected to result in a fair return to our shareholders.

The planning process is long, detailed, and tedious, and consists of two parts: strategic planning and budgeting. This process produces a meaningful plan that has the commitment of people at all levels throughout the company. The strategic planning process involves review of store openings in new and existing markets, business segment development, distribution implementation, supplier availability, personnel planning at market and store-support group levels, and information system requirements to support the company. The strategic plan aligns upper and middle management with PETsMART's direction for the coming year. The plan also sets the sales and profit boundaries for the budget.

The budgeting process begins in late October. It consists of the following phases: financial planning, store operating plan, and store-support group department budgets. A budget revision phase occurs in the last month of each quarter as we go through the year. Based on the strategic planning phase, senior management provides the necessary assumptions and targets for developing the budget.

The financial planning phase's objective is to estimate pretax quarterly earnings for the coming year. For these quarterly projections, people in finance, operations, merchandising, and marketing estimate sales. Department heads estimate sales mix, margins, and expenses for each quarter. Finance personnel develop budgets for new stores, using history for stores PETsMART opened in similar markets.

The store operating plan phase occurs in December and January. This plan provides a detailed operating budget by store, by department, and by month for the coming year. We expect that the aggregation of results by store will be as good or better than the financial planning stage's estimates. The budget assumes that currently opened stores will show a positive sales and profit trend. If estimates fail to support positive trends for sales and profits, then we sharpen our pencils to see if we can find them. If growth for a store does not exist, we must get the chief operating officer's approval before we can allow such performance to become part of the firm's budget. The operating budget represents the most accurate, nonpadded estimate of the coming year's operating pretax earnings.

The development of a store-support group budget occurs in November and December. This budget estimates the cost of general management, merchandising, real estate, marketing, information systems, human resources, training, accounting, and finance—activities necessary to support store operations. The board of directors sets maximum dollar amounts for the annual store-support budget. Within the budget, various costs are largely determined using historical or targeted percentage-of-sales ratios. The company's controller performs a detailed review of the budget and provides recommendations for any adjustments. We finalize the store-support group budget during a series of budget meetings that concludes in early January.

At this point we now have a detailed budget for the next fiscal year. However, because our market environment is dynamic, we revise store operating budgets on a quarterly basis. During the last month of each accounting quarter, we review and revise store operating budgets based on the latest business information available. The intent is to set new achievable standards for the remainder of the fiscal year. Any revisions must cover the store-support group budget and the targeted pretax earnings estimate we made in the financial planning phase.

opportunities. Management may conclude that the future growth rate of its market is below the growth rate required by the company. In such a case, management must determine what new industries it should consider as part of its strategic direction.

For example, assume that Mickelson Company has been in a growth industry throughout its existence. The industry is growing at a rate at least 5 percent greater than inflation. Mickelson has been able to maintain a growth posture fairly close to that of the industry, but current market research concludes that, in the future, the growth rate for the industry will be lower than the anticipated rate of inflation because of market saturation and lower consumer demand. Management must now consider the following options:

- Stay in the industry and capture a greater market share.
- Stay in the industry but consider alternative markets.
- Stay in the industry but grow in proportion to the market.
- Stay in the industry but gradually divest and identify other market potentials.

Each of these alternatives will influence the financial targets as well as the strategic direction the company adopts.

19.2.2 Cash Flow Goal

The overall strategic planning process includes a review of cash flows. Forecasted financial statements are the basis for determining expected cash flows. The forecasted cash flows allow management to see the expected cash impact of its planning decisions within the forecast period. Such a cash-planning approach connects each application of funds with one or more sources of capital; it shows that all funds generated from operations, debt, and equity have an ultimate use. Lending institutions often regard the cash-planning portion of a financial plan as one of the most important sections because it provides an excellent means of evaluating a company's financial strength.

To take advantage of an unusually high cash inflow in a long-range financial plan, management may consider alternatives such as increasing its growth expectations, expanding into other industries, increasing research and development efforts that would place the company into a more favorable competitive position, expanding through acquisition, or reducing high-interest debt financing. When evaluating the possible sources and uses of excess funds, the long-range cash plan must not only consider funds generated from operating profits but must also take into account anticipated sales of fixed assets, divestitures of businesses or product lines, and income from the company's investment portfolios of financial securities. On the other hand, cash planning must also consider the funds required to pay for debt obligations and dividends to stockholders.

19.2.3 Return on Equity

A company's return on equity (ROE) is a popular measure of financial performance among investors and senior managers. ROE is important because it is a measure of the efficiency with which management employs shareholders' capital. In developing a ROE requirement for the business plan, management must first prepare a multiyear sales forecast. A multiyear capital budgeting plan is made based on the sales forecast. This plan reflects the investments the firm must make to maintain and expand its business.

The next schedule is the multiyear pro forma income statement, which will include the projected depreciation from the capital budgeting program. A fourth schedule is the pro forma balance sheet, which shows a breakdown of investment into cash, accounts receivable, inventories, and fixed assets, among others, and the necessary financing to support these investments. It is at this point that forecasted ROE can be calculated.

Comprehension Check

1. Identify Porter's five strategic dimensions and eight competitive forces.
2. Why are targets for growth, cash flow, and return on equity important for the firm? What problems may management encounter in setting goals?

19.3 PLANNING ASSUMPTIONS

A company's strategic direction and the financial impact of assuming that direction comes before a quantification of financial goals, feeding into them and shaping them. The financial goals, when first established, must be considered tentative until the planning analyst develops pro forma financial statements based upon specific assumptions about growth, market segment, new-product development, growth in organization, cost improvements, acquisitions, divestitures, capacity, expansion, equipment needs, dividend plans, and any other key factors that affect profits, investment, and financing. Let's examine some of the key assumptions.

19.3.1 Product Life Cycle

Many of the goods and services a firm produces either have limited life or must be altered or enhanced to meet changing consumer demands. A number of factors may influence product life cycles: obsolescence (for example, cathode ray tubes); styling changes (automobiles); consumer requirements for greater value and safety (the demand for radial tires); changing consumer trends (light beer); and changes in packaging or improvements in quality (to stimulate sagging sales). Management changes some products or services to improve efficiency and reduce costs; for example, the fast-food concept allows some restaurants to handle a large volume of customers in a short period of time. Some products, such as personal computers, have a limited life cycle because the introduction of new technology influences both cost and function.

The business forecast must consider the product life cycle and how it will influence sales, product obsolescence, inventory obsolescence, and changes in costs, all of which may affect profitability. With respect to new products, additional special considerations include production startup costs, marketing costs necessary for generating consumer awareness, and costs associated with changes to improve original designs. In order to stabilize profitability and limit financial risk, these additional costs must be offset by operating cash flows generated by existing product lines.

Some industries, such as the fashion industry, constantly introduce new products and phase out obsolete ones. When a firm faces higher than expected introduction costs, faster phasing out of existing products, and lower market acceptance of maturing products than anticipated, a burdensome financial imbalance usually results. In such situations, financially strong companies can dip into their monetary resources for survival, whereas less fortunate companies may be threatened by takeover or bankruptcy.

19.3.2 Geographic Volume

Some managers of regional businesses maintain that because their businesses are neither international nor national in scope, they do not need sales information by geographic segments. Nevertheless, regional businesses must be aware of their customer base in order to take advantage of distribution methods, plant location, marketing presence, and influences of local or national competitors. The planning analyst, therefore, should analyze historical sales performance by geographic areas, and the strategic marketing plan should project how these markets will change in the future.

19.3.3 Line of Business Performance

Line of business performance may refer either to the product line or to the market segments for which the company intends the product. An example of a product line of a business is a group of household appliances, such as refrigerators, stoves, and dishwashers. An example of a market segment is family dwellings, which can be separated into single-family residential homes and multiple-family apartment complexes. Management must develop a strategic plan from a line of business perspective, since each product or market segment may have different operating and marketing characteristics. For example, management of General Electric's major appliance division may be misled if it studies the historical growth pattern of total family dwellings. In planning, management must recognize that single-family residents clearly dominate the industry's growth for large refrigerators, while smaller-sized refrigerators for apartments trail the overall industry growth.

Thus, it is necessary not only to study the various business segments but also to compile and analyze the historical financial performance of the company. Knowledge of historical trends helps define future expectations and focus attention on specific cost containment or improvement programs for each business segment.

19.3.4 Real Growth

To get a handle on real growth, let's briefly look at a hypothetical situation. A chief executive officer is receiving congratulations for leading the company to its first billion dollar sales level. Suddenly she realizes that the second billion dollar level will be achieved at an even faster rate. Why? Inflation. At the same level of performance, this CEO can achieve the second billion dollar milestone in seven years. This can be done without increasing output by simply raising prices 10 percent each year.[3]

The proper way to analyze a company's growth is to discount any price increases of its products and services throughout the company's historical performance. By monitoring and tracking the price increases, the analyst can measure the real growth of the company and compare the performance against similar real growth of the industry. Such analysis eliminates any false sense of security about whether market penetration achieved by the company is, in fact, real or merely the effect of inflationary dollars.

19.3.5 Cost Analysis

For a company engaged in a number of product lines, management should review not only the historical sales trend but also the cost pattern of each product line to identify

---

[3]A technique known as the *Rule of 72* provides a good approximation for calculating compound growth rates. Simply divide the number 72 by the interest rate. The result is the number of years it will take for the amount to double, given the stated interest rate: $72 \div 10 \approx 7$ years.

the profitability of each relative to the total company. These costs must be identified by function, such as production, service, sales, and marketing. Within each of these functions, costs should be further broken down between variable and fixed. This exercise provides insight into how these costs should change as sales and production levels change; also it is useful for estimating the breakeven sales level. Products or services that do not reflect an accounting profit should not automatically be candidates for elimination. Management must determine if such products or services are providing positive cash flow in excess of the opportunity cost of funds, similar to our capital budgeting discussion in Chapters 14 and 15.

 Comprehension Check

1. The financial plan depends on several key assumptions, notably assumptions pertaining to product life cycle, geographic sales volume, line of business performance, real growth, and cost analysis. Discuss the importance of each assumption to the financial plan.

 ## 19.4 PREPARATION OF THE FINANCIAL FORECAST

The preparation of forecasted (pro forma) financial statements involves several steps. The management must:

- Project sales revenue for the forecast period.
- Determine the capital expenditures necessary to meet the sales forecasts.
- Project operating expenses (cost of goods sold, selling and administrative, income taxes) and calculate projected operating income.
- Project the assets, liabilities, and shareholders' equity needed to support the level of operations projected in the first three steps.
- Derive the statement of cash flows from the forecasted income statement and the forecasted comparative balance sheets.

This five-step procedure is illustrated in the following pages.[4] Figure 19.3 outlines the process.

19.4.1 The Sales Forecast

Analysts should prepare the sales forecast with and without inflationary pricing so that management is able to distinguish real growth from nominal growth. Once sales projections are available, the firm's managers can compare these forecasts with the expected growth identified in the company's overall plan. If this comparison reveals an unfavorable variance with the growth goal, management must determine the strategy or strategies necessary to bring forecast and growth together. Should acquisitions be undertaken or should more product lines be introduced? What are the implications of these adjust-

---

[4]An additional step could be inserted before the final step. It would determine the cost of financing the capital structure derived in step 4 and then subtract the after-tax cost of this financing from operating income to obtain adjusted projected net income. We forego this step because of the complexity involved in ensuring asset, liability, and equity accounts change in the correct amounts to account for additional interest expense or income. Exclusion of this step does not lead to serious misrepresentation of the forecasts.

FIGURE 19.3

THE FORECASTING FLOW CHART

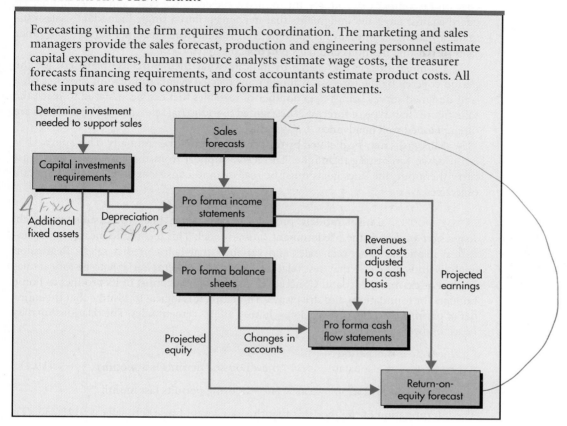

Forecasting within the firm requires much coordination. The marketing and sales managers provide the sales forecast, production and engineering personnel estimate capital expenditures, human resource analysts estimate wage costs, the treasurer forecasts financing requirements, and cost accountants estimate product costs. All these inputs are used to construct pro forma financial statements.

ments, for example, in terms of funding? Although these are open questions, one thing is certain. Under no circumstances should management arbitrarily force the sales projections to attain the growth goal, since this defeats the whole purpose of the planning process.

The sales forecast can be prepared from several methods, including *judgmental forecasts, causal analysis forecasts,* and *trend analysis forecasts.* Often the planning analyst relies on a combination of these methods.

JUDGMENTAL FORECASTS. **Judgmental forecasts** include *case history, intuitive judgments,* and *sales goals.* Case history techniques base forecasts on comparisons to similar products or past successes and failures. Such techniques are often used in sales forecasts for new-product introductions. For example, management of Mendenhall Manufacturing wants to introduce two new stereos. The last time the company introduced a stereo line, sales were lower than expected the first year. However, there was a definite sales uptrend around Christmas. Given this useful information, Mendenhall management might forecast sales for the new stereos using the historical trends.

Intuitive judgments are the judgments of executives and salespeople who, based on experience and knowledge of the firm and its products, may have excellent skills. Since sales representatives are close to a firm's customers, estimates by these employees can be a valuable source of sales information. For example, competitors regard the sales

Judgmental forecast. A nonstatistical technique that relies on the forecaster's experience or best estimate.

manager of Mendenhall as the most knowledgeable manager in the industry. Based on his insight, he puts together a sales forecast. In doing so, he brings together his knowledge of the company's products, the industry, the customer base, and the economy. To guard against any value judgments that may creep into a single individual's sales estimate, a manager compares his estimate with results from customer surveys and other sales forecasting methods and flags potential discrepancies.

Customer surveys ask clients to indicate what their purchase plans are for the period covered by the forecast. Although unexpected events can disrupt the forecast, a well-designed survey brings up a number of variables that can be analyzed to reach the sales figure. This type of forecast is best suited to industrial sales, in which purchases are often planned well in advance.

Sales goals may be dictated by top management of the company. This approach is a top-down forecasting technique. To receive support from the employees who must carry them out, the sales goals must be realistic and consistent with overall corporate objectives.

Causal model. Assumes that the factor to be forecast exhibits a cause-and-effect relationship with a number of other factors.

CAUSAL MODELS. **Causal models** provide an alternative sales forecasting approach. *Regression analysis* is the predominant causal model. This technique measures the statistical relationship between sales and variables that helps predict sales.[5] Regression analysis finds the curve that best relates a historical predictor variable to historical sales levels. For example, Portland Concrete Company may sell most of its product to home builders for foundations and driveways. Therefore, it is logical to assume that the number of permits issued to construct new houses affects cement sales. The relationship may be as follows:

$$\text{Cement sales this period} = \text{Constant} + \beta \times (\text{new housing permits last month}) \tag{19.1}$$
$$= 125,750 + 550 \times (\text{new housing permits last month})$$

The interpretation of the model is that the base level of monthly sales is $125,750. β is the slope of the line, and it indicates that each new housing permit issued last month should result in additional sales of $550 this month.

For this model, the relationship between sales and building permits is a curve that is represented by a straight line, as in Figure 19.4(a). This regression is known as *linear regression*. *Nonlinear regression,* as in Figure 19.4(b), fits a curved line to the data, and may provide a better fit. A representative nonlinear model would be:

$$\text{Cement sales this period} = \text{Constant} + \beta_1 \times (\text{new housing permits last month}) + \beta_2 \times (\text{new housing permits last month})^2 \tag{19.2}$$
$$= 125,750 + 550 \times (\text{new housing permits last month}) - 20 \times (\text{new housing permits last month})^2$$

This model indicates that sales increase as permits increase, but the increase is happening at a decreasing rate. The base level for sales is $125,750. To go from zero permits to one permit, sales are expected to be $125,750 + ($550 \times 1) - ($20 \times 1)^2 = $126,280$. Thus, sales increase $530 (= $126,280 - $125,750). As the number of permits increases to two, sales should be $125,750 + ($550 \times 2) - ($20 \times 2)^2 = $126,770$. Thus, sales change $490 (= $126,770 - $126,280) from the previous level.

[5]We briefly discussed regression analysis in Chapter 5.

FIGURE 19.4

USING REGRESSION ANALYSIS TO ESTIMATE SALES

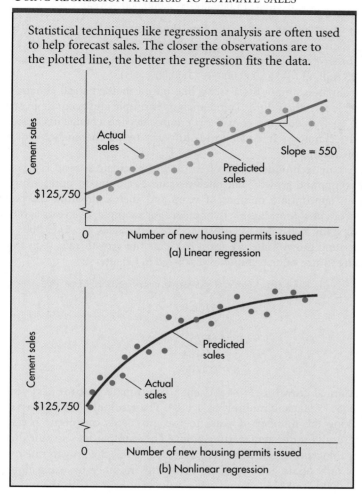

Statistical techniques like regression analysis are often used to help forecast sales. The closer the observations are to the plotted line, the better the regression fits the data.

Cement sales

Actual sales

Slope = 550

Predicted sales

$125,750

0 Number of new housing permits issued

(a) Linear regression

Cement sales

Predicted sales

Actual sales

$125,750

0 Number of new housing permits issued

(b) Nonlinear regression

In regression analysis, the analyst tries to minimize the deviations between the fitted curve and the actual data, which are indicated by the points in the graph. The derived relationship between sales and the variable used to predict sales is a probabilistic one; actual sales can differ from the amount predicted. However, the methodology assumes that any differences are expected to average out to zero over time.[6]

TREND ANALYSIS. **Trend analysis** is a regression technique commonly used to forecast future sales based on time.[7] The equation takes the form:.

> **Trend analysis.** A variable of interest is analyzed against time.

[6]A technique called *multiple regression analysis* allows the analyst to use several variables to predict sales. This topic is discussed in quantitative business analysis courses.

[7]*Time series analysis* is beneficial in predicting or forecasting sales that are a function of time. Time can be divided into three elements: *trend, cyclical,* and *seasonal.* The trend reflects the general change in sales over time; the cyclical component varies with the business cycle; and the seasonal component varies with the time of year. A separate forecast based on past patterns is required for each of the elements. The three forecasts are then totaled.

$$\text{Sales} = \text{Constant} + \beta \times \text{year} \qquad (19.3)$$

$$= 15{,}000{,}000 + 2{,}000{,}000 \times \text{year}$$

The constant of 15,000,000 means the firm should realize base sales of $15 million. β indicates the increase in sales for each year of the forecast. For example, sales for the first year of the forecast should be $17 million (year $= 1$), whereas sales for the third year should be $23 million ($= 17{,}000{,}000 + 2{,}000{,}000 \times 3$).

This technique simply fits a trend line into a mathematical equation and then projects the line into the future. Trend analysis is simple and accurate in stable industries, but the analysis does not consider economic decline, change in consumer habits, or improved technology. In order to identify any trend, the analyst requires a large number of observations.

An alternate technique that is often used to calculate a trend is a *point-to-point* estimate of compound growth. The analyst achieves a point-to-point growth estimate by picking an appropriate number of years and then estimating the compounded growth rate from one point in time to another. For example, five years ago Educational Software Company had sales of $100,000. This year sales are $175,000. To find an annual compound growth rate, we must calculate the growth rate, g, in the following equation using future value techniques discussed in Chapter 4:

$$\text{Sales this year} = (\text{Sales five years ago}) \times (1 + g)^5 \qquad (19.4)$$

Calculator
Clear
PV
100,000
FV
175,000
N
5
CPT
%i
Ans.: 11.84

$$\$175{,}000 = \$100{,}000 \times (1 + g)^5$$
$$1.75 = (1 + g)^5$$
$$(1 + g) = (1.75)^{1/5}$$
$$g = 1.1184 - 1$$
$$g = 0.1184$$

Compound annual growth is 11.84 percent.[8] To estimate sales for next year, take this year's sales of $175,000 and multiply by 1.1184. The resulting sales forecast is $195,720.

In picking the number of years to use, problems can occur because varying growth rates result for different starting points. For example, let's assume that sales four years ago for Educational Software were $125,000. Thus, the growth rate over the past four years is only about 8.78 percent. Verify this number by using Equation 19.4. Replace $100,000 with $125,000 and replace the exponent 5 with the number 4, since there are only four compounding periods.

Should the analyst use a growth rate of 11.84 percent or 8.78 percent in the sales forecast, or some other number? The appropriate starting point must be solved by the analyst's own judgment. If sales have grown at a reasonably steady rate in prior periods, then this growth rate can be projected into the future. If the historical growth rate has been significantly affected by a major acquisition or sale of part of the business in one year, then the effect of this event on the historical growth rate should be filtered out. The most difficult sales projections occur for firms with cyclical sales patterns (for example, a company such as Caterpillar Corporation which sells heavy machinery). Historical sales growth rates for these firms might reflect wide variations in both direction and amount from year to year.

[8]We can use the future value of $1 table to solve for g. First go down the period column to the fifth period. Next look across that row to find the table factor closest to 1.75. A factor of 1.762 is found under the 12 percent column. Without interpolating (discussed in an appendix to Chapter 8), we estimate the growth rate at slightly less than 12 percent.

With several alternative techniques to forecast sales, there are bound to be conflicts in the projections. To reconcile the sales figures, management must uncover the assumptions underlying each of the forecasts and determine which set of assumptions is most reasonable. But even if management can agree to a most likely forecast, conditions and sales can change. For this reason, it is best to predict a range of sales with the probability of attaining levels within the range. However, in order to simplify the discussion, Illustration 19.1 uses single-point sales forecasts.

ILLUSTRATION 19.1

Mendenhall's sales projections

Mendenhall Corporation, a manufacturer of stereo equipment, has current sales of $110 million. The company produces three product lines and plans to introduce two additional lines, one in two years and another in three years. The marketing manager believes that the firm can achieve an overall nominal growth rate of 17 percent, with inflation accounting for 10.5 percentage points of the growth.

The following table shows judgmental projections for each of the next five years as estimated by the marketing and finance managers. In arriving at the growth projections for existing products, the two managers used information received from sales representatives, as well as an analysis of recent sales trends. Forecasts for the new products are based on the company's experience when it initially introduced a product called Boom Box. The total sales amounts are based on a 17 percent compound growth rate. For instance, forecasted sales in year 1 of $128,700 are $1.17 \times$ current sales of $110,000; sales in year 2 are $(1.17)^2 \times \$110,000$; and so on.

SALES PROJECTIONS ($000)

Product	1	2	3	4	5	Growth
Audio II	$ 58,123	$ 63,935	$ 70,329	$ 77,362	$ 85,097	10.0%
Boom Box	49,685	55,850	62,442	69,492	77,032	11.6
Audio I	16,512	12,052	10,000	10,000	10,000	−11.8
Compac		7,030	9,400	11,300	15,500	30.2
Discman			4,500	7,500	12,400	66.0
Total	$124,320	$138,867	$156,671	$175,654	$200,029	12.6%
Variance	4,380	11,712	19,506	30,474	41,140	75.1
Total	$128,700	$150,579	$176,177	$206,128	$241,169	17.0%

(handwritten annotation: Sales ties to pg 762 Top of IN/ST)

After reviewing these sales projections, upper management concluded that existing and new-product lines only have the strength to achieve a compound growth rate of 12.6 percent, as opposed to the 17 percent target. Consequently, management must restudy its strategic options. Moreover, management believes the variance between the sales projections and the total sales needed to achieve the 17 percent growth target is sufficiently large so that it would be difficult to offset this variance with the introduction of more new products.

In Illustration 19.1, what are the options available to management? Normally, when a company faces variances of this magnitude, it looks for a major solution—acquisition. Certainly, an acquisition would be one option for Mendenhall. Other options would be to modify and enhance product line Audio I to improve its aging characteristics; to intensify the introduction of new lines Compac and Discman; to expand the company's market penetration; or to implement a combination of all three options and make an acquisition of moderate size.

19.4.2 The Capital Expenditure Plan

After completing and adopting the long-range sales projections, management's next step is to determine the capital expenditures required to sustain existing products and services and to introduce new products and services. Capital expenditure projections can be broken down into two categories, each of which indicates the reason for the expenditure: replacement and expansion. Net present value procedures (discussed in Chapters 14 and 15) should be used to justify the expenditures.

The review of forecasted capital expenditures is often less precise than the review of the sales projections. Instead of conducting detailed net present value analysis for each project, the analyst often simply conducts a review of past new investment versus annual depreciation, forecasted new investment versus cash flows anticipated, or historical capital expenditures per year versus future expenditures per year. However, the capital investment funding requirements may be difficult for management to assess until the analyst completes formal discounted cash flow analyses and shows how they influence the firm's profitability. Illustration 19.2 continues the Mendenhall example.

ILLUSTRATION 19.2

Mendenhall's capital expenditure forecast

Once Mendenhall's management agrees with the sales projections and how it will solve the variance in Illustration 19.1, its next step is to identify the capital expenditure requirements. After much review and analysis of investment proposals suggested by manufacturing and engineering personnel, management identifies the following expenditures as necessary to meet the business goals. An engineer for the company, working with a financial analyst, estimates the cost of these expenditures to be about $32.9 million over the five-year period. All expenditures are forecasted to realize positive net present values.

CAPITAL INVESTMENT REQUIREMENTS ($000)

Product	Reason	1	2	Years 3	4	5
Audio II	Replacement	$ 850	$ 500	$ 550	$ 700	$1,000
	Expansion	240	320	370	420	500
		$1,090	$ 820	$ 920	$1,120	$1,500
Boom Box	Replacement	$1,200	$1,000	$ 700	$1,100	$1,100
	Expansion	300	300	400	500	700
		$1,500	$1,300	$1,100	$1,600	$1,800
Audio I	Replacement	$ 500	$ 250	$ 300	$ 250	$ 250
	Expansion					
		$ 500	$ 250	$ 300	$ 250	$ 250

Compac	Replacement			$ 300	$ 700	$1,100
	Expansion	$3,000	$2,000	900	1,000	1,500
		$3,000	$2,000	$1,200	$1,700	$2,600
Discman	Replacement			$ 400	$ 600	
	Expansion	$2,000	$1,000	$2,000	850	1,200
		$2,000	$1,000	$2,000	$1,250	$1,800
	Total	$8,090	$5,370	$5,520	$5,920	$7,950

see Gross Fixed Assets Pg 764

19.4.3 The Pro Forma Income Statement

After checking the capital expenditure forecast for completeness and feasibility, the analyst's next step is to prepare a pro forma income statement. The information needed to prepare this statement comes from various sources, such as a detailed cost of goods schedule (which includes any objectives to improve labor efficiency and any equipment to improve productivity). It is comprised of forecasts of overhead cost, including added depreciation from additions of plant and equipment, transportation cost, advertising expenses to support the sales forecasts, sales and marketing expenses, and general and administrative expenses.

The analyst can use several different techniques to estimate the expenses. A typical approach is the common-size vertical analysis method we used in Chapter 18, where we estimate each expense item as a percent of sales. The percentages used can equal the company's most recent income statement items as a percentage of current sales or an average percentage computed over the past several years. Alternatively, the percentages can be based on managerial judgment, especially in the case of altering a ratio, such as the proportion of each sales dollar spent on advertising. However the analyst calculates the percentages, the percent-of-sales method assumes that each percentage remains constant.

The percent-of-sales method is a crude approach. The technique works best for companies with stable relationships between sales and expenses. If significant variations exist between sales and the various expense items, this method can introduce considerable error into the expense forecasts. Alternative approaches are the statistical concepts of regression or trend analyses and point-to-point estimates that we discussed earlier. Let's continue the Mendenhall example and develop the pro forma income statement in Illustration 19.3.

ILLUSTRATION 19.3

Mendenhall's pro forma income statement

The financial analyst for Mendenhall concludes that any relationship between sales and expenses is not stable enough to use either the percent-of-sales method or the point-to-point approach. A preliminary use of a regression model resulted in a poor statistical fit between historical sales and the various expenses items. As such, the pro forma income statement relies on managers' judgments as to the expected relationship of the income statement items with sales. For example, the sales manager thought that gross profit margin for the first year of the forecast should be 40 percent. Given the sales programs the marketing department expects to implement during the forecast period, the sales manager, in consultation with the manufacturing manager and chief financial officer, suggests that gross profit margin should improve one percentage point each year, becoming 44 percent in the fifth year.

Other expense items in the income statement were forecasted in consultation with other individuals in the company. For example, management expects general and administrative expenses to increase one tenth of a point each year during the planning period. The increases are largely for increased wages and benefits to employees. A tax rate of 46 percent was agreed upon after much deliberation. The federal government has been hinting at raising the income tax rate so it can fund proposed social programs.

Pro Forma Income Statement ($000)

	1	Years 2	3	4	5
Sales (Illustration 19.1)	$128,700	$150,579	$176,177	$206,128	$241,169
Cost of sales	77,220	88,842	102,183	117,493	135,055
Gross profit	$ 51,480	$ 61,737	$ 73,994	$ 88,635	$106,114
Operating expenses:					
Transportation	$ 3,861	$ 4,682	$ 5,932	$ 8,032	$ 9,542
Advertising	10,296	12,046	14,094	11,048	12,926
Sales and marketing	15,444	18,521	22,022	26,178	30,869
General and administrative	7,079	8,449	10,042	11,955	14,229
	$ 36,680	$ 43,698	$ 52,090	$ 57,213	$ 67,566
Income from operations	$ 14,800	$ 18,039	$ 21,904	$ 31,422	$ 38,548
Interest expense	1,800	1,200	900	600	300
Profit before taxes	$ 13,000	$ 16,839	$ 21,004	$ 30,822	$ 38,248
Taxes (46%)	5,980	7,746	9,662	14,178	17,594
Profit after taxes	$ 7,020	$ 9,093	$ 11,342	$ 16,664	$ 20,654

Common-Size Statement:

Sales	100.0%	100.0%	100.0%	100.0%	100.0%
Cost of sales	60.0	59.0	58.0	57.0	56.0
Gross profit margin	40.0%	41.0%	42.0%	43.0%	44.0%
Operating expenses:					
Transportation	3.0	3.1	3.4	3.9	3.9
Advertising	8.0	8.0	8.0	5.3	5.4
Sales and marketing	12.0	12.3	12.5	12.7	12.8
General and administrative	5.5	5.6	5.7	5.8	5.9
	28.5%	29.0%	29.6%	27.7%	28.0%
Income from operations	11.5%	12.0%	12.4%	15.3%	16.0%
Interest expense	1.4	0.8	0.5	0.3	0.1
Profit before taxes	10.1%	11.2%	11.9%	15.0%	15.9%
Taxes	4.6	5.2	5.5	6.9	7.3
Profit after taxes	5.5%	6.0%	6.4%	8.1%	8.6%
Depreciation expense included in cost of sales and general and administrative	$ 3,161	$ 3,621	$ 4,185	$ 5,137	$ 6,055

Profitability of sales, measured by the percentage of *profits after taxes* row, indicates strong improvement in performance during the forecast period. The improvement is primarily because of increasing gross profit margins and slower growth in advertising expenditures.

19.4.4 The Pro Forma Balance Sheet

A pro forma balance sheet forecasts how management expects to invest the firm's assets and how it expects to finance these assets using debt and equity capital. Actual balance sheet accounts are closely related to changes in sales. This is an important point because understanding the relationship provides a foundation for constructing a pro forma balance sheet. Inventory fits in as a good example. If management wants to increase sales, inventory most likely has to increase to accommodate the larger sales volume. The more the company sells, the more raw materials it will have to keep on hand, the more work-in-process it will generate, and the more finished goods it will maintain to meet anticipated sales increases. Accounts receivable is another example. The more a company sells, the more customers charge on account, thereby increasing the accounts receivable balance.

While the relationships between many other balance sheet accounts and sales may not be as obvious, these relationships do exist. An account that is directly related to sales is called *spontaneous*. A **spontaneous asset** is one that automatically increases or decreases when sales increase or decrease. A **spontaneous liability** is one that changes in the same direction as sales change. Management can prevent spontaneous assets or liabilities from changing in direct response to a change in sales, and in some instances may want to do just that. However, without management action, spontaneous assets and liabilities rise when sales rise and fall when sales fall.

Generally, forecasters consider cash, accounts receivable, and inventory to be spontaneous assets positively related to sales. On the other hand, marketable securities are not related to sales. Rather, marketable securities change when management makes a decision to invest excess cash or to sell off existing securities. Therefore, forecasters consider marketable securities and similar accounts to be nonspontaneous accounts.

Many times, forecasters treat fixed assets as partially spontaneous accounts. In reality, fixed assets do not automatically increase when sales increase. However, once a company reaches its productive capacity, it needs additional fixed-asset investment if sales are to increase. Expenditures for fixed assets generally are made in large lump-sum purchases, as our capital budgeting forecast in Illustration 19.2 shows. If management expects sales to increase a little each year over the next five years, it is not in the company's best interests to build several small factories during each of the next five years. A less expensive strategy for management to follow is to plan ahead and possibly build one factory to handle the growth for at least the next five years.

Spontaneous liability accounts include accounts payable, taxes payable, and accruals. These accounts are generally related to sales volume. As sales increase, a company's production usually increases, so its accounts payables and accruals also rise. If these new sales are profitable, taxes payable will rise. Management can prevent increases in these liabilities but unless it does so, the increases will occur. Liabilities that require specific negotiation with a lender are not spontaneous financing. Included in this category are notes payable, bank loans, and bonds. When these nonspontaneous liabilities change, they do so as a result of a management decision.

Shareholder equity accounts for common stock issued (including the stock issued at par account and the capital surplus account) are not spontaneous financing accounts. Changes in the common stock issued account requires specific management action, since increases in common stock do not occur spontaneously. The retained earnings

> **Spontaneous asset.** An asset that increases or decreases as sales increase or decrease.
>
> **Spontaneous liability.** A liability that increases or decreases as sales increase or decrease.

account is an equity account that is partially spontaneous. If sales increase, retained earnings likely increase. To figure out how much retained earnings change, we must add the forecasted net income and subtract the forecasted dividends paid to shareholders to the previous retained earnings balance. Illustration 19.4 provides an example of pro forma balance sheet preparation.

ILLUSTRATION 19.4

Mendenhall's pro forma balance sheet

The most recent year's balance sheet for Mendenhall follows along with the five-year forecast. The spontaneous accounts of cash, receivables, inventory, accounts payable, and accruals are readily identified. The company is currently operating at its fixed-asset capacity, so any sales increases require new fixed-asset investment as identified earlier in Illustration 19.2.

PRO FORMA BALANCE SHEET ($000)

	Current	1	2	3	4	5
				Years		
Cash	$ 385	$ 450	$ 527	$ 617	$ 722	$ 845
Marketable securities	0	0	0	0	0	0
Accounts receivable	5,135	6,008	7,029	8,224	9,622	11,258
Inventories	10,049	11,757	13,756	16,095	18,831	22,032
Current assets	$15,569	$18,215	$21,312	$24,936	$ 29,175	$ 34,135
Gross fixed assets	$61,500	$69,590	$74,960	$80,480	$ 86,400	$ 94,350
Accumulated depreciation	(20,150)	(23,311)	(26,932)	(31,117)	(36,254)	(42,309)
Net fixed assets	$41,350	$46,279	$48,028	$49,363	$ 50,146	$ 52,041
Total assets	$56,919	$64,494	$69,340	$74,299	$ 79,321	$ 86,176
Accounts payable	$10,438	$12,212	$14,288	$16,717	$ 19,559	$ 22,884
Accruals	6,958	8,141	9,525	11,144	13,038	15,254
Long-term debt payable	2,000	2,000	2,000	2,000	2,000	2,000
Current liabilities	$19,396	$22,353	$25,813	$29,861	$ 34,597	$ 40,138
Long-term debt	$18,000	$16,000	$14,000	$12,000	$ 10,000	$8,000
Common stock at par	$ 1,000	$ 1,000	$ 1,000	$ 1,000	$ 1,000	$ 1,000
Capital surplus	750	750	750	750	750	750
Retained earnings:						
Beginning balance	$12,788	$17,773	$22,943	$29,781	$ 38,385	$ 51,121
+ profits	6,785	7,020	9,093	11,342	16,664	20,654
− dividends	(1,800)	(1,850)	(2,255)	(2,738)	(3,928)	(4,819)
= ending balance	$17,773	$22,943	$29,781	$38,385	$ 51,121	$ 66,956
Total equity	$19,523	$24,693	$31,531	$40,135	$ 52,871	$ 68,706
Total financing	$56,919	$63,046	$71,344	$81,996	$ 97,468	$116,844
Assets minus total financing		$ 1,448	$(2,004)	$(7,697)	$(18,147)	$(30,668)
Increase marketable securities by:			$ 2,004	$ 7,697	$18,147	$ 30,668
Increase notes payable by:		$ 1,448				

Cash is the first account listed. Since management expects sales to increase by 17 percent, the analyst assumes that cash will increase by 17 percent as well. The predicted cash balance in year 1 of the forecast is $450,000, a 17 percent increase over the prior year. For each succeeding year, the cash balance increases 17 percent in line with sales growth.

Marketable securities is the next account listed. The analyst maintains marketable securities at their existing zero balance because this account is not spontaneous. The pro forma balances for receivables and inventories increase by 17 percent each year, since they are treated as spontaneous accounts. Gross fixed assets increase by the acquisition cost of capital expenditures (Illustration 19.2), whereas accumulated depreciation increases by the annual depreciation expense (Illustration 19.3).

Forecasted total assets for year 1 are $64,494,000. The estimated liabilities and equities must total to this amount. Because accounts payable and accruals are spontaneous, the analyst expects their balances to increase 17 percent annually, in line with the sales growth. The loan covenant requires the long-term debt to be repaid in the amount of $2000 annually. The analyst decides that the company will not need to issue common stock, at least according to what the analysis reveals to this point. Hence, the equity accounts for common stock issued and capital surplus will not change.

The current year's retained earnings balance is $17,773,000. The retained earnings balance of $22,943,000 for year 1 is derived by adding the forecasted profits of $7,020,000 and subtracting the forecasted dividends of $1,850,000. Future year's retained earnings are derived in a similar fashion.

When the analyst sums the liabilities and equities for the first year of the forecast, the total financing balance is $63,046,000, which is $1,448,000 short of the asset balance. The forecasted increase in assets is greater than the increase in liabilities and equities. The $1,448,000 difference is the estimate of the *external financing requirement* in the first year of the forecast.[9] The **external financing requirement (EFR)** indicates to management how much financing Mendenhall needs to raise in order to support the new projected asset base. The analyst explains to management that the EFR exists because sales growth is accompanied by growth in assets that is not offset by spontaneous growth in liabilities and equities. However, as shown by the negative EFR amounts, this problem is overcome in all future years of the forecast. Negative EFR means that excess funds exist that could be invested in marketable securities.

External financing requirement (EFR). The amount of funds that must be supplied by creditors or investors to satisfy financing needs.

[9] In order to simplify the problem, we ignore interest expense or income that would be realized on the external financing requirement. Thus, we understate any additional debt financing required and overstate profits because this additional debt would incur interest costs. Whenever total financing exceeds assets, as for years 2 through 5 of the forecast, we understate both investment in marketable securities and profits because these securities would earn interest income. Since all numbers are based on projections which have error associated with them, these misstatements should not be serious.

At this stage of the forecasting procedure, Mendenhall's management must decide how to raise the EFR. It could use either new long-term debt or a common stock sale. Alternatively, management could reduce the EFR by reducing the growth in assets. Since the financing needs are only for one year, management believes that it can negotiate a line of credit with the bank.

19.4.5 Pro Forma ROE Calculations

Upon completing the pro forma balance sheet, the planning analyst is now in a position to calculate return on equity. Illustration 19.5 discusses the calculations and results.

ILLUSTRATION 19.5

Mendenhall's ROE projections

Mendenhall's planning analyst uses the forecasted profits, assets, debt, and equity figures from Illustration 19.4 and sales figures from Illustration 19.3 to compute expected ROE for each period. He divides the projected profit by the estimated annual equity balance to determine the annual return-on-equity forecast.

RETURN-ON-EQUITY PROJECTIONS ($000)

	Years				
	1	2	3	4	5
Sales	$128,700	$150,579	$176,177	$206,128	$241,169
Assets	64,494	71,344	81,996	97,468	116,844
Debt	39,801	39,813	41,861	44,597	48,138
Equity	24,693	31,531	40,135	52,871	68,706
Profits	7,020	9,093	11,342	16,664	20,654
Return on equity	28.4%	28.8%	28.3%	31.5%	30.1%
Return on sales	5.5%	6.0%	6.4%	8.1%	8.6%
Asset turnover	2.0 ×	2.1 ×	2.1 ×	2.1 ×	2.1 ×
Financial leverage	2.6 ×	2.3 ×	2.0 ×	1.8 ×	1.7 ×

Note: Return on equity equals profits divided by equity, or alternatively, it equals the product of (return on sales) × (asset turnover) × (financial leverage). Any difference between the two calculations is because numbers are rounded to one decimal place.

Return on equity hovers around the 28 percent to 31 percent range. The decline in year 5 of the forecast appears to be a result of the relative decline in the use of debt financing.

19.4.6 The Pro Forma Cash Flow Statement

The next planning statement the analyst prepares is a pro forma cash flow statement. This statement breaks activities of the firm into three areas: operating activity, investing activity, and financing activity. The sum of the amounts for these three activities equals the change in the firm's cash account. Thus, the cash flow statement shows how cash was generated and how it was used. Information for the cash flow statement is taken from current financial statements and from the previously calculated pro forma income statement and pro forma balance sheet. (See Illustration 19.6.)

ILLUSTRATION 19.6

Mendenhall's pro forma cash flow statement

Mendenhall's planning analyst begins the exercise by treating profit, decreases in asset accounts, and increases in liability accounts as sources of cash. He treats increases in asset accounts and decreases in liability accounts as uses of cash. Because depreciation is a noncash expense item, he adds it to profits. Dividend payments use cash, and the analyst therefore subtracts them in determining cash flow. The only change in the equity accounts is in the retained earnings account; but the profit and dividend amounts account for these changes.

The cash flow statement illustrates the analyst's calculations. The sum of cash inflows and outflows balance to the ending cash balance shown in the pro forma balance sheet (see Illustration 19.4).

CASH FLOW STATEMENT ($000)

	Years				
	1	2	3	4	5
Operating activities:					
Profits after taxes	$ 7,020	$ 9,093	$ 11,342	$ 16,664	$ 20,654
Depreciation	3,161	3,621	4,185	5,137	6,055
Increase in receivables	(873)	(1,021)	(1,195)	(1,398)	(1,636)
Increase in inventories	(1,708)	(1,999)	(2,339)	(2,736)	(3,201)
Increase in payables	1,774	2,076	2,429	2,842	3,325
Increase in accruals	1,183	1,384	1,619	1,894	2,216
Cash flow from operations	$10,557	$13,154	$ 16,041	$ 22,403	$ 27,413
Investing activities:					
Capital expenditures	$(8,090)	$(5,370)	$ (5,520)	$ (5,920)	$ (7,950)
Marketable securities	0	(2,004)	(5,693)	(10,450)	(12,521)
Cash flow from investing	$(8,090)	$(7,374)	$(11,213)	$(16,370)	$(20,471)
Financing activities:					
Dividend payments	$(1,850)	$(2,255)	$ (2,738)	$ (3,928)	$ (4,819)
Notes payable	1,448	(1,448)			
Debt payments	(2,000)	(2,000)	(2,000)	(2,000)	(2,000)
Cash flow from financing	$(2,402)	$(5,703)	$ (4,738)	$ (5,928)	$ (6,819)
Net cash flow	$ 65	$ 77	$ 90	$ 105	$ 123
Beginning cash balance	385	450	527	617	722
Ending cash balance	$ 450	$ 527	$ 617	$ 722	$ 845

The pro forma cash flow statement indicates that after the first year Mendenhall is able to generate enough cash flow from operations to support its planned investing activities, pay down its obligation on the long-term debt, pay a dividend to shareholders, and still realize a positive cash flow. Indeed, the firm is able to generate large amounts of cash as the investment in marketable securities shows. The next step is for management to identify better uses for this cash.

Comprehension Check

1. Outline the five steps to prepare pro forma financial statements.
2. Distinguish between judgmental forecasts, trend analysis forecasts, and causal analysis forecasts.
3. Why are many accounts in the pro forma balance sheet estimated with a percent-of-sales approach? Why shouldn't the percent-of-sales approach be used to estimate expenditures for plant and equipment?
4. Discuss the benefit to management of having the cash flow statement identify operating, investing, and financing activities.

19.5 ANALYSIS OF THE FINANCIAL FORECASTS

Once the planning analyst prepares the pro forma statements, management must review them and compare the projections with the financial goals of the company. In the Mendenhall case, management sees significant improvements: nominal sales growth is 17 percent compounded annually with a real annual growth rate of 6.5 percent; cash needs change from an unfavorable position of $1,448,000 to a favorable position of $30,668,000 within five years; and return on equity improves from 28.4 percent in the first year of the forecast to 30.1 percent in the last year.

Although forecasts look favorable, management now must ask several important questions:

- What is the probability of attaining the sales levels? The profit levels? The projected ROEs?
- With the generation of significant cash flows in the last three years of the plan, should management consider alternative uses for the excess cash (other than to purchase marketable securities) to obtain further growth?
- Will stockholders accept such relatively small cash dividends?
- With such favorable results, is the company a viable candidate for an unfriendly takeover?
- Are the financial projections too optimistic when compared to historical performance?
- Should management begin to consider alternative courses of action in two or three years if the projections actually materialize?

The forecasts look fairly optimistic. What happens to the pro forma return on equity and the cash flow from operations projection if sales are less than expected or cost projections are more than expected? Management should identify contingency plans to address such possibilities. Contingency plans may include the following actions:

- Decrease expenses by implementing cost-reduction programs; improve sales by aggressive price cutting for products Audio II and Boom Box in an effort to stimulate sales volume and, hopefully, improve overall profits.
- Lessen funding needs by delaying expenditures associated with product Audio I; defer discretionary capital expenditures for new products Compac and Discman by one year.
- Carry less inventory for product Audio I, thereby improving inventory levels and turnover rates at the expense of stockouts.
- Offer major customers extended credit terms to see if such action increases sales.
- Lease some of the equipment instead of buying it.
- Decrease the dividend payout and issue stock dividends in order to conserve cash.
- Evaluate whether a different capital structure is better for improving firm value and shareholder wealth.

However, before incorporating any of these alternatives into final contingency plans, management must examine the potential long-term effects of these changes. For example, reducing inventory levels may result in permanent loss of customers; extended credit terms may put too much strain on cash flows; and the dividend decrease may cause capital markets to lose confidence in the company, thereby driving down stock and bond prices. And as a means of expansion, long-term leasing may be more expensive than purchasing and may limit long-term borrowing.

On the other hand, if these business policy changes have been well studied, they may, in fact, be sound business decisions. For example, reducing inventory levels of product Audio I may encourage Mendenhall to exit the declining business, thereby freeing resources for more profitable use. The extended payment terms may result in higher market share and more loyal customers. Leasing may provide a firm with more expansion flexibility and reduce the risk of overexpansion. And if these changes have positive influences on cash flows of the firm, the stock market will bid up the company's stock price. Such a result means increased shareholder wealth.

Once analysts compute the pro forma statements for income, capital expenditures, balance sheets, and cash flow statements, detailed ratio analysis can be conducted and results compared against the financial goals. If the results are inconsistent with the desired goals, either the planning assumptions must be modified or additional objectives must be added to the strategic plans to improve the expected financial results. A computerized financial modeling system can streamline the task significantly.

One method of evaluating the accomplishments of the firm is to measure the actual results against the established financial targets. However, this evaluation only determines the effectiveness of management in enhancing the wealth of the company by the way it controls the process. The process represents the implementation of ideas through the use of assets. The ideas must have a foundation that management can relate to the strategic goals of the company. The firm's capital budgeting process acts as the foundation. Management compares the anticipated financial results of each individual project against the quantified goals. In essence, if a project's business purpose compares favorably with the strategic business plan and the financial goals established, the project should be approved. Overall, management determines the projects to be undertaken. The implementation and management of the projects determine the success of the company.

Comprehension Check

1. Why is it important for management to analyze the forecast in detail?
2. What are contingency plans? Why are they important?

SUMMARY ▼▼▼▼▼▼▼▼▼▼▼▼

NONCONTROLLABLE AND CONTROLLABLE EFFECTS ON FINANCIAL PLANNING

- The objective of financial planning is to identify risks facing the company and plan actions to deal with them.
- Management must understand what factors it can and cannot control. For those aspects that it cannot control, management should try to comprehend how these factors influence firm decisions and outcomes.
- Meaningful financial measurements are those that guide management in maximizing shareholder wealth. The measurements should not cause conflicts among themselves.

PLANNING GOALS

- Financial targets related to revenue growth, cash flow generation, and return on equity should provide management with targets for meeting the objective of maximizing shareholder wealth.
- A realistic growth goal for sales can only be established once management understands its markets.
- A goal for generation of cash flow is based on realistic assumptions about sales, expenses, and capital expenditures required to support the plan.
- A goal for return on equity acts as a proxy for maximizing shareholder wealth. Higher return on equity should lead to higher stock price.

PLANNING ASSUMPTIONS

- The most critical part of the forecasting process is determining significant assumptions. The forecast is dependent on sales. Thus, the most significant assumptions relate to sales: the life cycle of the product, sales volumes, line of business performance, and real growth versus nominal growth.
- A breakdown of costs between variable and fixed components aids in projecting income statements.

PREPARATION OF THE FINANCIAL FORECAST

- The sales forecast can be prepared from judgmental forecasting methods, causal models, and trend models. A mixed use of these methods provides a way to cross check the methods.
- The capital expenditure forecast is based on identifying investments whose net present values are positive. These investments should be accepted.
- The pro forma income statement can be estimated using a percent-of-sales method, a judgmental approach, or a combination of these methods.
- The pro forma balance sheet usually is constructed through both a percent-of-sales approach and a judgmental approach. Spontaneous accounts, such as cash, receivables, inventories, payables, and accruals, change in direct response to changes in sales. Nonspontaneous accounts, such as fixed assets and long-term financing, do not change in response to sales.
- The pro forma cash flow statement shows how cash flows are expected to be generated and how they are expected to be used.

ANALYSIS OF THE FINANCIAL FORECASTS

- It is extremely important that management scrutinize the pro forma results. It is possible that some unrealistic assumptions were used to derive forecasted numbers.
- Management should identify contingency plans that can become operative if certain targets are missed. Contingency plans are meant to minimize any shortfalls from forecasts.

FURTHER READING ▼▼▼▼▼▼▼▼▼▼▼

Donaldson, Gordon, *Managing Corporate Wealth: The Operation of a Comprehensive Financial Goals System.* New York: Praeger Publishers, 1984. This book should be read and studied by business executives, educators, and students.

Katz, Robert L., *Cases and Concepts in Corporate Strategy.* Englewood Cliffs, NJ: Prentice Hall, Inc., 1970. This excellent book, written by a former executive, deals with the critical issues, decisions, and actions which determine a company's competitive posture.

Lee, Cheng F., *Financial Analysis and Planning: Theory and Application.* Reading, MA: Addison-Wesley Publishing Company, 1985. This book integrates both theoretical and practical corporate analysis and planning material.

SELF-TEST PROBLEMS ▼▼▼▼▼▼▼▼▼▼▼▼

ST19-1. The director of budgets and analysis for Fahlman Corporation is developing a sales forecast for next year. This year's sales are expected to be $1,050,000. Sales nine years ago were $510,000. Calculate forecasted sales to the nearest thousand dollars for next year assuming that sales will increase at the compound growth rate that has occurred over the past nine years.

ST19-2. As it begins a new year, the management of Robertson Wholesale is preparing a pro forma income statement for the year ahead. The company's most recent income statement follows. Management has found a reasonably stable relationship in expense items in relationship to sales over recent years. Therefore, except for interest (which is assumed to be a fixed expense) and income taxes (which are estimated to be 30 percent of taxable income), the percent-of-sales method will be used to create the pro forma income statement. The sales forecast is based on an increase of 10 percent above the current year's $2 million. Using these data, prepare a pro forma income statement for the coming year.

Robertson Wholesale, Inc.
Most Recent Income Statement

Net sales	$2,000,000
Cost of sales	1,060,000
Gross margin	$ 940,000
Operating expenses	600,000
Operating income	$ 340,000
Interest expense	100,000
Income before taxes	$ 240,000
Income taxes	72,000
Net income	$ 168,000

ST19-3. The financial analyst of Quick Fox Stores, Inc. has projected next year's sales to be $12 million with net income of $800,000. The firm's pro forma balance sheet for the end of next year is summarized as follows:

Total assets	$10,000,000
Total debt	$ 4,000,000
Total equity	6,000,000
Total financing	$10,000,000

Calculate expected return on equity for Quick Fox by first calculating return on sales, asset turnover, and financial leverage.

ST19-4. Wayland Corporation's balance sheet for this year and its pro forma balance sheet and income statement for next year follow. Sales are forecast to increase 12 percent next year. The company plans to spend $12,000 for machinery next year. The equipment will be financed with a three-year loan from the manufacturer. A payment of $5,000 is due on the company's long-term debt. Prepare a pro forma cash flow statement using the format of Illustration 19.6 in the chapter.

What is the projected change in cash for next year? Comment on the main sources and uses of funds shown in your pro forma cash flow statement.

Wayland Corporation
Balance Sheet

	This Year	Pro Forma	
Cash	$ 8,000	$ 16,400	*
Accounts receivable	30,000	33,600	+ 12%
Inventories	70,000	78,400	+ 12%
Current assets	$108,000	$128,400	
Gross fixed assets	$ 80,000	$ 92,000	+ $12,000
Accumulated depreciation	(48,000)	(56,000)	+ $8,000
Net fixed assets	$ 32,000	$ 36,000	
Total assets	$140,000	$164,400	
Accounts payable	$ 35,000	$ 39,200	+ 12%
Accruals	10,000	11,200	+ 12%
Current liabilities	$ 45,000	$ 50,400	
Long-term debt	$ 40,000	$ 47,000	+ $12,000 − $5,000
Common stock	$ 20,000	$ 20,000	
Retained earnings	35,000	47,000	+ $19,000 − $7,000
Total equity	$ 55,000	$ 67,000	
Total liabilities and equity	$140,000	$164,400	

*Balancing figure

Wayland Corporation
Pro Forma Income Statement

Sales	$336,000	Increase of 12%
Cost of goods sold*	168,000	50% of sales
Gross profit	$168,000	50% of sales
Operating expenses	141,000	42% of sales
Operating income	$ 27,000	8% of sales
Interest expense	3,000	Estimate
Taxable income	$ 24,000	
Income taxes (20%)	5,000	
Profit after taxes	$ 19,000	

Projected cash dividends: $7,000

*Includes depreciation of $8,000

PROBLEMS ▼▼▼▼▼▼▼▼▼▼▼▼

FORECASTING SALES

19-1. The manager of Jim's Plumbing & Air Conditioning is developing a sales forecast for the coming year. If the manager uses linear regression analysis, what is the sales forecast if the base level of sales is $300,000 and each building permit issued in the county results in additional sales revenue for Jim's of $600? The homebuilders' association has estimated that 800 houses will be built in the county next year.

19-2. A firm's financial officer is developing a sales forecast for the coming year using linear regression analysis. What is the sales forecast if the base level of annual sales is $2 million and each percentage point change in personal income for the region where the firm does business results in a sales change of $100,000? The U.S. Commerce Department forecasts an increase of 6 percent in personal income for the region next year.

19-3. The sales manager of Lee's Electronics is using linear regression to forecast sales for next year. What is the sales forecast if the base level of annual sales is $1.6 million and each percentage point change in personal income for the region where the firm does business results in a sales change of $80,000? Economists at the local university are forecasting an increase of 8 percent in personal income for the region next year.

19-4. In preparation of the company's financial plan for next year, a company's general manager uses linear regression analysis to forecast annual sales. The base level of annual sales is $15 million and each percentage point change in industrial production for the region where the firm does business results in a sales change of $150,000. Government economists forecast a decrease of 5 percent in the region's industrial production next year How much is the sales forecast for next year?

19-5. A firm's financial manager is developing the company's financial plan for next year. The first step is to forecast sales. Sales for the current year are expected to be $1.6 million; six years ago sales were $700,000. Management believes that sales next year will increase at the same compound annual rate as has existed for the past six compounding periods. Calculate forecasted sales for next year. Round your growth estimate to the nearest tenth of 1 percent.

19-6. The sales manager is developing a sales forecast for next year. Sales this year will be $2.5 million. Sales ten years ago were $1 million. Calculate forecasted sales for next year assuming that sales will increase at the same annual rate as the compounded growth rate over the past ten years.

19-7. A product manager is developing a sales forecast for next year. Six years ago, sales were $280,000; today they are $430,000. Calculate next year's forecasted sales to the nearest thousand dollars assuming that sales will increase at the same compounded growth rate as realized over the past six annual compounding periods.

19-8. What is the compound annual growth rate for sales over the past 12 years if recent sales were $237,860,000 and earliest sales were $75,840,000? Give your answer to the nearest whole percentage point.

19-9. Estimate the compound annual growth rate of sales over the past seven annual compounding periods if sales have increased from $312,000 to $830,000. Give your answer to the nearest whole percentage point.

19-10. If sales for a hardware manufacturer are expected to grow at a 13 percent rate compounded for the next four years, what will be the forecasted sales for each of the next four years if sales last year were $650,000?

19-11. If sales in the current year are $96,000, what are forecasted sales for the sixth year from now if sales are expected to increase at an annual compound growth rate of 16 percent?

19-12. If sales this year are $12.4 million, what are forecasted sales nine years from now if sales are expected to grow at an annual compound rate of 8 percent?

19-13. If sales this year are $118,000, what were sales five years ago if sales grew at a 7 percent annual compound rate?

19-14. Sales this year are expected to be $600,000. What were sales nine years ago if sales grew at a 10 percent annual compound rate over this period?

THE PRO FORMA INCOME STATEMENT

19-15. The management of Perfection Dieting, Inc. is preparing a pro forma income statement for the coming year. Following is the company's most recent unaudited income statement. Management has found a reasonably stable relationship in expense items in relationship to sales over recent years. Therefore, except for interest (which is assumed to be a fixed expense) and income taxes (which are estimated to be 35 percent of taxable income), management decides to use the percent-of-sales method to create the pro forma income statement. The sales forecast is based on an increase of 12 percent above the current year's $15 million. Using these data, prepare a pro forma income statement for the coming year.

Perfection Dieting, Inc.
Most Recent Income Statement

Net sales	$15,000,000
Cost of sales	6,000,000
Gross margin	$ 9,000,000
Operating expenses	4,500,000
Operating income	$ 4,500,000
Interest expense	1,200,000
Income before taxes	$ 3,300,000
Income taxes	1,155,000
Net income	$ 2,145,000

19-16. With preliminary accounting figures available for the end of its current year, Hair By Reynard's financial manager needs a pro forma income statement prepared for the coming year as part of her presentation to the bank for a loan. The company's most recent unaudited income statement follows. A stable percentage relationship exists for expenses in relation to sales. The manager wants the percent-of-sales method used to prepare the income statement. She treats interest as a fixed expense and estimates income taxes at 28 percent of taxable income. She bases the sales forecast on an increase of 7 percent above the current year's sales of $188,000. Prepare a pro forma income statement for the coming year.

Hair By Reynard's
Most Recent Income Statement

Net sales	$188,000
Cost of sales	96,000
Gross margin	$ 92,000
Operating expenses	64,000
Operating income	$ 28,000
Interest expense	3,000
Income before taxes	$ 25,000
Income taxes	7,000
Net income	$ 18,000

19-17. As the current year ended, Jennifer of Jennifer's Emporium needs a pro forma income statement for the coming year to present to the State Bank for extension of the store's line of credit. The company's income statement for the latest year follows. Jennifer expects next year's cost of goods sold and operating expenses to be about the same percentage of sales as for the year just ended. For forecasting purposes, interest is assumed to be $8000 next year. Next year's income tax rate is estimated at 30 percent. Using the percent-of-sales method, prepare the shop's pro forma income statement. Because of a new factory locating in the community, the owner expects sales to grow by 15 percent next year.

Jennifer's Emporium
Most Recent Income Statement

Net sales	$400,000
Cost of sales	220,000
Gross margin	$180,000
Operating expenses	116,000
Operating income	$ 64,000
Interest expense	6,000
Income before taxes	$ 58,000
Income taxes	17,500
Net income	$ 40,500

19-18. The financial analyst for Commercial Products Corporation is preparing a pro forma income statement for next year using the preliminary income statement for the current period. An upturn in the industry suggests that sales will increase 10 percent next year. Because of new equipment, the cost of sales is expected to decrease to 38 percent of sales. However, higher operating costs, including a new advertising program, are expected to increase operating expenses by $400,000 next year. For planning purposes, the analyst assumes interest expense will decline to $90,000. The firm's effective tax rate is estimated at 40 percent. Given these data, what should the analyst's pro forma income statement look like?

Commercial Products Corporation
Current Income Statement

Net sales	$8,500,000
Cost of goods sold	3,400,000
Gross margin	$5,100,000
Operating expenses	3,570,000
Operating income	$1,530,000
Interest expense	110,000
Income before taxes	$1,420,000
Income taxes	568,000
Net income	$ 852,000

19-19. Hank's Auto Parts expects sales next year of $750,000. The company's bank has requested a pro forma income statement before considering a request for an expansion loan. Competition in the auto parts business leads Hank's management to conclude that its gross profit margin next year will decline to 36 percent. Management also expects operating expenses to increase by $20,000 over current levels. In preparing the pro forma statement, interest expense is expected to double over the current year's $15,000. The firm's effective tax rate is estimated to be 25 percent. The current year's income statement follows. With these data, prepare Hank's pro forma income statement.

Hank's Auto Parts
Current Income Statement

Net sales	$700,000
Cost of goods sold	434,000
Gross margin	$266,000
Operating expenses	175,000
Operating income	$ 91,000
Interest expense	15,000
Income before taxes	$ 76,000
Income taxes	19,000
Net income	$ 57,000

19-20. The management of Star Stores expects sales to increase 10 percent next year and 8 percent the year after that. Management believes the gross profit margin will improve one percentage point each year from the present 45 percent. However, higher selling and administrative costs will raise operating expenses by one-half of one percentage point annually for the next two years. Interest expense will remain constant over the two years under the company's loan agreement. The company's effective tax rate is expected to be 34 percent. The current year's income statement follows. With these data, prepare Star's pro forma income statements for the next two years.

Star Stores
Current Income Statement

Net sales	$13,800,000
Cost of goods sold	7,590,000
Gross margin	$ 6,210,000
Operating expenses	4,140,000
Operating income	$ 2,070,000
Interest expense	470,000
Income before taxes	$ 1,600,000
Income taxes	544,000
Net income	$ 1,056,000

19-21. Because of the cyclical nature of its business, the management of Massey Machine Tools expects next year's sales to rise by 15 percent over this year's sales. However, sales are expected to drop the year after that by 10 percent from next year's level. The gross profit margin will improve next year by three percentage points over its current level of 50 percent. However, with sales declining in two years, the gross profit margin will decline by five percentage points from this year's level. Lower administrative costs will reduce operating expenses by one percentage point of sales annually for the next two years. Interest expense in dollars is expected to remain about the same over the next two years. The firm's effective tax rate is estimated to be 40 percent. The current income statement follows. Given these data, prepare Massey's pro forma income statements for the next two years with calculations to the nearest thousand dollars.

Massey Machine Tools
Current Year's Income Statement

Net sales	$234,000,000
Cost of goods sold	117,000,000
Gross margin	$117,000,000
Operating expenses	93,600,000
Operating income	$ 23,400,000
Interest expense	4,400,000
Income before taxes	$ 19,000,000
Income taxes	7,600,000
Net income	$ 11,400,000

THE PRO FORMA BALANCE SHEET

19-22. Cue & Card Corporation's balance sheet for the year just ended follows. Management has asked you to prepare a pro forma balance sheet for one year from now. Assume that sales will increase by 16 percent and that current assets must increase by that same proportion to support the higher sales. The company's gross fixed assets are not expected to change. Annual depreciation charges are 10 percent of gross fixed assets. Accounts payable and accruals will rise the same percentage as sales, but long-term debt will remain the same unless the company's management can negotiate any necessary increases with its bank. No sale of common stock is planned during the next 12 months. Expected net income is $12,000. The company has not been paying cash dividends.

What will be the increase in cash or the funds shortage one year from now?

Cue & Card Corporation
Balance Sheet
Year Just Ended

Cash	$ 5,000
Accounts receivable	25,000
Inventories	80,000
Current assets	$110,000
Gross fixed assets	$ 90,000
Accumulated depreciation	(50,000)
Net fixed assets	$ 40,000
Total assets	$150,000

Accounts payable	$ 20,000
Accruals	15,000
Current liabilities	$ 35,000
Long-term debt	$ 50,000
Common stock	$ 30,000
Retained earnings	35,000
Total equity	$ 65,000
Total liabilities and equity	$150,000

19-23. The balance sheet for the accounting period just ended for Young's Service Company follows. Prepare a pro forma balance sheet for one year from now. Assume that sales will increase by 20 percent and that current assets except for cash, which will remain the same, must increase by 25 percent to support the higher sales. The company is operating at capacity and will have to invest $50,000 in additional equipment, which will be added to gross fixed assets. Annual depreciation charges are 12 percent of gross fixed assets at the end of next year. Accounts payable and accruals will rise by the same percentage as sales. Long-term debt will decline by $10,000 because of a scheduled principal payment. No sale of common stock is planned during the next year. Expected net income is $20,000. The company has no plans to pay a cash dividend next year.

What will be the increase in cash or the funds shortage one year from now? Comment briefly on the company's pro forma condition.

Young's Service Company
Balance Sheet
Period Just Ended

Cash	$ 30,000
Accounts receivable	150,000
Inventories	120,000
Current assets	$300,000
Gross fixed assets	$130,000
Accumulated depreciation	(70,000)
Net fixed assets	$ 60,000
Total assets	$360,000
Accounts payable	$100,000
Accruals	60,000
Current liabilities	$160,000
Long-term debt	$ 40,000
Common stock	$ 50,000
Retained earnings	110,000
Total equity	$160,000
Total liabilities and equity	$360,000

19-24. Based on Nelson Corporation's most recent balance sheet as follows, prepare a pro forma balance sheet for one year from now. Assume that sales will increase by 10 percent and that current assets, except for marketable securities, must increase by 10 percent to support the higher sales. The company is operating below capacity and will not have to add to gross fixed assets over the year. Accumulated depreciation will increase by 10 percent of gross fixed assets. Accounts payable and accruals will rise by the same percentage as sales. Long-term debt will decline by $25,000 because of scheduled principal payments. No sale of common stock is planned during the next 12 months. Expected net income is $80,000. The company plans to pay a cash dividend during the next year of $30,000.

What will be the projected change in marketable securities one year from now? Comment briefly on the company's pro forma condition.

Nelson Corporation
Balance Sheet
Year Just Ended

Cash	$ 10,000
Marketable securities	125,000
Accounts receivable	340,000
Inventories	420,000
Current assets	$ 895,000
Gross fixed assets	$ 970,000
Accumulated depreciation	(560,000)
Net fixed assets	$ 410,000
Total assets	$1,305,000
Accounts payable	$ 280,000
Accruals	150,000
Current liabilities	$ 430,000
Long-term debt	$ 330,000
Common stock	$ 100,000
Retained earnings	445,000
Total equity	$ 545,000
Total liabilities and equity	$1,305,000

19-25. Based on Barland's most recent balance sheet as follows, prepare a pro forma balance sheet for one year from now. Assume that sales will drop by 10 percent and that current assets, except for marketable securities (which are not directly affected by sales), will decrease by 5 percent in view of a lower level of sales. The company will be operating below capacity and will not have to add to gross fixed assets over the year. Accumulated depreciation will increase by 10 percent from the year just ended. Accounts payable and accruals will decline by the same percentage as sales. Long-term debt will decline by $300,000 because of scheduled principal payments. No sale of common stock is planned during the next year. The company forecasts a loss after taxes next year of $100,000. The company does not plan to pay any cash dividends during the next year.

What will be the projected change in marketable securities one year from now? Comment briefly on the company's pro forma condition.

Barland Company, Inc.
Balance Sheet
Year Just Ended

Cash	$ 240
Marketable securities	500
Accounts receivable	5,600
Inventories	8,460
Current assets	$14,800
Gross fixed assets	$ 5,800
Accumulated depreciation	(2,600)
Net fixed assets	$ 3,200
Total assets	$18,000
Accounts payable	$ 4,900
Accruals	3,000
Current liabilities	$ 7,900
Long-term debt	$ 2,500
Common stock	$ 3,000
Retained earnings	4,600
Total equity	$ 7,600
Total liabilities and equity	$18,000

PRO FORMA RETURN ON EQUITY CALCULATIONS

19-26. Versions, Inc.'s financial analyst has projected next year's sales to be $14.4 million with net income of $1 million. The firm's pro forma balance sheet for the end of next year is summarized as follows:

Total assets	$12,000,000
Total debt	$ 8,000,000
Total equity	4,000,000
Total financing	$12,000,000

Calculate expected return on equity for Versions, Inc. by first calculating return on sales, asset turnover, and financial leverage. Show your work.

19-27. The financial officer for Four Star Enterprises projects next year's sales to be $275 million with net income of $3 million. The firm's pro forma balance sheet for the end of next year is summarized as follows:

Total assets	$25,000,000
Total debt	$20,000,000
Total equity	5,000,000
Total financing	$25,000,000

Calculate expected return on equity for Four Star by calculating the product of return on sales, asset turnover, and financial leverage. Show your work. Comment briefly on Four Star's return on equity.

19-28. The manager of Willis' Photos forecasts next year's sales to be $120,000 with net income of $30,000. The firm's pro forma balance sheet for the end of next year is summarized as follows:

Total assets	$100,000
Total debt	$ 20,000
Total equity	80,000
Total financing	$100,000

Calculate expected return on equity for Willis' Photos by multiplying return on sales, asset turnover, and financial leverage. Show your work. Comment briefly on Willis' return on equity.

19-29. A company's return on equity for the current year is 9 percent. Given the following financial data, calculate the company's projected return on sales, asset turnover, financial leverage, and return on equity for the next three years. Comment on your calculations.

PRO FORMA SUMMARIES ($000)

	Years		
	1	2	3
Sales	$180,000	$190,000	$220,000
Assets	40,000	45,000	60,000
Debt	10,000	15,000	20,000
Equity	30,000	30,000	40,000
Profits	3,000	4,000	6,000

19-30. A corporation that manufactures goods for the U.S. Department of Defense has return on equity for the current year of 30 percent. Given the following financial data, calculate the corporation's projected return on sales, asset turnover, financial leverage, and return on equity for each of the next three years. Comment on your results.

PRO FORMA SUMMARIES ($000)

	Years		
	1	2	3
Sales	$120,000	$108,000	$90,000
Assets	30,000	28,000	27,000
Debt	15,000	16,000	16,000
Equity	15,000	12,000	11,000
Profits	4,000	3,000	2,000

THE PRO FORMA CASH FLOW STATEMENT

19-31. Show-Me Corporation's balance sheet for this year and its pro forma balance sheet and income statement for next year follow. Prepare a pro forma cash flow statement using the format in Illustration 19.6 in the chapter.

What is the projected change in cash for next year? Comment on the main sources and uses of funds shown in your pro forma cash flow statement.

SHOW-ME CORPORATION
BALANCE SHEETS

	This Year	Next Year
Cash	$ 5,000	$ 14,800
Accounts receivable	25,000	29,000
Inventories	80,000	92,800
Current assets	$110,000	$136,600
Gross fixed assets	$ 90,000	$ 90,000
Accumulated depreciation	(50,000)	(59,000)
Net fixed assets	$ 40,000	$ 31,000
Total assets	$150,000	$167,600
Accounts payable	$ 20,000	$ 23,200
Accruals	15,000	17,400
Current liabilities	$ 35,000	$ 40,600
Long-term debt	$ 50,000	$ 50,000
Common stock	$ 30,000	$ 30,000
Retained earnings	35,000	47,000
Total equity	$ 65,000	$ 77,000
Total liabilities and equity	$150,000	$167,600

PRO FORMA INCOME STATEMENT
NEXT YEAR

Sales	$285,000
Cost of goods sold*	140,000
Gross profit	$145,000
Operating expenses	115,000
Operating income	$ 30,000
Interest expense	15,000
Taxable income	$ 15,000
Income taxes	3,000
Net Income	$ 12,000

*Includes depreciation of $9,000.

19-32. The balance sheet for the accounting period just ended for April's Company follows along with the pro forma balance sheet for one year from now. Next year's projected net income is $20,000. Annual depreciation charges are 12 percent of gross fixed assets at the end of next year. No sale of common stock is planned during the next year. The treasurer considers $30,000 to be the minimum cash balance, which should be maintained.

From these data, prepare a pro forma cash flow statement for the coming year. Prepare the statement using the format in Illustration 19.6 in the chapter. Comment briefly on this projected statement.

APRIL'S COMPANY
BALANCE SHEET

	This Year	Next Year
Cash	$ 30,000	$ 30,000
Accounts receivable	150,000	187,500
Inventories	120,000	150,000
Current assets	$300,000	$367,500
Gross fixed assets	$130,000	$180,000
Accumulated depreciation	(70,000)	(91,600)
Net fixed assets	$ 60,000	$ 88,400
Total assets	$360,000	$455,900
Accounts payable	$100,000	$120,000
Bank notes payable	0	53,900
Accruals	60,000	72,000
Current liabilities	$160,000	$245,900
Long-term debt	$ 40,000	$ 30,000
Common stock	$ 50,000	$ 50,000
Retained earnings	110,000	130,000
Total equity	$160,000	$180,000
Total liabilities and equity	$360,000	$455,900

19-33. General Plus Company's current balance sheet and its pro forma balance sheet for next year follow. Next year, the treasurer projects $400,000 depreciation, a loss after taxes of $300,000, and debt repayments of $500,000. The board of directors has stated that no cash dividends will be paid next year. The treasurer's policy is to have a minimum cash balance of $100,000 to provide a cushion against unexpected delays in cash inflows.

Prepare a pro forma cash flow statement for next year using the format in Illustration 19.6 in the chapter. Comment on the main cash flows shown in your pro forma cash flow statement.

GENERAL PLUS COMPANY, INC.
BALANCE SHEETS ($000)

	This Year	Next Year
Cash	$ 200	$ 100
Marketable securities	800	
Accounts receivable	6,000	5,700
Inventories	9,000	9,000
Current assets	$16,000	$14,800
Gross fixed assets	$ 7,000	$ 7,000
Accumulated depreciation	(2,600)	(3,000)
Net fixed assets	$ 4,400	$ 4,000
Total assets	$20,400	$18,800

Accounts payable	$ 6,000	$ 5,400
Accruals	2,000	1,800
Current liabilities	$ 8,000	$ 7,200
Long-term debt	$ 2,500	$ 2,000
Common stock	$ 2,000	$ 2,000
Retained earnings	7,900	7,600
Total equity	$ 9,900	$ 9,600
Total liabilities and equity	$20,400	$18,800

LIBRARY ASSIGNMENT

19-34. Using a corporation's balance sheet and income statement for the most recent available year from *Moody's Industrial Manual, Standard & Poor's Corporate Records,* or the company's annual report, prepare a pro forma balance sheet, income statement, and cash flow statement for the next year. Round dollar amounts to the nearest thousand dollars. State your assumptions about changes in sales, net income, depreciation, and balance sheet accounts in your pro forma statements. Comment on the company's forecasted situation as revealed by your projections.

COMPREHENSIVE PROBLEM ▼▼▼▼▼▼▼▼▼▼▼▼▼

19-35. Carol's Coffee Bar, located near the campus, has just completed its third year of operations. The coffee bar was an instant success and is popular with both students and faculty. Cash dividends have been paid annually beginning with the first year. Directors would like to pay a $40,000 cash dividend in year 4 (next year). The manager and the firm's accountant are developing financial projections for the firm's fourth year to present to Carol's banker for a planned expansion by knocking out the wall of a next-door vacant building. In the following problems, assume that the current year's data are for the year just concluded. Round dollar amounts to the nearest thousand dollars and percentages to the nearest tenth of 1 percent unless otherwise specified.

A summary of Carol's Coffee Bar, Inc. financial data since its opening follows:

INCOME STATEMENTS

	Years		
	1	2	3
Sales	$150,000	$195,000	$254,000
Cost of sales	53,000	68,000	89,000
Gross profit	$ 97,000	$127,000	$165,000
Operating expenses	70,000	80,000	90,000
Operating income	$ 27,000	$ 47,000	$ 75,000
Interest expense	1,000	1,000	1,000
Profit before taxes	$ 16,000	$ 46,000	$ 74,000
Taxes	3,000	7,000	14,000
Profit after taxes	$ 13,000	$ 39,000	$ 60,000

BALANCE SHEET
YEAR 3

Cash	$10,000
Accounts receivable	4,000
Inventories	31,000
Current assets	$45,000
Gross fixed assets	$60,000
Accumulated depreciation	(18,000)
Net fixed assets	$42,000
Total assets	$87,000
Accounts payable	$15,000
Accruals	7,000
Current liabilities	$22,000
Long-term bank loan	$10,000
Common stock	$10,000
Retained earnings	45,000
Total equity	$55,000
Total liabilities and equity	$87,000

a. Calculate forecasted sales to the nearest thousand dollars for year 4 if management assumes that sales will increase at the compound growth rate that has occurred over the past two years. (*Hint:* Use Equation 19.4 to determine the compound growth rate in sales.)

b. If management believes that sales will increase in year 4 by 25 percent over year 3, prepare a pro forma income statement for year 4. Use the percent-of-sales technique based on year 3's income statement. Assume that operating expenses will increase by $10,000; that interest expense is $20,000; and that the effective income tax rate is 20 percent.

c. Prepare a pro forma balance sheet for year 4. Assume that the minimum cash balance desired is $10,000. Any cash over $10,000 may be invested in marketable securities. The proposed expansion will require a $220,000 increase in gross fixed assets. Year 4's depreciation is estimated at $12,000 with the expansion. Accounts receivable are projected to rise by 50 percent. Inventories, accounts payable, and accruals will double with this year's expansion. Management is planning that long-term debt will increase to whatever is necessary to provide funding for the expansion and increase in current assets. Hopefully this would occur by the bank increasing its five-year loan.

d. Calculate Carol's return on equity for year 3 and the bar's projected return on equity for year 4 to the nearest whole percentage point. Do this by first calculating return on sales, asset turnover, and financial leverage. Show your work.

e. Prepare a pro forma cash flow statement for year 4 for Carol's Coffee Bar. Use the data given previously and your pro forma income statement and balance sheet for year 4.

f. Comment on your calculations for Carol's Coffee Bar. What significant changes are projected to occur in year 4? If you were the loan officer for the company's bank, how would you react to the request for the increase in the bank's long-term loan? What additional information would you want before making a recommendation to the bank's loan committee?

ST19-1. Use Equation 19.4 to determine the compound growth rate in sales:

$$\text{Sales this year} = \text{Sales nine years ago} \times (1 + g)^9$$
$$\$1,050,000 = \$510,000 \times (1 + g)^9$$
$$2.0588 = (1 + g)^9$$
$$(1 + g) = (2.0588)^{1/9}$$
$$g = 1.0835 - 1.0$$
$$g = 0.0835 \text{ or } 8.4 \text{ percent}$$

$$\text{Sales forecast} = \text{Sales this year} \times 1.084$$
$$\text{Sales forecast} = \$1,050,000 \times 1.084$$
$$= \$1,138,000$$

ST19-2.

ROBERTSON WHOLESALE, INC.
INCOME STATEMENT

	Most Recent Year		Next Year
Net sales	$2,000,000	100.0%	$2,200,000*
Cost of sales	1,060,000	53.0	1,166,000
Gross margin	$ 940,000	47.0	$1,034,000
Operating expenses	600,000	30.0	660,000
Operating income	$ 340,000	17.0	$ 374,000
Interest expense	100,000	5.0	100,000**
Income before taxes	$ 240,000	12.0	$ 274,000
Income taxes (30%)	72,000	3.6	82,200
Net income	$ 168,000	8.4%	$ 191,800

* 10% sales increase over current year.
** Interest assumed to be fixed.

ST19-3.

$$\text{ROE} = \text{Return on sales} \times \text{asset turnover} \times \text{financial leverage}$$

$$= \frac{\$800,000}{\$12,000,000} \times \frac{\$12,000,000}{\$10,000,000} \times \frac{\$10,000,000}{\$6,000,000}$$

$$= 0.0667 \times 1.2 \times 1.6667$$
$$= 0.1334 \text{ or } 13.3 \text{ percent}$$

$$\text{Check: ROE} = \frac{\text{Net income}}{\text{Equity}}$$

$$= \frac{\$800,000}{\$6,000,000}$$

$$= 0.1333 \text{ or } 13.3 \text{ percent}$$

ST19-4.

Wayland Corporation
Pro Forma Cash Flow Statement

Operating activities:	
Profit after taxes	$ 19,000
Depreciation	8,000
Increase in accounts receivable	(3,600)
Increase in inventories	(8,400)
Increase in accounts payable	4,200
Increase in accrued payables	1,200
Cash flow from operations	$ 20,400
Investing activities:	
Capital expenditures	$ (12,000)
Financing activities:	
Dividend payments	$ (7,000)
Equipment loan	12,000
Long-term debt payment	(5,000)
Cash flow from financing	$ 0
Net cash flow	$ 8,400
Beginning cash balance	8,000
Ending cash balance	$ 16,400

The cash account for Wayland Corporation is projected to increase by $8,400 next year. This change was primarily due to cash generated from cash flow from operations. The capital spending for equipment is offset by the loan from the equipment manufacturer. Cash is used for dividend payments and the scheduled payment on the company's long-term debt. If the projected cash balance is more than necessary for operations, excess funds could be temporarily invested in marketable securities, used to pay additional cash dividends, or used to reduce interest-bearing debt. This assumes that the company is current in its payments to suppliers and for various accrued payables.

Video Case 19

Frito-Lay Inventory

This video shows how one company, Frito-Lay, uses new technology to generate and analyze an enormous amount of data, which it then accesses for a variety of planning purposes. The information revolution has helped Frito-Lay more carefully manage its current assets, particularly inventories. Frito-Lay's information system also generates data used in strategic planning, as well as operation and production management. For Frito-Lay information is an important competitive tool. Not only does it reduce costs, it improves the company's ability to plan for the future.

As the video describes, Frito-Lay's information system begins at the store level with the salesperson generating data on sales by brand and location. Interestingly, data on competitors are also collected. The company then aggregates this information by region to examine inventory policies, changes in sales patterns, and the effect of promotions. Many companies would quit here, concentrating their efforts on inventory management. Certainly inventory management is important. According to the video, reducing the quantity of out-of-date snacks saved Frito-Lay $39 million in a single year! Other benefits of state-of-the-art inventory management include reduced stockouts and thus fewer lost sales, and lower storage and spoilage costs at the regional distribution centers.

While inventory management is important, Frito-Lay does much more with the information than just control inventory costs. By combining the data on brands with data from supermarket scanners, it can show store managers that assigning Frito-Lay products more shelf space will benefit the store. Shelf space can determine the success or failure of many grocery store items. Limited shelf space, or space on shelves out of shoppers' normal viewing range, hurts sales. Arguing successfully for additional shelf space almost always results in higher sales.

These data benefit the operation and production areas by allowing Frito-Lay to quickly reroute deliveries to respond to changes in sales and to better determine production plans and material purchases and deliveries. It also helps Frito-Lay evaluate marketing promotions and advertising campaigns. Utilizing the data in so many ways helps Frito-Lay cut costs and increase revenues, which translates into increased shareholder wealth.

Besides using the data to manage inventories and manufacturing, it contributes to Frito-Lay's strategic planning efforts. The quality of a company's long-range strategy depends on the quality of information. Accurate forecasts come from combining good information with an understanding of how the organization's operations interact. The immense amount of information that Frito-Lay collects and analyzes gives it important and early insights about changes in consumer tastes and spending patterns. Using this information Frito-Lay learns what type of products to develop, how to allocate advertising dollars, and, more generally, how resources can best be allocated to benefit the company's shareholders. Planning, strategy, and management all depend on accurate and timely information. Frito-Lay has developed information gathering and processing into a science, which may explain why it can sell $4.5 billion of snacks each year.

Study Questions

1. We usually think of companies as being very secretive, but Frito-Lay shares information with its customers. TQM (total quality management) also recommends information sharing. What types of information do you think companies should and should not share and why?

2. In the long-run will Frito-Lay's intense data collection and analysis strategy continue to be profitable? Why or why not? Be sure to consider what competitors are likely to do.

Glossary

A-B-C system. An *ad hoc* technique of monitoring inventory. *A*-items are high value, *C*-items are low value, and *B*-items fall between.

Accounting profit. Earnings amount derived from accrual accounting practices that correspond with generally accepted accounting principles.

Accounting rate of return. Nondiscounted profitability measure that divides accounting earnings by average investment.

Accounts receivable turnover ratio. Method of monitoring trends in customer payments; higher turnover is considered positive.

Add-on interest. Interest calculated on the amount of funds to be lent and added to loaned amount to determine loan's face value.

Adjustable-rate preferred stock (ARPS). A capital market security that periodically adjusts the dividend amount in the direction of interest rate movements.

Adjusted present value (APV). A value derived by evaluating financing cash flows separate from operating cash flows.

Agent. A person who performs activities for another person, called a *principal*. Managers are agents of the firm.

Aging schedule. Process of classifying accounts by the amount of time they have been outstanding. The schedule usually displays the percentage of receivables that are one month old, two months old, and so on.

American depository receipt (ADR). Receipt issued by bank; represents ownership of foreign company's common stock. The shares of the foreign companies are held in trust.

Amortizing term loan. A loan with serial payments for principal and interest.

Annual clean-up period. Period of time the bank wants the borrower to be free of bank credit or to have the balance below some agreed amount. The purpose is to show the bank that the firm does not need the loan as a source of permanent financing.

Annual operating cash flows. The cash outflows incurred for material, labor, and overhead; excludes all financing costs.

Annual percentage rate (APR). The rate per period times the number of periods per year.

Annual report. The formal financial statement issued yearly by a corporation. The annual report shows assets, liabilities, income, and how the company stood at the close of the business year. It usually also includes other information of interest to shareholders.

Annualized cost of a missed discount (ACD). The cost of foregoing cash discounts and paying at some date beyond the discount period.

Annuity due. A series of equal cash payments occurring at the beginning of each period with equal amounts of time between each payment.

Asked price. The lowest price at which a dealer offers to sell securities—the sell side of the bid-asked spread.

Average collection period (ACP). The amount of time accounts receivable are outstanding; used to evaluate the quality of the investment in accounts receivable.

Balance proportions. An accounts receivable monitoring technique that relates the outstanding balance to the sale that generated the receivable.

Balance sheet. Statement of a firm's financial position on a given date. Shows what the firm owns (its assets), what it owes (its liabilities), and the residual or equity of the owners (the net worth).

Bank discount rate method. Interest calculated on the face amount of the loan. Lender deducts the interest in advance.

Bankruptcy. A legal proceeding to decide whether to liquidate or reorganize a company and the administration thereof.

Bar chart. A graph of a period's high, low, and closing price. The price range is a vertical bar. The close is a short horizontal bar.

Basis point. One hundredth of a percentage point. Used to express changes in interest rates.

Baumol EOQ model. A mathematical model for calculating the optimal cash order size. The model minimizes the total ordering and holding costs.

Bearer bond. A bond issued without a record of the owner's name. Payment is made to whomever holds the bond.

Beta. A measure of a security's nondiversifiable risk; shows the relationship between an individual security's performance and the performance of a market index.

Bid price. The price at which a dealer offers to buy a security.

Bill (T-bill). Short-term (one year or less) security issued by the U.S. Treasury. T-bill is issued at a discount and pays no coupon.

Bond. Long-term (over ten years) security which pays a specified sum (called the principal) either at a future date or periodically over the length of a loan, during which time a fixed rate of interest may be paid on certain dates.

Bond market. Financial market for trading long-term debt instruments issued by firms and governments; bonds represent promises to repay specified amounts at a future time.

Book value of assets. Historical value of the assets adjusted for depreciation of fixed assets and other asset write-downs.

Business organization. An institution that buys material and labor and organizes them to produce and sell goods and services.

Business risk. The risk associated with the returns generated by a firm's assets as if the firm were financed entirely by equity. Risk associated with debt financing is ignored.

Business sector. Part of the economy that consists of units that produce and provide goods and services to households and other businesses.

Buy-and-hold strategy. Investment strategy of buying securities and holding them for a period of time. Opposite of trading in an attempt to sell at each market high and buy at each market low.

Buyout specialists. Organizations that use borrowed funds to buy public firms and privatize them.

Call provision. A feature of the trust indenture of a bond that allows the issuer to repurchase outstanding bonds at a given price from the holders after a given date.

Callable preferred stock. Preferential stock that can be retired by the issuer; unlike equity security, may not have infinite life.

Capital budgeting. Process of identifying, evaluating, and implementing approved capital expenditures.

Capital gain. Increase in value of a security over its original cost.

Capital gains tax. Tax on the excess of proceeds over cost from the sale of capital asset as defined by the Internal Revenue Code. The Tax Reform Act of 1986 made the capital gains tax rate the same as the tax on other income.

Capital investments. Expenditures of a firm for assets, such as plant and equipment.

Capital loss. Decrease in value of a security from its original cost.

Capital market line (CML). The relationship between risk and return in well-diversified portfolios.

Capital market. A market for securities with maturities beyond one year.

Capital rationing. A situation in which new investments are limited to less than those economically justifiable.

Capitalizing cash flows. The process of dividing future cash flow amounts by an interest rate representing the minimum return the cash flows should earn; for example, if future cash flow is $10 per year in perpetuity and the interest rate is 4 percent, the cash flows have a capitalized (economic) value of $10 \div 0.04 = \$250$. Chapter 4 discusses this and other types of calculations to capitalize cash flows.

Cash budget. A schedule of expected cash receipts and disbursements and the borrowing requirements for a given period of time.

Cash conversion cycle. The operating cycle less the accounts payable and accrued liabilities deferral period.

Cash dividend. Cash payment from the firm to its shareholders.

Cash inadequacy. Insufficient cash to meet current obligations.

Causal model. Assumes that the factor to be forecast exhibits a cause-and-effect relationship with a number of other factors.

Certainty equivalent (CE). A technique used to adjust uncertain cash flows downward to a level that the decision maker is indifferent between the risky unadjusted cash flows and the certain adjusted cash flows.

Collateral trust bond. A *bond* secured by pledges of stocks and bonds.

Common-size analysis. Accounting statements expressed as a percentage of net sales or total assets to aid comparison.

Compensating balance. A bank's requirement that the borrower maintain a minimum noninterest-bearing average balance; used to compensate banks for services; borrower pays interest on these balances.

Compound interest. Interest computed on both the principal sum and the interest earned by the principal sum as of a given date.

Compounding. Process by which a given amount is adjusted to yield a future value. Compounding is the opposite of *discounting*.

Concentration bank. A bank to which a company transfers all excess cash balances daily.

Contribution margin proportion. The proportion of each sales dollar left after paying *variable costs;* ratio of (sales – variable costs) ÷ sales.

Convertible bond. A bond that pays fixed interest payments and has a specified maturity, just like an ordinary bond, but differs in that it can be exchanged for a specified number of shares of common stock.

Correlation. Measure of the degree to which two variables move together.

Cost of capital. Minimum market rate of return on new investments required to maintain the value of the firm.

Cost of debt. *Yield to maturity* of the instrument.

Cost of equity. Market rate of return required by investors to hold the company's common stock.

Cost of preferred stock. Preferred stock dividend divided by the market price of the stock.

Covariance. A statistical term used to reflect the extent to which two variables move together. A positive value means that on average, they move in the same direction. The covariance depends not only on the correlation between the two variables but also the *standard deviations* of each variable.

Covenants. Restrictions placed on the borrower requiring specific standards be met, as verified by the trustee.

Credit. Arrangement that allows a customer to take goods or services and delay paying for them.

Credit standards. Criteria used to determine which customers receive credit. Usually encompasses an examination of the customer's credit rating, credit references, outstanding debt, and financial statements.

Credit terms. The payment provisions that are part of a credit arrangement.

Cumulative voting. A voting system in which a shareholder may cast votes equal to the number of shares owned times the number of directors to be elected. The votes may be cast for only one director but in any combination.

Currency risk. The risk that fluctuating exchange rates will adversely affect the investment.

Current assets. Assets that will turn into cash within the normal business cycle.

Current liabilities. Liabilities that are payable within the firm's business cycle.

Current ratio. A measure of liquidity, defined as current assets divided by current liabilities.

Debenture. A debt obligation not secured by specific property but backed by the general credit of the issuing company.

Debt security. Agreement to pay a specified sum (called the principal) either at a future date or over the course of a loan, during which time interest may be paid on certain dates.

Declaration date. The date the firm's directors issue a statement declaring a dividend. The dividend becomes a legally binding obligation of the corporation.

Default (credit) risk. The chance that interest or principal on a debt security will not be paid on a payment date and in the promised amount.

Default risk premium. The premium on a loan charged in case the borrower fails to make a contracted payment.

Defensive interval ratio. A measurement of the number of days of normal cash expenditures covered by quick assets.

Deficit (borrowing) units. Net borrowers, who spend more than they save. The business sector is considered a net deficit unit.

Degree of financial leverage (DFL). The percentage change in net income for a given change in earnings before interest and taxes.

Degree of operating leverage (DOL). The percentage change in earnings before interest and taxes for a given change in sales.

Degree of total leverage (DTL). The percentage change in net income for a given change in sales.

Dependency. The degree of association, or *correlation*, between two variables. Dependency is low for small levels of correlation and high for high levels of correlation.

Depository transfer check (DTC). An instrument used to transfer funds between bank accounts of the same firm. No signature is required. The DTC clears through the normal channels, similar to a check.

Direct send. The check clearing process bypasses at least part of the normal Federal Reserve collection system in an effort to accelerate collection of funds.

Discount. The amount by which a bond (or preferred stock) sells below its par value. The security trades at a discount when the coupon rate is lower than the market rate of interest.

Discount factor. Present value of $1 received at a stated future date.

Discount rate. Interest rate charged to member banks on their loans from the *Federal Reserve Banks*. It is so called because the interest on a loan is discounted when the loan is made, rather than collected when the loan is repaid.

Discounted cash flow analysis. The process of converting future cash flows to their present values. This process is the opposite of *future value analysis*.

Discounted payback period. A discounted cash flow technique that calculates the time it takes to recover the original investment.

Discounting. Process by which a given amount is adjusted at interest to yield a present value. Discounting is the opposite of *compounding*.

Diversifiable risk. The amount of risk that can be eliminated through proper *diversification*.

Diversification. Investing in more than one asset to reduce risk.

Dividend payout ratio. The proportion of earnings paid out in dividends.

Dow Jones Industrial Average. A price index of 30 listed stocks. The price of the stocks is added and divided by a number that adjusts for *stock splits*. An example of a stock split is when a share selling for $90 is split into two shares selling for $45 each.

Duration. A number which summarizes the various factors that affect a bond's price sensitivity to changes in interest rates.

Dutch auction. A process where investors submit bids for securities. The issuer ranks the bids from high to low and sequentially selects those bids that are most advantageous to the issuer.

Earnings available to common shareholders. Net income less dividends paid to preferred shareholders.

EBIT indifference level. The level of earnings before interest and taxes to which management is indifferent between financing alternatives.

Economic returns. Payments to a firm in excess of the economic costs, including normal profit.

Economic system. Relationship between the components of an economy (such as its households, firms, and government) and the institutional framework of laws and customs within which these components operate.

Economic value of assets. The expected value of an asset derived by capitalizing future cash flows at an appropriate interest rate. See *capitalizing cash flows*.

Economic value of cash. The expected return that a firm gives up when it invests in cash rather than in a risk-free security.

Effective annual rate (EAR). The true interest rate that is paid on a loan.

Efficiency ratios. Measures that portray how quickly assets or liabilities are used. The higher an efficiency ratio, the more efficient management is perceived in utilizing the resources committed to the measured activity.

Efficient financial market. Prices for traded securities embody all currently available relevant information. Characteristics of efficient markets include low transaction costs, freely accessible information, many investors, and quick price corrections.

Efficient frontier. The frontier is the boundary line marking off the best risk-and-return combinations available to the investor.

Efficient investment. An investment offering the best expected return for a given risk, or the lowest risk for a given expected return.

Efficient market. Market condition in which prices always fully reflect all available information. Adjustment to new information is virtually instantaneous.

Efficient market hypothesis (EMH). The concept that competition in the financial markets alerts investors to information so that prices adjust almost instantaneously to new information.

Electronic depository transfer check (EDTC). An electronic version of the *DTC*. Funds are transferred by wire.

Electronic wire transfer. A means of effecting the immediate transfer of funds from one bank account to an account at another bank.

EOQ model. A mathematical model for calculating the optimal inventory order size; it minimizes the total ordering and holding costs.

Equilibrium price. Price of a commodity or service determined in the market by the intersection of supply and demand; the price at which the market clears.

Equipment trust certificate (ETC). A bond issued to pay for new equipment; secured by a lien on the purchased equipment.

Equity security. Security which provides ownership in the firm issuing it. The security has no maturity date.

Equivalent annual annuity (EAA). An even cash flow that yields the same present value amount as the project's net present value.

Eurobond. An international debt instrument denominated in a currency different from the currency of the country in which it is sold.

Eurocapital market. An international market for debt and equity securities.

Eurocurrency loans. Loans by commercial banks denominated in currencies other than the currency of the country in which the bank resides.

Eurodollar market. A market for dollar-denominated deposits outside the United States.

Euroequity. An ownership financial instrument denominated in a currency different from the currency of the country in which it is sold.

Excess profits. Returns in excess of profits required to satisfy the investor for the amount of risk involved.

Excess reserves. Quantity of a bank's legal reserves over and above its required reserves. Excess reserves are the key to a bank's lending power.

Ex-dividend date. Date when ownership of the security is without the right to a dividend about to be paid by a firm.

Expected inflation premium. The premium investors require to compensate them for the expected eroding effect of inflation on the value of money.

Expected portfolio return. The weighted arithmetic average of all possible outcomes for the *portfolio,* where the weights are the probabilities that each outcome will occur.

Expected return. The weighted average of all possible outcomes, where the weights are the probabilities that each outcome will occur. It is the expected value or mean of a probability distribution.

Expected return-risk principle. Given the risk exposure, securities are priced to provide investors with a return that compensates for the risk.

External financing requirement (EFR). The amount of funds that must be supplied by creditors or investors to satisfy financing needs.

Factor. A company in the business of buying accounts receivable from other businesses at a discount to their face value.

Factoring. Selling accounts receivable at a discount to a financial institution. The *factor* usually bears the risk of collection.

Favorable financial leverage. Positive effects of debt financing on shareholders' claims on earnings.

Federal funds rate. Interest rate at which banks borrow excess reserves from other banks' accounts at the Fed, usually overnight, to keep required reserves from falling below the legal level. In general, the lower the volume of excess reserves, the higher the federal funds rate. Therefore, the federal funds rate is an important indicator that the Fed watches to decide whether to add to banks' reserves or take away from them.

Federal Reserve Bank (Fed). One of the 12 banks (and branches) which make up the Federal Reserve System. Each serves as a "banker's bank" for the member banks in its district by acting as a source of credit and a depository of resources.

Finance. The study and practice of making money-denominated decisions. As a discipline, finance can be classified into three areas: managerial, investments, and markets and institutions.

Finance subsidiary. A separate legal entity owned by the parent corporation that specializes in financing the company's sales.

Financial assets. Financial instruments with claims on *real assets.*

Financial (capital) lease. A long-term, noncancelable *lease* that has many characteristics of debt. The lease obligation is shown directly on the balance sheet.

Financial intermediaries. Financial institutions that serve as middlemen between lenders and borrowers. They create and issue financial claims against themselves in order to acquire financial claims against others. Examples: banks, savings and loans associations, and pension funds.

Financial intermediation. The process of wholesaling or retailing funds between lenders and borrowers by *financial intermediaries.*

Financial leverage. The effects of debt financing on shareholders' claims on earnings.

Financial leverage ratios. Measures that show how the use of debt affects the firm's ability to repay the obligations.

Financial markets. One of the three areas of finance. Markets of the economy in which both short-term and long-term securities are exchanged.

Financial risk. Variability in the earnings stream of a company that results from the use of debt.

Financial system. The channel through which the savings of surplus sectors flow to the deficit sectors that wish to borrow.

First-in, first-out (FIFO). A method of inventory accounting in which the oldest item in inventory is assumed to be sold first.

Fiscal policy. Deliberate exercise of government's power to tax and spend in order to achieve price stability, help dampen the swings of business cycles, and bring the nation's output and employment to desired levels.

Five C's of credit. An *ad hoc* approach for evaluating credit applicants that looks at the customer's character, capacity, capital, collateral, and conditions.

Fixed-charge coverage ratio. A risk ratio to measure the level of earnings available per dollar of interest, fixed charges, and principal payments. Does not reflect the true cash flows available to meet the obligations.

Fixed cost. A cost that remains relatively constant regardless of the volume of operations. Examples: rent, depreciation, and property taxes.

Fixed income securities. Debt and preferred stock securities which make fixed dollar payments to investors over their lives.

Float. Checks in the process of collection.

Floating-rate preferred. A preferential security whose dividend adjusts periodically to track changing interest rates.

Forward exchange rate. Foreign exchange bought (or sold) at a given time and at a stipulated current or "spot" price, but payable at a future date. By buying or selling forward exchange, importers and exporters can protect themselves against the risks of fluctuations in the current exchange market.

Forward rates. Future interest rates implied by currently available spot interest rates.

Fourth market. Direct trading of securities between institutions without the service of dealers or brokers.

Fractional reserve banking system. The practice of keeping only a fraction of the deposits of depository institutions as cash reserves.

Free reserves. Excess banking reserves minus reserves borrowed from the Federal Reserve by depository institutions.

Funding constraint. A fixed amount of money available for investments aggregating in excess of the amount.

Funds. Any means of payment.

Future value analysis. The determination of the future worth of a series of cash flows. This process is the opposite of discounted cash flow analysis.

Future value formula. The value of $(1 + r)^n$, where r is the interest rate and n is the number of time periods.

Future value of an annuity due. The value at a known future date of a series of constant cash flows for a known number of periods, with the cash flows occurring at the beginning of each period.

Future value annuity factor (FVIFA). The sum of the future value of $1 amounts, using the future value formula, which occurs in periods 1, 2, . . . , n.

General obligation bond (GO). A municipal bond for which the coupon and maturity payments are backed by the "full faith and credit" of the issuing municipality.

Geometric average. The nth root of the product of n observations.

Goodwill. The excess of the purchase price over the assessed value of the *tangible assets* acquired.

Hedge. To take an action to remove or reduce an exposure or a position.

Hedging strategy. The matching of asset and liability cash flows.

Holder-of-record date. The date as of which all shareholders listed in a company's records are noted to receive the declared cash or stock dividend when it is paid.

Holding-period rate of return. Rate of return earned from holding an asset during a given time period.

Horizontal analysis. Common-size analysis that compares the same accounts from year to year.

Household sector. Part of the economy that consists of units that consume and provide funds and labor to business sector. Households purchase goods and services from business sector.

Imperfect competition. A market type in which a large number of firms compete with one another by making similar but slightly different products; there is *asymmetrical information*—not all firms know what other firms are doing.

Income. Revenues for the period minus the costs for the period.

Income statement. Financial statement of a firm showing its revenues, costs, and profit during a given period. Also known as a profit-and-loss statement.

Incremental expense cash flow. Additional cash outflows for expenses that result from accepting a *capital budgeting* project.

Incremental investment. The additional investment the firm will encounter as a result of implementing a new credit policy.

Incremental operating cash costs. The additional cash operating costs that result from the acceptance of a *capital budgeting* project.

Incremental sales. The additional sales that result from the acceptance of a *capital budgeting* project.

Indenture. A contract specifying the legal requirements between the bond issuer and the bond holders.

Independence. No association, or *correlation*, exists between two variables.

Inflation. Rise in the general price level of all goods and services—or equivalently, a decline in the purchasing power of a unit of money (such as the dollar).

Informational signaling. An increase in the dividend signals positive information; a decrease signals negative information.

Insider trading. Process of trading in a company's stock to profit from information that is not available to the public.

Installed cash cost. Cash expenditure to buy, install, and make operative the item proposed by the *capital budgeting* proposal.

Interest coverage ratio. Measures the amount of earnings before interest and taxes available to pay interest. Its shortcoming is that earnings are not cash flow.

Interest rate. The price paid for borrowing money. It is the rate of exchange of present consumption for future consumption, or the price of current dollars in terms of future dollars.

Interest rate parity. An economic principle that holds that the differential in interest rates between countries is the only determinant of the difference between the spot and forward currency rates.

Interim loan. A bridge loan until permanent financing is arranged.

Internal rate of return (IRR). A time value of money technique that finds the interest rate that equates the present value of cash inflows with the present value of cash outflows.

Intraperiod interest rate. The annual interest rate divided by the number of compounding periods within one year.

Intrinsic value. The "real" value that a stock "should" have, based on fundamental factors affecting value.

Inventory turnover. A ratio used to evaluate the number of times average inventory has been sold during the period.

Investment banker. A financial organization that specializes in selling newly issued securities. Investment bankers also advise clients on financial matters, negotiate mergers and takeovers, and sell previously issued securities.

Investment decisions. Decisions pertaining to the selection and diversification of the purchase of assets.

Investment goods. Additions to the economy's real capital stock; that is, all final purchases of capital equipment (machinery, tools), all construction, both residential and nonresidential, and changes in inventory.

Investment grade rating. Bond ratings *BBB* (by S&P) or *Baa* (by Moody's) or above.

Investment opportunity schedule. A graph of the firm's investment projects ranked in order of their rates of return.

Investment tax credit (ITC). A tax deduction, approved by the federal income tax statutes, allowed corporations investing in equipment. Politicians approve it and repeal it depending on what they think is good for the economy.

Investment turnover. The amount of sales that each $1 of investment generates.

Investment-type cash flows. An initial cash outflow followed by positive cash inflows in future periods.

Investments. One of the three areas of finance. It deals with the commitment of funds toward the purchase of securities or assets issued by firms, governments, or individuals.

Irrelevant cash flow. Cash flow that does not change as a result of some specific action.

Judgmental forecast. A nonstatistical technique that relies on the forecaster's experience or best estimate.

Junk bonds. Bonds rated below investment grade—rated *BB* (by S&P) or *Ba* (by Moody's) or below.

Just-in-time (JIT) inventory system. A production and management system in which inventory is cut down to a minimum through adjustments to the time and physical distance between the various production operations.

Last-in, first-out (LIFO). A method of inventory accounting in which the newest item in inventory is assumed to be sold first.

Lease. A contractual agreement between the owner of an asset (lessor) and the user of the asset (lessee), which calls for the lessee to pay the lessor an established lease payment.

Line of credit. Prearranged agreement with a lender for short-term borrowings on demand under prespecified terms. There is no legal commitment on the part of the lender to provide the stated credit.

Liquidation. The termination of the firm. Assets are sold and the proceeds are paid to creditors. Any monies remaining after paying creditors is distributed to shareholders.

Liquidity. A characteristic of a security that refers to its risk, both credit risk and *market risk*, and its marketability. High liquidity requires low risk and high marketability.

Liquidity effect. The fall (rise) in the rate of interest caused by an increase (decrease) in the supply of money balances.

Loan-type cash flows. An initial cash inflow followed by cash outflows in future periods.

Lock box. A post office box address to which credit customers mail payments.

Long-term value index (LVI). The proportion of the stock price that is based on cash flows expected to be received after the first five years.

Majority voting. A voting system in which the number of votes a shareholder may cast for any director may not exceed the number of shares owned.

Managerial finance. One of the three areas of finance. It deals with management decisions relating to obtaining funds and assets for the firm, controlling costs, and managing the firm's cash flows.

Margin of safety. The amount long-term financing exceeds permanent asset investment in current and fixed assets.

Market anomalies. Situations in which the *efficient market hypothesis* is not supported.

Market portfolio. An imaginary *portfolio* that includes all risky assets in proportion to their market value.

Market risk. The risk inherent in the ownership of any security because the market fluctuates. This risk cannot be eliminated.

Market structure indicators. Factors that measure actions of the market in terms of highs and lows, breadth, volume, and strength.

Market timing. Strategy of varying the proportion of certain types of securities in a portfolio depending on where the investor views the market to be at a particular time.

Market value of assets. The value exchanged in an arm's-length transaction between a willing buyer and a willing seller.

Materials requirement planning (MRP). A computerized system for determining inventory requirements and when to place orders.

Maximize shareholders' wealth. The theoretical objective management should follow to increase the long-term value of the company's common stock.

Miller-Orr model. A cash management control limit model that allows irregular cash patterns in order to minimize costs of investing in cash.

Mini-muni. Municipal bond with a par value of less than $1000.

Monetary indicators. Factors that signal monetary changes in the economy which influence stock prices.

Monetary policy. Deliberate exercise of a country's monetary authority's (for example, Federal Reserve's) power to induce expansions or contractions in the money supply in order to help dampen the swings of business cycles and bring the nation's output and employment to desired levels.

Money market. A market for securities with less than one year to maturity. Typical securities are Treasury bills, repurchase agreements, negotiable certificates of deposit, and bankers' acceptances.

Money market preferred stock (MMPS). *Preferred stock* with a short life that trades in the money market.

Money supply. Money is a medium of exchange. The money supply measures the amount of the exchange medium available.

Mortgage bond. A bond secured with a lien on real property.

Multinational firm. A business with investments and operating facilities in more than one country.

Mutual fund. An investment company that issues redeemable shares (sometimes called units) to the public and invests the proceeds in a portfolio of securities.

Mutually exclusive. Either-or decision; take one project or the other.

Net advantage to leasing. The difference between the cost to purchase the asset and the present value of lease payments.

Net cash flow from financing (NCFFF). Shown in the Statement of Cash Flows as cash generated or reduced from the sales or repurchase of securities used to finance the business or the payment of dividends.

Net cash flow from investing (NCFFI). Shown in the Statement of Cash Flows as cash generated or reduced from the sales or purchases of investment in long-term securities or plant and equipment.

Net cash flow from operations (NCFFO). Shown in the Statement of Cash Flows as cash generated or consumed by the productive activities of a firm over a period of time; represents cash profits.

Net present value (NPV). A time value of money technique that nets the present value of cash inflows against the present value of cash outflows.

Net working capital. The excess of current assets over current liabilities. Alternatively, the excess of equity and long-term debt over fixed and other noncurrent assets. As it applies to capital expenditures, it is defined as current assets less noninterest bearing current liabilities that change as a result of a capital budgeting decision.

Net worth. The ownership interests of common and, perhaps, preferred shareholders in a company; on a balance sheet, equity equals total assets less all liabilities.

Neutral financial leverage. The effect of debt financing has no effect on shareholders' claims on earnings.

New York Stock Exchange Composite Index. Value-weighted price index based on all stocks traded on the New York Stock Exchange. *Value-weighted* means the market value of the firm's equity, relative to the aggregate equity market value of all firms traded on the exchange.

No-growth firm. Firm whose investment opportunities simply earn the required market rate.

Nominal interest rate. The observed rate of interest, uncorrected for inflation. *Nominal* means in name only, and thus is likely not the effective rate of interest.

Nonspontaneous financing. Financing that has either an explicit or an implicit cost associated with it.

Note. Medium-term (one to ten years) security. Note holder receives coupon payments.

Odd lot. The quantity of securities that is less than the established unit for trading.

Open market operations. Purchases and sales of government securities by the Federal Reserve System. Purchases of securities are expansionary because they add to commercial banks' reserves; sales of securities are contractionary because they reduce commercial banks' reserves.

Open market purchase. Purchase of shares on the exchanges or in the over-the-counter market without any public announcement.

Operating breakeven sales level. The point at which the firm's operating revenues equal its operating costs. To compute the breakeven point, costs are divided into fixed and variable components.

Operating costs. Expenses incurred in operating a business, excluding all financing expenses.

Operating cycle. The period of time between the acquisition of material, labor, and overhead inputs for production and the collection of sales receipts.

Operating lease. A lease in which the present value of the lease payments is less than 90 percent of the initial cost of the asset; the life of the lease is less than 75 percent of the economic life of the asset; no bargain purchase option exists in the lease; and no transfer of ownership of the lease asset to the user exists.

Operating leverage. The effect of fixed operating costs on earnings when sales revenue changes.

Operating loan. Bank credit used to finance a temporary need for working capital funds.

Operating return on assets. A measure of the productivity of assets on a before tax basis; defined as EBIT ÷ assets.

Ordinary annuity. A stream of cash flows of equal amount occurring at the end of each period for a specified number of periods.

Over-the-counter-market (OTC). Secondary markets conducted by dealers who supply buy-sell quotes on the securities in which they deal. If the securities are listed on an organized exchange, the market is called the *third market.*

Payback period. A nondiscounted cash flow technique that determines the estimated time it takes to recover the original investment.

Payment date. Date company actually mails out dividend checks to stockholders.

Perfect competition. A theoretical state that occurs in markets in which a large number of firms sell an identical product; there are many buyers; there are no restrictions on entry; firms have no advantage over potential new entrants; and all firms and buyers are fully informed about the prices of each and every firm.

Perpetuity. An investment offering a level stream of cash flows with no maturity date.

Point and figure chart. A charting device that records every price change of a certain minimum amount, rather than every price change.

Points. An up-front fee where one point is 1 percent of the value of the loan.

Portfolio. A combination of multiple securities that attempt to obtain the best balance between risk and return.

Portfolio beta. An index representing the undiversifiable risk of a group of stocks formed into a *portfolio.*

Portfolio risk. The variability associated with a collection of securities grouped into a *portfolio.*

Preemptive right. A provision in the corporate charter or in state law that allows the existing stockholders to purchase additional shares of stock before they are offered for sale to the public. This allows existing stockholders to maintain their proportionate ownership in the firm.

Preferred stock. Shares of stock that receive priority over common stock at a fixed rate in the distribution of dividends, or in the distribution of assets if the company is liquidated.

Premium. The amount by which a bond (or preferred stock) sells above its par value. The security trades at a premium when the coupon rate is above the market rate of interest.

Present value annuity factor (PVIFA). The sum of the present value of $1 amounts, using the *present value formula,* which occurs in periods 1, 2, . . ., n.

Present value formula. A formula showing how the current price of an asset is related to its expected future cash flows, through the use of a rate of interest. The formula is $1/(1 + r)^n$ where r is an interest rate and n is time periods.

Present value of an annuity due. The value today of a series of constant cash flows for a known number of periods, with the cash flows occurring at the beginning of each period.

Present value of growth opportunities (PVGO). Projects available to a firm that have an expected return in excess of the firm's required market return.

Primary market. The market in which the initial sale of securities occur.

Principal. An individual who establishes a compensation scheme to motivate an agent to choose activities advantageous to the principal. Shareholders are *principals* of the firm.

Principal. The face (or par) value of a bond that must be repaid at maturity.

Principal-agent problem. The possibility that an *agent* will act in her or his own self-interest to the detriment of the *principal* for whom she or he is acting.

Private placement. A securities issue offering made to institutional investors. The securities are not registered with the Securities and Exchange Commission.

Production opportunities. The diversion of some present wealth into activities which result in increased future wealth.

Profitability index. A discounted cash flow technique that compares the present value of future cash flows to the initial cash outflow.

Prospectus. A legal document provided to potential investors in a new securities issue detailing all pertinent facts concerning the securities to be offered.

Proxy. A document that a stockholder gives to another party for the purpose of voting the shares.

Purchasing power parity. A principle stating that comparable goods should sell for equivalent prices regardless of the currency used to price the goods.

Purchasing power risk. The risk that an investment's principal and income will lose their purchasing power because of *inflation*.

Pure time value of money. Theoretical interest rate on a long-term, riskless loan, where the interest payments are made solely for the use of someone else's money. In practice, this rate is often approximated by the interest rate on long-term negotiable government bonds.

Quick ratio (acid test ratio). A measure of liquidity, defined as cash, marketable securities, and accounts receivable divided by current liabilities.

Range. A crude measure of dispersion defined as the difference between the highest value and the lowest value in a data set.

Rate of return. In a financial framework, it is the interest rate that equates the present value of cash returns on an investment with the present value of the cash expenditures relating to the investment.

Ratio projection method. The historical proportion of cash to sales to estimate the amount of cash that should be held.

Real assets. Land, buildings, plant and equipment, inventories, and consumer durable goods.

Real interest rate. The observable *(nominal)* rate of interest minus the rate of *inflation*.

Recaptured depreciation. The difference between the selling price of a depreciable asset and its net book value, up to the original cost of the asset.

Registered bond. A bond issued with a record name of the owner. Payment is made directly to the registered owner of the bond.

Reinvestment (interest rate) risk. Uncertainty about the rate of return that will be earned by future cash flows from an investment.

Relevant cash flow. Cash flow that changes as a result of some specific action.

Reorganization. A legal process in which all financial claims against the company are settled to reflect the firm's intrinsic value. The firm continues its operations.

Reserve requirements. Minimum amount of legal reserves that a bank is required by law to keep behind its deposit liabilities.

Return on assets. An accounting based ratio showing the profitability of the book value of assets.

Return on beginning equity. An accounting profitability measure, which divides profits by beginning equity shown on the balance sheet.

Return on equity. An accounting based ratio showing the return on the book value of equity.

Return on sales. A measure of the proportion of each sales dollar that is left after meeting all expenses.

Revenue bond. A municipal bond for which the coupon and maturity payments are paid from revenues from a specific revenue-generating project, such as a toll road.

Revolving loan. Legally assured *line of credit* with a bank. Interest charged at one rate for the amount used and at a lower rate for the amount not used.

Risk. Quantitative measurement of an outcome, such as a gain or loss; the chance of an outcome.

Risk aversion. It is a dislike for risk. Higher risk requires higher expected return.

Risk-free rate. The interest rate for an asset that is virtually riskless. For example, debt issued by the government maturing in one year has a precisely predictable rate of return for one year.

Risk premium. The actual return on a security minus the risk-free rate of return.

Round lot. A unit of trading of a security.

S&P 500 Index. A value-weighted price index made up of 500 large companies traded on the New York Stock Exchange. *Value-weighted* means the market value of the firm's equity, relative to the aggregate equity market value of all firms traded on the exchange.

Salvage value. The resale value of an asset.

Salvage value tax adjustment. The calculation of income taxes on an asset that is sold for either more or less than its depreciated book value.

Secondary market. Securities markets that handle transactions in existing securities. Often contrasted with *primary market*.

Secured loan. Financing that is backed by the pledge of some asset. In liquidation, the secured creditor receives the cash from the sale of the pledged asset to the extent of the loan value.

Securitization of accounts receivable. Substitution of tradable financial securities for privately negotiated accounts receivable.

Security interest. A legal term meaning a lender has a secured interest in an asset. Unsecured lenders cannot look to the secured asset for repayment.

Semistrong-form efficiency. Market condition in which current prices not only reflect all informational content of historical prices but also reflect all publicly available knowledge about the firm under study.

Sentiment indicators. Factors that attempt to measure the buying and selling psychology of investors.

Shelf registration. Securities and Exchange Commission Rule 415, which allows companies to register all securities they plan to issue over the following two years. The companies then file short statements when they wish to sell any part of these securities during the period.

Simple discount. The difference between the future value and present value when simple interest is used.

Simple interest. Interest computed by multiplying the original principal by the percent of interest by the time period involved. It is paid when the loan matures.

Specialist. Broker to the brokers.

Sponsored ADR. *ADR* issued by a single depository institution.

Spontaneous asset. An asset that increases or decreases as sales increase or decrease.

Spontaneous financing. Those liabilities such as accounts payable and accrued wages that arise automatically, without negotiation, in the course of doing business.

Spontaneous liability. A liability that increases or decreases as sales increase or decrease.

Spot exchange rate. The rate at which one currency can be converted into another, or the price of one currency in terms of another. For example, if the price of the German mark were $0.25 per mark, it would require $0.25 to purchase one mark or four marks to purchase $1.

Spread. In *underwriting,* the difference between the price that the underwriter pays the company for the new securities and the price at which the securities are sold to the public or are privately placed.

Stakeholders. Claimants on cash flows of the firm.

Standard deviation. A statistic used to measure dispersion about an expected value. A high (low) standard deviation is associated with high (low) risk. It is the square root of the variance.

Standby credit. A *term loan* that matures at the expiration date of the loan. It cannot be paid down and reused again without being renegotiated.

Statement of cash flows. An accounting statement that traces the sources and uses of cash as a result of organizational activity.

Stock dividend. A dividend paid in securities rather than cash.

Stock exchange. A physical location where securities trade like at an auction. Securities are always bought by the highest bidders and sold by the lowest offerers.

Stock market. The financial market for trading claims (shares) of a firm.

Stock split. The division of a corporation's outstanding shares into a larger number of shares.

Straight bond value. That component of a callable bond that acts like an ordinary bond.

Strategic decisions. The set of decisions resulting in the formulation and implementation of strategies, or plans, designed to achieve the objectives of the organization.

Stretching accounts payable. Failing to pay within the prescribed trade credit period.

Strong-form efficiency. Market condition in which no information that is available, be it public or private, can be used to earn superior investment returns consistently.

Sunk costs. Cash flow expended in the past.

Surplus (saving) units. Net savers, who save more than they spend. The *household sector* is considered a net surplus sector.

Sustainable growth. Growth the firm can maintain over time given its dividend policy, financing policy, asset management performance, and profitability of sales.

Tactical decisions. The set of decisions designed to carry out daily activities so as to meet strategic objectives.

Tangible assets. Physical assets such as plant and equipment.

Tax-loss carryovers. Taxable losses carried forward into future years to offset tax liability of those years.

Tender offer. A publicly announced offer to buy the stock of a firm directly from its shareholders.

Term loan. A loan with a maturity greater than one year.

Term structure of interest rates. The relationship between yield and time to maturity of a debt security.

Terminal nonoperating cash flows. Cash flow occurring at the end of the investment's life; included are *salvage value,* taxes on sale of asset, and liquidation of all net working capital associated with the investment.

Terminal value. The value of cash flows compounded forward to some later time at an appropriate interest rate.

Third market. Over-the-counter trading of securities that are listed on organized exchanges.

Time deposit. Bank accounts and other deposits that earn a higher interest than savings accounts but which must be left on deposit for a specified period of time (their maturity).

Time preference rate. Human desire for a good in the present as opposed to the future. The rate is reflected by the price people are willing to pay for immediate possession of the good, as opposed to the price they are willing to pay for future possession.

Time value of money. A principle stating that dollars at different points in time can only be directly compared when they are first adjusted by the interest rate representing the opportunity cost of money.

Timeliness. Indicator used by Value Lines Investment Services to signify the potential price changes in stocks.

Total debt-to-equity ratio. A measure of financial leverage risk, defined as total debt divided by shareholders' equity.

Total risk. Diversifiable risk + nondiversifiable risk.

Trades on the equity. The use of debt to increase the expected return on equity.

Trading. The buying and selling of securities to take advantage of price swings.

Trading post. Place on the exchange floor where a company's stock trades.

Treasury stock. Common stock that has been repurchased by the company that originally issued it.

Trend analysis. A variable of interest is analyzed against time.

Treynor index. A measure of reward per unit of risk. It indicates the rate of return on the market index required to make the expected rate of return on a portfolio equal to the risk-free rate.

Underwriting. A guarantee by investment banking firms to an issuing corporation that a definable sum of money will be paid on a specified date for the issue of stocks or bonds.

Unfavorable financial leverage. Negative effects of debt financing on shareholders' claims on earnings.

Unlevered firm. A firm financed entirely with equity financing.

Unsecured loan. Financing that requires no assets as collateral but allows the lender a general claim against the borrower, rather than a lien against specific assets.

Unsponsored ADR. *ADR* issued by more than one depository institution.

Valuation. The worth of an economic asset.

Value of unlevered firm. Value of a firm that is financed entirely with equity.

Variable cost. A cost that moves directly with a firm's output, rising as output increases over a full range of production. Examples: Raw materials and sales commissions.

Variance. A statistic that measures dispersion about the expected value. A high (low) variance is associated with high (low) risk. It is the *standard deviation* squared.

Vertical analysis. Common-size analysis that compares accounts in the income statement to net sales and amounts in the balance sheet to total assets.

Weak-form efficiency. Market condition in which current prices reflect all information that is contained in the historical sequence of prices.

Weighted average cost of capital. The minimum rate of return that is acceptable on new nonrisk changing investments in order to maintain the value of the firm.

Window dressing. Making financial statements appear more favorable than they really are.

Yankee bond. A foreign bond denominated in U.S. dollars.

Yield curve. A pictorial representation of the *term structure of interest rates.*

Yield to maturity (YTM). Percentage figure reflecting the effective yield on a bond, based on the difference between its purchase and redemption prices, and any returns received by the bondholder in the interim.

Zero balance account (ZBA). A demand deposit account that has a zero balance at the end of the day. Checks presented against the account are covered by funds transferred from another account.

Zero coupon security. A note or bond that earns no annual interest payments. The difference between the purchase price and the par value at maturity represents interest to the holder.

Answer Key

CHAPTER 2:

2-31. a. $500
c. −$390
e. $250
g. −$200
i. $370

2-32. b. $50
d. $1500
f. −$40
h. $0
j. −$15

CHAPTER 3:

3-3. a. Time-preference of consumption
c. No

3-4. Consumption would change.

3-5. Rate of return: A = 10%, B = 20%,
C = 18.75%, D = 15%.

3-6. a. Accept projects B, C, and D.
b. Borrow to invest in all acceptable projects.

3-7. a. $32.57
b. $0
c. $30
d. $33.60
e. Better

3-8. a. B and D

b. $4,636,364 in total
c. $636,364

3-9. Maximum consumption this period:
$40,370; next period: $43,600.

3-10. Consumption today of $30,000 means
consumption next period of $11,200.

3-11. Rate = 25%

3-12. No, fails to earn market interest rate.

3-13. Consumption next period: $29,830.

3-14. a. Consume this period: $45,436
b. Borrow this period: $24,636
c. Consume next period: $0

3-16. Year 5: inflation = 8.7%, real rate = 3.04%

3-17. a. 9.18%
b. 9.14%
c. 11.24%
d. 31.44%
e. 2.88%
f. 3.59%

3-18. a. 11%
b. 4%

3-19. a. Moderate changes in business cycle;
maintain price stability

3-20. Open market operations; direct impact on
reserves

3-21. Banks must meet reserve requirements

805

3-22. a. Expansion = $83,333

3-23. a. No, $1 billion reserve deficiency
b. $1 billion; no effects
c. $10 billion; decrease $10 billion

3-24. After three transactions: $3,532.80; in total: $23,000

3-25. a. & b. Increase of $10 million
c. Expand $83.33 million

3-26. a. Reserves decrease $30 million; money supply decreases $300 million

3-27. Money supply decreases $4.545 billion

3-28. a. March's free reserves = $1105
b. Easy monetary policy

3-29. a. December's free reserves = –$540
b. Tight monetary policy

3-30. a. 24%
b. Low interest rate moves security prices up

3-34. a. Incentive to invest
b. Broaden range of opportunities
c. Investors borrow and lend at market rate
d. Loan to Howard; $240.38
e. Borrow against future cash inflows
f. Packard investment: 5.34%

3A-1. $2.77

3A-2. $251.96; pay in dollars

3A-3. 129.4 yen/dollar

3A-4. a. $0.00788
b. Yen: 1,583,856; dollars: $12,480
c. 126.91 yen/dollar

3A-5. a. Forward rates less than spot rates
b. U.S. dollar expected to weaken in future
c. Yen and Swiss franc at a discount
d. Weakened: Canadian dollar, New Zealand dollar, South African rand; strengthened: British pound, German mark; no change: Hong Kong dollar

3A-6. b. 1.49655 francs per dollar
c. Forward premium

CHAPTER 4:

4-1. a. $10,600
b. $11,200
c. $14,150.94
d. $11,538.46

4-2. $3000

4-3. $2.81

4-4. 7.5%

4-5. $12,000

4-6. 80%

4-7. a. $1190
b. $2380

4-8. a. $10,600
b. $11,236
c. $14,150.94
d. $11,208.87

4-9. a. 0.3759
b. 6%
c. 17%
d. 2.7731
e. 11.1111
f. Discount factor: 5.1317; present value amount: $5131.70; future value amount: $15,415.71
g. 16%
h. 0.0611
i. PV factor for $200 payments: 11.4699; PV of payments: $2293.98
j. FV factor for $200 payments: 36.7856; FV of payments: $7357.12
k. PV factor for receipts: 5.1968; PV of receipts: $1039.36

4-10. a. $0.3759
b. Factor = 0.89
c. 17%
d. 2.7731
e. 11.0140 (from Table)
f. 5.1317
g. 16%
h. 0.0611

4-11. a. $5157.07
b. $3157.07

4-12. a. $1650
b. $1996.50
c. $2415.75

4-13. $726.50

4-14. a. $17,865.24
b. 1.1910

4-15. Promise is worth $2222.22. No.

4-16. $1111.11

4-17. a. 5.06%

b. 11.46%

c. 17.35%

4-18. 7.72%

4-19. 12% (10.8% if you round too soon)

4-20. a. $712.74

b. $744.09

4-21. a. 0.8163; 0.7664

b. 1.2250; 1.3048

c. 2.6243; 7.7861

d. 3.2149; 10.1591

4-22. a. $30,744.90

b. $57,844.36

c. $132,877.70

d. $250,000

e. $32,282.15

4-23. $2569.68

4-24. $26,080.09

4-25. 10%

4-26. $4951.98

4-27. Yes, present value = $1,306,578.21

4-28. Borrow: $1750.34; factor: 3.8897

4-29. a. $11,274.19

b. $11,950.64

4-30. $11,505.54

4-31. $5640.24

4-32. a. $399,270.20

b. $885,185.20

c. $973,703.72

4-33. 19.5%

4-34. a. 8.5%

b. $5862.07

4-35. $113.33

4-36. $119.23

4-38. a. $48,000

b. $552,000

c. $652,173.91

4-39. a. $150,000

b. $1,850,000

c. $2,162,162.16

4-40. a. $2480

b. $2382.03

c. $2391.24

d. $2187.31

e. $544.51

4-41. a. $1649.95

b. $443.84

c. Four payments of $443.84 each

d. 12.196%

e. 1.178% monthly or 15.09% annually

f. $148.91

g. 8.16%

4-42. $57,238

CHAPTER 5:

5-1. 12.5%

5-2. 19%

5-3. $217.94

5-4. a. 7.5%

b. 13.3%

5-5. Expected return = 0.15833%; variance = 10.7526; standard deviation = 3.279%

5-6. Expected return = .166; variance = 0.0140; standard deviation = 0.1183

5-7. Expected value = $21.75; standard deviation = $7.68

5-8. a. Expected return = 10%; variance = 36% squared; standard deviation = 6%

b. Expected return = 8%; variance = 5% squared; standard deviation = 2.236%

c. Risk-to-reward ratio favors GE

5-9. a. 2.4 risk-to-reward ratio

5-10. 10.7%

5-11. a. Highly risk averse

b. Less risk averse

c. Risk seeking

d. Most likely risk averse

5-12. a. $1080

b. 10.8%

5-13. a. $5616

b. 15.4%

5-14. Perfectly and positively correlated

5-15. b.

Nos.	Variances	Covariances
1	1	0
2	2	1
3	3	3
10	10	45
100	100	4950
1000	1000	499,500

5-16. Expected return = 0.125; correlation has no effect on return. Variance = 0.0756 if correlation = 1; 0.0406 if correlation = 0; 0.0056 if correlation = −1

5-17. Variance = 0.0125 if correlation = 1; 0.0095 if correlation = 0.5; 0.0064 if correlation = 0

5-18.

	Stanford	Berkeley
Expected return	0.0800	0.1100
Variance	0.0216	0.0189
Standard deviation	0.1470	0.1375
Covariance	0.0162	

5-19.

	Portfolio			
	1	2	3	4
Expected return	0.20	0.125	0.115	0.075
Standard deviation	0.30	0.014	0.057	0.225

5-20.

	Security C	Security D
a. Expected return	0.07	0.0575
b. Variance	0.027	0.0147
c. Portfolio expected return = 0.0638		
d. Portfolio variance = 0.01939		

5-21. a. 13.67%
b. 6.6%

5-22. a. 0.1275
b. Variance = 0.028625

5-23.

	A	B	C
a. Expected return	5.4%	4.4%	4.7%
b. Variance	31.14	5.84	7.11
c. Correlation: A & B = 0.8729;			
A & C = −0.9395; B & C = −0.8815			

5-24. Yes, 20% in Contrarian and 80% in Optimistic.

5-25. a. Beta represents nondiversifiable risk
b. No.
c. No; fails to diversify diversifiable risk
d. Not likely.

5-26. 15% decrease

5-27. 7% decline

5-28. a. 6% increase
b. Portfolio value falls

5-29. a. 1.025

5-30. Beta = 1.71

5-31. a. 16%
b. 1.0667

5-32. a. 1.0725
b. 7.0

5-33. a. Aggressive = 7.6; Moderate = 8.5
b. Moderate provides superior returns

5-34. Fidelity = 12.5; Janus = 26; Vanguard = 18.8

5-40.

	T-bills	Market	Gate Co.	Central
a.	4%	8.45%	9%	7.7%
b.	0	5.617	9.198	1.453
c.	0	0.665	1.022	0.189
d. Beta = 0.775; return = 7.2875%				
e. Beta = 1.08; return = 8.48%				
f. Treynor (d) = 4.24; Treynor (e) = 4.15				
g. 4.02%				

CHAPTER 6:

6-1. When securities desired by savers are not the same as lenders want to issue

6-3. Increase liquidity; provide knowledge and diversification

6-5. Money markets mature in less than one year

6-6. Money is fluid; tied by continuity of instruments

6-7. Dollar-denominated deposits outside the U.S.; higher risk

6-9. Act as dealers and brokers

6-10. a. To avoid risk of selling the stock
b. Company willing to assume risk

6-11. a. Stockholders of company
b. Comparable risky firms

6-12. Preliminary prospectus

6-14. Rights have value

6-15. a. Secondary; 2nd
b. Primary
c. Primary
d. Secondary; 3rd
e. Secondary; 4th
f. Secondary; 1st

6-17. a. Provide centralized markets, among other factors
b. Banks, S&L, insurance companies, pension plans, REITs
c. Match savers and users; provide liquidity
d. Money market is short-term
e. Primary market is for issuing new securities
f. Perform specialized financial services
g. Shelf registrations, rights offerings, private placements
h. Provide liquidity
i. First, second, third, and fourth markets

Chapter 7:

7-1. a. Unconditional promise to pay; fixed maturity; market interest rate; debtholders have insignificant equity holdings
      b. Debt interest is tax deductible

7-2. Debenture is unsecured

7-6. $4,554,000

7-7. $5,280,000

7-8. Taxes paid with debt financing: $3,757,740; without debt financing: $4,356,800

7-9. a. After-tax income: Johnson $26,772; Roberts $22,425
      b. Effective tax rate: Johnson 46.46%; Roberts 55.15%

7-12. Price moves with interest rates; rating services interested in default risk

7-19. Allow individuals to buy U.S. treasury securities directly

7-20. Exempt from state and local taxes.

7-25. Inadequate cash flows

7-26. a. 6.67%
      b. 8.33%
      c. 8.96%

7-27. 7.879%

Chapter 8

8-1. a. Annual interest = $83.75
      b. 8.05%

8-2. a. 9.98%
      b. 18.39%
      c. 2.10%

8-3. a. Year 0: 7.29%; year 2: 7.11%
      b. HPR_1: 8.33%; HPR_3: 8.63%
      c. HPR_{0-2}: 17.19%; HPR_{1-3}: 17.53%

8-4. YTM = 5.347%

8-5. YTM = 12.838%

8-6. 12.68%

8-7. 9.76%

8-8. 5.625%

8-9. 9.859%

8-10. Interest rate increased; rate of default increased

8-11. a. 5%
      b. $50

8-12. $902.78

8-13. a.

	Maturity	
	5 years	30 years
4%	$1089.04	$1345.82
8%	920.16	774.87
12%	783.69	516.71
16%	672.56	382.23
20%	581.34	302.93

      b. 6%
      c. Longer maturity bond

8-14. a. 4%: $1156.22; 6%: $872.17; 8%: $679.76
      b. 4%: $1009.62; 6%: $990.57; 8%: 972.22
      c. 25-year bond is riskier.

8-15. a. 10%
      b. Year 3 forward rate = 12%; YTM over years 2 and 3: 11%

8-16. a. 9%
      b. 11.04%

8-18. Shortest duration is bond #4

8-19. a. 2.78 years
      b. Duration increases

8-20. a. 1.582 years
      b. −1.46%
      c. −1.44%

8-21. −0.97%

8-22. a. One-year bond: 75.65%; two-year bond: 8%
      b. Duration equals maturity
      c. 11.84%
      d. 10%
      e. 1.91 years

8-23. a. 20.41
      b. $19.23
      c. $908.25
      d. $29.40
      e. Not possible
      f. $15.68
      g. 10.1%
      h. $1030

8-24. a. $1125
      b. Investors believe bond will be converted
      c. Yes; price falls to the conversion price

8-25. a. $750
      b. $240

c. Current yield > coupon rate
d. Current yield = 5.71%; IRR = 20%; YTM approximation = 19.09%

8-26. a. $64
 b. $16 gain

8-27. a. $83.33
 b. Unlikely
 c. Likely

8-28. Between 18% and 19% (18.63%)

8-29. a. 3%
 b. $50

8-31. a. Current yield = 6.66%; AYTM = 5.97%;
 YTM = 6%
 b. $1104.14
 c. 3.53 years
 d. $25.55
 e. 8.216%

CHAPTER 9:

9-3. a. June 28
 b. No change in rate of return

9-6. $66.67

9-9. a. Cash outlay = $5130
 b. Cash inflow = $4861

9-10. a. Limit order
 b. Stop-loss order
 c. All-or-nothing order

9-11. a. 0.674%
 b. 19.55%

9-12. −3.3%

9-13. a. 1189 shares
 b. 13.5%

9-16. Company 1: $ 5.59; Company 2: $ 8.33;
 Company 3: $15.00; Company 4: $21.96

9-17. a. $39.375
 b. Undervalued relative to intrinsic value

9-18. 2.33%

9-19. a. $49.57
 b. 8.95%

9-20. a. Before: $10.60; After: $19.85
 b. Year 1: sell 10 shares; year 2: sell 9
 shares; year 3: sell 8 shares

9-21. a. $24.58
 b. $24.89
 c. No

9-22. $36.60

9-23. a. $173.636 million
 b. $39.825 million

9-24. a. $5.25
 b. $35.57
 d. $31.26
 e. 4.4%
 f. $32.75

9-25. a. $44.61
 b. $70.82

9-26. a. Price declines $2
 b. Price declines 10%

9-27. a. $0.50
 b. Price declines 5%

9-30. a. Budget of $15 million: $7 million
 dividends
 b. Budget of 19.6 million: $2.4 million
 dividends

9-31. a. Year 7: $3
 b. Year 1: Regular $1; extra $1

9-40. a. Ex-date: October 24
 b. October 21
 c. $20.17
 d. $104.40
 e. No gain or loss unless signaling happens
 f. Price increases if signaling happens

CHAPTER 10:

10-1. Consensus of opinion

10-2. No

10-3. Weak, semistrong, and strong forms

10-4. Numerous well-informed investors seeking
 profits

10-5. No

10-6. No

10-9. Search out information for pricing securities

10-10. Analysts contribute to making markets
 efficient

10-11. Should encourage

10-12. Past history

10-13. a. Not clear he is able to beat the market
 b. Not consistent with weak-form
 c. Not consistent with weak-form

10-14. Returns higher in January

10-15. a. Needs further testing
 b. Appears to beat the market

10-16. a. Semistrong form violated
 b. Bizarre rule

c. Semistrong form not contradicted; strong form is

10-17. Why bother being an analyst

10-19. a.

	Semistrong		Strong	
	State	West	State	West
Day 2	$2.00	$3.00	$3.00	$3.20
Day 4	3.00	2.67	3.00	3.20
Day 10	3.00	3.20	3.00	3.20
b. Day 2	$2.00	$3.00	$3.15	$3.15
Day 4	2.75	2.75	3.15	3.15
Day 10	3.15	3.15	3.15	3.15

10-24. a. Ignores transaction costs
b. Must use out-of-sample data to test
c. Failure to adjust for risk
d. Questionable fit.
e. Failure to account for dividends

CHAPTER 11:

11-5. $38 million

11-6. $16,250,000

11-7. $611 million

11-8. $2.628628 billion

11-9. a. Decline
b. Corporate rate fell, investor rate increased, or a combination
c. Increase in market interest rate

11-10. $168 million

11-11. $16.875 million

11-12. New market value = $3.2 million; old market value = $2.1333 million

11-13. a. 75%
b. $24 million; decreases
c. Assets earn less than market rate

11-14. 4%: $0.333; 12%: $1.00; 20%: $1.67

11-15. Value destroyed for 9% and 12%; value created for 18% and 21%

11-16. Decrease in firm value

11-17. Before: $5 million; after: $1 million

11-18. $35 million; increase

11-19. 40%

11-20. $20 million

11-21. $418.75 million

11-22. $18 million

11-23. 6.67%

11-24. $233,333

11-25. $3.91 million

11-26. $800,000

11-27. $914,286

11-28. $144,000

11-29. $1,866,667

11-30. $36,000

11-31. a. $7.875 million
b. Market rate > coupon rate

11-32. a. $28.33
b. $122.18
c. $382.50

11-33. a. $83,333
b. $58,333
c. Unlevered: $55,000; Levered: $38,500 equity and $63,500 firm

11-34. a. $13.60
b. $166.40

11-35. a. $106,061
b. $568,000
c. $368,000
d. Before: $100; After: $122.67
e. Before: 7.14; After: 6.19

11-36. a. Value of equity: $1,604,000
b. Value of equity: $1,643,600

11-37. a. $80.67
b. $75.04
c. $59.91

11-38. a. 4%
b. Value of firm: $5,340,000

11-39. a. Unlevered: $30 million; Levered: $34 million
b. $7.5 million for both firms
c. EPS unlevered: $1.50; EPS levered: $1.95

11-40. a. $100
b. $540
c. Before: $694; After: $586

11-41. a. $125 million
b. 19.6%
c. $18 million
d. $31.92

11-45. e. $191 million
g. $150 million
h. New value: $20 million; –$10 million decrease
i. Decline in firm value

j. $40 million

k. 15%

l. Annual tax savings: $324,000; PVTS = $3.6 million

m. $26 million

n. $12,727,273

Chapter 12:

12-1. 3.96%

12-2. 6.75%

12-3. 5.8%

12-4. 7.7%

12-5. 8%

12-6. 10.84%

12-7. RJR Nabisco is riskier

12-8. 12.5%

12-9. 12.36%

12-10. 13.25%

12-11. 13.4%

12-12. 15%

12-13. No

12-14. a. 15.79%
b. 16.58%

12-15. a. Firm 1 = 8.5%; Firm 3 = 13%; Firm 5 = 20.5%
b. Direct relationship

12-16. 18%

12-17. 2.0

12-18. 9%

12-19. 12.24%

12-20. 9.64%

12-21. 13.11%

12-22. 9.04%

12-23. 12.41%

12-24. 12.2%

12-25. a. 0%: 20%; 20%: 18.2%; 40%: 16.4%; 50%: 15.5%; 60%: 14.6%

12-26. a. Unlevered: $30 million; Levered: $34 million
b. $7.5 million for both firms
c. Unlevered: $4.5 million; Levered: $3.9 million

d. Cost of equity: 15% unlevered; 16.25% levered; WACC: 15% unlevered; 13.235 levered

12-27. a. $100
b. $540
c. Before: $694; After: $586
d. Before: 9.51%; After: 9.22%

12-28. a. $125 million
b. 19.6%
c. $18 million
d. $31.92
e. 25%
f. 17.133%

12-29. a. 36.9%
b. 15.48%

12-30. a. 23.3%
b. $8.4 million
c. 20.833%

12-31. No

12-32. a. $9 million
b. Debt: $9 million; equity: $7,349,845

12-33.

	Proportion of equity			
	100%	75%	50%	25%
Firm ($mill.)	$4.95	$5.29	$5.63	$5.97
Cost of capital	12.0%	11.2%	10.6%	9.9%

12-36. a. 5.94%
b. 8.4%
c. 17%
d. 13.928%
e. 13.9%

Chapter 13:

13-1. No, bankruptcy is costly

13-2. a. 2.50
b. 0.877

13-3. a. 4.00
b. 1.04

13-4. a. 3.70
b. 1.92

13-5. a. 8.00
b. 2.33

13-7. $2,280,000 taxes paid over 10 years

13-8. $1,650,000 taxes paid over 10 years

13-9. $2,190,000 taxes paid over 10 years

13-10. $840,000 taxes paid over 10 years

13-11. $300,000 taxes paid over 10 years

13-17. a. Company A: ROE = 8.125%; Company B: ROE = 8.883%; Both firms: ROA = 8.125%

13-18. a. Company C: ROE = 4.2%; Company D: ROE = 2.333%; Both firms: ROA = 4.2%

13-19. a. Both firms: ROA = ROE = 6%

13-20. ROE = 22.78%; ROA = 10.69%

13-21. 9.84%

13-22. 8.94%

13-23. a. $3,300,000
b. $1,166,667

13-24. a. Alternative A: ROA = 4.4%; ROE = 3.96%; Alternative B: ROA = 4.4%; ROE = 4.4%
b. Alternative A: ROA = 8.8%; ROE = 10.56%; Alternative B: ROA = 8.8%; ROE = 8.8%
c. $48,000

13-25. a. Net income = $11,715,000; ROA = 13.2%; ROE = 15.62%
b. Net income = $9,842,250; ROA = 13.2%; ROE = 21.87%
d. Yes; yes

13-26. a. $9,343,750
b. Capital structures A and B: ROA = 6.167%; ROE = 6.243%

13-27. a. $964,750

13-28. a. 0.333 debt-equity = 15.62%; 4 debt-equity = 13.2%
b. About 1.5
c. 4
d. Greater than 4

13-29. 25% debt = 16.18%; 66.7% debt = 19.82%; 150% = 27.08%; 400% debt = 48.88%

13-31. a. EBIT = $100,000; Net income = $28,000
b. 2
c. 2.5
d. 5

13-32. a. 3
b. 1.714
c. 5.14
d. $105,000
e. 75%

13-33. a. 1.1429
b. 1.3750
c. 1.5715

13-34. a. $274,560
b. DFL = 1.12; DOL = 1.32; DTL = 1.48
c. Risk decreases

13-35. a. $258,060
b. DFL = 1.14; DOL = 1.38; DTL = 1.58
c. Higher interest expense and fixed costs
d. DFL = 1.018; DOL = 0.958; DTL = 0.976

13-38. a. Interest coverage = 6.25; fixed charge coverage = 1.333
b. $1.2 million
c. ROA = 17.5%; ROE = 24.5%
d. 7 percentage points
e. DOL = 2.4; DFL = 1.19; DTL = 2.86

CHAPTER 14:

14-1. a. 10.5%
b. 16%

14-2. a. 33.3%
b. 10%

14-3. 36%

14-4. 6%

14-5. 1.5

14-6. 3

14-8. a. −$2138; reject
b. $1434.40; accept
c. $0.21; accept since it satisfies cost of capital

14-9. $9258; accept

14-10. $220; accept

14-13. Accept NIT = 11.2%; reject NAT = 28.8%

14-14. A = 12.3% – reject; B = 14.4% – reject; C = 18.6% – reject

14-15. $289; accept

14-16. a. $18,967; accept
b. −$50; reject
c. Neither may be

14-17. IRR

14-18. 10%; accept

14-19. IRR = 15%; accept

14-20. 1.104

14-21. 1.2; accept

14-22. a. #3,#2,#1
b. Project #2 if surplus can't earn more than $29

14-23. Not a wealth maximizing technique

14-24. a. 20%
b. Time value of money; profits and not cash flows

14-25. a. 2.5 years

14-26. a. 3.19 years

14-27. Payback = 5.67 years; discounted payback = 8.3 years

14-28. a. Project 1: 0% = $4000; 20% = –$939;
Project 2: 5% = –$2411; 10% = –$1095
b. Project 1: 5% = 1.24; 10% = 1.11;
Project 2: 0% = 0.60; 20% = 1.09
d. Project 2

14-29. a. 32%
b. $23,450; accept
c. IRR = 22.6%

14-30. a. 5.65 years
b. 12%

14-31. Rankings

	A	B	C	D
Payback	1	2	3	4
Discounted payback	4	1	2	3
ARR	4	1	2	2
NPV	4	3	1	2
IRR	4	2	1	3

14-32. a. NPV B = $19,527; NPV C = $9949;
IRR B = 28%; IRR C = 25%
b. NPV of B – C = $9582; invest in B

14-33. NPV of #1 – #2 = $6330; invest in #1

14-34. Alpha = $212,496; Beta = $223,600; select Beta

14-35. b. #1 = $9505; #2 = $10,368
c. PV #1 = $5627; PV #2 = $6138

14-36. a. A = $16,059; B = $17,205
b. A = 18%; B = 16%
d. B is preferred at low rates; A preferred at high rates.

14-37. a. $94,800
b. 10% = $148,421; 25% = $36,114; 40% = –$26,562
c. About 33%

14-38. b. Find cost of capital and discount cash flows

14-39. a. Project A and B
b. Accept F, replace D with E

14-40. a. Accept all positive NPVs
b. B, D, E, F, and G

14-42. a. 16.2%
b. 20% payout
e. NPV = $9405, accept
f. 15%
g. 2.5 years
i. All projects with NPV > 0
j. Chi, Kappa, Sigma, and Psi

14A-1. a. –$84,000
b. $80,000
c. –$4000

14A-2. a. –$87
b. –$71

14A-3. $240

CHAPTER 15:

15-1. Relevant flows: $100,000 expenditure & $125,000 revenues

15-2. As in Problem 15-1 plus $30,000 R&D

15-3. –$63,000

15-4. Recapture = $160,000; capital gain = $50,000

15-5. Total tax outflow = $57,000

15-6. a. Total tax liability = $32,500
b. IRS owes $10,500

15-7. a. –$12,369,200
b. Outflow reduced $400,000

15-8. –$1,577,500

15-9. –$271,000

15-10. $18,600

15-11. $23,500

15-12. $11,500

15-13. a. System #2
b. EAA #1 = $1599; EAA #2 = $734
c. System #2

15-14. EAA 4S4 = $5624; EAA 4XS = $6544

15-15. a. NPV #1 = –$431,425; NPV #2 = –$432,888
b. EAA #1 = –$119,674; EAA #2 = –$105,230
c. No; invest using plan #2

15-16. a. 1 year = $455; 4 years = $1830
b. EAA 2 years = $738; EAA 3 years = $708

15-17. 4 years; EAA for 4 years = $8536

15-18. EAA #1 = $7873; EAA #2 = $6176

15-19. NPV = $6

15-20. Initial = −$35,000; terminal = $5000; operating = $6500

15-21. Option #1 preferred; NPV #1 = $36; NPV #2 = $24

15-22. a. Initial = −$280,000; terminal = $7000; operating = $61,000
b. No, NPV = −$23,608

15-23. Initial = −$5400; terminal = $180; operating = $2120; NPV = $7

15-24. a. −$40,000
b. $6400
c. $9000
d. −$5655

15-25. a. Initial = −$10,600; terminal = $600; operating year 1 = $3400; operating years 2-5 = $4100
b. $4678; accept

15-26. Initial = −$1,150,000; terminal = $270,000; operating = $440,000; NPV = $685,710; accept

15-27. a. Initial = $600,000; terminal = $0; operating = $211,000; NPV = $160,655
b. Scenario 1: NPV = −$217,870; reject; Scenario 2: NPV = $34,480; accept; Scenario 3: NPV = $7926; accept

15-28. Initial = −$54,500; terminal = −$2500; operating year 1 excluding depreciation = $9960; operating years 2-6 excluding depreciation = $14,976; NPV = $12,488; accept

15-29. a. Initial = −$62,000; terminal = $3000
b. Operating excluding depreciation = $8400
c. NPV = $12,332; accept

15-30. NPV lease = −$7122; buy

15-31. NPV lease = −$3704; buy

15-32. Operating leases would be more attractive

15-33. a. NPV = −$9998; reject
b. NPV lease = $5331; lease

15-35. a. Yes
b. −$160,000
c. Years 1 thru 3 = $34,000
d. $40,000
e. $5813
f. Yes

CHAPTER 16:

16-1. $330,000

16-2. a. 9.5 days
b. $62.67

16-3. a. $1.1 million

16-4. a. $140,000 savings

16-5. a. $12,910
b. $22,361

16-6. a. $556,417
b. $278,209
c. $27,810
d. $27,821

16-7. a. $60,000
b. $30,000
c. 33% (rounded)
d. $5970

16-8. a. $10,392
b. $5196
c. $14,697

16-9. Return = $116,510; average = $122,013; upper = $149,530

16-10. a. Return = $1004; average = $1339; upper = $3012
b. Return = $932; average = $1243; upper = $2797
c. Return = $740; average = $986; upper = $2220
d. Return = $1594; average = $2125; upper = $4782
e. Return = $1825; average = $2433; upper = $5474
f. Return = $1645; average = $2194; upper = $4936

16-11. a. Return = $62,403; upper = $187,209; average = $83,204
b. $0; increase by $200,000

16-12. a. Return = $507,114; upper = $521,342; lower = $500,000
b. Return = $507,343; upper = $522,029; lower = $500,000
c. Return = $507,343; upper = $522,029; lower = $500,000
d. Return = $506,891; upper = $520,673; lower = $500,000
e. Return = $507,343; upper = $522,029; lower = $500,000

16-13. Return = $2605; upper = $7815; average = $3473

16-14. a. Return = $916,017; upper = $1,748,051; lower = $500,000
 b. Ending balance: Day 1 = $700,000; day 3 = $1,416,017; day 7 = $916,017

16-16. a. $400,000
 b. $280,000
 c. $22,400

16-17. NPV = $57,708; accept

16-18. a. $1,260,000
 b. $280,000 outflow
 c. −$580,000; reject

16-19. a. 78 days
 b. $20,400,000 outflow
 c. $139,600,000
 d. Accept
 e. $27,920,000

16-20. NPV = $321,528; accept

16-21. NPV = $17,508.40; implement

16-22. NPV = $42,188; liberalize

16-23. NPV A = $4,650,000; NPV B = −$3,405,000

16-24. NPV = −$42,880; reject

16-25. 775

16-26. 467

16-27. 3203

16-28. 5

16-29. EOQ = 4000

16-30. a. 240
 b. 100
 c. $120
 d. $120

16-31. a. 2000
 b. 20
 c. $200
 d. $200

16-32. a. EOQ = 3000; total costs = $1500
 b. Savings = $1225

16-33. a. 9000
 b. 8485

16-34. EOQ = 3200; orders = 62; average = 1600

16-35. a. Improvement
 b. May ACP = 14 days; July ACP = 37 days
 c. May sales outstanding end of June = $1.70
 d. Proportion of May's sales outstanding end of June = 21.25%

16-36. Aging schedule: January AR at end of March = 14.04%
 Balance proportion for January sales still outstanding at the end of March = 17.78%

16-37. a. For last 60 days = 54.9 days; for last 150 days = 80.2 days
 b. Two months ago = 25% of total
 c. Two months ago balance proportion = 44.5%

16-38. a. April balance = $330
 b. April aging: 45.5% from March; 54.5% from April
 c. ACP for April: last 30 days = 49.5; last 90 days = 47.9
 d. Balance proportions for February: January = 50%; February = 90%

16-39. a. February aging: November = 5%; January = 15%
 b. February
 c. Balance proportions January: October 8.33%; December = 20%

16-40. a. May balance = $900 from April + $10,000 from May
 b. May balance = 8.3% from April + 91.7% from May
 c. May: 32.7 for last 30 days; 50.3 for last 60 days

16-42. A-items = items 11, 13, 2; B-items = 15, 7, 14, 8, 5

16-46. a. $821,584
 b. $410,792
 c. $32,880
 d. $32,863
 f. Average = $233,887; upper = $401,245; return = $200,415
 g. ACP = 90 days; investment = $30.5 million; NPV = $340 million

16-47. a. Improvement
 b. November ACP = 46 days
 c. November balance = $28.8 from Nov. + $7.2 from Oct.
 d. November balance = 96.0% from Nov. sales & 32.7% from Oct. sales

CHAPTER 17:

17-1. a. $130,000
 b. $130,000
 c. $60,000 in June

d. Long term: $130,000; short term: $27,500

e. Add $10,000 to long-term financing needs

17-2. $63,000

17-3. $13,500

17-4. a. CR = 3.35; QR = 0.85; NWC = $2820

17-5. a. 77 days

17-6. a. −7 days

17-7. −5 days

17-8. a. 145 days

17-9. 127 days

17-10. 108 days

17-11. 0 days

17-12. $106,875

17-13. $26,677

17-14. 36.7%

17-15. 15%

17-16. a. 37.1%

b. 24.7%

17-17. a. 24.5%; $200

b. Borrowing saves $85.67

17-18. b. 18.56%

17-19. a. 55.7%

b. 31.8%

17-20. b. Cumulative bank loan as of Sept.: $24,400

17-21. a. Cumulative loan as of March: $32,000

b. $42,000 in February

c. February

d. April

17-22. a. Excess cash balance in June: $138,500

b. Isn't any

17-23. a. CR = 1.84; QR = 0.94; NWC = $2546;
D/E = 1.14; FCC = 14.5

17-24. a. CR = 0.88; QR = 0.43; NWC = −$4000

17-25. a. CR = 4.18; QR = 2.54; NWC = $25,100;
D/E = 0.34; FCC = 4.4

17-26. $15,582.01

17-27. $14,593.57

17-28. $843.86

17-29. a. $19,773.20

b. Year 3's interest = $3856.55

17-30. 10.23%

17-31. 8%

17-32. 10%

17-33. 8.83%

17-34. 9.278%

17-35. a. Bank = 14.29%

17-37. a. July: $400,000

b. Minimum long-term funds: $400,000;
maximum short-term funds: $180,000 in
November

c. Average short-term funds: $67,500

e. CCC = 56 days

f. 24.5%

g. June's cumulative borrowings = $93,200

h. CR = 1.88; QR = 1.04; NWC = $105,000;
D/E = 0.52; FCC = 3.4

i. $8,805.79

j. 9.5%

k. 8.9%

CHAPTER 18:

18-2. a. Cash: vertical this year = 20.5%;
horizontal = −5.1%

18-3. a. Cost of sales: this year = 81.7%;
horizontal = 14%

18-4. a. Net income this year = $900,000

b. Change in net income = −17%

18-6. Cash from operations = $38,400

18-7. Cash sales = $18,600; cash net income =
$4900

18-8. a. Cash flow from operating activities =
−$3000; cash flow from investing activities
= −$15,000; cash flow from financing
activities = −$4000

18-9. Cash sales = $613,000; cash cost of sales =
$365,000

18-11. a. This year: NWC = $160,000; QR = 0.74;
inventory days outstanding = 73.29

18-12. a. ACP year 1 = 90 days; inventory turnover
in year 1 = 3

b. Operating cycle = 282.46 days in year 3

c. Cash conversion cycle = 147.70 days in
year 2

18-15. This year: CR = 2.9; QR = 1.2; NWC =
$170,000; DI = 42.4 days

18-16. a. $150,000

b. $111,000

c. Current ratio = 4 before borrowing and
3 after borrowing

d. Dividend declared: 1.67 CR; dividend paid: 1.83 CR

18-18. a. 3.25

18-20. a. 12.25
b. 2.2

18-21. a. Sales = $89,583; units = 4479
b. $110,417
c. $116,666
d. Breakeven sales = $120,516

18-22. a. $1,728,000; 48,000 units
b. Incremental breakeven = $347,400 or 9650 units

18-23. a. Alpha = $20,000; Beta = $25,000
b. Alpha = –$1200; Beta = –$2800
c. Alpha = $4200; Beta = $800
d. Alpha = 80%; Beta = 93%

18-25. a. Both ROAs = 6.5%
b. ROE: Winn = 9.5%; Barter = 7.2%
c. EPS: Winn = $2.61; Barter = $1.80
d. Yes

18-26. a. ROA: A = 9%; B = 2.8%
b. ROE: A = 10.75%; B = 2.97%

18-27. 13.6%

18-28. a. Debt = $166,667; equity = $333,333
b. 6.4%
c. 39.4%
d. Turnover: New = 3.03; current = 2

18-30. CR: Penn = 2.7; Teller = 2.9
DI: Penn = 88.8; Teller = 127.9
AR T/O: Penn = 7.3; Teller = 7.1
Calculate other ratios as well.

18-31. a. CR year 1 = 1.33; CCC year 1 = 147.6 days; AR T/O year 2 = 4.83; DI year 3 = 60 days

18-33. a. Year 7 = 2.3
b. Year 7 = 0.93
c. Year 7 = 40.2%

18-35. a. $38,000 loss
b. Higher loss

18-36. a. This year: ROS = 17.1%; ROA = 21.4%; ROE = 42.1%

18-37. a. Decreasing cost of sales
b. Year 2 = 39.8%
c. Increased capital expenditures

18-38. Receivables = $30,000; total current assets = $123,750

18-39. Cash = $3900; prepaid expenses = $1430; bonds = $6500

18-40. a. 6.2

18-41. Income before taxes = $47,300

CHAPTER 19:

19-1. $780,000

19-2. $2.6 million

19-3. $2.24 million

19-4. $14.25 million

19-5. $1,836,800

19-6. $2.74 million

19-7. $461,820

19-8. 10%

19-9. 15%

19-10. Year 4 sales = $1,059,808

19-11. $233,894

19-12. $24,787,657

19-13. $84,132

19-14. $254,458

19-15. Pro forma net income = $2,496,000

19-16. Pro forma net income = $19,421

19-17. Pro forma net income = $45,920

19-18. Pro forma net income = $1,042,200

19-19. Pro forma net income = $33,750

19-20. Next year net income = $1242.7; net income in two years = $1421.0

19-21. Next year net income = $19,964; net income in two years = $7532

19-22. Cash increase = $9000

19-23. Finance shortage = $53,900

19-24. Marketable securities increase = $88,000

19-25. Marketable securities decrease = $215,000

19-26. ROE = 25%

19-27. ROE = 60%

19-28. ROE = 37.5%

19-29. ROE: year 1 = 10%; year 2 = 13.3%; year 3 = 15%

19-30. ROE: year 1 = 26.7%; year 2 = 25%; year 3 = 18.2%

19-31. Cash increase = $9800

19-32. No change in cash balance

19-33. Cash decrease = $100

19-35. a. Year 4's sales = $330,454

b. Net income = $70,000

c. Total assets = $328,000

d. ROE = 109%, year 3; 82.4%, year 4

e. Cash increase = $1000

Index

Compound Sum of $1 Received at End of Period: $(1 + r)^n$

Period	1%	2%	3%	4%	5%	6%	7%	8%	9%	10%	12%	14%	15%	16%	18%	20%	24%	28%	32%	36%
1	1.0100	1.0200	1.0300	1.0400	1.0500	1.0600	1.0700	1.0800	1.0900	1.1000	1.1200	1.1400	1.1500	1.1600	1.1800	1.2000	1.2400	1.2800	1.3200	1.3600
2	1.0201	1.0404	1.0609	1.0816	1.1025	1.1236	1.1449	1.1664	1.1881	1.2100	1.2544	1.2996	1.3225	1.3456	1.3924	1.4400	1.5376	1.6384	1.7424	1.8496
3	1.0303	1.0612	1.0927	1.1249	1.1576	1.1910	1.2250	1.2597	1.2950	1.3310	1.4049	1.4815	1.5209	1.5609	1.6430	1.7280	1.9066	2.0972	2.3000	2.5155
4	1.0406	1.0824	1.1255	1.1699	1.2155	1.2625	1.3108	1.3605	1.4116	1.4641	1.5735	1.6890	1.7490	1.8106	1.9388	2.0736	2.3642	2.6844	3.0360	3.4210
5	1.0510	1.1041	1.1593	1.2167	1.2763	1.3382	1.4026	1.4693	1.5386	1.6105	1.7623	1.9254	2.0114	2.1003	2.2878	2.4883	2.9316	3.4360	4.0075	4.6526
6	1.0615	1.1262	1.1941	1.2653	1.3401	1.4185	1.5007	1.5869	1.6771	1.7716	1.9738	2.1950	2.3131	2.4364	2.6996	2.9860	3.6352	4.3980	5.2899	6.3275
7	1.0721	1.1487	1.2299	1.3159	1.4071	1.5036	1.6058	1.7138	1.8280	1.9487	2.2107	2.5023	2.6600	2.8262	3.1855	3.5832	4.5077	5.6295	6.9826	8.6054
8	1.0829	1.1717	1.2668	1.3686	1.4775	1.5938	1.7182	1.8509	1.9926	2.1436	2.4760	2.8526	3.0590	3.2784	3.7589	4.2998	5.5895	7.2058	9.2170	11.703
9	1.0937	1.1951	1.3048	1.4233	1.5513	1.6895	1.8385	1.9990	2.1719	2.3579	2.7731	3.2519	3.5179	3.8030	4.4355	5.1598	6.9310	9.2234	12.166	15.916
10	1.1046	1.2190	1.3439	1.4802	1.6289	1.7908	1.9672	2.1589	2.3674	2.5937	3.1058	3.7072	4.0456	4.4114	5.2338	6.1917	8.5944	11.806	16.060	21.647
11	1.1157	1.2434	1.3842	1.5395	1.7103	1.8983	2.1049	2.3316	2.5804	2.8531	3.4785	4.2262	4.6524	5.1173	6.1759	7.4301	10.657	15.116	21.199	29.439
12	1.1268	1.2682	1.4258	1.6010	1.7959	2.0122	2.2522	2.5182	2.8127	3.1384	3.8960	4.8179	5.3503	5.9360	7.2876	8.9161	13.215	19.343	27.983	40.037
13	1.1381	1.2936	1.4685	1.6651	1.8856	2.1329	2.4096	2.7196	3.0658	3.4523	4.3635	5.4924	6.1528	6.8858	8.5994	10.699	16.386	24.759	36.937	54.451
14	1.1495	1.3195	1.5126	1.7317	1.9799	2.2609	2.5785	2.9372	3.3417	3.7975	4.8871	6.2613	7.0757	7.9875	10.147	12.839	20.319	31.691	48.757	74.053
15	1.1610	1.3459	1.5580	1.8009	2.0789	2.3966	2.7590	3.1722	3.6425	4.1772	5.4736	7.1379	8.1371	9.2655	11.974	15.407	25.196	40.565	64.359	100.71
16	1.1726	1.3728	1.6047	1.8730	2.1829	2.5404	2.9522	3.4259	3.9703	4.5950	6.1304	8.1372	9.3576	10.748	14.129	18.488	31.243	51.923	84.954	136.97
17	1.1843	1.4002	1.6528	1.9479	2.2920	2.6928	3.1588	3.7000	4.3276	5.0545	6.8660	9.2765	10.761	12.467	16.672	22.186	38.741	66.461	112.14	186.28
18	1.1961	1.4282	1.7024	2.0258	2.4066	2.8543	3.3799	3.9960	4.7171	5.5599	7.6900	10.575	12.375	14.463	19.673	26.623	48.039	85.071	148.02	253.34
19	1.2081	1.4568	1.7535	2.1068	2.5270	3.0256	3.6165	4.3157	5.1417	6.1159	8.6128	12.056	14.232	16.777	23.214	31.948	59.568	108.89	195.39	344.54
20	1.2202	1.4859	1.8061	2.1911	2.6533	3.2071	3.8697	4.6610	5.6044	6.7275	9.6463	13.743	16.367	19.461	27.393	38.338	73.864	139.38	257.92	468.57
21	1.2324	1.5157	1.8603	2.2788	2.7860	3.3996	4.1406	5.0338	6.1088	7.4002	10.804	15.668	18.822	22.574	32.323	46.005	91.592	178.41	340.45	637.26
22	1.2447	1.5460	1.9161	2.3699	2.9253	3.6035	4.4304	5.4365	6.6586	8.1403	12.100	17.861	21.645	26.186	38.142	55.206	113.57	228.36	449.39	866.87
23	1.2572	1.5769	1.9736	2.4647	3.0715	3.8197	4.7405	5.8715	7.2579	8.9543	13.552	20.362	24.891	30.376	45.008	66.247	140.83	292.30	593.20	1178.7
24	1.2697	1.6084	2.0328	2.5633	3.2251	4.0489	5.0724	6.3412	7.9111	9.8497	15.179	23.212	28.625	35.236	53.109	79.497	174.63	374.14	783.02	1602.9
25	1.2824	1.6406	2.0938	2.6658	3.3864	4.2919	5.4274	6.8485	8.6231	10.835	17.000	26.462	32.919	40.874	62.669	95.396	216.54	478.90	1033.6	2180.1
26	1.2953	1.6734	2.1566	2.7725	3.5557	4.5494	5.8074	7.3964	9.3992	11.918	19.040	30.167	37.857	47.414	73.949	114.48	268.51	613.00	1364.3	2964.9
27	1.3082	1.7069	2.2213	2.8834	3.7335	4.8223	6.2139	7.9881	10.245	13.110	21.325	34.390	43.535	55.000	87.260	137.37	332.95	784.63	1800.9	4032.2
28	1.3213	1.7410	2.2879	2.9987	3.9201	5.1117	6.6488	8.6271	11.167	14.421	23.883	39.204	50.065	63.800	102.96	164.84	412.86	1004.3	2377.2	5483.9
29	1.3345	1.7758	2.3566	3.1187	4.1161	5.4184	7.1143	9.3173	12.172	15.863	26.750	44.693	57.575	74.009	121.50	197.81	511.95	1285.6	3137.9	7458.1
30	1.3478	1.8114	2.4273	3.2434	4.3219	5.7435	7.6123	10.063	13.268	17.449	29.960	50.950	66.212	85.850	143.37	237.38	634.82	1645.5	4142.1	10143.
40	1.4889	2.2080	3.2620	4.8010	7.0400	10.286	14.974	21.725	31.409	45.259	93.051	188.88	267.86	378.72	750.38	1469.8	5455.9	19427.	66521.	*
50	1.6446	2.6916	4.3839	7.1067	11.467	18.420	29.457	46.902	74.358	117.39	289.00	700.23	1083.7	1670.7	3927.4	9100.4	46890.	*	*	*
60	1.8167	3.2810	5.8916	10.520	18.679	32.988	57.946	101.26	176.03	304.48	897.60	2595.9	4384.0	7370.2	20555.	56348.	*	*	*	*

*FVIF > 99,999.

Present Value of $1 Received at the End of Period: $1/(1 + r)^n$

Period	1%	3%	5%	6%	7%	8%	9%	10%	11%	12%	13%	14%	15%	16%	17%	18%	19%	20%	24%	28%
1	.9901	.9709	.9524	.9434	.9346	.9259	.9174	.9091	.9009	.8929	.8850	.8772	.8696	.8621	.8547	.8475	.8403	.8333	.8065	.7813
2	.9803	.9426	.9070	.8900	.8734	.8573	.8417	.8264	.8116	.7972	.7831	.7695	.7561	.7432	.7305	.7182	.7062	.6944	.6504	.6104
3	.9706	.9151	.8638	.8396	.8163	.7938	.7722	.7513	.7312	.7118	.6931	.6750	.6575	.6407	.6244	.6086	.5934	.5787	.5245	.4768
4	.9610	.8885	.8227	.7921	.7629	.7350	.7084	.6830	.6587	.6355	.6133	.5921	.5718	.5523	.5337	.5158	.4978	.4823	.4230	.3725
5	.9515	.8626	.7835	.7473	.7130	.6806	.6499	.6209	.5935	.5674	.5428	.5194	.4972	.4761	.4561	.4371	.4190	.4019	.3411	.2910
6	.9420	.8375	.7462	.7050	.6663	.6302	.5963	.5645	.5346	.5066	.4803	.4556	.4323	.4104	.3898	.3704	.3521	.3349	.2751	.2274
7	.9327	.8131	.7107	.6651	.6627	.5835	.5470	.5132	.4817	.4523	.4251	.3996	.3759	.3538	.3332	.3139	.2959	.2791	.2218	.1776
8	.9235	.7894	.6768	.6274	.5820	.5403	.5019	.4665	.4339	.4039	.3762	.3506	.3269	.3050	.2848	.2660	.2487	.2326	.1789	.1388
9	.9143	.7664	.6446	.5919	.5439	.5002	.4604	.4241	.3909	.3606	.3329	.3075	.2843	.2630	.2434	.2255	.2090	.1938	.1443	.1084
10	.9053	.7441	.6139	.5584	.5083	.4632	.4224	.3855	.3522	.3220	.2946	.2697	.2472	.2267	.2080	.1911	.1756	.1615	.1164	.0847
11	.8963	.7224	.5847	.5268	.4751	.4289	.3875	.3505	.3173	.2875	.2607	.2366	.2149	.1954	.1778	.1619	.1476	.1346	.0938	.0662
12	.8874	.7014	.5568	.4970	.4440	.3971	.3555	.3186	.2858	.2567	.2307	.2076	.1869	.1685	.1520	.1372	.1240	.1122	.0757	.0517
13	.8787	.6810	.5303	.4688	.4150	.3677	.3262	.2897	.2575	.2292	.2042	.1821	.1625	.1452	.1299	.1163	.1042	.0935	.0610	.0404
14	.8700	.6611	.5051	.4423	.3878	.3405	.2992	.2633	.2320	.2046	.1807	.1597	.1413	.1252	.1110	.0985	.0876	.0779	.0492	.0316
15	.8613	.6419	.4810	.4173	.3624	.3152	.2745	.2394	.2090	.1827	.1599	.1401	.1229	.1079	.0949	.0835	.0736	.0649	.0397	.0247
16	.8528	.6232	.4581	.3936	.3387	.2919	.2519	.2176	.1883	.1631	.1415	.1229	.1069	.0930	.0811	.0708	.0618	.0541	.0320	.0193
17	.8444	.6050	.4363	.3714	.3166	.2703	.2311	.1978	.1696	.1456	.1252	.1078	.0929	.0802	.0693	.0600	.0520	.0451	.0258	.0150
18	.8360	.5874	.4155	.3503	.2959	.2502	.2120	.1799	.1528	.1300	.1108	.0946	.0808	.0691	.0592	.0508	.0437	.0376	.0208	.0118
19	.8277	.5703	.3957	.3305	.2765	.2317	.1945	.1635	.1377	.1161	.0981	.0829	.0703	.0596	.0506	.0431	.0367	.0313	.0168	.0092
20	.8195	.5537	.3769	.3118	.2584	.2145	.1784	.1486	.1240	.1037	.0868	.0728	.0611	.0514	.0433	.0365	.0308	.0261	.0135	.0072
25	.7798	.4776	.2953	.2330	.1842	.1460	.1160	.0923	.0736	.0588	.0471	.0378	.0304	.0245	.0197	.0160	.0129	.0105	.0046	.0021
30	.7419	.4120	.2314	.1741	.1314	.0994	.0754	.0573	.0437	.0334	.0256	.0196	.0151	.0116	.0090	.0070	.0054	.0042	.0016	.0006
40	.6717	.3066	.1420	.0972	.0668	.0460	.0318	.0221	.0154	.0107	.0075	.0053	.0037	.0026	.0019	.0013	.0010	.0007	.0002	.0001
50	.6080	.2281	.0872	.0543	.0339	.0213	.0134	.0085	.0054	.0035	.0022	.0014	.0009	.0006	.0004	.0003	.0002	.0001	*	*
60	.5504	.1697	.0535	.0303	.0173	.0099	.0057	.0033	.0019	.0011	.0007	.0004	.0002	.0001	.0001	*	*	*	*	*

*The factor is zero to four decimal places.